ENCYCLOPEDIA OF SOFTWARE ENGINEERING

VOLUME 2

ENCYCLOPEDIA OF SOFTWARE ENGINEERING

VOLUME 2

John J. Marciniak, *Editor-in-chief*

A Wiley-Interscience Publication
John Wiley & Sons, Inc.

New York / Chichester / Brisbane / Toronto / Singapore

This text is printed on acid-free paper.

Library of Congress Cataloging in Publication Data:

Encyclopedia of software engineering / John J. Marciniak, editor.
p. cm.
Includes index.
ISBN 0-471-54004-8 (cloth : acid-free paper). — ISBN 0-471-54001-3 (v. I : only sold as a set). — ISBN 0-471-54002-1 (v. II : only sold as a set)
1. Software engineering—Encyclopedias. I. Marciniak, John J.
QA76.758.E53 1994
005.1'03—dc20 93-17387

Printed in the United States of America

10 9 8 7 6 5 4 3 2 1

O

OBJECT-ORIENTED DESIGN

INTRODUCTION

Work on what was to become "structured design" began in the early 1960s. Structured design, as a well-defined and named concept, did not achieve appreciable visibility until the publication of an article in the *IBM Systems Journal* in 1974 (Stevens and co-workers, 1974). Five years later, Prentice Hall published a book by Larry Constantine and Edward Yourdon (1979) that introduced structured design to the masses. (There were earlier published versions of this book, e.g., the so-called "orange book.") Even before 1979, variations on Constantine's version of structured design began to appear, e.g., Myers, 1975, 1976, and 1978. After 1979, software engineers could select from an ever increasing variety of approaches to structured design (Gomaa, 1984; Ward and Mellor, 1985; Hatley and Pirbhai, 1987; and Marca and McGowan, 1988). It should be obvious to even a casual observer that there is more than one way to accomplish a "structured design."

Like structured design, the term object-oriented design (OOD) means different things to different people. For example, OOD has been used to imply such things as:

- The design of individual objects, and/or the design of the individual methods contained in those objects (Taylor and Hecht, 1990).
- The design of an inheritance (specialization) hierarchy of objects.
- The design of a library of reusable objects (Coggins, 1990).
- The process of specifying and coding of an entire object-oriented application.

(What many people consider to be the first object-oriented programming language, Simula (Dahl and Nygaard, 1966), was introduced in 1966. The term object-oriented, however, did not come into use until around 1970, with many people crediting Alan Kay (Goldberg and Kay, 1976; Kay, 1969; 1977) as the person who coined the term.

It is not the purpose of this article to define basic object-oriented concepts. For these, the reader is referred to references such as Berard (1993), Blair and co-workers (1991), and Wegner (1990).

TWO DIFFERENT CULTURES

Part of the problem is the diversity within the so-called object-oriented community. Many object-oriented people seem to focus primarily on programming language issues. They tend to cast all discussions in terms of the syntax and semantics of their chosen object-oriented programming language. These people find it almost impossible to discuss any software engineering activity (e.g., analysis, design, and testing) without direct mention of some specific implementation language.

Outside of producing executable prototypes, people who emphasize programming languages seldom have well-defined techniques for analyzing their client's problems or describing the overall architecture of the software product. A great deal of what they do is intuitive. If they have a natural instinct/intuition for good analysis or good design, their efforts on small-to-medium, noncritical projects can result in respectable software solutions.

Programming language people use the terms *analysis* and *design* in a very loose sense. Analysis can mean listening to their customer, making some notes and sketches, thinking about both the problem and potential solutions, and even constructing a few software prototypes. Design can mean the code-level design of an individual object, the development of an inheritance (specialization) hierarchy, or the informal definition and implementation of a software product (e.g., identify all the objects, create instances of the objects, and have the instances send messages to each other).

Another group of object-oriented people are interested in formality and rigor. To these people, software engineering is largely very systematic, repeatable, and transferable. They view object-oriented software engineering as primarily an engineering process with well-defined, coordinated tasks, and well-defined deliverables. The quality of the resulting products (and the process itself) can be evaluated in a quantitative, as well as qualitative manner.

For members of this second camp, object-oriented programming (OOP) is primarily a coding activity, and object-oriented design did not exist until about 1980. The programming language people, on the other hand, often lay claim to all things object-oriented, including object-oriented design. Even though a well-defined, quantifiable, transferable, and repeatable process for object-oriented design did not exist until the early 1980s, in their minds OOD has existed at least since there were object-oriented programming languages, a process many people date from 1966 when Simula was first introduced.

As you might guess, there are significant cultural differences between these two groups of object-oriented people. For example, some of those that emphasize rigor and formality view the programming language people as chaotic, overly error prone, wasteful, and largely unpredictable. On the other hand, some of the programming language people consider the formality and rigor to be mere window dressing, at best adding nothing to the quality of the final product, and at worst increasing the cost of development while simultaneously delaying the delivery and lowering the quality of the resulting software product.

Even if one takes into account the widely different perspectives described above, there are still significant variations within each of these perspectives. Consider inheritance, i.e., the process whereby an object acquires characteristics from another object. (Note that object is used here in its most generic sense. Some people restrict the term object to mean only instances of classes.) A few object-oriented programming languages allow an object to inherit directly from only one other object (single inheritance). Other languages allow an object to inherit characteristics from more than one object (multiple inheritance). Someone who defines OOD in programming language terms may choose to include or exclude multiple inheritance from the design process based on whether or not their particular language supports the concept.

Other issues that arise in the programming language camp include the mixing of data and objects, the ability to have program elements that are not encapsulated within any object; and the use of exceptions, parameterized classes, metaclasses, and concurrency.

Within the formality and rigor group there is also a significant amount of diversity. Some try to portray object-oriented methods as slightly recast structured approaches (old wine in new bottles). Others advocate a more data-driven style, e.g., the extensive use of entity-relationship diagrams and other data modeling techniques. Still others seem to have successfully blended object-oriented thinking and rigorous software engineering. In effect, they have integrated the two without losing the benefits of either.

Almost everyone who advocates a formal approach views object-oriented design as only one part of the software development life cycle. It may be preceded by such activities as object-oriented analysis and feasibility studies, and followed by object-oriented programming (coding). Those accomplishing object-oriented design will also be expected to interact with testing, quality assurance, and management personnel. Only if the software problem is small, and of relatively low risk will object-oriented design be the first life-cycle activity, and even then it will be followed by object-oriented programming.

(The word *formal* is sometimes reserved for mathematical (or logically rigorous) approaches to software development. Examples of such approaches include Vienna Development Methodology (VDM) (Chedgey and co-workers, 1987; Jackson, 1985; and Jones, 1986), OBJ and its derivatives (Gallimore and co-workers, 1989; Goguen, 1984; and Grogono and Bennett, 1989); Z (Spivey, 1988, 1989); and C. A. R. Hoare's (1985) communicating sequential processes. In this article, we will use the word "formal" more in the sense of "a well-defined, step-by-step, repeatable process with accompanying guidelines, and defined deliverables.)

PROGRAMMING LANGUAGE (NONFORMAL) VIEWS OF OOD

We will use the term nonformal to describe approaches to OOD that are not well defined, step-by-step, or repeatable, such as those that emphasize the design of individual objects, specialization (inheritance) hierarchies, and libraries of objects. A survey of such approaches indicates that there may indeed be some repeatable rigor (and some sage advice) given for these approaches, but they are severely lacking when it comes to defining the software architecture of large and critical systems.

Nonformal OOD approaches usually exhibit many of the following characteristics:

- There is an overriding emphasis on identifying the objects that will make up the application, almost to the exclusion of understanding the overall application. For example, one nonformal approach defines the OOD approach as "identify and create the classes, create instances from the classes, and then have the instances send messages to each other."
- Because of the above, nonformal approaches are often bottom-up in nature. Specifically, one identifies, defines, and implements pieces of the solution, and then merges these pieces into a final or partial solution. (Note that a bottom-up approach need not be chaotic, and may be entirely appropriate for small and/or noncritical problems.)
- Nonformal approaches frequently address issues related to the internal design of individual objects and almost never discuss strategies for the design of the software architecture for the overall application.
- Often there is a blurring of the distinction between the design of an individual object and the design of the application at hand. Specifically, it is not unusual in such approaches to see objects containing application-specific information. (This, unfortunately, reduces the reusability of such objects and decreases the overall reliability of the application.)

Examples of nonformal approaches to OOD that are very close to coding are described in Jalote (1989), Mullin (1989), Scharenberg and Dunsmore (1991), and Taylor and Hecht (1990). Bailey (1989) and Clark (1987) describe informal techniques for designing individual objects, while Coggins (1990) discusses approaches to the design of a library of classes.

LIFE-CYCLE VIEWS OF OOD

We now shift our attention to those who view object-oriented design as one process among several in the development of software products. This view stipulates that, with the possible exception of simple, noncritical pieces of software several processes are involved in the creation of software products. These processes have commonly been referred to as methodologies. (There are those who point out that the -ology suffix on methodology should mean "the study of methods," but the term *methodology* will be used as it is usually understood.

There are many views how to partition the development part of the software product life-cycle. These views can be simple (e.g., design, followed by coding, followed by testing) or fairly involved (e.g., including feasibility studies, requirements analysis, high-level external design, etc.). Samples of different perspectives on the development part of the software life cycle see Bergland (1981), Birrell and Ould, (1985), Blank and co-workers (1983), Freeman and Wasserman (1980), Yau and Tsai (1986), and TBE (1987).

Virtually all life-cycle views of OOD assume the possibility of some form of analysis (establishing an understanding of the problem to be solved, sometimes coupled with a high-level external description of the solution). Only if the problem is simple, will the analysis phase become optional. Life-cycle views very often consider coding to be separate from "design." For example, it is not uncommon to hear statements such as, "no code will be produced until the design is complete."

Software engineers have known for some time that the divisions between various life cycle phases (e.g., between analysis and design and between design and coding) are not sharp. Older approaches tended to emphasize the divisions by using different techniques, deliverables, and viewpoints:

- Structured analysis (Connor, 1980; DeMarco, 1978; Gane and Sarson, 1977; and Marca and McGowan, 1988) emphasized understanding the way the client conducted business, data flow diagrams, and "the flow of data."
- Structured design (Hatley and Pirbhai, 1987; Ward and Mellor, 1985; and Yourdon and Constantine, 1979), on the other hand, stressed developing an acceptable software system architecture, structure charts, and "the flow of control."

With both increased experience in software development techniques and an emphasis on an object-oriented view point, the distinctions between various life cycle phases have become more blurred. Many people have observed that structured analysis, structured design, and structured programming had little in common other than a sense of formality and the adjective *structured.* Object-oriented techniques (e.g., object-oriented analysis, object-oriented design, and object-oriented programming), however, tend to be much more consistent with each other.

E. W. Dijkstra (1969) introduced the term, and basic concepts behind, "structured programming" in 1969. Although structured programming focused primarily on coding activities, it accelerated a movement that lead to the formalization of other life cycle phases, e.g., structured design and structured analysis. Object-oriented programming has had a similar effect on life-cycle phases.

One very important difference between the so-called "structured revolution" and the so-called "object-oriented revolution" is the much higher degree of consistency among object-oriented life-cycle phases. For example, the concept of inheritance (specialization) is much the same in object-oriented requirements analysis, in object-oriented design, and in object-oriented programming.

NONRIGOROUS OOD APPROACHES

Dave Bulman (1989) and others have observed that the mere identification and creation of objects is not a substitute for "design." It is important to realize that, by "design," Bulman means the establishment of a system architecture. This includes not only the identification of system components (objects), but also the definitions of their interactions and interrelationships as well.

Russell J. Abbott (1980, 1983) described an informal method for specifying the design of a software system. It involved writing a paragraph that described a solution to the problem at hand, and then identifying the nouns and noun phrases as candidate objects. The verbs in the paragraph could then be analyzed to suggest methods (operations) encapsulated within the objects. Of course, Abbott used the Ada programming language (ARM, 1983) to illustrate his points, and many people consider Ada to be "object-based," and not "object-oriented." (Wegner, 1990).

Grady Booch adopted the work of Abbott as a mechanism for bringing out the software engineering features of Ada (Booch, 1981, 1982, 1983a, 1983b). Initially making only a few changes in Abbott's approach, Booch referred to his technique as "object-oriented design." To be sure, Booch was also influenced by Smalltalk, object-oriented computer hardware, and semantic data modeling. One could say that Booch was probably the first person to significantly popularize the term "object-oriented design." It was not until the mid to late 1980s that people who focused primarily on object-oriented programming languages began using the term OOD with any frequency.

Many people did not understand Booch's intentions. They thought, for example, that OOD *always* required that one write a paragraph, and then underline nouns and verbs. Booch viewed the paragraph as a "crutch," i.e., one technique out of many which could be used to help identify and define objects.

By 1982, the author had begun to develop some Ada training courses. These courses included simple object-oriented design exercises. Later, in 1984, the author wrote a 300-page book on object-oriented design, i.e., *An Object-Oriented Design Handbook for Ada Software,* (Berard, 1985). Also in 1984, reports from people attempting to use Booch's approach on real projects began to emerge, (Mickel, 1984). By late 1985, both Booch and Berard had begun to incorporate more classic object-oriented thinking actively Smalltalk concepts) into courses, consulting, and articles.

MODERATELY FORMAL OOD APPROACHES

People who define approaches, guidelines, and techniques for various software engineering activities are commonly called "methodologists." People such as Grady Booch, Larry Constantine, and James Rumbaugh are examples of people who are often referred to as methodologists. As both the methodologists and the users of their methodologies become more experienced, they cause mutations (clarifications, modifications, and extensions) to the methodologies. In fact, it can be quite interesting to follow the evolution of a particular methodology over time. Almost invariably, methodologies become more formal as both their users and creators gain experience.

In February of 1986, Booch wrote an article (1986) describing his evolving thinking on object-oriented approaches. Realizing that object-oriented thinking is not limited to design and coding, Booch began to refer to his approach as "object-oriented *development.*" (Berard's approach to OOD, for example, has constantly been evolving, (Berard 1987; Richardson and co-workers, 1992). Sometimes adopters of a particular OOD methodology do their own tailoring (evolving) (ATC, 1989).

Some OOD approaches are strongly influenced by particular programming languages. For example, the influence of Ada is obvious in Lee and co-workers (1987) and Walters (1991). Although the proponents of "responsibility-driven design" (Wirfs-Brock and Wilkerson, 1989; Wirfs-Brock and co-workers, 1990) do not think of the approach as specific to a particular programming language, its Smalltalk roots are fairly obvious (Stroustrup, 1991, Chapt. 11).

As object-oriented technology increases in popularity, people who formerly advocated structured techniques have begun to modify their approaches to encompass object-oriented thinking. The degree of modification varies from author to author. Colbert, (1989); McIntyre and Higgins (1988); Nielsen and Shumate (1987), Pun and Winder, (1989); Shumate (1988), and Wasserman and co-workers, 1989, (1990) describe OOD approaches that are, to some degree, influenced by more traditional structured approaches.

One technique for creating a "new" methodology is to take one or more important principles from older approaches and then to recast new ideas (e.g., object-orientation) in terms of these principles. The Hierarchical Object-Oriented Design (HOOD) (Heitz, 1988; Vielcanet, 1989) stresses the importance of a top-down approach to software engineering, and places object-orientation within that framework. The General Object-Oriented Development (GOOD) approach advocated by Seidewitz and Stark (Stark and Seidewitz, 1987) stressed the importance of understanding a problem in more traditional terms (e.g., data modeling) before moving to an object-oriented perspective.

There are other views on OOD that have evolved from fairly unusual perspectives. (Jochem and co-workers, 1989) describes an approach that was influenced by computer integrated manufacturing (CIM). James Rumbaugh (Blaha and co-workers, 1988; Rumbaugh and co-workers, 1991) advocates an approach that is more closely based on data modeling than on object-oriented thinking. Peter Coad (Coad and Yourdon, 1991) describes a "multicomponent, multilayered" approach that is fairly unique.

MIXED PARADIGMS

There are methodologists that suggest mixing object-oriented approaches with other approaches, and giving each approach equal weighting. Bewtra and co-workers, (1990) suggests combining object-oriented technology with functional programming (Backus, 1978, 1982). Pendley, 1989) describes a combination of object-oriented thinking and information engineering (Finkelstein, 1989; Martin, 1989 1990a, and 1990b). Stream and formal object-oriented specification techniques are advocated in Toetenel and co-workers (1990).

MODIFYING OTHER APPROACHES TO ENCOMPASS OBJECT-ORIENTED THINKING

When moving from an older way of doing things to a newer way, it is seldom advisable to "throw out" everything connected with the old way. One often used strategy is to enlarge the older way so that it can encompass some or all of the aspects of the newer. Henderson-Sellers (1991), Henderson-Sellers and Constantine (1991), Li (1991), and Ward (1989) all suggest mechanisms for keeping much of traditional structured/functional-decomposition thinking while addressing object-oriented concerns. Birchenough and Cameron (1989), Hull and co-workers (1989), and Reed and Bynum (1989) all describe OOD within the context of Jackson System Development (JSD) (Jackson, 1983).

DIFFERENT PARADIGMS IN THE SAME LIFE CYCLE

Experience has shown that simply attempting to integrate object-oriented thinking into the more traditional methodologies (e.g., structured) is a Mistake. The major problem is that of localization, i.e., the placing of related items in close physical proximity to each other. Functional approaches, for example, tend to localize information around functions, whereas object-oriented approaches tend to localize information around objects. A functional decomposition "front end" to an object-oriented process, in effect, breaks up objects and scatters their parts. Later, these parts must be retrieved and relocalized around objects.

There have been quite a number of attempts to reconcile the output of a non-object-oriented process with the input requirements of an OOD process, e.g., (Alabiso, 1988; Brown and Dobbs, 1989; Gray, 1987, 1988; Khalsa, 1989; and Lukman, 1991). None of these scenarios are as clean and easy as using an object-oriented approach from the very beginning of the software life cycle.

Analysis of OOD Approaches

Since object-oriented programming has been with us for more than a quarter of a century, and OOD proper has been around for over a decade, it is not unusual that a number of attempts have been made to analyze the OOD process. See, e.g., (Gardner, 1988; Hruschka, 1990; Jaworski and LaVallee, 1990; Rine, 1986, 1987, 1991, Rosson and Gold, 1989; Vidale and Hayden, 1987; Wiener, 1991; and Wirfs-Brock and Johnson, 1990). While some of these analysis reveal potential problems with particular OOD approaches, none have advocated avoiding an object-oriented approach.

Comparisons

Comparisons of methodologies have been around since the 1970s. The first significant comparison of OOD with structured analysis/structured design and Jackson system development was done under the auspices of General Electric (Boehm-Davis and Ross, 1984). This study gave the same problem to three different groups of people, and had them all implement solutions using the same programming language. When compared with the other solutions, the researchers found that the OOD solutions:

- Were simpler (using control-flow complexity and numbers of operators and operands as metrics).
- Were smaller (using lines of code as a metric).
- Took less time to develop.
- Were better suited to real-time problems.

Some comparisons have been very informal (Boyd, 1987 and Jamsa, 1984), and others have been flawed because the authors did not fully understand what OOD was (Kelly, 1987).

OOD TECHNIQUES

A number of authors, while not describing complete OOD methodologies, have described techniques that can be used in the OOD process. Beck and Cunningham (1989), for example, describes Class-Responsibility-Collaboration (CRC) cards. The idea is to create one CRC card for every class involved in the problem or solution. The responsibilities (method interfaces) of the object are documented on one area of the card and the collaborations (other objects with which the object must interact) are placed on another area.

Byrne and Wiatrowski (1986) describe a graphical means of representing objects in an OOD process. In the same vein, Coleman and co-workers (1992) describes a variation on statecharts (Harel, 1987; Harel and co-workers, 1987) i.e., "objectcharts." Loomis and co-workers (1987) defines a graphical technique that is used in the OOD approach advocated by James Rumbaugh.

EXPERIENCES WITH OOD

One of the signs of a maturing technology is the emergence of "war stories," i.e., accounts of the experiences of those who have used the technology. Chedgey and co-workers (1987) describes an attempt to use a formal methodology (Vienna Development Method, Jones, (1986) with OOD. Meyer and co-workers (1989) talks about the experience of using an approach to OOD that mixes functional decomposition with more traditional object-oriented techniques. Davis and Irving (1989) presents a discussion of one of the most common uses of OOD, i.e., for real-time systems. Vlissides and Linton (1988) describes the use of OOD for the creation of a graphics application.

METRICS

Even before Tom Gilb wrote his landmark book on software metrics (Gilb, 1977), people had been interested in measuring software. While there are now numerous metrics for measuring non-object-oriented software (Arthur, 1985; Card and Glass, 1990; Conte and co-workers, 1986; Dreger, 1989; Ejiogu, 1991; Grady and Caswell, 1987; and Jones, 1991), there are relatively few discussions on metrics for object-oriented software.

Karl Lieberherr and his colleagues have written a number of articles on assessing the quality of the design of an individual object (Lieberheff and Riel, 1989). However, until very recently, there has not been much else published. Chidamber and Kemerer (1991) is probably the most comprehensive article to date on assessing the quality of an object-oriented design.

COMPUTER AIDED SOFTWARE ENGINEERING FOR OOD

Computer aided software engineering (CASE), once considered a luxury, is becoming increasingly necessary in today's software engineering arena. With the rising interest in object-oriented software engineering, it is only natural to ask, "Where are the CASE tools for object-oriented technology?"

One of the major obstacles to OOD CASE tools is the wide variety of approaches that we have presented in this article. Some OOD methodologists, or their organizations, have put out their own CASE tools, e.g., Rational's ROSE and Object International's OOATool. Some CASE vendors have chosen to automate the approaches from several different methodologists, e.g., Mark V Systems, Ltd.'s ObjectMaker and Protosoft Inc.'s Paradigm Plus. However, it will be some time before the object-oriented technology market becomes as focused as the so-called structured technology marketplace. (OOA Tool is a trademark of Object International, Inc. ObjectMaker is a trademark of Mark V Systems, Ltd. Paradigm Plus is a trademark of Protosoft, Inc. Rational is a registered trademark and Rational Rose is a trademark of Rational.) Those seeking more information on OOD case tools are advised to consult Anderson and co-workers (1989), Jeffcoate and Templeton (1991), and Salmons and Babitsky (1992).

CONCLUSION

Object-oriented technology has many different dimensions, viewpoints, and implementation strategies. Those considering using OOD on a project have many different options from which to choose. However, the "right choice" will require careful research.

Significant portions of this article are adapted from Edward V. Berard, *Essays on Object-Oriented Software Engineering,* vol. 1, Prentice Hall, chapts. 1 and 13. Used with permission.

BIBLIOGRAPHY

R. J. Abbott, "Report on Teaching Ada," *Technical Report SAI-81-313-WA,* Science Applications, Inc., McClean, Va., 1980.

R. J. Abbott, "Program Design by Informal English Descriptions," *Communications of the ACM* **26**(11), 882–884 (Nov. 1983).

B. Alabiso, "Transformation of Data Flow Analysis Models to Object-Oriented Design," *OOPSLA '88 Conference Proceedings, Special Issue of SIGPLAN Notices,* Vol. 23, No. 11, Nov. 1988, pp. 335–353.

J. A. Anderson, J. McDonald, L. Holland, and E. Scranage, "Automated Object-Oriented Requirements Analysis and Design,"

Proceedings of the Sixth Washington Ada Symposium, June 26–29, 1989, pp. 265–272.

Reference Manual for the Ada Programming Language, ANSI/MIL-STD 1815A (1983), United States Department of Defense, Feb. 1983.

L. J. Arthur, *Measuring Programmer Productivity and Software Quality,* John Wiley & Sons, New York, 1985.

Air Training Command, *Object-Oriented Design (Student Handout),* USAF Technical Training School, Keesler AFB, Miss., May 1989.

J. Backus, "Can Programming be Liberated From the von Neumann Style?: A Functional Style and Its Algebra of Programs," *Communications of the ACM* **21**(8), 613–641 (Aug. 1978).

J. Backus, "Function Level Computing," *IEEE Spectrum* **19**(8), 22–27 (Aug. 1982).

S. C. Bailey, "Designing With Objects," *Computer Language* **6**(1), 34–43 (Jan. 1989).

K. Beck and W. Cunningham, "A Laboratory for Teaching Object Oriented Thinking," *OOPSLA '89 Conference Proceedings, Special Issue of SIGPLAN Notices,* **24**(10), Oct. 1989, pp. 1–6.

E. V. Berard, *An Object-Oriented Design Handbook for Ada Software,* EVB Software Engineering, Inc., Frederick, Md., 1985.

E. V. Berard, "Object-Oriented Development," *Methodologies and Tools for Real-Time Systems Conference Proceedings,* National Institute for Software Quality and Productivity, Washington, D.C., March 1987, pp. E1–E27.

E. V. Berard, *Essays on Object-Oriented Software Engineering,* Vol. 1, Prentice Hall, Englewood Cliffs, N.J., 1993.

G. D. Bergland, "A Guided Tour of Program Design Methodologies," *IEEE Computer* **14**(10), 18–37 (Oct. 1981).

M. Bewtra, S. C. Balin, and J. M. Moore, "An Ada Design and Implementation Toolset Based on Object-Oriented and Functional Programming Paradigms," *Proceedings of the Seventh Washington Ada Symposium, June 25–28, 1990,* pp. 213–226.

A. Birchenough and J. R. Cameron, "JSD and Object-Oriented Design," *JSP & JSD: The Jackson Approach to Software Development,* IEEE Computer Society Press, Washington, D.C., 1989.

N. D. Biffell and M. A. Ould, *A Practical Handbook for Software Development,* Cambridge University Press, New York, 1985.

M. R. Blaha, W. J. Premerlani, and J. E. Rumbaugh, "Relational Database Design Using an Object-Oriented Approach," *Communications of the ACM* **31**(4), 414–427 (Apr. 1988).

G. Blair, J. Gallagher, D. Hutchison, and D. Sheperd, *Object-Oriented Languages, Systems and Applications,* Halsted Press, New York, 1991.

J. Blank and co-workers, *Software Engineering: Methods and Techniques,* John Wiley & Sons, New York, 1983.

D. Boehm-Davis and L. S. Ross, "Approaches to Structuring the Software Development Process," *General Electric Company Report Number GEC/DIS/TR-84-BIV-1,* Oct. 1984.

G. Booch, "Describing Software Design in Ada," *SIGPLAN Notices* **16**(9), 42–47 (Sept. 1981).

G. Booch, "Object Oriented Design," *Ada Letters* **I**(3), 64–76 (March– April 1982).

G. Booch, *Software Engineering with Ada,* Benjamin/Cummings, Menlo Park, Calif., 1983a.

G. Booch, "Object Oriented Design," *IEEE Tutorial on Software Design Techniques,* 4th ed., P. Freeman and A. I. Wasserman, eds., IEEE Computer Society Press, IEEE Catalog No. EHO205-5, IEEE-CS Order No. 514, 1983b, pp. 420–436.

G. Booch, "Object Oriented Development," *IEEE Transactions on Software Engineering* **SE-12**(2), 211–221 (Feb. 1986).

G. Booch, "On the Concepts of Object-Oriented Design," in P. A. Ng and R. T. Yeh, eds., *Modern Software Engineering: Foundations and Current Perspectives,* Van Nostrand Reinhold, New York, 1990, pp. 165–204.

G. Booch, *Object-Oriented Design With Applications,* Benjamin/Cummings, Menlo Park, Calif., 1991.

S. Boyd, "Object-Oriented Design and PAMELA: A Comparison of Two Design Methods for Ada," *Ada Letters,* Vol. 7, No. 4, July–August 1987, pp. 68–78.

R. J. Brown and V. Dobbs, "A Method for Translating Functional Requirements for Object-Oriented Design," *Proceedings of the Seventh Annual National Conference on Ada Technology,* March 1989, pp. 589–599.

D. Bulman, "Objects Don't Replace Design," *Computer Language,* Vol. **6**(8), 151–152 (Aug. 1989).

W. E. Byrne and E. Wiatrowski, "Object-Oriented Design With Graphical Abstraction," *Proceedings of the Third National Conference on Methodologies and Tools for Real-Time Systems,* National Institute for Software Quality and Productivity, Washington, D.C., Sept. 1986, pp. C-1–C-19.

D. N. Card and R. L. Glass, *Measuring Software Design Quality,* Prentice Hall, Englewood Cliffs, N.J., 1990.

G. Carlson, "Problems Encountered in Learning Object-Oriented Design Using Ada," *Proceedings of the Seventh Annual National Conference on Ada Technology,* March 13–16, 1989, pp. 209–212.

C. Chedgey, S. Kemey, and H.-J. Kugler, "Using VDM in an Object-Oriented Development Method for Ada Software," *VDM '87 VDM—A Formal Method At Work, Proceedings of the 1987 European Symposium,* Springer Verlag Lecture Notes On Computer Science, Number 252, pp. 63–76.

S. R. Chidamber and C. F. Kemerer, "Towards a Metrics Suite for Object-Oriented Design," *OOPSLA '91 Conference Proceedings, Special Issue of SIGPLAN Notices,* Vol. 26, No. 11, November 1991, pp. 197–211.

R. G. Clark, "Designing Concurrent Objects," *Ada Letters* **VII**(6), 107–109 (Fall 1987).

P. Coad and E. Yourdon, *Object-Oriented Design,* Prentice Hall, Englewood Cliffs, N.J., 1991.

D. Coleman, F. Hayes, and S. Bear, "Introducing Objectcharts or How to Use Statecharts in Object-Oriented Design," *IEEE Transactions on Software Engineering* **16**(1), 9–18 (Jan. 1992).

J. M. Coggins, "Designing C++ Class Libraries," *Proceedings of the C++ Conference, San Francisco, California, April 1990,* USENIX Association, Berkeley, Calif., 1990, pp. 25–35.

E. Colbert, "The Object-Oriented Software Development Method: A Practical Approach to Object-Oriented Development," *Proceedings of TRI-Ada '89—Ada Technology In Context: Application, Development, and Deployment, October 23–26, 1989,* Association for Computing Machinery, New York, pp. 400–415.

M. F. Connor, *SADT: Structured Analysis and Design Technique—Introduction,* SofTech, Inc., Waltham, Mass., May 22, 1980. (Submitted to *Guide 50,* Houston, Texas.)

S. D. Conte, H. E. Sunsmore, and V. Y. Shen, *Software Engineering Metrics and Models,* Benjamin/Cummings, Menlo Park, California, 1986.

O. J. Dahl and K. Nygaard, "SIMULA—an ALGOL-Based Simulation Language," *Communications of the ACM* **9**(9), 671–678 (Sept. 1966).

N. W. Davis and M. Irving, "Practical Experiences of Ada and Object-Oriented Design In Real-Time Distributed Systems,"

Ada: the Design Choice—Proceedings of the Ada-Europe Conference, Madrid 13–15 June 1989, Cambridge University Press, Cambridge, U.K., 1989, pp. 59–79.

T. De Marco, *Structured Analysis and System Specification,* Yourdon Press, New York, 1978.

E. Dijkstra, "Structured Programming," Presented at the 1969 NATO Science Committee Conference. Reprinted in Yourdon, (1979), pp. 113–125.

C. M. Donaldson, "Dynamic Binding and Inheritance in an Object-Oriented Ada Design," *Ada: the Design Choice—Proceedings of the Ada-Europe Conference, Madrid 13–15 June 1989,* Cambridge University Press, Cambridge, U.K., 1989, pp. 16–25.

J. B. Dreger, *Function Point Analysis,* Prentice Hall, Englewood Cliffs, N.J., 1989.

L. O. Ejiogu, *Software Engineering With Formal Metrics,* QED Technical Publishing Group, Boston, Mass., 1991.

C. Finkelstein, *An Introduction to Information Engineering: From Strategic Planning to Information Systems,* Addison-Wesley, Reading, Mass., 1989.

P. Freeman and A. I. Wasserman, *Software Development Methodologies and Ada (Methodman),* Department of Defense Ada Joint Program Office, Arlington, Va., 1982.

R. Gallimore, D. Coleman, and V. Stravridou, "UMIST OBJ: A Language for Executable Program Specifications," *Computer Journal* **32**(5),413–521 (Oct. 1989).

C. Gane and T. Sarson, *Structured Systems Analysis: Tools and Techniques,* Improved System Technologies, New York, 1977.

M. Gardner, "Successes and Limitations of Object-Oriented Design," *Journal of Pascal, Ada, and Modula-2* **7**(6), 30–41 (Nov./Dec. 1988).

T. Gilb, *Software Metrics,* Winthrop Publishers, Cambridge, Mass., 1977.

J. A. Goguen, "Parameterized Programming," *IEEE Transactions on Software Engineering* **SE-10**(5), 528–543 (Sept. 1984).

A. Goldberg and A. Kay, Editors, *Smalltalk-72 Instructional Manual,* Technical Report SSL-76-6, Xerox PARC, Palo Alto, Calif., March 1976.

A. Goldberg and D. Robson, *Smalltalk-80: The Language and Its Implementation,* Addison-Wesley, Reading, Mass., 1983.

H. Gomaa, "A Software Design Method for Real-Time Systems," *Communications of the ACM* **27**(9), 938–949 (Sept. 1984).

R. B. Grady and D. L. Caswell, *Software Metrics: Establishing a Company-Wide Program,* Prentice Hall, Englewood Cliffs, N.J., 1987.

L. Gray, "Procedures for Transitioning from Structured Methods to Object-Oriented Design," *Proceedings of the Conference on Methodologies and Tools for Real-Time Systems IV,* National Institute for Software Quality and Productivity, Washington, D.C., September 14–15 1987, pp. R-1–R-21.

L. Gray, "Transitioning from Structured Analysis to Object-Oriented Design," *Proceedings of the Fifth Washington Ada Symposium, June 27–30, 1988,* Association for Computing Machinery, New York, 1988, pp. 151–162.

P. Grogono and A. Bennett, "Polymorphism and Type Checking in Object-Oriented Languages," *SIGPLAN Notices* **24**(11), 109–115 (Nov. 1989).

D. Harel, "Statecharts: A Visual Formalism for Complex Systems," *Science of Computer Programming* **8**(3), 231–274 (June 1, 1987).

D. Harel, A. Pnueli, J. P. Schmidt, and R. Sherman, "On the Formal Semantics of Statecharts," *Proceedings of the Second IEEE Symposium on the Logic of Computer Science,* 1987, pp. 54–64.

D. J. Hatley and I. A. Pirbhai, *Strategies for Real-Time System Specification,* Dorset House Publishing Company, New York, 1987.

M. Heitz, "HOOD: A Hierarchical Object-Oriented Design Method," *Proceedings of the Third German Ada Users Congress,* Jan. 1988, Gesellschaft fur Software Engineering, Munich, West Germany, pp. 12-1–12-9.

M. Heitz and B. Labreuille, "Design and Development of Distributed Software Using Hierarchical Object Oriented Design and Ada," in *Ada In Industry: Proceedings of the Ada-Europe International Conference Munich 7–9 June, 1988,* Cambridge University Press, Cambridge, U.K., 1988, pp. 143–156.

B. Henderson-Sellers, "Hybrid Object-Oriented/Functional Decomposition Methodologies for the Software Engineering Lifecycle," *Hotline on Object-Oriented Technology* **2**(7), 1, 2–8 (May 1991).

B. Henderson-Sellers and L. L. Constantine, "Object-Oriented Development and Functional Decomposition," *Journal of Object-Oriented Programming* **3**(5), 11–17 (Jan./Feb. 1991).

C. A. R. Hoare, *Communicating Sequential Processes,* Prentice Hall, Englewood Cliffs, N.J., 1985.

P. Hruschka, "Towards An Object-Oriented Method for System Architecture Design," *Proceedings of the 1990 IEEE International Conference on Computer Systems and Software Engineering—EuroComp '90,* Tel-Aviv, Israel, May 8–10, 1990, pp. 12–17.

M. Hull, A. Zarea-Aliabadi, and D. Gutherie, "Object-Oriented Design, Jackson System Development (JSD) Specifications and Concurrency," *Software Engineering Journal* **4**(2), 79–86 (March 1989).

M. A. Jackson, *System Development,* Prentice Hall, Englewood Cliffs, N.J., 1983.

M. I. Jackson, "Developing Ada Programs Using the Vienna Development Method (VDM)," *Software Practice and Experience* **15**(3), 305–318 (March 1985).

P. Jalote, "Functional Refinement and Nested Objects for Object-Oriented Design," *IEEE Transactions on Software Engineering* **15**(3), 264–270 (March 1989).

K. A. Jamsa, "Object Oriented Design vs. Structured Design—A Student's Perspective," *Software Engineering Notes* **9**(1), 43–49 (Jan. 1984).

A. Jaworski and D. LaVallee, "Principles for Defining an Object-Oriented Design Decomposition in Ada," *Proceedings of the Seventh Washington Ada Symposium, June 25–28,* 1990, pp. 173–182.

J. Jeffcoate and A. Templeton, *Object Technology Sourcebook,* Ovum, Ltd., London, U.K., 1991.

R. Jochem, M. Rabe, W. Süssenguth, and P. Bals, "An Object-Oriented Analysis and Design Methodology for Computer Integrated Manufacturing Systems," *Technology of Object-Oriented Languages and Systems 1989 (TOOLS '89),* Paris, France, Nov. 13–15, 1989, pp. 75–84.

R. E. Johnson and B. Foote, "Designing Reusable Classes," *Journal of Object-Oriented Programming* **1**(2), 22–35 (July/Aug. 1988).

C. B. Jones, *Systematic Software Development Using VDM,* Prentice Hall, Englewood Cliffs, N.J., 1986.

C. Jones, *Applied Software Measurement: Assuring Productivity and Quality,* McGraw-Hill, Inc., New York, 1991.

A. Kay, *The Reactive Engine,* Department of Computer Science, University of Utah, Aug. 1969.

A. C. Kay, "Microelectronics and the Personal Computer," *Scientific American* **237**(3), 230–244 (Sept. 1977).

J. C. Kelly, "A Comparison of Four Design Methods for Real-Time Systems," *Proceedings of the 9th International Conference on Software Engineering,* March 30–April 2, 1987, pp. 238–252.

G. K. Khalsa, "Using Object Modeling to Transform Structured Analysis Into Object-Oriented Design," *Proceedings of the Sixth Washington Ada Symposium,* June 26–29, 1989, pp. 201–212.

K. J. Lee and M. S. Rissman, *An Object-Oriented Solution Example: A Flight Simulator Electrical System,* Technical Report CMU/SEI-89-TR-5, Software Engineering Institute, Pittsburgh, Pa., 1989.

K. J. Lee, M. S. Rissman, R. D. D'Ippolito, C. Plinta, and R. Van Scoy, *An OOD Paradigm for Flight Simulators,* Technical Report CMU/SEI-87-TR-43 (ESD-TR-87-206), Software Engineering Institute, Pittsburgh, Pa., 1987.

X. Li, "Integration of Structured and Object-Oriented Programming," in *Focus On Analysis and Design,* SIGS Publications, Inc., New York, 1991, pp. 54–60.

K. J. Lieberherr and A. J. Riel, "Contributions to Teaching Object-Oriented Design and Programming," *OOPSLA '89 Conference Proceedings, Special Issue of SIGPLAN Notices,* Vol. 24, No. 10, October 1989, pp. 11–22.

M. E. S. Loomis, A. V. Shaw, and J. E. Raumbaugh, "An Object Modeling Technique for Conceptual Design," *Proceedings of ECOOP '87: European Conference on Object-Oriented Programming,* Springer Verlag, New York, 1987, pp. 192–202.

J. T. Lukman, "Transforming the 2167A Requirements Definition Model Into an Ada-Object-Oriented Design," *Proceedings of the Ninth Annual National Conference on Ada Technology,* March 4–7, 1991, pp. 200–205.

D. A. Marca and C. L. McGowan, *SADT—Structured Analysis and Design Technique,* McGraw-Hill, New York, 1988.

C. D. Marable and C. C. Belgrave, "Designing an Ada Tutorial Using Object-Oriented Design," *Proceedings of the Eighth Annual National Conference on Ada Technology,* March 1990, pp. 19–20.

D. A. Marca and C. L. McGowan, *SADT—Structured Analysis and Design Technique,* McGraw-Hill, New York, 1988.

J. Martin, *Information Engineering, Book 1: Introduction,* Prentice Hall, Englewood Cliffs, N.J., 1989.

J. Martin, *Information Engineering, Book 2: Planning and Analysis,* Prentice Hall, Englewood Cliffs, N.J., 1990.

J. Martin, *Information Engineering, Book 3: Design and Construction,* Prentice Hall, Englewood Cliffs, N.J., 1990.

P. Masiero and F. S. R. Germano, "JSD As An Object-Oriented Design Method," *Software Engineering Notes* **13**(3), 22–23 (July 1988).

S. C. McIntyre and L. F. Higgins, "Object-Oriented Systems Analysis and Design: Methodology and Application," *Journal of Management Information Systems* **5**(1), 25–35 (Summer 1988).

K. McQuown, "Object-Oriented Design in a Real-Time Multiprocessor Environment," *Proceedings of TRI-Ada '89—Ada Technology In Context: Application, Development, and Deployment, October 23–26, 1989,* Association for Computing Machinery, New York, pp. 570–588.

C. Meyer, M. Wallis, and M. Meier, "Experiences in Applying the Layered Virtual Machine/Object-Oriented Development Methodology to an Ada Design Effort," *Proceedings of TRI-Ada '89—Ada Technology In Context: Application, Development, and Deployment, October 23–26, 1989,* Association for Computing Machinery, New York, pp. 416–425.

S. B. Mickell "Experiences With an Object-Oriented Method of Software Design," *Proceedings of the Third Joint Ada Europe/AdaTech Conference,* Cambridge University Press, Cambridge, U.K., 1984, pp. 271–280.

M. Mullin, *Object-Oriented Program Design: With Examples in C++,* Addison-Wesley Publishing Company, Reading, Mass., 1989.

G. J. Myers, *Reliable Software through Composite Design,* Van Nostrand Reinhold Company, New York, 1975.

G. J. Myers, *Software Reliability Principles and Practices,* John Wiley & Sons, New York, 1976.

G. J. Myers, *Composite/Structured Design,* Van Nostrand Reinhold Company, New York, 1978.

K. W. Nielsen and K. Shumate, "Designing Large Real-Time Systems With Ada," *Communications of the ACM* **30**(8), 695–715 (Aug. 1987).

J. Pendley, "Using Information Engineering and Ada Object-Oriented Design Methods in Concert—A Case Study," *Proceedings of the Sixth Washington Ada Symposium,* June 26–29, 1989, pp. 11–19.

W. W. Y. Pun and R. L. Winder, "A Design Method for Object-Oriented Programming," *ECOOP '89: Proceedings of the European Conference on Object-Oriented Programming, British Computer Society Workshop Series,* Cambridge University Press, Cambridge, U.K., 1989, pp. 225–240.

G. P. Reed and Donald E. Bynum, "Analyzing Systems for Object-Oriented Design," *Proceedings of the Sixth Washington Ada Symposium,* June 26–29, 1989, pp. 195–200.

J. E. Richardson, R. C. Schultz, and E. V. Berard, *A Complete Object-Oriented Design Example,* Berard Software Engineering, Gaithersburg, Maryland, 1992.

D. C. Rine, "A Brief Comparison of Ada and Object-Oriented Design Elements for Ada," *Proceedings of the Second Annual Conference on Artificial Intelligence and Ada,* 1986, pp. 10-1–10-10.

D. C. Rine, "A Common Error in the Object Structure of Object-Oriented Design Methods," *Software Engineering Notes* **12**(4), 42–44 (Oct. 1987).

D. C. Rine, "A Proposed Standard Set of Principles for Object-Oriented Development," *Software Engineering Notes* **16**(1), 43–49 (Jan. 1991).

M. B. Rosson and E. Gold, "Problem-Solution Mapping In Object-Oriented Design," *OOPSLA '89 Conference Proceedings, Special Issue of SIGPLAN Notices,* Vol. 24, No. 10, October 1989, pp. 7–10.

J. Rumbaugh, M. Blaha, W. Premerlani, F. Eddy, and W. Lorensen, *Object-Oriented Modeling and Design,* Prentice Hall, Englewood Cliffs, N.J., 1991.

J. Salmons and T. Babitsky, *1992 International OOP Directory,* SIGS Publications, Inc., New York, 1992.

M. E. Scharenberg and H. E. Dunsmore, "Evolution of Classes and Objects During Object-Oriented Design and Programming," *Journal of Object-Oriented Programming* **3**(5), 18–28 (Jan./Feb. 1991).

E. Seidewitz and M. Stark, "Towards a General Object-Oriented Software Development Methodology," ed., R. L. Brown, *Proceedings of the First International Conference on Ada Programming Language Applications for the NASA Space Station, Vol. II,* University of Houston—Clear Lake, June 1986 pp. D.4.6.1–D.4.6.14.

E. Seidewitz and M. Stark, *General Object-Oriented Software Development,* Document No. SEL-86-002, NASA Goddard Space Flight Center, Greenbelt, Md., 1986b.

K. Shumate, "Layered Virtual Machine/Object-Oriented Design," *Proceedings of the Fifth Washington Ada Symposium, June*

27–30, 1988, Association for Computing Machinery, New York, 1988, pp. 177– 190.

J. M. Spivey, *Understanding Z: A Specification Language and Its Formal Semantics,* Cambridge University Press, Cambridge, U.K., 1988.

J. M. Spivey, *The Z Notation: A Reference Manual,* Prentice Hall, Englewood Cliffs, N.J., 1989.

M. Stark and E. V. Seidewitz, "Towards a General Object-Oriented Ada Life-Cycle," *Proceedings of the Joint Ada Conference, Fifth National Conference on Ada Technology and Washington Ada Symposium,* U.S. Army Communications-Electronics Command, Fort Monmouth, N.J., 1987, pp. 213–222.

W. P. Stevens, G. J. Myers and L. L. Constantine, "Structured Design," *IBM Systems Journal* **13**(2), 115–139 (May 1974). Reprinted in P. Freeman and A. I. Wasserman, eds., *Tutorial on Software Design Techniques,* 4th ed., IEEE Computer Society Press (catalog number EHO205-5), Silver Spring, Md., 1983, pp. 328–352.

B. Stroustrup, *The C++ Programming Language,* 2nd ed., Addison-Wesley, Reading, Mass., 1991.

D. K. Taylor and A. Hecht, "Using CASE for Object-Oriented Design with C++," *Computer Language* **7**(11), 49– 57 (Nov. 1990).

Teledyne Brown Engineering, *Software Methodology Catalog,* Technical Report MC87-COMM/ADP-0036, Tinton Falls, N.J., Oct. 1987.

H. Toetenel, J. van Katwijk, and N. Plat, "Structured Analysis—Formal Design, Using Stream and Object-Oriented Formal Specification," *Proceedings of the ACM SIGSOFT International Workshop on Formal Methods in Software Development,* Special Issue of Software Engineering Notes, Vol. 15, No. 4, September 1990, pp. 118–127.

R. F. Vidale and C. R. Hayden, "A Student Project to Extend Object-Oriented Design," *Proceedings of the Ada Software Engineering Education and Training Symposium,* June 9–11, 1987, pp. 89–98.

P. Vielcanet, "HOOD Design Method and Control/Command Techniques for the Development of Realtime Software," *Proceedings of the Sixth Washington Ada Symposium,* June 26–29, 1989, pp. 213–219.

J. M. Vlissides and M. A. Linton, "Applying Object-Oriented Design to Structured Graphics," *Proceedings of the C++ Conference, Denver, Colorado, October 1988,* USENIX Association, Berkeley, Calif., 1988, pp. 81–94.

N. L. Walters, "An Ada Object-Based Analysis and Design Approach," *Ada Letters* **XI**(5), 62–78 (July/August 1991).

P. T. Ward, "How to Integrate Object Orientation with Structured Analysis and Design," *IEEE Software* **6**(2), 74–82 (March 1989).

P. T. Ward and S. J. Mellor, *Structured Development for Real-Time Systems,* Vols. 1, 2 and 3, Yourdon Press, New York, 1985.

A. I. Wasserman, P. Pitcher, and R. J. Muller, "An Object-Oriented Design Method for Code Generation," *Software Engineering Notes* **14**(1), 32–55 (Jan. 1989).

A. I. Wasserman, P. Percher, and R. J. Muller, "An Object-Oriented Design Notation for Software Design Representation," *IEEE Computer* **23**(3), 50–63 (March 1990).

P. Wegner, "Concepts and Paradigms of Object-Oriented Programming," *OOPS Messenger* **1**(1), 7–87 (Aug. 1990).

R. S. Wiener, ed., *Focus On Analysis and Design,* SIGS Publications, Inc., New York, 1991.

R. J. Wirfs-Brock and R. E. Johnson, "Surveying Current Research in Object-Oriented Design," *Communications of the ACM* **33**(9),105–124 (Sept. 1990).

R. Wirfs-Brock and B. Wilkerson, "Object-Oriented Design: A Responsibility-Driven Approach," *OOPSLA '89 Conference Proceedings, Special Issue of SIGPLAN Notices,* Vol. 24, No. 10, Oct. 1989, pp. 71–76.

R. Wirfs-Brock, B. Wilkerson, and L. Wiener, *Designing Object-Oriented Software,* Prentice Hall, Englewood Cliffs, N.J., 1990.

S. S. Yau and J. J.-P. Tsai, "A Survey of Software Design Techniques," *IEEE Transactions on Software Engineering* **SE-12**(6), 713–721 (June 1986).

E. N. Yourdon, ed., *Classics in Software Engineering,* Yourdon Press, New York, 1979.

E. Yourdon and L. L. Constantine, *Structured Design: Fundamentals of a Discipline of Computer Program and System Design,* Prentice Hall, Englewood Cliffs, N.J., 1979.

EDWARD V. BERARD
Berard Software Engineering, Inc.

OBJECT-ORIENTED DEVELOPMENT

HISTORICAL PERSPECTIVE

The object-oriented model for software development has become exceedingly attractive as the best answer to the increasingly complex needs of the software development community. What was first viewed by many as a research curiosity and an impractical approach to industrial strength software is now being enthusiastically embraced. Object-oriented versions of most languages have been or are being developed. Numerous object-oriented methodologies have been proposed. Conferences, seminars, and courses on object-oriented topics are extremely popular. New journals and countless special issues of both academic and professional journals have been devoted to the subject. Contracts for software development which specify object-oriented techniques and languages currently have a competitive edge. Object-oriented development is to the 1990s what structured development was to the 1970s, and the object-oriented movement is still accelerating.

Concepts like "objects" and "attributes of objects" actually date back to the early 1950s when they appeared in early works in Artificial Intelligence (Berard, 1993). However, the real legacy of the object-oriented movement began in 1966 when Kristen Nygaard and Ole-Johan Dahl moved to higher levels of abstraction and introduced the language Simula. Simula provided encapsulation at a more abstract level than subprograms; data abstraction and classes were introduced in order to simulate a problem. During approximately this same time frame, Alan Kay was working at the University of Utah on a personal computer that he hoped would be able to support graphics and simulation. Due to both hardware and software limitations, Flex, Kay's computer venture, was unsuccessful. However his ideas were not lost and surfaced again when he joined Xerox at Palo Alto Research Center (PARC) in the early 1970s.

At PARC he was a member of a project that espoused the belief that computer technologies are the key to improving communication channels between people and between people and machines. Based upon this conviction and influenced by the class concept in Simula; the turtle ideas LOGO provided in the Pen classes; the abstract data typing in CLU; and the incremental program execution of LISP; the group developed Smalltalk. In 1972, the first version of Smalltalk was released by PARC. About this time the term "object-oriented" was coined. Some people credit Alan Kay because he is said to have used the term to characterize Smalltalk. Smalltalk is considered to be the first true object-oriented language (Goldberg, 1983), and today Smalltalk remains the quintescential object-oriented language. The goal of Smalltalk has been to enable the design of software in units that are as autonomous as possible. Everything in the language is an object; that is, an instance of a class. Objects in this nascent Smalltalk world have been associated with nouns. The Smalltalk effort has supported a highly interactive development environment and prototyping. This original work has not been publicized and has been viewed with academic interest as highly experimental.

Smalltalk-80 was the culmination of a number of versions of the PARC Smalltalk, and was released to the non-Xerox world in 1981. The August 1981 issue of *Byte* featured the Smalltalk efforts. On the cover of the issue was a picture of a hot air balloon leaving an isolated island which symbolized the launch of the PARC object-oriented ideas. It was time to start publicizing to the software development community. The impact was gradual at first but mounted to the current level of flurry about object-oriented techniques and products. The balloon was in fact launched and there was an effect. The early Smalltalk research in environments led to window, icon, mouse and pulldown window environments. The Smalltalk language influenced the development in the early to mid 1980s of other object-oriented languages, most notably: Objective-C (1986), C++ (1986), Self (1987), Eiffel (1987), and Flavors (1986). The application of object-orientation was broadened. Objects no longer were associated just with nouns, but also with events and processes. In 1980, Grady Booch pioneered with the concept of object-oriented design (Booch, 1982). Since then others have followed suit, and object-oriented analysis techniques have also begun to be publicized. In 1985, the first commercial object-oriented database system was introduced. Most recently, object-oriented domain analysis, testing, metrics and management are being investigated.

MOTIVATION

Why has the object-oriented movement gained such momentum? In reality some of its popularity probably stems from the hope that it, like so many other earlier software development innovations, will address the crying needs for greater productivity, reliability, maintainability, and manageability. However, aside from the hope that object-orientation is in fact the "silver bullet," there are many other documented arguments to motivate its adoption.

Object-oriented development adds emphasis on direct mapping of concepts in the problem domain to software units and their interfaces. Furthermore, it is felt by some that based upon recent studies in psychology, viewing the world as objects is more natural since it is closer to the way humans think. Objects are more stable than functions; what most often precipitates software changes is change in required functionality, not change in the players, or objects. In addition, object-oriented development supports and encourages the software engineering practices of information hiding, data abstraction, and encapsulation. In an object, revisions are localized. Object-orientation results in software that is easily modified, extended, and maintained (Berard, 1993). Object-orientation extends across the life cycle in that a consistent approach is used from analysis through coding. The use of object-oriented development encourages the reuse of not only software but also design and analysis. Furthermore, object-oriented development facilitates interoperability; that is, the degree to which an application running on one node of a network can make use of a resource at a different node of the network. Object-oriented development also supports the concurrency, hierarchy and complexity present in some of today's software systems. It is currently necessary to build systems, not just black-box applications. These complex systems are often hierarchically composed of different kinds of subsystems. Object-oriented development supports open systems; there is much greater flexibility to integrate software across applications. Finally, use of the object-oriented approach tends to reduce the risk of developing complex systems, primarily because system integration is diffused throughout the life cycle (Booch, 1991).

OBJECT-ORIENTED MODEL

The object-oriented model is more than a collection of new languages: it is a new way of thinking about what it means to compute and about how information can be structured. In the object-oriented model, systems are viewed as cooperating objects which encapsulate structure and behavior and which belong to classes which are hierarchically constructed. All functionality is achieved by messages which are passed to and from objects. The object-oriented model can be viewed as a conceptual framework with the following elements: abstraction, encapsulation, modularity, hierarchy, typing, concurrence, persistence, reusability and extensibility.

The emergence of the object-oriented model does not mark any sort of computing revolution. Instead, object-orientation is the next step in a methodical evolution from both procedural approaches and strictly data-driven approaches. New approaches to software development have been precipitated by both programming language developments and increased sophistication and breadth in the problem domains for which software systems are being designed. While in practice the analysis and design processes ideally precede implementation, it has been the language innovations which have necessitated new approaches to design and then later, analysis. Language evolution in turn has been a natural response to enhanced architecture capabilities and the ever increasingly sophis-

object-oriented software development has followed this general trend. Figure 1 depicts the many contributing influences.

Perhaps the most significant influencing factors are the advances in programming methodology. Over the last several decades the support for abstraction in languages has progressed to higher levels. This abstraction progression has gone from address (machine languages), to name (assembly languages), to expression (First Generation languages, e.g., FORTRAN), to control (Second Generation languages, e.g., COBOL) to procedure and function (Second and early Third Generation languages, e.g., Pascal), to modules and data (late Third Generation languages, e.g.. Modula 2), and finally to objects (object-based and object-oriented languages). The development of Smalltalk and other object-oriented languages as discussed above has necessitated the discovery of different analysis, and design techniques.

These new object-oriented techniques are really the culmination of the structured and database approaches. In the object-oriented approach, the smaller scale concerns of data flow-orientation, like coupling and cohesion, are very relevant (Booch, 1992). Similarly, the behavior within objects of the object-oriented approach will ultimately require a function-oriented design approach. The ideas of the entity relationship (ER) approach to data modeling from the database technology are also embodied in the object-oriented model.

Likewise, advances in computer architecture, both in the increased capability combined with decrease in cost, and in the introduction of objects into hardware (capability systems and hardware support for operating systems concepts) have impacted the object-oriented movement. Object-oriented programming languages are frequently memory and MIPS intensive. They have required and are now utilizing added hardware power. And finally, philosophy and cognitive science have influenced the advancement of

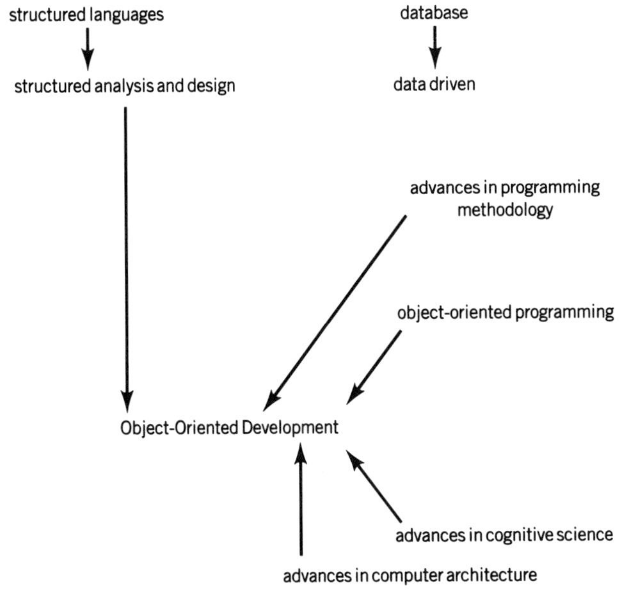

Figure 1. Influences in object-oriented development.

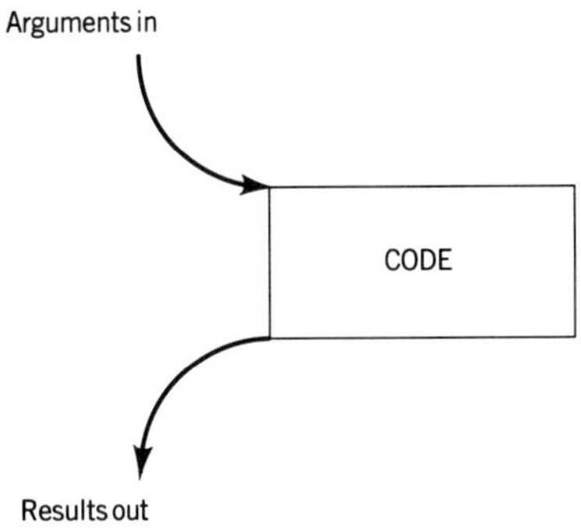

Figure 2. Procedural model.

the object-oriented model in their hierarchy and classification theories (Booch, 1991).

Because there are many and varied influences on object-oriented development and because this approach has not reached maturity, there is still considerable diversity in thinking and terminology and unfortunately confusion. All object-oriented languages are not created equal nor do they refer to the same concepts with consistent verbiage "across the board." Likewise there is no consensus on how to do object-oriented analysis and object-oriented design nor the symbology to use in order to depict these activities. Nevertheless, object-oriented development has already proven successful in many application areas including: air traffic control, animation, banking, business data processing, command and control systems, computer-aided design (CAD), computer integrated manufacturing, databases, document preparation, expert systems, hypermedia, image recognition, mathematical analysis, music composition, operating systems, process control, robotics, space station software, telecommunications, telemetry systems, user interface design, and VLSI design.

OBJECT-ORIENTED PROGRAMMING

Concepts

Since the object-oriented programming efforts predate the other object-oriented development techniques, it is reasonable to focus first on object-oriented programming. In object-oriented programming, programs are organized as cooperating collections of objects, each of which is an instance of some class and whose classes are all members of a hierarchy of classes united via inheritance relations (Booch, 1991). Object-oriented languages are characterized by the following: object-creation facility, message-passing capability, class capability and inheritance. While these concepts can and have been used individually in other languages, they complement each other synergistically in object-oriented languages.

Figure 2 illustrates the procedural programming model. To achieve functionality, arguments are passed to a procedure and results are passed back. Object-oriented languages involve a change of perspective. As depicted in Figure 3, functionality is achieved through communication with the interface of an object. An object can be defined to be an entity that encapsulates state and behavior; that is,

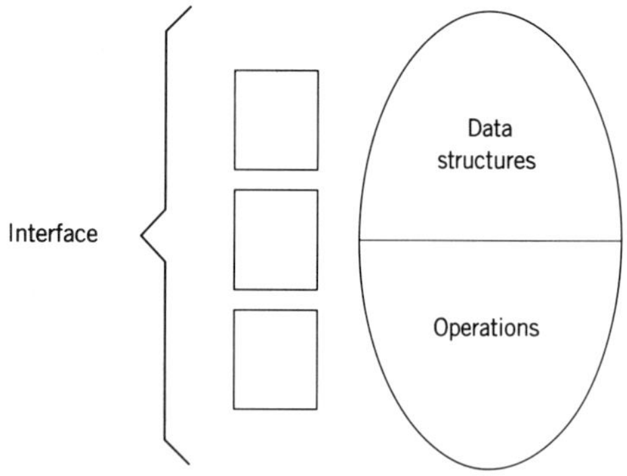

Figure 3. Object-oriented model.

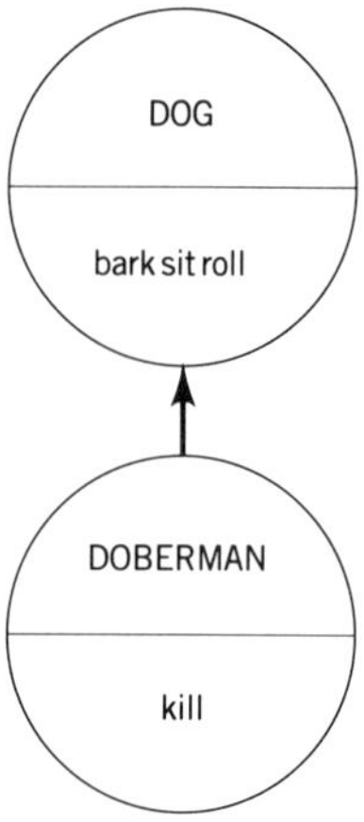

Figure 5. Inheritance.

data structures (or attributes) and operations. The interface, also called the protocol, of the object is the set of messages to which it will respond. Messaging is the way objects communicate and therefore the way that functionality is achieved. Objects respond to the receipt of messages by either performing an internal operation, also sometimes called a method or routine, or by delegating the operation to be performed by another object. All objects are instances of classes, which are sets of objects with similar characteristics or, from another viewpoint, a template from which new objects may be created. The method invoked by an object in response to a message is determined by the class of this receiver object. All objects of a given class use the same method in response to similar messages. Figure 4 shows a DOG class and objects instantiated from the dog class. All the DOG objects respond in the same way to the messages sit, bark, and roll. All DOG objects will also have the same state (data structures) though the values contained in what are typically called state variables can vary from DOG object to DOG object.

Classes can be arranged in a hierarchy. A subclass will inherit state and behavior from its superclass higher in the inheritance hierarchy structure. Inheritance can be defined as the transfer of a class' capabilities and characteristics to its subclasses. Figure 5 shows a subclass DOBERMAN of the original DOG class. An object of the DOBERMAN class will have the bark, sit, and roll behavior of the DOG class, but in addition, the kill behavior particular to the DOBERMAN class. When a message is sent to an object, the search for the corresponding method begins in the class of the object and will progress up the superclass chain until such a method is found or until the chain has been exhausted (when an error would occur). In some languages it is possible for a given class to inherit from more than one superclass. This capability is called multiple inheritance.

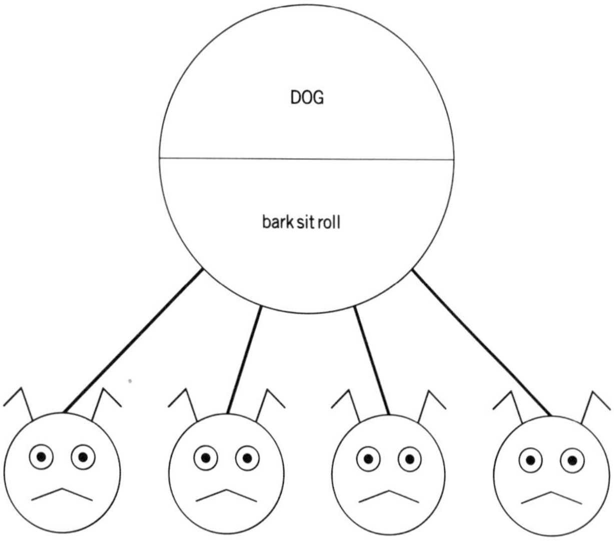

Figure 4. Instantiation of objects from a class.

When dynamic binding is present, inheritance results in polymorphism. Polymorphism essentially describes the phenomenon that a given message sent to an object will be interpreted differently at execution, based upon subclass determination. Figure 6 illustrates a superclass UNMEMBER with its subclasses. If the message "speak" is sent to an object, at execution time it will be determined where the appropriate speak method will be found based upon the current subclass association of the object. Thus the polymorphism means that the speak capability will vary and in fact will be determined at execution. It is possible for a method to not be actually defined in the superclass but still be included in the interface and hence be inherited by subclasses. One calls such a superclass an abstract class. Abstract classes do not have instances and are used only to create subclasses. For example, UNMEMBER would be an abstract class if the method for the message speak was not defined in UNMEMBER. Including speak in the interface of UNMEMBER, however, would dictate that speak would be a message common to all subclasses of UNMEMBER but the exact speak behavior would vary with each subclass. Abstract classes are used to capture commonality without determining idiosyncratic behavior.

Languages

There are essentially four branches of object-oriented languages: Smalltalk-based, C-based, LISP-based, and Pascal based. Simula is actually the common ancestor of all of these languages. The terminology and capability of the object-oriented languages varies considerably. A sampling of popular object-oriented languages in each branch is

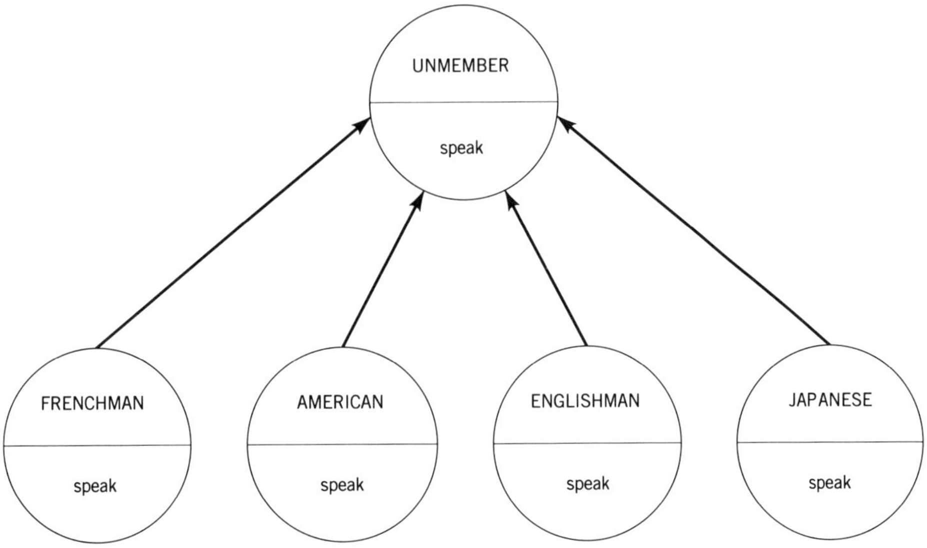

Figure 6. Polymorphism.

given in Table 1. The Smalltalk-based languages include the five versions, including Smalltalk-80, developed at PARC as well as Digitalk Smalltalk and other such versions. Smalltalk 80 is considered the truest object-oriented language although it and the others in this group do not have multiple inheritance capability.

In the C-based category are languages which are derived from C. Objective-C was developed by Brad Cox, has an extensive library and has been used successfully to build large systems (Saunders, 1989). C++ was written by Bjarne Stroustrup of AT&T Bell Labs. Cs STRUCT concept is extended in C++ to provide class capability with data hiding. Polymorphism is implemented by virtual functions which deviate from the normal C typing which is still resolved at compilation. C++ Version 2.0 includes multiple inheritance. C++ is a popular choice in many software areas, especially those where UNIX is preferred.

The many dialects including LOOPS, Flavors, Common LOOPS, and New Flavors, in the LISP-based branch have been precipitated by knowledge representation research. Common LISP Object System (CLOS) has been an effort to standardize object-oriented LISP. The Pascal-based languages have included, among others, Object Pascal and Turbo Pascal as well as Eiffel. Object Pascal has been developed by Apple and Niklaus Wirth for the Macintosh. The class library for Object Pascal is MacApp. Turbo Pascal, developed by Borland, has followed the Object Pascal lead. Eiffel has been released by Bertrand Meyer of Interactive Software Engineering, Inc. in 1987. Eiffel is a full object-oriented language that has an Ada-like syntax and operates in a UNIX environment.

There are also languages which are referred to as object-based. A sample of object-based languages appears in Table 2. Object-based languages differ from object-oriented languages extensibly in their lack of inheritance capability. It should be noted that while Ada is object-based, its successor, Ada 9X, will be object-oriented.

OBJECT-ORIENTED SOFTWARE ENGINEERING

Life Cycle

While the object-oriented languages are exciting developments, coding is not the primary source of problems in software development. Requirements and design problems are much more prevalent and much more costly to correct. The focus on object-oriented development techniques, therefore, should not be strictly on the programming aspects, but more appropriately on the other aspects of software engineering. The promise object-oriented methodologies hold for attacking complexity during analysis and design and accomplishing analysis and design reuse, is truly significant. If it is accepted that object-oriented development is more than object-oriented coding, then a whole new approach, including life cycle, must be adopted (Henderson-Sellers, 1990).

Table 1. Object-Oriented Languages

Smalltalk-80
Objective C
C++
Flavors XLISP
LOOPS
CLOS
Object Pascal
Turbo Pascal
Eiffel

Table 2. Object-Based Languages

Alphard
CLU
Euclid
Gypsy
Mesa
Modula
Ada

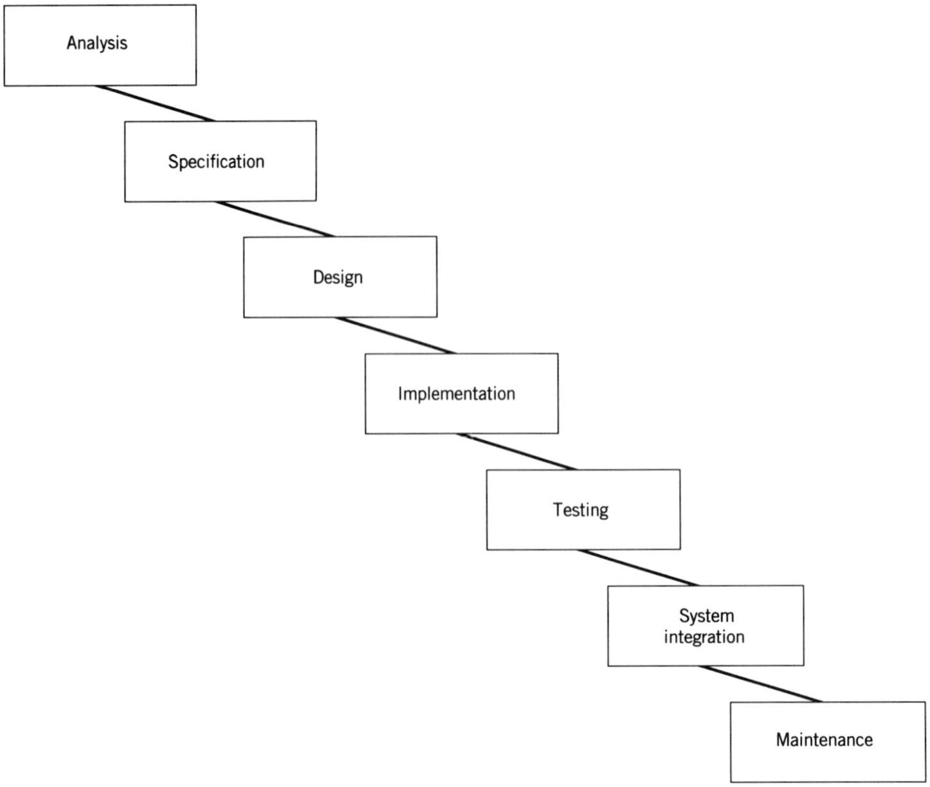

Figure 7. Waterfall life cycle.

The most widely accepted life cycle to date is the waterfall/structured life cycle (Lorenz, 1993). The waterfall organization has come into existence to stem the ad hoc approaches which had led to the software crisis as it was first noted in the late 1960s. A version of the waterfall life cycle is pictured in Figure 7. As is shown, the process is sequential; activities flow in primarily one direction. There is little provision for change and the assumption is that the system is quite clearly understood during the initial stages. Unfortunately, any software engineering effort will inherently involve a great deal of iteration, whether it is scheduled or not. Good designers have been described as practitioners who work at several levels of abstraction and detail simultaneously (Curtis, 1989). The waterfall life cycle does not accommodate real iteration. The waterfall/structured life cycle is also criticized for placing no emphasis on reuse and no unifying model to integrate the phases (Korson, 1990).

The object-oriented approach admits and supports iteration. Figure 8 illustrates a version of the water fountain life cycle which has been used to describe the object-oriented development process. The fountain idea conveys that the development is inherently iterative and seamless. The same portion of the system is usually worked on a number of times with functionality being added to the evolving system with each iteration. Prototyping and feedback loops are standard. The seamlessness is accounted for in the lack of distinct boundaries during the traditional activities of analysis, design, and coding. The reason for removing the boundaries is that the concept of object permeates; objects and their relationships are the medium of expression for each of analysis, design and implementation. There is also a switch of effort from coding to analysis and an emphasis on data structure before function. Furthermore, the iterative and seamless nature of object-oriented development makes the inclusion of reuse activities natural.

Object-Oriented Analysis (OOA) and Object-Oriented Design (OOD)

Since object-oriented technology is still relatively new, there is, as noted above, a number of approaches to Object-Oriented Analysis and Design. Most of them use graphics representation models, whose idea was likely inherited from structured methodologies. Object-oriented analysis builds on previous information modeling techniques, and can be defined as a method of analysis that examines requirements from the perspective of the classes and objects found in the vocabulary of the problem domain. Analysis activities yield black box objects which are derived from the problem domain. Frameworks have become very useful in capturing an object-oriented analysis for a given problem domain and making is reusable for related applications. Basically a framework is a skeleton of an application or application subsystem implemented by concrete and abstract classes. In other words, a framework is a specialization hierarchy with abstract super classes that depicts a given problem domain. One of the drawbacks of all current object-oriented analysis techniques is their universal lack of formality.

During object-oriented design the object focus shifts to the solution domain. Object-oriented design is a method

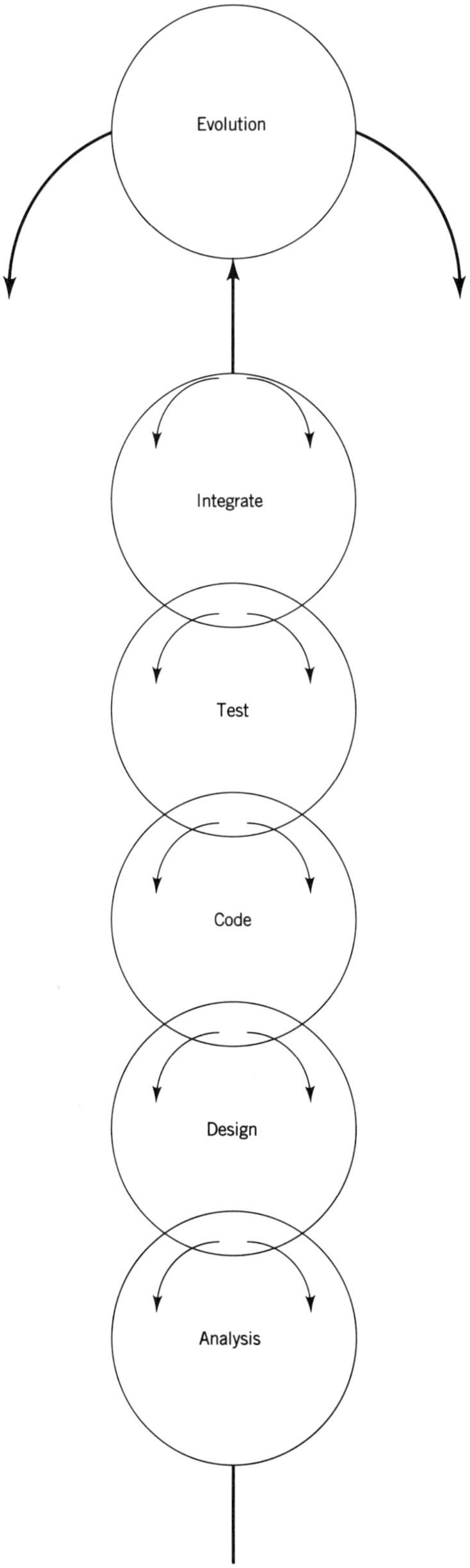

Figure 8. Water fountain life cycle for object-oriented software development.

of design encompassing the process of object-oriented decomposition and a notation for depicting both logical and physical as well as static and dynamic models of the system under design (Booch, 1991). OOD techniques have actually been defined before OOA techniques had been conceieved.

There is difficulty in identifying and characterizing current OOA and OOD techniques because, as described above, the boundaries between analysis and design activities in the object-oriented model are fuzzy. Given that problem, the following descriptions provide an overview to some of the OOA and OOD techniques being used.

Meyer uses language as a vehicle for expressing design. His approach is really not classifiable as an OOD technique (Meyer, 1988). Booch's OOD techniques extend his previous Ada work. He advocates a "round trip gestalt" process during which: objects are identified, semantics of the objects are identified, relationships are identified, implementation is accomplished, and iteration occurs. He uses class diagrams, class category diagrams, class templates, and object diagrams to record design (Booch, 1991). Wirfs-Brock's OOD technique is driven by delegation of responsibilities. Class responsibility cards (CRC) are used to record classes responsible for specific functionality, and collaborators with the responsible classes. The initial exploration of classes and responsibilities is followed by detailed relationship analysis and implementation of subsystems (Wirfs-Brock, 1990).

Rumbaugh and co-workers (1991) use three kinds of models to describe a system: the object model, which is a static structure of the objects in a system; the dynamic model, which describes the aspects of a system that change over time; and the functional model, which describes the data value transformations within a system. Object diagrams, state diagrams, and data flow diagrams are used to represent the three models, respectively (Rumbaugh and co-workers, 1991). Similarly, Shlaer and Mellor (1988) use three models: the information model, the state model and the process model to perform OOA.

In their OOA technique, Coad and Yourdon (1991) advocate the following steps: find classes and objects, identify structures and relationships, determine subjects, define attributes, and define services, to delineate a multi-layer object-oriented model. The layers corresponds to the steps, namely: class and object layer, subject layer, structure layer, attribute layer, and service layer, respectively. Their OOD technique is both multi-layer and multi-component. The layers are the same as in analysis. The components include: problem domain, human interaction, task management, and data management.

There are also other published OOA and OOD techniques as well as variations of the above which are not listed here.

Management Issues

As organizations begin to shift to object-oriented development techniques, the management activities which support software development will also necessarily have to change. The seamless, iterative, prototyping nature of object-oriented development eliminates traditional milestones. New milestones will have to be established. Also, some of the ways in which measurements were made seem less appropriate in an object-oriented context. LOC is definitely not helpful. Reuse measurements would be useful as would number of class-to-class relationships. Most work in object-oriented metrics is relatively new, but references are beginning to surface (Lorenz, 1993).

Resource allocation needs to be reconsidered as does team organization. Smaller development teams are suggested (Booch, 1991), as is cultivation of reuse experts. Incentives should be based on reuse, not LOC. A entirely new mind set is required if reuse is to really be operative. Libraries and application frameworks have to be supported and built along with contracted application software. Long term investment strategies are imperative.

Regarding quality assurance, typical review and testing activities are still essential, but their timing and definition must be changed. For example, a walkthrough could involve enacting a scenario of interacting objects proposed to effect some specific functionality. Testing of object-oriented systems is another area which is only recently being formally addressed. Release in terms of a steady stream of prototypes requires a flavor of configuration management which differs from that which is being used to control products generated using structured techniques. Another management concern ought to be appropriate tool support. An object-oriented development environment is essential. Also needed are: a browser for class library, an incremental compiler, debuggers that know about class and object semantics, graphics support for design and analysis notation and reference checking, configuration management and version control tools, and a database application that functions as a class librarian. Tools are beginning to be available, but because of the use of diverse techniques they are not always as useful as they might be.

Estimates can also be problematic until there is an object-oriented development history to substantiate proposed development estimates of resource and cost. Cost of current and future reuse must be factored into the equation. Finally, management must be aware of the risks involved in moving to an object-oriented approach. Also there are potential performance risks such as: cost of message passing, explosion of message passing, class encumbrance, paging behavior, dynamic allocation and destruction overhead. There are also start-up risks including: acquisition of appropriate tools, strategic and appropriate training, and development of class libraries.

OBJECT-ORIENTED TRANSITION

There are documented success stories, but there are also implicit recommendations. The transition has to progress through levels of absorption before assimilation into a software development organization actually occurs. This transition period can take considerable time. Training is essential. Pilot projects are recommended. Combinations of structured and object-oriented approaches are not recommended. There is growing evidence that success requires a total object-oriented approach for at least the following reasons:. traceability improvement, reduction in significant integration problems, improvement in conceptual integrity of process and product, minimization of need for objectification and deobjectification, and maximization of the benefits of object-orientation (Berard, 1993).

FUTURE TRENDS

In summary, object-oriented development is a natural outgrowth of previous approaches and has great promise for software development in many application domains. Object-oriented development is not, however, a panacea and has not yet reached maturity. While the future of object-oriented development cannot be defined, there have been predictions. It is likely that the movement will continue to gain in popularity, and techniques will mature significantly as experience increases. Class libraries and application frameworks will be readily available in the marketplace. Information access will be transparent across applications and environments. Object-orientation will provide environments in which users can communicate among applications. Integrated object-oriented multimedia tool kits will be available (Winblad, 1990). It is also likely that object-orientation will eventually be replaced or absorbed into an approach which deals at an even higher level of abstraction. Of course these are just predictions. In the not too distant future, talk about objects will no doubt be passé, but for now there is much information available to generate genuine enthusiasm.

BIBLIOGRAPHY

E. V. Berard, *Essays on Object-Oriented Software Engineering,* Vol. 1, Prentice-Hall, Inc., Englewood Cliffs, N.J., 1993.

G. Booch, "Object-Oriented Design," *Ada Letters,* **I**(3), 64–76 (Mar.–Apr. 1982).

G. Booch, *Object-Oriented Design with Applications,* The Benjamin/Cummings Publishing Company, Inc., Redwood City, Calif., 1991.

T. Budd, *An Introduction to Object-Oriented Programming,* Addison-Wesley Publishing Co., Inc., New York, 1991.

P. Coad and J. Nicola, *Object-Oriented Programming,* Prentice-Hall, Inc., Englewood Cliffs, N.J., 1993.

P. Coad and E. Yourdon, *Object-Oriented Analysis,* 2nd ed., Prentice-Hall, Inc., Englewood Cliffs, N.J., 1991.

P. Coad and E. Yourdon, *Object-Oriented Design,* Prentice-Hall, Inc., Englewood Cliffs, N.J., 1991.

B. J. Cox, *Object-Oriented Programming: An Evolutionary Approach,* Addison-Wesley, Reading, Mass., 1986.

B. Curtis, "...But You Have to Understand. This Isn't the Way We Develop Software At Our Company," Microelectronics and Computer Technology Corporation, Austin, Texas, 1989, *MCC Technical Report No. STP-203-89.*

A. Goldberg and P. Robson, *Smalltalk-80: The Language and Its Implementation,* Addison-Wesley, Reading, Mass., 1983.

B. Henderson-Sellers and J. M. Edwards, "The Object-Oriented Systems Life Cycle," *CACM,* 143–159 (Sept. 1990).

T. Korson and J. McGregor, "Understanding Object-Oriented: A Unifying Paradigm," *CACM,* 41–60 (Sept. 1990).

M. Lorenz, *Object-Oriented Software Development,* Prentice-Hall, Inc., Englewood Cliffs, N.J., 1993.

B. Meyer, *Object-Oriented Software Construction,* Prentice-Hall, Inc., Englewood Cliffs, N.J., 1988.

D. Monarchi and G. Puhr, "A Research Typology for Object-Oriented Analysis and Design, *CACM,* 35–47 (Sept. 1992).

R. Pressman, *Software Engineering A Practitioner's Approach,* 3rd ed., McGraw-Hill, Inc., New York, 1992.

J. Rumbaugh, M. Blaha, W. Premerlani, F. Eddy, and W. Lorensen, *Object-Oriented Modeling and Design,* Prentice-Hall, Inc., Englewood Cliffs, N.J., 1991.

S. Shlaer and S. J. Mellor, *Object-Oriented Systems Analysis: Modeling the World in Data,* Yourdon Press: Prentice-Hall, Englewood Cliffs, N.J., 1988.

A. L. Winblad, S. D. Edwards, and D. R. King, *Object-Oriented Software,* Addison-Wesley Publishing Company, Inc., Reading, Mass., 1990.

R. Wirfs-Brock, B. Wilkerson, and L. Wiener, *Designing Object-Oriented Software,* Prentice-Hall, Inc., Englewood Cliffs, N.J., 1990.

LINDA M. NORTHROP
Software Engineering Institute

OBJECT-ORIENTED LANGUAGES

See C++; OBJECT-ORIENTED PROGRAMMING; SMALLTALK.

OBJECT-ORIENTED MEASUREMENT OF SOFTWARE

INTRODUCTION

With all of the attention being paid to management uses of measurement, it is easy to forget that measurement can be a very useful software design tool. As software engineering matures as a discipline, practitioners are looking for ways to use measurement in the engineering of their products. As development technology changes, they find their measures must change as well.

This article focuses on the need for measures in the engineering of object-oriented software. It begins by building a framework for software measurement as a whole, placing technical measurement in context with other types of measurement. It discusses specific demands placed on measures by object-oriented software development, highlighting some of the fundamental differences between object-oriented and the more traditional structured development techniques. The article then presents some of the current and ongoing work in this fairly new field. Finally, the article notes some areas where no work is currently underway, providing opportunities for research.

TECHNICAL MEASUREMENT

The field of software measurement can be modeled using a three tiered framework. In the first tier, strategic measurement is concerned with the long term performance of an organization. Measures at this level must combine the results of many technologies and development environments, both across the organization and over time. Thus, these measures tend to be generic, and oriented towards management concerns such as productivity and performance. The primary user of strategic measures is the organization executive.

In the second tier, tactical measurement is concerned with the performance of an individual project. Measures at this level tend to be task oriented. Although some measures can be process oriented, they are usually concerned with the conformance of the actual process used on the project to a standard or preferred process. Further, a single project may include several products, each using somewhat different technologies and environments, especially on large projects or where outside developers are involved. So, too, these measures will tend to be generic, that is, not oriented to a specific technology or environment. The primary user of tactical measures is the project manager.

In the third tier, technical measurement is concerned with the details about a single product or process. Measures at this level are used to predict, estimate, or compare the attributes of a product, or to model, troubleshoot, and change a process. The primary user of technical measures is the software engineer.

By necessity, measures used lower on the framework are more sensitive to changes in the technology or environment than those used higher in the framework this is not necessarily true of measures based on attributes external to the product or process, such as the functionality delivered to the customer. Technical measures are the most sensitive to changes in the technology or environment. Small changes to either can render the current definition of a measure meaningless or obsolete. Even though the concept underlying the measure, such as complexity or coupling, does not change with the technology or environment, the meaning or semantics of that concept may change dramatically. For example, the concept of complexity can be used for the same purpose across technologies or environments: it is always something to be minimized or optimized. However, the source of complexity, or even the underlying meaning of complexity, in a structured application is not the same as for an object-oriented application. It is these changing semantics that force us to redefine a set of technical measures for each major new development technology or environment.

Nearly all of the uses of technical measures can be placed in one of the following six categories. The categories are based on the purpose for measuring. This purpose plays a significant role in the section of measures and the collection of the data. The categories are

1. Estimation—Measures derived from existing product documentation are combined with historical and environmental data to estimate the time and effort required to create future documents. For our purposes, "product documentation" is given the broadest possible interpretation. It includes such artifacts as the list of requirements, the functional specification,

high-level and detail design documents, source code, and test results. In addition, measures from an existing application can be combined with the same historical and environmental data to estimate the time and effort required to create a new, similar application. These same measures can be used to estimate the level of a future on-going activity per time period, such as using code complexity and other historical and environmental data to estimate the maintenance effort.

2. Prediction—Measures derived from existing documentation are used to predict the values of measures of future documentation. For example, data from testing can be used to predict the reliability of the application. Prediction differs from estimation in that prediction relies solely on the measures of the current product or process, and estimation is heavily dependent on data about the history of the organization and the environment.
3. Assessment—Measures from the product or process are compared to predetermined values set by standards, project-specific targets, or customer requirements to assess the conformance of the product or process to the standard, target, or requirement.
4. Comparison—Measures of a set of attributes from two or more products or processes are compared for the purposes of choosing one from among them, or for ranking them according to some scheme. This includes comparison or measures from an active project with those from historical projects.
5. Improvement—Measures from both the product and the process are used to investigate the cause and effect relationship between the two. These measurements, along with the cause and effect relationships, can be used to identify changes to be made to the process to influence the measured values of these or other characteristics of the product or process.
6. Investigation—Measures are taken of the product and/or process to support or refute a given hypothesis or to answer a specific question.

STRUCTURED VERSUS OBJECT-ORIENTED DEVELOPMENT

Practitioners and researchers alike are finding that technical measures based on structured, function-oriented development technologies are not well suited to object-oriented technologies. Although the concepts covered by these function-based measures, such as complexity, coupling, and cohesion, still have meaning in object-oriented software, the semantics of the measures themselves no longer hold (Roberts, 1992).

One theory set forth to explain this phenomenon is that object-oriented software development is very different from structured development (Chidamber and Kemerer, 1992). Structured development focuses on function first, then data, with the effect that the shape of the resulting application is skewed towards the functions performed. Michael Jackson's work (1975) focuses on data, then function, but the effect is the same—the resulting application is still shaped like the functions performed. Structured designs are blocks of function calling other blocks of function, with the connections between functions representing the passing of control (Page-Jones, 1980). Except for real-time systems, structured development methods rarely, if ever, model the behavior of the application under construction. In contrast, object-oriented development focuses on modeling the world in which the application is to operate, and tends to view data and function as a single package called an object. This object also has one or more states which model its behavior, both over time and in response to internal and external events. All of the published object-oriented development methods model the three dimensions of data, function, and behavior (Booch, 1991; Coad and Yourdon, 1991; Embley and co-workers, 1992; Page-Jones and Wiess, 1992; Rumbaugh and co-workers, 1991; Shlaer and Mellor, 1991; Wirfs-Brock and co-workers, 1990). The resulting application is shaped like the world in which it operates. Object-oriented designs are packages of data and function—objects passing messages to other objects. The connections between objects are either structural (object relationships such as inheritance) or communicational (message links).

Not surprisingly, the measures developed for structured development technologies tend to focus on the function-oriented characteristics of the application. Function length (lines of code), McCabe's (1976) Cyclomatic Complexity, and Halsted's (1977) Software Science, are all measures based on the content of function-oriented code. Measures such as fan-in or fan-out are based on module or function structure and interaction. Further, measures based on structured development provide no means to measure the effects of such object-oriented concepts as inheritance, encapsulation, message passing, and the internal and external structure of objects. These concepts can have significant influence on such factors as development time and effort, code size, the shape of the solution (the distribution of functionality), and the approach to solving the problem. Practitioners of object-oriented development are actively seeking ways to measure these concepts (Chidamber and Kemerer, 1992; Roberts, 1992; Whitmire, 1992).

CURRENT WORK IN TECHNICAL MEASUREMENT OF OBJECT-ORIENTED SOFTWARE

Several people have recently published work on measures specifically tailored to object-oriented software. Several more have work in progress.

Some have taken existing measures from structured development and extended them to cover object-oriented methods (Lieberherr and co-workers, 1988; Moreau and Dominick, 1989; Morris, 1988). Others developed new definitions of existing concepts, and new measures to go with them (Chidamber and Kemerer, 1992; Moreau and Dominick, 1989; Sheetz and co-workers, 1992; Whitmire, 1992). Still others have developed a set of measures during the process of accomplishing some other objective (Pfleeger and Palmer, 1990).

Perhaps the most comprehensive work to date, both in terms of the measures developed, and in terms of the research to validate them, is by Chidamber and Kemerer (1992). They present a set of measures covering many design concepts, including complexity, coupling, and cohesion. While comprehensive, their measures are not without weaknesses and criticisms, but are useful nonetheless (Roberts, 1992).

The reader is encouraged to explore these and more recent publications. This is a new field, and more information is published every month. Periodicals will be the best source for information about ongoing work because of shorter publication cycles.

AREAS NEEDING FUTURE WORK

In his book, *Object-Oriented Design With Applications*, Booch (1991) proposed several criteria for judging the quality of an object-oriented design. In addition to complexity, Booch suggested:

1. Coupling—The interconnectedness between objects, particularly the visibility of an object's components to other objects.
2. Cohesion—The degree of connectedness or strength of relationships between the components of an object.
3. Sufficiency—The degree to which the minimum number of characteristics of the real-world object are included in the model to make it useful to the application.
4. Completeness—The degree to which all of the necessary characteristics of the real-world object are captured by the model object.
5. Primitiveness—The degree to which the methods in the model object cannot be implemented efficiently without intimate knowledge of the internal structure of the object.

The criteria of complexity, coupling, and cohesion have been covered by some published and unpublished work (Chidamber and Kemerer, 1992; Roberts, 1992; Whitmire, 1992). The other areas are completely void of proposals or even work in progress as of the date of publication of this article.

CONCLUSION

The field of technical measures for object-oriented software development in undeveloped. There are many opportunities to advance the state of the art. Many of the concepts applicable to object-oriented designs are as yet undefined. Naturally, before they can be measured, they must be defined.

Furthermore, both the definitions and the measures must be tested against real-world experience to make sure they measure what they are purported to measure. This process will take time. It may be years before we have a set of common, validated measures to apply to object-oriented software. But unlike other development technologies, the measures for object-oriented technology will be developed concurrently with the technology itself. And, perhaps more important, these measures are in demand before they are available—a unique phenomenon in this field.

BIBLIOGRAPHY

G. Booch, *Object-Oriented Design with Applications,* Benjamin/Cummings, Redwood City, Calif., 1991.

S. R. Chidamber and C. F. Kemerer, *A Metrics Suite for Object-Oriented Design,* MIT Sloan School CISR Working Paper #249, 1992.

P. Coad and E. Yourdon, *Object-Oriented Analysis,* 2nd ed., Yourdon Press, Prentice Hall, Englewood Cliffs, N.J., 1991.

D. W. Embley, B. D. Kurtz, and S. N. Woodfield, *Object-Oriented Systems Analysis: A Model Driven Approach,* Yourdon Press/Prentice-Hall, Englewood Cliffs, N.J., 1992.

M. H. Halstead, *Elements of Software Science,* Elsevier North-Holland, New York, 1977.

M. Jackson, *Principles of Program Design,* Academic Press, London, 1975.

K. Lieberherr and co-workers, "Object-Oriented Programming: An Objective Sense of Style," *Third Annual ACM Conference on Object-Oriented Programming Systems, Languages, and Applications (OOPSLA),* 1988, pp. 323–334.

T. J. McCabe, "A Complexity Measure," *IEEE Transactions on Software Engineering* **SE-2**(4), 308–320 (1976).

D. R. Moreau and W. D. Dominick, "Object-Oriented Graphical Information Systems: Research Plan and Evaluation," *Journal of Systems and Software* **10,** 23–28 (1989).

K. Morris, *Metrics for Object-Oriented Software Development,* MIT Sloan School Masters Thesis, 1988.

M. Page-Jones, *The Practical Guide to Structured Systems Design,* Yourdon Press/Prentice-Hall, Englewood Cliffs, N.J., 1980.

M. Page-Jones and S. Wiess, "Object-Oriented Analysis and Design: The Synthesis Model," *Software Development '92,* Santa Clara, Calif., 1992.

S. L. Pfleeger and J. D. Palmer, "Software Estimation for Object-Oriented Systems," *1990 International Function Point User Group Fall Conference,* San Antonio, Texas, 1990, pp. 181–196.

T. Roberts, "Workshop on Metrics for Object-Oriented Software Development," unpublished report from OOPSLA, 1992.

J. Rumbaugh and co-workers, *Object-Oriented Modeling and Design*, Prentice-Hall, Englewood Cliffs, N.J., 1991.

S. D. Sheetz and co-workers, *Measuring Object-Oriented System Complexity,* University of Colorado Working Paper, 1992.

S. Shlaer and S. Mellor, *Object Lifecycles: Modeling the World in States,* Yourdon Press/Prentice-Hall, Englewood Cliffs, N.J., 1991.

S. A. Whitmire, "Measuring Complexity in Object-Oriented Software," *Third Annual Conference on the Application of Software Measurement,* La Jolla, Calif., 1992.

R. Wirfs-Brock, B. Wilkerson, and L. Weiner, *Designing Object-Oriented Software,* Prentice-Hall, Englewood Cliffs, N.J., 1990.

SCOTT A. WHITMIRE
Advanced Systems Research

OBJECT-ORIENTED REQUIREMENTS ANALYSIS

INTRODUCTION

Object-oriented requirements analysis (OORA) is a method of formulating the requirements for a software system in terms of objects and their interactions, based on an initial informal statement of requirements. The discipline has two origins. Shlaer and Mellor (1988) began using information modeling as part of the requirements analysis process, and this approach progressively became more object-oriented. At the same time, OORA was started by practitioners of object-oriented design (qv) who found that conventional process-oriented requirements analysis methods, such as structured analysis (deMarco, 1979; Gane and Sarsen 1978) and SADT (SofTech, 1978) , did not flow well into an object-oriented design. The difficulties in proceeding from structured analysis to object-oriented design stem from differences in the criteria for decomposing a system into subsystems and lower-level components. Converting a process-oriented decomposition (the result of a structured analysis) into an object-oriented decomposition frequently requires a great deal of reorganization (Seidewitz and Stark, 1986). Object-oriented requirements analysis seeks to decompose a system into interacting parts that represent the user's requirements as faithfully as conventional analysis methods but to do so in a way that is compatible with object-oriented design.

Compatibility with object-oriented design facilitates the transition from the requirements analysis to the design phase. It also simplifies the traceability of requirements throughout the development life cycle and makes less disruptive the process of iterating over requirements and design (ie, backtracking to the requirements analysis if the design implications are discovered to be infeasible).

Historically, OORA arose for these reasons. Some proponents of the approach argue that the object-oriented framework provides a more robust and accurate description of user requirements than the conventional approaches and is, therefore, to be preferred intrinsically over process-oriented analysis.

Distinguishing Characteristics of OORA

Object-oriented requirements analysis differs from conventional process-oriented methods in two respects: (1) the way in which a system is partitioned into subsystems and components and (2) the way in which the interaction between subsystems or components is described.

Partitioning a System into Objects. In a process-oriented approach, a system is described as a set of interacting processes. In the object-oriented approach, a system is described as a set of interacting objects. The first question that any newcomer to this approach will ask is, therefore, "What is an object?" The question of what constitutes an object is a difficult one. Determining what the objects are is one of the fundamental tasks of an object-oriented requirements analysis, and later of object-oriented design. Most simple answers tend to beg the question by saying that an object is a real-world entity or a thing as opposed to an action. These answers may be suggestive, but all they really do is replace one word (object) with another (entity or thing).

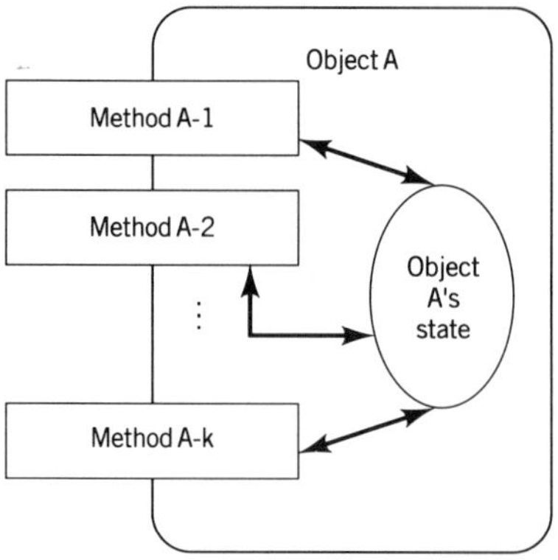

Figure 1. The structure of an object.

Despite the difficulty in defining precisely what an object is, there are frequently many obvious candidates during the requirements analysis phase. These are the major things about which one finds oneself talking when discussing the system. For example, in an air-traffic control system, one frequently refers to aircraft, sectors, controllers, weather, etc. Each of these is a candidate object. But there is no simple algorithm for identifying or selecting these and for precisely defining their interfaces. That is the task of the requirements analysis process.

As shown in Figure 1, each object encapsulates a set of services (also called functions or methods) and a state to which the services have read and write access. A fundamental goal in defining objects is to group datum items together with the functions that read or write to those items. This kind of grouping makes each object a cohesive set of functions and data. This approach to partitioning contrasts with the conventional functional or process-oriented approach, in which a system is decomposed into the primary services that it performs.

Describing Interaction. The basic idea in OORA is to represent system requirements in terms of interacting objects. Objects interact by sending messages or signaling events to each other; this typically results in the receiving object performing some service for the sending object. Messages may have both input and output arguments, through which data can be passed between the sender and the receiver of the message: input arguments specify the parameters of the service being requested and output arguments return the results. Messages may be received and processed immediately (i.e., synchronous communication) or queued and processed later (asynchronous communication). The basic paradigm is illustrated in Figure 2.

What is most significant about this paradigm is that each object provides a well-defined interface to its clients (other objects that will send messages to this object). The interface describes exactly what form of messages the object will accept. Another way to view the interface is that it describes what services the object provides, or what operations it is capable of performing. Thus an object encapsulates a set of services. The services provided by all the

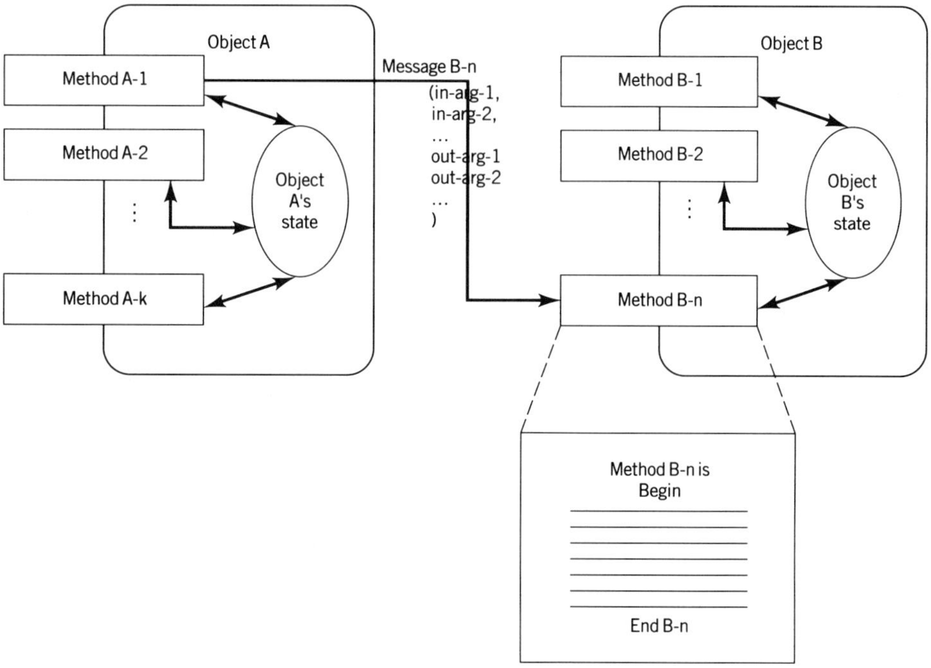

Figure 2. The object interaction paradigm.

objects, taken together, represent the functional requirements of the system. The primary goal of the analysis process is to determine how these services should be encapsulated, i.e., to determine what the objects are, what services they should provide, and how they should interact.

In contrast to the well-defined interfaces of the object-oriented approach, functional or process-oriented methods tend to rely on less precise data flow representations of system interfaces. The ambiguities of data flow models are well known. For example, when two flows are shown to enter a process, do they arrive at the same time (as distinct arguments passed to an operation that the process must perform) or are they independent, alternative means of activating the process? Through its more precise models, the object-oriented approach forces the analyst (and later the designer) to address important questions that might otherwise go unnoticed until implementation.

Outline

The next section presents the most important concepts of object-oriented requirements analysis in a notationally and methodologically open fashion, i.e., without trying to induce the reader to think in terms of a specific notation or a specific set of steps to be followed. In addition to the fundamental object-oriented concepts, it also introduces the most typical models that are used to describe system requirements in an object-oriented manner. These models are found in most of the published OORA methods, although the notations and the specific information captured may vary. The criteria for deciding when an object-oriented requirements analysis is (tentatively) complete also are discussed.

Later it is shown how several specific OORA methods apply the concepts previously discussed. The methods discussed are those of Coad and Yourdon (1991), Rumbaugh and co-workers (1991), Shlaer and Mellor (1992), Wirfs-Brock and co-workers (1990), Firesmith (1992), and Seidewitz and Stark (1992). In addition to showing how the common concepts appear in these methods, some of the unique aspects of each approach are pointed out. The intention here is to provide the reader with a sense of what each approach can offer, as a basis for choosing between them or incorporating aspects of them in a hybrid method.

Next the risks involved in an organization transitioning to OORA are discussed. These include methodological traps that are easy to fall into, technology acceptance issues, and issues concerning the relationship between system and software engineering. The last section summarizes the main areas of impact of object-oriented requirements analysis on software engineering practice.

FUNDAMENTAL CONCEPTS

The basic concepts of OORA also are those of object-oriented design and object-oriented programming:

- Objects.
- Classes.
- Relationships.
- Methods (also known as services or functions).
- Variables (also known as attributes).
- Inheritance.
- Polymorphism.
- Information hiding.
- Message passing (and the related issue of binding).

What distinguishes OORA from object-oriented design is the fact that OORA is concerned with *problem domain objects* and *problem domain classes*. In the design process, one is still concerned with these, but also with solution domain objects and classes. In object-oriented programming, one is concerned with ways of representing the objects and classes within a given programming language.

Objects

What is meant by problem domain objects? Commonly offered phrases, such as "entities that play a role in the problem to be solved," are suggestive but do not provide clear criteria for identifying objects. At the expense of some of this suggestiveness, an object can be defined precisely as follows: An object is data together with a collection of functions that act on, or refer to, the data. The data represent the current *state* of an object, or the current *attributes* of the object. The functions, which are called methods in object-oriented jargon, provide the means for setting or changing the object's state, for retrieving the current values that make up its state, for computing values derived from the current state, and for performing operations that require access (read, write, or both) to the current state.

An object is a *problem domain* object if its data and functions are intrinsic to the problem that the software is intended to solve. An object is a *solution domain* (design) object if its data or functions represent ways of solving the problem. Thus whether an object belongs to the problem domain or the solution domain is not so much a property of the object itself as of one's conception of the problem to be solved. Again, there are no ready-made answers: the boundaries between the problem and solution domains may be well defined; if they are not, then it is part of the requirements analysis process to decide where the boundaries lie. Typically considered as design objects are those whose sole purpose is to support the distribution of data between other objects or to schedule the activation of other objects' services. Design objects also include those that provide low-level services, such as communication or input–output, which are needed by other objects. It is helpful also to distinguish between problem or solution domain objects and *implementation artifacts*, such as modules or packages in a specific programming language, which may used to implement the objects.

The transition from OORA to OOD involves the introduction of solution domain objects. It may also involve the transformation of messages between problem domain objects. What was represented as a simple communication of a message in the requirements analysis may be realized by a relatively complex design mechanism, such as a message queue. For this reason, messaging in the problem domain, as represented in the OORA, may look quite different from messaging in the solution domain, as represented in the design. Nevetheless, there are usually explicit transformation rules for converting problem domain communications into solution domain communications.

The purpose of distinguishing between problem and solution domains is to prevent the analyst from prematurely ruling out useful alternative approaches to building the system. This does not imply that one finishes defining requirements before considering design. Throughout the analysis process, the design implications of the requirements (e.g., the feasibility of realizing them) should be considered. This may involve performing design in parallel with requirements analysis. Nevertheless, the distinction between the two activities, and their respective roles, should be maintained.

More on Objects and System Partitioning. The goal of cohesively grouping functions and data leads to criteria for partitioning a system (into objects) that are quite different from the traditional functional criteria. In the functional approach, a system is partitioned into the principal high level functions that it performs. Each of these functions is then decomposed into subfunctions, ie, the constituent steps or actions through which the high level function is achieved. Each subfunction can then be decomposed into subsubfunctions, etc.

Thus, in the functional approach, the analyst begins by asking, "What does the system have to do?" This leads to a set of functions $F_1 \ldots F_n$. For each such identified function F_i, the analyst then asks, "What needs to be done to accomplish F_i?" This process of functional decomposition continues until the lowest level of identified functions is considered to be defined well enough to permit a straightforward design and implementation.

A process-oriented approach to system partitioning follows the same overall criteria of functional decomposition, the only difference being that decomposing a process P into subprocesses $P_1 \ldots P_n$ does not necessarily mean that $P_1 \ldots P_n$ are performed successively. Instead, some or all of them may be performed in parallel.

In the object-oriented approach to analysis, one starts by asking "What are the key objects that play a role in this system?" Some objects may suggest themselves immediately. As a means of identifying other objects, one may ask the functional question, "What does the system have to do?" (In fact, this question *must* be asked during the requirements analysis process, whether one's approach is object-oriented or not; see below, Ignoring Behavioral Modeling.) From the resulting identification of the top-level services or functions, one might then ask "What state information or data do these functions act on or reference?" It is then possible to begin to identify key objects by grouping the top-level functions with the state information or data to which they belong. It is this grouping process that makes the approach object-oriented.

Classes

Classes are a means of organizing objects in terms of their similarities and differences. It is possible to group similar objects into a class that represents the shared aspects of those objects. For example, animals who share the characteristic that their body temperature remains nearly constant, regardless of changes in the environmental temperature, are grouped by zoologists into the class of "warm-blooded animals."

In a software system it is useful to identify a class when there will be several objects that are expected to behave similarly. By defining a class, it is possible to specify, and eventually to implement, requirements for the entire class; these requirements will then implicitly apply to each object in the class. Therefore, there are two criteria for the identification of classes:

- Multiple objects.
- Similar behavior.

In other words, it does not make sense to define a class that can only contain only a single object. Nor does it make sense to define a class of objects whose behaviors, within the system being developed, will be dissimilar from each other. In a software system, the behavior of an object is characterized by the services it provides and by its intrinsic attributes. Objects are similar to each other if they perform some of the same services or if they have some of the same attributes. For example, in an airline reservation system, one of the services (in fact, the key service) performed by an airplane might be *passenger flight*. Because this is a similarity in the behavior of all the airplanes represented in the reservation system, it makes sense to define a class of airplanes. In an air-traffic control system, not all of the airplanes represented will perform *passenger flight*, so it might make sense to distinguish the class of passenger airplanes from the class of commercial transport airplanes.

It is important to realize that the right classes may not be immediately apparent. There are usually many ways to organize objects into classes and subclasses, depending on what similarities and what differences are considered to be important. It is the task of the analyst to consider these alternatives and to choose among them according to the following criterion: which organization best represents the similarities and differences that are significant for this application? This is a process of choosing abstractions, and it is fundamental to the object-oriented approach in requirements analysis as well as in design and implementation.

Parent Classes and Subclasses. Classes themselves are organized into a structure of generalization and specialization: thus, warm-blooded animals are a special type of animal, ie, warm-blooded animals are a *subclass* of the class of animals, which is in turn a subclass of the class of all living beings (consisting of animals and plants). The structure of classes and subclasses can be understood in terms of the predicate *is a*. Every warm-blooded animal *is an* animal; every animal *is a* living being. Note that this is true in object-oriented requirements analysis but is not always true in object-oriented programming (qv). In object-oriented programming languages like C^{++}, in which one can distinguish between public and private subclasses, the latter are used to represent the predicate *is implemented by means of* rather than the predicate *is a*. It follows that a class can have several subclasses (e.g., warm-blooded animals and cold-blooded animals), and also that a class can be a subclass of several "parent" classes (animals are living beings, animals are also mobile entities). In its most general form, the structure of classes and subclasses is a lattice of the form shown in Figure 3, in which an arrow from A to B means that B is a subclass of A.

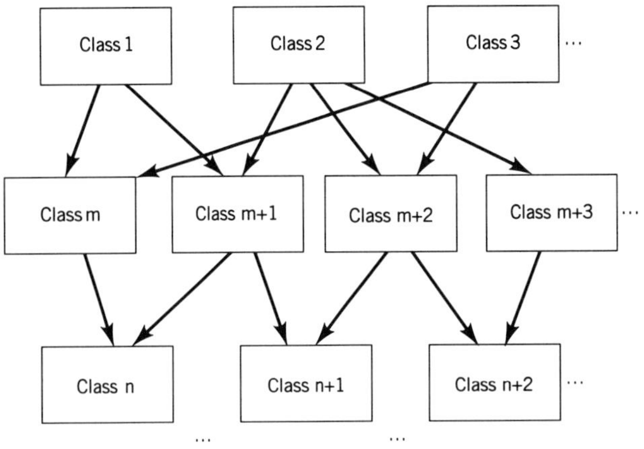

Figure 3. Lattice of classes and subclasses.

Relationships Between Objects

Objects interact with each other via messages in order to perform their functions. Sending and receiving messages is one way that objects in a system can be related to each other. There are two other basic kinds of relationships between objects: one object may *contain* another object as a part, e.g., an engine is a part of a car (see Whole Part Model, below), and one object may be *associated with* another object, e.g., a personnel record in a company is associated with an employee of the company, a library book is associated with its current borrower, etc. Identifying these relationships and describing their characteristics are key tasks in the object-oriented requirements analysis process. Entity-relationship models, as described in Chen (1976), are a convenient way to present this type of information.

Describing Objects and Classes

If an object belongs to a class, it is described implicitly through the description of that class. A class is described in terms of the services provided by, and the attributes inherent in, the objects of that class. A singular object, one that plays a unique role in the system and does not belong to any class (other than the universal class of all objects), is described in terms of the services *it* provides and the attributes that *it* possesses.

Methods or Functions of an Object Class. The methods of a class are the things that objects in the class can do. They are operations that an object in the class performs when called on to do so. These calls are made by the methods of other objects or in response to external events such as system initialization or the receipt of user input. It is in the methods of a system's classes that the functional capabilities of the system are realized. The methods can, therefore, consist of whatever kind of processing is needed. There are, however, certain standard types of methods that a class will frequently possess:

- Constructors and destructors.
- Set and get.

A constructor for the class C is a method whose job is to create instances of, i.e., new objects in class C. Constructors

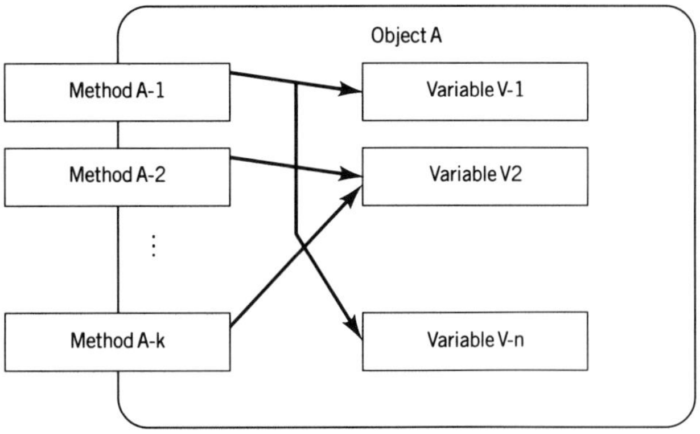

Figure 4. The variables of an object.

are used when objects must be created dynamically during system operation. A destructor for class C is a method that discards an instance of class C when it is no longer needed.

Set and get methods are used to update and access the state of an object. An object's state is determined by the values of its internal variables or attributes. For each such variable, there can be a *set* method, which allows users of the object to *change* the value of the variable, and a *get* method, which allows users of the object to *read* the value of the variable. Access to either or both of these methods may be restricted, and the methods need not be provided at all. Determining which variables should have set or get methods and how access to them should be controlled is the question of information hiding, discussed below.

Variables or Attributes of an Object Class. Typically, the state of an object is represented as a set of values that are assigned to the object's *variables* (sometimes called *attributes*). An object was described as consisting of data together with a set of functions associated with the data. The object's variables constitute its data (Fig. 4). Unlike methods, each object in a class has its own set of variables, which are used to represent the object's current state. It is also possible for certain variables to be associated with the class as a whole, rather than with any particular object in the class. For example, a class may keep track of the number of currently existing instances by means of a cardinality attribute. Such variables, which represent the state of the class itself, are known as *class variables*.

Just as with a class's methods, there are various levels of detail at which one can describe the variables of an object or class. At the most general level, they can simply be named, together with a short description of what each variable represents. More detail can be given by specifying the type of each variable. Finally, the visibility and modifiability of each variable can be specified in terms of which other objects in the system can read or update it.

Inheritance. The lattice of classes and subclasses was described in terms of the relation *is a*. Each member of a subclass *is a* member of the parent class as well. In object-oriented systems, the *is a* relation is realized through *inheritance*. Each member of a subclass inherits some of its characteristics from the parent class. Specifically, members of a subclass inherit the methods and variables of the parent class. That is, if method M is defined for class C_p, and class C_s is a subclass of class C_p, then every member of class C_s will have a method called M. The reason for this is clear: members of class C_s are also members of class C_p; because all members of class C_p provide method M, the members of C_s must also provide method M.

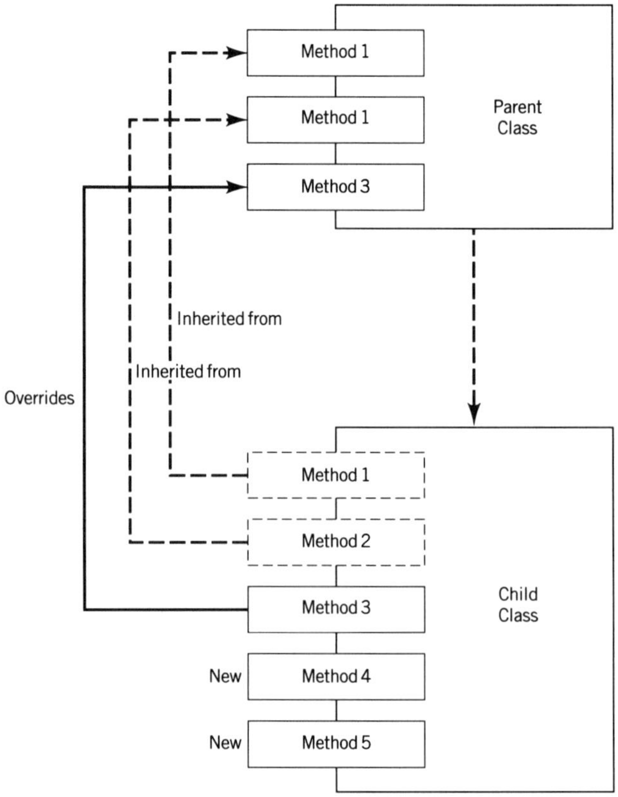

Figure 5. Specialization of a method from a parent to child class.

The method M that is provided by all members of class C_s will have the same name and the same signature (that is, input and output arguments) as the method M that is provided by class C_p, However, C_s may explicitly replace an inherited method with one that is appropriate specifically to that subclass. This is because members of class C_s may have additional characteristics, not found among other members of class C_p, which require special processing. For example, suppose C_p is the class of documents, and C_s is a subclass of documents that may contain embedded graphics. C_p might provide a print method that, as a default, assumes that the document contains only text. C_s might override this method to provide a print routine that can handle embedded graphics. The process of replacing a method M with a different version, which is appropriate for members of a subclass but not for all members of the parent class, is called *specialization* (Fig. 5). The capabilities of the parent class are *specialized* to reflect the additional characteristics of the subclass.

In some cases it may be impossible for a parent class to provide a default method for a certain capability, even though every member of the class *must* have that capability. In the case of the document class and the print method, eg, it may not be reasonable to assume text-only documents as the default; nevertheless, every document must be printable. In such cases, the parent class is defined as an *abstract class*. This means that every member of the parent class is also a member of some subclass; there are no objects that are just members of the parent class. In the document example, this would mean that there are no plain documents. Instead, every document object must be a member of some subclass of documents, e.g., text, graphics, etc. Each subclass of documents would have a print method that is appropriate to that subclass. It is still possible to say that the document class provides a print method, in the sense that every document can be printed. But it is only at the level of the subclasses that one can determine exactly what the appropriate print method is. The print method of the document class is really a placeholder that defines a uniform purpose and interface for all of the specific print methods. As such, it is known as a *virtual method*, or *virtual function*. Its importance is that it allows the analyst to discuss printing in a general, abstract manner.

When a subclass has several parents, as in Figure 3, it inherits the methods and variables of all its parents. This is known as *multiple inheritance*. Multiple inheritance can be a powerful tool for modeling real-world problems. Different properties of objects in the real world can be separated into different classes; eg, airborne objects might be in class C_a, whereas objects belonging to foreign countries might be in class C_f. An airplane belonging to France would then be a member of both of these classes. More generally, an object with certain properties would be a member of the classes that provide those properties. Multiple inheritance should be used with caution because it can be difficult to implement successfully. The difficulties tend to arise during the programming phase of development, and multiple inheritance need not be used in the implementation of these problem domain concepts. An awareness of the potential difficulties is appropriate during requirements analysis, however, to keep the transition to the later phases of development as smooth as possible.

Polymorphism. When different classes provide an identically named method, such as the print example above, the system is said to support polymorphism. Polymorphism means that a function, which is thought of as a single function at a conceptual level, takes different forms, depending on the type of object on which it is acting. The benefit of polymorphism is that the users of this function need not be concerned with the different behaviors required by the different types of objects. The virtual print function described above is an example of polymorphism.

Information Hiding. As noted, the description of a class requires decisions about which variables or attributes will be visible to users of the class and which are solely for internal use by the class's own methods. Similarly, update access to some variables may be provided to users of the class via a "set" or "put" function. More generally, for each method of a class, there is a choice between making the method available, to be called by users of the class, or keeping it private, to be called only by other methods in the same class. These decisions determine how much information about the class is available to the class's users. The decisions should be made on the basis of the concept that the class is supposed to represent. It is convenient, in this respect, to think of the objects in a class as *virtual machines* that provide a set of well-defined services to their users. The methods that are made available to users of a class should be only those that provide these services. Any additional methods that are needed only as supporting functions, to implement the services, should be kept private within the class. An argument can be made that during the analysis phase, one is not interested in these supporting functions, because they describe "how" the services of the virtual machine are to be implemented, rather than "what" the services of the virtual machine are.

Interaction Among Objects: Message Passing

The discussion has been on how classes and objects are described; the issue of how they interact with each other is now addressed. As mentioned above, objects interact by sending messages to each other. The messages that an object can accept correspond to the services that the object provides (Fig. 2). How does an object send a message to another object? Remember that all the activity of an object is carried out by its methods. Thus it is the *methods* of an object that will send messages to other objects, thereby invoking methods within those other objects. How, then, do things get started? Typically, some event external to the system will cause the activation of some method in some object within the system. From that point on, the objects interact via message passing.

Polymorphism was described as the ability of a system to execute conceptually the same function in different ways, depending on the object on which the function is acting. Thus printing a text document at a laser printer is different from printing a graphic at a color monitor, but polymorphism can allow one to treat these operations similarly, as manifestations of the single conceptual function *Print*. In an object-oriented system, polymorphism is achieved by having different classes provide an identically named method. The "decision" as to which class should process a polymorphic function call (e.g., which class's print function should be activated) is equivalent to deciding on the *destination* of the message requesting the print. This decision process is called *binding*: the message, or service request, is *bound* to a specific class. In an implementation of an object-oriented system, binding may occur at execution time (this is called dynamic binding) or at compile time (static binding). Although this distinction is an implementation issue, it may have implications for performance and fault tolerance, and it is, therefore, something that the analyst should understand.

Models Commonly Used in OORA

The ways in which the concepts described above are used to capture system requirements are now addressed. Typically, some or all of the basic concepts are applied to create a model, which expresses certain required aspects of the system to be built. The following types of models are commonly used in OORA:

- Whole-part (aggregation, assembly).
- Classification (is-a, inheritance).
- Class–object definition.
- Object interaction (communication, message flow, usage).
- State machine.

Whole Part Model. The whole part model is a way of describing how objects are composed of simpler objects. For example, a car consists of a body, an engine, a transmission, an exhaust system, etc. Each of these, in turn, consists of lower level objects. The ability to describe complex objects as a structure of interacting simpler objects is one of the key benefits of the object-oriented approach. The whole part model can be represented in a hierarchy diagram in which the boxes represent classes, and an arrow from A to B means that each object of type A (i.e., in class A) contains an object of type B. The whole-part model is sometimes called the *aggregation* model or the *assembly* model.

Classification Model. The classification model describes the inheritance relationships between classes. The classification model can be represented by a lattice diagram such as Figure 3. Alternatively, aggregation and inheritance relationships can both be shown in the same diagram, by using a different type of arc to represent the two different relations. Whatever notation is used, it is important to keep in mind the distinction between these relations. Aggregation refers to the situation in which one object *is a part of* another object. Classification refers to the situation in which objects of one class *are a kind of* object of a more inclusive class.

Class–Object Definition. At some point in the analysis process, it is necessary to specify what services are provided by the objects in each class. This effectively defines each class within the system. There are various levels of detail at which a classes's services, or methods, can be specified. At the most general level they can simply be named: with each class, one associates a list of the methods provided by that class. At a slightly greater level of detail, it is possible to identify the input and output arguments of each method and provide a concise description of what each method does. A more formal approach is to be precise about the *types* of the input and output arguments. Finally, a pseudocode or minispec presentation of the method's procedural logic can be provided. Choosing among these approaches one must take into account the novelty of the class (classes that perform standard, well-understood functions may not need to be described as fully as more novel ones), its importance in the system (how much risk is entailed by not specifying the details), and the completion criteria that are described below.

Object Interaction Model. An object-oriented model of a system must describe the way the objects interact. As discussed above, objects interact by sending message to each other. Thus, the object interaction model shows the message flow between objects. There are several ways that message flow can be shown, corresponding to different levels of detail. The analyst must choose which level of detail is appropriate to the current task (see below).

A detailed object interaction model would show each message that flows between each object, together with the method in the receiving object that each message activates.

A slightly less detailed representation would show each message, but would not explicitly show the methods that are activated.

A still less detailed form of this model would only show which objects send messages to other objects, without explicitly showing each message as a unique arc in the diagram.

This form of object interaction model can be thought of as showing the *usage relationships* between objects, ie, which objects make use of services provided by other objects.

State Model. In the state model, each object is modeled as a state machine. This is a form of behavioral modeling in which an object's behavior is described as a passage through different states. In dynamic systems, the creation of an object and its eventual disappearance from the system may also be modeled; the passage of the object from its creation through its various states to its destruction is called the object's *life cycle* (see the discussion of the Schaler-Mellor approach, below).

Objects are typically modeled as *finite* state machines. This means that there are only a finite number of states in which the object can exist. For most systems, such a model will be a significant abstraction from the actual behavior of the constituent objects. For example, an object that has *heat* as an attribute may eventually be implemented so that its heat is represented by a floating-point number. Thus there are virtually an infinite number of possible states, corresponding to the continuous range of possible temperatures. (The word *virtually* was used because in any computer implementation the accuracy of floating-point numbers is limited, so that really only a finite, but large, range of numbers can be represented.) For the purpose of modeling system requirements, however, it may suffice to describe the object as being at all times in one of the following three states:

- Temperature acceptable.
- Too hot (temperature above some limit).
- Too cold (temperature below some limit).

The state model describes the conditions under which the object passes from one state to another. These are called *state transitions*. In the case of an object with a heat attribute, eg, the transition from "acceptable" to "too hot" occurs when its heat rises above a maximum acceptable temperature T_{max}.

State models are usually specified in either a graphical or a tabular form. The graphical form is a state transition diagram (STD). Nodes in an STD represent possible states of the object. An arrow between two nodes represents a transition between those two states. An arrow is typically labeled with the name of the event, or condition, that causes the change in state. More detailed STDs may specify an action that the object performs when entering a state, or after it has entered the state, or when it is leaving a state. These actions are typically specified by means of a descriptive label (e.g., "Notify Controller of Excessive Temperature"). The label may, in turn, refer to a more detailed description of the activity in the form of pseudocode or, in structured analysis terminology, a minispec.

The tabular form of the state model is called a transition matrix, and it is equivalent in expressive power to a state transition diagram. In a transition matrix, each row corresponds to one of the object's states and so does each column. The entry in the jth row and kth column represents the transition from the jth state to the kth state.

Completion Criteria for an Object-Oriented Requirements Analysis

In fact, requirements analysis is never complete until the system has been retired. Until then, there is a continual need to reassess, or at least to reconfirm, the users' requirements. What is meant by *completion criteria* is, of course, more modest, namely, the conditions under which one decides to proceed with building (or modifying) a system that conforms to the requirements models. This represents the point at which the analyst's job is, for the time being, done. Although there may have been design activity during the analysis phase for purposes of understanding the implications of various requirements, the design activity now becomes primary: it begins the process of realizing the requirements by transforming the models into software.

The question is when this should happen. As in any transition from requirements analysis to design, the question can be answered with two considerations:

- Traceability.
- Absence of significant ambiguity.

That is, the analysis process is complete when (1) all of the original informally specified requirements can be traced to the models and (2) the models themselves are precise enough so that *any* realization of them will be acceptable.

The second item is a tall order. This is one reason why requirements must be continually revisited. Just as some design activity is necessary in the analysis phase, in order to explore the implications of the requirements, it is also true that some analysis activity is invariably needed during the design phase. This is because ambiguities that had not been previously recognized in the models may later appear, as one tries to "build to" the models.

The meaning of traceability and absence of ambiguity in the object-oriented approach is now considered. The initial requirements specification for a system is typically formulated in terms of *function* and *performance*, i.e., what the system must do and how quickly, accurately, and under what workload conditions it must do it. Traceability, therefore, requires that all functional capabilities identified in the initial specification must be mapped to objects. In the most straightforward cases, it is possible to map a required function to the object that provides that function as a method. Because of the encapsulated nature of objects, however, it is not always the case that a single object will suffice to perform an entire system-level function. There might, instead, be a chain of successive method invocations, involving several objects, that *together* perform the required function. This is the primary reason that modeling a system's end-to-end behavior is an important aspect of OORA.

One way to facilitate traceability is to structure the system so that every required function corresponds to an *interface method*. In this approach, the system itself is modeled as a large object providing certain services to the system's environment (which may consist of users or other systems). The required functional capabilities can be directly mapped to these system-level services. The system-level services can then be allocated to lower-level objects using the standard method of object decomposition–aggregation. The reader should note that even using this approach, end-to-end behavioral modeling is still necessary to guarantee that performance requirements will be met.

Absence of ambiguity means that the contents of the initially specified requirements have been sufficiently clarified so that any implementation of them will be acceptable. There is no easy way to ascertain this. Extensive discussion with the prospective users of the system together with prototypes of key features for user feedback are still the foundation of a successful requirements analysis. The object-oriented approach does help in one respect, however. Because there is a more direct relationship between the form of the OORA products and the eventual design and implementation, there is less of a chance of intentions becoming lost in the translation from requirements to design or from design to implementation. Moreover, because the requirements and design representations are similar in form, the iteration necessitated by a discovery of ambiguity is made easier.

COMPARISON OF SIX DIFFERENT APPROACHES

The models we described earlier in Models commonly used in OORA form the basis of all of the approaches that we now discuss. Thus, the various methods have a lot in common. They differ from each other in several respects:

- Emphasis (i.e., their view of which models are most important).
- Specific notations (e.g., additional information that can be provided in the models).
- Recommended steps to be followed in developing the models.

In this section we will concentrate on the differences —particularly the differences in emphasis and the kinds of information that each approach suggests putting into the models. The notational differences are fairly arbitrary and the reader should recognize that elements of the different methods can be combined, as appropriate, for modeling the most important information about a particular system's requirements.

The Coad-Yourdon Approach

Coad and Yourdon present an object-oriented analysis as consisting of five "layers." These layers are not layers of the system being described, but rather layers of the analysis itself. The development of each layer adds certain information to the resulting specification, and the analysis is complete when all five layers have been specified. The layers are

- Class-object.
- Structure.
- Subject.
- Attribute.
- Service.

The *class-object* layer consists of identifying the key classes and objects in the application. The *structure* layer consists of describing the whole-part (aggregation) and generalization-specialization (inheritance) relations between classes and objects. In the Coad-Yourdon notation, the whole-part and generalization-specialization relations can be presented together in a single diagram: different arc shapes are used to indicate the two different relations.

The *subject* layer consists of identifying what Coad and Yourdon call "subjects." These are high-level groupings of objects and/or classes into major areas, and are similar to what have conventionally been called "subsystems." The criteria for grouping objects and classes into subjects are less well-defined than those that govern the definition of classes (namely, strong internal coupling and well-defined service-based interfaces). The purpose of the subjects is to provide an easily comprehended top-level view of a system which is compatible with the more detailed enumeration of classes and objects.

The *attribute* and *service* layers are where the classes and objects of a system are described in detail. Also, in these layers, the analyst explores relationships between classes other than specialization and aggregation.

Coad and Yourdon suggest a number of questions that can help one identify a class's (or an object's) attributes. Once the attributes have been identified, they recommend identifying *instance connections* between objects. An instance connection is an association between two objects —essentially the same as a relationship in an Entity-Relationship model. Associations have cardinality constraints such as one-to-one, one-to-many, many-to-many, and optional. After the instance connections have been identified, Coad and Yourdon recommend checking for certain "suspect" connections; these are connections that "hide" additional classes, which should then be explicitly defined. Instance connections may be used to eliminate attributes with *repeating values*—for example, the attribute "car" of the class "owner" (an owner can have many cars). Such attributes can be replaced by classes in their own right—in our example, the class "car." An instance connection (e.g., "owner has car") can then be used to represent the relationship between the original class and what used to be the repeating attribute.

Finally, in the service layer, the analyst identifies the services that each class (or object) provides. The most notable feature of this step is the order in which Coad and Yourdon recommend describing system dynamics: first model each object as a *state machine,* then identify the *services* that each object provides, and then identify *message connections* between objects. Thus, the behavior of an object as a state machine provides a basis for identifying services. The elaboration of each service, in turn, provides a basis for identifying messages that flow between objects.

Services are classified into two high-level categories, *algorithmically simple* and *algorithmically complex.* Within the simple category, four types of services are identified: *create, connect, access,* and *release.* Within the complex category, there are two types of services: *calculate* and *monitor.* A *service diagram,* which is essentially a structured form of flow chart, is used to specify the procedural logic of each service.

The Shlaer-Mellor Approach

The Shlaer-Mellor approach differs from Coad-Yourdon in placing more emphasis on information modeling and state modeling, and less emphasis on modeling object interfaces. Shlaer and Mellor discuss three basic models and several supplementary models. The basic three are

- The *informational model* involves identifying and describing the *objects* of a system, the *relationships* between objects, and the *attributes* of the objects and relationships. This is essentially an entity–relationship–attribute model, borrowing ideas that were originally developed for database systems (Chen, 1976). (In the context of OORA, Shlaer and Mellor speak of *object instances* rather than entities. Unfortunately, the term *object* in Shlaer-Mellor is used to denote what most others refer to as a *class.*)
- The *state model* in the Shlaer-Mellor approach is treated in more depth and detail than in other OORA methods.
- The *process model* is a dataflow representation of each method of an object; it describes the processing performed by each method. (Shlaer and Mellor speak of an object's *actions* rather than methods.)

In the following paragraphs we discuss some of the highlights of these and the supplementary models.

Information Model. Shlaer and Mellor identify three types of attributes: descriptive, naming, and referential. *Descriptive* attributes identify the relevant properties of an object. The descriptive attributes of a physical object might, for example, include weight, heat, color, speed, etc. *Naming* attributes are identifiers that are used to locate specific objects; they include the names with which a system user would identify objects, as well as internal identifiers used by the system itself. A *referential* attribute is a reference within an object to another object. For example, in a vehicle registration system, the object type *car* might have the attribute *owner.* This is a referential attribute because it refers to another object in the system, namely the owner of the car.

Shlaer and Mellor specify a handful of rules for structuring the information model—these are derived from the standard rules for normalizing databases, and help to ensure the integrity of the system's data throughout its operation (Codd, 1970).

Relationships in the information model are classified as unconditional, conditional, and biconditional. An unconditional relationship is one that holds throughout the lifetime of the objects involved. A conditional relationship between objects arises dynamically when certain conditions are met. A biconditional relationship is one in which either object may or may not be involved. For example, the relationship *Driver owns Car* arises when a car is purchased. Since both a Driver and a Car can exist without being in such a relationship, this is a biconditional relation.

The Shlaer-Mellor approach supports the notion of *associative* objects, i.e., objects that represent specific relationships. For example, a *Title* object can be defined to represent the relationship *Driver owns Car.* Representing relationships as objects in their own right provides considerable flexibility to the information model. An associative object can, for example, enter into relationships with other objects. In particular, by identifying the "is-a" relationships between associative objects, the analyst can define a hierarchy of relationship types. For example, a hierarchy of purchase types may be defined by introducing the associative objects *Title, House Title,* and *Car Title,* where a *House Title* is-a *Title,* and similarly a *Car Title* is-a *Title.*

State Model. Shlaer and Mellor introduce the notion of an *object life-cycle* to describe the sequence of states that an object passes through from its creation to its disappearance. Certain life-cycle paradigms are described—for example, a *circular life-cycle* is one in which an object repeatedly passes through the same sequence of states, indefinitely. A *born-and-die life-cycle* is one in which an object is dynamically created during the system's operation, passes through a series of states, and then disappears from the system. In the Shlaer-Mellor approach, actions are associated with object states: that is, when an object is in a given state it will perform a specific action associated with that state. (The alternative, which is supported in the Rumbaugh approach described below, is to associate actions with transitions between states.) This implies the *same data rule:* all events that cause a transition into a particular state must carry the same event data.

The Shlaer-Mellor state model includes some unique constructs, such as:

- *Timer objects:* these are objects that generate events at specific time intervals. Shlaer and Mellor provide a generic state model for such objects.
- *Subtype migration:* This occurs when an object, through a change of state, also changes its type (i.e., the class that it belongs to). Subtype migration is not explicitly supported by any of the mainstream object-oriented programming languages. It is, however, consistent both with the object-oriented paradigm and with the concept of objects as state machines: in different states, an object will accept different messages, or will process the same messages differently. One way to represent such differences is to place the object in different subclasses when it is in these different states.

The Shlaer-Mellor approach is particularly strong in their treatment of *relationship dynamics.* They introduce the concepts of assigner objects and monitor objects for modeling competitive relationships—that is, relationships in which several objects compete for access to a limited set of resources. An *assigner object* is one whose purpose is to mediate such competition by serializing requests for resources and assigning resources to the requesting objects as they become available. A *monitor object* is a simple form of assigner: the monitor repeatedly cycles through the states "waiting for request," "waiting for resource," "assigning resource to request." More complex forms of assigner lifecycle are sometimes necessary: Shlaer and Mellor go into quite a bit of detail about different forms of competitive relationships and the kinds of assigner objects that are needed to mediate them.

System dynamics are described by means of an *object communication model* (OCM), which is essentially the object interaction model: Individual messages between objects are shown as arcs, but the services that they cause to be invoked are not explicitly shown. The OCM implies a layering of objects, wherein top-level objects issue messages, lowest-level objects receive messages, and middle-layer objects do both. Shlaer and Mellor adhere to the accepted wisdom that top-level objects are responsible for control, lowest-level objects perform common services, and middle level objects carry out functions specific to the application.

Another distinctive aspect of message passing in Shlaer-Mellor is that they explicitly accommodate asynchronous communication between objects. Messages (which are called *event signals* in their terminology) are buffered at their destination until the receiving object is available to process them. Moreover, objects can access the variables of other objects directly, when necessary, without sending *get* and *set* messages. This implies that the design of the software will require significant transformation of the requirements analysis models: in an object-oriented design, messaging is typically synchronous and data access is frequently mediated by *get* and *set* operations. Shlaer and Mellor have developed explicit procedures for transforming the analysis models into a design.

An important part of the Shlaer-Mellor approach is the dynamic modeling of individual *threads* in a system—a thread being the sequence of actions, across all objects, that occur in response to a given event. The Thread-of-Control chart is a graphical model of this behavior. Each object's sequence of states is shown in a column—one object per column. Interactions between objects in specific states are shown as arrows between the respective columns. This model is especially important because end-to-end modeling of system behavior is often ignored in the practice of OORA.

Process Model. The third basic model in the Shlaer-Mellor approach represents the processing performed by each object action (i.e., method). The decomposition of an action into subprocesses is shown by means of a dataflow diagram, enhanced with a notation for showing control flow and conditional outputs. In their discussion of the process model they identify several types of processes:

- Accessors, which access an object's data store (i.e., the object's variables).
- Event generators, which signal other processors.
- Transformations, which operate on input data and make the results available as output data.
- Tests, which check whether specific conditions hold and then cause control to be transferred appropriately.

Finally, the *object access model* is an abstraction of the process model: it shows dataflow between objects, and is thus complementary to the object communication model.

The Object Modeling Approach of Rumbaugh and Co-workers

Rumbaugh's approach shares with Shlaer-Mellor the use of three basic models, which in Rumbaugh's nomenclature are

- Object model.
- Dynamic model.
- Functional model.

These are roughly analogous to the information, state, and process models of Shlaer-Mellor. The two approaches emphasize different details in the basic models, and offer different kinds of supplementary models.

Object Model. In the Rumbaugh approach, the object model is the static model of a system. Like the Shlaer-Mellor information model, this static model is based on the idea of objects, classes of objects, and relationships between objects. Like the Coad-Yourdon model, classes are defined in terms of their attributes and their methods.

In Rumbaugh's terminology, a relationship between specific objects is called a *link;* the relation itself—that is, the set of all links of a given type—is called an *association.* Links are not necessarily between two objects; there can be ternary links, involving three objects, and higher-order links, involving more objects. Like objects, links can have attributes. Associations can be modeled as classes in their own right—this is similar to the associative objects in the Shlaer-Mellor approach.

In addition to objects, object classes, links, and associations, Rumbaugh and co-workers introduce the concept of a *module,* which is essentially a subsystem, i.e., a collection of objects that together perform an identifiable high-level system function. They also introduce the concept of *sheets,* which are essentially individual pages in a specification, showing some cohesive portion of the system being modeled.

Rumbaugh and co-workers go into some detail concerning the structure of the object model. Among the more distinctive constructs that they discuss are the following:

- Recursive aggregation: the idea of an object of class **A** containing a sub-object that is also of class **A.** This phenomenon is found, for example, in languages that may form part of an application. A command in a user interface language may consist of several subcommands.
- Propagation of operations through components of an object—or, more generally, through a network of linked objects. This concept is useful in modeling the end-to-end behavior of a system, and is similar in spirit to the thread-of-control charts in the Shlaer-Mellor approach.
- Distinction between abstract and concrete classes: abstract classes do not have any instances in their own right—they only have subclasses. Concrete classes do have instances. For example, we might consider *animal* to be an abstract class, since there is no such thing as a generic animal: every animal is a member of some species, e.g., *dog, cat, orangutan,* which are concrete subclasses of the abstract class *animal.*
- Metadata: the treatment of descriptors—that is, patterns whose purpose is to describe a set of objects—as objects in their own right. A class definition is a descriptor, since it describes a set of objects (namely, the instances of the class). Thus, the Rumbaugh approach accommodates treating a class definition as an object in its own right. For example, one might treat Car Models as objects in their own right. Each Car Model describes a set of cars (namely, the cars of that model), but treating the Car Model itself as an object provides additional flexibility in specifying the system.
- Candidate Keys: a candidate key is a minimal set of attributes that suffices to identify any object in a class uniquely.
- Constraints: these are assertions involving one or more objects and links, which must hold true in order for the system to operate correctly.

Dynamic Model. Like the Shlaer-Mellor approach, the Rumbaugh and co-workers approach emphasizes modeling each object as a state machine—the state of an object at any time is determined by the values of its attributes. System dynamics are modeled by relating the individual state diagrams to each other by means of shared events.

Rumbaugh and co-workers advocate a certain amount of system-wide dynamic modeling preceding the description of each state machine, in order to identify the significant events and to determine the dynamic relationships between objects. The first step in this process is to identify *scenarios,* which are sequences of related events. The next step is to identify the source and recipient of each event and represent this information in an *event trace.* An event trace is similar to the protocol diagrams frequently found in communication protocol specifications. Each object is represented by a vertical line, and events sent from one object to another are represented as horizontal arrows from the source object to the receiving object. Successive events appear underneath one another as shown in Figure 6.

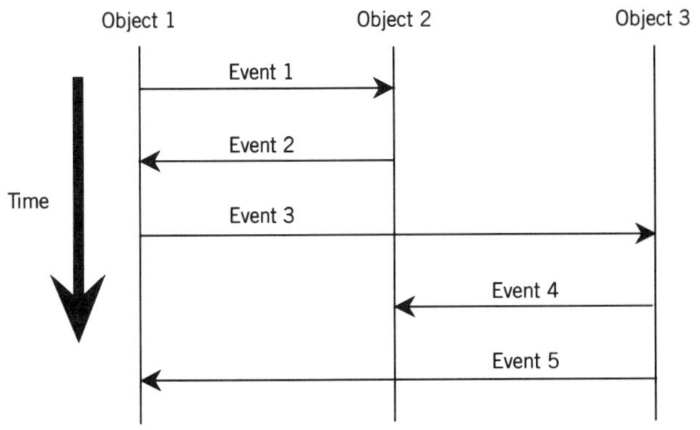

Figure 6. Event trace.

Event traces are similar to the thread-of-control charts in Shlaer-Mellor, except that specific states for each object are not yet identified.

Following the specification of event traces, each object that has a significant dynamic behavior is modeled as a state machine. The following are some of the more distinctive aspects of state diagrams as advocated by Rumbaugh and co-workers:

- A distinction between *activities,* which are performed while an object is in a given state, and *actions,* which are relatively instantaneous operations performed during a transition between states (or upon entry into, or exit from, a state).
- Nested state diagrams: this is a way of reducing the complexity of the state model. Several closely related states, say $\mathbf{S}_1$, $\mathbf{S}_2$ ... $\mathbf{S}_n$, can be aggregated, or generalized, into a higher level state **S**. Thus, an object is in state **S** if and only if it is in one of the states $\mathbf{S}_1$, $\mathbf{S}_2$ ... $\mathbf{S}_n$. In a similar manner, a generalization hierarchy of event types can be defined. These ideas were originally developed by Harel (1987, 1988).
- Concurrency of state machines: when an object consists of several subobjects (the whole-part relationship), the subobjects act as concurrent state machines —that is, each state machine operates in parallel with the others. Rumbaugh and co-workers also discuss the possibility of concurrent state machines within an undecomposed object, i.e., an object that has no subobjects. In this case, concurrency can sometimes be achieved by partitioning the object's attributes, and considering each partition as a state machine in its own right.
- Automatic transitions: these arise when the sole purpose of a state is to perform a certain activity. Once the activity is completed, a transition to a successor state occurs automatically.
- Sending events: Rumbaugh and co-workers provide an explicit notation in their state diagrams to show when one state machine sends an event to another state machine.
- Synchronization of concurrent activities: a notation is provided for showing concurrent activities within a single state. The transition to this state from a previous state involves a *splitting* of activity into two or more concurrent portions; the transition from this state to a successor state involves a *merging* of the concurrent activities.

Functional Model. Like the process model of Shlaer and Mellor, this is a dataflow model. Unlike the Shlaer-Mellor process model, high-level dataflow diagrams in the Rumbaugh and co-workers approach do not necessarily correspond to object methods. Instead, they represent *processes,* which are yet another view of the system. The lowest-level processes—those that appear in the lowest-level dataflow diagrams—do correspond to object methods. This relatively undefined relationship between the functional model and the other models in the Rumbaugh approach may be considered a weak point of the method.

The Wirfs-Brock and Co-workers Approach

Wirfs-Brock and co-workers offer their approach as a way of doing object-oriented design, but it is widely viewed as an analysis method as well. The distinguishing characteristic of this approach is its emphasis on *responsibilities, collaborations,* and *contracts.* The responsibilities of a class are the functions that it is intended to perform. Collaborations are the uses that one class—the client—makes of another class—the server—in performing its responsibilities. Contracts are the "agreements" or "protocols" that govern a collaboration between client and server. Ultimately a contract will be implemented by means of one or more messages between the classes.

The emphasis in the Wirfs-Brock approach is on clarifying each class's responsibilities, identifying the collaborations necessary to meet those responsibilities, and defining the contracts that will govern those collaborations. In studying the interaction between classes—specifically from the point of view of meeting the functional requirements of the system—this approach goes into more depth than the others considered here. The theme of collaborations is most closely related to Rumbaugh's discussion of propagating operations between classes. It is also manifested in Rumbaugh's Event Traces and Shlaer-Mellor's Thread-of-Control Diagrams. In the Wirfs-Brock approach, however, the theme of responsibilities, collaborations, and contracts takes center stage.

A *Collaborations Graph* is similar to the Object Interaction model in that each contract is shown as an arc between a point in the client class and a port in the server class. Wirfs-Brock and co-workers also recommend the use of a *Hierarchy Graph,* which is similar to the classification model shown in Figure 3, and also *Venn Diagrams* as a means of expressing common responsibilities of classes.

The emphasis on collaborations shows up in the Wirfs-Brock template for Class Specifications. As in the Coad-Yourdon and Rumbaugh approaches, these specifications identify the services performed by the class—i.e., its contracts. Unlike Coad-Yourdon and Rumbaugh, the Wirfs-Brock description of each contract includes a list of required collaborations—that is, collaborations that this class needs in order to meet its responsibility as defined by the contract. Thus, the Class Specification includes not only a list of services *provided* by the class, but also of services *used* by the class (and provided by other classes).

Wirfs-Brock and co-workers divide the specification process into two phases, which they call the *exploratory* phase and the *analysis* phase. The exploratory phase consists of identifying classes, responsibilities, and collaborations. They emphasize the process of looking for *abstract superclasses* by identifying common attributes in previously identified classes.

In the analysis phase, hierarchy graphs are developed in order to document inheritance between classes, and Venn diagrams are drawn to document shared responsibilities. Then, specific contracts are defined, and their protocols are elaborated. This phase also includes the identification of *subsystems,* which are collections of classes that collaborate closely with each other. Subsystems, in this sense, are similar to the *subjects* of Coad-Yourdon and the *modules* of Rumbaugh and co-workers.

The Firesmith Approach

The Firesmith approach, known as ADM-3, is the most detailed and complete of those that we consider. (A more recent version, called ADM-4, has been developed but has not yet been publicly documented.) This makes it more difficult to grasp as a whole—there is a plethora of diagramming and Ada-like textual notations—but also perhaps quite useful as a collection of practical techniques. The primary concern of ADM-3 is the development of very large software systems, i.e., systems containing millions of source lines of code. It is oriented towards the use of Ada as a programming language and the use of Government standards, such as 2167-A, for documentation.

Firesmith addresses OORA from several points of view:

- Models.
- Heuristics.
- Process.
- Specification language.
- Documentation guidelines.

Models. Each of the following models consists of several types of diagrams as well as textual specifications:

- Assembly model: Firesmith's notion of *assembly* is similar to the concept of *subject* in Coad-Yourdon, *module* in Rumbaugh, and *subsystem* in Wirfs-Brock. Taken together, the assemblies represent the highest-level of a system. An assembly model describes an assembly as a collection of subassemblies. It includes a Context Diagram showing relationships between the assembly and its environment, an Assembly Diagram showing the dependency relationships among the subassemblies, and a textual specification including the purpose and a description of each subassembly.
- Object model: This documents a subassembly as a collection of objects. A General Semantic Network (GSN) is used to show relationships between objects. The GSN is similar to the *instance connections* in Coad-Yourdon, the *information model* in Shlaer-Mellor, and the *links* in Rumbaugh and co-workers object model. An Interaction Diagram shows the messaging relationships between objects. Composition Diagrams show the aggregation relationships between objects. In addition, each object is described in terms of its operations and attributes and the exceptions that it can raise. Firesmith distinguishes between *modifier* operations, which can change the state of an object, and *presever* operations, which leave the state intact.
- Class model: This provides additional information to the object model, identifying classes of objects and the inheritance relationships between classes. Firesmith employs a more detailed version of the classification diagram illustrated in Figure 3.
- State model: Each object and class is described by means of a State Transition Diagram, a State Operation Table, and a textual description of each state. The State Operation Table is a way of describing the states in which each preserver operation can be invoked.
- Control model: Firesmith introduces the notion of a *scenario,* which is a possible sequence of operation calls and/or exception flows among or within objects and classes. A scenario is described by means of a Control Flow Diagram. This is a useful tool in modeling end-to-end system behavior, later. The control model also includes a specification of each operation of each object and class. Firesmith recommends use of a declarative specification of operations in terms of pre-conditions and post-conditions, but if this is impractical then a conventional algorithmic specification may be given.
- Timing model: A very specific notation is provided, under than name of Timing Diagrams, to specify performance requirements for sequences of operations. An alternative to the development of timing diagrams is to annotate the interaction diagrams, state transition diagrams, and/or control flow diagram with this information.

Heuristics. Firesmith devotes a significant amount of space to presenting guidelines for identifying objects and classes. Unlike the corresponding discussions in the other texts we have considered, Firesmith addresses the pros and cons of each guideline, and offers a set of "recommended" guidelines as well as a set of "conventional" guidelines that he views as less effective.

Process. Firesmith treats the OORA process largely from a program management perspective. As such, he goes beyond simply presenting, the modeling steps to be performed. There is, in addition to the modeling issues, a discussion of training requirements, team organization, prototype development, formal reviews, and integration. Of particular interest is the inclusion of a *project-specific domain analysis,* which Firesmith advocates under two conditions: (1) a multi-project domain analysis has not yet been performed (see below), and (2) the project is sufficiently large to warrant an intensive search for reuse opportunities.

Specification Language. In addition to the diagrams discussed above, Firesmith has developed an extensive textual specification and design language that is used to document assemblies, subassemblies, objects, classes, usage and inheritance relationships, messages, operations, attributes, and exceptions. A form pseudocode is provided to specify algorithms procedurally; a complementary *assertion* language— involving invariants, preconditions, and postconditions—allows operations to be specified in declarative form. The syntax of the specification language is similar to that of Ada. Specifications developed in this language can be straightforwardly extended, during system implementation, to become compilable Ada program units.

Documentation Guidelines. Firesmith provides a detailed table of contents for a software specification and design document, drawing on the models discussed above. This again reflects the origins of ADM-3 in very large-scale software system development. (It should be noted that Shlaer and Mellor (1992) also provide an explicit tailoring of the MIL-STD-2167A Software Requirements Specification outline.)

The Seidewitz-Stark Approach

The Seidewitz-Stark approach is noteworthy for its specifically Ada orientation. Although the concepts are quite similar to those discussed above, the notations have been developed to flow smoothly into Ada program unit definitions. The authors also provide brief summaries that compare and contrast their approach with other approaches, including some of those discussed above.

Seidewitz and Stark advocate a two-dimensional approach consisting of (1) static analysis and (2) dynamic analysis. Their method of static analysis is similar to the Shlaer-Mellor and Rumbaugh and co-workers approaches. It consists of identifying objects and their attributes, grouping objects into classes, and defining relationships and dependencies between objects. Particular attention is paid to the relationship between a *superclass* (i.e., parent class) and its subclasses, and the whole-part relationship between a *composite class* and its constituent parts.

It is in the dynamic portion of the analysis that Seidewitz and Stark introduce the operations (methods) of an object class. Operations are categorized as being either *constructors* or *selectors*. These terms are synonymous with Firesmith's *modifier* and *preserver* operations: constructors are those operations that can alter the value of an object's attributes. Selectors are those operations that only read an object's attributes. (This is a not quite standard use of these terms. The term "constructor" is frequently used for an operation that creates new instances of a class.) Within this high-level categorization, Seidewitz and Stark offer the taxonomy of operations shown in Figure 7.

Operations in the Seidewitz-Stark approach may be specified using a procedural pseudocode. Alternatively, they suggest using a declarative syntax that specifies the preconditions of the operation by means of a *requires* clause, and the postcondition of the operation by means of an *ensures* clause. Using the declarative syntax keeps the specification within the realm of requirements ("what") as opposed to algorithm design ("how").

The dynamic analysis may also include state transition diagrams—one for each class of objects—as in the other methods we have discussed. The Seidewitz-Stark approach resembles the Coad-Yourdon method in that the state model is considered a supplement to the (more essential) specification of a class's operations. Nevertheless, Seidewitz and Stark observe that developing the state transition model is often a good way to start specifying the dynamics of a class.

Dynamic analysis in the Seidewitz-Stark approach also involves an analysis of the required system-level functions. The analysis is placed in an object-oriented framework by describing the *system environment*, which consists of the following:

- External objects that will generate events for the system to process.
- The events generated by these external objects.
- The effects of the system on the external objects when these events occur.

Finally, Seidewitz and Stark pay more attention than the other approaches to the dynamic aspects of inheritance. In the approaches previously discussed, specification of the class-subclass hierarchy is considered to be part of the static model of a system. There is, however, an essential dynamic aspect to the class-subclass hierarchy. The dynamic aspect is manifested in the inheritance of operations from a parent class, and/or the overriding of such operations.

RISKS IN TRANSITIONING TO OORA

As a relatively new approach to software engineering the transition of an organization to OORA carries with it several risks. In this section, the following risk areas are discussed:

Management Risks

- Acceptance.
- Interface with systems engineering.
- Need for Domain Analysis.

Technical Risks

- Identifying objects.
- Ignoring behavioral modeling.
- Ignoring functional modeling.

Acceptance

Acceptance is an issue in all technology transfer. In the case of object-oriented methods, the situation is muddied by the sheer popularity of the term *object-oriented* and the

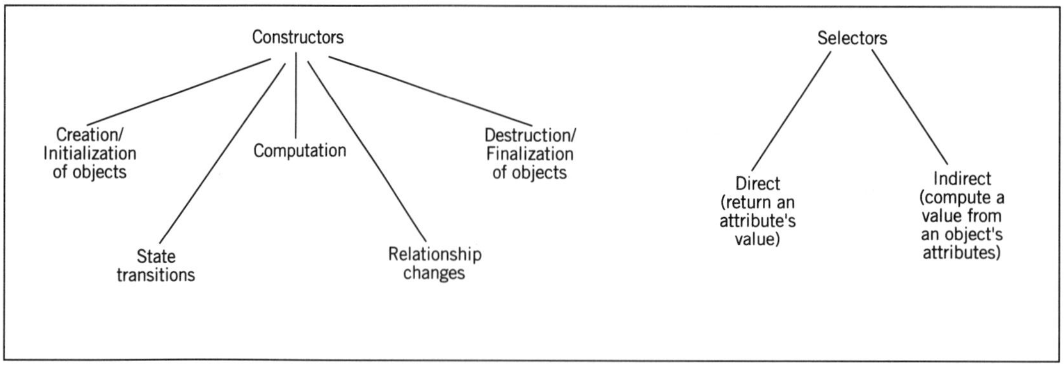

Figure 7. Taxonomy of object operations.

myths associated with it. Education in the basic concepts, as presented above, is essential in combating the resistance that stems from ignorance or misconceptions. The *reasons* for object-oriented partitioning criteria, and their impact on maintainability and reusability, should be emphasized and illustrated with examples. It may also be useful to point out that the underlying issues addressed by the object-oriented approach, such as cohesion, coupling, and information hiding, are not new, nor are the answers particularly surprising. Object-oriented development makes explicit the issues that the best engineers have always tackled. Thus OORA can be presented not as a radically new approach being imposed by fiat or as a result of fashion but rather as a sharpening of the basic principles of software engineering that have long been known.

Interface with Systems Engineering

In the conventional organization of a large development project, the systems engineering group produces a system design that allocates functions to a software and hardware and from which software requirements are derived. The allocation of functions to software frequently involves the identification of major software blocks, sometimes known as computer software configuration items or as software subsystems. There is a tremendous risk to this approach if the system design process has followed the traditional method of functional decomposition: the major blocks of software will not represent good object-oriented partitions, and the system design will force the software development team to compromise its application of object-oriented criteria. This, in turn, can lead to confused and poorly justified software design decisions and eventually to disillusionment with object-oriented methods on the part of the software team ("We tried it and it didn't work").

There are two measures that can prevent such situations: (1) integrate object-oriented partitioning principles into the system design process and (2) ensure early and ongoing interaction between the system design team and the software development team. The latter may be an easier measure to implement in the short term, but a commitment to object-oriented system development is probably necessary, in the long term, if the fun benefits of object-oriented software development are to be realized.

Need for Domain Analysis.

Although reuse and object-orientation are not synonymous, the culture of object-orientation is largely a culture of reuse, for two reasons: (1) objects, with their well-defined interfaces and encapsulated functionality, provide an effective vehicle for reuse and (2) good objects and classes are hard to define and arriving at them requires a significant investment. If this second point is not recognized by management, there will be unrealistic expectations for an early return on investment in object-oriented development.

A commitment to object-oriented development entails a commitment to a serious and ongoing analysis of what the "right" objects and classes are. This is nothing but domain analysis (qv). If an organization practices object-oriented development on a regular basis, it will be doing domain analysis whether it is aware of this fact or not. Awareness of the fact will enable an organization to employ, to its advantage, the methods and techniques that are now being developed for domain analysis.

Identifying Objects

Identifying objects is the technical counterpart to the risk area just discussed. Practitioners should not expect that their first attempt to identify the objects of an application will be optimal. The identification and definition of objects and classes involves trade-offs, the answers to which are not always clear until negative lessons have been learned through experience. A number of books on object-oriented programming provide guidance in this area (e.g., Meyer, 1992; Cargill, 1992), but the OORA literature is still fairly shallow on this point, probably because the field is new.

Ignoring Behavioral Modeling

With its emphasis on data encapsulation and information hiding, the literature on OORA has tended to emphasize static modeling: the definition of objects, classes, and their interfaces. Dynamic modeling, to the extent that it is addressed, tends to be limited to the behavior of individual objects, i.e., describing them as state machines or specifying each method in pseudocode. Interactions between objects are described in terms of the individual messages that flow between them. There is frequently an implicit assumption that if a system is implemented to meet such specifications, it is ensured to behave correctly.

This assumption is ill-founded and carries with it the risk that the required end-to-end behavior of the system (i.e., the behavior of the system as a whole) will not be sufficiently analyzed. A thorough requirements analysis must include some consideration of end-to-end processing, starting with the occurrence of an event that activates some system processing, following the succession of messages and activations of objects' services that occur in response to the event, and ending with a description of the system's steady state at the conclusion of this processing and of any output that results. The models described earlier must be verified against such scenarios, and the scenarios themselves must be checked for completeness with respect to the system requirements and operations concept.

Ignoring Functional Modeling

A related risk is the tendency in object-oriented development to ignore the functional aspects of a system and of the objects within a system. Although OORA leads one away from functional decomposition as a method of *structuring* a system, it does not relieve one of the obligation to analyze what the system is supposed to do. In the object-oriented approach, inputs and outputs are passed as arguments within messages exchanged between objects. This view tends to downplay their importance in comparison to the messages themselves. Nevertheless, it is through the conversion of inputs to outputs that the proper operation of each object, and of the system as a whole, will eventually be assessed. It is, therefore, necessary to describe the functional relationships between system-level inputs and outputs and between the input and output arguments of each object's methods. The *data flow* view can be useful in this connection, as long as (1) its purpose is understood (namely, to describe the functional properties of a system), (2) its limitations are recognized (ie, the need to complement it with the models described above), and (3) a well-defined relationship between the data flow models and the other models is established (i.e., it must be possible to map the data flow model into the others, eg, by considering data flow between *objects* rather than between some ill-defined kind of *processes*). Other ways of representing functions are also possible, e.g., using pre- and post-conditions as in the approach of Seidewitz and Stark.

CONCLUSION

The use of OORA reduces the amount of restructuring needed to create an object-oriented design from the requirements analysis products. In doing so, it improves the ability of developers and verifiers to trace requirements to designs. The emphasis on precise interface definitions should lead to more manageable development in the large and facilitate the eventual integration of independently developed blocks of software. Finally, by encouraging the specification of relatively self-contained subsystems, the use of object-oriented partitioning criteria in the requirements analysis phase should improve the reusability of requirements analysis products from one system to the next.

Little, if any, numerical evidence has been collected in support of these expectations, and it is perhaps not unfair to argue that the verdict on OORA is still out. Nevertheless, its practice appears to be growing, and its use in the successful development of operational (as opposed to prototype) systems has made it a serious competitor to the more process or function-oriented approaches.

BIBLIOGRAPHY

S. Bailin, "An Object-Oriented Requirements Specification Method," *Communications of the ACM* **32**(5) (May 1989).

P. Chen, "The Entity-Relationship Model—Towards a Unified View of Data," *ACM Transactions on Database Systems,* **1**(1) (March 1976).

P. Coad, "Object-Oriented Patterns," *Communications of the ACM* **35**(9) (Sept. 1992).

P. Coad. and E. Yourdon, *Object-Oriented Analysis,* 2nd ed., Yourdon Press, Prentice Hall, 1991.

E. Codd, "A Relational Model of Data for Large Shared Data Banks," *Communications of the ACM* **13**(6) (June 1970).

T. DeMarco, *Structured Analysis and Systems Specification,* Prentice Hall, 1979.

D. Embly, B. Kurtz, and S. Woodfield, *Object-Oriented Systems Analysis: A Model-Driven Approach,* Yourdon Press, 1992.

M. E. Fayad, L. J. Hawn, M. A. Roberts, and J. R. Klatt, "Using the Shlaer-Mellor Object-Oriented Analysis Method," *IEEE Software* **10**(2) (March 1993).

R. G. Fichman, and C. F. Kemerer, "Object-Oriented and Conventional Analysis and Design Methodologies," *IEEE Computer* **25**(10) (Oct. 1992).

D. G. Firesmith, *Object-Oriented Requirements Analysis and Logical Design,* John Wiley & Sons, New York, 1993.

C. Gane and T. Sarsen, *Structured Systems Analysis: Tools and Techniques,* Prentice Hall, 1978.

D. Harel, "Statecharts: a Visual Formalism for Complex Systems," *Science of Computer Programming* **8,** pp. 231–274 (1987).

D. Harel, "On Visual Formalisms," *Communications of the ACM* **31**(5), pp. 514–530 (May, 1988).

D. E. Monarchi and G. I. Puhr, "A Research Typology for Object-Oriented Analysis and Design," *Communications of the ACM* **35**(9) (Sept. 1992).

J-M. Nelson, "Applying Object-Oriented Analysis and Design," *Communications of the ACM* **35**(9) (Sept. 1992).

K. S. Rubin and A. Goldberg, "Object Behavior Analysis," *Communications of the ACM,* **35**(9) (Sept. 1992).

J. Rumbaugh, M. Blaha, W. Premerlani, F. Eddy, and W. Lorensen, *Object-Oriented Modeling and Design,* Prentice Hall, 1991.

E. Seldewitz and M. Stark, *Principles of Object-Oriented Software Development with Ada,* Millenium Systems Inc., Rockville, Md., 1992.

S. Shlaer and S. Mellor, *Object Lifecycles: Modeling the World in States,* Yourdon Press, Prentice Hall, New York, 1992.

S. Shlaer and S. Mellor, *Object-Oriented Systems Analysis: Modeling the World in Data,* Prentice Hall, New York, 1988.

SofTech, Inc., *An Introduction to SADT Structured Analysis and Design Technique,* Technical Report 9022-78R SofTech, Inc., Waltham, Mass., 1978.

R. Wirfs-Brock, B. Wilkerson and L. Wiener, *Designing Object-Oriented Software,* Prentice Hall, New York, 1990.

E. Yourdon and L. Constantine, *Structured Design,* Prentice Hall, New York, 1979.

SIDNEY C. BAILIN
CTA, Inc.

OPERATING SYSTEMS

BACKGROUND

Early Computers

Computers in the 1940s were programmed by connecting cables to establish a desired sequence of operations. Later computers performed computation sequences preprogrammed on a punched paper tape. By the early 1950s, the *stored program computer* had come into being. Programs and data were stored together in the computer's main memory. Input to and output from these early computers was by punched cards. The computer's memory was reloaded from a card reader for each new application program. With such limited hardware capabilities, there was no perceived need for operating systems as we understand them today.

Evolution of Storage Devices

In the early years of computing, software advances were often evoked by changes in hardware. The major hardware evolution that impelled development of operating systems was the adaptation of magnetic tape recording to the storage of digital data. Computers in the 1950s had minuscule memories, and punched cards were extremely bulky. The ability to store a few hundred characters per inch of half-inch-wide magnetic tape was therefore an immense improvement. Later, with thin layers of the same ferrimagnetic powder coated on circular disks, read and write access time was greatly reduced. Storage capacity per unit area was increased by many orders of magnitude as well.

These new mechanical devices required complex control commands: rewinding, searching for a particular numbered block, and reading or writing of data blocks from and to the magnetic surface. Disk storage access requires selection of: (**1**) a *head,* on one or more disks mounted on a common spindle; (**2**), a circular *track,* accessed by moving the head closer to or farther from the center of the disk; and (**3**) a *block* or *sector* of data read from a section of the track.

Storage access was not directly related to the applications being executed on the computer. It made good sense to have a utility program handle storage device operations. Operating systems originated as utilities to perform hardware-dependent operations that were identical (except for the data and location) for any program.

Early Operating Systems

Early operating systems handled routine hardware operations in the computer and its peripheral storage and other devices. They also made it feasible, for the first time, to queue a sequence of computer jobs, with their associated programs and data, to improve productivity greatly. Each job was automatically loaded, executed, and unloaded when completed. Until interactive computing showed up in the early 1960s, this so-called "batch" mode of operation was universal. It is still used today in routine applications.

A representative early operating system was IBSYS, a collection of programs designed to operate IBM's 7000 Series computers. In the early 1960s these systems were workhorses for scientific and engineering computations. Application programs were then usually written in FORTRAN, which used easy-to-remember mnemonics (names) in place of numeric values, for data locations and machine instruction codes. Programs were now translated into computer-usable form by a *compiler* (program) which produced machine code from source programs. A *linker* combined the parts of the user's program into a single *object program,* and *loader* transferred the resulting machine-code program into the computer's memory at execution time. Compilers were considered integral parts of early operating systems. This remains true today for computer designs produced in small quantities.

Evolution of Modern Operating Systems

Through the 1960s, development of operating systems had to keep step with ever-expanding arrays of hardware devices: storage drives, communications adapters, display terminals, event recorders, pointing devices, etc. Processing and memory capacity of computer hardware increased rapidly. It was no longer efficient to have a machine executing only one program at a time. Operating systems were then evolved to support *multitasking:* many program tasks in memory concurrently, but only one using the processor at any instant. These systems supported *multiprogramming,* wherein jobs for several independent users can be simultaneously resident in the system. Though this advance may now appear trivial, it greatly improved system efficiency. With it, the computer could be in use almost all of the time, rather than less than half the time, as before.

In early operating systems, *memory management* was merely a matter of loading a program and its data into memory. With the advent of multiprogramming, several programs had to compete for memory, and the operating system was assigned new tasks. More recently graphical user interfaces, especially in personal computers, have added major new operating system tasks, since the output console must be time- and area-shared between many applications.

Modern operating systems, even those designed for personal computers, can support these same operating system functions and more. Some handle a wide array of hardware peripherals and support many terminal users at once.

BASIC FUNCTIONS AND OPERATIONS OF OPERATING SYSTEMS

Figure 1 represents a processor, read-only memory containing basic input/output system software (BIOS), attached storage devices and other peripherals, and high-speed memory containing components of the operating sys-

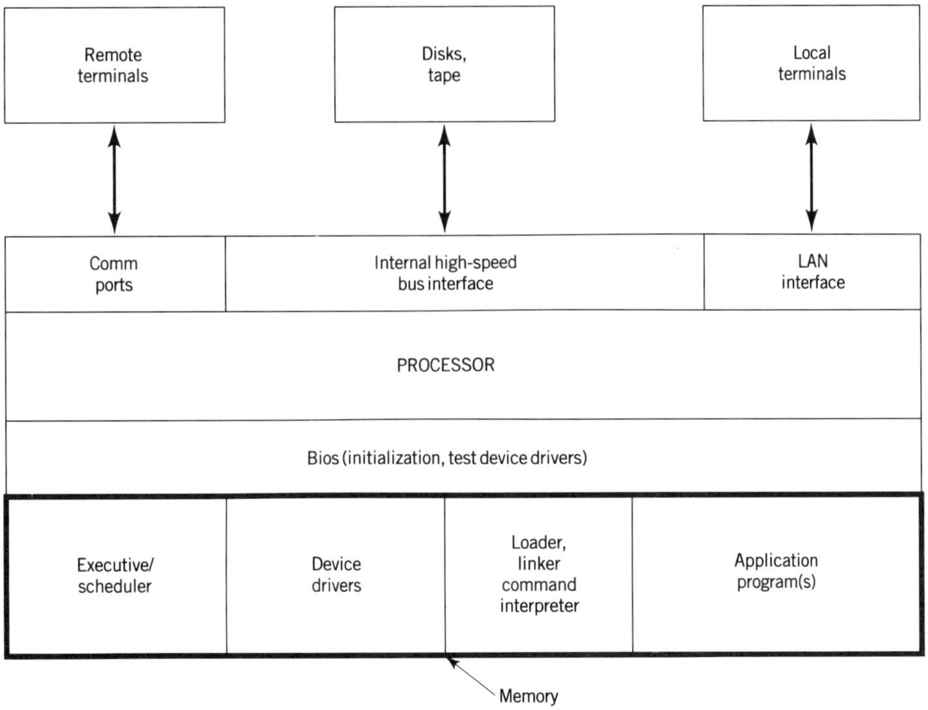

Figure 1. Elements of a computer and its operating system.

tem and currently executing application programs. There is no single "typical" operating system organization. However, the elements shown in Figure 1 and discussed below are common to a great many operating systems.

Most of these software elements are not computational wizards, but merely hardware resource managers. In operating system software, smaller (and faster) is better. Sophisticated software components such as graphic display interfaces are usually not in the core operating system, lest they defeat the objective of providing a simple and robust program interface.

Management of Memory, Storage Devices, and Other Peripherals

A primary function of any operating systems is management of the system hardware. A desirable objective is that users be shielded from the variety and complexity of the actual interfaces. The *logical interfaces* of a class of peripheral devices should be simple and as uniform as possible for all members of the class (storage devices, printers, etc.) A good operating system, in short, should do most of its work without the user and application program needing to be aware of it.

Memory Management. Memory management became an important operating system function after multiprogramming appeared. Because memory was now a shared resource, programmers were expected to request only as much memory as needed. The addition of dynamic memory allocation during program execution required the programmer of a well-behaved application to ask for more memory when needed, and to return it again when no longer needed. Random-length memory allocations at random times from a common pool of memory lead to fragmentation of that memory pool. Some computers determine all addresses by the addition of contents of two or more registers. In this case, the operating system can defragment memory by moving programs' memory during intervals when it is not in use.

Some computers support virtual memory in fixed-length pages of a few kilobytes or more. The address of each page is independently and automatically translated so that physically fragmented memory assignments appear continuous to a program. In these systems, operating systems make allocations and keep track of them, while hardware does the actual translation.

Storage Device Management. Storage device management by operating systems, once limited to reading magnetic tapes, now requires dealing with (**1**) the hardware peculiarities of the devices, (**2**) translating a physically fragmented storage space into continuous files, and (**3**) managing multiple streams of read and write requests. Over the years, special terms evolved to describe these important functions. If the storage media are removable, e.g., reels of tape or "disk packs," each reel, disk pack, or diskette is referred to as a *volume.* A volume may contain a machine-readable label, but there is nothing to guarantee that this agrees with the handwritten or printed label that identifies the volume physically.

The first step in using a volume is its *mounting* by an operator and the final step its *demounting*, physical removal of the medium from the storage drive. These same terms are sometimes used, even where no physical operation takes place: data becomes usable when it is mounted, and can no longer be accessed when demounted. A volume may contain a *hierarchy of directories,* each of which contains a number of individual files. Typically, files and directories are given alphanumeric mnemonic names. In large storage volumes shared via a network, individual users may be assigned specific directories. A file located in a sub-directory is located by its compound path name. For example, the character string D:\TREE LIMB\BRANCH\TWIG\LEAF.FIL could describe the location of a file LEAF.FIL whose immediate directory is TWIG and which is located deep in a hierarchy of file on the drive identified by letter D. Each directory is itself a file containing file name, size, location data, and date and time of file creation or changes.

Modern multiprogramming operating systems and network managers control read and write access to individual files. This is done in such a way as to avoid having a file changed independently by two users. While write authority usually limits file access to a single user, any number may obtain read access to a file. Large database files may be controlled at the level of an individual *record.*

Demountable storage volumes (e.g., disk packs, digital tapes or diskettes) usually have ways to *write-protect* information. For example, a movable plastic tab or adhesive strip scanned by a simple photo detector can positively prevent changing of volume contents.

In magnetic tape storage devices, a single directory is usually at the start of the tape. Magnetic disks are preformatted to lay out data in circular tracks, each containing the same number of fixed-length *sectors* or *blocks.* Error detection and correction schemes are implemented independently for data in each sector. Allocation schemes are designed for efficient use of recording surface while ensuring rapid access to the data. Generally, file space is allocated in fixed numbers of sectors. In large volumes, the smallest allocation may be 4k or 8k bytes. Although this is wasteful if average file size is less than one allocation unit, the alternative of smaller minimum allocations requires larger numbers of allocation units and more lengthy searching. The directory entry for a file may list all space allocations it owns, or merely point to a table that links the sequence of allocations in a chain of disk addresses. Internal disk addresses usually identify disk surface, cylinder (track number), and sector number.

Managing Input and Output. In addition to controlled processor, memory, and storage, all operating systems manage the flow-through of executing programs and related data. In the earliest computers, each program was executed independently and the system reset between programs. The was soon replaced by *job streams* comprising independent programs and some of their data, all punched into paper cards or paper tape. The operating system was directed by additional cards containing commands that called for operating system services, sent a message to an operator to mount or demount a tape, and identified the user, priorities, etc. In the single job stream environment, printed output emerged in job-input sequence from the system printer. It was usually identified by printing identifiers, in large letters, on a cover page.

With multiprogramming operating systems, each job concurrently executing in the system usually requests input, and produces output, in short spurts. While this could be handled through multiple input devices and multiple printers, a more efficient sharing technique was evolved; it became known as *spooling.* Input program and data was stored to a random access magnetic storage device (usually a disk file) well ahead of execution, then read into memory in blocks as requested during execution; output for each job was likewise collected in a file on a storage disk. After execution of a particular job was complete, its spooled output was sent to the printer. Spooling ensures that the input reader and printer's slow speeds do not delay the processor. In some systems, spooled output on a magnetic tape was taken to a separate computer whose function was to drive one or more printers. Though input spooling is still common for managing long-running programs on large machines, growth of interactive applications forced programs and data to be spooled on high speed random-access storage units. Spooling of printer output is widely used to share printers on local area networks.

Working with Files. In using a file under operating system control, a program must first request the system to *open* the file: for reading, writing, or adding data. When opened, a file has a logical *seek pointer* that locates the first character in the file. The pointer can be *moved* by commands to the operating system. It may be moved past the end of the existing file to prepare to add chronological data to the file. *Rewinding* to the start of the file requires only setting the seek pointer to the beginning. When the program has finished working with the file, it issues a command to the operating system to close it. This results in certain housekeeping: memory buffers are written to file, directory and space allocation are updated to reflect changes in file length, and the date and time are recorded in the file's directory entry. Modern operating systems automatically close files left open by an application when it terminates.

Task and Job Management

A second essential activity carried out by a modern operating system is management of executing tasks. Evolution from a single spooled job stream to multiple job streams—each potentially supporting multiple on-line terminal tasks—drastically changed operating system job and task management. Mainframe and minicomputer operating systems have evolved, since the late 1950s, into multitasking, multiprogramming operating systems. Some are capable of handling multiple processors. While most of these supported a single manufacturer's products, the UNIX operating system was developed at AT&T Bell Laboratories in the 1970s as a multitasking, multi-user operating system, capable of easy portability to different processor hardware. Likewise, from the first, operating systems for Apple Corporation's Macintosh personal computers have supported multiple concurrent program execution.

Task and job management functions include operations preliminary to execution: locating the program in storage, allocating memory, reading the program into memory, changing program parameters dependent on the memory addresses occupied, initializing the processor, and branching to the program's starting address. An operating system maintains resource tables in memory to record the resources allocated to each program and each "child" task it may create.

Each time an application invokes a system service, say for disk file access or printing of output, the operating system is called to action. In some systems, to gain space for additional programs or data in memory, the operating system may "roll out" another program temporarily to disk storage. Each time a task completes, the operating system steps in to tidy up.

Finally, when the program terminates—whether successful or not—the operating system closes files and updates its resource listings. It may also prepare accounting records by which users are charged for system services.

System Initialization and Failure Handling

At time of power-up or major reset (*booting* or *rebooting*) of the system, first steps are taken by the hardware, driven from a read-only *boot program*. Presuming appropriate responses to hardware tests by the boot program, an initial part of the operating system program is next read from storage.

The operating system may make limited tests of external devices; for example, it may test to determine if a system printer is on-line. It usually cannot attempt comprehensive tests of peripherals, for in many cases a human would be required to verify that the peripheral responded correctly.

Most operating systems read configuration files to determine system and user options, since few can be deduced from electrical measurements. Some key configuration parameters, for example the amount and type of installed memory, are "read" by invoking inputs from electrical switches set up during installation.

Initialization can become a lengthy process, including loading utility programs, updating activity logs, and reading parameters from configuration files. If the system operates unattended, startup may include transmitting status data to some attended site.

Batch or Job Control Languages: Command Interpreters

Computers that are to operate in a batch mode, or are continuously unattended, are usually sequenced through stored commands. These commands constitute a simple job control or batch language. These are typically simpler and operate at higher levels than programming languages used to manipulate application data.

Where systems can be operated directly from a human-interface terminal, program execution can be commanded by merely typing the proper command on the terminal. The operating system software routine responsible for reading and interpreting individual commands, or the sequence of commands in a batch program, is sometimes termed the *Command Interpreter*.

Command initiation may be further simplified through a *graphic user interface* (GUI). Here, the user may need to do nothing more than move a pointer on a screen over a graphic symbol (icon) representing a desired program, and press a button. Software for supporting the GUI may be part of the operating system itself, or it may be a separate *shell* program through which the user communicates with the operating system and with applications.

Interrupt Handling and Direct Memory Access

Many of the tasks handled by operating system programs are routine, neither unexpected nor time-critical. Certain operations, such as those of high-rate external input devices, are time-critical, and their timing is unpredictable—or, at least, not synchronized with the computer's cycle. Modern computers contain special hardware features to deal with them, the two most common being interrupts and direct memory access. Both are important in the design of operating systems, since the operating system manages peripheral hardware.

A processor capable of *interrupt* handling is interrupted by applying a voltage step or pulse to a particular input point. Typically the processor disables response to further interrupt signals and completes the instruction under way when the interrupt occurred. It then saves to memory its *machine state.* This usually involves saving only a few bytes, mode switches, and the binary "flags" that store the results of mathematical or logical operations (zero flag, carry flag, etc.). The processor then determines the source of the interrupt, which may be done in a variety of ways. Processors designed especially for rapid responsiveness (real-time operation) receive, from the interruption source, a digital input that identifies the source; for example, an 8-bit identifier can distinguish 256 interrupt sources. This identifier is commonly a pointer to a location in memory holding the starting address of to an interrupt handier (routine) stored in memory. Since the interrupt pointers and routines are in memory, they can be changed dynamically by the operating system or by application programs requiring real-time responsiveness.

In systems where no interruption-source identifier is available to the processor, the interrupt source may have to be identified by querying each possible source. This is a slow process, and not a suitable choice for real-time computers.

When the interrupt handler routine begins, it may again enable interrupts to accommodate processes more urgent than itself. Values of processor registers used in the interrupt program are then saved (usually pushed on the current stack). The required *interrupt processing,* for instance storage of one input data byte, is then completed. The final steps include restoration of original register contents followed by an *interrupt return* instruction. This restores machine-state flags, and branches back to the interrupted program's next instruction in sequence. There is but a slight delay of the executing program while the interrupt routine performs its urgent work.

Interrupts are used, especially with multitasking, to signal completion of peripheral-device operations to the operating system. Consider an operating system that directs a storage disk drive to *seek cylinder 20.* Since both the disk and its control hardware are separate from the processor, there is no need for the processor to stop all execution while this seek takes place. Some task that is not waiting for I/O may be executing during the disk seek. At completion of the seek, a brief interrupt sequence, set up in advance, can launch the disk control into the next phase of operations.

In a single-task operating system, such as Microsoft Corporation's *DOS,* there is in principle nothing else to be done concurrently, hence in principle the entire system waits while the disk seeks cylinder 20.

In practice, there may also be output to a printer or I/O to some other device. Interrupts are crucial for operating communications interfaces, even in single task stream operation. If a remote input source sends data at a continuous high data rate, the processor must pause to write data to storage each time a block of 512 bytes (or some greater length) is received. If the remote source cannot be halted, input data may be lost while writing data to the disk.

Interrupt processing can overcome this problem. The receiving device is arranged to interrupt the processor when each character arrives, even while disk operations are under way. The interrupt handling routine needs only to store one data byte and to locate the next available memory buffer whenever the previous one is filled. The main program's function is now only to check if a storage buffer is full. In that case, it should direct its contents be written to storage. When the main program regains control after the write operation, it merely marks the buffer as available for more input. Of course, the rate at which data can be stored to the disk must exceed the input rate.

Interrupts are critical to multiprogramming operating systems which "time-slice" to assign processing intervals to applications. An external timer independent of the computer signals when time allocated to a task is completed.

Direct memory access is a hardware technique that permits simple input or output while the main processor executes other tasks. High speed storage disks receive and deliver data at rates as high as millions of bits per second. One way to handle this data rate would be to dedicate the processor to the transfer, but that is self-defeating. Instead, an elementary processor called a direct memory access device is connected to the I/O circuit and to the main memory. Prior to a multibyte data transfer, it receives the memory address of a buffer for the data and a count of data bytes expected. It can then operate independently to transfer data between the storage I/O interface and the computer memory. For each byte transferred, its internal counter is decremented. When that much data has been transferred, the DMA device typically interrupts the main processor to indicate its completion. This scheme works because the processor itself uses only a portion of the memory read or write cycles. DMA devices which serve input-output devices that cannot wait, are given highest priority access to memory. Typical modern main memory has an access time of 0.1 microseconds or less, i.e., a data rate of 10 million computer *words* per second. Only a fraction of its bandwidth is needed to handle needs of a typical disk storage unit. There is usually no problem if DMA devices occasionally used nearly all memory access cycles; executing programs would merely run more slowly. However, if the combination of transfers between memory and several time-critical DMA devices exceeded memory bandwidth (data transfer rate), one or more data transfers would fail.

EXTENDED OPERATING SYSTEM FUNCTIONS

Multitasking, Multiprogramming, and Time Sharing

Simple multitasking systems may be limited to a few tasks and usually have tight limitations on memory. Large multitasking operating systems can support hundreds of tasks. When total memory demands exceed capacity, the operating system may "roll out" of physical memory those tasks whose memory needs cannot currently be supported. Later, the tasks are "rolled in" to continue their execution. One result can be a significant reduction in system performance because of the overhead involved in frequently moving programs and data between memory and storage. *Virtual memory* systems are organized to routinely move data and programs between memory and disk storage in fixed-length pages. When too heavily loaded they enter a regime known as thrashing," where almost all available processor time is taken up in handling moves between memory and storage.

Multitasking is done in one of two ways: In *nonpreemptive multitasking,* each task retains control of the processor until it initiates some operating system function such as a disk read or write; at this point, the operating system takes control and can assign the processor to some other task.

In *preemptive multitasking,* often called *time-sharing* or *time-slicing,* each task is allowed a short "time slice" of processor time, which is terminated by a timer interrupt that allows the operating system to regain control and assign the processor to another task. If no other task is ready to execute, the processor continues executing the same task.

Multitasking operating systems lose a certain amount of processing time to necessary housekeeping duties during *context switching* between tasks. Registers, flags, and stack pointers must be saved and restored, and status of tasks examined for the transfer. This overhead is independent of the time slice length. Efficiency is better with longer time slices. Time slices on the order of 50 milliseconds are typical.

When several independent jobs may run concurrently in one system, additional issues arise. Since applications are usually unaware of each other, protection must be provided to avoid contention if several tasks seek to alter the same file. Input and output streams must be separate for each program or job, as discussed earlier. The operating system must also be able to initiate new jobs while other jobs continue their execution.

Priority and prescheduling features are common features of multiprogramming operating systems. It may be desirable to execute certain work immediately while other work is delayed until night-time hours when it will not delay applications such as on-line terminal data entry.

Multiprocessing

Multiprocessing operating systems manage more than one processor as a system resource. A traditional multiprocessor configuration shares one large memory between all processors, through a multiport memory interface or by *interleaving.* In the latter, *low order bits* in the memory address select from two, four, eight, or more independent memory banks that are independently accessible, reducing effective memory access time by the same factor.

In this type of multiprocessor, the operating system resides in the common memory. Executing on whatever processor is currently available, it assigns each processor to tasks needing them when processors become available.

A large variety of multiprocessor configurations have been studied, many less actually built, and a handful built in significant quantities. Some share common memory, while some share only magnetic storage devices. Some share one or more high speed data buses, while others are coupled through dynamically switched communications networks. Many have been designed to operate with processors arranged as an array, performing vector math. Others, known as *data flow processors,* factor complex algorithms into elementary parts and move operands through the system in preset paths to carry out repetitive digital signal processing.

As a group, these machines' influence on operating system concepts and design has been small. This was, in part, because none of these systems led the way to universal or lasting system concepts, but also because each was principally a study in hardware architecture with a relatively basic operating system. Work continues toward more effective combination of hundreds of thousands of single-chip computers. Because huge applications such as weather modeling or numerical wind tunnels are so different from one another, the most important obstacles are perceived to be in algorithmic representation, or programming language design, rather than those of operating systems.

Virtual Machine Operating Systems

Computer applications that can operate successfully in conventional multitasking and multiprogramming environments must be well-behaved; that is, they should not have faults that cause them to stray into memory or other resources assigned to other programs.

Virtual machine operating systems are designed to provide, among other things, a high degree of separation between tasks executing concurrently in a system. These operating systems may isolate each application as if it were the only task executing on that computer system. They serve a variety of useful purposes. They may be designed to execute programs written for computers no longer available, by emulating the earlier machine's instructions and other characteristics. Properly designed, they can prevent even the most error-ridden program from disturbing other programs executing on the same system.

Virtual machine operating systems are primarily mimics of system hardware that pretend to be several independent systems at once. Each partition executing concurrently usually contains in memory, a private copy of a conventional operating system. The virtual machine operating system is an interface between the real actual system hardware and these separate operating systems. Virtual memory, where pages of memory are moved between physical memory and external storage, is a common feature of virtual machine systems.

Systems running virtual machine operating systems are also excellent vehicles for applications that place stringent demands on interprocess isolation. One such is *multilevel security,* where it is desired to segregate sets of users and the data to which each set may have access.

Storage Protection

Storage protection, which might better be termed memory protection, is the selective ability to prevent an executing task from writing or reading memory allocated to another task. While correct, well-behaved programs should not violate memory assigned to others, real programs frequently have errors that allow them to do so. When storage protection is implemented, through software alone or a combination of hardware and software, each active task is assigned an identifier. Allocation in some systems is in fixed-length pages, while in others variable-length segments may be allocated. When a task is allocated more memory by the operating system, an allocation record is marked with the task's identifier and data indicating the type of protection to be enforced (read-only, etc.). If a task attempts to break the rules enforced for the particular page or segment, an error occurs. This feature in a system can make much easier the locating of programming errors that lead to incorrect memory access.

Network Support

An operating system may support the interface between its processor and an external network of independent computers. Prior to development of high speed local networking of personal computers and workstations, economy dictated that most networks be coupled only when data was actually being transmitted. Most networks used common-carrier telephone transmission systems. Network support programs were tailored to the needs of individual networks. Networking was not supported by operating systems.

Growing numbers of personal computers spurred development of Local Area Networks (LANS) in the early 1980s. In the 1990s, operating system developers begin incorporating LAN support, by which time LANs had become well-established through add-on software and hardware.

LANs are intended for use within ranges up to a few thousand feet. A simple LAN may require only a transmission line connecting the network, with an interface adapter circuit installed in each computer. More complex networks may include special hardware, such as bridging hardware used to couple several networks. Software implements the LAN features. The most common is the ability for a computer on the network to make use of storage in network computers running software that configures them as *network servers.*

Large local networks usually dedicate one or more servers provided with large storage drives and high speed printers. Since the effect of the LAN is that the remote peripheral appears to be connected directly to one's computer, calls to its operating system must be interpreted in a network context. A popular LAN feature is electronic mail, which permits computer users to communicate whether or not the message recipient is currently at a computer console. Few networks support direct computer-to-computer communication. Communicating through exchange of files on network servers is more efficient and relieves the network software and system designers of the need to minimize response times while handling large numbers of short messages.

Where operating systems do not support networking explicitly, they may support related capabilities such as *file sharing* and *file locking*. This makes it simpler to support file protection mechanisms with add-on network software. Network applications such as electronic mail and printer spooling can be either network features or add-ons.

Access Control

The growth of networks, both as LANs and remote communications between widely distributed computers, has increased users' concerns over unauthorized access to network data and the risk of inserting destructive programs such as *viruses* and *worms*. Most multiuser operating systems provide some kind of password control whereby users may be required to identify themselves using private passwords. Commercial and governmental systems may require additional steps to gain access to critical data or programs. Techniques such as *call-back*, where the secure computer responds to calls on the public phone network by dialing the number associated with the caller, have been developed to enhance security. A useful analogy to security features is multiple locks on a door. Good security requires multiple independent security checks and frequent changing of keys and passwords.

Most computer operating systems were designed originally to provide easy and rapid access to system resources, not to inhibit it. As such, they have often had shortcuts, bypasses, or other features through which users could evade security. Those systems providing the most stringent access control are characterized by small *kernel* control programs through which *all* requests for data and other protected system resources must pass. This permits a uniform level of stringency not possible in a system with many routes through which system resources can be accessed.

Some operating systems, in particular, *virtual machine operating systems,* are very effective in separating users from one another. They have been used as bases for building trustworthy computer systems. Even so, the problems are severe: for example, hardware failures or errors may seriously reduce the security of a system that, if operating correctly, appears impregnable.

OPERATING SYSTEM RELATIONSHIPS TO APPLICATION PROGRAMS

Almost any computer can be programmed to execute applications without the presence of an operating system. Processors embedded in electronic controllers or other apparatus usually don't need one. The tradeoffs are determined by how much the application needs of what an operating system can provide. Typical services provided, as noted earlier, are program loading and relocation, handling data on storage devices, operating a display, allocating memory, and managing multiple tasks.

Operating systems usually provide these services in a flexible way, for example, managing hierarchies of file directories, variable numbers of tasks occupying different amounts of memory, or sharing a display screen between many applications. This flexibility has attendant costs in memory and processing time utilization. If an application is important enough, its needs simple, or available operating system features inadequate, it may provide some or all of these services internally. While the design of mainframe computers evolved to virtually ensure that they would be managed by an operating system, minicomputers entered the market in the late 1960s as programmable controllers. This opened the door to many special applications, and ultimately to the development of operating systems intended for use on a variety of computers.

Obtaining Operating System Services for Application Programs

During execution of application programs there may be frequent need for operating system services such as: finding, opening, reading, writing, and closing files; outputting data to a printer or display; accepting input from a keyboard; or initiating a subtask. At these times the application program invokes the operating system, much as it would call a subprogram. The information required by the operating system, typically a command identifier and data, are moved to proper locations in memory, registers, and/or on a stack. The operating system is called and performs the service, returning results in memory, registers, or the stack. If the operation was unsuccessful, the results will include information indicating why it failed.

The actual programming interface depends on the operating system and on the programming language used. If the programming medium is assembly language, the programmer sets up registers and/or memory areas, then issues a service call or *software interrupt* instruction to invoke operating system services. When using higher order languages, operating system functions are invoked in the same way as user-written subroutines, requiring certain arguments in a particular order.

In efficient multitasking operating systems, operating system functions are usually multitasked to improve performance. However, several application tasks may concurrently request usage of the same resource, for example disk-file read and write operations. Tasks whose object involves a common hardware resource can be better optimized by handling them as a group. This makes it possible to service several file requests to a common cylinder before moving the read and write heads to another cylinder. Managed effectively, this can greatly improve system performance.

In nonpreemptive or preemptive multitasking, an application that invokes the operating system typically loses control of the processor until all other ready-to-execute tasks of equal or higher priority have had their turns at it. Multitasking systems will allow an application that has requested operating system services to continue execution, if no other applications need the processor. The developer of an application can, in this situation, achieve a gain in processing speed by generating tasks that can usefully occupy processor time while another task is awaiting input or output.

An application that, for example, manages operation of numbers of data entry terminals must perform operating system-like functions. Efficient multiprogramming operating systems provide programming hooks for this sort of application.

If the operating system cannot comply with a request, for example if a requested file does not exist or cannot be read, an *error condition* should be returned. This may be interpreted by the application to determine what it should do next. An experienced programmer will interpret and respond to any error condition that could affect execution following the event. Depending on the application and the circumstances when the error occurs, a programmer might determine to abort or to carry out a selected recovery procedure. If the program is responding to a terminal user, that individual may be requested to select an alternative.

Peripheral Drivers; Direct Manipulation of External Hardware; BIOS Interfaces

It is quite common for program developers to discover that some desired manipulation of a peripheral device was not anticipated by the designers of an operating system. The particular device may not have been available when the operating system was developed, or it might be intended for a special and limited market. Examples are temperature sensors for a building's comfort control system, or serial I/O device chips with different properties from those anticipated during operating system design.

This problem may be approached with either broad or narrow objectives, depending on economic factors. If the special device is expected to be widely used, a comprehensive set of special functions may be created. Operating systems may provide for this in various ways: *service-call identifiers* reserved for application use, and *driver interfaces* through which programs can access program routines to manipulate special peripheral devices. If needed by only one or a few users, *ad hoc* software functions can be written by a hardware-knowledgeable programmer. That the operating system is bypassed need be of little concern so long as the special hardware is accessed only by the special software. If the application is multiprogrammed, and several concurrent applications may invoke these functions, additional protection or resource management mechanisms may be needed.

If a peripheral *device driver* program is to be the vehicle for dealing with special hardware, it will be necessary to have detailed descriptions of (**1**) the functions the operating system expects to be performed through such drivers, (**2**) the format of commands and associated data passed by the operating system to the driver program, (**3**) any special data formats required by the device, and (**4**) a logical description of control, response, and states of the special hardware. Peripheral drivers may be simple programs that merely send a few control bits to an external device. They may be as complicated as the large printer driver programs required to convert printed-page descriptions into PostScript, a powerful programming language understood by PostScript printers.

A special driver, to be fully integrated with the operating system, should couple to the error reporting structure so it can return notice of successful and unsuccessful operations.

Operating systems intended for use with a variety of processors usually require transitional firmware drivers and converters to map between their generalized interfaces and the specific ones of the system hardware. UNIX, CP/M, MS-DOS, and PC-DOS operating systems are of this character. Where target hardware employs different instruction sets, as with UNIX, the operating system must be written in a language that is compiled to produce equivalent results on each machine. In personal computers, the transitional firmware has been referred to as the *BIOS (Basic Input-Output System)*. This software must be designed so that the interfaces to the operating system proper are independent of any hardware differences. This permits the cost of the operating system software to be shared by many small manufacturers of similar though not identical computer systems.

In a given personal computer application, peripheral hardware might be operated in one of three ways: (**1**) driving it directly from the application, (**2**) programming the BIOS interface, or (3) invoking an operating system service. *Maximum performance* is almost invariably achieved by direct manipulation, while greatest *program portability* is achieved if external devices can be manipulated using only operating system functions. Limited-capability operating systems such as CP/M or MS-DOS leave no alternative to driving hardware directly to achieve acceptable performance from slow early microprocessors.

SPECIAL REQUIREMENTS FOR INTERACTIVE AND REAL-TIME OPERATING SYSTEMS

Interactive applications are operated principally by users at keyboard-display or graphics terminals. These include personal computers as well as the more powerful workstations. However, some large computers support interactive applications on large numbers of terminals concurrently. This is principally for applications where the same data must be used by all terminals, as in airline reservation, bet-taking, or banking systems.

A distinctive requirement is that the system must respond to terminal inputs rapidly, say within a second or two, even at peak loading. This criterion would not be particularly difficult for a personal computer using data from its own storage. It becomes much more demanding when a central system must respond to hundreds or even thousands of terminals in hundreds of locations up to thousands of miles away.

These multiterminal interactive systems are, for the most part, application-unique. They may employ standard operating systems for storage access but implement terminal service using unique service routines for handling request and response queues.

Graphics Display. There is a great difference between terminal support software to deal only in ASCII text, and that required to handle high-resolution graphics. A monochrome text display usually contains fewer than 2000 characters (bytes). A 768- by 1024-pixel display with 24-bits/pixel—a likely standard for the year 2000—contains almost 2,400,000 bytes!

So imposing are the problems of creating and refreshing this class of display that powerful processors are now dedicated to nothing other than display support for personal computers. At the currently favored refresh rate of 72 Hertz, date rate between the processor and display could, in principle, reach 1.4 *gigabits/second,* orders of magnitude greater than standard television image data rates.

Techniques for displaying high-resolution graphics, not surprisingly, emphasize reducing the data rate. Since only those objects that move or change need refreshing on the display, most images require much lower data rates. The remarkable imagery produced by many video games is accomplished via techniques that produce strong visual effects using modest resources.

Real-Time Operating Systems. Real-time operating systems are expected to be capable of responding to input signals within short time periods. The specific needs depend on the application. A robot's controller may require that its internal computer respond to a stimulus in less than one millisecond, while in refinery control or flight simulation a 40 millisecond response may be acceptable.

The ability of computer hardware and operating system to respond rapidly depends mainly on interrupt handling and processing delays. If a stimulus arrives in the form of an interrupt, but the computer must examine hundreds of potential sources before it can react correctly, there will be substantial delay. Qualitatively, for economical real-time operation, the interrupt process should begin executing *source-unique instructions* within a few instructions after interrupt occurs. It follows also that processing required to respond to an input event must not take longer than the allowable response time. Even though overall processing loads may be small, in a real-time system, interrupt response time often determines the class of processor required.

Operating systems to support real-time applications, in addition to enabling rapid interrupt processing, may provide special support for large numbers of "discrete" (binary signals or switches), and the control of analog to digital converter peripheral devices.

OPERATING SYSTEM IMPLICATIONS FOR SOFTWARE ENGINEERING

Software engineering is concerned with software development tools and the processes by which software is designed and tested. The characteristics of an operating system can either ease or impede software developments using that system, or the software developed to run on that system.

Choice of Operating Systems

Selection of a computer or a family of software-compatible computers usually implies a limited selection of operating systems, often only one. This is especially true in the case of large computers (mainframes and super computers). Not only are operating systems for complex machines and peripherals expensive to build, their cost must often be distributed over relatively few machines.

The choice of operating systems is limited for personal computers as well. Application programs interface the computer and other hardware, at least in part, through the operating system. They are developed so as to achieve operating system compatibility rather than compatibility with particular hardware. A new operating system incompatible with those for which applications exist must have superior qualities, or it cannot hope to attract application developers to use it.

Traditionally, the manufacturer of a mainframe computer developed an operating system, compiler, and other software tools as essential accessories. Without them, few users could use, or would purchase, the hardware. Some of these mainframe operating systems have evolved for more than a quarter-century. This tradition of matching hardware with operating system continued when minicomputers appeared. Two significant events broke that tradition. One was the decision by IBM Corporation, a relative late-comer in the personal computer field, to develop a new personal computer incorporating a processor chip developed independently by Intel Corporation. The computer would use an operating system that its developer, Microsoft Corporation, would also sell to other personal computer builders. Possibly for the first time in the computer's commercial history, processor and operating system were both designed, and openly sold, by firms other than the system integrator/marketer.

The second salient development was a new concept in operating systems, UNIX, developed by Bell Laboratories in the 1970s. Unlike its predecessors, it was not wedded to a single processor family, but designed for easy portability to a wide range of computers. From the outset UNIX was designed as a multitasking, multiprogramming, multiuser, interactively operated operating system. (Only in later versions did it claim real-time capabilities.) Earlier operating systems had been written in machine language, but UNIX was written largely in the higher-order programming language *C*. A departure from long-time programming language evolution toward more "natural" languages, C commands translated economically into machine language algorithms important to efficient operating systems. It could be "ported" to a new processor family by development of hardware interface code and a C compiler just capable enough to compile the full compiler. It was designed by technologists, primarily for their own use, and reflects this in sometimes-inconsistent syntax and oddly named utility functions. It has rapidly grown in popularity, especially among technical users, and is available for use on a wide range of computers.

The term *open systems* is used to describe the sort of *de facto* standardization that resulted from IBM's decision not to develop a proprietary processor and operating system for its personal computer. IBM's strong reputation in computer systems encouraged others to copy the IBM/PC's largely unpatented features. The open systems approach, in retrospect, turned out to be IBM's gift to the fledgling personal computer industry, because others—especially Microsoft—in the end profited to a greater extent than IBM.

Other Operating System Features

Though they may have relatively little variety, different operating systems have many features in addition to those previously discussed.

Comprehensiveness. Some operating systems are bare-boned, offering no more than an executive program, loader, and utilities supporting input, output, and storage. Others, of which UNIX is an outstanding example, are equipped with numerous utilities for the creation and editing of programs and document files, listing programs, file backup and restore, and management and maintenance of the system. Most operating systems do not include so wide a range of utilities, although popular operating systems accumulate a wide variety of extra-cost programs and utilities. Many free (public domain) programs also accumulate—some of high quality— when an operating system is widely used.

Operator Control. Most operating systems support a *control console* from which programs can be initiated or scheduled, operating parameters altered, and system status indicators read. Some provide these services only at a terminal connected directly to the processor. Others can direct most system control functions to a remote terminal. Operating systems vary considerably in regard to how much control a system operator has over applications initiated by users. Operating systems supporting batch job-input streams from remote terminals usually allow a system operator to turn these streams on and off and to adjust their priorities.

Software Development Tools. Operating systems may include compilers, source linkers, debugging aids, and a variety of analysis programs that can characterize a program's internal connectivity, tabulate use of stored data, or record its actual sequence of operations. The variety and power of software development tools are still evolving. The most novel tools seldom emerge from the operating system developers. One must look elsewhere for syntax-checking program editors, consistency checkers, software version management utilities, and most software now judged to be important in software engineering.

Operations Management Tools and Hooks. Computer systems used for high-production applications—for example, manufacturers' repair parts data systems or airline reservation systems—must be measured and adjusted regularly for optimal performance. Two ways to measure performance are: (**1**) to instrument each application program, and (**2**) to measure the system through special software *hooks* in its operating system. The latter is cheaper, all-encompassing, and should be more consistent. Some necessary operating data cannot be captured through an application program. Typical operating system hooks permit system events such as completion of tasks or jobs to be recorded on a system log file. The recorded data can later be analyzed using general-purpose or *ad hoc* utility programs.

Special Peripheral Support. In addition to conventional peripheral devices, some operating systems provide support for terminals with special graphic display capabilities, communications multiplexers permitting a computer to support hundreds of telephone lines to remote terminals, point-of-sale recorders, factory-floor recorders, or other devices intended for particular applications. If suitable software support is not already available for some peripheral device or terminal, hardware cost might represent a small fraction of the cost of putting it to work. For this reason, special-purpose peripheral devices may be designed to be controlled by software that handles some other, standardized, class of peripherals.

Portability

Portability, in this context, refers to what must be done to transfer an existing operating system to a processor having different instruction sets or differences in other interface characteristics.

An operating system's designers can often extend its use to processors having expanded instruction sets, by using only the most basic subset of instructions. The hierarchy of operating system features may mimic the hardware hierarchy, so addition of a higher-speed peripheral interface in the hardware family can be paralleled by a software module supporting that interface.

Some adjustment may be adaptive. On starting, the operating system may probe the hardware system that it occupies, testing memory and other features, then alter itself appropriately. This works only if the dimensions and directions of hardware evolution are clear from the start which is seldom the case. The most reliable method of adaptation is to supply a configuration file, though this puts an extra onus on system installers.

A principal concern of most system users is that the need to functionally expand their system does not force a change of operating system, especially one that alters the application program interface and demands replacement of large amounts of software. The operating system developer's viewpoint is often somewhat different. A user can be induced to purchase a new, or updated operating system only if the perceived benefit exceeds the perceived conversion cost. Accordingly, the usual pattern of operating system evolution is to offer new features while retaining compatibility with all but the oldest applications.

Software Development and Modification Support

Some operating systems provide far more assistance to software development than do others. Virtual machine operating systems, discussed earlier, constitute an environment in which even the most egregious software errors need not disturb other users of the machine. An operating system that includes storage protection mechanisms can assist greatly in program development if it can identify and store the sources of incorrect memory access requests. Most but not all operating systems provide an automatic date and time stamp when files are created or altered. Though this may appear trivial, it is an essential element of software version control.

Multitasking operating systems can greatly assist program debugging. A monitor program can operate as a separate task and, by masquerading as a part of the operating system, can assume memory and storage access authority that enable it to examine the program under test. With some assistance from the processor's memory protection hardware, a monitor task can report when data in memory locations of interest is changed, without materially delaying program execution.

As software engineering practices are further refined, it is certain that hardware and operating systems will evolve additional ways to support important software engineering needs.

DESIGN AND IMPLEMENTATION OF OPERATING SYSTEM SOFTWARE

Full-featured operating systems are complex and costly to develop. The original OS/360, developed by IBM in the 1960s, reportedly cost $80 million for its 8 megabytes of object programs. Since most operating systems continue to evolve over many years, total development costs can be enormous. Users, from the start, expect wide-ranging and error-free capabilities in an operating system. Thus unless one is marketing very special hardware such as a super computer, it is not reasonable to offer only basic operating system elements initially. In other words, design cost is "up front." The announcement of a new full-featured operating system is still a rare event.

Software programs providing some of the elements of operating systems are introduced more frequently. Most are add-on programs. For example, Microsoft Windows provides limited multitasking plus a sophisticated graphic display interface on top of the relatively simple DOS operating system. Windows in turn spawned add-ons: displaying and printing font characters at any desired size, performing numerous utility functions, managing the display screen more effectively, maintaining a personal calendar, and many other nontraditional computer applications. By riding on the coattails of widely used operating systems, such products can be brought to market at reasonable cost.

Software tools, which in years past were closely integrated with operating systems, are now almost exclusively developed and marketed separately; this illustrates how few system users develop their own software.

Operating Systems for New Computers. Operating system design and implementation is greatly increased in difficulty when the complementary computer hardware is simultaneously under development. This was the usual rule during the first two decades of computer system development. Assembly language (machine language) was central to early operating system development principally because, prior to C, high level programming languages were not well-suited to operating system design. Software tools are inevitably limited, or even nonexistent, at the outset of new processor and operating system codevelopment.

In approaching a new operating system design, traditionally the designers would begin with what they called the *control program.* This provides basic processor and memory resource management and task switching. *Basic input-output* also received early attention, as did a primitive program loader. These few elements provided a basis that could be used to support tests of additional software elements, and of hardware features not fully testable with small test programs. Additional operating system functions could readily be integrated on this framework.

In this chicken-and-egg situation, early testing was necessarily primitive. It relied primarily on hardware to start and stop the processor, load registers and memory, and examine contents of registers and memory. As more and more of the hardware and operating system elements were integrated, the process grew in its sophistication.

Evolution in Operating System Design. For all but the largest processors, many traditional system design processes have been supplanted by reliance on computer simulations and emulations. This permits parts of the operating system to be developed in parallel, following top-level design, interface definition, and specification phases.

Since processor design became a role for semiconductor chip makers, few operating systems are designed concurrently with new processor hardware. The UNIX ideal of universal operating system portability makes this unnecessary and probably even undesirable. As always, operating system designers face an essential decision: make it fast and simple, or slow and flexible? Perceptions of market forces have repeatedly shaped responses to that question. Competitive forces ultimately determined their success and failure.

BIBLIOGRAPHY

The most comprehensive descriptions of actual operating systems, especially those designed for specific mainframes or super computers, are available from their developers in technical manuals. These are good sources for the reader who wants to understand design of operating systems, and may usually be obtained for a modest charge from the manufacturer. Textbooks deal more usefully alternative design approaches. As is true throughout the digital systems field, books more than ten years old reflect earlier periods in which different tradeoffs were favored, than are correct today.

S. Coffin, *UNIX System V Release 4: The Complete Reference,* Osborne/McGraw-Hill, Berkeley, Calif., 1990. [Concentrates on the terminal user interface to UNIX, which has collected over the years a huge number of associated utility programs.]

H. M. Deitel, *An Introduction to Open Systems,* Addison-Wesley Publishing Co., Inc., Reading Mass., 1989.

S. Coffman and P. Denning, *Operating Systems and Theory,* Prentice-Hall, Inc., Englewood Cliffs, N.J., 1973.

R. Duncan (general ed.) and co-workers, *The MS-DOS Encyclopedia,* Microsoft Press, Redmond, Wash., 1988. [A wide variety of books dealing with the user interface of DOS from various levels of technical complexity; Microsoft manuals for each version of the programs. A comprehensive description of the programmer interface, detailing the evolution of MS-DOS from versions 1.0 through 3.nn.]

T. Hogan, *Osborne CPIM User Guide,* 2nd ed., Osborne/McGraw-Hill, Berkeley, Calif., 1982. [Deals with terminal operation, utility programs, programmer interfaces, and some technical details of the relatively simple CP/M operating system for Intel 8080 and Zylog Z-80 microprocessors.]

S. E. Madnick and J. J. Donovan, *Operating Systems,* McGraw-Hill Book Co., Inc., New York, 1974.

WALTER R. BEAM
Consultant

OPERATIONAL PROFILE

See LOGARITHMIC NHPP MODEL; SOFTWARE RELIABILITY ENGINEERING; RANDOM TESTING.

OPERATIONAL TESTING

Operational testing (OT) is conducted at the system level by an organization that is independent of the developers. It is normally performed in phases, each of which are keyed to a decision review in the material acquisition process. OT is conducted with typical users in realistic and operational environments. It provides decision authorifies with an estimate of the: utility, operational effectiveness, and suitability of the new system; system desirability, considering systems already available, and the operational benefits or burdens associated with the new system; the need for modifications to the new system; and the adequacy of doctrine, organizations, operating techniques, and training for employment of the system; and the adequacy of maintenance support for the system. Operational test is conducted in keeping with principles of objectivity and an impartial evaluation to provide to the decision authority, prior to each major milestone review, the operational information necessary to resolve critical operational issues. OT typically focuses on three principles: the amount of data and realism of test conditions must be sufficient the resolution of critical operational issues; test planning, control of test events, and treatment of data must make the operational information clear and accurate; and test conduct and data handling must be separated from external influence and personal self-interest (Department of Defense Instruction 5000.2, *Defense Acquisition Management Policies and Procedures,* Feb. 23, 1991).

OPERATIONS AND MAINTENANCE

See MAINTENANCE; SOFTWARE-RELIABILITY ENGINEERING.

ORACLES

See RANDOM TESTING; TESTING.

OULD, MARTYN A. (1948–)

Martyn Ould took a degree in mathematics at Cambridge University and in 1970 joined ICL where he worked on the GEORGE operating system. After a brief spell in medical computing, he joined software house Logica where he worked principally in software development for clients in real-time and related areas, including sonar, radar, communications, and digital television. In 1983 he co-founded an internal initiative into software engineering within the company world-wide. In 1985 he joined software engineering company Praxis where he is currently Quality & Technical Director, responsible for its overall quality and technical strategy.

His work in the software process has led him to develop practical techniques for planning the development with particular reference to risk and quality management. Most recently he been working in the area of business process modeling, applying techniques developed in the mid-1980s for modeling the software process. He is a Fellow of the British Computer Society and Chartered Engineer.

BIBLIOGRAPHY

M. A. Ould, *Modelling Business Processes,* John Wiley, Chichester, England, 1994 planned.

—*Strategies for Software Engineering,* John Wiley, Chichester, England, 1990.

—with C. Unwin, eds., *Testing in Software Development,* Cambridge University Press, Cambridge, England, 1986, 1989.

—with N. D. Birrell, *A Practical Handbook for Software Development,* Cambridge University Press, Cambridge, England, 1985, 1988).

OUTPUT SPACE

See SOFTWARE RELIABILITY.

P

PARALLEL PROCESSING IMPLICATIONS FOR SOFTWARE ENGINEERING

INTRODUCTION

This article considers parallel systems to be a broader topic than the mapping of single algorithms to parallel processors. This strategy allows for a discussion of general principles, rather than the techniques that apply to specific machines. Much of the present parallel hardware industry provides machines that do not support a parallel machine model as needed for software engineering practices, therefore, this strategy is necessary. Massively parallel machines are organized for selected algorithm approaches that attain high performance at the sacrifice of software productivity because unacceptable application constraints result when building complete parallel systems with multiple algorithms and application domains. For these machines the goals of software engineering practices cannot be met; for instance, efficiency, productivity, long-term support, portability, reuse, predictable performance, sometimes even deterministic or consistent behavior. Some parallel machines do support a suitable parallel machine model for software engineering, but these have a maximum processor count which limits peak performance. To better discuss parallel systems two styles are introduced: *intensive* and *extensive* (see Table 1).

Extensive concurrent applications are those that are too complex and interrelated to have a recognizable and predictable response structure. Fortunately, extensive programming methods derived from the virtual concurrent view used in operating system development, can be effectively used. Parallel machines suited for extensive programming are widespread but typically have a smaller processor count than the intensive ones.

Intensive algorithms are those that have predictable data and control flow paths. Intensive algorithms are selected for mapping to intensive style parallel machines. They have predictable data locations as well as structured control flow, and typically have a small component of input or output.

Both styles require software engineering methods and tools and are sufficiently different from each other so that the style must be stated for any rational and reasonable discussion.

THE PARALLEL SYSTEM DEFINED

For this article a parallel system is a large, complex, hardware and software entity that operates at all levels of the hierarchy of data organization—data, information, and intelligence—at all phases of data linkages and information fusion. This definition assumes that the parallel system is composed of subsystems that are themselves homogenous parallel components. The parallel system has a long life that requires continued support and upgrades over irregular periods. Performance (minimum time spent in reaching a solution), operational optimization and efficiency (constraints on hardware costs or physical parameters), and development and long term optimization (software costs), are considered as the driving factors in the development.

The reasons for the use of parallel computing in the system are to increase performance, to achieve fault tolerance, and to share resources or information. In many cases parallel designs may be the only way of reaching required performance or minimum response time. Software engineering is necessary to achieve these goals with a minimum of performance risk as well as minimum capital, development, and long term operational costs. Note that this system definition does not include computer centers where maximum use is more important than performance; nor a network of processors coupled to take economical advantage of night-time resource usage; nor a system distributed due to geographic reasons, although the methods may be applicable.

STATUS OF SOFTWARE ENGINEERING FOR PARALLEL SYSTEMS

Software engineering for parallel systems is at least a generation behind that for sequential systems because of unpredictability of performance and the failure of hardware systems to adequately support a widely available machine model.

The discipline of engineering requires, at each level of development, that the subsystems, functions and behavior of any system be defined and a prediction be made of system performance. The discipline requires that the implementation consist of established, predictable, and timed modules that make up an infrastructure on which the system is engineered. The engineering discipline requires a well established process tied to the product complexity so that risk, cost, and schedule can be defined in advance. In nonparallel software engineering the discipline of software engineering has not solved these problems but has identified many of the steps necessary to achieving a discipline status.

Status of Extensive Solutions and Systems. The extensive style has a widely used parallel machine model. The advantage of the extensive style is that it works for all classes of applications, including intensive ones. However, as the number of processors grows, the hardware methods necessary to both support the model and provide high performance become saturated at a relatively low processor count. The processor count is limited because the automatic mechanisms for cache coherency, intertask communications, and resource allocation have been limited due to design complexity and costs. The result is that very large extensive software systems have no adequate hardware base. However, success of the extensive method and the parallel machine model has been demonstrated for

Table 1. Methods of Solution and Machine Attributes

Parallel Systems: Problem, Programming and Machine Separation	
Extensive Problem Attributes	*Intensive Problem Attributes*
Task interaction	Task Interaction
Complex	Regular
Frequent	Infrequent
Any other task	Nearest neighbor (as mapped)
Unpredictable Paths	Predictable computation path
Data dependent path	No data dependency
Task dependent path	Structure known
Scheduling	Scheduling
No optimum scheduling solution	Uniform sequential module size
	Schedule computable
Data	*Data*
Location Indeterminate	Location Predicted
Size indeterminate	Fits Node Memory
Ratio of sequential module size to communication size is small	Ratio of sequential module size to communication size is large
Extensive Development Style	*Intensive Programming Style*
Operating system techniques	Task mapped to physical processor
Shared variables	Data mapped to physical processor
Semaphores	Message passing techniques
Monitors	synchronous and asynchronous
	remote procedure call
	rendezvous
Extensive Machine Attributes	*Intensive Machine Attributes*
Shared memory	Distributed memory (shared nothing)
Balanced bandwidth (constant bandwidth per processor to all processors)	Scalable bandwidth (fixed bandwidth per processor to nearest neighbors)
Virtual resources	

transaction processing and mainframe applications when communications with other transactions are limited. In that situation, large systems have been successfully built. Extensive method software tools are provided by both independent (e.g., Scientific Computing Associates—Linda) (Carriero and Gelernter, 1989) and individual vendors (operating system synchronization call libraries), and published books on how to program the tool sets (Andrews, 1991).

Parallel machine support for extensive style has recently been advanced significantly by extending the cache coherency (Lenoski, 1992) and use of threads for task management. (Anderson, 1991). The use of threads lowers software overhead of parallel intertask communication and synchronization significantly and reduces the parallel instruction time. Directory based cache coherency methods and performance—enhancing, memory-consistency operations extend the number of processors for extensive applications (Lenoski, 1992). Coupled with increases in-processor power of individual general purpose microprocessors, a large fraction of the parallel market could be captured by the extensively-oriented, general-purpose parallel computer using such facilities. Therefore, research in extensive methods is centered around methods to design hardware for extending cache coherency, memory consistency, and software for extending the threads models for better synchronization, communication, and resource allocation (Lenoski, 1992). By identifying a set of primitive instructions for threads, the efficiency for large processor count may be extended further, providing robust and predictable performance for extensively programmed problems (Sullivan, 1992). Multithreading techniques which provide more efficient operation also contribute to the performance and efficiency provided by parallel machines for extensively programmed applications.

The list below gives details on threads-based systems. A thread is one of many single sequential flows of control within a process.

Properties

- Shared-resources and file descriptions
- Separate stack, timers, and scheduling
- Faster response to application task demands
- Finer grain allows higher concurrency to be expressed

Support

- Low level: Shared memory, synchronization primitives
- High level: creation, priority scheduling, exception and interrupt handling, fine grain scheduling, protected I/O and capabilities

Requires

- Higher communications bandwidth
- Multithreading to improve processor efficiency

Thread examples are C lightweight processes, CMA, Chorus, Ultrix, OS/2, Pthreads(Posix).

Status of Intensive Problems and Systems. For the intensive style the inability to support software engineering is due to the absence of a virtual parallel machine model for the system designer, programmer, and computer architect. Such a model, when coupled with hardware support, might eliminate the high degree of mapping and the resulting lack of portability and reuse. An architecturally independent model cannot be created for intensively oriented machines because their interconnect structure can be overwhelmed by arbitrary problem complexity. The present intensive style is to map and reduce complexity in order to avoid use of the network.

The intensive style (selected algorithms mapped on a minimized set of hardware) is less concerned with the algorithm analysis, design, programming, and integration effort than extensively oriented methods. The intensive effort required is necessary for sparsely coupled and nonbandwidth-balanced machines. In the intensive style, mapping to explicit hardware structures is required at all stages of development; thus, even algorithm analysis and selection is determined by the details of the target hardware. The adverse symptom in software engineering for the intensive style is that small deviations in the algorithm structure from that of the hardware, lead to the violation of bandwidth balance constraints and a non-proportional decrease in performance. Since the algorithm may be based on a specific intensive machine, changes due to obsolescence may put the process back to the algorithm analysis stage. Although called "scalable," the intensively oriented computers are not, in fact, useful across a wide range of processor numbers (Bell, 1992). Different algorithms are often more efficient and necessary as the processor count varies across an order of magnitude. There are special cases where algorithms are scalable; that is, for larger sizes they grow in compute requirements without corresponding growth in communications or system demands. Such algorithms map in order to provide high efficiency on the intensive style machine.

Present software engineering research for intensive oriented parallel systems is directed towards languages and compiler back-ends. The language approach allows intensive problems to be data mapped and written in a high level language (front-end) and ported to different parallel machines by re-compiling with a new back-end that creates efficient code for each different intensive style architecture. All structure expressed by the originator of the algorithm or system designer and expressed in the code by a programmer must be preserved in the intermediate interface between the two ends because the matching of structure is critical to performance gains.

Parallel software development tools are provided by both independents (e.g., Parasoft—EXPRESS™) and individual vendors for aid in the creation of architectural dependent message-passing primitives from an independent higher level expression. This procedure provides a degree of portability for well chosen algorithms where the user avoids the detailed mapping from machine to machine. However, the parallel industry frequently makes radical architectural changes and "improvements" that inhibit attempts to improve its support for software engineering for intensive problems.

PARALLEL MACHINE MODEL: THE CRITICAL COMPONENT

A widely accepted and hardware supported parallel machine model is the most critical component of software engineering in parallel systems. Additionally, the tool set required must provide additional supporting features, especially in performance prediction and modeling, and testing and debugging.

Serial Machine Model. The basis for extensive software in sequential systems is the von Neumann random access machine (Cook and Reckhow, 1973). The von Neumann machine model is constantly present in sequential "von Neumann" computers and implied at all levels of operation. For example, superscalar processors perform out-of-order execution but guarantee that the von Neumann machine model is preserved in the user view. The von Neumann model allows algorithm inventors, programmers, and architecture developers to work independently and is the primary supporting component that makes conventional software engineering feasible. The serial machine model, the von Neumann random access machine (RAM) model, provides both the implementation foundation and performance estimation. In this model each instruction (arithmetic, logic, branch, memory access, etc.) has a timing model based upon an unlimited memory (Cook and Reckhow, 1973). Sequential languages, such as Fortran, are based upon this model and basic programming concepts are taught using it. At any design level—algorithm, program, or machine architecture—the performance of an algorithm can be estimated from timing and weighing analysis of instructions by count. The latest computer architectures are said to be quantitatively designed using this approach (Patterson and Hennessy, 1990).

Parallel Machine Model. Having a parallel machine model is as critical for parallel software engineering as in the sequential case. However, parallel software adds an element of coordination between processors that is not found in sequential systems. Unfortunately, parallel hardware developers often compromise and adjust their operating model to attain higher performance. This compromise is one of the primary difficulties in providing robust software engineering for parallel systems.

The parallel machine model for extensive programming is the parallel random access model (PRAM). The PRAM model extends the RAM model to parallel systems by adding a processor whenever required by the application (i.e., data is ready). The not needed processor is removed (i.e., data is not ready). An unlimited number of virtual processors is available. The memory is accessible to each processor and is unlimited in size. Each task, having its own virtual processor, is internally consist with the von Neumann model for the timing of ordinary instructions. Each parallel memory access instruction type has its own timing value. The functions of the PRAM model may be represented by communicating sequential processes (Hoare), which provide the formal basis for writing operating systems and very complex system functions; hence, its close relationship to the extensive style for multiprocessors.

Use of the PRAM is limited because physical parallel processors do not closely represent the model, as sequential processors do for the von Neumann RAM model. For example, practical parallel computers do not have the constant timing for the parallel memory access instructions required in the PRAM. A necessary condition for a practical PRAM is that the bandwidth available to any processor be independent of the number of processors. This precondition may be achieved by the network design, combining, and hashing techniques found in some extensive style machines. However, the timing is still dependent on the number of processors by $\log_2 p(n)$ (Skillicorn, 1991). When using the realizable PRAM model the number of processors and the level of concurrency is used to predict performance when the parallel timing is known. The concurrency excess over the number of processors (slackness) can be used to increase the multiprocessor efficiency in extensive programming, with a slackness of $\log_2 p(n)$ required to increase the efficiency to within a constant multiplier of the processor count. The constant multiplier, η, is given by equation 1, where G is the granularity, T_p is the average timing of the parallel instruction and T_o the average timing of the ordinary instructions (Sullivan, 1992).

$$\eta = \frac{1}{1 + \frac{1}{G} * \frac{T_p}{T_o}} \tag{1}$$

Thus, for properly designed extensive machines, the PRAM model can be realized and performance predicted. Performance prediction is the most critical element in a parallel machine model, in order to accomplish software engineering in parallel systems.

Since arbitrary communication patterns are allowed in this model, it is not suitable for intensive style machines. In those machines both the bandwidth between processors and the parallel instruction timing are dependent upon the number of processors. As a result, timing cannot be predicted unless the program structure is known or the communications limited. It is a modified PRAM with restricted communications and thus, a model that allows the communication to be limited (XPRAM or bulk synchronous model, allows the user a model that fits specific architectures built into the model (Valiant). It has the following parameters:

- One specifies the number of processors p(n)
- The model provides for a local memory and a globally shared memory
- One constrains the frequency of access to the shared memory and uses that in performance estimation
- One ensures that bandwidth is adequate for the application (a necessary condition for validity)

Time will determine if such models are generally useful since each intensive machine would require a new set of constraints. The XPRAM could be useful for some stages of parallel engineering as a starting point for project specific performance prediction tools and as a constraint definition to guide programmers. By using standard restrictions for intensive programming it is feasible to allow some applications to be programmed in higher level language.

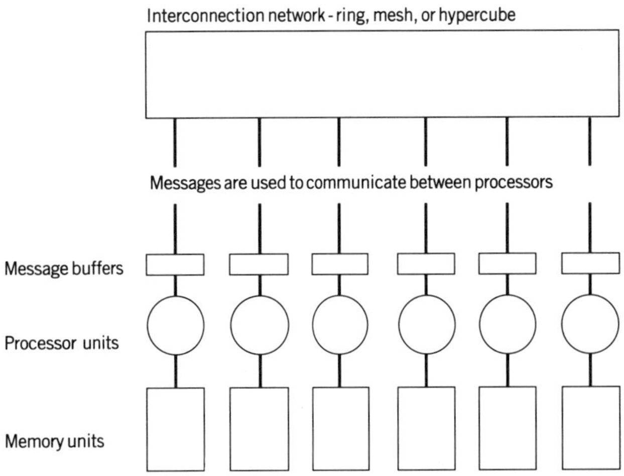

Figure 1. Intensive styles in parallel systems.

- High performance and efficiency are attained when data are partitioned and placed in local memory units and processes of equal size are placed on associated processors.
- Programming is intensive style with compiler support for libraries of common algorithms.
- Cannot use extensive programming style.
- Communication constraints on the application and on the programmer are required to avoid excessive stress on the interconnection.
- Cache coherence and memory consistency are resolved since each processor is an ordinary sequential processor.
- Bandwidth is "scalable" or equal bandwidth between nearest neighbors for any processor count.

TYPES OF PARALLEL COMPUTERS

The two styles of machines, intensively and extensively oriented, are shown in Figures 1 and 2. The software engineering goals are: to solve the application in a time that is considered short compared to that on a single processor; to use the parallel resources efficiently to maintain cost effectiveness; and to allow effective software engineering of the project to keep software and long term support costs low.

Intensively Oriented Machines. These machines are typically connected in mesh or ring arrangements and have local memories that are expected to contain the entire code and data context for the program. Input and output are performed at special nodes on the edges of the configuration where the program and data are loaded. The machine-use pattern is as a dedicated machine to a single application. High performance and efficiency result from placing the data in the local memory, selecting algorithms that increase computational requirements with respect to communication when expanded, and doing architecturally dependent mapping to the machine. Figure 3 shows typical interconnection configurations for intensive style ma-

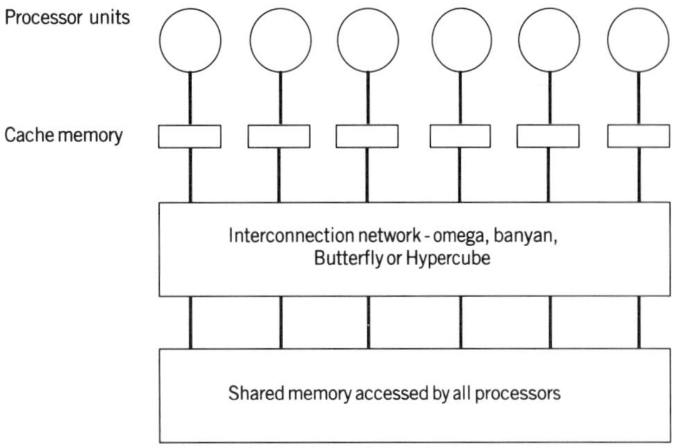

Figure 2. Extensive styles in parallel systems.

- High performance and efficiency are best when caches are large enough to act as local memory; network latency interfers otherwise.
- Bandwidth balance required: equal bandwidth to all processors no matter what the processor count.
- Multithreading and multitasking are used to overcome memory latency or delay in accessing shared memory.
- Extensive programming style used; but intensive style may be used for performance enhancements (as in von Neumann model).
- Extensive programming requires efficient cache coherency mechanism; this typically limits the number or processors.
- Sequential memory consistency model is sometimes relaxed to increase performance, requiring intensive control of memory access in critical regions.

chines. Algorithms and software for these machines are machine dependent. The structure and number of processors determine the optimum algorithm or programming approach. The appeal of the intensively oriented machine is that selected algorithms match the machine, allowing for impressive efficiencies. An advantage in these architectures is that the peak performance can be increased by adding processors at approximately a constant cost per processor rate. However, performance loss from the peak is typically significant if the problem cannot be mapped to obtain negligible communication with other than the nearest neighbors. The risk is that the required application cannot be mapped; that is, data cannot be partitioned and communication cannot be reduced for any one of the algorithms required to gain the needed high performance or efficiency. Amdahl's law applies to this single failure limiting the speed-up. Successful mapping leads to a high peak performance capability.

The disadvantage is that the algorithms must be intensively programmed and nonportable software results. The intensive style fits continuum model problems well but deviations from perfect mapping restrict the applications domain (Stone, 1987).

Extensively Oriented Machines. These machines represent an approximate model of the parallel machine model provided by the PRAM. The bandwidth is balanced. Figure 4 shows some example networks that could be built from two input, two output switches. Included in the useful configurations are hypercubes, omega, banyan, butterfly, and optimized chordal rings. Each configuration attempts to achieve a constant bandwidth between any two arbitrary processors for all processor counts, keeping the average diameter (number of links that must be traversed) and maximum diameter low. The latency of access for shared memory operations is longer than local data access. The latency also affects the smallest average granularity that can be allowed in the application. Performance is increased by caches, at the processors, which are significantly larger than conventional ones. These caches capture the context (code and data) of application and reduce use of the network for task local data. As the cached memory size is increased, the machine takes on the performance level gained through programmer specific data partitioning. Each processor looks like a local memory computer when operating on the locally cached code and data. Software labor is reduced since data partitioning is automatically performed by a caching mechanism. With an efficient cache mechanism, tasks can be placed at processors automatically. If slackness is adequate, tasks are swapped out when blocked and replaced with an unblocked one. Thus, performance and efficiency on very large data partitionable problems can approach that of the intensive application oriented machines without the necessity of mapping.

The advantage is that when communication or synchronization is required between tasks, the bandwidth is adequate for these arbitrary demands. The limitations are that large configurations require the additional bandwidth, additional hardware for cache coherence, and additional hardware to multiplex tasks into and out of the processors. Extensive-style, large-processor solutions that provide the complete parallel machine model, do not presently attain the peak speeds of intensive style machines due to processor count limits.

PERFORMANCE AND PROGRAMMABILITY IN PARALLEL SYSTEMS

Software engineering is feasible for extensively oriented machines because there is a parallel machine model. How-

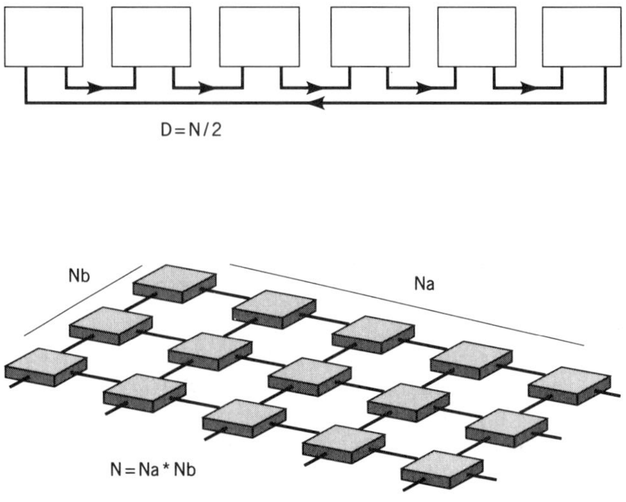

Figure 3. Intensive style networks.

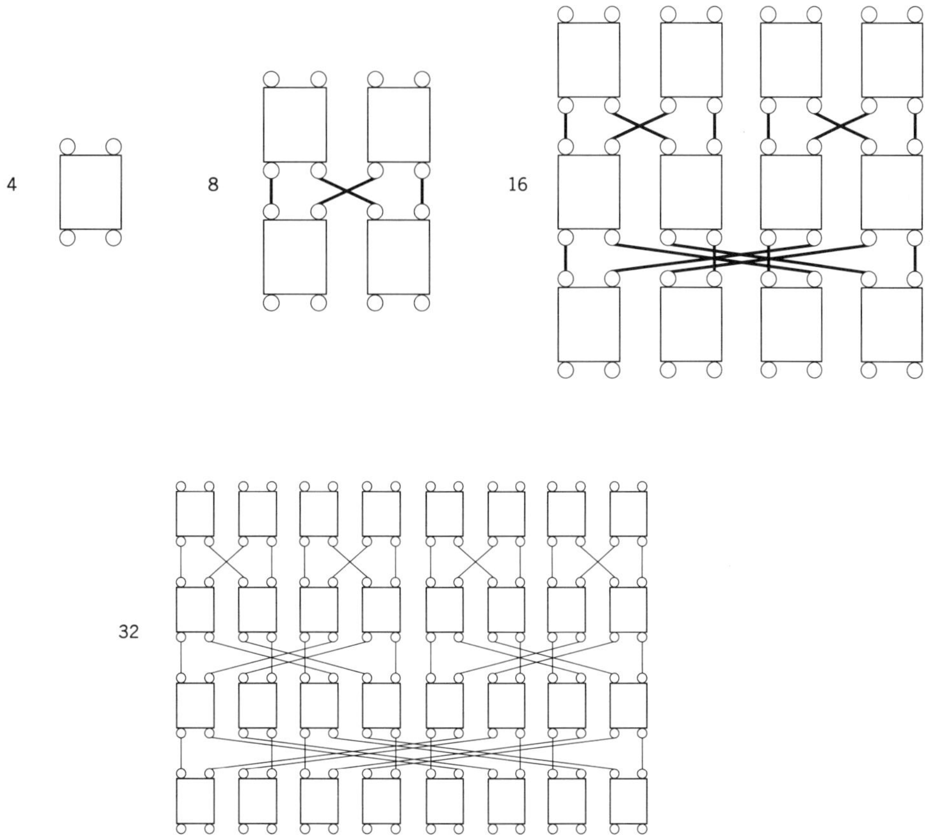

Figure 4. Extensive style networks using two by two switch.Omega network example: A two input by two output switching unit may be used to build networks for different numbers of processors. The time across the network increased as log *p(n)*. The bandwidth is balanced, that is remains a constant between any two processors no matter what the number of processors.

ever, the processor count is limited by hardware constraints. Reasonable performance and efficiency can be obtained as long as the hardware supports the parallel machine model. To extend this performance, extensive oriented machines, like von Neumann machines, can be intensively programmed to improve performance. For example, the programmer may have to signal the form of memory consistency to be used to allow processors to proceed without obtaining a result from shared memory, or physical locations may require that certain tasks be mapped to specific processors, for example, input and output interface to disks. Extensive oriented machines provide a less fragile implementation than intensive oriented ones since the parts of the parallel system that are not intensively programmed are well supported by extensive style hardware.

Some algorithms may be recognized as intensive; that is, their algorithm and data can be organized and structured to allow mapping to intensive style machines. Software engineering for intensive applications leads to restrictions on the programmer that are machine dependent. In that case software tools can aid. This approach is appropriate when ultra high performance is required; the algorithm matched to available parallel machine and the software effort of mapping is believed to be worth the investment and risk of high-cost, long-range support.

SOFTWARE ENGINEERING PARALLEL SYSTEM DEVELOPMENT LEVELS

As long as the extensive style is used a parallel system can be built in a series of stages, each with a finer level of detail expression. The software engineering approach is to build each stage, analyze or run it, estimate performance and efficiency, and refine it. Experiments on elements in the following stages are often made to provide timing estimates. At each stage, specific design decisions are made. The development stages and the design decisions made at each are given in Table 2.

The stages of software engineering in parallel systems are similar and consistent with those of other engineering approaches. However, the greater differences in results and sensitivity to choices in parallel systems over sequential ones, adds to the process complexity. The stages of analysis, design, implementation, integration, qualification and long term support are impacted by the decision point at which architectural and specific machine decisions are made. In sequential systems, the differences between sequential machines have only a moderate impact on the development's progression. In parallel systems the critical factor at each level is that the bandwidth capability demanded by the implementation remains well below that

Table 2. Software Engineering Levels in Parallel Systems

System Analysis	*Intensive Implementation*
Algorithm selection	Identification of component
Language/compiler selection	Structure
Parallel machine model	Identification of data partitions
System model analysis	Evaluation of granularity
Performance prediction	Match to architecture
	Select intensive architecture
	Scheduling and mapping
System Design	*Intensive Integration*
System model and emulation	Intensive machine operation
Bandwidth verification model	Performance and efficiency
Data, control, and input/output flow	Profile
Library functions (monitors, barriers, ...)	Debugging
Synchronization primitives, timing	Operations visualization
Performance estimation	
Extensive Implementation	*System Integration, Test and Debugging*
Primitives code	System operation
Library code	Performance and efficiency
Applications code	Profile
Threads modification	Debugging
	Operations visualization
Extensive Integration	*Qualification and Validation*
Extensive machine operation	System environmental testing
Performance and efficiency	Test case expansion
Profile	Validation
Debugging	
Operations visualization	
	Long-Term Support
	Bandwidth constraint attention
	Obsolescence
	New requirements

provided by the parallel machine. Correct system analysis requires an interprocessor bandwidth guarantee, a factor often ignored in the software analysis effort.

In parallel systems the decision to switch the design from extensive (targeted toward general parallel machines) to intensive (targeted toward a specific architecture or machine) has a greater impact than in sequential systems. Ideally each stage in development can be completed and only major changes in requirements would cause a complete redesign. However, in intensive style parallel systems the design can be so fragile that new algorithm analysis and selection may be required if the target hardware is changed. Not only can the code be non-portable but the analysis and design can be non-portable as well. Therefore, the software engineering process must be designed to delay the specific architecture selection for as long as possible, building the system in extensive style, and reverting to intensive methods for bottleneck components. Because of the close coupling between the software and the hardware, software engineering must take a system engineering role when the intensive decision is made, ensuring that the machine bandwidth constraints are followed. In parallel systems the software engineering process must be much more akin to that used in large complex circuit designs where the entire system is simulated and performance evaluated at behavioral, register-transfer, gate and transistor levels.

Analysis Level

The goal of the analysis stage is to determine the algorithms that are to be integrated to solve the parallel system requirements. Critical to this analysis are the performance (time allowed to reach a result), the efficiency (minimize resource constraints), fault tolerance (availability), and support impacts (time to perform necessary system functions that are off-line to the primary performance goal). A system model is made using data flow and bandwidth estimates. The model must include input and output of data and information interaction with external systems. If subsystems are identified, the flow of information between them must be established. Analysis of the algorithm set is performed with respect to this system model. To accomplish this analysis a parallel machine model with timing of ordinary and parallel instructions is used. The efficiency impacts of both sequential and parallel language compiler selection and timing impacts of executive or operating system calls are included in the analysis. The speed-up promised by the parallel system can be compromised by not

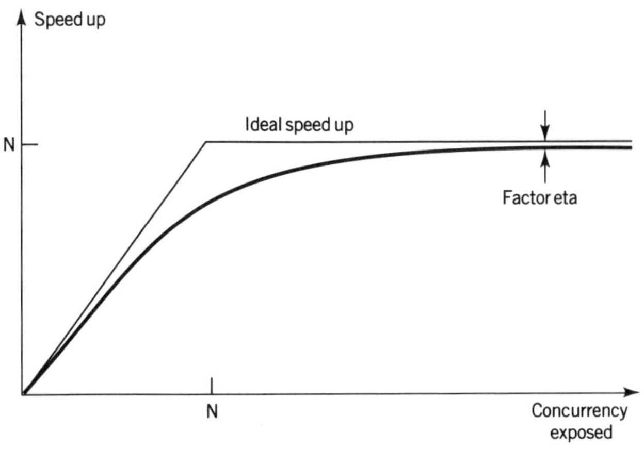

Figure 5. Speed-up limits. The use of slackness allows the machine to approach the limit within the multiplying factor η.

providing for concurrent performance of even very small portions of the system. Therefore, it is more important that the parallel analysis include all components. The speed-up impact is called Amdahl's Law (Amdahl, 1967). The equation below shows this law for one sequential and one parallel subsystem for use in the analysis stage, however, this configuration must be expanded to include each operation in the system in order to be used.

$$speedup_{\text{system}} = \frac{1}{(1 - fraction_{\text{par}})} + \frac{fraction_{\text{par}}}{speedup_{\text{par}}} \qquad (2)$$

Where $speedup_{\text{system}}$ is the speed gain due to the enhanced function *par*, $speedup_{\text{par}}$ is the ratio of the speed of the parallel component to the speed of the sequential component, and $fraction_{\text{par}}$ is the fraction of the application that is sped up. The only way to avoid this speed-up limit for a chosen parallel enhancement is to increase the concurrency by increasing the term $fraction_{\text{par}}$. Some applications provide the necessary computational expansion as they can be increased in size to attain a higher $fraction_{\text{par}}$ allowing speed-ups close to one. Slackness is used to make $fraction_{\text{par}}$ nearer to 1 by programming for a higher level of concurrency than the number of processors. More detailed analysis can be performed on extensive approaches when bandwidth is proven adequate. For this example the worst case curve shown in Figure 5 results. The factor η, dependent upon average instruction timing and granularity, is defined in equation 1, reduces the computed performance. Performance and efficiency prediction are the critical decision parameters in the analysis level. The analysis and choice of algorithm should be made without consideration of the architecture to the maximum degree possible. However, if it is necessary to make the selection of an architecture or a specific machine at this stage, then it is important to isolate the intensive selection to a subsystem and to consider the impacts of the hardware availability over a long time span. Otherwise the system is subject to repeating of analysis and design when the underlying hardware arrangement or the system requirements change. The risk and cost impact of intensive choice of architecturally dependent subsystems is magnified over those costs in sequential systems. An extensive analysis style is much more robust.

Design Level

In the parallel system design stage the detail of the analysis is expanded. All data flow, control flow, and input or output flows are defined in detail. Layers in the system are defined to isolate and provide autonomy of each component from other components. The following three parallel support levels are designed, modeled, coded and timed:

- Library algorithms—defined for the frequently used, compute intensive elements of the system (examples are: Fourier transforms, linear algebra and matrix operations or parallel SQL data base calls).
- Synchronization and communication—The critical intertask synchronization and communication component layer provides the applications programmer with a common set of interprocess communications, resource allocation, and reliable services for system development (examples are: Monitors, Barriers, or Message passing tools).
- Primitive thread interface to hardware—Threads methods or hardware adaptation are often used for the primitive operations layer interface to the hardware.

All primitive and synchronization or communication level operations should be verified to be correct. This means that they are kept small and combinations should be functionally tested in allowable combinations. Assertive methods of design and test planning are recommended for implementing both the primitive and frequent synchronization and communication components (Andrews, 1991). The assertive approach should be applied to the most critical and primitive elements of the system. The effort in assertive approach is placed in the design and expression of the test, and is most consistent with the goals of software engineering practitioners. The results are a set of proven basic primitives and synchronization modules upon which the remainder of the system is built. These modules provide the foundation from which software engineering processes are used to build the system.

Performance Analysis

The frequency of use and timing of each of these components is counted or estimated. To accomplish this task, a system scenario driver may be built to generate these values or an analysis of similar systems can be used. The most frequent and time critical intertask communications components are built, verified, and tested with hardware emulators if necessary. This information and the design provide the timing and use frequency that are necessary to make both a performance and efficiency evaluation as well as an operational evaluation of the design. The selection of the architecture is re-evaluated and shown to have adequate bandwidth, validating the design. The use of the levels of library, synchronization and communications component, as well as primitive hardware calls, is important as portability insurance. This added dimension to the software development layers may restrict impacts to lower layers when requirements are changed that mismatch the selected architecture or if the machine architecture is changed due to obsolescence.

Extensive Implementation Level. For the extensive implementation, the library, synchronization and communication, and primitive hardware interfaces are used to build the relationships between each system applications component. Overlapping of operations is necessary to avoid the impact of loss of system speed-up due to Amdahl's law effects. At this phase, performance profiles are measured to prove the functionality, resource demands, performance, and efficiency of the subsystems. In addition, debugging and operation visualization tools are necessary at this stage to understand the interaction between the subsystems. Extensive programming requires a set of tools and programming methods that allow each task to be programmed autonomously and independent of architecture. This style reduces the complexity and allows portable parallel code to be developed. However, the performance (time to complete) or the efficiency (speed-up on a number of processors) may be lost if the hardware does not support the extensive method effectively over an adequate processor count. Any performance or efficiency shortfall correction depends upon the identification of bottlenecks and the redesign of library or synchronization techniques in the program to eliminate the bottleneck. Many architectures require the substitution of intensive methods at this point. Testing and debugging is required to determine the existence, location, and correction of consistency errors, determinism errors, and synchronization sequence errors.

Functional testing should be performed on the interaction of parallel support level modules of the system. In functional testing a subset collection of methods are integrated to accomplish testing of each of the functions of a program over the function's important test cases and error cases. Parts of the program, which correspond to the essential ideas used in building the program, are tested in a stand-alone environment. Many faults, whose existence is difficult to detect in a fully integrated fashion, are found by testing in partially integrated form (Howden). Functional testing requires that the program be viewed as being constructed from subsets of functions that are combined to accomplish the overall functionality. Two steps are necessary to apply functional testing: synthesis and testability. To be practical a testing method must have accomplished the following:

- a systematic procedure for selection of test
- means of determining that test has ended
- classes of errors must be specific and explicitly described

Functional testing provides the methods to view programs as a meld of new functions from smaller functions, to separate the different ways of thinking about the joining together, to establish specific error classes to be investigated for each function, and to systematically investigate those errors.

The synthesis at different levels is applied to derive detail level functionality for small functions and abstract level for more complicated functions. There are four kinds of synthesis commonly used: algebraic, conditional, iterative, and control (Howden, 1985). Testability requires an oracle (external test statement) to decide if the output of testing is correct; that is, that the output is the same as if the function's output is the same as the "correct" function.

Intensive Implementation Level. The intensive style requires that the algorithm structure be known, processes be located on specific processors, and data location be defined by the programmer. The expected speed-up on an algorithm from intensive style machines must be very large to justify the expensive and non-portable effort of mapping. Typically the algorithm is restricted to the continuum model that allows only communications between nearest neighbors in the machine. For this style the software engineering infrastructure is based on library subroutines as provided by the vendor or built specially for each algorithm. In this approach the programmer calls the appropriate primitives of the underlying library. All message passing operations and executive or operating system interactions should be library calls. The basis for good performance is that the problem has a recognized structure that matches the machine organization. This matching minimizes communication and reduces non-nearest neighbor communication to a minimum. The program and data are then directly mapped to the specific architecture. In some architectures the mapping includes elimination of branches and schedule dependencies because the instruction—driving mechanism must perform every branch and path in a separate sequence, reducing concurrency and efficiency. Data partitioning programming requires that each of the processes be of nearly the same length to allow scheduling to be intensive. Since scheduling can be an extensive operation, this simplification is necessary.

The intensive system must be built from a collection of algorithm components, each matching the machine constraints. Since each algorithm is mapped to the processor it may be necessary to either transform or move data between algorithm component steps. Any performance gain from using intensive style machines must be large enough to overcome the overhead of data movement between algorithms steps. When algorithms have inadequate granularity for intensive style machines the tasks must be combined to reduce intertask communications. This step reduces the available concurrency and reduces the speed-up potential. Thus, bandwidth management, performance and efficiency are the responsibility of the programmer in intensive style machines. If making the problem larger is beneficial, then higher efficiency can often be obtained if the algorithm is such that the computation expands without corresponding increase in communications. In this manner arbitrarily large granularity can be provided and higher efficiencies obtained. Slackness is reduced but is not typically used in the intensive style to gain higher speed-up.

Table 3. Parallel System Performance Evaluation Factors

Factor	Mechanisms Observed	Comment
Bandwidth balance	Deliver same bandwidth between any arbitrary processor no matter the processor count	Must support bandwidth requirements during I/O in addition to pair interprocessor communications
Bandwidth efficiency	Hashing and combining to avoid hot spots; queuing and flow control	Performance prediction requires hashing, queuing network with combining
Latency avoidance mechanisms	Cache for distributed local memory	Automatic data partitioning by cache loading
Task creation efficiency	Threads or automatic hardware for allocation	Increases efficiency by lowering the parallel overhead instruction time; allows smaller granularity
Context preservation and migration	Migration for sparse completion; end-game only	Migration destroys cache context

Integration and Debugging. The problems of parallel debugging go beyond those conventionally considered in sequential debugging. Parallel architectures are rapidly changing and the model of parallel operation supported can change, reducing once acceptable synchronization methods on one machine to chaos on another. Architectural errors can fail to provide the advertised memory model. Programmers may also misunderstand the memory consistency provided if it is not the standard von Neumann one. Some parallel systems provide a weaker memory consistency model, expecting the user to employ an intensive style synchronization technique to compensate for the architectural deficiency (Gharachorloo and co-workers, 1989). This additional burden is placed on the programmer in the desire to attain higher speed, and the user is allowed to control the degree of synchronization needed to match a level of comfort in reliability, consistency, and determinism. Some sequential processors have similar problems with determinism. For example, one popular high performance computer chip has no interlocks on its pipes, although the standard von Neumann model requires prevention from two instructions with dependencies being in the pipe at the same time. Coders are expected to recognize these dependencies and insert no-ops to prevent this error.

The integration of parallel programs is exacerbated by the lack of a clear consensus on the methodology necessary. A complete integration requires three levels in parallel testing:

- test cases—enumeration of possible histories and verification of acceptability (heuristic)
- functional testing with operational reasoning—consider the ways operations of each process might be interleaved to consider all possible histories (exhaustive test analysis) (Howden, 1985)
- assertive reasoning—formulas of predicate logic (assertions) are used to characterize the sets of states wherein actions are viewed as predicate transforms that change the state from one satisfying one predicate to another (Andrews, 1991)

Qualification and Validation. Qualification and validation are similar to normal sequential software engineering practices. In-service tests and effort in this phase are based upon external demands that are independent of the form of processing. There are performance and integrity factors that should be measured and tracked in the system. Errors in design may have larger impacts in parallel systems than in conventional sequential systems. Table 3 gives the performance factors to be considered in the parallel system. The integrity features are given in Table 4.

Long Term Support

The additional burden placed upon long term support is that the programmer must adhere to bandwidth balance or bandwidth constraints in consideration of any change to the system. The knowledge necessary to follow the constraints may not be available during long term support. A systematic approach must be followed to preserve the information from the algorithm analysis, system design, implementation, and qualification stages. A test bed may be necessary to preserve the design constraints.

CONCLUSION

Software engineering in parallel systems has two styles: *intensive* and *extensive*. For the intensive style communications, restricted algorithms are mapped to match hardware capabilities and structure. For the extensive style, arbitrary applications without communications restrictions may use a widely accepted parallel machine model. The extensive style works for all cases of applications, including intensive ones. This method allows algorithm analysis, design, implementation, and system architecture to be developed independently. However, higher processor counts are available if the parallel machine model is not supported by the machine, thus leading to use of the intensive style. The intensive style is often inconsistent with the goals of software engineering practices.

Because to the lack of machine support for acceptable parallel machine models, software engineering in parallel

Table 4. Integrity Features in Parallel Systems

Feature	Purpose or Advantage
Cache coherence	Maintain existing load/store methods
Memory consistency	Preservation of order; minimum blocking of SEND, STORE, and hardware synchronization instructions
Synchronizing Instructions: test&set: match&replace: fetch&add	Efficient synchronization for building monitors and barriers in software
Communication Instructions: RECEIVE and SEND; many RECEIVEs for single SEND	Allows macrodata flow programming; several tasks wait for a single SEND for efficient software and data flow control
Multiple waiting RECEIVEs	Required for fast tree transversal support and other decision systems
Broadcast	Effective communications: used only when necessary for operating system support
System wide processor interrupts	Control of processor for task swapping, debugger aid
Job interaction	Multiple partitions, dynamic partitioning, real time and specialized functions

systems is not as mature as it is for sequential machines. However, the prognosis is good. Changes in parallel machines to match the parallel machine model for large processor-counts extensive programming, are underway. Parallel machine models with reduced communications limits are being developed that would allow software engineering development stages for the intensive style.

Software engineering in parallel systems has the standard stages of algorithm analysis, design, implementation, integration, qualification and long term support. A widely accepted and hardware supported parallel machine model is the most critical component of software engineering in parallel systems. A parallel machine model must provide performance prediction. For software engineering to succeed the subsystems, functions and behavior of a system must be defined and a prediction be made of system performance.

The basis for the extensive style in sequential systems is the von Neumann random access machine. (Cook and Reckhow, 1973). The von Neumann RAM model allows algorithm inventors, programmers, and architecture developers to work independently and is the primary supporting component that makes conventional software engineering feasible. The parallel machine model for extensive programming is the parallel random access model (PRAM). The PRAM model extends the RAM model to parallel systems by allowing an unlimited number of virtual processors. Parallel instruction times are added to the ordinary von Neumann ones. Valiant has proposed the XPRAM with restricted communications for the intensive style. In parallel systems the critical factor at each level is that the bandwidth capability demanded by the implementation remains well below that provided by the parallel machine.

The infrastructure for software engineering for the extensive style is three levels of engineering for each stage of development. These levels are algorithm library, synchronization and communication, and primitive interface to the machine. The algorithm library level is defined by the frequently used, compute intensive elements of the system. The synchronization and communication level provides the applications programmer with a common set of interprocess communications, resource allocation, and reliable services for system development. At the primitive interface level, threads methods or hardware support perform any machine dependent operations. At each stage in the software engineering process the frequency of use and timing of each of these components is counted or estimated. This information and the design provide the timing and use frequency necessary to make a performance, efficiency, and operational evaluation of the design.

For the intensive style software engineering is more difficult because small mismatches between algorithm and hardware structure may lead to the violation of bandwidth balance constraints and a nonproportional decrease in performance. This hazard leads to different choices of algorithms or designs for different target machines, requiring revisiting of development stages when requirements or machines change. As a result, the intensive style tends to be direct implementation oriented rather than following software engineering stages of algorithm analysis, design, programming, and integration effort as found in extensively oriented methods. Bandwidth management, performance and efficiency are the responsibility of the programmer in the intensive style. Constraints on communications are a key part of the implementation controls. The software engineering infrastructure is based on library subroutines that meet the target machine constraints. All message passing operations and executive or operating system interactions are library calls. Since each algorithm is mapped to the processor it may be necessary to either transform or move data between algorithm component steps. Any performance gain from using intensive style machines must be great enough to overcome the overhead of data movement between algorithm steps.

BIBLIOGRAPHY

G. M. Amdahl, "Validity of the Single Processor Approach to Achieving Large Scale Computing Capabilities," *Proceedings AFIPS Spring Joint Computer Conf.*, Atlantic City, N.J. **30,** 483–485 (April 1967).

T. E. Anderson, "Operating System Support for High Performance Multiprocessing," *Technical Report No. 91-08-10,* Department of Computer Science and Engineering, University of Washington, Seattle, Wash., Aug. 1991.

F. André, D. Herman, and J-P. Verjus, *Synchronization of Parallel Programs,* The MIT Press, Boston, Mass., 1985.

G. R. Andrews, *Concurrent Programming,* The Benjamin/Cummings Publishing Co., Redwood City, Calif., 1991.

G. Bell, "Utracomputers: A Teraflop Before Its Time," *Science* **256,**6 (Apr. 1992); "Ultracomputers A Teraflop Before Its Time, *Communications of the ACM* **35**(8), 27–47, (Aug. 1992).

J. Boyle and co-workers, *Portable Programs for Parallel Processors,* Holt, Rinehart and Winston, Inc., New York, 1987.

N. Carriero and D. Gelernter, "Linda in Context," *Comm. ACM,* **32**(4), 444–458 (April 1989).

K. M. Chandy and J. Misra, *Parallel Program Design: A Foundation,* Addison-Wesley Publishing Co., Inc., Reading, Mass., 1988.

S. A. Cook and R. A. Reckhow, "Time Bounded Random Access Machines," *J. of Computer and Systems Sciences* **7,** 354–375, (1973).

D. DeWitt and J. Gray, "Parallel Database Systems: The Future of High Performance Database Systems," *Comm. ACM* **35**(6), 85–98 (June 1992).

D. Gelernter and N. Carriero, "Coordination Languages and Their Significance," *Comm. ACM,* **35**(2) (Feb. 1992).

K. Gharachorloo and co-workers, *Memory Consistency and Event Ordering in Scalable Shared-Memory Multiprocessors,* Technical Report, Stanford University, Computer Systems Laboratory, Nov. 21, 1989.

C. A. R. Hoare, *Communicating Sequential Processes,* Prentice-Hall International, Englewood Cliffs, N.J. 1985.

W. E. Howden, "The Theory and Practice of Functional Testing," *IEEE Software,* 6–17 (Sept. 1985).

D. Lenoski and co-workers, "The Stanford Dash Multiprocessor," *Computer,* 63–79 (Mar. 1992).

G. Lindemood, *Projections of Supercomputer Market for the 1990's,* Presentation: Research Consortium, Inc., Annual Management Meeting, Washington, D.C., Dec. 1991.

D. Nussbaum and A. Agarwal, "Scalability of Parallel Machines," *Comm. ACM,* **34**(3), 57–61 (Mar. 1991).

C. M. Pancake, "Software Support for Parallel Computing: Where Are We Headed?," *Comm. ACM,* **34**(11), 53–64 (Nov. 1991).

D. A. Patterson and J. L. Hennessy, *Computer Architecture A Quantitative Approach,* Morgan Kauftnann Publishers, Inc., 1990.

D. B. Skillicorn, "Practical Concurrent Programming for Parallel Machines," *The Computer Journal* **34**(4), 302–310 (Aug. 1991).

H. S. Stone, *High-Performance Computer Architecture,* Addison-Wesley Publishing Co., Inc., Reading, Mass., 1987.

H. Sullivan, *On the Performance of Multiprocessors—Analytic Results,* CHoPP Computer Corporation, La Jolla, Calif., August 1992, Technical Report.

L. G. Valiant, "General Purpose Parallel Architectures," in J. van Leeuwen, ed., *Handbook of Theoretical Computer Science,* Elsevier Science Publishing Co., New York, pp. 944–971.

CARL G. MURPHY
CHoPP Computer Corporation

PARALLEL PROGRAMMING IN 2001

In the last decade, the parallel computer has surpassed the raw power of traditional vector supercomputers to become an important tool in science, engineering, and business. Its popularity is growing in scientific computation, decision-support activities, financial analysis, and database systems. Yet the parallel computer remains the exception, while the sequential computer is the norm.

The next decade may see that reversed, however, as advances continue in VLSI, parallel software, and communication technology. It will be less difficult to develop an efficient parallel program, and fewer programmers will seek sequential solutions. Obstacles like the cost of translating a sequential program to a parallel one and the difficulty of using parallelism in general will become less overwhelming. In some applications, parallel computing will be the only solution.

Software technologies will change to meet these challenges. Reactive programs will play a larger role in program development as cooperative processing becomes more popular. Also, as the struggle to debug parallel programs continues, expect to see more widespread acceptance of formal methods for reasoning about a program's correctness. Technologies that will be vital to parallel programming's success are theories, methods, and notations that deal with program composition. Operating systems will also take on more responsibility for resource management, including process allocation and load balancing. Virtual-memory management across distributed memories will become commonplace.

PROGRAMMING PREDICTIONS FOR 2001

- Reactive systems and hence reactive programs will be ubiquitous.
- Programmers, tired of debugging difficulties, will use design methods that produce correct programs as well as formal methods of proving correctness and methods of integrating proofs and testing.
- Reactive and transformational programs will be integrated, which will give rise to methods and notations suitable for developing both types of programs.
- Because heterogeneous networks of workstations and servers will be common, programming systems will also be heterogeneous. Programmers will be able to compose programs of different types and languages into single entities.
- There will be more programming systems that let you manipulate different kinds of large data structures as atomic operations. The parallelism inherent in manipulating these structures will be implicit rather than explicit SIMD notations will evolve into the parallel composition of different data-parallel operations.
- Driven by the need for reusable templates, programmers will turn more towards higher order declarative programming and the use of object-oriented features such as inheritance and operator overloading.
- Parallel I/O and the need to manage heterogeneous networks will give operating systems more responsibilities, such as managing process creation and balancing load.

GROWTH FACTORS

One factor driving the growth of parallel computing is the economy of scale in chip design and production. It costs less to get raw computing power by concurrent execution on commodity chips than by sequential execution using special-purpose hardware.

Another factor is the increased use of networked workstations. A network can be viewed as a potential parallel computer that offers a great deal of power. Moreover, this power is generally not used at night or during off-peak periods.

Advances in communications technology will also contribute to the growth of parallel computing, particularly advances in optical fiber technology, improvements in protocol design, and the availability of faster and cheaper switches. These developments, plus the potential of optical switching, will make it economical to interconnect many processors.

The demand for more power will also stimulate the use of parallel computing. Some applications, such as weather forecasting, require so much computation in so little time that even the most powerful sequential computers are inadequate. As supercomputing becomes a bigger part of scientific research, parallel computing will grow. It will become the only option for some applications.

There will also be more demand for reactive systems, systems that interact with their environment rather than simply compute an answer in isolation. Cooperative processing, in which teams of people collaborate on a common project using local area networks is already becoming more popular as concurrent engineering concepts take hold. Systems that support this cooperative processing must be reactive programs that interact with their environment.

CONSTRAINTS

A number of factors inhibit the growth of parallel computing. One is the considerable investment in sequential programming. It can cost a lot to convert programs developed for sequential computers to execute efficiently on parallel machines. Compilers that automatically restructure sequential programs to reduce, if not eliminate, the cost of a sequential-to-parallel transformation have not been universally successful.

On the other hand, dealing with parallelism directly can be difficult. Developing efficient programs for parallel computers is harder than it is for sequential computers. Exploiting parallel computers can mean developing completely new algorithms, and most programmers are trained to develop sequential algorithms. Indeed, most education in programming teaches students how to design a sequence of operations to achieve some goal.

There is also a considerable investment in sequential-programming tools to aid in program testing, execution profiling, and interactive debugging. Because far fewer tools support parallel programming, the cost of developing these programs is higher than for sequential programs.

Another problem is the lack of a single, predominant, parallel architecture. Many different kinds of parallel computers are available today, and we may see an even richer variety in the next 10 years. Since successful programs last for many years, an investment in developing a program that will execute particularly well on only one kind of parallel computer can be risky.

By contrast, the basic sequential architecture — the von Neumann machine—has remained unchanged for decades. Programmers are typically isolated from variations in sequential computers by high-level compilers and industry-standard operating systems such as Posix. Such uniformity does not yet exist for parallel computers, which makes them less attractive platforms for software development.

ARCHITECTURE

The impact of advances in communication, VLSI technology, and embedded systems on parallel architecture will introduce special challenges and opportunities to parallel processing.

Communication Architecture

Advances in switching and networking will enable the interconnection of 10,000 to 100,000 high-performance processors. Current system architectures support up to 8,048 full-featured processors, with most common configurations having fewer than 1,000 processors, or 64,000 small processors limited to integer arithmetic.

The challenge for the coming decade is to develop methods of efficient distributing and managing the computations taking place on many processors.

Advances in communication may also allow truly distributed, possibly heterogeneous, supercomputing environments with elements specialized for visualization, I/O, and different kinds of computing. Most parallel supercomputers are mainframes, in the sense that they are packaged in a single, connected set of frames, and stored in a single room. In the future, a single program will run on a network of specialized, parallel supercomputers distributed across many institutions.

The challenge will be to distribute computing and data across several heterogeneous processors. The resource-management problem is compounded, because several programs—each with its own set of resource needs—can use a distributed supercomputer concurrently.

Designing reliable multicomputers distributed across many buildings, institutions, and even countries will be more of a challenge than designing fault-tolerant mainframe systems.

VLSI Technology

One model of parallel computing dictates that you get the best price-to-performance ratio with many processors, each with a small amount of memory. Computers would thus have tens or hundreds of thousands of processors, but less memory per processor than current multicomputers. These arguments support what is called small-grain parallel computing, with granularity measured as memory per processor.

Another model dictates that medium-size processors offer the best processor cost-performance ratio; very-low and very-high end processors cost too many dollars per delivered Flops. Likewise, the commodity memory market dictates the optimal amount of memory. These arguments support medium-grain parallel computing, computers with up to thousands of high-performance processors, each with many megabytes of memory.

The challenge to small-grain parallel computing is how to partition data effectively across tens of thousands of small memory units and use many processors concurrently. Medium-grain parallel computing needs effective ways to handle latency, which is the time required to access or fetch data from remote nodes. The overall programming challenge is to develop notations, methods, and theories that are efficient over a wide range of processor granularities.

Networks of Multiprocessors

In the next 10 years, shared-memory multiprocessors each with two to eight processors will become a basic building block of large-scale parallel computers. Regardless of how individual multiprocessors are interconnected to form large machines, communication among them will take much longer than communication within a multiprocessor. The challenge is to manage the communication hierarchy efficiently.

Embedded Systems

Distributed computing elements are controlling systems from cars and airplanes to power plants. As this distributed-control trend continues, the challenge will be to get complete and correct specifications, develop correct distributed programs, include time constraints when reasoning about correctness, and design systems that accommodate faults.

SOFTWARE TECHNOLOGY

The challenges of parallel computing will force software technologies to change in the coming decade.

Languages and Compiler Technology

High-level notations are closer to problem-specification notations and further from machine language than low-level notations. Because architecture-specific details of communication and concurrency are hidden, high-level notations place most of the burden of efficient execution on compilers.

For several reasons, high-level notations for parallel computers will gain more acceptance in the coming decade:

- They are more amenable to reasoning about correctness, which win help reduce dependence on debugging.
- They reduce the time it takes to develop and maintain parallel programs. Because parallel programming does not have sequential programming's large libraries or many experts, high productivity in parallel-program development is critical.
- No one knows for sure what types of parallel machines will be prevalent in 2001, so programs must be transportable across many parallel architectures without too heavy a performance penalty.
- Compiler technology and tools will continue to improve to the point that executing high-level notations will be almost as efficient as executing low-level notations.

Guaranteeing Program Correctness

Debugging parallel programs is usually more difficult than debugging sequential programs because testing for all possible interactions between concurrently executing processes is at best impractical, at worst impossible. Because it is so difficult to identify errors in parallel programs, methods for designing error-free programs will become attractive, even if such methods require discipline, formal methods, and a great deal of time. The coming decade will see wider applications of disciplines that help in designing error-free parallel programs, thus reducing dependence on debugging.

Programming Environments

Much of the effort in developing sequential-programming tools will help parallel programming as well. Examples include tools for

- Managing program libraries
- Managing multiple product releases
- Composing (Unix make file) different program releases
- Incorporating documentation, assertions, and tests into programs
- Improving efficiency

Some aspects of program development and execution are unique to parallel programs. These include managing non-determinism (when a program exhibits more than one behavior for the same input), controlling interprocess interactions, distributing data and processes across processors, and monitoring program execution.

Programmers in 2001 will have tools to deal with these special aspects of parallel programming, which will simplify the development of efficient and reliable parallel programs.

Operating Systems

Operating systems for parallel computers are complex because architectures vary widely, and managing resources for multiple heterogeneous processors is difficult. We expect to see open systems for managing these computers in the next decade.

TYPES OF PARALLEL PROGRAMMING

Parallel programs fail into two broad categories: transformational programs and reactive programs.

Transformational Programs

A transformational program reads data then computes and outputs a result. Transformational programs are specified as functions from inputs to outputs. Programming as taught in most schools deals primarily with developing transformational programs that will execute on sequential machines. Most efforts in parallel supercomputing—for example, fluid dynamics, climate modeling, and DNA sequence matching—are concerned with the development of transformational programs.

The current approaches to expressing parallel transformational programs include

- Conventional notations for sequential programming (like Fortran-77) that are automatically made parallel for execution on target parallel computers.
- Sequential notations with operations for modifying large data structures like arrays and relations. These include the so-called data-parallel languages.
- Extensions of sequential languages with parallel constructs like Doacross. These include object-oriented languages in which objects (processes) are written in a sequential language extended with primitives for passing messages, locking shared data values, or using monitors.
- Declarative notations that are well suited for parallel execution, including those based on functional programming or logic programming.

We expect all these approaches to be more effective—and consequently more popular—in the next decade. To date, no one approach solves all practical problems in the development of transformational parallel programs. Therefore, we expect to see programming notations that combine several methods in one framework.

Reactive Programs

A reactive program interacts with its environment while the program is executing. In general, you cannot specify a reactive program as a function from input to output because the program can receive input while it is executing. Its behavior thus depends on the program's state when the input arrives. Reactive programs are operating, command and control, and real-time systems.

Reactive systems are inherently parallel. The designer of a reactive system must consider at least two concurrently executing components: the reactive system itself and the environment with which it reacts. Reactive systems are usually non-deterministic. Much computer-science research is concerned with the systematic design of reactive systems.

The most popular notations for reactive systems use processes with some explicit mechanism for communication. Many notations for cooperative processes use explicit primitives for cooperation (see parallel-programming notation, below).

Alternatives include notations with implicit communications like concurrent-logic programming notation.

Today the term parallel programming is often defined exclusively in terms of developing transformational programs for parallel computers. We believe that the importance of reactive systems will grow, but not to the exclusion of transformational elements. By 2001 programmers will be developing integrated systems with both transformational and reactive components. Systems to control vehicles in space have both components even today.

The first step in realizing these integrated systems is to stop thinking of transformational and reactive systems as different. They do have differences—you can neither use transformational notations to express reactive computations, nor gracefully express transformational computations with a reactive notation—but we expect to see them merged into a unified framework by 2001. Compositional programming techniques will become more common. These techniques focus on defining interfaces that let you put different notations and styles together.

PARALLEL-PROGRAMMING NOTATION

Notations are classified in terms of how they use program variables and composition operators. Program variables are either mutable or definition. Composition operators, which are constructs to compose basic operations into a program, are either choice, sequential, or parallel.

Variables

Mutable variables can be assigned values an arbitrary number of times during program execution. An example is a Fortran variable. In parallel execution, you must use locks or monitors to explicitly synchronize operations on mutable variables. If you store the same mutable variable on more than one processor, you must ensure copy consistency.

Definition variables, also called single-assignment variables, do not have these problems. Their initial value is a special symbol, undefined, and you can assign a value to them only once during program execution. Therefore, the only possible copy inconsistency is an undefined variable in one copy and a defined one in the other. In this case, a program with an undefined copy waits for the variable to become defined. You do not need to explicitly synchronize operations on definition variables.

Definition variables are in concurrent logic programming and functional and dataflow languages.

Composition

Composition is the means by which statements combine to form a program. Choice composition is the construct in if-then-else or case statements or guarded commands. You use it to select program blocks according to a Boolean condition.

Sequential composition is the familiar composition operator of imperative languages, while the parallel-composition operator specifies that composed programs are to execute concurrently.

Notation for Transformational Programs

You can express transformational programs in five ways:

Making Sequential Programs Parallel. On the surface, using a compiler to form sequential languages like Fortran-77 or C into parallel programs would seem ideal. However, this automatic transformation can be done only with great difficulty.

First, sequential programs use only mutable variables and choice and sequential composition. You must execute assignment statements to change variable values.

Second, because a sequential program may overspecify the order in which statements execute, the compiler has to reverse-engineer the program by removing the overspecification—a convoluted and expensive process. In simplistic terms, the compiler identifies any loops in the program whose iterations can execute concurrently without altering the results of the program and arranges for their parallel execution. The result generally executes in single-program, multiple-data mode—the same program executes on each available processor. The input data to each copy of the program is a subset of all the input data.

Thus, the difficulty of transforming sequential programs into non-SPMD programs plus being forced to represent fundamentally parallel programs in sequential notations for reverse engineering make this method of expression uneconomical.

Although compilers for sequential-to-parallel transformation are likely to improve (much progress has already been made), they do not as yet offer a complete solution for parallel-program development. Parallel execution of transformational programs in Fortran, C, and other sequential notations on computers with up to 30 processors is feasible now. But we do not believe that completely automatic sequential-to-parallel transformation will offer a general solution for computers with thousands of processors.

Sequential Programs with Assignments to Complex Data Structures. Fortran-90, Connection Machine Fortran, A Programming Language, and Structured Query Language provide operations on arrays and relations. Compilers can partition these operations into parts that can execute concurrently. An example of a matrix multiply that uses this feature is given below.

The array index 1: n tells the compiler that it can perform n operations in parallel.

The advantage of this program type is that you can reason about program behavior in the same way you would reason about conventional sequential-program behavior. The only difference is that you are dealing with assignments to data structures, not assignments to elementary units like numbers and characters. These programs use only mutable variables and sequential and choice composition.

However, even with Fortran-90, the compiler's analysis to derive the most parallelism from a program is significant. In the matrix multiply in Fortran-90 below, for the outer loop to execute in parallel, the compiler must detect that all j index values are independent. Although this task appears easy for the matrix multiply in the figure, it is, in practice, very difficult.

```
   DO 20J=1, N
     DO 10 K=1, N
       A(1:N,J)=
         A(1:N,J)+B(1:N,K) * C(K,J)
 10 CONTINUE
 20 CONTINUE
```

Sequential Notations with Parallel Constructs. As an alternative to requiring a compiler to detect the potential for parallel execution, you can explicitly state which program elements can execute in parallel. The most common approach is to extend sequential languages like Fortran by including primitives for parallel execution.

You can think of a parallel program as a sequential program with parallel versions of a few sequential primitives. An example of this is replacing sequential do loops with parallel Doall or Doacross loops. It is typically your responsibility to specify dependencies between loop iterations. Parallel programs developed using such notations can have many synchronizing operations that must participate among several processes.

Below is an example of a Doall (a parallel do loop). In a Doall, you extend the matrix multiply routine by explicitly specifying that the outer loop can execute in parallel.

```
   DOALL 20 J=1, N
     DO 10 K=1, N
       A(1:N,J)=
         A(1:N,J)+B(1:N,K) * C(K,J)
 10  CONTINUE
 20 CONTINUE
```

Constructs like parallel loops simplify the expression of SPMD programs. SPMD programs with parallel loops have not only both sequential and choice composition, but also a parallel-composition operator.

This type of SPMD program has three levels of blocks: low, middle, and top. A low-level block is a sequential program like Fortran-77. A middle-level block is a parallel composition of low-level blocks. The middle-level block uses parallel constructs like Doacross, fork/join, and parbegin/parend. The top-level block is a sequential program in which the statements are middle- or low-level blocks.

Restricting parallel composition to the middle-level block simplifies program development. Thus, developing an SPMD program is like dealing with a conventional sequential program except for the middle-level block.

Declarative Languages. These languages are based on formal mathematical systems like predicate logic. They have elegant semantics and provide ample opportunity for parallel execution. Because the semantics are inherently parallel, you can express algorithms cleanly and succinctly. The drawback is having to learn mathematical and logical notation if you are familiar only with conventional imperative notation.

A subset of declarative languages is functional programming notation. A functional program is a set (conjunction) of functional definitions. Languages based on applying functions are attractive because they are mathematically elegant, and data dependencies exist only between the function producing a value and the functions using that value.

You can assign functional values to a variable (as in lambda calculus), but you can do so only once—which makes them, in effect, definition variables. As such they share the advantage of definition variables: Once you produce functional values, you can copy them without worrying about consistency.

Another advantage of functional programs is that functional semantics allow you to determine the exact dependency graph in a straightforward manner. Parallelism in a functional program is relatively easy to detect and exploit; it is not as difficult as trying to extract dependency information from sequential programs, for example.

Functional programs are not without drawbacks, however. One problem is that many scientific programs and database applications modify small parts of large data structures. For example, suppose you want to modify one element of a large array A, say $A[0,0,0]$. You can treat the modification as if you were modifying a mutable structure in state-based notation or you can do it as if you were defining a new array A' in functional notation. (In the latter case, A' and A are identical except for the [0,0,0] elements.) Which approach is better remains to be seen. We cannot predict whether computational scientists and programmers will find it simpler to reason and develop programs in a functional style or an imperative style.

A matrix multiply in the functional language Sisal is shown below (Cann and co-workers, 1990). A disadvantage of Sisal is that you have to create a new logical, if not physical, copy of the array. Dataflow languages have advanced significantly in the last 10 years, and we expect them to advance even more and be more widely used in the next decade.

```
for J in 1, N
  NewA:=
   for initial
    K:=1
    while K<N repeat
     A:=
      for L in 1, N
       returns array old A(L,J)+B(L,K) * C(K,J)
      end for;
     K:=old K+1;
  returns
   array of A
  end for;
 returns
  array of NewA
end for;
```

Reactive Programs

Reactive programs are not that different from informational programs as far as notation is concerned. You can use reactive-system notations for transformational programs as well. The relationship between the two becomes clearer if you think of a transformational program as a special case of a reactive program. In a transformational program, the system interacts with its environment only at the beginning of the program, when it reads data from the environment and at the end, when it writes data. In a reactive program, on the other hand, the system is constantly interacting with its environment.

The most popular notations for reactive systems use processes with some explicit mechanism for communication—whether that is sending and receiving messages, using remote procedure calls, invoking methods in remote objects (object-oriented terminology), or explicitly using monitors. In alternative notation, communication among program components takes place implicitly through the use of abstractions the shared memory.

Thus, a reactive system is a process that is either waiting or active (Kesselman, 1991). Its state depends on the value of a process variable called the input channel. The input channel's value is determined, in turn, by the queue of messages in the channel. When the queue has no messages, the process is called a *waiting* process. Values of all process variables other than the input channel remain unchanged while the process is waiting.

A waiting process remains in that state until its input channel receives a message. A finite number of steps later the wanting process becomes *active*, removes a message from its input channel and copies the contents of the message into other process variables. It then

- Modifies its variables and/or
- Sends messages (appends messages to the tails of queues that are input channels) and/or
- Creates processes.

The process then either becomes waiting again or stops executing. Once a process becomes active, its computation is independent of other processes. Message sending, in particular, is asynchronous. That is, a process can send a message regardless of the receiver's state.

You can modify the input channel's value for, say process p, in only one of two ways: Any process can append a message to the end of the queue, and p can delete any message at the head of the queue.

A process continues execution until it becomes waiting. When a process becomes waiting, other processes on the processor are scheduled for execution.

This scheme has many variations:

- Message-passing can occur when communicating processes rendezvous, as in Ada.
- You can send messages on ports rather than directly to processes, as in Occam.
- You can connect ports statically or dynamically. In other words, you can break down and reestablish connections between ports and have processes cooperate through shared variables.

Linda (Ahuja and co-workers, 1986) is a novel approach to reactive programming, in which a sequential language is augmented by a shared structure, called a tuple space.

You manipulate the tuple space from the sequential language by using a subroutine library. The result is an architect-independent abstraction for process creation, interprocess communication, synchronization, and data sharing.

Concurrent-Logic Programming. Definition variables are the basis of logic-programming derivatives for parallel languages like Strand88, Flat Concurrent Prolog, and Guarded Horn Clauses.

A program is a relation between variables. The equation $x=f(y)$ is a special-case relation of x and y. You can specify a nondeterministic program as a relation: For instance, z is an interleaving of sequences x and y. Because x and y can have many interleavings, the specification is a relation and not a function.

Programs based on definition variables suffer the same problem as functional programming: To represent a modification in a program's state, you have to define a new state, which is inconvenient when you are making small modifications to large data structures like arrays.

You can derive these programs from specifications using predicate calculus, which is an advantage.

Compositional Programming. Program Composition Notation (Chandy and Taylor, 1991) is an example of a compositional notation. With this notation, you can write programs in either a functional, relational, or imperative style, and you can compose programs in different notations like C and Fortran.

PCN uses all three composition operators—choice, parallel, and sequential—and both mutable and definition variables. Array operations, like those in Fortran-90, and operations on data structures like sets are permitted in some compositional notations. The question remains whether compositional theory can be made simple enough to let you reason about programs composed from diverse parts.

Below is an example of a compositional program for a matrix multiply. The outer block of the program is a parallel composition, while the inner block is a sequential composition. You need sequential composition to sequence update operations on A, which is a mutable variable.

```
{||J in <1...N>
  {; K in <1...N>
   A(1:N,J):=A(I:N,J)+B(1:N,K) * C(K,J)
  }
}
```

You can design PCN programs either top-down or bottom-up, depending on what you start with. If you start with a specification, the top-down method is better. If you start with a sequential program, the bottom-up method is better.

In top-down design, you use predicate calculus to refine a specification into a convenient form, which is then transformed mechanically into a declarative PCN program.

Almost all this work is in predicate calculus and is thus largely independent of the target language.

If the declarative program is not efficient enough, you can use performance tools to determine the major sources of inefficiency. To modify parts of the program that most contribute to inefficiency, you can replace definition variables with mutable variables and sequence updates to new variables by substituting sequential composition for parallel composition. Because a small part of a program is usually responsible for most of the execution time and memory use, you need to optimize only that small part.

In bottom-up design, you start with a sequential program in Fortran-77 or C and partition it into blocks. Often the blocks correspond to Fortran subroutines or C functions.

You can then compose the blocks using the parallel-composition operator, with blocks communicating through shared definition variables. You can use PCN's proof rules to demonstrate the composed program's properties.

The biggest advantage of compositional notation is that you can use the collection of programming paradigms that best fits your problem, whether that is functional, relational, or SPMD.

TEMPLATES AND LIBRARIES

Sequential-programming libraries are a big part of sequential-program development. In parallel programming, libraries (of parallel programs) should have an even bigger part because parallel-program development is more difficult and hence has more catching up to do.

Much has been written about reusing sequential programs. Experience suggests that parallel programmers should try to reuse programming idioms as well. A few programming idioms are used repeatedly to develop many parallel programs. These idioms deal not only with the algorithmic program structures but also with resource-management issues like determining when to offload part of a computation to a different processor.

By 2001, programmers will have theories, methods, and tools that will let them define their own idioms, including resource-management idioms. These idioms, called templates or stencils, will significantly increase programmer productivity because programmers will be able to develop parts of programs simply by filling in the templates.

Programmers will also have tools to help them browse through template and program libraries. They will use these tools to insert programs from the program library into templates from the template library. In this way, templates and libraries will help educate a generation of parallel programmers.

REASONING ABOUT PARALLEL PROCESSES

A major problem in designing parallel software is how to design it correctly and efficiently, yet inexpensively. Reasoning about parallel processes is essential if you are going to develop and test reliable parallel systems. However, reasoning about parallel processes (and debugging parallel processes) can be more difficult than reasoning about sequential programs because parallel processes interact and are non-deterministic.

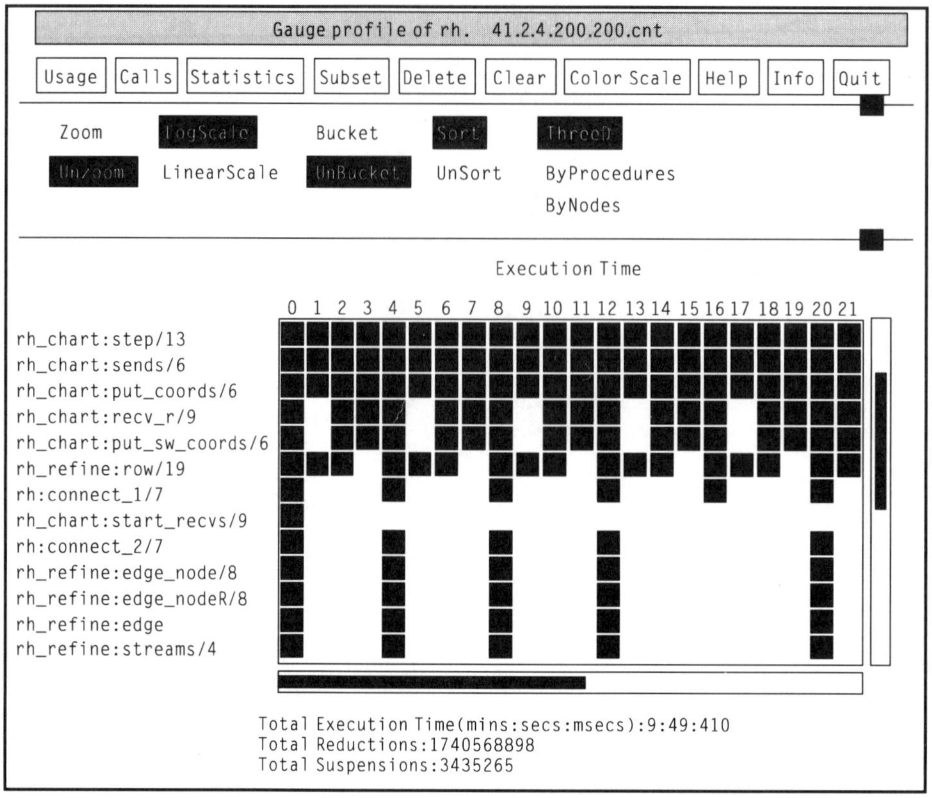

Figure 1. A parallel execution profile using the Gauge performance-visualization system.

One of the advantages of automatically making Fortran-77 parallel is that you can use conventional methods of reasoning about the programs. Sequential programming notations with array operations use similar conventional methods of reasoning. All you have to add are the rules for assignment statements that assign values to more than one variable in parallel.

Reasoning about cooperating processes adds a new dimension, however. How do you reason about how process executions interleave? One way is to reason about each process separately and to prove that process x does not interfere with the reasoning (proof) of process y. Another way is to reason about the properties of the collected processes as a whole by using simple proof rules based on temporal logic. Unity uses this approach (Chandy and Misra, 1988).

You can avoid reasoning about how process executions interleave if you are designing transformational systems —just program in sequential notations—but you cannot avoid the problem if you are designing a reactive system.

Formal methods for reasoning about the correctness of programs will play an increasing role in the coming decade. The notation that is most restrictive yet still appropriate for the problem will provide the simplest correctness arguments.

PROGRAMMING ENVIRONMENT

Very few tools are available for developing program on parallel computers. Although parallel programs will benefit from advances in development tools for sequential programs, parallel programming requires special programming tools, particularly to support functional and performance debugging. Visual methods of presentation will be integral to these tools.

Functional Debugging

Functional debugging is the focus of much research today, but there is no consensus on debugging methods for parallel programs. Right now you usually resort to inserting print statements into a program to figure out what is going on.

The challenge of debugging a parallel program comes from monitoring it. Monitoring can change the behavior of the program, making it difficult to duplicate the erroneous behavior. Furthermore, it is difficult to integrated the monitored behaviors of many concurrent processes into a single system behavior for use in debugging.

In the most promising approaches to debugging parallel programs, the capabilities are similar to those in sequential interactive debuggers. The difference is that parallel debuggers must deal with determinacy issues.

A debugging technique known as instant replay is an example of one way to debug parallel programs. Instant replay captures elements of the program state as the program executes. Enough state is recorded to allow portions of the computation to reexecute, yet you maintain the order of interaction between concurrently executing program segments, even if debugging slows down part of the execution. The disadvantage of instant replay is the difficulty in identifying which state elements need to be recorded.

Testing based on proof rules is an alternative approach that is being pursued in the context of compositional notations. In this method, you use proof rules associated with composition to compile in checks for a program's invariant and progress properties. Although proof-based testing is just starting to be used, we believe it will be a valuable complement to trace-based debugging.

Performance Debugging

The primary reason for writing a parallel transformational program is to enhance performance, yet little specialized support is available for measuring that performance. Performance debugging—determining why a program's efficiency is inadequate on a target parallel computer—will become a critical area in the coming decade.

Within the next 10 years, performance will become an integral part of parallel programming. Gauge, a performance-visualization system (Kesselman, 1991), represents the state of the art today. Gauge has been used to improve the performance of programs executing on computers as large as the 500-node Intel Touchstone Delta system.

Figure 1 shows a parallel-execution profile produced by PCN and Gauge. The program's procedures are on the horizontal axis, the processor number is on the vertical axis, and the execution time is indicated by the level of gray in the corresponding square.

By 2001 programmers will have tools to help them improve the performance of programs executing on thousands of processor's.

OPERATING-SYSTEM SUPPORT

Operating-system support will improve, making parallel programs more portable and easier to program. Looking back, as virtual-memory management became widely accepted, operating systems took away the responsibility of managing memory resources. Likewise, we expect to see them take away the responsibility for processing resources in parallel computers as data distribution and load balancing become simpler.

The most advanced operating-system capabilities are on shared-memory computers. The Mach operating system (Accetta and co-workers) is one such system, which supports simple load balancing and memory management. Within the next 10 years, we expect multiprocessing operating systems to be commonplace.

The Convex C2 computer and operating system has more sophisticated capabilities, including a feature to allocate processor subsets to subtasks and dynamically adjust task granularity, and balance load.

Distributed-memory computers have less support. You have to determine how processors will be allocated and implement that allocation through a mechanism called space sharing. Space sharing allocates a subset of processors to a computation for its duration. This mechanism is limited today in that you cannot adjust the size of this subset during computation. Moreover, you are solely responsible for problem partitioning, load balancing, and memory management.

Some improvement is on the horizon. Research is ongoing to extend the concept of virtual memory across processors. With distributed virtual memory (Li and Schaefer, 1989), you will have transparent access to all computer memory. In addition, this mechanism provides for some degree of sharing.

Operating systems in 2001 will manage many of the details that parallel programmers have to deal with today, including resource management. They will manage resources in a way that hides distinctions between shared-memory and distributed-memory parallel computers.

In the coming decade, parallel programs will be called on to carry out many functions, including reacting with the environment, performing repeated data-parallel operations on large data structures, and managing concurrent activities.

Purely data-parallel notations, such as Fortran-90 and purely declarative notations will be used for certain kinds of programming problems. We think it is unlikely that any one style will offer a complete solution. Just as the trend in architecture is to focus on the composition of heterogeneous servers to form multicomputer's—how they are put together and packaged to obtain single computing engines —so too, the trend in software architecture is likely to be program composition—how programs, perhaps in different languages and exploiting different architectures, can be put together to get a single, efficient program.

This article is reprinted from *IEEE Software* 11–20 (Nov. 1991) with the permission of the IEEE. IEEE, 1991. The work reported here is supported by the US Air Force—Office of Scientific Research under contract AFOSR-91-0070.

BIBLIOGRAPHY

M. Accetta and co-workers, "Mach: A New Kernel Foundation for UNIX Development," *Unix Review,* 37–39 (Aug. 1986).

S. Ahuja, N. Carriero, and D. Gelernter, "Linda and Friends," *Computer,* 26–34 (Aug. 1986).

D. C. Cann, J. T. Feo, and T. M. DeBoni, "Sisal 1.2: High-Performance Applicative Computing," *Proc. Symp. Parallel and Distributed Processing,* IEEE CS Press, Los Altamitos, Calif., 1990, pp. 612–616.

K. M. Chandy and J. Misra, *Parallel Program Design,* Addison-Wesley, Reading, Mass., 1988.

K. M. Chandy and S. Taylor, *An Introduction to Parallel Programming,* Bartlett and Jones, Boston, 1991.

L. Foster and S. Taylor, *Strand: Concepts in Parallel Programming,* Prentice Hall, Englewood Cliffs, N.J., 1989.

C. Kesselman, *Tools and Techniques for Performance Measurement and Performance Improvement in Parallel Programs,* Tech. Report UCLA-CS-TR-91-03, Univ. of Calif. at Los Angeles, 1991.

K. Li and R. Schaefer, "A Hypercube Shared Virtual Memory System," *Proc. Int'l Conf. Parallel Processing,* Pennsylvania State Univ. Press, University Park, 1989, pp. 125–132.

C. Seitz, *Developments in Concurrency and Communication,* chapter 5, Addison-Wesley, Reading, Mass., 1991, pp. 131–201.

K. Mani Chandy
Carl Kesselman
California Institute of Technology

PARALLEL SYSTEMS

INTRODUCTION

A parallel system can be simply defined as any system in which more than one action may happen at once. In human terms this it is a concept similar to sharing dish washing, "You wash and I'll dry," or a squad of soldiers marching along to the commands of their leader, "Left, right, left, halt." In computer terms a parallel system is made up of a number of processes cooperating on a job. The execution of the processes is mapped on to physical processors and the cooperation between the processes must be carefully planned and programmed (Almasi and Gottlieb, 1989). There are a number of programming models that can be used to represent parallel systems, these programming models can be seen to be similar to the underlying architectural model of the appropriate parallel processors. However, it is not necessary that a particular parallel system be executed on a corresponding architecture, it is possible to map any model of parallel processing on to any other model.

CLASSIFICATION OF PARALLEL SYSTEMS

Parallel systems can be categorized according to the underlying architectural model to which they are most matched, alternatively they can be categorized according to the way in which the parallelism is represented in the software. For a real understanding of a parallel system it is necessary to use both.

Flynn's Classification

An early classification of parallel systems (Flynn, 1966) divided them into four distinct groups:

1. *SISD.* The single instruction stream single data stream is the conventional serial computer that executes one instruction at a time.
2. *SIMD.* The single instruction stream multiple data stream is a system in which many identical processors simultaneously execute the same instruction on different data.
3. *MISD.* The multiple instruction stream single data stream is a system in which many processors simultaneously execute different instructions on the same data.
4. *MIMD.* The multiple instruction stream multiple data stream is a system in which many processors execute their own instructions on their own data.

These classifications are useful for discussion in general terms, e.g., if one wishes to talk about whether a problem is well suited to a SIMD or MIMD solution. However there is confusion as to which category to place some parallel systems in, the pipeline model has been placed in all four categories, and for the MIMD group more information is required to separate the vast number of different systems (e.g., interconnection topology).

Hockney and Jesshope's Classification

Hockney and Jesshope (1988) have proposed a much more detailed classification of parallel systems based on a structural notation consisting of five headings:

1. *Units.* The basic processors, peripherals or memory comprising a computer, e.g., a floating point unit.
2. *Connections.* Units can be connected in various ways and this heading clarifies that relationship, e.g., units may be connected in a multidimensional array.
3. *Comments.* These are used to clarify any meaning not obvious from the notation.
4. *Control.* Each computer is defined to have at least one instruction unit that can be programmed, the notation allows indication as to which instruction units are grouped with other units.
5. *Examples.* Showing how different computers may be described, an array processor such as the AMT DAP may be described by:

$$I[n^d\{B_b-M\}]_1^{c-nn}$$

This notation may be considered to be more detailed than is necessary for discussion of parallel systems.

Williams's Classification

A compromise between the two extremes is to study systems currently in use and identify distinct models that can be readily recognized. Such models will be applicable to both hardware and software. Williams (1990) suggests the following models:

1. *Sequential.* The conventional model.
2. *Array.* Reflecting large numbers of stupid processors obeying a controller.
3. *Pipeline.* A line of specialist processes down which information can flow.
4. *Shared Memory.* A number of processes working on a pool of shared data.
5. *Message Passing.* Many processes working together but communicating according to a well-defined protocol.

Other models include object-oriented and functional ones.

Parallel Constructs

A number of programming language constructs have been proposed for representing parallelism in programs. Essentially, to represent parallelism within a program it is necessary to be able to do the following:

- Specify, initiate, and terminate a process.
- Coordinate and dictate the interaction of processes.

Many constructs have been proposed and their syntax is varied (Trew and Wilson, 1991). For a particular model, the varied programming constructs have a general form that can be seen to be characteristic for that type of parallel system. In the following sections the constructs for representing parallelism are discussed in relationship to the models of parallel systems.

SPECIFICATION, INITIATION, AND TERMINATION OF PROCESSES

The execution of a conventional sequential program on a single processor is sometimes called a process, and it is this concept that is used when trying to define a parallel process, ie, a division of the job into parts that could each be executed on separate single processor (although they may not be).

Processes in Sequential Programs

Currently, the most well known model of processing is the sequential one, sometimes called the von Neumann approach. Essentially one instruction is executed at a time, when that instruction terminates the *next* instruction starts, all instructions are executed in a sequential manner. The semicolon separating two Modula-2 statements can usually be translated to :transfer control from statement to the next.

```
first:=old+1;
second:=first+2;
third:=first/second;
```

In this example the first statement is an assignment to a variable called first this is achieved by finding the value of old adding 1 to it and storing the result in the memory location associated with first.On completion of this, control passes to the assignment to second statement, and after that to the evaluation of third. With each of these example statements the variable first is used. The programmer is assured that the value of first accessed in the second and third statements is the one evaluated in the first.

Loops and conditionals alter the flow of control in a deterministic manner, ie, it is always possible to see that control will be passed to a specific statement. Similarly, procedure and function calls alter the flow of control in a predictable hierarchical manner. The same is true even with recursive calls. The whole of a sequential program can be considered to be a process; alternatively, the program can be divided into smaller partitions (eg, statements, loops, or procedures) and each of these can be called a process.

Coroutines

The concept of coroutines is not available in all procedural languages, but they provide a sequential mode of computation. Coroutines are similar to procedures except control is passed symmetrically rather than hierarchically. The use of coroutines is sometimes called concurrent programming; however, only one statement is executed at a time in a *consecutive* manner. Consider the following example.

```
coroutine patient            coroutine doctor
    :                            :
patient.1                    doctor.1
    :
    :
resume doctor                    :
    :                        resume patient
    :                            :
patient.2                    doctor.2
    :                            :
    :                        resume patient
resume doctor                    :
    :                            :
patient.3
    :
```

Given that control starts with patient, the program will execute the code labeled patient.1; when it first reaches resume doctor, control will pass to doctor, and the code labeled doctor.1 will then be executed. On reaching resume patient, control returns to patient immediately below the point it relinquished control and the code labeled patient.2 is executed. In all, the statements will be executed in this order:

```
    :
patient. 1
    :
doctor.1
    :
patient.2
    :
doctor.2
    :
patient. 3
    :
```

The concept of coroutines is found in a number of simulation languages such as SIMULA (see SIMULA) and in some procedural languages such as Modula-2 (see MODULA)

Array Processes

The array processing model consists of a single controller directing a number of processes on which to perform a single operation; each process has its own private data (Figure 1). Each process is one of a number of identical processes performing the same operations on different data. Problems usually have at least some parts that are not well suited to array processing, so even in the best cases a problem will consist of parts that can be divided into sets of array processes and other parts that are inherently sequential processes. When such problems are executed on an array processor the sequential parts are usually executed on the controller.

Array processors are sometimes programmed using conventional languages such as Fortran. Compiler techniques can be used to detect processes that can be executed in parallel (Zima and Chapman, 1991). Alternatively, conventional languages are extended to allow constructs to represent processes that can be executed in parallel (Flanders, 1979). Some special-purpose languages have been devel-

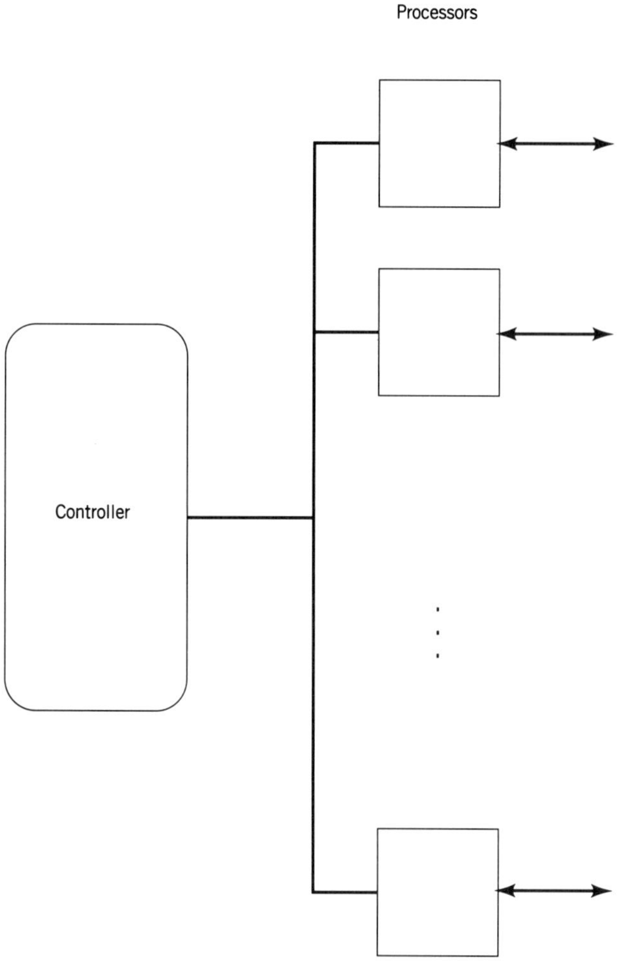

Figure 1. Array processor.

oped (Perrot and Zarea-Aliabadi, 1986); these, however, are not widely used.

All such parallelism is found within loops and so the general form is

FORALL control variable=lower TO upper DO
process (control variable)

The FORALL, or similar statement, indicates that the process below is to be executed simultaneously a number of times. The process body indicates the statements that are to be executed by each of these identical processes, and the control variable indicates the different data sets to be used. Processes are delimited as the body of a loop. All processes are executed in lockstep synchronous mode, i.e., all processes are executing the same statement at the same time. So all processes start together and terminate together.

Pipeline Processes

The concept of pipelining is commonly seen in factories such as car manufacturing plants were cars proceed along, stopping at a number of stations where different tasks take place (e.g., place engine or insert seats). Indeed, the name *pipeline* is derived from the petroleum industry where various products flow down a physical pipeline.

A piece of work may be divided into a number of distinct processes that can be executed one after the other, when the first process has completed operating on its data it can pass its results to the second process (Fig. 2). The first process can then commence work on the next set of data while the second is working on the first set of data and so on (Fig. 3). Pipeline processing takes some time during which some processes are idle, but once all processes are primed there is a large degree of parallelism.

The techniques for representing parallelism within programs for pipeline processors are similar to those for array processors; indeed, some of the language extensions and specialist languages are the same. However, it is usual for conventional sequential languages to be used to program pipeline machines (Quinn, 1987). This leads programmers to adopt a special style of programming that they know will help the compiler, although this will be ameliorated by improvements in compilation techniques (e.g., Aiken and Nicolau, 1990). All processes within a pipeline can be executing at the same time but they are carrying out different operations on different items of data.

Shared Memory and Message Passing Processes

Processes for shared memory and message passing models can be delimited in similar ways with the same effect. When programming these models, authors sometimes use conventional languages and apply compiler techniques to detect processes that can be executed in parallel. Alternatively, conventional languages are extended to allow constructs to represent processes that can be executed in parallel. Some special-purpose languages have been developed that allow the user to indicate processes and the relationships between them, eg, the programming language occam-2 (INMOS, 1988).

Three general forms of such construction of processes can be identified:

1. COBEGIN is a structured way of representing the parallel execution of a set of processes. The general form of this statement is

```
COBEGIN
   process 1,
   process 2,
   :
   :
   process n
COEND
```

   Processes in this example are separated by commas to highlight the difference from the semicolon separator that dictates sequentiality. COBEGIN and COEND can be considered to bracket the processes together; following the COBEGIN, all of the processes may start and all processes must have terminated before the COEND is reached. Variants on COBEGIN include the PAR of occam and PAR of Algol 68.

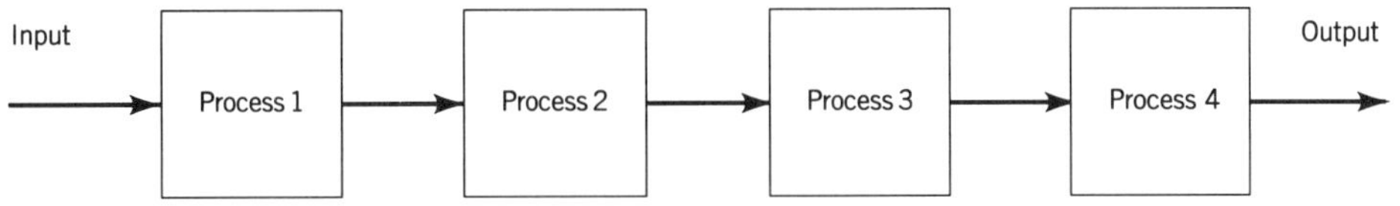

Figure 2. Pipeline processing.

2. FORK and JOIN were suggested as constructs for representing parallelism in the 1960s (Anderson, 1965) and are still in use today. Essentially, FORK allows the current execution of a program to be continued along with another strand of program (process) that is branched to. JOIN statements are used to bring together processes. The syntax of FORKs and JOINs vary from system to system but all can be used in an unstructured manner (Williams, 1990). The general form is

```
m:FORK a            a:process 2
  process 1           JOIN m
  JOIN a
```

Following a FORK, the next process in sequence can be executed along with the one forked to; the joining of processes is not always undertaken in a synchronous manner.

3. Parallel loops can be implemented in the same manner as for array processors, to indicate the same processing is to be applied a number of times. However, this does not usually indicate that all the processes must be executed simultaneously, rather that the same processing will be repeated a number of times. All processes must terminate before the loop terminates.

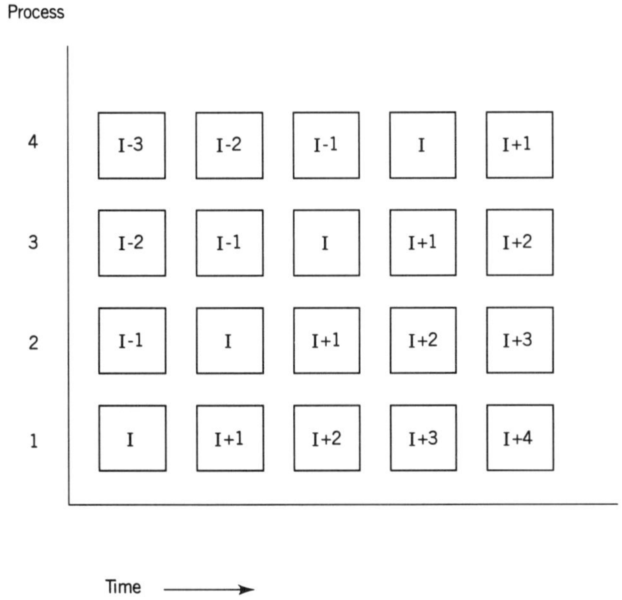

Figure 3. Flow of work along a pipeline.

COORDINATING PROCESSES

When a program consists of a number of processes, it is necessary to have mechanisms for ordering their execution and allowing processes to share information. The order of execution of processes is part of their specification, for example the FORALL of array processors; this does not address how separate processes can communicate.

Guarded Commands

Most sequential systems are deterministic, ie, given a set of inputs it is possible to determine the order of execution of statements (or processes) and predict the outputs. Even when using coroutines, the order of execution of processes is deterministic. Nondeterminism can be introduced into sequential programs by the use of guarded commands (Dijkstra,1975). If the choice of executing x or y is nondeterministic, then not even the most detailed study of the environment should reveal which will be chosen, nor is there anything to be discovered about which will be executed by looking at previous executions.

A guarded command consists of a guard and the associated command. The guard should be able to be evaluated to give a Boolean condition, whereas the command may be a list of statements. A set of guarded commands are executed by evaluating all the guards, choosing one that is true in a nondeterministic manner, and then executing all the commands associated with that guard. The evaluation of the guards can take place in parallel; the execution of the statements within the associated command will take place sequentially.

Communication between Array Processes

The execution of array processes in lockstep means that they must all be executed together. However, it is often necessary to communicate partial results and other data from one process to another. Individual processes can be envisaged to be closely linked to some processes called their nearest neighbors. Other processes can only be communicated with via a series of communications to nearest neighbors. For instance, array processes can be envisaged to be linked in a hypercube or on a two-dimensional grid. Although it is possible to model an array process using any interconnection topology, if it is necessary to map the program to an array processor with a different topology, there may be performance penalties.

Coordination of Pipelined Processes

Within a pipeline, data flows from one process to the next. A process will only output its data when execution has terminated, and a process is only willing to accept new

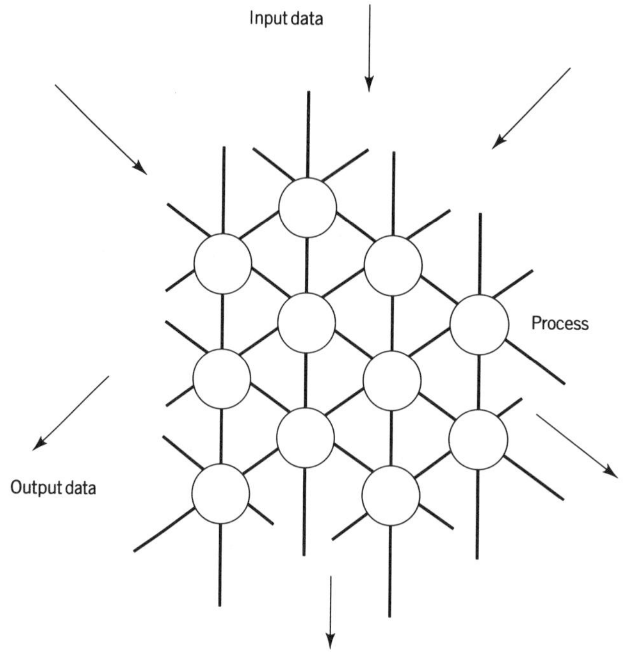

Figure 4. Flow of data through a systolic array.

input if the previous execution has terminated. This can lead to bottlenecks. For instance, if in the pipeline in Figure 2, processes 1, 2, and 4 took one time unit but process 3 took two time units, the whole pipeline would only be able to work at a speed of two time units, because process 4 would only receive its inputs every two time units and process 2 would not be able to pass on its outputs until after two time units (when process 3 would be ready). Similarly, process 1 would be waiting two time units for process 2 to be ready. Process 3 has created a bottleneck, slowing down the rate of all other processes in the pipeline. It may be possible to remove or reduce the bottleneck by dividing the work of process 3 between two processes or mapping the execution of these processes on to appropriate processors.

Systolic Arrays

A systolic array can be considered to be multidimensional pipeline, data flowing through each of the dimensions in only one direction (Fig. 4). Each process uses data from a number of fixed different directions and passes data out in a number of directions. The data are pumped through the systolic array (like blood through the heart) in a lock-step synchronous mode.

Shared Memory

The shared memory model refers to many processes that share a single memory (Fig. 5). This is perhaps the most intuitive model of a parallel processing system. The principal problem with this model is offering protection to data that are shared to ensure their integrity. Processes can be specified to work in parallel, using constructs such as COBEGIN, but they also specify other relationships among groups of processes, such as the following.

1. Sequential, for which the first process must be complete before the next can commence (the conventional model).
2. Commutative, for which the following processes can be run in any order, but once a process has started it must run to completion and no two processes may run at the same time.
3. Synchronous, for which all processes must execute together and not on their own.

It is also possible to build up hierarchies of processes, i.e., a group of processes linked together sequentially may be able to run commutatively with another group of processes that can run in parallel.

A number of mechanisms are available to help users protect data. This may be offered by the system or implemented by the user. Ben-Ari (1990) fully discusses techniques for offering mutual exclusion when accessing data. Briefly the techniques include the following extremes:

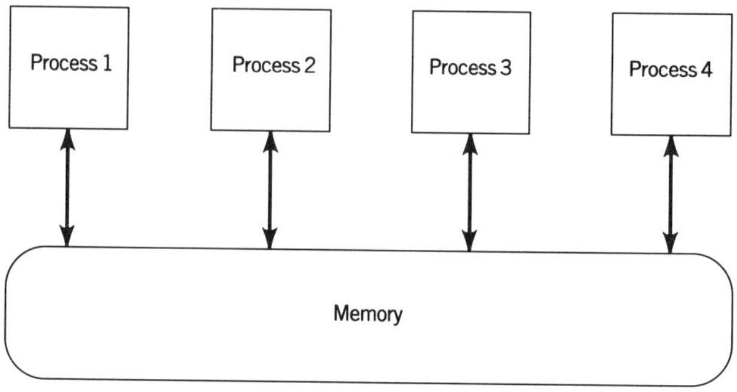

Figure 5. Shared memory processing.

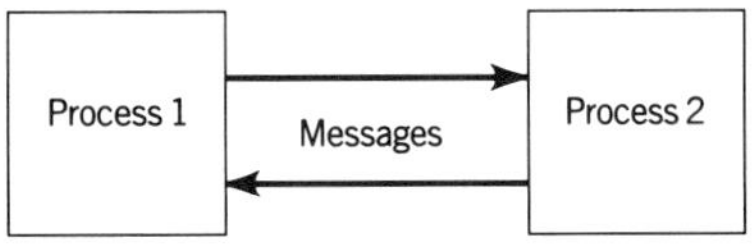

Figure 6. Message passing processes.

1. Semaphores based on two primitives, allowing mutual exclusion while executing critical parts of code.
2. Monitors that define and protect shared data structures, blocking access as necessary.

Message Passing Coordination

As with shared memory processes, the execution of message passing processes can be dictated by sequencing constructs, such as sequential and commutative ones. Data are considered private to a specific process. Data are shared in one of two ways: either by passing them as messages along channels (Figure 6) or by using a rendezvous as Ada does (see ADA). There are a number of ways in which message passing can be achieved in both synchronous and asynchronous manners. Hoare's (1985) communicating sequential processes (CSPs) and the related language occam are based on named channels that connect processes. Data are sent down a channel like this:

```
channel1 ! output data
```

and received by another process like this:

```
channel1 ? input data
```

Because of the synchronous nature, both processes must be running in parallel, otherwise the whole system would deadlock.

FUTURE PARALLEL SYSTEMS

The future success of parallel systems lies with their ease of use. Currently, parallel systems are seen as closely related to the hardware model and so expert knowledge of parallel processing is needed to program them. When parallel systems become more oriented toward the problem domain, they will become easier to design. This implies that there will be a much more distinct layer between the hardware architecture and the parallel systems. This will mean the development of techniques for mapping from the conceptual system to the real architecture.

BIBLIOGRAPHY

A. Aiken and A. Nicolau, "Fine-grain Parallelization and the Wavefront Method," in D. Gelernter, A. Nicolau, and D. Padua, eds., *Languages and Compilers for Parallel Computing*, Pitman, London, 1990, pp. 1–16.

G. S. Almasi and A. Gottlieb, *Highly Parallel Computing*, Benjamin/Cummings, Redwood, 1989.

A. Anderson, "Program Structures for Parallel Processing," *CACM* **8**, 786–788 (1965).

M. Ben-Ari, *Principles of Concurrent and Distributed Programming*, Prentice Hall International, Hemel Hempstead, 1990.

E. W. Dijkstra, "Guarded Commands, Non-determinism and Formal Derivation of Programs," *CACM* **18**, 453–457 (1975).

P. M. Flanders, "Fortran Extensions for a Highly Parallel Processor," in R. W. Hockney and C. R. Jesshope, eds., *Supercomputers*, Vol. 2, Infotech International Ltd., Maidenhead, 1979, pp. 118–133.

M. J. Flynn, "Very High Speed Computing Systems," *Proceedings of the IEEE* **54** 1901–1909 (1966).

C. A. R. Hoare, *Communicating Sequential Processes*, Prentice Hall International, Hemel Hempstead, 1985.

R. W. Hockney and C. R. Jesshope, *Parallel Computers 2*, Adam Hilger, Bristol, 1988.

INMOS Limited, *occam 2 reference Manual*, Prentice Hall International, Hemel Hempstead, 1988.

M. J. Quinn, *Designing Efficient Algorithms for Parallel Computers*, McGraw Hill, International, 1987.

R. H. Perrot and A. Zarea-Aliabadi, "Supercomputer Languages," *ACM Comput. Surv.* **18**(1), 5–22 (1986).

A. Trew and G. Wilson, eds., *Past, Present, Parallel,* Springer-Verlag., Berlin, 1991.

S. A. Williams, *Programming Models for Parallel Systems,* John Wiley & Sons, Inc., New York, 1990.

H. Zima and B. Chapman, *Supercompilers for Parallel and Vector Computers,* ACM Press, New York, 1991.

SHIRLEY A. WILLIAMS
University of Reading

PARNAS, DAVID LORGE (1941–)

Dr. David Lorge Parnas is a Professor in the Department of Electrical and Computer Engineering at McMaster University in Hamilton, Ontario. He is a member of the Communications Research Laboratory and Principal Investigator for both the Telecommunications Research Institute of Ontario, and the Canadian Institute for Telecommunications Research. Previously he was Lansdowne Professor of Computer Science at the University of Victoria, Victoria, British Columbia. He has also been a member of the faculty at Carnegie Mellon University, The University of Maryland, the Technische Hochschule Darmstadt, and the University of North Carolina at Chapel Hill. He has also had non-academic positions, including Philips Computer Industry and the United States Naval Research Laboratory in Washington, D.C. where he was Principal Investigator of the Software Cost Reduction Project for several years.

The author of more than 150 papers and reports, Dr. Parnas is interested in most aspects of computer system engineering. His special interests includes precise abstract specifications, real-time systems, safety-critical software, program semantics, language design, software structure, process structure, and process synchronisation. He initiated and led an experimental redesign of a hard-real-time system, the onboard flight program for the U.S. Navy's A-7 aircraft, in order to evaluate a number of software engineering principles. More recently, he has advised the Atomic Energy Control Board of Canada on the use of safety-critical real-time software at the Darlington Nuclear Generation Station. Dr. Parnas seeks to find a "middle road" between theory in practice, emphasizing theory that can be applied to improve the quality of our products.

Professor Parnas received his Ph.D. in Electrical Engineering from Carnegie Mellon University, and an honorary doctorate from the ETH in Zurich. He won the ACM "Best Paper" Award in 1979, and a "Most Influential Paper" award from the International Conference on Software Engineering in 1991. Deeply concerned that computer technology be applied to the benefit of society, Dr. Parnas was the first winner of the "Norbert Wiener Award for Professional and Social Responsibility". He was recently elected a Fellow of the Royal Society of Canada.

PASCAL

See PROGRAMMING LANGUAGES.

PATH ANALYSIS

Analysis of a computer program to identify all possible paths through the program, to detect incomplete paths, or to discover portions of the program that are not on any path (IEEE).

PATH TESTING

Testing designed to execute all or selected paths through a computer program (IEEE).

PATHOLOGICAL COUPLING

A type of coupling in which one software module affects or depends upon the internal implementation of another (IEEE).

PDL

See PROGRAM DESIGN LANGUAGES.

PERFORMANCE

The degree to which a system or component accomplishes its designated functions within given constraints, such as speed, accuracy, or memory usage (IEEE).

PERFORMANCE ENGINEERING

Software performance engineering (SPE) is a method for constructing software systems to meet performance objectives. The process begins early in the software life cycle and uses quantitative methods to identify satisfactory combinations of requirements and designs and to eliminate

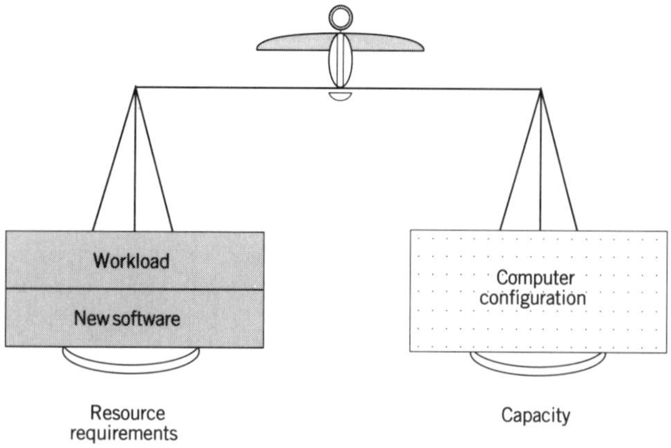

Figure 1. Performance balance.

those that are likely to have unacceptable performance, before developers begin implementation. SPE continues through the detailed design, coding, and testing stages to predict and manage the performance of the evolving software and to monitor and report actual performance against specifications and predictions. SPE methods cover performance data collection, quantitative analysis techniques, prediction strategies, management of uncertainties, data presentation and tracking, model verification and validation, critical success factors, and performance design principles.

In this article, performance refers to the response time or throughput as seen by the users. For real-time, or reactive, systems, it is the time required to respond to events. Reactive systems must meet performance objectives to be correct. Other software has less stringent requirements, but responsiveness limits the amount of work processed, so it determines a system's effectiveness and the productivity of its users.

The performance balance in Figure 1 depicts a balanced system: resource requirements match computer capacity, thus software meets performance objectives. With SPE, analysts assess the balance *early in development.* If demand exceeds capacity, quantitative methods support cost–benefit analysis of hardware solutions versus software requirements or design solutions versus a combination of the two. Developers select software or hardware solutions to performance problems before proceeding to the detailed design and implementation stages.

SPE is a software-oriented approach; it focuses on architecture, design, and implementation choices for managing performance. Other approaches have been proposed. For example, system-oriented approaches that focus on scheduling (Sha and Goodenough, 1990; Xu and Parnas, 1991), resource allocation, operating system executives (Stankovic and Ramamritham, 1991), total system approaches (Kopetz and Merker, 1985; Kopetz and co-workers, 1991; Levi and Agrawala, 1990; Popspischil and co-workers, 1992; Shin and co-workers, 1992), and so on are viable, supplemental methods for managing performance of real-time systems but are outside the scope of the SPE approach defined here. Similarly, techniques that focus on timing requirements using temporal logic or fault-tree analysis (Gabrielian and Franklin, 1990; Jaffe and co-workers,

1991; Jahanian and Mok, 1987) are not within this SPE definition.

This article first covers the evolution of SPE, then it gives an overview of the SPE process and the SPE methods. It presents the general principles for performance-oriented design, then it introduces the quantitative techniques for predicting and analyzing performance. The SPE techniques used throughout the software life cycle follow. Finally, the conclusion reviews the status and future of SPE.

THE EVOLUTION OF SPE

Performance was typically considered in the early years of computing. Knuth's (1968, 1973) early work focused on efficient data structures, algorithms, sorting, and searching. The space and time required by programs had to be carefully managed to fit them on small machines. The hardware grew, but rather than eliminating performance problems, it made larger, more complex software feasible and programs grew into systems of programs. Software systems with strict performance requirements, such as flight control systems and other embedded systems used detailed simulation models to assess performance. Consequently, creating and solving them was time-consuming, and updating the models to reflect the current state of evolving software systems was problematic. Thus the labor-intensive modeling and assessment were cost-effective only for systems with strict performance requirements.

Authors proposed performance-oriented development approaches (Bell and co-workers, 1977; Graham and co-workers, 1973; Riddle and co-workers, 1978; Sholl and Booth, 1975), but most developers of nonreactive systems adopted the fix-it-later approach. It advocated concentrating on software correctness, deferring performance considerations to the integration testing phase, and (if performance problems were detected then) procuring additional hardware or tuning the software to correct them. Fix-it-later was acceptable in the 1970s, but in the 1980s the demand for computer resources increased dramatically. System complexity increased, while the proportional number of developers with performance expertise decreased. This, combined with a directive to ignore performance, made the resulting performance disasters self-fulfilling prophecies. Many of the disasters could not be corrected with hardware, because platforms with the required power did not exist. Neither could they be corrected with tuning, as corrections required major design changes, and thus reimplementation. Meanwhile, technical advances led to the SPE alternative.

SPE uses models to predict performance, tools to formulate and solve models, and methods to prescibe how and when to conduct performance studies. The SPE techniques developed in the 1980s focused on models that could be solved with analytic techniques because the tools and the speed of the processors made analytic techniques more desirable than simulation techniques for early life cycle design trade-off studies. Consequently, the following sections on the SPE evolution focus on these analytic techniques, tools, and methods. Later, recent developments are presented that make other models, tools, and adaptations of the methods viable.

MODELING FOUNDATIONS

In 1971, Buzen proposed modeling systems with queuing network models and published efficient algorithms for solving some important models. In 1975, Baskett, and co-workers defined a class of models that have efficient analytic solutions. The models are an abstraction of the computer systems they model, so they are easier to create than general-purpose simulation models. Because they are solved analytically, they can be used interactively. Since then, many advances have been made in modeling computer systems with queuing networks, faster solution techniques, and accurate approximation techniques (Jain, 1990; Lazowska and co-workers, 1984; Molloy, 1989; Sauer and Chandy, 1981).

Queueing network models are commonly used to model computer systems for capacity planning. A capacity-planning model is constructed from specifications for the computer system configuration and measurements of resource requirements for each of the workloads modeled. The model is solved and the resulting performance metrics (response time, throughput, resource utilization, etc.) are compared with measured performance. The model is calibrated to the computer system. Then it is used to study the effect of increases in workload and resource demands and of configuration changes.

Initially, queueing network models were used primarily for capacity planning. For SPE they were sometimes used for feasibility analysis: request arrivals and resource requirements were estimated and the results assessed. More precise models were infeasible because the software could not be measured until it was implemented.

The second SPE modeling breakthrough was the introduction of analytical models for software (Beizer, 1978; Booth, 1979a, 1979b; Booth and Wiecek, 1980; Sanguinetti, 1978; Smith and Browne, 1979; Trivedi, 1982). With them, software execution is modeled, estimates of resource requirements are made, and performance metrics are calculated. Software execution models yield an approximate value for best, worst, or average resource requirements (such as CPU usage or number of I/O operations). They provide an estimate for response time; they can detect response time problems, but because they do not model resource contention, they do not yield precise values for predicted response time.

The third SPE modeling breakthrough was combining the analytic software models with the queueing-network system models (Smith, 1980; Smith and Browne 1980). Combined models more precisely model the execution. They also show the effect of new software on existing work and on resource utilization. They identify computer device bottlenecks and the parts of the new software with high use of bottleneck devices. By 1980, the modeling power was established and modeling tools were available (many new tools are now available). Thus it became cost-effective to model large software systems early in their development.

SPE METHODS

Early experience with a large system confirmed that sufficient data could be collected early in development to predict performance bottlenecks (Smith and Browne, 1982). Unfortunately, despite the predictions, the system design was not modified to remove them and upon implementation (approximately 1 year later) performance in those areas was a serious problem, as predicted. SPE methods were proposed (Smith, 1981) and later updated (Smith 1990) to address the reasons that early predictions of performance problems were disregarded. Key parts of the process are methods for collecting data early in software development and critical success factors to ensure SPE success. The methods also address compatibility with software engineering methods, what is done, when, by whom, and other organizational issues. SPE methods are described below.

SPE DEVELOPMENT

The 1980s brought advances in all facets of SPE. Software model advances were proposed by several authors (Beizer, 1984; Booth and co-workers, 1986; Estrin and co-workers, 1986; Qin, 1989; Sahner and Trivedi, 1987; Smith, 1982, 1990; Smith and Loendorf, 1982). Martin (1988) proposed data-action graphs as a representation that facilitates transformation between performance models and various software design notations. Opdahl and Sølvberg (1992) integrate information system models and performance models with extended specifications. Rolia (1992) extends the SPE models and methods to address systems of cooperating processes in a distributed and multicomputer environment with specific applications to Ada. Woodside (1986, 1989) proposes stochastic rendezvous networks to evaluate performance of Ada systems, and Woodside and coworkers incorporate the analysis techniques into a software engineering tool (Buhr and co-workers, 1989; Woodside and co-workers, 1991). Opdahl (1992) describes SPE tools interfaced with the processes, phenomena, and programs (PPP) CASE tool and the IMSE environment for performance modeling; both are part of the Esprit research initiative. Lor and Berry (1991) automatically generate systems architects apprentice (SARA) models from an arbitrary requirements specification language using a knowledge-based design assistant.

Other tools that incorporate features to support SPE modeling are reported by numerous authors (Bagrodia and Shen, 1991; Beilner and co-workers, 1988; Goettge, 1990; Nichols, 1990; Nichols and Oman, 1991; Pooley, 1991; Smith, 1991; Smith and Williams, 1990). Extensive advances have been made in computer system performance modeling techniques. A complete list of references is beyond the scope of this article.

Bentley (1982) proposes a set of rules for writing efficient programs. A set of formal, general principles for performance-oriented design is reported by Smith (1986, 1988a, 1990). Software architects who are experts in formulating requirements and designs and developers who are experts in data structure and algorithm selection use intuition to develop their systems. The rules and principles formalize that expert knowledge. Thus the expert knowledge developed through years of experience, can be easily transferred to software developers with less experience. Additional information on the rules and principles and related work is presented later.

Fox (1987, 1989) describes middle, life cycle SPE activities. He emphasizes that models alone are insufficient and that measurement and analysis of evolving software are essential to meeting performance objectives. Bell and Falk (1987) advocate techniques for system performance engineering.They cover middle life cycle techniques and focus on the overall system, not just the software. Numerous authors relay experience with SPE (Alexander, 1986; Alexander and Brice, 1982; Anderson, 1984; Bell, 1988; Bell and co-workers, 1987; Fox, 1987, 1989; Paterok and co-workers, 1991; Smith, 1985, 1988b). The *Proceedings of the Computer Measurement Group Conferences* contain SPE experience papers each year.

SPE has also been adapted to real-time process control systems. When these systems must respond to events within a specified time interval, they are called *reactive systems.* As mentioned earlier, much of the previously reported work on real-time systems is outside the scope of SPE's software-oriented work. Howes (1990) prescribes principles for developing efficient reactive systems. Goettge (1990) applies SPE to a reactive system, using a performance engineering tool with an expert system for suggesting performance improvements. Smith and Williams (1993) describe the SPE process for a case study of a reactive system. Sholl and Kim (1986) adapt the computation–structure approach to real-time systems, and LeMer (1982) describes a methodology and tool. Joseph and Pandya (1986) claim a computationally efficient technique for finding the exact worst-case response time of real-time systems. Chang and coworkers (1989) use petri net model extensions to evaluate real-time systems. Baldasarri and coworkers (1989) integrate a petri net design notation into a CASE tool that provides performance results. After the descriptions of SPE in the next four sections, the final section mentions additional related work that shows SPE trends for the future.

THE SPE PROCESS

Figure 2 depicts the SPE process, which will be discussed below. First, developers define the specific SPE assessments for the current software life cycle phase. Assessments determine whether planned software meets its performance objectives, such as acceptable response times, throughput thresholds, and constraints on resource requirements. A specific, quantitative objective is vital if analysts are to determine concretely whether that objective can be met. A crisp definition of the performance objectives lets developers determine the most appropriate means of achieving objectives and avoid spending time overachieving them.

Business systems specify performance objectives in terms of responsiveness as seen by the system users. Reactive systems specify timing requirements for event responses. Both the response time for a task and the number

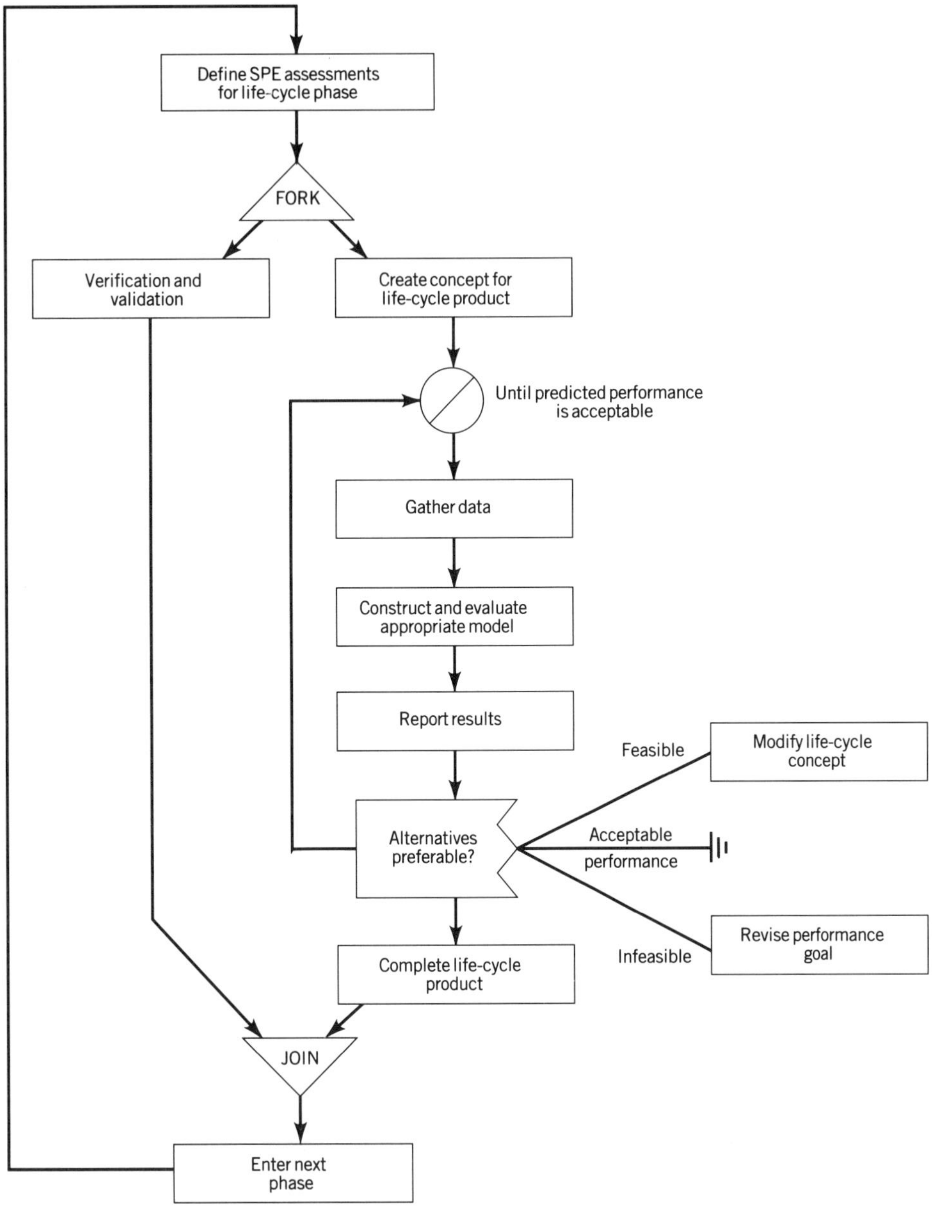

Figure 2. Software performance engineering process.

of work units processed in a time interval (throughput) are measures of responsiveness. Responsiveness does not necessarily imply efficient computer resource usage. Efficiency is addressed only if critical computer resource constraints must be satisfied.

After defining the goals, designers create the concept for the life cycle product. For early phases the concept is the functional architecture, the software requirements and the high level plans for satisfying requirements. In subsequent phases the concept is a more detailed design, the algorithms and data structures, the code, etc. Developers apply SPE's general principles (described later) to create responsive functional architectures and designs.

Once the life cycle concept is formulated, analysts gather data sufficient for estimating the performance of the concept proposal. First analysts need the projected system workload: how it will *typically* be used. They also need an explanation of the current design concept. Early in development, analysts use the general system architecture; later models incorporate the proposed decomposition into modules; still later, analysts add the proposed algorithms and data structures. Early analysis of reactive systems also examines typical usage; later analyses examine worst-case and failure scenarios. Estimates of the resource usage of the design entities complete the specifications. More details on data requirements and techniques for gathering specifications are present later.

Because the precision of the model results depends on the precision of the resource estimates and because these are difficult to estimate early in software development, a best- and worst-case analysis strategy is integral to the methodology. Analysts use estimates of the lower and upper bound when there is high uncertainty about resource requirements. Using them, the analysts produce an estimate of both the best- and worst-case performance. If the best-case performance is unsatisfactory, they seek feasible alternatives. If the worst-case performance is satisfactory, they proceed with development. If the results are between the two extremes, models identify critical components whose resource estimates have the greatest effect, and focus turns to obtaining more precise data for them. A variety of techniques provides more precision, such as further refining the design concept and constructing more detailed models, or constructing performance benchmarks and measuring resource requirements for key elements.

An overview of the construction and evaluation of the performance models is presented below. If the model results indicate that the performance is likely to be satisfactory, developers proceed. If not, analysts report quantitative results on the predicted performance of the original design concept. If alternative strategies would improve performance, reports show the alternatives and their expected (quantitative) improvements. Developers review the findings to determine the cost-effectiveness of the alternatives. If a feasible and cost-effective alternative exists, developers modify the concept before the life cycle product is complete. If none is feasible, e.g., when the modifications would cause an unacceptable delivery delay, developers explicitly revise the performance goal to reflect the expected degraded performance.

Vital and ongoing activities of the SPE process are to verify that the models represent the software execution behavior and to validate model predictions against performance measurements. Reports compare the model specifications for the workload, software structure, execution structure, and resource requirements to actual use and software characteristics. If necessary, analysts calibrate the model by adjusting model parameters until they represent the system behavior for a variety of loading conditions. They also examine discrepancies to update the performance predictions and to identify the reasons for differences, to prevent similar problems occurring in the future. They produce reports comparing system execution model results (response times, throughput, device utilization, etc.) to measurements. Analysts study discrepancies, identify error sources, and calibrate the model as necessary. Model verification and validation should begin early and continue throughout the life cycle. In early stages, focus is on key performance factors; prototypes or benchmarks provide more precise specifications and measurements as needed. The evolving software becomes the source of the model verification and validation (V&V) data. This discussion outlined the steps for one design-evaluation pass. The steps repeat throughout the life cycle. For each pass, the goals and the evaluations change somewhat. A later section discusses the life cycle stages and the questions to be considered.

GENERAL PRINCIPLES FOR CREATING RESPONSIVE SYSTEMS

Engineering new software systems is an iterative process of refinement. At each refinement step, engineers understand the problem, create a hypothetical solution, describe or represent the proposed product of the creation step, and then evaluate that product's appropriateness. The evaluation assesses a design's correctness (adherence to specification), feasibility (cost, time, and technology to implement), and the preferability of one solution over another (simplicity, maintainability, usability, and so on). Responsiveness may be a correctness assessment (for reactive systems) or a feasibility assessment (will the architecture support the performance requirements) or a preferability assessment (when other requirements are met, engineers and users prefer a more responsive alternative).

Several software engineering methods advocate a software design process with these steps (Alford, 1985; Baldassari and co-workers, 1989; Bell and co-workers, 1977; Riddle and co-workers, 1978; Winchester and Estrin, 1982). Lampson (1984) presents an excellent collection of hints for computer system design that addresses effectiveness, efficiency, and correctness. His efficiency hints are the type of folklore that has until recently been informally shared. Kopetz (1986) presents principles for constructing real-time process control systems; some address responsiveness; all address performance in the more general sense.

Alter (1979) and Kant (1981) take a different approach; they use program optimization techniques to generate efficient programs from logical specifications. Search techniques identify the best strategy from various alternatives for choices such as data set organizations, access methods, and computation aggregations.

Authors address program efficiency from three perspectives: efficient algorithms and data structures (Bentley, 1982; Knuth, 1968, 1973), efficient coding techniques (Jalics, 1977; McNeil and Tracy, 1980; Van Tassel, 1978), and techniques for tuning existing programs to improve efficiency (Bentley, 1982; Ferrari, 1978; Ferrari and co-workers, 1983; Knuth, 1971). The program efficiency techniques evolved first. Later, the techniques evolved to address large-scale systems of programs in early life cycle stages when developers seek requirements and design specifications that will lead to systems with acceptable responsiveness (Smith, 1986, 1988a, 1990). During early stages, it is seldom the efficiency of machine resource usage that matters; it is the system responsiveness. Another distinction between system design and program tuning approaches is that program tuning transforms an inefficient program into a new "equivalent" program that performs the same function more efficiently. In system design, developers can transform what the software is to do as well as how it is to be done.

SPE uses both the early life cycle system principles and the later life cycle program design techniques. A summary follows of general principles that apply to the requirements and design creation steps to identify alternatives that are likely to meet responsiveness objectives and to refine concepts that require improved responsiveness. Principles that apply to implementation steps to identify desirable algorithms and data structures will also be discussed. Performance tuning in later life cycle stages is covered in a later section. To experienced performance analysts, Lampson's hints and these synthesis principles are not revolutionary new prescriptions. They are, however, a generalization and abstraction of the expert knowledge that performance specialists use in building or tuning systems. The principles supplement performance assessment rather than replace it. Performance improvement has many trade-offs; a local performance improvement may adversely affect overall performance. The quantitative methods provide the data required to evaluate the net performance effect to be weighed against other aspects of correctness, feasibility, and preferability.

EARLY LIFE CYCLE PERFORMANCE PRINCIPLES

Smith (1990) defines the following seven principles. A quantitative analysis of the performance results of three of them has been published (Smith, 1986) and extensive explanations and examples for each principle have been given (Smith, 1988a, 1990).

Fixing-Point Principle

Fixing connects the desired action or function to the instructions that accomplish the action. Fixing also connects the desired result to the data used to produce it. The fixing *point* is a point in time. The latest fixing point is during execution immediately before the instructions or data are required. Fixing could establish connections at several earlier points: earlier in the execution, at program initiation time, at compilation time, or outside the software system.

Suppose users need summary data of (multiple) account detail records. The latest fixing point summarizes the data at the time users request summary-data screens; earlier fixing updates the summary data as account detail records arrive. The principle is as follows:

> *Fixing-point Principle: For responsiveness, fixing should establish connections at the earliest feasible point in time, such that retaining the connection is cost-effective.*

It is cost-effective to retain the connection when the savings realized with it offset the retention cost. In the summary data example, the retention cost is the cost of the storage to hold summary data. Assume that the data are saved for other purposes anyway, then there is no additional retention cost. The operational costs are roughly the same: to summarize on request, the software must locate and read each detail record, then write one summary record. To update summary data as detail records arrive, there is one locate and one write per detail record. Thus, in this case, early fixing is warranted because the responsiveness is better; users do not have to wait for the summary data calculation.

Locality-Design Principle

Locality refers to the closeness of desired actions, functions, and results to physical resources. For example, if a desired screen result is identical to the physical database row that produces it, the locality is good. According to *Webster's*, *close* means being near in time, space, effect (that is, purpose or intent), or degree (that is, intensity or extent). The dictionary specification for *close* leads to four types of locality design for performance engineering. These are illustrated in the following example. Consider the logical task to sort a list of names. Temporal locality is better if the names are all sorted at the same time rather than sorting a few, adding a few more names to the list, and sorting again. Spatial locality is better if the names are near the processor that conducts the sort, such as in the processor's local memory, rather than on a disk drive attached to a different machine. The sort can execute on different types of physical processors; effectual locality is better if the processor can sort long character strings directly, rather than breaking strings into smaller "processor-size" pieces (such as words or bytes). Degree locality is better if the entire list of names fits in memory rather than requiring intermediate storage on disk. The principle is as follows:

> *Locality-design Principle: Create actions, functions, and results that are close to physical computer resources.*

Processing Versus Frequency Trade-off Principle

The next principle addresses the amount of work done per processing request, and its impact on the number of requests made. The trade-off looks for opportunities to reduce requests by doing more work per request and vice versa. The principle is as follows:

> *Processing Versus Frequency Trade-off Principle: Minimize the processing times frequency product.*

When software adds many rows to a database, two design alternatives are (1) to execute the database load commands once per row and (2) to collect the changes then execute the database load command once for the entire batch. The processing versus frequency trade-off principle compares the total cost of the alternatives. If the software executes on a client platform and the database resides on a server, the communication overhead processing is part of the total cost.

Shared-Resource Principle

Computer system resources are limited, thus processes compete for their use. Some resources may be shared: multiple processes can use the resource at the same time. Other resources require exclusive use: processes take turns; each process has exclusive use of the resource, one at a time. Exclusive use affects performance in two ways: the additional processing overhead to schedule the resource and the possible contention delay to gain access to the resource. The contention delay depends on how many processes request exclusive use and the time they hold the resource. The shared-resource principle is of the synergistic type: it improves overall performance through cooperation to reduce contention delays, rather than by reducing individual processing like the first three *independent-type* principles. The general principle is as follows:

> *Shared-resource Principle: Share resources when possible. When exclusive access is required, minimize the sum of the holding time and the scheduling time.*

Resource sharing minimizes both the overhead for scheduling and the wait to gain access (there may be a wait if another process already has exclusive access even though the requester is willing to share). A database organization that keys on date and clusters transactions entered on the same date, does not promote sharing when possible, because all additions during the day must lock the same portion of the database.

Parallel Processing Principle

Processing time can sometimes be reduced by partitioning a process into multiple concurrent processes. The concurrency can either be real concurrency in which the processes execute at the same time on different processors, or it can be apparent concurrency in which the processes are multiplexed on a single processor. For real concurrency, the processing time is reduced by an amount proportional to the number of processors. Apparent concurrency is more complicated: although some of the processing may be overlapped (one process may use the CPU while another accesses the disk), each process may experience additional wait time. Both real and apparent concurrency require processing overhead to manage the communication and coordination between concurrent processes. The principle is as follows:

> *Parallel Processing Principle: Execute processing in parallel (only) when the processing speedup offsets communication overhead and resource contention delays.*

The parallel processing principle is another synergistic principle. SPE performance models assess speedup, contention delays, and communication delays.

Centering Principle

The five previous principles provide guidance for creating software requirements and designs. Their application improves the performance of the part of the system to which they are applied. Centering is different in that it leverages performance by focusing attention on the parts of software systems that have the greatest impact on responsiveness. Centering is based on the folkloric "80–20 rule" for the execution of code within programs, which claims that $\leqq 20\%$ of a program's code accounts for $\geqq 80\%$ of its computer resource usage. Centering identifies the subset ($\leqq 20\%$) of the system functions that will be used most ($\geqq 80\%$) of the time. These frequently used functions are the dominant workload functions. The dominant workload functions also cause a subset ($\leqq 20\%$) of the programs or modules in the software system to be executed most ($\geqq 80\%$) of the time, and the code within modules, and so forth. Performance enhancements made to these key areas of the software system thus greatly affect the overall responsiveness of the system. The principle is as follows:

> *Centering Principle: Identify the dominant workload functions and minimize their processing.*

That is, create special, streamlined execution paths for the dominant workload functions that are customized and trimmed to include only processing that *must* be part of the function. Use the five previous principles to minimize processing of the special paths. Create separate transactions for the workload functions that are used less frequently.

Design the dominant workload functions first to increase the likelihood that the data organization matches the access patterns. Even though the dominant workload functions are usually trivial transactions (not the essence of the software design) they will likely have the greatest effect on the overall responsiveness of the system. Thus they require early resolution.

Instrumenting Principle

Instrumenting software means inserting code at key probe points to enable the measurement of pertinent execution characteristics. The principle is

> *Instrumenting Principle: Instrument systems as you build them to enable measurement and analysis of workload scenarios, resource requirements, and performance goal achievement.*

This principle does not in itself improve performance, but is essential to controlling performance. It has its foundations in engineering, particularly process control engineering. The rule of thumb in engineering is, "if you can't measure it, you can't control it." Data collection mechanisms are part of the system requirements and design; it is much more difficult to add it after implementation. This is because of limitations in instrumenting technology; most external measurement tools collect system-level data, such as program execution time, rather than functional data, such as end-to-end response time (for business units of work that require multiple transactions). To collect functional data, programmers must insert code to call system timing routines and write key events and pertinent data to files for later analysis. Define these probe points when defining the functions.

Heuristics for Real-Time Systems Design

Howes develops design heuristics for "demonstrably efficient" real-time systems to be implemented in Ada. Howes and Weaver (1989) introduce the following principle.

> *Structuring Principle of Physical Concurrency: Introduce concurrency only to model physically concurrent objects or processes.*

This is a specific instance of the earlier, more general parallel processing principle. This principle provides guidance to real-time system developers for the efficient use of Ada rendezvous. It is an alternative to maximum concurrency that advocates concurrency as a goal in itself and conceptual concurrency that uses concurrency to simplify a design. The authors compare the efficiency of the three concurrency approaches.

Howes (1990) introduces the following principle.

> *Tuning Principle: Reduce the mean service time of cyclic functions.*

This is also a specific instance of the more general centering and processing versus frequency principles. It guides real-time system developers to identify the functions that execute at regular, specific time intervals and minimize their processing requirements. Howes (1990) applies both principles to a small design problem and compares the results with those achieved with other design heuristics that do not address performance. Howes's conclusion indicates that the investigation of other performance principles is under way.

Summary

A quantitative analysis of the performance effect of the fixing-point, processing versus frequency trade-off, and centering principles is in Smith. Although these three can be evaluated with simple, back-of-the-envelope calculations, the others require more sophisticated models. The quantitative methods for evaluating responsiveness of alternatives are reviewed later.

IMPLEMENTATION PRINCIPLES

These principles apply during the detail-design stage to guide the selection and implementation of proper data structures and algorithms for the critical modules. These topics are covered by a variety of data structure texts (eg, Knuth, 1968, 1973; Schneider and co-workers, 1978; Standish, 1980). Bentley (1982) provides a systematic methodology and specific efficiency rules for implementing the data structures and algorithms. Bentley proposes two sets of rules: the first set trades space for time; the second trades time for space. His rules are summarized below.

Data Structure Augmentation Rule: Augment structures with extra information or change the structure so that it can be accessed more easily.

For example, save pointers for ready access to data.

Store Precomputed Results Rule: Compute the results of expensive functions once, store the results, and satisfy subsequent requests with a table look-up.

Bentley (1982) covers examples such as storing distances between points, evaluations of board positions, and others.

Caching Rule: Store data that are accessed most often to make them cheapest to access.

Bentley (1982) cites examples of hardware caches, caching the last item retrieved (Jalics, 1977), and moving each item found closer to the beginning of a list (Knuth, 1973).

Lazy Evaluation Rule: Postpone evaluation until an item is needed.

Kernighan and Plauger (1978) applied this rule to defer calculation of line width in a text editor until it was required (rather than after each character was input).

Bentley's (1982) next two rules trade time for space:

Packing Rule: Use dense storage representations to decrease storage cost by increasing the time required to store and retrieve data.

File compression techniques use the packing rule to reduce the amount of disk space required for a file.

Interpreter Rule: Represent common sequences of operations compactly and interpret as required.

Subroutines are represented once and called when needed. Table-driven algorithms also implement the interpreter rule.

Bentley also points out that all rules can be applied in the opposite direction to reverse the time and space trade-off. He cites a rich set of examples from the literature for each of his rules and quantifies the benefits of many of the rules. He also describes rules for modifying code to be more efficient. Those rules apply to performance tuning in later life cycle stages.

QUANTITATIVE METHODS FOR SPE

The quantitative methods prescribe the data required to conduct the performance assessment and techniques for gathering the data, the performance models and techniques for adapting them to the system evolution, and techniques for verification and validation of the models.

DATA REQUIREMENTS

To create a software execution model analysts need performance goals, workload definitions, software execution characteristics, execution environment descriptions, and resource usage estimates. An overview of each follows. Performance goals (precise, quantitative metrics) are vital to determine concretely whether or not performance objectives can be met. For business applications, both on-line performance goals and batch window objectives must be met. For on-line transactions, the goals specify the response time or throughput required. Goal specifications define the external factors that impact goal attainment, such as the time of day, the number of concurrent users, whether the goal is an absolute maximum, a 90th percentile, and so on. For reactive systems, timing constraints specify the maximum time between an event and the response. Some reactive systems have throughput goals for the number of events processed in a time interval.

Workload definitions specify the key scenarios of the new software. For on-line transactions scenarios (initially) specify the transactions expected to be the most frequently used. Later in the life cycle, scenarios also cover resource intensive transactions. On-line workload definitions identify the key scenarios and specify their workload intensity: the request arrival rates or the number of concurrent users and the time between their requests (think time). Batch workload definitions identify the programs on the critical path, their dependencies, and the data volume to be processed. Reactive systems represent scenarios of time-critical functions and worst-case operating conditions.

Software execution characteristics identify components of the software system to be executed for each workload scenario. The software execution scenario identifies software components most likely to be invoked when users request the corresponding workload scenario, the number of times they are executed or their probability of execution, and their execution characteristics, such as the database tables used and screens read or written. Reactive systems initially specify the likely execution paths and later add less likely, but feasible, execution paths.

The execution environment defines the computer system configuration, such as the CPU, the operating system, and the I/O subsystem characteristics. It provides the underlying queueing network model topology and defines resource requirements for frequently used service routines. This is usually the easiest information to obtain. Performance modeling tools automatically provide much of it, and most capacity and performance analysts are familiar with the requirements.

Resource use estimates determine the amount of service required of key devices in the computer system configuration. For each software component executed in the workload scenario, analysts need the approximate number of instructions executed (or CPU time required); the number of physical I/Os; and use of other key devices such as communication lines (terminal I/Os and amount of data), memory (temporary storage, map, and program size), etc. For database applications, the database management system (DBMS) accounts for most of the resource use, so the number of database calls and their characteristics are usually sufficient. Early life cycle requirements are tentative, difficult to specify, and likely to change, so SPE uses upper and lower bound estimates to identify problem areas or software components that warrant further study to obtain more precise specifications.

The number of times a component executes, or its resource use, may vary significantly. To represent the variability, analysts identify the factors that cause the variability, use a data-dependent variable to represent each factor, and specify the execution frequency and resource usage in terms of the data-dependent variables. Later, the models study the performance sensitivity to various parameter values.

It is seldom possible to get precise information for all these specifications early in the software's life cycle. Rather than waiting to model the system until it is available (i.e., in detailed design or later), SPE suggests gathering guesses, approximations, and bounded estimates to begin, then augmenting the models as information becomes available. This approach has the added advantage of focusing attention on key workload elements to minimize their processing (as prescribed by the centering principle). Otherwise, designers tend to postpone these important performance drivers in favor of designing more interesting but less frequently used parts of the software.

Because one person seldom knows all the information required for the software performance models, performance walk throughs provide most of the data (Smith, 1990). Performance walk throughs are closely modeled after design and code walk throughs. In addition to software specialists who contribute software plans they bring together users, who contribute workload and scenario information, and technical specialists, who contribute computer configuration and resource requirements of key subsystems such as DBMS and communication paths. The primary purpose of a performance walk through is data gathering rather than a critical review of design and implementation strategy.

PERFORMANCE MODELS

Two models provide the quantitative data for SPE: the software execution model and the system execution model. The software execution model represents key facets of software execution behavior. The model solution quantifies the computer resource requirements for each workload scenario. The system execution model represents computer system resources with a network of queues and servers. The model combines the workload scenarios and quantifies overall resource utilization and consequent response times of each scenario.

Execution graph models are one type of software execution model. They are not the only option but are convenient for illustration. A graph represents each workload scenario. Nodes represent functional components of the software; arcs represent control flow. The graphs are hierarchical, with the lowest level containing complete information on estimated resource requirements (Smith, 1990).

A static analysis of the graphs yields mean, best- and worst-case execution times of the scenarios. The static analysis makes the optimistic assumption that there are no other workloads on the host configuration competing for resources. Simple, graph–analysis algorithms provide the static analysis results (Beizer, 1978; Booth, 1979a, 1979b; Smith, 1990). Next, the system execution model solution yields the following additional information:

- The effect of resource contention on response times, throughput, device utilizations and device queue lengths.
- Sensitivity of performance metrics to variations in workload composition.
- Effect of new software on service level objectives of other existing systems.
- Identification of bottleneck resources.
- Comparative data on performance improvements to the workload demands, software changes, hardware upgrades, and various combinations of each.

To construct and evaluate the system execution model, analysts first represent the key computer resources with a network of queues, then use environment specifications to specify device parameters (such as CPU size and processing speed). The workload parameters and service requests come from the resource requirements computed from the software execution models. Analysts solve the model and check for reasonable results, then examine the model results. If the results show that the system fails to meet performance objectives, analysts identify bottleneck devices and correlate system execution model results with software components. After identifying alternatives to the software plans or the computer configuration, analysts evaluate the alternatives by making appropriate changes to the software or system model and repeating the analysis steps.

System execution models based on the network of queues and servers can be solved with analytic techniques in a few seconds. Thus analysts can conduct many tradeoff studies in a short time. Analytic solution techniques generally yield utilizations within 10% and response times within 30% of actual. Thus they are well suited to early life cycle studies when the primary objective is to identify feasible alternatives and rule out alternatives that are unlikely to meet performance goals. The resource usage estimates that lead to the model parameters are seldom sufficiently precise to warrant the additional time and effort required to produce more realistic models. Even reactive systems benefit from this intermediate step; it rules out serious problems before proceeding to more realistic models.

Early studies typically use simple SPE models. The SPE goal is to find problems with the simplest possible model. Experience shows that simple models can detect serious performance problems very early in the development process. The simple models isolate the problems and focus attention on their resolution (rather than on assumptions used for more realistic models). After they serve this primary purpose, analysts augment them as the software evolves to make more realistic performance predictions.

SPE calls for matching the modeling effort to the precision of the available data. The effort depends on the sophistication of the modeling tools available and their solution speed. As new tools become available and processor speeds increase, the shift from simple, optimistic models to more detailed, realistic models is adapted accordingly. Likewise, the shift from analytic to simulation solutions is adapted accordingly. Analytic solutions produce mean-value results that may not adequately reflect a system's performance if it has periodic problems or unusual execution characteristics.

Advanced system execution models are usually appropriate when the software reaches the detail-design life cycle stage. Even when it is easy to incorporate the additional execution characteristics earlier, it is better to defer them to the advanced system execution model. It is seldom easy, however, and the time to construct and evaluate the advanced models usually does not match the input data precision early in the life cycle.

The modeling difficulty arises from several sources. They are described next. First, advances in modeling technology follow the introduction of new hardware and operating system features. So accurate models of new computer system resources are active research topics. For example, I/O subsystems may have channel reconnect, path selection when multiple channel paths are available, disk cache controllers, etc. Models of these resources are evolving.

The second modeling difficulty is that special software features such as lock–free, acquire–release, etc., require passive resources, i.e., resources that are required for processing but that do no work themselves. They are held while the software uses one or more active resources; the queueing delays for active resources influence the duration of passive resource usage. The impact of these passive resource delays is twofold. The response of jobs forced to wait on the passive resource will be slower, but because these waiting jobs do not use active resources while they wait, other jobs may execute at a faster rate due to the decreased contention. Passive resource delays are difficult to quantify with analytic queueing network models: quantitative data for queueing delays requires a queue-server node, but its service time depends on the time spent in other queue or servers.

A third modeling difficulty is that computer system environment characteristics (such as distributed processing, parallel processing, concurrent and multithreaded software, and memory management overhead) challenge model technology. They either use passive resources, have complex model topologies, or couple tightly the models of software and system execution.

These three facets of execution behavior are represented in the advanced system execution model. It augments the elementary system execution model with additional types of constructs. Then procedures specify how to calculate corresponding model parameters from software models and how to solve the advanced models. SPE methods specify checkpoint evaluations to identify those aspects of the execution behavior that require closer examination (Smith, 1990a).

Recent modeling research results have simplified the analysis of advanced system execution models with passive resources (Rolia, 1992; Woodside, 1989; Woodside and co-workers, 1991). Details of these models are beyond the scope of this article. Information on system and advanced system execution models is available (Jain, 1990; Lazowska and co-workers, 1984; Molloy, 1989; Sauer and Chandy, 1981). The *Proceedings of the ACM SIGMETRICS Conferences* and the *Performance Evaluation Journal* report recent research results in advanced systems execution models. The *Proceedings of the Performance Petri Net Conferences* also reports relevant results.

VERIFICATION AND VALIDATION

Another vital part of SPE is continual verification of the model specifications and validation of model predictions. V&V begins early, particularly when model results suggest that major changes are needed. The V&V effort matches the impact of the results and the importance of performance to the project. When performance is critical, or major software changes are indicated, analysts identify the critical components, implement or prototype them, and measure. Measurements verify resource usage and path execution specifications and validate model results.

Early V&V is important even when predicted performance is good. Performance specialists influence the values that developers choose for resource usage estimates, and specialists tend to be optimistic about how functions will be implemented, and about their resource requirements. Resource usage of the actual system often differs significantly from the optimistic specifications.

Performance engineers interview users, designers, and programmers to confirm that usage will be as expected and that designed and coded algorithms agree with model assumptions. They adjust models when appropriate, revise predictions, and give regular status reports. They also perform sensitivity analyses of model parameters and determine thresholds that yield acceptable performance. Then, as the software evolves and code is produced, they measure the resource usage and path executions and compare with these thresholds to get early warning of potential problems. As software increments are deployed, measurements of the workload characteristics yield comparisons of specified scenario use to actual use and show inaccuracies and omissions. Analysts calibrate models and evaluate the effect of model changes on earlier results. As the software evolves, measurements replace resource estimates in the verification and validation process.

V&V is crucial to SPE. It requires the comparison of multiple sets of parameters, for heavy and light loads, to corresponding measurements. The model precision depends on how closely the model represents the key performance drivers. It takes constant vigilance to make sure they match (See VERIFICATION AND VALIDATION).

LIFE CYCLE SPE

The previous sections outline the SPE steps: define objectives, apply principles to formulate performance-oriented concepts, gather data, model, evaluate, and measure to verify model fidelity, validate model predictions, and confirm that software meets performance objectives. The steps are repeated throughout the life cycle. The goals and the evaluation of the objectives change somewhat for each pass. System performance engineering techniques evaluate the overall end-to-end performance to ensure that performance objectives will be met when all subsystems are combined. Systems with complex combinations of software, networks, and hardware have many potential pitfalls in addition to application software choices.

ADAPT THE METHODS TO THE LIFE CYCLE STAGE

Table 1 contains a synopsis of the SPE considerations in each life cycle stage. The first evaluation occurs during the requirements definition and the initial formulation of the software design; it assesses the feasibility and desirability of the functional architecture to detect infeasible plans. The requirements may be prescribed before development begins and many developers perceive them to be nonnegotiable. It is nevertheless prudent to verify that the requirements can be met with reasonable cost and performance. The next evaluation determines the computer configuration required to support the new product, that is, the power of the supporting hardware, operating system software, and network capacity. These are not independent issues: the design depends on the requirements, and the configuration will vary with the design. Therefore, analysts evaluate several combinations of requirements, designs, and configurations to determine the best combination.

After establishing a feasible set of requirements, the functional architecture of the software, and the supporting configuration requirements, the focus of SPE changes. Analysts identify components of the overall system that are critical with respect to meeting performance goals, and implement them first. This identification of critical components maximizes the impact of the performance efforts and yields early measurement data of actual resource requirements to produce more precise predictions. In the middle stages of the life cycle, SPE incorporates additional design details as they evolve, and design changes as they occur. Continued analysis helps to detect problems as soon as possible. At this stage, SPE studies provide data for developers to select appropriate data structures, algorithms, and system decomposition strategies. Models incorporate details of operating system overhead for memory management, data management, resource management and communication. As implementation proceeds, analysts add implementation details, refine the resource requirements estimates, and use more detailed models to produce more precise predictions.

During the maintenance stage, SPE evaluates both major and minor revisions that correct defects or add functions. Minor changes use mid–life cycle techniques to incorporate changes into the models and assess their performance impact. Major revisions use early life cycle techniques to assess the feasibility and desirability of the revised requirements and functional architecture, and follow the major revision project with standard SPE steps. Maintenance evaluations require much less effort than original studies when the SPE models are current and complete and can be used as the basis for the analysis.

SPE PERFORMANCE MEASUREMENT

Performance measurements drive the SPE process in the following ways:

- Measurements from existing systems augment SPE models.
- Measurements of experiments or prototypes provide model specifications.
- Measurements of evolving software replace earlier specification estimates, provide verification and validation data, and demonstrate performance goal achievement or specific problems requiring improvement.

Extensive literature describes performance measurement concepts. Some excellent introductory references are available (Bouhana, 1985; Ferrari and co-workers, 1983; Nutt, 1975; Svoboda, 1977). The *Conference Proceedings and Transactions of the Computer Measurement Group* is also an excellent source of recent publications on measurement tools, techniques, and concepts. Applied Computer Research publishes an annual review of performance measurement products.

Even though performance measurement concepts are well known, and many measurement tools exist, they seldom provide exactly the data required and in the form

Table 1. Synopsis of the Performance Engineering Considerations

Life Cycle Stage	Performance Considerations
Requirements analysis and functional architecture	What are typical user tasks? How will the software be used? What are the performance goals for the software usage scenarios? Can the requirements be achieved with acceptable performance? Approximately how much computer power is required to support it?
Preliminary design	Does the expected performance of this design meet specifications? Is the proposed configuration adequate? Excessive?
Detailed design	Have changes occurred that affect earlier predictions? What is a more realistic estimate of the projected performance?
Implementation and integration testing	How does the performance of the implementation alternatives compare? Have any unforeseen problems arisen? What are the resource requirements of the critical components? Are the performance requirements met?
Maintenance and operation	What is the effect of the proposed modifications? What are the long-range configuration requirements to support future use?

required for SPE. Software instrumentation provides much of the data (refer to the instrumenting principle defined earlier). Table 2 summarizes the performance metrics needed for SPE and the primary techniques used to collect the data (Smith, 1990).

Most of the existing measurement tools are for traditional computer architectures. Koskela and Simmons (1990) provide a compilation of results in performance instrumentation and visualization. Haban and Wybranietz (1990) propose a hybrid monitor that combines the analysis of behavior and performance of distributed systems. Penny and coworkers (1986) describe a technique for monitoring response times for systems with many independent, concurrent tasks.

PERFORMANCE TUNING

Performance tuning is a process for transforming code that fails to meet performance objectives into more responsive code that performs an equivalent function. Tuning is usually conducted late in development or postdeployment when improvements must be made immediately. The tuning process prescribes strategies and techniques for maximizing the performance and capacity payoff of tuning efforts. With the limited time available for tuning and the extent of improvements necessary, it is vital to identify and focus on those areas with the highest potential payoff (rather than to expend effort on improvements that have a negligible overall effect).

The systematic approach begins with measurement studies to quantify the problems and identify their causes. The steps are as follows:

1. Prepare test plans that identify objectives and how they will be accomplished:
   - Identify peak (or near peak) periods and other performance problem scenarios to be studied.
   - Characterize the properties of the workload: number and type of users or number and type of external devices.
   - Identify system workload requests that are representative of peak or performance problem operational usage (such as transaction or customer-call volumes, screens displayed, database requests, sensor sampling rates, control signal rates, etc.).
   - Define reports and results to be produced and measurements required to produce them (see step 3, below).
   - Identify the measurement tools needed and specific procedures for their use (parameter settings, startup procedures, etc.).
2. Conduct measurement studies under the desired operational conditions and document the workload characteristics. The systematic study produces a comprehensive report with data such as the following: CPU utilization, disk utilization, CPU–I/O overlap, I/O rates and average I/O service time by device, communication line utilization, traffic rates, message sizes, number of processes active, process execution time, CPU usage by process (system and application), number of file accesses (for primary files), their location, block size and file size, memory usage statistics, number of page faults, number of program swaps, and lock information (or time processes are blocked and why).
3. Identify the bottleneck device(s). This step uses the quantitative data to identify problems and the potential payoff of correcting them. One can always find potential problems in software that can be corrected

Table 2. Performance Data Collection Techniques

Performance Metrics	Data Collection Technique				
	System Monitor	Program Monitor	System Event Recorder	External Program Event Recorder	Internal Event Recorder
Workload Data					
Requests for each function			X		X
request rate			X		
request patterns					X
Data Characteristics					
Volume (number of entries of each type)					X
size of each					X
access locality					X
Execution Characteristics					
Resource requirements					
scenario resource usage	X	X	X		X
component level, resource usage		X			X
Support software services					
types requested, resources required	X	X			X
elapsed execution time			X		X
Path characteristics					
Execution probabilities, loop repetitions		X		X	X
Computer System Usage					
Response time, throughput, resource service times and wait times, resource utilization and throughput, and queue lengths	X		X		

with tuning. This step replaces speculation and random observation of problems with a systematic approach that focuses on vital problems.

4. Produce the heavy hitters list for the bottleneck device(s): the processes that are the heaviest users of the resource during the peak or performance-problem period. Usually 10% or fewer of the processes use 90% or more of the resource.
5. Evaluate the relative payoff of tuning the overall system versus tuning the software. Changes made to operating system parameters, file placements, and so on are usually easier and they do not require changes to code and the associated debugging and testing. More information on system tuning is available (Ferrari, 1978; Ferrari and co-workers, 1983; Jain, 1990).
6. To evaluate the benefits of tuning code, profile the heavy hitters to identify the hot spots within the processes. A profile is created by running the program (e.g., with a program monitor) under the desired operational conditions and periodically "sampling" the program to determine what it is doing: if using the CPU, find out which instruction, if executing an I/O, capture the characteristics, if handling a page fault, which page, etc. If the sampling interval is set appropriately the results are representative of the detailed behavior. The 90–10 rule of thumb (in step 4) usually applies within programs as well. The overall magnitude of improvements to hot spots is far greater than that of random improvements. Profiling the heavy hitters is difficult. The profiles require operational loading conditions, but the measurement overhead may perturb the system. One alternative is to collect trace tapes that record operational activity on a live system, and later drive a laboratory system with the operational data traces to facilitate measurement studies and (later) performance testing of improvements.
7. Identify performance remedies and quantify their performance improvement, development effort, maintenance impact, and other risks. Performance remedies range from low cost (and usually low payoff) automatic optimization options to high cost (potentially high payoff) software re-creation. Software that is re-created without SPE may have worse performance and other problems. Brooks (1975) describes this second-system effect. Intermediate options include changing algorithms and data structures using the implementation principles covered earlier (Bentley, 1982; Knuth, 1968, 1973) and modifying program code to use more efficient language constructs (Jalics, 1989; Knuth, 1971, 1973; Van Tassel, 1978).

8. Select appropriate remedies, implement, and conduct performance stress tests to quantify the improvement and produce measurements for capacity planning model studies.

CAPACITY MANAGEMENT

Capacity management is the process of characterizing future workloads, forecasting workload volumes and their computer resource requirements, planning the acquisition of computer resources to support the demand, and controlling the future resource requirements through SPE. Planning uses quantitative methods, usually system execution models similar to those described earlier. The modeling process is as follows:

- Measure current resource usage.
- Characterize homogeneous workloads.
- Construct and calibrate the system execution model to match measurements.
- Forecast demands of new software.
- Update the models, and explore sensitivity to forecast parameters and alternate scenarios of future demands.

Refer to Computer Measurement Group publications for more information on capacity management.

STATUS AND FUTURE OF SPE

Since computers were invented, the attitude persists that the next hardware generation will offer significant cost–performance enhancements, so it will no longer be necessary to worry about performance. There was a time, in the early 1970s, when computing power exceeded demand in most environments. The cost of achieving performance goals, with the tools and methods of the era, made SPE uneconomical for many batch systems; its cost exceeded its savings. Today's methods and tools make SPE the appropriate choice for many new systems. Will tomorrow's hardware solve all performance problems and make SPE obsolete? It has not happened yet. Hardware advances merely make new software solutions feasible, so software size and sophistication offset hardware improvements. There is nothing wrong with using more powerful hardware to meet performance objectives, but SPE suggests evaluating all options early and selecting the most effective one. Thus hardware may be the solution, but it should be explicitly chosen and early enough to enable orderly procurement. SPE still plays a role.

The three primary elements in SPE's evolution are the models for performance prediction, the tools that facilitate the studies, and the methods for applying them to systems under development. With these, the use of SPE increases and new design concepts develop that lead to high performance systems. Future evolution in each of these five areas will change the nature of SPE but not its underlying philosophy to build performance into systems. The following paragraphs speculate on future developments in each of these areas.

Both research and development will produce the tools of the future. We seek better integration of the models and their analysis with software engineering tools such as specification languages, CASE tools, and automatic program generators. Then software changes automatically update prediction models. Simple models can be transparent to designers; designers could click a button while formulating designs and view automatically generated performance predictions. Expert systems could suggest performance improvements (Goettge, 1990). Visual user interfaces could make analysis and reporting more effective. Software measurement tools could capture, reduce, interpret, and report data at a level of detail appropriate for designers. Measurement tools could automatically generate performance tests and compare specifications to measurements, compare predictions to actual performance, and report discrepancies. Each of these tools could interface with an SPE database to store evolutionary design and model data and support queries against it.

While simple versions of each of these tools are feasible with today's technology, research must establish the framework for fully functional versions. For example, if a CASE tool supports data flow diagrams and structure charts, how does software automatically convert them to software models? How should performance models integrate with specification languages or automatic program generators—should one begin with models and generate specifications or code from them, or should one write the specifications and let underlying models select efficient implementations, or some other combination? How can expert systems detect problems? Can software automatically determine from software execution models where instrumentation probes should be inserted? Can software automatically reduce data to appropriate levels of detail? Can software automatically generate performance tests? Each of these topics represents extensive research projects.

Performance models currently have limits in their ability to solve analytic models of tomorrow's complex environments. Models of extensive parallel or distributed environments must be hand crafted, with many checkpoint evaluations tailored to the problem. More automatic solutions are desired. Second, the analytic queueing network models yield only mean value results. Analysts need to model transient behavior quickly and easily for studying periodic behavior or unusual execution characteristics. For example, averaged over a 10-hr period, locking effects may be insignificant, but there may be short 1-min intervals in which locks cause all other active jobs to log jam, and it may take 30 min for the log jam to clear. Mean value results do not reflect these aftereffects; transient behavior models could. Petri nets and simulation offer more of the desired capabilities than analytical methods. Finally, as computer environments evolve, model technology must also develop. Thus research opportunities are rich in software and computer environment models.

Technology transfer suggests that the use of SPE is likely to spread. More literature documenting SPE experiences is likely to appear. As it is applied to new, state-of-the-art software systems, new problems will be discovered that require research solutions. Future SPE applications will require skills in multiple domains and offer many new learning opportunities. As quantitative models evolve, so will the use of SPE for new problem domains. For example, models of software reliability have matured enough to be integrated with other SPE methods. Similarly, models can also support hardware–software codesign and enable software versus hardware implementation choices early in development (Frank and co-workers, 1985).

The concepts for building high performance systems will evolve as SPE use spreads. Experience will lead to many examples illustrating the difference between high and low performance software that can be used to educate new software engineers. SPE quantitative techniques should be extended to build in other quality attributes, such as reliability, availability, testability, maintainability, etc. Research in these areas is challenging, e.g., do existing software metrics accurately represent quality factors? Can one develop predictive models? What design data will drive the models? What design concepts lead to improved quality?

SPE methods should undergo significant change as its usage increases. The methods should be better integrated into the software development process, rather than an add-on activity. SPE should become better integrated into capacity planning as well. As they become integrated, many of the pragmatic techniques should be unnecessary (how to convince designers there is a serious problem, how to get data, etc.). The nature of SPE should then change. Performance walk throughs will not be necessary for data gathering; they may only review performance during the course of regular design walk throughs. The emphasis will change from finding and correcting design flaws to verification and validation that the system performs as expected. Additional research into automatic techniques for measuring software designs is needed, for calibrating models, and for reporting discrepancies.

SPE methods need to evolve from a general methodology with numerous examples (many in the business systems area) to a more exhaustive set of procedures based on system types. For a particular type of system: Is a standard set of performance requirements appropriate? Which performance metrics are relevant? Which design principles and rules of thumb are most important? What specific SPE steps should be conducted at each life cycle stage? Which modeling techniques and tools are most appropriate to represent pertinent system characteristics? What specific measurements are needed and which tools provide the data?

For certain real-time systems, particularly those with mission-critical or safety-critical performance requirements, SPE procedures must be rigorously defined. The SPE results must also be defined and reviewable so inspectors can determine that SPE was properly conducted and the system will meet its performance requirements (Smith, 1992).

Thus, the research challenges for the future are to extend the quantitative methods to model the new hardware–software developments, to extend hardware–software measurement technology to support SPE, and to develop interdisciplinary techniques to address the more general definition of performance. The challenges for future technology transfer are to automate the sometimes cumbersome SPE activities, and to evolve SPE to make it easy and economical for future environments.

BIBLIOGRAPHY

C. T. Alexander, *Performance Engineering: Various Techniques and Tools,* paper presented at the Computer Measurement Group Conference, Las Vegas, Dec. 1986.

W. Alexander and R. Brice, *Performance Modeling in the Design Process,* Proc. National Computer Conference, Houston, June 1982, pp. 264–267.

M. Alford, "SREM at the Age of Eight: The Distributed Computing Design System," *IEEE Comput.* **18**(4), 257–262 (Apr. 1985).

S. Alter, "A Model for Automating File and Program Design in Business Application Systems," *Commun. ACM* **22**(6), 345–353 (June 1979).

G. E. Anderson, "The Coordinated Use of Five Performance Evaluation Methodologies," *Commun. ACM* **27**(2), 119–125 (Feb. 1984).

R. L. Bagrodia and C. Shen, "MIDAS: Integrated Design and Simulation of Distributed Systems," *IEEE Trans. Software Eng.* **17**(10), 1042–1058 (Oct. 1991).

M. Baldassari and co-workers, *PROTOB: A Hierarchical Object-Oriented CASE Tool for Distributed Systems,* paper presented at the European Software Engineering Conference, Coventry, UK, Sept. 1989.

F. Baskett and co-workers, "Open, Closed, and Mixed Networks of Queues with Different Classes of Customers," *J. ACM* **22**(2), 248–260 (Apr. 1975).

H. Beilner, J. Mäter, and N. Weissenburg, "Towards a Performance Modeling Environment: News on HIT," in *Proceedings of the 4th International Conference on Modeling Techniques and Tools for Computer Performance Evaluation,* Plenum Publishing, Corp., New York, 1988.

B. Beizer, *Micro-Analysis of Computer System Performance,* Van Nostrand Reinhold Co., Inc., New York, 1978.

B. Beizer, "Software Performance," in C. R. Vicksa and C. V. Ramamoorthy, eds., *Handbook of Software Engineering,* Van Nostrand Reinhold Co., Inc., New York, 1984, pp. 413–436.

T. E. Bell, guest ed., "Software Performance Engineering Special Issue," *Computer Measurement Group Trans.* 60, (Spring 1988).

T. E. Bell, D. X. Bixler, and M. E. Dyer, "An Extendible Approach to Computer-aided Software Requirements Engineering," *IEEE Trans. Software Eng.* **3**(1), 49–59 (Jan. 1977).

T. E. Bell and A. M. Falk, *Performance Engineering: Some Lessons from the Trenches,* Proc. Computer Measurement Group Conference, Orlando, Fla., Dec. 1987, pp. 549–552.

J. L. Bentley, *Writing Efficient Programs,* Prentice-Hall, Inc., Englewood Cliffs, N.J., 1982.

T. L. Booth, "Performance Optimization of Software Systems Processing Information Sequences Modeled by Probabilistic Languages," *IEEE Trans. Software Eng.* **5**(1), 31–44, (Jan. 1979).

T. L. Booth, *Use of Computation Structure Models to Measure Computation Performance,* Proc. Conference on Simulation, Measurement, and Modeling of Computer Systems, Boulder, Colo., Aug. 1979b, pp. 173–182.

T. L. Booth, R. O. Hart, and B. Qin, *High Performance Software Design,* Proc. Hawaii International Conference on System Sciences, Honolulu, Jan. 1986, pp. 41–52.

T. L. Booth and C. A. Wiecek, "Performance Abstract Data Types as a Tool in Software Perfromance Analysis and Design," *IEEE Trans. Software Eng.* **6**(2), 138–151 (Mar. 1980).

J. P. Bouhana, *Software Systems Instrumentation: An End-to-End View,* paper presented at the Hawaii International Conference on System Sciences, Honolulu, Jan. 1985.

F. P. Brooks, *The Mythical Man Month,* Addison-Wesley Publishing Co., Inc., Reading, Mass., 1975.

R. J. Buhr and co-workers, "Software CAD: A Revolutionary Approach," *IEEE Trans. Software Eng.* **15**(3), 234–249 (Mar. 1989).

J. P. Buzen, *Queueing Network Models of Multiprogramming,* doctoral dissertation, Harvard University, Cambridge, Mass., 1971.

C. K. Chang and co-workers, "Modeling a Real-Time Multitasking System in a Timed PQ Net," *IEEE Trans. Software Eng.* **6**(2), 46–51 (Mar. 1989).

G. Estrin and co-workers, "SARA (System ARchitects' Apprentice): Modeling, Analysis, and Simulation Support for Design of Concurrent Systems," *IEEE Trans. Software Eng.* **SE- 12**(2), 293–311 (Feb. 1986).

D. Ferrari, *Computer Systems Performance Evaluation,* Prentice-Hall, Inc., Englewood Cliffs, N.J., 1978.

D. Ferrari, G. Serazzi, and A. Zeigner, *Measurement and Tuning of Computer Systems,* Prentice-Hall, Inc., Englewood Cliffs, N.J., 1983.

G. Fox, *Take Practical Performance Engineering Steps Early,* Proc. Computer Measurement Group Conference, Orlando, Fla., Dec. 1987, pp. 992–993.

G. Fox, *Performance Engineering as a Part of the Development Lifecycle for Large-Scale Software Systems,* Proc. Eleventh International Conference on Software Engineering, Pittsburgh, Pa., May 1989, pp. 85–94.

G. A. Frank, C. U. Smith, and J. L. Cuadrado, *Software / Hardware Codesign with an Architecture Design and Assessment System,* Proc. Design Automation Conference, Las Vegas, Nev., 1985, pp. 417–424.

A. Gabrielian and M. K. Franklin, *Multi-Level Specification and Verification of Real-Time Software,* Proc. Twelfth International Conference on Software Engineering, Nice, France, Apr. 1990, pp. 52–62.

R. T. Goettge, *An Expert System for Performance Engineering of Time-Critical Software,* Proc. Computer Measurement Group Conference, Orlando, Fla., 1990, pp. 313–320.

R. M. Graham, G. J. Clancy, and D. B. DeVaney, "A Software Design and Evalation System," *Commun. ACM* **16**(2), 110–116 (Feb. 1973).

D. Haban and D. Wybranietz, "A Hybrid Monitor for Behavior and Performance Analysis of Distributed Systems," *IEEE Trans. Software Eng.* **16**(2), 46–51 (Feb. 1990).

N. R. Howes, *Toward a Real-Time Ada Design Methodology,* paper presented at the Tri-Ada 90, Baltimore, Md., Dec. 1990.

N. R. Howes and A. C. Weaver, "Measurements of Ada Overhead in OSI-Style Communications Systems," *IEEE Trans. Software Eng.* **15**(12), 1507–1517 Dec. 1989).

M. S. Jaffe and co-workers, "Software Requirements Analysis of Real-Time Process Control Systems," *IEEE Trans. Software Eng.* **17**(3), 241–258 (Mar. 1991).

F. Jahanian and A. K. L. Mok, "A Graph-Theoretic Approach for Timing Analsis and its Implementation," *IEEE Trans. Computers* **C-36**(8), 961–975 (Aug. 1987).

R. Jain, *Art of Computer Systems Performance Analysis,* John Wiley & Sons, Inc., New York, 1990.

P. J. Jalics, "Improving Performance the Easy Way," *Datamation* **23**(4), 135–148 (Apr. 1977).

P. J. Jalics, "Realizing the Performance Potential of COBOL," *IEEE Software* **6**(5), 70–79 (Sept. 1989).

M. Joseph and P. Pandya, "Finding Response Times in a Real-Time System," *Comput. J.* **29**(5), 390–395 (1986).

E. Kant, *Efficiency in Program Synthesis,* UMI Research Press, Ann Arbor, Mich., 1981.

B. W. Kernighan and P. J. Plauger, *The Elements of Programming Style,* 2nd ed., McGraw-Hill Book Co., Inc., New York, 1978.

D. E. Knuth, *The Art of Computer Programming, Vol. 1: Fundamental Algorithms,* Addison-Wesley Publishing Co., Inc., Reading, Mass., 1968.

D. E. Knuth, "An Empirical Study of FORTRAN Programs," *Software Prac. Exper.* **1**(2), 105–133 (Apr. 1971).

D. E. Knuth, *The Art of Computer Programming, Vol. 3: Sorting and Searching,* Addison-Wesley Publishing co., Inc., Reading, Mass., 1973.

H. Kopetz, *Design Principles of Fault Tolerant Real-Time Systems,* Proc. Hawaii International Conference on System Sciences, Honolulu, Jan. 1986, pp. 53–62.

H. Kopetz and W. Merker, "The Architecture of Mars," in *Proceedings FTCS 15,* IEEE Press, Ann Arbor, Mich., June 1985, pp. 274–279.

H. Kopetz and co-workers, "The Design of Real-Time Systems: From Specification to Implementation and Verification," *Software Eng. J.,* 72–82 (1991).

R. Koskela and M. Simmons, eds., *Parallel Computer Systems: Performance Instrumentation and Visualization,* ACM Press, 1990.

B. W. Lampson, "Hints for Computer System Design," *IEEE Software* **2**(1), 11–28 (Feb. 1984).

E. D. Lazowska and co-workers, *Quantitative System Performance: Computer System Analysis Using Queuing Network Models,* Prentice-Hall, Inc., Englewod Cliffs, N.J., 1984.

E. LeMer, *MEDOC: A Methodology for Designing and Evaluating Large-Scale Real-Time Systems,* Proc. National Computer Conference, 1982, Houston, 1982, pp. 263–272.

S. Levi and A. K. Agrawala, *Real-Time System Design,* McGraw-Hill Book Co., Inc., New York, 1990.

K. Lor and D. M. Berry, "Automatic Synthesis of SARA Design Models from System Requirements," *IEEE Trans. Software Eng.* **17**(12), 1229–1240 (Dec. 1991).

C. R. Martin, *An Integrated Software Performance Engineering Environment,* masters thesis, Duke University, 1988.

M. McNeil and W. Tracy, "PL/I Program Efficiency," *SIGPLAN Notices* **15**(6), 46–60 (June 1980).

M. K. Molloy, *Fundamentals of Performance Modeling,* Macmillan, New York, 1989.

K. M. Nichols, "Performance Tools," *IEEE Software* **7**(3), 21–30 (May 1990).

K. M. Nichols and P. Oman, guest eds., "Special Issue in High Performance" *IEEE Software,* **8**(5) (Sept. 1991).

G. Nutt, "Computer System Monitors," *IEEE Comput.* **8**(11), 51–61 (Nov. 1975).

A. Opdahl, *A CASE Tool for Performance Engineering During Software Design,* paper presented at the Fifth Nordic Workshop on Programming Environmental Research, Tampere, Finland, Jan. 1992.

A. Opdahl and A. Solvberg, *Conceptual Integration of Information System and Performance Modeling,* paper presented at the Working Conference on Information System Concepts: Improving the Understanding, 1992.

M. Paterok, R. Heller, and H. deMeer, *Performance Evaluation of an SDL Run Time System—A Case Study,* Proc. Fifth International Conference on Modeling Techniques and Tools for Computer Performance Evaluation, Torino, Italy, Feb. 1991, pp. 86–101.

J. P. Penny, P. J. Ashton, and A. L. Wilkenson, "Data Recording and Monitoring for Analysis of System Response Times," *Computer J.* **29**(5), 396–403 (1986).

R. Pooley, *The Integrated Modeling Support Environment,* Proc. Fifth International Conference on Modeling Techniques and Tools for Computer Performance Evaluation, Torino, Italy, Feb. 1991, pp. 86–101.

G. Pospischil and co-workers, "Developing Real-Time Tasks with Predictable Timing," *IEEE Software* **9**(5), 35–50 (Sept. 1992).

B. Qin, "A Model to Predict the Average Response Time of User Programs," *Perform. Eval.* **10,** 93–101 (1989).

W. E. Riddle and co-workers, "Behavior Modeling during Software Design," *IEEE Trans. Software Eng.* **SE-4**(4), 283–292 (1978).

J. A. Rolia, *Predicting the Performance of Software Systems,* Ph.D. Thesis University of Toronto, 1992.

R. A. Sahner, and Kishor S. Trivedi, "Performance and Reliability Analysis Using Directed Acyclic Graphs, *IEEE Trans. Software Eng.* **13**(10), 1105–1114 (Oct. 1987).

J. W. Sanguinetti, *A Formal Technique for Analyzing the Performance of Complex Systems,* paper presented to the Performance Evaluation Users Group 14, Boston, Oct. 1978.

C. H. Sauer and K. M. Chandy, *Computer Systems Performance Modeling,* Prentice-Hall, Inc., Englewood Cliffs, N.J., 1981.

G. M. Schneider, S. W. Weingart, and D. M. Perlman, *An Introduction to Programming and Problem Solving with Pascal,* John Wiley & Sons, Inc., New York, 1978.

L. Sha and J. B. Goodenough, "Real-Time Scheduling Theory and Ada," *IEEE Comput.* **23**(4), 53–62 (Apr. 1990).

K. G. Shin and co-workers, "A Distributed Real-Time Operating System," *IEEE Software* **9**(5), 58–68 (Sept. 1992).

H. Sholl and S. Kim, *An Approach to Performance Modeling as an Aid in Structuring Real-time, Distributed System Software,* Proc. Hawaii International Conference on System Sciences, Honolulu, Jan. 1986, pp. 5–16.

H. A. Sholl and T. L. Booth, "Software Performance Modeling Using Computation Structures," *IEEE Trans. Software Eng.* **1**(4) (Dec. 1975).

C. U. Smith, *The Prediction and Evaluation of the Performance of Software from Extended Design Specifications,* Ph.D. dissertation, University of Texas, 1980.

C. U. Smith, *Software Performance Engineering,* Proc. Computer Measurement Group Conference XII, Dec. 1981, pp. 5–14.

C. U. Smith, *A Methodology for Predicting the Memory Management Overhead of New Software Systems,* Proc. Hawaii International Conference on System Sciences, Honolulu, Jan.1982, pp. 200–209.

C. U. Smith, guest ed., "Special Issue on Software Performance Engineering," *Comput. Measurement Group Trans.* **49** (1985).

C. U. Smith, "Independent General Principles for Constructing Responsive Software Systems," *ACM Trans. Comput. Sys.* **4**(1), 1–31 (Feb. 1986).

C. U. Smith, "Applying Synthesis Principles to Create Responsive Software Systems," *IEEE Trans. Software Eng.* **14**(10), 1394–1408 (Oct. 1988).

C. U. Smith, "Who Uses SPE?" *Comput. Measurement Group Trans.,* 69–75 (Spring 1988b).

C. U. Smith, *Performance Engineering of Software Systems,* Addison-Wesley, Publishing Co., Inc., Reading, Mass., 1990.

C. U. Smith, *Integrating New and "Used" Modeling Tools for Performance Engineering,* Proc. Fifth International Conference on Modeling Techniques and Tools for Computer Performance Evaluation, Torino, Italy, Feb. 1991, pp. 148–158.

C. U. Smith, *Software Performance Engineering in the Development of Safety-Critical Systems,* No. 92-03, Performance Engineering Services, Nov. 1992.

C. U. Smith and J. C. Browne, *Performance Specifications and Analysis of Software Designs,* Proc. ACM Sigmetrics Conference on Simulation Measurement and Modeling of Computer Systems, Boulder, Colo., Aug. 1979, pp. 173–182.

C. U. Smith and J. C. Browne, *Aspects of Software Design Analysis: Concurrency and Blocking,* Proc. ACM Sigmetrics Conference on Simulation Measurement and Modeling of Computer Systems, Toronto, Ontario, May 1980, pp. 245–253.

C. U. Smith and J. C. Browne, *Performance Engineering of Software Systems: A Case Study,* Proc. National Computer Conference, Houston, June 1982, pp. 217–224.

C. U. Smith and D. D. Loendorf, *Performance Analysis of Software for an MIMD Computer,* Proc. ACM Sigmetrics Conference on Measurement and Modeling of Computer Systems, Seattle, Aug. 1982, pp. 151–162.

C. U. Smith and L. G. Williams, "Why CASE Should Extend into Software Performance," *Software Mag.* **10**(9), 49–65 (1990).

C. U. Smith and L. G. Williams, "Software Performance Engineering: A Case Study with Design Comparisons," *IEEE Trans. Software Eng.,* (Summer 1993).

T. A. Standish, *Data Structure Techniques,* Addison-Wesley Publishing Co., Inc., Reading, Mass., 1980.

J. A. Stankovic and K. Ramamritham, "The Spring Kernel: A New Paradigm for Real-Time Systems," *IEEE Software* **8**(3), 62–72 (Mar. 1991).

L. Svoboda, *Computer Measurement and Evaluation Methods: Analysis and Applications,* Elsevier, Science Publishing Co., Inc., New York, 1977.

K. S. Trivedi, *Probability and Statistics with Reliability, Queueing, and Computer Science Applications,* Prentice-Hall, Inc., Englewood Cliffs, N.J., 1982.

D. Van Tassel, *Program Style, Design, Efficiency, Debugging, and Testing,* Prentice-Hall, Inc., Englewood Cliffs, N.J., 1978.

J. W. Winchester and G. Estrin, *Methodology for Computer-based Systems,* Proc. National Computer Conference, Houston, Texas, 1982, pp. 369–379.

C. M. Woodside, *Throughput Calculation for Basic Stochastic Rendezvous Networks,* Technical Report, Carleton University, Ottawa, Canada, Apr. 1986.

C. M. Woodside, "Throughput Calculation for Basic Stochastic Rendezvous Networks," *Perform. Eval.* **9** (1989).

C. M. Woodside and co-workers, "The CAEDE Performance Analysis Tool," *Ada Lett.* **11**(3) (Spring 1991).

J. Xu and D. L. Parnas, *On Satisfying Timing Constraints in Hard Real-Time Systems,* Proc. ACM SIGSOFT 91 Conference on Software for Critical Systems, New Orleans, La., 1991, pp. 132–145.

CONNIE U. SMITH
Performance Engineering Services

PERFORMANCE TESTING

See CATEGORIES OF TESTING.

PERT

PERT, or Project Evaluation and Review Technique, is a scheduling technique based on a network of events or activities, and nodes which signal the completion of the activity. Each event is classified by a minimum, average, and maximum time to complete. The connected network, the interconnection of all nodes, shows the relationship of all activities in the development. The path through the network with the longest expected time to complete is called the "critical path". By identifying this critical path, management and engineering focus can be applied to assure that the schedule is met by dealing with risks and issues that are identified through use of the technique. The technique is highly amenable to automation. As actual event completion times are recorded the computer can recalculate the critical path through the network and furnish schedule reports. This technique is also referred to as PERT-CPM for PERT-Critical Path Method. [J. J. Marciniak, *Software Acquisition Management,* Wiley, New York, 1990, p. 99.]

PERT/CPM

See PERT PROJECT MANAGEMENT.

PETRI NET

An abstract, formal model of information flow, showing static and dynamic properties of a system. A Petri net is usually represented as a graph having two types of nodes (called places and transitions) connected by arcs, and marking (called tokens) indicating dynamic properties (IEEE).

PHASED DEVELOPMENT

See DESIGN; PROCESS MODELS IN SOFTWARE ENGINEERING.

PIPELINE PROCESSING

See PARALLEL SYSTEMS.

PL/I

See PROCEDURAL LANGUAGES.

POSIX

POSIX is a suite of operating system interface standards being developed by the IEEE Computer Society and ISO/IEC JTC1. These standards define implementation conformance (for operating system products) and application conformance for applications software. The objective of this standards work is to provide for portability of properly engineered applications between a wide variety of computer systems. One engineering management task that is gaining increasing importance is to engineer software to meet a business objective of "portability." The POSIX standards are one of the building blocks that address this objective. To see how this building block is being used in conjunction with other standards to provide a rich application environment see PROFILES.

The POSIX standards are based on AT&T's UNIX operating system, although any operating system could implement these interfaces. The work is divided into 6 major areas: system interface specifications, Shell and Utility specifications, system administration, test methods, language bindings, and application environment profiles. These standards are in various stages from early development to full ISO/IEC International Standard acceptance. These projects in the IEEE all have numbers in the range P1003.0 to P1003.18, where the 1003 indicates the "POSIX family" of standards projects. Copies of the approved standards can be obtained from the IEEE, and copies of drafts in progress from the IEEE Computer Society. Participation in the development or approval of these is open to all interested professionals through the Computer Society. IEEE approval indicates acceptance by all industry segments, users and producers. ISO/IEC approval indicates acceptance by all national standards bodies. U.S. Government Federal Information Processing Standard (FIPS) 151-1 specifies the POSIX system interfaces for Federal agency procurements, and similar guidelines are being adopted by both the public and private sectors worldwide.

The POSIX system interface work consists of a number of standards and projects. The base services are the most mature POSIX project (IEEE Std. 1003.1-1990; ISO/IEC IS 9945-1:1990). This defines C-language application interfaces for services such as: file management for byte-stream files, directory management, process management, signals (asynchronous conditions), and access to system information (time, options, users). The P1003.4 work for real-time services extends this to provide for shared memory management, interprocess communications, event handling, synchronous and asynchronous I/O. contiguous files, and multithread operations. The P1003.6 extensions address security services (access control, audit logging, . . .).

An additional set of system interface standards address extensions for distributed operations. The P1003.8 (Transparent File Access) defines how 1003.1 file services are provided in a network. The P1003.12 (Protocol Independent Interface) provides a program interface to control network communications that is independent of the underlying protocol stack (OSI or TCP/IP for example). The P1003.17 (Directory Services) defines the interface for 1003.1 directory services in a network environment including X.400.

Extension beyond the C-language interfaces are defined in the P1003.5 work, for Ada language interfaces, and P1003.9 work for Fortran 77 language interfaces.

The Shell is a command line interpreter that can interface directly to interactive users, or can be driven from parameterized files called shell scripts. The basis for the P1003.2 shell is the UNIX Bourne Shell, with Korn Shell extensions. In addition to the shell environment, the P1003.2 defines a large number of utilities based on existing UNIX systems work. These include trivial operations such as "cp" (copy) to more advanced functions like sort, as well as functions unique to the UNIX heritage such as "grep" and "awk". An additional set of user portability extensions are also defined, including "vi," which is a full-screen text editor. The P1003-15 extensions provide for batch services in response to this need in the supercomputing environment.

System administration, covered in P1003.7, is the third major element of an operating system environment. Here the lack of a consistent heritage, and the need to address a distributed multi-vendor environment, has resulted in committee development as opposed to building on existing practice. The system administration services will use an object-oriented model compatible with the OSI network management work. This will include services such as printing, backup, recovery, and user-management.

The test methods work (P1003.3) focuses on how to test for implementation compliance. Conformance tests and procedures have been developed by the U.S. Government and are under development in Europe. NIST has established accredited test laboratories and operating system implementations can be certified by these labs. Conformance to the POSIX standards entails services, interactions and conditions that cannot be tested, and this limitation needs to be understood. Applications conformance testing has not yet been addressed in the standards process, although some private firms are developing tools for this purpose. Guidance on developing POSIX applications is available in the commercial press.

The last area of POSIX projects are application environment profiles. These describe a combination of the POSIX standards, with options and parameters, as well as other standards needed to address some specific functional objective. (See PROFILES). This work is particularly relevant to identifying a useful set of standards as a target environment for applications development. Environments being defined by the POSIX effort include: P1003.10 Supercomputing, P1003.11 Transaction Processing, P1003.13 Real Time, P1003.14 Multiprocessing, and P1003.18 POSIX Platform. The POSIX Platform work defines the traditional UNIX environment in terms of the formal standards: 1003.1. 1003.2, and the C language.

JAMES ISAAK

PRECOMPILER

A computer program or routine that processes source code and generates the equivalent code that is acceptable to a compiler. For example, a routine that converts structured FORTRAN to ANSI-standard FORTRAN (IEEE).

PRELIMINARY DESIGN

(1) The process of analyzing design alternatives and defining the architecture, components, interfaces, and timing and sizing estimates for a system or component. (2) The result of the process in (1) (IEEE).

PRIVACY AND SECURITY

The information age has extended the means to catalog and dossier electronically individuals on a scale unimaginable to those who kept paper records some fifty years ago. The "seamless" nature of computer systems and telecommunications networks has enabled the transmission of countless data on every aspect of an individual's life: medical status, employment history, economic station, political leaning, leisure interests, etc. Therefore, many people have begun to take an active interest in regulating the negative effects of technology on the privacy of individuals. This interest has resulted in the enactment of data privacy/data protection legislation in many countries, provinces and states; the organization of citizens' groups dedicated to information privacy and the development of technological data security safeguards to protect the privacy of sensitive personal data.

HISTORY

Throughout ancient and modern history there has been an interest by political, religious and commercial authorities in maintaining detailed records on individuals. China's authorities began collecting detailed personal records on its citizens as early as 246 BC during the Chin Dynasty. The Chins established a system in which groups of households were organized for purposes of spying on one another. People who were suspected of "evil practices" were reported to the authorities. The Han Dynasty instituted a system called "ren shi dang an" in which promotions of army officers were based on detailed records of their wartime performance (Madsen, 1993). The Roman Empire had a relatively sophisticated method that supplemented census and taxation records with information on real or imagined threats to the empire. In some cities in Greece and Egypt, public record offices maintained very detailed information culled from the annual census, land deeds and commercial contracts for property. After the Norman invasion of England in 1086, the scribes of William the Conqueror swept through England collecting detailed information on the incomes of residents. This information was compiled in the "Domesday Book" (Madsen, 1992). In more recent times, Soviet Russia and Nazi Germany engaged in particularly intrusive record keeping practices. The Soviet Communists, through their security services (the NKVD and later the KGB) kept detailed data on many Soviet citizens. The records were maintained at KGB Headquarters in Moscow and information was gathered from a complex network of informants throughout the Soviet Union. The smaller versions of the KGB that existed in Soviet satellite countries kept similar personal records on those considered to be enemies of the state or just merely suspicious. The most significant surveillance programs were those run by the East German Stasi and the Romanian Securitate (see below) (Madsen, 1992).

The Nazis, upon invading another country, seized as many public and private records as they could find. These records were transported to Germany where analysts of the Security Service of the Gestapo (SD) closely examined records and transcribed useful information to color-coded cards that were placed in revolving cylinders for easy retrieval. Relational information was examined to establish the political leanings, ethnic origin, and religious affiliation of individuals. In most cases this information was passed to units of the Gestapo who then rounded up suspected individuals for transport to concentration camps (Madsen, 1992). Cards as information media were first used during the 1890 U.S. Census when Herman Hollerith developed a system by which information could be recorded by punching holes in cards. These holes could then be read by spring-activated pins. The Hollerith tabulating machines and the German SD mechanical card retrieval systems were the precursors of today's automated information systems. It is noteworthy that both systems were initially developed to record personal data on individuals.

PROTECTION OF COMPUTERIZED PERSONAL DATA

Personal files are maintained for a variety of legitimate purposes such as law enforcement, granting of credit, taxation, health care administration, and licensing. However, personal data are also kept for a number of dubious reasons including political harassment, religious and ethnic discrimination, intrusive target marketing and surreptitious surveillance.

The advent of the computer and the information age has resulted in an increase in the capability to retain large numbers of personal data files. One of the first references to privacy in relation to computer-based data systems can be found in a 1965 paper written by Paul Baran of the RAND Corporation. The paper addressed the impact of computer technology on communications and people. Baran's closing paragraph contains the statement: "It may seem a paradox, but an open society dictates a right of privacy among its members, and we [computer professionals] will have thrust upon us much of the responsibility of preserving this right" (Baran, 1965). High-speed data networks, data base management systems, data storage technology and the relative low cost of computer hardware and software have all contributed to an explosion of information systems that process, store and transmit billions of bytes of name-linked personal data around the world on a daily basis. While various nations are addressing the need to protect such information by introducing or revising privacy legislation, one fact remains constant in almost every country: people ("data subjects") are becoming more concerned about how information on them is collected, used and disseminated. Legislation is but one method of countering threats to data privacy. Laws are supplemented by traditional computer and communication security countermeasures ensuring both confidentiality and integrity. Many data protection laws are primarily concerned with data privacy. However, they also address requirements for data security and accuracy. It can be argued that data protection is a subset of privacy. Government agencies that make wrong or unfair decisions based on erroneous data are violative of data protection principles but not necessarily invasive upon personal privacy.

Security controls that ensure confidentiality (or privacy) include those measures required to limit access to only those authorized persons who have a lawful or otherwise valid purpose in examining personal information. Authorized purposes include law enforcement, public health and safety, social work, employee management, licensing, taxation and voter registration. Integrity controls provide data subjects with the assurance that information held on them is relevant (has a lawful purpose) and accurate.

In the field of computer security, confidentiality and integrity controls are extended to include availability resources. Availability assures that information is provided in a timely manner and that it is protected from damage or destruction. In data privacy, availability has a somewhat different connotation. Although personal data must be backed-up in order to prevent loss, they must also be provided to data subjects in a timely and comprehensible manner ("freedom of information," FOI). In this regard, data subjects are able to ensure both the accuracy and relevancy of their data.

THE AMERICAN APPROACH TO DATA PRIVACY: A SECTORAL PATCHWORK

By the 1970s practically one-half of all personal data were stored in computer systems. The ubiquitous nature of computerized personal data necessitated the enactment of data protection legislation. Europe and the United States took fundamentally different approaches to the protection of personal data. Each approach is based on unique traditions of government involvement in private business as well as experiences with totalitarian abuses of power.

The American policy is to rely on business and government to ensure data privacy with minimal government intervention. Privacy legislation in the United States is considered by many experts to be arcane and ill-suited for application to the modern information age. In the United States, the Social Security Act of 1935 introduced the first widespread numerical identifier for American citizens, the nine-digit Social Security Number (SSN). Although the SSN was originally designed only as a reference number to administer the payment of social security benefits to Americans, its use was gradually expanded to include taxpayer information. The Tax Reform Act of 1976 extended the use of the SSN to the administration of welfare programs and for use by state and local governments for various purposes, including licensing of motorists (Linowes, 1989).

Although it was never intended to be a personal identification number, the SSN has, by common practice, become a de facto national identifier. The increased use of computers by Federal, state and local governments has promoted the SSN's popularity as an identification mechanism. Although numbers rather than names are more conducive to digital processing, there are inherent data integrity problems with the use of the SSN. The primary difficulty arises from the fact that the nine-digit SSN is shared by more than one user. In a database environment, information on two different individuals holding the same SSN could become intermixed.

The U.S. Department of Health, Education and Welfare (HEW) (now the Department of Health and Human Services) was the first Federal government agency to address the importance of data privacy in 1973. The 1973 Report of the Department of HEW's Secretary's Advisory Committee on Automated Personal Data Systems ("Records, Computers and the Rights of Citizens) introduced five Fair Information Principles. These are

1. There must be no personal data record-keeping systems whose very existence is secret.
2. There must be a way for an individual to find out what information about him/her is in a record and how it is used.
3. There must be a way for an individual to prevent information about him/her obtained for one purpose from being used or made available for other purposes without his/her consent.
4. There must be a way for an individual to correct or amend a record of identifiable information about him/her.
5. Any organization creating, maintaining, using, or disseminating records of identifiable personal data must assure the reliability of the data for their intended use and must take reasonable precautions to prevent misuse of the data. (Privacy Protection Study Commission, 1977)

These Fair Information Principles were significant in that they were to form a basis for the requirements of the 1974 Privacy Act as well as other Federal legislation in later years. These principles also form a cornerstone of data protection principles found in many European data protection laws.

Interest in data privacy in the United States was raised at a Congressional level in the early 1970s after revelations that the Nixon Administration had been ordering law enforcement and intelligence agencies to obtain personal data on American citizens illegally. The Watergate Affair eclipsed the interest President Nixon had in examining the income tax records of his political opponents. The political intelligence gathering also involved the burglarizing of a psychiatrist's office to acquire confidential medical data on Defense Department official Daniel Ellsberg, a critic of the administration's Vietnam War policies. There were also lingering concerns about the Federal Bureau of Investigation's (FBI) personal data keeping practices that had existed since the days of Senator Joseph McCarthy's "blacklists" in the 1950s. These concerns were exacerbated by suspicions regarding FBI Director J. Edgar Hoover's "secret files" on the personal lives of many noted and not-so-noted American citizens (Madsen, 1992).

The Privacy Act was signed by President Ford on 31 December 1974. The Privacy Act applies only to Federal government agency records dealing with personally identifiable data held in both manual and automated form. The act ensures that information held about individuals is accurate, timely, complete and relevant. The Privacy Act also grants individuals the right to inspect files held on them by Federal agencies. There is a wide range of exemptions from inspection granted to certain Federal agencies like the FBI, Central Intelligence Agency (CIA) and other elements concerned with intelligence and law enforcement. The Privacy Act had been preceded by two narrowly focused laws dealing partly with data privacy and freedom of information. These were the Fair Credit Reporting Act (FCRA) and Fair Credit Billing Act (FCBA). These laws apply to credit grantors and companies that maintain credit information on individuals ("credit reporting agencies") and are narrow in their scope and application. In 1974, the Family Education Rights and Privacy Act (FERPA) was passed that granted access to student records to students over the age of 18 or, when younger, to their parents. Passage of the Privacy Act, FCRA, FCBA and FERPA was to begin a process in the US Congress and state legislatures of passing extremely sectoral privacy legislation that would later resemble a "patchwork quilt" of privacy laws. Aggrieved citizens would have to rely on the courts to hear privacy complaints against government and business. Many Americans, especially those at the bottom of the social ladder, would find such an option financially prohibitive. This would be a major criticism of the American approach to data privacy to be later leveled by Europeans and others against the United States.

The Privacy Act failed to create a permanent Federal Privacy Commission. The law did authorized the creation of a temporary Privacy Protection Study Commission that issued a report in 1977. However many of the report's recommendations were relatively unheeded by the administrations of Presidents Carter and Reagan. It was the failure by the United States to establish a permanent Federal Privacy Commission, a recommendation of the Privacy Study Commission, that ultimately led to the wide differences in data protection policy between the US and Europe that were to develop in the latter 1980s.

Throughout the 1980s, Federal agencies continued to develop extensive information systems that processed various details on American citizens. The advent of high-speed data networks and sophisticated relational database management systems (RDBMSs) allowed agencies to build "electronic dossiers" of individually-identifiable information. Many of these systems involved law enforcement information. Examples of these systems include the Customs Service's Treasury Enforcement Communications System (TECS), Treasury's Financial Crimes Enforcement Network (FINCEN), the Securities and Exchange Commission's Electronic Data Gathering, Analysis and Retrieval (EDGAR) system and the Interior's Department's Law Enforcement Incident Reporting System (LEIRS). Many of these systems were to be connected to the National Crime Information Center upgrade (NCIC 2000) (see below) (Madsen, 1992).

THE LAW ENFORCEMENT DATA WEB

Law enforcement data, a major portion of the Federal government's personal data files, are exempted by the Privacy Act. According to a 1988 estimate by the US Congress's Office of Technology Assessment (OTA), non-intelligence/law enforcement agencies of the Federal government alone accounted for nearly 290 million computerized data files on some 114 million Americans. Intelligence and law enforcement computer systems of the Departments of Defense, Treasury, Justice and State held several hundred million additional personal data files. Moreover, the OTA reported that data accuracy statistics could not be produced by any of the 142 Federal agencies analyzed by the OTA (Forester and Morrison, 1990). Other OTA reports have stated that the Department of Justice's National Crime Information Center (NCIC) was seriously plagued by inaccurate and incomplete criminal data, unauthorized use of criminal justice data and the failure to establish a formal policy on interstate exchange of criminal history data. A 1984 audit of Illinois's Criminal Justice Information System (which uploads data to NCIC) revealed that up to 20% of the data was inaccurate and 50% failed to include case disposition data. While much of NCIC's data concerns tangible property such as vehicles, unregistered firearms, boats, license plates and heavy equipment, it is the Computerized Central History (CCH) database that contains the bulk of personal data. Since a wide variety of users are permitted to query and modify the data contained in the CCH, security and privacy becomes problematic (Van Duyn, 1991).

The NCIC upgrade, NCIC 2000, is designed to maintain records on as many as 40 million people and will have the capability to be accessed from 72,000 domestic law enforcement agencies. NCIC 2000 will introduce a new database that will identify the membership of groups to which a wanted individual belongs. This poses a significant threat to personal privacy because innocent people could potentially become suspect merely by association with wanted individuals with whom they happen to share membership in a group or association. This was a hallmark of the McCarthy era when membership in a union, trade association, or political group that may have contained communists resulted in all members of the group becoming suspect by the FBI.

Any misuse of NCIC data has merely been subject to strictures contained in nonstatutory "user agreements" between law enforcement agencies. Considering repeated cases of "information brokering" between law enforcement agencies, private investigators and corporate security departments, these informal agreements have proven to be an ineffective privacy control.

CREDIT REPORTING AND DIRECT MARKETING: ASSAULT ON CONSUMERS' PRIVACY

The credit reporting and direct marketing industries capitalized on information technology in order to improve their operations. These two industries, more than any other, did much to raise the issue of data privacy with the general public. In the United States the credit reporting industry is dominated by three key players: TRW Credit Data Services, Equifax and Trans Union. Customer information files held by these companies contain a variety of personal details on individuals who perform financial transactions using credit. These credit reporting agencies provide over 450 million credit reports per year to credit grantors. The FCRA authorizes access to credit reports to anyone with a "legitimate business need." The FCRA, FCBA, and the Fair Debt Collection Act give data subjects a vague right of access to their credit reports. In some cases the credit reporting agencies charge a fee for a copy of the report. Some privacy experts argue that by merely requesting a copy of one's credit report he or she becomes a credit suspect and as a result unfavorable data is entered in their report. However it is the credit score on which the credit industry maintains a close veil of secrecy. The credit score rates consumers as to their credit worthiness. The score is based on such variables as income, age and number of years at current residence. The secrecy surrounding the credit score arises from accusations that the credit reporting industry includes other elements to determine the score. These include race, gender, marital status, number of children, etc. This personal information can be supplemented by data collected from direct marketing firms many of which have established close business relationships with the credit reporting industry (Rothfeder, 1992).

In 1991 these relationships led to law suits against TRW by more than five states. TRW was sued for selling personal credit data to direct marketing firms without the consent of the data subjects and for failing to correct erroneous credit reports (Madsen, 1992). The Federal Trade Commission (FTC) took further action in 1993 by forcing two of the big three credit reporting agencies to stop selling sensitive credit data to target marketing firms. The two firms, TRW and Trans Union, had been selling databases on "elite retail shoppers," "highly affluent consumers," and "premium bank card holders" to direct marketing firms (Miller, 1993). There were several attempts in the late 1980s and early 1990s to amend the FCRA to give greater rights to consumers to exercise more control over their personal financial data. Immense lobbying by the credit and banking industries prevented passage of the amendments.

The direct marketing industry also increased its use of information technology to gather an enormous amount of personal data on consumers. Much data are gathered from consumers who are, in many cases, unaware of the ultimate use of the data they provide. Consumers provide data for seemingly innocent reasons such as registering a warranty for an appliance with a manufacturer, signing up for a supermarket bonus and discount program, entering a sweepstakes run by a magazine publishing consortium or merely calling a toll-free number for information. When such transactions occur, consumers' data files are activated and personal data are passed between all types of direct marketers for a variety of purposes. The introduction of calling number identification (CNI) by the telephone companies allowed direct marketers operating 800 toll-free services to automatically identify the calling party without the consent of the caller. The privacy implications of this technology becomes sensitive when dealing with anonymous "tip" hotlines designed to report cases of physical abuse and fraud.

In the case of CNI consumers are forced to pay a fee in order to "opt out" of being automatically identified. In normal cases, consumers pay for something if they want it. In the case of CNI, however, consumers are asked to pay for something if they do not want it (Ware, 1991). Such corporate presumptuousness was apparent in 1990 when practically every consumer in the United States was included in a marketing database without their knowledge. Lotus Development Corporation (the developer of the Lotus 1-2-3 spreadsheet software) and Equifax jointly offered a database on a compact disk (CD) called Lotus Marketplace that combined personal financial data with information culled from public data sources such as the census and public deed records. The database allowed direct marketers to target their customers based on such parameters as income level, age, marital status and purchasing characteristics. The public furor that resulted convinced the companies to discontinue the product. Nevertheless, other direct marketers are able to obtain private financial data from a host of sources including credit reporting services and financial services companies like American Express.

MEDICAL INDUSTRY: GENETIC + GENEALOGICAL DATA = EUGENICS

The International Human Genome Project is an effort by scientists in the United States, Canada, Europe and Japan to map the human genome or "genetic map." There are 3.3 billion base pairs in human DNA. Together these base pairs make up some 100,000 human genes (Privacy Commission of Canada, 1992). By December 1990, 50 million base pairs had been sequenced. Human Genome Project scientists state that their goal is to identify those genetic sequences that may indicate particular fatal diseases and other genetic traits that could be passed on to off-spring (Kevles, 1992). However, it was such research by the Nazis in Germany that led to the science of eugenics, the combination of genealogical and genetic data. This "research" was used by the Nazis to justify their extermination of certain races and types of people whom they considered to be "sub-human." Millions of Jews, Gypsies, Slavs, and mentally disturbed and retarded people were herded off to camps for extermination as a fulfillment of the goals of eugenics.

Many skeptics of the Human Genome Project wonder about the "slippery slopes" inherent in such research. Conservative policy-makers are concerned about the effect of such research on prenatal preferences and the risk of abortion. Liberal politicians are concerned about the government's involvement in genetic affairs (Kevles, 1992).

Law enforcement is actively using DNA fingerprinting in criminal investigations. This technique is known as restriction fragment length polymorphism (RFLP) analysis. RFLP patterns, which look like universal product codes on supermarket items, are matched with genetic samples taken from a crime scene. Matching samples are used as evidence in trials (Privacy Commission of Canada, 1992). The major problem for consumers arises not from legitimate criminal investigations but from the value of genetic data to private businesses such as insurance companies. The mere fact that an individual's genome may contain genetic pairs indicating the presence of the Duchenne dystrophy or the Parkinson's disease gene could result in that individual's inability to obtain life or health insurance. Companies involved in the Human Genome Project may be willing to sell personal genetic data to insurance and pharmaceutical firms much like the credit reporting industry sells personal financial data to direct marketers.

Dangerous liaisons have been conducted between Human Genome researchers and genealogists. In the 1980s the National Institutes of Health, the major center for the Human Genome Project, and the Church of Jesus Christ of Latter-Day Saints (the Mormons) matched genetic and genealogical data. Data on more than one million Mormons, contained in a database separated into a quarter million family pedigree schema, was combined with Utah's state death certificate database and the U.S. Public Health Service's Utah Cancer Registry. The result was that several thousands of Utahans were identified as being prone to cancer, heart disease and diabetes (Coates, 1991). While such research was undoubtedly beneficial to those identified as high-risk for future medical problems, the fact that the research was conducted between a religious group and the Federal government raised suspicions about eugenics creeping back as an acceptable field of study.

For about thirty years, the Mormons have engaged in a program of microfilming public and parish registers on a worldwide scale. This activity has been undertaken in some 100 countries including the United States, Canada, France, Ireland, South Africa, Australia, New Zealand, Germany and the United Kingdom by the Genealogical Society of Salt Lake City, operated as a component of the Mormon Church.

The Mormons currently maintain computerized records of 14 billion deaths. These are stored along with support information inside a grotto in the heart of the Rocky Mountains. The primary reason for this operation is religious: the Mormons want to administer to their own ancestors a retroactive baptism. It has been said that these retroactive baptisms are not only practiced on the ancestors of the Mormons but also on all of humanity for purposes of "final salvation." While such collection practices for religious purposes, by themselves, seem harmless, genealogical data becomes useful for geneticists interested in identifying familial traits. However, what is useful for geneticists becomes dangerous for those who could be victimized by the study of eugenics. The legal and ethical implications of the Human Genome Project will be at the forefront of the data privacy debate well into the next century.

An extensive medical database already exists in the United States. The Medical Information Bureau (MIB), located near Boston, maintains extremely detailed medical information on some 15 million Americans and Canadians. The information is routinely shared between insurance companies (Madsen, 1992). The medical data is not regulated by an explicit Federal statute. Further concerns about medical data privacy have been raised as part of the plan to institute a national health care system in the United States. In 1993 many privacy advocates voiced their concerns over plans by President Clinton's Health Care Task Force to assign the Social Security Number as a patient identifier on a national health care identity card. There has also been alarm in Britain over the Government's mooted plans to create a DNA database for the whole male population of the United Kingdom, something the UK Data Protection Registrar warned might be rife with inaccuracies because, he stated, "the percentages of certainty are not quite as high as are being stated" (Privacy Commission of Canada, 1992, p. 47).

CENSUS "GEO-CODING"

The U.S. Census has engendered a great amount of public concern about government personal data collection practices. Once every ten years every American is required, by law, to provide the government with various data concerning themselves, their families, and place of residence. Most Americans are unaware of what ultimately becomes of the data they provide. Distributed database systems and large memory computers permit government statisticians to "geo-code" households. Geo-codes are organized according to geographic area codes that are based on census tracts and block numbers. Geo-coded data represents inferential statistical data which are data that have been aggregated to represent particular geographical units or segments of the population (Davies, 1992). U.S. Census geo-coding serves as a baseline which permits third-party users to determine the average statistics for a minimum of ten households. The narrowing down of census data is aided by organizing the geo-codes according to the nine-digit postal "ZIP" codes.

Although census data, by law, is anonymous and confidential, value-added marketing research firms can "overlay" data from other sources (credit bureaus, deed offices, manufacturers) on top of inferential census data to narrow down statistics such as income level, number and names of children, number and types of automobiles, and real estate value to individual families. The value-adding process results in anonymous census data becoming individually-identifiable information.

A Census Bureau database known as the TIGER (Topologically Integrated Geographic Encoding and Referencing) system contains geo-coded data for every county in the United States as well as administrative areas in Puerto Rico, Guam, American Samoa, Northern Marianas, Palau, Midway Island and the now independent countries of the Marshall Islands and the Federated States of Micronesia. The average size of a census file for an entire state is about 500 megabytes (small states are approximately 4 megabytes while larger states like California are 1800 megabytes). The entire TIGER database is 25,000 megabytes. Therefore, many small states can be combined on a single CD-ROM (for example, Maine, Massachusetts, New Hampshire and Vermont are found on a single CD-ROM). Seven large states are contained or more than one CD-ROM (for example, California and Nevada are included on three CD-ROMS). CD-ROMs are relatively inexpensive for users ($250 per disc) (U.S. Census Bureau, 1991). The availability of theses CD-ROMs makes it advantageous for many firms to combine the census data with other personal data to target specific consumers. U.S. privacy laws provide no means for data subjects to have their names removed from the electronic dossiers that are built from combining census data with marketing information.

Many Americans are relatively sanguine about providing census information to their government. In comparison, Europeans are more suspicious about supplying such data. Census data has been used by many European totalitarian regimes in the past to suppress certain ethnic and political groups. Proposed censuses in Germany and the Netherlands were canceled in the 1980s because of opposition from the public (Netherlands and Germany) and judicial intervention (Germany).

AN AMERICAN SURVEILLANCE SOCIETY

The National Security Agency (NSA) was established in 1952 to protect classified United States government communications. Over the years its role has been expanded to include protection of classified government and contractor information systems. The NSA's major role has been the development of cryptographic systems to protect classified information. Its other role is to break the cryptographic codes used by other nations in order to obtain communications intelligence for use by Federal agency policy-makers and military components. Many privacy experts have for many years been concerned about NSA's immense control of cryptographic use by the civilian and commercial sectors. In the 1970s, the U.S. National Bureau of Standards (NBS) in concert with IBM developed the Data Encryption Standard (DES), a means to standardize encryption using a 56-bit key. The DES was embraced by many civilian agencies and commercial institutions as a favored means for encrypting communications. Many skeptics were convinced that the DES could have been an even stronger encryption method but that the NSA forced the NBS/IBM team to scale down the key length from 128 bits to its ultimate 56 bit length. The NSA critics contend that the NSA was unable to break higher key lengths in the time necessary to make any intelligence gleaned from interceptions useful. During the 1980s, some commercial users began using other encryption systems such as the RSA (named for its founders, Rivest, Shamir and Adleman, three Massachusetts Institute of Technology mathematicians). RSA is a public-key encryption system for which key lengths of over 200 bits can be set by the user. By 1990 the issue of public-key encryption alarmed the intelligence community so much that it began to formulate three new communications policy initiatives with dramatic constitutional consequences.

The first initiative was to try convincing government and industry to adopt a new encryption scheme to replace the DES. The NSA, using as a screen the National Institute for Standards and Technology (NIST) (formerly the NBS), attempted to have an encryption system known as the Digital Signature Standard (DSS) adopted as a Federal standard. Many critics contended that the DSS was inadequate since it only provided a means for digital authentication and not data encryption. Many cryptographic experts including MIT's Ron Rivest and Stanford's Martin Hellman concluded that the DSS was an effort to accede to demands by the NSA to have a weak cryptographic standard in place in order to make it's job of monitoring communications that much easier (Rotenberg, 1993).

The second initiative involved permitting the intelligence and law enforcement community to gain more authority over unclassified government and commercial computer and telecommunications systems. This policy was first broached in 1984 when President Reagan, by authority of his National Security Decision Directive 145 (NSDD-145), attempted to bring unclassified public and private information system security under the aegis of the NSA. The subsequent Computer Security Act of 1987 split responsibilities for classified and unclassified information system security between the NSA and NIST, respectively. As a result, NSDD-145 was withdrawn. In 1991 the FBI attempted to enact legislation in Congress that would have essentially provided it with instantaneous access to the nation's digital telecommunications system (Madsen, 1992). The FBI contended that the intricacies of telecommunications software prevented it from exercising its wiretapping operations under the provisions of the Omnibus Crime Control Act of 1968 (Title 111). The FBI, in particular, recognized that digital communications provided new means to eavesdrop on individuals. CNI automatically provides the called party with the number of the caller, facsimile transmissions display the number of the calling facsimile machine and electronic mail provides the electronic address of the originator as well as his or her host computer (Rotenberg, 1993). The FBI, through a piece of legislation, known as the "Digital Telephony Amendment," attempted to coop the telecommunications carriers into providing it with "turn-key" access to the national digital networks. Increased costs would then be passed on to the consumers while normal public utility commission hearings on rate increases would be closed to public scrutiny.

The third initiative was the April 1993 announcement by the Clinton administration of a new encryption system to be used by the Federal government. The Clipper Chip would be embedded in all Federal communications systems and, as hoped by the administration, in all telecommunication vendors' units. When the government wished to conduct a court-ordered wiretap it would obtain separate 40-bit keys from two independent entities who would hold the keys in escrow. When combined, the keys would allow the government to eavesdrop on any communications session using the Clipper Chip system for encryption. Many critics contended that such an embedded "trap door" weakens the security of the Clipper Chip encryption scheme (Markoff, 1993).

The late 1980s and early 1990s witnessed an increase in the use of digital communications by many companies, universities, libraries, political parties, and social activist groups around the world. The expansion of "cyberspace" as an international ethereal playing field for the exchange of ideas and information has attracted the attention of intelligence and law enforcement agencies. Intelligence and law enforcement agencies claim they are merely monitoring cyberspace activities in order to identify possible computer crime and other illicit enterprises. In 1993 a U.S. Federal court ruled that the U.S. Secret Service's monitoring of an electronic bulletin board called "Illuminati" and its subsequent seizure of computer software and hardware from Steve Jackson Games of Austin, Texas, was a violation of Federal law. The court specifically stated that the seizure of documents and equipment from Steve Jackson Games, a magazine publisher, was a violation of the Privacy Protection Act of 1980 which explicitly protects the press from unreasonable searches and seizures. With the advent of the proposed National Information Infrastructure, Integrated Services Digital Networks (ISDNs) and asynchronous transfer mode (ATM) communications, private individuals and organizations will increase their use of digital communications for the exchange of data, facsimile, voice and video images. As a consequence, more sensitive information will be exposed to illegitimate eavesdroppers. Some computer networks like Prodigy and Compuserve are already monitoring and controlling information on their networks and are therefore limiting free speech on their various electronic forums to avoid running afoul of defamation lawsuits as well as obscenity sanctions from the Federal Communications Commission (FCC) (Godwin, 1993). NASA disciplined some Ames Research Center scientists in 1993 for engaging in spirited debate over Most Favored Nation (MFN) status for China over the Internet. NASA was tipped off about the electronic conversations by the FBI which had been monitoring the Internet as part of its foreign counterintelligence mission. Technology can provide security countermeasures, but legislation will be necessary to restrain overzealous government intelligence agencies from wanton snooping.

DATA PROTECTION: THE EUROPEAN DIMENSION

Europe's approach to data privacy has been molded by its recent history. Unlike the United States, Europe has experienced the worst forms of data privacy invasion. The exploits of the Gestapo, KGB and security services of Spain, Greece and eastern Europe sensitized Europeans to the need for strict data protection legislation. Europe's social democratic tradition also opened the way for the private sector to be subject to data protection legislation. The Organization for Economic Cooperation and Development (OECD) was the first international organization to address the issue of privacy of information in computerized databanks as early as 1963. This ultimately led to the issuance of a set of non-binding OECD guidelines dealing with privacy in 1980. The OECD Guidelines on the Protection of Privacy and Transborder Flows of Personal Data serve as the basis for data privacy legislation in European countries as well as Canada, Australia, New Zealand, Japan and other countries.

The OECD efforts coincided with national and subnational data privacy legislation in some European countries. The German state of Hesse was the first jurisdiction to adopt modern data protection legislation in 1970. Sweden followed suit with its own Data Act in 1973. The Council of Europe began to take up the issue of data protection in the same year. By the end of the 1970s, Austria, Denmark, France, the Federal Republic of Germany, Iceland, Luxembourg and Norway had joined Sweden in adopting data protection legislation. In 1981, the Council of Europe's (COE) deliberations on data protection resulted in the adoption of Convention 108 on the Protection of Individuals with Regard to Automatic Processing of Personal Data. Convention 108 requires COE members to enact data privacy laws and create oversight bodies ("Data Protection

Commissions") to administer the provisions of the laws. This binding statutory convention came fully into force in 1985 after it had been ratified by five member nations of the COE (France, Federal Republic of Germany, Norway, Spain and Sweden).

In 1979 the European Community (EC) began to look into the issue of data protection when the European Parliament issued its "Report on the Protection of the Individual in the Face of the Technical Developments in Data Processing" (also known as the "Bayerl Report"). The various supranational data protection efforts of the COE and EC led to additional European countries passing data protection legislation: Belgium (1993), Czech and Slovak Federal Republic (1992), Faeroes (1984), Finland (1987), Guernsey (1986), Hungary (1993), Isle of Man (1986), Ireland (1988), Jersey (1987), Netherlands (1988), Portugal (1991), Slovenia (1989), Spain (1992), Switzerland (1993) and the United Kingdom (1984). Other nations amended their data protection legislation in the 1980s: Germany (1990) (including the states of the former German Democratic Republic), Iceland (1989), Norway (1987) and Sweden (1982) (Madsen, 1992). There were concerns that the failure of some countries to adopt legislation might result in the creation of "data havens" that would lure data processing enterprises wanting to avoid cumbersome notification, registration and licensing procedures in their home nations. In fact, during the early 1990s Czechoslovakia began attracting such enterprises from neighboring Austria and Estonia became an advantageous site for Finnish companies trying to avoid Finland's restrictions on personal data processing. Europe's consolidation in 1993 resulted in many data havens losing their beneficial allure. Andorra, Estonia, Czech Republic, Liechtenstein, Monaco, San Marino, and Slovakia, all potential data havens, had either become, or announced plans to become, full members of the Council of Europe, thus coming under the statutory provisions of Convention 108.

Although there are some significant differences between the various European data protection laws, there are some elements common to all the legislation. These are

1. Personal data shall be obtained legally and fairly (the OECD's Collection Limitation Principle).
2. Personal data shall be stored for specific and legitimate purposes (the OECD's Purpose Specification Principle).
3. Personal data shall be relevant and not excessive to their purpose (the OECD's Data Quality Principle).
4. Personal data shall be accurate and current (up-to-date) (the OECD's Data Quality Principle).
5. Except where there are legal provisions and safeguards, personal data of a sensitive nature (racial, political, religious, health or sexual life) may not be processed by automated means (Article 6 of COE Convention 108).
6. Personal data shall be protected by appropriate security measures (OECD's Security Safeguards Principle).
7. Personal data shall be subject to the inspection, completion, rectification or deletion by the data subject when circumstances warrant such action (OECD's Individual Participation Principle).
8. Notification of the existence of automated personal data processing systems to an oversight body (OECD's Accountability Principle) (Madsen, 1992).

The major differences in European legislation involve such matters as data protection for "legal persons" such as corporations in addition to "natural" persons (legislation in Austria, Denmark, France and Luxembourg cover corporations); inclusion of manual data in data protection legislation (legislation in Ireland and the UK apply only to automated data); extent of the accountability principle (some nations like Austria, Denmark, France and the UK require prior registration of personal data processing systems with a government agency, while Ireland only requires registration of certain personal data processing systems and Germany merely requires a notification of the existence of personal data processing systems); restrictions on communications of data to other countries (some nations like Austria, Denmark, France and Sweden prohibit the transfer of personal data to other countries without either a legal obligation or consent of the data subject whilst the United Kingdom's Data Protection Registrar is empowered to issue a "Transfer Prohibition Notice" embargoing data transfers to other countries) and "informed consent" (some countries like France and Germany require that the data subject be given the reason for personal data collection at the time of collection). There are also strict provisions regarding third-party access to personal data. For example, data given to an agency for one expressed purpose is not to be used for other purposes. There have been cases involving foreigners who present a visa office with a bank statement having their financial data disclosed to tax collection agencies in the applicants' home country because of Mutual Tax Assistance Treaties. Third-party rules on use of personal data prohibit such sharing without either a judicial warrant or the consent of the data subject.

In an attempt to harmonize European data protection laws, the EC, in 1990, issued a Draft Directive on Data Privacy. While the directive generally followed the main aspects of the French and German data protection laws, it specifically addressed two major subjects that resulted in consternation among European trading partners. The first of these restrictions addressed the transborder data flow (TDF) of personal information to non-EC nations lacking adequate data protection laws. The second restriction applied to the "prior consent" of the data subject to transfer personal data to third parties before such transactions actually occurred. Many banks argued that international automated teller machine (ATM) networks would be plagued by problems if bank computers in other countries were denied access to the account balances of Europeans because of the prior consent clause.

Europeans are generally emotional about the creation of computer files that contain "sensitive" data. These files are mainly created for purposes of law enforcement and national security. Many European nations prohibit the collection and storage of data pertaining to an individual's ethnicity, religious affiliation or political opinions. Such data can only be collected and stored with the expressed written consent of the data subject. On the other hand, United States law authorized the collection of such data when it involves criminal investigations and intelligence missions. Such differences in approach pose legal problems for the unhindered flow of "sensitive" data between Europe and the United States. However, some experts feel that the level of sensitive data flow between Europe and the United States is far greater than many imagine since it is carried out between intelligence and law enforcement agencies on both sides of the Atlantic. Much of this data, the experts claim, is collected from clandestine signals intelligence (SIGINT) operations operated by an alliance of the United Kingdom, the United States, Canada, Australia and New Zealand (UK-USA Agreement) (Bamford, 1985; Richelson and Ball, 1990). Traditional SIGINT practices are also being applied to the collection of digital data. Several nations have initiated programs to gather sensitive data from data networks. Responsibilities have been assigned to national intelligence agencies. Germany, Israel, Japan and France are at the forefront of such digital eavesdropping and on-line intelligence gathering (Schweizer, 1993; Cornwall, 1991; and Madsen, 1991). Reports that SIGINT agencies were involved with eavesdropping on politicians surfaced during the early 1990s in France, Ireland, Greece, Hungary, Norway and the United Kingdom. The French scandal involving wiretapping of opponents to President Francois Mitterand partially led to the defeat of France's Socialist government in March 1993 elections.

As a result of European Community attempts to drop most border restrictions between member states, European national police forces are sharing law enforcement information to a far greater degree. There are concerns about how such information is treated by national police where nations have different laws concerning the collection and use of criminal information. In 1985 representatives of France, Germany, Netherlands, Luxembourg and Belgium met in Schengen, Luxembourg, to set up a system to exchange police intelligence between the five countries. What became known as the Schengen Accord eventually served as a basis for creation of the Schengen Information System, a computerized law enforcement data system modeled after the NCIC in the United States. East Germany (upon German reunification), Italy, Spain and Portugal eventually became parties to the Schengen Accord. In some cases, the police themselves questioned the wisdom of granting unrestricted access to national criminal intelligence. The Netherlands voiced concern over the possible presence of former East German Ministry of State Security ("Stasi") agents in the German law enforcement establishment (Madsen, 1992). Danish police voiced misgivings about joining such a police data network. One Danish police officer was quoted as asking "What's the point of working in Rome with corrupt Italian police?" (*The European*, 1993). The Channel Tunnel between the United Kingdom and France also pointed to problems associated with exchanging police data. British police units will be stationed on French soil with computer terminals linked to the French police information system. French police will have similar units established on British territory with terminals linked to Britain's Police National Computer 2 (PNC2). Questions have been raised regarding the applicability of national data protection laws in such extraterritorial situations.

The other major European issue affecting data protection is found in the former Soviet bloc states of Eastern Europe. After the downfall of Eastern Europe's communist regimes, new governments were perplexed over questions of what to do with the millions of personal dossiers compiled by the communist apparatuses' secret services. The East German "Stasi" alone maintained about six million files on East Germans. In some cases as many as 80,000 individual items were held on a single individual. The Stasi employed some 100,000 agents with about 6,000 of those dedicated to electronic eavesdropping operations (Einwag, 1991). Upon reunification of Germany, the Federal German Data Protection Commissioner was faced with the monumental task of deciding how to handle such volumes of raw and unverified sensitive data. The German Data Protection Commissioner estimated that the Stasi files, if laid end-to-end, would be some 202 kilometers long. The German Bundestag separated the Stasi files into four main categories:

1. Files on subjects of spying (victims).
2. Files on those employed by the East German Ministry of Security (with a distinction made between full-time employees and part-time informers).
3. Files on beneficiaries (those who received support from the Stasi such as terrorists).
4. Files on other persons (for example, West German citizens).

The German government passed a special law dealing with the Stasi files. Individuals in the first category were permitted to access their files at offices throughout the former German Democratic Republic.

Other Eastern European countries were confronted with similar problems concerning the invasive files of their former secret services. Some countries like Poland and Czechoslovakia began to use the files to screen potential government officials pursuant to lustration (screening) laws adopted by their parliaments. During the two years following the overthrow of President Ceausescu, the Romanian Intelligence Service (RIS) destroyed and altered old files and fabricated new files for political purposes (Ionescu, 1992). Many individuals were faced with denunciation as collaborators if they were the subject of secret police files and were forced to resign their government positions. The Eastern European press began to print lists of "informers" culled from unvetted secret police files. The Polish Interior Ministry released a partially-fabricated list of suspected communist collaborators directly to the Polish Parliament in June 1992. The list contained as many as 100 members of parliament suspected of being informants. President Walesa denounced the circulation. Former secret police officials admitted that they often assigned code names to innocent people as a disinformation tactic.

Based on secret police files, Presidents Walesa of Poland and Havel of Czechoslovakia as well as former Romanian Prime Minister Petre Roman were accused of being informants. The accusations were based on unsubstantiated data. As opposed to Western Europe, data protection in the East is concerned with properly disposing of data files containing intimate details on the lives of hundreds of thousands of people. Whilst Germany decided to open Stasi files to the data subjects concerned, the Czechoslovak government announced in February 1992 that most of the former STB (security police) files had been destroyed with only fragments left intact. A Romanian law on the files of the former Securitate forbids them to be released to the public for thirty years. A Bulgarian law permitted every Bulgarian citizen to be granted access to his or her secret police files, with the files of those wishing to hold political office or civil servant jobs being made public. By the end of 1992, four Eastern European countries (Poland, Czech Republic, Hungary and Bulgaria) had joined the Council of Europe and were considering legislation to comply with Convention 108. Their respective data protection laws were to consider the problems associated with the secret police files. The proposed legislation also took an unfavorable approach to exemption clauses. Police and security services were not to be exempt from compliance with the data protection laws.

DATA PRIVACY IN THE PACIFIC RIM AND CANADA

Data privacy laws in the Commonwealth countries of Australia, Canada and New Zealand, while more advanced than those of the United States, fall somewhat behind the European laws in scope and strength. In one respect the Australians, Canadians and New Zealanders have adopted a quasi-American style approach to ensuring privacy of data. Aside from the Australian credit reporting industry, the private sector is free to self-regulate their adherence to privacy standards of conduct. However, Quebec has been considering extending its privacy legislation to cover the insurance sector and New Zealand is considering to what extent its 1991 Privacy Act might extend to the private sector. All three countries have established national Privacy Commissions that act in an ombudsman capacity. They hear complaints about governmental privacy abuses. They also advise government on the creation of new legislation for emerging technologies. For example, the Canadians have been at the forefront of addressing issues surrounding genetic data. This has occurred at both the Federal and provincial levels. In all three countries concern has been voiced by the general public over the use of identification numbers as universal national identifiers. The Canadian Privacy Commission has been instrumental in curtailing the abuse of Canada's Social Insurance Number (SIN), a number adopted in 1964 solely for purposes of administering social insurance benefits (Madsen, 1992). Governments in Australia and New Zealand came under heavy fire for trying to propose national identity cards for citizens. Plans to adopt an Australian Card and a New Zealand "Kiwi" Card were denounced as an invasion of privacy by several public advocacy groups and politicians across the political spectrum. Many Australians are convinced that the later introduction of the Tax File Number (TFN) was merely a clever ploy to issue a de facto national identification number (Davies, 1992). Australia was faced with the ever-growing problem of the illegal trafficking of personal data between government agencies and private sector organizations. What started as an anticorruption probe into allegations that personal data was being sold by the New South Wales Police and the Roads and Traffic Authority of New South Wales blossomed into a full-blown probe into such activities at a national level. What was code-named "Operation Tamba" resulted in the revelation that similar practices were being conducted by police departments, credit reporting agencies, private investigators, information brokers and government agencies all over Australia (Davies, 1992). In 1992 a similar network was uncovered in the United States. Several government employees and information brokers were charged by Federal authorities with violating numerous privacy statutes by selling and buying personal data from government databases.

Privacy does not have a strong traditional basis in the culture of Japan. Therefore, Japan was relatively late in addressing the privacy concerns of the Western countries. The adoption of the OECD Guidelines in 1980 and subsequent international legislation on data protection resulted in a fear by Japan that it would be cut off from important financial and communications links with Western countries if it did not adopt some form of data privacy legislation. In 1988, Japan adopted a Data Protection Act covering only government data files. Some 300 Japanese municipalities have adopted their own data protection ordinances. Japanese consumers are becoming much more aware of the potential for personal data abuse. Therefore, the Ministry for International Trade and Industry (MITI) encouraged private firms to comply with its 1989 guidelines titled, "Protection of Personal Data Processed by Computers in the Private Sector" (Madsen, 1992).

Hong Kong's colonial government issued a set of voluntary data protection guidelines in 1988. Hong Kong's government feared that its failure to address the issue of data protection might adversely affect its trading relationships with the European Community and the OECD countries. Efforts were underway in 1992 and 1993 to transform the guidelines into a law. The most significant question looming over Hong Kong is the possible effect that its return to Chinese sovereignty in 1997 will have on any data protection regime for the territory.

THE DEVELOPING WORLD

The developing countries of the world are beginning to use automation throughout their societies. They are facing somewhat unique problems associated with the introduction of computer systems. Many totalitarian governments see computer technology as but one more tool they can use to suppress various sectors of their populations. Western firms have sold sophisticated computer technology including relational database management systems to countries with less than stellar human rights records. Many countries, especially some in Asia, became enamored with the possibility of issuing "smart" identity cards to citizens, thus allowing a near real-time surveillance capability. Thailand proposed a system that would combine such elements as medical status, voting eligibility, and religious and ethnic

Table 1. Status of International Data Protection Legislation[a]

Country	Type of Law	Year Passed(Year Revised)	Sectoral Coverage
Australia	Privacy Act	1988	Public and private[b]
Austria	Data Protection Act	1978	Public and private
Belgium	Data Protection Act	1993	Public and private
Canada	Privacy Act	1982	Public
Czech-Slovak Federation[c]	Data Protection Act	1992	Public and private
Denmark	Data Protection Acts	1978 (1988)	Public and private
Faeroes	Data Protection Act	1984	Public and private
Finland	Data Protection Act	1987	Public and private
France	Data Protection Act	1978	Public and private
Germany	Data Protection Act	1978 (1990)	Public and private
Guernsey	Data Protection Act	1986	Public and private
Hungary	Data Protection/FOI Act	1993	Public and private
Iceland	Data Protection Act	1989	Public and private
Isle of Man	Data Protection Act	1986	Public and private
Israel	Privacy Act	1981	Public and private
Japan	Data Protection Act	1988	Public
Jersey	Data Protection Act	1987	Public and private
Kalaalit Nunaat (Greenland)	Data Protection Act	1979	Public and private
Luxembourg	Data Protection Act	1979	Public and private
Netherlands	Data Protection Act	1988	Public and private
New Zealand	Privacy Act	1991	Public
Norway	Data Protection Act	1978 (1987)	Public and private
Portugal	Data Protection Act	1991	Public and private
Spain	Data Protection Act	1992	Public and private
Slovenia	Data Protection Act	1989	Public and private
Sweden	Data Protection Act	1973 (1982)	Public and private
Switzerland	Data Protection Act	1993	Public and private
United Kingdom	Data Protection Act	1984	Public and private
United States	Privacy Act	1974	Public (Federal)

[a] The following countries are considering data protection legislation: Andorra, Belarus, Bulgaria, Croatia, Cyprus, Czech Republic, Estonia, Greece, Hong Kong, Italy, Republic of Korea, Kyrgyzstan, Latvia, Liechtenstein, Lithuania, Malta, Mexico, Moldova, Monaco, Poland, Romania, Russian Federation, San Marino, Singapore, Slovakia, South Africa, Turkey and Ukraine. [b] Privacy Amendment Act 1990 extended coverage to credit reference industry. [c] Federation dissolved 31 December 31, 1992. Federal laws no longer apply to the independent republics of Czechia and Slovakia.

affiliation on a single chip embedded in a national identity card. Other nations like the Philippines, Taiwan, Singapore, Brunei, Malaysia and Indonesia expressed an interest in developing similar systems (Madsen, 1993). In fact, Malaysia is currently manufacturing one of the more advanced smart cards (Davies, 1992).

Israeli authorities have for several years required Palestinian residents of the West Bank and Gaza to carry bar-coded identity cards. The bar-codes contains detailed personal information on the bearer and are read by portable units carried by Israeli authorities. The information is then uploaded to IBM computers in Jerusalem for matching and vetting purposes (Madsen, 1992).

In 1992 Pakistan announced that it was planning to issue modern identity cards that would contain the religious affiliations of its citizens. Because Pakistan's government is of a fundamentalist Islamic tilt, many non-Muslims and Muslims expressed concern over the use of such information. The small Christian community and the Ahmadi sect (an Islamic off-shoot) were worried that such information could be used by the government as a new form of suppression and discrimination. Such potential problems exist in other ethnically diverse countries planning to introduce modern means of identification.

Many developing nations emulate larger industrialized nations by creating immense intelligence infrastructures that use the latest in electronic and computerized surveillance systems. Seemingly innocuous data like census data is often used to identify certain religious, ethnic and other minorities for persecution. (Madsen, 1993) India has created a particularly large surveillance infrastructure in the form of its Joint Intelligence Committee (JIC) which combines the resources of Research and Analysis Wing (RAW), the Directorate of Revenue Intelligence (DRI), the Intelligence Bureau (IB), the Central Bureau of Investigation (CBI), and the three military intelligence branches. This large surveillance organization routinely taps the telephones of opposition politicians and ethnic minorities. Detailed personal files are maintained on hundreds of thousands of individuals (Vaughn, 1993). India, like many other developing countries with similar surveillance structures, has not passed any form of data protection or freedom of information legislation. The experiences of Argentina, Chile, and Uruguay serve as stark examples of what sinister motives may often lie behind the accumulation of such files. During the military rule these countries experienced, thousands of individuals who were identified in secret computerized data files were rounded up by police and most were never heard from again (Madsen, 1992).

Some developing nations, especially those in Africa, are concerned about data privacy but for their countries as a whole. Some nations reliant on Western assistance are expressing concern about having industrialized nations indiscriminately browsing their government data bases and uploading data to computers in the West (Madsen, 1990). There are also concerns about geographic information systems (GIS) capturing sensitive data from satellite sensors without ever being screened by national authorities. Many developing countries have voiced their apprehension about possible loss of sovereignty.

Recent United Nations initiatives to adopt "Guidelines for the Regulation of Computerized Data Files" would, if adopted, extend a non-statutory data privacy umbrella over the 184 member nations (as of July 1993) of the United Nations. A draft resolution was adopted by the General Assembly in 1990 but the draft was sent back to the special rapporteur, Louis Joinet of France, for redrafting. Many developing countries, eager to protect their own sovereignty by adhering to controls of trans-border flows of data, supported the initiative.

Table 1 gives the status of international data protection legislation.

SUMMARY

Privacy protection in the information age is a vexing issue. Solutions are easy to imagine but hard to implement. Data privacy concerns everyone because every person in the United States is the subject of data files (Ware, 1991). It is almost impossible to divorce oneself from his or her digital "alter ego." Computer professionals are at the forefront of the privacy battle. They can either participate as conscious or unwitting players in the development of more sophisticated means to electronically invade the privacy of the individual. Or they can use their experience and talent to develop technical means to guard individual privacy. Government holds the key to introducing legislation that addresses the privacy problems introduced by new technology. Relational data base management systems that permit uncontrolled data matching, genetic data bases, high-resolution geographic information systems (GIS), calling number identification (CNI), electronic monitoring in the workplace, computerized voting and census tallying, and digital eavesdropping all point to the need for contemporaneous legislation. The ultimate goal of such vigilance is to ensure that individuals continue to control technology rather than having technology control individuals.

BIBLIOGRAPHY

J. Bamford, *The Puzzle Palace,* Penguin Books, New York, 1985.

P. Baran, "Communications, Computers and People," *AFIPS Conference Proceedings*, Vol. 27, part II, Spartan Books, Washington, D.C., 1967.

J. M. Carroll, *Confidential Information Sources* 2nd ed., Butterworth-Heinemann, Boston, 1991.

J. Coates, *In Mormon Circles,* Addison-Wesley Publishing Co., Inc., Reading, Mass., 1991.

H. Cornwall, *The Industrial Espionage Handbook*, Random Century, Ltd., London, 1991.

S. Davies, *Big Brother,* Simon and Schuster Australia, East Roseville, NSW, Australia, 1992.

A. Einwag, Data Protection Commissioner of Germany, Speech to the Data Protection Commissioners Conference, Strasbourg, Oct. 4, 1991.

T. Forester and P. Morrison, *Computer Ethics,* Basil Blackwell, Ltd., Oxford, UK, 1990.

M. Godwin, "New Frontiers: A Visitor's Guide," *Index on Censorship* **22**(2), 11–13 (Feb. 1993).

D. Ionescu, "Romania's Public War Over Secret Police Files," RFE/RL Research Report, Vol. I, issue 29, July 17, 1992, pp. 9–15.

D. Kevles "Out of Eugenics: The Historical Politics of the Human Genome" in D. Kevles and L. Hood, eds., *The Code of Codes: Scientific and Social Issues of the Human Genome Project,* Harvard University Press, Cambridge, Mass., 1992.

D. F. Linowes, *Privacy in America,* University of Illinois Press, Urbana, 1989

W. Madsen, "African Nations Emphasizing Security," *Datamation* **1,** 104-2–104-8 (May 1990).

W. Madsen, "Data Privacy: Legislation and Intelligence Agency Threats," *Computer Security and Information Integrity,* North Holland, Amsterdam 1991.

W. Madsen, *Handbook of Personal Data Protection,* Stockton Press, New York, 1992.

W. Madsen, "Protecting Privacy in a Digital World: Developments in the Asia-Pacific Region," *Media Information Australia,* (67), 40–50 (Feb. 1993).

J. Markoff, "New Communication System Stirs Talk of Privacy vs. Eavesdropping," *The New York Times,* A1, A18 (April 16, 1993).

M. W. Miller, "FTC Takes Aim at Trans Union, TRW Mail Lists," *Wall Street journal,* **13,** B1 (Jan. 1993).

Privacy Commission of Canada, *Genetic Testing and Privacy*, Ministry of Supply and Services, Ottawa, 1992.

Privacy Protection Study Commission, *Personal Privacy in an Information Society: Report of the Privacy Protection Study Commission,* US Government Printing Office, Washington, D.C., July 1977.

J. T. Richelson and D. Ball, *The Ties That Bind,* Unwin Hyman, Boston, 1990.

M. Rotenberg, "To Tap or Not to Tap," *Communications of the ACM* **36**(3), 36–39 (March 1993).

J. Rothfeder, *Privacy for Sale,* Simon and Schuster, New York, 1992.

P. Schweizer, *Friendly Spies,* Atlantic Monthly Press, New York, 1993.

The European, (April 15–18, 1993).

U.S. Bureau of the Census, *TIGER Questions and Answers,* Sept. 1991.

J. Van Duyn, *Automated Crime Information Systems,* TAB Books, Blue Ridge Summit, Pa., 1991.

B. Vaughn, "The Use and Abuse of Intelligence Services in India," *Intelligence and National Security* **8**(1), 1–22 (Jan. 1993).

W. Ware, "Contemporary Privacy Issues," *Proceedings of the National Conference on Computing and Values (NCCV)*, Research Center of Computing and Society, Southern Connecticut University, New Haven, Conn., Aug. 12–16, 1991.

WAYNE MADSEN
Computer Sciences Corporation

PROBABILITY MODEL/OPERATIONAL PROFILE TESTING

INTRODUCTION

Software testing is the process of executing software products against a set of defined inputs to verify that product execution results in a set of predefined outputs. Testing is performed at several points in the software development life cycle by software developers, by testers, and by customers. One form of software testing, structural testing (Ntafos, 1988), is performed primarily by the software developers to verify that the implemented software matches its design. It is typically accomplished in the three steps of unit, string, and integration testing. A second form of software testing, functional testing (Howden, 1986), is performed primarily by independent testers and customers to verify that the software design and implementation deliver the required capability. Functional testing is typically accomplished with some number of qualification and acceptance tests.

The focus of this article is to address software functional testing and, in particular, the use of the operational profile method. Functional testing views the software product as a black box and is primarily concerned with verifying the correct mapping of software inputs to expected outputs (the software externals). The internal structure of the software is not explicitly addressed because that is the focus of the developer-conducted structural tests. The requirements addressed through functional testing are the functional capability of the software, its performance, its reliability, its installability, and its other operational characteristics. Essentially any product characteristic defined in a software requirements specification and of interest to the customer is considered a candidate for functional testing.

Functional testing is typically performed as a systematic process of identifying the capabilities (i.e., requirements) to be verified, creating the appropriate test materials, executing the software against those test materials, and reporting the test results. A test plan is generally created to identify which requirements within a specification are to be verified and by what verification method. Inspection, analysis, demonstration, and test are the methods from which the tester chooses. The size and complexity of a particular software development will determine the number and hierarchy of requirements specifications which are needed to scope the development effort. The test plan is further elaborated in test procedures (cases) that identify the steps to be executed in a test, the discrete data values to be used as inputs to the software, the expected output values from the software execution, and the pass-fail criteria for deciding whether the software execution was correct. These test procedures are run against the software in a predefined environment, the execution outputs are recorded, and results are summarized in the test report.

In general, it is impractical to attempt the verification of every specified requirement under every possible combination of input data. The effort to define, execute, and analyze the results from the required number of tests is prohibitive, except in a few exceptional cases, such as the testing of language compilers (Bird and Munoz, 1983). The more common challenge facing the tester is how best to select or sample the requirements and software input data to organize test procedures which verify the software implementation to an acceptable level of confidence. The sheer number of requirements and the number of discrete tests which should be run to verify an individual requirement present significant challenges to the functional tester.

Typically, the requirements with which the tester must verify come, initially, from the customer's statement of work (SOW), are refined and expanded in the vendor's proposal, and are finalized after contract award in requirements specifications. Data from an aircraft system development (Dyer, 1992) illustrates the numbers problem that can be encountered in this process of requirements discovery for medium- to large-sized software systems. In the particular customer's SOW a requirement was identified for an avionics subsystem to provide the aircraft's electronics capability. Within the subsystem, flight software would provide the interface between the various aircraft systems and the flight crew. Some dozen components within the flight software were also identified, one of which was the navigation component for which 16 discrete requirements were identified. At proposal time the requirements for the navigation component were further refined and resulted in the identification of 250 discrete requirements. With the completion of the software requirements specification for the flight software, the number of discrete requirements reached 459.

In the test process, procedures are defined to execute the software which implements specific requirements. Appropriate problem data must be used by these procedures, which requires an analysis of the problem data domain. This analysis differentiates legal and illegal data values, identifies subsets of frequently used values, and uncovers relationships and dependencies between data values. The total human effort that is needed to define, execute, and analyze the results for a single test procedure is typically measured in terms of hours (e.g., 2–4 hours). When that per-procedure effort is matched against the total number of requirements for a product, the resulting test effort can be significant. In the case of the navigation component, the effort for a single test of each requirement would require some 250–500 hours (roughly 6–12 weeks). This is not an attractive prospect since something better than a single test per requirement is generally required and the navigation software accounts for a small fraction of the total system requirements in this case.

To alleviate this problem, some form of sampling must be introduced to select the contents (requirements and data inputs) for the functional test procedures. Two approaches have been defined which can be loosely classified as either deterministic or statistical. In the deterministic approach, test data is selected through a systematic analysis of the requirements specification and/or the software design and implementation. A variety of domain partitioning and data flow analysis methods have been defined to support the deterministic approach. In the statistical approach, test data is randomly selected based on probability distributions defined across the test input domain. Surveys of functional methods for software testing (Beizer, 1983; Coward, 1990) indicate that most research has focused on the deterministic approach.

STATISTICAL TESTING OVERVIEW

Statistical methods for software testing (Duran and Ntafos, 1984; Ince and Hekmatpoor, 1984) have been discussed in the technical literature, but the literature has generally focused on software structural testing. The reported statistical methods generate test procedure contents by a random sampling of what is considered a uniformly distributed set of input data values. In the reported experience, the methods for this random test procedure generation compared favorably with other structural test methods (e.g., branch and path testing) in terms of their coverage of the program structure.

More recently, statistical methods have been introduced into functional testing. In this case, the random sampling is not uniform but is driven by probability distributions that are defined across the requirements and data input domains. These methods rely on the probability distributions for defining profiles on the use of the software capabilities (requirements) and the associated input data during software operation.

The cleanroom software development research (Dyer, 1992a) was the first reported attempt to base functional testing on statistical methods that generated representative samples of software usage. In the cleanroom case, functional testing based on operational profiles was defined to ensure a statistical test environment for making reliability projections in terms of software mean time to failure (MTTF). The underlying objective of the cleanroom method is to develop and certify software products with known MTTF reliability.

A subsequent comparison of testing strategies (Ehrlich, Emerson, and Musa, 1988) for use in software reliability measurement also reported benefits from test strategies based on operational profiles. The reported study was a simulation analysis of the testing of different usage patterns of the Unix system. The use of different test strategies was simulated to determine which were effective in achieving reliability growth in the software. A strategy based on operational profiles and one based on straight random sampling proved to be the more effective.

A Markov Chain technique has been recently introduced (Whittaker and Poore, 1992) for estimating operational profiles directly from the software requirements and design. A usage analysis is conducted to establish the set of usage states within the software and the ordering of this set. Analytical stopping rules are identified for determining when sufficient testing has been conducted, and a discrete software reliability model is defined which does not require assumptions about the distribution of failures within the software. This method would be particularly effective when no data exists on software usage (historical or projected) from which to construct distributions.

Statistical testing methods have also been identified for testing the general class of fault tolerant software (Thevenod-Fosse, 1988). In this case, statistical testing is shown to be effective for both error removal and error forecasting, with a role suggested for deterministic testing to ensure satisfactory requirements coverage. Statistical methods have also been identified for the testing of multiple equivalent versions of software (Vouk, 1990), with the potential of offering an approach to analyzing expected outputs for large volumes of tests. More recently, the use of statistical techniques has been reported in a robust testing experiment (Brownlie, Prowse, and Phadke, 1992), using orthogonal array ideas from the Taguchi method (Taguchi and Konishi, 1987). An orthogonal array tool was developed which helped to convert product requirements from specifications into a concise set of tests, which represented a smaller but more effective test sample than available with deterministic sampling techniques.

AN OPERATIONAL PROFILE TESTING METHOD

The first reported (Mills and Dyer, 1981) use of a statistical testing method based on operational profiles was as part of the cleanroom software development methodology (Dyer, 1992). A three step process was used which involved (*1*) defining probability distributions on the use of the software functions and software inputs, from an analysis of operational requirements; (*2*) encoding the probability distributions into a data base; and (*3*) generating test samples for functional testing from the database. The last two steps imply the availability of a tool for test sample generation (Gerber, 1986), which is needed for the statistical testing of software with any reasonable complexity.

The first step in this particular process starts with an analysis of the software requirements specification to gather the requirements to be verified in the functional testing. The specification analysis addresses the total set of requirements and all of the constraints, dependencies, relationships, and interactions between and among those requirements. For software products embedded in larger systems, other considerations, such as the different modes of the system operation, the system reconfiguration strategies for failure work-arounds, and the system philosophy on operation with partial capabilities, must also be addressed in the analysis. An analysis for the software requirements is always performed, regardless of whether a statistical or a deterministic approach to functional testing is used. However, the second step of requirements analysis is unique to statistical approaches and involves the identification of the probability distributions for each requirement and its associated data. Figures 1 and 2 illustrate the requirements analysis performed for the navigation component of the flight software and excerpt a set of data which is used to demonstrate the process application.

If the functions and input data for a given software product are equally likely to occur, then a uniform probability distribution would be defined for all selection of test procedure contents. This is a very unlikely case but is also the one which is mistakenly interpreted to characterize all sampling strategies for statistical testing. This uniform

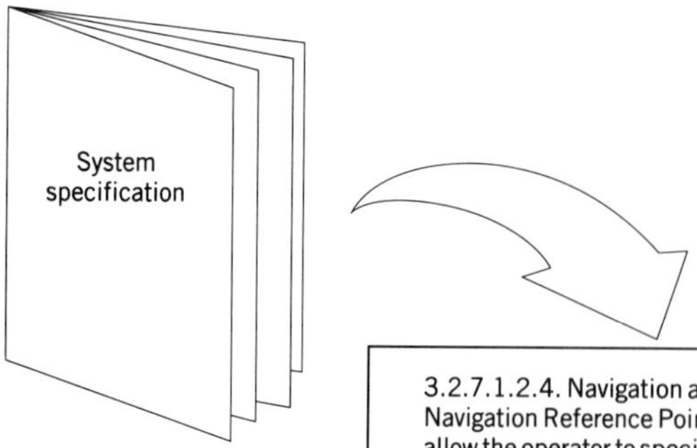

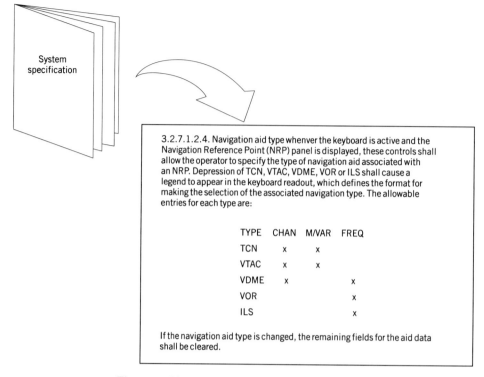

3.2.7.1.2.4. Navigation aid type whenever the keyboard is active and the Navigation Reference Point (NRP) panel is displayed, these controls shall allow the operator to specify the type of navigation aid associated with an NRP. Depression of TCN, VTAC, VDME, VOR or ILS shall cause a legend to appear in the keyboard readout, which defines the format for making the selection of the associated navigation type. The allowable entries for each type are:

TYPE	CHAN	M/VAR	FREQ
TCN	x	x	
VTAC	x	x	
VDME	x		x
VOR			x
ILS			x

If the navigation aid type is changed, the remaining fields for the aid data shall be cleared.

Figure 1. Identifying the navigation requirements.

distribution is not appropriate for describing most situations in which software is involved, since the software was introduced to handle the variability in the system operation.

For software functional testing, the goals of the testing effort must be clearly established at the outset since they dictate the basis for the probability distributions. In the cleanroom work (Dyer, 1992a), the goal is certifying the reliability of the software product, so probability distributions should provide a picture of the operational usage of the product. In another case the goal might be determining software adequacy within a safety-critical application or its adequacy in handling the performance drivers within a particular application. Operational usage would not be

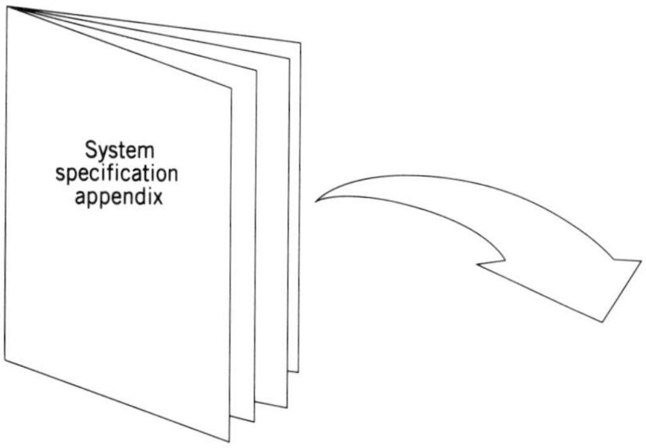

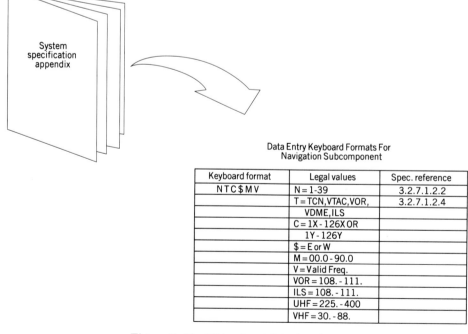

Data Entry Keyboard Formats For Navigation Subcomponent

Keyboard format	Legal values	Spec. reference
NTC$MV	N = 1-39	3.2.7.1.2.2
	T = TCN, VTAC, VOR,	3.2.7.1.2.4
	VDME, ILS	
	C = 1X - 126X OR	
	1Y - 126Y	
	$ = E or W	
	M = 00.0 - 90.0	
	V = Valid Freq.	
	VOR = 108. - 111.	
	ILS = 108. - 111.	
	UHF = 225. - 400	
	VHF = 30. - 88.	

Figure 2. Identifying input data domains.

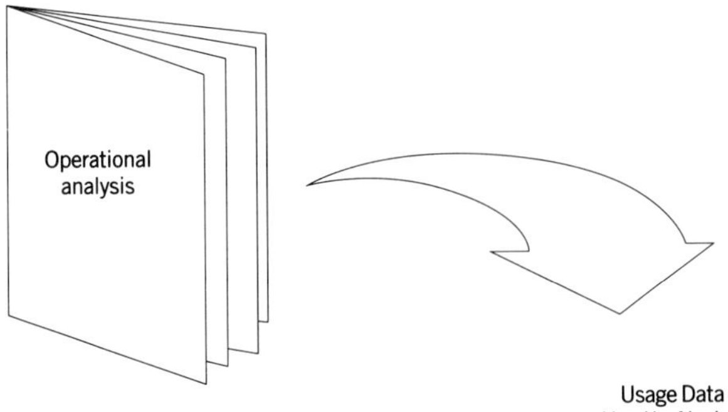

Usage Data on Display Panel
Used by Navigation Subcompent

Uses/Mission	Function key	Processing
80	L1	Next NRP
80	L2	Previous NRP
16	L3	TCN selection
16	L4	VTAC selection
16	L5	VDME selection
16	L6	VOR selection
16	L7	ILS selection
80	L8	Control exit

Figure 3. Defining the probability distributions.

the correct perspective in these cases, where safety incidents and stress loads would be more appropriate probability drivers. In many cases there may be different goals to be achieved, which would require the definition of a family of probability distribution.

All the information for developing probability distributions is generally not contained completely within the software requirements specification but must be extracted from other project-documentation which deals with the software's operating environments. Figure 3 shows the frequency data that was used in creating probability distributions for the navigation component. In this particular application, the flight software was activated by pilot actions through a keyboard/display device. Programmable function keys were displayed to the pilot through a series of display panels that would allow access to all of the avionics systems functions. Probability data was determined by considering the frequency at which panels and their function keys were accessed during the aircraft's different missions. The frequency data was normalized into function key "uses per mission" to define the probabilities for function execution and data value usage within the aircraft's mission envelope. In the illustrated case (Figure 3), there would be some probability for the navigation component panel appearing and, when that panel was displayed, some probability for using each of the programmable function keys. The uses/mission data give the function key probabilities, and probabilities associated with panels appearing would be a composite of the function key actions necessary on a succession of panels to have the navigation panel accessed. The particular system initializes and resets to a standard panel configuration.

The second step in the statistical test process is converting the probability distribution data into a form that is convenient for test procedure generation and also acceptable to a test generation support tool (Gerber, 1986). In the cleanroom work, a tool was built to support the generation of test procedures. A list notation was defined for describing the function definitions, the data definitions and the data relationships and a minimal set of terminal, macro, and pseudo commands were invented to support the data encoding. The pseudo commands provided operations on members of lists, the macros supported navigation through the sets of list definitions, and the terminals permitted the formatting of test procedures to meet the specific requirements of a given application. The particular generator tool provided many test functions, the first of which was organizing a database for the list notation that defined the skeletal form of the test procedure. The data on probability distributions was also encoded within the skeletons to simplify and speed up the subsequent test procedure generation.

Figure 4 gives a snapshot of the database encoding which supported the functional testing of the navigation component of the flight software. In the illustration two skeletons (NAV Panel Selection and NAV Panel Candidates) reflect the paths taken through the database to get to the function to be tested (TCN Selection Options). The first two skeletons identify various options within panels (reflecting uses/mission probabilities), which can be taken when navigating through the data base.

The third step in the statistical test process is the generation of realistic and representative test procedures. With the test generator tool, test procedures are created by sequencing through the database for a particular software product and selecting skeletons with filled-in contents of representative operational data. Both the skeleton selection and their data content are randomly determined based

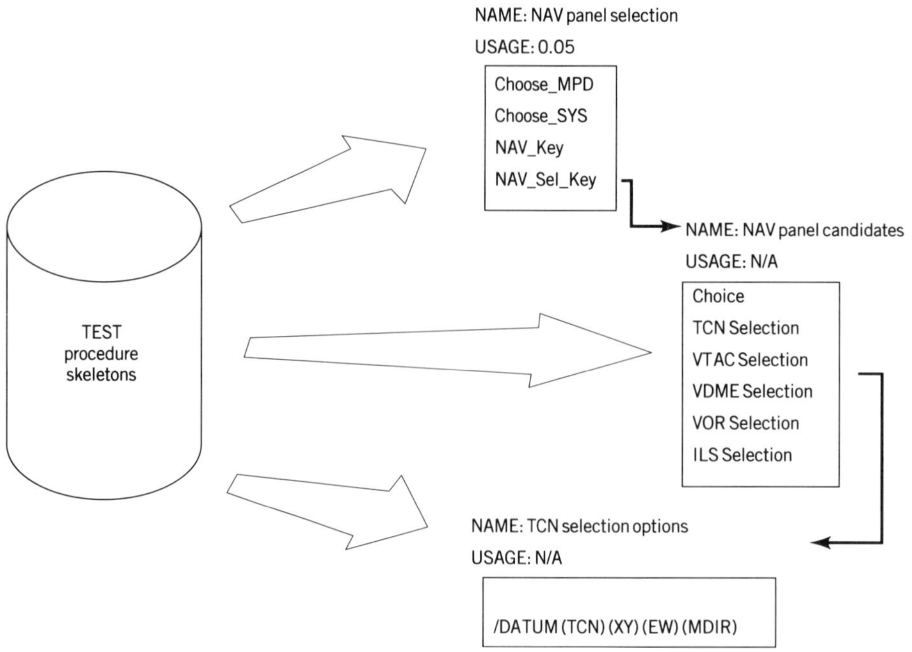

Figure 4. Encoded database content.

on the probability distribution information encoded in the database. Table 1 gives a sample test procedure for the navigation component testing, where the initialization and verification steps within the test procedure are created with representative usage data and in the proper display/keyboard formats. As discussed earlier, the pilot navigates through a series of display panels to activate the software functions. In the illustrated case, the test procedure is attempting to verify that the TCN navigation aid with appropriate settings can be selected by the pilot. The last two steps in the procedure would perform this selection, through the appropriate programmed function key (PF Key) action and keying the settings (i.e., 086 X). The first three steps in the procedure simulate a path that the pilot could take in getting the navigation panel on a display to make the TCN selection. Again, this is accomplished through a series of function key actions.

AUTOMATION (CASE) SUPPORT

The test case generator developed for the cleanroom method (Gerber, 1986) is a menu-driven editor that supports the entry of definitions and probability data for test skeletons. The skeletons for a particular software product are organized into a database from which representative operational test samples are generated. Standardized formats and a table-driven design were used within the generator in order to accommodate most software test applications.

The functions of the generator are interactive construction of test skeleton data bases and the automatic creation of representative test samples. The processing flow for the particular generator (Gerber, 1986) is shown in Figure 5. Three primary editing functions are available to the user in organizing a test skeleton database:

- Adding new test skeletons
- Updating existing test skeletons
- Updating input data definitions.

A report generation feature is also selectable, which allows on-line browsing and/or hardcopy printing of the database for a particular software product. Selection of the test generation function results in the automatic generation of a test sample for the particular software product. User selection of run-time overrides is supported for changes to

Table 1. Randomly Generated Test Procedure for TCN Requirement in Navigation Component

Case	Selected actions	PF key	Expected result	Comments
1	1. copilot display			start with copilot display
	2. hit IR key	T1	get initial panel	callup IR menu to
	3. hit NRP key	R5	NRP panel selected	select NRP
	4. hit TCN key	L3	TCN selected	select TACAN AID
	5. enter 086 X		channel selected and tuned.	supply channel data

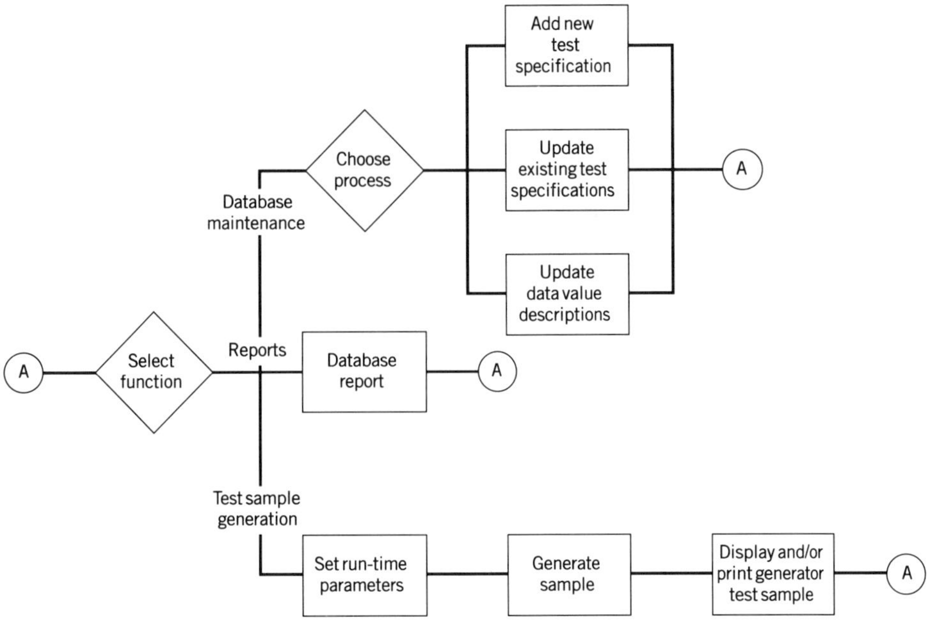

Figure 5. Test generator flow.

database probabilities, hardcopy headings, and the seed for the random number generator.

As shown in Figure 6, the generator was implemented as three separate PL/I programs, which total some 2,500 PL/I statements. An additional 1,000 PL/I statements were required for utility routines to handle report preparation, data conversions, and random number generation.

STATISTICAL TESTING EXPERIENCE

The particular statistical test method (Dyer, 1992a) and its test generation tool (Gerber, 1986) have been used in a dozen different application areas, including the testing of the generator itself. In each case, the test personnel were able to identify probability distributions for the re-

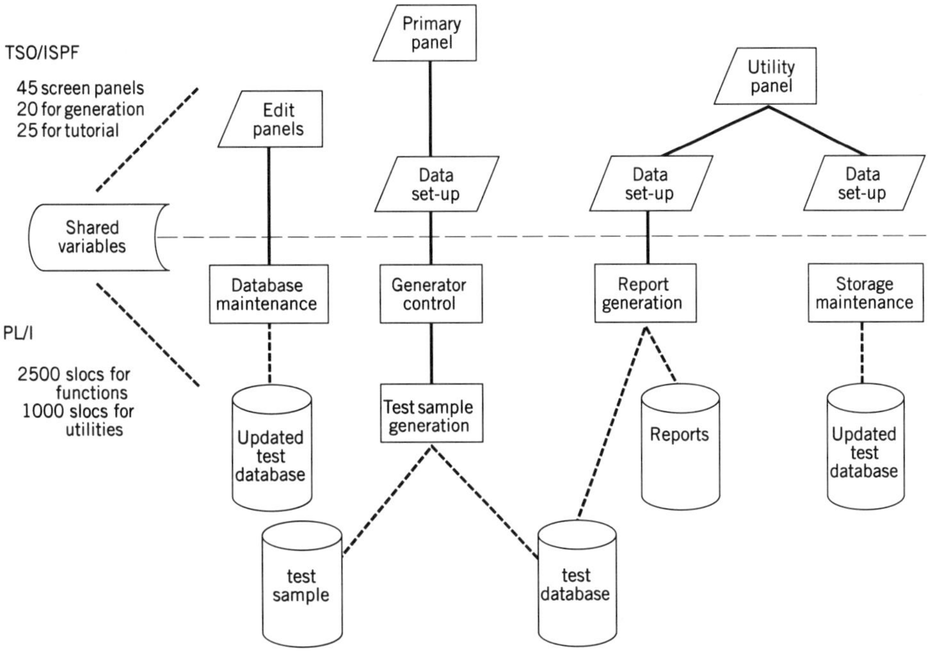

Figure 6. Test generator implementation.

quirements to be verified. The information was efficiently encoded into a database from which realistic and representative tests procedures were generated. The operational profiles for embedded software within avionics, surveillance, and space applications presented additional challenge to the testers. The method still proved effective in these applications with inherent system complexity, environment constraints, and heavy interaction with human operators.

Statistical test methods, while not widely used in functional testing, provide a more formal and objective basis for verifying the correctness of a product and for mitigating risks in product release. The underlying concerns with statistical test methods have arisen from a perception of significant technical complexity and from a misapprehension on test coverage completeness. The complexity concern stems from the challenge of defining the operational profile and from the need to compute expected outputs for randomly generated inputs.

Defining probability distributions is definitely a new task for testers and is work that cannot be performed without support from other engineering disciplines. In many software developments, performance and loading analyses are typically performed with models (prototypes) that assess the adequacy of the proposed problem solution. The inputs that drive these analyses (function execution, input traffic, operational scenarios, etc.) are exactly the data needed for statistical testing. The testers have a new role of working with systems engineers, operational analysts, and customers to define the distributions that reflect the planned usage of the software. This analysis of distributions does introduce additional resource requirements but, if viewed as an extension of the loading and performance analysis, should not introduce additional development complexity.

To define the expected outputs for each test procedure in order to decide the success of the test execution is a normal test responsibility. Computing these outputs may require various levels of analyses, from simple pencil and paper calculations to complicated mathematical simulations. When using deterministic methods, the tester has the liberty of selecting input values for which output values are known or can be readily defined. When using statistical methods, the input values are randomly selected by a generator tool, and the calculation of expected outputs will require more effort. Computing the test outputs is the price that must be paid for introducing realism into the test procedures. The full impact of this effort depends on the problem complexity and on the nature of the expected output for a pass/fail determination (i.e., an on/off light indication versus satellite coordinates to six decimal point precision).

The coverage concern arises from a misconception of the application of statistical methods to functional testing. It is not the case that test inputs are randomly selected based on a uniform distribution (each test input is as likely to occur as any other), which will produce haphazard, large, and costly test samples. It is the case that the statistical methods (Dyer, 1992; Ehrlich, Emerson, and Musa, 1988; Whittaker and Poore, 1992; Thevenod-Fosse, 1988; Vouk, 1990) for software testing define requirement and input data selection as directly controlled by probability distributions which reflect a best understanding of the software's operational use. No problem with requirements coverage has materialized in the existing experience with the use of the statistical testing method embodied in the cleanroom technique (Dyer, 1992).

A concern related to using probability distributions in test has been raised as to whether only requirements and input values with higher probabilities will be selected. The concern is that many requirements and input values which are significant to the application but statistically insignificant may go unselected and untested. It is the case that items with low probability are less likely to be selected, but that does not preclude their consideration within the test program. Whenever there are items which are critical in some application sense, special consideration is required. In the flight software example (Dyer, 1992), there were many flight situations which, if they arose, would be life threatening (e.g., loss of propeller blades). While the probability of these situations occurring is very unlikely, it would be foolhardy not to include these situations within the testing, prior to system delivery. A fault tree analysis is a useful tool for characterizing the life threatening situations and their likelihoods of occurring. A separate probability distribution for this subset of requirements and input values should be created for testing the system from a safety rather than a reliability perspective. Using a probability distribution approach ensures both objectivity and rigor in the testing from these special interest perspectives.

BIBLIOGRAPHY

D. Bird and C. Munoz, "Automatic Generation of Random Self-Checking Test Cases," *IBM Systems Journal* **22**(3), (1983).

B. Beizer, *Software Testing Techniques,* Van Nostrand Reinhold Co., Inc., New York, 1983.

R. Brownlie, J. Prowse, and M. S. Phadke, "Robust Testing of AT&T PMX/StarMAIL Using OATS," *AT&T Technical Journal,* May/June 1992.

P. D. Coward, "Software Testing Techniques," *The Software Life Cycle,* Butterworth & Co. Ltd., Kent, UK, 1990.

J. W. Duran and S. C. Ntafos, "An Evaluation of Random Testing," *IEEE TSE SE* **10,** (July 1984).

M. Dyer, *The Cleanroom Approach to Quality Software Development,* John Wiley & Sons, Inc., New York, Jan. 1992a.

M. Dyer, *IBM FSC Technical Report #86-9209, Statistical Approaches to Software Testing,* Apr. 1992b.

W. K. Ehrlich, R. J. Emerson, and J. Musa, "Effect of Test Strategy on Software Reliability Measurement," in *Proceedings of the International Research Conference on Reliability,* 1988.

J. J. Gerber, *IBM TR 86.0008, Cleanroom Test Case Generator,* 1986.

W. E. Howden, "A Functional Approach to Program Testing," *IEEE TSE* **12** (10), (1986).

D. Ince and S. Hekmatpoor, *UK Open University TR 84/7, An Evaluation of Some Black Box Testing Methods,* 1984.

S. C. Ntafos, "A Comparison of Some Structural Testing Strategies," *IEEE TSE* **14**(6), (1988).

H. D. Mills and M. Dyer, *Cleanroom Approach to Reliable Software Development,* Research Triangle Institute Report, Research Park, North Carolina, Nov. 1981.

G. Taguchi and S. Konishi *Orthogonal and Linear Graphs*, American Supplies Institute (ASI) Press 1987.

P. Thevenod-Fosse, Statistical Testing of Software: A Survey, LAAS Research Report No. 88-355, Dec. 1988.

M. A. Vouk, "Using Back to Back Testing for a Regression Test and Porting," in *Proceedings of the Testing Computer Software Conference,* June 1990.

J. A. Whittaker and J. H. Poore, "Statistical Testing for Cleanroom Software Engineering," in *HICSS-25 Proceedings,* Jan. 1992.

MICHAEL DYER
IBM Federal Systems Company

PROBLEM STATEMENT LANGUAGE/ PROBLEM STATEMENT ANALYZER

INTRODUCTION

The Problem Statement Language (PSL) and the Problem Statement Analyzer (PSA) were first described in 1971 (Teichroew and Sayani, 1971). PSL™ was introduced in that paper as the equivalent of a blueprinting language for an information systems "factory," and PSA™ as the software to support its usage. This first version (1) was used mainly by the sponsors of the Information Systems Design and Optimization System (ISDOS) project at the University of Michigan. A more widely introduced version, 2. 1, was described in an IEEE paper in 1977 (Teichroew and Hershey, 1977).

Our goal in this article is to describe PSL/PSA, to lend a perspective to the chances that have taken place in the PSL/PSA system over 15 years, to examine its acceptance by the information systems community, to portray a scenario of usage, and to comment on the trends in the industry that not only affect PSL/PSA but also similar productivity tools that are now becoming available in the industry.

DESCRIPTION OF PSL/PSA

Problem Statement Language

PSL is based on the concept of the Entity-Relationship-Attribute (ERA) model, although at the time of its design the ERA terminology had not been coined. PSL's underpinnings allow up to four Entity-types to participate in a Relationship. Entities may have Attributes and may play roles in a relationship. Because these relationship-roles are not formalized, they cannot have Attributes assigned to them.

The designers of PSL felt that a specification language user must be supplied with constructs appropriate for the task at hand. Therefore, PSL has a set of predefined classes of Entities (e.g., PROCESS, INPUT, ELEMENT, EVENT), Relationships (e.g., EMPLOYS, UPDATES, TRIGGERS), Attributes (e.g., TRACEKEY) and a set of rules (the constructs of the language) which permit only prescribed combinations. One can think of PSL/PSA, therefore, as an application built on top of a generalized Entity Relationship Attribute Management System (ERAMS) with a predefined data definition. However, many of the reports produced by PSA do have semantic knowledge of PSL, e.g., the Contents Reports recognizes Completeness in the context of PSL's data structuring features.

PSL has three levels of formality to describe a system:

- Very formal: using only predefined Entity-types and Relationships
- Semiformal: adding user-defined properties
- Informal: attaching free form text to entities.

This three-level approach offers users controlled extensibility of the language while still providing the functionality of PSA.

PSL has about 19 Entity-types and about 100 Relationship-types. It helps in understanding PSL to group the types by the "aspect" of system description. Figure 1 summarizes these aspects. Some PSA reports work at the lower granularity of Entities and Relationships while others require the specification of the higher granularity of aspects.

PSL statements are written in free-form and recognized by keywords. Examples of these will be shown later.

Problem Statement Analyzer

PSA is the software package that manages PSL statements. It can be thought of as a data-based application with the following categories of functionality:

- The *modification* of the database, including the updating and changing of its contents. The database is modified without compromising the integrity of the underlying language.
- The *display* of information in the database as predesigned reports; the display, feature includes an ad hoc query system.
- The *analysis* of information in the database, this analysis focuses on errors of omission and on the production of numeric and cross-referenced summaries.
- It permits *control* of the PSA environment.

The actual commands, summarized by these categories, are described in Figure 2.

The core architecture of PSL/PSA is summarized in Figure 3.

PSA may be used with varying degrees of interaction. The major modes are:

- *Interactive:* PSA commands typed at the terminal and PSA prompts, error messages, and reports received on the terminal.
- *Batch:* PSA executing commands from a file containing a sequence of commands and without prompting; writing error messages and reports to a file or designated printer.
- *Monitored:* similar to batch mode but echoing the commands being executed and displaying messages on the terminal.

- Aspects Applicable to All Principal PSL Objects:
- *Properties and Characteristics*
  - parametric (user extensible) and textual
- *Project Management*
  - provides cross-reference and assignment of definitional responsibilities
- *Requirements Traceability*
  - allocation of requirements to specific components

Information Flow Aspects:
- *System Boundary and Input/Output Flow*
  - shows how the system exchanges data with its environment
- *Data Derivation and Flow*
  - depicts transformation of data within the system
  - allows specification of "right to know"

Architectural Aspects:

- *System Structure*
  - architectural relationships between major components
- *Data Structure*
  - detailed relationships between data objects
  - includes architectural, relational (as in ERA) and security

Behavioral Aspects:
- *System Dynamics*
  - response of system to recognized happenings, changes in situations, and time triggers
- *System Control*
  - shows precedence of Processes and their invocation by others

Performance Aspects:
- *Quantification and Resource Usage*
  - addresses performance and size related specifications

Project Convenience Aspects:
- *Generic Structure*
  - makes it convenient to group, link, or name objects in an ad hoc fashion.

Figure 1. Facets of systems development with appropriate aspects provided by PSL

Modification Commands

CHANGE NAME
CHANGE NAME TYPE
COMBINE
DELETE NAME
DELETE TEXT ENTRY

INPUT LAYOUT
LANGUAGE PROCESSOR

PROBLEM NAME
REPLACE TEXT ENTRY

Analysis Commands

ACCESS RIGHTS ANALYSIS
ASSERTION CONSISTENCY
CONTENTS ANALYSIS
CONTENTS COMPARISON
DATA ACTIVITY INTERACTION
DYNAMIC INTERACTION
ELEMENT PROCESS ANALYSIS
ELEMENT PROCESS USAGE
IDENTIFIER ANALYSIS
RESOURCE CONSUMPTION ANALYSIS
SUBSET ANALYSIS
UTILIZES ANALYSIS

Display Commands

ACTIVITY FLOW DIAGRAM
ATTRIBUTE
CONTENTS
DATA DIVISION
DATABASE SUMMARY
DICTIONARY
EXTENDED PICTURE
FREQUENCY
FUNCTION FLOW DATA DIAGRAM
KEYWORD IN CONTEXT
LAYOUT
LIST CHANGES
NAME LIST
NAME SELECTION
NETWORK
PICTURE
PROCESS CHAIN
PROCESS SUMMARY
QUERY SYSTEM
RELATION STRUCTURE
SELECTED FORMATTED STATEMENTS
STRING SELECTION
STRUCTURE
UNIT STRUCTURE
WRITE TEXT ENTRY

Control (of environment) Commands

COMMAND
DISPLAY
EXPAND
HELP
LIST
LOOP
MACRO
SET
STOP

SYSTEM

Modification Commands

CHANGE NAME
CHANGE NAME TYPE
COMBINE
DELETE NAME
DELETE TEXT ENTRY
INPUT LAYOUT
LANGUAGE PROCESSOR
PROBLEM NAME
REPLACE TEXT ENTRY

Figure 2. Summary of PSA commands by category.

Examples of PSL/PSA

Figure 4 shows a context diagram of the type suggested by the Structured Analysis Methodology (Yourdon, 1989). This diagram is a graphic specification of the top-level view of a system. The PSL statements in Figure 5 are a linguistic equivalent of the graphic.

The three "DEFINE" paragraphs, "sections" in PSL, can be specified in any order; similarly the non-DEFINE statements may be rearranged within a (DEFINE) section. These PSL statements would fit into PSL/PSA's Information Flow aspect of system specification.

Further refinement of the system, the specification of a hierarchy of functions underlying the Greenbelt-Distribution-System, would be part of PSL/PSA's System Structure aspect. The PSA Structure report would depict this as shown in Figure 6. The actual PSA command is shown just before the report output.

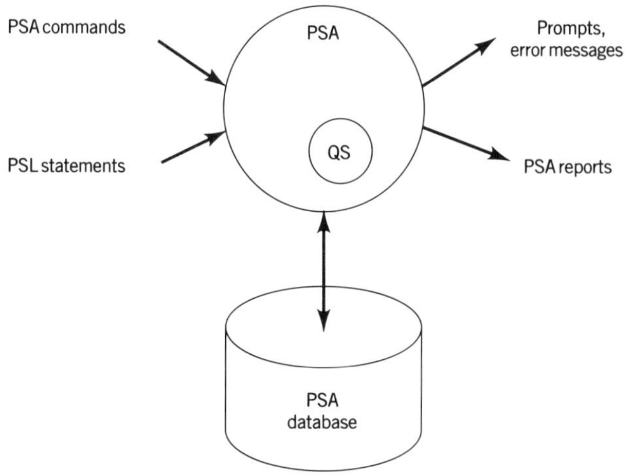

Figure 3. Core architecture of PSL/PSA.

If the Data Derivation and Flow aspect had been specified at these lower levels of refinement, it could be displayed as the Activity Flow Diagram of Figure 7.

The structure of data can also be specified, and the System Structures (macro view) and Data Structure (micro view) aspects of the system's specification is portrayed in Figure 8.

The behavior of the system can be described by PSL statements of the System Dynamics aspect. The Process-Chain Report could illustrate these specifications graphically (Fig. 9).

Entities described in the database can be selected by user-specified criteria and can be presented in an order specified through the Name Selection command as shown in Figure 10.

An encyclopedic view of any Entity can be obtained with the Selected-Formatted Statements command as shown in the italicized type in Figure 11.

Finally, a Query System permits ad hoc queries about any information in the database. Figure 12 illustrates three queries with the italics indicating the intent of the queries.

In this section we have described the architecture and capabilities of the core PSL/PSA which can play a key role in a larger environment with the addition of ancillary tools and access (bridges) to other tools. To appreciate this larger architecture, we now present a brief history of the evolution of PSL/PSA.

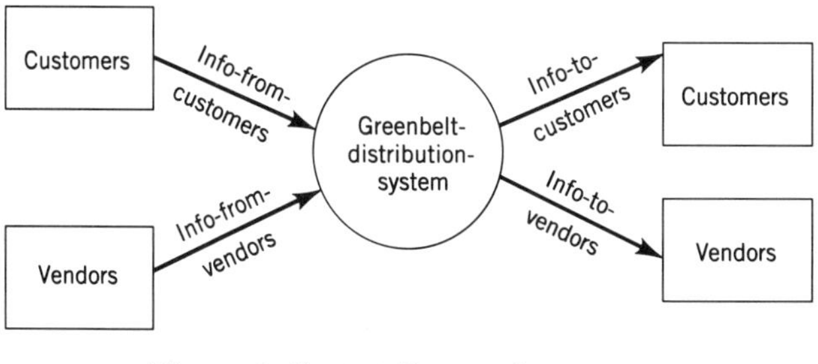

Figure 4. Context diagram for a system.

EVOLUTION OF PSL/PSA

Since its inception in 1968 at the ISDOS project at the University of Michigan (earlier work had been done by graduate students Nunamaker, Tremblay, and McCusky it Case Western Reserve University under Dr. Daniel Teichroew's guidance), PSL/PSA has evolved in response to pressures from the market. Figure 13 shows a quick snapshot of major events.

PSL/PSA was introduced before the acronym "CASE" (Computer-Aided Software Engineering) was coined. The various changes that have affected PSL/PSA are not unique and, in fact, may be a model for the evolution of many such high-technology products. In this section, we give a chronology of the versions, the organizational changes, changes in the language (PSL), the software (PSA), the advent of "add-on" tools, new interfaces to the PSL/PSA system, and the type of support available to its users.

As mentioned earlier, PSL/PSA Version 1 was introduced as a component of automated systems development (Teichroew and Sayani, 1971) envisioned by the ISDOS Project. The PSA software was designed along the lines of standard compilers, namely, it had an in-memory symbol table that was populated with appropriate attributes of objects and their relationships to other objects as these were recognized in PSL statements. The ISDOS project's underlying philosophy was that all developments be made available to supporting sponsors, which included Fortune 100 companies and various Government agencies, both civilian and DOD. Thus Version 1 was actually used on real applications. As a result of these "real world" applications, one of the first realizations was that the symbol table concept had to be replaced by a disk-based database management system (dbms). Version 2.0 included an in-house developed network-model dbms called "ADBMS." With some changes, this version of PSL/PSA became known as Version 2.1 and was introduced to a wider audience in 1974.

PSL/PSA was initially designed to capture the logical, or "essential," requirements of an Information System. However, the Electronic Systems Division of the Air Force needed to extend PSL/PSA to address physical, or "allocation," modeling. They contracted for a special version of the PSL/PSA system which in effect would have been Version 3. However, to give it organizational affinity, this version of PSL was called the User Requirements Language (URL) and PSA was called User Requirements Analyzer (URA). Major additions to URL included the concept of "Resources," and the specification of Resource Consumption by Processes. The software (URA) permitted a static analysis of the Resources that would be consumed by the proposed system based on the structure of the system and frequency with which Processes were invoked. The Air Force also needed to produce DOD documentation in approved format from the database, so the software, called the Automated Documentation System (ADS™) (Sayani, 1978) was developed to do this. URL/URA also went through some evolution from Version 3.0 through Version 3.3. The acceptance of URL/URA is an interesting story in itself! However, we will not delve into that here.

PSL Statements for Greenbelt-Distribution System

DEFINE PROCESS	Greenbelt-Distribution-System;
RECEIVES	Info-from-Customers,
	Info-from-Vendors;
GENERATES	Info-to-Customers,
	Info-to-Vendors;
DEFINE INTER-FACE	Customers;
GENERATES	Info-from-Customers;
RECEIVES	Info-to-Customers;
DEFINE INTER-FACE	Vendors;
GENERATES	Info-from-Vendors;
RECEIVES	Info-to-Vendors;

Figure 5. Context level view of a system.

Concurrent with the URL/URA development, improved Versions of PSL/PSA, 4.0 and later, 4.2, were developed and released around 1976. The enhancements made in the URL/URA Version (including ADS) were incorporated into Version 5.0 of PSL/PSA, which was introduced around 1977. Version 5.0 was followed by Version 5.2 around 1979.

Finally, in 1988, the current version, 6.0, was introduced. It includes changes in both the Language and the Analyzer. These changes will be discussed later. The 1980s also saw the development of auxiliary software designed either to improve the interface to PSL/PSA (e.g., graphic front-end) or to add new functionality (e.g., ability to design a target database from PSL specifications). This too will be described later.

structure relations=subparts name=Greenbelt-Distribution-System nostatistics - noobject-types norelation-types noline-numbers

1	Greenbelt-Distribution-System
2	accounting
3	accounts-receivable
4	prepare-customer-invoices
4	receive-customer-payments
4	review-receivables
3	accounts-payable
4	receive-vendor-invoices
4	schedule-payments
4	send-payments-to-vendors
3	general-ledger
3	process-customer-order
4	evaluate-customer-credit
4	authorize-shipment
4	send-letter-to-customers
3	reconcile-inventory
2	receiving
2	stocking
2	shipping

Figure 6. Hierarchy of the system.

The above evolution is interesting from the perspective of time taken from the germination of an idea, to its introduction, and evolution into an accepted way of doing business—over 21 years!

Changes in the Organizational Structure

Around 1983, a facet of the ISDOS project was "spun out" as a profit-making entity. ISDOS Inc. was formed in Ann Arbor, Michigan. The remaining (research) aspects of the project at the University were retitled Program for Research in Information Systems Engineering (PRISE). This change was precipitated not only by the University's dual desires of keeping the University work at a research plane and demonstrating that the University could be a good incubator, but also by pressure from users of the PSL/PSA who wanted a commercial level of support. ISDOS Inc. was organized along traditional business lines and sought to make PSL/PSA more of a commercial product than just a research/academic tool.

In 1986 Dr. Teichroew turned over operational control to Dr. Richard Welke, the Canadian distributor of PSL/PSA, who changed the name of the organization to Meta Systems, Ltd. This change brought about further restructuring of the day-to-day operations and a new version of PSL/PSA, Version 6. Special attention was also paid to updating documentation to be more thorough and comprehensive.

In today's environment of venture-funded technology development, it is interesting to note that PSL/PSA has followed a path from university research to a commercial entity without venture funding.

Changes to the Problem Statement Language (PSL)

Since the chronology of specific chances to PSL is not particularly interesting to other than those intimately, involved with PSL/PSA, we will attempt to summarize the changes that have taken place since the last article on PSL/PSA was published in the *IEEE Transactions on Software ware Engineering* in 1977 (Teichroew and Hershey).

The evolution in the language has amounted to introduction of new Entity-types, removing existing Entity-types, adding new Relationship-types, modifying existing Relationship-types, and similarly altering Attribute-types. These changes have either been requested by users, or have been introduced to support some of the structured methodologies; other changes have been influenced by work done in other phases of the information systems development life cycle, such as the need to "reverse engineer" program code (Sayani, 1988).

The decision as to which demand for language enhancement should be acceded to and which one accommodated by clever modeling has always been a delicate one. The language could range from the simplicity of using very few Entity-types to coming close to natural language (e.g., Structured Analysis uses EXTERNAL, PROCESS, DATA STORE and DATA FLOW, whereas PSL further distinguishes DATA FLOW: EXTERNAL to PROCESS is called an INPUT, PROCESS to EXTERNAL is called in OUTPUT, while a PROCESS to PROCESS DATA FLOW is called an ENTITY). PSL philosophy requires that a specifi-

activity-flow-diagram name=Greenbelt-Distribution-System

Data-In		Greenbelt-Distribution- System		Data-Out
notification-of-parts-accepted invoices from-vendors requests-to-reorder orders-from-customers payments-from-customers packing-slips-to-customers-cpy	→	accounting	→	authorizations-to-ship orders-to-vendors-copy file-on-customers
orders-to-vendors-copy packing-slips-from-vendors	→	receiving	→	notification-of-parts-accepted notification-of-parts-to-stock
requests-for-parts notification-of-parts-to-stock	→	stocking	→	responses-from- stocking requests-to-reorder file-on-parts
responses-from-stocking authorizations-to-ship	→	shipping	→	requests-for-parts packing-slips-to-customers-cpy

Figure 7. Hierarchy of Inputs, Outputs and Processes.

cation must also be communicable and this can only be achieved if the scope of the language is kept under control and is limited to few key constructs. One way to solve this communication/simplicity dilemma was introduced in Version 6, allowing the user to "SUBTYPE" instances of a particular Entity-type as another type. For example, PSL Version 6 allows a user to specify that a PROCESS at the top level will be called SYSTEM. The user can also decide to classify PROCESSes at the second level as FUNCTIONs, and those at the third level as TASKs. Hence, while the software thinks of them all as PROCESSes, they are presented to the user with user-defined designations of SYSTEM, FUNCTION, and TASK in the PSA reports. This facility is further enhanced in an interface called QuickSpec™, which will be referred to later in section 3.5.2: Non graphic Interfaces to PSL/PSA.

This works well up to a point; however, when the usage of PSL needs to be extended beyond its natural domain, the user must distort the usage of the predefined language constructs to suit the situation. It is the equivalent of using a DBMS with a predefined schema to model a situation not designed to be covered by that schema. When such distortions become intolerable, an organization may seek an alternative mechanism for modeling.

Changes to the Problem Statement Analyzer Software

In this section, we will concentrate on the changes made to PSA itself rather than describe external software that has been developed to either make it easier to use or to provide added functionality.

The utility of most software can be measured in terms of three major noneconomic characteristics: functionality, performance and user interface. If these characteristics are paired with the evolution of the usage of the software, an interesting correlation can be discovered. When CASE-type tools were first introduced, the uppermost issue was the functionality. Would they be able to model, say, a real-time system? As the tools were accepted and used on large projects, users demanded sprightly performance. Would they handle 20,000 objects in a reasonable time? Finally, as the tools were put to everyday usage by individuals who were merely doing a job, the ease of use became the issue. It is important to note also that, at any given time, there will be a mix of users, some at each of these three stages of evolution. Hence, the direction of technology evolution depends on the user-mix that the developer is willing to serve (the "market"). Limited resources may therefore be assigned to improve one or more characteristics at the expense of others.

In the last 15 years PSL/PSA has also evolved along this path. While it was housed at the University, emphasis was placed on the functionality. When it was first commercialized, performance became important. Lately, with the competition from other PC-based tools, the interface and "user friendliness" have received considerable attention as described in section 3.5: New Interfaces to PSL/PSA.

Improvement in PSA Functionality. Initially, PSA had a core of simple mechanisms to populate a database, to retrieve information from it, and to present the results in the form of a limited number of reports. As its use began to grow, there was increased demand to retrieve information in many different ways. The retrieval mechanism increased in functionality from the ability to select certain types of Entities, to selecting Entities with certain Attributes, to selecting those participating in certain Relationships. The options for this retrieval mechanism grew in an ad hoc fashion. Finally, realizing that such growth could make the retrieval mechanism very difficult to team (and support) a generalized Query System (QS™) was added. QS permitted the retrieval of instances of any Entity-type, by any Attribute, or role played in any Relationship(s).

Similarly, the reporting mechanisms also grew. First, there were requests to see the database information in specific new forms. Many of these requests were handled by increasing the functionality of existing reports with additional parameters, and designing some new reports. Next, recognizing that there was a great deal of informa-

```
structure relations=subparts name=info-from-customers nostatistics - noobject-types norelation-types nolinenumbers
1          info-from-customers
 2           payments-from-customers
 2           orders-from-customers


contents name=orders-from-customers

1 *(INPUT)       1 orders-from-customers
 1(GROUP)          2 order-form-num+date-of-order
 2(ELEMENT)          3 order-form-number
 3(ELEMENT)          3 date-of-order
 4(ELEMENT)        2 date-of-order
 5 (GROUP)         2 customer-name
 6 (ELEMENT)         3 first-name
 7 (ELEMENT)         3 middle-name
 8 (ELEMENT)         3 last-name
 9(GROUP)          2 customer-address
10 (ELEMENT)         3 customer-street-no-and-name
11 (ELEMENT)         3 mail-stop (optional)
12 (ELEMENT)         3 customer-city
13 (ELEMENT)         3 customer-state
14 (ELEMENT)         3 customer-zip
15 (GROUP)         2 order-line (repeats)
16 (ELEMENT)         3 part-number-ordered
17 (ELEMENT)         3 quantity-ordered
18 (ELEMENT)         3 description-of-part-ordered
19 (ELEMENT)         3 total-of-part-ordered
20 (ELEMENT)       2 sub-total-of-this-order
21 (ELEMENT)       2 handling-and-postage
22 (ELEMENT)       2 TOTAL-this-order
23 (GROUP)         2 credit-card-info (may-be-blank)
24 (ELEMENT)         3 type-of-credit-card
25 (ELEMENT)         3 customer-card-number
26 (ELEMENT)         3 date-of-expiration
27 (GROUP)         2 catalog-reference-number
28 (ELEMENT)         3 retail-reference-price
29 (ELEMENT)         3 retail-original-price
30 (ELEMENT)         3 retail-sale-price
31 (ELEMENT)       2 retail-price
```

Figure 8. Macro and micro view of selected input.

tion in the database, there were requests to perform certain analyses and highlight only that information that was either incomplete or potentially in conflict. Still other reports were requested to support certain methodologies. The number of reports and their parameters began to approach an unmanageable size. This coincided with some work being done on a large Navy Procurement Contract (CAEDOS, 1981) where it was mandated that the Navy requirements be modelled in PSL/PSA for accuracy, then sent out as a Request for Proposal. The traditional batch of PSA reports, or even the scripted output from the Automated Documentation System, was considered inadequate. Hence, a generalized Report Specification Interface (RSI™) was developed. This permitted the user to write a program in the Report Programming Language (RPL), which could algorithmically retrieve, manipulate, and format the results in the desired form. This mechanism allows users to design and write reports that are peculiar to their needs. It also permits users to distort PSL to suit their applications and to produce reports that reflect their view of the model. The functionality of retrieval and reporting is now essentially unlimited.

Improvement in PSA Performance. Because the research into PSL/PSA was being funded by various organizations, the ISDOS project felt obligated to produce software that ran on diverse hardware systems that the sponsors possessed. The result was that there was hardly any medium-to-large computer system to which PSA was not ported. This of course diverted finite resources to the porting and maintenance effort, distracting from improvements in the speed with which PSA could perform.

With the commercialization of PSA, some pragmatic, although not always popular, decisions were made to restrict the porting to targeted hardware systems. Improved quality control and performance were results of this policy. Underlying systems (e.g., ADBMS) were improved by rewriting code in a more modern programming language; access and storage strategies were improved. Commonality among reports was recognized and reports were consolidated, thereby reducing the size of the system and permitting additional focus on the remaining code.

Added Functionality with External Tools

One of the advantages of having a predefined set of Entities, Relationships, and Attributes that comprise a language such as PSL is that it provides a stable base for both the original developer and for third parties to write additional software, providing functionality not originally present in the software.

An example of added functionality is that of designing a database from the specifications of requirements. Two such packages were developed: one, the View Integration System (VIS™) from Meta Systems, Ltd., and LdbD™ from ASTEC in Maryland. While the two design packages had differences in philosophy, both allowed the user to take the requirements database and produce a third normal form schema to be used in the design phase.

PSL/PSA users matured in their usage of the tool from small projects with limited number of analysts, to larger teams of analysts needing to merge their separate PSA databases describing the target system. PSA has a rather straightforward way of synthesizing the statements made at various times. If the later statements do not contradict the earlier statements, they are accepted and the database enhanced appropriately. If later statements conflict, they are rejected. It is not possible to override the prior statements or to provide rules by which to accept modifications to them. The Structured Architect Integrator (SAI™), introduced by Meta Systems Ltd., has been at the leading edge in solving this dilemma. SAI can play the role of the arbiter between various users and support the data administrator responsible for coordinating the development of the PSA database.

Process-chain=customer-orders-initialization no message arrows

```
Name=customer-orders-initialization                                   Page 1 of 1


                                                               /- -PROCESS- -\
                                                               |  authorize-  |
                                                         . . . >|  shipment    |
                                                         .      |              |
@- - -EVENT- - -@       /- -PROCESS- -\      ?- - -COND- - - -?  .    \TRIG WHEN T/
|   customer-    |      |  evaluate-   |      |    good-       |  .
|   orders-ini-  |. . . . . . .> |  customer-   |. . . . . .> |  credit-risk   |. . . .
|   tialization  |      |   credit     |      |                |  .
@- - - - - - - - - - - @      \-TRIGGERED-/      ?- -CHANGED- -?    .    /- -PROCESS- -\
                                                          .      |    send-     |
                                                          . . . . >|  letter-to-   |
                                                                 |  customers   |
                                                               \TRIG WHEN F/
```

Figure 9. Behavior of a system in response to event

Many developers, tiring of having to develop every system from a blank slate, have wanted to start with an existing system, and to modify or enhance it as dictated by new requirements. Here it is convenient to have existing programs reverse engineered into PSL and to store the programs in a PSA database. REVENGG (Sayani, 1988b) is such a tool; it can accept COBOL, FORTRAN, some JCL and DBMS statements and can convert them into PSL. The designers can then manipulate this database and use it either to understand the system for maintenance purposes, or as a base for moving to the next evolutionary step in the information system.

name-selection selection='match=?customer?' order=alpha

1	customer-address	GROUP
2	customer-card-number	ELEMENT
3	customer-city	ELEMENT
4	customer-invoice-number	ELEMENT
5	customer-name	GROUP
6	customer-number	ELEMENT
7	customer-order-date	ELEMENT
8	customer-order-history	GROUP
9	customer-order-history-ytd	GROUP
10	customer-order-number	ELEMENT
11	customer-orders-initialization	EVENT
12	customer-purchase-order-number	ELEMENT
13	customer-shipment-number	ELEMENT
14	customer-state	ELEMENT
15	customer-street-no-and-name	ELEMENT
16	customer-zip	ELEMENT
17	customers	INTERFACE
18	evaluate-customer-credit	PROCESS
19	file-on-customers	SET
20	info-about-customers	ENTITY
21	info-from-customers	INPU
22	info-to-customers	OUTPUT
23	invoices-to-customers	OUTPUT
24	num-of-customer-shipment	SYSTEM-PARAMETER
25	orders-from-customers	INPUT
26	packing-slips-to-customers	OUTPUT
27	packing-slips-to-customers-cpy	ENTITY
28	payments-from-customers	INPUT
29	prepare-customer-invoices	PROCESS
30	process-customer-order	PROCESS
31	receive-customer-payments	PROCESS
32	send-letter-to-customers	PROCESS

Figure 10. All objects that deal with "Customer".

New Interfaces to PSL/PSA

The linguistic input to PSA, PSL statements, can be awkward for some users. Many prefer the pictorial interface provided by graphic tools such as DesignAid® (Nastec)

process-chain name=customer-orders-initialization nomessage arrows

selected-formatted-statements name=info-about-customers

```
DEFINE ENTITY    info-about-customers;
 /* DATE OF LAST CHANGE - Jul 10, 1989, 13:22:21 */
 SYNONYMS ARE: cust-info;
 DESCRIPTION;
Contains key customer information and year-to-date order history.
;
 KEYWORDS ARE: 'Marketing Info';
 RESPONSIBLE-PROBLEM-DEFINER IS:
              'Kaisler Hudson Solomon';
 SOURCE IS: 'interview with BWT, 8-22-85';
 COLLECTED IN: file-on-customers;
 CONSISTS OF:
   customer-name,
   customer-address,
   customer-number,
   credit-line,
   principal-contact,
   customer-order-history-ytd;
 IDENTIFIED BY: customer-number;
 SECURITY IS: 'Organization Security';
 CARDINALITY IS:
              300;

EOF EOF EOF EOF EOF
```

Figure 11. Encyclopedic report about a selected object.

Find all Processes that produce data but do not take any in.
Set Name: ** not defined **
Query: PROCESS and ? DERIVES ! and not ? EMPLOYS !
The Number of Objects is: 3
The Objects are:

Object Name	*Object Type*
prepare-customer-invoices	PROCESS
receive-customer-payments	PROCESS
review-receivables	PROCESS

Find all data Elements that do not have their "type" declared.
Set Name: ** not defined **
Query: ELEMENT and not ? ATTRIBUTE type !
The Number of Objects is: 3
The Objects are:

Object Name	*Object Type*
customer-invoice-number	ELEMENT
delinquent-account	ELEMENT
valid-account-number	ELEMENT

Find the lowest level (primitive) Processes and find those that do not have Procedures (mini-specs) defined for them.
Set Name: ** not defined **
Query: PROCESS and not ? SUBPARTS ARE ! and not has PROCEDURE
The Number of Objects is: 13
The Objects are:

Object Name	*Object Type*
authorize-shipment	PROCESS
evaluate-customer-credit	PROCESS
general-ledger	PROCESS
receive-customer-payments	PROCESS
receive-vendor-invoices	PROCESS
receiving	PROCESS
reconcile-inventory	PROCESS
review-receivables	PROCESS
schedule-payments	PROCESS
send-letter-to-customers	PROCESS
send-payments-to-vendors	PROCESS
shipping	PROCESS
stocking	PROCESS

Figure 12. Checking completeness with ad hoc queries.

and Excelerator™ (Index Technology). Still other users feel that they want to be "walked through" the input process, as in an interview where a series of questions, posed in the user's terms, would elicit the information needed to produce the required PSL statements. Both of these approaches are available and will be described next.

Graphical Interfaces to PSL/PSA. The PSL/PSA family of tools now includes Structured Architect (SA™), a PC-based drawing tool that models the concepts of Structured Analysis. It also provides a set of local reports that lets the user browse through the system described by using SA. Further, it can produce output that can be synthesized through SAI (which can produce PSL statements), or can be sent directly to PSA as PSL statements.

However, by the time SA was made available, users were requesting functionality beyond its scope, namely, extensions to handle Real-Time systems, and to draw Structure Charts and Entity-Relationship Diagrams. So many users opted for other PC-based graphics packages such as Design-Aid or Excelerator (/RTS) even though they recognized the advantage of using PSL/PSA to synthesize the work products of these tools. ASTEC has developed bridges between these front-end tools and PSL/PSA to accommodate these users. Some of these bridges have been one-way (going from the graphic tool to PSL/PSA) and others have been two-way (also going from PSL/PSA back to the graphic tool).

Nongraphic Interfaces to PSL/PSA. EntrySpeed™ was developed by ASTEC to allow casual users to specify a system by answering queries. Entryspeed questions can follow any of several different methodologies. The user's responses to questions can be represented to the user as text, or PSL can be generated from them. By having the user respond to questions posed in a familiar language, any contorted use of PSL/PSA is hidden. This technique also permits the application of a standard "style-sheet" for the usage of PSL/PSA.

Similarly, PSA-SA was developed by (then) ISDOS Inc. It could also produce a packet of reports designed especially for the interface.

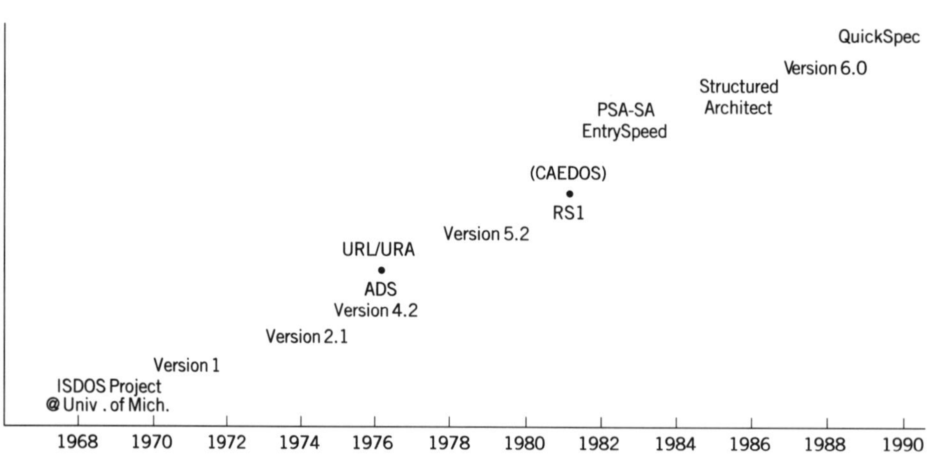

Figure 13. Evolution of PSL/PSA. Scale approximate.

Neither of these interfaces is being promoted very aggressively. Nor have users appreciated that such interfaces are particularly suited to the casual user. Although expert users often prefer to write PSL statements directly, users who have been away from PSL for a while could easily reorient themselves using this interface until they achieve their previous level of proficiency.

QuickSpec, a current product of Meta Systems Ltd., takes advantage of the Windows environment of MS-DOS. It allows the user to import a selected portion of a central PSA database, presented in the user's terms through a filter provided as part of Quickspec. The user can browse, modify, or add information and export data back to the central database.

Finally, reverse engineering output is another non-graphic way to populate PSA databases. With the use of a two-way bridge to a graphic front end, this information may now be examined graphically if desired. An example of a software engineering environment, including the tools described above, is discussed later.

Support of PSL/PSA Users

In the early days of PSL/PSA in the University of Michigan, the users (sponsors) received enthusiastic if eccentric support from the ISDOS Project. There was one standard course that was essentially a vendor dump of everything that PSL/PSA could do.

When the author cofounded ASTEC in 1978, an extensive set of courses, seminars, and workshops was developed for various audiences at various levels. Instructors have been available as consultants and also undertake to perform contractual services by using the PSL/PSA family of tools, and there is an annual conference sponsored by Meta Systems, Ltd. to discuss new developments, to suggest improvements, and to share experiences in the use of the PSL/PSA family of tools.

ACCEPTANCE OF PSL/PSA

An organization can be said to have accepted a technology when it employs that technology as its normal way of doing business (i.e., all work in that area is performed by using that technology and the loss of this technology would cripple their capability for work). Using this definition of acceptance, the PSL/PSA family of tools has not been widely accepted. There never was a "band wagon" (such as, for example, for Object-Oriented Design) and most users embraced its usage almost reluctantly, often because their clients required it. That is not to say that organizations that geared up to bring PSL/PSA successfully into their organizations did not benefit from it. Indeed, there are several large projects that function productively today because they have the PSL/PSA tool set. The recent RFP for the Reserve Component of the Army (RCAS) (U.S. Army, 1989) was presented to potential bidders in the form of a PSA database.

Most organizations do not appreciate the subtle nuances involved in technology transfer. Typically, there has to be some pressure (often the need to increase productivity) that a technology could alleviate; a receptive climate must be nurtured in the receiving organization. From the perspective of the technology vendor, the opportunity to make the technology known and to be able to aggressively promote it and support its transfer is small. In many ways, PSL/PSA suffered because of its university origins in not being widely marketed when it could have been regarded as a cutting-edge tool. Having lost that initial opportunity, the improved marketing strategies now being brought to bear are chasing after a market distracted by rapidly changing technology and buffeted by organizational myopia. PSL/PSA is being used less by application developers (commercial usage is minuscule) and more by belabored contract monitors in the government who have recognized the potential for its use in the management of various contracts.

Some of the lackluster acceptance can also be laid at the door of an immature information systems industry. For example, while methodologists frequently talk about how to accomplish the tasks of a particular phase in the development life cycle, one hears very little about how to make the transition between one phase and the next, or how to trace back to earlier work, all feasible when using PSL/PSA. Even worse, managers are not even sure what flavor of the development life cycle they should be following! Since PSL/PSA does not explicitly support any particular life-cycle development method (it expects the users to cast their methodology in PSL/PSA terms), inadequacies are ascribed to PSL/PSA, rather than to the methodologies that lack guidelines for transition between lifecycle phases.

Another roadblock to acceptance is that the use of technology such as PSL/PSA often requires a major cultural shift in the user organization. These shifts can go quite deep, into the very way the analysts and designers think about systems; such change does not occur easily. This problem, along with other distractions discussed below, have impeded the widespread acceptance of PSL/PSA.

Factors Affecting the Acceptance of PSL/PSA

Various other factors, discussed below, inhibit the acceptance of PSL/PSA, or for that matter, any similar technology.

Support of Methods. During the original design of PSL, there was much discussion as to whether PSL should be made to follow a particular strategy for building systems (e.g., top-down versus bottom-up, outside-in versus inside-out) or whether particular types of information systems should be addressed (e.g., real-time versus administrative versus data-centered). The decision made was to allow the client organization to choose its own methodology and to enable the specification of any type of information system in PSL/PSA. However, the advent of methods such as Structured Analysis has changed that perspective. Whether supporting tools such as PSL/PSA should rigidly enforce methodologies or should allow for local variations is still a subject for debate; and all the debate is delaying the performance of real work.

Influence of Platforms. The blossoming of the PC as a cheap platform (cheaper than, say, that used for CAD/CAM applications) made it feasible for many organizations to provide PCs to their analysts and designers of information systems. However, the mind set that accompanied the PC was often that of a cottage industry instead of a modern automated factory. This type of thinking and the obvious limitations of the PC have caused a great deal of turmoil in the systems departments of organizations. The arrival of "friendly" CASE tools, often no more than toys, also distracted the attention of systems developers. Seduced by the ease of usage of these tools, developers were often blind to the limitations in describing large systems or working as a group. PSL/PSA has been capable of doing both those, but has not been seriously considered, lacking the glittter of color graphics, pop-up menus and a port to the PC. Today, systems departments are struggling with the alternatives of changing from existing PCs to workstations (at a hefty expenditure) or waiting for more powerful PC operating systems. In the meantime, decisions about the selection of technology, methodology, software, etc., are deferred.

PSL Limitations. While PSL presents a good-sized set of the needed constructs in defining information systems, other constructs that are not supported (e.g., the calling sequence in a program) need to be modelled by "creative" use of the language. Hence, PSL is perceived as being a limited, hard-to-use language, although some experience with flexibly definable "cultures" does point out that too much flexibility can result in monstrously unwieldy languages. Some of the limitations in the choice of terms in PSL can be surmounted by constructs in Version 6 (the "SUBTYPE" referred to earlier) and by the use of the interface QuickSpec also described earlier.

Some limitations have more to do with how PSL/PSA has been viewed rather than how it functions. Some organizations, recognizing that PSA plays the role of a higher level (Entity as opposed to Data) management system, instead of actually using PSA, have attempted to emulate it by using tools such as relational database management systems (RDBMS). Most of these organizations have come to the conclusion that such emulations are, at best, cumbersome, very expensive to build on top of the popular RDBMS platform and still unsatisfactory to those who were not party to the development. Such attempts to develop an "emulated PSA" shift focus and resources away from the main objective of building systems. Further, the failure in developing an effective tool and in producing the target system seems to stiffen an organization's resistance to any other new tools in a backlash effect that has been observed to persist for as long as five years.

CONFIGURING A SOFTWARE ENGINEERING ENVIRONMENT WITH PSL/PSA

An organization planning to use software engineering tools would do well to configure an environment required to perform the tasks. An environment would be most viable if the organization selected methodologies and tools in a top down fashion.

First, a Life Cycle Methodology (LCM) would be picked. This methodology would describe the phases of the development process, the deliverables required of each phase and the traceability (to prior and post phases) that needs to be maintained. Ideally, the LCM would also specify how to move from one phase to the next.

Next the methodologies for individual phases would have to be picked. Here the organization would have to make sure that the products suggested by the phase-methodologies dove-tail into the requirements of the LCM.

Only after having picked the methodologies for the phases should the organization shop for tools to support the selection. This is where the organization may run into problems posed by the immaturity of the information systems industry. Products of individual tools, selected because of specific desirable features, may be difficult to consolidate into one software engineering environment. Hence, the organization should be prepared to "bridge" tools as necessary.

Finally, the organization must set standards and practices for the use of the methodologies and tools that have been chosen. Different roles and responsibilities (e.g., librarian, tool-smith, data administrator) must be defined. Appropriate training and support assistance must be acquired. When all of this is in place, one can claim to have a workable software engineering environment.

An Example of a Software Engineering Environment (SEE)

Figure 14 shows an example of a SEE with PSL/PSA as a central tool. The figure is best read in layers (rows) from top to bottom. Unshaded boxes represent the Meta System tool set; shaded boxes show some of the tools available from third parties that are usable with PSL/PSA.

The very top row of the diagram shows which methodologies are supported by the tools shown in the boxes in the second row. For example, if the organization was working in the requirements analysis phase and had picked the Structured Analysis method, all but one of the tools would be feasible (the exception being the right-most tool, REVENGG, which expects that a system already has programs written in, say, COBOL or FORTRAN).

If the user wished to use a graphics front-end, SA, DesignAid, or Excelerator (all CASE tools) would support the drawing of data flow diagrams. If the user wanted to use the recent Real-Time extensions to structured analysis, then either DesignAid or Excelerator would be appropriate. (Note: at this time there are over 50 such graphic tools; we are only picking the ones known to have viable bridges to PSL/PSA.)

Assuming that the user had picked, say, Excelerator, and had drawn diagrams on a PC or appropriate workstation, these diagrams could be analyzed, reports produced from them, and checks made for completeness. When the user teams were ready to integrate individual work into a composite, project-wide database supported by PSA, they could use XL-XPRESS to convert their local databases (on the PCs or workstations) to PSL statements.

Had SA been appropriate for the graphic front-end (i.e., no extensions needed for Real-Time), then several analysts could have been assigned portions of the work to be done on their individual workstations. This work could have been synthesized by using SAI. When there were no conflicts, SAI would be asked to generate PSL statements to

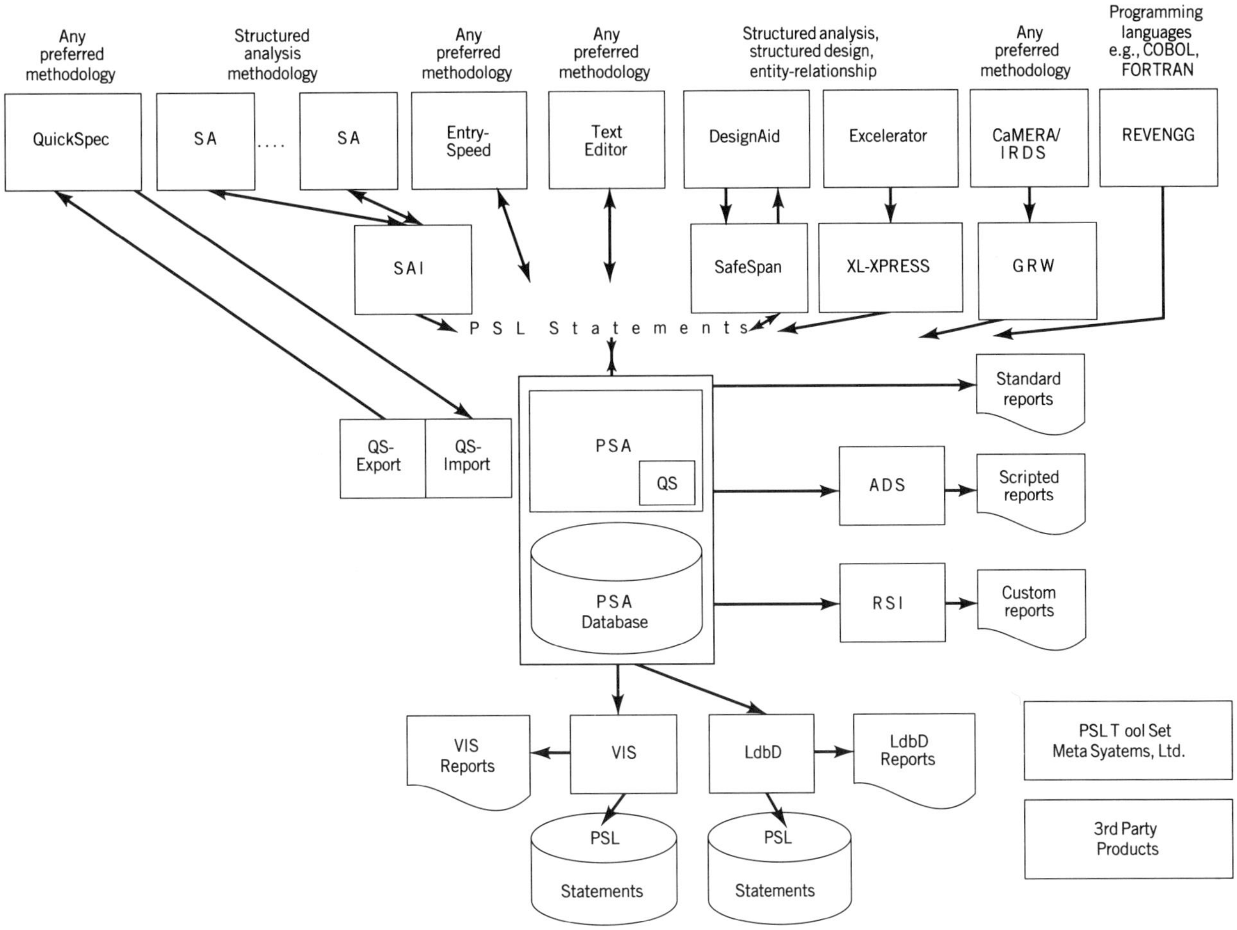

Figure 14. Software engineering environment using PSL/PSA and auxiliary tool set.

send to PSA. (Alternatively, and not shown in the figure, SA could also generate PSL statements but then there would be no adjudication of conflicts provided by SAI).

Alternatively, an organization's style may be more linguistic rather than graphic. In this case, they may opt to use a regular text editor and directly type PSL statements. Or, they might prefer to have questions asked (as in an interview) and to supply responses that would then be converted to PSL statements. In this case, they might use a tool such as EntrySpeed.

The PSL statements could be presented to PSA to populate the database. Inconsistencies among individual databases would surface at this point and would be attended to by the individual specifiers, and the translation process repeated (if appropriate) until an "error-free" (i.e., free of conflicts) PSA database was produced.

Now, the project could examine the composite PSA database for errors of omission and for disjoint components in the system specification. The PSA mechanisms that could be used include standard PSA reports, the Query System, or even customized reports by using the Report Specification Interface. An example of such a report produced for use with REVENGG does type-checking of data in calling sequences to supplement compilers that do not enforce strong type-checking. The errors could either be corrected back at the individual databases and the process repeated or the PSA modifier commands could be used to correct the database as necessary.

When the PSA database is certifiably complete and correct, the project can produce deliverable reports by using the standard reports and/or customized reports (from RSI) and can opt to embed these in a script of introductory text by using the Automated Documentation System (ADS).

Any comments obtained from the readers of these reports could be accommodated as above.

After finishing the requirements analysis phase, when the project wished to move to the design phase, they could take advantage of available tools such as VIS or LdbD to automatically generate third normal forms of relevant data found in the requirements analysis phase. The resulting design is produced in the form of PSL statements that could be used to populate the design database. Similarly, the using organization could itself program some algorithms, by using RSI, to automatically convert selected Processes found in the requirements phase to modules in the design phase.

Variations in the Classic Methodology

If the organization was working with an existing system (say, a suite of FORTRAN programs) and wished to ensure that none of the old functionality was dismissed without examination, it could choose to reverse engineer these programs into PSL statements, by using REVENGG, and could populate a database representing the system as it exists today. This database could be modified to reflect the desired changes and the development could be continued as before.

Or, if the organization were required to use the standard Information Resource Dictionary System (IRDS) (ANSIS, 1988) for one of its earlier phases and they had used a tool based on an Extended Entity, Relationship Attribute model (Sayani, 1988a), they could use its GRW interface to produce PSL statements.

Often, the methodology used by an organization is dictated by the client. For example, many applications in the Department of Defense require that the 2167A set of documents be produced. These deliverables imply both a lifecycle methodology and a set of phase-specific methodologies. Many of the popular commercial methodologies such as Structured Analysis and Structured Design are acceptable for appropriate phases. The user organization must nevertheless, develop standards and practices for the use of these methodologies and the tools to produce the deliverables. When the specification is produced in the form of PSL statements, the production of the required documents is relatively simple by using RSI and ADS.

CONCLUSIONS

Development tools appear to have come full cycle: from PSL/PSA to CASE tools to the recognition of the repository as the important component of the systems development environment. The ANS/X3H4 committee developed a standard for Information Resource Directory Systems (ANSIS, 1988). Their proposal is now a U.S. standard. Its usage in software engineering environments will be obviously encouraged. In light of its binary (as opposed to a potential four-part in PSL) model of the entity-relationship-attribute, perhaps PSL/PSA's capabilities will be appreciated.

However, issues of technology transfer persist. There are organizations standing along the sidelines waiting for the perfect tool to come along, while others flit from tool to tool hoping for the same. Neither of these problem-solving techniques promote good system development. And some small organizations do not want to make a "risky" investment until they see a universally accepted tool or some client forces them into a decision. What is needed is a concerted push for pro-active technology transfer. The time and effort required for transferring a technology, such as the PSL/PSA tool set, and institutionalizing that technology, costs as much as the initial purchase of the tools. If organizations fail to approach systems development as an engineering problem and not an art form, and fairly quickly, systems development as we know it will no longer be a viable option for impatient managers. There are several technologies, such as reuse and vertical packaging, emerging to take the place of "stick-built" custom systems.

PSL/PSA is sometimes dismissed as showing its age, although the counter could be that it has matured with experience; it has improved its user interface and there is a great deal of auxiliary software available to use with it. PSL/PSA has obvious potential as a repository and we look forward to widened interest in its use.

PSL/PSA is a registered trademark of Meta Systems, Ltd., MI.
QuickSpec, SA, SAI, ADS, RSI, VIS, and QS are Trade Marks of Meta Systems, Ltd., MI.
REVENGG, EntrySpeed, SafeSpan, XL/XPRESS, XL/XPRESS/RTS, LdbD, CaMERA, and GRW are trademarks of Advanced Systems Technology Corp. (ASTEC), MD.
DesignAid is a registered trademark of Nastec Corporation, MI.
Excelerator, Excelerator/RTS are trademarks of Index Technology Corporation (Intech), MA.
Through work in information technology consulting, ASTEC (in Greenbelt Maryland) has supported organizations in exploiting technology to build systems more productively and with improved quality; so we can look at PSL/PSA® from the perspective of someone who has worked with it in several capacities, including training, support, technology transfer, and actual usage on contracts. Also, while a faculty member at the University of Maryland, the author supported its use on the university computer system for students in the Information Systems Management Department.
This article is reprinted from IEEE, 1990

BIBLIOGRAPHY

American National Standard for Information Systems: *Information Resource Dictionary System,* (X3, 138-1988) X3 Secretariat/CBEMA, Washington, D.C., July 1988.

CAEDOS Interactive Graphics Specification: an RFP issued by the Naval Regional Contracting Office, Long Beach, Calif., Sept. 1981.

H. Sayani, "The Automated Documentation System," in *Tools for Improved Computing in the 80's,* National Bureau of Standards, Gaithersburg, Md., June 15, 1978, pp. 147–153.

H. Sayani: "Enlarging the Base for Case Tools," in *Advance Working Papers, Vol 1., Second International Workshop in Computer-Aided Software Engineering* (*CASE '88*), Cambridge, Mass., July 12–15, 1988a, pp. 6.35–6.38.

H. Sayani, "Reverse Engineering: An Aid in Understanding" in *Proceedings of the Thirteenth Annual Software Engineering Workshop,* NASA, Washington D.C., Nov. 30, 1988b.

D. Teichroew and H. Sayani, "Automation of System Building," *Datamation,* 25–30 (Aug. 15, 1971).

D. Teichroew and E. A. Hershey, III, "PSL/PSA: A Computer-Aided Technique for Structured Documentation and Analysis of Information Processing Systems," *IEEE Transactions on Software Engineering,* **SE-3**(1), 41–48 (Jan. 1977).

E. Yourdon, *Modern Structured Analysis,* Prentice-Hall, Englewood Cliffs, N.J., 1989.

US Army Information Systems Selection and Acquisition Agency, Draft Request for Proposals (DRFP) Describing the Requirements for the Reserve Component Automation System (RCAS) Project, ATTN: ISSA-ABA (RCAS), 2461 Eisenhower Avenue, Hoffman I, Alexandria, VA 22331-0700, June 1989.

HASAN H. SAYANI
Advanced Systems Technology Corp.

PROCEDURAL LANGUAGES

INTRODUCTION

This article addresses procedural, or imperative, programming languages, i.e., languages that focus the programmer's attention on the definition of algorithms, through the composition of individual commands or statements, representing elementary computational steps combined into larger units. Fine-grain composition is achieved by means of control structures, such as sequencing, selection, and iteration, and coarse-grain composition by encapsulating a composite statement within a program unit, such as blocks, functions, and procedures.

This article provides a historical view of imperative languages and starts by providing a definition of imperative programming languages. It then discusses how the development of programming languages has evolved from machine dependence to a greater orientation to the humans involved in software production, i.e., toward higher levels of abstraction. Early high level imperative languages also are covered, and data, control, and programming-in-the-large features are discussed. Modern high level imperative languages are examined, and types and newer in-the-large issues (such as exception handling, concurrency and distribution, and object-oriented decomposition) are presented.

WHAT MAKES A LANGUAGE PROCEDURAL?

The structure of conventional machines dates back to the historical model of the von Neumann computer architecture. The von Neumann architecture is based on the idea of a memory that contains data and instructions, a control unit, and a processing unit. The control unit is responsible for taking instructions out of memory, one at a time. Machine instructions are low level. Basically, they require that the data be taken out of memory, manipulated by the processing unit, and that the results be copied back to some memory cells. Conventional computers have retained the philosophical principles of the von Neumann architecture, even though there have been dramatic technological improvements in the way the architecture is implemented.

Programming a von Neumann machine by directly using its machine language is cumbersome and error prone. Moreover, programs are tightly coupled to the machine on which they are to be executed and must be reimplemented if they must be moved to a different machine. Consequently, the need arose to provide languages that supported concepts closer to those used by humans in their reasoning and linguistic constructs that were closer to those used by humans to communicate.

High level imperative programming languages were invented to meet these requirements. Although the basic philosophy of the behavior of the von Neumann machine was retained, these languages progressively provided higher levels of abstractions. That is, they moved away from the fine-grain details of the behavior of a machine by providing language features closer to human needs. The closer the language is to the humans', the higher its abstraction level. The history of language development may be described by showing its progressive evolution toward higher abstraction levels. This is the viewpoint followed in this article.

All imperative programming languages share a common conceptual approach to program design; this is often phrased by saying that they provide a common programming paradigm, or style. According to such a paradigm, programs are defined by suitable composition of elementary statements, representing elementary computational steps, through special control structures that govern the control flow through them. Computations proceed by sequences of state changes, i.e., changes in the values of the data associated with the variables, representing the abstract machine's memory. What varies from language to language is the power of statements, the kinds of data that can be manipulated, the way control structures assemble instructions together, and the way they are encapsulated into larger units.

Note, however, that there is another development stream of programming languages that does not follow the imperative paradigm. This includes functional and logical programming languages, which represent radical departures from the von Neumann architecture. In fact, they do not represent programs as step-by-step sequences of state modifications, but rather their foundations are rooted into such mathematical concepts as function theory and logic.

ABSTRACTION IN IMPERATIVE LANGUAGES

Abstraction is a key concept in computer science. It is especially useful in this context to understand and compare the different language features provided by different programming languages. Abstraction means ignoring irrelevant details and focusing attention on the main features of the phenomenon being examined. Real-life phenomena are often difficult to analyze, understand, and describe because of their complexity. Abstraction is the main conceptual tool to control such complexity.

In the case of imperative programming languages, by abstracting away from the low level details of a specific machine language, the programmer can concentrate attention on the problem being solved and better dominate the complexity of algorithm construction. This, in turn, improves program reliability. Abstractions provided by imperative programming languages may be grouped into three main categories: *data, operations,* and *control*.

In the case of data, high level imperative languages moved away from storage-level models to the higher level concepts of built-in types, data constructors, types, abstract data types, and strong typing. The initial steps of this evolution and more recent achievements are illustrated below.

Machine-level statements consist of simple data movement operations from memory to registers (and vice versa) and simple manipulation of data stored in registers. High level languages do not distinguish between data stored in registers and data stored in memory; in addition, they allow complex expressions to be written to compute new values and provide assignment statements to assign the value of an expression to a variable. Assignment statements are the basic consituents provided by high level imperative languages (input–output statements may also be viewed as assignment statements for which the source and the target, respectively, of the operation are found in the external environment). As a consequence of executing an assignment statement, the program state changes.

Hence computations proceed through sequences of state changes.

Imperative programming languages also offer a variety of schemes (control structures) to combine individual statements into larger structures. The resulting composite statements, in turn, can be combined by means of control structures to provide even more complex commands. These control structures may be referred to as control structures in-the-small, because they support the combination of elementary units (statements) by defining how control flows through them during execution.

In addition, high level imperative languages offer control structures in-the-large. Program fragments may be encapsulated into units (such as blocks, procedures, and functions), and a suitable control flow may be established among these units. Modern languages have pushed this issue even further, by defining other kinds of units and by establishing newer forms of control flow among such units. These issues are discussed below, and modularization constructs supporting exception handling, concurrency, distribution, and classes are analyzed.

EARLY HIGH LEVEL IMPERATIVE LANGUAGES

Early high level imperative languages date back to the mid-1950s and early 1960s. Among the principal achievements are Fortran, Cobol, and Algol 60. Not only were most of the fundamental concepts of imperative languages introduced by these languages but some of them, such as Fortran and Cobol, have been evolving through years and are still in widespread use. In what follows, the main features offered by these early languages will be surveyed by examing data facilities, control structures in-the-small, and control structures in-the-large.

Data Abstraction

Machine languages view data as sequences of bits that may be manipulated by the operations provided by the machine, such as shifting the binary string, complementing it, adding it to another binary string, etc. Data are accessed by addressing the cells in which their value is stored. A first abstraction level is introduced by assembly languages, which allow data to be accessed by means of a symbolic name, instead of a numeric address, and operations to be specified by mnemonic codes (such as ADD or MOVE) instead of numeric codes. Mnemonic codes and symbolic names make programs more readable. Symbolic names also make program changes easier to apply. For example, inserting a new datum or instruction does not require the existing program to be changed (e.g., by modifying the address fields of existing instructions within a sequence of statements).

High level languages push data abstraction even further by introducing the concept of data type. Machine- and assembly-level data are simply sequences of bits organized as words or bytes. On the other hand, high level languages allow programmers to refer to the data as integers, reals, strings of characters, Booleans, etc., and provide specialized operations to manipulate them. For example, arithmetic operators are provided to manipulate reals and integers, string manipulation operations are provided for strings, and logical operators are provided to manipulate Booleans.

Early high level procedural languages introduced a fixed, built-in set of data types. For example, Fortran introduced INTEGER, REAL (in simple and double precision), COMPLEX, and LOGICAL. The choice of the features provided for each language depended on the application area the language intended to address. For example, Fortran was mainly oriented to numerical applications and thus offered special features to support numerical calculus. On the contrary, Cobol was oriented to symbolic data manipulation in business applications and thus offered special features to manipulate files and handle input–output.

By introducing the notion of data type, the language abstracts away from the physical representation of the data, which is no more visible to the programmer. For example, if one knows how integer numbers are represented in binary form and how binary arithmetic works, one may choose to double an integer number by shifting its binary representation one position to the left. The disadvantages of accessing the physical representation of data are twofold. First, programs are awkward and difficult to read and understand. Second, programs are tied to a specific machine architecture. If the language provides data types, however, data are manipulated only through the high level operations defined for the type, and the implementation of the data type on a specific machine architecture is taken care by the language implementation.

The notion of data type provides the further advantage of allowing programs to be type checked statically by the translator. If a datum is defined to belong to a given data type, it may only be manipulated through the operations defined for the type. Any inadvertent incorrect access through operations not defined for the type may be caught before execution. Unfortunately, this notion is only partially supported by early high level languages.

A new generation of high level imperative programming languages was introduced in the 1960s. Among them are PL/I, Pascal, Simula 67, and Algol 68. Simula 67 and Algol 68 are historically important but are no longer in use. The use of Pascal, however, has been constantly increasing over the years. A brief assessment of the data facilities offered by Pascal is now provided.

An important feature offered by Pascal is the concept of typed pointers. Pointers were offered by other earlier languages, such as PL/I, as a mechanism to define complex data structures (such as lists, trees, and graphs). Pointers, however, have been often criticized for being a low level mechanism. For example, a PL/I pointer is just a memory address, and through it one may access any stored value in an unconstrained fashion. Thus pointers are so powerful that programmers may easily misuse them, and little or no control may be enforced on their correct use by the compiler. Pascal enforces a discipline in the use of pointers. Pointers may not be used to refer to the storage area allocated for a named variable; they may only be used to access unnamed data that are dynamically allocated. Moreover, if a pointer is declared to refer to data of type T, it is guaranteed to refer only to data of such type.

Pascal also introduced the concept of user-defined data types through the type declaration. This feature allows programmers to extend the set of built-in data types by defining new application-dependent data types. New data types are introduced by using type constructors to define a data structure and then associating a name to such data structure. Pascal data constructors include enumerations, subranges, arrays, records, sets, files, and pointers.

Once a new data type has been introduced, variables may be declared of that type. To manipulate such variables, however, it is then necessary to access the data representation. This is the most notable difference between built-in types and user-defined types. In the former case, the data representation is hidden and suitable high level operations are provided to manipulate the variables. In the latter, the representation is accessible: the user has the option of defining suitable high level operations to manipulate the data by means of procedures and functions, but access to the data is not forced to occur through such high level operations.

The next evolutionary step, in which new data types are introduced by associating operations with the newly introduced types and in which all implementation details remain hidden to the users of the type, leads to the concept of abstract data types. Abstract data types are supported by a class of modern high level imperative languages: object-oriented languages. A step in this direction is also taken by languages that offer advanced modularization facilities.

Control Abstraction

Machine language provides limited ways of expressing control flow. Instructions are executed sequentially (i.e., by successive addresses of the cells in which they are stored); if one wishes to alter the sequential control flow, an explicit jump may be used to transfer execution to the instruction stored at a specified address other than the next. Assembly languages offer the same facilities, but abstract away from the physical address of instructions. The target of a jump is a symbolic address (or label), which may be used to name the location in some meaningful way.

Since early high level procedural languages, further abstractions were provided to specify control flow among instructions. For example, in Fortran, the implicit sequential flow and the explicit control transfer (known as GOTO) were retained, but explicit structures to specify selection of alternative branches based on a test (IF statement) and iteration (DO statement) were also provided.

In the late 1960s, seminal research studies laid the foundations of the field of programming methodologies, and programming languages were critically evaluated in the light of their support of a disciplined approach to programming. Programs written by using GOTOs as a main mechanism to structure control flow (the so-called spaghetti programs) were shown to be hard to understand, verify, and maintain. This criticism, based on methological motivations, was further corroborated by a theoretical result (known as Boehm-Jacopini theorem), which proved that any algorithm can always be programmed using only three basic control structures: sequences, IF statements, and WHILE statements. Much research activity was, therefore, directed toward investigating better control structures to be incorporated in a new geration of programming languages.

A language like Pascal can be viewed as practical response to these concerns about the relationship between the programming language and the programming methodology that should guide its use. The language was defined to support a disciplined program development, and much attention was paid to the choice of the control structures provided by the language. For example, a multiple branching mechanism (CASE statement) was added to the conventional two-way branching mechanism (IF statement). Three kinds of loops were provided: loops for which the number of iterations is known a priori (DO loops), loops for which termination is checked before executing the body (WHILE statement), and loops for which termination is checked after executing the body (REPEAT statement).

Although the debate on the best set of control structures to be provided by a programming language continued to be active for a while, the focus of the research on programming methodologies moved on to the more general and crucial themes of language support to modularity and control structures in-the-large, which will be discussed below.

Program Units

Large programs are often decomposed into smaller components, hereafter called units. Early high level procedural languages introduced two kinds of units: blocks and subprograms. A block, as introduced by Algol 60, is any (composite) statement within which one may declare local variables, whose visibility scope corresponds to the block itself. The block is executed as it is encountered during the sequential progress of execution: its boundaries define a conceptual abstract operation.

Subprograms are the key construct for structuring large programs. A subprogram defines an abstract operation, which is separately defined from the program and can be explicitly called by it. The subprogram call is a kind of control structure in-the-large. The calling unit names the subprogram to be invoked and transfers the actual parameters on which the subprogram must operate. When the subprogram terminates, control is implicitly and automatically transferred back to the caller, at the point where the call was previously issued.

Parameters are the principal way of exchanging information between the caller and the callee. In addition, the callee may have access to other data that are not explicitly specified as parameters of the invocation but rather are made visible to the callee by the scope rules of the language. If any such data are modified by the subprogram while it is executed, a side effect is said to occur. Side effects are often criticized on the grounds of good programming style, because they tend to make programs obscure, hard to understand, verify, and modify. In fact, the possible effects of a subprogram call are not explicit in the call but can only be identified by examining the body of the subprogram.

Parameters are usually exchanged in two ways: (*1*) by copying their value from the caller into the callee's formal parameters acting as local variables (call by value) and possibly back from the callee to the caller (call by result), or (*2*) by transferring the address of actual parameters to the callee (call by reference). In call by value, when the callee accesses a parameter, it actually accesses a local variable that was initialized with the value of the corresponding actual parameter at the point of call. In call by reference, it accesses the corresponding actual parameter. For example, Fortran is usually implemented by using call by reference; Pascal offers both call by reference and call by value.

There are two kinds of subprograms: procedures and functions. Functions return a value (the result of the function); parameter modifications as well as any other kind of side effects should be avoided. Procedures achieve their effects through parameters: if any effect is to be communicated to the caller, this should occur by means of parameters (by result or by reference).

Subprograms are the main tool provided by early procedural languages to modularize large programs. During design, the program is progressively decomposed into lower level abstract operations. When one reaches the point where abstract operations are simple enough and do not deserve further decomposition, they may be implemented by a subprogram.

When the program to be implemented is large, design and implementation cannot be a single person's responsibility, but require a programming team. It is thus crucial that only after reaching a common agreement on general design decisions (module interfaces) that the various members of the team proceed in the implementation in an independent fashion. The language may support this if the modules, which may be implemented by different programmers, may be developed and tested in isolation before the system is integrated. This requirement was initially recognized by Fortran, which offered the ability to compile subprograms separately and independently.

Separate and independent compilation, as offered by Fortran, is an effective (although rather naive) way of supporting independent development; it also has the drawback of permitting inconsistent module interfaces to be implemented. For example, one can write a subprogram with three formal parameters and call such subprogram from another unit with only two actual parameters. Because the two are compiled separately, the error remains unchecked in the object code, and thus a failure may occur later during execution, when it may be impossible to recover from it. Later languages (like Modula 2 and Ada) offered a modified scheme, called separate but not independent compilation.

MODERN HIGH LEVEL IMPERATIVE LANGUAGES

The 1970s were characterized by research and experimentation in the field of programming languages. Programming languages were no longer seen simply as languages for implementing algorithms but rather as languages for structuring large systems. Much emphasis was devoted to providing language support to design methodologies emphasizing design for change, separation of interface from implementation, and information hiding. At the same time, reliability issues became more important. Software was increasingly used in critical applications for which the effect of failures could be extremely serious. Therefore, languages were defined with the goal of supporting the discovery of the largest possible number of errors before program execution, thus reducing the chance of unforseen run-time failures.

Most of the language experiments made in the 1970s never evolved into widely used languages. Nevertheless, they had a strong influence on later languages, like Modula 2, Ada, and more recent object-oriented languages, such as C^{++} and Eiffel. Among these experiments, are CLU, Alphard, and Gypsy.

This section reviews the principal achievements of modern high level procedural languages, with special emphasis on Modula 2 and Ada. Object-oriented languages also are discussed. Before starting this discussion, however, a major language achievement of the 1970s, the C programming language, should be mentioned.

C combines high level language features with lower level facilities that make its implementation extremely efficient. C may be considered a high level language for systems programming (operating systems, compilers, software development tools, and other kinds of general utilities). The availability of low level features allows the programmer to behave in an unstructured manner. On the other hand, it allows the disciplined programmer to benefit from the use of a high level language when dealing with efficiency-critical applications.

Types

Programming languages in which the type of every variable must be declared a type and the type of every expression may be determined by static analysis (i.e., at compile time) are said to be strongly typed. This property protects the programmer from inadvertent errors; it guarantees that all acceptable programs will run without type errors. For example, it allows the compiler to check that a variable of a given type will never be assigned a value of the wrong type, and that a formal parameter of a given type will never be matched by an actual parameter of the wrong type in a subprogram call.

The ability to perform static program checking provides powerful support to program reliability. The errors discovered and removed before execution are guaranteed not to occur at run time, whereas run-time checking is not guaranteed to result in a failure for all errors present in a program, because the failure depends on the choice of the test data. Therefore, delaying error detection to run time decreases program reliability.

Early high level procedural languages are not fully strongly typed. Therefore, the effectiveness of static checking is limited. Later languages, like Ada, provide a better approximation to a strongly typed language; therefore, they allow for enhanced ability to support static program validation.

Improved Modularity

Modern high level procedural languages have been paying increasing attention to providing language support to the design and construction of large systems, by offering powerful modularization constructs (other than procedures and functions) and by supporting separate development of modules and incremental integration.

Ada offers a construct, called package, for enclosing a group of declarations (types, variables, and subprograms) and an initialization statement within a lexical boundary. Packages may be nested according to the scope rules of the language. However, they find their full justification and use as ways of structuring large systems as a set of external units. External units are subprograms (representing abstract operations) or packages (representing general information hiding modules). Packages are discussed here as external units.

The package is composed of two parts: the interface, specifying which of the defined items are visible from outside the module and which of the other modules are used by the current module, and the body, specifying the internal details of the module. Consequently, the package construct provides explicit support to applying the principles of information hiding and abstract interface to a module. By encapsulating in the implementation part all possible changeable parts, the construct also supports the goal of design for change.

A package can be used to implement an abstract data type. In fact, an interface may define an exported type as a private type, which means that the details of its structure are not visible by the user modules. The interface of a module implementing an abstract data type should thus contain a private type and the header of all the procedures and functions that implement the operations provided to manipulate the type. User modules may declare variables of the newly defined abstract data type but can only manipulate them by using the associated operations.

The interface and the body parts may be defined and compiled separately from each other. In particular, one may assume that interfaces are defined (and compiled) in the design stage, whereas bodies are provided later in the implementation stage. The language, however, forces programmers to follow a partial order in their compilation that ensures that no interface errors will ever arise. Compilation is thus separate but not independent. In particular, interfaces must be compiled before the corresponding bodies; the interface of a module must be compiled before any unit using it.

Internal subprograms or packages may also be defined (and compiled) separately. In such a case, if X contains a separately defined module Y, X must be compiled before Y. This corresponds to the conventional notion of top-down development and integration and may be used to replace easily a module Y with a stub (for testing purposes).

Ada provides further support to modularization by allowing modules (packages and subprograms) to be parameterized (with values, types, and procedures), using the generic mechanism. A generic package or subprogram acts as a template and cannot be directly used. Rather, a particular instance must be generated at compile time by instantiation. Such a parameterization mechanism offers a powerful abstraction tool that allows the programmer to capture the essentials of a set of actual modules by providing a single generic module to be instantiated. A sophisticated compiler can then share the object code among instances of the same generic template. CLU, Chill, and Modula 2 offer similar facilities to those offered by Ada to support modularization.

Exception Handling

Inevitably, no matter how carefully a programmer behaves when writing a program and no matter how thoroughly its verification is carried out, errors remain in the program and program execution may result in a failure. The program may fail because the code contains a logical error, because unexpected values are supplied as input data, or because the hardware detects a fault (such as an overflow in an arithmetic expression). If the failure occurs during testing, the system is stopped and the error is traced and removed. But if the system is running in the target environment, it is usually impossible to stop it by simply printing out some diagnostic message. For example, think of the control system for a rocket, or a real-time control system for a chemical plant; more generally, think of any typical embedded computer applications. The programming language may provide a framework for detecting and then handling faults so that the program either fails gracefully or continues to work after some remedial action has been taken to recover from the error. Such linguistic framework is usually called exception handling.

Among the features offered by programming languages to support exception handling are the following.

1. The ability to distinguish the normal control flow from the exception handling flow to make the structure of the program clear.
2. The ability to detect faults as they occur in the program, not only by explicitly raising an exception but also by implicitly raising it on account of the run-time environment (e.g., when an array is indexed with a value that exceeds the declared bounds). Both kinds of faults should be handled uniformly.
3. The ability to transfer control to a programmer-definable exception handler when the fault is detected. The language should specify the rules by which a detected fault is bound to its corresponding exception-handling routine.
4. The ability to specify how control flows after the exception handler is executed, i.e., whether one can resume execution from the point at which it left off (in the case of successful recovery) or whether the program should gracefully fail.

Most early programming languages do not provide specific features for exception handling but rather use the normal language constructs to implement it. For example, a common strategy is to write subprograms that return error codes via a special parameter or as the value returned by the function. This strategy is widely used in the interface with libraries or the operating system (e.g., the C interface with the UNIX operating system). Obviously, this and other ad hoc methods do not satisfy the requirements listed above.

PL/I was the only widely used early language to provide comprehensive facilities for exception handling. Such features, however, were elaborate and complicated. They were difficult to use and understand. They were also difficult to implement in a reasonably efficient way. Therefore, they were seldom used in practice. As a consequence, modern high level imperative languages have adopted simpler but more effective strategies.

Exception-handling features are offered by Ada, a language whose primary target is the class of embedded computer applications. In Ada, an exception handier may be attached to any block, subprogram (i.e., procedure or function), or package. Exceptions may be raised either explicitly (by means by the RAISE statement) or implicitly (by the run-time system or the hardware). After an exception is raised, the appropriate handler must be found to handle the exception. First, the handler is sought in the block where the exception was raised; if it is not found there, enclosing scopes are orderly examined until either a handler is found (in which case, execution procedes from there, after exiting all the necessary nested scopes) or the end of a subprogram is reached without finding a handler. At this point, the exception is propagated along the dynamic calling sequence: the subprogram is exited, and the search for a handler procedes from the call to the subprogram that raised the exception. Eventually, if no handler is found, the program (or task) terminates.

Exception handling in Ada satisfies points 1 through 3 listed above. The language, however, does not permit a retry after recovery of the operation that caused the raising of the exception. Thus it does not fully satisfy point 4.

Slightly different exception-handling features are offered by other modern languages, such as Chill, CLU, and Mesa. Modula 2 does not offer any specific exception-handling constructs. However, a recent new version of the language, called Modula 3, offers comprehensive exception-handling facilities, similar to those offered by Ada.

Eiffel offers an interesting solution to exception handling by coupling it with the assertion facilities that may be used to annotate programs with the expected state at critical points. If the assertion is violated, an exception is raised. In addition, the language allows the programmer to specify both graceful failure (called organized panic in the Eiffel context) and retry after recovery.

Concurrency and Distribution

A von Neumann machine is intrinsically sequential: execution starts at the first statement of the program, and then each statement defines its unique successor either implicitly (next statement) or explicitly (in the case of jumps). A unit of code having this behavior is often called a process, or task. Other models of computation that do not follow the von Neumann paradigm usually are intrinsically highly parallel. This means that there is not a total ordering in the execution, ie, at any time there may be a large number of ready-to-be-executed instructions.

This section presents the way concurrency has been embedded in programming languages that still rely on an underlying von Neumann paradigm. A concurrent von Neumann program may be abstractly viewed as a set of loosely coupled processes, each representing a purely sequential von Neumann abstract machine. Each process evolves sequentially but may occasionally interact with other processes to cooperate or to avoid interference. This behavior may be achieved in two ways:

1. By multiprogramming, i.e., multiplexing, through time, the processes on a single processor.

2. By allocating each process to a processor. If the processors share a common memory, this architecture is called a multiprocessing. If they do not, and the processors are connected by a network (e.g., Ethernet), it is called distributed processing.

To achieve cooperation and avoid interference, processes must communicate and synchronize. Communication may be achieved by the use of shared variables or by message passing. Synchronization is then necessary to ensure that communication occurs at appropriate points in time.

Early languages provided limited support to concurrency by means of coroutines. Coroutines may be viewed as a way of implementing multiprogramming. In fact, coroutines are a set of processes for which the pattern of process switching is predetermined. Each coroutine executes for a while, then transfers control to another coroutine, and eventually, is resumed by some other coroutine from the state in which it previously left off. Coroutines are provided by Simula 67. They are also provided by Modula 2 and can be used as a way of implementing higher level mechanisms.

A popular way of dealing with concurreny is through operating system calls. For example, in C one may do so by executing the Unix fork and join operations. This solution, however, is neither clean nor elegant, because it does not fully amalgamate concurrency within the language.

In early experiments (such as the introduction of processes and semaphores in PL/I and Algol 68) concurrency was basically an afterthought: the language was essentially conceived as a sequential notation and constructs supporting concurrency were added afterward. In such languages, concurrency had limited application.

Concurrent Pascal was the first example of a programming language for which concurrency was the primary issue. The underlying abstract architecture of Concurrent Pascal consists of a set of processes that cooperate by communicating through shared data. Shared data are defined as instances of abstract data types with controlled access, implemented by the MONITOR construct. As in an abstract data type, the monitor exports a type (but not its implementation) and a set of operations to access the instances of the type. The monitor guarantees that each operation on an instance of the abstract data type is executed in mutual exclusion, ie, no two processes are allowed to execute the internal code of the instance at the same time. In addition, monitors provide mechanisms (condition variables and queues) to synchronize the access to the shared data. For example, if a monitor instance represents a buffer, these mechanisms provide a way to suspend any process attempting to store data if the buffer is full; similarly, they can suspend any process that tries to extract data from the buffer if the buffer is empty. The WAIT operation suspends a process in queue. The process can then be resumed by the SIGNAL operation.

The run-time concurrency model of Concurrent Pascal is based on a set of active entities (processes) and a set of passive encapsulated data objects (monitor instances). A different view is taken by Ada, which views a system as composed of all active entities, called TASK. Ada tasks may communicate by accessing shared nonlocal data. The primary communication mechanism, however, is based on the notion of message passing, which makes concurrency naturally implementable also on a distributed system.

Message passing in Ada takes the form of the pair (entry call, accept statement) that matches in a RENDEZVOUS. Entry calls are syntactically similar to a (remote) procedure call; accept statements are syntactically similar to procedures. A task X wishing to communicate with task Y issues a call to an entry y of Y, and suspends itself until Y accepts the entry and executes the corresponding accept statement. When Y does so, the rendezvous occurs, and after execution of the accept statement, the two tasks procede concurrently. Tasks suspended on a given entry are handled in a fifo fashion.

From the above, it is clear that both the call and the accept may block the task if the other task is not ready to accept or issue the call. Such an eventuality may be avoided if the caller uses a conditional entry call or a timed entry call. For example, the timed entry call specifies a time-out for the entry call; if the rendezvous does not occur within the specified time, the request to communicate is withdrawn and an alternative execution path is followed. The block can also be avoided by the callee by embedding accept statements in a select statement. The select statement enables a task to check if any one of a set of entries has a pending request. If more than one entry has pending requests, one of them is nondeterministically served. If none of them has pending requests, the task can, e.g., do other actions or suspend itself for a given period of time.

Occam is another language that adopts message passing for interprocess communication. Occam is designed as a high level assembly language to program transputers and thus exploits directly parallelism in the hardware. The architecture goes far beyond the classical von Neumann paradigm, but the language used to program processes is imperative, and its concurrency features are based on CSP.

Among other modern concurrent languages are Edison, a multiprocessor language, and Argus, a language for distributed processing. Many other interesting languages are also being developed as research experiments.

Object-oriented Imperative Languages

Object-oriented imperative languages take a radical viewpoint in the choice of the modularization mechanisms offered to structure programs: they provide only the CLASS construct, by which programs may be designed as a collection of abstract data type implementations. Instead of following the traditional decomposition of a system into abstract operations (implemented as procedures and functions) and information hiding modules, object-oriented languages enforce a system decomposition in terms of abstract data type implementations.

Object-oriented languages also differ from traditional high level languages in the way modules may be structured. Traditional languages either provide a flat structure (a system is composed of a set of external modules, as in Fortran), a tree-structured hierarchy (a system is organized as a set of nested components as in Algol 60 or Pascal), or a combination of them (external modules may be internally tree structured, as in Ada). Based on this structure, the scope rules of the language define the set of nonlocal entities that are visible from any given module. Object-oriented languages add a new powerful structuring facility: inheritance among modules.

A class Y inheriting from a class X is said to be a subclass, and X is said to be Y's parent class. A language is said to support multiple inheritance if a class Y can inherit from more than one parent class; if there is at most one parent class, the language is said to support simple inheritance. Different object-oriented languages differ in the way they support inheritance. The analysis here is restricted to a simple case. The goal here is to show how the class of procedural object-oriented languages arises as an evolution of the field of procedural languages.

Inheritance may be used to define a subtype of the parent type. For example, class RECTANGLE can be defined to be a subclass of class POLYGON. A subclass defines only what is different in the subclass from the parent class: all the rest is inherited. A subclass can add new attributes to its parent class (e.g., additional operations); some of the parent's operations may also be redefined. For example, the class RECTANGLE may export a further operation called DIAGONAL, which yields the value of the rectangle's diagonal. It may also redefine operation AREA, instead of inheriting the general way of computing the area for polygons.

If p is a variable declared to refer to a polygon, it may also be assigned a rectangle: indeed, a rectangle is a special kind of polygon. The opposite, however, is not possible and results in an error. After p is assigned as a value an instance of class RECTANGLE, if operation AREA is invoked on p, the implementation for the operation redefined for rectangles is chosen, not the one defined for polygons. This feature is known as dynamic binding: although p is statically defined to refer to polygons, the operations to be executed when they are invoked on p are chosen, depending on the kind of value associated to p at run-time.

Dynamic binding potentially conflicts with static type checking, unless suitable restrictions are imposed by the language. Smalltalk supports a liberal viewpoint, i.e., no restrictions are imposed and the checking is delayed to run time. At the other extreme, Eiffel adopts a strict viewpoint: the restrictions are such that no errors should arise at run time as result of dynamic binding. Further facilities offered by object-oriented languages include the ability to define generic classes (implementing generic abstract data types) and the ability to define abstract classes (classes that have no instances but are just used to factor the common behavior of a number of classes, which are then defined as subclasses).

Object-oriented languages are becoming extremely popular. Object-oriented features are also added on top of nonprocedural languages (such as functional or logic languages). The concepts of class and inheritance, however, date back to an earlier seminal language: Simula 67. These concepts have been rediscovered, and offered in a more advanced way, by recent object-oriented languages. The importance of these concepts has been emphasized by the increasingly important issue of software reusability. Through classes and inheritance it is possible to organize software in a way that favors reusability. As the language is used in more and more applications, libraries of reusable components can progressively be built. Furthermore, when new applications are designed, it is possible to extract components from the library, possibly adapt them, by defining a subclass, and then reuse them in the new application.

The field of object-oriented languages is still evolving: new experimental languages are defined and new commercial products are brought to the market. C^{++} is one of the best known and most-widely used object-oriented languages. C^{++} uses an evolutionary approach, i.e., it introduces object-oriented concepts on top of the C programming language. Other languages adopt a more radical attitude and result in cleaner and more elegant notations. Smalltalk and Eiffel represent two extremes. The former is highly dynamic in nature and naturally supports rapid prototyping and exploratory system development. The latter emphasizes sound software engineering principles, such as program correctness and systematic program development, by supporting static checking, program annotation with assertions, and exception handling.

CONCLUSIONS

Programming languages have been evolving over the past 30 yr, and promise to do so in the future. Modern languages are no longer languages for "programming" but rather powerful tools for "software construction." By this it is meant that the emphasis is no longer on how to structure algorithms but on how to structure large software systems. The sharp distinction between design and implementation notations, which was largely the result of the low level concepts provided by earlier languages, tends to disappear. The programming language offers linguistic support to describing designs not just to describing fine-grain notions like data declarations or procedures. A modular language like Ada and current object-oriented languages illustrate this point quite clearly.

In the future, programming languages will move even higher to provide linguistic support to specification. Executable specification languages are being investigated and several running prototypes are described in the literature. One may conceive a wide-spectrum language that contains a "specification" component, a "design" component, and an "implementation" component. At an intermediate step of development, the system might be partly specified and partly implemented, but it could still be executable.

Other challenges will arise in the future due to the evolution in the architectures. Architectures will depart more and more from the original von Neumann paradigm. Massively parallel architecture will become widely available, and the need for suitable programming languages will arise to provide effective exploitation of the benefits of such architectures.

BIBLIOGRAPHY

General References

A. Ambler and co-workers, "Gypsy: A Language for Specification and Implementation of Verifiable Programs," *SIGPLAN Not.* **12**(3), 1–10 (Mar. 1977).

American National Standards Institute, *American National Standard Programming Language Cobol* (ANS X3.23-1974), ANSI, New York, 1974.

American National Standards Institute, *American National Standard Programming Language PL/I (ANS X3.53-1976), ANSI, New York, 1976.*

American National Standards Institute, *American National Standard Programming Language Fortran* (ANS X3.9-1978), ANSI, New York, 1978.

ANSI/MIL-STD-1815A, *Reference Manual for the Ada Programming Language,* U.S. Department of Defense, Washington, D.C., Jan. 1983.

G. M. Birtwistle, O.-J. Dahl, B. Myraug, and K. Nygaard, *SIMULA Begin,* Petrocelli/Charter, New York, 1973.

P. Brinch-Hansen, *The Architecture of Concurrent Programs,* Prentice-Hall, Inc., Englewood Cliffs, N.J., 1977.

P. Brinch-Hansen, "Edison: A Multiprocessor language," *Software Prac. Exper.* **11,** 325–362 (1981).

C. M. Gesche and co-workers, "Early Experience with MESA," *Comm. ACM* **20**(8), 540–553 (June 1975).

C. Ghezzi and M. Jazayeri, *Programming Language Concepts,* 2nd ed., John Wiley & Sons, Inc., New York, 1987.

A. Goldberg and D. Robson, *Smalltalk-80: The Language and Its Implementation,* Addison-Wesley Publishing Co., Inc., Reading, Mass., 1983.

C. A. R. Hoare, "Communicating Sequential Processes," *Comm. ACM* **21**(8), 666–677 (Aug. 1978).

INMOS Ltd, *OCCAM Programming Manual,* Prentice-Hall, Inc., Englewood Cliffs, N.J., 1984.

K. Jensen and N. Wirth, *The Pascal User Manual and Report,* 3rd ed., Springer-Verlag, New York, 1985.

B. W. Kernighan and D. M. Ritchie, *The C Programming Language,* Prentice-Hall, Inc., Englewood Cliffs, N.J., 1978.

C. H. Lindsay and S. G. van der Meulen, *An Informal Introduction to Algol 68,* 2nd ed., North Holland, 1977.

B. Liskov and co-workers, *CLU Reference Manual,* Springer Verlag, New York, 1981.

B. Liskov and co-workers, *Implementation of Argus,* paper presented at the Eleventh ACM Symposium on Operating Systems Principles, 1987.

B. Meyer, *Object Oriented Software Construction,* Prentice-Hall International, Englewood Cliffs, N.J., 1988.

P. Naur, ed., "Revised Report on the Algorithmic Language ALGOL-60," *Comm. ACM* **6** 1–17 (Jan. 1963).

M. Shaw, ed., *Alphard: Form and Content,* Springer-Verlag, New York, 1981.

C. H. Smedema and co-workers, *The Programming Languages Pascal, Modula, CHILL, and Ada,* Prentice-Hall, Inc., Englewood Cliffs, N.J., 1983.

B. Stroustrup, *The C++ Programming Language*, Addison-Wesley Publishing Co., Inc., Reading, Mass., 1985.

N. Wirth, *Programming in Modula 2*, 3rd ed., Springer-Verlag, New York, 1983.

CARLO GHEZZI
Politechnico di Milano

PROCESS ABSTRACTION

See ABSTRACTION.

PROCESS MATURITY MODEL

OVERVIEW

The Software Process Maturity Model (CMM) deals with the capability of software organizations to produce high quality products consistently and predictably. It is closely related to such topics as software process, quality management, and process improvement. The drive for improved software quality is motivated by technology, customer need, regulation, and competition. Although industry's historical quality improvement focus has been on manufacturing, software quality efforts must concentrate on product development and improvement.

Process *capability* is the inherent ability of a process to produce planned results. A capable software process is characterized as mature. The principal objective of a mature software process is to produce quality products to meet customers' needs. For such human-intensive activities as software development, the capability of an overall process is determined by examining the performance of its defined subprocesses. As the capability of each subprocess is improved, the most significant causes of poor quality and productivity are thus controlled or eliminated. Overall process capability steadily improves and the organization is said to mature.

It should be noted that capability is not the same as performance. The performance of an organization at any specific time depends on many factors. Although some of these factors can be controlled by the process methods, others cannot. Changes in user needs or technology surprises cannot be eliminated by process methods. Their effects, however, can often be mitigated or even anticipated. Within organizations, process capability may also vary across projects and even within projects. It is theoretically possible to find a well-controlled and -managed project in a chaotic and undisciplined organization, but it is not likely. The reason is that it takes time and resources to develop a mature process capability. As a consequence, few projects can build their process while they simultaneously build their product.

The term *maturity* implies that software process capability must be grown. Maturity improvement requires strong management support and a consistent long-term focus. It involves fundamental changes in the way managers and software practitioners do their jobs. Standards are established and process data are systematically collected, analyzed, and used. The most difficult change, however, is cultural. High maturity requires the recognition that managers do not know everything that needs to be done to improve the process.

The software professionals often have more detailed knowledge of the limitations of the processes they use. The key challenge of process management is to continuously capture and apply this knowledge.

Process maturity improvement is a long-term incremental activity. In manufacturing organizations, the development and adoption of effective process methods typically has taken 10 to 20 years. Software organizations could easily take comparable periods to progress from low to high process maturity. U.S. management is generally impatient for quick results and not accustomed to thinking in terms of long-term continuous process improvement. Once the cultural, organizational, and managerial obstacles are removed, the needed technical and procedural actions can often be implemented quite quickly. Although history demonstrates that such changes can take a long time, it also demonstrates that, given a great enough need and broad consensus on the solution, surprising results can be produced quite quickly. The challenge is thus to define the need and achieve broad consensus on the solution. This is the basic objective of the Software Process Maturity Model and the Software Process Assessment method.

The focus on the software process has resulted from a growing recognition that the traditional product focus of organizational improvement efforts has not generally had the desired results. Many management and support activities are required to produce effective software organizations. Inadequate project management, for example, is often the principal cause of cost and schedule problems. Similarly, weaknesses in configuration management, quality assurance, inspection practices, or testing generally result in unsatisfactory quality. Typically, projects do not have the time nor resources to address such issues and thus a broader process improvement focus is required.

It is now recognized that traditional engineering management methods work for software just as they do for other technical fields. There is an increasing volume of published material on software project management and a growing body of experience with such topics as cost and size estimation, configuration management, and quality improvement. While hardware management methods can provide useful background, as shown in Table 1, there are key differences between hardware and software. Hardware managers thus need to master many new perspectives to be successful in directing software organizations.

The Shewhart cycle provides the foundation for process improvement work. As shown in Table 2, it defines four steps for a general improvement process (Deming, 1982).

The cycle begins with a plan for improving an activity. Once the improvement plan is completed, the plan is implemented, results are checked, and actions taken to correct deviations. The cycle is then repeated. If the implementation produced the desired results, actions are taken to make the change permanent. In the Software Engineering

Table 1. Hardware and Software Differences

- •Software is generally more complex.
- •Software changes appear relatively easy to make.
- •Many late-discovered hardware problems are addressed through software changes.
- •Because of its low reproduction cost, software does not have the natural discipline of release to manufacturing.
- •Software discipline is not grounded in natural science and it lacks ready techniques for feasibility testing and design modeling.
- •Software is often the element that integrates an entire system, thus adding to its complexity and creating exposures to late change.
- •Software is generally most visible, thus most exposed to requirements changes and most subject to user complaint.
- •Because software is a relatively new discipline, few managers and executives have sufficient experience to appreciate the principles or benefits of an effective software process.

Institute's (SEI) process strategy, this improvement plan is the principal objective of a Software Process Assessment.

The Shewhart approach, as espoused by W. E. Deming, was broadly adapted by Japanese industry in the 1950s and 1960s. The key element of the remarkable success of Japanese industry has been the sustained focus on small incremental process improvements. To enroll the employees in the improvement effort, quality control circles were formed and given considerable authority and responsibility for instituting change. Japanese management's basic strategy, followed to this day, is to focus on quality improvement in the belief that the desired productivity and profit improvements will naturally follow.

Based on these principles, the Software Process Maturity Model was designed by the author and his associates to provide a graduated improvement framework of software capabilities. Each level progressively adds further enhancements that software organizations typically master as they improve. Since some capabilities depend on others, it is important to maintain an orderly improvement progression. Because of its progressive nature, this framework can be used to evaluate software organizations to determine the most important areas for immediate improvement. With the growing volume of software process maturity data, organizations can also determine their relative standing with respect to other groups.

Table 2. The Shewhart Improvement Cycle

1. Plan
    - Define the problem
        - Establish improvement objectives
2. Do
    - Identify possible problem causes
        - Establish baselines
        - Test change
3. Check
    - Collect data
        - Evaluate data
4. Act
    - Implement system change
        - Determine effectiveness

This article describes the background of the Software Process Maturity Model: what it is, where it came from, how it was developed, and how it is being improved. Its major applications are also described, including the users, application methods, and the general state of software practice. Future developments are then described, including improvement trends, likely application issues, and current research thrusts. Finally, the conclusion outlines the critical issues to consider in applying these methods.

BACKGROUND

With the enormous improvements in the cost-performance of computers and microprocessors, software now pervades most facets of modem life. It controls automobiles, flies airplanes, and drives such everyday devices as wrist watches, microwave ovens, and VCRs. Software is now often the gating element in most branches of engineering and science. Our businesses, our wars, and even our leisure time have been irretrievably changed. As was demonstrated in the Gulf War in the Middle East, "smart" weapons led to an early and overwhelming victory. The "smart" in modem weapons is supplied by software.

While society increasingly depends on software, software development's historical problems have not been addressed effectively. Software schedules, for example, are uniformly missed. An unpublished review of 17 major DOD (Department of Defense) software contracts found that the average 28 month schedule was missed by 20 months. One four year project was not delivered for seven years; no project was on time. Deployment of the U.S. Air Force B1 bomber was delayed by a software problem and the $58 billion U.S. Navy A12 aircraft program was cancelled partly for the same reason. Although the military has its own unique problems, industry does as well. In all spheres, however, one important lesson is clear: large software content means trouble.

There are many reasons for this slow rate of improvement. Until recently, software project management methods have not been defined well enough to permit their inclusion in university curricula. They have thus generally been learned by observation, experience, or word of mouth. Second, few managers have worked in organizations that effectively manage software. This lack of role models means these managers must each learn from their own experiences. Unfortunately, these experiences are often painful and the managers who have learned the most are often associated with failed projects. By searching for an unblemished hero who can "clean up the mess," management generally picks someone who has not been tested by a challenging software project. Unfortunately, this generally starts another disastrous learning cycle.

The most serious problems in software organizations are not generally caused by an individual manager or software team. They typically concern organizational procedures and cultural behavior. These are not things that individual managers can generally fix. They require a comprehensive and longer term focus on the organization's software process.

PROCESS MATURITY MODEL DEVELOPMENT

The U.S. Department of Defense recognized the urgency of these software issues and, in 1982, formed a joint service task force to review software problems in the U.S. Department of Defense. This resulted in several initiatives, including the establishment of the Ada Program, the Software Engineering Institute at Carnegie Mellon University, and the STARS (Software Technology for Adaptable Reliable Systems) Program. Examples of U.S. industrial efforts to improve software practices are the Software Productivity Consortium (qv) and the early software work at the Micro-Electronics and Computer Consortium (qv). Similar initiatives have been established in Europe and in Japan, although they are largely under government sponsorship.

The Software Engineering Institute was established at Carnegie Mellon University in December of 1984 to address the need for improved software in U.S. Department of Defense operations. As part of its work, SEI developed the Software Process Maturity Model for use both by the Department of Defense and by industrial software organizations. The Software Capability Evaluation Project was initiated by the SEI in 1986 at the request of the U.S. Air Force.

The Air Force sought a technically sound and consistent method for the acquisition community to use in order to identify the most capable software contractors. The Air Force asked the MITRE Corporation to participate in this work and a joint team was formed. They drew on the extensive software and acquisition experience of the SEI, MITRE, and the Air Force Electronic Systems Division of Hanscom Air Force Base, MA. This SEI-MITRE team produced a technical report that included a questionnaire and a framework for evaluating organizations according to the maturity of their software processes (Humphrey, 1987). This maturity questionnaire is a structured set of yes–no questions that facilitates objective and consistent assessments of software organizations. The questions cover three principal areas.

1. *Organization and Resource Management.* This deals with functional responsibilities, personnel, and other resources and facilities.
2. *Software Engineering Process and its Management.* This concerns the scope, depth, and completeness of the software engineering process and the way in which it is measured, managed, and improved.
3. *Tools and Technology.* This deals with the tools and technologies used in the software engineering process and the effectiveness with which they are applied. This section is not used in maturity evaluations or assessments.

Some sample questions from the maturity questionnaire are

- Is there a software engineering process group or function?
- Is a formal procedure used to make estimates of software size?
- Are code and test errors projected and compared to actuals?

There have been many contributors to this work and many companies have participated in early questionnaire reviews. The basic ideas behind the maturity model and the SEI assessment process come from several sources. The work of Phil Babel and his associates at ASD at Wright-Patterson Air Force Base provided a useful model of an effective Air Force evaluation method for software-intensive acquisitions. In the early 1980s, IBM initiated a series of assessments of the technical capabilities of many of its development laboratories. An IBM software quality and process group then coupled this work with the maturity framework used by Phil Crosby in his Quality College (Crosby, 1979). The result was an assessment process and a generalized maturity framework (Radice, 1985). SEI then extended this work to incorporate the Deming principles and the Shewhart concepts of process management (Deming, 1982). The addition of the specific questions developed by MITRE and SEI resulted in the Software Capability Maturity Model (Humphrey, 1987, 1989).

As part of its initial development, SEI and MITRE held many reviews with individuals and organizations experienced in software development and acquisition. During this process it became clear that software is a rapidly evolving technology and that no static criteria could be valid for very long. Since this framework must evolve with advances in software technology and methods, the SEI maintains a continuing improvement effort. This work has broad participation by experienced software professionals from all branches of U.S. industry and government. There is also growing interest in this work in Europe and Japan.

In 1991 SEI produced the Capability Maturity Model for Software (CMM) (Paulk, 1991). This was developed to clarify the structure and content of the maturity framework. It identities the key practice areas for each maturity level and provides an extensive summary of these practices. To ensure that this work properly balances the needs and interests of those most effected, a CMM Advisory Board was established to review the SEI work and to advise on the suitability of any proposed changes. This board has members from U.S. industry and government.

THE PROCESS MATURITY MODEL

The five-level improvement model for software is shown in Figure 1. The levels are designed so that the capabilities at the lower levels provide a progressively stronger foundation on which to build the upper levels.

These five developmental stages are referred to as maturity levels, and at each level, the organization has a distinct process capability. By moving up these levels, the organization's capability is consistently improved.

At the initial level (level 1), an organization can be characterized as having an *ad hoc,* or possibly chaotic, process. Typically, the organization operates without formalized procedures, cost estimates, and project plans. Even if formal project control procedures exist, there are no management mechanisms to ensure that they are followed.

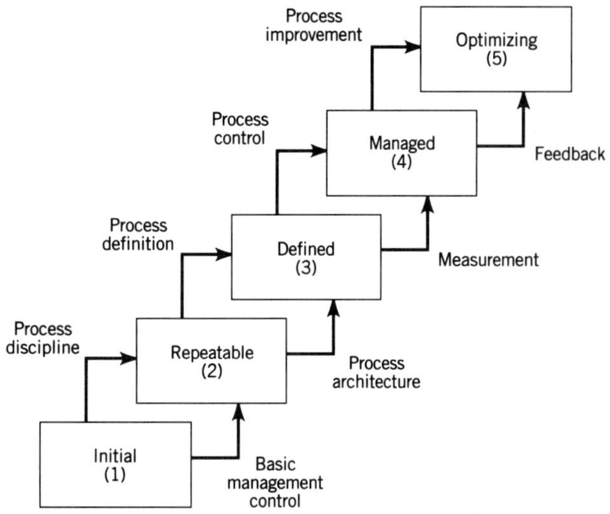

Figure 1. The five levels of software process maturity.

Tools are not well integrated with the process, nor are they uniformly applied. Change control is generally lax and senior management is not exposed to or does not understand the key software problems and issues. When projects do succeed, it is generally because of the heroic efforts of a dedicated team rather than the capability of the organization.

An organization at the repeatable level (level 2) has established basic project controls: project management, management oversight, product assurance, and change control. The strength of the organization stems from its experience at doing similar work, but it faces major risks when presented with new challenges. The organization has frequent quality problems and lacks an orderly framework for improvement.

At the defined level (level 3), the organization has laid the foundation for examining the process and deciding how to improve it. A Software Engineering Process Group (SEPG) has been established to focus and lead the process improvement efforts, to keep management informed on the status of these efforts, and to facilitate the introduction of a family of software engineering methods and technologies.

The managed level (level 4) builds on the foundation established at the defined level. When the process is defined, it can be examined and improved but there is little data to indicate effectiveness. Thus, to advance to the managed level, organizations must establish a set of quality and productivity measurements. A process database is also needed with analysis resources and consultative skills to advise and support project members in its use. At level 4, the Shewhart cycle is used to continually plan, implement, and track process improvements.

At the optimizing level (level 5) the organization has the means to identify its weakest process elements and strengthen them, data are available to justify applying technology to critical tasks, and evidence is available on process effectiveness. At this point, data gathering has at least been partially automated and management has redirected its focus from product repair to process analysis and improvement. The key additional activity at the optimizing level is rigorous defect cause analysis and defect prevention.

These maturity levels have been selected because:

- They reasonably represent the historical phases of evolutionary improvement experienced by software organizations.
- They represent a reasonable sequence of achievable improvement steps.
- They suggest interim improvement goals and progress measures.
- They make obvious a set of immediate improvement priorities, once an organization's status in this framework is known.

While there are many aspects to the advancement from one maturity level to another, the basic objective is to achieve a controlled and measured process as the foundation for continuous improvement. Some of the characteristics and key challenges of each of these levels are shown in Figure 2. A more detailed discussion is included in (Humphrey, 1989).

Because of their impatience for results, organizations occasionally attempt to reach level 5 without progressing through levels 2, 3, or 4. This is counterproductive, however, because each level forms a necessary platform for the next. Consistent and sustained improvement also requires balanced attention to all key process areas. Inattention to one key area can largely negate advantages gained from work on the others. For example, unless effective means are established for developing realistic estimates at level 2, the organization is still exposed to serious overcommitments. This is true even when important improvements have been made in other areas. Thus, a crash effort to achieve some arbitrary maturity goal is likely to be unrealistic. This can cause discouragement and management frustration and lead to cancellation of the entire improvement effort. If the emphasis is on consistently making small improvements, their benefits will gradually accumulate to impressive overall capability gains.

Similarly, at level 3, the stability achieved through the repeatable level (level 2), permits the process to be examined and defined. This is essential because a defined engineering process cannot overcome the instability created by the absence of the sound management practices established at level 2 (Humphrey, 1989). With a defined process, there is a common basis for measurements. The process phases are now more than mere numbers; they have recognized prerequisites, activities, and products. This defined foundation permits the data gathered at level 4 to have well-understood meaning. Similarly, level 4 provides the data with which to judge proposed process improvements and their subsequent effects. This is a necessary foundation for continuous process improvement at level 5.

USES OF THE MATURITY MODEL

The major uses of the maturity model are in process improvement and evaluation:

- In assessments, organizations use the maturity model to study their own operations and to identity the highest priority areas for improvement.

Level	Stabilize	Key process areas	Result
5 Optimizing	Continuous process improvement	Defect prevention Technology innovation Process change management	Productivity and quality
4 Managed	Product and process quality	Process measurement and analysis Quality management	
3 Defined	Engineering process	Organization process focus Organization process definition Peer reviews Training program Intergroup coordination Software product engineering Integrated software management	
2 Repeatable	Project management	Software project planning Software project tracking Software subcontract mgt. Software quality assurance Software configuration mgt. Requirements mgt.	
1 Initial			Risk

Figure 2. The key process challenges.

- In evaluations, acquisition agencies use the maturity model to identify qualified bidders and to monitor existing contracts.

The assessment and evaluation methods are based upon the maturity model and use the SEI questionnaire. It provides a structured basis for the investigation and permits the rapid and reasonably consistent development of findings that identify the organization's key strengths and weaknesses. The significant difference between assessments and evaluations comes from the way the results are used. For an assessment, the results form the basis for an action plan for organizational self-improvement. For an evaluation, they guide the development of a risk profile. In source selection, this risk profile augments the traditional criteria used to select the most responsive and capable vendors. In contract monitoring, the risk profile may also be used to motivate the contractor's process improvement efforts.

Software Process Assessment

An assessment is a diagnostic tool to aid organizational improvement. Its objectives are to provide a clear and factual understanding of the organization's state of software practice, to identify key areas for improvement, and to initiate actions to make these improvements. The assessment starts with the senior manager's commitment to support software process improvement. Since most executives are well aware of the need to improve the performance and productivity of their software development operations, such support is often readily available.

The next step is to select an assessment coordinator who works with local management and the assessing organization to make the necessary arrangements. The assessment team is typically composed of senior software development professionals. Six to eight professionals are generally selected from the organization being assessed and one or two coaches who have been trained in the SEI assessment method. While the on-site assessment period takes only one week, the combined preparation and follow-on assessment activities generally take at least four to six months. The resulting improvement program should then continue indefinitely.

Software Process Assessments are conducted in accordance with a signed assessment agreement between the SEI-licensed assessment vendor and the organization being assessed. This agreement provides for senior management involvement, organizational representation on the assessment team, confidentiality of results, and follow-up actions. As described in the section on other assessment methods, SEI has licensed a number of vendors to conduct assessments.

Software Process Assessments are typically conducted in six phases. These phases are

1. *Selection Phase.* During the first phase, an organization is identified as a candidate for assessment and the SEI or other qualified assessing organization conducts an executive level briefing.
2. *Commitment Phase.* In the second phase, the organization commits to the full assessment process. An assessment agreement is signed by a senior executive of the organization to be assessed and the assessment vendor. This commitment includes the personal participation of the senior site manager, site representation on the assessment team, and agreement to take action on the assessment recommendations.
3. *Preparation Phase.* The third phase is devoted to preparing for the on-site assessment. An assessment team receives training and the on-site period of the assessment process is fully planned. This includes

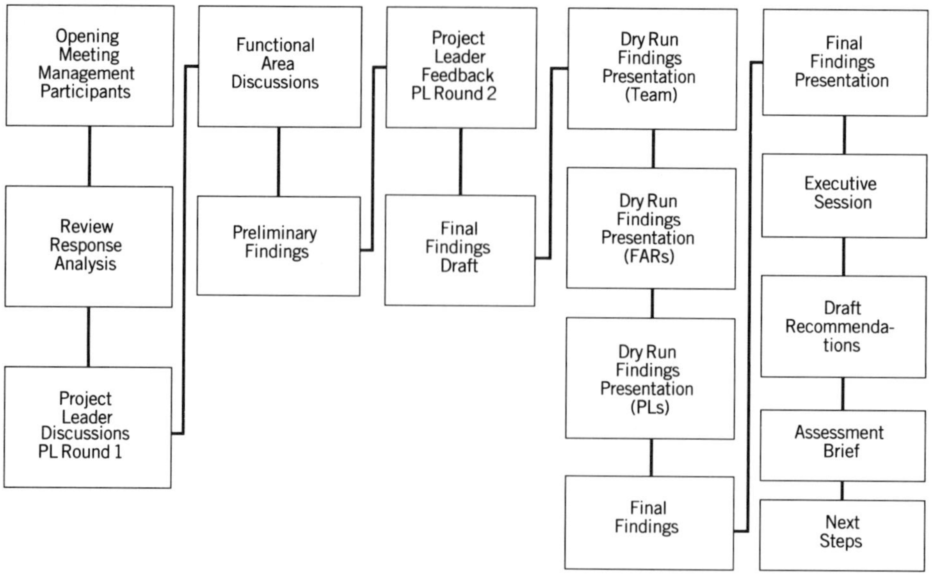

Figure 3. SEI on-site assessment process flow.

identifying all the assessment participants and briefing them on the process, including times, duration, and purpose of their participation. The maturity questionnaire is also filled out at this time.

4. *Assessment Phase.* In the fourth phase, the on-site assessment is conducted. The general structure and content of this period is shown in Figure 3. On the first day, senior management and assessment participants are briefed as a group about the objectives and activities of the assessment. The team then holds discussions with the leader of each selected project to clarify information provided from the maturity questionnaire. On the second day, the team holds discussions with the functional area representatives (FARs). These are selected software practitioners who provide the team with insight into the actual conduct of the software process. At the end of the second day, the team generates a preliminary set of findings. Over the course of the third day, the assessment team seeks feedback from the project representatives to help ensure that they properly understand the issues. A final findings briefing is then produced by the team. On the fourth day, this briefing is further refined through dry run presentations for the team, the FARs, and the project leaders. The findings are revised and presented to the assessment participants and senior site management on the fifth day. The assessment ends with an assessment team meeting to formulate preliminary recommendations.
5. *Report Phase.* The fifth phase is for the preparation and presentation of the assessment report. This includes the findings and recommendations for actions to address these findings. The entire assessment team participates in preparing this report and presenting it to senior management and the assessment participants. A written assessment report provides an essential record of the assessment findings and recommendations. Experience has shown that this record has lasting value for the assessed organization.
6. *Assessment Follow-Up Phase.* In the final phase, a team from the assessed organization formulates an action plan. This should include members from the assessment team. There may be some support and guidance from the assessment vendor during this phase. Action plan preparation typically takes from three to nine months and requires several person-years' professional effort. After approximately 18 months, the organization should do a reassessment to assess progress and to sustain the software process improvement cycle.

To conduct assessments successfully, the assessment team must recognize that their objective is to learn from the organization. Consequently, 50 or more people are typically interviewed to learn what is done, what works, where there are problems, and what ideas the people have for process improvement. Most of the people interviewed are non-management software professionals.

Software Capability Evaluation

Software capability evaluations (SCE), are typically conducted as part of the Department of Defense or other government or commercial software acquisition process. Many U.S. government groups have used SCE and several commercial organizations have also found them useful in evaluating their software contractors and subcontractors. A software capability evaluation is applied to the site where the proposed software work is to be performed. While an assessment is a confidential review of an organization's software capability largely by its own staff, an evaluation is more like an audit by an outside organization.

The software capability evaluation method helps acquisition agencies understand the software management and engineering processes used by a bidder. To be fully effective, the SCE evaluation approach should be included in the Source Selection Plan and the key provisions described in the request for proposal. After proposal submission and SCE evaluation team training, site visits are planned with each bidder. The acquisition agency then selects several representative projects from a set of submitted alternatives, and the project managers from the selected projects are asked to fill out a maturity questionnaire.

The on-site evaluation team visits each bidder and uses the maturity questionnaire to guide selection of the representative practices for detailed examination. Information is generally gained through interviews and documentation reviews. By investigating the process used on the bidder's current projects, the team can identity specific records to review and quickly identity key risk areas. The risk categories considered in these evaluations are of three types:

- The likelihood that the proposed process will meet the acquisition needs.
- The likelihood that the vendor will actually install the proposed process.
- The likelihood that the vendor will effectively implement the proposed process.

Because of the judgmental nature of risk evaluations, it is essential that each evaluation use consistent criteria and a consistent method. The SCE method provides this consistency.

Integrating the evaluation method into the acquisition process involves four steps:

1. Identifying the maturity of the contractor's current software process.
2. Assessing program risks and how the contractor's improvement plans alleviate these risks.
3. Making continuous process improvement a part of the contractual acquisition relationship.
4. Ongoing monitoring of software process performance.

Evaluations take time and resources. To be fully effective, the evaluation team must be composed of qualified and experienced software professionals who understand both the acquisition and the software processes. They typically need at least two weeks to prepare for and perform each site visit. Each bidder must support the site visit with the availability of qualified managers and professional staff members. Both the government and the bidders thus expend considerable resources in preparing for and performing evaluations for a single procurement. Software capability evaluations should thus be limited to large-scale and/or critical software systems, and they should only be performed after determining which bidders are in the competitive range.

A principal reason for this SCE evaluation approach is to assist during the source selection phase of a project. No development project has yet been established to do the work, so other representative projects must be examined. The review thus examines the development practices used on several current projects because these practices are likely representative of those to be used on the new project. The SCE evaluation thus provides a basis for judging the nature of the development process that will be used on a future development.

Because of the audit nature of the evaluation process, it must follow a somewhat different approach from that used with assessments. The organizations tend to use more managers to provide information and the evaluation team is more concerned with insuring that the information is complete and accurate.

Contract Monitoring

The SCE method can also be used to monitor existing software contracts. Here, the organization evaluates the maturity of the development work being done on the current contract. While the process is similar to that used in source selection, it is somewhat simpler. During the site visit, for example, the evaluation team typically only examines the project under contract. To facilitate development of a cooperative problem-solving attitude, some acquisition agencies have found it helpful to use combined acquisition-contractor teams and to follow a process that combines features of assessments and evaluations. As more experience is gained it is expected that contract monitoring techniques will evolve and improve as well.

Other Assessment Methods

Self-assessments are another form of SEI assessment, with the primary distinction being assessment team composition. Self-assessment teams are composed primarily of software professionals from the organization being assessed. It is essential, however, to have one or two software professionals on the team who have been trained in the SEI method. The context, objective, and degree of validation are the same as for SEI-assisted assessments.

Vendor-assisted assessments are SEI assessments that are conducted under the guidance of commercial vendors who have been trained and licensed to do so by the SEI. The assessment team is trained by the vendor and consists of software professionals from the organization being assessed plus at least one vendor professional who has been licensed by the SEI. By licensing commercial vendors, SEI has made software process assessments available to the general software community.

During the early development of the assessment method, SEI conducted a number of assessment tutorials. Here, professionals from various organizations learned about process management concepts, assessment techniques, and the SEI assessment methodology. They also supplied demographic data on themselves and their organizations as well as on a specific project. The did this by completing several questionnaires. This format was designed to inform people about the SEI assessment methodology and to get some early data on the state of the software practice.

Assessment and Evaluation Considerations

The basic purposes of the Software Process Maturity Model, assessment method, and capability evaluation method are to foster the improvement of U.S. industrial software capability. The assessment method assists industry in its self-improvement efforts and the capability evaluation method provides acquisition groups with an objective and repeatable basis for determining the software capabilities of their vendors. This in turn helps to motivate software organizations to improve their capabilities. Generally, vendors cannot continue to invest in efforts that are not valued by their customers. Unless a software vendor's capability is recognized and valued by its customers, there can thus be little continuing motivation for process improvement. The SCE approach facilitates sustained process improvement by establishing process quality criteria, making these criteria public, and supporting software acquisition groups in their application.

One common concern with any evaluation system concerns the possibility that software vendors could customize their responses to achieve an artificially high result. This concern is a consequence of the common misconception that questionnaire scores alone are used in SCE evaluations. Experience with acquisitions demonstrates that the SCE method makes this strategy impractical. When properly trained evaluators look for evidence of sound process practices, they have no difficulty in identifying organizations with poor software capability. Well-run software projects leave a clear documented trail that less competent organizations are incapable of emulating. For example, an organization that manages software changes has extensive change review procedures, approval documents, and control board meeting minutes. People who have not done such work are incapable of pretending that they do. In the few cases where such pretense has been attempted, it was quickly detected and caused the evaluators to doubt everything else they had been told. To date, the record indicates that the most effective contractor strategy is to actually implement a software process improvement program.

STATE OF SOFTWARE PRACTICE

One of the most effective quality improvement methods is called benchmarking. Here, an organization identifies one or more leading organizations in an area and then consciously strives to match or surpass them. Benchmarking has several advantages. First, it clearly demonstrates that the methods are not theoretical and that they are actually in use by a leading organization. Second, when the benchmarked organization is willing to cooperate, it can be very helpful in providing guidance and suggestions. Third, a benchmarking strategy provides a real and tangible goal and the excitement of a competition. SEI has established state-of-the-practice data and has urged leading software organizations to identity themselves to help introduce the benchmarking method to the software development community.

While no statistically constructed survey of software engineering practice is available, SEI has published data drawn from the assessments they have conducted from 1987 through 1991 (Kitson). This includes data on 293 projects at 59 software locations together with interviews of nearly a thousand software managers and practitioners. The bulk of these software projects were in industrial organizations working under contract to the U.S. Department of Defense (DOD). A smaller set of projects was drawn from U.S. commercial software organizations and U.S. government software groups. While there are insufficient data to draw definitive conclusions on the relative maturity of these three groups, SEI has generally found that industrial DOD software contractors have somewhat stronger software process maturity than either the commercial software industry or the government software groups.

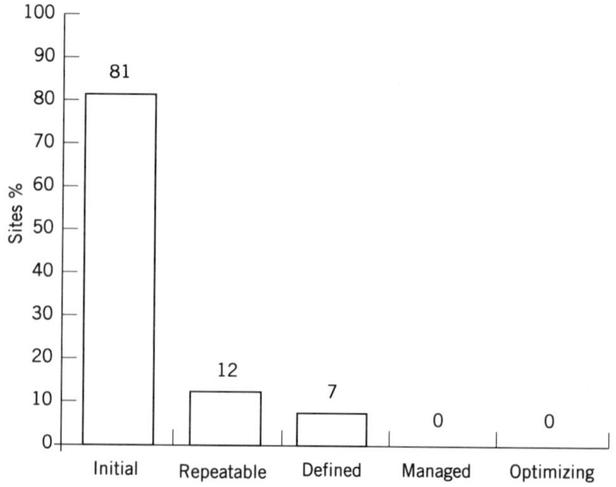

Figure 4. U.S. assessment maturity level distribution.

Figure 4 shows the data that SEI had obtained as of January 1992 on the maturity distribution of U.S. software sites assessed. Those results indicate that the majority of the respondents reported projects at the initial level of maturity with a few at levels 2 and 3. No sites were found at the managed level (level 4) or the optimizing level (level 5) of software process maturity.

While these results generally indicate the state of the software engineering practice in the U.S., there are some important considerations relating to SEI's data gathering and analytical approach.

First, these samples were not statistically selected. Most respondents came from organizations affiliated with the SEI. Second, the respondents also varied in type and degree of involvement with the projects on which they reported.

These results are also a mix of SEI-assisted and self-assessments. While the assessment methods were the same in all cases, the selection process was not. SEI focused primarily on organizations whose software work was of particular importance to the DOD or organizations that were judged to be doing advanced work. Figure 5 shows these two distributions. Here, the SEI-assisted assessments covered 63 projects at 13 sites and the self-assessments covered 233 projects at 46 sites.

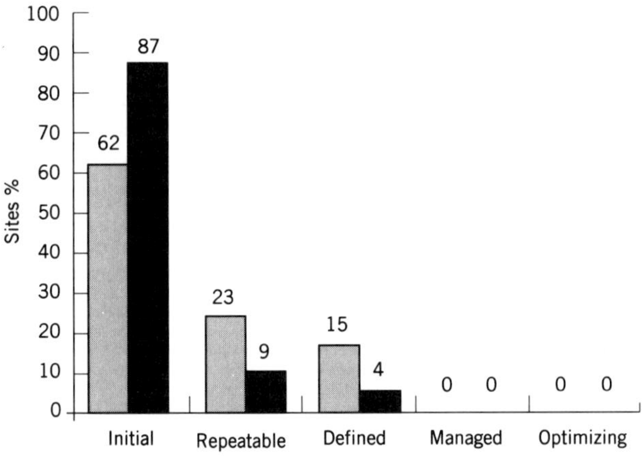

Figure 5. U.S. SEI-assisted assessment maturity level, distribution by assessment type. Thirteen sites encompassing 63 projects conducted SEI-assisted assessments; 46 sites encompassing 233 projects conducted self assessments dark box. SEI-assisted assessments; screen box, self-asssessments.

PROCESS MATURITY AND CASE

CASE systems are intended to help automate the software process. By automating the routine tasks, labor is potentially saved and sources of human error are eliminated. It has been found that a more effective way to improve software productivity is by eliminating mistakes rather than by performing tasks more efficiently (Humphrey, 1989b). This requires an orderly focus on process definition and improvement.

For a complex process to be understood, it must be relatively stable. W. Edwards Deming, who inspired the post war Japanese industrial miracle, refers to this as statistical control (Deming, 1982). When a process is under statistical control, repeating the work in roughly the same way will produce roughly the same result. To get consistently better results, statistical methods can be used to improve the process. The first essential step is to make the software process reasonably stable. After this has been achieved, automation can be considered to improve its efficiency.

Consistent and sustained software process improvement must ultimately utilize improved technology. Improved tools and methods have been helpful throughout the history of software; but once the software process reaches maturity level 5 (optimizing), organizations will be in a far better position to understand where and how technology can help.

In advancing from the level 1 (chaotic) process, major improvements are made by simply turning a crowd of programmers into a coordinated team of professionals. The challenge faced by immature software organizations is to learn how to plan and coordinate the creative work of their professionals so they support rather than interfere with each other. The first priority is for a level 1 organization to establish the project management practices required to reach level 2. It must get its software process under control before it attempts to install a sophisticated CASE system. To be fully effective, CASE systems must be based on a common set of policies, procedures, and methods. If these systems are used with an immature process, automation will generally result in more rapid execution of chaotic activities. This may or may not result in improved organizational performance. This conclusion does not apply to individual task-oriented tools such as compilers and editors, where the tasks are reasonably well understood.

Table 3. On-Board Shuttle Software

	1982	1985
Early error detection, %	48	80
Reconfiguration time, weeks	11	5
Reconfiguration effort, person-years	10.5	4.5
Product error rate, errors per 1000 lines of code	2.0	0.11

IMPROVEMENT EXPERIENCE

Of the many organizations that have worked with SEI on improving their software capability, some have described the benefits they obtained. At Hughes Aircraft, for example, a process improvement investment of $400,000 produced an annual savings of $2,000,000. This was the culmination of several years work by some experienced and able professionals, with strong management support (Humphrey, 1991). Similarly, Raytheon found that the cost benefits of software process improvement work reduced their testing and repair efforts by $19.1 million in about four years (Dion, 1992). While the detailed results of their improvement efforts have not been published, it is understood that their costs were of the same general order of magnitude as that at Hughes Aircraft.

A similar and longer term improvement program was undertaken at IBM Houston by the group that develops and supports the on-board software for the NASA space shuttle. Using these quality principles, and with the aid of IBM's earlier assessment efforts, they achieved the results shown in Table 3 (Kolkhorst, 1988).

FUTURE DIRECTIONS

Future developments with the SEI maturity model must be intimately related to the future developments in software technology and software engineering methods. While many relevant developments are covered in other encyclopedia articles, the major themes discussed in the following paragraphs will likely govern future work with the software capability maturity model.

As the SEI works to evolve and improve the software process maturity model, it will likely focus on organizations in the U.S. but both the Europeans and Japanese are showing considerable interest. With proper direction, this work should evolve into an internationally recognized framework for process improvement. This would likely require broader and more formal review and approval mechanisms to involve all interested parties.

Historically, almost all new developments in the software field have resulted in multiple competing efforts. This has been highly destructive in the cases of languages and operating systems and appears likely to be a serious problem with support environments as well. While each competing idea may have some nuance to recommend it, the large number of choices and the resulting confusion has severely limited the acceptance of many products and has generally had painful economic consequences as well. The SEI has attempted to minimize such a risk by inviting broad participation in the development and review of the CMM and questionnaire improvement efforts. Several hundred software professionals from many branches of industry and government have participated in this work and the SEI change control system now has several thousand recorded comments and suggestions. It is thus hoped that anyone with improvement suggestions will participate in this work rather than start their own. Such separate efforts would dilute the motivational and communication value of the current software process maturity model and make it less effective for process improvement. The need is to evolve the instrument and framework to meet the needs of all interested parties. This would assure maximum utility of the maturity model and retain its credibility in the eyes of managers and acquisition groups.

Several divisions of the U.S. Department of Defense acquisition community are beginning to adopt the SCE method, with the CMM as its basis, as a routine practice for evaluating its major software vendors. This work has been started with the support of the SEI and, as of 1992, more than 500 government personnel had been trained in SCE and more than 45 such acquisitions have been conducted. Roughly 88% of the personnel trained and 75% of the acquisitions conducted were during 1991–1992. This is indicative of the increasing user perception and acceptance of the SCE method as a viable acquisition tool. The anecdotal evidence from these acquisition experiences have been consistently positive for the users, and increased usage is likely.

The greatest risk with SCE is its accelerated use. In their eagerness to address the current severe problems with software acquisition, management could push its application faster than capability evaluation teams could be trained and qualified. If this results in an overzealous audit mentality, industry's improvement motivation will likely be damaged. The result could easily be another expensive and counterproductive step in an already cumbersome and often ineffective acquisition process.

More generally, several research efforts in the U.S. and Europe are addressing various aspects of process modeling and process definition. This work has recognized that processes are much like programs and that their development requires many of the same disciplines and technologies (Osterweil, 1987; Kellner, 1988). This body of work is building improved understanding of the methods and techniques for defining and using processes. This in turn will likely facilitate work on improved automation support of the software process.

CONCLUSIONS

Software is pivotal to U.S. industrial competitiveness, and improved performance of software groups is required for the U.S. to maintain its current strong position. As has happened in many industries, an early U.S. technological lead can easily be lost through lack of timely attention to quality improvement. With proper management support, dedicated software professionals can make consistent and substantial improvements in the performance of their organizations. The SEI Capability maturity model has been helpful to managers and professionals in motivating and guiding this work.

[This work was sponsored by the U. S. Department of Defense.]

BIBLIOGRAPHY

P. B. Crosby, *Quality is Free,* McGraw-Hill, New York, 1979.

W. E. Deming, *Out of the Crisis,* MIT Center for Advanced Engineering Study, Cambridge, Mass., 1982.

R. A. Dion, "Elements of a Process Improvement Program," *IEEE Software, 83–85 (July 1992).*

W. S. Humphrey, *Managing the Software Process,* Addison-Wesley, Reading, Mass., 1989.

W. S. Humphrey, T. R. Snyder, and R. R. Willis, "Software Process Improvement at Hughes Aircraft," *IEEE Software* (July 1991).

W. S. Humphrey and W. L. Sweet, *A Method for Assessing the Software Engineering Capability of Contractors,* Software Engineering Institute Technical Report CMU/SEI-87-TR-23, Carnegie Mellon University, Pittsburgh, Pa., 1987.

M. I. Kellner, "Representation Formalism for Software Process Modeling," *Proceedings of the 4th International Software Process Workshop,* ACM Press, 1988, pp. 93–96.

D. H. Kitson and S. Masters, *An Analysis of SEI Software Process Assessment Results 1987–1991,* Software Engineering Institute Technical Report CMU/SEI-92-TR-24, ADA253351, Carnegie Mellon University, Pittsburgh, Pa., 1992.

B. G. Kolkhorst, and A. J. Marcina, "Developing Error-Free Software," *Proceedings of Computer Assurance Congress '88,* IEEE Washington Section on System Safety, June 27–July 1, 1988, pp. 99–107.

L. Osterweil, "Software Processes are Software Too," *Proceedings of the 9th International Conference on Software Engineering,* Monterey, Calif., IEEE Computer Society Press, 1987, pp. 2–13.

M. C. Paulk, B. Curtis, and M. B. Chrissis, *Capability Maturity Model for Software,* Software Engineering Institute Technical Report CMU/SEI-91-TR-24, Carnegie Mellon University, Pittsburgh, Pa., Aug. 1991.

R. S. Radice, J. T. Harding, P. E. Munnis, and R. W. Phillips, "A Programming Process Study," *IBM Systems Journal,* **24**(2) (1985).

WATTS S. HUMPHREY
Software Engineering Institute

PROCESS MODELS IN SOFTWARE ENGINEERING

INTRODUCTION

Software systems come and go through a series of passages that account for their inception, initial development, productive operation, upkeep, and retirement from one generation to another. This article categorizes and examines a number of schemes for describing or modeling how software systems are developed. First will be some background and definitions of traditional software life cycle models, which dominate most textbook discussions and current software development practices. This is followed by a more comprehensive review of the alternative models of software evolution that have been recently proposed and used as the basis for organizing software engineering projects and technologies.

BACKGROUND

Explicit models of software evolution date back to the earliest projects developing large software systems in the 1950s and 1960s (Benington, 1983; Hosier, 1961; Royce, 1970). Overall, the apparent purpose of these early software life cycle models was to provide an abstract scheme for rationally managing the development of software systems. Such a scheme could, therefore, serve as a basis for planning, organizing, staffing, coordinating, budgeting, and directing software development activities.

For more than three decades, many descriptions of the classic software life cycle (often referred to as the waterfall chart) have appeared (Benington, 1983; Royce, 1970; Boehm, 1976; Distaso, 1980; Scacchi, 1984; Fairley, (1985).Such charts are often employed during introductory presentations to people who may be unfamiliar with what kinds of technical problems and strategies must be addressed when constructing large software systems. These classic software life cycle models usually include some version or subset of the following activities:

- *System Initiation–Adoption.* Where do systems come from? In most situations, new systems replace or supplement existing information processing mechanisms whether they were previously automated, manual, or informal.
- *Requirement Analysis and Specification.* Identifies the problems a new software system is suppose to solve, its operational capabilities, its desired performance characteristics, and the resource infrastructure needed to support system operation and maintenance.
- *Functional Specification or Prototyping.* Identifies and potentially formalizes the objects of computation, their attributes and relationships, the operations that transform these objects, the constraints that restrict system behavior, and so forth.
- *Partition and Selection (Build Versus Buy Versus Reuse).* Given requirements and functional specifications, divide the system into managable pieces that denote logical subsystems, then determine whether new, existing, or reusable software systems correspond to the needed pieces.
- *Architectural Configuration Specification.* Defines the interconnection and resource interfaces between system modules in ways suitable for their detailed design and overall configuration management.
- *Detailed Component Design Specification.* Defines the procedural methods through which each module's data resources are transformed from required inputs into provided outputs.
- *Component Implementation and Debugging.* Codifies the preceding specifications into operational source code implementations and validates their basic operation.
- *Software Integration and Testing.* Affirms and sustains the overall integrity of the software system architectural configuration through verifying the consistency and completeness of implemented modules, verifying the resource interfaces and interconnections against their specifications, and validating the performance of the system and subsystems against their requirements.
- *Documentation Revision and System Delivery.* Packaging and rationalizing recorded system development descriptions into systematic documents and user guides, all in a form suitable for dissemination and system support.
- *Deployment and Installation.* Providing directions for installing the delivered software into the local computing environment, configuring operating systems parameters and user access privileges, running diagnostic test cases to ensure the viability of basic system operation.
- *Training and Use.* Providing system users with instructional aids and guidance for understanding the system's capabilities and limits to use the system effectively.
- *Software Maintenance.* Sustaining the useful operation of a system in its host–target environment by providing requested functional enhancements, repairs, performance improvements, and conversions.

What Is a Software Life Cycle Model?

A software life cycle model is either a descriptive or prescriptive characterization of how software is or should be developed. Typically, it is easier and more common to articulate a prescriptive life cycle model for how software systems should be developed. This is possible because most such models are intuitive or well reasoned. In turn, this allows these models to be used as a basis for software project organization. This means that many idiosyncratic details for how to organize a software development effort can be ignored, generalized, or deferred for later consideration. This, of course, should raise concern for the relative validity and robustness of such life cycle models when developing different kinds of application systems, in different kinds of development settings, using different programming languages, with differently skilled staff, etc. However, prescriptive models are also used to package the development tasks and techniques for using a given set of software engineering tools or environment during a development project.

Descriptive life cycle models, on the other hand, characterize how particular software systems were actually developed in specific sellings. As such, they are less common and more difficult to articulate for an obvious reason: one must observe or collect data throughout the life cycle of a software system, a period of elapsed time often measured in years. Also, descriptive models are specific to the systems observed and only generalizable through systematic comparative analysis. This suggests that the prescriptive software life cycle models will dominate attention until a sufficient base of observational data is available to articulate empirically grounded descriptive life cycle models.

These two characterizations suggest that there are a variety of purposes for articulating software life cycle models. These characterizations serve as

- A guideline to organize, plan, staff, budget, schedule, and manage software project work over organizational time, space, and computing environments.
- Prescriptive outlines for what documents to produce for delivery to client.
- A basis for determining what software engineering tools and methodologies will be most appropriate to support different life cycle activities.
- Frameworks for analyzing or estimating patterns of resource allocation and consumption during the software life cycle (Boehm, 1981).
- Comparative descriptive or prescriptive accounts for how software systems come to be the way they are.
- A basis for conducting empirical studies to determine what affects software productivity, cost, and overall quality.

What Is a Software Process Model?

In contrast to software life cycle models, software process models often represent a networked sequence of activities, objects, transformations, and events that embody strategies for accomplishing software evolution (IEEE, 1984, 1986; Wileden and Dowson, 1986). Such models can be used to develop more precise and formalized descriptions of software life cycle activities. Their power emerges from their use of a sufficiently rich notation, syntax, or semantics, often suitable for computational processing.

Software process networks can be viewed as representing multiple interconnected task chains (Kling and Scacchi, 1982; Garg and Scacchi, 1989). Task chains represent a nonlinear sequence of actions that structure and transform available computational objects (resources) into intermediate or finished products. By nonlinear it is meant that the sequence of actions may be nondeterministic, iterative, accommodate multiple–parallel alternatives, and be partially ordered to account for incremental progress. Task actions in turn can be viewed a nonlinear sequences of primitive actions that denote atomic units of computing work, such as a user's selection of a command or menu entry using a mouse or keyboard. Winograd and Flores (1986) have referred to these units of cooperative work between people and computers as "structured discourses of work."

Task chains can be employed to characterize either prescriptive or descriptive action sequences. Prescriptive task chains are idealized plans of what actions should be accomplished and in what order. For example, a task chain for the activity of object-oriented software design might include the following task actions:

- Develop an informal narrative specification of the system.
- Identify the objects and their attributes.
- Identify the operations on the objects.
- Identify the interfaces between objects, attributes, or operations.
- Implement the operations.

Clearly, this sequence of actions could entail multiple iterations and nonprocedural primitive action invocations in the course of incrementally progressing toward an object-oriented software design.

Task chains join or split into other task chains resulting in an overall production lattice (Kling and Scacchi, 1982). The production lattice represents the organizational production system that transforms raw computational, cognitive, and other organizational resources into assembled, integrated, and usable software systems. The production lattice, therefore, structures how a software system is developed, used, and maintained. However, prescriptive tasks chains and actions cannot be formally guaranteed to anticipate all possible circumstances or idiosyncratic foulups that can emerge in the real world of software development (Gerson and Star, 1986; Gasser, 1986; Scacchi, 1989; Mi and Scacchi, 1990). Thus any software production lattice will in some way realize only an approximate or incomplete description of software development. As such, articulation work will be performed when a planned task chain is inadequate or breaks down. The articulation work can then represent an open-ended nondeterministic sequence of actions taken to restore progress on the disarticulated task chain, or else to shift the flow of productive work onto some other task chain (Bendifallah and Scacchi, 1987; Mi and Scacchi, 1990, 1991). Thus descriptive task chains are employed to characterize the observed course of events and situations that emerge when people try to follow a planned task sequence. Articulation work in the context of software evolution includes actions people take that entail either their accommodation to the contingent or the anomalous behavior of a software system, or negotiation with others who may be able to affect a system modification or otherwise alter current circumstances (Bendifallah and Scacchi, 1987; Mi and Scacchi, 1990, 1991). This notion of articulation work has also been referred to as software process dynamism.

TRADITIONAL SOFTWARE LIFE CYCLE MODELS

Traditional models of software evolution have been around us since the earliest days of software engineering. Four are identified here. The classic software life cycle (or waterfall chart) and stepwise refinement models are widely instantiated in just about all books on modern programming practices and software engineering. The incremental release model is closely related to industrial practices where it most often occurs. Military standards based models have also reified certain forms of the classic life cycle model into required practice for government contractors. Each of these four models use coarse-grain, or macroscopic characterizations when describing software evolution. The progressive steps of software evolution are often described as stages, such as requirements specification, preliminary design, and implementation; these have usually have little or no further characterization other than a list of attributes that the product of such a stage should possess. Furthermore, these models are independent of any organizational development setting, choice of programming language, software application domain, etc. In short, the traditional models are context free rather than context sensitive. But as all of these life cycle models have been in use for some time, they are referred to as the traditional models; each will be characterized in turn.

Classic Software Life Cycle

The classic software life cycle is often represented as a simple waterfall software phase model, for which software evolution proceeds through an orderly sequence of transitions from one phase to the next in order (Royce, 1970). Such models resemble finite state machine descriptions of software evolution. However, such models have been perhaps most useful in helping to structure, staff, and manage large software development projects in complex organizational sellings, which was one of their primary purposes (Royce, 1970; Boehm, 1976). Alternatively, these classic models have been widely characterized as poor descriptive and prescriptive models of how software development "in the small" or "in the large" can or should occur.

Stepwise Refinement

In this approach, software systems are developed through the progressive refinement and enhancement of high level system specifications into source code components (Wirth, 1971). However, the choice and order of which steps to choose and which refinements to apply remain unstated. Instead, formalization is expected to emerge within the hueristics and skills that are acquired and applied through increasingly competent practice. This model has been most effective and widely applied in helping to teach individual programmers how to organize their software development work. Many interpretations of the classic software life cycle thus subsume this approach within their design and implementations.

Iterative Enhancement, Incremental Development, and Release

Developing systems through incremental release requires first providing essential operating functions, then providing system users with improved and more capable versions of a system at regular intervals (Basili and Turner, 1975; Tully, 1984). This model combines the classic software life cycle with iterative enhancement at the level of system development organization. It also supports a strategy periodically to distribute software maintenance updates and services to dispersed user communities. This in turn accommodates the provision of standard software maintenance contracts. It is, therefore, a popular model of software evolution used by many commercial software firms and system vendors. More recently, this approach has been extended through the use of software prototyping tools and techniques (described later), which more directly provide support for incremental development and iterative release for early and ongoing user feedback and evaluation (Graham, 1989). Last, the Cleanroom software development method (used in IBM and NASA laboratories) provides incremental release of software functions and subsystems (developed through stepwise refinement) to separate inhouse quality assurance teams that apply statistical measures and analyses as the basis for certifying high quality software systems (Selby and co-workers, 1987; Mills and co-workers, 1987).

Industrial and Military Standard Models

Industrial firms often adopt some variation of the classic model as the basis for standardizing their software development practices (Royce, 1970; Boehm, 1976; Bistaso, 1980; Scacchi, 1984, 1986). Such standardization is often motivated by the need to simplify or eliminate complications that emerge during large software development or project management. Many government contractors organize their software development activities according to military standards such as that embodied in MIL-STD-2167A (Department of Defense 1988). Such standards outline not only a variant of the classic life cycle activities but also the types of documents required by clients who procure either software systems or complex platforms with embedded software systems. Military software system are often constrained in ways not found in industrial or academic practice: they (1) require the use of military standard computing equipment (which is often technologically dated and possesses limited processing capabilities), (2) are embedded in larger systems (e.g., airplanes, submarines, missiles, command and control systems) that are mission-critical (i.e., untimely failure could result in military disadvantage and life-threatening risks), (3) are developed under contract to private firms through cumbersome procurement and acquisition procedures that can be subject to public scrutiny and legislative intervention, and (4) many embedded software systems for the military are among the largest and most complex systems in the world. In a sense, military software standards are applied to simplify and routinize the administrative processing, review, and oversight required by such institutional circumstances. However, this does not guarantee that delivered software systems will be easy to use or maintain. Nor does it necessarily indicate what decisions, processes, or trade-offs were made in developing the software so as to conform to the standards, to adhere to contract constraints, or to ensure attainment of contractor profit margins. Thus these conditions may not make software development efforts for the military necessarily the most effective or well engineered.

In industrial settings, standard software development models often provide explicit detailed guidelines for how to deploy, install, customize, and tune a new software system release in its operating application environment. In addition, these standards are intended to be compatible with provision of software quality assurance, configuration management, and independent verification and validation services in a multicontractor development project. Recent progress in industrial practice has been described (Humphrey, 1985; Radice, 1985; Yacobellis, 1984). However, neither such progress nor the existence of such standards within a company necessarily implies to what degree standards are routinely followed, whether new staff hires are trained in the standards and conformance, or whether the standards are considered effective.

Alternatives to the Traditional Software Life Cycle Models

There are at least three alternative sets of models of software development. These models are alternatives to the traditional software life cycle models. These three sets focus attention to either the products, production processes, or production settings associated with software development. Collectively, these alternative models are finer grained (often detailed to the point of computational formalization), more often empirically grounded, and in some cases, address the role of new automated technologies in facilitating software development. Although most of these models are not in widespread use, each set of models is examined in the following sections.

SOFTWARE PRODUCT DEVELOPMENT MODELS

Software products represent the information-intensive artifacts that are incrementally constructed and iteratively revised through a software development effort. Such efforts can be modeled using software product life cycle models. These product development models represent an evolutionary revision to the traditional software life cycle models. The revisions arose as a result of the availability of new software development technologies such as software prototyping languages and environments, reusable software, application generators, and documentation support environments. Each of these technologies seeks to enable the creation of executable software implementations either earlier in the software development effort or more rapidly. Therefore, in this regard, the models of software development may be implicit in the use of the technology rather than explicitly articulated. This is possible because such models become increasingly intuitive to those developers whose favorable experiences with these technologies substantiates their use. Thus detailed examination of these models is most appropriate when such technologies are available for use or experimentation.

Rapid Prototyping

Prototyping is a technique for providing a reduced functionality or a limited performance version of a software system early in its development (Balzer and co-workers, 1982; Squires and co-workers, 1982; Boehm, 1984, 1986; Hekmatpour, 1987; Connell and Shafer, 1989). In contrast to the classic system life cycle, prototyping is an approach whereby more emphasis, activity, and processing is directed to the early stages of software development (requirements, analysis, and functional specification). In turn, prototyping can more directly accommodate early user participation in determining, shaping, or evaluating emerging system functionality. As a result, this up-front concentration of effort, together with the use of prototyping technologies, seeks to trade-off or otherwise reduce downstream software design activities and iterations as well as simplify the software implementation effort.

Software prototypes come in different forms, including throwaway prototypes, mockups, demonstration systems, quick-and-dirty prototypes, and incremental evolutionary prototypes (Connell and Shafer, 1989). Increasing functionality and subsequent evolvability is what distinguishes the prototype forms on this list. Prototyping technologies usually take some form of software functional specifications as their starting point or input, which in turn is either simulated, analyzed, or directly executed. As such, these technologies allow software design activities to be initially skipped or glossed over. In turn, these technologies allow developers to rapidly construct easy or primitive versions of software systems that users can evaluate. These user evaluations can then be incorporated as feedback to refine the emerging system specifications and designs. Furthermore, depending on the prototyping technology, the complete working system can be developed by continually revising and refining the input specifications. This has the advantage of always providing a working version of the emerging system, while redefining software design and testing activities to input specification refinement and execution. Alternatively, some prototyping approaches are best suited for developing throwaway or demonstration systems or for building prototypes by reusing part or all of some existing software systems.

Assembling Reusable Componentry

The basic approach of reusability is to configure and specialize preexisting software components into viable application systems (Biggerstaff and Perlis, 1984; Neighbors, 1984; Goguen, 1986). Such source code components might already have specifications and designs associated with their implementations as well as have been tested and certified. However, it is also clear that software specifications, designs, and test case suites may themselves be treated as reusable software development components. Therefore, assembling reusable software components is a strategy for decreasing software development effort in ways that are compatible with the traditional life cycle models.

The basic dilemmas encountered with reusable software componentry include (1) how to define an appropriate software part naming or classification scheme, (2) collecting or building reusable software components, (3) configuring or composing components into a viable application (Allen and Lee, 1989); and (4) maintaining and searching a components library (Wood and Sommerville, 1988). In turn, each of these dilemmas is mitigated or resolved in practice through the selection of software component granularity.

The granularity of the components (ie, size, complexity, and functional capability) varies greatly across different approaches. Most approaches attempt to use components similar to common (textbook) data structures with algorithms for their manipulation as small-grain components. However, the use–reuse of small-grain components in and of itself does not constitute a distinct approach to software development. Other approaches attempt to use components resembling functionally complete systems or subsystems (e.g., user interface management system) as large-grain components. The use–reuse of large-grain components, guided by an application domain analysis and subsequent mapping of attributed domain objects and operations onto interrelated components, does appear to be an alternative approach to developing software systems (Neighbors, 1984), and thus is an area of active research.

There are many ways to use reusable software components in evolving software systems. However, the cited studies suggest their initial use during architectural or component design specification as a way to speed implementation. They might also be used for prototyping purposes if a suitable software prototyping technology is available.

Application Generation

Application generation is an approach to software development similar to reuse of parameterized, large-grain software source code components. Such components are configured and specialized to an application domain via a formalized specification language used as input to the application generator. Common examples provide standardized interfaces to database management system applications, and include generators for reports, graphics, user interfaces, and application-specific editors (Horowitz and coworkers, 1985).

Application generators give rise to a model of software development whereby traditional software design activities are either all but eliminated or reduced to a database design problem. The software design activities are eliminated or reduced because the application generator embodies or provides a generic software design that is supposed to be compatible with the application domain. However, users of application generators are usually expected to provide input specifications and application maintenance services. These capabilities are possible because the generators can usually only produce software systems specific to a small number of similar application domains, usually those that depend on a database management system.

Software Documentation Support Environments

Much of the focus on developing software products draws attention to the tangible software artifacts that result. Most often, these products take the form of documents: commented source code listings, structured design diagrams, unit development folders, etc. These documents characterize what the developed system is suppose to do, how it does it, how it was developed, how it was put together and validated, and how to install, use, and maintain it. Thus a collection of software documents records the passage of a developed software system through a set of life cycle stages.

It seems reasonable that there will be models of software development that focus attention to the systematic production, organization, and management of the software development documents. Furthermore, as documents are tangible products, it is common practice when software systems are developed under contract to a private firm, that the delivery of these documents is a contractual stipulation as well as the basis for receiving payment for development work already performed. Thus the need to support and validate conformance of these documents to software development and quality assurance standards emerges. However, software development documents are often a primary medium for communication between developers, users, and maintainers that spans organizational space and time. Thus each of these groups can benefit from automated mechanisms that allow them to browse, query, retrieve, and selectively print documents (Garg and Scacchi, 1990). As such, do not be surprised to see construction and deployment of software environments that provide ever-increasing automated support for engineering the software documentation life cycle (Penedo and Stuckle, 1985; Horowitz and Williamson, 1986; Choi and Scacchi, 1989; Garg and Scacchi, 1990).

Program Evolution Models

In contrast to the preceding four prescriptive product development models, Lehman and Belady (1985) sought to develop a descriptive model of software product evolution. They conducted a series of empirical studies of the evolution of large software systems at IBM during the 1970s. Based on their investigations, they identify five properties that characterize the evolution of large software systems:

1. *Continuing Change.* A large software system undergoes continuing change or becomes progressively less useful.
2. *Increasing Complexity.* As a software system evolves, its complexity increases unless work is done to maintain or reduce it.
3. *Fundamental Law of Program Evolution.* Program evolution, the programming process, and global measures of project and system attributes are statistically self-regulating with determinable trends and invariances.
4. *Invariant Work Rate.* The rate of global activity in a large software project is statistically invariant.
5. *Incremental Growth Limit.* During the active life of a large program, the volume of modifications made to successive releases is statistically invariant.

However, it is important to observe that these are global properties of large software systems, not causal mechanisms of software development.

SOFTWARE PRODUCTION PROCESS MODELS

There are two kinds of software production process models: nonoperational and operational. Both are software process models. The difference between the two primarily stems from the fact that the operational models can be viewed as computational scripts or programs: programs that implement a particular regimen of software engineering and development. Nonoperational models, on the other hand, denote conceptual approaches that have not yet been sufficiently articulated in a form suitable for codification or automated processing.

Nonoperational Process Models

There are two classes of nonoperational software process models of the great interest. These are the spiral model and the continuous transformation model. There are also a wide selection of other nonoperational models that, for brevity, have been labeled as miscellaneous models. Each is examined in turn.

The Spiral Model. The spiral model of software development and evolution represents a risk-driven approach to software process analysis and structuring (Boehm, 1986). This approach incorporates elements of specification-driven, prototype-driven process methods together with the classic software life cycle. It does so by representing iterative development cycles as an expanding spiral, with inner cycles denoting early system analysis and prototyping and outer cycles denoting the classic software life cycle. The radial dimension denotes cumulative development costs, and the angular dimension denotes progress made in accomplishing each development spiral.

Risk analysis, which seeks to identify situations that might cause a development effort to fail or go over budget or schedule, occurs during each spiral cycle. In each cycle, it represents roughly the same amount of angular displacement, whereas the displaced sweep volume denotes increasing levels of effort required for risk analysis. System development in this model therefore spirals out only as far as needed according to the risk that must be managed. Alternatively, the spiral model indicates that the classic software life cycle model need only be followed when risks are greatest and after early system prototyping as a way of reducing these risks, albeit at increased cost. Finally, efforts to prototype and develop operational versions of the spiral model are being pursued (AMC, 1988).

Continuous Transformation Models. Continuous transformation models propose a process whereby software systems are developed through an ongoing series of transformations of problem statements into abstract specifications into concrete implementations (Wirth, 1971; Basili and Turner, 1975; Bauer, 1976; Balzer, 1981). Most of these models propose a scheme whereby there is no traditional life cycle or separate stages, but instead there is an ongoing series of reifying transformations that turn abstract specifications into more concrete programs (Lehman, 1984). In this sense then, problem statements and software systems can emerge somewhat together and thus can continue to coevolve.

Continuous transformation models also accommodate the interests of software formalists who seek the precise statement of formal properties of software system specifications. Accordingly, the specified formalisms can be mathematically transformed into properties that a source implementation should satisfy. The potential for automating such models is apparent, but it still the subject of ongoing research (see below).

Miscellaneous Process Models. Many variations of the non-operational life cycle and process models have been proposed, and appear in the proceedings of four software process workshops (IEEE, 1984, 1986; AMC, 1988; Wileden and Dowson, 1986). These include fully interconnected life cycle models that accommodate transitions between any two phases subject to satisfaction of their preconditions and postconditions as well as compound variations on the traditional life cycle and continuous transformation models. However, the cited reports indicate that, in general, most of these software process models are exploratory, so little experience with these models has been reported.

Operational Process Models

In contrast to the nonoperational process models, many models are now beginning to appear that codify software engineering processes in computational terms, as programs or executable models. Three classes of operational software process models can be identified and examined.

Operational Specifications for Rapid Prototyping. The operational approach to software development assumes the existence of a formal specification language and processing environment (Bauer, 1976; Balzer and co-workers, 1982, 1983a; Zave, 1984). Specifications in the language are coded, and when computationally evaluated, they constitute a functional prototype of the specified system. When such specifications can be developed and processed incrementally, the resulting system prototypes can be refined and evolved into functionally more complete systems. However, the emerging software systems are always operational in some form during their development. Variations within this approach represent efforts in which either the prototype is the end sought or specified prototypes are kept operational but refined into a complete system.

The power underlying operational specification technology is determined by the specification language. Simply stated, if the specification language is a conventional programming language, then nothing new in the way of software development is realized. However, if the specification incorporates (or extends to) syntactic and semantic language constructs that are specific to the application domain, which usually are not part of conventional programming languages, then domain-specific rapid prototyping can be supported.

An interesting twist worth note is that it is generally within the capabilities of many operational specification languages to specify systems whose purpose is to serve as a model of an arbitrary abstract process, e.g., a software process model. In this way, using a prototyping language and environment, one might be able to specify an abstract model of some software engineering processes as a system that produces and consumes certain types of documents as well as the classes of development transformations applied to them. Thus, in this regard, it is possible to construct operational software process models that can be executed or simulated using software prototyping technology. Humphrey and Kellner (1989) describe one such application and give an example using the graphic-based state-machine notation provided in the STATECHARTS environment.

Software Process Automation and Programming. Process automation and programming are concerned with developing formal specifications of how a (family of software system(s) should be developed. Such specifications, therefore, should provide an account for the organization and description of various software production task chains, how they interrelate, when then can iterate, etc as well as what software tools to use to support different tasks and how these tools should be used (Hoffnagel and Peregi, 1985; Huseth and Vines, 1986; Osterweil, 1987). Focus then converges on characterizing the constructs incorporated into the language for specifying and programming software processes. Accordingly, discussion then examines the appropriateness of language constructs for expressing rules for backward and forward chaining (Kaiser and co-workers, 1988), behavior (Williams, 1988), object type structures, process dynamism, constraints, goals, policies, modes of user interaction, plans, off-line activities, resource commitments, etc. across various levels of granularity. This in turn implies that conventional mechanisms such as operating system shell scripts (e.g., Makefiles on Unix) do not support the kinds of software process automation these constructs portend.

Lehman (1987) and Curtis and co-workers, (1987) provide provocative critiques of the potential and limitations of the early proposals for software process automation and programming. Their criticisms, essentially point out that many process programming proposals (as of 1987) were focused almost exclusively to those aspects of software engineering that were amenable to automation, such as tool sequence invocation. They point out how such proposals often fail to address how the production settings and products constrain and interact with how the software production process is defined and performed, as revealed in empirical software process studies (Bendifallah and Scacchi, 1987, 1989; Curtis and co-workers, 1988).

Knowledge-Based Software Automation. Knowledge-based software automation (KBSA) attempts to take process automation to its limits by assuming that process specifications can be used directly to develop software systems and to configure development environments to support the production tasks at hand. The common approach is to seek to automate some form of the continuous transformation model (Bauer, 1976; Balzer, 1985; Lowry and McCartney, 1991). In turn, this implies an automated environment capable of recording the formalized development of operational specifications, successively transforming and refining these specifications into an implemented system, assimilating maintenance requests by incorporating the new or enhanced specifications into the current development derivation, then replaying the revised development toward implementation (Balzer and co-workers, 1983b; Balzer, 1985). However, progress has been limited to demonstrating such mechanisms and specifications on software coding, maintenance, project communication, and management tasks (Balzer and co-workers, 1983b; Balzer, 1985; Cheatham, 1986; Kedzjerski, 1984; Santi and co-workers, 1985, 1986; Mi and Scacchi, 1990; Lowry and McCartney, 1991) as well as more recently to software component catalogs and formal models of software development processes (Ould and Roberts, 1988; Wood and Sommerville, 1988). Last, recent research has shown how to combine different life cycle, product, and production process models within a process-driven framework that integrates both conventional and knowledge-based software engineering tools and environments (Mi and Scacchi, 1992).

CONCLUSIONS

In conclusion, the central thesis of this article is that contemporary models of software development must account for software the interrelationships between software products and production processes as well as for the roles played by people and tools. Such models can thus use features of traditional software life cycle models as well as those of automatable software process models.

BIBLIOGRAPHY

ACM, ed., *Proceedings of the Fourth International Software Process Workshop,* Devon, UK, ACM Press, 1988.

B. P. Allen and S. D. Lee, *A Knowledge-based Environment for the Development of Software Parts Composition Systems, paper presented at the Eleventh International Conference on Software Engineering, 1989.*

R. Balzer, "Transformational Implementation: An Example," *IEEE Trans. Software Eng.* **SE-7**(1), 3–14 (1981).

R. Balzer, "A 15 Year Perspective on Automatic Programming," *IEEE Trans. Software Eng.* **SE-11,** (11) 1257–1267 (Nov. 1985).

R. Balzer, T. Cheatham, and C. Green, "Software Technology in the 1990's: Using a New Paradigm," *Computer* **16**(11), 39–46 (Nov. 1983b).

R. Balzer, D. Cohen, M. Feather, N. Goldman W. Swartout, and D. Wile, "Operational Specifications as the Basis for Specification Validation," in G. Ferrari, *Theory and Practice of Software Technology,* North-Holland, Amsterdam, 1983a pp. 287–301.

R. Balzer, N. Goldman, and D. Wile, "Operational Specifications as the Basis for Rapid Prototyping," *ACM Software Eng. Notes* **7**(5), 3–16 (1982).

V. R. Basili and A. J. Turner, "Iterative Enhancement: A Practical Technique for Software Development," *IEEE Trans. Software Eng.* **SE-1**(4), 390–396 (Dec. 1975).

F. L. Bauer, *Programming as an Evolutionary Process,* paper presented at the Second International Conference on Software Engineering, Jan. 1976.

S. Bendifallah and W. Scacchi, "Understanding Software Maintenance Work," *IEEE Trans. Software Eng.* **SE-13**(3), 311–323 (Mar. 1987).

S. Bendifallah and W. Scacchi, "*Work Structures and Shifts: An Empirical Analysis of Software Specification Teamwork,* paper presented at the Eleventh International Conference on Software Engineering, 1989.

H. D. Benington, "Production of Large Computer Programs," *Ann. History Comput.* **5**(4), 350–361 (1983).

T. Biggerstaff and A. Pedis, eds., "Special Issues on Software Reusability," *IEEE Trans. Software Eng.* **SE-10**(5) (Sept. 1984).

B. Boehm, "Software Engineering," *IEEE Trans. Comp.* **C-25**(12), 1226–1241 (Dec. 1976).

B. W. Boehm, *Software Engineering Economics,* Prentice-Hall, Inc., Englewood Cliffs, N.J., 1981.

B. W. Boehm, "A Spiral Model of Software Development and Enhancement," *ACM Software Eng. Notes* **11**(4), 22–42 (1986).

B. W. Boehm, T. Gray, and T. Seewaldt, *Prototyping vs. Specifying: A Multi-project Experiment,* paper presented at the Seventh International Conference on Software Engineering, 1984.

R. Budde, K. Kuhlenkamp, L. Mathiassen, and H. Zullighoven, *Approaches to Prototyping,* Springer-Verlag, New York, 1984.

T. Cheatham, *Supporting the Software Process,* paper presented at the Nineteenth Hawaii International Conference on Systems Sciences, 1986.

S. Choi and W. Scacchi, "Assuring the Correctness of Configured Software Descriptions," *ACM Software Eng. Notes* **17**(7) 67–76 (1989).

J. L. Connell and L. B. Shafer, *Structured Rapid Prototyping,* Yourdon Press, Prentice-Hall, Englewood Cliffs, N.J. 1989.

B. Curtis, H. Krasner, and N. Iscoe, "A Field Study of the Software Design Process for Large Systems," *Commun. ACM* **31**(11), 1268–1287 (Nov. 1988).

B. Curtis, H. Krasner, V. Shen, and N. Iscoe, *On Building Software Process Models under the Lamppost,* paper presented at the Ninth International Conference of Software Engineering, Apr. 1987.

Department of Defense, *DRAFT Military Standard: Defense System Software Development,* DOD-STD-2167A, DOD, Washington, D.C., 1988

J. Distaso, "Software Management—A Survey of Practice in 1980," *Proc. IEEE* **68**(9), 1103–1119 (1980).

R. Fairley, *Software Engineering Concepts,* McGraw-Hill Book Co., Inc., New York, 1985.

P. K. Garg and W. Scacchi, "ISHYS: Design of an Intelligent Software Hypertext Environment," *IEEE Expert* **4**(3), 52–63 (1989).

P. K. Garg and W. Scacchi, "A Hypertext System to Manage Software Life Cycle Documents," *IEEE Software* **7**(2), 90–99 (1990).

L. Gasser, L. "The Integration of Computing and Routine Work," *ACM Trans. Office Info. Sys.* **4**(3), 205–225 (1986).

E. Gerson and S. L. Star. "Analyzing Due Process in the Workplace," *ACM Trans. Office Info. Sys.* **4**(3) (1986).

J. Goguen, "Reusing and Interconnecting Software Components," *Computer* **19**(2), 16–28 (Feb. 1986).

D. R. Graham, "Incremental Development: Review of Nonmonolithic Life-Cycle Development Models," *Info. Software Technol.* **31**(1) 7–20 (Jan. 1989).

S. Hekmatpour, "Experience with Evolutionary Prototyping in a Large Software Project," *ACM Software Eng. Notes* **12**(1) 38–41 (1987).

G. F. Hoffnagel and W. Beregi, "Automating the Software Development Process," *IBM Sys. J.* **24**(2), 102–120 (1985).

E. Horowitz, A. Kemper, and B. Narasimhan, "A Survey of Application Generators," *IEEE Software* **2**(1), 40–54 (Jan. 1985).

E. Horowitz and R. Williamson, "SODOS: A Software Documentation Support Environment—Its Definition," *IEEE Trans. Software Eng.* **SE-12**(8), 849–859 (1986).

W. A. Hosier, "Pitfalls and Safeguards in Real-Time Digital Systems with Emphasis on Programming," *IRE Trans Eng. Manage.* **EM-8**, 99–114 (June 1961).

W. S. Humphrey, "The IBM Large-Systems Software Development Process: Objectives and Direction," *IBM Sys. J* **24**(2), 76–78 (1985).

W. S. Humphrey and M. Kellner, *Software Process Modeling: Principles of Entity Process Models,* paper presented at the Eleventh International Conference on Software Engineering, 1989.

S. Huseth and D. Vines, *Describing the Software Process,* paper presented at the Third International Software Process Workshop, 1986.

IEEE, ed., *Software Process Workshop,* Los Alamitos, Calif., IEEE Computer Society, 1984.

IEEE, ed., *Third International Software Process Workshop,* Los Alamitos, Calif., IEEE Computer Society, 1986.

G. Kaiser, P. Feiler, and S. Popovich, "Intelligent Assistance for Software Development and Maintenance," *IEEE Software* **5**(3) (1988).

B. I. Kedzierski, *Knowledge-Based Project Management and Communication Support in a System Development Environment,* paper presented at the Fourth Jerusalem Conf. Info. Technology, 1984.

R. Kling and W. Scacchi, "The Web of Computing: Computer Technology as Social Organization," *Adv. Comput.* **21** 1–90 (1982).

M. M. Lehman, *A Further Model of Coherent Programming Processes,* paper presented at the Software Process Workshop, 1984.

M. M. Lehman, *Process Models, Process Programming, Programming Support,* paper presented at the Ninth International Conference on Software Engineering, April, 1987.

M. M. Lehman and L. Belady, *Program Evolution: Processes of Software Change,* Academic Press, Inc., New York, 1985.

M. M. Lehman, V. Stenning, and W. Turski, "Another Look at Software Development Methodology," *ACM Software Eng. Notes* **9**(2), 283–294 (1984).

M. Lowry and R. McCartney, eds., *Automating Software Design,* AAAI and MIT Press, Menlo Park, Calif., 1991.

P. Mi and W. Scacchi, "A Knowledge Base Environment for Modeling and Simulating Software Engineering Processes," *IEEE Trans. Knowledge Data Eng.* **2**(3), 283–294 (1990).

H. D. Mills, M. Dyer, and R. C. Linger, "Cleanroom Software Engineering," *IEEE Software* **4**(5), 19–25 (1987).

P. Mi and W. Scacchi, *Modeling Articulation Work in Software Engineering Processes,* paper presented at the First International Conference on Software Process, 1991.

P. Mi and W. Scacchi, "Process Integrations for CASE Environments," *IEEE Software* **9**(2), 45–53 (1992).

J. Neighbors, "The Draco Approach to Constructing Software from Reusable Components," *IEEE Trans. Software Eng.* **SE-10**(5), 564–574 (Sept. 1984).

L. Osterweil, *Software Processes Are Software Too,* paper presented at the Ninth International Conference on Software Engineering, Apr. 1987.

M. A. Ould and C. Roberts, "Defining Formal Models of the Software Development Process," P. Brererton, ed., in *Software Engineering Environments,* Ellis Horwood, Chichester, UK, 1988, pp. 13–26.

M. H. Penedo and E. D. Stuckle, *PMDB—A Project Master Database for Software Engineering Environments,* paper presented at the Eighth International Conference on Software Engineering, 1985.

R. A. Radice, N. K. Roth, A. L. O'Hara, Jr., and W. A. Ciarfella, "A Programming Process Architecture," *IBM Sys. J.* **24**(2), 79–90 (1985).

W. W. Royce, *Managing the Development of Large Software Systems,* paper presented at the Ninth International Conference on Software Engineering, 1987.

A. Sathi, M. S. Fox, and M. Greenberg, "Representation of Activity Knowledge for Project Management," *IEEE Trans. Patt. Anal. Mach. Intell.* **PAMI-7**(5), 531–552 (1985).

A. Sathi, T. Morton, and S. Roth, "Callisto: An Intelligent Project Management System," *AI Mag.* **7**(5), 34–52 (1986).

W. Scacchi, "Managing Software Engineering Projects: A Social Analysis," *IEEE Trans. Software Eng.* **SE-10**(1), 49–59 (Jan. 1984).

W. Scacchi, "Shaping Software Behemoths," *UNIX Rev.* **4**(10), 46–55 (Oct. 1986).

W. Scacchi, "Designing Software Systems to Facilitate Social Organization," in *Work with Computers, Vol. 12A, Advances in Human Factors and Ergonomics,* G. Salvendy, ed., Elsevier, Amsterdam, The Netherlands, 1989, pp. 64–72.

R. W. Selby, V. R. Basili, and T. Baker, "CLEANROOM Software Development: An Empirical Evaluation," *IEEE Trans. Software Eng.* **SE-13**(9), 1027–1037 (1987).

S. Squires, M. Barnstad, and M. Zelkowitz, eds., "Special Issue on Rapid Prototyping," *ACM Software Eng. Notes* **7**(5) (Dec. 1982).

C. Tully, *Software Development Models,* paper presented at the Software Process Workshop, 1984.

J. Wileden and M. Dowson, eds., "Second International Workshop on Software Process and Software Environments," *ACM Software Eng. Notes* **11**(4) (1986).

L. Williams, *Software Process Modeling: A Behavioral Approach,* Tenth International Conference on Software Engineering, IEEE Computer Society Press, Los Alamitos, Calif., 1988, pp. 174–200.

T. Winograd and F. Flores, *Understanding Computers and Cognition: A New Foundation for Design,* Ablex Publishers, 1986.

N. Wirth, "Program Development by Stepwise Refinement," *Commun. ACM* **14**(4), 221–227 (April 1971).

M. Wood and I. Sommerville, "A Knowledge-Based Software Components Catalogue," P. Brererton, ed., *Software Engineering Environments,* Ellis Horwood, Chichester, UK, 1988, pp. 116–131.

R. H. Yacobellis, *Software and Development Process Quality Metrics,* paper presented at COMPSAC 84, 1984.

P. Zave, "The Operational Versus the Conventional Approach to Software Development," *Commun. ACM* **27,** 104–118 (Feb. 1984).

WALT SCACCHI
University of Southern California

PRODUCTIVITY

INTRODUCTION

For more than a hundred years the standard economic definition of productivity has been "goods or services produced per unit of labor and expense" (Garb, 1981). This basic concept proved remarkably difficult to apply to software because of the lack of an acceptable definition of goods or services when associated with a software product. Two types of surrogate definitions for productivity were used. They were abstract definitions which did not the define goods or services at all, and fallacious definitions which used invalid or unacceptable definitions for software's goods or services.

A typical example of an abstract productivity definition which fails to define either goods or services is "projects produced on time and within budget." Note that what constitutes a project or on time or within budget is left to the imagination. Such abstract definitions have no value in economic studies and are too vague to convey useful information.

The most troublesome example of an invalid productivity definition is the well-known concept that productivity can be expressed in terms of lines of source code produced per time unit. Equally troublesome is the corollary definition that deals with costs rather than effort, i.e., cost per source line. The problem with code-based definitions is that lines of source code are not economic commodities. That is, lines of code are neither the primary goods or services of software projects, nor are they directly consumable by users and clients.

Due to the impact of fixed costs and noncoding tasks such as paperwork, lines of source code produced per time unit is decoupled from economic productivity. There are instances where economic productivity will improve at the same time that lines of source code rates decrease and cost per source line rises. The underlying mathematical reason for this paradox was worked out for manufacturing processes more than two hundred years ago but was first published for software only in 1978 (Jones, 1978). Prior to the understanding of the paradox associated with lines of code, many topics of software research were severely handicapped. For example, it is impossible to evaluate the productivity impact of high level programming languages using lines of source code.

In October of 1979 IBM published a description of a new metric termed function points (Albrecht, 1979) (see FUNCTION POINTS).

SOFTWARE MANUFACTURING AND THE PRESENCE OF FIXED COSTS

Outside the domain of software, manufacturing managers have understood that if a manufacturing process involves a substantial percentage of fixed costs, and there is a decline in the number of units manufactured, then the cost per unit must go up.

Software, as it turns out, involves a substantial percentage of fixed or inelastic costs that are not associated with coding. Thus, when more powerful programming languages are used, the result is to reduce the number of units that must be produced for a given program or system. However, the requirements, specifications, user documents, and many other cost elements tend to behave like fixed costs, and hence they cause metrics such as cost per line of source code to move paradoxically up instead of down.

Following is a simplified example showing two versions of a military software project delivering the same functions

Table 1. The Paradox of Source Code Metrics and Economic Productivity

	Case A	Case B	Difference
	Assembler Version (100,000 lines)	*Ada Version (30,000 lines)*	
requirements	20	20	0
analysis and design	30	30	0
coding	100	30	−70
testing	50	30	−20
documentation	20	20	0
management	30	20	−10
total effort	*250*	*150*	*−100*
total costs	*$1,250,000*	*$750,000*	*−$500,000*
cost per line	*$12.50*	*$25.00*	*+$12.50*
lines per month	*400*	*200*	*−200*

[a]In person-months of effort.

to end users. One version was written in basic assembler language and required 100,000 source code statements. The second was written in the more powerful Ada language, and required only 30,000 source code statements. Assume $5,000 as the monthly burdened salary rate in both cases.

The Ada version of the application cost $500,000 less than the Assembler language version that delivered the same functions. Plainly, Ada improves economic productivity in this example. Indeed, for this example there is a savings associated with Ada of 40% in terms of real economic productivity compared to Assembler language. Yet, paradoxically, the cost per source line metric favors the Assembler language version by 2 to 1, and the overall lines of code rate is twice as high for Assembler as for Ada.

This paradox is clearly due to the impact of the noncoding activities which tend to act like fixed costs. Since Ada is a more powerful language than Assembler, what is happening is that the number of source code units required to produce the application is reduced with Ada. When the number of units is reduced in the presence of fixed costs, the cost per unit must go up and the number of units produced per person month must go down. Clearly, lines of source code is a misleading and deceptive metric which violates the basic assumptions of economic productivity.

Note that in neither Case A nor Case B is coding the only cost element. For economic purposes, goods or services should both serve as a cost and resource accumulator and serve as deliverable to clients or users. Lines of code violates both criteria.

FUNCTION POINTS AS THE GOODS OR SERVICES OF SOFTWARE PROJECTS

In the middle 1970s the position was taken that the economic output unit of software projects should not be based on lines of code, and should represent topics of concern to the users of the software (Albrecht, 1979). In short, the functionality of software was to be measured.

Table 2. Function Points for the Assembler and Ada Examples

Count	Element		Weight	Totals
8	input	×	4 =	32
17	output	×	5 =	85
12	inquiry	×	4 =	48
5	data file	×	10 =	50
5	interface	×	7 =	35
	unadjusted total			*250*
	complexity adjust			*1.2*
	function points			*300*

[a](IFPUG, 1990).

It was considered that the visible external aspects of software which could be enumerated accurately consisted of five things: the inputs to the application, the outputs from it, inquiries by users, the data files that would be maintained and used by the application, and the interface files used from other applications.

Empirical weighting factors were developed for the five items through trial and error. The number of inputs was weighted by 4, outputs by 5, inquiries by 4, data file updates by 10, and interfaces by 7. These weights represent the relative functional size and the underlying processing of each of the five items.

In October of 1979 the results of this new software measurement technique, termed function points, were presented at a joint SHARE/GUIDE/IBM conference in Monterey, California. This marked the first time in the history of the computing era that economic software productivity could be measured.

Consider the two versions of the projects shown in Table 1 in terms of the function point technique. Since both versions provide the same functionality, their function point totals will be identical. Table 2 shows an abbreviated calculation sequence for counting function points.

Since the functionality of the application remains constant regardless of coding language, the function point total becomes the economic output unit. Both function points per person month and cost per function point are the normal metrics that result. A third alternative, work hours per function point, is also frequently encountered but need not be illustrated since it is merely a mathematical variation.

Function points satisfy both of the criteria stated for economic measures, i.e., they can be used to accumulate costs, and they serve as deliverable units of interest to consumers.

Note that the function point total for the application is not affected by the choice of programming language and hence is constant for both versions of the examples (Tables 1, 3). Note also that function points are synthetic metrics, rather than actual or tangible deliverables. The use of synthetic or calculated metrics is very common, as may be illustrated by the fact that horsepower is a standard unit for measuring electric, diesel, and internal combustion engines and works perfectly well with all of them.

Now let us reconsider the two projects shown in Table 1 using function points rather than source lines as the economic normalization method, assuming 300 function points.

Table 3. The Convergence of Function Points and Economic Productivity

	Case A[a]	Case B[a]	Difference
	Assembler Version	*Ada Version*	
requirements	20	20	0
analysis and design	30	30	0
coding	100	30	−70
testing	50	30	−20
documentation	20	20	0
management	30	20	−10
total effort	*250*	*150*	*−100*
total costs	*$1,250,000*	*$750,000*	*−$500,000*
cost per function point	*$4167*	*$2500*	*−$1667*
function points per person month	*1.2*	*2.0*	*+0.8*

[a]In person-months of effort and 300 Function Points.

As may readily be seen, function point metrics are far superior to the source line metrics for dealing with economic productivity data. As real costs decline, cost per function point also declines. As real economic productivity goes up, function points per staff month also goes up. Thus with function points, it is possible to explore the factors which influence software projects for better or for worse. Entirely new fields of research, such as measuring the impact of high level languages, are starting to be explored.

THE THREE ELEMENTS OF SOFTWARE PRODUCTIVITY MEASUREMENT

Function points is one element and provides a basic metric for economic studies. Additionally, the activities or chart of accounts used to collect resource data and the factors or attributes which influence software projects must also be carefully considered and controlled.

The chart of accounts shown in Tables 1 and 3 contains resource data for six activities which include requirements, analysis and design, coding, testing, documentation, and management. These six levels of granularity are marginally adequate for serious productivity studies, although it would be desirable to expand the chart of accounts to a greater level of detail. For example, the testing activity might be expanded to include unit test, new function test, regression test, stress test, system test, and user acceptance test as separate items in the chart of account.

There is currently no standard chart of accounts in use for software engineering, nor even any standards that define the basic work content of common activities such as unit test. Therefore, productivity researchers should carefully define both the chart of accounts and the work contents of the activities included so that their productivity data can be replicated and validated. This task is made complex because military software, systems software, and information systems typically carry out a number of different activities and do not have internal consistency. For example, a military software project of some nominal size such as 300 function points may be required by military specifications to carry out more than twice as many activities as a civilian information systems project of the same size.

The smallest chart of accounts that can be applied uniformly without ambiguity to information systems, systems software, and military software contains eight phases, 25 primary activities, and expands to 140 discrete tasks (Jones, 1991).

The third element is the ways of evaluating the factors or attributes which influence software projects. More than 200 factors that can cause changes in software productivity by as much as 1% have been identified (Boehm, 1981; Jones, 1986; DeMarco and Lister, 1987; and Humphrey, 1989).

The major factors that can exert changes in excess of 10% in net productivity include the skills and experience of the project managers and staff, volatility of requirements, the methods used, programming languages, available tools, response time and computer power, geographical dispersal of the staffs, organization structures, the physical office environments, the structural complexity of a project, and the novelty of the project to the team assigned. These factors will vary in significance as they interact with the characteristics of the software projects themselves. For example, the factors which influence large military software projects are not the same as the factors which influence small civilian information system projects. Active research is underway in the domain of measuring attributes and influential factors. The best current practices tend to evaluate more than a hundred attributes by means of multiple choice questionnaires administered to project teams and then analyzed using multiple regression techniques.

OBSERVED RANGES OF SOFTWARE PRODUCTIVITY

One of the difficulties facing productivity researchers is the selection of the most appropriate way to express productivity results. For example, productivity rates tend to vary with the size of the projects measured (i.e., large systems, medium applications, and small programs), with the class (i.e., military projects, systems software, or information systems projects), and with the nature (i.e., new projects or enhancements to existing systems).

Both the arithmetic mean and the mode of productivity data tend to favor small projects. The harmonic mean and median tend to a bias toward the larger, less productive projects. The total range of observed productivity and the interquartile range (width which half of the projects will reside) appear to give the best fit to the current data.

The following data is based on observations and reconstructions of some 2500 projects developed between 1980 and 1990 (Jones, 1991). The data is only provisional, and the sample size required to actually construct U.S. norms would be at least 10 times larger. Nonetheless, the information provides a glimpse of software productivity rates when a full chart of accounts is used.

Information Systems Productivity Ranges

Information systems are defined as software projects intended to provide useful information to human users. Such systems typically have higher productivity rates than either systems software or military projects. Examples of information systems include accounting software, payroll software, banking applications, and insurance claims handling software. The observed range for information systems runs from a low of 0.75 to a high of 140 function points per staff month. The interquartile range, width which half of all projects may be found, runs from about 4 to 16 function points per staff month.

Systems Software Productivity Ranges

Systems software projects are defined as software directly controlling and interacting with physical devices. Such systems are typically less productive than information systems. Examples of systems software include operating systems, public switching systems, and process control software. The observed range for systems projects is from a low of 0.35 function points per staff month to a high of 30 function points per staff month. The interquartile range for systems software is from about 2 to 10 function points per staff month.

Military Software Productivity Ranges

Military software projects are defined as those constrained to follow military specifications such as 2167(A) or 2168. Such projects usually have the lowest productivity rates for their size due to the enormous volume of paperwork associated with military specifications. The observed range for military projects is from 0. 15 to 25 function points per staff month. The interquartile range for military projects is from about 1 to 7 function points per staff month.

CONCLUSION

Since the original 1979 publication, the usage of function points has extended internationally, and function points are likely to become the standard metric for information systems within a few years. Systems and military software have lagged behind in adopting function points, but extended forms of function points are attracting increased attention within these domains.

Active research programs are now underway in exploring the factors which influence productivity. Thus programs are underway to explore the impact of software processes, staff skills, tools, languages, and even programming office environments.

Active research is also underway in refining and extending the function point metrics themselves. Unlike any previous software metric, function points are supported by an international association (IFPUG, the International function point Users Group) with an active standards committee.

Now that the economic productivity of software can be measured, it can also be improved. Thus measurement is on the critical path to achieving tangible improvements in one of the most complex human activities of the twentieth century.

BIBLIOGRAPHY

A. J. Albrecht, "Measuring Application Development Productivity", *Proceedings of the Joint IBM / SHAREGUIDE Application Development Symposium,* Monterey Calif., Oct. 1979, pp 83–92.

B. Boehm, *Software Engineering Economics,* Prentice-Hall. Inc., Englewood Cliffs, N.J., 1981.

T. DeMarco and T. Lister, *Peopleware,* Dorset House Press, New York, 1987.

G. Garb, *Micro-Economics: Theory, Application, Innovations,* Macmillan Publishing Company, New York, 1981, pp. 88–110.

W. Humphrey, *Managing the Software Process,* Addison-Wesley, Inc., Reading, Mass., 1989.

IFPUG Counting Practices Manual Release 3.0, International Function Point Users Group, Westerville, Ohio, Apr. 1990.

T. C. Jones, "Measuring Programming Quality and Productivity", *IBM Systems Journal* **17**(1), 39–63 1978.

C. Jones, *Programming Productivity,* McGraw-Hill Publishing Company, New York, 1986.

C. Jones, *Applied Software Measurement,* McGraw-Hill Publishing Company, New York, 1991, Chapt. 2, 3.

CAPERS JONES
Software Productivity Research, Inc.

PROGRAM DESIGN LANGUAGE (PDL)

A specification language with special constructs and, sometimes verification protocols used to develop, analyze, and document a program design (IEEE).

PROGRAM INSPECTIONS

See INSPECTIONS.

PROGRAM LIBRARY

See SOFTWARE DEVELOPMENT LIBRARY.

PROGRAM SYNTHESIS

The use of software tools to aid in the transformation of a program specification into a program that realizes that specification (IEEE).

PROGRAM SLICING

Program slicing is a family of program decomposition techniques based on extracting statements relevant to a computation in a program. Program slicing as originally defined produces a smaller program that reproduces a subset of the original program's behavior (Weiser, 1984). This is advantageous because the slice can collect an algorithm for a given calculation that may be scattered throughout a program, excluding irrelevant statements. It should be easier for a programmer interested in a subset of the program's behavior to understand the corresponding slice than to deal with the entire program. The utility and power of program slicing comes from the potential automation of tedious and error-prone tasks. Program slicing has applications in program debugging, program testing, program integration, parallel program execution, and software maintenance. Several variations on this theme have been developed, including program dicing, dynamic slicing and decomposition slicing.

PROGRAM SLICING

Static Slicing

The original definition of program slicing is now called static program slicing, because the slice is found by static dataflow analysis on the flow graph of the program. A slicing criterion for a program slice is a tuple <*i,v*>, where *i* is a statement in the program and *v* is a subset of the program variables. A slice of a program is computed *on v, at* statement *i*. A program slice of a program *P* for a given slicing criterion, <*i,v*>, is an executable program obtained by deleting zero or more statements from *P* such that the values of the variables in *v* are the same when execution reaches statement *i* for both *P* and the slice on *P*. Figure 1 shows an example of program slicing for the criterion <21,**avg**>.

Dynamic Slicing

Dynamic program slicing was introduced to reduce significantly the size of static slices when using slicing as a software testing and debugging aid (Korel, 1988). Dynamic slices are computed from a program trajectory or execution trace for some input. A dynamic slicing criterion for a program *P* executed on input *x* is a triple $C=(x, I^q, V)$ where I^q is q^{th} instruction in the program trajectory and V is a subset of program variables. Dynamic slices are often much smaller than static slices when programs include programming language features such as arrays, structures and dynamic objects. An alternative formulation of dynamic slicing using program dependence graphs was developed by Agrawal and Horgan (1990).

Decomposition Slicing

Program slicing can be used to decompose a program in such a way that all statements that affect any state of some given variable can be removed. This set of statements, called a decomposition slice, is an executable program preserving the computations on the given variable. A decomposition slice captures all the computation on a given variable, without regard to any specific program location, by taking the union of all static slices on a given variable. The decomposition yields a second component called the complement that captures all the other computations in the program. These two components have the property that if the decomposition slice is maximal (not contained in another decomposition slice) then any statements in the decomposition slice that are not also in the complement are independent of the computations in the complement and can be safely changed without danger of an unexpected linkage (side effect) in the complement. Using these results on decomposition slicing yields a set of rules for safely making changes to the code of a decomposition slice and for merging the slice back with the complement. If a maintenance programmer follows these rules for making changes in the decomposition slice, then regression testing for any output in the complement can be eliminated because all effects of the change are confined to the decomposition slice (Gallagher and Lyle, 1991).

Integrating Noninterfering Versions of Programs

Program slicing has also been applied to the task of integrating several related, but slightly different, variants to a base version of a program. The problem is to produce automatically a new program that preserves the new behavior of all the variants and also preserves behavior that was not changed in any of the variants (Horwitz and co-workers, 1989). Program slices are used to find the program statements that might be involved in the computation of variables potentially affected by the integration of the variants.

Properties of Program Slices

Slices often exhibit a number of useful properties that can be exploited:

1. The union of two slices is a slice with a slicing criterion that is the union of the respective slicing criteria. A program can be viewed as the union of slices computed for each output variable (output slices). Any statement not in this union must be useless (dead) code because it does not contribute to the calculation of any program output.
2. The intersection of two slices is a slice with a slicing criterion that is related to the intersection of the respective slicing criteria. Using intersections, each output slice can be further partitioned into two parts: a backbone slice, the union of all intersections with other output slices, and the set of statements not included in the backbone slice (called the residual set). This partitioning of the program is useful in program debugging.
3. Program slices fit in with the way programmers understand programs, because after trying to understand an unfamiliar program, programmers recognize slices from the program better than other chunks of code from a program (Weiser, 1982).

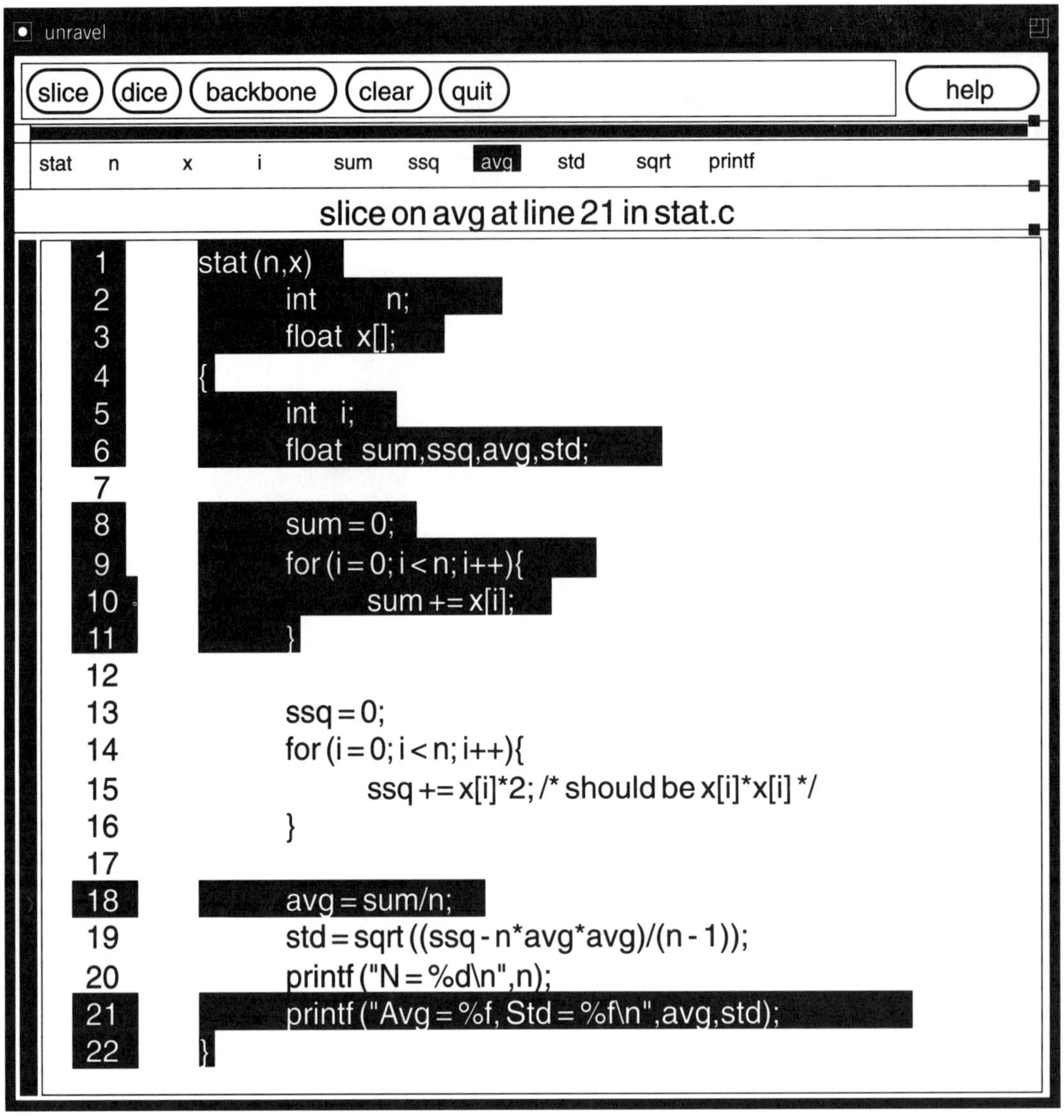

Figure 1. Slice on **avg.**

4. Slices are not unique because any statement that does not affect the variables of a slicing criterion can be included in a slice.
5. Because the utility of program slicing comes from reducing the number of statements to be examined, the smaller the slice, the better. However, finding statement-minimal slices is equivalent to solving the halting problem.

Computing Slices

An informal definition of a program slice at statement n on variable v is all statements that might affect the value that v has just before control reaches statement n. Two helpful definitions for discussing slicing are defs(n), the set of variables assigned a value at statement n (the left side of an assignment statement), and refs(n), the set of variables referenced at statement n (the right side). The values of the variables in defs(n) after statement n is executed depend on the values of the variables in refs(n) before statement n is executed.

A slicing algorithm for programs in a simple language that has no **if** or **loop** statements but contains only assignment statements, print statements, and expressions is easy to construct. Let v be some program variable name, n be some statement, and $succ(n)$ be a function returning the statement following n.

Recursive Slicing Algorithm

$$S_{<M=succ(n),v>} = \begin{cases} \{n\} & \text{if } v \in \text{defs}(n) \text{ \& refs}(n)=0 \\ S_{<n,v>} & \text{if } v \notin \text{defs}(n) \\ \{n\} \cup S_{<n,x>} \forall x \in refs(n) & \text{if } v \in \text{defs}(n) \text{ \& refs}(n) \neq 0 \end{cases}$$

This slicing algorithm is, for a given slicing criterion, to include in the slice the statement immediately before the

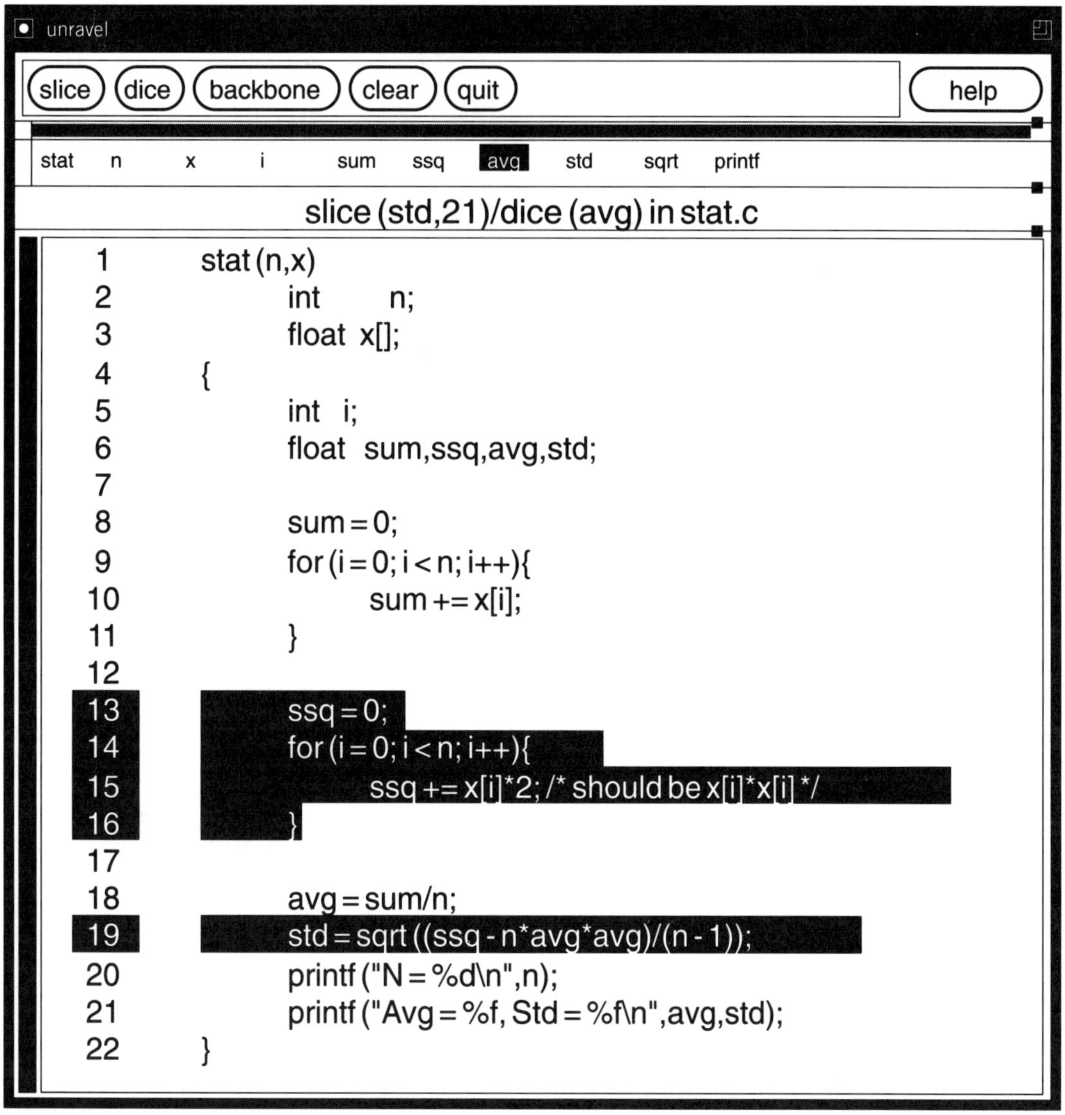

Figure 2. Slice on **std** diced with **avg**.

criterion statement, if the statement assigns a value to the criterion variable. If a statement is included in a slice, then slices on any variables referenced by the included statement should also be added to the slice. If a slicing criterion does not include the previous program statement in the slice, apply the slicing criterion to the previous statement. The above slicing algorithm can be extended for loops and other conditional statements such as **if** and **case** statements that contain one or more blocks of statements and an expression controlling execution of the blocks. For any program statement, define a set (called requires) of directly enclosing conditional statements. Then the slicing rule for the condition if $v \in \text{defs}(n)$ & $\text{refs}(n) = 0$ becomes

$$S_{<n,v>} = \{n\} \cup S_{<n,x>} \forall x \in \text{refs}(n) \cup (\{y\} \cup S_{<y,x>} \forall x \in \text{refs}(y) \forall y \in \text{requires}(n))$$

The extended slicing algorithm is, for any statement included in a slice, to include any enclosing conditional statement and add the slices of any variables referenced in the condition.

Two other approaches to slicing algorithms are Bergeretti and Carré, 1985) and (Ferrante and co-workers, 1987). Bergeretti and Carré, using the information flow relations, defines the notion of a partial statement on a variable, which is essentially a program slice on that variable. The other algorithm, using program dependence graphs, is widely used because a slice can be obtained in linear time from the program dependence graph. Program dependence graphs are also useful for interprocedural program slicing (Horwitz, 1990).

USING PROGRAM SLICING IN DEBUGGING

The basic scenario for detecting the existence of a program bug is for the programmer to run the program being tested against sets of test data until a result fails to match the

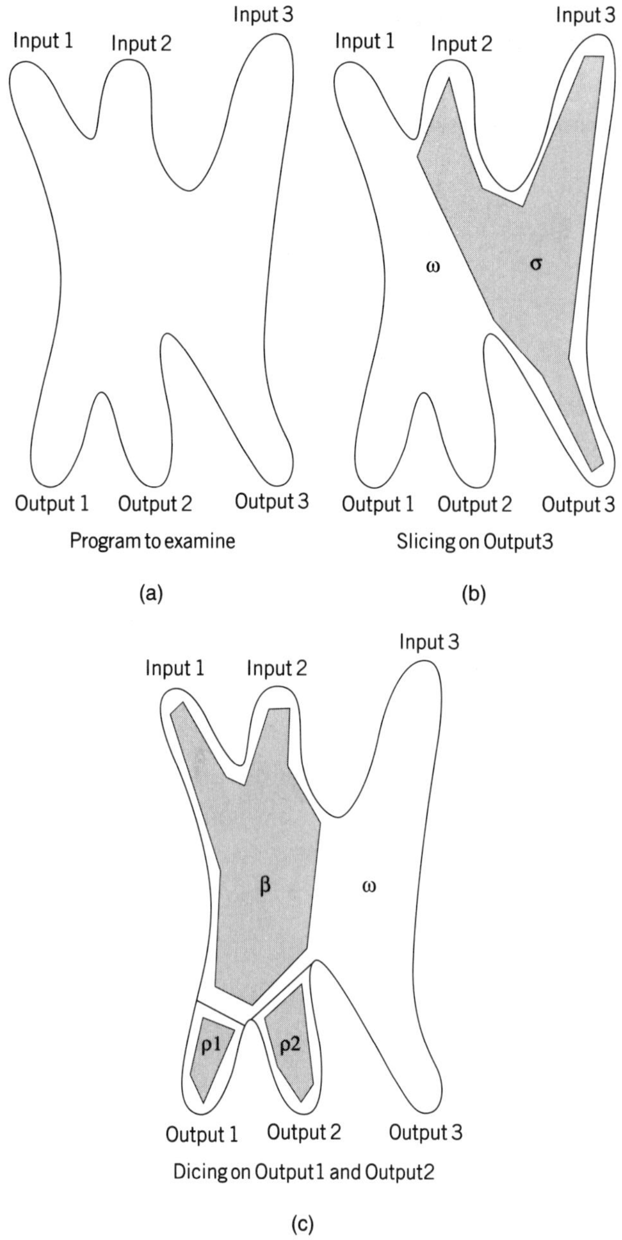

Figure 3. Slide-based model of program structure.

expected value. Then the programmer attempts to locate the cause of the discrepancy by finding a point in the program where the actual implementation departs from a correct implementation. To find the bug, the programmer must try to understand what the program actually does as well as what the program should be doing. The programmer typically tries to understand a program by sorting through a wealth of information about the program by reading program text, reading program documentation, ad

Table 1. Predicted Bug Locations

a	*b*	$B \subseteq A$	$A \subseteq B$	$A \not\subseteq B$ & $B \not\subseteq A$
pass	fail	B	$B \cap \neg A$	$B \cap \neg A$
fail	pass	$A \cap \neg B$	A	$A \cap \neg B$
fail	fail	B	A	$A \cap B$

hoc testing with different inputs, or conducting dynamic tracing. Program slicing is used to address this information overload problem in three ways. A static program slice extracts all the statements that might be relevant to a computation. A dynamic program slice extracts all the statements that are relevant to a computation for a given set of data. Program dicing (of either static or dynamic slices) exploits all the information learned from testing a program, not just what went wrong but also what the program is doing right.

Program Dicing

Program dicing uses the information that some variables fail some test sets and other variables pass all test sets to isolate the bug automatically to a set of statements likely to contain the bug (Lyle, 1986). These statements are those in the slice on an incorrectly valued variable minus any statements in the slice on a variable that appears to be correctly computed. If two outputs are incorrect and a common cause is suspected, then the bug is likely to be found in the intersection (backbone slice) of the two output slices. In the case of one correct and one incorrect output, the bug should be searched for in the residual set of the slice on the incorrect output. Figure 2 shows an example of program dicing. The highlighted lines are the residual set of a slice on **std** after removing the backbone slice between a slice on **avg** and a slice on **std**.

Dicing depends on the assumptions that an error always propagates to an output, all incorrectly computed variables are identified, and no program bug masks another bug. Let *a* and *b* be output variables of a program. Let *A* and *B* be slices on *a* and *b* at their respective output statements. Table 1 summarizes where to look for a bug based on the correctness of the test outputs for *a* and *b* and whether one slice is a subset of the other.

Slice-based Model of Program Structure

From unions and intersections of slices, a slice-based model of program structure can be built that has applications to program debugging. Figure 3a represents a programmer's view of an unfamiliar program. The programmer sees some inputs, some outputs, and a shapeless mass of code with unknown connections among inputs and outputs. Figure 3b represents the programmer's knowledge after computing a slice on *Output3*. He or she knows that to answer questions about the computation of *Output3*, it is necessary to examine the slice on *Output3* (the shaded region labeled σ, the slice) and to ignore statements not in the slice (unshaded region ω, of other statements). Figure 3c shows how the slice-based model can further refine the programmer's knowledge about the program. The backbone slice relative to *Output1* and *Output2*, β, is the intersection of the respective slices. If the programmer suspects that a single bug is causing both outputs to be incorrect, then he or she should examine the backbone slice. However, if the programmer has some confidence that one output is correctly computed, he or she should look for a bug among the statements of the residual set of the other computation. For example, if *Output1* fails some set of test data but *Output2* appears to be correct, then the programmer should look for the error among the statements unique to *Output1*, the residual set ρ_1.

BIBLIOGRAPHY

H. Agrawal and J. R. Horgan, "Dynamic Program Slicing," *Proceedings of the ACM SIGPLAN '90 Conference on Programming Language Design and Implementation,* 246–256 (June 20–22, 1990).

J. Bergeretti and B. A. Carré, "Information-Flow and Data-Flow Analysis of while-Programs," *ACM TOPLAS* **7**(1), 37–61 (Jan. 1985).

J. Ferrante, K. Ottenstein, and J. Warren, "The Program Dependence Graph and its Use in Optimization," *ACM TOPLAS* **9**(3), 319–349 (July 1987).

K. B. Gallagher and J. R. Lyle, "Using Program Slicing in Software Maintenance," *IEEE Transactions on Software Engineering* **17**(8), 751–761 (Aug. 1991).

S. Horwitz, J. Prins, and T. Reps, "Integrating Noninterfering Versions of Programs," *ACM TOPLAS* **11**(3), 345–387 (July 1989).

S. Horwitz, T. Reps, and D. Binkley, "Interprocedural Slicing Using Dependence Graphs," *ACM TOPLAS* **12**(1), 26–60 (Jan. 1990).

B. Korel and J. Laski, "Dynamic Program Slicing," *Information Processing Letters* **29**(3), 155–163 (Oct. 1988).

M. Weiser, "Programmers Use Slices When Debugging," *CACM* **25**(7), 446–452 (July 1982).

M. Weiser, "Program Slicing," *IEEE Transactions on Software Engineering* **SE-10**(4), 352–357 (July 1984).

M. Weiser and J. R. Lyle, "Experiments on Slicing-Based Debugging Aids," E. Soloway and S. Iyengar, eds., *Empirical Studies of Programmers,* Ablex Publishing Corporation, Norwood, N.J., 1986, pp. 187–197.

JAMES R. LYLE
National Institute of Standards and Technology

PROGRAM VISUALIZATION

INTRODUCTION

It is well-known that conventional programming languages are difficult to learn and use, requiring skills that many people do not have (Lewis and Olson, 1987). However, there are significant advantages to supplying programming capabilities in the user interfaces of a wide variety of programs. For example, the success of spreadsheets can be partially attributed to the ability of users to write programs (as collections of *formulas*).

As the distribution of personal computers grows, the majority of computer users now do not know how to program. They buy computers with packaged software and are not able to modify the software even to make small changes. In order to allow the end-user to reconfigure and modify the system, the software may provide various options, but these often make the system more complex and still may not address the users' problems. Easy-to-use software, such as *direct manipulation* systems (Schneiderman, 1983) actually make the user-programmer gap worse since more people will be able to use the software (since it is easy to use), but the internal program code is now much more complicated (due to the extra code to handle the user interface).

Therefore, we must find ways to make the programming task more accessible to users. One approach to this problem is to investigate the use of graphics as the programming language. This has been called *visual programming* or *graphical programming.* Some visual programming systems have successfully demonstrated that nonprogrammers can create fairly complex programs with little training (Halbert, 1984).

Another class of systems tries to make programs more understandable by using graphics to illustrate the programs after they have been created. These are called *program visualization* systems and are usually used during debugging or when teaching students how to program.

This paper, which is updated and revised from Myers (1986; 1988b), attempts to provide a more formal definition of these terms, and discusses why graphical techniques are appropriate for use with programming. Then the various approaches to visual programming and program visualization are illustrated through a survey of relevant systems. This survey is organized around three taxonomies. Finally, some general problems and areas for further research are addressed.

DEFINITIONS

Programming

In this article, a computer *program* is defined as "a set of statements that can be submitted as a unit to a computer system and used to direct the behavior of that system" (Oxford, 1983). While the ability to compute everything is not required, the system must include the ability to handle variables, conditionals, and iteration, at least implicitly.

Interpretive vs. Compiled

Any programming language system may either be *interpretive* or *compiled.* A compiled system has a large processing delay before statements can be run while they are converted into a lower-level representation in a batch fashion. An interpretive system allows statements to be executed when they are entered. This characterization is actually more of a continuum rather than a dichotomy since even interpretive languages like Lisp typically require groups of statements (such as an entire procedure) to be specified before they are executed.

Visual Programming

Visual programming (VP) refers to any system that allows the user to specify a program in a two-(or more)-dimensional fashion. Although this is a very broad definition, conventional textual languages are not considered two-dimensional since the compilers or interpreters process them as long, one-dimensional streams. Visual programming does *not* include systems that use conventional (linear) programming languages to define pictures, such as Sketchpad (Sutherland, 1963), CORE, PHIGS, Postscript

(Adobe, 1985), the Macintosh Toolbox (Apple, 1985), or X-11 Window Manager Toolkit (McCormack and Asente, 1988). It also does not include drawing packages like Apple Macintosh MacDraw, since these do not create *programs* as defined above.

Program Visualization

Program visualization (PV) is an entirely different concept from visual programming. In visual programming, the graphics are used to create the program itself, but in program visualization, the program is specified in a conventional, textual manner, and the graphics are used to illustrate some aspect of the program or its run-time execution. Unfortunately, in the past, many program visualization systems have been incorrectly labeled visual programming (as in Grafton and Ichikawa (1985)). Program visualization systems can be classified using two axes: whether they illustrate the *code, data,* or *algorithm* of the program, and whether they are *dynamic* or *static. Data visualization* systems show pictures of the actual data of the program. Similarly, *code visualization* illustrates the actual program text by adding graphical marks to it or by converting it to a graphical form (such as a flowchart). Systems that illustrate the 'algorithm' use graphics to show *abstractly* how the program operates. This is different from data and code visualization, since with algorithm visualization the pictures may not correspond directly to data in the program and changes in the pictures might not correspond to specific pieces of the code. For example, an algorithm animation of a sort routine might show the data as lines of different heights, and swaps of two items might be shown as a smooth animation of the lines moving. The *swap* operation may not be explicitly in the code, however.

Dynamic visualizations refers to systems that can show an animation of the program running, whereas *static* systems are limited to snapshots of the program at certain points.

If a program created using visual programming is to be displayed or debugged, clearly this should be done in a graphical manner, which might be considered a form of program visualization. However, it is more accurate to use the term visual programming for systems that allow the program to be *created* using graphics, and program visualization for systems that use graphics *only* for illustrating programs after they have been created.

Visual Languages

Visual languages refer to all systems that use graphics, including visual programming and program visualization systems. Although all these terms are somewhat similar and confusing, it is important to have different names for the different kinds of systems, and these are the names that are conventionally used in the literature.

Example-Based Programming

A number of visual programming systems also use *example-based programming.* Example-based programming refers to systems that allow the programmer to use examples of input and output data during the programming process. There are two types of example-based programming: *programming by example* and *programming with example.* Programming by example refers to systems that try to guess or *infer* the program from examples of input and output or sample traces of execution. This is often called *automatic programming* and has generally been an area of Artificial Intelligence research. Programming with example systems, however, requires the programmer to specify everything about the program (there is no inferencing involved), but the programmer can work out the program on a specific example. The system executes the programmer's commands normally, but remembers them for later reuse. Halbert (1984) characterizes programming with examples as 'Do What I Did' whereas inferential programming by example might be 'Do What I Mean'.

Of course, whenever code is executed in any system, test data must be entered to run it on. The distinction between normal testing and Example-Based Programming is that in the latter the system requires or encourages the user to provide the examples *before* programming begins, and then applies the program to the examples as it develops.

ADVANTAGES OF USING GRAPHICS

Visual programming and program visualization are very appealing ideas for a number of reasons. The human visual system and human visual information processing are clearly optimized for multi-dimensional data. Computer programs, however, are conventionally presented in a one-dimensional textual form, not utilizing the fun power of the brain. Two-dimensional displays for programs, such as flowcharts and even the indenting of block structured programs, have long been known to be helpful aids in program understanding (Smith, 1977). A number of program visualization systems (Baeker, 1981; Brown and Sedgewick, 1984; Myers, 1983; Myers, Chandhok, and Sareen, 1988) have demonstrated that two-dimensional pictorial displays for data structures, such as those drawn by hand on a blackboard, are very helpful. Clarisse (Clarisse and Chang, 1986) claims that graphical programming uses information in a format that is closer to the user's mental representations of problems, and will allow data to be processed in a format closer to the way objects are manipulated in the real world. It seems clear that a more visual style of programming could be easier to understand and generate for humans, especially for nonprogrammers or novice programmers.

Another motivation for using graphics is that it tends to be a higher level description of the desired actions (often deemphasizing issues of syntax and providing a higher level of abstraction) and may therefore make the programming task easier even for professional programmers. This may be especially true during debugging, where graphics can be used to present much more information about the program state (such as current variables and data structures) than is possible with purely textual displays. Also, some types of complex programs, such as those that use concurrent processes or deal with real-time systems, are difficult to describe with textual languages so graphical specifications may be more appropriate.

The popularity of *direct manipulation* interfaces (Shneiderman, 1983), where there are items on the computer screen that can be pointed to and operated on using a mouse, also contributes to the desire for visual languages. Since many visual languages use icons and other graphical objects, editors for these languages usually have a direct manipulation user interface. The user has the impression of more directly constructing a program rather than having to abstractly design it.

Smith (1977) discusses at length many psychological motivations for using visual displays for programs and data.

TAXONOMIES OF VISUAL LANGUAGES

This article presents three taxonomies. The first is for systems that support programming, and classifies them as to whether they use visual programming or example-based programming. The second lists the various ways that visual programming systems have represented the program. The third taxonomy is for program visualization systems, and shows whether the systems illustrate the code, data, or algorithm of programs.

Of course, a single system may have features that fit into various categories, and some systems may be hard to classify, so these taxonomies attempt to characterize the systems by their most prominent features. Also, the systems discussed here are only representative; there are many systems that have not been included (additional systems are described (Berztiss, 1988; Chang, Ichikawa, and Ligomenides, 1986; Jungert, 1987; Korfhage, 1986; Shu, 1988)). Since there are so many visual language systems, it would be impossible to survey them all in a single article, but hopefully the 50 or so discussed here will give the reader an overview of the work that has been done.

TAXONOMY OF PROGRAMMING SYSTEMS

Table 1 shows a taxonomy of some programming systems divided into eight categories using the orthogonal criteria of:

- Visual programming or not;
- Example-based programming or not; and
- Interpretive or compiled.

Not EBP, Not VP, Compiled, and Interpretive

These are the conventional textual, linear programming languages that are familiar to all programmers, such as Pascal, Fortran, and Ada for compiled, and LISP and APL for interpretive.

Not EBP, VP, Compiled

One of the earliest visual representations for programs was the flow chart. Grail (Ellis, Heafner, and Sibley, 1969) could generate programs directly from computerized flowcharts, but the contents of boxes were ordinary machine language statements. Since then, there have been many flowchart languages. For example, FPL (First Programming Language) is reported to be "particularly well suited to helping novices learn programming" because it eliminates syntactic errors (Cuniff, Taylor, and Black; 1986). Other flowchart languages are IBGE (Taylor and Burton, 1986) for the Macintosh, and OPAL (Harel, 1988), which allows doctors to enter knowledge about cancer treatments into an expert system (see Fig. 1). OPAL handles iterations, conditionals, and concurrency in an easy-to-understand manner. The GAL system (Albizuri-Romero, 1984) uses a flowchart-variant called Nassi-Shneiderman flowcharts (Nassi and Shneiderman, 1973) and is compiled into Pascal.

An early effort that was not based on flowcharts was the AMBIT/G (Christensen, 1968) and AMBIT/L (Christensen, 1971) graphical languages. They supported symbolic manipulation programming using pictures. Both the programs and data were represented diagramatically as directed graphs, and the programming operated by pattern matching. Fairly complicated algorithms, such as garbage collection, could be described graphically as local transformations on graphs.

A new variant on graphs is called *HiGraphs* (Harel, 1988), which allows the nodes to contain other nodes, and allows the arrows to split and join (see Figure 2). HiGraphs can also be restricted to certain forms to create specific visual programming languages. For example, Miro (Maimone, Tygar, and Wing, 1988) is a HiGraphs language for defining security constraints in operating systems (for determining which users can access which files). Another application is the programming of computer user interfaces in StateMaster (Wellner, 1989).

You might think that a system called *Query by Example* would be a *Programming by Example* system, but in fact, according to this classification, it is not. Query by Example (Zloof and de Jong, 1977) allows users to specify queries on a relational database using two-dimensional tables (or forms), so it is classified as a visual programming system. The examples in QBE are what Zloof called variables. They are called examples because the user is supposed to give them names that refer to what the system might fill into that field, but they have no more meaning than variable names in most conventional languages. The ideas in QBE have been extended to mail and other nondatabase areas of office automation in *Office by Example* (OBE) (Zloof, 1981). A related forms-based database language is FORMAL (Shu, 1985), which explicitly represents hierarchical structures.

The MOPS-2 system (Ae and co-workers, 1986) uses colored Petri nets to allow parallel systems to be constructed and stimulated in a visual manner. Petri nets may help when programming real-time software, as described in Ae and Aibara (1987). Berztiss (1987) discusses how to lay out Petri nets automatically.

Another interesting way to present program constructs is using tiles that look like jigsaw pieces and will only fit together in ways that form legal programs. One version of this is Proc-BLOX (Glinert, 1987), shown in Figure 3.

Table 1. Classification of Programming Systems by Whether They Are Visual or Not, Whether They Have Example-Based Programming or Not, and Whether They Are Compiled or Interpretive[a]

VP Status	Compiled	Interpretive
Not example-based programming		
not VP	all conventional languages: Pascal, Fortran, etc.	LISP, APL, etc.
VP	Grail (Ellis, Heafner, and Sibley, 1969)	Graphical program editor (Sutherland, 1966)
	AMBIT/G/L (Christensen, 1968; 1971)	Spreadsheets
	Query by example (Zloof and de Jong, 1977; Zloof, 1981)	PIGS (Pong and Ng, 1983; Pong, 1986)
	FORMAL (Shu, 1985)	Pict (Glinert and Tenimoto, 1984)
	GAL (Albizuri-Romero, 1984)	PROGRAPH (Pietrzykowski, Matwin, and Muldner, 1983; Pietrzykowski and Matwin, 1984)
	FPL (Cunniff, Taylor, and Black, 1986)	State transitions UIMS (Jacob, 1985)
	IBGE (Taylor and Burton, 1986)	PLAY (Tanimoto and Runyan, 1986)
	MOPS-2 (Ae and co-workers, 1986)	Action graphics (Moshell and co-workers, 1987
	OPAL (Musen, Fagen, and Shortliffe, 1986)	Forms (Ambler, 1987)
	Proc-BLOX (Glinert, 1987)	VERDI (Graf, 1987)
	HiGraphs (Harel, 1988)	LabView (National Instruments)
	Miro (Maimone, Tygar, and Wing, 1988)	SIL-ICON (Chang and co-workers, 1989)
	StateMaster (Wellner, 1989)	
	MPL (Yeung, 1988)	
Example-based programming		
not VP	I/O pairs[a] (Shaw, Swartout, and Green, 1975)	Tinker (Lieberman, 1982)
		Editing by example [b](Nix, 1985)
VP	Traces[a] (Bauer, 1978)	Pygmalion (Smith, 1977)
		Smallstar (Halbert, 1984; 1981)
		Rehersal World (Gould and Finzer, 1984a; 1984b)
		Graphical thinglab (Borning, 1986)
		Music system (Desain, 1986)
		HI-VISUAL (Hirakawa and co-workers, 1987)
		ALEX [b](Kozen and co-workers, 1987)
		Peridot[a] (Myers, 1987; 1988)
		InterCONS (Smith, 1988)
		Fabrik (Ludolph and co-workers, 1988)

[a]The systems are listed in approximate chronological order. [b]Systems have inferencing (programming by example, other example-based programming systems use programming with example).

The MPL system (Yeung, 1988) allows graphical representations of matrices to be combined with conventional Prolog programs. The program is entered with a modified text editor that allows symbolic representations of the matrices to be drawn graphically, and then the resulting file is compiled and run. This is a good example of combining the use of graphics with text.

Not EBP, VP, Interpretive

Probably the first visual programming system was William Sutherland's Graphical Program Editor (Sutherland, 1966), which represented programs somewhat like hardware logic diagrams that could be executed interpretively. Some systems for programming with flowcharts have been interpretive. Pict (Glinert and Tanimoto, 1984) uses conventional flow charts, but is differentiated by its use of color pictures (icons) rather than text inside the flowchart boxes. PIGS (Pong and Ng, 1983) uses Nassi-Shneiderman flow charts and has been extended to handle multiprocessing in Pigsty/I-PIGS (Pong, 1986). Another variant of flow charts is used by the PLAY system (Tanimoto and Runyan, 1986), which allows children to create animations by using a "comic strip" representation of the actions to be performed. The VERDI system (Graf, 1987) uses a form

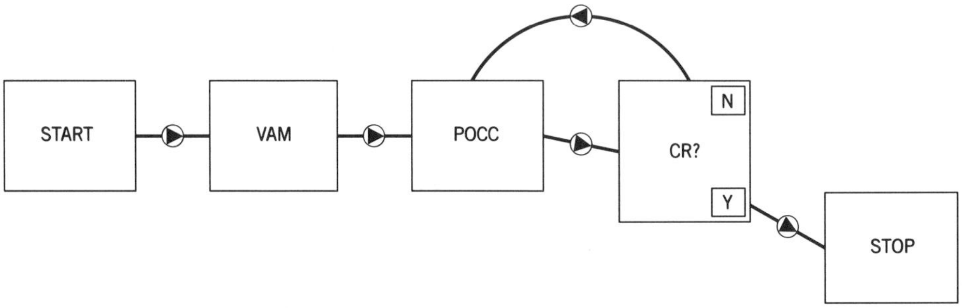

Figure 1. An OPAL program for defining a single cycle of VAM chemotherapy followed by cycles of POCC chemotherapy until the parameter CR (complete response) becomes true (Musen, Fagen, and Shortliffe, 1986).

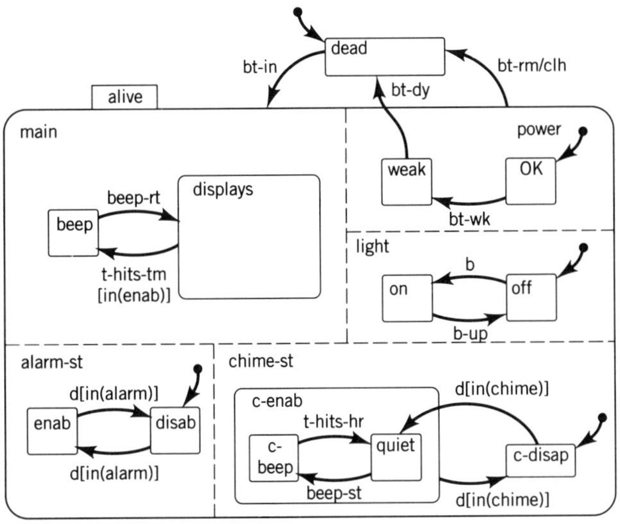

Figure 2. A HiGraphs Program describing the operation of a digital watch (Harel, 1988).

of Petri nets to specify distributed systems. With VERDI, the user can see an animation of the program running by watching tokens move around the network.

A number of visual programming systems use *dataflow diagrams*. Here the operations are typically put in boxes, and the data flows along the wires connecting them. One example is PROGRAPH (Pietrzykowski, Matwin, and Muldner, 1983), which is a structured, functional language that claims to alleviate the usual problem with functional languages where "the conventional representation in the form of a linear script makes it almost unreadable" (Pietrzykowski and Matwin, 1984). Another data flow language is Lab-VIEW, which is a commercial product running on Apple Macintoshes for controlling external instruments. LabVIEW provides procedural abstraction, control structures, and many useful primitive components such as knobs, switches, graphs, and arithmetic and transcendental functions (see Fig. 4).

A number of systems for automatically generating user interfaces for programs (User Interface Management Systems (Myers, 1989), allows the designer to specify the user interface in a graphical manner. An example of this is the slate transition diagram editor by Jacob (1985). Most other UIMSs require that designers; specify the programs using some textual representations, so they do not qualify as visual programming systems.

Spreadsheets, such as those in VisiCalc or Lotus 1-2-3, were designed to help nonprogrammers manage finances. Spreadsheets incorporate programming features and can be made to do general purpose calculations (Kay, 1984) and therefore qualify as a very high level visual programming language. Some of the reasons that spreadsheets are so popular are the following (Ambler, 1987; Lewis and Olson, 1987):

1. The graphics on the screen use a familiar, concrete, and visible representation which directly maps to the user's natural model of the data
2. They are nonmodal and interpretive and therefore provide immediate feedback
3. They supply aggregate and high-level operations
4. They avoid the notion of variables (all data is visible)
5. The inner world of computation is suppressed
6. Each cell typically has a single value throughout the computation
7. They are nondeclarative and typeless
8. Consistency is automatically maintained
9. The order of evaluation (flow of control) is entirely derived from the declared cell dependencies

The first point differentiates spreadsheets from many other visual programming languages including flowcharts, which are graphical representations derived from textual (linear) languages. With spreadsheets the original representation is graphical, and there is no natural textual language.

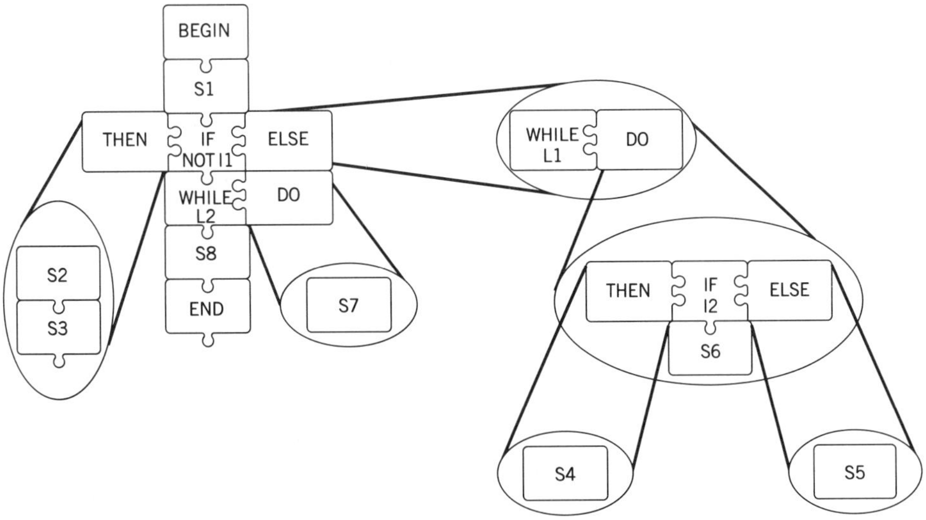

Figure 3. A Proc-BLOX display for some Pascal-like program constructs (Glinert, 1987). The jigsaw puzzle pieces will only fit together in ways that form legal program.

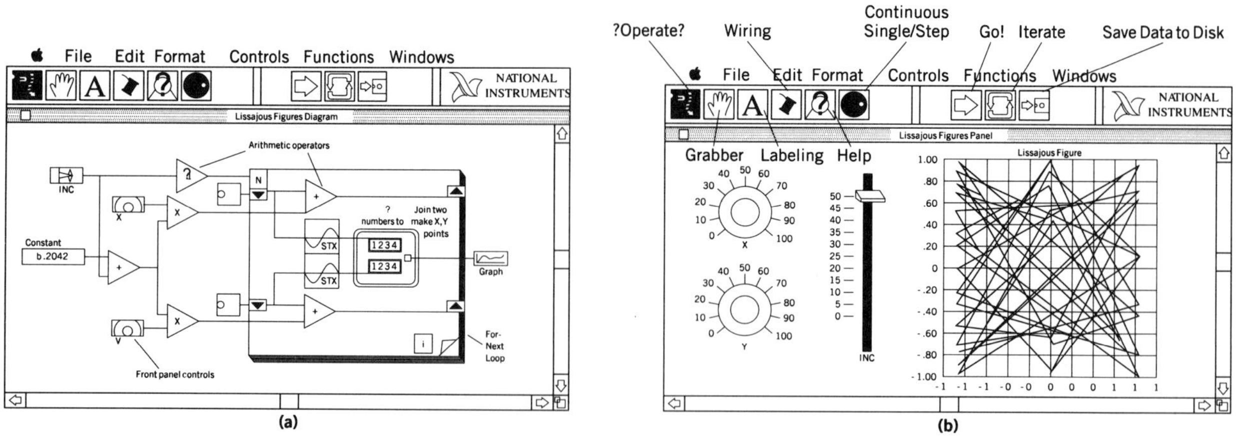

Figure 4. A LabVIEW window (**a**) in which a program to generate a graph has been entered. The resulting user interface after the program has been hidden is shown in (**b**).

Action graphics (Moshell and co-workers, 1987) uses ideas from spreadsheets to try to make it easier to program graphical animations. The *forms* system (Ambler, 1987) uses more a more conventional spreadsheet format, but adds subsheets (to provide procedural abstraction) which can have an unbounded size (to handle arbitrary parameters).

A different style of system is SIL-ICON (Chang and co-workers, 1989), which allows the user to construct "iconic sentences" consisting of graphics arranged in a meaningful two-dimensional fashion, as shown in Figure 5. The SIL-ICON interpreter then parses the picture to determine what it means. The interpreter itself is generated from a description of the legal pictures, in the same way that conventional compilers can be generated from BNF descriptions of the grammar.

EBP, Not VP, Compiled

Some systems have attempted to infer the entire program from one or more examples of what output is produced for a particular input. One program (Shaw, Swartout, and Green, 1975) inferred simple recursive LISP programs from a single I/O pair, such as (A B C D)→(D D C C B B A A). This system was limited to simple list processing programs, and it is clear that systems such as this one cannot generate all programs or even be likely to generate the correct program (Biermann, 1976).

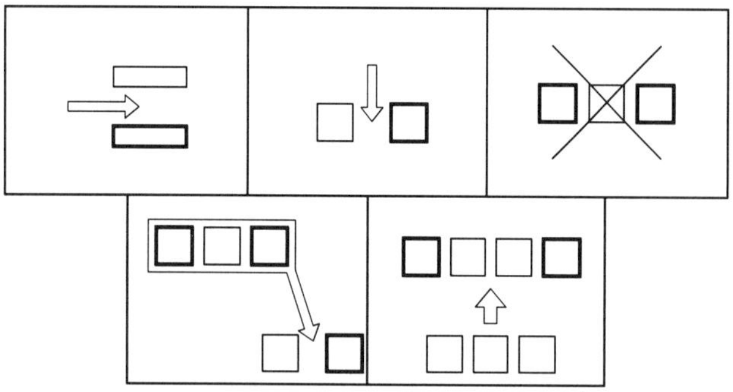

Figure 5. Five different 'iconic sentences' that SIL-ICON can interpret. They mean: insert a line, insert a string, delete a string, move a string to a new place, and replace a string. The user constructs these pictures from primitives such as rectangles, lines and arrows (Chang and co-workers, 1989).

EBP, Not VP, Interpretive

Tinker (Lieberman, 1982) is a *pictorial* system that is not classified as VP. The user chooses a concrete example, and the system executes Lisp statements on this example as the code is typed in. Although Tinker uses windows, menus, and other graphics in its user interface, it is not a VP system since the user presents all of the code to the system in the conventional, linear, textual manner. For conditionals, Tinker requires the user to give two examples: one that will travel down each branch. Tinker notices that two contradictory paths have been specified and prompts the user to type in a test of distinguish when each branch is desired.

The Editing by Example (EBE) system (Nix, 1985) is based on ideas from input/output pairs. Here, the system generates a small program that describes a sequence of editing operations. This program can then be run on any piece of text. The system compares two or more examples of the editing operations in order to deduce what are variables and what are constants. The correct programs usually can be generated given only two or three examples, and there are heuristics to generate programs from single examples. EBE creates the programs from the *results* of the editing operations (the input and output), rather than *traces* of the execution, to allow the user more flexibility and the ability to correct small errors (typos) while giving the examples. EBE seems to be relatively successful, chiefly because it limits the domain in which it performs inferencing.

EBP, VP, Compiled

Some inferencing systems that attempt to cover a wider class of programs than those that can be generated from I/O pairs have required the user to specify the data structures and algorithms and then run through a computation on a number of examples. The systems attempt to infer where loops and conditionals should go to produce the shortest and most general program that will work for all of the examples. One such system is by Bauer (1978), which also decides which values in the program should be constants and which should be variables. It is visual since the user can specify the program execution using graphical traces. Unfortunately, these systems tended to create incorrect programs, and it was difficult to check what the system had done without studying the generated code.

EBP, VP, Interpretive

Pygmalion (Smith, 1977) was one of the seminal VP and EBP systems. It provides an 'iconic' and 'analogical' method for programming: concrete display images for data and programs, called icons, are manipulated to create programs. Pygmalion is also credited with inventing the use of icons in computer interfaces. Icons were later used by Smith and others in commercial products such as the Xerox Star and Apple Lisa and Macintosh. The emphasis is on "doing" pictorially, rather than "telling." Thinglab (Borning, 1979; 1981) was designed to allow the user to describe and run complex simulations easily. A VP interface to Thinglab is described by Borning (1986). Here the user can define new constraints among objects by specifying them graphically. Also, if a class of objects can be created by combining already existing objects, then it can be programmed by example in Thinglab.

Smallstar (Halbert, 1984; 1981) uses EBP to allow the end user to program a prototype version of the Star office workstation (Smith and co-workers, 1982). When programming, the user simply goes into program mode, performs the operations that are to be remembered, and then leaves program mode. The operations are executed in the actual user interface of the system, which the user already knows. Since the system does not use inferencing, the user must differentiate constants from variables and explicitly add control structures (loops and conditionals). This is done on a textual representation of the program created while the user is giving the example. Halbert reports that Star users were able to create procedures for performing their office tasks with his system.

The goal of Rehersal World (Gould and Finzer, 1984) is to allow teachers who do not know how to program to create computerized lessons easily. Interactive graphics are heavily used to provide a "collaborative, evolutionary and exploratory" environment where programming is "quick, easy and fun". The metaphor presented to the user is a *theatre,* where the screen is the *stage* and there are predefined *performers* that the user can *direct* to create a *play.* The teacher developing the program sees at every point exactly what the student-user of the play will see. In addition, the teacher can have additional performers in the *wings* (so the student will not see them) that provide auxiliary functions such as flow control. Everything is made visible to the teachers, however, which allows their thinking to be concrete, rather than abstract as in conventional programming environments. When a new performer is needed, often its code can be created using examples, but when this is not possible some Smalltalk code must be written. The static representation for all performers is Smalltalk code, which can be edited by those who know how.

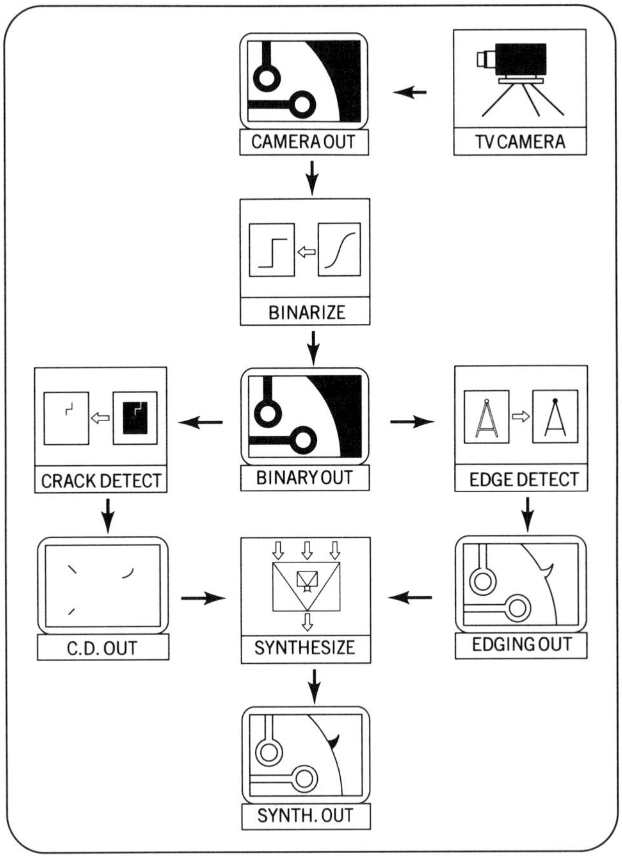

Figure 6. A HI-VISUAL program for performing image processing (Hirakawa and co-workers, 1987).

HI-VISUAL (Hirakawa and co-workers, 1987) allows the user to construct data flow programs out of iconic pictures (see Fig. 6). It is classified as EBP because the user supplies sample data before programming starts, and the system executes the program on the data as each icon is added to the program.

A related system uses direct manipulation to configure icons and circuit diagrams to define sound processing systems (Desain, 1986). This system is classified as Programming With Example because the resulting sound is continuously played while the circuit is being constructed.

The ALEX system (Kozen and co-workers, 1987) allows matrix manipulation algorithms to be specified by example. The user points to a typical element, row, or column in graphical presentation of a sample matrix, and then specifies how to process it. The system then generalizes this operation to operate on the entire array.

Peridot (Myers, 1987; 1988a) is a tool for creating user interfaces by demonstration without programming. The user draws a picture of the desired interface and the system generalizes this picture to produce a parameterized procedure (see Fig. 7). The user gives example values for any parameters so the system can display a concrete instance of the user interface. Peridot allows a nonprogrammer to create menus, scroll-bars, buttons, sliders, etc., and it can create most of the interaction techniques in the Apple Macintosh Toolbox.

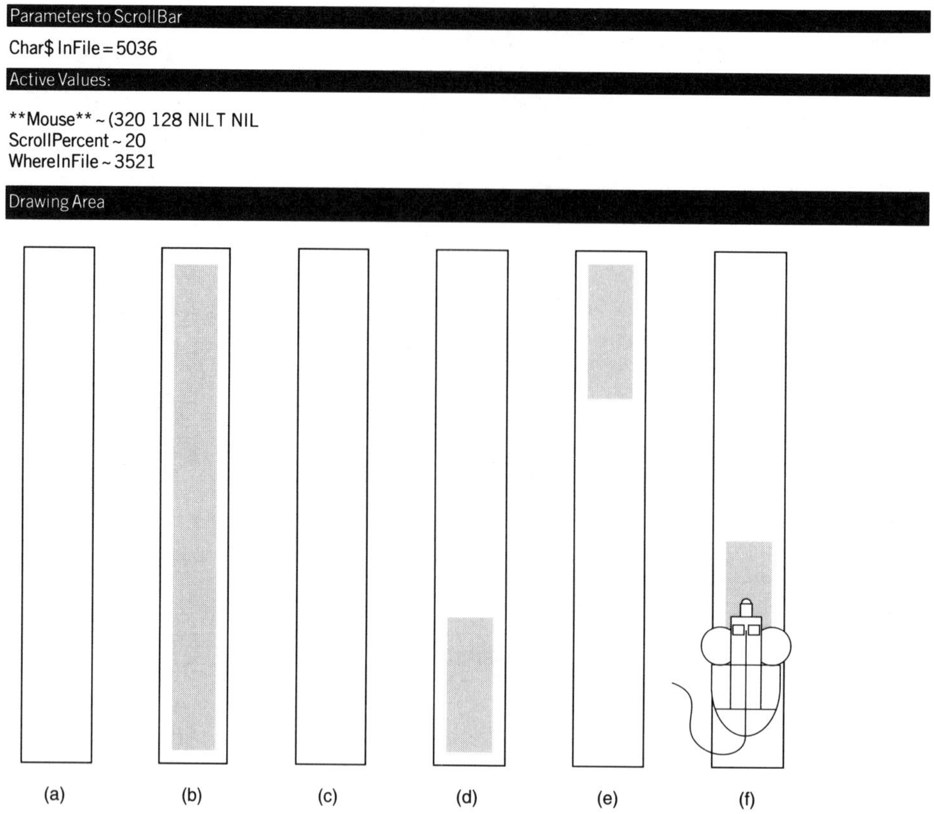

Figure 7. Creating a scroll bar using Peridot. In (**a**), the background graphics have been created. The grey bar will represent percent of file visible in the window. The two extremes of the full file (**b**) and none of the file (**c**) are demonstrated. This will depend on the active value *ScrollPercent* which ranges from 100 to 0 (**d**). Next, the two extremes of seeing the end of the file (**d**) and the beginning of the file (**e**) are demonstrated. The active value *WhereInFile* (which varies from tie value of the parameter *CharsInFile* down to one) controls this (**f**). The designer then demonstrates (**f**) that the bar should follow the mouse when the middle button is down using the 'simulated mouse' (Myers, 1987).

Two data flow systems support Programming with Example. InterCONS (Smith, 1988) and Fabrik (Ludolph and co-workers, 1988) both were developed in Smalltalk and allow the user to wire together low-level primitives like arithmetic operators and higher-level user interface elements like scroll bars and buttons. These systems allow the user to input sample data as the program input, and they continually adjust the output data based on the input and the program constructed thus far. Fabrik also handles undefined values on wires by drawing them with dotted lines. Figure 8 shows an example of an InterCONS program for a calculator.

CLASSIFICATION BY SPECIFICATION TECHNIQUE

Another way to classify programming systems is by what kind of representation they use for the code. Table 2 lists the systems discussed here by what specification technique they use. As new visual programming systems are designed, this list is likely to grow, since new forms for the specification can be invented.

Discussion

Many of the categories listed in Table 2 should be clear, but some need additional explanation.

The "textual language" specification style is clearly used by all conventional programming languages. It is also used by Tinker since it is not a visual programming language. Smallstar is a example-based-programming system, and the system generates the appropriate code while the user is demonstrating the program. Smallstar uses a textual language (augmented with a few decorative icons) to record the user's program. Many of the other example-based-programming systems are listed in the figure as having no textual language. This is because they generate code in a conventional computer language (e.g., Lisp for I/O Pairs and Peridot), which is not shown to the users.

The *iconic sentences* are a separate category because here the positions of the picture are meaningful, and not just in regard to how they are connected with arrows as with flow charts and graphs.

In *demonstrational* systems, the program is defined by graphics that change in time. The meaning and behavior of the icons is demonstrated temporally, and the system

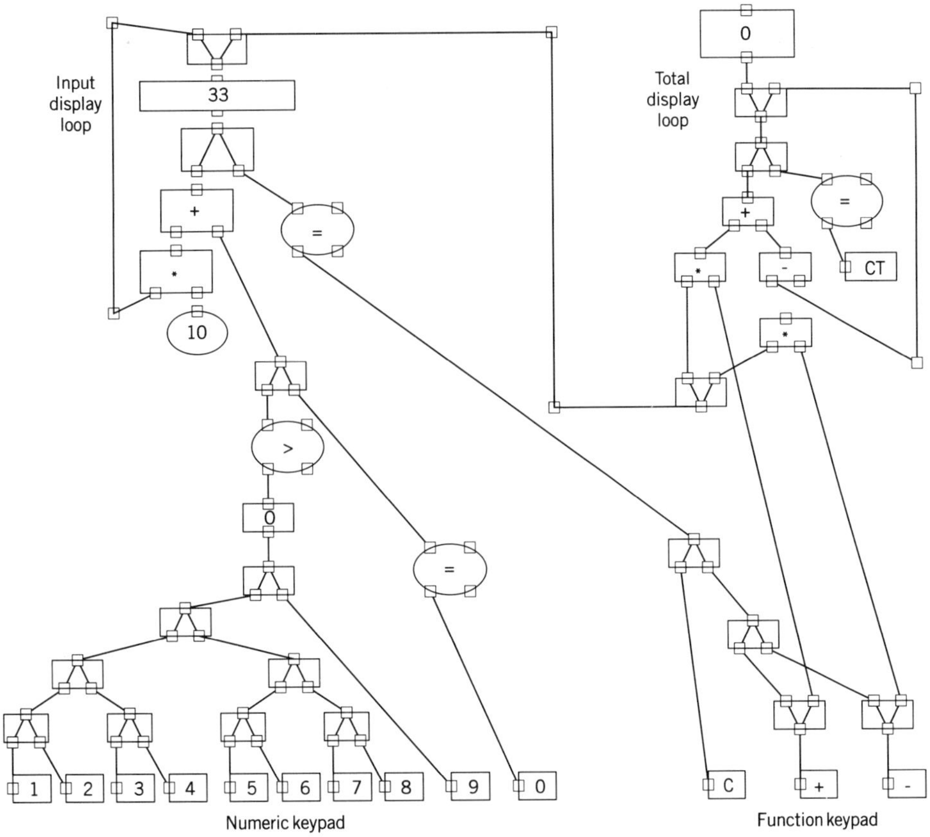

Figure 8. A desk calculator program in InterCONS (Smith, 1988).

Table 2. Classification of Programming Systems by Specification Style[a]

Specification Technique	Systems
	Pascal, Ada, Fortran, Lisp, Ada, etc.
Textual languages	Tinker, Smallstar
Flow charts	Grail, Pict, FPL, IBGE, OPAL
Flow chart derivatives	GAL, PIGS, SchemaCode, PLAY
Petri nets	MOPS-2, VERDI
	Graphical Program Editor, PROGRAPH,
Data flow graphs	Graphical Thinglab, Music System, HI-VISUAL,
	LabVIEW, Fabrik, InterCONS
Directed graphs	AMBIT/G/L, State Transition UIMS, Bauer's Traces
Graph derivatives	HiGraphs, Miro, StateMaster
Matrices	ALEX, MPL
Jigsaw puzzle pieces	Proc-BLOX
Forms	Query by Example, FORMAL
Iconic sentences	SIL-ICON
Spreadsheets[b]	VisiCalc, Lotus 1-2-3, Action graphics, "Forms"
Demonstrational[b]	Pygmalion, Rehersal World, Peridot
None[b]	I/O Pairs, Editing by Example

[a]References for these systems are shown in Table 1.
[b]Classification shows data, rather than code, primarily.

remembers what the user has done. For example, in Pygmalion, to demonstrate that 3 should be added to the value in a variable, the user would drag the icon for the variable into one of the input slots of the adder icon, and a 3 to the other input slot. There is no visible representation of the actions.

The systems classified as using demonstrational, spreadsheets, and no language ("none") actually show the *data* of the program, rather than the code. The current values of the data is visible on the screen, and the code that caused the data to get to be that way is hidden. Sometimes, but not often, there is a way to discover previous states of the data. This is in contrast to most other systems (including data flow diagrams), where the code of the program is represented and the data is implicit. The AMBIT languages are somewhat unique however, because here both the code and data are shown in a pictorial manner.

TAXONOMY OF PROGRAM VISUALIZATION SYSTEMS

The systems discussed in this section are not *programming* systems since code is created in the conventional manner. Therefore, none of the systems discussed below appears in the previous sections. Graphics are used here to *illustrate* some aspect of the program after it is written. Table 3 shows some program visualization systems classified by whether they attempt to illustrate the code, data, or algorithm of a program, and whether the displays are static or

Table 3. Classification of Program Visualization Systems by Whether They Illustrate the Code, Data, or Algorithm, and Whether They Are Static or Dynamic

Classification	Static	Dynamic
Code	flow charts (Haibt, 1959 SEE visual compiler (Baecker and Marcus, 1986) PegaSys (Moriconi and Hare, 1985)	BALSA (Brown and Sedgewick, 1984) PV prototype (Brown and co-workers, 1985) MacGnome(Chandhok and co-workers, 1985) Object-oriented diagrams (Cunningham and Beck, 1986)
	TPM (Eisenstady and Brayshaw, 1987)	TPMEisenstady and Brayshaw, 1987)
Data	TX2 display files (Baecker, 1968) Incense (Myers, 1988; Myers,1980)	Linked lists (Knowlton, 1966) MacGnome (Myers, 1983)
		two systems (Baecker, 1975)
Algorithm	Stills(Bentley and Kernighan, 1987)	sorting out sorting (Baecker,1981) BALSA (Brown and Sedgewick, 1984; Brown, 1988) Animation kit (London and Duisberg, 1985) PV Prototype (Brown and co-workers, 1985) ALADDIN (Hyrskyakari and raiha, 1987) Animation by demonstration (Duisberg, 1987) TANGO (Stasko, 1989)

dynamic. Some systems fit into multiple categories because they illustrate multiple aspects or have different modes.

Static Code Visualization

The earliest example of a visualization is undoubtably the flowchart. As early as 1959, there were programs that automatically created graphical flowcharts from Fortran or assembly language programs (Haibt, 1959). An entirely different approach is taken by SEE (Baecker and Marcus, 1986), which attempts to make conventional program text easier to read by adding multiple fonts, nice formatting, and other graphics.

In PegaSys (Moriconi and Hare, 1985), pictures are formal documentation of programs and are drawn by the user and checked by the system to ensure that they are syntactically meaningful and, to some extent, whether they agree with the program. The program itself, however, must still be entered in a conventional language (Ada).

The Prolog logic-programming language has a quite different execution model than conventional languages. In order to try to make it more understandable, TPM (the Transparent Prolog Machine) (Eisenstadt and Brayshaw, 1987) generates pictures of the execution of Prolog programs. TPM will produce nicely formatted pictures after a program has completed (so it is classified as 'static'), but it will also show an animation of the code executing on less well-formatted pictures (so it is also listed as "dynamic"). Figure 9 shows a sample of a TPM picture.

Dynamic Code Visualization

Most systems in this class do not actually animate the code itself, but rather dynamically show what parts of the

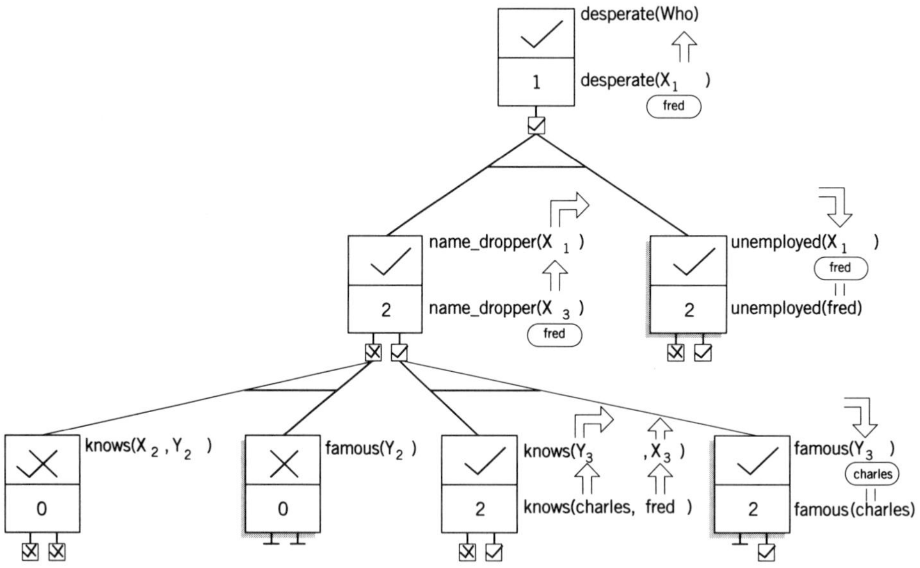

Figure 9. A Prolog program visualized by TPM (Eisenstadt and Brayshaw, 1987).

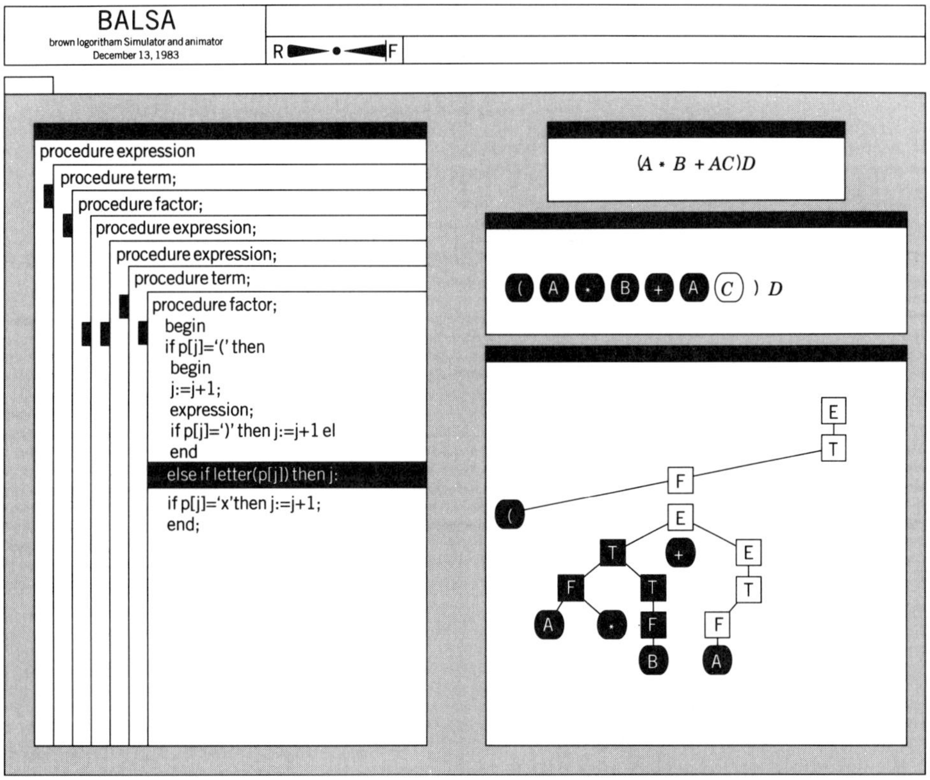

Figure 10. On the left is a code visualization from BALSA showing the highlight bar that follows the execution and the recursive nesting of procedures. On the right is the algorithm animation (Brown and Sedgewick, 1984).

code are being executed as the program is run using some sort of highlighting. Examples are BALSA (Brown and Sedgewick, 1984), PV Prototype (Brown and co-workers, 1985), and MacGnome (Chandhok and co-workers, 1985). Figure 10 shows the BALSA highlighting the execution of a recursive procedure.

The Object-Oriented Diagraming system (Cunningham and Beck, 1986) has a somewhat different focus. It is aimed at illuminating the message-passing structure in object-orientated programs. The system displays objects as boxes (see Fig. 11), and arrows show whether the message is handled by the object class or by one of its super-classes.

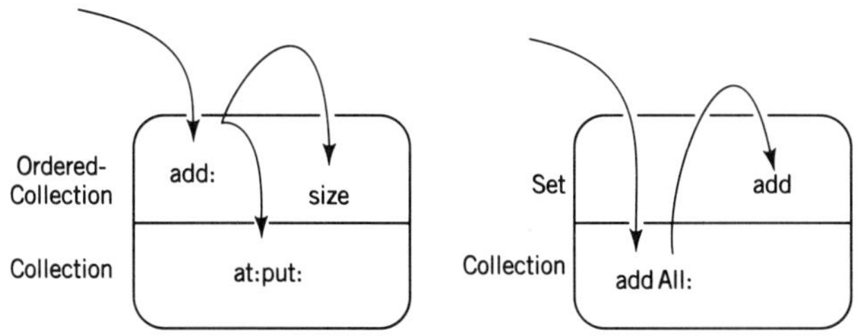

Figure 11. Display of message passing from Cunningham and Beck(1986). Each rounded box is one object instance, and super-classes are shown below sub-classes. The arrows show whether the message was handled by the object class itself (e.g., *add:* which calls *at:put:* of its parent class) or whether it is handled by the super-class (e.g., *addAll:*).

Static Data Visualization

A very early system for the TX-2 computer could produce static pictures of the display file to aid in debugging (Baecker, 1968). Incense (Myers, 1983; 1980) automatically generated static pictorial displays for data structures. The pictures included curved lines with arrowheads for pointers and stacked boxes for arrays and records, as well as user-defined displays (see Fig. 12). The goal was to making debugging easier by presenting data structures to

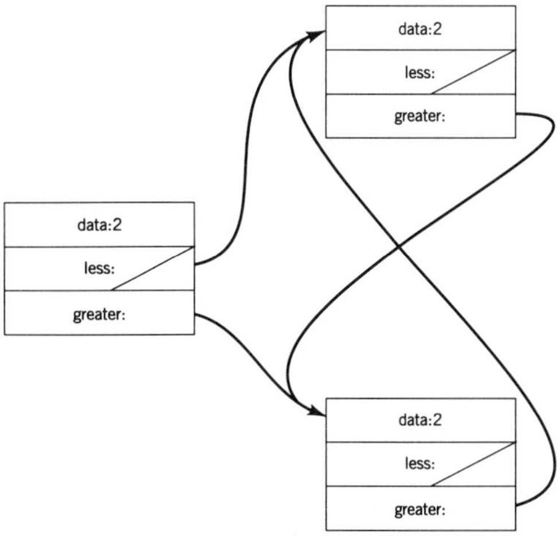

Figure 12. A display produced automatically by Incense of three records containing pointers (Myers, 1980).

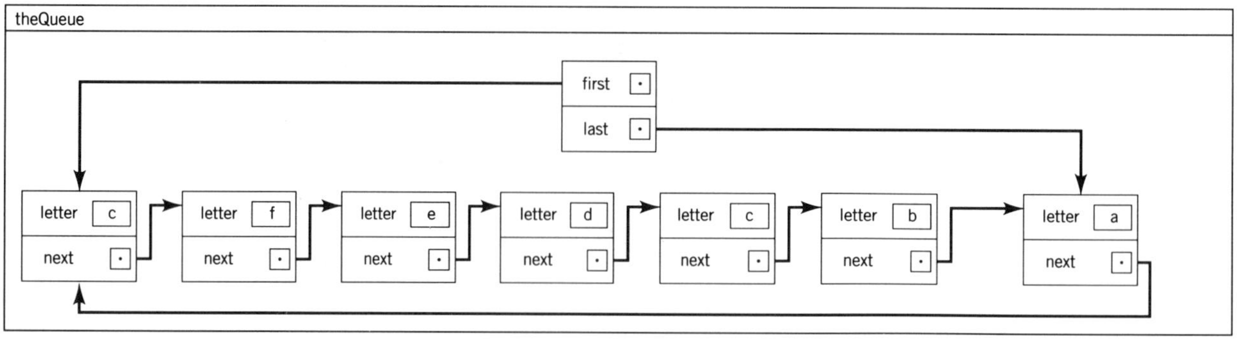

Figure 13. A data visualization automatically produced by MacGnome (Myers, Chandhok, and Sareen, 1988) of a queue of characters implemented as a linked list of records.

programmers in the way that they would draw them by hand on paper.

Dynamic Data Visualization

One of the earliest data visualization systems was the L6 movie of list manipulations (Knowlton, 1966). This system actually falls between dynamic and static, since the software created frames that were filmed. The hardware was not fast enough to animate the structures changing. The MacGnome system, however, shows the pictures changing as the data is modified (Myers, Chandhok, and Sareen, 1988). It runs on the Macintosh, and is similar to Incense in that it automatically produces displays for data structures from the types of the variables; no extra code is needed to generate the pictures. The user simply points to a variable with the mouse, and a picture of its data is automatically displayed (see Fig. 13).

Static Algorithm Visualization

A visualization system that produces static snapshots of the algorithm is Stills (Bentley and Kernighan, 1987). The user added special commands to the source algorithm, and the system generated troll output which could be sent to printers.

Dynamic Algorithm Visualization

Most algorithm visualizations systems are dynamic since they produce animations of the algorithm in action. The first few systems in this class, like the early data visualization systems, created movies of the algorithms (e.g., sorting) and were used for teaching computer science algorithms (Baecker, 1975; 1981).

Unlike data visualization systems, all algorithm animation systems require that the programmer explicitly add information to the code to control the animations. In the famous BALSA system from Brown University (Brown and Sedgewick, 1984), special instructions were added to the code to signal important events. This system was designed to teach students about programming, and produces the illustrations in real time on an Apollo personal workstation (see Fig. 10). An updated version, called BALSA-II, runs on the Macintosh and allows the user to control the animation using Macintosh-style menus (Brown, 1988). The code of the algorithm must still be augmented to tell the system about important events.

The 'PV Prototype' (Brown and co-workers, 1985) was designed to aid in debugging and program understanding, and it supports dynamic displays of data and easier construction of user-defined displays. Another system, called Animation Kit, has similar goals. It is written in Smalltalk and features smooth transitions from one state to another (London and Druisberg, 1985).

A recognized problem with these systems is that it is difficult to specify what the data animations should look like. ALADDIN (Hyrskyakari and Raiha, 1987) attempts to alleviate this problem by allowing a declarative specification of the desired views using a catalog of pre-defined graphical and animation primitives. A different approach was used by Duisberg (Duisberg, 1987) in the Animation by Demonstration system, which allows the desired animations to be specified by demonstration. The user draws a sample picture and then demonstrates an example of the animation to be performed. This animation can then be triggered when a message is sent to an object in the underlying Smalltalk environment. The system uses gestures and a music-like score editor to control the timing of the animations. TANGO (Stasko, 1989) uses a similar approach and allows much of the animations to be created using a graphical editor instead of by writing code.

EVALUATION OF VISUAL PROGRAMMING AND PROGRAM VISUALIZATION

Although there is a great deal of excitement about visual programming and program visualization, as well as a large number of working systems, there is still a lot of skepticism about the success and prospects of the field. For example, Frederick Brooks wrote:

"A favourite subject for PhD dissertations in software engineering is graphical, or visual, programming—the application of computer graphics to software design. ... Nothing even convincing, much less exciting, has yet emerged from such efforts. I am persuaded that nothing will. In the first place, ... the flowchart is a very poor abstraction of software structure .... It has proved to be useless as a design tool. ... Second, the screens of today are too small, in pixels, to show both the scope and the resolution of any seriously detailed software diagram. ... More fundamen-

tally, ... software is very difficult to visualize. Whether one diagrams control flow, variable-scope nesting, variable cross-references, dataflow, hierarchical data structures, or whatever, one feels only one dimension of the intricately interlocked software elephant." (Brooks, 1987, pp. 15–16, emphasis added)

In a similar vein, referring to the MacGnome system, Edsger Dijkstra wrote:

"I was recently exposed to ... what ... pretended to be educational software for an introductory programming course. With its "visualizations" on the screen, it was ... an obvious case of curriculum infantilization. ... We must expect from that system permanent mental damage for most students exposed to it." (Dijkstra, 1989)

Visual languages are new paradigms for programming, and clearly the existing systems have not been completely convincing. The challenge clearly is to demonstrate that visual programming and program visualization can help with real-world problems. The key to this, in my opinion, is to find appropriate domains and new domains to apply these technologies to. For general-purpose programming by professional programmers, textual languages are probably more appropriate. However, we will find new domains and new forms of visual language where using graphics will be beneficial. The systems discussed in this paper show that some successful areas so far include, for visual programming:

- Helping to teach programming (FPL, Pict, etc.)
- Allowing non-programmers to enter information in limited domains (OPAL, spreadsheets)
- Allowing nonprogrammers to construct animations (PLAY) and simple computerized lessons for computer-aided instruction (Rehearsal World)
- Helping with the construction of user interfaces (Peridot, State Transition UIMS)
- Most significantly, financial planning with spreadsheets

and for program visualization:

- Helping to teach algorithms involving data structures (Sorting out Sorting, BALSA),
- Helping to teach program concepts, such as Prolog code execution (TPM), and
- Helping to debug programs (MacGnome).

GENERAL PROBLEMS AND AREAS FOR FUTURE RESEARCH

As described in the previous section, the largest area for future research is to prove that visual languages will actually help users. In addition, there are a number of more technical problems that most of these systems share.

All Visual Languages

The problems mentioned in this section apply to many visual programming and program visualization systems.

Difficulty with Large Programs or Large Data. Almost all visual representations are physically larger than the text they replace, so there is often a problem that too little will fit on the screen. This problem is alleviated to some extent by scrolling and various abstraction mechanisms.

Need for Automatic Layout. When the program or data gets to be large, it can be very tedious for the user to have to place each component, so the system should lay out the picture automatically. Unfortunately, for many graphical representations, generating an attractive layout can be difficult, and generating a perfect layout may be intractable. For example, generating an optimal layout of graphs and trees is NP-Complete (Johnson, 1982). More research is needed, therefore, on fast layout algorithms for graphs that have good user interface characteristics, such as avoiding large scale changes to the display after a small edit.

Lack of Formal Specification. Currently, there is no formal way to describe a visual language. Something equivalent to the BNFs used for textual languages is needed. This would provide the field with a "hard science" foundation, and may allow tools to be created that will make the construction of editors and compilers for visual languages easier. Chang (Chang and co-workers, 1987; 1989), Glinert (Glinert and Gonczarowski, 1987) and Selker (Selker and Koved, 1988) have made attempts in this direction, but much more work is needed.

Tremendous Difficulty in Building Editors and Environments. Most visual languages require a specialized editor, compiler, and debugger to be created to allow the user to use the language. With textual languages, conventional, existing text editors can be used, and only a compiler and possibly a debugger needs to be written. Currently, each graphical language requires its own editor and environment, since there are no general purpose visual language editors. These editors are hard to create because there are no "editor-compilers" or other similar tools to help. The "compiler-compiler" tools used to build compilers for textual languages are also rarely useful for building compilers and interpreters for visual languages. In addition, the language designer must create a system to display the pictures from the language, which usually requires low-level graphics programming. Other tools that traditionally exist for textual languages must also be created, including pretty-printers, hard-copy facilities, program checkers, indexers, cross-referencers, pattern matching and searching (e.g., 'grep' in Unix), etc. These problems are made worse by the historical lack of portability of most graphics programs.

Lack of Evidence of Their Worth. There are not many visual languages that would be generally agreed are "successful," and there is little in the way of formal experiments or informal experience that shows that visual languages are good. It would be interesting to see experimental results that demonstrated that visual programming techniques or iconic languages were better than good textual methods for performing the same tasks. Metrics might include learning time, execution speed, retention, etc. Fortunately, preliminary results are appearing for the advantages of using graphics for teaching students how to program (Cuniff, Taylor, and Black, 1986).

Poor Representations. Many visual representations are simply not very good. Programs are hard to understand once created and difficult to debug and edit. This is especially true once the programs get to be a non-trivial size.

Lack of Portability of Programs. A program written in a textual language can be sent through electronic mail and used, read, and edited by anybody. Graphical languages require special software to view and edit; otherwise they can only be viewed on hard copy.

Specific Problems for Visual Programming

A primary problem for many visual programming languages is that they are "unstructured" in the software engineering sense. This is because many of them:

- Use Gotos and explicit transfer of control (often through wires)
- Only have global variables
- Have no procedural abstraction
- If they have procedural abstraction, they may not have parameters for the procedures
- Have no place for comments

Another problem is that many visual programs do not integrate with programs created in different languages, such as text. A visual program might be appropriate for some aspects of the programming task but not others. An exception is MPL, which uses a visual language for matrices and a textual language for everything else. Another approach is for the compiler for the visual programming language to generate conventional computer programs (e.g., in C), so they can be combined with other programs.

Specific Problems for Program Visualization

Difficulty in Specifying the Display. Newer program visualization systems are beginning to ease the task of specifying the display, but it can still be very difficult to design and program the desired graphics. Some systems, such as BALSA-II make it easy to choose from a predefined set of displays, but creating other displays can still be very difficult because it involves making low-level calls to the graphics primitives.

Problem of Controlling Timing. For dynamic data visualization, it is difficult to specify when the displays should be updated. Issues of aesthetics in timing are very important to produce useful animations.

CONCLUSIONS

Visual programming and program visualization are interesting areas that show promise for improving the programming process, especially for non-programmers, but more work needs to be done. The success of spreadsheets demonstrates that if we find the appropriate paradigms, graphical techniques can *revolutionize* the way people interact with computers.

Reprinted from B. A. Myers, "Taxonomies of Visual Programming and Program Visualization," in S. K. Chang and S. Levialdi, eds., *Journal of Visual Languages and Computing* **1,** 97–123 (1990), by permission of Academic Press, Ltd., Harcourt Brace Jovanovich, Publishers, London, UK.

BIBLIOGRAPHY

Adobe Systems, Inc., *Postscript Language Reference Manual,* Addison-Wesley, Menlo Park, Calif., 1985.

T. Ae and co-workers, "Visual User-Interface of a Programming System: MOPS-2," in Korfhage, 1986, pp. 44–53.

T. Ae and R. Aibara, "A Rapid Prototyping of Real-Time Software Using Petri Nets," in Jungert, 1987, pp. 234–241.

M. B. Alibizuri-Romero, "GRASE—A Graphical Syntax-Directed Editor for Structured Programming," *SIGPLAN Notices* **19,** 28–37(1984).

A. L. Ambler, "Forms: Expanding the Visualness of Sheet Languages," in Jungert, 1987, pp. 105–117.

Apple Computer, Inc., *Inside Macintosh,* Addison-Wesley, Menlo Park, Calif., 1985.

R. M. Baecker, "Experiments in On-Line Graphical Debugging: The Interrogation of Complex Data Structures," (summary), *First Hawaii International Conference on the System Sciences,* Jan. 1968, pp. 128–129.

R. M. Baecker, "Two Systems Which Produce Animated Animated Representations of the Execution of Computer Programs," *SIGCSE Bulletin* **7,** 158–167(1975).

R. M. Baecker, *Sorting out Sorting,* 16 mm color, sound film, 25 minutes Dynamics Graphics Project, Computer Systems Research Institute, University of Toronto, Ontario, Canada, presented at ACM SIGGRAPH 1981, Dallas, Tex., Aug. 1981.

R. Baecker and A. Marcus, "Design Principles for the Enhanced Presentation of Computer Program Source Text," *Human Factors in Computing Systems: Proceedings SIGCHI 1986,* Boston, Mass., Apr. 13–17, 1986.

M. A. Bauer, *A Basis for the Acquisition of Procedures,* PhD dissertation, Department of Computer Science, University of Toronto, Ontario, Canada, 1978.

J. L. Bentley and B. W. Kernighan, *A System for Algorithm Animation: Tutorial and User Manual,* AT&T Bell Laboratories Computing Science Technical Report No. 132, Murray Hill, N.J., Jan. 1987.

A. T. Berztiss, "Specification of Visual Representations of Petri Nets," in Jungert, 1987, pp. 225–233.

A. S. Berztiss, ed., *1988 IEEE Workshop on Visual Languages,* IEEE Computer Society Press, Los Angeles, Calif., Oct. 10–12, 1988.

A. W. Biermann "Approaches to Automatic Programming," in *Advances in Computers,* M. Rubinoff and M. C. Yovitz, eds., Academic Press, New York, 1976, pp. 1–63.

A. Borning, *Thinglab—A Constraint-Oriented Simulation Laboratory,* Xerox Palo Research Center Technical Report SSL-79-3, July, 1979.

A. Borning, "The Programming Language Aspects of Thinglab: A Constraint-OrientedSimulation Laboratory," *Transactions on Programming Language and Systems* **3,** 353–387, (1981).

A. Borning, "Defining Constraints Graphically," *Human Factors in Computing Systems: Proceedings SILGCHI 1986,* Boston, Mass., Apr. 13–17, 1986.

F. P. Brooks, Jr., "No Silver Bullet: Essence and Accidents of Software Engineering," *IEEE Computer* **20,** 10–19(1987).

G. P. Brown and co-workers, "Program Visualization: Graphical Support for Software Development," *IEEE Computer* **18,** 27–35(1985).

M. H. Brown, "Exploring Algorithms Using Balsa-II," *IEEE Computer* **21**(5), 14–36(1988).

M. H. Brown and R. Sedgewick, "A System for Algorithm Animation," *Computer Graphics, SIGGRAPH 1984 Conference Proceedings* **18,** 177–186(1984).

R. Chandhok and co-workers, "Programming Environments Based on Structure Editing: The Gnome Approach," *Proceedings of the National Computer Conference* (NCC 1985), AFIPS, 1985.

S.-K. Chang, T. Ichikawa, and P. A. Ligomenides, eds., *Visual Languages,* Plenum Press, New York, 1986.

S.-K. Chang and co-workers, "Icon Purity—Toward a Formal Theory of Icons," in Jungert, 1987, pp. 3–16.

S. K. Chang and co-workers, "A Visual Language Compiler," *IEEE Transactions on Software Engineering,* May 1989, pp. 506–525.

C. Christensen, "An Example of the Manipulation of Directed Graphs in the AMBIT/G Programming Language," in M. Klerer and J. Reinfelds, eds., *Interactive Systems for Experimental Applied Mathematics,* Academic Press, New York, 1968, pp. 423–435.

C. Christensen, "An Introduction to AMBIT/L, A Diagramatic Language for List Processing," *Proceedings of the Second Symposium on Symbolic and Algebraic Manipulation,* Los Angeles, Calif., March 23–25, 1971, pp. 248– 260.

O. Clarisse and S.-K. Chang, "VICON: A Visual Icon Manager," *Visual Languages,* Plenum Press, New York, 1986, pp. 151–190.

N. Cunniff, R. P. Taylor and J. B. Black, "Does Programming Language Affect the Type of Conceptual Bugs in Beginners' Programs? A Comparison of FPL and Pascal," *Proceedings SIGCHI 1986: Human Factors in Computing Systems,* Boston, Mass., Apr. 13–17, 1986, pp. 175–182.

W. Cunningham and K. Beck, "A Diagram for Object-Oriented Programs," OOPSLA 1986 Proceedings, Portland, Oreg., Sept. 29–Oct. 2, 1986, *SIGPLAN Notices* **21**(11), 361–367(Nov. 1986).

P. Desain, "Graphical Programming in Computer Music," *Proceedings of the International Computer Music Conference,* Royal Conservatory, The Hague, Netherlands, Oct. 20–24, 1986, pp. 161–166.

E. W. Dijkstra, "On the Cruelty of Really Teaching Computing Science, The SIGCSE Award Lecture, *CACM* **32,** 1403– 1404(1989).

R. A. Duisberg, "Visual Programming of Program Visualizations," in Jungert, 1987, pp. 55–56.

M. Eisenstadt and M. Brayshaw, "The Transparent Prolog Machine: an Execution Model and Graphical Debugger for Logic Programming," *Journal of Logic Programming,* Human Cognition Research Laboratory Technical Report No. 21a, The Open University, Milton Keynes, UK, Oct. 1987.

T. O. Ellis, J. F. Heafner, and W. L. Sibley, *The Grail Project: An Experiment in Man-Machine Communication,* Rand Report RM-5999-Arpa, 1969.

E. P. Glinert, "Out of Flatland: Towards 3-D Visual Programming," in Korfhage, 1987, pp. 283–290.

E. P. Glinert and J. Gonczarowski, "A (Formal) Model for (Iconic) Programming Environments," *Human-Computer Interaction —Interact 1987,* Elsevier Science Publishers, North Holland, 1987, pp. 283–290.

E. P. Glinert and L. Tanimoto, "Pict: An Interactive Graphical Programming Environment," *IEEE Computer* **17,** 7–25(1984).

L. Gould and W. Finzer, *Programming by Rehersal,* Xerox Palo Alto Research Center Technical Report SCL-84-1, May 1984.

L. Gould and W. Finzer, "Programming by Rehersal," *Byte* **9,** 187–210.

M. Graf, "A Visual Environment for the Design of Distributed Systems," in Jungert, 1987, pp. 330–344.

R. B. Grafton and T. Ichikawa, eds., *IEEE Computer,* Special Issue of Visual Programming **18,** 6–94(1985).

L. M. Haibt, "A Program to Draw Multi-Level Flow Charts," *Proceedings of the Western Joint Computer Conference,* San Francisco, Calif. **15,** 131–137 (Mar. 3–5, 1959).

D. C. Halbert, *An Example of Programming by Example,* MS dissertation, Computer Science Division, Department of Electrical Engineering and Computer Science, University of California, Berkeley, and Xerox Corporation Office Products Division, Palo Alto, Calif., June 1981.

D. C. Halbert, *Programming by Example,* PhD dissertation, University of California, Berkeley, 1984.

D. Harel, "On Visual Formalisms," *CACM* **31**(5), 514–530(May 1988).

M. Hirakawa and co-workers, "HI-VISUAL Iconic Programming," in Jungert, 1987, pp. 40–45.

A. Hyrskyakari and K.-J. Raiha, "Animation of Algorithms Without Programming," in Jungert, 1987, pp. 40–45.

R. J. K. Jacob, "A State Transition Diagram Language for Visual Programming," *IEEE Computer* **18,** 51–59 1985.

D. S. Johnson, "The NP-Completeness Column: An Ongoing Guide," *Journal of Algorithms* **3,** 89–99(1982).

E. Jungert, ed., *1987 Workshop on Visual Languages,* Linkoping, Sweden, IEEE Computer Society, Aug. 19–21, 1987.

A. Kay, "Software," *Scientific American* (Sept. 1984).

K. C. Knowlton, *L6: Bell Telephone Laboratories Low-Level Linked List Language,* Black and White Shoud Files, Bell Laboratories, Murray Hill, N.J., 1966.

R. R. Korfhage, ed., *1986 IEEE Workshop on Visual Languages,* Computer Society Order Number 722, Dallas, Texas, IEEE Computer Society Press, Los Angeles, Calif., June 25–27, 1986.

D. Kozen and co-workers, "ALEX—An Alexical Programming Language," in Jungert, 1987, pp. 315–329.

C. Lewis and G. M. Olson, "Can Principles of Cognition Lower the Barriers to Programming?" *Empirical Studies of Programmers* Vol. 2, Ablex, 1987.

H. Lieberman, *Constructing Graphical User Interfaces by Example,* Graphics Interface 1982, Toronto, Ontario, Mar. 17–21, 1982. pp. 295–302.

R. L. London and R. A. Druisberg, "Animating Programs in Smalltalk," *IEEE Computer* **18,** 61–71(1985).

F. Ludolph and co-workers, "The Fabrik Programming Environment, " in Berztiss, 1988, pp. 222–230.

M. W. Maimone, J. D. Tygar, and J. M. Wing, "Miro Semantics for Security," *1988 IEEE Workshop on Visual Languages,* Pittsburgh, Pa., Computer Society Order Number 876, IEEE Computer Society Press, Los Angeles, Calif., Oct. 10–12, 1988, pp. 45–51.

McCormack and P. Asente, "An Overview of the X Toolkit," *Proceedings of the ACM SIGGRAPH Symposium on User Interface Software,* Banff, Alberta, Canada, ACM Press, Oct. 17–19, 1988, pp. 46–55.

M. Moriconi and D. F. Hare, "Visualizing Program Designs Through PegaSys," *IEEE Computer* **18,** 72–85(1985).

J. M. Moshell and co-authors, "A Spreadsheet-Based Visual Language for Freehand Sketching of Complex Motions," in Jungert, 1988, pp. 94–104.

M. A. Musen, L. M. Fagen, and E. J. Shortliffe, "Graphical Specification of Procedural Knowledge for an Expert System," in Korfhage, 1986, pp. 167–178.

B. A. Myers, *Displaying Data Structures for Interactive Debugging,* Xerox Palo Alto Research Center Technical Report CSL-80-7, June, 1980.

B. A. Myers, "Incense: A System for Displaying Data Structures, Computer Graphics," *SIGGRAPH 1983 Conference Proceedings* **17,** 115–125(1983).

B. A. Myers, "Visual Programming, Programming by Example, and Program Visualization: A Taxonomy," *Proceedings SIGCHI 1986: Human Factors in Computing Systems,* ACM Press, Boston, Mass., 1986, pp. 59–66.

B. A. Myers, "Creating Interaction Techniques by Demonstration," *IEEE Computer Graphics and Applications* **7**, 51–60(1987).

B. A. Myers, *Creating User Interfaces by Demonstration,* Academic Press, Boston, Mass., 1988.

B. A. Myers, *The State of the Art in Visual Programming and Program Visualization,* Carnegie Mellon University Computer Science Department, Technical Report No. CMU-CS-88-114, 1988.

B. A. Myers, "User Interface Tools: Introduction and Survey," *IEEE Software* **6,** 15–23(1989).

B. A. Myers, R. Chandhok, and A. Sareen, "Automatic Data Visualization for Novice Pascal Programmers," in Berztiss, 1988, pp. 192–198.

I. Nassi and B. Shneiderman, "Flowchart Techniques for Structured Programming," *SIGPLAN Notices* **8,** 12–26(1973).

National Instruments, *LabVIEW,* Austin, Tex.

R. P. Nix, "Editing by Example," *ACM Transactions on Programming Languages and Systems* **7,** 600–621(1985).

T. Pietrzykowski and S. Matwin, *PROGRAPH: A Preliminary Report,* University of Ottawa Technical Report TR-84-07, Apr. 1984.

T. Pietrzykowsk, S. Marwin, and T. Muldner, "The Programming Language PROGRAPH: Yet Another Application of Graphics," *Graphics Interface 1983,* Edmonton, Alberta, Canada, May 9–13, 1983, pp. 143–145.

M.-C. Pong, "A Graphical Language for Concurrent Programming," in Korfhage, 1986, pp. 26–33.

M. C. Pong and N. Ng, "Pigs—A System for Programming with Interactive Graphical Support," *Software—Practice and Experience* **13,** 847–855(1983).

T. Selker and L. Koved, "Elements of Visual Language," in Berztiss, 1988, pp. 38–43.

D. E. Shaw, W. R. Swartout, and C. C. Green, "Inferring Lisp Programs from Examples," *Fourth International Joint Conference on Artificial Intelligence,* Tbilisi, Republic of Georgia **1,** 260–267(Sept. 3–8, 1975).

N. C. Shu, "FORMAL: A Forms-Oriented Visual-Directed Application Development System, *IEEE Computer* **18,** 38–49(1985).

N.-C. Shu, *Visual Programming,* Van Nostrand Reinhold Co., Inc. New York, 1988.

D. C. Smith, *Pygmalion: A Computer Program to Model and Stimulate Creative Thought,* Birkhauser, Basel, Switzerland, Stuttgart, Germany, 1977.

D. N. Smith, "Visual Programming in the Interface Construction Set," in Berztiss, 1988, pp. 109–120.

D. C. Smith and co-workers, "Designing the Star User Interface," *Byte Magazine,* 242–282(Apr. 1982).

J. T. Stasko, *TANGO: A Framework and System for Algorithm Animation,* Technical Report No. CS-89-30, PhD dissertation, Department of Computer Science, Brown University, Providence, R.I., May 1989.

I. E. Sutherland, "SketchPad: A Man-Machine Graphical Communication System," *AFIPS Spring Joint Computer Conference* **23,** 329–346(1963).

W. R. Sutherland, *On-Line Graphical Specification of Computer Procedures,* Lincoln Labs Report TR-405, PhD dissertation, MIT, Cambridge, Mass., 1966.

S. L. Tanimoto and M. S. Runyan, "PLAY: An Iconic Programming System for Children," *Visual Languages,* Plenum Press, New York, 1986, pp. 191–205.

T. H. Taylor and R. P. Burton, "An Icon-Based Graphical Editor," *Computer Graphics World* **9,** 77–82 (1986).

P. D. Wellner, "Statemaster: A UIMS Based on Statecharts for Prototyping and Target Implementation," *Proceedings SIGCHI 1989: Human Factors in Computing Systems,* Austin, Tex., Apr. 30–May 4, 1989, pp. 177–182.

R. Yeung, "MPL—A Graphical Programming Environment for Matrix Processing Based on Logic and Constraints," in Berztiss, 1988, pp. 137–143.

M. M. Zloof, "QBE/OBE: A Language for Office and Business Automation," *IEEEComputer* **14**(5), 13–22(May 1981).

M. M. Zloof and S. Peter de Jong, "The System for Business Automation (SBA): Programming Language," *CACM* **20**(6), 385–396(June 1977).

BRAD A. MYERS
Carnegie Mellon University

PROGRAMMING LANGUAGES: MODELS AND PROGRAMMING STYLES

INTRODUCTION

'When I use a word,' Humpty Dumpty said, in rather a scornful tone, 'it means just what I choose it to mean—neither more nor less'. 'The question is,' said Alice, 'whether you can make words mean so many different things.' 'The question is,' said Humpty Dumpty, 'which is to be master—that's all.'

Through The Looking Glass, Lewis Carroll.

In any discipline, ideas and terminology proliferate together. Unfortunately, the relationship of one to the other is not always clearly defined; labels and expressions infiltrate common parlance often before their meanings are precise, so that discussions are ill-founded and ambiguous. Computer science is no exception; terminology covering programming paradigms—even the use of "paradigm"—is disputed.

In this article we try to clarify the nature and usage of programming languages in order to understand the qualities driving classification. Viewing coding as a translation process, we consider the accessibility of the models between which translations must be accomplished. Hence, we examine the computational models which underlie programming languages and consider at what level—language surface or implementation— computational mechanisms are evident and at what level algorithmic decisions are defined. This examination guides our re-appraisal of the terminology, starting with our notions of 'specification' and 'program', and culminating in a series of questions which highlight the significance of 'imperative' and 'declarative'. We find that, in this formulation, the languages form a continuum, and we present a simple map.

Terminology

We start by giving the following short, "garden variety" definitions as a base for our examination:

Imperative. Imperative languages express sequences of operations required to achieve a calculation. These languages are 'state-oriented'; they imply an underlying machine manipulated explicitly by a programmer's commands.

Declarative. Declarative languages emphasize what is to be calculated rather than how the calculation should proceed. How the calculation is performed depends on the implementation, which embodies algorithmic information not found directly in the language. A declarative program is a statement of constraints on the solution which can be read 'declaratively' as a description of the solution set. These constraints coerce the algorithmic engine embedded in the language implementation to produce a solution or set of solutions.

"Imperative" and "declarative" are the major classes on which we focus our appraisal. The following terms govern subclasses or styles, and their meanings are less problematic:

Procedural. A subclass of imperative languages, procedural languages incorporate language constructs for modularizing source code in the form of procedures or functions which are called with parameters and which return control to the caller.

Object-Oriented. A subclass of imperative languages, object-oriented languages view computation as interaction among active data objects. All data are objects, all objects are treated uniformly, and all processing is done by passing messages among objects. Each object embodies operations defined for it, and 'control' takes the form of requests ('messages') sent to data objects to transform themselves. Data abstraction is sustained, and the internals of objects are hidden. Similar objects can be grouped in a hierarchy of classes, with classes able to "inherit" common attributes form their superclasses.

Logic. A subclass of declarative languages, logic programming languages provide constructs for defining atomic relationships among values by asserting facts and rules about them in the form of "implications" in which at most one conclusion derives from the conjunction of zero or more conditions. The logic used is of first order; the clauses that constitute a program are mutually independent but cannot be treated as objects in their own right. Programs are 'interrogated' to elicit truths about individuals and their relationships. The engine for "resolving" and "unifying" these relationships is wholly within the language implementation. Programs generate sets of answers, not necessarily single answers. Serialization of the set generation is usually handled by the user interface.

Functional. A subclass of declarative languages, functional languages specify output as a function, in the mathematical sense, of the input. These languages are "value-oriented"; there is no implied state and hence no changes of state or "side-effects." These languages incorporate 'referential transparency'; the value of a function is determined solely by the values of its arguments, so a function called with the same arguments will always yield the same values.

Applicative. Treated here as a synonym for "functional," this term emphasises that effects are achieved by composing functions and applying them recursively. This term is used elsewhere as a stricter label the sense of "purely applicative," that is, referential transparency is maintained for all expressions.

Computational Model

Underlying all programming is some notion of a machine. However a solution is pursued, the vehicle is the computer. Abstraction from specific machine operations—the evolution of high-level languages—has made it possible to characterise different models of computation compatible with actual processing. Embodied in each language is such a computational model, a view of the actions and interactions by which solutions are achieved. Moreover, some of the structure originally imposed at the hardware level—actually "wired in"—is now provided within language implementations, so that the machine-level model is simpler, and sophistication is introduced in the computational models underlying high-level languages. We will examine our terminology for languages in terms of the distinctions or similarities among the embedded views of the computational world.

Between conception and computation are translations; of strategies to code, of source code to machine code, of instructions to actions. The introduction of levels of abstraction, i.e., intermediate models, implies additional translations. These are introduced to bring the model of computation closer to the user by reducing the translation distance between the top layers of translation. In compensation, the translation distance between underlying layers —between the language implementation and machine instructions—lengthens. In fact, in recognition of the improvements in language technology, machine instructions have become more rudimentary. Less structure is imposed at the level of machine instructions, making the hardware more amenable to the imposition of various computational models, with the consequence that the machine language

Computation Conception

1. In the beginning, there was machine code:

(..........Machine..........) (.................Mind..................)

2. Assembly language provided a computational model closer to the programmer.

(..........Machine..........) (Assembler) (..........Mind..........)

3. The high level languages further reduced the user-end translation distance:

(..........Machine..........) (Assembler) (Compiler) (..........Mind..........)

4. Attempts were made to make the hardware simpler but without changing the boundary between hardware and software. An extra level was introduced: microcode programs were held in ROM and called firmware:

(..........Machine..........) (Microcode) (Assembler) (Compiler) (..........Mind..........)

5. Attempts were also made to make the hardware much more sophisticated and so directly able to support the high level languages:

(..........Machine..........) (Compiler) (..........Mind..........)

6. The current RISC idea is a return to the simple hardware of 4 but requiring the compiler to provide the sophistication for the user; there is no manufacturer-supplied-software level:

(..........Machine..........) (Assembler) (.......Compiler.......) (..........Mind..........)

7. The above are all compilation models. There are also interpreters which are software machines, programs that act like hardware computers:

(..........Machine..........) (..........Interpreter..........) (..........Mind..........)

Figure 1. Translation distances.

is even further from the user. The lengthened translation gap is bridged by the high-level language compiler. Figure 1 shows these changes of translation distance over time.

The priorities of programming language development are clear: the translation distance from the user mind to the user language must be minimized; the rest is technology. The distance of the hardware model from the user is irrelevant, as long as a translation path that preserves semantics exists from the user's computational model to the machine model. It is the translation distance between the top layers—between the user's perception of the language model and the computational model embedded in the language—that is critical.

Efficacy of programming depends on the continuity of translation between these top layers and so is concerned not only with how well the model captures computation but also with how accessible the model is to the user. In order for programs to succeed, the programmer's perception of the model must reflect the language with some accuracy.

Some tolerance is required in this discussion. The perimeter of a language is not strictly defined, and so the underlying computational model, although stable in principle, has blurred edges. Mechanisms such as procedure and data abstraction define new words which become part of the language. They enable extensions to a language in the language, which confuses the borders of both language and model.

Moreover, a program implies a model which is related to the language's computational model. A program selects from the language model in the sense that it exercises only portions of the model. Yet it also extends the model of computation by composing and defining new items using language constructs.

Thus, it is not a single computational model which governs effective programming, but the interactions of several. The compatibility of the model embodied by the program, the model inherent in the language, and the programmer's perception of both of these are issues of translation distance.

CHARACTERIZATION OF MODELS UNDERLYING STYLES

Our willingness to classify languages (i.e., to exercise the terminology under discussion) implies that we acknowledge some commonality of models among languages of a style or class, even if we reject that those computational models are equivalent. Thus, models inherent in languages considered declarative share characteristics not found in models embodied in imperative languages, and so on. For the purposes of this discussion, we will treat a style as having an inherent computational model which is the general distillation of attributes shared by models underlying the languages of the style.

The Imperative Model

The imperative computational model is reflected by the notion of the von Neumann machine, which was for many years the model for all digital computers. The basic von Neumann machine has two components: a memory and a single processor. Programs, like all other data, are stored in memory, from where they are retrieved for execution for the processor. The processor performs two sorts of functions: it can access any memory location to retrieve or modify the contents, and it can execute instructions, which exercise its simple logic operations, one at a time in a sequence defined by the program. Thus, memory and a single processor combine into a model of a global environment, which undergoes incremental changes.

The imperative model incorporates these von Neumann machine characteristics in the notions of assignment, state, and effect. Values are assigned to variables, which are seen as 'boxes' whose contents are mutable. Procedures operate by modifying their parameters or global variables. Hence, the machine comprises objects (variables) which can change over time. Collectively, the values of the variables at a given time describe the state of the machine. This model of operation, by change of state and by calculation and alteration of variable values, yields the notion of "computation by effect".

Under this model, algorithms are conveyed as a consequence of changes of state. The subject languages contain explicit control structures for guiding the flow of execution.

The closeness of this computational model to the hardware model is a matter of evolution. Programming languages began as strings of machine-specific binary codes corresponding to individual machine operations. These machine language instructions comprised two parts, resembling the von Neumann model: operation code and memory location. Next, the assembly languages introduced mnemonics to represent the binary instructions and removed the need for programmer control of storage locations but necessitated translation of this symbolic code into machine code and 'assembly' of the variously stored program components (subroutines). Although some mnemonics represented more than one machine instruction, translation remained mainly 1:1. The so-called high-level languages abstracted from assembly language, becoming machine independent and incorporating composite constructs. These languages require more sophisticated translation ("compilation") from their portable form into machine-specific code. These high-level languages, as abstractions from machine codes, still reflect basic machine operations. Developments of structure and style reflect the consideration of programming languages in their own right instead of as versions of machine code, that is, as mere extensions of hardware.

This closeness of language to machine model is reflected in practical ways, e.g., the good control afforded by many imperative languages over machine aspects such as memory allocation and I/O. However, the strength of correspondence means that imperative languages embody hardware-based restrictions, so that pragmatics may intrude upon expression. It may be impossible to express structures whose bounds are not defined or whose characteristics may change at runtime.

The Declarative Model

The declarative model is divorced from the von Neumann machine, from explicit sequential control, from state and from what John Backus (1978) labelled "the von Neumann bottleneck"-assignment. This is a model of "computation by value". Functions, rather than causing the 'effects' of modifying parameters or variables, return values. Data items are immutable; there is no sense of updatable memory accessible by instruction.

There is no sense of instruction, instead there is a "script" which defines what is to be computed. The manipulations by which this objective is achieved are not explicitly part of the model. Indeed, David Turner (1985) introduced the term "script" for the programs written in his functional languages to emphasize that such programs were qualitatively different from their imperative counterparts.

Distance from machine operations is achieved by declarative languages at the cost of certain practicalities, those which govern performance. Input/output can be awkward, and matters such as garbage collection and efficiency cannot be addressed directly by the programmer. What is gained in exchange is release (in concept and notation) from some hardware-based restrictions, so that it is possible to express explicitly structures which potentially cannot be evaluated. This useful conceptual freedom is said to facilitate reasoning about strategies without pragmatic clutter.

The interpreter adopts the burden of pragmatism. It intervenes to constrain the program into conformance with the underlying (imperative) machine model, so that what is declaratively conceived becomes imperatively computable.

DECLARATION IMPLIES SPECIFICATION

The crux of the distinction between declarative and imperative languages is the "declarative reading" afforded by the former in addition to, or instead of, the operational reading provided by the latter. The declarative reading epitomises the shift of emphasis of "program" from prescription of operations to be performed, to definition of the objects to be computed, that is, from computer behavior to solution properties.

The intention, in the terms used in the declarative programming literature is "to separate logic from control components (Kowalski, 1979), so that the solution logic or properties can be investigated thoroughly without commitment to a particular realization and without reference to the behavior of the machine. "Control" or computational issues governing machine behavior are handled within the language implementation. The declarative reading of the program is essentially a solution specification.

The literature treats "specification" as related to but distinct from the "program" that results from it. "Specification" is taken to mean characterizing what the solution entails, whereas "program" means determining how the solution is to be reached. It seems as though declarative programming blurs the distinction between specification and program. Rather, the alignment of declarative program with specification reflects the disalignment of declarative program and imperative program; it is the use of the term "program" which has lost precision. The consequence of "separating logic from control"—of relegating control of computation from program to language implementation—is that the declarative language implementation injects information not in the program. Whereas an imperative language compiler does a reasonably direct translation between program and machine instructions, a declarative language translator disambiguates the program and chooses among possible realizations. In declarative programming, operational or algorithmic decisions are not avoided but are deferred to the language implementation.

Just as the declarative program is not complete without the language implementation, the language surface— the bits of language visible as lexicon and syntax which are used by the programmer—does not reflect completely the computational model underlying the language. Since imperative programs are explicitly a list of instructions, where syntactic units correspond roughly to psychological ones, imperative languages imply the computational model in the syntax. In contrast, aspects of a declarative model are inaccessible from the syntax and reside solely in the implementation. The "declaration" alone cannot anticipate behavior or performance; it has no 'hooks' into actual computation.

Declaration, by nature, excludes algorithm: the 'process or rules for (esp. machine) calculation . . . .' How, then, can we characterize languages that bear both a declarative and an operational reading? Clearly, programs in these languages entail more than declaration; they must contain some expression of algorithmic intent.

Levels of Information

It is possible to view these issues in terms of an approach to programming, so that classification reflects successive levels of information captured in a complete program. In this view, the programmer considers a problem and establishes the properties of its solution set. Methods for actualizing the solution are appraised, and some strategy is elaborated. The programmer then fits the algorithm to the framework of control employed by the machine.

Consider as an analogy, the problem: 'Find me an aardvark.' Under the above view, the searcher first asks: 'What is an aardvark?' That is, what constitutes a solution? An aardvark is a nocturnal mammal, native to the grasslands of Africa, with long ears and snout, that feeds on termites. Next the searcher asks: 'How can I find an aardvark? ' That is, what strategy produces the solution? To find an aardvark, its habitat must be identified and located, its spoor distinguished and followed until an individual is found. Finally, the searcher expresses the strategy in terms of the available 'machinery,' in this case, acquiring funding, making arrangements for visas, transportation, guides, and so on.

Each stage of the approach adds a level of information, so that the progression can be viewed as a shift of orientation from solution specification to solution pursuit, or as an incremental translation that gradually constrains intention into conformance with operation. With respect to terminology, this view emphasizes the continuity from declaration to instruction, so that the questions guiding language classification are: How much of the computational model is explicit in the language surface? Where is the transition from specification to instruction undertaken? Is the solution critically dependent on the language implementation?

Under this view, languages bearing both declarative and operational readings occupy a logical middle ground between declaration alone and machine control. They express both the solution space and algorithmic intent. Programs in such languages are specifications that inform execution; in the continuum between specification and program, these may be called executable specifications. The computational models underlying these languages are partially hidden; the general algorithm is available in the code, although it employs mechanisms concealed in the language implementation.

The Need to Reason about Behavior

If we accept that declaration implies specification and excludes algorithm, how appropriate is the category "declarative language" for languages which afford both declarative and operational readings? Does calling them "declarative" obscure their nature, emphasizing that they have a declarative reading at the risk of implying that they have only a declarative reading?

The value of executable specifications (which enhance declaration with algorithmic information) lies in the fact that, just because a language may reduce the degree to which a user must conform to the underlying machine and may hide matters of machine control, does not mean that all keys to program behavior are expendable. Actually, there are computational issues (including aspects of efficiency) that are critical to the programmer, so that reasoning about algorithm behavior is part of reasoning about the solution. A specification that admits only a declarative reading is in this sense incomplete.

Further, the issue extends beyond what the language affords, to how it is used. In a local, informal survey of functional programmers, we found that their typical approach is process-oriented. Although these programmers recognize and defend the declarative semantics, all agree that they exercise the operational semantics as well. Typically, they write their programs algorithmically and discuss them in operational terms.

We give an example drawn from experimentation, where (not unusually) the programmer demonstrated operational use of the functional language Miranda by exploiting his/her knowledge about a discrepancy between the language definition and the implementation used: although the order of evaluation of guards is not defined in the language, the implementation causes a textual order evaluation. The example function determines whether a given year is a leap year or not:

```
leapyear x=True, x mod 400=0
          =False, x mod 100=0
          =True, x mod 4=0
          =False, otherwise
```

The definition is clearly intended as an ordered sequence; indeed, if the evaluation occurs in any other order, the function probably gives an incorrect result. Further, there is a hint of operational bias in the language design; the 'otherwise' implies a final catch-all. Only when all others have been tried and failed, choose this one.

Even with the more orthodox version, where all guards are mutually exclusive:

```
leapyear x=True, x mod 400=0
           =False, x mod 400=0 & x mod 100=0
           =True, x mod 100 =0 & x mod 4=0
           =False, x mod 4=0
```

the guarded definitions are read as a sequence, perhaps with a tendency towards the if-then view, and the whole definition is read as a process of testing to determine which result is appropriate.

It may be worth noting that there is a process bias even in mathematical discussion, as in a formal proof. Whereas the mathematician recognizes that all relationships hold at once (i.e., recognizes the declarative nature of the proof), it is usual to read the proof as a process.

Declarativeness and the Accessibility of the Computational Model

The declarative reading is a by-product of hiding portions of the computational model in the implementation so as to shift the emphasis of 'program' from solution strategy to solution specification. Those languages which also afford an operational reading, admit the expression of algorithmic intent so that less is hidden in the implementation and more of the computation is available at the language surface. The basis of the distinction between declarative and imperative languages (and hence the appropriate basis for classification) lies in the significance of the particular implementation, that is, in where the computational model resides and in the closeness of the computational model to the language surface.

We propose that the directness of accessibility of the computational model (the degree to which it is reflected in the language surfacer) is the important dimension for classifying languages. It is more instructive to treat "imperative" and "declarative" as poles on a language class continuum than as strictly distinguished categories.

We have accumulated a set of related questions that draw out the relative placements of languages along this imperative-declarative continuum: how great is the translation distance between the language that the programmer sees and the computational model that makes it executable? How hidden is the computational model? Where is algorithmic intent introduced? How difficult is it to deduce the principal computational mechanisms from the language surface? How complex are the computational mechanisms provided in the language implementation? The more important the language implementation, the greater its role in providing algorithmic information and realizing the program, the farther the language is along the continuum toward the declarative extreme.

THE CONTINUUM OF LANGUAGES

In this section, we explore this continuum of languages by reviewing critical features of a few popular programming languages. We show where these languages are sited on this continuum and present some examples coded in the various languages to highlight our argument. For the examples, we have chosen the problem of calculating the factorial of a number. The examples illustrate, in the shift from imperative tɔ declarative style, the withdrawal first of explicit control and then of algorithmic information, leaving the injection of such information to the implementation.

Before offering the examples, we should point out that factorial is only defined for non-negative integers. Also, in many implementations, there will be restrictions caused by the finite range of computer numbers. For instance, our C solutions work only if the result is less than the maximum unsigned integer the machine will hold.

FORTRAN

FORTRAN is about as close as high-level language can get to assembler; it has few varieties of control structure, few data types, and poor data structuring tools. FORTRAN is definitely an iterative, imperative language; recursion is not permitted. FORTRAN is strongly typed but allows variables to be declared implicitly by usage on the left hand side of an assignment. FORTRAN treats functions as distinct from data items.

Factorial: A FORTRAN solution.

```
integer function factorial (number)
integer number
integer loopcounter, totalizer
if (number .lt. 0) then
   factorial=0
   return
endif
totalizer=1
do 10 loopcounter=2, number
   totaliser=totalizer+loopcounter
continue
factorial=totalizer
return
end
```

C

C is a flexible imperative language that affords good machine control, including input–output, good data structuring features, and (to a certain extent) higher level features, such as the construction of higher-order functions. C is a typed language, but there are many exceptions and faults. C supports recursion and pointer manipulation. In consequence of the range of expression offered, much C code is resistant to machine verification. Also, C programming depends heavily on the construction and use of good libraries.

Factorial: An iterative solution in C (a decidedly imperative solution):

```
unsigned int
factorial(number)
unsigned int number;
{
   unsigned int result=1;
   unsigned int count;
   for (count=2; count<=number; count++)
     result*=count;
```

```
    return result;
}
```

Factorial: A recursive solution in C (which looks more like a functional program):

```
unsigned int
factorial(number)
unsigned int number;
{
    returned (number==0)?1:number*factorial(number -1);
}
```

Although the above solution appears 'functional,' control remains explicit in the 'return' statement.

LISP

LISP is a language based on function evaluation but which employs imperative constructs to control the process of expression evaluation. The list is its essential data structure. There are good function abstraction features but poor data abstraction features. Modern variants of LISP, e.g., Scheme, have introduced much stronger type checking and also lexical scoping of names to help in the production of modular software.

Factorial: A recursive solution in Scheme:

```
(define (factorial x)
  (if (=x 0)
   1
   (* x (factorial (-x 1)))))
```

Making use of the 'setq' (in Scheme 'set!')feature, the iterative solution can also be coded, but most LISP programmers would use the above functional algorithm.

Miranda

Miranda is a strongly but implicitly typed functional language with good pattern matching facilities. Functions use recursion and guarded commands. It also has implementation features such as tail recursion and lazy evaluation, which programmers often use explicitly to make scripts cause efficient execution. Unfortunately, input–output is achieved using functions that are not referentially transparent.

Factorial: A Miranda implementation (definitely functional) based on guarded commands:

```
factorial      x=1 ,            x=0
               =x*factorial     otherwise
               (x-1),
```

An alternative Miranda implementation (equally functional) based on pattern matching:

```
factorial 0              =1
factorial (x+1)          =(x+1)* factorial x
```

The first implementation in Miranda, although functional, exhibits control features directly. The guards force explicit choice between the options available, and this is exhibited explicitly. Selection is hidden in the second Miranda example. The mechanism of selection is pattern matching; the implementation chooses the relevant part of the definition of factorial by a mechanism not explicit in the code. The programmer is responsible for writing mutually exclusive patterns, hence the '(x+1)'. If this is not the case, an implicit rule, such as textual ordering, is invoked, so that the program can be executed. We consider this latter implementation of factorial more concise and more declarative.

PROLOG

PROLOG is inspired by first-order predicate logic. The major computational controls lie within the PROLOG implementation, whose computational model is unification. Backtracking is also required, as the essential feature of unification is searching. PROLOG has many control features for the programmer (for example, the cut operator) which allow the programmer to interfere with the searching of the implementation for particular pieces of software. Further, the user interface supplies implicit control of the program and, inscrutably, governs input–output. Procedure call facilities to other languages are usually provided. The order of rules is important to control; PROLOG systems always search rules in textual order. Also the and operator ',' provides sequencing. For example, all values must already be known before they can be used in an 'is' expression; the order of the comma-separated expression in the example is critical.

Factorial: Perhaps the only the implementation in PROLOG:

```
factorial (0,1).
factorial (X, F):-XP is X-1, factorial (XP, FP), F is X*FP.
```

This example highlights a number of hidden control-oriented features:

1. The unnecessary PROLOG variable 'XP' appears because PROLOG does not allow expressions as parameters to functions.
2. All arithmetic expressions must be evaluable, i.e., must contain no unknowns. This leads to the necessary feature that, although ',' is the Boolean and operation, it also provides sequencing: the predicate on the left must be dealt with before the predicate on the right.
3. There are two assignment predicates: '=' and 'is'. The difference between the two is that the 'is' predicate forces evaluation and assignment immediately, whereas with '=' it may be delayed.

Obj

Obj is a executable subset of Clear. Obj specifications are written with the knowledge that the order of statements is important to the underlying implementation; statement order determines search order for the underlying term re-write system. Obj specifies functions in terms of their inputs and outputs and their relationships to other functions. Specification statements may use recursion and guarded commands.

The following Obj specifications assume an object Natural, defining the sort 'nat' and the functions 'succ,' 'pred,' and 'mult,' and including an object Boolean, defining the function 'not'.

Factorial: An Obj specification using guarded statements:

```
obj Factorial/Natural
ops
  factorial: nat->nat
vars
  n: nat
eqns
    (factorial(n)=1 if                          (n==0))
    (factorial(n)=mult(n, factorial(pred(n)))if not(n==0))
jbo
```

Factorial: An Obj alternative using pattern matching:

```
obj Factorial/Natural
ops
  factorial: nat->nat
vars
  n: nat
eqns
  (factorial(0)=1)
  (factorial(succ(n))=mult(succ(n), factorial(n)))
jbo
```

VDM

VDM is a specification language based on predicate logic, which captures specifications in terms of pre- and post-conditions. A computational model is defined, and VDM specifications can be made executable. However, the specification itself makes no statement about how the function is implemented, only about the state of the computation before and after the function has been executed.

Factorial: A VDM specification:

$$\text{factorial}: N \rightarrow N$$
$$\text{pre-factorial}(n) = TRUE$$
$$\text{post-factorial}(n,r) = r = n!$$

It is important to note here that the definitions of the predicates are statements in mathematics, not in a computer language. In particular in this example, the ! (factorial) symbol is the mathematically defined one.

Z

Z is a specification language based on set theory. It is a mathematical system for reasoning about things for which no computational model has yet been constructed, although we understand such a thing is possible. Z specifications are captured in terms of pre- and post-conditions rather like VDM.

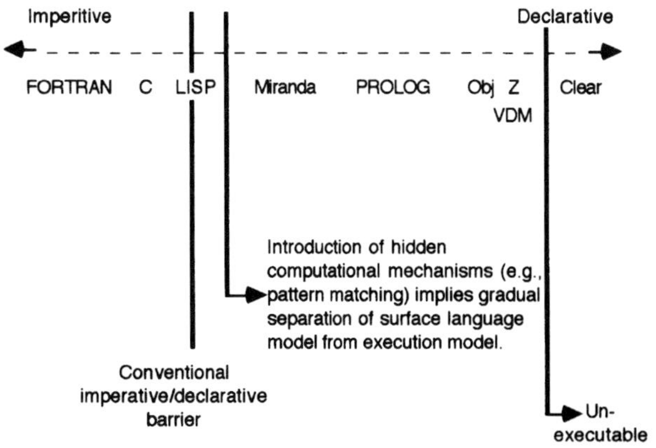

Figure 2. The continum of languages.

Factorial: A Z specification:

$factorial: N \rightarrow N$

$factorial\ 0 = 1$

$\forall n \varepsilon N \mid n > 0 \bullet$

$factorial\ n = n * factorial\ (n-1)$

Clear

Clear is a mathematical system for reasoning about things based on universal algebra. This specification language includes constructs considered mathematically sound and useful but for which a computational engine cannot be defined. Therefore, only a subset (Obj) of this language can be made executable.

Figure 2 presents a map, siting these example languages on the continuum between 'imperative' and 'declarative'.

The specification languages (Clear, VDM, Z, OBJ) are concerned with solutions rather than with computation. They are based on models formalized in mathematics. These models are not really available at the language surface but must be learned elsewhere. Further since they are concerned only with the outcome of computation, these borrowed models are incomplete; usually they do not embody strategies to drive the computation. The languages can be made executable by the addition of some computational model. Hence the user must apply his or her own additional computational information, or, to enable execution, the model as interpreted and embedded in the language implementation must be enhanced (e.g., by combining set theory with some set resolution mechanism) or constrained in order to construct a computation engine. Such enhanced models are usually complex and different from the models inherent in the language.

The Z specification given above can be shown to be satisfied by all the language implementations. The specification, in this form, describes neither the time/ space behavior nor the efficiency of the implementation. Therefore the specification cannot help us choose between implementations.

As with the specification languages, Miranda, LISP, and PROLOG are based on a computational model distinct from the von Neumann machine, i.e., lambda calculus and first order predicate logic. Unavailable at the language surface, these models can nevertheless be learned from other sources without necessitating forays into language implementation details. Confusion may arise, however, where the borrowed model has been adapted for use in the language, and the mechanisms which drive computation may still be obscure.

CONCLUSION

The declarative philosophy, as expressed in the literature and reflected in current terminology, is, we believe, mis-oriented. The basic difference between programming styles lies in the hiding of the computational model. The distinction between imperative and declarative, so evangelistically touted, is not exclusive but gradual, and the characterization of both terminology and classification, reoriented in this way, is more powerful and more satisfying. Moreover, it emphasizes that programmers will not be freed from implementation details until language designers provide comprehensive, workable reasoning models of their languages, models which accommodate reasoning about program behavior.

This article is reprinted from *The Computer Journal* **33**(2), 173–180 (1990) with the permission of Oxford University Press.

BIBLIOGRAPHY

J. Backus, "Can Programming Be Liberated From the von Neuman Style? A Functional Style And Its Algebra Of Programs," *Communications Of The ACM* **21,** 613–641 (1978).

R. Kowalski, "Algorithm=Logic+Control," *Communications Of The ACM* **22,** 424–436 (1979).

D. A. Turner, "Miranda: A Non-Strict Functional Language With Polymorphic Types," in *Proceedings Of The IFIP International Conference On Functional Programming Languages And Computer Architecture,* Springer Verlag Notes In Computer Science-201, Nancy, France, 1985.

MARIAN PETRE
R. WINDER
University College, London

PROGRAMMING SUPPORT ENVIRONMENT

See CASE; SOFTWARE ENGINEERING ENVIRONMENTS.

PROGRAMMING TEAMS

See CHIEF PROGRAMMER TEAM.

PROFILES

Profiles are a method for documenting a suite of standards and how they are required to operate together to provide an environment that supports a functional objective. This concept of "functional standards" was formalized in ISO when it became clear that the 140+ standards that fit into the 7 layer OSI model were unlikely to be combined in the same way on different systems. By defining the specific standards at each level, and related options and implementation parameters, the functional objective of interoperability could be achieved. OSI profiles may be adopted as international standardized profiles (ISPs) by ISO/IEC JTC1, or may be adopted by other specification sources such as the U.S. Government OSI Profile (GOSIP). In addition to formal standards and government use, Profile definition can be a conscious or *ad hoc* activity of industry associations, corporations or even projects within a department of a corporation.

Profiles can also describe a set of standards to meet objectives such as portability and interoperability of applications for a specific industry or application domain. These profiles are called "Application Environment Profiles" or "Open System Environment Profiles." The development of such profiles is encouraged by work at the ISO/IEC level as both an aid to applications portability and to guide future standards work.

Software engineering for open systems requires "proper engineering." This means managing software to standards conformance where portability, interoperability, or consistency of user interaction is an objective. The development of profiles to accomplish this is described in IEEE POSIX project P1003.0. A single standard such as the C language, or C plus the POSIX standards, provides a limited range of functions. With a more diverse set of standards, such as GKS for graphics and SQL for database access, a wider range of applications can be supported to meet open system objectives.

Efforts to define such profiles are occurring within the formal standards efforts (see POSIX). The U.S. Government is defining a Application Portability Profile, and various industry associations are developing similar profiles, for example the X/Open Common Application Environment, the Open Software Foundations Application Environment Specification, and the Petrotechnical Open Software Corporation's work.

This approach parallels the traditional definition of an application environment in terms of proprietary products, such as "NVS with IBM Cobol and DB2," "VMS with DEC/Fortran and RDB," or "KS/DOS with Microfocus Cobol and DBASE." However, the objective is to define these in terms of multivendor standards such as "POSIX with ANSI C and SQL." In complex applications, additional services beyond the standards may be needed. From a software management perspective, the use of these extensions needs to be documented and isolated in the code. A profile may need to indicate these required extensions, and this is guidance for both future revision of standards and also future selection of target environments.

JAMES ISAAK

PROJECT MANAGEMENT

INTRODUCTION

This article is about software engineering project management, the universality of a five-element management model, and the application of the five-element model to software engineering project management.

Management involves the activities undertaken by one or more persons for the purpose of planning and controlling the activities of others in order to achieve objectives that could not be achieved by the others acting alone. The five-element management model categorizes management functions into planning, organizing, staffing, leading, and controlling.

A project is a one-time effort having well-defined objectives and occurring within a specific time frame. A project plan is prepared, people are assigned to the project, resources are allocated, and success criteria are specified. A software engineering project is a project in which the objective is to produce a software product, on schedule and within budget, that satisfies a set of requirements.

Project management is a system of management procedures, practices, and know-how needed to manage a project successfully. Know-how, in this case, means the skill, background, and experience required to apply knowledge to practical situations. If the product of a project is software, then the act of managing the project is called software engineering project management. The manager of a software engineering project is called a software engineering project manager, a software project manager, or in many cases just project manager.

Software engineering projects are frequently part of larger, more comprehensive projects that include equipment (hardware), facilities, personnel, and procedures, as well as software. Examples include aircraft systems, accounting systems, radar systems, inventory control systems, railroad switching systems. These system engineering projects are typically managed by one or more system project managers (sometimes called program managers) who manage projects comprised of engineers, experts in the field of the application, scientific specialists, programmers, support personnel, and others. If the software to be delivered is a "stand-alone" software system (a system that does not involve development of other nonsoftware components) the software engineering project manager may be called the system project manager.

The five-element management model comes from management science (Koontz and O'Donnell, 1972; Fayol, 1949). It is a universal model in the sense that:

- Management performs the same functions (planning, organizing, staffing, leading, and controlling) regardless of position in the organization or the enterprise managed.
- Management functions are characteristic duties of managers; management practices, methods, activities, and tasks are particular to the enterprise or job managed.

The universality of this management model allows us to apply it to software engineering project management (Thayer and Pyster, 1984).

The importance of software project management is best illustrated by the following paragraphs extracted from two Department of Defense (DOD) reports.

A report from the STARS initiative (STARS: Software Technology for Adaptable, Reliable Systems) states, "The manager plays a major role in software and systems development and support. The difference between success or failure—between a project being on schedule and on budget or late and over budget—is often a function of the manager's effectiveness." (DOD Software Initiative, 1982).

A Report to the Defense Science Board Task Force on Military Software, states that " ... today's major problems with software development are not technical problems, but management problems" (Brooks, 1987).

This article describes a comprehensive set of software engineering project management functions, activities, and tasks that should be undertaken by any manager who is assigned the responsibility of managing a software engineering project. It covers the management functions of planning, organizing, staffing, leading, and controlling software projects and the detailed activities and specific tasks of project management that are necessary to successfully manage a software engineering project. The universal functions of management are decomposed into a detailed list of management activities.

Additional information on software project management can be obtained from the cited references. A comprehensive collection of software engineering project management papers can be found in Thayer (1988).

FUNCTIONS AND ACTIVITIES OF MANAGEMENT

This article presents a top-down approach to describing software engineering project management responsibilities, activities, and tasks that should be undertaken by any manager who is assigned the responsibility of managing a software engineering project. A top-down approach is used to partition and allocate top-level functions to lower-level activities and tasks.

The universal management model allows us to use the elements of the model as the top-level activities of software engineering project management. The classic management model is portrayed by well-known authors in the field of management (Koontz, O'Donnell, and Weihrich, 1984; Cleland and King, 1972; and MacKenzie, 1969).

According to this model, management is partitioned into five separate functions or components: planning, organizing, staffing, leading, and controlling (see Table 1 for definitions or explanations of these functions). All the activities of management, such as budgeting, scheduling, establishing authority and responsibility relationships, training, communicating, monitoring, etc., fall under those five headings.

In earlier editions of textbooks such as Koontz and O'Donnell (1972), the function "leading" was called "directing." The newer terminology has been adopted in this article.

Each of the five principal functions of management can be further partitioned into a set of more detailed management activities (see Table 2) which in turn can be further divided into more detailed tasks. These activities are the characteristic duties of managers and can be applied to the management of any organization or activity.

Table 1. Major Functions of Management

Activity	Definition of Explanation
Planning	Predetermining a course of action for accomplishing organizational objectives
Organizing	Arranging the relationships among work units for accomplishment of objectives and the granting of responsibility and authority to obtain those objectives
Staffing	Selecting and training people for positions in the organization
Leading	Creating an atmosphere that will assist and motivate people to achieve desired end results
Controlling	Measuring and correcting performance of activities toward objectives according to plan

The detailed activities and tasks that are particular to a software engineering project are defined and discussed later. The management activities in Table 2 are partitioned into one or more levels of detailed tasks, which are then discussed and/or illustrated in the appropriate section.

PLANNING A SOFTWARE ENGINEERING PRODUCT

Introduction and Definitions

Planning a software engineering project consists of the management activities that lead to selection, among alternatives, of future courses of action for a project and a program for completing those actions. Thus, planning involves specifying the *goals* and *objectives* for a project and the *strategies, policies, programs,* and *procedures* for achieving them. "Planning is deciding in advance what to do, how to do it, when to do it, and who is to do it" (Koontz and O'Donnell, 1972). Every software engineering project should start with a good plan. Uncertainties and unknowns, both within the software project environment and from external sources, make planning necessary. The act of planning focuses attention on project goals, objectives, uncertainties, and unknowns.

Major Issues in Planning a Software Project

The major issues in planning for a software engineering project are

- Software requirements are difficult to determine and document.
- Planning is not done or is poorly done.
- Accurate software cost and schedule estimates are hard to prepare.
- Selecting the appropriate analysis, design, testing, and management methodologies for a project is difficult.

Preparing software requirements that are correct, complete, and unambiguous is difficult (Davis, 1990). As a result, the project may have unclear or incomplete objectives. This vagueness can result in poor cost and schedule estimates. However, more importantly, planning for a software project is often not done or is poorly done. Plans, if done, are often neglected and not updated as conditions change. Software project plans are usually not deliverable items. Therefore, to some managers, planning appears to be an unnecessary activity that is best discarded, and the money saved, used for programming and testing. Even in Department of Defense (DOD) projects, where a planning document is usually required 30 days after award of contract, the project plan may receive only a superficial review and, in many cases, is allowed "to gather dust on a shelf" after it is produced.

Table 2. Major Activities of Management Planning

Management Functions	Management Activities
Planning	Set objectives or goals Develop strategies Develop policies Determine courses of action Make decisions Set procedures and rules Develop programs Forecast future situations Prepare budgets Document project plans
Organizing	Identify and group required tasks Select and establish organizational structures Create organizational positions Define responsibilities and authorities Establish position qualifications Document organizational structures
Staffing	Fill organizational positions Assimilate newly assigned personnel Educate and train personnel Provide for general development Evaluate and appraise personnel Compensate Terminate assignments Document staffing decisions
Leading	Provide direction Supervise personnel Delegate authority Motivate personnel Build teams Coordinate activities Facilitate communications Resolve conflicts Manage changes Document directing decisions
Controlling	Develop standards of performance Establish monitoring and reporting systems Measure results Initiate corrective actions Reward and discipline Document controlling methods

Accurate budgets and schedules are hard to prepare. Numerous software cost and schedule models are available (Bailey and co-workers, 1986); however, most estimation

Table 3. Planning Activities for Software Projects

Activity	Definition or Explanation
Set objectives and goals	Determine the desired outcome for the project.
Develop strategies	Decide on major organizational goals and develop a general program of action for reaching those goals.
Develop policies	Make standing decisions on important recurring matters to provide a guide for decision making.
Determine possible courses of action	Develop and analyze different ways to conduct the project.
Make planning decisions	Evaluate and select a course of action from among alternatives.
Set procedures and rules	Establish methods, guides, and limits for accomplishing the project activities.
Develop project plans	Establish policies, procedures, rules, tasks, schedules, and resources necessary to complete the project.
Prepare budgets	Allocate estimated costs to project functions, activities, and tasks.
Conduct a risk assessment	Anticipate possible adverse events and problem areas; state assumptions; develop contingency plans, predict results possible courses of action.
Document project plans	Record policy decisions, courses of action, budget, program plans, and contingency plans.

Table 4. Types of Plans for Software Projects

Type of Plan	Definition of Explanation
Objectives	The project goals toward which activities are directed.
Strategic Plan	The overall approach to a project which provides guidance for placing emphasis and using resources to achieve the project objectives.
Policies	Directives that guide decision making and project activities. Policies limit the freedom in making decisions but allow for some direction.
Procedures	Directives that specify customary methods of handling activities; guides to actions rather than decision making. Procedures detail the exact manner in which a project activity must be accomplished and allow very little discretion.
Rules	Requirements for specific and definite actions to be taken or not taken with respect to particular project situations. No discretion is allowed.
Program Plan	An interrelated set of goals, objectives, policies, procedures, rules, work assignments, resources to be used, and other elements necessary to conduct a software project.
Budget	A statement of constraints on resources, expressed in quantitative terms such as dollars or staff-hours.

methods are based on estimated size of the software product (e.g., lines of code, function points) (Boehm 1987; Kemerer 1987). Accurate size estimates are extremely difficult in the planning stage of a software project and often result in inaccurate budget and schedule estimates for the project. However the major reason for inaccurate estimates is lack of relevant historical data on which to base the estimates.

Despite the large number of software engineering development methods and automated tools available, very little data are available to indicate which are the best or most cost-effective technologies, and which types of projects are amenable to which types of methods and tools. Software engineering project managers are faced with the difficult tasks of selecting the methods and tools to be used, and convincing their corporate leaders and project sponsors that their choices provide a cost-effective approach.

Planning Activities and Tasks

Table 3 provides an outline of the planning activities that must be accomplished to plan a software project. As indicated in Table 3, numerous types of planning activities must be conducted. Table 4 contains a list of different types of management plans for software engineering projects. The balance of this section provides greater detail on the activities outlined in Table 3.

Set Goals and Objectives. The first step in planning for a software engineering project is to determine what the project must accomplish, when it must be accomplished, and what resources are necessary. Typically, this endeavor involves analyzing and documenting the system and software requirements. In addition, the management requirements and constraints must be determined. Management constraints are often expressed as resource and schedule limitations.

Success criteria must also be specified. Success criteria should always include delivery of a software system that satisfies the requirements, on time and within costs. However, there may be other criteria. For instance, success could include winning a follow-up contract. Other criteria might include increasing the size and scope of the present contract, or increasing the profit margin by winning an incentive award.

Develop Project Strategies. Another planning activity is to develop and document a set of management strategies (sometime called strategic policies) for a project. Strategies are general approaches to achieving project goals and are usually developed at a corporate level; however, a software project team can have strategic plans within an individual project. This circumstance is particularly true if it is a large project. An example of a strategic plan might be to develop a new area of expertise for the organization by conducting a project in that area.

Develop Policies for the Project. *Policies* are predetermined guidelines for making management decisions. The software project manager may establish policies for the project to provide guidance to supervisors and individual team members in making routine decisions. For example, it might be a policy of the project that status reports from team leaders are due in the project managers office by the close of business each Thursday. Policies can reduce the need for interaction on every decision and provide a sense of direction for the team members. In many cases, the project manager does not develop new policies for the project, but follows the policies established at the corporate level.

Determine Possible Courses of Action. In most software projects there is more than one way to conduct the project —but not with equal cost, equal schedule, or equal risk. Various approaches that could achieve the project objectives and satisfy the success criteria must be examined. For example, one approach might be very costly in terms of staff-hours of effort and computer time, but would reduce the schedule dramatically. Another approach might reduce both schedule and cost but face a severe risk of being unable to deliver a satisfactory system on schedule and within budget. A third approach might be to stretch the schedule, thereby reducing the overall cost of the project. Each course of action must be examined to determine advantages, disadvantages, risks, and benefits. (See the paper by Boehm (1987) for a description of a software development life-cycle model that incorporates risk-analysis procedures.)

Make Planning Decisions. The project planning team, in consultation with higher level management, the customer, and other appropriate parties, is responsible for choosing among the many possible courses of action that are most appropriate for meeting project goals and objectives. The planning team is also responsible for making tradeoff decisions involving cost, schedule, design strategies, and risks.

Methods, tools, and techniques, both technical and managerial, by which the product will be developed and the project be managed, must be selected. For example, will the requirements be documented using "structured analysis" methods or "Warnier-Orr" charts? Will testing be done top-down, bottom-up, or both? Which tools, techniques, and procedures will be used in planning the development schedule: PERT, CPM, workload chart, work breakdown chart (WBS), or Gantt chart (Cori, 1985)?

Set Procedures and Rules for the Project. The software project planning team establishes procedures and rules for a project. In contrast to policies, *procedures* specify customary methods and provide detailed guidance for project activities. For example, there may be a procedure for conducting design reviews. In contrast, a *rule* establishes specific and definite actions to be taken or not taken with respect to a given situation. A rule allows no discretion. For example, a rule might require two people to be on duty in the computer room at all times. *Process standards* (in contrast to *product standards*) can be used to establish procedures. Process standards may be adopted from corporate standards or written for a particular project. Process standards might cover topics such as reporting methods, reviews, and documentation requirements.

Develop a Software Project Plan. A software project plan specifies all of the actions necessary to successfully deliver a software product.

Typically, the plan specifies:

1. The *tasks* to be performed by the software development staff in order to develop and deliver the final software product. This endeavor requires partitioning of the project activities into small, well-specified work packages. The work breakdown structure (WBS) is a useful tool for representing the partitioned and decomposed project tasks.
2. The *cost* and resources necessary to accomplish the overall project and each project task (Boehm, 1984).
3. The project *schedule* which specifies the duration of tasks, dependencies among tasks, and establishes project milestones.

For further discussion of project planning see Miller, (1978).

Prepare a Budget. *Budgeting* is the process of allocating estimated costs to project tasks. Cost is the common denominator for all elements of the project plan. Requirements for staffing, computers, travel, office space, equipment, and so forth can only be compared and cost-tradeoffs made when these requirements are measured in terms of their monetary value.

The budget is allocated to the various tasks in the project. In many large projects, each major activity is allocated a portion of the budget and given the authority to spend it to accomplish the goals of that activity.

Conduct a Risk Assessment and Prepare Contingency Plans. Risk factors must be identified and forecasts of situations that might adversely impact the software project must be prepared. Risk assessment is accomplished in two steps: The first step involves identification of risk factors and the second is impact analysis. The impact of a risk factor is the negative consequence that would result, should the adverse situation occur. Examples of risk factors include unavailability of qualified staff, late delivery of new computer hardware, or a major change in requirements without a corresponding modification of the schedule and/or budget. Contingency plans specify the actions to be taken should a risk (a potential problem) become a real problem. A risk becomes a problem when a risk-indicator metric crosses a predetermined threshold. For example, the schedule overruns by more than 10% or the memory budget is overrun by more than 12% (Boehm, 1989).

Document the Software Project Plan. The project planning team is responsible for documenting the project plan (Fairley, 1987) and for preparing other plans such as the software quality assurance plan, software configuration management plan, staffing plan, and the test plan. The project plan is the primary means of communicating with other entities that interact with the project.

ORGANIZING A SOFTWARE ENGINEERING PROJECT

Introduction and Definitions

Organizing a software engineering project involves itemizing the project activities required to achieve the objectives of the project and then grouping these activities into logical clusters. It also involves assignment of groups of activities to various organizational entities, establishing the authority and responsibility relationships among the tasks and entities, and assigning responsibilities and delegating authority needed to carry out the activities. The purpose of an organizational structure is to "focus the efforts of many on a selected goal" (Donnelly, Gibson, and Ivancevich 1975).

Major Issues in Organizing for a Software Project

The major issues in organizing a software engineering project are

- It is difficult to determine the best organizational structure for a particular project (e.g., project, functional, matrix).
- The organizational structure may leave responsibilities for some project activities and tasks undefined or unclear.
- The matrix structure presents special challenges to both the organization and the individuals assigned to the organization.

The best organizational structure for a project and for the organization conducting the project is difficult to determine. According to Youker (1977), there is a spectrum of organizational techniques for software projects ranging from the project format to the functional format to the matrix format. The project format creates centralized control over the project and makes the project manager responsible for all aspects of the project. Conversely, the functional organization distributes authority and control of a project among the functional elements involved. The matrix organization incorporates elements of project and functional formats. Project managers are given authority over the project; the project members are drawn from their functional "homes" and assigned to the project for as long as needed. In a matrix structure, conflicts can arise between the project manager, who is responsible for the project, and the functional managers, who provide the software engineers to the project. Matrix structures require special attention to overcome this "two-boss" phenomenon.

Papers by Stuckenbruck (1982), Youker (1977), and Mantei (1981) provide criteria for selecting the appropriate organizational structure for a software project. Both Stuckenbruck and Youker indicate the need for top management to provide a clear charter for the matrix organization in order to define responsibilities and authority for the project manager as well as in the roles of the functional departments.

Table 5. Organizing Activities for Software Projects

Activity	Definition or Explanation
Identify and group project function, activities and tasks	Define, size, and categorize the project work.
Select organizational structures	Select appropriate structures to accomplish the project and to monitor, control, communicate, and coordinate.
Create organizational positions	Establish title, job descriptions, and job relationships for each project role.
Define responsibilities and authority	Define responsibilities for each organizational position and the authority to be granted for fulfillment of those responsibilities.
Establish position qualifications	Define qualifications for persons to fill each position.
Document organizational decisions	Document titles, positions, job descriptions, responsibilities, authorities, relationships, and position qualifications

Organizing Activities

Table 5 provides an outline of the activities that must be accomplished to organize a software project. The remainder of this section provides greater detail concerning the activities outlined in Table 5.

Identify and Group Required Tasks. The software product requirements must be mapped into work tasks to be accomplished, and the tasks must be sized and grouped into logical entities. Task names are assigned to the groupings of tasks; for example, analysis tasks, design tasks, coding tasks, and testing tasks. Groupings are mapped into organizational entities. This information enables the project planning team to select an organizational structure to monitor and control these groups. See Table 6 for an example of task identification and grouping.

Supporting tasks, both internal and external to the project, must also be identified. Examples of internal support tasks are secretarial support, word processing support, financial monitoring, and project administration. External to the project, there may be tasks associated with travel requirements, motor pools, security guards, computer operation support, and so on.

Select an Organizational Structure. After identifying and grouping project tasks, an organizational structure must be specified. Organizing a software development project may involve several different and overlapping organizational issues. For example:

- The organization structure—line or staff organization.
- The project structure—functional, project, or matrix.
- The team structure—democratic, chief programmer, or hierarchical.

The planning team may not have the luxury of selecting the best organization structure or project structure, since

Table 6. A Set of Software Engineering Project Tasks That Have Been Grouped and Assigned an Organizational Entity

Project Tasks	Group Identifier
Partition and allocate software requirements to software components Implement standards and practices Collect and evaluate technical performance measurements Audit software components for quality	Software system engineering
Prepare software test documents Conduct software tests Support system tests	Software test engineering
Maintain software development library Install vendor supplied software Provide technical support on system software	System software support
Analyze software components for type 1 requirements Design components of type 1 Implement type 1 software components Prepare documents Support testing	Software engineering applications group 1
Analyze software components for type 2 requirements Design components of type 2 Implement type 2 software components Prepare documents Support testing	Software engineering applications group 2

this configuration may be determined by policy at the corporate level. Regardless of how it is selected, an organizational structure and project structure that matches the needs and goals of the project and facilitates communication between organizational entities, should be selected.

Conventional Organizational Structures. A *line* organization has the responsibility and authority to perform the work that represents the primary mission of the larger organizational unit. In contrast, a *staff* organization is a group of functional experts that has responsibility and authority to perform special activities that help the line organization do its work. All organizations in a company are either line or staff.

Project Structures. A project structure is a special organizational form that has been established for the purpose of developing and building a system that is too big to be done by one or, at most a few people. In a software engineering project, the system to be built is a software system. A project structure can be superimposed on a line or staff organization. For example, a functional software engineering project can be either a line or staff organization. Figure 1 illustrates the use of five line organizations as software engineering functional organizations. Figure 1 is the organizational structure for the example in Table 6.

Functional Project Organization. One type of project organization is a *functional* organization; a project structure built around a software engineering function or group of similar functions. A project is accomplished either within a functional unit or, if multifunctional, by two or more functional units. In a functional-by-phase project, the project is accomplished by passing the work products from functional unit to functional unit as the product evolves through the life-cycle phases. Figure 2 illustrates the tasks and lines of authority of a functional organization used to develop a software product.

In Figure 2, the software requirements specifications, are prepared by the *software systems engineering group* under the supervision of the group leader. When finished, the system engineering group transfers the requirement specifications to the *software engineering applications group* that is most familiar with the application. The software engineering applications group, using the requirement specifications, designs the software system under the supervision of the software engineering applications group leader. In this illustration, the applications group also programs the software system and then passes the finished code to the *software test engineering group* for testing. Tools and system support are provided by the *system software support group*.

To continue the example illustrated in Figure 2, Project 1 is under the control and supervision of the software engineering manager and Project 2 reports to top management. Each project is monitored by a "user liaison." The user liaison does not supervise the staff or control the project. This project coordinator usually does not have the responsibility to hire, discharge, train, or promote people within the project. The user liaison coordinates the project, monitors the progress (reporting to top management when things do not go according to plan), and acts as a common interface with the user. Note that one engineer in SE Application Group 1 is shared by two projects.

Project Organization. Another type of project organization is built around each specific project; a project manager is given the responsibility, authority, and resources for conducting the project (Middleton, 1967). (The project organization is sometimes called a *projected* organization to get away from the term "project-project organization."). The project manager is responsible for meeting the project goals within resource and schedule constraints. In the project format, the project manager usually has the responsibility and authority to hire, discharge, train, and promote people within the project. Figure 3 illustrates the tasks and lines of authority of a project organization. Note that the software project manager has total control over the project and the assigned software personnel.

Matrix Project Organization. The third project organization is the *matrix* organization (sometimes called matrix project organization); it is a composite of the functional

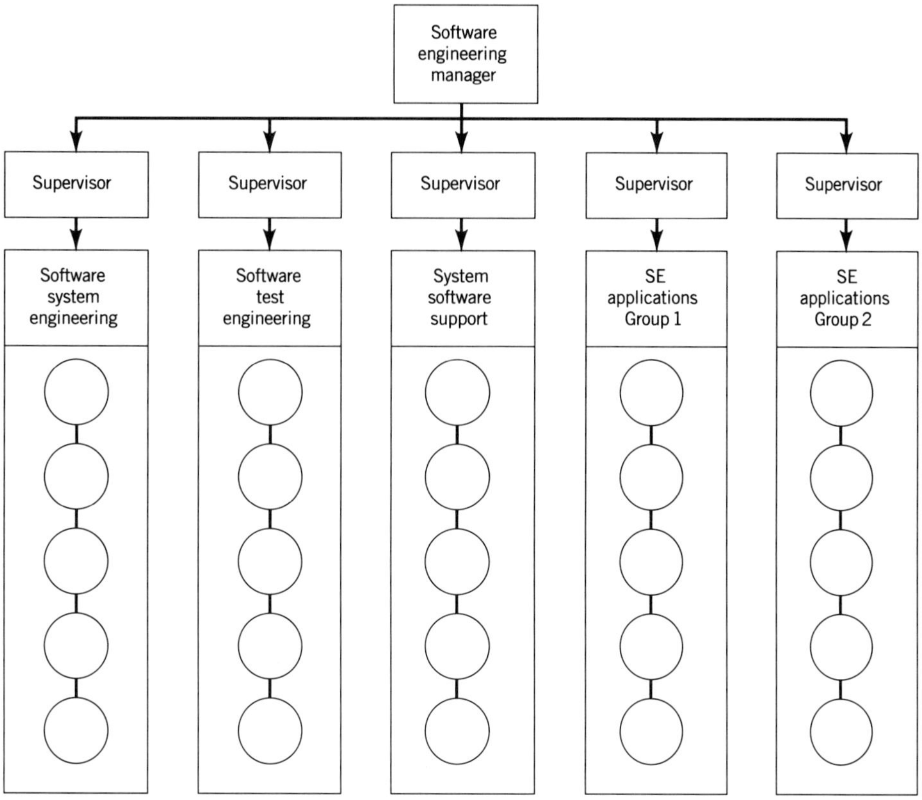

Figure 1. Line organizations used as software engineering functional organizations.

organization and the project organization (Stuckenbruck, 1981). The project manager is given responsibility and authority for the project. The functional managers provide the resources needed to conduct the project. In a matrix organization, the project manager usually does NOT have the authority to hire, discharge, train, or promote personnel within the project. Figure 4 illustrates the tasks and lines of authority in a matrix organization.

In Figure 4, each project is supervised by a project manager who supervises functional workers. Typically the software project manager is responsible for the day-to-day supervision of the software project members and the functional manager is responsible for the career, training, and well-being of those people.

Note also in Figure 4, that one engineer in the system support group is shared by two projects—a common occurrence in a matrix organization.

Software Project Team Structures. Within the larger organizational structures discussed above, a software development project is typically organized around a number of software engineering teams. These teams usually consist of five to seven members. Examples of structures for these teams include *egoless programming teams, chief programmer teams,* and *hierarchical teams* (Mantei, 1981).

- *Egoless Programming Team.* The egoless team structure was introduced by Dr. Gerald Weinberg (1971). An egoless team typically consists of 10 or 12 members. Discussions and decisions are made by consensus. Group leadership rotates; there is no permanent central authority.
- *Chief Programmer Team.* The chief programmer team was first used by IBM in the now-famous New York Times Morgue Project. The team consists of three or four permanently assigned team members—chief programmer, backup programmer, and program librarian—plus other auxiliary programmers and/or analysts who are added as needed. The chief programmer manages all the technical aspects and makes all the managerial and technical decisions. The librarian maintains all documents, code and data, and performs all administrative work (Cooke, 1976).
- *Hierarchical Team.* A hierarchical team is a structure in which the project leader manages team leaders and team leaders manage individual contributors. On large software projects there may be a layer of subsystem managers between the project manager and the team leaders. On system projects involving both hardware and software, the software project manager may report to the system (or program) manager. This structure is called "hierarchical" because of the top-down flow of authority and task assignments.

Strengths and Weaknesses of Project OrganizationStructures. Most importantly, the needs of the project should be matched to the appropriate organization type. The list below displays the strengths and weaknesses of the three organizational structures (functional, project, matrix).

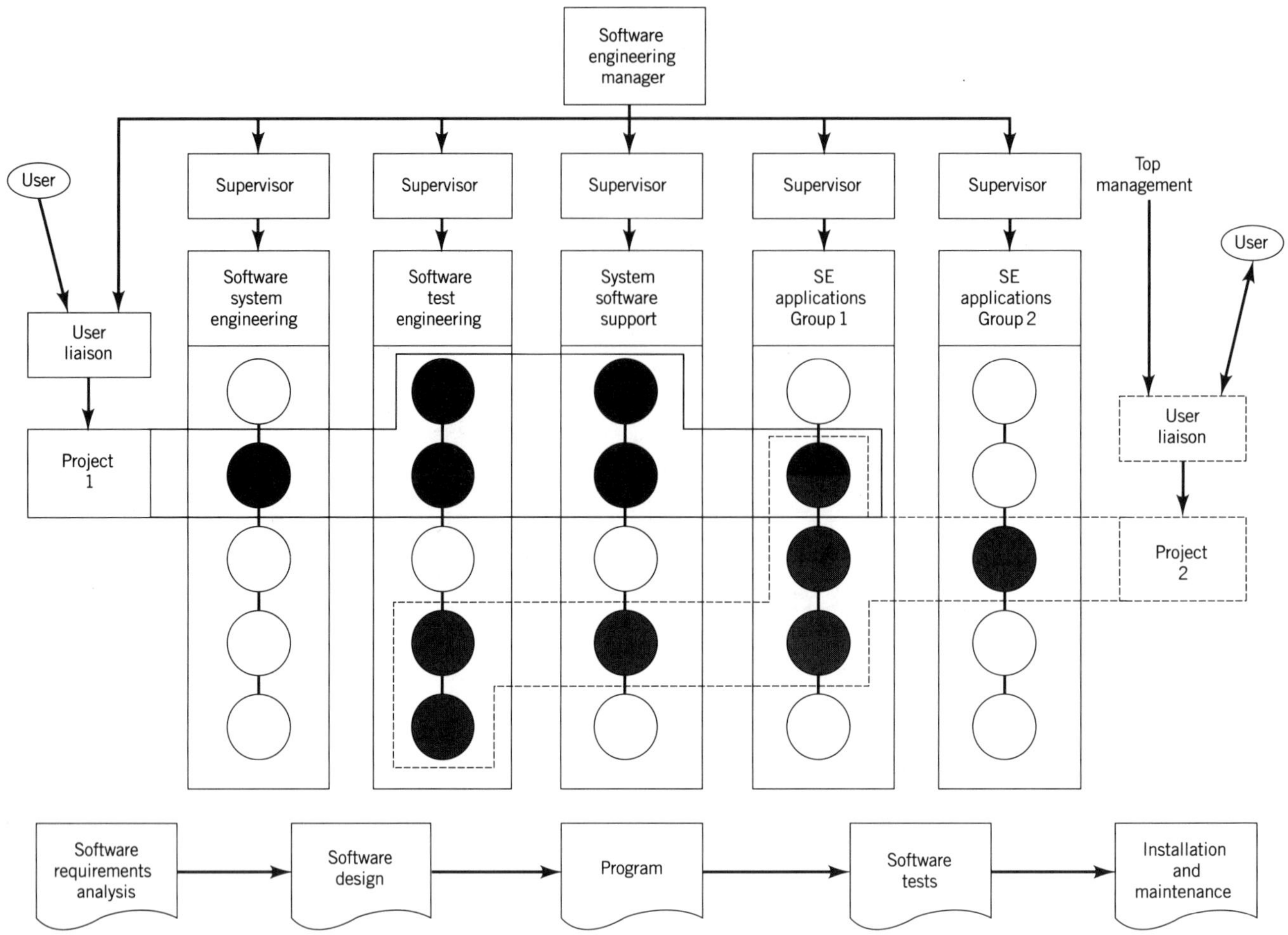

Figure 2. Tasks and lines of authority of software engineering functional organizations used to develop a project.

Functional Project Organization

Strengths

Organization already exists (quick start-up and phase-down).

Recruiting, training, and retention of functional specialists are easier.

Policies, procedures, standards, methods, tools, and techniques, are already established.

Weaknesses

No central point of complete responsibility or authority for the project.

Interface problems are difficult to solve.

Projects are difficult to monitor and control.

Project Organization

Strengths

A central position of responsibility and authority for the project.

Central control over all system interfaces.

Decisions can be made quickly.

Staff motivation is typically high.

Weaknesses

Team must be formed for each new project.

Recruiting, training, and retention of functional specialists may be more difficult than for functional format.

Policies, procedures, standards, methods, tools, and techniques, must be tailored for each project.

Matrix Project Organization

Strengths

Improved central position of responsibility and authority compared to functional format.

Interfaces between functions can be controlled more easily than in functional format.

Recruiting, training, and retention may be easier than in project format.

Easier to start and end a project than in project format.

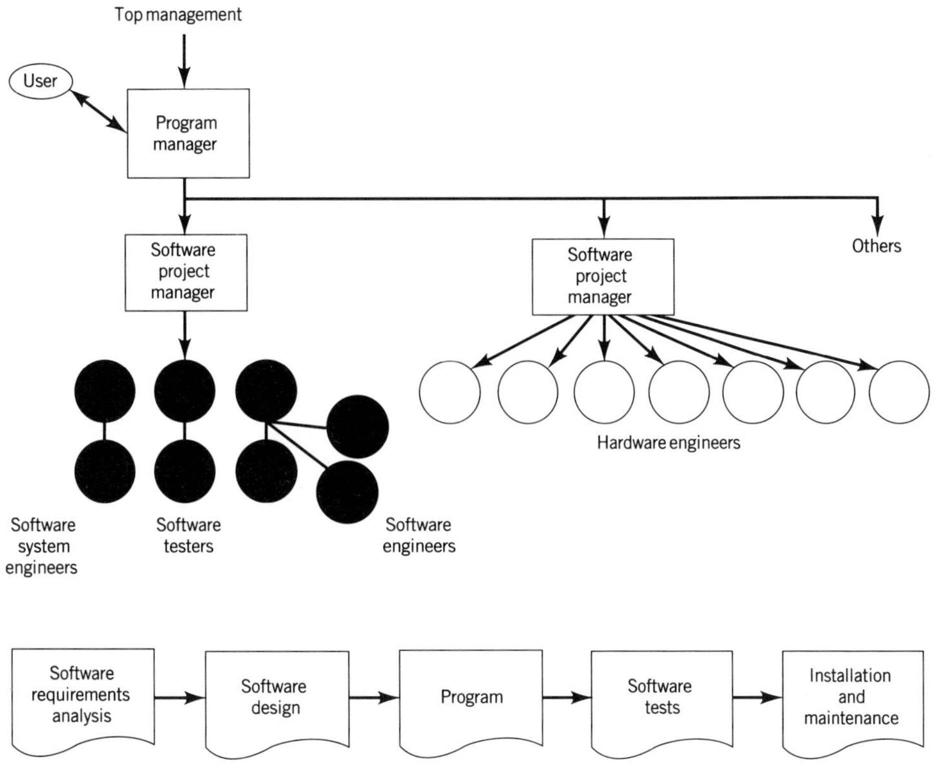

Figure 3. Tasks and lines of authority of project organization used to develop a project.

Policies, procedures, standards, methods, tools, and techniques already established; unlike project organization.

More flexible use of people than in project or functional formats.

Weaknesses

Responsibility for and authority over individual project members is shared between two or more managers: unlike project or functional formats.

Too easy to move people from one project to another: unlike project or functional formats.

More organizational coordination is required than in project or functional formats.

Greater competition for resources among projects than in project or functional formats.

Each software engineering project exists within a *line* or *staff* organization. It must be determined whether the project will operate as a functional, project, or matrix structure and whether the project will use egoless, chief programmer, or hierarchical project teams. (The chief programmer and egoless teams are seldom used). However, the librarian concept from the chief programmer team and the egoless technical reviews (walkthroughs) are frequently used by software engineering project teams. The majority of software engineering projects in the aerospace industry use the matrix organization with hierarchical project teams. A few companies use the term "chief programmer team" to mean a hierarchical team.

Create Organizational Positions for the Software Project. Once the tasks are identified, sized, and grouped, and the organizational structure has been specified, job titles and position descriptions must be created. Personnel will be recruited for the project using the job titles and position descriptions. Some short examples of typical software engineering titles and position descriptions are illustrated below (EDP, 1987):

- *Project managers*—responsible for system development and implementation within major functional areas; direct the efforts of software engineers, analysts, programmers, and other project personnel.
- *Software engineers*—design and develop software to drive computer systems; Develop firmware, drivers, specialized software such as graphics, communications controllers, operating systems and user friendly interfaces. Work closely with hardware engineers and applications and systems programmers, requiring understanding of all aspects of the product.
- *Scientific/engineering programmers, programmer-analysts*—perform detailed program design, coding, testing, debugging, and documentation of scientific/engineering computer applications and other applications that are mathematical in nature; may assist in overall system specification and design.

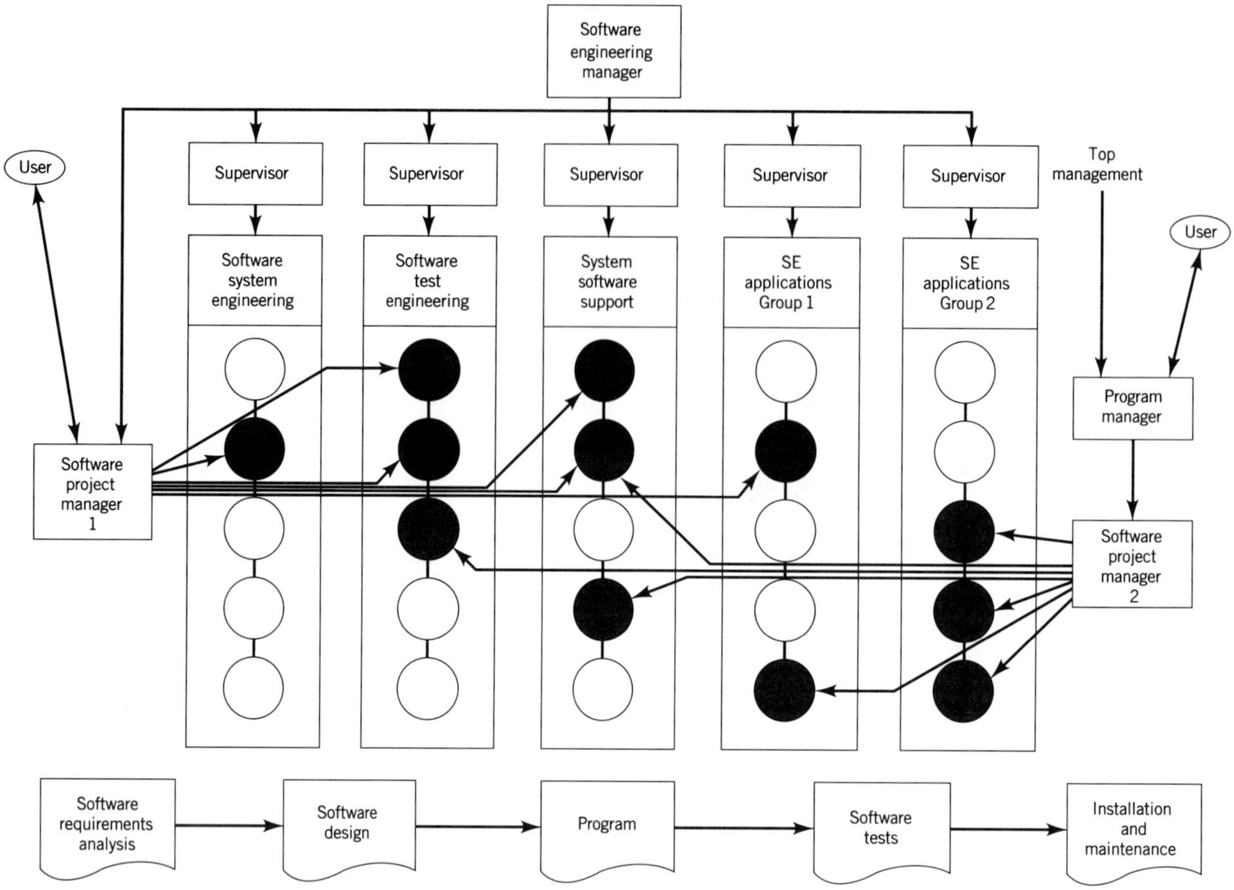

Figure 4. Tasks and lines of authority of matrix organization used to develop a project.

Define Responsibilities and Authorities. *Responsibility* is the obligation to fulfill commitments. *Authority* is the right to make decisions and exert power. It is often stated that authority can be delegated, but responsibility cannot. Koontz and O'Donnell (1972) support this view by defining responsibility as "the obligation owed by subordinates to their supervisors for exercising authority delegated to them in a way to accomplish results expected." Responsibility and authority for organizational activities or tasks should be assigned to the organizational position at the time the position is created or modified. The project manager is first assigned and in turn assigns the responsibilities and the corresponding authorities to the various organizational positions within the project.

Establish Position Qualifications. Position qualifications must be identified for each position in a software project. Position qualifications are established by considering issues such as: What type of individuals are needed for the project? How much experience is necessary in the area of the application? How much education is required: BS in computer science, MS in artificial intelligence? How much training is required, either before or after the project is initiated? Does the applicant need to know FORTRAN, Lisp, or some other programming language? Establishing proper position qualifications makes it possible to correctly staff the project.

Some short examples of typical position qualifications for software engineering titles and positions are illustrated below (EDP, 1987):

- *Project managers*—background in successful systems implementation; advanced industrial knowledge; awareness of current computer technology; intimate understanding of user operations and problems; and proven management ability. Minimum requirements are 4 years of significant system development and project management experience.
- *Software engineers*—four years experience in aerospace applications designing real-time control systems for embedded computers. Experience with Ada preferred. BS in Computer Science, Engineering, or related discipline.
- *Scientific/engineering programmers, programmer–analysts*—3 years experience in programming aerospace applications, control systems, and/or graphics. One year minimum with FORTRAN, Assembler, or C programming languages. Large-scale or mini/micro hardware exposure and system software program-

ming experience desired. Minimum requirements include undergraduate engineering or math degree.

Document Organizational Decisions. Lines of authority, tasks, and responsibilities should be documented in the project plan. Justifications for decisions must be well documented and made available to guide staffing of the project.

STAFFING A SOFTWARE ENGINEERING PROJECT

Introduction and Definitions

Staffing a software engineering project consists of all the management activities that involve filling (and keeping filled) the positions that were established within the project organizational structure. This initiative includes selecting candidates for the positions and training or otherwise developing candidates and incumbents to accomplish their tasks effectively. Staffing also involves terminating project personnel when necessary.

Staffing is not the same as organizing; staffing involves filling the roles created in the project organizational structure through selection, appraisal, and development of personnel. The objective of staffing is to ensure that project roles are filled by personnel who are qualified (both technically and temperamentally) to occupy them.

Principal Issues in Staffing a Software Project

The principal issues in staffing for a software engineering project are

- Productivity of programmers, analysts, and software engineers varies greatly from individual to individual.
- Project managers are frequently selected for management positions without the benefit of management training.
- Universities are not producing a sufficient number of computer science graduates who understand the software engineering process.

One of the major issues in staffing for a software project is that productivity of programmers and software engineers varies widely from individual to individual. In a study by Sackman and co-workers, the difference in productivity between programmers was as high as 26 to 1 (Sackman and co-workers, 1968). In his book *Software Engineering Economics,* Boehm (1981) reports differences in productivity due to personnel/team capability as high as 10 to 1. The inability to accurately predict the productivity of project personnel undermines ability to accurately estimate the cost and schedule of a software project.

Software project managers frequently are assigned to their jobs without management training. It is common practice today to make project managers of those programmers and software engineers who have excelled at their technical activities. Training should be, but seldom is, provided to these proven software engineers so that they will be capable of managing a software engineering project.

Table 7. Staffing Activities for Software Projects

Activity	Definition or Explanation
Fill organizational positions	Select, recruit, or promote qualified people for each project position.
Assimilate newly assigned personnel	Orient and familiarize new people with the organization, facilities, and tasks to be done on the project.
Educate or train personnel	Make up deficiencies in position qualifications through training and education.
Provide for general development	Improve knowledge, attitudes, and skills of project personnel.
Evaluate and appraise personnel	Record and analyze the quantity and quality of project work as the basis for personnel evaluations. Set performance goals and appraise personnel periodically.
Compensate	Provide wages, bonuses, benefits, or other financial remuneration commensurate with project responsibilities and performance.
Terminate assignments	Transfer or separate project personnel as necessary.
Document staffing decisions	Record staffing plans, training plans and achievements, appraisal records, and compensations recommendations.

Universities are not producing sufficient numbers of software engineers. Most of the computer science programs in the United States do not sufficiently emphasize the procedures, tools, and techniques of software engineering. Most industry personnel and others involved in hiring, seek graduates of computer science programs who have education and experience in developing software systems—that is, software engineering skills (McGill, 1984).

Staffing a Software Project

Table 7 provides an outline of the activities and tasks that must be accomplished to staff a software project. The remainder of this section provides greater detail on the activities and tasks outlined in Table 7.

Fill Organizational Positions. Job positions established during organizational planning for a software project must be filled with qualified personnel. The following factors should be taken into consideration when filling organizational positions (i.e., staffing the project). Deficiencies in any of the following factors can be offset by strengths in other areas. For example, deficiencies in education can be offset by better experience, a particular type of training, or enthusiasm for the job. Serious deficiencies should be cause for corrective action.

- *Education*—Does the candidate have the level of education needed for the job? Does the candidate have the educational background for future growth in the company?

- *Experience*—Does the candidate have an appropriate level of experience? Is it the right type and variety of experience?
- *Training*—Is the candidate trained in the language and methodology to be used, on the equipment to be used, and the application area of the software system?
- *Motivation*—Is the candidate motivated to do the job, work for the project, work for the company, and take on the assignment?
- *Commitment*—Will the candidate demonstrate loyalty to the project, the company, and to the decisions made?
- *Self motivation*—Is the candidate a self-starter, willing to carry a task through to the end without excessive direction?
- *Group affinity*—Does the candidate fit in with the current staff? Are there potential conflicts that need to be solved?
- *Intelligence*—Does the candidate have the capability to learn, to take difficult assignments, and adapt to changing environments?

Powell and Posner (1984) provides additional information on filling organizational positions.

Sources of Qualified Individuals. Transfer of personnel from within the project itself can be one source of qualified individuals. It is the project manager's prerogative to move people from one task to another within a project. Another source is transfers from other projects within the organization. These transfers can be done anytime but often happen when another software engineering project is either phasing down or cancelled. Other sources of qualified personnel are new hires from other companies through such methods as job fairs, referrals, headhunters, want ads, and unsolicited resumes. New college graduates can be recruited through interviews on campus and through referrals from recent graduates who are now company employees. If the project manager is unable to obtain qualified individuals to fill positions, one option is to hire unqualified but motivated individuals and train them for those vacancies.

Selecting a Productive Software Staff. Two metrics may indicate a productive software staff member:

1. *Amount of experience*—An experienced staff member is usually more productive than an inexperienced person (Boehm, 1984). Some of the best experience comes from having worked on software projects similar to the project being staffed.
2. *Diversity of experience*—Diversity of experience is a reasonable predictor of productivity (Kruesi, 1982). Better that the individual under consideration has done well in several jobs over a period of time rather than one job for the same time period.Other qualities indicative of a highly productive individual are communications skills (both oral and written), a college degree (preferably in a technical field), being a self-starter, and experience in the application area of the project.

Assimilate Newly Assigned Personnel into the Project. The management team (project manager, team leaders, higher level management) is responsible for familiarizing newly assigned personnel with any project procedures, facilities, or plans necessary to assure their effective integration into the project. In short, the management team is responsible for introducing new employees to the company and the company to the employees.

Many large companies have formal orientation programs lasting several days. An orientation program may include the features and history of the company; the products or services that are the main sources of revenue for the company; general policies and procedures; organizational structure; company benefits; and the availability of in-company service organizations.

Educate or Train Project Personnel as Necessary. The recruitment or transfer of employees with exactly those skills needed for a particular project is not always possible. Therefore, the personnel assigned to the project must be educated and/or trained to ensure that they can fulfill their roles in the project.

Education differs from training. *Education* involves teaching the basics, theory, and underlying concepts of a discipline with a view toward a long-term payoff. *Training* involves teaching a skill or knowledge of how to use, operate, or make something. The skill is typically needed in the near future and has a short term payoff. For example, managers should be educated in the management sciences and business techniques. They should be trained in management techniques and the duties of administration. Engineers, on the other hand, are educated in science, physics, and mathematics but must be trained in the application domain of the project, state-of-the-art and company-specific techniques, and software engineering procedures used in the project. Training methods include on-the-job training, formal company courses, courses through local universities and schools (Mills, 1980), self-study, and in-house lectures. Each individual within an organization must have a *training plan* that specifies career education and training goals and the steps to be taken in achieving those goals. Training programs must be actively supported by top management. Another technique is retraining into software engineering (sometimes called "retreading") of long-time, valuable employees with somewhat obsolete skills (Ben-David and co-workers, 1984; McGill 1984).

Provide for General Development of Project Staff Members. In addition to providing job-specific education and training, the organization must ensure that project staff grow with the project and company. One purpose of providing general development for the project member is to improve organizational effectiveness. For example, courses and degree programs at the local university in any worthwhile skill, funded by the company, will improve employee morale, aid in retaining employees, and, in general, broaden the skill base available to the company. Even indirect skills such as typing and communication can be enhanced.

Evaluate and Appraise Project Personnel. The project manager is responsible for periodically evaluating and appraising personnel. An appraisal provides feedback to staff members concerning the positive and negative aspects of their performance. This feedback allows the staff member to strengthen good qualities and improve weak ones. Appraisals should be done at regular intervals and should concentrate on the individual's performance and not on personality, unless personality issues interfere with performance (Moneysmith, 1984).

One well-known evaluation technique that can be applied to software project personnel is "management by objectives" (Maslow, 1954). At the beginning of the appraisal period, the individual and the project manager (or perhaps the team leader) establish a set of measurable goals that the individual believes can be met during the next reporting period. These measurable goals form the basis of the next appraisal. This approach is superior to evaluation by personal traits and work characteristics, such as promptness, neatness, punctuality, golf scores, and so on.

Compensate Project Personnel. The software project manager—sometimes directly, sometimes indirectly—is responsible for determining compensation of project personnel. Compensation includes salary and perquisites. Perquisites ("Perqs") take on many forms. Most are monetary or can be equated to money. These include stock options, a company car, first class tickets for company trips, or a year-end bonus. Some perqs are not monetary but appeal to the self-esteem of the individual; examples are combat medals in the military, a reserve parking place at the company plant, or an impressive title on the door.

Terminate Project Assignments. The software project manager is not only responsible for hiring people, but must also terminate assignments as necessary. "Terminate" includes reassignment of personnel at the end of a successful project (a pleasant termination) and dismissal of personnel due to project cancellation (an unpleasant termination). Termination can also occur by firing when an employee is determined to be unsatisfactory.

Document Project Staffing Decisions. Staffing plans, training policies, and compensation procedures should be documented and available for everyone to read. Each individual on the project should have a personal training plan reflecting course work needed and progress made. Other staffing documents produced include orientation plans and schedules, salary schedules, and promotion policies. The project manager and each individual employee should have a copy of his or her current performance objectives signed by the individual and the project manager.

LEADING A SOFTWARE ENGINEERING PROJECT

Introduction and Definitions

Leading a software engineering project consists of the management activities that involve motivational and interpersonal aspects by which project personnel come to understand and contribute to the achievement of project goals. Once project personnel are trained and assimilated into the project, the management team has a continuing responsibility for clarifying their assignments, guiding them toward improved performance, and motivating them to work with enthusiasm and confidence toward project goals.

Leading, like staffing, involves people. Leading is sometimes considered to be synonymous with directing (compare reference Koontz and O'Donnell (1972), with reference Koontz, O'Donnell, and Weihrich (1984)). Leading a project involves day-to-day supervision of project personnel, delegating authority to lower organizational entities, coordinating activities of the project members, facilitating communications between project members and those outside the project, resolving conflicts, managing change, and documenting important decisions.

Major Issues in Leading a Software Project

The major issues in leading a software engineering project are

- Current methods of specifying requirements, designing systems, or planning projects sometimes present a communication barrier among individuals and groups.
- Money alone is not a sufficient motivator for software developers.
- The use of modern methods, tools, and techniques, which are motivators for software developers, may not be encouraged by the leadership team (project manager, team leaders, higher level management).

One of the major goals of software engineering is to improve communication among the many organizations that may be involved in developing a software system. Most software engineering documents are written in the English language, which is imprecise and ambiguous. Research in software engineering is concerned, in part, with developing tools and techniques to ease communication of requirements specifications, design documents, and other software engineering artifacts.

Most software engineers are well paid, work in pleasant surroundings, and are reasonably satisfied with their position in life. Therefore, in accordance with Maslow's hierarchy of unfulfilled needs, the average software engineer is high on the ladder of satisfied needs (Maslow, 1954). Most software engineers are at the "esteem and recognition" level and are occasionally reaching to the "self-actualization" level. At this level money alone is not a strong motivator. Thus, one of the issues that management faces is the question of how to motivate software engineers to produce more and better software (called *software psychology* in some circles), since money alone is not sufficient. The opportunity to use modern tools and techniques is a strong motivator for many software engineers. However, management may not support the use of new methods and techniques for the following reasons:

- The leadership team may be reluctant to introduce unfamiliar methods and tools because it may increase the risks to their projects.
- The use of unfamiliar methods and tools may make it more difficult for the leadership team to estimate project cost and schedule.

Techniques for improving the transfer of new technology into a software project are discussed later in "Manage Change."

Leading the Project Team

Table 8 provides an outline of leadership activities and tasks that must be accomplished by the project leadership (project manager and team leaders). The remainder of this section discusses and provides greater detail on the activities outlined in Table 8.

Provide Leadership. The leadership team provides direction to project members by interpreting plans and requirements to ensure that everyone on the project team is working toward common goals. A good leader is able to align the personal goals of subordinates with organizational goals of the project. Leadership results from the power of the leader and his or her ability to guide individuals. Leadership power can be derived from the organizational position of the leader; this is called *positional power*. A leader's power can also be derived from "charisma," which is the leaders ability to motivate on the basis of personality and charm; this is called *personal power*. Problems can arise when a leader who has only positional power comes into conflict with a subordinate who has personal power over the project members. For a discussion on different uses of power by leaders see (Boyatzis, 1971).

Table 8. Leading Activities for Software Projects

Activity	Definition or Explanation
Provide leadership	Create an environment in which project members can accomplish their assignments with enthusiasm and confidence.
Supervise personnel	Provide day-to-day instructions, guidance, and discipline to help project members fulfill their assigned duties.
Delegate authority	Allow project personnel to make decisions and expend resources within the limitations and constraints of their roles.
Motivate personnel	Provide a work environment in which project personnel can satisfy their psychological needs.
Build teams	Provide a work environment in which project personnel can work together toward common project goals. Set performance goals for teams as well as for individuals.
Coordinate activities	Combine project activities into effective and efficient arrangements.
Facilitate communication	Ensure a free flow of correct information among project members.
Resolve conflicts	Encourage constructive differences of opinion and help resolve the resulting conflicts.
Manage changes	Stimulate creativity and innovation in achieving project goals.
Document directing decisions	Document decisions involving delegation of authority, communication and coordination, conflict resolution, and change management.

Supervise Project Personnel. The leadership team is responsible for overseeing the project members' work and providing day-to-day supervision of the personnel assigned to the project. It is the leader's responsibility to provide guidance and, when necessary, discipline project members to ensure that they fulfill their assigned duties. Supervisory responsibilities can involve such mundane tasks as "clocking in" the employees at the beginning of the work day, approving vacation time, reprimanding an individual for a missed appointment, or approving a deviation from company policy. At other times, the leader can provide a crucial decision on a software design approach; make a well-reasoned argument to top management which results in procurement of better tools and work space; or be a sympathetic listener to a project member's personal problems.

Delegate Project Authority. The leadership team of a software engineering project is also responsible for delegating authority to the project staff. Tasks are assigned to subgroups, teams, and individuals, and authority is delegated to these teams so that they can accomplish their tasks in an efficient and effective manner. Typically, a good leader will delegate authority down through the lowest possible level of the project (Raudsepp, 1981).

Proper delegation of authority can free leaders from time-consuming routine supervision tasks, thus enabling them to concentrate on the important aspects of the project. Leaders should ensure that individual project members understand what authority is delegated for what responsibility. Project members should also clearly understand the scope, limitations, and purpose of the authority.

Motivate Project Personnel. Project leaders must motivate personnel and inspire them to do their best. Several motivational techniques from mainstream management are applicable to software engineering projects, such as: management by objective, Maslow's hierarchy of needs (Maslow, 1954), Herzberg's hygiene factors (Herzberg, Mausner, and Snyderman 1959), and the charisma of the leader. A leader should always acknowledge the special needs of the highly qualified, technically trained engineers and scientists who staff the project. Money will attract good software engineers to a company; money alone will not keep them. For a further discussion on motivating software development personnel see Fitzenz (1978). For another paper with a unique method of motivating computer people, see Powell and Posner (1984).

The following paragraphs summarize several motivation techniques (see also Table 9):

Hierarchy of Needs (Maslow): Satisfied needs are not motivators. For example, an individual who has adequate job security cannot be motivated by increased job security. Maslow's hierarchy of human needs in order of importance is listed below (Maslow, 1954):

- *Biological survival needs:* basic needs to sustain human life—food, water, shelter, etc.
- *Security and safety needs:* freedom from physical danger.
- *Social needs:* need to belong; to be accepted by others.
- *Esteem and recognition needs:* to be held in esteem by themselves and by others.
- *Self-actualization needs:* to maximize one's potential and to accomplish something or significance.

McGregor's Theories X and Y: McGregor presented two theories concerning human nature called Theory X and Theory Y (McGregor, 1960). It should be noted that contrary to popular belief, McGregor did not favor one view over the other. He did not say that Theory Y was a better view than Theory X, only that there were two theories.

Table 9. Motivational Theories

Motivation Model	Definition or Explanation
Frederick Taylor	Workers will respond to an incentive wage.
Elton Mayo	Interpersonal (group) values override individual values. Personnel will respond to group pressure.
Kurt Lewin	Group forces can overcome the interests of an individual.
Douglas McGregor	Managers must understand the nature of people in order to be able to motivate them.
A. H. Maslow	Human needs can be categorized in a hierarchy. Satisfied needs are not motivators.
Frederick Herzberg	A decrease in environment factors is dissatisfying; an increase in environment factors is NOT satisfying. A decrease in job content factors is NOT dissatisfying; an increase in job content factors is satisfying.
Chris Argyris	The greater the disparity between company needs and individual needs the greater the dissatisfaction of the employee.
Rensis Likert	Participative management is essential to personal motivation.
Arch Patton	Executives are motivated by the challenge of work, status, the urge to achieve leadership, the lash of competition, fear, and money.
Theory Z	A combination U.S. and Japanese management styles. People need goals and objectives, otherwise they can easily impede their own progress and the progress of their company.

Theory X Assumptions:

- Human beings have an inherent dislike of work and will avoid it if they can.
- Because of this dislike of work, most people must be coerced, controlled, directed, and threatened with punishment to get them to put forth adequate effort toward the achievement of organizational objectives.
- Human beings prefer to be directed, wish to avoid responsibility, have relatively little ambition, and want security above all.

Theory Y Assumptions

- The expenditure of physical and mental effort in work is as natural as in play or rest.
- External control and the threat of punishment are not the only means for achieving organizational objectives. People will exercise self-direction and self-control in the attainment of objectives to which they are committed.
- Commitment to objectives is a function of the rewards associated with their achievement.
- Motivated human beings not only accept responsibility but will also seek it.

Theory Z. Theory Z is a combination of U.S. and Japanese management styles (Ouchi, 1981). The basic principles of Theory Z are (Arthur, 1983):

- People need goals and objectives. Goals help to keep one on a forward track while minimizing the time lost to nonproductive activities.
- Motivation is essential for good performance and must be both positively and negatively reinforced by management. Optimal motivation is derived from both peer and managerial recognition and, to a lesser extent, from promotion and monetary reward.
- Merely having goals and motivation will not prevent people from making mistakes. Managers must correct their movement along paths that are in the best interests of the company.
- The best interests of any given company are achieved when each individual's work is standardized to ensure that similar goals are attained by similar means. In turn, any suggested improvement in one particular area of work automatically is incorporated into related areas.
- Goals must change as working conditions and corporate needs change. In anticipation of such change, Theory Z provides the mechanism for gradual change.

Job Factors for Computer Personnel: The list below provides factors, in order of declining importance, that motivate computer personnel toward taking a job (left-hand column), and a list of factors that make a job dissatisfying to the job-holder (right-hand column).

Job Attractors	Job Dissatisfiers
Salary	Company mismanagement
Chance to advance	Poor work environment
Work environment	Little feeling of accomplishment
Location	Poor recognition
Benefits	Inadequate salary
Facilities/equipment	Poor change to advance
Job satisfaction	Poor facilities/equipment
Company management	Poor benefits
Job responsibility	Poor career path definition

Build Project Teams. Team building is the process of improving the relationships among team members to improve the efficiency and effectiveness of the team as a whole. Techniques such as team building exercises, "off-site" meetings and group dynamics can be used to improve the capabilities of the team to be more productive as a group than the team members would be as individuals in isolation.

Coordinate Project Activities. Coordination is the arrangement of project entities to work together toward common goals with minimum friction. Documents, policies, and procedures are viewed differently by different people. The task of the leadership team is to reconcile differences in approach, effort, and schedule, and to resolve these differences for the benefit of the project.

Facilitate Communication. Along with coordination, the leadership team is responsible for facilitating communication both within the project and between the project and other organizations. *Facilitate* means to expedite, ease, and assist in the progress of communication. *Communication,* in turn, is the exchange of information among entities that are working toward common goals. For example, the project manager should disseminate the staffing plans and project schedule throughout the organization as soon as practical. Nothing can destroy the morale of an organization faster than false and misleading rumors. A good leader will ensure that the project staff is kept well-informed so that rumors are quickly dispelled.

Quality Circles: Quality circles are an excellent means for improving project communication. One company, for example, has used quality circles to involve the software engineering team members in selecting the software engineering methodologies for the company.

Although the practice of using quality circles originated in the United States, it is widely implemented only in Japan. Using quality circles, employees meet periodically in small groups to develop suggestions for quality and productivity improvements. To implement a quality circle (Arthur, 1983) it is necessary to:

- Train managers, project leaders, and higher level management on the effectiveness of quality circles. Training must include such organizational techniques as agendas, worksheets, checklists, and, most importantly, group participation.
- Hold quality circle meetings as part of the company's working agenda, on company time and in company facilities. This strategy reinforces the company's commitment to each circle. Quality circle membership should be voluntary so as to be viewed as an opportunity rather than a requirement.
- Organize the meetings so as to not waste the members' time. Suggestions should be acted upon and those ideas which appear most beneficial for the company's and members' betterment should be pursued.

For a further discussion on quality circles applied to software projects see Couger (1983).

Resolve Project Conflicts. The leadership team is responsible for resolving conflicts among project staff members and between project staff and external organizations, in both technical and managerial matters. A leader is not expected to be an expert in all aspects of the project. However, he or she should have the good judgment to recognize the best possible approach in solving a particular technical or managerial problem when conflicts must be resolved. The leader should control the opportunity for future conflict over non-technical issues by removing potential sources of disagreement whenever possible, e.g., team members with somewhat equal positions should have equal benefits, access to management, parking places, and so forth. Another type of conflict that the leadership team should watch for is the conflict between the employee's work activities and personal life. When this conflict reaches epic proportions it is called "burnout" (Cherlin, 1981).

Manage Change. The leadership team should encourage independent thought and innovation in achieving project goals. A good leader must always accommodate change, when change is cost-effective and beneficial to the project (Kirchof and Adams, 1986).

The leadership team must control change and not discourage cost-effective changes. Requirements will change, the design will change, and the needs of the application area for which the software is built will change. There will be social changes. What is acceptable to build or the procedures to build at one time will not necessarily be acceptable at another time. People change; newly graduated engineers will have new ideas, as they have been taught new ways to develop software systems. The bottom line is not to eliminate change but to control it. Yourdon (1987) presents a simple step-by-step plan for the transfer of a new software technology (a change) into a software development organization:

- Explain the risks and benefits of the new method, tool, or technique.
- Provide training for the project team.
- Prototype the technique before it is used.
- Provide technical support throughout the project.
- Listen to the users' concerns and problems.
- Avoid concentrating on the technology at the expense of the project.

As another example of controlling (taking advantage of) change, staff turnover is usually considered a problem in most software development organizations. The paper by Bartol and Martin (1983) discusses how to make positive use of staff turnover.

Document Leadership Decisions. The leadership team must document all assignments of authority and responsibility and the outcomes of conflict resolution. In addition, all decisions concerning lines of communication and coordination must be documented.

CONTROLLING A SOFTWARE ENGINEERING PROJECT

Introduction and Definitions

Controlling techniques for software engineering projects include the collection of management activities used to ensure that the project goes according to plan. Performance is measured against plans, deviation are noted, and corrective actions are taken to ensure conformance of plans and actuals. Control requires status information on how well the project is going. Is the project on schedule? Is it within cost? Are there any potential problems that will cause slippages in meeting the requirement within the budget and schedule? The control process also requires well-defined lines of communication and coordination. Who is responsible for assessing progress? Who will take action on reported problems?

Controlling methods and tools must be objective; status information must be quantified. The methods and tools used must point out deviations from plans without regard to the particular people or positions involved. Control methods must be tailored to individual environments and managers. The methods must be flexible and adaptable to deal with the changing environment of the organization. Control also must be economical; the cost of control should not outweigh its benefits. Lastly, control must lead to corrective action—either to bring actual status back to the plan, to change the plan, or to terminate the project.

Major Issues in Controlling a Software Project

The major issues in controlling a software engineering project are:

- Many methods of controlling a software project rely on budget expenditures for measurement of "progress" without consideration of work accomplished.
- Often, standards for software development and project management are not written or, if written, not enforced.
- The body of knowledge called software metrics (used to measure the productivity, quality, and progress of a software product) is not fully developed or widely applied.

A major issue in controlling a software project involves reliance on budget expenditures as the key indicator of progress. For instance, when a project manager is asked for the status of a software project, he or she will typically look at the resources expended. If three-quarters of project funds have been expended, the project manager will report that the project is three-quarters completed. The obvious problem is that the relationship between resources consumed and work accomplished is only a rough measure at best and completely incorrect at worst. One possible solution is the earned-value method of monitoring software projects. A description of this method is contained in the paper by Howes (1984).

Standard methods of measuring progress are often not written or, if written, not enforced. Standards are sometime felt to be detrimental to software projects because they "stifle creativity." Therefore, it is not unusual for entire projects, including the project manager, to ignore standards in favor of local, ad hoc, and frequently inadequate, project control systems.

The body of knowledge known as software metrics is not fully developed. For example, software-quality metrics used to measure reliability, maintainability, usability, safety, and security of a software product are not widely understood or applied. Because knowledge of how to do *a priori* design of software systems that, when implemented, will have the desired quality attributes, is incomplete, emphasis is placed on the processes of software engineering in the belief that sound development processes will result in high quality products.

Table 10. Controlling Activities for Software Projects

Activity	Definition or Explanation
Develop standards of performance	Set goals that will be achieved when tasks are correctly accomplished.
Establish monitoring and reporting systems	Determine necessary data, who will receive it, and when they will receive it, and what they will do with it to control the project.
Analyze results	Compare achievements with standards, goals, and plans.
Apply corrective actions	Bring requirements, plans, and actual project status into conformance
Reward and discipline	Praise, renumerate, and discipline project personnel as appropriate
Document controlling methods	Document the standards, of performance, monitoring and control systems, and reward and discipline mechanisms.

Controlling Activities and Tasks for Software Projects

Table 10 provides an outline of the project management activities that must be accomplished to control software projects. The remainder of this section discusses the activities outlined in Table 10.

Develop Standards of Performance. Standards of performance and procedures for determining the status of performance, must be specified for each software project. Standards and procedures can be specially developed for the project; for example, adopted from standards developed by the parent organization; or standards developed by the customer or a professional society (IEEE Software Engineering Standards (1993). A standard is a documented set of criteria used to specify, and determine the adequacy of, an action or object. A *software engineering standard* is a set of procedures that define the processes for developing a software product and/or specify the quality of a software product. See Buckley (1987) for a discussion of implementing software engineering standards in a company. Process and product standards are both important to the task of developing high-quality software. Software engineering is primarily concerned with the *process* of developing software. This is because software product metrics (measuring such quality attributes as software reliability, maintainability, portability, and other "-ilities") is not a well developed science, and tools and techniques that do an effective job of measuring the quality of a software product are not generally available. Therefore, most software engineering standards are concerned with process.

In addition to providing a gauge by which to measure the software engineering process, software engineering standards offer substantial advantages for a software project:

- Standardized procedures and measures of performance reduce the need to retrain engineers, designers, and programmers.
- Communications among team members can be improved.
- Transferring staff among project activities can be eased.
- Experiences and project history can be more readily shared if software development is based on common processes.
- The best experience of successful projects can be uniformly applied.
- Software implementation and software maintenance can be standardized.
- Standardized performance measures and procedures can be controlled, resulting in controlled projects.
- Standard quality assurance procedures can be applied.

Software Quality Assurance: Software quality assurance (SQA) is "a planned and systematic pattern of all actions necessary to provide adequate confidence that the item or product conforms to established technical requirements" (IEEE Glossary, 1983). SQA is one of the major control techniques for software projects.

Establish a Monitoring and Control System. A monitoring and control system must be specified in order to determine and maintain project status. Project status is needed to determine whether the project is proceeding according to plan. The type, frequency, originators, and recipients of project reports must be specified. Status reporting tools must provide visibility of progress, and not just resources used or time passed.

The baseline management system is one of the most effective monitoring and controlling methods for a software project. A *baseline* is a work product that has been reviewed, accepted, and placed under change control procedures. A work product under baseline control cannot be changed without agreement of the involved parties. The baseline management system integrates a series of life-cycle phases, reviews, and baselined documents into a project management framework. Specifically, baseline management:

- Partitions the project into manageable phases: requirements, design, implementation, and test.
- Establishes milestones, documents, and reviews at the end of each phase.
- Establishes baselines at periodic intervals.
- Uses configuration management to control the baselines.

The purpose of a milestone is to allow partitioning of a project into measurable work units, each of which results in one or more work products that can be evaluated according to objective criteria. Examples of milestones are: the completion of a software requirement specification; the completion of a software design; the completion of code; and of course, the major milestone, the completion of the project.

Milestone reviews are analyses of project processes and products, by customer, user, and management, in order to assess progress. A milestone review is held at the end of each life-cycle phase of a software project. For example, a preliminary design review (PDR) is held at the completion of the preliminary design phase. Milestone reviews are usually chaired by the customer or by higher level management. The project manager presents: the current status and progress, the work done to date, the money expended, the current schedule, and any management and technical problems that may have surfaced since the last review. The review is judged a success when the customer or top management gives permission for the project team to proceed to the next phase.

Milestone reports play a major role in the controlling process for software projects. A milestone is a discrete event; achievement of a milestone must be based on completion of one or more tangible work products, subject to objective evaluation criteria.

Other techniques that aid in monitoring and controlling of a software project are work breakdown structures, PERT and CPM methods, workload charts, and Gantt charts (Cori 1985). The Howes paper (1984) presents the earned-value method of tracking a software engineering project. Table 11 summarizes some typical monitoring and reporting techniques. Table 12 lists examples of the types of reports that can be generated by a project control system.

Other techniques for monitoring and controlling a software project are described below.

The *unit development folder* (UDF) is a specific form of development notebook which has proven to be useful and effective in collecting and organizing software products as they are produced. The purpose of the UDF is to provide an orderly approach to the development of a program unit

Table 11. Methods of Monitoring Software Projects

Method	Definition or Explanation
Baseline management Paradigm	A management strategy that is used to control the work products of a software project.
Budget reviews	A comparison of estimated budget with actual expenditures by customers, developers, and managers in order to determine compliance with or deviations from plan.
Independent auditing	An independent examination of a software project for the purpose of determining compliance with plans, specifications, and standards.
Formal (milestone) reviews	Periodic, preplanned reviews of work products by developers, customers, users, and management in order to assess progress.
Process standards	Mechanisms that define the procedures or operations to be used in developing a software product.
Software quality assurance (SQA)	A planned and systematic pattern of all actions necessary to provide adequate confidence that the development process and the work products of a software project conform to established standards.
Unit development folder (UDF)	A specific form of development notebook which provides an orderly approach to the development of a programming unit and provides management visibility and control over the development process.
Configuration management (CM)	A method for controlling and reporting on the status of work products generated by a software project.
Testing	The controlled exercise of the program code in order to expose errors.
Verification and validation	The process of assuring that each phase of the development life cycle correctly implements the specifications from the previous phase and that each software work product satisfies its requirements.
Walkthroughs and inspections	Systematic examination of software work products by the producer's peers, conducted for the purpose of finding errors.

and to provide management visibility and control over the development process (Ingrassia, 1987).

Walkthroughs and inspections are reviews of software work products (design specifications, code, test procedures, etc.) conducted by peers of the author (Weinberg and Freedman, 1984). Walkthroughs are examinations of software products by the producer's peers for the purpose of finding errors. The inspection system is another peer review developed by Michael Fagan (Fagan, 1976, 1986) of IBM in 1976. Inspections are typically more formal than walkthroughs.

The *software project audit* is a review of a software project to determine compliance with software requirements, specifications, baselines, standards, policies and software quality assurance plans. An *independent audit* is an audit done by an outside organization not associated with the project (Bernstein, 1981); (Walters 1987). On the positive side, an independent team can provide a totally unbiased opinion. In case of a need for expert knowledge, the independent team can supplement existing talent. However, be aware that an independent audit team will have to become familiar with the project and will require ongoing involvement in order to be effective.

Table 12. Types of Reports for Software Projects

Type of Report	Definition or Explanation
Budget report	Compares budget with expenditures and provides a basis for making estimates of cost-to-complete and updating of budgets.
Schedule report	Provides status of milestones achieved versus planned milestones, reasons for missed milestones and corrective actions.
Staff-hours by activity	Compares planned versus actual amount of effort for each project activity.
Progress report	Provides the status of progress during a stated time interval and a list of activities accomplished
Action item report	Itemizes current action items, priorities, responsible parties, and due dates
Trend chart	Shows trends in such areas as budget, lines of code produced per month, number of errors found in the system, staff hours of sick leave, and so on. Trend reports are extrapolated to predict future status.
Significant change report	Records exceptions to plans and significant changes in report plans, both good and bad. Normally used to report inadequate progress.

Software configuration audits provide the mechanism for determining the degree to which the current software system mirrors the software system contained in the baseline specification and the requirements document (Bersoff, 1984).

A method for determining whether a software product is correct, is: verification and validation (V&V). Verification assures that each phase of the life cycle correctly interprets the specification from the previous phase. Validation assures that each completed work product satisfies its requirements (Wallace and Fuji, 1989).

Initiate Corrective Actions. Corrective actions must be initiated when plans and requirements are not being met. Corrective action techniques include changing the plans or descoping the requirements (i.e., delivering less than originally planned). Changing plans might involve a larger budget, more people, or more checkout time on the development computer. Plans might also be changed; for example, reducing the number of peer reviews from reviewing all software modules to only reviewing the critical software modules.

Sometimes, to get back on plan corrective action can involve compensation in different operations of the plan. For example, it is sometime possible to get back on schedule, without descoping the product, by increasing the number of personnel. This adjustment increases the resource plan. Another way to hold on to the original budget by stretching out the schedule or by reducing the functionality of the software system. Descoping the requirements involves delivering software without a full complement of supporting documents or software that does not meet completely all the functional requirements that have been laid out in the original software requirements specifications.

PROJECT MANAGEMENT TOOLS

An automated project management tool is a software system (along with its accompanying system software, hardware, and procedures) that can increase the productivity, efficiency, and quality of project managements activities, such as, planning, scheduling, communicating and controlling. Like other software, project management tools can either be custom made for a particular project, or purchased as a software product (commonly called "packages"). In the recent DOD software technology initiative called STARS (Software Technology for Adaptable, Reliable Systems) it was stated that "it is generally accepted that productivity increase is derived from capital intensive rather than labor intensive activity" (DOD Software Initiative, 1982). The use of project management tools fits the description of a capital intensive activity .

Reasons for Using Project Management Tools

The single, most important benefit from project management tools is the ability to plan the project and play the "what if" games in order to pick the best possible course of action for the project. These tools can:

- Enable the manager to "try", numerous approaches to cost, schedule, task assignments, etc. to find the project plan with the lowest cost or least risk.
- Reduce the time and effort in determining what changes can be made in a project to keep it on schedule and within the limitations of the budget.

Tools can also help the manager plan, track, and shape a project. They can:

- Reduce cost and schedule of software engineering projects
- Increase accuracy and timeliness of the various project management reports
- Reduce the effort in or eliminate boring, tedious jobs, e.g., manually tracking project status
- Increase interest in or willingness to perform management tasks because of the support given by automation, e.g., collecting weekly progress reports to obtain total project status
- Propagate standards

Types of Project Management Tools

The project management tools that can support a project can be divided into two groups. One group of tools supports the project manager as an individual (sometimes called personal information manager). These are the same tools that would support any "high-tech" worker.

The second group of tools support the software project assisting in such activities as project scheduling, budget tracking, manhour accounting, configuration control, etc. Examples of both are given below.

Tools for the individual:

- Word processing, outliners
- Notepads, autodialers, appointment schedulers
- Automated Calendars

Tools for the project:

- Electronic mail
- Automatic cost models
- Task schedulers
- Configuration management (accounting, control, security)
- Tracking tools
- General project management tools (all-in-one scheduling, resource allocation, and tracking)

Features of a General Purpose Tool

General purpose project management tools should encompass the following features:

- Covers the entire life cycle
- Provides multiple views of the project master schedule (critical path method, PERT, Gantt chart)
- Supports multiple projects and sub-projects
- Determines critical path, slack-time, lead-time, and lag-time
- Aids in the commitment of resources (usually people) to project tasks
- Performs automatic resource leveling
- Tracks the use of resources
- Produces fixed format and tailored project reports

Advantages of Using a Project Management Tool

The use of an automated tool has many advantages over a manual approach. For instance:

- Allows accurate tracking of tasks for very large projects—project management tools can compare actual against planned tasks completed and resources used.
- Assists in developing PERT, CPM (network) and WBS charts—Many analysis tools are built around these procedures.
- Allows the automatic updating of multiple views. Example: a change to an activity network will automatically change the Gantt chart.
- Computes the critical path—automatically identifies those tasks on the critical path.
- "What if" processing—allows planners to determine the impact of various proposed requirement and/or

project changes to the overall project schedule and resource utilization.

- Provides project visibility—provides insight into actual progress of work accomplished and resources spent.
- Provides a standard notation and representation method—improves communications between project members.
- Increases productivity—replaces the circle-template and ruler edge for producing charts and documents and the hand calculator for computing cost and schedule.
- Provides automatic computations of resources and schedules—rolls up total cost and schedule from incremental data.
- Supports automatic production of project reports—produces fixed format and tailored project reports.
- Assists in verifying resource utilization and costs—the tool data base allows verification of resource utilization.

Disadvantages of Using a Project Management Tool

- Learning a project management tool is time consuming.
- New project management methods may require change —in order to adopt a particular project management tool companies must adopt the tools and reports used and produced by the project management tool.
- Difficult to integrate into the project—getting people to accept any new procedure, including a new project management technique, is difficult.
- Project management tools are more complex than the manual system they replace and tools are very complex making it difficult to sort out which techniques and reports are best.
- Special reports must be customized—a time-consuming effort.
- Costs money—the cost of the tool coupled with the cost of learning may be greater than the benefits.

Considerations in Selecting a Project Management Tool

A few of the external factors that should be considered are

- Are Users' manual and/or reference guide available?
- Is technical support available (in house or through contract)?
- Can tools be reused and can that skill be taught?
- Are courses of instruction available (in house or through contract)?
- Are the tools portable and expandable?

A few of the internal things that should be considered are

- Current project management methods
- Experience of the software engineering staff
- Requirements of the reports to upper management or the customer
- Type, complexity, and size of the software product
- Staff availability for training
- Host machine architecture
- Cost effectiveness of the project management tool

SUMMARY

In this article and in many other documents the terms, "management," "project management," and "software engineering project management" are used interchangeably because the management of a software engineering project and other types of projects require many of the same tools, techniques, approaches, and methods of mainstream management. The functions and general activities of management are the same at all levels; only the detailed activities and tasks are different.

Implementing all of the project management functions, activities, and tasks, described in this article does not guarantee a successful project. A good project team can sometimes overcome deficiencies in organization, staffing, budgets, standards, and other areas. A poor team stumbles over every problem, real or imaginary; no number of rules, policies, standards, or techniques will help. The methods and techniques discussed in this article, in the hands of competent leadership and team members, can significantly improve the probability of a successful project.

BIBLIOGRAPHY

An earlier version of this article appeared in R. H. Thayer, ed., *Tutorial: Software Engineering Project Management,* IEEE Computer Society Press, Los Alamitos, Calif., 1988. References listed below marked with an asterisk were also reprinted in the Tutorial, 1987.

ANSI/IEEE Std. 729–1983, *IEEE Standard Glossary of Software Engineering Terminology,* IEEE, Inc., New York, 1983.

L. J. Arthur, *Programmer Productivity: Myths, Methods, and Murphology,* John Wiley & Sons, Inc., New York, 1983.

E. K. Bailey, T. P. Frazier, and J. W. Bailey, *A Descriptive Evaluation of Automated Software Cost-Estimation Models,* Institute for Defense Analysis, IDA Paper P-1979 Oct. 1986.

K. M. Bartol and D. C. Martin, "Managing the Consequences of DP Turnover: A Human Resources Planning Perspective," *Proceedings of the 20th ACM Computer Resources Planning Perspective,* ACM Inc., New York, 1983, pp. 79–86*.

A. Ben-David, M. Ben-Porath, J. Loeb, and M. Rich, "An Industrial Software Engineering Retraining Course: Development Considerations and Lessons Learned," *IEEE Transactions on Software Engineering,* **SE-10**(1) 748–755 (Nov. 1984).

L. Bernstein, "Software Project Management Audits," *The Journal of Systems and Software,* 281–284 (1982).

E. H. Bershoff, "Elements of Software Configuration Management," *IEEE Transactions on Software Engineering* **SE-10**(1) 79–87 (Jan. 1984)*.

B. W. Boehm, *Software Engineering Economics,* Prentice-Hall, Englewood Cliffs, N.J. 1981.

B. W. Boehm, "Software Engineering Economics," *IEEE Transactions on Software Engineering,* **SE-10**(1), 4–21, (Jan. 1984).

B. W. Boehm, "A Spiral Model of Software Development and Enhancement," R. H. Thayer, ed., *Tutorial: Software Engineering*

Project Management, Computer Society of the IEEE, Washington, D.C., 1987.

B. W. Boehm, *Tutorial: Software Risk Management,* IEEE Computer Society Press, Washington, D.C., 1989.

R. E. Boyatizis, "Leadership: The Effective Use of Power," *Management of Personnel Quarterly,* Bureau of Industrial Relations 1971, pp. 1–8*.

F. J. Buckley, "Establishing Software Engineering Standards in an Industrial Organization," R. Thayer, ed., *Tutorial: Software Engineering Project Management,* Computer Society of the IEEE, Washington, D.C., 1987.

M. Cherlin, "Burnout: Victims and Avoidances," *Datamation,* 92–99 (July 1981).

D. Cleland and W. King, *Major Management Functions as Seen by Various Authors, from Management: A Systems Approach,* McGraw-Hill Book Co., Inc., New York, 1972.

L. H. Cook, Jr., "The Chief Programmer Team Administrator," *Datamation,* 85–85 (June 1976).

K. A. Cori, "Fundamentals of Master Scheduling for the Project Manager," *Project Management Journal,* 78–89 (June 1985).

J. D. Cougar, "Circular Solutions," *Datamation,* 135–142 (Jan. 1983).

A. M. Davis, "The Analysis and Specification of System and Software Requirements," in R. H. Thayer and M. Dorfman, eds., *System and Software Requirements Engineering,* IEEE Computer Society Press, Los Alamitos, Calif., 1990.

J. H. Donnelly, Jr., J. L. Gibson, and J. M. Ivancevich, *Fundamentals of Management: Functions, Behavior, Models,* rev. ed., Business Publications, Inc., Dallas, Tex., 1975.

M. E. Fagan, "Design and Code Inspections to Reduce Errors in Program Development," *IBM Systems Journal,* **15**(3), 182–211 (1976).

M. E. Fagan, "Advances in Software Inspections," *IEEE Transactions on Software Engineering,* **SE-12**(7) 744–751 (July 1986).*

R. E. Fairley, "A Guide for Preparing Software Project Management Plans," in R. H. Thayer, ed., *Tutorial: Software Engineering Project Management,* Computer Society of the IEEE, Washington, D.C., 1987.

J. Fitz-enz, "Who is the DP Professional?," *Datamation,* 125–128 (Sept. 1978).*

F. Herzberg, B. Mausner, and B. B. Snyderman, *The Motivation to Work,* John Wiley & Sons, Inc., New York, 1959.

N. R. Howes, "Managing Software Development Projects for Maximum Productivity," *IEEE Transactions on Software Engineering,* **SE-10**(1) 27–35 (Jan. 1984).*

F. S. Ingrassia, "The Unit Development Folder (UDF): A Ten-Year Perspective," R. H. Thayer, ed., *Tutorial: Software Engineering Project Management,* Computer Society of the IEEE, Washington, D.C., 1987.

C. F. Kemerer, "An Empirical Validation of Software Cost Estimation Models," *Communication of the ACM,* **30**(5) 416–429 (May 1987).

N. S. Kirchof and J. R. Adams, "Conflict Management for Project Managers: An Overview," Extracted from *Conflict Management for Project Managers,* Project Management Institute, Feb. 1986, p. 1–13*.

H. Koontz and C. O'Donnell, *Principles of Management: An Analysis of Managerial Functions,* 5th ed., McGraw-Hill Book Co., Inc., New York, 1972.

H. Koontz, C. O'Donnell, and H. Weihrich, Management, 8th ed., McGraw-Hill Book Co., New York, 1984.

B. Kruesi, *Software Psychology,* California State University, Sacramento, Fall 1982, Seminar.

R. A. MacKenzie, "The Management Process in 3-D," *Harvard Business Review,* **47**(6), 80–87 (Nov.–Dec. 1969)*

M. Mantei, "The Effect of Programming Team Structures on Programming Tasks," *Communications of the ACM,* **24**(3) 106–113 (Mar. 1981).*

A. H. Maslow, *Motivation and Personality,* Harper & Brothers, New York, 1954.

J. P. McGill, "The Software Engineering Shortage: A Third Choice," *IEEE Transactions on Software Engineering,* **SE-10**(1) 42–48 (Jan. 1984).*

D. McGregor, *The Human Side of Enterprise,* McGraw-Hill Book Co., Inc., New York, 1960.

C. J. Middleton, "How to Set Up a Project Organization," *Harvard Business Review,* 73–82 (Nov.–Dec. 1967).*

W. B. Miller, "Fundamentals of Project Management," *Journal of Systems Management* **29**(11), 22–29 (Nov. 1978).*

H. D. Mills, "Software Engineering Education," *Proceedings of the IEEE,* **68**(9), 1158–1162 (Sept. 1980).

M. Moneysmith, "I'm OK—and You're Not," *Savvy,* 37–38 (Apr. 1984).*

W. Ouchi, *Theory Z: How American Business Can Meet the Japanese Challenge,* Addison-Wesley, Reading, Mass., 1981.

G. N. Powell and B. Z. Posner, "Excitement and Commitment: Keys to Project Success" *Project Management Journal* 39–46 (Dec. 1984).*

E. Raudsepp, "Delegate Your Way to Success," *Computer Decisions,* 157–164 (Mar. 1981).*

H. Sackman, W. J. Erikson, and E. E. Grant, "Exploratory Experimental Studies Comparing On-Line and Off-Line Programming Performance," *Communication of the ACM,* **11**(1) 3–11 (Jan. 1968).*

Software Engineering Standards, IEEE, New York, 1993.

Source EDP, *Computer Salary Survey and Career Planning Guide,* San Francisco, Calif., 1987.

Strategy for a DOD Software Initiative, Department of Defense Report, Oct. 1982 (A public version was published in *Computer* (Nov. 1983).

L. C. Stuckenbruck, "The Matrix Organization," *A Decade of Project Management,* Project Management Institute 1981, pp. 157–169.*

R. H. Thayer, ed., *Tutorial: Software Engineering Project Management,* Computer Society of the IEEE, Washington, D.C., 1987.

D. R. Wallace and R. U. Fujii, *Software Verification and Validation: Its Role in Computer Assurance and Its Relationship with Software Project Management Standards,* National Computer Systems Laboratory, National Institute of Standards and Technology, Gaithersburg, Md., 1989, NIST Special Publication 550–165.

G. Weinberg, *The Psychology of Computer Programming,* Van Nostrand Reinhold Co., New York, 1971.

G. M. Weinberg and D. P. Freedman, "Reviews, Walkthroughs, and Inspections," *IEEE Transactions on Software Engineering,* **SE-10**(1) 68–72 (Jan. 1984)*.

G. F. Walters, "Investigative Audit for Controlling Software Development," in R. Thayer, ed., *Tutorial:Software Engineering Project,* 1987.*

P. Youker, "Organizational Alternatives for Project Management," *Project Management Quarterly* **VIII**(1), 18–24 (Mar. 1977).*

E. Yourdon, "A Game Plan for Technology Transfer," in R. Thayer, ed., *Tutorial:Software Engineering Project,* 1987.*

RICHARD H. THAYER
California State University, Sacramento

RICHARD FAIRLEY
Software Engineering Management Associates, Inc.

PROJECT MONITORING AND CONTROL

See PROJECT MANAGEMENT.

PROJECT PLANNING

See PROJECT MANAGEMENT.

PROPAGATION-ORIENTED TESTING

See UNIT TESTING.

PROTOCOL

A set of conventions that govern the interaction processes, devices, and other components within a system.

PSL/PSA

See PROBLEM STATEMENT LANGUAGE/PROBLEM STATEMENT ANALYZER.

PSEUDO CODE

A combination of programming language constructs and natural language used to express a computer program design. For example:

```
IF the data arrives faster than expected,
  THEN reject every third input.
  ELSE process all data received.

ENDIF
```

(IEEE).

PUTNAM, LAWRENCE H.

Lawrence Putnam received his B.S. from the U.S. Military Academy at West Point in 1952, his M.S. in physics from the U.S. Naval Postgraduate School in 1961, and undertook MBA studies at George Washington University from 1973 to 1976.

Mr. Putnam is the founder and has been President of Quantitative Software Management, Inc. since 1978. Before establishing QSM, Mr. Putnam was the Manager of Systems and Technologies at the General Electric Company for one year and was responsible for developing software cost estimating systems and performing cost estimates for GE and its clients.

Prior to joining GE, Mr. Putnam served over twenty-five years as an Army Officer and retired with the rank of Colonel. He has over fifteen years of software and hardware resource planning, estimating, and allocation.

For the past fifteen years Mr. Putnam has been teaching public seminars in software cost estimating throughout the United States, Western Europe, Japan and Australia. He conducted five-day software cost estimating courses for the Department of Defense (at the Department of Defense Computer Institute) approximately four times a year for the period 1980–1984. Mr. Putnam has taught a two day software management and cost estimating course internally within IBM Corporation 6–10 times per year over the last eight years.

Fifteen years ago, Mr. Putnam developed SLIM (Software Life-Cycle Management) Model, (a quantitative management tool for software development) and has been refining and expanding its capabilities ever since. SLIM is used widely throughout the U.S. Department of Defense, U.S. Federal Government and private industry in the United States and abroad.

During the period 1978 to the present, he has participated in and has led software cost estimates for more than seventy five projects of national level importance. A significant number of these have been within the Department of Defense. Mr. Putnam has worked with other government agencies, such as the U.S. Postal Service, Department of Labor, U.S. Geological Survey, General Accounting Office, Federal Aviation Agency, NASA, and the U.S. Veterans Administration.

Commercial organizations that he has done software productivity measurement and estimating for include: The Hartford Insurance Group, General Electric, ITT, IBM, Burroughs, NCR, Sperry, Honeywell, GTE Data Services, General Telephone of California, Schlumberger, Electronic Data Systems, Eastman Kodak, Nippon Telegraph and Telephone, British Telecom, Motorola, Alcatel Network Systems, and AT&T.

Mr. Putnam was the first recipient of the Freeman award for sustained superior performance in parametric estimating covering a ten-year period. This award is the highest level award made by the International Society of Parametric Analysts.

BIBLIOGRAPHY

L. H. Putnam, "A Macro-Estimating Methodology for Software Development," *Digest of Papers, Fall COMPCON '76,* Thirteenth IEEE Computer Society International Conference, Sept. 1976, pp.138–143.

—"ADP Resource Estimating A Macro-Level Forecasting Methodology for Software Development," *Proceedings of the Fifteenth Annual U.S. Army Operations Research Symposium,* Oct. 26–29, 1976, Forher, Va. pp. 323–327.

—"A General Solution to the Software Sizing and Estimating Problem", as presented at the *Life Cycle Management Conference,* American Institute of Industrial Engineers, Washington, D.C., Feb. 8, 1977.

—with R. W. Wolverton, "Quantitative Management: Software Cost Estimating", *A Tutorial for COMPSAC '77, the IEEE Computer Society's First International Computer Software and Applications Conference,* Chicago, Nov. 8–10, 1977.

—with A. Fitzsimmons, "Estimating Software Costs," *DATAMATION,* Sept., Oct., Nov., 1979, pp. 312–315, 316–320, 321–323.

—Tutorial, *Software Cost Estimating and Life Cycle Control: Getting the Software Numbers,* IEEE Computer Society, New York, 1980.

—"The Real Economics of Software Development," *The Economics of Information Processing,* John Wiley & Sons, Inc., 1982, pp. 167–176.

—with D. T. Putnam and L. P. Thayer, "Software Equation Computes Characteristics—Programmer Productivity," *Software News, 26–36 (Oct. 1983).*

—with D. T. Putnam and L. P. Thayer, "A Tool for Planning Software Projects," *Systems and Software,* 147–154 (Jan. 1984).

—with D. T. Putnam and L. P. Thayer, "Theory Can Measure Effective Productivity," *Data Base Monthly,* 22–26 (Jan. 1984).

—with D. T. Putnam, "A Data Verification of Software Fourth Power Trade Off Law" in the *Proceedings of the Sixth Annual Conference the International Society of Parametric Analysts,* San Francisco, May 13–18, 1984.

—with R. M. Cline, "The SLIM Software Cost and Schedule Estimating Model," in the *Proceedings of the 1984 Summer Computer Simulation Conference,* Boston, July 23–25, 1984.

—with D. T. Putnam and L. P. Thayer, "Assessing the Proficiency of Software Developers," in the *Ninth Annual Software Engineering Workshop (NASA-Goddard) on Software Metrics,* Greenbelt, Md., Nov. 28, 1984.

—with D. T. Putnam and L. P. Thayer, "Quality in Software is Free", in the *proceedings of the Seventh Annual Conference of the International Society of Parametric Analysts,* Orlando, Fla., May 7–9, 1985.

—"Software Cost and Quality Management," published in *Proceedings of the Software Cost and Quality Management Conference of The National Institute for Software Quality and Productivity, Inc.,* Sheraton Hotel, Tyson's Corner, Virginia, Oct. 29–30, 1986.

—"QSM's Size Planner: A Front End Software Sizing Tool," presented at the Software Cost & Quality Control Conference of The National Institute for Software Quality and Productivity, Inc., Radisson Mark Plaza Hotel, Alexandria, Va., Sept. 22, 1987.

—with J. Greene and G. Bingham, *PEP Paper 5, Managing Productivity in Systems Development,* Butler Cox & Partners Limited, Productivity Enhancement Program (PEP), London, U.K., April 1988.

—"Managing Software Productivity" *paper presented at the Conference on Managing Software Quality Improvement sponsored by NASA and the Jet Propulsion Laboratory at the Pasadena Convention Center,* Pasadena, Calif., June 7, 1989.

—"Strategic Issues in Managing Software Cost and Quality," *Engineering Management Journal,* **1**(4), (Dec. 1989).

—"Using Measurement to Support TQM Practices in Software Control", *paper presented at the Sixth Conference on Improving Productivity in System Development sponsored by ACR,* in Phoenix, Ariz., Jan. 27–31, 1992.

—*Measures for Excellence: Reliable Software On Time, Within Budget,* Prentice Hall, Inc., 1992.

PYSTER, ARTHUR B. (1950–)

Arthur B. Pyster is best known for advancing the state of software engineering practices worldwide. He is the Senior Vice President and Chief Technical Officer of the Software Productivity Consortium, one of the most successful consortia in the United States.

Pyster earned his Bachelor of Science from the University of Illinois in 1971; his Masters of Science (1973) and Doctorate (1975) in Computer and Information Sciences, both from the Ohio State University.

From 1976 to 1982, as a professor at the University of California, Santa Barbara, Pyster developed much of the curriculum during the early years of their computer science program. There he completed *Compiler Design and Construction,* a popular textbook on compilers and published several articles on software engineering, formal languages, and programming languages.

From 1981 to 1984, Pyster served as Manager of Systems Engineering for the Software Productivity Project at TRW. This project, led by Dr. Barry Boehm, was an ambitious effort to improve TRW's software productivity by introducing CASE tools, UNIX, local area networks, laser printers, and office automation at a time when these technologies were novel.

From 1984–1987, at Digital Sound Corporation, Pyster helped create voice processing products such as voice mail. Pyster then went to the Software Productivity Consortium, where he is responsible for all aspects of the technical program. Consortium technologies are used on over 100 projects including the F-22 advanced tactical fighter, Boeing 777, Comanche Helicopter, and the advanced information system for the Patent and Trademark Office. *Ada Quality and Style: Guidelines for the Professional Programmer* is the most widely used Ada style guide in the United States. The Consortium's approaches to software reuse, real-time requirements and design, and process improvement are among the most comprehensive and widely used in the aerospace and defense communities.

Pyster speaks worldwide on advanced technology in software engineering. He is a member of the ACM, American Management Association, Northern Virginia Technology Council, and National Council on Systems Engineering. He is a senior member of the IEEE, serves on the Technical Council of the Electronic Industries Association, is a member of the advisory committee of the Computer and Information Sciences Department of Ohio State University, is a distinguished alumnus of the Engineering College of the Ohio State University, and is a program evaluator for the Computer Sciences Accreditation Board.

BIBLIOGRAPHY

A. B. Pyster, "The Synthesis process for software development," *IEEE Tutorial on Systems and Software Requirements Engineering,* 1990.

—*Compiler Design and Construction,* 2nd ed., Van Nostrand Reinhold, New York, 1988, 1st ed., 1980.

—with B. Boehm, M. Penedo, E. D. Stuckle and R. Williams, "An Environment for Improving Software Productivity," *Computer* (1984).

—with B. Boehm, M. Penedo, E. D. Stuckle and R. Williams, "The TRW Software Productivity System," *Proceedings of 6th International Conference on Software Engineering,* Tokyo, Japan, Sept. 14–16, 1982, selected as best paper.
—with R. Thayer and R. Wood, "Validating Solutions to Major Problems in Software Engineering Project Management," *Computer* **15**(8) 65–77 (1982).

PROOFS OF CORRECTNESS

INTRODUCTION

A proof of correctness is a mathematical proof that a computer program or a part thereof will, when executed, yield correct results, i.e. results fulfilling specific requirements. Before proving a program correct, the theorem to be proved must, of course, be formulated. The hypothesis of such a correctness theorem is typically a condition that the relevant program variables must satisfy immediately *before* the program is executed. This condition is called the precondition. The thesis of the correctness theorem is typically a condition that the relevant program variables must satisfy immediately *after* execution of the program. This latter condition is called the postcondition. Thus a correctness theorem usually has the following form: "If the condition V is true before execution of the program S, then the condition P will be true after execution of S." V is the precondition; P is the postcondition. Such a correctness theorem is usually written $\{V\}S\{P\}$. One sometimes sees the notational form $V\{S\}P$, especially in the earlier literature. Alternatively, the thesis of a correctness theorem may be a statement that the final values of the program variables are a particular function of their initial values.

By interpreting the term *program variable* sufficiently broadly to include input and output data, e.g., data entered via a keyboard, displayed on a screen, or printed on paper, essentially any externally observable aspect of the program's execution may be covered by the precondition and postcondition.

The various approaches to proving a program correct can be categorized in different ways. Often a distinction is made between those that (**1**) view the program as a transformation between preconditions and postconditions and (**2**) view the program as a function mapping the initial values of the relevant program variables to their final values. Although this distinction is in principle clear, in practical application it often becomes blurred. For example, if one allows a postcondition to refer also to the initial values of the program variables (as is sometimes desirable and useful in practice), a functional relationship between initial and final values of the program variables can be incorporated within the postcondition. Then, the distinction referred to above loses significance.

The weaker the hypothesis and the stronger the thesis of a mathematical theorem are, the stronger the theorem is. A strong correctness theorem $\{V\}S\{P\}$ will, therefore, have a weak precondition V and a strong postcondition P. For this reason, one is sometimes interested in the weakest precondition or the strongest postcondition of a program statement.

Especially in practice, it is important to distinguish between two situations: (**1**) the program in question terminates (i.e., its execution proceeds to the end in finite time) and yields a correct result (i.e., a result fulfilling the postcondition) and (**2**) the program in question may or may not terminate, but if it does, then the result is correct. A program of the first type above is said to be totally correct; a program of the second type, partially correct. If one proves that a program is partially correct and then, in a separate step, proves that it terminates, then one has obviously proved that it is totally correct. A proof of total correctness is usually separated into these two parts to simplify the proof. Typically, quite different types of arguments are appropriate for these two proofs.

Another approach to proving a program correct is to prove that it is equivalent in some appropriate sense to another program that was assumed, has been defined, or has been proven to be correct. Such an approach can be useful when the program in question is the result of a series of refinement steps.

Note that the precondition and postcondition of a program together effectively constitute a specification of that program.

The definition of correctness need not be a single one but may take on the form of a hierarchy of specifications. For example, one may be concerned with two aspects of the behavior of a program: its functionality and the safety of its use. The functional specification, i.e., the correctness theorem dealing with its full functionality, will typically be much stronger and more detailed than the safety specification, i.e., than the correctness theorem dealing only with safety-related aspects of its behavior. The safety relevant correctness theorem, being mathematically weaker than the functional correctness theorem, will typically be easier to prove.

APPLICATION AREAS

The most obvious use of a correctness proof is to show that a program will yield correct results in all cases of interest or concern not just in those cases included, e.g., in a test. Another, frequently overlooked, application area is program design. The steps in a correctness proof give rise to certain requirements that the various parts of a program being designed must satisfy. These requirements can be generalized and used as guidelines for the design phase. This may very well be the potentially most valuable aspect of correctness proofs in practice.

HISTORICAL OVERVIEW

The seminal paper of the contemporary literature on correctness proofs provided a basis for formal definitions of the meanings of programs (Floyd, 1967). To each connection in the program's flow chart Floyd assigned a proposition that was asserted to be true whenever control passed along that connection. He then defined the meaning of each program statement type (e.g., assignment statement, if statement, loop, etc.) in terms of a relationship between its preconditions and postconditions. Generally, Floyd's article works from the beginning of the program to the end, emphasizing the strongest postcondition, whereas current practical applications tend to work backward from the end of the program to the beginning, emphasizing the weakest precondition instead.

Hoare (1969) and Dijkstra (1976) built on the ideas presented by Floyd (1967) in fundamentally important ways. Hoare viewed a program statement as a transformation between preconditions and postconditions, defining each program statement type in terms of an axiom about its precondition–postcondition transform. Dijkstra emphasized the weakest precondition and presented rules for deriving the weakest precondition for a given program statement or construct and for a given postcondition.

The theoretical basis of program correctness proofs was developed further and in detail (Loeckx and Sieber, 1984) and was presented in somewhat more application-oriented forms (Gries, 1978). Linger, Mills and co-workers (1979) developed a contrasting approach, directing attention more to the function (in the mathematical sense) realized by a program.

This work was also theoretically based, but more motivated by practical application, especially in cleanroom software development. *Cleanroom* is an approach to large-scale software development based on correctness proof approaches to program design and statistical testing. Significant success in reducing the error rate in software has been claimed for this approach (Mills and co-workers, 1987; Selby and co-workers, 1987).

Another example of theoretically based and application-motivated work in correctness proof techniques is the Vienna Development Method (VDM) (Jones, 1986). This approach is based on the precondition–postcondition view of a program, but appears to be motivated fundamentally by needs arising when developing programs in contrast to verifying them.

A major criticism of all of the above approaches raised by typical software development practitioners is that the mathematical knowledge and ability required are too extensive. This criticism, however, is probably more the result of the form of the relevant literature than of its fundamental content. The language and notational forms used by logicians are not well known among practicing software developers, engineers, technicians, etc. and make this material appear to these readers to be more complicated and difficult than it really is. In an attempt to make this material more easily accessible to these groups and to facilitate its practical application, Baber (1987, 1991a) recast much of it in mathematically simpler language, using notational forms borrowed from typical engineering mathematics.

A considerable number of software tools for proving programs correct have been developed and employed in research environments. Typically, they consist of two parts: a verification condition generator and a theorem prover. The verification condition generator decomposes the correctness theorem to be proved into a number of lemmas whose truth guarantees the truth of the correctness theorem. The theorem prover is then applied to each lemma. A number of these tools employ the Boyer–Moore theorem prover or variants thereof. Only a few commercial products for supporting correctness proofs have been marketed to date, but more are expected to appear in the near future.

One of the first areas in which correctness proof techniques were applied in practice was the development of secure systems for the military. Because such work is classified, little information about these efforts and their results has been made public.

The theory of proving programs correct is well developed and has become a recognized and established part of computing science. Its practical application is still, however, in an early stage of development. Some significant successes have been reported in the literature (Mills and co-workers, 1987; Selby and co-workers, 1987), including the verification of a small multitasking operating system kernel written in machine language (Bevier, 1989). Other unpublicized practical applications have been successful, i.e., have saved more effort than they required and have led to software with an atypically low error rate being delivered to customers. While the absolute number of such successes is significant, they represent only a very small fraction of software development projects in commercial practice. The trend appears to be slowly but surely in the direction of increasing use of correctness proof techniques in software development practice. Especially the stringent requirements of safety-critical systems will lead to an increasing demand to employ such approaches. For example, the British Ministry of Defence (1991) has published an interim standard calling for the use of correctness proofs when developing safety critical software.

FUTURE DEVELOPMENTS

It seems clear that correctness proofs will play an increasing role in software development. It is less clear how rapid this trend will be and how extensive this role will ultimately become. If software development is to become a true engineering discipline, then a mathematical foundation for the field such as that provided by Newton's laws for mechanical engineering, Maxwell's equations for electrical engineering, etc. is required. That body of knowledge variously referred to as correctness proofs, formal methods, etc. provides such a foundation for the work of the software engineer, and its widespread application is a prerequisite for the truly engineering practice of the field (Baber, 1991b).

CLOSELY RELATED AREAS

Symbolic execution of a program is a method of analyzing its executional behavior and leads to similar results as a proof of correctness; on the spectrum of verification methods it lies between formally proving correctness and testing. Research on program semantics has contributed to the development of the theory of proving program correctness, e.g., the work on denotational semantics by Scott and Strachey. Correctness proofs and the development of formal specification languages (e.g., Estelle, Larch, Lotos, OBJ, RSL, and Z) have mutually influenced each other (Spivey, 1989; Turski and Maibaum, 1987). The notion of developing the correctness proof and the program together is being extended and formalized with the aim of deriving a program automatically from the (ideally also automatically generated) proof of its consistency with the formal specification (Manna and Waldinger, 1992).

Research on theorem proving has provided the basis for the software tools mentioned earlier for proving the correctness of programs. Theorem proving is (and presumably will remain) the primary technical bottleneck in the development of these tools. Significant advances in theorem proving can be expected, therefore, to lead to corresponding advances in the state of the art of software tools for supporting correctness proofs.

Correctness proof concepts, especially preconditions, postconditions, and invariants, have had some influence on certain features of several specification and programming languages. For example, the object-oriented language Eiffel provides for a precondition and a postcondition for each routine, in support of the concept of programming by contract (Meyer, 1988). Eiffel also provides for several types of invariants, including a class invariant.

PROOF RULES

When proving a correctness theorem, i.e., that some condition V is a precondition of a postcondition P with respect to a program segment S (symbolically, $\{V\}S\{P\}$), the same types of arguments specific to the several types of program statements and constructs repeatedly occur. Therefore, general theorems are formulated and applied when proving particular programs correct. These generally applicable theorems are often called proof rules. Many proof rules deal with the relationship between preconditions and postconditions for a certain type of program statement, much as Ohm's, Faraday's and Henry's laws deal with the relationships between voltage and current for a resistor, capacitor, and inductor, respectively. Similarly, the mechanical engineer has mathematical formulas dealing with the relationships between force and position for a mass, a spring, and a viscous damper.

Typically, the application of a proof rule decomposes a proof task into one or more smaller ones. This process is repeated iteratively until only logical algebraic expressions remain; the truth of each is verified by algebraic manipulation. The following is a basic collection of proof rules for a structured language consisting of the assignment statement, the if construct, the while loop, and the sequence of statements.

From the definition of preconditions and postconditions, it follows that any condition stronger than a known precondition is also a precondition and that any condition weaker than a known postcondition also is a postcondition. This reasoning leads to

Proof Rule 1: If $V \Rightarrow V1$, $\{V1\}S\{P1\}$ and $P1 \Rightarrow P$, then $\{V\}S\{P\}$

Consider an assignment statement of the form $x{:=}E$, where the expression E may contain references to x as well as other program variables. The value of x after execution of this assignment statement is the same as the value of E before. The values of variables other than x remain unchanged (no side effects). Thus if one replaces every occurrence of x in P (the desired postcondition) by E (enclosed in parentheses), the newly formed condition (written $P^x{}_E$) will have the same truth value before execution of the assignment statement as P afterward. The newly formed condition is, therefore, a precondition of P with respect to the assignment statement in question. This important observation is

Proof Rule 2: $\{P^x{}_E\}x{:=}E\{P\}$

Note that the expression E comes from the program text. Operators appearing in E represent, therefore, functions as implemented in the programming language, not the standard mathematical functions that they approximate. When manipulating expressions involving these operators in subsequent steps in the correctness proof, only properties of those operations as actually implemented may be used. For example, if the symbol + in E represents floating-point addition, one may not use the associative law when manipulating expressions involving this operator, e.g., simplifying $(x + y) - y$ to x is not permitted. Using different symbols for the machine and standard mathematical versions of such functions (e.g., $\oplus$ for floating point addition, + for the usual addition in mathematics) helps to avoid such pitfalls.

Proof Rule 2 also applies to an assignment to an array variable, i.e., to a statement of the form $x(i){:=}E$. In such cases one must be careful to replace *all* references to $x(i)$ in the postcondition P by E. For example, a reference to $x(j)$ in P must be replaced by E if $i = j$, but not otherwise. Several different (but logically equivalent) ways of avoiding this potential pitfall when applying Proof Rule 2 to assignments to an array variable are given in Baber (1987, 1991a) and Gries (1978).

The combination of Proof Rules 1 and 2 is frequently useful in practice:

Proof Rule 3: If $V \Rightarrow P^x{}_E$, then $\{V\}x{:=}E\{P\}$

By applying Proof Rule 3, one reduces the task of proving a correctness proposition about an assignment statement to verifying an implication, which involves only logical algebraic manipulation. Many other proof rules also enable one to decompose a proof task into smaller ones, eg, the following proof rule for the if construct (Fig. 1).

Proof Rule 4: If $\{V \wedge B\}S1\{P\}$ and $\{V \wedge \neg B\}S2\{P\}$,
then $\{V\}$ **if** B **then** $S1$ **else** $S2$ **endif** $\{P\}$

A slightly reformulated version of Proof Rule 4 is suitable for deriving a precondition with respect to an if construct:

Proof Rule 5: If $\{V1\}S1\{P\}$ and $\{V2\}S2\{P\}$,
then $\{(V1 \wedge B) \vee (V2 \wedge \neg B)\}$ **if** B **then** $S1$ **else** $S2$ **endif** $\{P\}$

Thus, to derive a precondition for an if construct, one finds preconditions for the **then** and **else** parts separately and then combines these two preconditions as indicated above. Here again, a proof task has been decomposed into proof tasks involving smaller program segments.

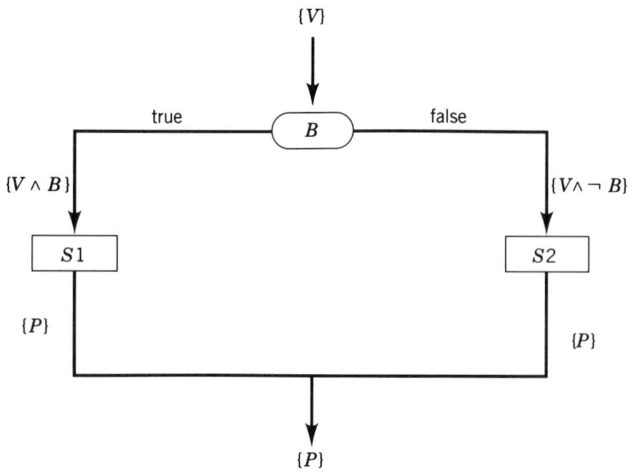

Figure 1. Proof Rule 4 for the if statement.

When a sequence of statements ($S1$; $S2$) is executed, the program state resulting from the execution of $S1$ is used as the starting point for the execution of $S2$. The postcondition of $S1$ will be the precondition of $S2$. This observation gives rise to

Proof Rule 6: If $\{V\}S1\{P1\}$ and $\{P1\}S2\{P\}$, then $\{V\}S1;\ S2\{P\}$

To derive a precondition with respect to a sequence of statements, one works backward through the sequence. The precondition with respect to the first statement is also the precondition with respect to the entire sequence.

To verify a correctness proposition about a sequence of statements, one applies Proof Rule 6 to decompose the proposition to be proved into correctness propositions about the individual statements. To do this, the intermediate condition ($P1$ above) is required. If it is not given, it must be derived by applying the proof rule appropriate for the statement type in question, e.g., Proof Rule 2 for an assignment statement and Proof Rule 5 for an if construct.

The assumption underlying Proof Rule 6 (that the program state resulting from the execution of one statement is the starting point for the execution of the following statement) can be violated in a concurrent programming environment. Therefore, a proof of correctness for a sequential program may not apply when that program is executed concurrently with other programs. The subject of proving correctness in an environment involving concurrent execution has been investigated in depth by a number of researchers (Apt and Olderog, 1991; Andrews, 1991).

If a condition I is true before a while loop is executed and if the body of the loop preserves the truth of I, then I will be true when (and if) the loop terminates. Furthermore, the while condition will be true immediately before each execution of the body of the loop. The while condition will be false on termination. These observations lead to

Proof Rule 7: If $\{I \wedge B\}S\{I\}$,
then $\{I\}$ **while** B **do** S **endwhile** $\{I \wedge \neg B\}$

The condition I is called the loop invariant; it expresses the principal design decision underlying a loop and is the key to understanding and proving the correctness of a loop. It should be specified by the designer of the loop. If it is not, that design step must be repeated when proving the correctness of the loop. A suitable loop invariant can usually be determined by generalizing the initial and final conditions, each of which is a special case of I.

Preceding almost every loop is an initialization, whose *only* purpose is to establish the prior truth of the loop invariant I. It is, therefore, convenient to have a proof rule for a while loop with initialization. Combining Proof Rules 1, 6 and 7 leads to Proof Rule 8 (Fig. 2).

Proof Rule 8: If $\{V\}$init$\{I\}$, $\{I \wedge B\}S\{I\}$ and $I \wedge \neg B \Rightarrow P$,
then $\{V\}$ init; **while** B **do** S **endwhile** $\{P\}$

The above proof rules deal with partial, not total, correctness. As mentioned earlier, it must be proved separately that the program will execute to the end in finite time with a defined result. Among other things (e.g., no overflow, values of expressions defined, etc.) one must prove that a loop does not execute indefinitely, i.e., that the while condition B will eventually become false. For this purpose one often defines a numerical expression whose value is decreased (or increased) by at least a fixed amount by each execution of the loop body and for which a lower (or upper) bound is known. The bound can follow either from the while condition B or from the loop invariant I. Such a numerical expression is called a loop variant.

The above set of proof rules forms a basic collection with which the correctness of a large class of programs can be proved. Still others can be formulated for calls to subprograms, breaking lengthy preconditions and postconditions

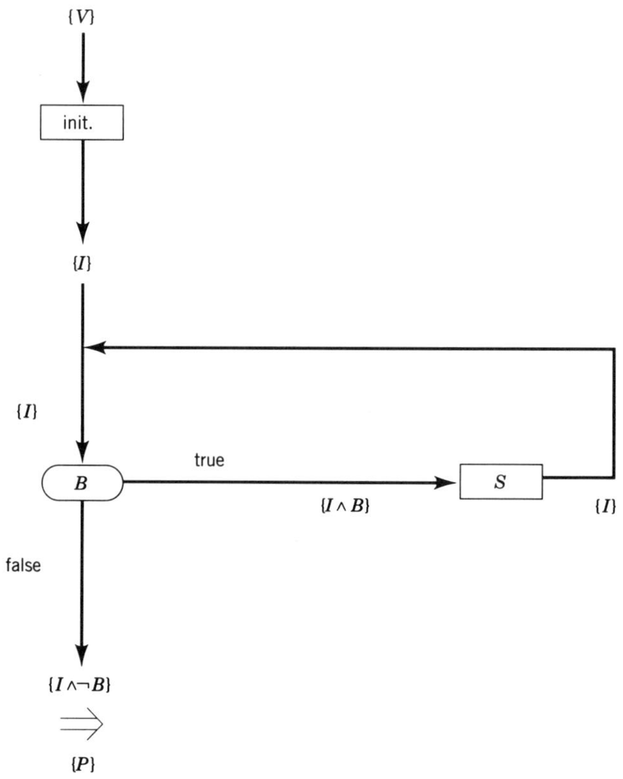

Figure 2. Proof Rule 8 for the while loop with initialization.

down into subexpressions for easier manipulation, etc. (Baber, 1991a; Gries, 1978).

The proof rules have useful implications for designing a program. In particular, the hypotheses of the various proof rules represent requirements that the designer must satisfy. For example, consider the design of a while loop with initialization. Given are the precondition V and the postcondition P. The designer's first task is to specify the loop invariant, eg, by suitably generalizing V and P or minor variations thereof. Once I and P are known, the designer determines B so that $I \wedge \neg B \Rightarrow P$. Often, this can be done mechanistically by manipulating the expressions for I and P appropriately. After determining B, the body S of the loop is designed so that $\{I \wedge B\}S\{I\}$. Only two considerations are of relevance here: maintaining the truth of I and ensuring progress toward P to guarantee termination. The initialization is designed so that $\{V\}$ init $\{I\}$. Thus the proof rules, used as design guidelines, serve to decompose the design task into smaller, independent tasks. Satisfying the requirements of the proof rules ensures that the individual program sections will fit together properly, i.e., so that the overall specification (precondition and postcondition) will be met.

ADDITIONAL ASPECTS OF PROVING CORRECTNESS

Recursive programs are typically proved correct by induction, using proof rules such as those given above together with one or more rules for invoking a subprogram. An operationally motivated approach is illustrated in Baber (1987). If the precondition is not given but is to be derived, a straightforward approach leads to an expression for the precondition that contains a reference to itself; the least fixed point of this expression is the precondition sought. Loops, being logically equivalent to recursion, are amenable to the same approach.

Correctness proofs for concurrently executing programs are based on the same concepts outlined above, but due consideration must be given to their interactions (see the comments on Proof Rule 6, above). In addition to partial and total correctness as described earlier, one must consider deadlock. Andrews (1991) gives an extensive treatment of these topics.

Especially in real-time applications it may be desirable or necessary to include timing considerations in a specification and the correctness proof. A simple approach is to model each program statement by appending an assignment statement that increments an auxiliary variable representing time. Timing requirements are then incorporated in the precondition, postcondition, and appropriate intermediate conditions. Alternatively, one may employ temporal logic, in which conditions are defined over traces (sequences of program states) rather than over individual program states only.

EXAMPLE OF A CORRECTNESS PROOF

Prove the correctness of a given program that sums the array elements $x(1), \ldots x(n)$ to the variable s. Specifically allow the array x to be empty, i.e., the value of the integer variable n to be 0. The formal specification of correctness consists of the precondition V and postcondition P:

$$V: \{0 \le n\}$$
$$P: \{s = \Sigma_{j=1}{}^{n} x(j)\}$$

The given program is as follows:

$i{:=}0$; $s{:=}0$; **while** $i<n$ **do** $i{:=}i+1$; $s{:=}s+x(i)$ **endwhile**

for which the designer specified the loop invariant

$$I: \{0 \le i \le n \wedge s = \Sigma_{j=1}{}^{i} x(j)\}$$

Thus the correctness theorem to be proved is

$\{0 \le n\}$ $i{:=}0$; $s{:=}0$;
while $i<n$ **do** $i{:=}i+1$; $s{:=}s+x(i)$**endwhile**
$\{s = \Sigma_{j=1}{}^{n} x(j)\}$

By Proof Rule 8 for the while loop with initialization, the above correctness theorem will be true if all of the following three propositions are true:

$$\{0 \le n\} i{=}0;\ s{:=}0\ \{I\} \quad (1)$$
$$\{I \wedge i<n\} i{:=}i+1;\ s{:=}s+x(i)\ \{I\} \quad (2)$$
$$I \wedge \neg i<n \Rightarrow s = \Sigma_{j=1}{}^{n} x(j) \quad (3)$$

By Proof Rules 6 (for the sequence of statements), 2 (for the second assignment statement), and 3 (for the first assignment statement), proposition 1 above will be true if

$$0 \le n \Rightarrow [I^{s}{}_{0}]^{i}{}_{0} \quad (1.1)$$

which is easily shown by replacing s and i by 0 in I and simplifying the resulting expression.

Similarly, by Proof Rules 6, 2, and 3, proposition 2 above will be true if

$$I \wedge i<n \Rightarrow [I^{s}{}_{s+x(i)}]^{i}{}_{i+1} \quad (2.1)$$

which can be proved by first replacing s by $(s + x(i))$ and then i by $(i + 1)$ in I and simplifying the resulting expression.

Proposition 3 above, already in the form of a logical implication, is proved by straightforward algebraic manipulation. The loop invariant I contains the term $i \le n$. Together with $\neg i<n$, this implies that $i=n$, in which case the second term in I becomes the postcondition P.

Finally, termination of the loop must be proved. Each execution of the body of the loop increases i by 1. But i is bounded above (see both the loop invariant and the while loop condition), so the loop cannot continue to repeat indefinitely. Formally, an appropriate loop variant would be $(n - i)$, the value of which is reduced by 1 during each iteration of the loop. As soon as $n - i \le 0$, the loop obviously terminates.

To prove total correctness, one must, strictly speaking, also show that each program statement will execute each time without run-time error, e.g., overflow, etc. Such considerations will lead to requirements on the prior declarations of the variables i and s and the range of index values for which the array x is defined. For example, i must be declared in such a way that all values from 0 to n, inclusive, are permitted (cf. the loop invariant I).

In the above proof of correctness, in particular at one place in the proof of proposition 2.1, it is necessary to verify that $s=\Sigma_{j=1}^{i}x(j) \Rightarrow s+x(i+1) = \Sigma_{j=1}^{i+1}x(j)$. If the symbols + and Σ both refer to addition as normally defined in mathematics, this implication obviously applies. It will also apply if the symbols + and Σ refer to the same floating point addition and if the sequence of the additions in Σ is suitably defined. If, however, the symbol + refers to floating point addition, but the symbol Σ refers to mathematical addition, then the implication is not justified and the correctness proof cannot be completed. In this case, the program will not, in general, establish the truth of the postcondition (see the comments on Proof Rule 2, above).

BIBLIOGRAPHY

G. R. Andrews, *Concurrent Programming—Principles and Practice,* Benjamin/Cummings, Redwood City, Calif., 1991.

K. R. Apt and E.-R. Olderog, *Verification of Sequential and Concurrent Programs,* Springer-Verlag, New York, 1991.

R. L. Baber, *The Spine of Software: Designing Provably Correct Software—Theory and Practice,* John Wiley & Sons, Inc., Chichester, UK, 1987.

R. L. Baber, *Error-free Software: Know-how and Know-why of Program Correctness,* John Wiley & Sons, Chichester, UK, 1991a.

R. L. Baber, "Epilogue: Future Developments," in J. McDermid, ed., *Software Engineer's Reference Book,* Butterworth-Heinemann, Oxford, UK, 1991b.

W. R. Bevier, "Kit: A Study in Operating System Verification," *IEEE Trans. Software Eng.* **15**(11), 1382–1396 (Nov. 1989).

E. W. Dijkstra, *A Discipline of Programming,* Prentice-Hall, Inc., Englewood Cliffs, N.J., 1976.

R. W. Floyd, "Assigning Meanings to Programs," *Proceedings of the Symposium of Applied Mathematics,* Vol. 19, American Mathematical Society, Providence, R.I., 1967, pp. 19–32.

D. Gries, *The Science of Programming,* Springer-Verlag, New York, 1978.

C. A. R. Hoare, "An Axiomatic Basis for Computer Programming," *Commun. ACM* **12**(10), 576–580, 583 (Oct. 1969).

C. B. Jones, *Systematic Software Development Using VDM,* Prentice-Hall, Inc. Englewood Cliffs, N.J., 1986.

R. C. Linger, H. D. Mills and B. I. Witt, *Structured Programming: Theory and Practice,* Addison-Wesley, Reading, Massachusetts, 1979.

J. Loeckx and K. Sieber, *The Foundations of Program Verification,* B. G. Teubner, Stuttgart, 1984.

Z. Manna and R. Waldinger, "Fundamentals of Deductive Program Synthesis," *IEEE Trans. Software Eng.* **18**(8), 674–704 (Aug. 1992).

B. Meyer, *Object-oriented Software Construction,* Prentice-Hall, Inc., Englewood Cliffs, N.J., 1988.

H. D. Mills, M. Dyer, and R. C. Linger, "Cleanroom Software Engineering," *IEEE Software* **4**(5), 19–25 (Sept. 1987).

Ministry of Defence, UK, *Interim Defence Standard 00-55, The Procurement of Safety Critical Software in Defence Equipment, Part 1: Requirements and Part 2: Guidance,* Ministry of Defence, Directorate of Standardization, Glasgow, Apr. 5, 1991.

R. W. Selby, V. R. Basili, and F. T. Baker, "Cleanroom Software Development: An Empirical Evaluation," *IEEE Trans. on Software Eng.* **SE-13**(9), 1027– 1037 (Sept. 1987).

J. M. Spivey, *The Z Notation, A Reference Manual,* Prentice-Hall, Inc., New York, 1989.

W. M. Turski and T. S. E. Maibaum, *The Specification of Computer Programs,* Addison-Wesley Publishing Co., Inc., Wokingham, UK, 1987.

Robert L. Baber
Management Consultant

PROSPECTS FOR AN ENGINEERING DISCIPLINE OF SOFTWARE

The term "software engineering" was coined in 1968 as a statement of aspiration— a sort of rallying cry. That year, the North Atlantic Treaty Organization convened a workshop by that name to assess the state and prospects of software production. Capturing the imagination of software developers, the NATO phrase "software engineering" achieved popularity during the 1970s. It now refers to a collection of management processes, software tooling, and design activities for software development. The resulting practice, however, differs significantly from the practice of older forms of engineering.

WHAT IS ENGINEERING?

"Software engineering" is a label applied to a set of current practices for development. But using the word "engineering" to describe this activity takes considerable liberty with the common use of that term. The more customary usage refers to the disciplined application of scientific knowledge to resolve conflicting constraints and requirements for problems of immediate, practical significance.

Definitions of "engineering" abound. Although details differ, they share some common clauses:

- *Creating cost-effective solutions* ... Engineering is not just about solving problems; it is about solving problems with economical use of all resources, including money.
- *... to practical problems* ... Engineering deals with practical problems those solutions matter to people outside the engineering domain—the customers.
- *... by applying scientific knowledge* ... Engineering solves problems in a particular way: by applying science, mathematics, and design analysis.
- *... to building things* ... Engineering emphasizes the solutions, which are usually tangible artifacts.
- *... in the service of mankind* ... Engineering not only serves the immediate customer, but it also develops technology and expertise that will support the society.

Engineering relics on codifying scientific knowledge about a technological problem domain in a form that is directly useful to the practitioner, thereby providing answers for questions that commonly occur in practice. Engineers of ordinary talent can then apply this knowledge to solve problems far faster than they otherwise could. In this way, engineering shares prior solutions rather than relying always on virtuoso problem solving.

Engineering practice enables ordinary practitioners so they can create sophisticated systems that work—unspectacularly, perhaps, but reliably. The history of development is marked by both successes and failures. The successes have often been virtuoso performances or the result of diligence and hard work. The failures have often reflected poor understanding of the problem to be solved, mismatch of solution to problem, or inadequate follow-through from design to implementation. Some failed by never working, others by overrunning cost and schedule budgets.

In current software practice, knowledge about techniques that work is not shared effectively with later projects, nor is there a large body of development knowledge organized for ready reference. Computer science has contributed some relevant theory, but practice proceeds largely independently of this organized knowledge. Given this track record, there are fundamental problems with the use of the term "software engineer."

Routine and Innovative Design

Engineering design tasks are of several kinds. One of the most significant distinctions separates routine from innovative design. Routine design involves solving familiar problems, reusing large portions of prior solutions. Innovative design, on the other hand, involves finding novel solutions to unfamiliar problems. Original designs are much more rarely needed than routine designs, so the latter is the bread and butter of engineering.

Most engineering disciplines capture, organize, and share design knowledge to make routine design simpler. Handbooks and manuals are often the carriers of this organized information. But current notations for software designs are not adequate for the task of both recording and communicating designs, so they fail to provide a suitable representation for such handbooks.

Software in most application domains is treated more often as original than routine—certainly more so than would be necessary if we captured and organized what we already know. One path to increased productivity is identifying applications that could be routine and developing appropriate support.

The current focus on reuse emphasizes capturing and organizing existing knowledge of a particular kind: knowledge expressed in the form of code. Indeed, subroutine libraries—especially of system calls and general-purpose mathematical routines—have been a staple of programming for decades. But this knowledge cannot be useful if programmers do not know about it or are not encouraged to use it. Furthermore, library components require more care in design, implementation, and documentation than similar components that are simply embedded in systems.

Practitioners recognize the need for mechanisms to share experience with good designs. This cry from the wilderness appeared on the Software Engineering News Group, a moderated electronic mailing list:

"In Chem E, when I needed to design a heat exchanger, I used a set of references that told me what the constants were ... and the standard design equations. ...

"In general, unless I, or someone else in my [software] engineering group, has read or remembers and makes known a solution to a past problem, I'm doomed to recreate the solution. ... I guess ... the critical difference is the ability to put together little pieces of the problem that are relatively well known, without having to generate a custom solution for every application. ...

I want to make it clear that I am aware of algorithm and code libraries, but they are incomplete solutions to what I am describing. (There is no Perry's Handbook for Software Engineering.)

This former chemical engineer is complaining that software lacks the institutionalized mechanisms of a mature engineering discipline for recording and disseminating demonstrably good designs and ways to choose among design alternatives. (*Perry's Chemical Engineering Handbook,* published by McGraw-Hill, is the standard design handbook for chemical engineering; it is about four inches thick and printed in tiny type on 8.5″×11″ tissue paper.)

Model for the Evolution of an Engineering Discipline

Historically, engineering has emerged from *ad hoc* practice in two stages: First, management and production techniques enable routine production. Later, the problems of routine production stimulate the development of a supporting science; the mature science eventually merges with established practice to yield professional engineering practice. Figure 1 shows this model.

The exploitation of a technology begins with craftsmanship: A set of problems must be solved, and they get solved any which way. They are solved by talented amateurs and by virtuosos, but no distinct professional class is dedicated to problems of this kind. Intuition and brute force are the primary movers in design and construction. Progress is haphazard, particularly before the advent of good communication; thus, solutions are invented and reinvented. The transmission of knowledge between craftsmen is slow, in part because of underdeveloped communications, but also because the talented amateurs often do not recognize any special need to communicate.

Nevertheless, *ad hoc* practice eventually moves into the folklore. This craft stage of development sees extravagant use of available materials. Construction or manufacture is often for personal or local use or for barter, but there is little or no large-scale production in anticipation of resale. Community barn raisings are an example of this stage: so is software written by application experts for their own ends.

At some point, the product of the technology becomes widely accepted and demand exceeds supply. At that point, attempts are made to define the resources necessary for systematic commercial manufacture and to marshal the expertise for exploiting these resources. Capital is needed

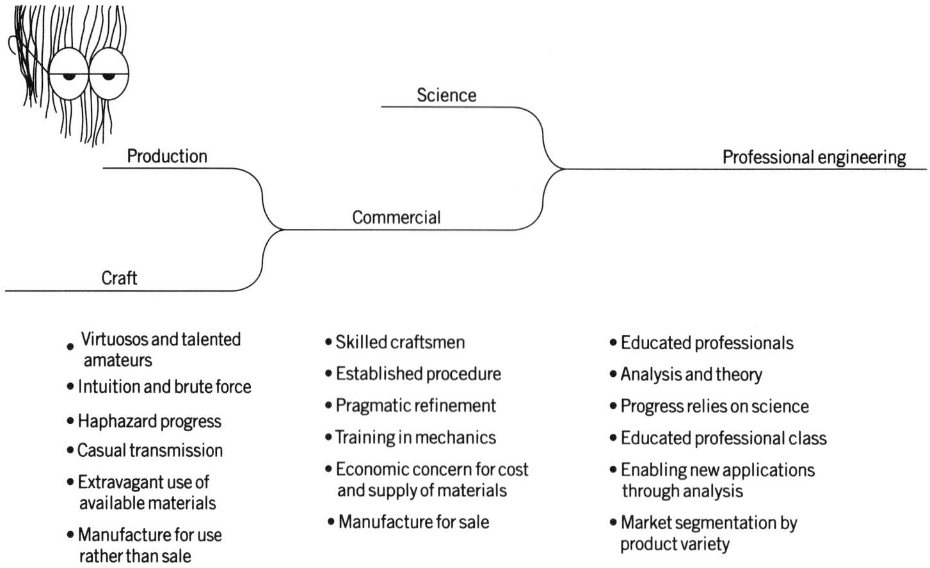

Figure 1. Evolution of an engineering discipline. The lower lines track the technology, and the upper lines show how the entry of production skills and scientific knowledge contribute new capability to the engineering practice.

in advance to buy raw materials, so financial skills become important, and the operating scale increases over time.

As commercial practice flourishes, skilled practitioners are required for continuity and for consistency of effort. They are trained pragmatically in established procedures. Management may not know why these procedures work, but they know the procedures *do* work and how to teach people to execute them.

The procedures are refined, but the refinement is driven pragmatically. A modification is tried to see if it works, then incorporated in standard procedure if it does. Economic considerations lead to concerns over the efficiency of procedures and the use of materials. People begin to explore ways for production facilities to exploit the technology base; economic issues often point out problems in commercial practice. Management strategies for controlling development fit at this point of the model.

The problems of current practice often stimulate the development of a corresponding science. There is frequently a strong, productive interaction between commercial practice and the emerging science. At some point, the science becomes sufficiently mature to be a significant contributor to the commercial practice. This marks the emergence of engineering practice in the sense that we know it today—sufficient scientific basis to enable a core of educated professionals so they can apply the theory to analysis of problems and synthesis of solutions.

For most disciplines, this emergence occurred in the 18th and early 19th centuries as the common interests in basic physical understandings of natural science and engineering gradually drew together. The reduction of many empirical engineering techniques to a more scientific basis was essential to further engineering progress. And this liaison stimulated further advances in natural science. "An important and mutually stimulating tie-up between natural and engineering science, a development [that] had been discouraged for centuries by the long-dominant influence of early Greek thought, was at long last consummated," wrote historian James Kip Finch (1951).

The emergence of an engineering discipline lets technological development pass limits previously imposed by relying on intuition; progress frequently becomes dependent on science as a forcing function. A scientific basis is needed to drive analysis, which enables new applications and even market segmentation via product variety. Attempts are made to gain enough control over design to target specific products on demand.

Thus, engineering emerges from the commercial exploitation that supplants craft. Modern engineering relies critically on adding scientific foundations to craft and commercialization. Exploiting technology depends not only on scientific engineering but also on management and the marshaling of resources. Engineering and science support each other. Engineering generates good problems for science, and science, after finding good problems in the needs of practice, returns workable solutions. Science is often not driven by the immediate needs of engineering; however, good scientific problems often follow from an understanding of the problems that the engineering side of the field is coping with.

The engineering practice of software has recently come under criticism for lacking a scientific basis. The usual curriculum has been attacked for neglecting mathematics (Dykstra, 1989) and engineering science (Parnas, 1990). Although current software practice does not match the usual expectations of an engineering discipline, the model described here suggests that vigorous pursuit of applicable science and the reduction of that science to practice *can* lead to a sound engineering discipline of software.

Examples from Traditional Engineering. Two examples make this model concrete: the evolution of engineering disciplines as demonstrated by civil and chemical engineering. The comparison of the two is also illuminating, because they have very different basic organizations.

Civil Engineering: a Basis in Theory. Originally so-called to distinguish it from military engineering, civil engineering included all of civilian engineering until the middle of the 19th century. A divergence of interests led engineers specializing in other technologies to break away, and today civil engineers are the technical expense of the construction industry. They are concerned primarily with large-scale, capital-intensive construction efforts, like buildings, bridges, dams, tunnels, canals, highways, railroads, public water supplies, and sanitation. As a rule, civil-engineering efforts involve well-defined task groups that use appropriate tools and technologies to execute well-laid plans.

Although large civil structures have been built since before recorded history, only in the last few centuries has their design and construction been based on theoretical understanding rather than on intuition and accumulated experience. Neither the artisans of the Middle Ages nor of the ancient world showed any signs of the deliberate quantitative application of mathematics to determine the dimensions and shapes that characterizes modern civil engineering. But even without formal understanding, they documented pragmatic rules for recurring elements. Practical builders had highly developed intuitions about statics and relied on a few empirical rules.

The scientific revolution of the Renaissance led to serious attempts by Galileo Galilei, Filippo Brunelleschi, and others to explain structures and why they worked. Over a period of about 200 years, there were attempts to explain the composition of forces and bending of a beam. However, progress was slowed for a long time by problems in formulating basic notions like force, particularly the idea that gravity could be treated as just another force like all the others. Until the basic concepts were sorted out, it was not possible to do a proper analysis of the problem of combining forces (using vector addition) that we now teach to freshmen, nor was it possible to deal with strengths of materials.

Around 1700, Pierre Varignon and Isaac Newton developed the theory of statics to explain the composition of forces and Charles Augustan de Coulomb and Louis Marie Henri Navier explained bending with the theory of strength of materials. These now provide the basis for civil engineering. By the middle of the 18th century, civil engineers were tabulating properties of materials.

The mid-18th century also saw the first attempts to apply exact science to practical building. Pope Benedict ordered an analysis of St. Peter's dome in 1742 and 1743 to determine the cause of cracks and propose repairs; the analysis was based on the principle of virtual displacement and was carried out precisely (although the model is now known to fail to account properly for elasticity). By 1850, it was possible for Robert Stephenson's Britannia Tubular Bridge over the Menai Strait between Wales and England to be subjected to a formal structural analysis.

Thus, even after the basic theories were in hand, it took another 150 years before the theory was rich enough and mature enough to have direct utility at the scale of a bridge design.

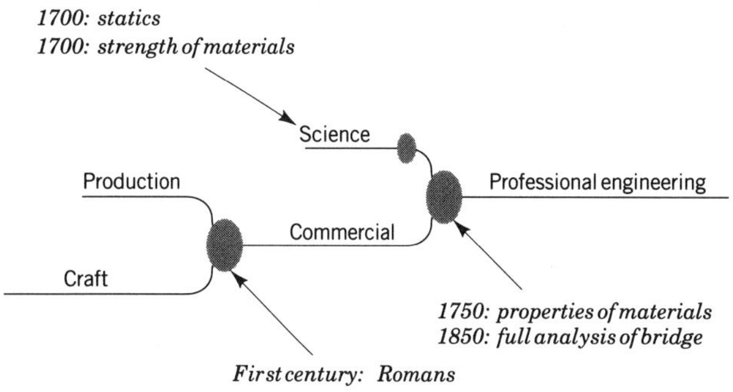

Figure 2. Evolution of civil engineering.

Civil engineering is thus rooted in two scientific theories, corresponding to two classical problems. One problem is the composition of forces: finding the resultant force when multiple forces are combined. The other is the problem of bending: determining the forces within a beam supported at one end and weighted at the other. Two theories, statics and strength of materials, solve these problems; both were developed around 1700. Modern civil engineering is the application of these theories to the problem of constructing buildings.

"For nearly two centuries, civil engineering has undergone an irresistible transition from a traditional craft concerned with tangible fashioning, towards an abstract science, based on mathematical calculation. Every new result of research in structural analysis and technology of materials signified a more rational design, more economic dimensions, or entirely new structural possibilities. There were no apparent limitations to the possibilities of analytical approach; there were no apparent problems in building construction [that] could not be solved by calculation," wrote Hans Straub (1964) in his history of civil engineering.

You can date the transition from craft to commercial practice to the Romans' extensive transportation system of the first century. The underlying science emerged about 1700, and it matured to successful application to practice sometime between the mid-18th century and the mid-19th century. Figure 2 places civil engineering's significant events on my model of engineering evolution.

Chemical Engineering: a Basis in Practice. Chemical engineering is a very different kind of engineering than civil engineering. This discipline is rooted in empirical observations rather than in a scientific theory. It is concerned with practical problems of chemical manufacture; its scope covers the industrial-scale production of chemical goods: solvents, pharmaceuticals, synthetic fibers, rubber, paper, dyes, fertilizers, petroleum products, cooking oils, and so on. Although chemistry provides the specification and design of the basic reactions, the chemical engineer is responsible for scaling the reactions up from laboratory scale to factory scale. As a result, chemical engineering depends as heavily on mechanical engineering as on chemistry.

Until the late 18th century, chemical production as largely a cottage industry. The first chemical produced at industrial scale was alkali, which was required for the manufacture of glass, soap, and textiles. The first economical industrial process for alkali emerged in 1789, well before the atomic theory of chemistry explained the underlying chemistry. By the mid-19th century, industrial production of dozens of chemicals had turned the British Midlands into a chemical-manufacturing district. Laws were passed to control the resulting pollution, and pollution-control inspectors, called alkali inspectors, monitored plant compliance.

One of these alkali inspectors, G. E. Davis, worked in the Manchester area in the late 1880s. He realized that, although the plants he was inspecting manufactured dozens of different kinds of chemicals, there were not dozens of different procedures involved. He identified a collection of functional operations that took place in those processing plants and were used in the manufacture of different chemicals. He gave a series of lectures in 1887 at the Manchester Technical School. The ideas in those lectures were imported to the U.S. by the Massachusetts Institute of Technology in the latter part of the century and form the basis of chemical engineering as it is practiced today. This structure is called *unit operations*; the term was coined in 1915 by Arthur D. Little.

The fundamental problems of chemical engineering are the quantitative control of large masses of material in reaction and the design of cost-effective industrial-scale processes for chemical reactions.

The unit-operations model asserts that industrial chemical-manufacturing processes be resolved into a relatively few units, each of which has a definite function and each of which is used repeatedly in different kinds of processes. The unit operations are steps like filtration and clarification, heat exchange, distillation, screening, magnetic separation, and flotation. The basis of chemical engineering is thus a pragmatically determined collection of very high-level functions that adequately and appropriately describe the processes to be carried out.

"Chemical engineering as a science ... is not a composite of chemistry and mechanical and civil engineering, but a science of itself, the basis of which is those unit operations [that] in their proper sequence and coordination constitute a chemical process as conducted on the industrial scale. These operations ... are not the subject matter of chemistry as such nor of mechanical engineering. Their treatment is in the quantitative way, with proper exposition of the laws controlling them and of the materials and equipment concerned in them," the American Institute of Chemical Engineers Committee on Education wrote in 1922 (van Antwerpen, 1980).

This is a very different kind of structure from that of civil engineering. It is a pragmatic, empirical structure—not a theoretical one.

You can date the transition from craft to commercial practice to the introduction of the LeBlanc process for alkali in 1789. The science emerged with the British chemist John Dalton's atomic theory in the early 19th century, and it matured to successful merger with large-scale mechanical processes in the 1890s. Figure 3 places chemical engineering's significant events on my model.

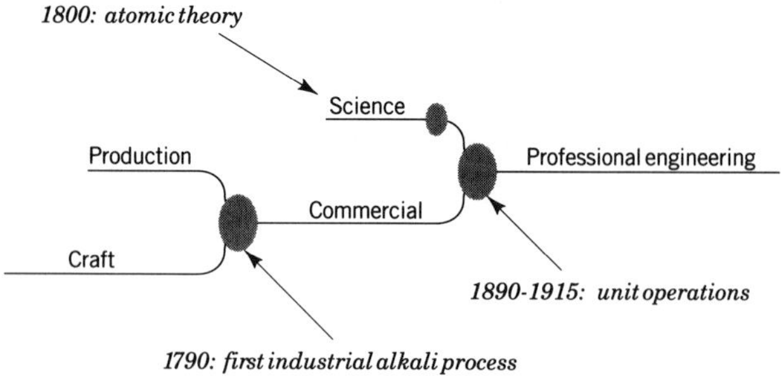

Figure 3. Evolution of chemical engineering.

SOFTWARE TECHNOLOGY

Where does software stand as an engineering discipline? For software, the problem is appropriately an engineering problem: creating cost-effective solutions to practical problems, building things in the service of humanity.

Information Processing as an Economic Force

The U.S. computer business—including computers, peripherals, packaged software, and communications— was about $150 billion in 1989 and was projected to be more than $230 billion by 1992. The packaged-software component is projected to grow from $23.7 billion to $37.5 billion in this period, according to the Data Analysis Group's fourth-quarter 1989 forecasts. Services, including systems integration and in-house development, are not included in these figures.

Worldwide, software sales amounted to about $65 billion in 1989. This does not include the value of in-house development, which is a much larger activity. World figures are hard to estimate, but the cost of in-house software in the U.S. alone may be in the range of $150 billion to $200 billion (CSTB, 1990). It is not clear how much modification after release (so-called "maintenance") is included in this figure. Thus, software is coming to dominate the cost of information processing.

The economic presence of information processing also makes itself known through the actual and opportunity costs of systems that do *not* work. Examples of costly system failures abound. Less obvious are the costs of computing that is not even tried; development backlogs so large that they discourage new requests, gigabytes of unprocessed raw data from satellites and space probes, and so on. Despite very real (and substantial) successes, the litany of mismatches of cost, schedule, and expectations is a familiar one.

Growing Role of Software in Critical Applications

The U.S. National Academy of Engineering recently selected the 10 greatest engineering achievements of the last 25 years (National Academy of Engineering, 1989). Of the 10, three are informatics achievements: commun-ications and information-gathering satellites, the microprocessor, and fiber-optic communication. Two more are direct applications of computers: computer-aided design and manufacturing and the computerized axial tomography scan. And most of the rest are computer-intensive: the Moon landing, advanced composite materials, the jumbo jet, lasers, and the application of genetic engineering to produce new pharmaceuticals and crops.

The conduct of science is increasingly driven by computational paradigms standing on equal footing with theoreti-

Table 1. Significant Shifts in Research Attention

Attribute	1960±5 years: Programming any-which-way	1970±5 years: Programming-in-the small	1980±5 years: Programming-in-the-large
Characteristic problems	Small programs	Algorithms and programming	Interfaces, management system structures
Data issues	Representing structure and symbolic information	Data structures and types	Long-lived databases, symbolic as well as numeric
Control issues	Elementary understanding of control flows	Programs execute once and terminate	Program assemblies execute continually
Specification issues	Mnemonics, precise use of prose	Simple input/output specifications	Systems with complex specifications
State space	State not well understood apart from control	Small, simple state space	Large, structured state space
Management focus	None	Individual effort	Team efforts, system lifetime maintenance
Tools, methods	Assemblers, core dumps	Programming language, compilers, linkers, loaders	Environments, integrated tools, documents

cal and experimental paradigms. Both scientific and engineering disciplines require very sophisticated computing. The demands are often stated in terms of raw processing power—"an exaflop (10^{18}) processor with teraword memory," "a petabyte (10^{15}) of storage," as one article put it (Leven, 1989)—but the supercomputing community is increasingly recognizing development, not mere raw processing, as a critical bottleneck.

Because of software's pervasive presence, the appropriate objective for its developers should be the effective delivery of computational capability to real users in forms that match their needs. The distinction between a system's computational component and the application it serves is often very soft—the development of effective software now often requires substantial application expertise.

Maturity of Development Techniques

Our development abilities have certainly improved over the 40 or so years of programming experience. Progress has been both qualitative and quantitative. Moreover, it has taken different forms in the worlds of research and practice.

One of the most familiar characterizations of this progress has been the shift from programming-in-the-small to programming-in-the-large. It is also useful to look at a shift that took place 10 years before that, from programming-any-which-way to programming-in-the-small. Table 1 summarizes these shifts, both of which describe the focus of attention of the software research community.

Before the mid-1960s, programming was substantially *ad hoc;* it was a significant accomplishment to get a program to run at all. Complex software systems were created—some performed very well—but their construction was either highly empirical or a virtuoso activity. To make programs intelligible, we used mnemonics, we tried to be precise about writing comments, and we wrote prose specifications. Our emphasis was on small programs, which was all we could handle predictably.

We did come to understand that computers are symbolic information processors, not just number crunchers—a significant insight. But the abstractions of algorithms and data structures did not emerge until 1967, when Donald Knuth showed the utility of thinking about them in isolation from the particular programs that happened to implement them.

A similar shift in attitudes about specifications took place at about the same time, when Robert Floyd showed how attaching logical formulas to programs allows formal reasoning about the programs. Thus, the late 1960s saw a shift from crafting, monolithic programs to an emphasis on algorithms and data structures. But the programs in question were still simple programs that execute once and then terminate.

You can view the shift that took place in the mid-1970s from programming-in-the-small to programming-in-the-large in much the same terms. Research attention turned to complex systems whose specifications were concerned not only with the functional relations of the inputs and outputs, but also with performance, reliability, and the states through which the system passed. This led to a shift in emphasis to interfaces and managing the programming process.

In addition, the data of complex systems often outlives the programs and may be more valuable, so we learned that we now have to worry about integrity and consistency of databases. Many of our programs (for example, the telephone switching system or a computer operating system) should *not* terminate; these systems require a different sort of reasoning than do programs that take input, compute, produce output, and terminate. In systems that run indefinitely, the sequence of system states is often much more important than the (possibly, undesirable) termination-condition.

The tools and techniques that accompanied the shift from programming-any-which-way to programming-in-the-small provided first steps toward systematic, routine development of small programs; they also seeded the development of a science that has matured only in the last decade. The tools and techniques that accompanied the shift from programming-in-the-small to programming-in-the-large were largely geared to supporting groups of programmers working together in orderly ways and to giving management a view into production processes. This directly supports the commercial practice of development.

Practical development proceeded to large complex systems much faster than the research community did. For example, the Sage missile-defense system of the 1950s and the Sabre airline-reservation system of the 1960s were successful interactive systems on a scale that far exceeded the maturity of the science. They appear to have been developed by excellent engineers who understood the requirements well and applied design and development methods from other (like electrical) engineering disciplines. Modern development methodologies are management procedures intended to guide large numbers of developers through similar disciplines.

The term "software engineering" was introduced in 1968 to name a conference convened by NATO to discuss problems of software production. Despite the label, most of the discussion dealt with the challenge of progressing from the craft stage to the commercial stage of practice. In 1976, Barry Boehm (1976) proposed the definition of the term as "the practical application of scientific knowledge in the design and construction of computer programs and the associated documentation required to develop, operate, and maintain them." This definition is consistent with traditional definitions of engineering, although Boehm noted the shortage of scientific knowledge to apply.

Unfortunately, the term is now most often used to refer to life-cycle models, routine methodologies, cost-estimation techniques, documentation frameworks, configuration-management tools, quality-assurance techniques, and other techniques for standardizing production activities. These technologies are characteristic of the commercial stage of evolution—"software management" would be a much more appropriate term.

Scientific Basis for Engineering Practice

Engineering practice emerges from commercial practice by exploiting the results of a companion science. The scientific results must be mature and rich enough to model practical problems. They must also be organized in a form that is useful to practitioners. Computer science has a few models and theories that are ready to support practice, but the packaging of these results for operational use is lacking.

Maturity of Supporting Science. Despite the criticism sometimes made by software producers that computer science is irrelevant to practical software, good models and theories *have* been developed in areas that have had enough time for the theories to mature.

In the early 1960s, algorithms and data structures were simply created as part of each program. Some folklore grew up about good ways to do certain sorts of things, and it was transmitted informally. By the mid-1960s, good programmers shared the intuition that if you get the data structures right, the rest of the program is much simpler. In the late 1960s, algorithms and data structures began to be abstracted from individual programs, and their essential properties were described and analyzed.

The 1970s saw substantial progress in supporting theories, including performance analysis and correctness. Concurrently, the programming implications of these abstractions were explored; abstract-data-type research dealt with such issues as:

- Specifications: abstract models and algebraic axioms.
- Software structure: bundling representation with algorithms.
- Language issues: modules, scope, and user-defined types.
- Information hiding: protecting the integrity of information not in the specification.
- Integrity constraints: invariants of data structures.
- Composition rules: declarations.

Both sound theory and language support were available by the early 1980s, and routine good practice now depends on this support.

Compiler construction is another good example. In 1960, simply writing a compiler at all was a major achievement: it is not clear that we really understood what a higher level language was. Formal syntax was first used systematically for Algol-60, and tools for processing it automatically (then called compiler compilers, but now called parser generators) were first developed in the mid-1960s and made practical in the 1970s. Also in the 1970s, we started developing theories of semantics and types, and the 1980s have brought significant progress toward the automation of compiler construction.

Both of these examples have roots in the problems of the 1960S and became genuinely practical in the 1980s, It takes a good 20 years from the time that work starts on a theory until it provides serious assistance to routine practice. Development periods of comparable length have also preceded the widespread use of systematic methods and technologies like structured programming, Smalltalk, and UNIX, as Sam Redwine and colleagues have shown (1984). But the whole field of computing is only about 40 years old, and many theories are emerging in the research pipeline.

Interaction between Science and Engineering. The development of good models within the software domain follows this pattern:

We engineers begin by solving problems any way we can. After some time, we distinguish in those *ad hoc* solutions things that usually work and things that do not usually work. The ones that do work enter the folklore: People tell each other about them informally. As the folklore becomes more and more systematic, we codify it as written heuristics and rules of procedure. Eventually, that codification becomes crisp enough to support models and theories, together with the associated mathematics. These can then help improve practice, and experience from that practice can sharpen the theories. Furthermore, the improvement in practice let us think about harder problems—which we first solve *ad hoc,* then find heuristics for, eventually develop new models and theories for, and so on. Figure 4 illustrates this cycle.

The models and theories do not have to be fully fleshed out for this process to assist practice: The initial codification of folklore may be useful in and of itself.

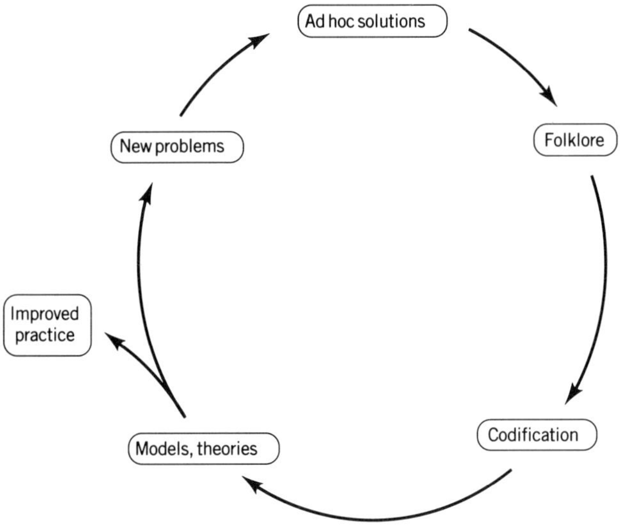

Figure 4. Cycle of how good software models develop as a result of the interaction between science and engineering.

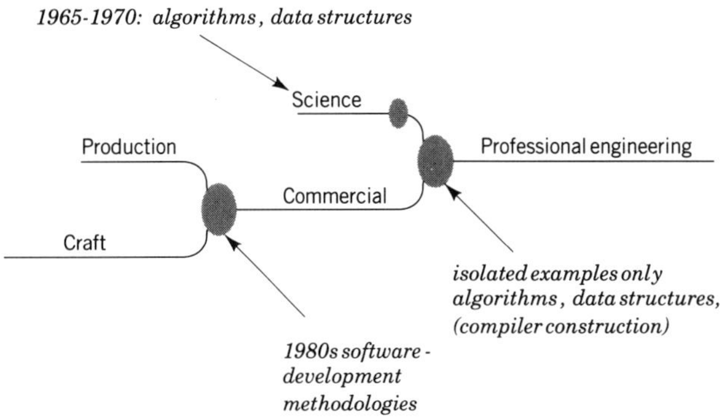

Figure 5. Evolution of software engineering.

This progression is illustrated in the use of machine language for control flow in the 1960s. In the late 1950s and the early 1960s, we did not have crisp notions about what an iteration or a conditional was, so we laid down special-purpose code, building each structure individually out of test and branch instructions.

Eventually, a small set of patterns emerged as generally useful, generally easy to get right, and generally at least as good as the alternatives. Designers of higher level languages explicitly identified the most useful ones and codified them by producing special-purpose syntax. A formal result about the completeness of the structured constructs provided additional reassurance.

Now, almost nobody believes that new kinds of loops should be invented as a routine practice. A few kinds of iterations and a few kinds of conditionals are captured in the languages. They are taught as control concepts that go with the language, people use them routinely, without concern for the underlying machine code.

Further experience led to verifiable formal specifications of these statements' semantics and of the programs that used them. Experience with the formalization in turn refined the statements supported in programming languages. In this way, *ad hoc* practice entered a period of folklore and eventually matured to have conventional syntax and semantic theories that explain it.

Where is software? Where, then, does current software practice lie on the path to engineering? It is still in some cases craft and in some cases commercial practice. A science is beginning to contribute results, and, for isolated examples, you can argue that professional engineering is taking place. (Figure 5 shows where software practice fits on my model.)

That is not, however, the common case. There are good grounds to expect that there will eventually be an engineering discipline of software. Its nature will be technical, and it will be based in computer science. Although we have not matured to that state, it is an achievable goal.

The next tasks for the software profession are

- To pick an appropriate mix of short-term, pragmatic, possible purely empirical contributions that help stabilize commercial practice and
- To invest in long-term efforts to develop and make available basic scientific contributions.

The profession must take five basic steps on its path to becoming a true engineering discipline:

Understand the Nature of Expertise

Proficiency in any field requires not only higher order reasoning skills but also a large store of facts together with a certain amount of context about their implications and appropriate use. Studies have demonstrated this across a wide range of problem domains, including medical diagnosis, physics, chess, financial analysis, architecture, scientific research, policy decision making, and others, as Herbert Simon described in the paper "Human Experts and Knowledge-Based Systems" presented at the 1987 IFIP Working Group 10.1 Workshop on Concepts and Characteristics of Knowledge-Based Systems.

An expert in a field must know about 50,000 chunks of information, where a chunk is any duster of knowledge sufficiently familiar that it can be remembered rather than derived. Furthermore, in domains where there are full-time professionals, it takes no less than 10 years for a world-class expert to achieve that level of proficiency (Redwine, 1984).

Thus, fluency in a domain requires content and context as well as skills. In the case of natural-language fluency, E. D. Hirsch has argued that abstract skills have driven out content; students are expected (unrealistically) to learn general skills from a few typical examples rather than by a "piling up of information"; and intellectual and social skills are supposed to develop naturally without regard to the specific content (Hirsch, 1989).

However, Hirsch wrote, specific information is important at all stages. Not only are the specific facts important in their own right, but they serve as carriers of shared culture and shared values. A software engineer's expertise includes facts about computer science in general, software design elements, programming idioms, representations, and specific knowledge about the program of current interest. In addition, it requires skill with tools: the language,

Table 2. Cost Distributions for the Ways to Get a Piece of Information

Method	Infrastructure cost	Initial-learning cost	Cost of use in practice
Memory	Low	High	Low
Reference	High	Low	Medium
Derivation	Medium-high	Medium	High

environment, and support software with which this program is implemented.

Hirsch provided a list of some 5000 words and concepts that represent the information actually possessed by literate Americans. The list goes beyond simple vocabulary to enumerate objects, concepts, titles, and phrases that implicitly invoke cultural context beyond their dictionary definitions. Whether or not you agree in detail with its composition, the list and accompanying argument demonstrate the need for connotations as well as denotations of the vocabulary.

Similarly, a programmer needs to know not only a programming language but also the system calls supported by the environment, the general-purpose libraries, the application-specific libraries, and how to combine invocations of these definitions effectively. The programmer must be familiar with the global definitions of the program of current interest and the rules about their use. In addition, a developer of application software must understand application-area issues.

Simply put, the engineering of software would be better supported if we knew better what specific content a software engineer should know. We could organize the teaching of this material so useful subsets are learned first, followed by progressively more sophisticated subsets. We could also develop standard reference materials as carriers of the content.

Recognize Different Ways to Get Information

Given that a large body of knowledge is important to a working professional, we as a discipline must ask how software engineers should acquire the knowledge, either as students or as working professionals. Generally speaking, there are three ways to get a piece of information you need: You can remember it, you can look it up, or you can derive it. These have different distributions of costs, as Table 2 shows.

Memorization requires a relatively large initial investment in learning the material, which is then available for instant use.

Reference materials require a large investment by the profession for developing both the organization and the content; each student must then learn how to use the reference materials and then do so as a working professional.

Deriving information may involve *ad hoc* creation from scratch, it may involve instantiation of a formal model, or it may involve inferring meaning from other available information. To the extent that formal models are available, their formulation requires a substantial initial investment. Students first learn the models, then apply them in practice. Because each new application requires the model to be applied anew, the cost in use may be very high (Shaw and co-workers, 1989).

Each professional's allocation of effort among these alternatives is driven by what he has already learned, by habits developed during that education, and by the reference materials available. Today, general-purpose reference material for software is scarce, although documentation for specific computer systems, languages,and applications may be extensive. Even when documentation is available, however, it may be underused because it is poorly indexed or because developers have learned to prefer fresh derivation to use of existing solutions. The same is true of subroutine libraries.

Simply put, software engineering requires investment in the infrastructure cost—in creating the materials required to organize information, especially reference material for practitioners.

Encourage Routine Practice

Good engineering practice for routine design depends on the engineer's command of factual knowledge and design skills and on the quality of reference materials available. It also depends on the incentives and values associated with innovation.

Unfortunately, computer-science education has prepared developers with a background that emphasizes fresh creation almost exclusively. Students learn to work alone and to develop programs from scratch. They are rarely asked to understand software systems they have not written. However, just as natural language fluency requires instant recognition of a core vocabulary, programming fluency should require an extensive vocabulary of definitions that the programmer can use familiarly, without repeated recourse to documentation.

Fred Brooks (1986) has argued that one of the great hopes for software engineering is the cultivation of great designers. Indeed, innovative designs require great designers. But great designers are rare, and most designs need not be innovative. Systematic presentation of design fragments and techniques that are known to work can enable designers of ordinary talent to produce effective results for a wide range of more routine problems by using prior results (buying or growing, in Brooks's terms) instead of always building from scratch.

It is unreasonable to expect a designer or developer to take advantage of scientific theories or experience if the necessary information is not readily available. Scientific results need to be recast in operational form; the important information from experience must be extracted from examples. The content should include design elements, components, interfaces, interchange representations, and algorithms. A conceptual structure must be developed so the information can be found when it is needed. These facts must be augmented with analysis techniques or guidelines to supports selection of alternatives that best match the problem at hand.

A few examples of well-organized reference materials already exist. For example, the summary flow chart of William Martin's (1971) sorting survey captured in one page the information a designer needed to choose among the then-current sorting techniques. William Cody and William Waite's (1980) manual for implementing elementary mathematical functions gives for each function the basic strategy and special considerations needed to adapt that strategy to various hardware architectures.

Although engineering has traditionally relied on handbooks published in book form, a software engineers' handbook must be on line and interactive. No other alternative allows for rapid distribution of updates at the rate this field changes, and no other alternative has the potential for smooth integration with on-line design tools. The online incarnation will require solutions to a variety of electronic-publishing problems, including distribution, validation, organization and search, and collection and distribution of royalties.

Simply put, software engineering would benefit from a shift of emphasis in which both reference materials and case studies of exemplary software designs are incorporated in the curriculum. The discipline must find ways to reward preparation of material for reference use and the development of good case studies.

Expect Professional Specifications

As software practice matures toward engineering, the body of substantive technical knowledge required of a designer or developer continues to grow. In some areas, it has long since grown large enough to require specialization—for example, database administration was long ago separated from the corresponding programming. But systems programming has been resistant to explicit recognition of professional specialties.

In the coming decade, we can expect to see specialization of two kinds:

- Internal specialization as the technical content in the core of software grows deeper and
- External specialization with an increased range of applications that require both substantive application knowledge and substantive computing knowledge.

Internal specialties are already starting to be recognizable for communications, reliability, real-time programming, scientific computing, and graphics, among others. Because these specialties rely critically on mastery of a substantial body of computer science, they may be most appropriately organized as postbaccalaureate education.

External specialization is becoming common, but the required dual expertise is usually acquired informally (and often incompletely). Computational specializations in various disciplines can be supported via joint programs involving both computer science and the application department; this is being done at some universities.

Simply put, software engineering will require explicit recognition of specialties. Educational opportunities should be provided to support them. However, this should not be done at the cost of a solid foundation in computer science and, in the case of external specialization, in the application discipline.

Improve the Coupling between Science and Common Practice

Good science is often based on problems underlying the problems of production. This should be as true for computer science as for any other discipline. Good science depends on strong interactions between researchers and practitioners. However, cultural differences, lack of access to large, complex systems, and the sheer difficulty of understanding those systems have interfered with the communication that supports these interactions.

Similarly, the adoption of results from the research community has been impeded by poor understanding of how to turn a research result into a useful element of a production environment. Some companies and universities are already developing cooperative programs to bridge this gap, but the logistics are often daunting.

Simply put, an engineering basis for software will evolve faster if constructive interaction between research and production communities can be nurtured.

Acknowledgments. This article benefited from comments by Allen Newell, Norm Gibbs, Frank Friedman, Tom Lane, and the other authors of articles in this special issue. Most important, Eldon Shaw fostered my appreciation for engineering. Without his support, this work would not have been possible, so I dedicate this article to his memory.

This work was supported by the U.S. Defense Dept. and a grant from Mobay Corp. 1990 IEEE. Reprinted with permission from *IEEE Software,* 15–24 (Nov. 1990).

BIBLIOGRAPHY

B. W. Boehm, "Software Engineering," *IEEE Trans. Computers,* **1**,226– 1241 (Dec. 1976).

F. P. Brooks, Jr., "No Silver Bullet: Essence and Accidents of Software Engineering," *Information Processing 86,* pp. 1,069–1,076.

W. J. Cody, Jr., and W. M. Waite, *Software Manual for the Elementary Functions,* Prentice-Hall, Englewood Cliffs, N.J. 1980.

Computer Science and Technology Board, National Research Council, *Keeping the U.S. Computer Industry Competitive,* National Academy Press, Washington, D.C., 1990.

E. W. Dijkstra, "On the Cruelty of Really Teaching Computing Science," *Comm. ACM,* 1,398–1,404 (Dec. 1989).

J. K. Finch, *Engineering and Western Civilization,* McGraw-Hill, New York, 1951.

E. D. Hirsch, Jr., *Cultural Literacy: What Every American Needs to Know,* Houghton Mifflin, Boston, 1989.

E. Levin, "Grand Challenges to Computational Science," *Comm. ACM,* 1,456–1,457 (Dec. 1989).

W. A. Martin, "Sorting," *ACM Computing Surveys,* 147–174 (Dec. 1971).

National Academy of Engineering, *Engineering and the Advancement of Human Welfare: 10 Outstanding Achievements 1964–1989,* National Academy Press, Washington, D.C., 1989.

D. L. Parnas, "Education for Computing Professionals," *Computer,* 17–22 (Jan. 1990).

S. T. Redwine and co-workers, "DoD-Related Software Technology Requirements, Practices, and Prospects for the Future," *Tech. Report P-1788,* Inst. Defense Analyses, Alexandria, Va., 1984.

M. Shaw, D. Giuse, and R. Reddy, "What a Software Engineer Needs to Know I: Vocabulary," *tech. report CMU/SEI-89-TR-30,* Carnegie Mellon Univ., Pittsburgh, Aug. 1989.

Software Engineering: Report on a Conference Sponsored by the NATO Science Committee, Garmisch, Germany, 1968, P. Naur and B. Bandell, eds., Scientific Affairs Div., NATO, Brussels, 1969.

H. Straub, *A History of Civil Engineering: An Outline from Ancient to Modern Times,* MIT Press, Cambridge, Mass., 1964.

F. J. van Antwerpen, "The Origins of Chemical Engineering," in W. F. Further, ed., *History of Chemical Engineering,* American Chemical Society, Washington, D.C., 1980, pp. 1–4.

MARY SHAW
Carnegie Mellon University

Q

QUALIFICATION TESTING

Qualification testing (QT) is a process that allows the contracting agency to determine whether a configuration item complies with the allocated requirements for that system component prior to operational test. It is normally peculiar to software that the government procures under contract using DOD-STD-2167A, and is similar to the later stages of phased acceptance test for commercial applications. QT includes stressing the software at the limits of its specified requirements. It is normally conducted on each software configuration item to make it easier to isolate errors. For some applications involving closely linked software configuration items, or in instances where thread testing is advisable, software configuration items may be combined for qualification test. In order to be predictable and repeatable, the QT process requires: documenting in detail the test to be performed on the software configuration items and performing the tests in the presence of agents of the contracting agency. For nondevelopmental software, items may be documented as formal products, but more often are documented as informal, internal products. The types of QT information for this category may include items such as design trade studies results, other design rationales, prototyping results, and test information. (Department of Defense Instruction 5000.2, *Defense Acquisition Management Policies and Procedures,* Feb. 23, 1991; DOD-STD-2167A, *Defense System Software Development,* Feb. 29, 1988.)

QUALITY ASSURANCE

HISTORY

Many of the precepts of software quality assurance (SQA) can be traced to the formative years of software engineering. As a discipline, however, SQA is rooted in practices traditionally identified with industrial quality control. Moreover, like much of quality control, SQA's growth has largely been fostered by concerns of the U.S. Military for better software and better control of software development projects.

The beginnings of modern industrial quality control (QC), however, were in industry, not the military. Formal quality programs were established at Bell Laboratories as early as 1916. During the two decades that followed, as mass production decreased the responsibility of individual workers for finished products, industry turned toward standardization and inspection to maintain quality standards. As manufacturing processes became more complex and more productive, statistical quality control was introduced in the 1940s to keep manufacturing processes within specifications. Most significantly for software, in the 1950s and 1960s QC moved beyond manufacturing to encompass formal programs covering all facets of design and development. (Dunn and Ullman, 1982, pp. 4, 5) W. Edwards Deming introduced his concepts of QC to Japan in the 1950s and 1960s. Joseph Juran published his first quality control handbook in 1951. Armand Feigenbaum published his first piece on "Total Quality Control" in 1957, a forerunner of his more recent work (Feigenbaum, 1983).

Thus, the quality control heritage of SQA. The history of SQA, itself, is marked by the ambiguity that attends the very term software quality assurance. Who is assured? More substantively, is SQA an organization, a philosophy, or a set of activities? People have applied the term to all three meanings. Any telling of the history of SQA has to deal with all three.

Starting with the late 1960s, several IBM locations were occasionally using the term software quality assurance, generally within the context of final product testing. Also, from time to time during the 1960s and early 1970s, requests for proposals for complex military equipment and systems would contain a paragraph under the rubric "Software Quality Assurance." The paragraph would require the contractor to conduct a careful test program for any software embedded in the product. Initial definition of a larger sense of SQA, one consonant with the still evolving formal programs directed to hardware design and development, appears to be first documented in a 1974 Army Specification, MIL-S-52779 (AD), *Software Quality Assurance Program Requirements.*

Influence of the DOD, Its Agencies, and the Services

MIL-S-52779 (AD) required that contractors address various aspects of software development and its management:

- The contractor's tools, techniques, and methods believed to influence the quality of the developed software
- Methods that the contractor would use to evaluate design and design documentation
- Internal approval of completed work
- Documentation of the contractor's standards governing the work performed under the contract
- Library control procedures for code and related data
- Reviews and audits, especially with regard to ensuring that the software, as it went through successive stages of development, would at all times reflect performance and other contractual requirements
- Connections between SQA and configuration management
- Testing, including plans, analysis of external specifications to make sure they were testable, test criteria, test control, certification of test results, test repeatability, and reviews of test documentation
- The means of detecting, documenting, and correcting software problems
- Control of the software of subcontractors

Matters such as preparation of software for delivery to the government were also addressed in a manner derived from standard military QC practices. With the notable exception of quality improvement, a topic not easily adapted to a single instance of development, MIL-S-52779 outlined the scope of SQA practices followed to this day. The specification did not identify the techniques, methods, practices, and tools that contractors were expected to follow. It simply said that these matters had to be thought out in advance and monitored to ensure their use during development. In short, MIL-S-52779 abstracted the essence of a software quality program, leaving the contractor with new record-keeping and reporting burdens but free to develop software as the contractor saw fit.

MIL-S-52779 and its later versions served as the model for several other specifications or standards: The FAA's FAA-STD-018, NATO's AQAP-13, and QSTAG 710, the last published by the ABCA (United States, Great Britain, Canada, Australia) Armies. In 1979 the IEEE issued P730, *Software Quality Assurance Plans* for trial use. P730 covered much the same ground as MIL-S-52779, although with greater emphasis on documentation, use of formal reviews reflecting the military waterfall development model, an implied reliance on verification and validation (V&V), and deliberate omission of testing procedures. A later version of P730, IEEE/ANSI Std 730-1984, intersects with IEEE standards covering V&V, test plans, configuration management, and the like.

These early documents dealt extrinsically, not intrinsically, with the attainment of software quality. It was not their purpose to prescribe tools and techniques for preventing defects, methods of conducting code reviews, test philosophy and technology, or the use of data to improve the quality of future releases. The intersection with other aspects of software engineering had only to do with monitoring the processes of software development and release. In short, the role of SQA was tacitly defined as that of a police or arbiter, certainly not as a direct agent to promote craftsmanship of inherent quality.

Moreover, following the usual practices of government contractors, MIL-S-52779 and its look-alikes were likely to come first to the attention of QC departments, reaching programming departments only if so routed by the QC people. Few QC departments knew how to interpret the new specifications. The rhythms (e.g., "Review of corrective measures ...") seemed familiar, but QC had never before danced to such odd music. Some help was offered by Lockheed's Richard Foster (Foster, 1973). His outline for a software quality assurance Program Plan looked familiar enough to anyone who had looked at the table of contents of MIL-S-52779 to reassure the reader that help was at hand. The real help came in an explanation of what software configuration management was all about, brief descriptions of certain kinds of software design documentation (e.g., flow charts), succinct definitions of some typical test methods, and similar programming matters heretofore regarded as foreign to quality professionals.

If few quality professionals were prepared to deal with the new SQA standards, few software engineers of the mid-1970s were impressed by them. Rather than saying how one could achieve higher degrees of quality, the standards focused on how one should document practices affecting software quality and evidence of quality problems. Many in the military, itself, felt the standards wanting. Mostly, the standards required contractors to generate a plan of how they would carry out a SQA program. The standards did not, however, define minimum acceptable standards. Conventional wisdom among cognizant DOD and Agency people was coming around to the view that the process orientation of SQA had to extend to a level of specificity unusual for quality programs mandated by the Government. Indeed, many in the military felt that the only remedy for the recurring problem of software project control lay in standardizing software processes. This was seen in MIL-STD-1679 (NAVY), of which more shortly, issued in 1978.

In April 1979, under the leadership of Gen. Donald Lasher of the Army, the Computer Software Management Subgroup (CSM) of the Joint Logistics Commanders (JLC) Joint Policy Coordinating Group on Computer Resource Management (JPCG-CRM) held a four-day workshop at the Naval Postgraduate School in Monterey, California. In later years referred to as Monterey I (A Monterey II workshop was held two years later, but dealt with a largely different agenda), the workshop was held for the express purpose of recommending methods for standardizing the software acquisition and development procedures of the Army, Air Force, and Navy. The JLC invited approximately 80 people from industry and government (both civilians and uniformed personnel) to take part in fashioning the recommendations. The 80 were divided into four panels: Software Acquisition/Development Standards, Software Documentation, Standards for Software Quality, and Software Acceptance Criteria. That a quarter of the workshop on software standardization should be devoted to quality issues suggests the importance with which the military viewed the problems of quality.

The software quality panel, chaired by the author, reviewed existing government quality standards dealing with software quality. MIL-S-52779 (AD) was one, of course. Of the other documents, the most pertinent was MIL-STD-1679 (Navy). Unlike MIL-S-52779, the focus of the 1978 Navy standard was on development techniques and the management of them. The Navy standard prescribed a diversity of programming particulars, although in a curiously uneven level of detail. Quality figured in several of these, including the requirement that the contractor's quality assurance organization "include provisions for addressing all the following facets of quality assurance." The facets were

- A QA organization outside that of development
- Participation in audits
- Participation in design reviews
- Auditing and examination of performance requirements and detailed design
- Examination of source code
- Witnessing of tests
- Procedures to assure contractual correctness of all deliverables (The actual wording was equally vague)

- Reporting of quality-related activities and follow-up of problems
- Escalation to mutually higher authority in the event of conflicts with other organizations (most notably, engineering)

Unlike the Army's MIL-S-52779, which was used for several procurements by the other services, use of MIL-STD-1679 was confined to the Navy, and not to many Navy contracts at that. Also, although a number of aggressive contractor QA managers welcomed government direction to overcome the reluctance of engineering in accepting QA's intrusion into the software development process, the standard was generally unpopular with industry managers. Still, at its release in 1978, MIL-STD-1679 was the only government document to tie quality activities to specified development methods. That is, it provided the specificity many in the Government believed necessary. In that respect, it was useful as a model to the Monterey I panels dealing with development standards and quality.

In the end, the panel on quality standards recommended that a modified version (rewritten on the spot) of MIL-S-52779 be adopted as an interim tri-service standard. The revised standard was released four months later as MIL-S-52779A. For the long run, the panel felt that a new quality standard should be prepared to track the development standard that would ultimately result from the recommendations of the Panel on Software Acquisition/Development Standards. The quality panel did not, of course, know exactly what such a development standard would look like, other than that it would be certain to reflect the documentation-driven top-down development process implicit in such military standards as MIL-STD-1679. The process to produce and release the standards was a lengthy one. DOD-STD-2167, which defined the development process, was not released until June 1985. Not until ten months after the February 1988 release of the next version, DOD-STD-2167A, was the quality standard released.

The quality standard, DOD-STD-2168, bears the title, *Military Standard, Defense System Software Quality Program.* It is officially designated as the successor to MIL-STD-52779A. The essence of DOD-STD-2168 is that contractors must establish a program to ensure that software projects are under management and configuration control, that the artifacts of development (e.g., design data) are evaluated with respect to quality, and that the final product is properly qualified for use. Interestingly, early drafts of the standard, the earliest of which were known as Software Quality Assessment and Measurements (SQAM), had emphasized evaluation of whether a contractor's development process was adequate to produce quality software (Baker and Fisher, 1982). We may also note with interest that nowhere does the standard expressly require the contractor to have a SQA organization.

During the drawn-out process leading to the 1988 release of DOD-STD-2168, the military continued to use and amplify MIL-S-52779A. One of the recommendations of the Monterey I panel called for preparation of a handbook to expand on the requirements of the specification. Under the title *Evaluation of A Contractor's Software Quality Assurance Program,* the handbook was released as MIL-HDBK-334 in July 1981. While the title implies that the handbook addresses the government personnel who audit contractors, it is in the nature of government handbooks that they find a larger audience in industry. Not only did MIL-HDBK-334 warn industry of what the Government would look for (or, at least, was supposed to look for) in auditing contractors' software quality programs, it provided industry with definitive interpretations of the sometimes cryptic provisions of MIL-S-52779A. (While authoritative interpretation was welcomed by industry, the fact that some of the interpretations extended the requirement of MIL-S-52779A was not.) As a crude measure of the extent to which the handbook amplifies the specification, the ratio of the volume of the two is about four to one.

Also, in the eight years between the release of MIL-S-52779A and DOD-STD-2168, the application of MIL-S-52779A to weapons system contracts became the rule rather than the exception. One after another major defense contractor established a SQA organization, usually within the quality assurance directorate, not because the Government expressly required it but for two practical reasons:

- A single point contact on SQA issues simplified dealing with government auditors and reduced the diversion of developers from creative work.
- It was less costly and more effective to use software quality engineers, rather than developers, to handle the various bookkeeping functions of SQA: tracking items needing correction, collecting defect data, and the like.

We can fairly state that the government initiatives during the evolution of SQA as a discipline, if sometimes regarded as much misguided as productive, were the most conspicuous agents for producing an awareness of SQA throughout all of industry, including the large part of industry not associated with defense work.

Beyond the Defense Industry

Notwithstanding the advantage that accrues to having a standard for SQA that tracks a standard for development, we have to recognize that the military standard for development, itself, was unlikely to be embraced by companies for whom the standard was not mandated. MIL-STD-2167A and MIL-STD-2168 were based on the military software life cycle model. While the model outlines a supremely controllable development process, it does not accurately reflect the way engineers and programmers actually design embedded software. For example, in no way does the rigid top-down military model recognize that designers, at the start of a project, attempt first to identify the kernels of the problem, next find solutions to them, and then build the system around the solutions, breaking the faith with top-down programming whenever necessary to ensure inclusion of the previously programmed critical elements. This failing of the military model was widely understood in both industry and government. Quoting the report of a Defense Science Task Force, "[MIL-STD-2167] reinforces exactly the document-driven, specify-then-build approach that lies at the heart of so many DOD software problems" (Defense, 1987).

Accordingly, it was not surprising that outside the defense industry the development of SQA, while still following the model of the military requirements with respect to the scope of SQA activities, branched out in several directions. (Ironically, the professional initiative that one would expect to have the greatest influence was surprisingly faithful to the military standards. The aforementioned P730 Trial Use Standard developed by the IEEE's Computer Society reads as though it were a military document. This can be explained by noting that the members of the committee that developed the standard were mostly employees of defense contractors.)

The main thrust of the military and IEEE models of SQA was in overseeing the efforts of software developers and designers, analogous to the traditional role of quality control. Yet QC, itself, was being reassessed by industrial management. Flirting with total quality management (TQM), Industry was coming to realize that the goal of quality was best served not simply by inspecting or testing products after the fact, or even after each manufacturing step. Quality had to be built into the immediate processes of planning, modeling of requirements, and designing.

The same holds for software quality. Although the MIL-S-52779 and DOD-STD-2168 emphasis on proper planning and conformance with plans would always remain pillars of SQA practice, attainment of quality was a larger management issue. We can see where the thinking of the late 1970s was going by looking at some of the chapter titles in a collection of articles on software quality management: (Cooper and Fisher, 1979)

- An Introduction to Software Quality Metrics (James McCall)
- Applications of Metrics to a Software Quality Management Program (Gene Walters)
- Software Acceptance Criteria (John Cooper and Matthew Fisher)
- The Applicability of Hardware Reliability Principles to Computer Software (Norman Schneidewind)
- Design Practices to Effect Software Quality (Lawrence Peters)
- Programming Practices for Increased Software Quality (John Brown)
- Software Quality Assurance Tools and Techniques (Donald Reifer)

The mid-1970s was also the period in which software reliability, certainly one of the prime attributes of quality software, started to attract as much attention as programmer productivity and project control. The attainment of software reliability was usually seen as the result of diligent implementation of the prevailing precepts of software engineering, with emphasis on development project planning, requirements modeling, design techniques, reviews, documentation, test case selection, configuration management, and test conduct. SQA played little or no part. A well-received book (Myers, 1976) on software reliability does not mention SQA at all. Three years later, Glass' book on software reliability (Glass, 1979) devotes four pages to SQA, but only in the context of SQA organizations, giving them the role of coordinating software control activities.

The 1970s conferences and symposia dealing with software reliability offered an opportunity for the fledgling SQA discipline to find an audience. A prominent 1973 conference on software reliability sponsored by the IEEE featured papers on reliability modeling, software modularity, change control, testing, error effects analysis, structured programming, and similar aspects of software engineering; and also two articles on SQA. The first of these, dealing with Bell Laboratory's development of the ESS 1 switch, used the term software quality control, rather than software quality assurance. Apart from the terminology, Bell Labs context of software quality control is enlightening: "... A set of rules and procedures used to guide the development, administration, maintenance, and improvement of the ESS program" (Bloom and co-workers, 1973). In a gross sense, this view conforms closely with the then emerging, larger, sense of quality control remarked earlier.

The other of the two papers on SQA dealt with an army development project. Interestingly, we learn that the project office, whose existence preceded release of MIL-STD-52779 (AD), believed that its contractors should establish quality assurance offices; moreover that the personnel of the offices can best evaluate emerging designs if they are directly involved with and participating in the design work. (Keezer, 1973). While generally this view has not prevailed to the present, the implication that quality engineers require high technical competence differed from the perception, which one could infer from the later military SQA standards, that SQA people were simply auditors and bean-counters.

In 1980 the state of SQA was more influenced by the quality management facets of its QC heritage than by such QC technology as reliability engineering. Although an attempt to map traditional quality control random sampling methods onto software test planning was published in 1980 (Cho, 1980), and some software quality engineers were attempting to use software growth reliability models in the late 1970s and early 1980s, most of the SQA activity was given to establishing and enforcing standards for ensuring circumspect bug detection, change control, documentation, and project control.

A view of SQA was published in 1982 that extended well beyond project control and the like to stress built-in quality, software measurement, and quality improvement (Dunn and Ullman, 1982). The book focused on SQA as a management tool, although it failed to clearly distinguish the tool from SQA organizations. Nevertheless, as a tool, the published vision of SQA, giving SQA's roots in software engineering as much importance as its roots in QC, showed consonance with recent developments-in design assurance.

The ambiguity between SQA as a set of activities—call it a management tool, an approach, or a philosophy—and SQA as a functional organization was common. Contrast Alberts' use of "SQA" as a set of fault detection techniques and tasks (Alberts, 1976) and Shooman's use of "SQA" exclusively with respect to an organization. (Shooman, 1983, pp. 413–414) In any case, the staffing of SQA organizations had drawn the attention of no few quality managers. Some saw SQA as another facet of design reliability assurance, and expected that their quality engineers could gracefully migrate to SQA as they had earlier migrated from, say, the quality of discrete electronic circuitry to that of integrated circuits. Still other quality managers viewed SQA as an opportunity to preserve the jobs of inspectors made obsolete by automated inspection equipment.

Whatever the expectations of quality managers, industry had many quality engineers, inspectors, and programmers on the payroll, but the professional software quality engineer was still an unknown save for the few who had qualified themselves through observation and study of the still slim literature of SQA. Dunn and Ullman (1982) made the case that, while one may increase the staff of SQA organizations with non-programmers, the kernel of a new SQA organization had to comprise software engineers who thoroughly understood the technology they would have to deal with. Not the least of the reasons for this was the need for software quality engineers to win the respect and cooperation of development people, who heretofore had run their own "skunk works" without interference from outside.

Although in the 1970s and 1980s one was most likely to find SQA in companies dealing with software embedded in their products, SQA had begun to find a home in systems programming and management information systems (MIS), the term that now includes not only dissemination of information but the programming of ordinary commercial applications. (Other current terms are IS (MIS without the M) and Information Resource Management.) As noted earlier, IBM units had from time to time since the 1960s referred to SQA. More to the point, within IBM one could find—at one location or another—all the activities lying at the intersection of software engineering and quality control. Capers Jones of the Santa Teresa Laboratories wrote about defect measurements (Jones, 1977) and the effectiveness of techniques (specification reviews, unit tests, etc.) for finding software faults (Jones, 1978). Michael Fagan of the Kingston laboratories had published the results of IBM's experiments in formal design and code inspections (Fagan, 1974 and 1976), a technique that has since been emulated in many companies. Albert Endres of IBM's German laboratories published remarkable findings on the distribution of program faults in the structure of large systems (Endres, 1975). Although he did not refer to it as such, Endres had used a standard QA tool, Pareto Analysis, to identify the few troublesome modules from the well-behaved many. These are but a few examples of IBM's ventures into work now associated with software quality programs and SQA.

Within applications programming, the greatest contribution to poor quality, especially for software developed by in-house programming departments, was inadequate testing. Indeed, it was not uncommon for some developers to consider software ready for use if the program could compile and load. Drawing on a 1982 experience, a Wall Street company called in the author to investigate the cause of recurring problems in an application package customized for the firm by an established software house. The author shortly learned that other than a check to make certain that the program could be loaded and terminated, none of the customized software had been tested before delivery. Quoting the project manager, "We expect our customers to find any bugs."

Not surprisingly, the meaning of SQA, when heard at all in the MIS world, generally referred to increased testing effort, particularly as applied to the deliverable package. Within this context, a SQA organization came to mean a test team separate from the programming team, occasionally the managers of beta test programs.

Verification and validation (V&V) was yet another meaning often ascribed to SQA during its formative years. Since progressive reviews (or inspections) and tests are common to both software quality programs and V&V, one can easily understand the confusion. When viewed from the perspective of V&V, SQA was usually synonymous with an organization rather than a management tool: "The quality assurance organization functions as an independent audit and evaluation agent to review all products for compliance to quality standards" (Deutsch, 1982).

Whether apart from organizational implications or intertwined with them, SQA by the mid-1980s had come to take on three distinct meanings:

- A comprehensive approach to improving software, the process of programming, and the control of software projects
- Diligent testing
- Verification and validation

A variant of the first, a view much influenced by the concepts of TQM, bypasses the organization-management tool confusion: "Software quality assurance does not assure [anyone of] the quality of software; it ensures the planning and execution of a quality program involving all three elements of the technology-people-management 3-tuple, the last recursively." (Dunn, 1990b).

During the 1980s, the first of the three meanings ascribed to SQA led to increased emphasis on analyzing the attributes of software structure (e.g., complexity) and accumulating and analyzing fault data. The current practices of data collection and analysis that gradually developed during the growth of SQA are described in the next section. Nevertheless, it is worth our noting here that reliance on data is intrinsic to total quality control (Feigenbaum, 1983), and is the substance of one of the seven categories of criteria for the Malcolm Baldrige National Quality Award (Baldrige, 1991).

We see data collection and analysis as one of the nine elements of a software quality program conceived by Bell Communications Research (commonly, Bellcore) in 1985. Bellcore, the research and engineering company jointly owned by the Regional Bell Operating Companies, analyzes the performance of telecommunications products (central office and other switches, digital multiplexers, and other elements of our complex telecommunications system) and the capabilities of the companies that supply them. Reflecting the critical need for reliability, maintainability, and other quality characteristics in telecommunications, Bellcore includes quality in its analyses. With the more complex equipments increasingly becoming software-driven, Bellcore initially based its analyses of software quality on nine criteria (Bellcore, 1985):

- Software life cycle plan
- Management commitment and organization
- Development support environment
- Documentation
- Verification and validation procedures
- Configuration management
- Problem reporting and corrective action
- Data collection, analysis, and use
- Customer engineering and operations

The criteria have since been increased in number, with some rearrangement as well (Bellcore 1989), but we may note that Bellcore's 1985 view of a software quality program conforms more closely with the broad precepts of both software engineering and TQM than the analogous standards published by the DOD and the IEEE.

Complex telephone switches are now based on up to 10 million lines of code. Certain software-driven military equipments also run to several million lines of code. Operating and database management systems often run over a million lines of code. More code is written for MIS software than the sum of all other applications. We would not expect the explosion of software volume during the 1970s and 1980s to have escaped the attention of senior management. Plainly, SQA, in all its several guises, as we know it today did not spring from the head of Zeus. SQA has evolved through trial, error, and intellectual energy in parallel with that of the other subdisciplines of software engineering.

CURRENT PRACTICES

Notwithstanding the precepts of TQM, which translate into assurance that quality attaches to every process involved in a business, the emphasis of traditional QC remains on measuring or estimating the quality of delivered goods and services. We see less of this emphasis in SQA, which increasingly is focussing on process rather than product. (However, most hands-on work performed by software quality engineers is directed to product.) We can attribute the departure of SQA from its parent to the essential distinctions between hardware and software:

- Hardware degrades with time, while software has the potential, if not obstructed by poor maintainability, of improving. Hence, attaining objectives of mean-time-to-failure (MTTF) for software has to do not with the specification of components and the like, but with quality improvement programs.
- Manufacturing quality is largely a matter of ascertaining how well a design has been copied. Copying software is trivial. Any preshipment inspection of a software product need merely be directed to making certain that the product contains the correct set of software components ordered by the customer.
- Hardware often warns of imminent failure. Software offers no warning, nor can quality engineers work out a program of preventive maintenance to improve the reliability of software. SQA must rely on the excellence of its defect detection and removal processes.
- Hardware can be built of components whose quality characteristics are known. Not until the reuse of software components reaches a higher plane than the present level can one estimate the quality of new software based on the characteristics of its constituents.
- The repair of hardware restores its original condition. The repair of software (i.e., removal of a bug) results in a new product baseline, and must be attended by change control procedures. The loss of configuration integrity can be as devastating to software quality as the loss of gauges would be to hardware measurements.
- Most hardware (dense VLSI circuits are a notable exception) can be tested over the entire spectrum of expected operational conditions. Not so with software, where the number of discrete program states is astronomically great. The result is that one can never know that software products are entirely free of significant defects. This list is based on one published in 1982 (Dunn and Ullman, 1982, pp. 8, 9).

Emphasis on Removing Defects

The last of the itemized differences between hardware and software leads in to the emphasis SQA places on defect removal. We can divide all defect detection activities into two categories, passive and active (Dunn 1990a, p. 80). Apart from the taxonomical distinction, wherein passive defect detection does not require execution of product code, the segregation of methods into the two categories distinguishes direct detection of defects (passive methods) from indirect detection (active methods) wherein only the presence of defects is indicated and further diagnosis is required.

Passive Methods	Active Methods
Reviews of requirements and design	Functional testing
Analysis of pseudolanguage design	Structural testing
Static analysis	
Code reviews	
Formal verification	

Note that formal verification, which usually translates to axiomatic proofs of correction (Hoare, 1969; Boyer and Moore, 1981), seldom plays a part in software quality assurance. For all our fascination with them, proofs are tedious, usually incomplete, and themselves error-prone.

Of the remaining passive methods, the last two apply to the removal of defects from code, as do both active methods.

Although it has been known for many years that the cost of removing a defect increases dramatically with the length of time the defect remains in the evolving software product (Boehm, 1976), few methods are in common use to detect defects in the artifacts of development before code is produced. Simply put, the representations of requirements-models and designs do not lend themselves to defect detection as readily as either source or executable code. Accordingly, with the exception of tools to analyze (perhaps simply display) the logic and semantics of designs couched in an artificial language, we are left with little other than manual reviews (or inspections) of requirements definitions and design decisions. At that, even the use of such tools is often limited to the more detailed levels of design. Nevertheless, software quality programs may include plans for the acquisition and use of such tools, and may include audits of their use by an SQA organization.

Given limited techniques for finding defects before they find their way to code, software quality programs generally include requirements and design reviews, usually conducted as peer reviews, but sometimes with the participation of software quality engineers.

Owing to their effectiveness at finding bugs, equal to and sometimes exceeding (Fagan, 1976) that of testing, use of code reviews or inspections is widespread. Static analysis of code, whether performed by compilers, special analysis tools, or both, augments but does not replace the practice of code reviews.

Despite the effectiveness of passive defect removal methods, testing is the sine qua non of SQA. Indeed, in MIS environments, SQA is sometimes synonymous with testing. In the context of SQA, in-house testing involves planning, design of test cases, often the preparation of test scripts or procedures, execution of the test cases, recording of results, and logging of any unexpected results or discrepancies. Software quality programs require that products be qualified through testing before release to the marketplace. (For software developed under contract, qualification may be replaced by acceptance testing.)

We might note that within the context of SQA, beta testing, distribution of a provisional product release to selected users for their evaluation before general release, is directed more to the evaluation of the usability of code, its robustness in ordinary use, and documentation (and possibly the adequacy of support) than the removal of defects. When part of a software quality program, beta testing involves criteria other than those supplied by marketing for selecting beta test sites. SQA also calls for meticulous change control and analysis and evaluation of results.

Where used exclusively within the context of defect removal, the term SQA is used with and without reference to an organization specific to SQA. Where an SQA organization is in place, it may mean any of the following, individually or in combination:

- An independent test team, usually taking over after integration testing
- Independent reviewers
- An independent group of people to oversee the review process
- An audit team to make certain that in-house and beta testing follow company standards

The first two of these represent the hands-on approach to SQA, while the last two are included in process-oriented SQA programs. Of course, SQA programs may include all four.

The prominent place that defect removal holds in SQA has, from the first, given rise to considerable confusion between the terms SQA and V&V. To confound matters, the distinction between verification and validation is often misunderstood. Boehm provides a succinct clarification: "Verification is doing the job right and validation is doing the right job" (Boehm, 1982, p. 728). The confusion between SQA and V&V is well-founded. Many defect detection activities are common to programs established under both rubrics. To clarify matters, the defect removal aspects of IEEE/ANSI Std 730-1984, a standard for SQA Plans, are largely relegated to reviews of V&V plans and methods, now described in IEEE/ANSI Std 1012-1986. Similarly, much of DOD-STD-2168 on software quality programs has to do with making certain that V&V activities (called "product evaluations") stipulated by DOD-STD-2167A actually happen. In short, both the IEEE and DOD standards on software quality emphasize monitoring aspects of quality control.

Elements of Comprehensive Software Quality Programs

Apart from SQA devoted exclusively to defect removal, more elaborate software quality processes are in place with the expectation that SQA will have favorable effect on

- Delivery of reliable, eminently usable, and maintainable products
- Control of programming projects to reduce risk of late delivery and cost overrun
- A general improvement in the quality of future software products.

The driving force for a software quality process embracing these three aspects of SQA is customer satisfaction. However, the last two additionally have appeal to senior management, who also are concerned with maintaining project control and minimizing development and maintenance cost. In this regard, we should note that the third aspect concomitantly entails improvement in programmer productivity, partly because the technology of quality improvement (as in CASE tools) also improves productivity, and partly because quality improvement implies reduction of rework.

Plainly, a software quality program addressing all three must be involved with all aspects of software development. As valuable in establishing and helping to carry out comprehensive quality systems as SQA organizations are, they are not intrinsic to software quality. As the principles of TQM put it, "A quality system is the agreed on, companywide and plantwide operating work structure, documented in effective, integrated technical and managerial procedures, for guiding the coordinated actions of the people,

Table 1. Elements of a Software Quality Program

Training programming staff in new techniques, methods, and tool use
Evaluation of effectiveness of current development methods and tools
Project, quality program, and test program planning as policy or standards dictate
Use of reviews, analysis tools, and tests to find defects at the earliest possible time
Library control, change control, distribution, and storage per project plan and relevant policies or standards
Recording of all defects found and follow-up to make certain they are corrected
Collection of defect data and subsequent analysis of defect, fault detection, and failure modality
Use of defect data to improve processes
Generation and analysis of various data for early indication of adverse product or project control trends
Product qualification
Gathering, analyzing, and evaluating user feedback
Survey of potential software vendors and surveillance of their performance
Objective evaluation of the fidelity with which plans and applicable standards are followed
Empowerment of staff to prevent defective code, artifacts of development, and user documentation from being entered into the system or delivered.

the machines, and the information of the company and plant in the best and most practical ways to assure customer quality satisfaction and economical costs of quality" (Feigenbaum, 1983, p. 14).

So too, for software, where quality is determined by the technology used, the caliber of the people using the technology, and the management disciplines applied to the entire process. In this context, Table 1 defines the elements of software quality programs as they have been found in companies committed to total quality control. Technically, Table 1 addresses software quality processes, not programs. Programs have defined end points; processes are continuous. However, programs is what they are called.

The last two items of Table 1 provide a rationale for establishing an independent SQA organization, but more on this later.

Each of the elements of Table 1 has been implemented at one company or another, and always in combination with several of the others. The elements of Table 1 also support upgrading processes to higher levels of the Capability Maturity Model published by the Software Engineering Institute. (Humphrey and Sweet, 1987) Level 3, the minimum defense contractors are expected to achieve, requires a defined and institutionalized process and people designated to lead process improvement. Level 4 requires a measured process and an analysis of process data. Level 5, the highest, requires that improvement be fed back into the process and also requires a rigorous defect-cause analysis and defect prevention.

SQA Techniques

Not only has SQA borrowed philosophy from its quality control parent, it has adapted a number of the parent's techniques as well to implement comprehensive software quality programs. This section discusses several of these techniques, selected to give the flavor of the entire set currently in use.

Pareto Analysis. The first of the techniques was, itself, adapted by QC from another discipline. In 1906 the Italian economist Vilfredo Pareto published a treatise on skewed distributions of wealth among various peoples. Decades later the quality expert J. M. Juran seized on Pareto's work to describe the process of separating the "vital few" from the "trivial many," as he put it. (Juran, 1964, p. 49) In Juran's adaptation, if the quality of a product mostly derives from only a few of the many processes required to produce it, these few processes should be the focus of any failure analysis and improvement effort. The conclusion seems obvious, but finding the vital few often is not.

The previous section on history noted the work of IBM's Albert Endres in finding that a remarkably small number of modules in a large system produced most of the errors. In particular, of 422 distinct modules, three modules (0.7%) were responsible for 15% of the faults, 10% of the modules accounted for 24%, etc. (Endres, 1975). Plainly, one would start an improvement project with the three worst actors, later moving on to the next lower tier of troublesome modules.

As another example of Pareto analysis, we can take an analysis of data published on fault type occurrences (Rubey and co-workers, 1975). Of some ten fault categories, two (erroneous data accessing and erroneous decision logic or sequencing) were found to account for 45% of all serious occurrences.

In 1989, in conjunction with a study to determine how to improve the quality of service to users of an overloaded data processing system, the author and an associate performed an (unpublished) analysis of the usage of the library of applications programs. Of 170 programs used during one month, ten accounted for 76% of all computer resource consumption. Obviously, the ten applications were the first ones earmarked for streamlining.

Pareto analysis can be used to determine if there are any parts of a software system that take an untoward time to modify (probably too complex a structure), or if only a few data fields are responsible for most of the revisions required of a database structure (more flexibility required). The literature describes still other uses for Pareto analysis within SQA (McCabe and Schulmeyer, 1987).

Of course, Pareto analysis does not always yield the answer that analysts hope for: the distribution of causes with respect to effects may be disappointingly uniform. In the absence of skewed distributions, analysts cannot assign priorities to improvement efforts.

Trend Data. SQA has adopted another standard QC technique, the detection and analysis of process variables related to quality and process control. The classic tool used in QC is the control chart (Deming, 1982), wherein one plots variation of a product, process, or service and compares the plot between constant limits. If the height of the nap of individual tennis balls rolling off the line frequently falls outside a specified pair of limits, adjustments need to be made. Since software management has few statistically

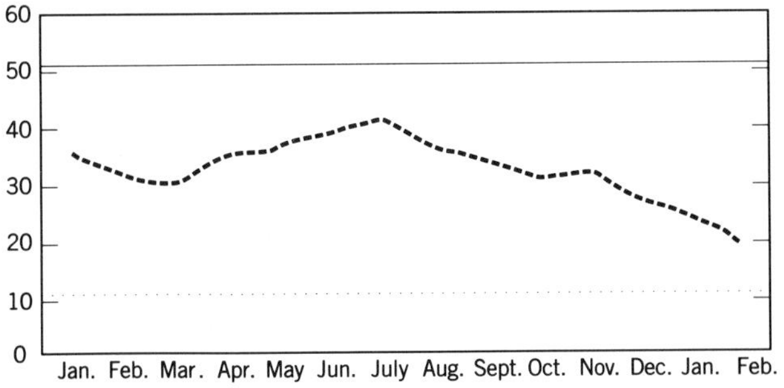

Figure. 1. Bugs/KLOC found in all integration testing: (—)Upper limit; (---)actuals; (·····)lower limits.

distributed variables to contend with, control charts are rarely used in SQA. For that matter, much of what passes for statistical quality control in manufacturing is actually statistical quality monitoring. Perhaps the most common use, if still seldom seen, is in the evaluation of defect removal results. For example, a code inspection that results in a density of detected errors greater than a given upper limit suggests disturbingly faulty code, while a density less than the lower limit may be symptomatic of an ineffective inspection (Christenson, 1990).

While not true control charts, though often mistakenly called that, a variety of trend charts that bear specified upper and lower bounds are used by SQA. The bounds reflect either experience or objectives. Figure 1, based on the author's own data, depicts the number of bugs per KLOC found in integration testing among all the projects of a company over a period of some months. Fault (or bug) density, rather than the actual number of bugs, is plotted to account for differences in test activity from month to month. A fault density falling below the lower bound suggests that integration testing is no longer carried out as assiduously as at earlier times. If the fault density rises above the upper bound, defect prevention and earlier defect removal methods (e.g., reviews and lower level tests) come under suspicion. The downward trend of Figure 1 would give rise to an investigation to determine whether integration testing is really falling short of expectations, or if, happily, the software presented to the integration testers actually contains decreasing fault densities.

Unlike charts of, say, failure rates, which indicate trend in the quality of a product, perhaps the widest use of trend charts in SQA is in the control of software projects, as in Figures 2, 3, and 4 (Dunn, 1990a, pp. 129, 133).

In Figure 2 we see the 95% completion syndrome, usually thought of as a testing phenomenon, exhibited much earlier in the course of a project. Brought to the attention of project management, the trend data demonstrate that remedial action (increasing staff, rethinking design strategies, etc.) is needed before the project becomes hopelessly behind schedule.

Figure 3 shows that testing is progressing more slowly than planned. Moreover, the rate of successful tests fails to compensate for the slower than expected test execution rate. Corrective action might take the form of adding a second test shift.

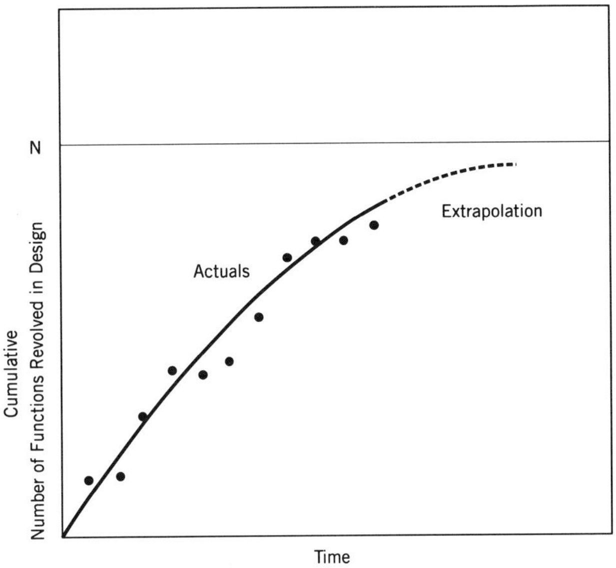

Figure 2. The 95% syndrome during design.

Figure 4 depicts a common problem in software development: ever-increasing estimations of machine resources. By the conclusion of Subsystem C design, management knows that it has a memory problem. The upper limit is not a statistical control limit, but an absolute limit. The chart shows that history makes no new estimate credible. Worse, the increments of additional memory required at each design stage are themselves growing monotonically. Remedial action in this case might take the form of redesign of the database, use of a more efficient compiler, or whatever; perhaps even abandonment of the project before more money is spent.

Various other trend charts have been used for SQA. Examples, all as a function of time, include cumulative numbers of reported and fixed problems, number of prob-

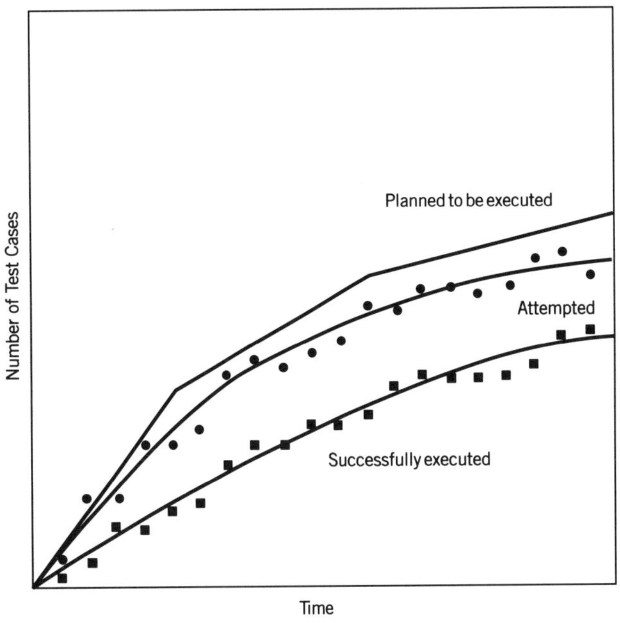

Figure 3. Testing: Plan and reality.

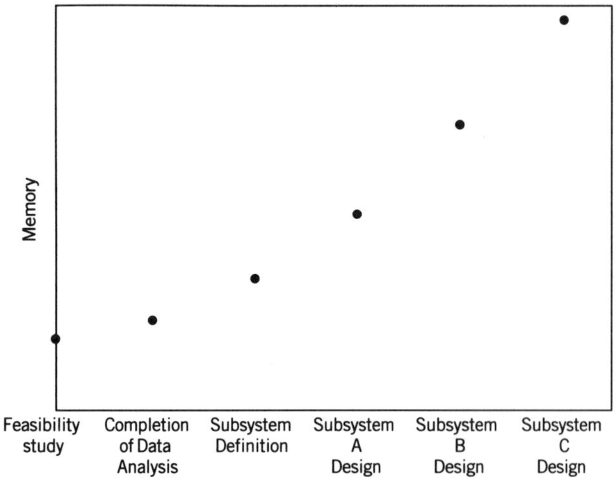

Figure 4. Growth in estimated memory requirements.

lems awaiting correction over several releases, planned and actual staff build-up, and the number of successfully and unsuccessfully tested functions or executed test cases.

Audits. Quality control has always relied on audits to confirm compliance with approved procedures. Among the audits used for SQA we can find both in-process audits and examinations of product. Examples include

- Records of procedures for control of code
- Documents audited to make certain that approved changes, and no other, have been made
- Minutes of reviews or walk-throughs, inspected to ensure adequate participation and correct logging of detected defects
- Test logs, examined for correct procedure and logging of bugs
- Change control documents, correlated with dissemination of the approved action or disapproved request
- Build sheets or files used for final product preparation, audited to ensure that the delivery has the ordered components (and none other)
- User manuals audited to ensure compliance with standards of format and inclusion of boiler plate information
- Project configuration management, and test plans; all audited for completeness, consistency, and conformance with applicable policies or standards

Reviews, which hold an established position within software engineering, are actually elements of software quality programs, whether or not such programs are conscious undertakings. Where reviews are held without the participation of software quality engineers, audits of the minutes of the reviews are held, as noted above. The material most commonly reviewed are planning documents and artifacts resulting from the processes of defining software requirements and designing to the requirements. Formats vary from the formal reviews demanded by the military or defined by IEEE standards (e.g., Critical Design Review) through highly structured inspections in the sense of Fagan (1976) to peer walk-throughs of technical design data or code. Formal reviews generally emphasize project status and customer comment on design decisions, while inspections and peer reviews focus on defect detection.

Within SQA, in-process audits are sometimes confused with reviews. Audits, however, are directed to seeing that things are being done in the correct way, while reviews focus on the substance of the material under review.

Many companies employ *phase exit criteria* to help control the progression of development steps. These companies inhibit the start of a given stage of development until the criteria for properly concluding all preceding steps are satisfied (or, alternatively, satisfaction is consciously waived). Audit reports often contribute to the judgment of whether such criteria have been met.

Failure Analysis. Failure analysis, a standard technique of reliability engineering, has found its way also to SQA. Software analysts look for common failure modes, correlation of failure with operating conditions, and the like. The results of the analysis of a failure or set of failures are used to correct the problem causing failure. Additionally, after they understand the cause of a failure, analysts assign it to one of several fundamental, rather than specific, failure causes (e.g., deficiency in defining operational requirements in a requirements model). Technical management draws upon such data to provide direction for quality improvement efforts.

User Feedback. Many companies have attempted to make it easy for customers to comment on the level of quality they find in the product or service they have bought. Examples are the service check-off card found in hotel rooms, quality-of-service questionnaires mailed by automobile manufacturers, and spaces left for comments on warranty registration cards. Similarly, software quality programs often include an aggressive effort to solicit customer or user comment on software products and service. Techniques in use include direct telephone or salesperson polling, semi-annual questionnaires sent to in-house users, and complaints from the floor heard at user group meetings. All of these, of course, antedate formal software quality programs, but SQA provides added value by tabulating comments, ensuring that unfavorable comments are followed up, and reporting comment trends. Determining the real needs of customers is somewhat different from learning their opinions of current product offerings, yet customer requirements also lend themselves to quantification (Gilb, 1988).

The most elaborate technique for soliciting user comment is beta testing. Again, beta testing exists outside of SQA, but SQA ensures that attention is paid not only to reported deficiencies but also to comments on usability.

Closely allied with customer feedback on quality, we have SQA's monitoring of customer assistance programs. Various statistics are compiled: waiting time on a toll-free hot-line, length of time to rectify a reported problem, number of times the same assistance is required (e.g., configuring a desktop computer application for hardware peripherals), and the like. Direct connection between customer assistance and the software quality program means that both favorable and disquieting trends in the customer interface will be detected and reported to the people who can either take action where needed or confirm that revised methods have resulted in improved service.

Direct Measurements of Software Products. Product measurements, a mainstay of quality control, play a major role in SQA also. Software measurements fall into two main areas: goodness and structure. Goodness is mostly a matter of the number of defects, graded by severity, known to be in a released product and its documentation. Plainly, no software producer permits truly severe defects, once discovered, to remain in a product. However, problems for which operational workarounds can be constructed or for which one has only subjective evidence are legion in operational software, fixed when time permits or perhaps not fixed at all for fear of generating bugs of even greater severity. An SQA imperative is to know the number of such bugs and to keep track of the trend of their population from release to release.

While one can conceive other measures of goodness, such as the time required to fix a bug (maintainability) or the time taken by a data entry operator to perform a given repetitive task (usability), none are currently standard in software quality programs. Staff of the Boeing Aerospace Company have proposed a number of quality indexes based on ratios. For example, usability would be rated as the ratio of "labor-days to use" to "labor-years to develop" and portability as the ratio of "effort to transport" to "effort to develop" (Bowen, 1985). While some of the ratios have intuitive appeal, they have not come into general use because of the difficulty in acquiring the necessary data.

The most popular structural measure in use is that of complexity. Though software complexity is a matter of one's perception (i.e., no absolute standards exist), and though most of the evidence of the relation between any complexity measure with software quality is anecdotal, opinion is fairly uniform that complexity is inimical with goodness. Typical complexity measures include McCabe's graph-theoretic calculation (McCabe, 1976), knot calculations (Woodward, 1979), and measures derived from Halstead's "software science" (Halstead, 1977). The first two are directed to control flow, while the last is a function of size and the number of tokens in a program.

Although less frequently encountered than complexity, measures of module coupling and cohesion have also found their way into software quality programs (Brandl, 1990). The metrics for these measures count the number of calling parameters, global flags, etc. One can posit other structural measurements related to quality, (e.g., data complexity and modularity), but such measures have not yet found their way into SQA. Indeed, the literature of software engineering has little to say on quantifying either of the two postulated measurements.

Statistical Methods. SQA employs fewer statistical methods than hardware QC. Nevertheless, some are used. One use of statistics attempts to compensate for the impossibility of completely testing programs. To avoid human bias in the design of test cases, a predetermined number of test data are often selected to randomly cover the input or output domain of the program. Carrying random sampling a step further, one can design sampling plans analogous to those used by QC for incoming inspection (Cho, 1980).

In addition to attempting to exercise the input or output domains through random data, one can use randomness to determine the extent that the program's structure has been exercised. Although not a common SQA practice, one can deliberately seed a program with faults before the start of testing and later use the number of seeds found during testing as a gauge of the extent to which the tests have covered the domain of the program. The procedure, of course, assumes random seeding. The key metric is the ratio of recovered seeds to total seeds. Going further, one can estimate the number of faults (including seeds) at the start of testing from the equation

$$\hat{N}=\frac{A\times B}{C}$$

where A=the number of planted seeds, B=the total number of bugs that were found, C=the number of recovered seeds. The effectiveness of seeding, itself, can be estimated from the ratio

$$E=\frac{B-A}{\hat{N}-A}$$

Testing normally yields batches of bugs. Each batch will produce an E_i and B_i. A line passed through the scatter diagram of the pairs (E_l, B_l) (E_i, B_i) ... (E_n, B_n) with a high correlation coefficient suggests that the seeds are being recaptured more or less in proportion to the total number of detected bugs, lending credibility to the estimate of N (Dunn, 1990a, pp. 131–132).

One can also compute the joint probability of finding exactly a of A planted seeds and n of N real faults from

$$q(a, n, A, N)=\frac{\binom{A}{a}\binom{N}{n}}{\binom{A+N}{a+n}}$$

which can be used to place confidence limits about a given estimate of N (Duran and Wiorkowski, 1981).

With or without seeding, bug detection rates during testing generally decrease in time when the mode of testing is such that one part of the system is as likely to be exercised as any other. After an initial unstable interval during which the rate of bug detection, loosely failure rate, may actually increase (possibly the result of the inefficiency often attending the start of a new activity), the rate often approximates an exponential decay. The exponential decay is usually attributed to the ever-decreasing number of bugs left to be exposed. That is, assuming that bugs are removed when found and that the instantaneous failure rate is proportional to the number of bugs subject to test, the failure rate will decay exponentially, asymptotically approaching zero (Shooman 1983, pp. 301–304). As a practical matter, since one cannot wait an indefinably long interval for a zero failure rate, one considers that zero has been reached when the time between failures exceeds some predetermined interval. For certain products (e.g., operating systems), perfection is considered unattainable and management is willing to settle for some suitably low failure rate. SQA cannot, however, accept that testing may be concluded simply because failure rates have reached an acceptable rate. The rate of finding new bugs may temporarily decrease for a variety of reasons having nothing to do with the total number of remaining bugs. To guard against premature termination of testing, SQA demands that no product be released until the trend of bug detection shows a steady decrease, if not necessarily an exponential one.

One can go further in interpreting failure rate trends by fitting confidence bounds to one's estimate. The technique is to attempt to model the growth of reliability (reliability function = 1 − failure function) such that an underlying statistical distribution can be determined. A number of reliability growth models have been fashioned, and in some companies models have found their way to routine use for estimating the results of further test activity (Musa, 1987).

Regression Testing. The repair of software is often attended by the generation of unwanted side effects; at best, unplanned changes in the user interface; at worst, new bugs. Software quality programs generally insist on a defined procedure to prevent such side effects from reaching users. A common method requires that all tests used earlier to qualify the product be executed anew after the repair itself has been checked out. If rerunning all the tests is impractical, a set of test cases representative of all parts of the program domain is used.

Without automating execution of the regression tests, as they are called, even the last may be impractical, especially if a fix must be delivered as quickly as possible to users. Automated regression test systems store both test scripts and previous results, run the tests in sequence, and compare the new results with those on file. A report is issued to mark any differences. Only if no differences are found, or if the differences can be waived, will the revised program be released to the user community.

Other Techniques and Tools. Quite nearly every software quality program uses a device of one sort or another to make certain that all discrete external specifications of the product are subject to test, perhaps in each of several test series. Traceability tools, as they are called, usually in the form of tables or directed charts indexed to elements of the requirements model, trace requirements to test cases. Frequently, the tools are used also to trace discrete requirements to specific design elements, although this is a less clean application since a given requirement may be implemented by several structural elements, some of which may also serve to implement other requirements.

Considerable detail attaches to the tracking of needed corrections, whether of software defects or deviations from approved practices. Usually, status is maintained through use of a database log of "correction items," to use the common, if unwieldy, locution. Typical of the database fields are reference number of the item, description of the defect or a pointer to the document where the problem is described, date and means of problem detection (review, customer problem report, etc.), person or organization to which investigation is assigned, date of correction, and date correction is confirmed.

Many quality managers have turned to Ishikawa cause and effect, or *fishbone,* diagrams to depict the possible causes of an undesirable effect. Ishikawa's diagram, fashioned with manufacturing processes in mind, has five main control points: man, method, machine, measurement, and material (Ishikawa 1985, pp. 63, 64). The diagrams have proved useful to focus the efforts of working groups investigating process problems. An example of such a group is a quality circle (Schulmeyer, 1987). In an SQA application, one needs to translate Ishikawa's five main control points to elements more appropriate for software. In the example of Figure 5, which has to do with the analysis of a hypothetical software maintenance process, we see man replaced by staff, machine by software development environment (SDE), and material by product definition (i.e., definition of the maintained software). Method remains method and measurement remains measurement.

To focus on a particular area, a fishbone diagram can be exploded iteratively by letting each element of a diagram give rise to a diagram of its own.

Cause and effect comes into play also in devising test strategies and individual cases. Although cause and effect techniques can be used to dissect external specifications at the most detailed "cause" level to derive test cases, as in Myers' cause-effect graphing (Myers, 1976, pp. 218–227), the role of the technique in SQA more generally is confined to specifications of greater scope. When dealing with less detailed specifications, as in the specification "Empty the queue into the track buffer when radar lock-on is confirmed," one is more likely to speak of stimulus and response than cause and effect. However, the idea is the same. The interactions of various stimuli and the responses to them, including responses not directly output from the computer, are graphed in any of several ways. An example is the System Verification Diagrams (SVD) devised by Computer Sciences Corp. (Deutsch, 1982, pp. 51–68). Each functional requirement gives rise to a graphical token consisting of the element and its associated stimuli and responses. Construction of a SVD leads to assurance that all functions will be tested; moreover, that they will be tested in predicted sequences—each dependent on input stimuli and each having predicted responses.

Various techniques have been employed to evaluate the quality of software products at given stages of development and at project completion. When fed back to development staff, such summaries serve much the same purposes as report cards, but to the end of improving products and processes rather than attention to studies. Indeed, *AYUMI,* which means report card in Japanese, is the name given the elaborate scheme used by the Telecommunications Systems Group of Fujistsu Limited (Toyama and co-workers, 1990).

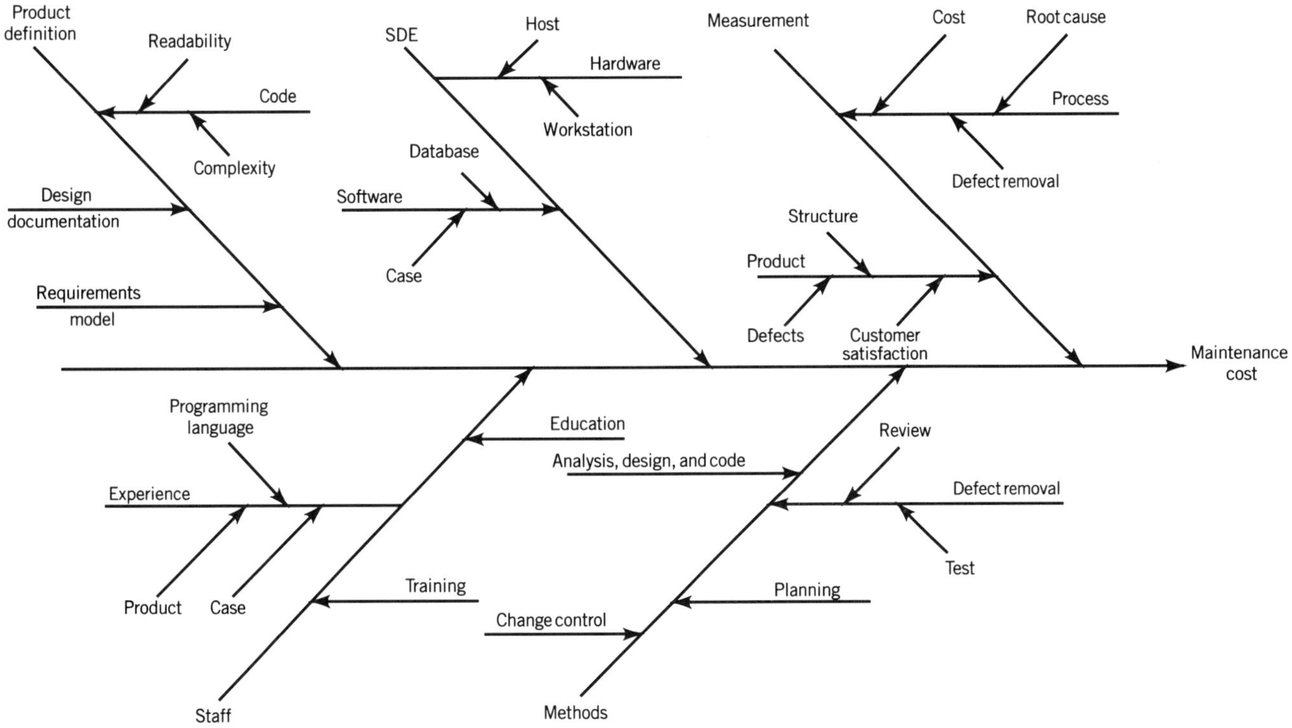

Figure 5. Process cause and effect.

Software Quality Organizations and Their Staffing

The various techniques of SQA have been applied by personnel having a diversity of assignments. However, many companies have seen fit to establish a separate organization for SQA. We may note that current quality thinking has cast doubt on the net worth of separate quality organizations, but more on that toward the end of the next section, The Future of SQA.

In the simple case discussed much earlier, where SQA is equated with a level of formality in testing, the SQA organization is an independent test team responsible for test planning and execution. An independent test organization almost always reports to technical management. This is an example of the hands-on type of SQA function in contrast to the QA programs in which SQA functions organize, implement, and monitor quality programs carried out largely by development staff. In more ambitious hands-on SQA organizations, software quality engineers also examine design artifacts, perhaps, also code, to detect faults. Most commonly, such independent review focuses on detecting deviations from approved design and coding standards rather than on program faults. Tajima and Matsubara (1984) describe the operation of such a program at Hitachi Software Engineering Co.

Whether hands-on or process-oriented, we find those SQA organizations involved in *all* development and maintenance activities in both technical and quality directorates. Placing SQA under technical management eases the problem of finding competent SQA staff at the expense of potentially concealing serious problems from senior management. Placing SQA under quality management ensures that disagreement between technical staff and SQA staff can be escalated to levels of management common to both directorates, but an SQA organization can be so located only at the expense of a potentially more difficult staffing problem. Undoubtedly, placement of SQA functions under technical or quality management has also been influenced by which directorate took the initiative to start a SQA operation.

However an SQA organization is implemented, Management expects a return on its investment in the organization. One of the most conspicuous measurements is the count of defects. Defect counts generally decrease markedly after SQA organizations go into operation. For example, Comer cites the experience of two projects that had a defect improvement ratio of approximately $2^1/_2$ to 1 (Comer, 1988).

The professional staff of an SQA organization are commonly referred to as software quality engineers. Industry has had more than a few problems in filling the staff requirements of SQA organizations. The fundamental staffing problem is that software quality engineers need to have skills in both software engineering and quality engineering. Either, of course, can be taught. Assuming that a candidate for a position as a software quality engineer has one of the two sets of skills, the candidate can be taught the other. In either case, the accepted premise is that software quality engineers must have technical credibility; not simply the ability to program in one or another language, but an understanding of software technology. Still, simple knowledge of software technology is no assurance of a seasoned staff. "Quality engineers can be taught programming concepts and methods, but they lack the essential ingredient of experience required to have an impact on the programming process" (Knight, 1979).

Not surprisingly, most software quality engineers are converted programmers. In a typical staffing operation, programmers interested in SQA as a management track position have received on-the-job training to qualify for their new position gradually. Technical has not always been willing to give up productive programmers, nor have enough programmers always been attracted to SQA. To get around this problem, several companies have instituted a rotation policy, wherein technical personnel have transferred into the SQA organization for a limited period of time. Rotation, or for that matter any transfer of personnel from development to SQA, requires earnest cooperation of technical management, who may be tempted to make their poorest performers available for quality assignments. It is interesting to observe that in Japan, which makes little of quality professionalism, engineers are generally rotated through the QC function on their way to or from design, manufacturing, and other divisions (Ishikawa 1985, pp. 23, 24).

The long-term solution to the staffing problem may well come from Academe. Several institutions offer, or plan to offer, degrees in software quality assurance. Examples are Mesa College in San Diego (AA degree), Wichita State University (BS degree), and University of New Mexico (BS). Other institutions (e.g., Arizona State University) offer courses in SQA, if not a degree.

Roles Played by Software Quality Engineers

While few words are required to describe the job of a programmer (e.g., analyst, designer, coder, tester, documenter), SQA staff take on a more diverse set of responsibilities. A 1983 survey specific to SQA in electronic data processing reported no fewer than nine categories of responsibility: system certification, enforcement of standards, three separate review categories, development of systems and programming standards, testing, development of control standards, and training. (Perry, 1987).

Without attempting to describe tasks applicable to any one specific software arena, software quality engineers have been found to play five different roles in industry (Dunn 1990a, pp. 159–173). These roles are described below, using the nomenclature of the cited reference.

Peacekeeper. More often, management uses "cop on the beat" to refer to the role of quality control in ensuring compliance to standards. However, *peacekeeper* suggests that software quality engineers not only ensure compliance, they also act constructively in helping to fashion standards that technical staff can follow without unnatural contrivance. The SQA technique of audits comes into play here as the basic element of determining compliance. Software quality engineers, of course, employ meticulous record-keeping to make certain that violations of standards are followed up.

Not uncommonly, standards are not followed because technical staff finds adherence to them impractical. In such cases, the resulting action may be to modify the approved practice, an action in which software quality engineers often participate. At the other extreme, technical management may disagree with the SQA finding, in which case the matter must be escalated to a higher authority. (We see the value of separating SQA from Technical here, since objective adjudication will be more likely if the problem is brought to the attention of management outside the technical directorate.)

Recall the earlier reference to phase exit criteria. Not uncommonly, forms are provided requiring the signature of a member of the SQA staff, along with other signatures, before a new phase of development may proceed.

In determining whether individual steps have been completed according to standards, SQA tacitly evaluates the status reports of programming supervisors. An element of design, for example, may be reported as complete, but an audit report may say that a number of problems were found that have yet to be corrected. Enough such reports will influence technical management's appraisal of the status of the entire project, perhaps in time for remedial action.

Surrogate. The primary concern of SQA is product quality: reliability, usability, and maintainability. (Each of these has several attributes. For example, maintainability includes ease of repair or modification, ease of adaptation to new operating systems, capability of expansion, and the like.) In this, software quality engineers have much in common with the ultimate users of the product. Through their involvement in reviews and testing, software quality engineers can see if the "ilities" are being built in and if the pursuit of defect removal is as thorough as standards demand. This is what the user would do if it were possible. Notwithstanding high level customer reviews for software developed under contract, users cannot participate in the process of producing software. Software quality engineers become their de facto surrogates.

Software quality engineers are most conspicuous in protecting the interest of users when software is qualified for release, whether release to beta test sites or to the general marketplace. Software quality engineers may have full responsibility for planning qualification tests and will certainly have a role in conducting the test. Participation during testing may be limited to control, as in confirming the integrity of test loads or seeing that test scripts are diligently followed, or participation may mean actual test conduct. Further hands-on activity may include direct examination of design and code artifacts. Whatever the extent to which software quality engineers are entrusted with the specifics of qualification, they invariably have authority to hold up release if they decide the product is not ready for release. As a manager of Israeli Aircraft Industries Ltd put it, "SQA authority shall as a minimum include release approval of all deliverable items ..." (Livson, 1988).

When software is purchased from an outside source, software quality engineers may act as surrogates for the users within their own companies. This activity is most prominent when custom software is procured under contract. Software quality engineers

- Review the contract or request for proposal to make certain that it contains appropriate clauses for
  - Quality of product and its support
  - Purchaser participation in the review process
  - Warranty
- Participate in in-process audits
- Assist in planning for acceptance tests
- Witness or participate in acceptance tests

Collector. Data fuel the engines of modern quality control. Most of the data that enter into a software quality program fall into five main categories: costs, defects, test status, product, and customer support. Most cost data can be gathered through the task accounting provisions of payroll systems. The other data are seldom collected in the absence of a software quality program.

When not the actual gatherers of all non-cost data, software quality engineers oversee the process of collection. In any case, data are their responsibility. Defect data—classified by source, detection method, modality, and the like—are gathered from the minutes or logs of reviews, output of static analyzers, programmer notebooks, test logs and reports, and customer reports. Test records, ranging from reports of test activity to seed recapture information, supply the information required for analyzing the progress of test operations. Product data include complexity and other direct measurements, the number of bugs known to be in a release, and (assuming use of a test coverage analyzer) the percentage of structure actually exercised in test. Customer data may include hot-line response time, completed service questionnaires, or whatever is appropriate to the product and the environment in which it is used.

Analyst. While we can scarcely say that the analysis of data arising from the software development and support processes is exclusive to SQA, it remains that software quality engineers are more likely than others to analyze data and evaluate the results as a routine part of their job.

The earlier discussion under *SQA Techniques* suggests the diversity of analyses found in software quality programs. Most analysis is directed to the purposes of improving products and processes and controlling projects. Additionally, however, software quality engineers are from time to time required to predict the quality of fielded software products, particularly with regard to reliability, but also with regard to structural attributes. For example, suppliers of telephone operating companies are advised not only to report the numbers of patches added each month to their software, but also to predict, for the forthcoming year, the number they expect to add each month (Erickson, 1990)

Although the experience of earlier products or releases usually influences predictions of faults and failures, software quality engineers also use measurements made of the product itself. Complexity domains of structure and size, for example, have been found to correlate with fault rates (Khoshgoftaar and Munson, 1990), and software reliability models have been used to predict future failure rates based on experience during testing (Musa, 1987).

Planner. Software quality engineers obviously are responsible for preparing and maintaining standards documents for SQA. Less obviously, in the preparation and maintenance of all other standards governing software processes, they assist in the preparation or review the standards or do both. When serving as coauthors, software quality engineers are more likely to focus on control rather than technological or managerial matters.

Software quality engineers generally produce unique quality plans for large projects, such plans often largely consisting of pointers to the specific application of company standards and documented practices. As with the generation and maintenance of company standards, software quality engineers have a hand in the preparation or review of such other project-peculiar plans as configuration management plans and test plans.

Quality improvement takes planning, too, and software quality engineers spend some time in recommending process changes based on the results of their data analyses. Less formally, software quality engineers comment on plans for technical staff training. They may, themselves, train programmers in such quality-oriented tasks as the performance of design and code reviews or inspections. In some companies, quality engineers have helped to start quality circles, sometimes serving as facilitators.

In a different sense of planning, we should also include the pre-award vendor surveys conducted in anticipation of the acquisition of software. Such surveys are often supplemented by carefully maintained records of past performance.

SQA Costs

The cost of SQA is only part of the total cost of software quality. Taking a leaf from traditional QC, we can break software quality costs into three categories:

- Prevention: actions taken to prevent defects in products
- Appraisal: inspections, tests, and other evaluations used to detect defects; alternatively, also the cost of removing defects before product shipment
- Failure: correction of defects; alternatively, only the correction of defects in released products

One may avoid the question raised by the alternative definitions by dividing failure into two categories: internal and external. In any case, SQA costs enter into all three (or four). As examples, prevention includes the cost of planning, appraisal includes the cost of testing, and failure includes the cost of tracking the correction of problems. In theory, spending money on prevention reduces the costs of both appraisal and failure, and spending money on appraisal reduces the cost of failure; hence, "quality is free" (Crosby, 1979).

While we see obvious value to tabulating quality costs to better weigh the merit of tool acquisition or the addition of personnel to certain tasks, the collection of such data is often difficult. Cost accounting systems linked to a payroll system are the most accurate and dependable sources for collecting labor costs, but not all such systems have the capability for task breakdowns congruent with one's quality cost itemization scheme. Nor can one always devise meaningful quality cost categories congruent with the capabilities of the payroll system. Put succinctly, "The Development Department is not in control of the costs of quality, the Accounting Department is." (Mandeville, 1990) It is even more difficult to collect the costs associated with specific defects, a theoretically useful ambition if one wants to determine the cost ranking of defect types and modality. However, special defect cost accounting systems have been fashioned for this purpose (Mandeville, 1990).

We can gauge some costs from published guidelines and experience. For example, one guide for a large switching system cites, for code reviews, individual preparation time of 125 statements per hour and total review meeting time of 150 statements per hour (Gannaway and Sabor, 1983). An example out of telecommunications experience speaks of 60 minutes as the approximate time to check a module manually, with an average result of 2 errors per module (Silva, 1986).

The cost of an SQA staff is a major factor in management's decision to implement an SQA organization. Most of the time, such costs seem to range between two percent and eight percent of technical staff, the range a function of both the extent to which a comprehensive quality program is undertaken and the extent to which SQA staff are responsible for the program's activities. On a project basis, project complexity, risk, and total cost also bear on the cost of quality programs. The costs of quality programs may range from as little as 1% for a simple project costing under $500K to 10% for a risky complex project costing over $2000K (Marciniak and Reifer, 1990).

FUTURE OF SQA

We can foretell some of the future of SQA directly from current trends in its practice. Other parts of the future we must infer from developments within other areas of software engineering that have yet to exert much effect on SQA. We start by extrapolating from current trends.

Much of SQA has to do with ensuring adherence with local standards for software development and maintenance (Dunn 1990a, p. 95).

> *There are three distinct levels of standards: The practices "everyone knows," documented standards, and the standards implied by the tools in use. The first of these have no place in a process directed to quality. The last represent the highest level, since they are integral to the process.*

With the ever-increasing use of CASE, especially for generating concurrent documentation of design decisions, we should expect a shift in the material audited. For example, rather than examining documentation files for compliance with documentation standards, software quality engineers, if they bother at all, will simply check to make certain that the documentation was produced by the approved tool. We have seen this in the past, when system build tools replaced the tedious checking once necessary to make certain that delivered program loads contained only the updated versions of each logic and data component.

We see a trend, also, in increased emphasis on the quality of direct customer support. This may, of course, result from the increased attention paid to total quality management. TQM places a premium on customer satisfaction, and the need for good support of customers seems especially acute for software customers. In any case, while SQA in its formative years was exclusively concerned with development and maintenance, and while today's practices still focus on getting software to market, the future will demand increased assurance of the quality of service. Such efforts to improve customer service as now exist were discussed under *User Feedback* in the Current Practices section above. We shall see more of this activity in the future.

Beyond extrapolating from current customer quality activities, SQA is likely to become involved in an entirely new sphere of activity; namely, recent developments in the use of telecommunications for customer support. For example, we may expect to see SQA activity directed to remote, on-line, diagnosis of software problems as the most direct and most rapid way to help customers in trouble. Similarly, we can expect SQA monitoring of direct on-line downloading of software updates, particularly with regard to ensuring that applicable updates, and only those, go to each customer subscribing to the service.

Interest in object-oriented programming continues to grow. SQA practices within O-O environments will have to conform to the O-O programming paradigm. For example, dynamic binding places a different face on the control of data. O-O programming lends itself to composition development models; those in which design starts with a set of defined pieces rather than ending with descriptions of pieces that need to be implemented. Composition models represent the epitome of software reusability. Plainly, SQA applied to composition models (whether or not in an O-O environment) will have to forge phase exit criteria different from those implicit in present day decomposition models.

If industry adopts the use of operational development models, we can expect major effect on SQA. The transformations that eventually produce code from executable specifications would, presumably, obviate the need to make certain that each development step implements the decisions of the previous step. On the other hand, one might have to deal with the problem of *ad hoc* substitutions of hand-written code.

The use of fourth generation languages should permit the shift of SQA resources from the verification of design and code to ensuring the correctness of the requirements model. This trend is opposite to another that we should expect very high level languages (VHLLS) to produce: The use of VHLLs for rapid prototyping allows a shift of SQA resources from the requirements model to design and code.

None of these trends in the technology of software development changes the fundamental role of SQA in helping to catch problems at the earliest possible time and in maintaining control of interim and final software products. As an example, there is no intrinsic difference between SQA applied to O-O's methods and messages and SQA applied to procedures and function calls of conventional programming.

The future of SQA will encompass more structural measurement than we find currently practiced. Consider modularity. The early years of SQA saw the average size of modules used as a metric for modularity; plainly, not a very good one. In the extreme case, for example, where a 10KLOC program comprised only four discrete components, one could speak of a low level of modularity. Later, SQA recognized that the average quantified complexity of the modules in a system provided a better estimation of modularity. Other measurements, such as statistics of the number of procedure call arguments, were also used as modularity indicators. None of these directly measures the essence of modularity, the sense in which the elements of a system are articulated. Research into truly meaningful metrics continues. For example, a *design stability metric* has been proposed based on the number of modules that can be affected by changes to the internal specifications of other modules in the system (Yau and Collofello, 1985).

Current industrial-strength analysis tools even now provide structural measurements that were largely impractical a few years ago. We now see the use of automatically generated program graphs, where-used tables, and the like. The use of such measurements, which add to the effectiveness of reviews or reduce the time they take, will become more widespread in the future. Similarly, structural test coverage as reported by dynamic test coverage tools will make common the use of coverage criteria in determining test sufficiency. Some programming shops do so today, but we can expect that structural coverage criteria will enter into nearly all SQA policies by the twenty-first century.

Looking at an entirely different force driving software engineering, we can expect the influence on military contractors exerted by the SEI's Capability Maturity Model (CMM) to spill over into civilian markets as well. There is, after all, nothing intrinsically military about the model, which in fact is ".. based on principles enunciated by W. A. Shewhart at the Bell Telephone Laboratories in the 1930s and further promulgated by W. E. Deming and J. M. Juran in their process-improvement work in Japan and the US after World War II" (Humphrey and Curtis, 1991). The emphasis of CMM on process and measurement encourages the measurements, defect prevention, and process improvement aspects of SQA as framed by Table 1.

These same aspects are also reinforced by the prevention orientation of the Malcolm Baldridge National Quality Award, with its concomitant emphasis on process and measurement and analysis. Beyond the companies that actually apply for the award, a far greater number of companies are using the Award's examination criteria for self-assessment.

Continuing to posit trends in the future, the farthest reaching ones may have nothing to do with technology or process, as have those above. Management philosophy may have even greater effect. Industry is beginning to look at the Japanese model of TQM (The Baldrige Award was inspired by, if not modeled after, Japan's Deming Award), which distributes responsibility for quality among the workers of all the operating divisions of the company, unlike the western concept of a separate quality organization staffed by quality professionals. The Cadillac company, for example, which won the Baldrige Award in 1990, disbanded its quality department in 1988. If a trend toward the Japanese model takes hold, we should expect a reversal of the current trend toward establishing SQA organizations where none had been before. Of course, the activities of measurement, analysis, defect removal, and so forth will still be performed.

Whether having a Japanese or a Western flavor, the growing acceptance of TQM principles will demand a more compelling view of SQA than is now common. While most current SQA programs fall short of fulfilling all the activities of Table 1, individual offices picking and choosing as they see fit, the present trend in industry toward more pervasive quality programs will result in an ever-increasing number of SQA programs that implement not a subset, but all the elements of Table 1.

BIBLIOGRAPHY

D. Alberts, "The Economics of Software Quality Assurance," *Proceedings 1976 NCC Conference,* Vol. 45, AFIPS Press, New York, 1976.

1991 Application Guidelines, Malcolm Baldrige National Quality Award Office, National Institute of Standards and Technology, Gaithersburg, Md. 1991.

E. Baker and M. Fisher, "A Software Quality Framework," *Concepts,* Vol. 5, No. 4, Defense Systems Management College, Fort Belvoir, Va., Autumn 1982, pp. 95–107.

Bellcore, *Software Quality Program Analysis Criteria,* Technical Advisory TA-TSY-000179, Bell Communications Research, Red Bank, N.J., Feb. 1985.

Bellcore, *Software Quality Program Generic Requirements (SQPR),* Technical Reference TR-TSY-000179, Bell Communications Research, Red Bank, N.J., July 1989.

S. Bloom, M. McPheters, S. Tsiang, "Software Quality Control," *Record 1973 IEEE Symposium on Computer Software Reliability,* IEEE, New York, Apr.–May 1973, pp. 107–116.

B. Boehm, "Software Engineering," *IEEE Transactions on Computers,* Vol C-25, Dec. 1976, pp. 1226–1241.

B. Boehm, *Software Engineering Economics,* Prentice Hall, Englewood Cliffs, N.J., 1982.

T. Bowen, G. Wigle, and J. Tsai, *Specification of Software Quality Attributes,* Report RADC-TR-85-37, Boeing Aerospace Company, Seattle, Feb. 1985.

R. Boyer and J. Strother Moore, *The Correctness Problem in Computer Science,* Academic Press, London, 1981.

D. Brandl, "Quality Measures in Design," *Software Engineering Notes,* Vol. 15, ACM Press, 1990, pp. 68–72.

C. Cho, *An Introduction to Software Quality Control,* Wiley, New York, 1980.

D. Christenson, S. Huang, and A. Lamperez, "Statistical Quality Control Applied to Code Inspections," *IEEE Journal on Selected Areas in Communications,* **8,** 196–200 (Feb. 1990).

E. Comer, "Software Quality Engineering: Making the Myth a Reality," *Proceedings: Annual National Joint Conference on Software Quality and Reliability,* NSIA, Washington, 1988, pp. 329–338.

J. Cooper and M. Fisher, *Software Quality Management,* Petrocelli, New York/Princeton, 1979.

P. Crosby, *Quality is Free,* McGraw-Hill Book Co., Inc., New York, 1979.

Defense 1987, *Report on Military Software,* Defense Science Task Force, U.S. Government Printing office, Washington, D.C., 1987.

W. E. Deming, *Quality, Productivity, and Competitive Position,* MIT Press, Cambridge, 1982.

M. Deutsch, *Software Verification and Validation: Realistic Project Approaches,* Prentice-Hall, Englewood Cliffs, N.J., 1982.

R. Dunn, *Software Quality: Concepts and Plans,* Prentice-Hall, Englewood Cliffs, N.J. 1990a.

R. Dunn, "SQA: A Management Perspective," in E. Yourdon, *American Programmer,* 21–25 (Nov. 1990b).

R. Dunn and R. Ullman, *Quality Assurance for Computer Software,* McGraw-Hill, New York, 1982.

J. W. Duran and J. J. Wiorkowski, "Capture-Recapture Sampling for Estimating Software Error Content," *IEEE Transactions on Software Engineering,* **SE-7**, 147–148 (Jan. 1981).

A. Endres, "An Analysis of Errors and Their Causes in System Programs," *IEEE Transactions on Software Engineering,* **SE-1,** 140–19 (Jan. 1975).

R. Erickson, D. Saxena, and G. Brush, "A View of Reliability and Quality Measurements for Telecommunications Systems, *IEEE Journal on Selected Areas in Communications* **8,** 219–223 (Feb. 1990).

M. Fagan, "Design and Code Inspections and Process Control in the Development of Programs," *Technical Report tr 21.572,* IBM Corp., Kingston, Dec. 1974.

M. Fagan, "Design and Code Inspections to Reduce Errors in Program Development," *IBM Systems Journal,* No. 3, 1976, pp. 182–211.

A. Feigenbaum, *Total Quality Control* 3rd ed., McGraw-Hill Book Co., Inc., New York, 1983.

R. Foster, *Introduction to Software Quality Assurance,* published by the author, San Jose, 1973.

A. Gannaway and W. Sabor, "Establishing a Software Quality Assurance Group," *Proceedings, ITT Conference on Programming Productivity & Quality,* ITT Corp., New York, June 1983, pp. 104–108.

T. Gilb, *Principles of Software Engineering and Management,* Addison-Wesley, Wokingham, U.K., 1988.

R. Glass, *Software Reliability Handbook,* Prentice-Hall, Englewood Cliffs, N.J., 1979.

M. Halstead, *Elements of Software Science,* Elsevier-North Holland, New York, 1977.

C. A. R. Hoare, "An Axiomatic Basis for Computer Programming," *CACM* **12,** pp. 576–583 (Oct. 1969).

W. Humphrey and B Curtis, "Comments on 'A Critical Look'," *IEEE Software,* 42–48 (July 1991).

W. Humphrey and W. Sweet, "A Method for Assessing the Software Engineering Capability of Contractors," *Tech. Report CMU/SEI-87-TR-23,* Software Engineering Institute, Carnegie Mellon University, Pittsburgh, Pa., 1987.

K. Ishikawa, *What Is Total Quality Control? The Japanese Way,* translated by D. Lu, Prentice Hall, Englewood Cliffs, N.J., 1985.

C. Jones, "Program Quality and Programmer Productivity," *IBM Technical Report TR 02.76,* IBM Corp., San Jose, 1977, pp. 42–78.

C. Jones, "Measuring Programming Quality and Productivity," *IBM Systems Journal* **17,** 39–63 (1978).

J. M. Juran, *Managerial Breakthrough,* McGraw-Hill, New York, 1964.

E. Keezer, "Practical Experiences in Establishing Software Quality Assurance," *Record 1973 IEEE Symposium on Computer Software Reliability,* April–May 1973, pp. 132–35.

T. Khoshogoftaar and J. Munson, "Predicting Software Development Metrics Using Software Complexity Metrics," *IEEE Journal on Selected Areas in Communications* **8,** 253–261 (Feb. 1990).

B. Knight, "Organizational Planning for Software Quality," in J. Cooper and M. Fisher, eds., *Software Quality Management,* Petrocelli Books, New York, 1979, pp. 83–99.

B. Livson, "A Practical Approach to Software Quality Assurance," *Software Engineering Notes,* **13,** ACM Press, 1988, pp. 45–48.

W. Mandeville, "Software Costs of Quality," *IEEE Journal on Selected Areas in Communications,* **8,** 315–318 (Feb. 1990).

J. Marciniak and D. Reifer, *Software Acquisition Management: Managing the Acquisition of Custom Software Systems,* John Wiley & Sons, New York, 1990, p. 228.

T. McCabe, "A Complexity Measure," *IEEE Transactions on Software Engineering* **SE-2,** 308–320 (Dec. 1976).

T. McCabe and G. Schulmeyer, "The Pareto Principle Applied to Software Quality Assurance," in G. Schulmeyer and J. McManus, eds., *Handbook of Software Quality Assurance,* G. Schulmeyer and J. McManus, eds., Van Nostrand Reinhold, New York, 1987, pp. 178–210.

J. Musa, A. Iannino, and K. Okumoto, *Software Reliability: Measurements, Prediction, Application,* McGraw-Hill, New York, 1987.

G. Myers, *Software Reliability: Principles and Practices,* Wiley-Interscience, New York, 1976.

W. Perry, "Effective Methods of EDP Quality Assurance," G. Schulmeyer and J. McManus, eds., *Handbook of Software Quality Assurance,* Van Nostrand Reinhold, New York, 1987, pp. 408–430.

R. Rubey, J. Dana, and P. Biche, "Quantitative Aspects of Software Validation," *IEEE Transactions on Software Engineering* **SE-1,** 150–155 (Jan. 1975).

G. G. Schulmeyer, "Software Quality Lessons from the Quality Experts," G. Schulmeyer and J. McManus, eds., *Handbook of Software Quality Assurance,* Van Nostrand Reinhold, New York, 1987, pp. 25–45.

M. Shooman, *Software Engineering: Design, Reliability, and Management,* McGraw-Hill Book Co., New York, 1983.

M. Silva, "Introducing Software Quality Engineering into Telecommunications Development Environment," *IEEE Journal on Selected Areas in Communications,* **7,** pp. 1026–1031 (Oct. 1986).

D. Tajima and T. Matsubara, "Inside the Japanese Software Factory," *Computer,* 34–43 (March 1984).

M. Toyama, M. Sugawara and K. Nakamura, "High-Quality Software Development System—AYUMI," *Selected Areas in Communications* **8**(2), 201–209 (Feb. 1990).

M. Woodward and co-workers, "A Measure of Control Flow Complexity in Program Text," *IEEE Transactions in Software Engineering,* **SE-5,** 45–50 (Jan. 1979).

S. Yau and J. Collofello, "Design Stability Measures for Software Maintenance," *IEEE Transactions in Software Engineering,* **SE-11,** 849–856 (Sept. 1985).

Robert H. Dunn
Systems for Quality Software

QUALITY FACTORS

INTRODUCTION

All engineering disciplines have some basis in measurement. Software quality measurement frameworks have

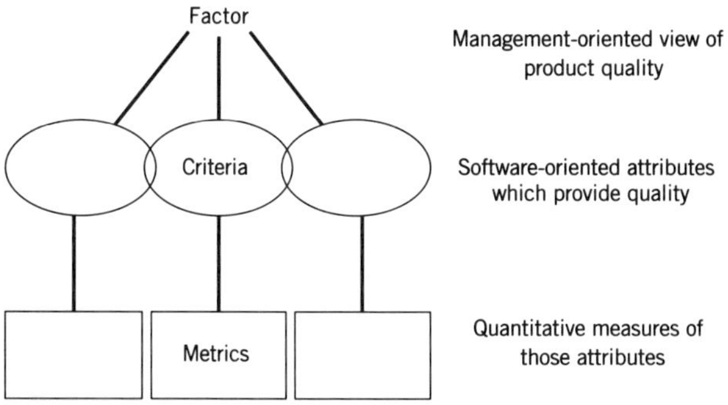

Figure 1. Software quality framework.

been developed to provide a measurement approach for software engineering.

The frameworks have a common structure illustrated in Figure 1. At the highest level of the framework are quality factors. These quality factors comprise a definition of software quality and represent attributes or characteristics of the software that a user, or customer of the software product, would relate to its overall quality. The second level of the framework provides the criteria or software attributes that relate to the factors, and their existence provides the related characteristics of quality. The third level provides the "metrics" or measurements that measure the degree to which those attributes exist.

The quality factors provide:

- A goal-oriented methodology for measuring software quality,
- Another dimension by which software requirements can be addressed complimenting the traditional, functional, schedule and budgetary requirements, typically specified, for a software product,
- A life cycle perspective to software, ie, identifying attributes important in a software product that will have impact later in its life cycle,
- A basis for process improvement (TQM).

HISTORY

The concept of quality factors originated in the late 1970s in conjunction with the research and development of software measurement technology. The focus on quality and measurement were complimentary to the "structured programming revolution" that was in process at that time. The factors provide the definitions of quality required of a software product. The software measurements, or "metrics," provide the technology by which the factors could be measured. Early work was done by Boehm (Boehm, 1978), sponsored by the then National Bureau of Standards, McCall, Walters and Richards (McCall, 1977), and Cavano and McCall (Cavano, 1978), sponsored by the U.S. Air Force Rome Air Development Center. These efforts had much in common, identifying sets of factors or characteristics, related attributes and criteria, and metrics. Boehm took a utility view in identifying seven characteristics of quality while McCall and co-workers took a life-cycle view in identifying 11 factors of quality. These perspectives and their related sets of quality factors are shown in Figure 2. The McCall work also had extended the concept of metrics from measures of code characteristics to also include measurements early in the development phases (requirements and design) and in later phases (testing and maintenance). Further development by Bowen (Bowen, 1985), Murine (Murine, 1983), and others (Grady, 1980), (Deutsch, 1988), (Evans, 1985), (Arthur, 1985), have refined the factors or added additional factors to consider. Table 1 compares factors identified by other efforts.

In each case, the factors are given formal definitions. Table 2 provides the definitions offered in McCall (1977). Less formal definitions are shown in Figure 3, which relates the factors to a life cycle perspective. For example, a customer or user of a newly developed software product is initially concerned, from a quality viewpoint, with how well that product operates. For example, does it perform the functions desired correctly, reliability, as efficiently as required, so that the user can operate it well, and in some cases, securely? If the product is going to be used for any

Table 1. Example Quality Factors

McCall, 1977	Boehm, 1978	Bowen, 1985	Murine, 1983	Others[a]
Correctness		Correctness	Correctness	Correctness
Reliability	Reliability	Reliability	Reliability	Reliability
Efficiency	Efficiency	Efficiency	Efficiency	Efficiency
Usability	Human Engineering	Usability	Usability	Usability
Integrity		Integrity	Integrity	Integrity
Maintainability	Understandability	Maintainability	Maintainability	Maintainability
Flexibility	Modifiability	Flexibility	Flexibility	Flexibility
Testability	Testability	Verifiability	Testability	Testability
Portability	Portability	Portability	Portability	Portability
Reusability		Reusability	Reusability	Reusability
Interoperability		Interoperability	Interoperability	Interoperability
		Survivability		Survivability
			Intraoperability	Safety
		Expandability		Manageability
				Functionality
				Supportability

[a] Grady and Caswell (1987); Deutsch and Willis (1988); Evans and Marciniak (1985); Arthur (1985).

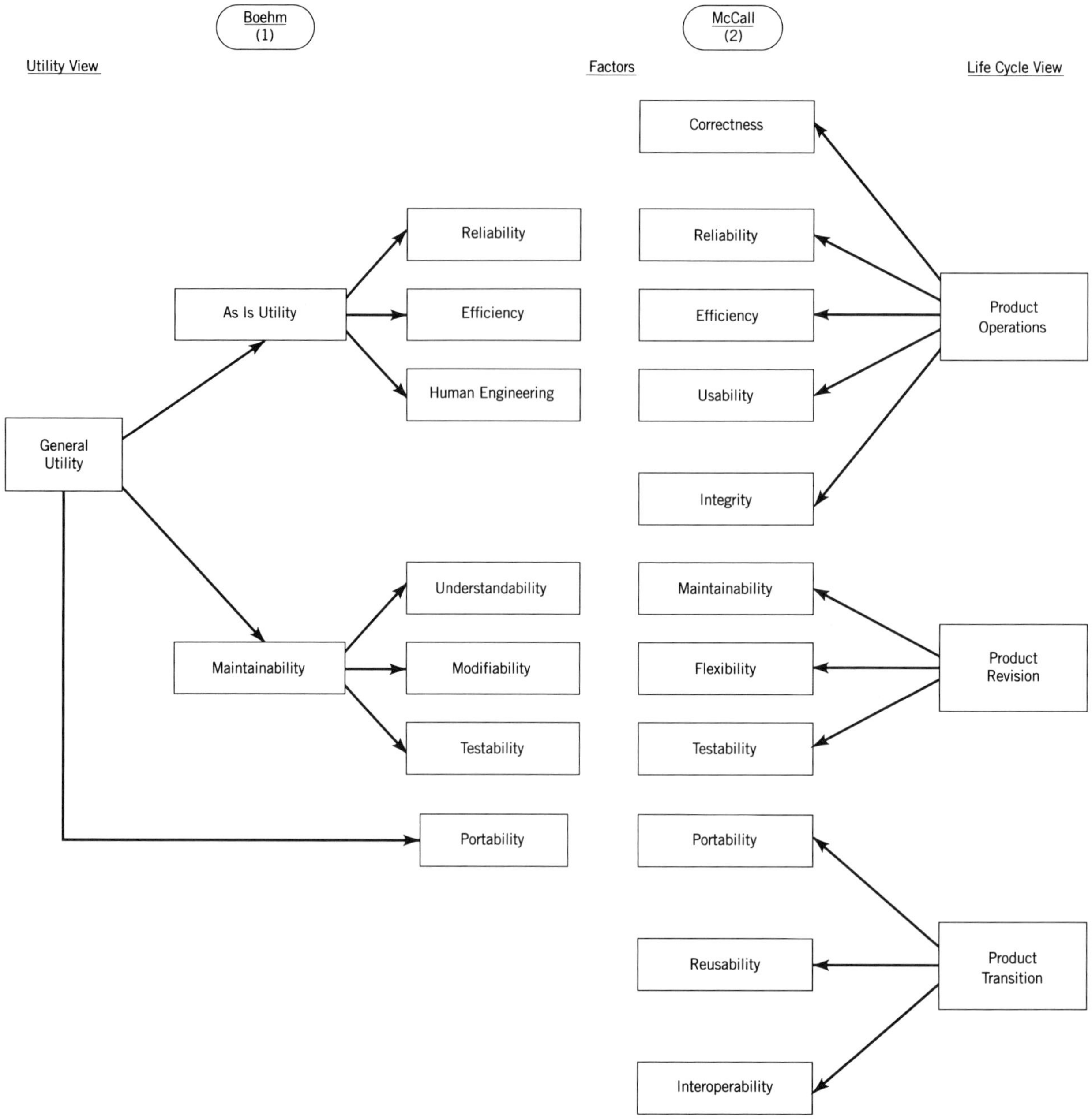

Figure 2. Quality factors perspectives.

length of time, then the concern becomes whether it is easy to maintain, change, and test to see if the fixes and changes have been made correctly. Longer life-cycle implications include how easy the product is to port to another environment or a new version of an operating system or a new hardware suite, how easy will it be to reuse when a new generation of the system is built, and how easy is it to interface with other systems? This quality focus relates to the effort required to develop and support the software during its life cycle. Bowen (Bowen, 1985) refined this concept further by organizing the factors by:

- Product performance: how well does the software function in its normal environment?
- Product design: how valid (appropriate) is the design with respect to requirements, verification and maintenance?
- Product adaptation: how easy it is to adapt the software for use beyond its original intended use?

Table 3 defines these factors, similar to Table 2, and adds a rating approach for each factor. This rating quantifies the quality factor. These ratings are examples of the types of quantitative quality goals that can be established using the quality measurement framework.

The above quality factors represent a management-oriented view of software quality. To introduce a dimension of quantification, this management orientation is translated into a software-related viewpoint. This translation is accomplished by defining a set of criteria or attributes for each factor. These criteria further define the quality factor and help describe the relationships between factors since one criterion can be related to more than one factor. The criteria are independent attributes of the software, or the software production process, by which the quality can be judged, defined, and measured. These attributes, related to the quality factors in Table 2, are shown in Figure 4.The factors are identified in ellipses and the criteria are identified in rectangles. The definitions of these criteria are provided in Table 4.

These criteria, or attributes, are the basis for recognizing the relationships between factors as quality goals for a development effort. Figure 5 illustrates an analysis of the factors relative to one another. The factor to factor trade-offs, which have an open circle, are examples of factors that have synergistic goals. For example, a development for which reliability is important will also generally result in software that is easier to test or vice versa. In some cases, indicated by a filled-in circle, goals can conflict, or better stated, can be more costly to achieve together. For example, highly efficient software is often achieved using lower level languages, system utilities, or programming techniques that make the software harder to understand and therefore more difficult to maintain. This analysis does not suggest that a highly efficient system that is also easy to maintain is unachievable, but instead means that a system with these two quality factors as goals is more difficult or costly to achieve.

Table 2. Definition of Software Quality Factors

Correctness	Extent to which a program satisfies its specifications and fulfills the user's mission objectives
Reliability	Extent to which a program can be expected to perform its intended function with required precision
Efficiency	The amount of computing resources required by a program to perform a function
Integrity	Extent to which access to software or data by unauthorized persons can be controlled
Usability	Effort required to learn, operate, prepare input, and interpret output of a program
Maintainability	Effort required to locate and fix an error in an operational program
Testability	Effort required to test a program to ensure it performs its intended function
Flexibility	Effort required to modify an operational program
Portability	Effort required to transfer a program from one hardware configuration and/or software system environment to another
Reusability	Extent to which a program can be used in other applications—related to the packaging and scope of the functions that programs perform
Interoperability	Effort required to couple one system with another

For each set of factors, related criteria and metrics are identified. The metrics are measurements of whether the attributes (criteria) exist or not and to what degree. The metrics can be *checklists* that "grade" the software for a particular attribute; *inspection guidelines* that evaluate the software and its documentation for specific attributes and information; or *quantitative measures* of characteristics such as size, complexity, independence, calling relationships, data usage, etc. The set of metrics (qv) related to (McCall, 1977) and extended by (Bowen, 1985) are listed in Table 5. The metrics provide actual measurement or indications of the quality of the software. The relationship of the metrics to quality ratings is derived through empirical studies.

The key contribution of the work done in software quality factors to software engineering is the established framework. The framework facilitates quality goals (factors) of a software product to be identified, relates the goals to the software product in terms of attributes and criteria for their existence, and then provides measurements to assure they are being built into the software product as it evolves. This goal-oriented approach provides a quality focused control system to the development effort, augmenting the traditional quality assurance practices. Two other significant references on software measurement frameworks take a goal/question/metric paradigm (Basili, 1992) and an experimentation perspective (Basili and co-workers, 1986).

CURRENT PRACTICE

The current state-of-the-art practice in the software industry involves the use of the quality factors within the software development methodology utilizing the associated software measurements to provide an evaluation or assessment mechanism. Methodologies such as those found in Bowen, (1985), Deutsch, (1988) or McCall, (1987) provide a complete implementation scheme for identifying quality goals, establishing required software attributes, and identifying measurements to assess the attainment of these goals.

These application approaches start by using the factors to identify user quality requirements. Each system has unique requirements affected by the type of application, expected life cycle, risk of use, performance requirements, etc. The user must evaluate these characteristics and identify which quality factors are important to emphasize or specify within the context of the development methodology. Table 6 provides guidance for selection of important quality factors.

Once the important factors are identified, they are then specified as requirements of the system development. This specification is done by including them as requirements, providing their definition, identifying supporting criteria (software attributes) and, in the most thorough applications, providing measurements to assess their attainment.

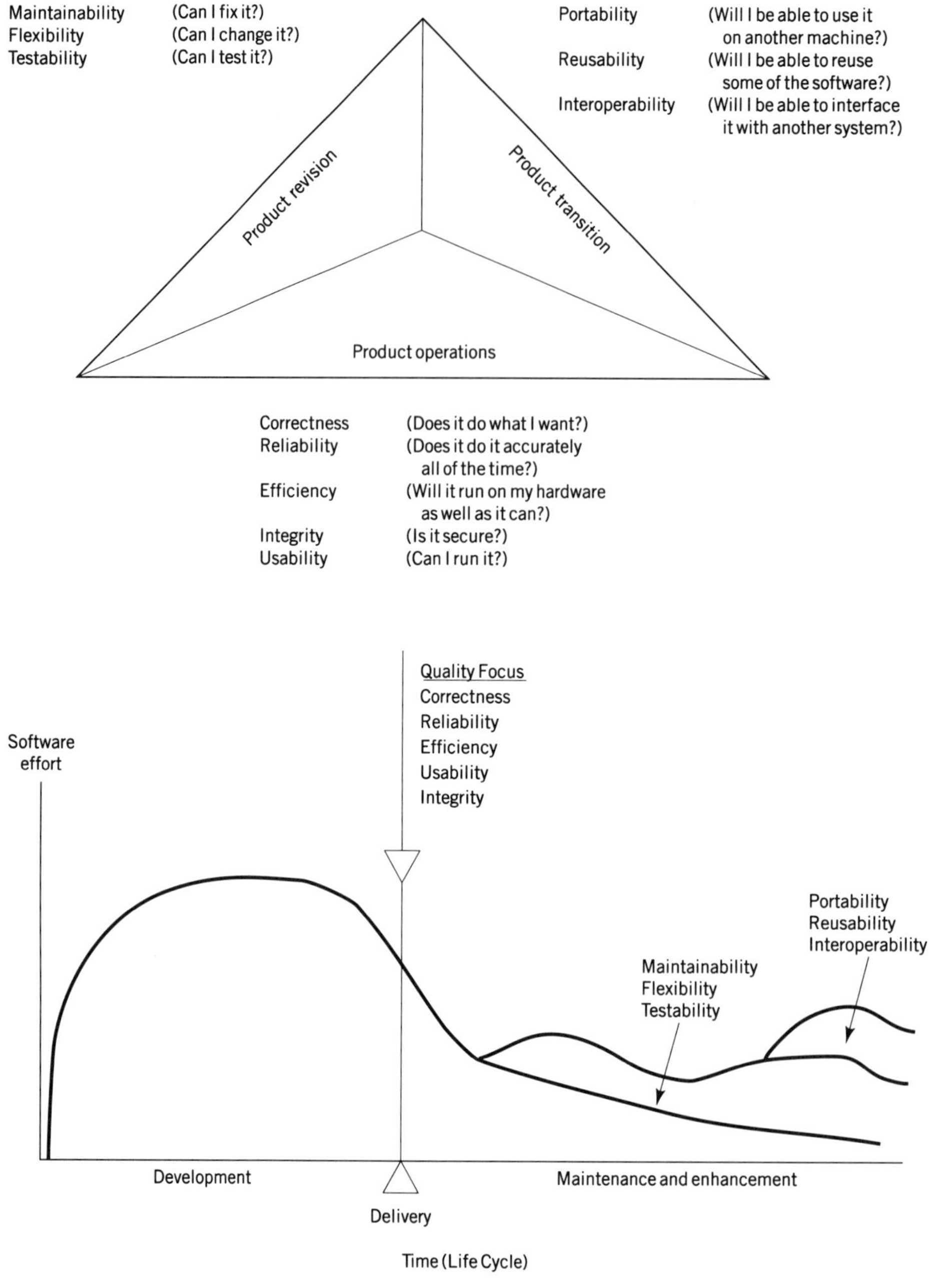

Figure 3. Allocation of software quality factors to life cycle activity.

This type of application of quality factors is now common in requests for proposals, statements of work, system specifications, software contracts, and design documents. A typical process is illustrated in Figure 6. The quality factors and associated metrics are contractually included in the following ways:

- As one of the determinants of incentive fees or award fees
- As part of the Software Quality Assurance Program
- Embedded in the Software Development Plan and Programming Standards
- As part of a Maintainability or Reliability Demonstration
- As checklists to be addressed at each formal review
- As part of the acceptance criteria/acceptance testing of the product

References AFSCP 800-43 (1987); AFSCP800-14 (1987); and Schultz (1988) are examples of how software acquisition organizations utilize the concept of software quality factors and measurements to state requirements for reporting metrics and quality status during developments. These same concepts are identified in (Paulk, 1991) relative to the maturity of a software organization's capabilities. Grady (Grady, 1987) describes how these concepts were introduced in a company and expands them for process improvement (Grady, 1992).

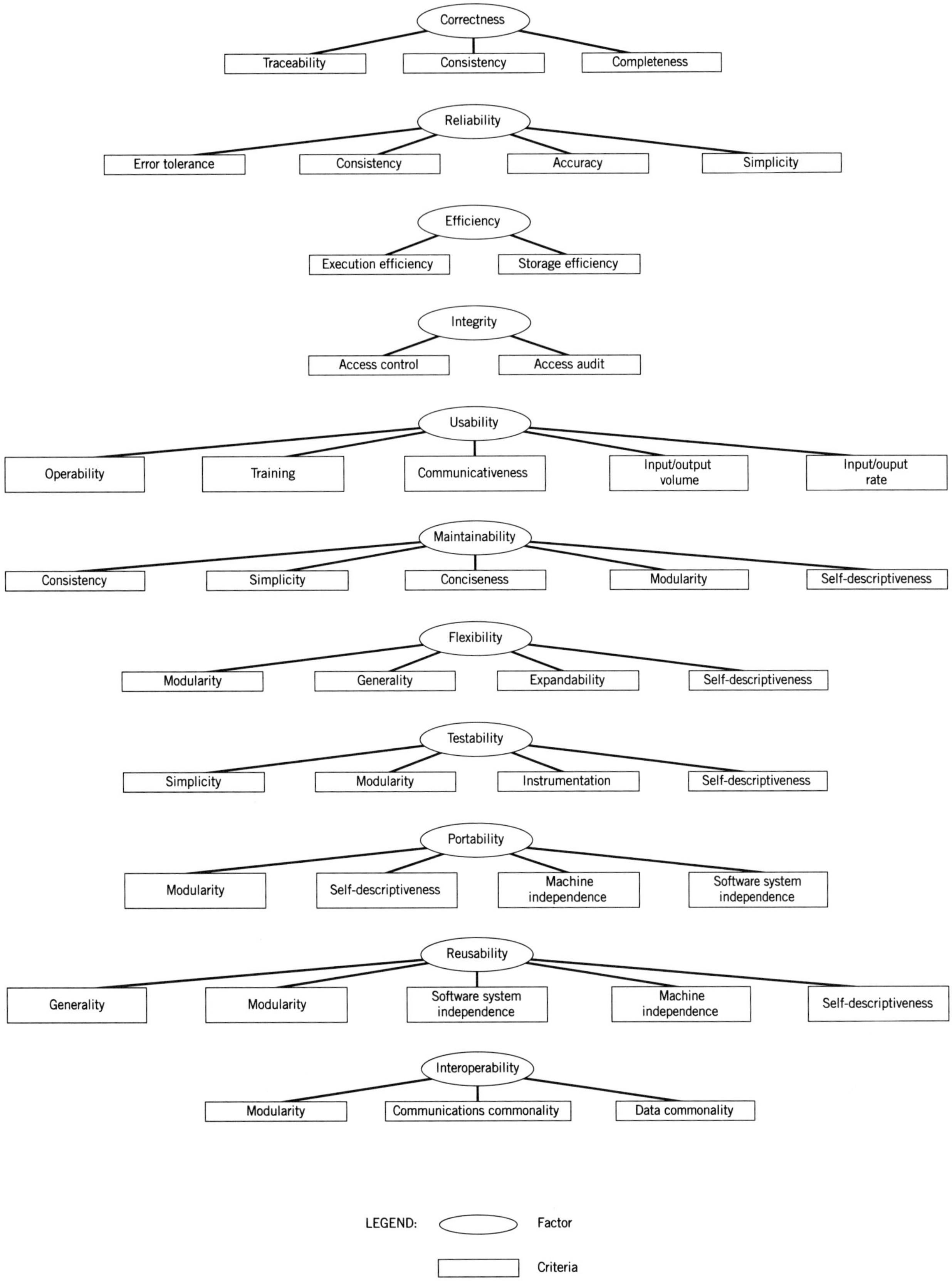

Figure 4. Relationship of criteria to software quality factors.

Table 3. Quality Factors and Rating Scheme[a]

Acquisition Concern	Quality Factor	Definition	Rating Formula	Rating Information[b]			
	Efficiency	Relative extent to which a resource is utilized (i.e. storage space, processing time, communication time)	$1-\frac{\text{Actual resource utilization}}{\text{Allocated resource utilization}}$	Value % utilization	0.1 90%	0.3 70	0.5 50%
	Integrity	Extent to which the software will perform without failures due to unauthorized access to the code or data within a specified time period	$1-\frac{\text{Errors}}{\text{Lines of code}}$	Value Errors/LOC	0.9995 5/10,000	0.9997 3/10,000	0.999 1/10,000
Performance	Reliability	Extent to which the software will perform without any failures within a specified period of time	$1-\frac{\text{Errors}}{\text{Lines of code}}$	Value Errors/LOC	0.995 5/1,000	0.997 3/1,000	0.999 1/1,000
	Survivability	Extent to which the software will perform and support critical functions without failures, within a specified time period when a portion of the system is inoperable	$1-\frac{\text{Errors}}{\text{Lines of code}}$	Values Errors/LOC	0.9995 5/10,000	0.9997 3/10,000	0.9999 1/10,000
	Usability	Relative effort using software (training and operation) (e.g. familiarization, input preparation, execution, output interpretation)	$1-\frac{\text{Labor-days}}{\text{Labor-years to develop}}$	Value Days/years	0.5 5/10	0.7 6/20	0.9 10/100
	Correctness	Extent to which the software conforms to its specifications and standards	$1-\frac{\text{Errors}}{\text{Lines of code}}$	Value Errors/LOC	0.9995 5/10,000	0.9997 3/10,000	0.9999 1/10,000
Design	Maintainability	Ease of effort for locating and fixing a software failure within a specified time period	$1-0.1$ (Average labor-days to fix)	Value Average labor-days	0.8 2.0	0.9 1.0	0.95 0.5
	Verifiability	Relative effort to verify the specified software operation and performance	$1-\frac{\text{Effort to verify}}{\text{Effort to develop}}$	Value % effort	0.4 60%	0.5 50%	0.6 40%
	Expandability	Relative effort to increase the software capability or performance by enhancing current functions or by adding new functions or data	$1-\frac{\text{Effort to expand}}{\text{Effort to develop}}$	Value % effort	0.8 20%	0.9 10%	0.95 5%
	Flexibility	Ease of effort for changing the software missions, functions, or data to satisfy other requirements	$1-0.05$ (Average labor-days to change)	Value Average labor-days	0.8 40	0.9 20	0.95 10
Adaptation	Interoperability	Relative effort to couple the software of one system to the software of another system	$1-\frac{\text{Effort to couple}}{\text{Effort to develop}}$	Value % effort	0.9 10	0.95 5	0.99 1
	Portability	Relative effort to transport the software for use in another environment (hardware, configuration and/or software system environment)	$1-\frac{\text{Effort to transport}}{\text{Effort to develop}}$	Value % effort	0.9 10	0.95 5	0.99 1
	Reusability	Relative effort to convert a software component for use in another application	$1-\frac{\text{Effort to convert}}{\text{Effort to develop}}$	Value % effort	0.4 60	0.6 40	0.8 20

[a] Bowen, 1985.
[b] The rating value range is from 0 to 1. If the value is less than 0. The rating value is assigned to 0.

Table 4. Criteria Definitions for Software Quality Factors

Criterion	Definition	Related Factors
Traceability	Those attributes of the software that provide a thread from the requirements to the implementation with respect to the specific development and operational environment.	Correctness
Completeness	Those attributes of the software that provide full implementation of the functions required.	Correctness
Consistency	Those attributes of the software that provide uniform design and implementation techniques and notation.	Correctness Reliability Maintainability
Accuracy	Those attributes of the software that provide the required precision in calculations and outputs.	Reliability
Error tolerance	Those attributes of the software that provide continuity of operation under non-nominal conditions.	Reliability
Simplicity	Those attributes of the software that provide implementation of functions in the most understandable manner. (Usually avoidance of practices which increase complexity).	Reliability Maintainability Testability
Modularity	Those attributes of the software that provide a structure of highly independent modules.	Maintainability Flexibility Testability Portability Reusability Interoperability
Generality	Those attributes of the software that provide breadth to the functions performed.	Flexibility Reusability
Expandability	Those attributes of the software that provide for expansion of data storage requirements or computational functions.	Flexibility
Instrumentation	Those attributes of the software that provide for the measurements of usage or identification of errors.	Testability
Self-descriptiveness	Those attributes of the software that provide explanation of the implementation of a function	Flexibility Maintainability Testability Portability Reusability
Execution efficiency	Those attributes of the software that provide for minimum processing time.	Efficiency
Storage efficiency	Those attributes of the software that provide for minimum storage requirements during operation.	Efficiency
Access control	Those attributes of the software that provide for control of the access of software and data.	Integrity
Access audit	Those attributes of the software that provide for an audit of the access of software and data.	Integrity
Operability	Those attributes of the software that determine operation and procedures concerned with the operation of the software.	Usability
Training	Those attributes of the software that provide transition from current operation or initial familiarization.	Usability
Communicativeness	Those attributes of the software that provide useful inputs and outputs which can be assimilated.	Usability
Software system independence	Those attributes of the software that determine its dependency on the software environment (operating system, utilities, input/output routines, etc.).	Portability Reusability
Machine independence	Those attributes of the software that determine its dependency on the hardware system.	Portability Reusability
Communications commonalty	Those attributes of the software that provide the use of standard protocols and interface routines.	Interoperability
Data commonalty	Those attributes of the software that provide the use of standard data representations.	Interoperability
Conciseness	Those attributes of the software that provide for implementation of a function with a minimum amount of code.	Maintainability

Another similar use of the quality factors is as an assessment of what quality characteristics are being emphasized in the development. Murine (Murine, 1983) has applied Quality Factors to Software Development Plans and System Specifications, allocating each itemized requirement within these documents to one of the factors, thereby demonstrating what quality factors are emphasized, implicitly or explicitly specified, and identifying where inconsistencies and lack of attention are a concern. Traceability of these specified goals throughout the development to demonstrable acceptance criteria should be a goal of all software development efforts.

Table 5. Quality Metrics Summary

Criterion	Metric
Accuracy	Accuracy checklist
Anomaly management (error tolerance)[a]	Error tolerance/control
	Improper input data
	Computational failures
	Hardware faults
	Device errors
	Communications errors
	Node/communication failures
Application independence	Data base management implementation independence
	Data structure
	Architecture standardization
	Microcode independence
	Functional independence
Augmentability (expandability)	Data storage expansion
	Computation extensibility
	Channel extensibility
	Design extensibility
Autonomy	Interface complexity
	Self-sufficiency
Commonality (communication, data commonality)	Communications commonality
	Data commonality
	Common vocabulary
Completeness	Completeness checklist
Consistency	Procedure consistency
	Data consistency
Distributedness	Design structure
Document accessibility	Access to documentation
	Well-structured documentation
Effectiveness communication (communicativeness)	Communication effectiveness measure
Effectiveness processing (execution efficiency)	Processing effective measure
	Data usage effectiveness measure
Effectiveness storage (storage efficiency)	Storage effectiveness measure
Functional overlap	Functional overlap checklist
Functional scope	Function specificity
	Function commonality
	Function selective usability
Generality	Unit referencing
	Unit implementation
Independence (software system, machine independence)	Software independence from system
	Machine independence
Modularity	Modular implementation
	Modular design
Operability	Operability checklist
	User input communicativeness
	User output communicativeness
Reconfigurability	Restructure checklist
Self-descriptiveness	Quantity of comments
	Effectiveness of comments
	Descriptiveness of language
Simplicity	Design structure
	Structured language or preprocessor
	Data and control flow complexity
	Coding simplicity
	Specificity
	Halstead's level of difficulty measure
System accessibility (access control, audit)	Access control
	Access audit
System clarity	Interface complexity
	Program flow complexity
	Application functional complexity
	Communication complexity
	Structure clarity

Table 5. *(Continued).*

Criterion	Metric
System compatibility	Communication compatibility
	Data compatibility
	Hardware compatibility
	Software compatibility
	Documentation for other system
Traceability	Cross reference
Training	Training checklist
Virtuality	System/data independence
Visibility (instrumentation)	Unit testing
	Integration testing
	CSCI Testing

[a]The criterion in parentheses relates to differences in terminology used by McCall (1977) vs Bowen (1985).

The use of the quality factors and associated measurements throughout the life cycle of a software system and as an organizational process standard, provides the basis for continuous improvement and also facilitates software being an integral part of an organization's Total Quality Management (TQM) process. As data is collected across projects within an organization, the process and measurements can also be used as the basis for risk assessment and cost estimation (Boehm, 1981; Putnam, 1992). The quality factors support the identification of risk areas. The measurements provide the mechanism for monitoring progress toward mitigating those risks (see also TOTAL QUALITY MANAGEMENT).

FUTURE DIRECTIONS AND CONCLUSION

The use of software quality factors and metrics has become a common practice in the industry, although the applications are not consistent, systematic or typically applied across projects or organizations. Future applications, motivated by software improvement activities and more consistently applied auditing practices by government acquisition agencies, will become more consistent and systematic throughout organizations. With this consistency, corporate quality measurement databases will facilitate further analysis of the cost issues/tradeoffs between factors and the costs to achieve various levels of quality.

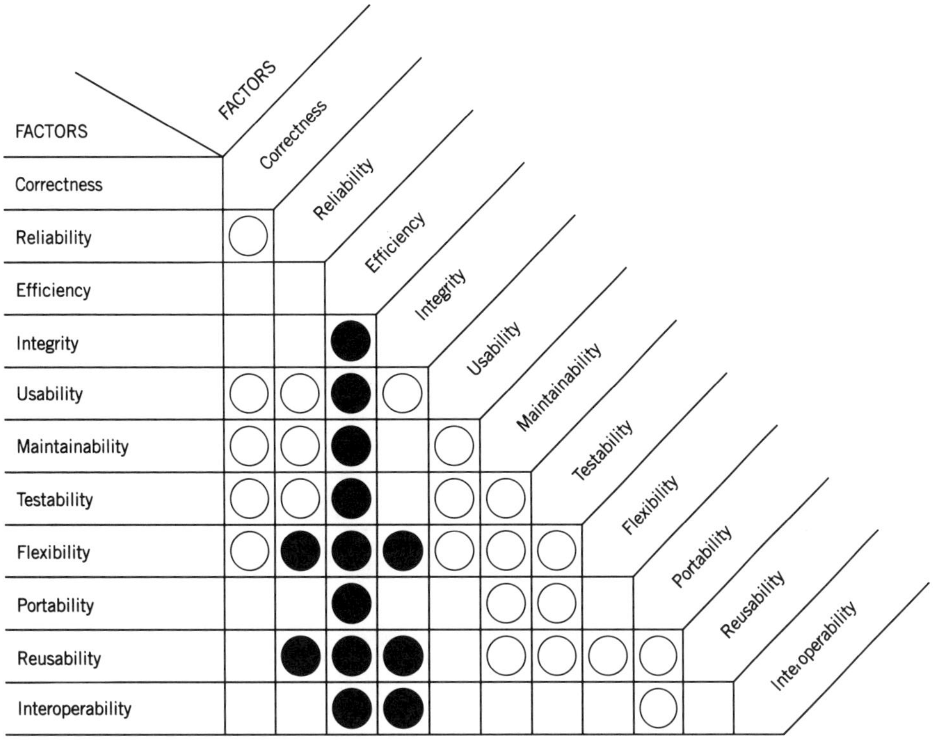

Figure 5. Relationships between software quality factors. If a high degree of quality is present for factor, what degree of quality is expected for the other. Light circle=high; dark circle=low. Blank=no relationship or application dependent.

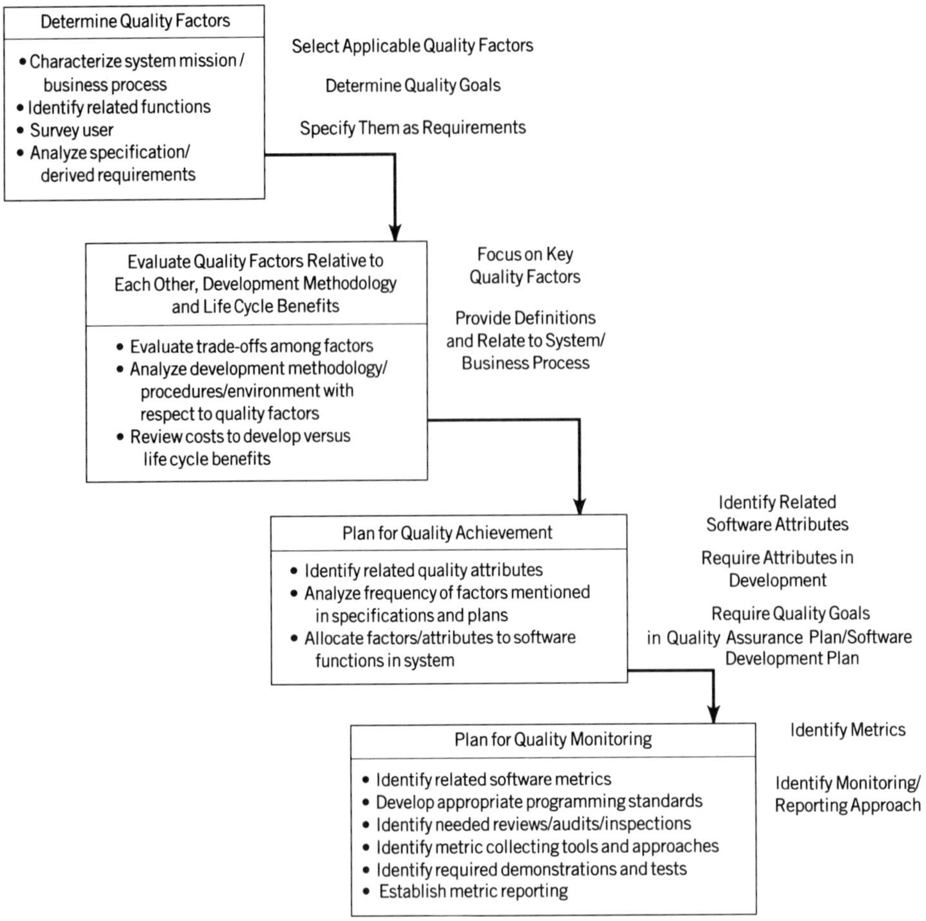

Figure 6. Quality factor specification process.

Table 6. Quality Factors Related to System Characteristics

	Related Quality Factor												
User's need/ system characteristic	Correctness	Reliability	Efficiency	Useability	Integrity	Maintainability	Flexibility	Testability	Portability	Reuseability	Interoperability	Safety	Supportability
Human lives affected	X	X						X				X	
Real time application	X	X	X										
Business critical application	X	X			X								
Classified/private data processing					X								
Interrelated with other systems											X		
Hazardous material handling	X	X										X	
Long life cycle						X	X	X	X	X			X
Continuously changing regulations							X						X
Specific user qualifications				X			X						X
Continuous operation		X				X							X
On-line usage	X	X	X	X		X							

Consequently, quality factors will be used more consistently in specifications, quality assurance plans, in test plans and acceptance test procedures. Software reliability and maintainability demonstrations will become an accepted contractual requirement.

Research and data collection efforts to support validation efforts will continue with the goal of refining the quantitative measurements of the quality factors. These efforts will continue to provide empirical data upon which to evaluate new developments. Use of measurement frameworks to support software engineering experimentation will continue (Curtis, 1980; Basili, 1986), aimed at empirically demonstrating improved techniques, programmer performance, effects of environment, and process improvement.

More wide-spread application of the qualify factors and associated measurements will occur as the technology is built into Computer-Aided Software Environment (CASE) tools, supporting the identification of quality factors in the requirements specification and then tracing and reporting their evolution though the CASE tool utilization.

Reuse libraries and certified software programs will contain quality certifications in the future. The reuse of libraries will not only contain specification, design and code documentation, but also performance data and code characteristics (metrics).

The author wishes to acknowledge the support of his wife, Carol, and his children, Andy, Julianne, Chris and Ashley, who bring quality to his life.

BIBLIOGRAPHY

L. Arthur, *Measuring Programmer Productivity and Software Quality,* John Wiley & Sons, New York, 1985.

V. Basili, *Software Modeling and Measurement: The Goal/Question/Metric Paradigm,* University of Maryland Computer Science Technical Report, CS-TR-2956, Sept. 1992.

V. Basili, R. Selby, and D. Jutchens, "Experimentation in Software Engineering," *IEEE Transactions on Software Engineering* **SE-12**(7) (July 1986).

B. Boehm, *Software Engineering Economics,* Prentice-Hall, Inc. Englewood Cliffs, N.J., 1981.

B. Boehm and co-workers *Characteristics of Software Quality,* North Holland Publishing Co., New York, 1978.

T. Bowen and co-workers, *Specification of Software Quality Attributes,* 3 vol., RADC Report TR-85-37, Feb., 1985.

J. Cavano and J. McCall, "A Framework for the Measurement of Software Quality," *Proceedings of the Software Quality Assurance Workshop,* Nov. 1978.

B. Curtis, "Measurement and Experimentation in Software Engineering," *Proceedings of the IEEE* **68**(9) (Sept. 1980).

M. Deutsch and R. Willis, *Software Quality Engineering A Total Technical and Management Approach,* Prentice Hall, Inc., Englewood Cliffs, N.J., 1988.

L. Ejiogu, *Software Engineering with Formal Metrics,* QED Technical Publishing Group, Boston, 1991.

M. Evans and J. Marciniak, *Software Quality Assurance and Management,* John Wiley & Sons, New York, 1985.

R. Grady, *Practical Software Metrics for Project Management and Process Improvement,* Prentice Hall, Inc., Englewood Cliffs, N.J., 1992

R. Grady and D. Caswell, *Software Metrics: Establishing a Company-Wide Program,* Prentice Hall, Inc., Englewood Cliffs, N.J., 1987.

M. M. Halstead, *Elements of Software Science,* Elsevier North Holland, New York, 1977.

T. McCabe, "A Complexity Measure," *IEEE Transactions on Software Engineering* **SE-2**(4) (Dec. 1976).

T. McCabe, "Air Force Systems Command Software Management Indicators," AFSCP 800-43, Jan. 1987.

T. McCabe, "Air Force Systems Command Software Quality Indicators," AFSCP 800-14, Jan. 1987.

J. McCall, P. Richards, and G. Walters, "Factors in Software Quality," 3 vol., NTIS AD-A049-015, 015, 055, Nov. 1977.

J. McCall and co-workers, "Methodology for Software Reliability Prediction," 2 vol., RADC Report TR-87-171, Nov., 1987.

G. Murine and C. Carpenter, "Applying Software Quality Metrics," *1983 ASQC Quality Congress Transactions,* Boston, 1983.

M. Paulk and co-workers, *Capability Maturity Model,* CMU/SEI-91-TR-24, ESD-TR-91-24, Software Engineering Institute, Carnegie Mellon University, Pittsburgh, Pa., Aug. 1991.

L. Putnam and W. Myers, *Measures for Excellence: Reliable Software On-Time, Within Budget,* Yourdon Press, Englewood Cliffs, N.J., 1992.

C. Schultz, "Software Management Metrics," ESD/Mitre, 1988.

JAMES A. MCCALL
Science Applications International Corp.

QUALITY INSPECTIONS

See REVIEWS AND AUDITS.

QUALITY MANAGEMENT

See QUALITY ASSURANCE; TOTAL QUALITY CONTROL.

QUERY LANGUAGE

A language used to access information stored in a database (IEEE).

R

RADATZ, JANE W. (1944–)

Jane Radatz is a Senior Program Manager with Logicon, Inc. She obtained her B.A. and M.S. in Mathematics from the University of Michigan in 1966 and 1967, respectively, and joined Logicon in 1975. Since 1979 she has supported the U.S. Department of Defense (DOD) and the IEEE in the development of software engineering standards. She played a key role in the development of DOD-STD-2167A (Defense System Software Development), DOD-STD-2168 (Defense System Software Quality Program), and the DOD handbooks on applying these standards. She is currently supporting the DOD in the development of MIL-STD-498 (Software Development and Documentation). She designed the DOD's expert system for tailoring DOD-STD-2167A and automated tools for performing other aspects of software acquisition. She has written guidebooks for the U.S. Air Force, Army, and Navy on software verification, testing, metrics, and software acquisition, and she performed a study for the Air Force quantifying the effects of independent verification and validation on software reliability, maintainability, and productivity. Ms. Radatz chairs the IEEE working group on software engineering terminology and led the development of IEEE Std 610.12-1990 (Standard Glossary of Software Engineering Terminology).

BIBLIOGRAPHY

J. Radatz, *A Prediction of Computer Technology,* Logicon, 1975.

—with co-workers, *Reliable Microprogamming,* RADC-TR-79-173, 1979.

—*Analysis of IV&V Data,* RADC-TR-81-145, 1981.

—with co-workers, *A Guidebook to Independent Verification and Validation,* Logicon, 1981.

—with M. Chern, *Verification and Validation Handbook,* Logicon, 1983.

—with co-workers, *Software Quality Engineering Handbook,* Logicon, 1984.

—with co-workers, "A Standard Dictionary of Computer Terminology: Project 610," *Computer,* (Feb. 1988).

—(chair) IEEE Std 610.12-1990, *Standard Glossary of Software Engineering Terminology,* IEEE, 1990.

RANDOM TESTING

INTRODUCTION

In computer science, originally where centered around artificial intelligence laboratories at Stanford and MIT, the adjective *random* is slang with a number of derogatory connotations ranging from "assorted, various" to "not well organized" or "gratuitously wrong" (Steele and co-workers, 1983). *Random testing* of a program in this sense describes testing badly or hastily done, the opposite of *systematic* testing such as functional testing or structural testing. This slang meaning, which might be rendered *haphazard testing* in normal parlance, is probably the common one, as in the sentence, "Random testing is the most used and least useful method." In contrast, the technical, mathematical meaning of random testing refers to an explicit lack of "system" in the choice of test data, so that there is no correlation among different tests. (There is dispute over the usefulness of random testing in this technical sense; however, it is certainly not the most used method.) If the technical meaning contrasts "random" with "systematic," it is in the sense that fluctuations in physical measurements are random (unpredictable or chaotic) versus systematic (causal or lawful).

Why is it desirable to be "unsystematic " on purpose in selecting test data for a program?

1. Because there are efficient methods of selecting random points algorithmically, by computing pseudorandom numbers; thus a vast number of tests can be easily defined.
2. Because statistical independence among test points allows statistical prediction of significance in the observed results.

In the sequel it will be seen that (1) may be compromised because the required result of an easily generated test is not so easy to generate. Reason (2) is the more important quality of random testing, both in practice and for the theory of software testing. To make an analogy with the case of physical measurement, it is only random fluctuations that can be "averaged out" to yield an improved measurement over many trials; systematic fluctuations might in principle be eliminated at their source, but if their cause (or even their existence) is unknown, they forever invalidate the measurement. The analogy is better than it seems: in program testing, with systematic methods we know what we are doing, but not what it means; only by giving up all systematization can the significance of testing be known.

Random testing at its best can be illustrated by a simple example. Suppose that a subroutine is written to compute the (floating-point) cube root of an integer parameter. The method to be used has been shown to be accurate to within 2×10^{-5} for input values in the interval $X=[1, 10^7]$. Assuming that all values in this range are equally likely (that is, the *operational profile* that describes how the subroutine will be used, has a uniform distribution), a random test of 3000 points can be performed as follows: Generate 3000 uniformly distributed pseudorandom integers in the interval X. Execute the subroutine on each of these, obtaining output z_t for input t. For each t, compute z_t^3, and compare with t. The process can be automated by writing a driver program incorporating the pseudorandom-number generator and the output comparison. If any of the 3000 outputs fails to be within 2×10^{-5} of the desired result the subroutine must be corrected, and the test repeated, but without reinitializing the input generator. That is, the pseudorandom sequence is continued, not restarted. Suppose that eventually the subroutine passes the test by computing 3000 correct values. As will be shown in the sequel, the probability that the subroutine could fail one or more times in 1000 subsequent runs is less than about 0.05. Roughly, it is 95% certain that the subroutine is going to be correct 999 times out of 1000. The ability to quantify the significance of a test that does *not* fail is unique to random testing.

Along the way to a successful random test, there may be many cycles of finding a program failure, and sending the software back for repair. It is to be expected that random testing is less good at exposing software defects than systematic methods designed for just that purpose. However, as discussed in the section, Efficacy of Random Testing for Finding Failures, the deficiency is not so severe as might be imagined—a great deal of effort may be invested in systematic testing without realizing much advantage.

The example above is unrealistic in two important ways, ways that show the weakness of random testing in practice. First, it is seldom so easy to calculate random test inputs. The input values may be more complicated than integers confined to a given interval. Worse, the operational profile may be unknown, so that predictive random inputs cannot be found at all. The second (and more damning) unrealistic feature of the example is that it is seldom possible to check the program's results against what it is supposed to do. In the usual case the comparison with correct behavior is hard because the requirements are imprecisely stated; in the worst case the required behavior is so complex that checking it at all presents formidable problems.

THE RANDOM-TESTING METHOD

The example in the Introduction indicates how random testing is done: the input domain is identified, test points are selected independently from this domain, the program under test is executed on these inputs (they constitute a random test set), and the results compared to the program specification. The test is a failure if any input leads to incorrect results; otherwise it is a success. To make this description precise requires a discussion of program and test types, of the input-selection criterion, and of the output comparison.

Program and Test Variations

The cube root subroutine of the Introduction might be used directly by a person to calculate and print roots, with a driver program that is very similar to the test harness already described. The predictions of its quality then refer to human use in which it is no more likely that one cube root will be requested than another. The random test is a system test in this case, and its intent would be twofold: to uncover as many failures as possible; and finally, when no more are found, to predict the future behavior of the software.

On the other hand, the cube root routine might be part of a library, and testing it in isolation is an example of unit testing. For unit testing, the predictive feature of random testing is lost, because a subroutine may have entirely different usage when incorporated in a variety of software systems. If in system P the cube roots requested are concentrated in the input interval [1,100], while for system Q they range over the whole interval $[1,10^7]$, then the test of the Introduction better applies to Q than to P. Since the system usage of a general routine is arbitrary ("random" in the slang sense!), statistical prediction is not possible. Furthermore, in some system R, most system functions might not require cube roots at all, so that even if an accurate prediction were available for the root routine, it would have little to do with a corresponding prediction for R itself. Random system testing of P, Q, and R themselves would be needed to make predictions about their behaviors. However, random testing is still used at the unit level, because it is surprisingly competitive with systematic methods in failure-finding. The uniform input distribution is used in the absence of any information about the location of failure points in the input domain. (This topic is discussed in detail below under EFFICACY OF RANDOM TESTING FOR FINDING FAILURES).

At the system-test level, the simplicity of random testing is also complicated by the several ways in which programs may be used, which influences the way they should be tested.

1. Batch programs are purely functional in nature: a batch program treats one input at a time, and its output depends only on that input. The sequencing of successive inputs is irrelevant. Each test of a batch program starts from scratch, so random testing such a program is straightforward—the tests have nothing to do with each other.
2. Interactive programs are in operation more or less continuously, but repeat an interactive cycle of reading input, computing, and writing output. At the head of the cycle, there may be a long wait for input, as a human user thinks, goes to lunch, etc. However, each interaction is not like a batch run, because an interactive program typically has a memory. Results from one interaction may influence subsequent interactions. It is typical for an interactive program to have a number of modes into which it is thrown by certain inputs, and to behave entirely differently in different modes. Random testing of interactive programs must take account of input *sequences*.
3. Some programs, like operating systems, telephone switches, or other real-time control programs, operate continuously, receiving input and producing output in bits and pieces over time. When such a program is slowed down and given a simple input pattern, it may appear to act like an interactive program, but in normal operation the situation is much more chaotic. Random testing of a real-time program requires multiple input streams, for which not only the input values and their sequence, but also their spacing and overlap in time, are significant.

Most of the theory of random testing applies easily only to batch programs.

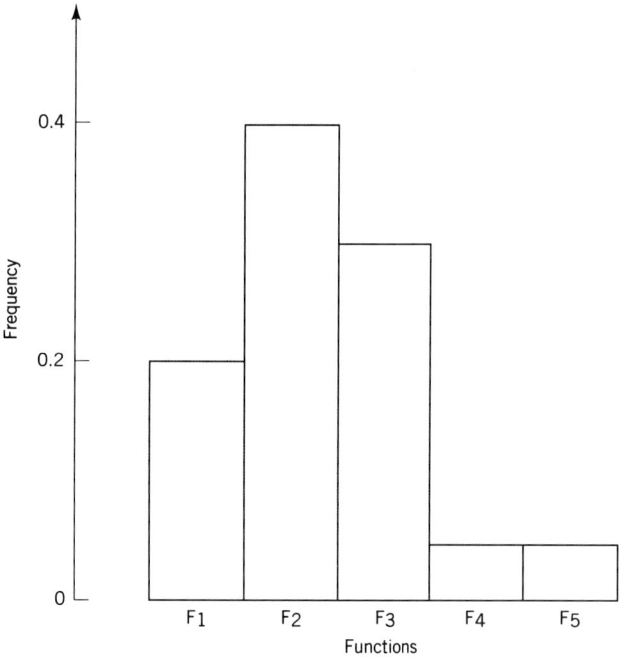

Figure 1. An operational profile.

The Operational Profile

Every testing method (except exhaustive testing for batch programs) is less than perfect. It is altogether possible that success will be observed on some test data, yet in fact the software contains defects not brought to light. It has therefore been suggested (Musa, 1988) that the choice of test points take into account use patterns the software will encounter in its intended environment. The argument is that by testing according to use, the failures found by imperfect methods are more likely to be the important ones, i.e., the ones most users would first encounter. In statistical prediction, the argument for tests mimicing usage is even more compelling: unless random tests are drawn as the software will be actually used, the tests are not a representative sample and all statistical bets are off.

Strictly speaking, the operational environment for a program is one part of the software requirements. An *operational profile* can be obtained in practice by partitioning the input space, and assigning to each subdivision D of the partition a probability that in normal use, the input will come from D. The name comes from representing the frequencies as a histogram whose bars form a "profile" of typical usage frequency versus subdivision. Any partitioning scheme may be used, but the most common is a functional partition that groups inputs for which the software is required to perform the same function. The input space may also be divided into equal-sized chunks without regard for function, or features of the program structure may be used to define input classes. However, the requirements are usually not helpful in assigning frequencies except for the functional partition. Figure 1 shows an illustrative operational profile for a program for which five functions $F_1, \ldots, F_5$ are required, with usage frequencies 0.2, 0.4, 0.3, 0.05, 0.05 respectively.

In the limit as the partition is refined to smaller subdivisions, the operational profile becomes a probability density function giving the probability that each input point will arise in use. In practice, the software requirements provide no way to refine the partition except to assume that the probability of choosing a point is constant within each subdomain. By arbitrarily subdividing subdomains according to some scale, the probability can be apportioned accordingly. For example, if in Figure 1 the input space is the integer interval [0, 100], and the subdomains occupy respectively intervals of length 20, 10, 40, 10, and 20 in order, then the density function has the appearance of Figure 2. (The density is discrete, but the Figures do not show this.) The probability amplitudes are 1/100, 1/25, 3/400, 1/200, 1/400, respectively. (For example, 0.3 of the points are to be chosen in the interval [30,69] for F_3, where there are 40 possibilities, making the probability of choosing each point 0.3/40 = 0.0075.)

Rather than the density function f, it is usual to work with the distribution function

$$F(t) = \int_{-\infty}^{t} f(x)\,dx$$

(for the case of a continuous density f; for a discrete density a sum replaces the integral). Figure 3 shows the operational distribution corresponding to Figure 2.

To select test inputs according to an operational profile for a batch program, choose uniformly distributed pseudorandom numbers in the intervals corresponding to the requirements partition, each interval considered its proper fraction of the time. In the example above, to sample F_3 properly, 0.3 of all test points should be uniformly distributed in [30,69]. Or, if an operational distribution F is given, start with uniformly distributed pseudorandom real numbers $r \in [0,1]$, for which the corresponding $F^{-1}(r)$ are distributed according to F.

For interactive or real-time programs, the choices are more complicated, because input sequences must be chosen. Often, the requirements are silent about the probability of one input following another, so the only possibility is to order choices uniformly. Or the input space can be expanded to include variable(s) representing stored infor-

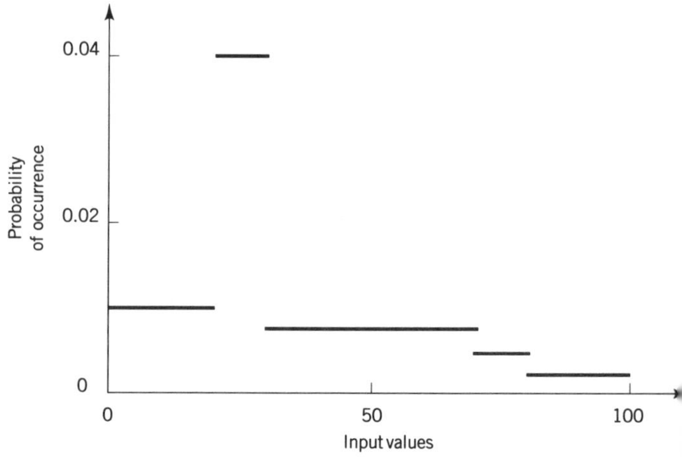

Figure 2. A probability density.

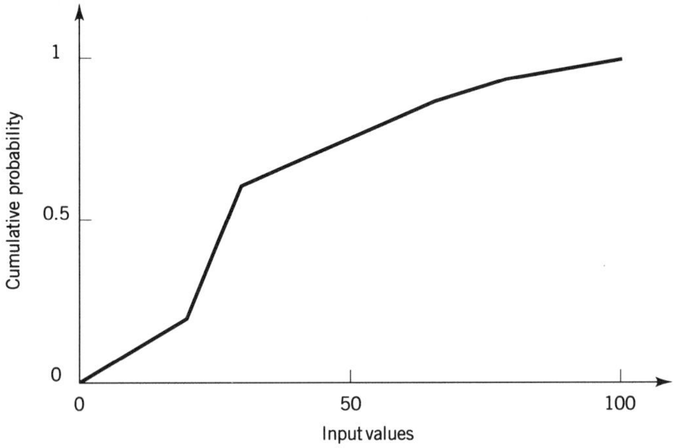

Figure 3. An operational distribution.

mation, whose values are taken to be uniformly distributed. Neither choice is satisfactory if it cannot be supported by the requirements document.

The Specification Oracle

Any testing method must rely on an oracle to judge success or failure of each test point. To be useful in testing, the oracle must be effective, i.e., there must be a mechanical means of judging the correctness of any program result. Testing theory usually assumes that an oracle is given, but in practice this false assumption has more influence than is usually admitted. It is responsible for the bias that a better testing method requires fewer test points. (In that case the oracle, which is likely to be hand calculation, has less to do.) The assumption is also responsible for testing done with trivial values, which may distort the ability of systematic methods to uncover failures. (With trivial values, hand calculation is easier.) Random testing cannot be attempted without an effective oracle, however. A vast number of test points are required, and they cannot be trivialized to make things easier for a human oracle.

Description of the Method

For batch programs whose operational profile is known, for whose domain a pseudorandom number generator is available, and for which there is an effective oracle, random testing is straightforward. A test set size N is selected. N may be based on a desired reliability (as indicated in the Introduction, and discussed in detail in the following section); however, in practice it is more likely to be chosen to reflect available resources for testing. Using the operational profile with K subdomains $D_1, D_2, \ldots, D_K$, these points are apportioned according to the corresponding probabilities $P_1, P_2, \ldots, P_K$ that input will be in each subdomain. The pseudorandom number generator is used to generate N_i test points for subdomain D_i, $N_i = p_i N$, for $1 \le i \le K$. These N points together form the test set. The program is executed, and the oracle used to detect any failures. If failures are found, the software is corrected and the test repeated with a new pseudorandom test set. Random testing ends when no failures are detected for the size-N test set.

In unusual cases, the requirements document will describe expected usage for an interactive or real-time program so that a partition is defined for sequences of inputs. That is, the operational profile will describe classes of input sequences, and the above procedure can be used to select a random test set (of sequences). Or the inputs may be available from a physical system like a radar, or from a simulation of such a system, so that random test sets are available by just recording them as they occur. (The question of selecting a time interval to record is often a difficult one, particularly when the resulting test set varies widely with time.) But the usual situation, particularly for real-time programs, is a requirements document that gives little information about input sequences and overlaps, because the use information is unknown. (A few constraints may be available, e.g., that certain events will not occur too frequently.) Thus in the usual case, the operational profile is not available, because it is sequences of values that constitute actual input, not single values.

When the operational profile is not available, random testing can still be used with a uniform distribution. But the predictive power of a successful test is compromised, because if actual usage concentrates on some inputs, the predictions for such inputs will be overly optimistic, and observed behavior may be arbitrarily worse than expected. For batch programs, all inputs are taken to be equally likely; this is equivalent to taking the whole input space as a single subdomain that occurs with probability 1. For an interactive program, sequences of inputs can be constructed by selecting each member of a sequence according to an operational profile for single inputs. It may happen that imprecise requirements nevertheless reject certain sequences constructed without regard for the probability that one input will follow another. For example, in a transaction-processing system, it may be known that certain combinations of transactions seldom or never occur. For a realtime system, test sets are multiple concurrent sequences of inputs. The relative time position of inputs in each sequence can be chosen using a standard distribution (e.g., the Poisson distribution), but without some help from the requirements about distribution parameters, such sequences are unlikely to have any connection to reality, even if individual-value probabilities and sequence probabilities are available. (In the real-time case, it may happen that overlap requirements are better understood than sequencing requirements.)

It should be evident that the application of random testing to interactive and realtime systems requires far more knowledge about these systems' usage than is usually available. It can be argued that the absence of usage data is a critical deficiency in the requirements phase of development: insofar as the necessary operational profile information is not available to construct accurate random test sets, the application has not been sufficiently analyzed to attempt a computer solution. To proceed without this information would be considered unprofessional negligence in most branches of engineering. Because "software can do anything," engineers are led to attempt general solutions to difficult problems, resulting in software that cannot be tested as it will be used, which can fail because of design flaws excited by the (unspecified) circumstances of its special use. Other branches of engineering are more aware of their limitations.

Reliability and Random Testing

It is the primary strength of random testing that the significance of a successful random test can be statistically predicted. Subject only to the availability of an accurate operational profile and to the validity of certain independence assumptions, a successful random test of program P can justify statements such as, "It is 99% certain that P will fail no more than once in 10,000 runs" (for a batch program) and; "It is 99% certain that P will have a mean time to failure of greater than 10,000 hours of continuous operation" (for a real-time program). The validity question will be considered elsewhere; here the conventional theory behind such statements will be derived.

Consider first the batch case in which previous inputs cannot influence the outcome of a test of program P. It is usual to postulate that P has a constant *failure rate* (or *hazard rate*) θ. Then on a single test, the probability that P will fail is θ, or $1\text{-}\theta$ that P will succeed. On N independent tests drawn according to the operational profile, the probability of universal success is $(1\text{-}\theta)^N$, or probability $e = 1\text{-}(1\text{-}\theta)^N$ that at least one failure be observed. e is the upper confidence bound that a failure will occur no more often than once in $1/\theta$ runs. Solving for $1/\theta$, which is also the mean time to failure (MTTF) in the constant-hazard-rate case,

$$\frac{1}{\theta} \geqq \frac{1}{1 - (1 - e)^{1/N}}$$

The number of tests required to attain confidence e in this MTTF is

$$\frac{\log(1 - e)}{\log(1 - \theta)}$$

The example in the Introduction had $N = 3000$, MTTF 1000 runs, so $e \approx 0.9503$.

The cases of interactive or real-time programs are the same, if the more complex operational profiles these programs require are available. In the case of real-time programs, if inputs arrive at an average rate of λ, then both MTTF and test-run count N can be converted into time units because λt inputs arrive in time t. For example, 90% confidence in a MTTF of 10^6 h requires testing for about 2.3×10^6 h.

It should be emphasized again that although these formulas can be used in the case that an unknown operational profile (or one that is inadequate for the interactive or real-time cases) is replaced by a uniform distribution, the results can be arbitrarily inaccurate, and the error is always in the optimistic direction of predicting a greater confidence in a better MTTF than actually is justified.

As the unique testing method for which test success can be quantified in meaningful software quality terms (i.e., confidence in MTTF), random testing has an important theoretical and experimental role. It serves as the standard of comparison by which other methods should be evaluated. For all the difficulties the method presents, this touchstone role remains of great importance.

EFFICACY OF RANDOM TESTING FOR FINDING FAILURES

Most systematic testing methods arose in practice, from the idea of coverage. In systematic testing, some aspect of a program is identified as a potential source of failure, and the method attempts to make sure that this aspect is not neglected in testing. For example, if a statement has never been executed during testing, it could be radically wrong, yet its fault would not show. Or, a required software function could be implemented very badly (perhaps not implemented at all) yet the error will not be detected if testing fails to invoke that function. Random testing, on the other hand, makes no claims to cover anything, except insofar as chance dictates. It is therefore unexpected that random testing can compete with systematic testing in its ability to expose failures. But that is exactly what studies have shown: under assumptions not unfavorable to systematic methods, they are not much better at finding failures than is random testing (Duran and Ntafos, 1984, Hamlet and Taylor, 1990).

The comparison of systematic methods with random testing is a useful exercise in its own right, because it has the potential for evaluating the systematic method to the random-testing standard. Systematic methods are often intuitively appealing, but their significance is in doubt, because they have not been analyzed in precise terms meaningful for software quality. To take an all-too-common example, some test standards require that (say) 80% of program paths (making some special provision for loops) be executed during testing. Yet there is no information on the effectiveness of 80% coverage at finding failures nor on the significance of an 80% coverage test that happens to succeed. The test standard is made from whole cloth, without any scientific basis beyond the intuition that covering 80% of something is better than nothing. If, on the other hand, a comparison with random testing were available, it might help us to write better standards, or to improve the significance of systematic methods.

The two studies cited above contrast partition testing with random testing. A partition test is an abstraction of any systematic method that divides the input space into disjoint subdomains, and requires that tests be selected from each subdomain. Path testing is such a method, because the equivalence classes of inputs defined by the relation "execute the same path" are a partition. Assuming that the software under test has a constant failure rate (see above), the probability of finding at least one failure by random testing depends only on the number of test points. The probability of finding at least one failure by partition testing depends also on the distribution of failures over the subdomains, which is in general unknown. But by making empirical choices for this distribution, the methods can be compared. The results are

1. It is difficult to force partition testing to be radically better than random testing, no matter how the sub-

domains fall relative to random choices of test points. That is, in general there is little to choose between the failure-finding ability of the methods.

2. Partition testing is typically better at uncovering failures; however, the difference is reversed by a modest increase in the number of points chosen for random testing. Typically, by taking 20% more points in a random test, the advantage a partition test might have enjoyed is wiped out.
3. The only way to give partition testing a clear advantage over random testing is to choose a partition in which some of the subdomains have substantially higher failure rates than the others, i.e., good partition testing concentrates failures within its subdomains.

If partition testing is about the same as random testing, then the systematic testing methods in common use are not much good for improving our trust in tested software. Typical systematic unit tests have on the order of 100 points in a test set. If such a test set were random, it would guarantee a MTTF of only about 62 runs (80% confidence level)—not very high quality.

The advice to seek partitions with high failure rate subdomains sounds like no advice; if the tester knew where failures lurked, no testing would be needed. But it does imply that subdividing the input space "for subdivision's sake" is not wise. If a partition is refined just to make the subdivisions smaller, without reason to believe that failures are being isolated in the smaller subdivisions, then the systematic method is not improved. It also suggests that potential flaws in development methods are a good source of subdomains for systematic testing. For example, specification changes that affect a software unit are likely to make that unit suspect (particularly if the change comes late in the development cycle and involves the interface). A partition can be defined that isolates the use of the unit to a subdomain in which the failure rate may be very high.

There is an intuitive explanation for the surprising success of random testing relative to its systematic competitors. Systematic methods are more subjective than they appear, because in most cases there are an infinite number of ways to satisfy the method, and the choice is usually made by a human being. There are good and bad choices, relative to finding failures. Random testing can be viewed as replacing human choice with chance selection, including the possibility of no selection at all. For example, randomly selected test points may cover all functions, all statements, etc., but the possibility always exists that some such elements could be missed. These random choices are not necessarily inferior to the ones made by human beings, because in practice a person may not have the information or skill to make a wise choice. The systematic method may not even be helpful to the human tester, because the coverage it requires may not be useful in exposing failures. It might, e.g., be better to try some functions many times, even if this means missing others all together. Random testing can make such choices, whereas systematic testing cannot.

CRITIQUE OF RANDOM TESTING

Random testing has only a specialized niche in practice, mostly because an effective oracle is seldom available but also because of difficulties with the operational profile and with generation of pseudorandom input values. It is beginning to be used in theoretical studies, which requires critical attention to its assumptions.

Practical Issues

It can be argued that an operational profile is an essential but neglected part of practical system requirements analysis and that if proper attention were paid to this aspect of program development, random testing would benefit along with the developer, who would have a much better idea of what the system must handle. For unit testing, this argument is invalid—it is an essential feature of many software components, particularly those designed for reuse, that *any* usage is acceptable. Conventional random testing is inappropriate for such units, because its predictions are in general incorrect. The best one can do is test with a uniform distribution, and in some unanticipated application, the unit may be subjected to a usage profile that concentrates heavily on part of the input space, for which the predictions can be arbitrarily over-optimistic. Random unit testing may still be used to uncover failures, as described earlier. However, existing testing theory indicates that unit testing to establish software quality is inferior to a combination of formal and informal inspection methods.

On the other hand, the other practical drawback of random testing, the oracle problem, is not one that better requirements analysis should necessarily address. It is not always the business of a software end-user to know the answers so that the software can be checked. In some cases, it behooves a user to conduct an extensive acceptance test of software, e.g., by running an accounting program in parallel with a system it is to replace. But such tests are not random. If the user had an efficient means of calculating "any" result, the program being tested would not be needed. This argument applies to all testing, but to random testing with particular force, because the number of test points is large in random testing. Thus it cannot be argued that the user's ability to calculate expected results by hand (which is surely enough to be able to say that the application is well understood), constitutes an oracle. Similarly, a simple, slow algorithm is not an oracle for a faster production program, because there is not time to use it. In short, in many applications the user wants a few results, with high confidence that they are correct; random testing can guarantee this only by using a large test set, for which the only fast enough computation comes from the application program itself.

In special cases, however, an oracle does exist:

1. The program to be tested may be a replacement for a trusted program. The latter can then be used as an oracle.
2. Checking the results of a calculation may be easier than making the calculation, both in the sense of

computational complexity, and in the sense of intellectual control. For example, the program for solving an equation is typically slower and harder to understand than a program that substitutes solutions into an equation to check them. Yet the latter is an oracle for the former.

3. Some computations are paired with their inverses, as in code/decode and protocol applications. An "end-to-end" test can then be conducted by applying both functions and insisting that the input be reproduced as result. This procedure can be incorrect, because compensating failures can occur in computation and inverse, but a combination of program inspection and random testing can make it unlikely that such failures exist.
4. In multiversion programming, several programs to solve a common problem are developed independently. It is not correct to run these programs against each other as oracles, because all might fail at the same test point. Nevertheless, many failures are not common, and the more programs there are, the less likely that all will agree accidently.
5. Some formal specifications, notably for abstract data types, can be mechanically executed to provide an oracle (Antoy, 1992). This is the most general solution to the oracle problem, but also the most problematic, since the executable specification is usually very inefficient, and it may produce results in a domain difficult to compare with that of a conventional program.
6. Sometimes a physical system can be constructed to model the results of a computation, and measurements of this system can serve as an oracle. An interesting special case is the use of human vision as oracle for pictorial output. A person can "tell at a glance" if a complex colored picture is substantially correct, and this ability can be used in random testing of graphics programs (Taylor, 1989).

When an oracle exists, random testing is a possibility; without an oracle, it is not.

The final difficulty in applying random testing concerns generating pseudorandom values. Every computer program input is actually limited to a finite number of possibilities, because inputs use some medium of limited size for storage or expression. But in practice the limits are so large that subdomains might as well be infinite. For such large spaces, it is not clear what a pseudorandom value means.

An example will illustrate the difficulty. Suppose that one is testing a compiler, so that inputs are programs. What constitutes a "random" program? The problem is partly that of the operational profile in disguise: one must have information about what programs will in fact be compiled, and in particular about the proportion of correct programs, those with syntax errors, the range of sizes to be expected, etc. The obvious solution of sampling the actual input stream to an existing compiler is not promising. At what time of day should the samples be taken? Should programs that are trivial modifications of each other (as may occur when a clueless student is doing an assignment by trial and error) be excluded? And no matter how samples are obtained, they will be suspect because of peculiarities in the particular installation's workload, and it will prove very difficult to collect enough data points.

The alternative to collecting programs from the input stream is to try to generate test programs according to constructed usage information. But no matter how detailed this usage information is, the subdomains of the operational-profile partition will be large and somewhat vaguely defined. For example, for programming assignments in an undergraduate language class, the following might be about right: "Small programs of 100–200 statements, containing mostly simple assignment statements and conditionals, with less than 20 simple variables." There seems no possibility of generating such programs at random but to define as many small, orthogonal intervals as possible, make a succession of uniform pseudorandom choices from each interval, and observe constraints among them. In the example, one might select a size from 100 to 200 (say 163), a number of assignments from 130 to 150, (say 137), a number of conditionals from 2 to 26 (say 20), a sequence of 6 other statement types from {i/o, loop}, and a number of variables from 3 to 20 (say 7). These parameters involve a number of relationships and arbitrary choices for the intervals. However, there is still a long way to go before a test program is obtained: one must choose particular identifiers for the variables, the form of assignments, etc., and the whole must be a syntactically correct program (or should it be "slightly" incorrect?!). It seems unreasonable to insist that distributions be provided in the necessary detail; but if they are not, it is impossible to believe that the resulting tests will be random in any sense but the slang one that introduced this article. Thus random testing may be precluded by an inability to make reasonable pseudorandom choices.

The pseudorandom number generators provided with most languages and systems usually compute word-sized bit patterns that can be interpreted as approximations to reals $r \in [0,1]$. Other floating-point intervals can be obtained by scaling and offsetting r. A pseudorandom integer in $[n,m]$ can be obtained as $r \bmod (m-n+1)+n$. A caution is in order, however. Many systems do not provide an adequate pseudorandom number generator, and deficiencies are not documented. For example, the generator may have short cycles or even fixedpoints in the sequence it generates; the low-order bits may not themselves form a random sequence (so the use of the mod function to obtain integer sequences is unwise), etc. Knuth (1981) describes both the generation and testing of pseudorandom sequences.

In summary, the best practical application of random testing, one that can supply a plausible reliability figure for software from a successful test, requires the following:

1. The test is at the system level.
2. There is both an operational profile and the ability to generate intuitively representative pseudorandom values in its subclasses. (Or, equivalently, an operational distribution on the input space is known.)
3. An effective oracle is available.

When these conditions do not exist in the testing situation, not only is random testing counterindicated, but testing of any kind cannot provide a plausible prediction of software quality. Tests may uncover failures so that many defects are fixed, but confidence that the software will behave properly in normal use is attainable only by using methods other than testing.

Theoretical Deficiences

Most criticism of random testing is really objection to misapplication of the method using inappropriate input distributions, as indicated earlier. Using a uniform distribution because the operational profile is not available, or because no single profile is appropriate, may represent the best a tester can do, but when its predictions fail, the fault does not lie with the random-testing theory. Similarly, testing interactive or realtime software as if it were batch software, is simply engaging in wishful thinking. Unfortunately, the practical character of testing and its weak theoretical foundations encourage the idea that much effort is a substitute for well-founded techniques. The software must be tested, so we do the best we can and hope for the best. The worst misuse of testing theory occurs when random testing is not used at all; a systematic method is used, and claims for reliability (or even correctness!) are based on its success.

However, fundamental theoretical issues cloud even the most careful use of random testing. These issues can all be traced to the program input space, and the use of an operational profile there.

It was argued earlier that for certain unit tests, notably those of reusable components, no operational profile is appropriate. It is tempting to argue that this lack excuses the use of a uniform test distribution, perhaps with more than the usual number of test points. But a large input domain and an application that emphasizes only a small part of it, make this position untenable. The uniform-distribution test predictions can be wrong by many orders of magnitude—the random test might just as well not have been done. (Put another way, orders of magnitude more uniform-distribution tests will be required to make accurate predictions about the application. But there are already too many points in the random test sets to be practical.) The same argument can unfortunately be applied at the system level. Each human user may have a quite different profile for software use; and, each person's profile may change over time, quite discontinuously. When one profile has been used for random testing, the results may be arbitrarily incorrect for another profile. A simple example contrasts "novice" and "expert" users, who utilize the same software in quite different ways. It is a common experience that a novice can immediately break software that experts have been using for a long time without problems. The novice's first attempt is an input far outside the experts' operational profile. ("What did you do that for?! No one is dumb enough to try that!") Again it is tempting to use a uniform test distribution or some other compromise between possible profiles. But for general-purpose software, it may be a better description of reality to treat each user, perhaps each input from each user, as a unique special case rather than a sample from a distribution. And again the practical difficulties will not permit orders-of-magnitude over-testing to compensate for the wrong distribution.

The second difficulty is more fundamental, and illuminates the problems with an operational distribution. The inputs selected according to an operational distribution may not be independent in the sense needed for random testing, thus invalidating any prediction of the reliability theory presented in the section on Reliability and Random Testing. The difficulty is that the process by which failures result from software defects is not really a random one, but systematic, so that failures cannot be treated statistically.

We might suspect that there is a mismatch between the statistical theory and actual software failures, because the theory fails to predict important observed facts. For example, a software "law" that is observed empirically is that larger programs have more defects in rough proportion to their size (measured in source statements). This observation is easy to account for intuitively, since the defects result from errors made by human designers and programmers, and such errors occur when people are overwhelmed by complexity. Thus program size should enter the reliability model as a parameter, but as shown earlier, it does not. The theory predicts exactly the same reliability for a 10-line program computing roots of a quadratic equation as for a 100,000-line accounting system, if each is tested with the same number of points. The result seems intuitively wrong because there are more nooks and crannies in larger programs, which should take more test data to explore.

For the phenomenon of software failure to be treated as a random process relative to test inputs, there can be no failure correlation between inputs. To take the most extreme case, when a random phenomenon is being sampled, repeating a sample is meaningful because no two samples are really the same; the random variations that are being sought may act to make them different. But software is not random in this sense, and intuitively it does not give more confidence in a lower predicted failure rate to repeat the same test over and over. Unfortunately, apparently independent inputs can constitute "the same test" for the purposes of exposing a failure.

Consider the simple situation in which there is a fault in an arithmetic expression within a large program. The integer variable X is incorrectly used in the expression, so that for some values of X the expression takes the wrong value, and hence the program fails. X happens to be an input variable restricted to nonnegative values, but it also suffers a "state collapse" just before its use in the faulty expression. A state collapse (Voas, 1990) occurs when a program statement vastly reduces the potential values for X. For example

$$X := X \bmod 5$$

reduces the possible values for X to the set $\{0,1,2,3,4\}$. Of these, suppose that only 0 excites the fault in the following X expression. Then all of the X input values in (say) $\{5z+2 \mid z \geqq 0\}$ are the same relative to this fault (they do not excite it), yet the input distribution may select many "independent" values from this set. Intuitively, success on many such "independent" inputs gives false increments in confidence that the program will not fail.

Many similar examples can be constructed, in which relative to a particular program fault, many inputs are "the same test." Consider the faulty code as a "unit." Its use within the system has a peculiar operational distribution, very different from whatever distribution is applied as system input. Thus the predictions from the input distribution are incorrect, just as predictions from a unit test using one distribution are incorrect for an application in which the unit has a different usage distribution. Since the random testing method continues to send software back for repair until a test set succeeds, the correlated points, ones which are really the same relative to any undetected failures that remain, are finally all success points, so the predictions are always overly optimistic.

CURRENT AND FUTURE RESEARCH

In this section research ideas that will likely influence the theory and practice of random testing in the future are mentioned briefly.

A theory of uniformly sampling the program's entire state space, that is, the possible values of all its variables throughout execution, has been proposed (Hamlet, 1988). This theory is still subject to criticism like that that ends the section on Theoretical Deficiencies (Morell, 1990), because state values may also be correlated. To sidestep many of the difficulties connected with the operational distribution for programs, it has been proposed that program states be randomly perturbed and the change in results observed (Miller and co-workers, 1992). When results resist change through perturbations of a state, that state is called "insensitive." An insensitive state suggests that testing cannot detect failures there, so test points are likely to be correlated. Voas has combined sensitivity analysis with random testing to give a plausible theory of "statistical correctness" (Hamlet and Voas, 1993).

Successful application of probabilistic ideas to calculation and proof hold promise for testing in the future, testing that may use statistical methods, but will differ profoundly from what we now call random testing. The theoretical drawback in random testing, is that test success in the presence of potential failure is not necessarily an unlikely event, nor are multiple tests that miss a failure necessarily unlikely. In contrast, the probabilistic proof that a number is prime, by each probe that fails to show a number composite, substantially reduces the probability that it is composite. Thus a few probes can demonstrate a high probability that the number is prime. In testing, it is difficult to contrive a method for which probabilities behave in this desirable way. One suggestive research project is investigating "self-checking" algorithms (Blum and Raghavan, 1989), ways of invoking a program redundantly so its multiple consistent results make it very unlikely that any is wrong.

Finally, it has been suggested that the definition of *random* in testing be changed to the Kolmogorov notion of "difficult to recognize algorithmically." A test that is truly random in this sense, can be shown to be foolproof (Podgurski, 1991).

BIBLIOGRAPHY

S. Antoy and R. G. Hamlet, "Self-Checking Against Formal Specifications, *Proc. Int. Conf. on Computing and Information,* Toronto, May 1992, pp. 355–360.

M. Blum and P. Raghavan, "Program Correctness: Can One Test for It?," in G. X. Ritter, ed., *Proc. IFIP '89,* North-Holand, 1989, pp. 127–134.

R. W. Butler and G. B. Finelli, The Infeasibility of Experimental Quantification of Life-Critical Sofware Reliability, *Proc. ACM SIGSOFT Conference on Software for Critical Systems,* New Orleans, Dec. 1991, pp. 66–76.

J. Duran and S. Ntafos, "An Evaluation of Random Testing," *IEEE Trans. Software Eng.* **SE-10**, 438–444 (July 1984).

R. G. Hamlet, "Probable Correctness Theory," *Info. Proc. Letters* **25,** 17–25 (April, 1987).

R. G. Hamlet and R. Taylor, "Partition Testing Does Not Inspire Confidence," *IEEE Trans. Software Eng.* **SE-16,** 1402–1411 (Dec. 1990).

R. G. Hamlet and J. M. Voas, "Faults on its Sleeve, Amplifying Software Reliability Testing," *Int. Symposium on Software Testing and Analysis,* Boston, June, 1993 pp. 89–98.

D. L. Knuth, *The Art of Computer Programming,* vol 2: *Seminumerical Algorithms,* 2nd ed., Addison Wesley, Reading, Mass., 1981.

K. Miller, L. Morell, R. Noonan, S. Park, D. Nicol, B. Murrill, and J. Voas, "Estimating the Probability of Failure when Testing Reveals no Failures," *IEEE Trans. Software Eng.* **SE-18,** 33–44 (Jan. 1992).

L. J. Morell and J. M. Voas, "Inadequacies of Datastate Space Sampling as a Measure of Trustworthiness," *Software Engineering Notes,* 73-74 (1991).

J. D. Musa, "Faults, Failures, and a Metrics Revolution," *IEEE Software,* 85, 91 (March, 1989).

D. L. Parnas, A. van Schouwen, and S. Kwan, "Evaluation of Safety-Critical Software," *CACM* **33**, 636–648 (June, 1990).

A. Podgurski, "Reliability, Sampling, and Algorithmic Randomness," *Proc. Symposium on Software Testing, Analysis, and Verification (TAV4),* Victoria, B.C., Oct. 1991, pp. 11–20.

M. L. Shooman, *Software Engineering, Design, Reliability, and Management,* McGraw-Hill, New York, 1983.

G. L. Steele, Jr. and co-workers, *The Hacker's Dictionary,* Harper & Row, New York, 1983.

R. Taylor, "An Example of Large Scale Random Testing," *Proc. Seventh Annual Pacific Northwest Software Quality Conference,* Portland, Ore., Sept. 1989, pp. 339–348.

J. M. Voas, "Preliminary Observations on Program Testability, *Proc. Ninth Annual Pacific Northwest Software Quality Conference,* Portland, Ore., Oct. 1991, pp. 235–247.

RICHARD HAMLET
Portland State University

RAPID PROTOTYPING

INTRODUCTION: WHY RAPID PROTOTYPING IS NEEDED

Explicit process models for software development have evolved in response to a variety of problems encountered in the development of large, complex software systems.

These problems include cost/schedule overruns and production of systems that do not operate as specified or do not meet customer needs. Process models have converged on rapid prototyping methods to reduce risks of software misdevelopment.

Before process models had been made explicit, software development suffered from chaotic implementation without much prior requirements analysis or design. The waterfall model has introduced a phased approach that produces a series of documents containing requirements, specifications, and designs before detailed implementation and testing of the software. Realizations of this model such as DOD-STD-2167 include review processes for these documents that are supposed to detect and correct errors before implementation, when they are relatively inexpensive to correct. The main problem with this approach is the assumption that system requirements can be discovered and frozen before implementation. This assumption has often been found to be invalid in practice, especially for first-of-a-kind systems. Significant project risks are associated with detecting requirements errors in the testing phase, near the end of the project when there is not enough time and money left to correct the errors.

Formulating requirements that accurately represent the customers' needs is a limiting factor in producing useful software, particularly for large systems that serve diversified user communities. Different people have partially overlapping and sometimes contradictory viewpoints on different aspects of the problem that are associated with their particular job functions. Analysts must create precise, formal models of unfamiliar problems, based on imprecise communication with people, each of whom has only a partial understanding of the system requirements. The situation is worst for new applications of computers because the proposed system may fundamentally redefine the job functions of the customers so that the introduction of the system can cause changes in its own requirements. The full impact of a proposed software requirement can therefore be very difficult to predict and assess.

The transition from fluctuating informal views of the problem to a fixed formal model is fundamentally uncertain. Reasonably accurate models can be created using an iterative guess/check/modify cycle that relies on prototype demonstrations and customer feedback to converge to a consensus about the requirements. The purpose of software prototyping is to help customers understand and criticize proposed systems and to explore the new possibilities that computer solutions can bring to their problems in a timely and cost effective manner (Luqi, 1991; Luqi and Royce, 1992). Measurements of prototypes can reduce uncertainty about the properties of a proposed design before it is implemented, supporting assessments of suitability, feasibility, and performance.

The main incentive for using prototypes is economic: scale models and prototype versions of most systems are much less expensive to build than the final versions. Prototypes should therefore be used to evaluate proposed systems if acceptance by the customer or the feasibility of development is in doubt. The need for software prototyping has become more urgent as systems being developed have grown more complex, more likely to have requirements errors, and more expensive to implement. Case studies illustrating this dilemma can be found in (Connell and Shafer, 1989).

WHAT IS RAPID PROTOTYPING?

Prototyping is a class of software development methods that use software prototypes of the envisioned system. A prototype is an executable model of a proposed system that accurately reflects a chosen subset of its properties, such as display formats, computed results, or response times. Prototypes are useful for formulating and validating requirements, resolving technical design issues, and supporting computer aided design of both software and hardware components of proposed systems. Rapid prototyping refers to the capability to create a prototype with significantly less effort than it takes to produce an implementation for operational use. Rapid prototyping usually implies some degree of automated code generation.

Relation to the Final System

Prototypes can be developed either to be thrown away after producing some insight, or to evolve into the product version of the software. Each of these approaches has its benefits and disadvantages, and the most appropriate choice depends on the context of the effort.

A software prototype may not satisfy all of the constraints on the final version of the system. For example, the prototype may provide only a subset of all the required functions, it may be expressed in a more powerful or more flexible language than the final version, it may run on a machine with more resources than the proposed target architecture, it may be less efficient in both time and space that the final version, it may have limited capacity (databases may be implemented in main memory), it may not include full facilities for error checking and fault tolerance, and it may not have the same degree of concurrency as the final version. Such simplifications are often introduced to make the prototype easier and faster to build. To be effective, partial prototypes must have a clearly defined purpose that determines what aspects of the system must be faithfully reproduced and which ones can safely be neglected.

The Throw-Away Approach. The main advantage of the throw-away approach is that it enables use of special-purpose languages and tools even if they introduce limitations that would not be acceptable in an operational environment or even if they are not capable of addressing the entire problem. The throw-away approach is most appropriate in the project acquisition phase where the prototype is used to demonstrate the feasibility of a new concept, and to convince a potential sponsor to fund a proposed development project. In such a context, available resources are skimpy and the ability to communicate the advantages of a new approach via a very low cost demonstration can be critical for creating a new project.

The most apparent disadvantage of a throw-away prototype is spending implementation effort on code that will not contribute directly to the final product. There is also the temptation to skip or abbreviate documentation for throw-away code. This temptation is harmful because the lessons learned from the prototyping effort may be lost if they are not recorded, and because lack of documentation and degradation of the initial design simplicity may block the evolution of the prototype, before it reaches a form that captures the customer's needs with respect to the scope of the prototyping effort. The throw-away approach can be a stopgap for an inadequate level of technology, and is most appropriate for rough system mock-ups used at the very earliest stages of a project.

The Evolutionary Build Approach. The evolutionary build approach produces a series of prototypes in which the final version becomes the software product. This approach depends on special tools and techniques because it is usually not possible to put a prototype into production use without significant changes to its implementation to optimize the code and to complete all of the details. The conceptual models and designs contained in a prototype can usually be used in the final version. Precise specifications for the components of a prototype and clear documentation of its design are therefore critical for effective software prototyping, as are tools for transforming and completing designs and implementations. The technology needed to support this approach is beginning to emerge (Budde and coworkers).

Relation to the Software Evolution Process

Rapid prototyping should be an integral part of the software development and evolution process. In recognition of this position, the 2167A standard for development of software for the U.S. government has been adjusted to include tailoring to ensure that only cost effective requirements are cited in defense solicitations and contracts (DOD, 1988). Prototyping can reduce the amount of maintenance effort spent on correcting requirements errors after systems have been delivered. However, prototyping is difficult to retrofit into a waterfall model, and requires explicit planning for iterations.

Relation to Software Automation

To be effective, prototypes must be constructed and modified rapidly, accurately, and cheaply. They do not have to be efficient, complete, portable, or robust, and they do not have to use the same hardware, system software, or implementation language as the delivered system. Automated construction of programs is needed to support the evolutionary approach to rapid prototyping, and such tools can be very useful in this context even if the resulting programs are not very efficient. Rapid prototyping is a high leverage area for the application of emerging technologies for computer-aided software development.

A RAPID PROTOTYPING PROCESS MODEL

An evolutionary software prototyping process is illustrated in Figure 1. The initial prototype is produced based on a requirements analysis of the customer's problem. This

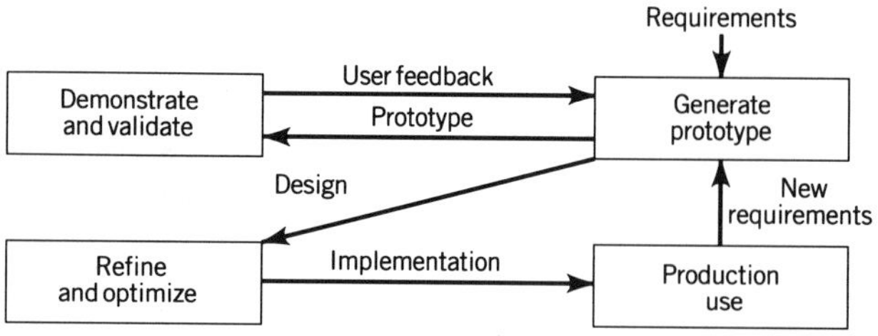

Figure 1. The prototyping process.

analysis is needed to ensure that the initial version of the prototype is close enough to what the customers need to enable them to provide meaningful evaluations and criticisms. Each succeeding version of the prototype is produced based upon an analysis of the customer's reaction to demonstrations of the previous version, and should be a better approximation to the final system. Delivered products are derived from prototypes that are accepted by customers via an optional optimization process. Maintenance activities are sparked by new customer requirements, which restart the prototyping process and extend the series of prototypes until a new stable point is reached and a new version of the product is produced by another instance of the optimization process. The spiral model is well known because it combines the common knowledge of waterfall model, incremental method and process model work into an attractive notation, even with less specific variation of this process.

Sometimes generating several small partial prototypes to answer different kinds of questions, rather than creating one large prototype, can be useful. For example, one prototype can be used to explore user interface requirements, while others can be used to refine requirements on system behavior and system performance. In such a case, each prototype presents a faithful model of the proposed system only for the selected aspects of the system. For example, the user interface prototype may have a high fidelity model of the display, including menu entries, shapes and placement of buttons and windows, colors, printing styles, and so on, but the displayed system responses may be randomly generated or drawn from a fixed data file.

Some advantages of this approach are that prototypes of different aspects of the system can be developed concurrently and independently, that each fragment is relatively small, simple, and easy to change, and that different tools and environments can be used for different aspects. The last property can be important in the short term, if tools are available for solving different parts of the problem, but these tools have not been integrated together into a comprehensive prototyping environment.

USER'S VIEW OF AN INTEGRATED PROTOTYPING ENVIRONMENT

The main functions that should be provided by an integrated prototyping environment are a convenient interface for formulating and viewing the specifications and design of a prototype, execution and analysis capabilities, support

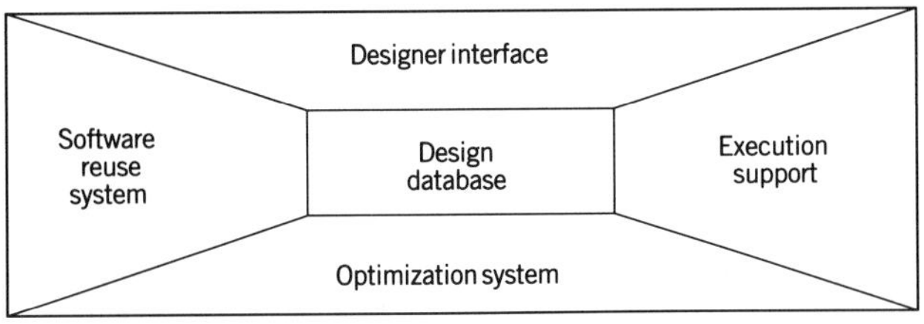

Figure 2. An integrated prototyping environment.

for evolution and reuse, and optimization capabilities, as illustrated in Figure 2.

The user interface should support both graphical and textual design representations. Graphical representations are useful for structural information, while text forms are appropriate for behavioral and performance specifications. The designer interface should also provide decision support functions for the designer and a high level model of the decisions that the designer must make, so that major choices can be picked from menus and implied details can be supplied by the design management system. Such facilities are essential for reducing the amount of detail that a prototype designer must explicitly consider. Static analysis tools should help the designer assess prototype properties such as type consistency, feasibility of timing constraints, consistency between the levels of a hierarchical description, preconditions on input parameters and generic parameters, constraints on relative rates of producer and consumer processes, absence of deadlocks in distributed and parallel systems, absence of unhandled exceptions, etc.

Execution support should include methods for executing incomplete specifications, and facilities for controlling, monitoring, measuring, and summarizing the results of execution as well as debugging facilities. Reusable components are needed to realize specified behavior if details of algorithms and data structures have not been given by the designer.

The design database should support the evolution of the prototype by managing the dependencies between the requirements and the prototype design, supporting change impact analysis, recording the history of the prototype development, coordinating concurrent updates to the design, and providing facilities for combining design alternatives in different combinations. Meaning-changing transformations are also important for supporting evolution (Berzins and co-workers, 1993).

Optimization facilities are needed to support the transition from the prototype version to the software product. In an integrated environment, such optimizations should be performed by a computer-aided process. Such a process can be supported by transformational implementation systems (Bauer and co-workers, 1989). This optimization process can be partially automatic and can be partially guided by the designer via annotations that provide implementation advice. Such annotations enable the details of the code to be generated automatically from the same source as the prototype, while allowing designers to tune the performance of the implementation by selectively overriding the default implementation methods used during prototype execution. Such facilities are essential for a mature integrated prototyping environment because they preserve the flexibility inherent in the prototype description to support system maintenance and rederivation.

SUPPORTING TECHNOLOGY FOR EFFECTIVE PROTOTYPING

Computer-aided prototyping depends on the development of several new technologies, and is gradually migrating into practical use as these technologies mature. The needed technologies involve

1. Prototyping languages
2. Execution support
3. Software reuse
4. Computer-aided design

Prototyping Languages

Rapid prototyping languages are used to create software prototypes, which are mechanically processable and executable descriptions or simplified models of proposed software systems. They are also used to document, analyze, and adjust the models. A prototyping language is used by both people and the software tools in a prototyping environment such as CAPS (Luqi and Ketabchi, 1988). To support the human users, a prototyping language should be easy to write, understand, and modify. To support the tools, the language should be easy to analyze and transform. An example of a prototyping language is PSDL (Luqi and co-workers). PSDL provides a simple representation of system decompositions using data flow diagrams augmented with non-procedural control constraints and timing constraints (maximum response times, maximum execution times, minimum inter-stimulus periods, periods, and deadlines). The language models both periodic and data-driven tasks, and both discrete (transaction-oriented) and continuous (sampled) data streams. The CAPS system provides automated tools for generating static schedules to guarantee hard real-time constraints as well as an execution support system that generates code for adapting, interconnecting, and controlling the execution of reusable software components.

A prototyping language should provide a simple computational model and primitives that match the problem domain as closely as possible. This can be done either via domain-specific prototyping languages or by providing domain-specific components and toolkits.

In addition to an execution capability, languages used in prototyping must simplify the description of software and capture specifications and requirements. Specifications and links to requirements are needed to record which aspects of the prototype are system requirements, so that they can be distinguished from accidental consequences of execution support mechanisms. This distinction affects the presentation and analysis of prototype demonstrations and the transformation of stable prototypes into software products.

Execution Support Technology

Ordinary compiler technology is insufficient for execution of a prototyping language. Conventional translation techniques must be coupled with transformations and application-specific techniques for automatically generating programs to allow the execution of incompletely specified facilities and with processes for scheduling to meet real-time constraints (Chang and co-workers).

Real-Time Scheduling. Prototyping of embedded software presents special challenges because such software is often associated with real-time constraints that must be met under all operating conditions. Explicit control over the scheduling of parallel tasks is usually necessary to guarantee that such hard real-time constraints can be met, since the scheduling capabilities provided by most operating systems are somewhat removed from the level of support needed for implementing hard real-time systems. The execution support system for a prototyping language that addresses real-time systems should therefore provide higher level facilities for scheduling real-time operations. Such facilities can be classified as on-line (done at run-time) and off-line (done prior to execution). There is no universally accepted approach to real-time scheduling. Optimal scheduling algorithms are very time consuming, and generally cannot be carried out on-line, while off-line approaches are inflexible and do not handle overload situations very well. Thus the execution support system for a prototyping language should provide the designer with several choices of scheduling methods, and should generate the code structures necessary to realize those methods in practice.

Program Transformations. Transformations are needed to execute incompletely specified components. Such transformations should supply reasonable default values for attributes necessary for execution if the designer does not explicitly specify them. This is essential for testing and demonstrating partially completed prototypes. Default values can be explicitly overridden to produce more accurate models of the system or to improve its performance. Default implementations can be created by simple or increasingly sophisticated techniques, such as interactively asking the user to supply values, using random selections from a fixed set of responses, using logic programming to simulate black-box specifications, or using transformation techniques to generate efficient implementations from the black-box descriptions.

Automated Program Construction. The most powerful systems currently in use are designed for specific problem domains. Some problem domains for which computer-aided prototyping tools have been developed include business information processing, user interfaces, computer languages, and real-time systems.

Generators for business information systems provide graphical interfaces to databases to define database schemas, queries, and reports by graphically defining table layouts. There are many commercially available tools in this category.

Generators for language processors are mostly based on attribute grammars. These systems can generate various tools for computer languages based on a context free grammar for the language, augmented with equations defining computed attributes for the nodes of the parse tree (Herndon and Berzins, 1988). This technology can be used to prototype tools for computer languages, including translators, interpreters, pretty printers, type checkers, data-flow analyzers, and so forth. Applications span programming languages, specification languages, data definition languages for databases, hardware description languages, and command languages for applications programs. Attribute grammar processors have been coupled to generators for syntax-directed editors (Reps and Teitelbaum, 1988) and program transformation systems (Abraido-Fandino, 1987).

Interface generation systems (Linton and co-workers, 1989) generate graphical user interfaces based on a set of predefined components such as windows, menus, scroll bars, and buttons. These components are placed and adapted interactively via a mouse and menu interface.

A knowledge-based approach is needed to provide adequate execution support for a prototyping language without requiring excessive algorithmic detail. This can be done via knowledge base support for finding realizations of common operations in the application domain.

The environment should assist the designer in retrieving reusable components, and in tailoring and combining available components to fulfill queries that do not exactly match any of the reusable components explicitly stored in the software base.

Software Reuse Technology

Software reuse is essential for rapid prototyping, because it can enable the designer to avoid many details that have been considered previously. Reuse can be applied at the levels of code (algorithms and data structures), design (system decompositions), and requirements models (domain specific concepts). Most of the work on reuse has focused on the code level. A framework for reuse at the specification and requirement levels is described in (Berzins and Luqi, 1991). Reuse has been difficult to put into practice because a large software base of components is needed to cover an appreciable part of the prototyping effort, and the difficulties of searching increase with the size of the software base. Manual examination of reusable components must be avoided or limited to very small sets to keep search effort from swamping the potential benefits of reuse. The use of specifications in retrieval can help because reading specifications is less work than reading code.

Automated support is essential to realize the potential benefits of reuse. Specifications are needed to help people and tools assess components without analyzing the code (Rollins and Wing, 1990; Steigerwald and co-workers, 1991). The Draco project has explored domain specific software reuse based on domain models and code generation

(Neighbors, 1989). Specifications can also capture behavioral aspects of components, and can thus provide much better discrimination and smaller candidate sets than informal methods based on keywords and faceted classification (Prieto-Diaz, 1991). This approach is attractive in the context of prototyping because specification information must be developed to document the design, so that there is little additional effort required to use this information for retrieval of reusable components as well.

Computer-Aided Design

The environment should contain models of common design activities and common classes of design decisions, to allow prototypes to be expressed in the conceptual framework of the designer rather than that of the machine. If the system is aware of the choices faced by a designer at each point in the design, it can present compact representations of the choices using menus.

The tools should provide decision support to the designer, and should be able to fill in details of the design that are implied by decisions explicitly entered by the designer. Examples of decision support include feasibility analysis for real-time constraints, performance assessment with respect to different hardware architectures, and static analysis to detect inconsistencies and incomplete aspects of the design.

Computer-aided design relevant to prototyping includes configuration management, integration of subsystems, high level debugging, explanations, and optimization.

Configuration Management. Configuration management systems record dependencies between different versions of a structured set of documents, record evolution history, help determine the impact of a change, and may help recombine different versions of different parts of a system.

System Integration. Different subsystems of large software products are often developed by different teams or different contractors. Integration tools can aid this process by supporting validation of the decomposition prior to dividing up the work, and can be used for comparison purposes when assessing whether delivered subsystems conform to their requirements. Both testing and proof technologies are relevant to checking soundness of a decomposition.

High Level Debugging. Errors and failures during prototype execution should be mapped from the programming language level to level of the prototyping language, to keep programming details from intruding when the designer tests and demonstrates the prototype.

Explanations. Justifications for decisions made by the tools should be available to provide feedback to the designer in cases where automated design completion procedures fail. Such a facility is needed to support systematic computer-aided design in situations where complete automation is not possible. This requires an expert system with a substantial knowledge base.

Optimization. The transformations for optimizing a prototype version of a system to produce a production version should be performed with minimum interaction with the designer.

Computer-aided prototyping of real-time systems is supported by the prototyping language PSDL (Luqi and co-workers, 1988) and the associated prototyping system CAPS (Luqi and Ketabchi, 1988). CAPS uses software base of reusable components, a program generator, a static scheduler, and a dynamic scheduler to realize systems containing both functions with hard real-time constraints and non-time-critical functions.

Other efforts to create computer-aided software design environments that can be used to support prototyping are the GIST system (Cohen, 1983), the PDS system (Cheatham and co-workers, 1984), the knowledge-based software assistant project (RADC, 1987), the programmer's apprentice (Rich and Waters, 1990), the EPROS prototyping system based on executable specifications (Hekmatpour and Ince, 1988), and the OBSERV system based on logic programming (Yehudai and Tyszberowitcz, 1990).

CONCLUSION

In the future, prototyping will be integrated with final implementation. To produce deliverable software, prototyping tools must be extended with optimization capabilities to produce programs whose efficiency is comparable to the designs of competent programmers. The beginnings of the required technologies are visible: correctness-preserving transformations and performance estimation techniques to guide derivation strategies. Work on reasoning support and methods for interactively supporting software engineers, such as the Programmer's Apprentice effort, are also critical for achieving the next level of automation in prototyping.

A new kind of language may be needed to smoothly integrate rapid prototyping with final implementation. Such a language should combine the flexibility of an interpreted language with a powerful set of features for selectively declaring various kinds of compile-time constraints as consistent refinements. Some critical aspects of such a language are support for a mixture of interpreted and compiled code, smooth integration of optional explicit storage management policies with a default policy of garbage collection, optional explicit synchronization policies with a default of mutual exclusion on multiprocess interactions, optional compile-time method resolution for types with subtypes with a default of run-time method selection for each instance, and optional explicit type declarations with defaults based on type inference procedures. These facilities will support refinement of the prototype into the final version by supplying additional information, and automatically transforming frequently used components to improve efficiency. Initially this process will be done via optional implementation advice supplied by software engineers, in analogy to the pragmas in the programming language Ada.

In the longer term, prototyping systems will have reasoning capabilities and extensive knowledge bases which may include generic models of the problem domain, common goals of customers, common system structures, and generators producing specifications and code for classes of software components. Facilities for supporting formal verification of prototype decompositions are desirable to ensure that proposed decompositions are viable, especially if the subcomponents are to be built by different contractors.

BIBLIOGRAPHY

L. Abraido-Fandino, "An Overview of REFINE 2.0," in *Proceedings of the Second International Symposium on Knowledge Engineering,* Madrid, Spain, April 8–10, 1987.

F. Bauer, B. Moller, H. Partsch, and P. Pepper, "Formal Program Construction by Transformations—Computer-Aided, Intuition-Guided Programming,"*IEEE Trans. on Software Eng.* **15**(2), 165–180 (Feb. 1989).

V. Berzins and Luqi, *Software Engineering with Abstractions,* Addison-Wesley, Reading, Mass., 1991.

V. Berzins, Luqi, and A. Yehudai, "Using Transformations in Specification-Based Prototyping," *IEEE Trans. on Software Eng.* **19**(5) (May 1993).

R. Budde, K. Kautz, K. Kuhlenkamp, and H. Züllighoven, *Prototyping An Approach to Evolutionary System Development,* Springer-Verlag, New York, 1992.

S. Chang, J. Stankovic and K. Ramamritham, "Scheduling Algorithms for Hard Real-Time Systems," in *Tutorial on Hard Real-Time Systems,* IEEE, 1988, pp. 150–173.

T. Cheatham, J. Townley, and G. Holloway, "A System for Program Refinement," in *Interactive Programming Environments,* McGraw-Hill, 1984, pp. 198–214.

D. Cohen, "Symbolic Execution of the Gist Specification Language," in *Proceedings of the Eighth International Joint Conference on Artificial Intelligence,* 1983, pp. 17–20.

J. Connell and L. Shafer, *Structured Rapid Prototyping,* Yourdon Press, 1989.

Defense System Software Development, DOD-STD-2167A, Department of Defense, Feb. 1988.

S. Hekmatpour and D. Ince, *Software Prototyping, Formal Methods and VDM,* Addison-Wesley, Reading, Mass., 1988.

R. Herndon and V. Berzins, "The Realizable Benefits of a Language Prototyping Language," *IEEE Trans. on Software Eng.* **SE-14**(6), 803–809 (June 1988).

M. Linton, J. Vlissides, and P. Calder, "Composing User Interfaces with InterViews," *IEEE Computer* **22**(2) (Feb. 1989), 8–22.

Luqi and M. Ketabchi, "A Computer Aided Prototyping System," *IEEE Software* **5**(2) 66–72 (March 1988).

Luqi, V. Berzins, and R. Yeh, "A Prototyping Language for Real-Time Software," *IEEE Trans. on Software Eng.* **14**(10) 1409–1423 (Oct., 1988).

Luqi, "Computer-aided Software Prototyping," *IEEE Computer* **24**(9) 111–112 (Sept. 1991).

Luqi and W. Royce, "Status Report: Computer-Aided Prototyping," *IEEE Software,* 77–81 (Nov. 1992).

J. Neighbors, "Draco: a Method for Engineering Reusable Software Systems," in T. Biggerstaff and A. Perlis, eds., *Software Reusability,* ACM Press, 1989, pp. 295–320.

R. Prieto-Diaz, "Implementing Faceted Classification for Software Reuse," *Comm. of the ACM* **34**(5), 88–97 (May 1991).

T. Reps and T. Teitelbaum, *The Synthesizer Generator: A System for Constructing Language-Based Editors,* Springer-Verlag, New York, 1988.

C. Rich and R. Waters, *The Programmer's Apprentice,* Addison Wesley, Reading, Mass. 1990.

E. Rollins and J. Wing, *Specifications as Search Keys for SW Libraries: A Case Study Using Lambda Prolog,* CMU, Computer Science Department, Carnegie-Mellon University, Pittsburgh, PA, CMU-CS-90-159, Sept. 1990.

Proceedings of the 2nd Annual RADC Knowledge-Based Software Assistant Conference, Rome Air Development Center, Utica, N.Y., Aug. 1987.

R. Steigerwald, Luqi, and J. McDowell, "A CASE Tool for Reusable Software Component Storage and Retrieval in Rapid Prototyping," *Information and Software Technology* **38**(11) (Nov. 1991).

A. Yehudai and S. Tyszberowitcz, "OBSERV—A Prototyping Language and Environment Combining Object Oriented Approach, State Machines, and Logic Programming," in *Proceedings of the 23rd Annual Hawaii International Conference on System Science,* IEEE Computer Society, Jan. 1990, pp. 247–256.

Luqi
Naval Postgraduate School
Raymond Yeh
International Software Systems, Inc.

RATE-MONOTONIC ANALYSIS

INTRODUCTION

Real-time computing systems are critical to an industrialized nation's technological infrastructure. Modem telecommunication systems, automated factories, sophisticated defense systems, power plants, aircrafts, airports, space stations and high energy physics experiments cannot operate without them. Indeed, real-time computing systems control the very systems that keep us productive, and enable us to explore new frontiers of science and engineering.

In real-time applications, the correctness of a computation depends not only upon its results but also upon the time at which its outputs are generated. The measures of merit in a real-time system include:

- Predictably fast response to urgent events.
- High degree of schedulability: Schedulability is the degree of resource utilization at or below which the timing requirements of tasks can be satisfied. It can be thought of as a measure of the number of *timely*-transactions per second.
- Stability under transient overload: When the system is overloaded by events and it is impossible to meet all the deadlines, the deadlines of selected critical tasks must still be guaranteed.

Generalized Rate-Monotonic Scheduling (GRMS) theory allows developers of real-time systems to meet application timing requirements by managing system concurrency and timing constraints at the level of tasking and message passing. In essence, GRMS theory guarantees that all tasks will meet their deadlines if the total system utilization of these tasks lies below a known bound, and these tasks are scheduled using appropriate algorithms. This analytic, engineering basis makes real-time systems considerably easier to develop, modify and maintain.

The generalized rate-monotonic scheduling theory begins with the pioneering work of (Liu and Layland, 1973) in which the rate-monotonic algorithm was introduced for scheduling independent periodic tasks. The rate-monotonic scheduling (RMS) algorithm gives higher priorities to periodic tasks with higher rates. RMS is an optimal static priority scheduling algorithm for independent periodic tasks when task deadlines are at period boundaries. The optimality of RMS is in the sense that if any static priority scheduling algorithm can schedule a set of independent periodic tasks with end of period deadlines, then RMS can also schedule the task set. RMS theory has since been generalized to analyze the schedulability of aperiodic tasks with both soft deadlines and hard deadlines (Sprunt and co-workers, 1989), interdependent tasks that must synchronize (Sha and co-workers, 1990b; Rajkumar and co-workers, 1988; Rajkumar, 1991), tasks with deadlines shorter than the periods (Leung and Whitehead, 1982), tasks with arbitrary deadlines (Lehoczky, 1990), and single tasks having multiple code segments with different priority assignment (Harbour and co-workers, 1991). An RMS-based technique called "period transformation" allows a task set to meet its critical deadlines even under overload conditions as long as the utilization of the critical tasks is below the schedulability bound (Sha and co-workers, 1986). RMS has also been extended to analyze scheduling of wide area networks (Sha and co-workers, 1992). RMS has also been applied to improve response times of aperiodic messages in a token-ring network (Strosnider and Marchok, 1989). The implications of RMS to Ada scheduling rules are discussed in (Sha and Goodenough, 1990), and the schedulability analysis of input/output paradigms have been treated in (Klein and Ralya, 1990). The theory has also been applied in the development of the ARTS real-time operating system (Tokuda and co-workers, 1987) and the Real-Time Mach operating system (Tokuda, 1991). Processor cache designs for real-time systems using RMS were developed in Kirk and Strosnider, 1990. Schedulability models for different operating system paradigms have been developed in Katcher and co-workers, 1991. RMS has also been applied to recover from transient hardware faults (Ramos-Thuel and Strosnider, 1991). The rate-monotonic scheduling algorithm with all its extensions is referred to as Generalized Rate-Monotonic Scheduling (GRMS).

Because of its versatility and ease of use, GRMS has gained rapid acceptance. For example, it is used for developing real-time software in the NASA Space Station Freedom Program (Gafford, 1990), the European Space Agency (ESA, 1990), and is supported by the IEEE Futurebus+ Standard (Futurebus+, 1990) and IEEE POSIX.4 (POSIX, 1991). A review of the basic results follows and then these results are illustrated with example applications.

OVERVIEW OF GENERALIZED RATE MONOTONIC SCHEDULING

The scheduling of independent periodic and aperiodic tasks begins this article. Then the issues of task synchronization and the effect of having task deadlines before the end of their period boundaries is addressed.

Scheduling Independent Periodic Tasks

A periodic task τ_i is characterized by a worst-case computation time C_i and a period T_i. Unless mentioned otherwise, assume that each instance of a periodic task must finish by the end of its period boundary when the next task instance arrives. Tasks are *independent* if they do not need to synchronize with each other. The following theorem (Liu and Layland, 1973) can be used to determine whether a set of independent periodic tasks is schedulable.

Theorem 1. A set of n independent periodic tasks scheduled by the rate-monotonic algorithm will always meet their deadlines for all task start times, if

$$\frac{C_1}{T_1} + \frac{C_2}{T_2} + \ldots + \frac{C_n}{T_n} \leqq n(2^{1/n} - 1)$$

where C_i is the worst-case execution time and T_i is the period of task τ_i.

C_i / T_i is the *utilization* of the resource by task τ_i. The bound on the total schedulable utilization, $n(2^{1/n}-1)$, rapidly converges to ln 2=0.69 as n becomes large.

The bound of Theorem 1 is the least upper bound of schedulable processor utilization for the rate-monotonic scheduling algorithm. It is very pessimistic because the worst-case task set is contrived and highly unlikely to be encountered in practice. The actual boundary for task sets encountered in practice is often over 90%. The remaining utilization can still be used by background tasks with low priority. An exact schedulability test based on the *critical zone* theorem rephrased from (Liu and Layland 1973) can be used to determine whether a set of tasks having utilization greater than the bound of Theorem 1, can meet all its deadlines.

Theorem 2. For a set of independent periodic tasks, if a task τ_i meets its *first* deadline $D_i \leq T_i$, when all the higher priority tasks are started at the same time, then it can meet all its future deadlines with any task start times.

It is important to note that Theorem 2 applies to any static priority assignment, not just rate-monotonic priority assignment. The following procedure (Lehoczky and co-workers, 1989) verifies if a task can meet its first deadline. Consider any task τ_n with a period T_n, deadline $D_n \leq T_n$, and computation C_n. Let tasks τ_1 to τ_{n-1} have higher priorities than τ_n. Suppose that all the tasks start at time $t=0$. At any time t, the total cumulative demand on CPU time by these n tasks is:

$$W_n(t) = C_1 \left\lceil \frac{t}{T_1} \right\rceil + \ldots + C_n \left\lceil \frac{t}{T_n} \right\rceil = \sum_{j=1}^{n} C_j \left\lceil \frac{t}{T_j} \right\rceil$$

The term $\lceil t/T_j \rceil$ represents the number of times task τ_i arrives during interval [0, t] and therefore $C_j \lceil t/T_j \rceil$ represents its demand during interval [0, t]. For example let $T_1=10, C_1=5$. When $t=9$, task τ_1 demands 10 units of execution time. When $t=11$, task τ_1 has arrived again, and the cumulative demand becomes 15 units of execution.
Suppose that task τ_n completes its execution exactly at time t before its deadline D_n. This means that the total cumulative demand from the n tasks up to time t, $W_n(t)$, is exactly equal to t, that is, $W_n(t)=t$. A method for finding the completion time of task τ_i; that is, the instance when $W_i(t)=t$ is given below.

$$\text{Set } t_0 \leftarrow \sum_{j=1}^{i} C_j$$
$$t_1 \leftarrow W_i(t_0);$$
$$t_2 \leftarrow W_i(t_1);$$
$$t_3 \leftarrow W_i(t_2);$$
$$\vdots$$
$$t_k \leftarrow W_i(t_{k-1});$$
$$\text{Stop when } (W_i(t_k) = t_k)$$

This procedure is referred to as the *completion time* test. If all the tasks complete before their deadlines, then the task set is schedulable. For example:

Example 1. Consider a task set with the following independent periodic tasks with end of the period deadlines:

- Task τ_1: $C_1=40$; $T_1=100$
- Task τ_2: $C_2=40$; $T_2=150$
- Task τ_3: $C_3=100$; $T_2=350$

The total utilization of tasks τ_1 and τ_2 is 0.67 which is less than 0.828, the bound for two tasks given by boundary Theorem 1. Hence these two tasks are schedulable. However the utilization of these three tasks is 0.90 which exceeds 0.779, Theorem 1's bound for three tasks. Therefore, apply the completion time test to determine the schedulability of task τ_3.

$$t_0=C_1+C_2+C_3=40+40+100=180$$

Tasks τ_1 and τ_2 are initiated one additional time in the interval (0, 180). Taking this additional execution into consideration,

$$t_1=W_3(t_0)=2C_1+2C_2+C_3= 80+80+100=260$$

Tasks τ_1 and τ_2 are initiated three and two times in the interval (0, 260), respectively. Taking this additional execution into consideration,

$$t_2=W_3(t_1)=3C_1+2C_2+C_3=120+80+100=300$$

Tasks τ_i and τ_2 are still initiated three and two times in the interval (0, 300), respectively. Taking this additional execution into consideration,

$$t_3=W_3(t_2)=3C_1+2C_22+C_3= 120+80+100=300=t_2$$

Thus, task τ_3 completes at time 300 and it meets its deadline of 350. Hence the completion time test determines that τ_3 is schedulable even though the test of Theorem 1 fails.

Scheduling Periodic and Aperiodic Tasks

A real-time system typically consists of both periodic and aperiodic tasks. The scheduling of aperiodic tasks can be treated within the rate-monotonic framework of periodic task scheduling. The completion time test is illustrated in the following example.

Example 2. Suppose that there are two tasks. Let τ_1 be a periodic task with period 100 and execution time of 99. Let τ_2 be a server for an aperiodic request that randomly arrives once within a period of 100. Suppose 1 unit of time is required to service each request. If the aperiodic server can execute only in the background, i.e., only after the completion of the periodic task, then the average response time for the aperiodic request is about 50 units. The same can be said for a polling server that provides one unit of service time in a period of 100. On the other hand, deposit one unit of service time in a "ticket box" every 100 units of time; when a new "ticket" is deposited, the unused old tickets, if any, are discarded. With this approach, no matter when the aperiodic request arrives during a period of 100, it will find there is a ticket for one unit of execution time at the ticket box. Server task τ_2 can be allowed to use the ticket to preempt, and execute immediately when the request occurs. In this case, τ_2's response time is precisely one unit and the deadlines of τ_1 are still guaranteed.

This is the idea behind a class of aperiodic server algorithms (Lehoczky and co-workers, 1987) that can reduce aperiodic response time by a large factor (a factor of 50 in this example). The key is to allow the aperiodic servers to preempt the periodic tasks for a *bounded* duration that is allowed by the rate-monotonic scheduling formula. An aperiodic server algorithm called the *Sporadic Server* that handles hard deadline aperiodic tasks is described in (Sprunt and co-workers, 1989). Instead of refreshing the server's "ticket-box budget" periodically, at fixed points in time, replenishment is determined by when requests are serviced. In the simplest approach, the budget is refreshed one period after it has been exhausted, but earlier refreshing is also possible.

A sporadic server is only allowed to preempt the execution of periodic tasks as long as its computation budget is not exhausted. When the budget is used up, the server can continue to execute at background priority if time is available. When the server's budget is refreshed, its execution can resume at the server's assigned priority. There is no overhead if there are no requests. Therefore, the sporadic server is especially suitable for handling emergency aperiodic events that occur rarely but must be serviced quickly.

An effective way to implement a sporadic server is as follows: When an aperiodic request arrives, the system registers the request time. The capacity consumed by this request is replenished one sporadic server period from the request time. This replenishment approach guarantees that the aperiodic response time is no greater than the sporadic server period, provided that the system is schedulable and sufficient server capacity is available. That is, the worst-case aperiodic demand request within a duration of the sporadic server period is no more than the server capacity. In contrast, the worst-case response time for an aperiodic request serviced by a polling server is bounded by twice the period of the polling server. This situation occurs when the request arrives just after the poll. It waits one period for the next poll and up to another period to complete its execution. From a schedulability viewpoint, a sporadic server is equivalent to a periodic task that performs polling, except that it provides better performance.

Task Synchronization

Tasks have been, so far, assumed to be independent of one another. Tasks, however, do interact, and GRMS can be applied to real-time tasks that need to interact. Common synchronization primitives include semaphores, locks, monitors, and Ada rendezvous. Although the use of these or equivalent methods is necessary to protect consistency of shared data or to guarantee the proper use of nonpreemptable resources, their use may jeopardize the system's ability to meet its timing requirements. In fact, a direct application of these synchronization mechanisms may lead to an indefinite period of *priority inversion,* which occurs when a high priority task is prevented from executing by a low priority task. Unbounded priority inversion can occur as shown in the following example.

Example 3. Let τ_1, τ_2 and τ_3 be three tasks listed in descending order of priority. In addition, tasks τ_1 and τ_3 share a resource guarded by a binary semaphore S. Consider the following sequence of events:

1. τ_3 obtains a lock on the semaphore S and enters its critical section to use a shared resource.
2. τ_1 becomes ready to run and preempts τ_3, Next, τ_1 tries to enter its critical section by first trying to lock S. But S is already locked and hence τ_1 is blocked and moved from ready queue to the semaphore queue.
3. τ_2 becomes ready to run. Since only τ_2 and τ_3 are ready to run, τ_2 preempts τ_3 while τ_3 is in its critical section.

One might expect that, τ_1 being the highest priority task, will be blocked no longer than the time for τ_3 to complete its critical section. However, the duration of blocking is, in fact, unpredictable. This unpredictably is because τ_3 is preempted by the medium priority task τ_2. As a result, task τ_1 will be blocked until τ_2 and any other pending tasks of intermediate priority are completed. The duration of priority inversion becomes a function of task execution times and is not bounded by the duration of critical sections, thus the name, "unbounded priority inversion."

The unbounded priority inversion problem can be avoided by using a *priority inheritance protocol* (Sha and co-workers, 1990b). The simplest such procotol is called the *basic priority inheritance* protocol, which requires that any task preventing one or more higher priority tasks from executing must inherit (use) the highest priority of the tasks it blocks. This simple priority, inheritance can still lead to relatively long durations of blocking for higher priority tasks. It also does not address the question of deadlocks. Unbounded priority inversion is avoided and minimized by another priority inheritance protocol called the *priority ceiling protocol.* The priority ceiling protocol is a real-time synchronization protocol with two important properties.

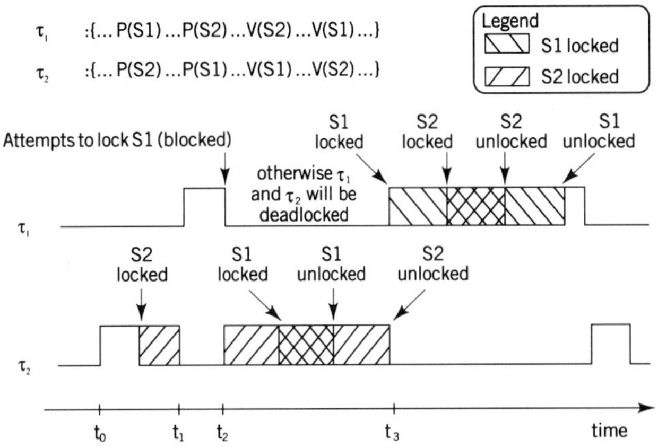

Figure 1. Example of deadlock prevention.

Theorem 3. The priority ceiling protocol prevents mutual locks between tasks. In addition, under the priority ceiling protocol, a task can be blocked by lower priority tasks for at most one critical section.

The protocol works as follows: The *priority ceiling* of a binary semaphore S is defined to be the highest priority of all tasks that may lock S. When a task τ attempts to execute one of its critical sections, it will be suspended unless its priority is higher than the priority ceilings of all semaphores currently locked by tasks other than τ. If task τ is unable to enter its critical section for this reason, the task that holds the lock on the semaphore with the highest priority ceiling is said to be blocking τ and hence inherits the priority of τ. As long as a task τ is not attempting to enter one of its critical sections, it will preempt every task that has a lower priority. The following example illustrates the deadlock avoidance property of the priority ceiling protocol:

Example 4. Suppose that there are two tasks τ_1 and τ_2 (see Fig. 1). In addition, there are two shared data structures protected by binary semaphores S_1 and S_2 respectively. Suppose task τ_1 locks the two semaphores in nested fashion in the order S_1, S_2, while τ_2 locks them in the reverse order. Further, assume that τ_1 has a higher priority than τ_2. Since both τ_1 and τ_2 use semaphores S_1 and S_2, the priority ceilings of both semaphores are equal to the priority of task τ_1. Suppose that at time t_o, τ_2 begins execution and then locks semaphore S_2. At time t_1, task τ_1 is initiated and preempts task τ_2, and at time t_2, task τ_1 tries to enter its critical section by attempting to lock semaphore S_1. However, the priority of τ_1 is *not* higher than the priority ceiling of *locked* semaphore S_2. Hence, task τ_1 must be suspended

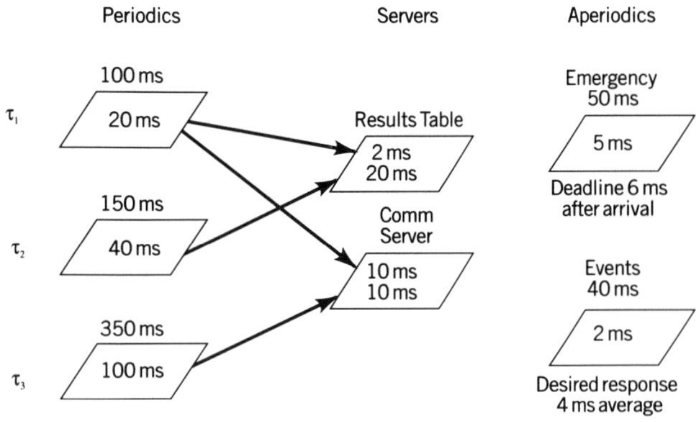

Figure 2. Task interactions for example 5. λ_2's deadline is 20 ms before the end of each period.

without locking S_1. Task τ_2 now *inherits* the priority of task τ_1 and resumes execution. Note that τ_1 is blocked outside its critical section. As τ_1 is not given the lock on S_1 but suspended instead, the potential deadlock involving τ_1 and τ_2 is prevented. Once τ_2 exits its critical section, it will return to its assigned priority and immediately be preempted by task τ_1. From this point on, τ_1 will execute to completion, and then τ_2 will resume its execution until its completion.

There is a simplified implementation of the priority ceiling protocol referred to as the ceiling semaphore protocol (Rajkumar and co-workers, 1988) or as priority ceiling emulation (Sha and Goodenough, 1990a). In this approach, once a task locks a semaphore, its priority is immediately raised to the level of the priority ceiling. The avoidance of deadlock and block-at-most once result still hold provided that the following restriction is observed: a task cannot suspend its execution within the critical section. (The full implementation permits tasks to suspend within a critical section.) The priority ceiling protocol has been extended to deal with dynamic deadline scheduling (Chen and Lin, 1990) and mixed dynamic and static priority scheduling (Baker, 1991).

The schedulability impact of task synchronization can be assessed as follows. Let B_i be the duration in which task τ_i is blocked by lower priority tasks. The effect of this blocking can be modeled as though task τ_i's utilization is increased by an amount B_i/T_i.

Example Application

Consider the following simple example which illustrates the application of the scheduling theory.

Example 5. Consider the following task set (see Fig. 2)

1. Emergency handling task: execution time=5 ms.; worst case interarrival time=50 ms.; deadline is 6 ms. after arrival.
2. Aperiodic event handling tasks: average execution time=2 ms. (assume that it is uniformly distributed between 1 ms. to 3 ms).; average inter-arrival time=40 ms.; fast response time is desirable but there are no hard deadlines.
3. Periodic task τ_1: execution time=20 ms.; period=100 ms.; deadline is at the end of each period. In addition, τ_3 may block τ_1 for 10 ms. by using a shared communication server, and task τ_2 may block τ_1 for 20 ms. by using a shared data object.
4. Periodic task τ_2: execution time=40 ms.; period=150 ms.; deadline is 20 ms. before the end of each period.
5. Periodic task τ_3: execution time=100 ms.; period=350 ms.; deadline is at the end of each period.

Solution: First, create a sporadic server for the emergency task, with a period of 50 ms. and a service time 5 ms. Since the server has the shortest period, the rate monotonic algorithm will give this server the highest priority. It follows that the emergency task can meet its deadline.

Since the aperiodic tasks have no deadlines, they can be assigned a low background priority. However, since fast response time is desirable, we create a sporadic server executing at the second highest priority. The size of the server is a design issue. A larger server (i.e., a server with higher utilization) needs more processor cycles but will give better response time. In this example, choose a large server with a period of 100 ms. and a service time of 10 ms. There are now two tasks with a period of 100 ms.—the aperiodic server and periodic task τ_1. The rate-monotonic algorithm allows us to break the tie arbitrarily, and hence let the server have the higher priority.

Now check if the three periodic tasks can meet their deadlines. Since under the priority ceiling protocol a task can be blocked by lower priority tasks at most once, the maximal blocking time for task τ_1 is B_1=max(10 ms., 20 ms.)=20 ms. Since τ_3 may lock the semaphore S_c associated with the communication server and the priority ceiling of S_c is higher than that of task τ_2, task τ_2 can be blocked by task τ_3 for 10 ms. At this point, directly apply the appropriate theorems. However, the number of steps in the analysis can be reduced by noting that period 50 and 100 are harmonics and treating the emergency server mathematically as if it had a period of 100 ms. and a service time of 10 ms., instead of a period of 50 ms. and a service time of 5 ms. There are now three tasks with a period of 100 ms. and an execution time of 20 ms., 10 ms., and 10 ms. respectively. For the purpose of analysis, these three tasks can be replaced by a single periodic task with a period of 100 ms. and an execution time of 40 ms. (20+10+10). Now there are the following three equivalent periodic tasks for analysis:

- Task τ_1: $C_1=40$; $T_1=100$; $B_1=20$; $U_1=0.4$
- Task τ_2: $C_2=40$; $T_2=150$; $B_2=10$; $U_2=0.267$
- Task τ_3: $C_3=100$; $T_3=350$; $B_3=0$; $U_3=0.286$

Note that B_3 is zero since a task can only be blocked by tasks of lower priority. Since τ_3 is the lowest priority task, it cannot be blocked. Apply the completion time test and Theorem 2.

Task τ_1: $t_0 = C_1+B_2 = 60$, which is less than the deadline 100.

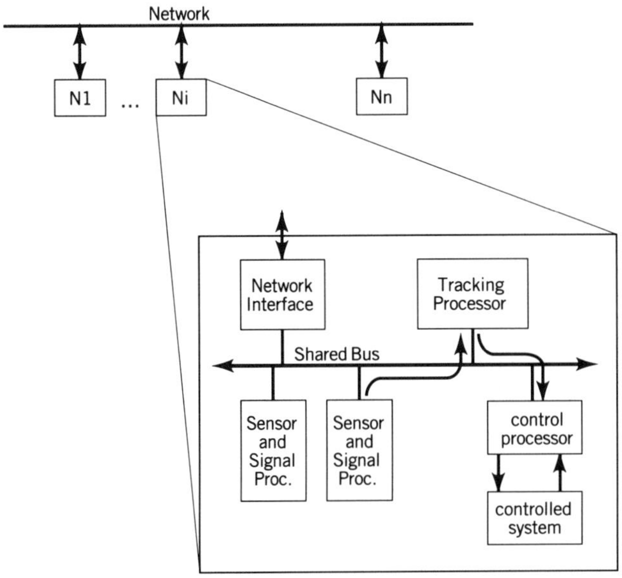

Figure 3. Distributed system configuration.

Task τ_2: $t_0=C_1+C_2+B_2=40+40+10=90$ and $W_2(t_0)=90=t_0$. That is, task τ_2 finishes at 90 which is earlier than its deadline 130 (150−20).

Task τ_3: The analysis here is identical to the analysis for Task 3 of example 1. It follows that all three periodic tasks can meet their first deadlines. By Theorem 2, they will meet all their deadlines.

The response time for the aperiodics can be determined. The server capacity is 10% and the average aperiodic workload is 5% (2/40). Because the emergency task rarely runs and most of the aperiodic arrivals can find "tickets," a good response time would be expected. Indeed, simulation indicates that the average 4 msec response-time requirement can be satisfied. The results derived for this example, show how the scheduling theory puts real-time programming on an *analytic engineering* basis.

End-to-End Delays in Distributed Systems

Consider the system in Figure 3 which uses a message-passing architecture for communication. Assume that the network used is FDDI, and a prioritized backplane such as the IEEE Futurebus+ is used. The sensor makes periodic observations, and a signal processing task processes the incoming signals and averages it every 4 cycles before sending it to the tracking processor. A tracking processor task processes the data and sends the result to the control processor. Task τ_3 on the control processor uses the tracking information. The unit of time in this example is milliseconds.

It is required that the end-to-end latency of the dataflow pipeline from the sensor to the control processor be no more than 785. Let the task set on the control processor be specified as given below:

- Aperiodic event handling with an average execution time of 10 and an average interarrival time of 100. Create a sporadic server task as follows: Task τ_1: $C_1=20$; $T_1=100$.
- A periodic task for handling local feedback control with a computation requirement and a given period. Task τ_2: $C_2=78$; $T_2=150$.
- A periodic task that utilizes the tracking information received. Again the computation time and period are given. Task τ_3: $C_3=30$; $T_3=160$.
- A periodic task responsible for reporting status across the network with a given computation time and period. Task τ_4: $C_4=10$; $T_4=300$.

Assigning Message and Task Deadlines

An integrated approach to assigning deadlines to tasks and interprocessor messages is to be used. Let the sensor take an observation every 40. The signal processing task processes the signal averaging every 4 cycles and sends it to the tracking processor every 160. The tracking processor task with a period of 160 sends a message to the control processor. Task τ_3 on the control processor uses the tracking information and has $C_3=30$ and $T_4=160$ as given above. Recall that the end-to-end latency for the control processor to respond to a new observation by the sensor needs to be less than 785.

Assume for the moment that the end-to-end delay is the sum of the period for each resource. Since the signal processor averages four cycles, each 40 long, its delay is up to 160. Each of the other resources including the back plane has a delay up to one period which is 160. That is, the total delay using rate-monotonic scheduling is bounded by 4*40+160+160+ 160+160=800. However, the specified maximum allowable latency is 785. Hence, some tasks may have to be assigned deadlines earlier than their period boundaries. From a software engineering viewpoint, it is advisable to give a full period delay for global resources such as the bus or the network since their workload is more susceptible to frequent changes. Since there are two bus transfers involved, attempt to assign a full period to each. Also attempt to assign a full period to the signal and tracking processors. Hence the required completion time of the control processor task τ_3 should be no greater than $785-4\times(160)=145$.

Scheduling Tasks on the Control Processor

The scheduling analysis of the control processor tasks is similar to that presented in the Example of Figure 3 except for one variation. The task set on the control processor is as described earlier with task τ_3 modified to have a deadline of 145. The completion time test for τ_3 shows that its completion time is 148. In order to meet the deadline of 145 imposed by the maximum allowable latency requirement, assign τ_3 a higher priority than τ_2 which has an end-of-period deadline of 150. This priority assignment is known as the deadline monotonic algorithm, an optimal generalization of RMS when deadlines are earlier than the periods (Leung and Whitehead, 1982). If deadline-monotonic priority assignment is different from the rate-monotonic assignment, Theorem 1 cannot be used directly. However, the completion time test can be used without modification for the deadline-monotonic priority assignment. Its application shows that τ_3 now meets its deadline of 148. A similar test shows that tasks τ_2 and τ_4 are also schedulable.

Scheduling Messages across a Network

The problem of guaranteeing message deadlines in the FDDI network has been addressed in (Agrawal and co-workers, 1992). FDDI employs a timed-token protocol that results in a bounded token rotation time. A protocol parameter called Target Token Rotation Time (TTRT) is negotiated at network initialization. Time-critical messages must only use synchronous mode of transmission, and each station can transmit once every TTRT for an amount equal to an assigned synchronous capacity H_i. The capacity to each station is allocated proportionally using the following formula (Agrawal and co-workers, 1992):

$$H_i = \frac{U_i}{U}\,(TTRT - D)$$

where H_i is the capacity allocated to station S_i, U_i is the network bandwidth utilized by station S_i, $U = U_1 + \ldots + U_n$, and D is the token round-trip propagation delay when the network is idle.

Consider three periodic messages to be transmitted on an FDDI network with the default TTRT of 8 ms. Let the token propagation delay D be 1 ms.

- Message τ_1: $C_1=7$; $T_1=100$.
- Message τ_2: $C_2=10$; $T_2=145$.
- Message τ_2: $C_3=15$; $T_3=150$.

The utilization of the above message set, $U=0.239$. Applying the above formula $H_1=2.05$, $H_2=2.02$, $H_3=2.93$.

The schedulability analysis can then be carried out as follows. Let there be at least four message priority levels. The messages are first processed in the Network Operating System (NOS), that executes on the end stations. The total application-level delay is the sum of the processing delay at the sender's NOS, the delay in the FDDI ring, and the processing delay in the receiver's NOS.

The requirements on the application-level delays are given in the table below. There are four message types with the following timing requirements.

For meeting the timing requirements, polling or sporadic servers for each level can be created. For example, to meet the average timing requirement, four polling servers can be created with periods T_1, T_2, T_3, and T_4, given by 7 ms, 8 ms, 10 ms and 16 ms respectively. Each server has a full period at the sending NOS, the FDDI and the receiving NOS. If the total traffic is schedulable according to the RMS formula, then the delays are expected to be under 21 ms, 24 ms, 30 ms and 48 ms most of the time. The absolute worst-case delays are 42 ms, 48 ms, 60 ms and 96 ms since polling guarantees a responsiveness of twice the period. If a sporadic server is used, the worst-case performance will be 21 ms, 24 ms, 30 ms and 48 ms.

For schedulability analysis, consider four message-processing tasks at the NOS level. Let task M_i have a processing requirement of C_i per period T_i. This sequence is determined by the number of messages the task processes per period. For example, assume that the processing of one message in task M_i takes 0.5 ms, and there are three messages to be processed per period. Hence $C_1=1.5$. Since the NOS executes on the host processor, the message processing tasks (C_1, T_1), (C_2, T_2), (C_3, T_3) and (C_4, T_4) are scheduled along with other application tasks if any. The schedulability analysis on the processor side and in the receiving NOS correspond to standard rate-monotonic analysis.

For message scheduling on FDDI, there can be four message transmission tasks with transmission time C_i for task with a period of T_i. For example, if 4 Kbyte packets are used, each packet will take 0.33 ms to transmit. If a message task M_1 has to transmit 3 packets its transmission time C_1 is 0.99 ms.

Consider the scheduling of messages in a particular station S_i. Let the capacity allocated to the station be H_i. The station can transmit for up to H_i ms every TTRT. This can be treated as having another high priority task with message transmission time (TTRT$-H_i$) and period TTRT. This task is referred to as the Token Rotation task M_{tr}. Suppose TTRT=6 ms and $H_i=2$ ms, then $M_{tr}=(C_{tr}=4, T_{tr}=6)$. The task set for station S_i is then (4, 6), (C_1, T_1), (C_2, T_2), (C_3, T_3) and (C_4, T_4). This task set can be analyzed in the standard rate-monotonic framework.

Finally, note that although the token rotation task behaves like the highest priority task at each station, it actually may be comprised of the transmission of lower priority messages from other stations. In this sense, it constitutes priority inversion and limits the schedulable utilization of the network.

Table 1. Latency Metrics

Message	Type	Average Latency, ms.
M_1	Emergency	21 ms
M_2	Alert	24 ms
M_3	Fast	30 ms
M_4	Normal	48 ms

CONCLUSION

The rate-monotonic scheduling theory and its generalizations provide an analytic engineering basis for building predictable real-time systems. This framework has been adopted by national high-technology projects such as the Space Station and have recently been supported by major open standards such as the IEEE Futurebus+ and IEEE POSIX. This article summarizes the basic elements of the theory and illustrates them with examples. Extensive references are provided for further study.

BIBLIOGRAPHY

G. Agrawal, B. Chen, W. Zhao, S. Davari, "Guaranteeing Synchronous Message Deadlines in High Speed Token Ring Networks with Timed Token Protocol," *Proceedings of IEEE International Conference on Distributed Computing Systems,* 1992.

T. Baker, "Stack-Based Scheduling of Realtime Processes," *Journal of Real-Time Systems,* **3**(1) 67–100 (Mar. 1991).

M. Chen and K. J. Lin, "Dynamic Priority Ceilings: A Concurrency Control Protocol for Real-time Systems," *Journal of Real-Time Systems,* **2**(4) 325–346 (Nov. 1990).

ESA, "Statement of Work, Hard Real-Time OS Kemel," *On-Board Data Division, European Space Agency,* July, 1990.

Futurebus+ P896.1 Specification, Draft 1.0, IEEE, New York, 1990. (Prepared by the P896.2 Working Group of the Microprocessor Standards Committee)

J. D. Gafford, "Rate Monotonic Scheduling," *IEEE Micro* (June 1990).

M. G. Harbour, M. H. Klein, and J. P. Lehoczky, "Fixed Priority Scheduling of Periodic Tasks with Varying Execution Priority," *Proceedings of IEEE Real-Time Systems Symposium,* Dec. 1991.

D. Katcher, H. Arakawa, and J. K. Strosnider, "Engineering and Analysis of Fixed Priority Schedulers," Center for Dependable Systems, Carnegie Mellon University, Pittsburgh, Pa., December 1991, Tech report CMUCDS-91-10.

D. Kirk and J. K. Strosnider, "SMART (Strategic Memory Allocation for Real-Time) Cache Design Using MIPS R3000," *Proceedings of IEEE Real-Time Systems Symposium,* 1990.

M. H. Klein and T. Ralya, "An Analysis of Input/Output Paradigms for Real-Time Systems," *Tech. report CMU/SEI-90-TR-19, ADA226724,* Software Engineering Institute, July 1990.

J. P. Lehoczky, L. Sha and J. Strosnider, "Enhancing Aperiodic Responsiveness in A Hard Real-Time Environment," *IEEE Real-Time System Symposium,* 1987.

J. P. Lehoczky, L. Sha, and Y. Ding, "The Rate Monotonic Scheduling Algorithm—Exact Characterization and Average Case Behavior," *Proceedings of IEEE Real-Time System Symposium,* 1989 Tech. report.

J. P. Lehoczky, "Fixed Priority Scheduling of Periodic Task Sets with Arbitrary Deadlines," *IEEE Real-Time Systems Symposium,* Dec. 1990.

J. Leung and J. Whitehead, "On the Complexity of Fixed-Priority Scheduling of Periodic, Real-Time Tasks," *Performance Evaluation* (2), 1982.

C. L. Liu and J. W. Layland, "Scheduling Algorithms for Multiprogramming in a Hard Real Time Environment," *JACM,* **20**(1), pp. 46–61 (1973).

IEEE Standard P1003.4 (Real-time extensions to POSIX), IEEE, New York, 1991.

R. Rajkumar, L. Sha, and J. P. Lehoczky, "Real-Time Synchronization Protocols for Multiprocessors," *Proceedings of the Real-Time Systems Symposium,* IEEE, Huntsville, Ala., Dec. 1988, pp. 259–269.

R. Rajkumar, L. Sha, J. P. Lehoczky, "An Experimental Investigation of Synchronization Protocols," *Proceedings of the IEEE Workshop on Real-Time Operating Systems and Software,* May, 1988.

R. Rajkumar, *Synchronization in Real-Time Systems: A Priority Inheritance Approach,* Kluwer Academic Publishers, 1991.

L. Sha, J. P. Lehoczky, and R. Rajkumar, "Solutions for Some Practical Problems in Prioritized Preemptive Scheduling," *IEEE Real-Time Systems Symposium,* 1986.

L. Sha and J. B. Goodenough, "Real-Time Scheduling Theory and Ada," *IEEE Computer* (Apr. 1990a).

L. Sha, R. Rajkumar, and J. P. Lehoczky, "Priority Inheritance Protocols: An Approach to Real-Time Synchronization," *IEEE Transaction On Computers* (Sept. 1990b).

L. Sha and S. Sathaye, "Distributed System Design Using Generalized Rate Monotonic Theory," *The Proceedings of The 2nd International Conference on Automation, Robotics, and Computer Vision,* 1992.

L. Sha, S. Sathaye, and J. Strosnider, "Scheduling Real-Time Communication on Dual Link Networks," *Proceedings of the IEEE Real-Time System Symposium,* 1992.

B. Sprunt, L. Sha, and J. Lehoczky, "Aperiodic Task Scheduling for Hard Real-Time Systems," *The Journal of Real-Time Systems,* (1), 27–60 (1989).

J. K. Strosnider and T. E. Marchok, "Responsive, Deterministic IEEE 802.5 Token Ring Scheduling," *Journal of Real-Time Systems,* **1**, 133–158 (1989).

S. Ramos-Thuel and J. Strosnider, "The Transient Server Approach to Scheduling Time-Critical Recovery Operations," *Proceedings of IEEE Real-Time Systems Symposium,* Dec. 1991.

H. Tokuda, L. Sha, and J. P. Lehoczky, "Towards Next Generation Distributed Real-Time Operating Systems," *Abstracts of IEEE Fourth Workshop on Real-Time Operating Systems,* 1987.

H. Tokuda, "The Real-Time Mach Operating System," Tech. report, Carnegie Mellon University, Pittsburgh, Pa., Sept. 1991.

LUI SHA
RAGUNATHAN RAJKUMAR
Software Engineering Institute
Carnegie Mellon University

RAULT, JEAN-CLAUDE (1937–)

Jean-Claude Rault ranks among French key pioneers in software engineering to which he contributed seminal work and which he helps by promoting through consulting, publishing and organizing conferences.

He is currently chairman of the EC2 company, a consulting and publishing firm he founded in 1987. EC2 is dedicated to software engineering, natural language processing, system and software dependability, CAD-CAM and CIM, an advanced information processing technologies such as neural networks, fuzzy systems, or genetic algorithms.

In this context, he is editor of several authoritative technical magazines and information newsletters in the French language, namely the quarterly *Génie Logiciel* (Software Engineering), *La Lettre de l'IA* (The AI Letter); he also is the publisher of the *PCTE Newsletter.* He is the founder and chairman of two successful yearly major European events, namely the Toulouse Conference (since 1988), the Avignon Conference (since 1981) dedicated to the industrial applications of, respectively, software engineering and artificial intelligence. He consults, on an international basis, for industrial companies, and government departments and international programs such as Esprit and Eureka.

From 1980 to 1987 he was with Agence de l'Informatique, a French Government Agency, with similarities with ARPA, NIST, and NSF, where he was responsible for R&D and technology transfer regarding software engineering, artificial intelligence, and CAD/CAM. In this capacity he is known to have been instrumental in launching several key projects, in promoting within French industry technologies such as Ada, Prolog, Lisp and, more generally, software engineering. In particular, he has been the initiator of the early work which gave birth in 1991 to the PCTE standard.

His interest for software engineering began in the mid-1960 while he was developing CAD tools for the design of integrated circuits and later while participating in the development of an early graphical station. While with the Thomson-CSF Group in the late 1960s, he introduced the concept of rapid prototyping, in particular by using the APL language, and performed the first studies conducted in France on software reliability and software testing. These studies led him to develop in the early 1970s, theoretical and practical work on software complexity and random software testing.

Jean-Claude Rault has authored around 50 papers on software engineering and has co-authored four books respectively on the APL language, expert systems, CAD, and software reliability.

RAYLEIGH MODEL

Initially software development managers regarded manpower and time as simplistically interchangeable. For instance, if managers wanted to complete a project in half the time, they employed twice as many people. During the 1970s research had indicated that this approach does not work and that the relationships between the factors that influence productivity are not simple linear functions:

- Fred Brooks showed, in his book *The Mythical Man Month,* published in 1975, that manpower and time are indeed not interchangeable.
- Peter Norden of IBM showed that hardware development projects are composed of overlapping phases, and that these phases have a well-defined manning profile that matches a mathematical function: the Rayleigh curve.
- In 1976 Joel Aron of IBM recognized that the manpower in large developments builds up in a characteristic pattern and identified complexity and duration as key elements affecting development productivity.
- In 1977 Walston and Felix of IBM collected consistent data on 60 completed software developments. They show that the variables of interest appear as complex power functions of the size of the system.
- Larry Putnam of Quantitative Software Management extended the earlier work by Peter Norden of IBM on hardware development to software projects. He found that the Rayleigh curve also fitted not only the individual components of a software development project but the entire project. He also refined the power functions described by Felix and Walston.

All this research was empirically based.

HOW THE RAYLEIGH APPROACH IS DERIVED

The Rayleigh approach divides development projects into three basic phases. These phases can accommodate the development processes in most organizations. The three basic phases are

- *Feasibility study,* which stops at the point where the outline requirements specifications and the project plans, are approved. The data recorded in this phase are time and effort.
- *Functional design,* which continues to the point when all functional design specifications, test plans, and management plans are approved. It can overlap the main build phase. In this phase, time, effort, peak staffing, and overlap with the main build phase are recorded.
- *Main build,* which begins at the start of detailed logic design and ends when the system reaches full operational capability. Full operational capability is defined to be the point at which all system and integration tests are successfully completed. In the main build phase a substantial amount of data can be recorded. Key items are time, effort, peak staffing, size of the system, and errors from the start of integration test to first operational capability.

Once the system is operational, additional data may be collected. (This situation is sometimes referred to as the maintenance and operational phase.) The data includes mean-time-to-defect, errors in the first month after first operational use, and cumulative time and effort spent by the development staff in operations and maintenance.

In this approach, the engineering analysis is applied to the main build phase, where, on average over 75 percent of the development effort is expended.

Quantitative Software Management uses an empirical approach to identify the relationships between the key management numbers. This approach is the most useful way of analyzing the data to relate the six project measures to the size of the project, expressed as effective source lines of code (ESLOC) or as function points. These measures are

- Duration, the time taken in months
- Effort, in person-months (cost)
- Average manpower, defined as effort divided by duration
- Average code production rate, in ESLOC per month or average function point rate, in function points per month
- Error rate
- Productivity, in ESLOC per person-month or function points per person-month.

Figures 1 to 3 show the development project duration, effort and errors plotted as a function of system size for a wide variety of projects.

These graphs are plotted against logarithmic scales to accommodate the wide range of values and the nonlinear relationships involved.

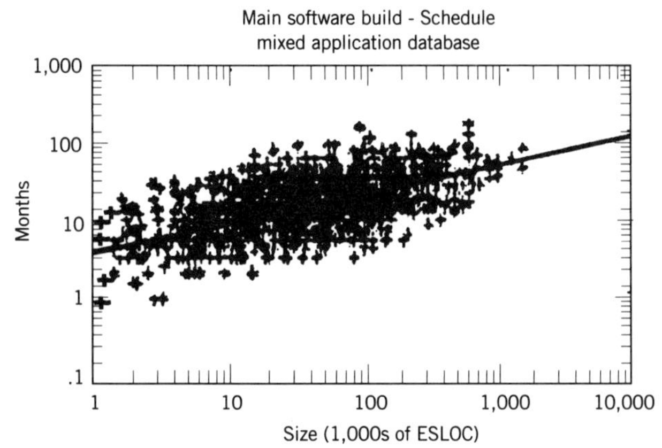

Figure 1. Software development schedule for main software construction phase. The time taken increases with the size of the system, but there is a large variability in time for any given size.

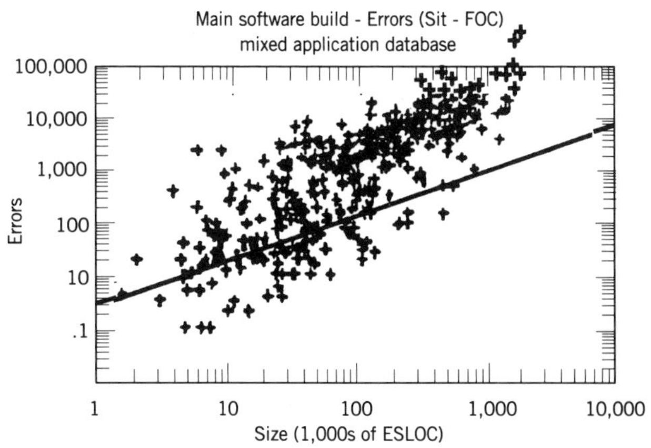

Figure 3. Errors discovered from start of systems integration testing through full operational capability. The number of errors increases with the size of the system, but there is wide variability.

The slopes of the trend lines demonstrate that there are nonlinear relationships between the dependent variables and the independent variable, system size.

The graphs also show the wide variability on the data for any given size of system, and indicate the absence of any simple pattern based on a small number of variables. This arrangement is because of the great variation in application types and the time period of the developments. However, a large database can be partitioned to eliminate some of the major sources of variation including application type, time, and developer efficiency. The list below shows the 9-system application types used to partition the database.) These results show that when this technique is done, very useful behavior patterns do emerge.

Microcode systems
Real-time embedded systems
Avionics systems
Command and control systems
Process control systems
Telecom systems
Systems code systems
Scientific systems
Business systems

Figure 4 shows the correlation between effort and system size for an application type in the form of a trend line together with two other lines. The middle line represents the least squares best fit. The upper line is plus one standard deviation and the lower line is minus one standard deviation. If the variability follows a normal distribution, 68 percent of the data will be expected to lie between plus and minus one standard deviation. This arrangement has been empirically verified with many data sets.

Standard slopes for the trend lines have been determined using a combination of statistical curve fitting and bootstrap statistical simulation. The intercepts are determined directly from the appropriate data set. Slopes and intercepts are then verified for reasonable closeness of fit from all the available data in the specified data set.

This procedure is necessary because pure curve fitting may produce poor results when the data set is sparse, noisy, poorly distributed, and so on-all quite common. The trend lines have been verified by independent data sets, worldwide, over a period of ten years. The trend lines con-

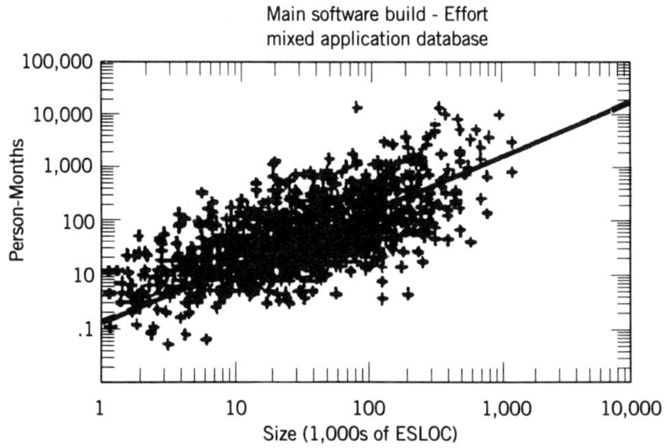

Figure 2. Development effort for main software construction phase. The effort increases with the size of the system, but there is a wide variability in effort for any given size.

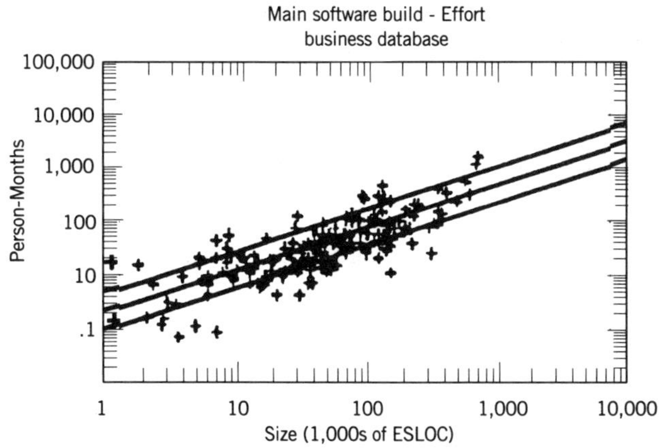

Figure 4. Correlation between effort and system size for a single application type. Better correlation is obtained once the data is partitioned into different kinds of systems.

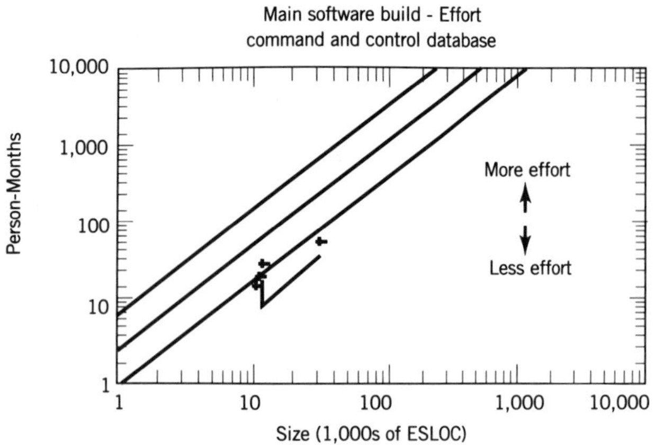

Figure 5. Four completed projects of different size positioned relative to the trend lines are shown. They required about one standard deviation less effort than the average.

tinue to be refined. They are reliable and represent well software behavior within our current recording and measurement accuracy.

All six measures have a distinct characteristic behavior as system size increases. Duration, cost, manpower, code production, and errors all increase with size. Productivity, expressed as ESLOC/person month, decreases with system size. All these relationships are nonlinear.

Since these six project measures vary significantly with system size, it follows that all comparisons should take size into account. Figure 5 shows four projects of different sizes positioned with respect to the trend lines.

Quantitative Software Management concludes that these four projects were done with about one standard deviation less effort than the average for other systems of the same size in the database. Similar comparisons for duration, manpower, code production rate, productivity, and error rate, can be made.

The trend lines also dispel myths about common rules-of-thumb that abound in the industry and are simplistically used to make multimillion-dollar decisions. The rules-of-thumb invariably assume some constant ratio between lines of code and effort based on a very small data sample. For example, a programming productivity of 180 ESLOC per personmonth might be used. Yet because of the strong variation of ESLOC per person month with size, this conclusion would be reasonably valid only for a small range of sizes. When the nonlinear nature of the software development process and the nonlinear tradeoff between time and effort is added, it is clear that this measure cannot account for all the complexities of software management. Most of the rules-of-thumb are dangerously wrong, especially ESLOC per personmonth. Do not trust them!

THE SOFTWARE EQUATION

Research shows that the software development process is driven by the production of source code (or other units of functionality) and the creation and discovery of defects, both of which follow synchronized Rayleigh-shaped rate curves. Figure 6 shows a graph of a Rayleigh curve. The Rayleigh curve is characterized by a rather steep buildup as coding begins, followed by a long tapering-off period before the system is ready for delivery. In many successful software development projects, the resource profile (the people assigned to the project) also follows a Rayleigh pattern, but may not be synchronized in time with code and defects for a variety of reasons. The curve shown could represent coding, discovery of defects, or manpower assigned to a project, and the area under the curve would be the number of valid lines of code written, defects discovered and fixed, or, in some cases, person-months. The proper system delivery date is when 95 percent of the area under the defect elimination curve has been realized.

The ratio of code to defects has a strong parallel in communications engineering, where the signal to noise ratio has a very important role in transmission quality. In software engineering, the ratio of code to defects often represents to management the impacts of environmental influences, eg, accelerated schedules, too many people, or primitive tools and techniques.

Using this insight into the Rayleigh-shaped profile of software development, it is possible to derive a mathematical relationship between the size of a project and the time and effort needed to complete it. The relationship is nonlinear, and involves a parameter which is a measure of productivity. From the software equation, a computational formula for a productivity measure which allows us to compare the productivities of different development projects can be obtained, even if the projects are of different size or duration. It is of the form

$$\text{Productivity measure} = \frac{\text{Size}}{(\text{Effort}/B)^{1/3} * (\text{Time})^{4/3}}$$

where time is in years, effort is in person-years, and B is a special skills factor directly related to size. The list below shows how B, the special skills factor, varies with system size.

Size (ESLOC)	B
5-15K	0.16
20K	0.18

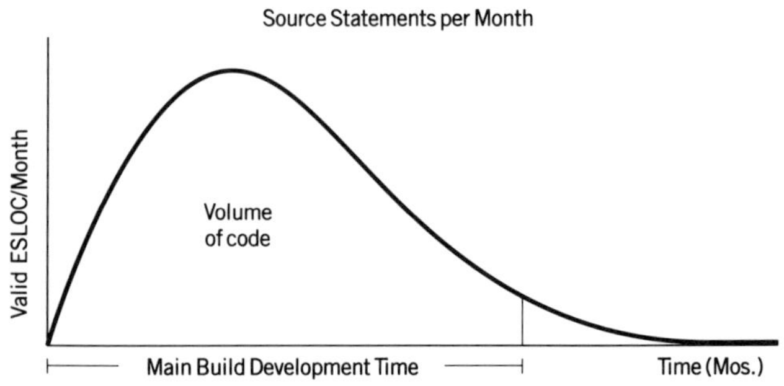

Figure 6. Rayleigh curve. Code generation follows a Rayleigh-shaped curve. The curve also describes rate of defect discovery (with area under the curve giving the total number of defects discovered). It also represents application of people to the project (with area under the curve being total effort applied to the project).

30K	0.28
40K	0.34
50K	0.37
≧70K	0.39

Given a certain level of productivity, the equation may be rearranged to calculate the effort required to complete a project of a given size.

$$\text{Effort} = \frac{B * \text{Size}^3}{\text{Time}^{4} * (\text{Productivity measure})^3}$$

This equation shows that the effort required for a project depends on the duration as well as the size, and on the productivity measure that applies in that particular development environment. The measure accounts for all the factors operating in the development environment. Both the effect of changes in productivity and compressing, or extending the scheduled time for a project, have dramatic effects on the effort and cost required.

Because the productivity measure can take a very wide range of absolute values, these values are represented as a Productivity Index (PI) using numbers in the range 1 to 40. The translation table for integer PIs up to 40, is shown in Table 1. The table shows the translation from the productivity measures to productivity indices. This table is more convenient to use than the measure in the equation, as smaller numbers can be visualized and remembered more easily.

Observe that only readily available information is required to calculate the PI for completed projects and those in progress:

- The number of new and modified source lines of code or function points (which also allows us to determine B).
- Total person-months of effort.
- Total elapsed calendar months.

Low values of the PI are generally associated with low productivity environments or highly complex projects. High values are associated with high productivity environments, good management, and well-understood straightforward projects.

Table 2 shows an analysis of a database of over 2000 completed systems by application type, calculating the average and variability of PI. The applications are arranged in order of decreasing complexity. This table shows the average PI and standard deviation by application type as of 1990. These averages are expected to go up slowly over time. Accuracy is given to closest integer value.

What Increases in the Productivity Index Mean

Any positive movement in the PI has a dramatic impact on the time, total effort, and hence total cost of development. The PI embraces all environmental factors impacting development. If you have a low PI, you may find there are bottlenecks that are acting as brakes to efficient production. Table 3 shows a simple example of the economic value of a PI increase. Note that the economic value is

Table 1. Productivity Index (PI) and the Association Productivity Measure

Productivity measure	PI
764	1
972	2
1234	3
1573	4
2001	5
2545	6
3238	7
4119	8
5240	9
6665	10
8478	11
10785	12
13719	13
17452	14
22200	15
28240	16
35923	17
45697	18
58129	19
73944	20
94062	21
119654	22
152207	23
193618	24
246295	25
313304	26
398543	27
506974	28
644905	29
820362	30
1043556	31
1327473	32
1688634	33
2148056	34
2732471	35
3475886	36
4421560	37
5624520	38
7154766	39
9101342	40

Table 2. Industry PI Base Lines

Application type	Average	Std. deviation
Microcode systems	2	2
Real-time systems	7	2
Avionic systems	6	2
Command and control systems	10	3
Process control systems	10	4
Telecom/Msg switchingsystems	11	3
System code systems	11	3
Scientific systems	12	4
Business systems	16	4

Table 3. Impact of Changing PI[a]

PI	Person-months	Time, mo	Cost, $
9	156	17.1	$1,365,000
10	115	15.4	$1,006,250
11	84	13.9	$735,000

[a] This figure shows the financial and time impact of increasing the PI on a modest system of 30,000 COBOL SLOC. The burdened Labor rate is $105,000 per person year.

high. An increase of one PI for a 30,000 line COBOL system saves more than $200,000. When you invest in tools, techniques, and management practices that relieve bottlenecks, PI goes up. The effects of high and low PI values are summarized in Table 4.

Figure 7 shows the effect on resources and errors of a capital investment boosting PI from 8 to 10. Clearly the PI is a measurement that management needs to understand and exploit for its impact on a company's profitability. The PI is the capital investment measure for software.

The Manpower Buildup Index (MBI) Reflects Time Pressures

The software equation also accounts for compression or extension of the project schedule. The software equation shows that when you compress the schedule for a project, the effort increases substantially. One of the reasons for this relationship is that as you overlap tasks, you need more staff to work on the project, which means more communications paths and more overhead. The effect of time compression is represented using a measure which is called the Manpower Buildup Index (MBI). (In engineering terms, this is the manpower acceleration).

MBI parameter is defined as Effort/(B $\times$Time^3) where effort is in man-years, time is in years, and B is the same special skills factor as in the software equation. As with the PI, the MBI is expressed as a simple value (level) which is more readily appreciated by business managers. The relationship between the MBI parameter and some integer MBI levels is shown below.

MBI parameter	**MBI level**
8	1
16	2
32	3
64	4
128	5
256	6

Table 4. General PI Impact

High PI	Low PI
Less time	More time
Less effort	More effort
Fewer people	More people
Fewer defects	More defects
Higher MTTD	Lower MTTD
More SLOC/month	Less SLOC/month
More SLOC/personmonth	Less SLOC/personmonth

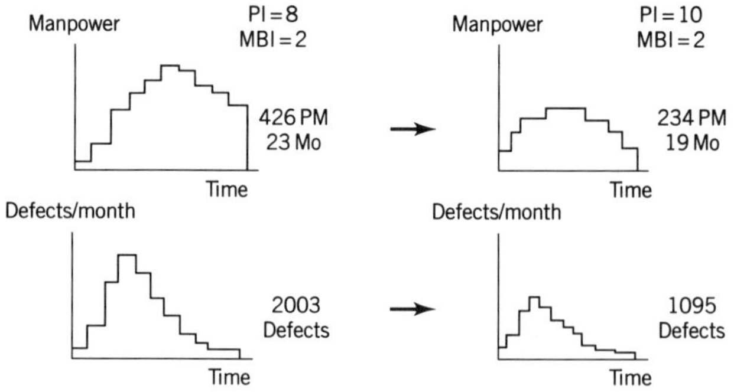

Figure 7. Impact of capital investment on resources and defect profiles. The reduction in resources and defects is a result of investments in process improvements which raise the PI from 8 to 10 for a product of a given size.

Level 1 represents a slow staff buildup. The project will take the longest and cost the least. Usually, this correlation reflects a limited number of staff available for development. Level 6 can be described as the "throw people at it" or "Brute Force" approach, and is characterized by attempting totally parallel task execution, with no staff or money limitations, and assumes all design issues are well understood from the outset.

The list below shows the economic impact of an increase in the MBI. If the MBI were to be increased from one to three in an effort to compress the schedule, the MBI increase would more than double the effort, and hence cost.

(30,000 COBOL ESLOC; PI =11).

MBI	**Time, mo**	**Effort,MM**
1	15.3	57
2	13.9	84
3	12.6	125
4	11.4	186
5	10.3	276
6	9.3	410

Figure 8 shows why the cost increases so dramatically. The number of human communication paths for the Level

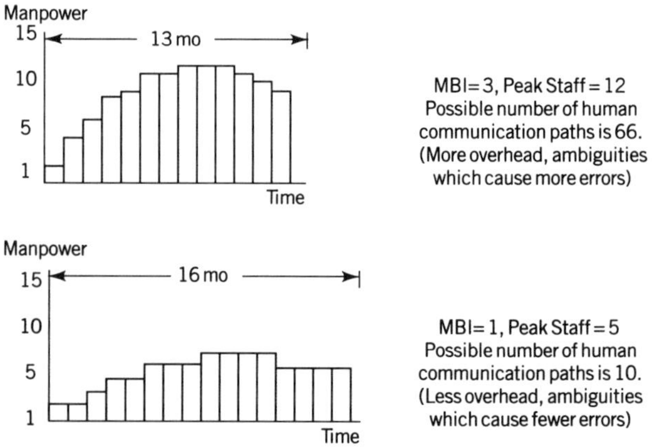

Figure 8. Human communication. An illustration why the cost increases so dramatically with changes in MBI.

3 MBI is about six times that for a Level 1 MBI. This alignment also manifests itself directly in quality terms by causing exponentially more defects.

Clearly, schedule compression is very expensive. Schedule compression is important to recognize because it is very commonly done, with little appreciation of the consequences. The list below summarizes the effects of high and low values of the MBI. The MBI is a parameter that managers can influence enormously since it is within their immediate control with no capital investment required.

Low MBI	High MBI
More time	Less time
Less effort	More effort
Fewer people	More people
Fewer defects	More defects
Higher MTTD	Lower MTTD
Less SLOC/month	More SLOC/month
More SLOC/personmonth	Less SLOC/personmonth

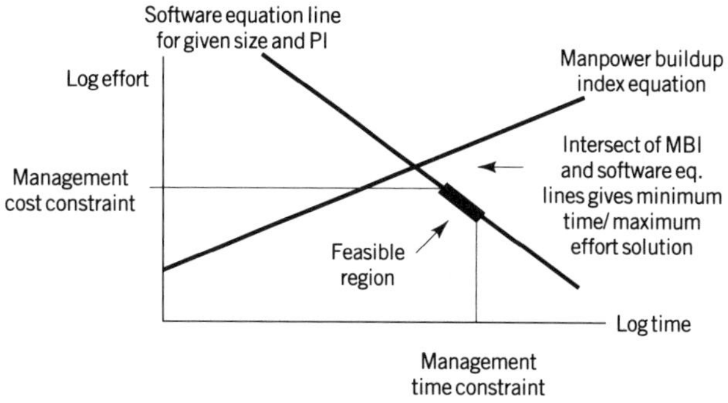

Figure 9. Minimum time calculation. The minimum development time concept for a particular size development at a given PI and MBI are shown. The intersection of the software equation line and the MBI line gives the minimum time/maximum effort solution. Also shown are maximum time and effort constraints imposed by management. Calculation of possible solutions with constraints is a simple linear programming problem, which is automated in the QSM software product SLIM.

USE PI AND MBI TO PLAN PROJECTS

The Productivity Index (PI) and the Manpower Buildup Index (MBI) are calculated using the basic data of development time, effort and size from completed projects.

Using the PI and MBI as inputs to the software equation together with the estimated size, you can plan the development time and effort for new projects. You can also use "what if" analyses to investigate management actions such as the effects of shortening or lengthening the schedule.

To determine the development time and effort requires three parameters:

- The PI, determined from the PI calculated for similar projects completed within the organization's development environment
- The MBI, which reflects the typical rate of manpower buildup on previous projects, or that proposed for the new project
- The size of the system to be developed, in ESLOC or Function Points, or some other reasonable quantification of the functionality, including estimates of the upper and lower limits of the expected size.

Figure 9 shows how these parameters can be used to graph equations relating effort to time, both for the software equation and for the MBI. Where they intersect represents the absolute minimum development time consistent with the known PI, MBI, and expected size. The project can be planned to take longer with consequent reduction in effort and cost.

The software equation line (illustrated in Fig. 9) is determined by the estimated mean size of the software and a PI that is calculated from completed past projects. In addition, Monte Carlo simulation (random sampling based on different sizes within the uncertainty range) can be used to determine a series of possible time and effort results. This approach enables the uncertainty in size to be mapped through to uncertainties in estimating development time and effort. Software development always involves uncertainty and risk. Monte Carlo simulations quantify risk during the early development stages as the estimates of size are updated periodically as the project moves along in time.

"What if?" Analysis

Having determined the minimum time for a given project, an examination of a number of practical alternatives to the development plan and their effects on costs, quality, and schedule can be decided. For example:

- Setting new schedules beyond the minimum time to exploit the time/effort/quality trade-off
- Imposing management constraints on time, cost, and resources to determine if development is feasible within these constraints
- Determining the size of system that can be developed in a shorter time frame
- Quantifying the uncertainty in the plans to ensure the software can be developed within a given time period at a specific level of risk
- Specifying reliability goals, since the software equation is also directly related to software errors
- Evaluating the joint probability of the software development being completed within the planned budgeted time and price.

Comparing project estimates with appropriate reference data (similar projects completed) can alert the manager when plans are moving outside normal development limits.

Set Realistic Target Dates

Our experience has shown that plans can be wildly unrealistic. Over-optimistic plans are the most common, but we also frequently find examples of over-conservative plans.

Using the software equation, realistic target dates and effort for the main build phase that are consistent with achievable productivity and project size should be identified, taking into account management constraints, reliability, and risk.

Key milestone dates in the main build phase include:

- Reviewing all design elements, including detailed program logic
- Completing the initial coding (when all code can be expected to be written but not yet unit tested, integrated, and system tested)
- Beginning the systems testing of the integrated software units
- Beginning the user-oriented system test
- Installing the software on the operational hardware
- Achieving full operational capability (Based on empirical analysis, this level is the point at which 95% of software errors have been found and fixed.)
- The points at which 99% and 99.9% of the total software errors have been found and fixed.

Once the development is planned at the macro level, the project manager must break down and allocate the work to individual team members. The milestones provide a framework for drawing up the detailed plan using any of the popular detailed project scheduling packages.

Monitor/Control Progress

The plans can be used to track progress and exercise high-level control. Quantifying the uncertainty in the plans can help track performance within these uncertainty bounds. Where the reported actuals exceed the uncertainty bounds, then actions can be taken either to replan the development or get the project back on track.

Milestones are essential for project tracking. If you miss a milestone, it is often very difficult to catch up without reducing the functionality of the system. Replanning the project based upon the actual milestone achieved can help evaluate the consequences in terms of the impending time and cost overruns. Then a decision on whether to reduce functionality can be made.

Milestone slippage is often caused by a substantial growth in the requirements specification that has not been taken into account in estimating the size range.

Parameters you should track are

- Monthly staffing
- Cumulative cost
- Monthly software defects
- Cumulative code production.

The data needed to track these measures is usually readily available from the project managers on a monthly basis, without incurring any additional cost or effort. Provided the monthly and cumulative values are within the uncertainty bounds, and the milestones are met, the project can be expected to be completed within the upper limits set on the schedule and budget.

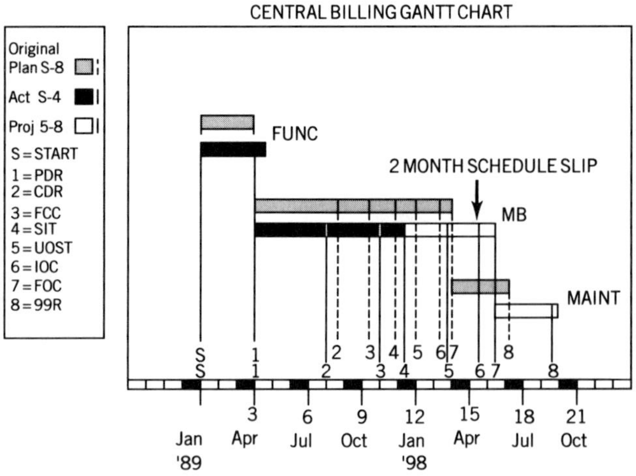

Figure 10. Updated schedule estimate based on actual performance. In this example, schedule was slipping and is projected to slip by two months by the end of the main build. The original plan is shown by the lightly shaded bars, and actual progress is shown with heavily shaded bars. The white bars represent a replan based on the rate of progress to date and months from beginning of project actual start month.

Do Adaptive Forecasting

Significant deviations between actual data and plans are indications that progress is not being made as forecasted. If the deviations are favorable, the implication is that the project will be under schedule and under budget. If the deviations are unfavorable (which is most common) the indication is that the project will not meet the planned schedule and budget.

In these situations the project manager will want to find out what the ultimate project schedule, cost and quality is going to be. Curve fitting techniques can be used to determine the "in process" PI being achieved. This actual PI along with a current estimate of the size and peak staffing, allow the forecasting of a new schedule, budget and quality projections. These new projections are then used to update the plan and monitor again in the future.

Figures 10–14 show a replan of a system called Central Billing based on actual accomplishment to date. Figures 10–14 are from QSM's SLIM-Control® software product. This project was not meeting its original plan in any of the metrics listed above. A replan shows the staffing and cost that will be necessary to complete the project.

A TQM Approach to Software Development

Ultimately these techniques lead to a corporate Total Quality Management (TQM) (qv) approach to software development.

The TQM idea has caught on and it is important to all segments of the economy. The Japanese refinement of this philosophy has been going on for forty years so the TQM concept is not new. What is new is applying these principles and those of W. Edwards Deming to the software manage-

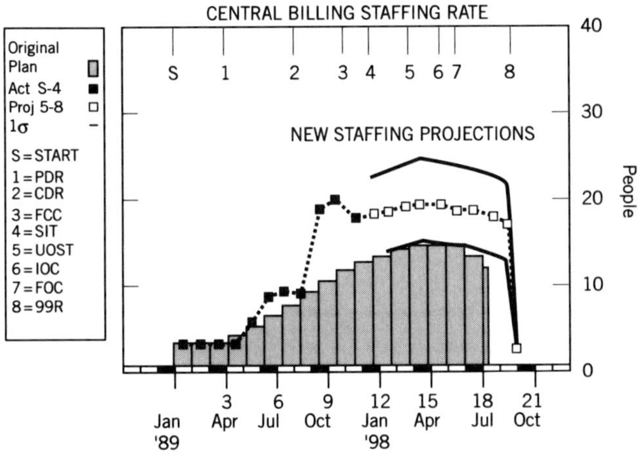

Figure 11. Updated staffing estimate. The planned staffing rate is shown by the shaded bars. Actual staffing (shown by the black squares) jump up much higher than planned as progress on coding was failing behind schedule. In the replan (shown by the white squares), staffing levels will remain higher than originally planned. The lines on either side of the staffing projections show a range of statistical possibilities.

ment process. Organizations that focus on broadly improving the software development process, by investment, education and management attention to process measurement and control, do improve the quality of their software products and produce those products faster. They produce them less expensively, with fewer people. These gains can only be achieved, however, with a continuous, long-term improvement effort across the whole spectrum of software development activities.

Excellent companies have, for more than ten years, done these things year-in, year-out and have made great progress. They measured so that they knew how they were doing. They focused their investment and education on the weaker spots and improved their process. As a result, their rate of improvement in reducing time and cost is twice the industry average. Needless to say, they produce a much better product.

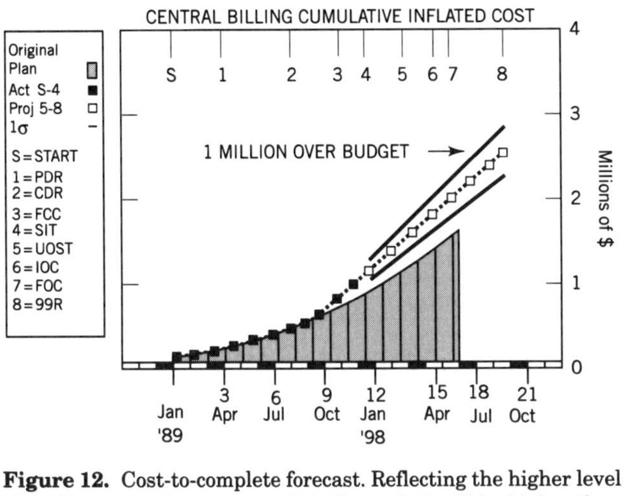

Figure 12. Cost-to-complete forecast. Reflecting the higher level of staffing, actual cost to complete the project will be higher than initially projected. Again, the original plan is shown by shaded bars, actual costs incurred to date are shown by black boxes, and projected costs are shown by white boxes.

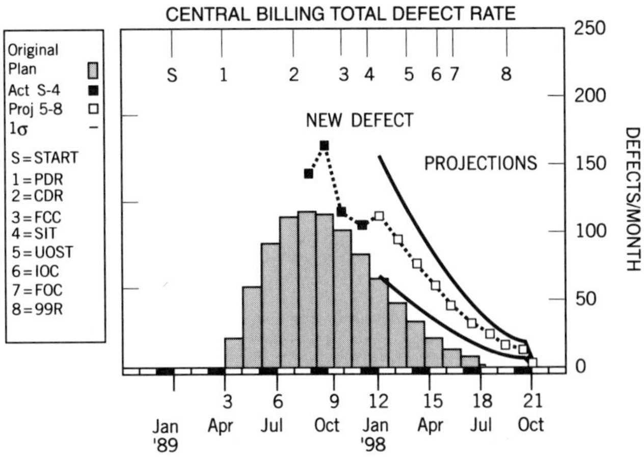

Figure 13. Updated defect projections. At the same same staffing increased substantially (Fig. 11), defects discovered jumped up. This often happens as a sharp increase in the number of people working on a project causes communications problems, resulting in more defects and eventual need to rework code.

One of the keys to TQM in software management is using Statistical Process Control on projects while they are underway. This approach applies statistical techniques coupled with the simple metrics outlined earlier to the management process traditionally governed by "gut feel," or intuition. Data-driven improvement is a critical component of TQM and makes ongoing measurement essential.

Developers should implement an "Early Warning System" to reduce risk of overrun and slippage. This system will allow them to predict accurately the outcome of a project based on real progress data. If the predicted outcome based on the real data appears unacceptable, correc-

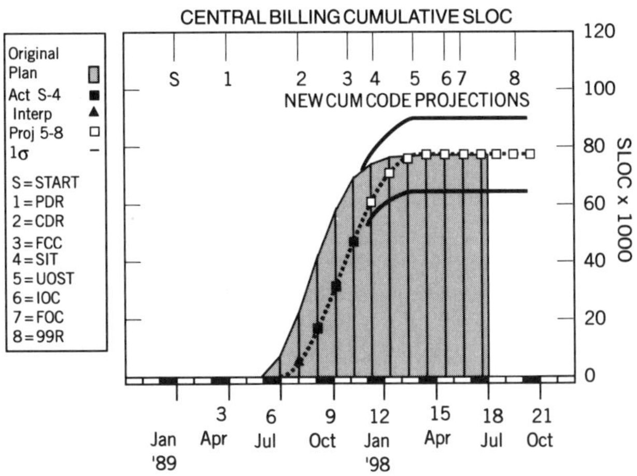

Figure 14. Updated code production rate. Actual code production had fallen behind plan by more than a month to this point in time. The coding is projected to be completed later than scheduled even though the final size of the system is not expected to be greater than planned. Because the development will require more time and effort than planned to produce the same amount of code, the software equation will show that the actual PI achieved on this project will be lower than the PI originally planned.

tive action can be identified early enough to have a beneficial effect.

Control offices and indicators should be established to measure, plan and control projects. For instance, each month all ongoing projects submit their actual data to the control office. Variance analysis is performed and projects are given a status rating of Green, Amber or Red:

- Green status is awarded to projects that are within their control bounds for schedule, effort, defects and cumulative function indicating they are on track.
- Amber status is given to projects that have limited excursions outside planned control bounds indicating that the project should be monitored closely for further deviations from planned performance.
- Red status means the project is consistently falling outside of its control bounds for three of the four progress measures listed above. These projects are given priority management attention to get them back on track.

If a red project is too far along to get it back on track, a revised plan is adopted using the adaptive forecasting technique and this updated plan becomes the new basis for monitoring progress.

The goal of this approach is to reduce the number of amber and red projects as the monthly project, "health check," becomes ingrained as part of the corporate development methodology. Benefits can be expected from using a common approach which will reduce management effort and facilitate improved project communication.

An added benefit of such a measurement system is that at the end of a project the "post mortem" is already complete and all the historical project data is available for collection by the control office. This historic data is used to:

- Measure productivity improvements over time
- Measure return on investment
- Measure performance against industry statistics

Using these insights, the control office can generate realistic, consistent work plans for schedule, cost, staffing, code production and defect prediction. The office can also act as a center of expertise in resource management available to all project teams.

Executive managers should begin to take a part in software development because these systems are now strategic to the organization. Such managers will expect and will be able to get good answers to the management questions: How long is it going to take? How many people? How much is it going to cost? What savings am I getting? What is the return on investment? Will it be good enough to satisfy my best customer? Can I optimize these factors to get the best value for my money?

CONCLUSION

The entire approach to managing software development described above has stemmed from our study of the Ray-leigh profile for code production and defect discovery. This, in turn, drives the demand for resources in the software development process. The software equation and the PI and MBI measures are obtained directly from the Rayleigh function and parameters. The result is a powerful macro-level system for taking control of the software development process.

Using the software equation to create plans and the Rayleigh profiles to monitor progress on your software developments, you will know where you've been, where you are, and most importantly *where you're going!*

Lawrence H. Putnam
Quantitative Software Management, Inc.

RCS

The Revision Control System, a suite of UNIX operating system programs for tracking and control of versions of text files (see W. Tichy, "RCS—A System for Version Control," *Software Practice and Experience* **15** (7), 637–645, (July 1985).

REENGINEERING

Reengineering is a term applied to software development where an existing or legacy) system is undergoing some degree of redevelopment. Synonyms are Software-Renewal and Software-Renovation.

INTRODUCTION

It was common, in the 1960s, and 1970s, to describe the evolution of software systems in two phases: development or production, followed by an operations and maintenance phase. In development or production, the popular model used was the waterfall life-cycle development model wherein development activities preceded in a sequential manner from requirements analysis through test and integration (see Process models in software engineering). Systems being developed were new, or unprecedented. That is, there was no existing automated system. Once the system was produced, it was accepted by a user or customer and the operational phase began. Maintenance performed during operation was described as the correction of latent defects in the software product that were discovered in operational use. This definition evolved to one that included changes to the software of two types: the enhancements to increase operational utility through the addition of user features and the addition of capabilities based on new functional requirements (perfective maintenance), and the need to respond to changing environmental conditions (adaptive maintenance) (see Maintenance). With these enhancements the software system began to evolve. Thus, the evolution of systems became a nominal happenstance. In today's world the situation is even more complex, giving rise to the term "software evolution" (see Software evolution).

Systems were upgraded in two ways. The first way was by completely rebuilding, thus replacing the initial system. As technology advanced, both in hardware and software capability, the capability to enhance software gracefully was improved and became more cost effective. New hardware was developed to be "upward compatible" from prior systems, thus, enabling moving to a new generation of hardware while rehosting existing software. Software portability was enhanced through the effective use of high order languages, cross compilers, and standard interfaces to operating system support environments. In addition, the investment in software was becoming so great that rewriting the system was not cost effective. A combination of these and other circumstances gave rise to the reengineering of software that is common in today's business environment.

Changes to systems are driven by customer and user demands. As a system becomes old hardware performance becomes an issue. Existing hardware may be one to two generations old in terms of that which is currently available, and maintenance of the hardware may be costly. In some situations the original vendor may have gone out of business or dropped support for the system. The user may be completely satisfied with the existing software and may wish to simply replace the hardware with a modem system. For example, the flight simulator for an existing aircraft where system flight characteristics are stable, would not require new software. In another example, the software may be becoming old in the sense that it has undergone extensive upgrade and maintenance is difficult and costly. Or, the original software may not have been engineered well, with poor or missing documentation describing its operation and construction. The user may wish to correct this situation, developing new documentation at the same time upgrading the system to new hardware. This was a common occurrence in the eighties as users were concerned with the maintenance and support of systems.

REENGINEERING ENVIRONMENT

Reengineering of software intensive systems has a spectrum of possibilities. Both hardware and software can be reengineered, either by themselves or in some combination. In a hardware reengineered project, the hardware is normally swapped out with new equipment, and the software may not be modified at all. Or, the hardware may be held constant and the software reengineered.

The extremes are shown on the left and the right in Figure 1. On the left we have the stable condition where nothing is changed. (Some would contend that even this situation is not realistic since software changes as a result of maintenance are a form of evolution.) On the right we see that both hardware and software are replaced, the essence of a complete new and unprecedented system development. (The so-called precedented and unprecedented systems are described in UNPRECEDENTED SYSTEMS). There are two other singular type of reengineering projects: that where the software is held constant and hardware is redeveloped, and that where the hardware is held constant and the software is reengineered. While these may appear to be common, they are not. In fact, when hardware is being replaced or upgraded it commonly requires software changes of varying degree. The more probable circumstance is one where the hardware is held constant and the software is reengineered.

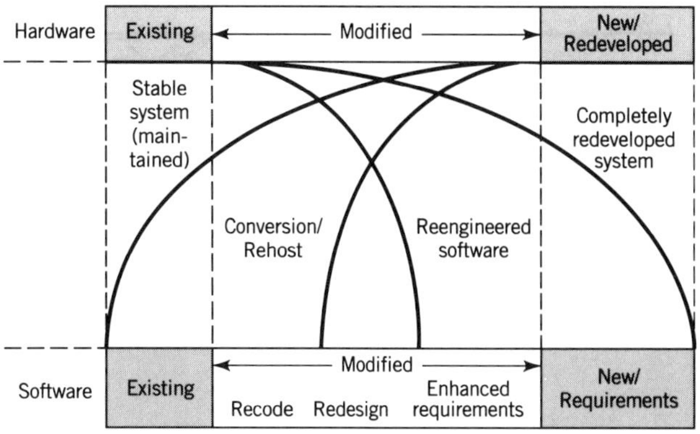

Figure 1. Reengineering environment.

In this latter case there are varying degrees of change. At one end of the spectrum the software may be only rehosted to a new hardware environment. At the other end, the software may be completely rebuilt to a new expanded set of requirements. As we see there is a wide divergence of reengineering possibilities in the evolution of software, Reengineering of a system has one requisite: that there has to be at least one constant) whether it is the hardware or a part of the software such as the requirements or design. If everything is changed, it simply means a new, engineered, system.

EXAMPLES OF REENGINEERING

The reengineering of the DST shareholder accounting and record keeping services for mutual funds systems. The system had evolved to the point where it was seriously under performing and had to be upgraded. Redevelopment was ruled out due to the prohibitive cost, therefore, there was no alternative except to reengineer. The software was rewritten at a cost of 12 million dollars over a period of approximately one year with a cost savings over redevelopment of approximately 40 million dollars (I/S Analyzer, 1991a).

Mellon Bank's trust application (InfoServ) system. In order to achieve higher productivity through high level languages, Mellon Bank decided to convert their software to utilize an application generation tool. The On-line programs were manually converted, with the remaining 400 plus batch programs converted in a two-week period using a tool called Recoder from Technology Inc. Mellon bank felt that the use of the Recoder tool made the project feasible (I/S Analyzer, 1991b).

CTA INCORPORATED had a project with the DOD (USAF) to reengineer a navigator training simulator system. The objective was to rewrite the software while upgrading to new hardware, while keeping existing functional requirements constant. Over 300,000 lines of assembly were rewritten to Ada and FORTRAN. The project was successful, however, an important lesson learned was that reengineering is different than new development. Recommendations included more analysis of existing code and familiarity with the processes: methodology, tools, and languages (Ardrey, 1993).

Westinghouse Electronic Systems Group reported on several projects to include a Processor upgrade for a 25-year old program. They converted approximately 10,000 lines of assembly to Ada over a three-year period. A commercial forward engineering tool had to be abandoned and Westinghouse wrote several tools to include a utility to count Ada SLOC and a requirements trace tool. Success was due to a highly motivated team and an efficient Ada compiler. Lessons from other reengineering projects included the need for an interactive tool to browse, edit, and navigate through the software, the need for good test tools, the need for tool support for variable analysis, and the availability of domain expertise (Mosley, 1993).

The National Institute of Standards and Technology (NIST) took on a case study of a reengineering project to investigate the feasibility and cost-effectiveness of reengineering existing code (NIST, 1991a). They selected a structured COBOL application system from the Internal Revenue Service. The system, the IRS Centralized Scheduling Program (CSP), was written in 1983 using structured COBOL 74 for a UNISYS 1100 computer. The purpose of the project was to migrate the system to a more disciplined, open environment. Approximately 50,000 lines of COBOL along with some miscellaneous code were rewritten. Conclusions reached included that the effectiveness of a reengineering approach is dependent on the variables of corporate and system goals, condition of current application system and documentation, and available resources (automated tools support and personnel).

The Union Bank of Switzerland (UBS) has taken over a number of smaller banks as well as other leasing and credit companies, most of which had existing software systems. One of the objectives of the takeovers was to obtain these applications. Following the takeover the software was analyzed in regard to its functionality and quality. If the scores were high enough the software was then submitted to a two-phase reengineering effort. In the first phase the programs and the data were restructured and converted to the environment of the UBS. The objective of this phase was to improve technical quality while preserving the original functionality. In the second phase the data structures were enhanced and the programs altered to include the additional functionality required by the UBS. With the additional functionality the UBS was able to fulfill its software requirements without having to develop new software. since 1989 the UBS has established a reengineering center which has already conducted a number of projects, some of which have been reported on (Sneed, 1991a).

ENGINEERING MODEL

Reengineering is viewed as two separate but closely related, phases: reverse engineering, and forward engineering. Reverse engineering is usually performed to gain a better understanding of the system; forward engineering is performed to upgrade a part of the system (Fig. 2).

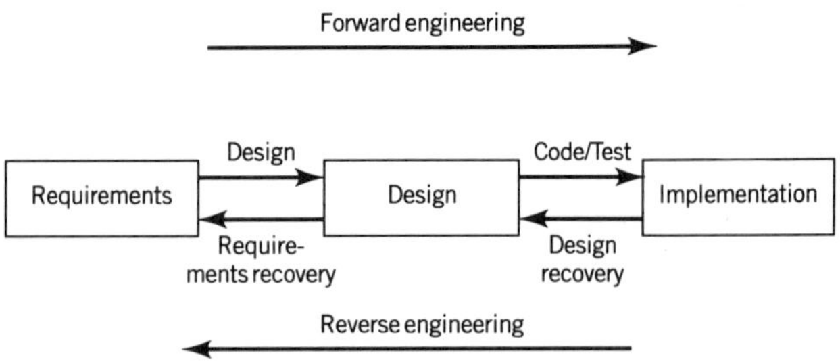

Figure 2. Reengineering model.

Reverse engineering is a normal engineering effort in a reengineering project. According to Chikofsky, "reverse engineering is a general term that refers to a process of analysis, supported by methods and tools, to investigate an existing system, its components, and their interrelationships, regardless of the implementation and ownership of the system" (see REVERSE ENGINEERING). Reverse engineering is an analysis process whereby the engineer discerns information about the system in order to: provide understanding; rebuild design specifications; and rebuild requirements, normally to reconstruct a prior abstraction of development and set the stage for "forward" engineering. It is common in a reengineering project that total information about the system is not present. The requirements and/or design may not be adequately documented.

The source code may have been changed without properly documenting previous changes, thus, existing documentation may be inconsistent with the system as currently implemented. These circumstances require that a reverse engineering effort be undertaken before the rebuilding of the system can begin. For further understanding of these processes, and reverse engineering, see the article REVERSE ENGINEERING.

The effort required to reverse the system also determines the effort required to "forward" engineer the system. Although forward engineering appears to be a straight forward development, there are differences. Each of these contribute to the effort and risk associated with the reengineering effort. Let us examine some of the more common engineering issues.

1. *Requirements.* One cannot assume that the requirements are stable, even if they are held constant by the customer. If the system is being reengineered to the same requirements, there are still important issues. First, are the requirements completely and accurately documented? Will the requirements have to be adjusted due to hardware changes that might require a different implementation then the existing system? Does the reengineering team understand the requirements?

2. *Adequacy of documentation.* Is there existing documentation and does the documentation accurately reflect the design of the system. A through audit should be performed at the onset of the project to determine the adequacy and accuracy of existing documentation.

3. *Code integrity.* Is the code readable? It is possible to have a reengineering project where the code is the best

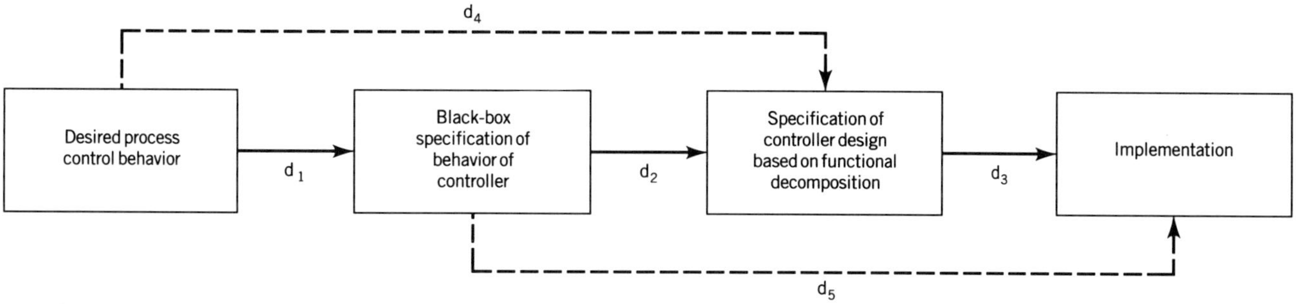

Figure 3. Semantic distance. Reprinted with the permission of the National Security Industrial Association (1993).

representation of the system. In this case reverse engineering tools will have to be employed to discern understanding of the system design. Even if code or product documentation exists the code may implement a system that is not reflected in either requirements or the design.

Software reengineering involves new techniques, especially tools. Reverse engineering tools are applied to aid understanding of the code or the design in order, for example, to recreate documentation. So-called programming aids may be built to dissect the existing code, at either the source or object levels to facilitate understanding in order to create a new design instantiation, or document requirements. There are at least two classifications of tools that can be applied. First, there may be some low level tools that may have to be built to discern information about code. For example, if code is in some low level form, such as assembly or pseudo code, a scanner may have to be built to gain information about the system such as data variables. If the code is in a higher level form, reverse engineering tools provided by companies such as Mark V systems (Object maker) or Interactive Development Environments (Software through Pictures) can be applied to aid design recovery. For more information about reverse engineering tools see REVERSE ENGINEERING.

The complexity of the project and associated risk are dependent on a number of factors. Among these are the degree of change, both of hardware and software, the state of documentation, and the extent of reverse engineering. Leveson described the concept of "semantic distance" at a workshop on reengineering held in Ridgecrest, California. (Leveson, 1993). In this concept, the greater the semantic distance, the greater the difficulty and risk that would be involved in a reengineering effort. Figure 3 shows this concept.

MANAGEMENT ISSUES

Some of the more global or broader issues that are important for reengineering projects are put forth by Lance Eliot (1993) in CASE trends. In this paper Eliot mentions five critical issues that should be considered when initiating a reengineering project:

1. *Placement of Reengineering Specialists.* This primarily deals with the organizational issue of where reengineering specialists are placed in the organization. However, it touches on another issue, that is, the need for reengineering specialists. As mentioned above, one cannot assume that reengineering is just like forward development. There are other engineering issues, for example, familiarity with reverse engineering techniques. In order to perform reengineering, personnel familiar with and trained in reengineering techniques are necessary.

2. *Mode of Reengineering being pursued.* Eliot discusses the extent of reengineering undertaken and its effect on the organization. Clearly, the extent of the project will determine cost since risks will be higher with a more extensive project. Decisions about what will be held constant, e.g., requirement's, design, are important ones, especially where the choices are not straightforward.

3. *Organization of the reengineering project.* Recognizing that the organization is involved in reengineering is the first step to properly organizing for the project. Placement of reengineering specialists is a consideration that was mentioned above. Eliot discusses this in the context of the composition of the reengineering group and its position in the organization.

4. *Direction of the reengineering effort.* This issue deals with how the project will be managed and perceived within the organization. Clearly, recognition that the project is a reengineering one will require that management adjust their mechanisms to provide for the appropriate resources and review of the project.

5. *Preparation for reengineering activities.* Preparation is probably the most important activity. It involves planning for the project by assembling the appropriate specialists, tools, and techniques. While it may not be possible to assemble a team that is totally composed of reengineering specialists, having the proper seed of personnel is important.

ECONOMICS

The economics of reengineering are different than for a normal development project. Differences are code may be converted, or rehosted, thus the factors for cost estimation are different; there are tradeoffs between continuing to use the existing system versus reengineering; the traditional understanding of resource expenditure in the life cycle is different. To illustrate this last point we again turn to the NIST case study.

The NIST example reported the following steps and effort per step (NIST, 1991b):

Step 1 Baseline current system, 19.76%

Step 2 Extract/analyze information, 43.26%

Step 3 Produce documentation, 4.05%

Step 4 Generate new code, 26.34%

Step 5 Execute and test new code, 6.59%

Two points are of interest when examining these data: first, the amount of time that was necessary for extraction and analysis of data, and second, the small amount of time that was used to produce documentation. As one can see this allocation does not neatly fit into a traditional waterfall life cycle development model.

An issue is whether one should reengineer, do nothing, or redevelop. Sometimes the issue is clear: the existing system is just not able to provide the degree of functionality that is required for a modern operation. Or, support for the current system is just not available. But the choices are difficult. The circumstances of the system will provide some insight into this issue. If the requirements are still valid then a reengineering effort is worth exploring. However, if the requirements are distinctly different from the existing system a redevelopment may be warranted. Once these considerations are explored, and a tentative direction is decided, then the costs of redevelopment versus reengineering, or simply doing nothing should be explored.

In his paper, Software Reengineering Strategies and Economics, Sneed identifies the three different situations for reengineering (Sneed, 1991b):

-A, when the existing application system has become technically obsolete, and must be replaced,
-B, when there are severe technical problems with the existing system,
-C, when it might be expedient to upgrade the existing system.

In each of these cases Sneed presents arguments and discussion for choosing an approach, whether it is an upgrade, redevelopment, or reengineering. He presents cost benefit analyses based on the value and costs of maintenance of the existing system versus the value and cost of redevelopment or reengineering system. In the first case (-A) he compares the reengineering cost (the value of the old system discounted by reengineering cost) with the redevelopment cost (the value of a new development discounted by development risk). The risk factor would have to be greater than 1 for the formula to be viable. Then:

$$\text{Re-engineering Benefit} = [\text{Old Value} - (\text{Re-eng.Cost} * \text{Re-eng.Risk})] - [\text{New-Value} - (\text{Dev.Cost} * \text{Dev.Risk})]$$

Notice that the element of risk is introduced into the benefit determination. Clearly, this is a subjective judgment. Thus, the higher the risk is with respect to new development versus reengineering then the benefit might be negative. In addition, the user must calculate the value of the new and old system. This might be some combination of the value of the hardware, software, and the functionality provided.

In the second case (-B) Sneed points out that there is a spectrum of possibilities ranging from replacement with a standard package, redevelopment, reengineering or the status quo. Here he uses the following equation to determine benefit:

$$\text{Re-engineering Benefit} = [\text{Old-Maint.Cost} - \text{Re-eng.Maint.Cost}] + [\text{Old-Value} - (\text{Reeng.Cost} * \text{Re-eng.Risk})] - [\text{New-Value} - (\text{Dev.Cost} * \text{Dev.Risk})]$$

Again, the second set of brackets refer to the discounted value of a reengineered system, whereas the third set refers to the discounted value of a new development.

In the third case (-C) the cost of maintenance is the dominant consideration and Sneed cites the work of Robert Figliolo (1989) presented at the Software Maintenance Association Conference in Atlanta. Sneed sums up the costs and benefits of reengineering in the following four factors:

1. Costs of reengineering relative to the costs of redevelopment and the costs of maintenance.
2. Added value of reengineering relative to the value of a new system and the value of the present system.
3. Risk of reengineering relative to the risk of a new development and the risk of doing nothing.
4. Life-expectancy in time of the existing system relative to the time required to reengineer it and the time required to redevelop it.

SUMMARY

Software reengineering is already a common form of endeavor in software engineering practice. At this point in time reverse engineering has received more attention, however, as the field of reengineering becomes more recognized in the context of software evolution there will be greater emphasis in academia and the commercial marketplace. We can expect to see more tools and methods, and a better elucidation of the process itself.

The author wishes to thank Harry M. Sneed for his comments and contributions to this article.

BIBLIOGRAPHY

R. Ardrey, "Case Experiences in Re-engineering," *Proceedings of the National Security Industrial Association and Embedded Computing Institute,* Ridgecrest, Calif., Jan. 12–14, 1993, pp. 71–86.

L. Eliot, "Re-engineering Roll-Out," *CASE Trends,* 31–32 (June 1993).

R. Figliolo, "Benefits of software re-engineering," *Proceedings of Software Maintenance Association Conference,* N. Zwetginzor ed., Atlanta, Ga., May, 1989.

I/S Analyzer (formerly EDP Analyzer), *Re-engineering Existing Systems,* **29**(10), 1–3 (Oct. 1992a).

I/S Analyzer (formerly EDP Analyzer), *Re-engineering Existing Systems,* **29**(10), 9–10 (Oct. 1992b).

N. Leveson, "Reverse Engineering TCAS System Requirements," *Proceedings of the National Security Industrial Association and Embedded Computing Institute,* Ridgecrest, Calif., Jan. 12–14, 1993, pp. 279–314.

V. Mosley, "Integrated Tools for Re-engineering," *Proceedings of the National Security Industrial Association and Embedded Computing Institute,* Ridgecrest, Calif., Jan. 12– 14, 1993, pp. 343–364.

National Security Association (NSIA), *Proceedings of the National Security Industrial Association and Embedded Computing Institute,* workshop on Reengineering, Ridgecrest, Calif., Jan. 12–14, 1993.

H. M. Sneed, "Reengineering Bank Applications at the Union Bank of Switzerland," *Prtoceedings of the Software Maintenance Conference*, IEEE Press, Sorrento, Italy, 1991a.

H. M. Sneed, "Economics of Software Re-engineering," *Journal of Software Maintenance: Research and Practice,* **3**(3) pp. 163–191 (Sept. 1991b).

U.S. Department of Commerce, National Institute of Standards and Technology, *Software Reengineering: A Case Study and Lessons Learned*, NIST Special Publication 500-193, Gaithersburg, Md., Sept. 1991a.

U.S. Department of Commerce, National Institute of Standards and Technology, *Software Reengineering: A Case Study and Lessons Learned,* NIST Special Publication 500-193, Gaithersburg, Md., Sept. 1991b, p.10.

JOHN J. MARCINIAK
CTA INCORPORATED

REACTIVE PROGRAMMING

INTRODUCTION

A reactive system is a system that is in charge of maintaining a permanent interaction with its environment at a pace that is governed by this environment. A reactive program is a program that drives a reactive system. This comparatively recent unifying concept covers a number of domains that were considered as quite distinct in the past but bear actually more similarities than differences: real-time process control, hardware and software controllers, communication protocols, systems and man–machine interface drivers, and signal processing. The priviledged but nonexclusive application field of reactive programming is that of embedded computing, where computers drive plants, transportation middles, house appliances, and ever more and more everyday's life objects. In these domains, it is clear that program quality and safety are very crucial concerns.

Reactive programming has always shown up to be a technically difficult area. Even small programs require considerable efforts to be specified, written, and debugged. It is easily seen that reactive programming has two essential requirements: *concurrency* and *determinism.* Concurrency is mandatory since the natural architecture of most reactive programs has the form of logically related but well-individualized concurrent components, a structure that should be preserved to obtain good quality source code; for example, a digital watch contains a timekeeper, an alarm, and a stopwatch that should be kept separated at programming level and individually written to be reusable. Determinism means that a program placed twice in the same environment should react twice in the same way, a constraint that is clear in most of the aforementioned applications—think again of a watch.

TRADITIONAL TOOLS

Among the conventional tools currently used to program reactive systems we can cite sequential programs made concurrent by calling operating systems primitives (tasking), high-level concurrent programming languages such as ADA, MODULA, or OCCAM, finite-state machines, block diagrams, or Petri-Net based formalisms. Unfortunately, none of these tools support both concurrency and determinism. A brief discussion of two extreme points of the above list: concurrent languages and finite state machines follows.

Concurrent languages of course support concurrency, but they lead to nondeterministic programs because their processes are loosely coupled. Intuitively, communication between concurrent processes can involve an arbitrary delay between the desire for a communication and its actual achievement, just as with mail systems. Consider a very basic reactive program such as "every 60 seconds, signal a minute". The minute transmission from the source process to the target process can in principle take any amount of time, which is certainly not what the programmer intends. Sequencing constructs can also consume time. Such defects are studied in details in (Berry, 1989). These defects show the intrinsic limitation of asynchronous concurrent languages to reactive and real time programming: one can write programs that look good, but they do not mean what they say. (Rendezvous communication is often called synchronous; we definitely prefer to call it "synchronizing" because only the final handshake is really synchronous, its preparation being fully asynchronous.)

On the exact opposite, finite state machines, also called automata, support determinism but exclude concurrency, which makes writing and reading nontrivial programs almost impossible because of state-space explosion: for example, waiting for the last of n events yields an automaton of size 2^n. Asynchronous networks of finite state machines or Petri Nets try to bring in concurrency, but they suffer the same problems as asynchronous languages.

PERFECT SYNCHRONY

The recent family of perfectly synchronous formalisms brings a new point of view on reactive programming. The main idea is to consider ideal reactive systems that need no time to compute their outputs when they are given their inputs. Clearly, this is what we would really desire: to show the right time, a watch should simply react instantly to the quartz signals and user commands. At first glance, perfect synchrony seems to be a mess since no such ideal system can be built. But this hypothesis really does simplify programming and its practical validity is checkable in most cases. Before showing this in more detail, notice that perfect synchrony is just a transposition to computer science of the principle of Newtonian mechanics, which supposes that body interaction is instantaneous. It is known that Newtonian mechanics is wrong at very high speeds, but this has really no importance in the vast majority of applications.

Perfectly synchronous reactive programs are purely passive and input-driven: they wait for events coming from its environment and react instantaneously to them. There is no "internal time" as in asynchronous programs. Concurrent processes behave in a tightly coupled way; they communicate instantaneously with each other, communication being generally based on instantaneous broadcast. Since concurrent processes share the same information at the same time, programming is made much simpler and determinism and concurrency can be reconciled.

The main synchronous languages are ESTEREL, LUSTRE, SIGNAL, STATECHARTS (Harel, 1987), and SML, the last two formalisms adopting perfect synchrony only partly. The first four languages are developed on industrial bases and used industrially. ESTEREL, STATECHARTS, and SML are imperative and well-adapted to control intensive applications such as controllers and drivers. LUSTRE and SIGNAL are data-flow oriented and better adapted to signal processing or continuous process control applications. We refer to the individual language presentations for their technical exploitation of perfect synchrony, which leads to particularly elegant programming styles (see Berry and Benveniste, 1991).

All the mentioned languages are rigorously defined by mathematical semantics written in various styles. Their authors unanimously think that this is the only way to guarantee program safety. Perfect synchrony actually leads to novel and interesting mathematical developments. The semantical definitions are no academic games: the various compilers are entirely based on the mathematical semantics. They produce a variety of targets, ranging from hardware circuits to programs written in conventional programming languages, in the forms of straight-line codes or finite state machines. These codes are extremely efficient and of predictable performance, a property that is very important in practice: perfect synchrony is reasonably approximated as soon as the rate of inputs is slower that the output computation time. Notice that this is exactly the functioning hypothesis of hardware digital circuits. Distributed implementations are currently under study, as well as formalisms unifying the asynchronous and synchronous approaches.

The rigor of the mathematical semantics makes it possible to perform real verifications on synchronous programs. The properties of interest are generally safety properties that ensure that nothing bad can happen, e.g., that a lift cannot travel with a door open. Most synchronous language compilers are linked with automatic verification systems, which can be based on automata manipulation techniques, temporal logics, or static assertion verifications algorithms.

The perfect synchrony hypothesis is studied and compared with asynchrony in Berry (1989).

BIBLIOGRAPHY

G. Berry, "Real-Time Programming: General Purpose or Special-Purpose Languages," in G. Ritter, ed., *Information Processing 98,* Elsevier Science Publishers, 1989, pp. 11–17.

G. Berry and A. Benveniste, eds., "Another Look at Real Time Programming, *Proceedings of the IEEE 79,* 1991.

D. Harel, "a Visual Approach to Complex Systems," *Science of Computer Programming* **8,** 231–274 (1987).

GÉRARD BERRY
Ecole des Mines de Paris

REAL-TIME LANGUAGES

A Real-Time Language (RTL) is a programming language used to implement an information processing system that can respond to externally generated stimuli within a finite and specifiable delay. Real-time languages are typically used to program embedded computer systems that interface directly to physical equipment and are dedicated to monitoring and operating that equipment in a larger information-processing system. The type of stimuli, the length of the delay, and the type of response depend on the application context. A delay of 15 seconds may be acceptable in an ATM transaction, but intolerable when flying an advanced fighter such as the F-18. Because the definition of "real time" varies so widely, the features of real time languages also vary widely.

Real-time software is usually comprised of multiple processes that are executed concurrently and interact, where necessary, to synchronize on events and exchange information. Real-time software must be extremely reliable, must be capable of responding to a wide variety of events with differing, but guaranteed, response times, and must be able to interface with a variety of non-standard I/O devices as well as conventional peripherals. It is not sufficient to verify that real-time software performs its function correctly, but that it does so in a predictable, timely manner.

REAL-TIME LANGUAGE FEATURES

To meet the requirements of real-time systems, an RTL requires both conventional programming constructs such as abstract data types, structured and dynamic data types, and classical program control structures, as well as specific features to support real-time programming (Young, 1982). To produce real-time software with predictable timing properties, a real-time language must provide, among other things, features for: specifying time constraints, estimating resource requirements, and providing predictable synchronization mechanisms (Halang, 1990).

In real-time systems, application deadlines are met by using scheduling and allocation techniques that are based either on compile-time scheduling (Xu, 1990) or run-time scheduling coupled with pre-run-time verification (Lehoczky, 1989). Both techniques require pre-run-time information about the timing constraints, maximum execution time, and other resource requirements of the program. Schedulability analysis (Halang, 1991) is a method for analyzing a program to extract timing information for each compilable unit. Using this information, an analyzer can compute the minimum response times of the program to specific events. It also can predict guaranteed response times to selected events. The feasibility of this approach has been demonstrated in the experimental language, Real-Time Euclid (Kligerman, 1986; Stoyenko, 1987).

Estimating Execution Time

Execution time of a program can be obtained in three ways: instrumentation and profiling, simulation, and estimation. The first two methods require considerable expertise and effort beyond writing the program to achieve useful results. Estimation is carried out using the programs themselves. Estimation can provide timing information as well as feedback about the nature of the program. Estimating the execution time of programs is complicated by the presence of high-level language features such as conditions, loops, recursion, and synchronization. The estimation process must consider the target code generated by the compiler, the timing characteristics of the operating system primitives, and the timing characteristics of the hardware instructions (Park, 1991). Most real-time languages do not support estimation of execution time. Those that do, restrict language constructs. Real-time Euclid (Kligerman, 1986; Stoyenko, 1987) allows only loops with constant bounds, but does not allow recursion or dynamic data structures. Other tools require the programmer to specify the worst-case execution path (Park, 1991). A recent thesis by Nirkhe (Nirkhe, 1992) demonstrates how to use the technique of partial evaluation to estimate the execution time of hard real-time programs.

Specifying Timing Constraints

Timing constraints for real-time systems are usually imposed by external decisions or requirements. It may not be possible to change the timing constraints without changing the behavior of the system. Timing constraints include delay intervals and delay between two processes, starting and ending times, and periodicity of actions. Because enforcement of timing constraints is essential to the successful operation of real-time systems, many RTLs provide mechanisms for expressing timing constraints. Some use hard-wired timing constraints while others use assembly language routines to provide accurate timing information. Synchronous languages such as ESTEREL (Boussinot, 1991), LUSTRE (Halbwachs, 1991), and SIGNAL (Guernic, 1991) use a model called "perfect synchrony" based on synchronous communication and atomic computation in which timing constraints are expressed implicitly through the flow of events. Some RTLs, such as PEARL (Martin, 1978) and RTC++ (Ishikawa, 1990) provide high-level constructs for explicitly specifying timing constraints. Ada-based systems (ANSI, 1983) use external timing specifications to implement real-time systems. The specification of timing constraints and resource requirements is affected by shared resource and synchronization mechanisms.

Synchronization

Large real-time systems, which have been decomposed in multiple processes, require synchronization to support scheduling and resource allocation. Resource requirements depend upon such factors as the number of processors and the schedule. For example, the execution time of two non-interfering concurrent processes allocated to separate processors, is the maximum of their execution times. Synchronization among cooperating processes affects the temporal behavior of the cooperating processes. The timing characteristics of synchronization primitives and the process ordering imposed by the scheduling algorithm, must be considered when determining the temporal behavior of concurrent processes. It is difficult to predict the timing characteristics of synchronization primitives since their performance depends upon the number of processes contending for the scheduling algorithm. A few languages, such as Real-Time Euclid, account for synchronization by using the worst case blocking time in estimating execution times. RTC (Wolfe, 1991) allows a programmer to specify a set of actions that may not overlap each other. At run-time the system acquires all required resources before the set of actions can occur.

AVAILABILITY OF RTLS

Beginning in the early 1960s, numerous RTLs had been designed and developed for a variety of applications. They can be divided into two categories: general purpose RTLs, which are used for programming non-real-time systems as well, and special purpose RTLs, including hard RTLs, which are used for specific applications and hardware suites (Benveviste, 1991).

Algol-60 was an early general purpose language used as an RTL. An Algol-60 variant, ECPL, was used to implement Burrough's MCP operating system for its B5xxx/6xxx/7xxx family of computers. RTL/2, a simplification of Algol-60, was developed by J. Barnes (Barnes, 1972) in the early 1970s in Britain. Algol's successors, including JOVIAL, Pascal, Modula, and Ada, have all been used to implement real-time systems.

The explicit rationale for Ada (qv) was to develop a language for implementing real-time embedded computer systems (Young 1982; ANSI, 1983). Although somewhat complex, Ada has several advantages: it is well-structured, readable, modular, and strongly typed. Ada makes explicit provisions for direct hardware access, task synchronization through asynchronous rendezvous, error handling, and system- and user-defined exceptions. Ada has been mandated as the development language by the U.S. Department of Defense for all new embedded computer systems.

Ada does not provide mechanisms for specifying timing constraints or allowing the programmer to define the scheduling of tasks (Mahjoub 1981; Halang 1990). Timing constraints must be imposed by an external executive. Ada does provide the "delay" construct which specifies a lower bound on the time a task may be delayed, but the actual delay may be larger, even unbounded. Dynamic task preemption and the non-deterministic rendezvous make it difficult to determine whether any deadline will be met.

Many conventional, general-purpose programming languages have been extended to support real-time applications. For example, FORTRAN (ACM, 1981) has defined extensions for industrial computer systems. FORTH (Brodie, 1981) was developed for real-time control of telescopes and is used to implement new device drivers for Sun Microsystems' SparcStation SBUS. C has been used to develop many real-time systems including, notably, many of those produced by AT&T for telecommunications switching. BASIC has been used extensively for real-time programming in laboratory instrumentation and measurement systems. Hewlett-Packard has developed an extensive library of BASIC routines and device drivers for controlling its measurement systems.

Real-Time Euclid (Kligerman, 1986; Stoyenko, 1987) consists of a compiler, a schedulability analyzer, and a run-time system. It restricts the use of high-level language constructs such as only allowing loops with constant bounds and forbidding recursion and dynamic data structures. A program in Euclid is decomposed into a set of blocks of code. The programmer specifies: the starting time of a task, the maximum time to wait on a semaphore, the maximum number of loop iterations, and the initiation and synchronization of concurrent tasks. Using the execution time for individual blocks, the execution time of the whole program is determined. The schedulability analyzer determines whether or not a program is schedulable before being executed. If the semaphore is not released before this time expires, the waiting process is automatically released. This maximum time is used in determining the worst-case execution time of a process.

ESTEREL (Boussinot, 1991) was one of the first languages to use the concept of "perfect synchrony" to develop reactive systems. ESTEREL is based on synchronous communication and atomic computation mediated by the flow of events. Events that mark the initiation and termination of actions, such as clock ticks, are used to synchronize processes. The computation performed in an ESTEREL module is both deterministic and atomic, i.e., no two instances of computation overlap. Because a unique output is produced for every input and, during execution, no interaction with the external environment takes place, communication and computation are assumed to take no time.

PEARL (Martin, 1978) is a general-purpose real-time programming language developed for process automation. PEARL provides mechanisms for the creation of concurrent tasks and the specification of timing constraints, including delays, starting and ending times, and periodicity of tasks. A run-time scheduler uses this information, coupled with event-synchronization information and process priorities, to schedule tasks.

RTC (Wolfe, 1991) addresses the problem of mutual exclusion for real-time transaction processing systems. A programmer is allowed to specify actions, or sets thereof, that may not overlap each other. At run time, the system acquires all of the required resources before an action or set of actions is executed.

RTC++ (Ishikawa, 1990) extends C++ with an active object which incorporates timing constraints at the statement level. Syntactic extensions to C++ allow the programmer to specify the starting time of an operation, a deadline for when the operation must complete, an ending time, and whether or not it is a periodic task. A schedulability analyzer uses these timing constraints to analyze the schedulability of the task set (see also C++).

THE FUTURE OF RTLS

To be properly designed and developed, real-time systems will require real-time languages that facilitate the verification of critical timing constraints and resource requirements. The easiest method for developing such languages is to design in the real-time features. However, since the bulk of the world's real-time software is written in general-purpose programming languages such as FORTRAN, extensions to these languages are necessary to support the development of real-time software.

Partial evaluation (Nirkhe, 1992) is a method for estimating resource requirements and execution time. Partial evaluation permits the use of some high-level constructs, such as recursion, unrestricted looping, and concurrent execution. Nirkhe demonstrates that partial evaluation gives tighter estimates of execution than previous methods based on worst-case estimation and leads to more accurate scheduling with higher resource utilization.

Future RTLs must provide high-level timing constructs instead of requiring programmers to use low-level timing mechanisms in order to provide for portability, reusability, and modifiability. Synchronization mechanisms must be developed to prevent nondeterministic interactions and to make possible the determination of resource requirements from compile-time data. Such mechanisms must also provide information for pre-scheduling analysis to ensure the ability to meet resource integrity constraints. Schedulability analysis must take into account timing constraints, resource requirements, and synchronization constraints in determining the execution time of real-time applications.

BIBLIOGRAPHY

ACM, Draft Standard on Industrial Real Time FORTRAN of the International Purdue Workshop on Industrial Computer Systems, ACM SIGPLAN Notices, Vol. 16(7), 1981, pp. 45–60.

ANSI/MIS-STD 1815, Ada Reference Manual, U.S. Printing Office, Washington, D.C., 1983.

J. Barnes, *RTL/2: Design and Philosophy,* Heyden, London, 1972.

J. Barnes, "Real Time Languages for Process Control," *Computer Journal,* **15,** 15–17 (1972).

A. Benveviste and G. Berry, *The Synchronous Approach to Reactive and Real-Time Systems,* IEEE Proceedings, **79**(9), 1270–1282, (1992).

F. Boussinot and R. de Simone, "The ESTEREL Language," *IEEE Proceedings* **79**(9), 1293–1304 (1991).

L. Brodie, *Starting Forth,* Prentice-Hall, Englewood Cliffs, N.J., 1981.

P. Guernic, T. Gauntier, M. le Borgne, and C. le Maire, "Programming Real-Time Applications with SIGNAL," *IEEE Proceedings,* **79**(9), 1321–1336 (1991).

W. Halang and A. D. Stoyenko, "Comparative Evaluation of High-Level Real-Time Programming Languages," *Real-Time Systems Journal* **2**(4), 365–382 (1990).

W. A. Halang and A. D. Stoyenko, *Constructing Predictable Real-Time Systems,* Kluwer Academic, Boston, 1991.

N. Halbwachs, P. Caspi, and co-workers, "The Synchronous Data Flow Programming Language LUSTRE," *Proceedings of the IEEE,* **79**(9), 1305–1320 (1991).

Y. Ishikawa, H. Tokuda, and C. Mercer, "Object-Oriented Real-Time Language Design: Constructs for Timing Constraints," *OOPSLA '90, SIGPLAN Notices* **25**(10) 289–298 (1990).

E. Kligerman and A. D. Stoyenko, "Real-Time Euclid: a Language for Reliable Real-Time Systems," *IEEE Transactions on Software Engineering* **SE-12**(9) 941–949 (1986).

J. Lehoczky, L. Sha, and Y. Ding, "The Rate Monotonic Algorithm: Exact Characterization and Average Case Behavior," *10th IEEE Real-Time Systems Symposium,* 166–171 (1989).

A. Mahjoub, "Some Comments on Ada as a Real-Time Programming Language," *ACM SIGPLAN Notices,* **16** (1981).

T. Martin, *The Real-Time Programming Language PEARL—Concepts and Characteristics,* COMPSAC 78, 1978.

V. M. Nirkhe, *Application of Partial Evaluation to Hard Real-Time Programming,* University of Maryland, UMIACS-TR-92-58, May 1992.

C. Y. Park and A. C. Shaw, "Experimenting with a Program Timing Tool Based on Source-Level Timing Schema," *IEEE Computer,* 48–57 (May 1991).

A. D. Stoyenko, "A Schedulability Analyzer for Real-Time Euclid," *8th IEEE Real-Time Systems Symposium,* 218–227 (1987).

V. Wolfe, S. Davidson, and I. Lee, "RTC: Language Support for Real-Time Concurrency," *12th IEEE Real Time Systems Symposium* (1991).

J. Xu and D. L. Parnas, "Scheduling Processes with Release Times, Deadlines, Precedence, and Exclusion Relations," *IEEE Transactions on Software Engineering* **SE-16**(3), 360–369 (1990).

S. J. Young, *Real Time Languages: Design and Development,* Ellis Horwood Limited, Chichester, UK 1982.

Stephen H. Kaisler
Laurel, Maryland

REAL-TIME OPERATING SYSTEMS

INTRODUCTION

Real-time computing systems play a vital role in our society. These systems control many types of applications that include simple ones such as laboratory experiments and automobile engines, as well as very complex applications such as nuclear power plants, flight control systems, manufacturing processes, and teams of robots working in hazardous environments. In real-time computing the correctness of the system depends not only on the logical result, but also on the time at which the results are produced. Building and analyzing real-time systems is difficult because these systems explicitly deal with time (usually via direct control of equipment that is, in turn, controlling or operating in some larger environment). One important component in producing an effective real-time system is the *real-time operating system.* There are many commercial and research oriented real-time operating systems. In discussing real-time operating systems it is possible to categorize them into three general classifications: small, fast, proprietary kernels; real-time extensions of commercial operating systems; and research oriented operating systems.

SMALL, FAST, PROPRIETARY KERNELS

Existing practices for designing, implementing, and validating real-time systems of today are still rather *ad hoc.* Software engineering practices that advocate modularity and the use of abstract data types are not usually pursued throughout the real-time software production process due to their perceived conflict with real-time requirements. This attitude has permeated the small, proprietary kernels —both commercially available ones and special *one-time* kernels found in many systems. The practice of building one's own kernel is diminishing, but is still sometimes required to meet especially difficult performance requirements. In most cases, proprietary kernels are used for small embedded systems when fast and highly predictable execution time must be guaranteed (Ready, 1986). To achieve speed and predictability, these kernels are stripped down and optimized as versions of timesharing operating systems. To reduce the run-time overheads incurred by the kernel and to make the system *fast,* kernel features are listed below:

- has a fast context switch
- has a small size (with its associated minimal functionality)
- is provided with the ability to respond to external interrupts quickly
- minimizes intervals during which interrupts are disabled
- provides fixed or variable sized partitions for memory management (i.e., no virtual memory) as well as the ability to lock code and data in memory
- provides special sequential files that can accumulate data at a fast rate.

To deal with timing requirements, the kernel

- bounds the execution time of its primitives (system calls)
- maintains a real-time clock
- provides a priority scheduling mechanism
- provides for special alarms and timeouts
- tasks can invoke primitives to delay by a fixed amount of time and to pause/resume execution

In general, the kernels also perform multitasking and intertask communication and synchronization via standard, well-known primitives such as mailboxes, events, signals, and semaphores. While these additional features are designed to be fast, fast is a relative term and not sufficient when dealing with real-time constraints. For example, even if each of these additional primitives is predictable, they can cause unpredictable blocking resulting in a very difficult analysis problem when attempting to verify that timing constraints of application tasks will be met. Nevertheless, for lack of a good alternative, many real-time system designers use these features as a predictable basis upon which to build real-time systems. Since these kernels provide little direct support for solving the difficult timing problems, the cost of maintaining real-time systems has generally been high. Research is being done to develop more sophisticated tools and kernels that directly address timing and fault tolerance constraints so that costs are lower and there is greater confidence that the system actually meets the requirements.

REAL-TIME EXTENSIONS TO COMMERCIAL OPERATING SYSTEMS

A second approach to real-time operating systems is the extension of commercial products, e.g., extending UNIX to RT-UNIX (Furht and co-workers 1991) or MACH to real-time MACH. The real-time version of a commercial operating system is generally slower and less predictable than the proprietary kernels, but have greater functionality and better software development environments. For example, one advantage of RT-UNIX is that it is based on a set of familiar interfaces (standards) that speed development and facilitate portability. However, since many variations of UNIX have evolved, a new standards effort, called POSIX (qv), has defined a common set of user level interfaces for operating systems. In particular, the POSIX P.1003.4, subcommittee is defining standards for real-time operating systems. To date, the effort has focussed on eleven important real-time related functions: timers, priority scheduling, shared memory, real-time files, semaphores, interprocess communication, asynchronous event notification, process memory locking, asynchronous I/O, synchronized I/O, and threads.

Various problems exist when attempting to convert a non real-time operating system to a real-time version. These problems can exist both at the system interface as well as in the implementation. For example, in UNIX interface problems exist in process scheduling due to the *nice* and *setpriority* primitives and the round robin scheduling policy. In addition, the timer facilities are too coarse, memory management (of some versions) contains no method for locking pages into memory, and interprocess communication facilities do not support fast and predictable communication. The implementation problems include intolerable overhead, excessive latency in responding to interrupts, partly but very importantly, due to the non-preemptability of the kernel, and internal queues are FIFO. These and other problems are then solved to result in a real-time operating system that is used for both real-time and non real-time processing. However, users must be careful not to use certain non real-time features that might insidiously impact the real-time tasks.

RESEARCH OPERATING SYSTEMS

While many real-time applications will be constructed with these commercial real-time operating systems, significant problems still exist. In particular, the commercial offerings emphasize speed rather than predictability. Research in real-time operating systems is emphasizing predictability and argues that totally different approaches are required. Three brief examples are given as representative of the current research.

The Spring kernel (Stankovic and Ramamritham, 1991) contains real-time support for multiprocessors and distributed systems. It uses on-line, dynamic planning and retains a significant amount of application semantics at run time. These features are integrated to provide direct support for achieving both application and system level predictability. A novel aspect of the work is the integration of real-time cpu scheduling and resource allocation. Another aspect is the use of global replicated memory to achieve predictable distributed communication.

The MARS kernel (Kopetz and co-workers, 1989) offers support for controlling an application based entirely on time events rather than asynchronous events from the environment. Emphasis is placed on an *a priori* design (including static scheduling) and analysis to demonstrate that timing requirements are met. An important feature of this system is that flow control on the maximum number of events that the system handles is automatic and this fact contributes to the predictability analysis.

The CHAOS system (Schwan and co-workers, 1990) represents an object-based approach to real-time kernels. This approach allows easy creation of a family of kernels, each tailored to a specific hardware or application. This is important because real-time applications vary widely in their requirements and it would be beneficial to have one basic paradigm for a wide range of applications. The family of kernels is based on a core that supports a real-time threads package. This core is the machine dependent part. Virtual memory regions, synchronization primitives, classes, objects, and invocations all comprise additional support provided in each kernel.

BIBLIOGRAPHY

B. Furht, D. Grostick, D. Gluch, G. Rabbat, J. Parker, and M. Roberts, *Real-Time Unix Systems,* Kluwer Academic Publishers, Norwell, Massachusetts, 1991.

H. Kopetz, A. Demm, C. Koza, and M. Mulozzani, "Distributed Fault Tolerant Real-Time Systems," *IEEE Micro* 25–40 (Feb. 1989).

J. Ready, "VRTX: A Real-Time Operating System for Embedded Microprocessor Applications," *IEEE Micro* 8–17 (Aug. 1986).

K. Schwan, A. Gheith, and H. Zhou, "From CHAOSbase to CHAOSarc: A Family of Real-Time Kernels," *Proceedings of the Real-Time Systems Symposium,* 82–91 (Dec. 1990).

J. Stankovic and K. Ramamritham, "The Spring Kernel: A New Paradigm for Hard Real-Time Operating Systems," *IEEE Software* 62–72 (May 1991).

JOHN A. STANKOVIC
University of Massachusetts

REAL-TIME RESOURCE MANAGEMENT TECHNIQUES

INTRODUCTION

Real-time systems are of ever increasing importance to modern society. These systems are used to monitor and control complex physical processes ranging from the civilian problems of aircraft traffic control, manufacturing and space flight, to the military applications that arise with modern warfare systems. Unlike general purpose computer systems, where resources must be managed to provide adequate system responsiveness for all tasks on the average, the underlying physical processes being controlled by a real-time system impose explicit timing requirements on the tasks processed by the computer system. These timing requirements are an integral part of the correctness and safety conditions of a real-time system. Although real-time systems must manage many resources including memory, I/O, files, etc., it is the management of time which distinguishes real-time systems from ordinary computer systems. In this article, we address resource management for real-time uniprocessor-based systems and focus exclusively on time management as applied to processor scheduling.

Proper resource management, to ensure that tasks meet their timing requirements, is a vital aspect of a real-time system design where failure to meet a task timing requirement causes a timing fault to occur. Although tempting to think that speed (e.g., processor or communication media speed) would be the sole ingredient to meeting system timing requirements, speed alone is not enough. Proper resource management techniques must also be used, for example, to prevent situations in which long, low priority tasks block higher priority tasks with short deadlines. A guiding concern in real-time system resource management is *predictability,* the ability to determine for a given set of tasks whether the system will be able to meet all of the timing requirements of those tasks. Predictability calls for the development of scheduling models and analytic techniques which can be used to determine *a priori* whether or not a real-time system can meet its timing requirements. Moreover, these techniques must be computationally efficient. The distinctions between real-time systems and ordinary computer systems are discussed by Stankovic (Stankovic, 1988). Finally, real-time systems must be highly fault tolerant and behave properly in the presence of timing faults or transient system overloads.

Embedded real-time systems must schedule diverse activities to meet the timing requirements imposed by the physical environment. While this issue may be a difficult problem, the real-time system developer works in a tightly constrained environment and, typically, has the advantage of knowing the entire set of tasks that are to be processed by the system and the conditions under which each might be run. An algorithmic-based scheduling methodology allows the developer to combine task-set characterization data with the associated timing requirements, to determine through the use of schedulability criteria whether or not the task set can be scheduled to meet its timing requirements. Consequently, a scheduling theory can make the timing properties of the system predictable. This methodology allows the determination, analytically, as to whether the timing requirements of a task set will be met, and if not, which task-timing requirements will fail. An iterative process can then be used to modify certain tasks to achieve the schedulability of the entire task set.

CLASSIFICATION OF REAL-TIME TASKS

There are two types of tasks that are commonly encountered in real-time systems that are designed for monitoring and control functions. If a computer system must monitor a physical system or process, then it must sample it and react to the data gathered. This regular sampling gives rise to a periodic task. A periodic task refers to a single task with an infinite series of regular invocations (jobs), beginning with an initial invocation at some relative initiation time, I. Subsequent invocations occur periodically, every T time units. Each of these invocations has a computation requirement of C units which may be deterministic or stochastic. If the computation time is stochastic, then C often denotes the upper bound (or worst case) computation time. Each task invocation will have an explicit timing requirement. The most common requirement is that a task invocation must be completed within D time units after it is ready: a timing requirement which is often referred to as a hard deadline. Thus the first invocation must be completed by time I+D, the second by I+T+D, etc. Periodic tasks are usually invoked by internal timers with the periodicity chosen to ensure that the latency is short enough to react to event or changes in the underlying physical process being monitored.

A second and closely related type of task is the sporadic task. A sporadic task differs from a periodic task only in the times between invocations. Whenever a sporadic task is invoked, the next invocation cannot occur any sooner than T time units later. A sporadic task is often triggered by an external event rather than by an internal timer with a restriction on the times between invocations. The times between task invocations may be stochastic but have a lower bound of T. In the worst case (in the sense of the largest possible processor demand), a sporadic task will place exactly the same demand as a periodic task on the processor. A sporadic task will also have a timing requirement which is often a deadline, D. This restraint means that the task must be completed D time units after it is invoked.

Tasks in the third category are referred to as aperiodic or asynchronous tasks. These tasks have stochastic arrival times with only the long run arrival rate being known, perhaps only approximately. The processing times may also be stochastic. Aperiodic tasks can also be classified according to their timing requirements. Some aperiodic tasks will have hard deadlines meaning that they must be completed by a fixed time, D, once they are invoked, or a timing fault occurs. An example of an aperiodic task with a hard deadline is an alert condition which must be dealt with immediately. A second example would be a software fault that has occurred in the execution of a periodic or sporadic task. The task must be reprocessed and completed before the original deadline; thus, this aperiodic request will have a hard deadline. Other aperiodic tasks will have soft deadlines. Here, the task will have no specific completion time, but a system design goal will be to minimize the completion time of these tasks, subject to meeting all the hard deadlines of any other tasks.

Some consideration has been given to more sophisticated timing requirements for real-time systems: the assumption being that each task has an associated value function. This function gives the relative value associated with completing that task at any particular time and seeks to maximize the total system value which is defined as the sum of the values attained by each of the tasks (Locke, 1987). While a wide range of timing requirements can be expressed through value functions, to date no comprehensive theory of value function scheduling has been developed. Nevertheless, this topic is receiving increased attention, particularly in the case of processor overload. For the special case of hard deadlines with processor utilization in excess of 1, Baruah and co-workers (1992) developed a bound on the best value that any on-line algorithm can achieve relative to the optimum off-line algorithm. Koren and Shasha (1992) have presented an algorithm, D^{OVER}, which achieves this bound.

CLASSIFICATION OF SCHEDULING ALGORITHMS

Initially, distinguishing between *on-line* and *off-line* scheduling algorithms is useful. The distinction lies in the input available for use by the scheduling algorithm. An off-line algorithm assumes that the entire task set, all invocation times, computation times and deadlines are known. A schedule can then be computed and a time-line constructed. This procedure results in a static, deterministic schedule which is not changed over time. An off-line algorithm has the potential of being optimal; however, there are other, more important concerns to be discussed later that must also be considered. On-line algorithms can not only use information about the past and the general structure of the scheduling problem, but can also react to changes in the environment within which the system is operating. A scheduling algorithm is optimal among a collection of algorithms if it can find a schedule satisfying all task timing requirements when such a schedule is possible using some algorithm in the collection considered.

Some real-time systems are sufficiently simple, static and involve relatively few tasks; therefore, they can be scheduled with the execution sequence being laid out on a time-line. For example, if the task set consists solely of periodic tasks, then once the first invocation has been determined, all future invocations times can be determined exactly. For the case in which periodic tasks are being scheduled, the resulting off-line schedule is called a cyclic executive. These schedules can be efficient, can reduce overhead from task swapping and can offer a simple method to enforce mutual exclusions. They do, however, have major problems. Any change in the task set, including modifications to the tasks themselves, will require that a new time-line be drawn and then fully tested. The method also requires that the task set be relatively small. Further, cyclic executives are not well suited to handling mixtures of periodic and aperiodic tasks. Consequently, cyclic executives do not offer as good a response time for aperiodic tasks as can be achieved by other methods. To efficiently implement a cyclic executive, the task periods should be as close to harmonic as possible to create a short schedule. This method may force tasks to be executed more frequently than their required or natural periods, creating unnecessary task utilization with a longer aperiodic response. Finally, a cyclic executive cannot easily respond to environmental changes. For these reasons, in this article, the focus is only upon on-line priority-based scheduling algorithms.

There are several classifications for on-line scheduling algorithms. An important dichotomy exists with the distinction between preemptive and non-preemptive scheduling algorithms. Preemptive algorithms assume that any process can be suspended by the scheduler, essentially instantly, and later resumed from the point of suspension. The most common reason for preemption is when a higher priority task becomes ready to run. Non-preemptive scheduling algorithms do not permit running processes to be suspended. Non-preemptive schedulers are relatively easy to implement, but can cause high priority tasks to miss their deadlines when they are blocked by a long, lower priority task. Nevertheless, partial non-preemptivity can be effectively used for concurrency control; for example, in enforcing critical sections. Furthermore, it may sometimes not be possible to preempt; for example, when interrupts on behalf of lower priority tasks are not masked or when the scheduler or other operating system functions are executing. While much of the scheduling literature deals with the non-preemptive case, most modern computer systems allow task preemption with little, if any, time loss. Thus in this article, the focus is primarily on the preemptive case.

A second important classification of scheduling algorithms is *static priority* versus *dynamic priority* algorithms. A static priority scheduling algorithm will preassign a single priority to each task (and the same priority to every invocation of that task). This priority is not changed, no matter what the circumstances. Dynamic algorithms allow a task to change its priority at any point in time between its readiness and its completion time. In addition, different invocations of a periodic task can have different priorities. Dynamic algorithms can also change task priorities if there are changes in the environment in which the system is functioning.

The task scheduling problem has been extensively studied in the operations research and computer science literature. The focus of that literature tends to be on optimal scheduling methods and their computational complexity.

Most realistic real-time scheduling problems which incorporate practical issues such as task blocking and transient overloads are NP-hard. As such, optimal methods will often not be useful in real-time systems. Garey, Graham, and Johnson (1978) summarize the situation as follows:

> *Unfortunately, although it is not difficult to design optimization algorithms (e.g., exhaustive search is usually applicable), the goal of designing efficient optimization algorithms has proved much more difficult to attain. In fact, all but a few schedule-optimization problems are considered insoluble except for small or specially structured problem instances. For these scheduling problems no efficient optimization algorithm has yet been found and, indeed, none is expected. This pessimistic outlook has been bolstered by recent results showing that most scheduling problems belong to the infamous class of NP-complete problems.*

For real-time systems it is more important to use algorithms which, while not optimal, will be predictable and guarantee high levels of schedulable utilization. There are two scheduling algorithms that are especially important for scheduling real-time systems: the *rate monotonic* scheduling algorithm and the earliest deadline scheduling algorithm. The former is an on-line but static priority algorithm which assigns periodic task priorities in inverse relation to the task periods. The latter is a dynamic priority algorithm in which highest priority is accorded to the ready task with the nearest deadline. A comprehensive scheduling theory has been developed for the rate monotonic algorithm and its generalizations which are capable of handling many of the practical problems that arise with real-time systems. The remainder of this article describes much of that theory. To a lesser extent, there is a scheduling theory associated with the earliest deadline algorithm. Some of the results are briefly described at the end of this article.

THE RATE MONOTONIC SCHEDULING ALGORITHM

The problem of scheduling periodic tasks was first addressed analytically by Serlin (1972) and by Liu and Layland in 1973. Liu and Layland provided the most comprehensive treatment of the periodic task scheduling problem. They considered both static priority and dynamic priority scheduling algorithms and studied this scheduling problem under idealized circumstances by assuming:

- A1: Tasks are periodic, are invoked at the start of each period, and do not suspend themselves during their execution. Tasks have known, deterministic execution times.
- A2: Tasks are independent and can be instantly preempted. All overhead for scheduling and context swapping is ignored.
- A3: Tasks are independent in the sense that they cannot block each other.
- A4: Task deadlines are at the end of the task period.

Under these rather stringent assumptions, Liu and Layland were able to derive very important results concerning both static and dynamic priority scheduling algorithms. In particular, they showed that the earliest deadline scheduling algorithm can schedule any periodic task set with task deadlines at the end of the task period having total utilization up to 100%. With respect to static priority scheduling, Liu and Layland showed that the rate monotonic algorithm, in which each invocation of a single task receives an identical priority and priorities are assigned in an inverse relation to the tasks periods, is the optimal static priority algorithm in the sense that any task set that can be scheduled by some static priority algorithm can also be scheduled by the rate monotonic algorithm. Both Serlin and Liu and Layland derived a simple sufficient condition to determine if a periodic task set can be scheduled by the rate monotonic algorithm. The next task is to formulate the static priority scheduling problem, summarize the Liu and Layland rate monotonic scheduling theory and present its more recent extensions.

Consider a set of n periodic tasks, $\tau_1, \ldots, \tau_n$. Each task is characterized by four components (C_i, T_i, D_i, I_i), $1 \le i \le n$ where

$$C_i = \text{computation requirement of each invocation of } \tau_i,$$

$$T_i = \text{period of } \tau_i$$

$$D_i = \text{deadline of } \tau_i$$

$$I_i = \text{phasing of } \tau_i \text{ relative to some fixed time origin}$$

Each periodic task creates an infinite sequence of invocations. The jth invocation of τ_i occurs at time $I_i+(j-1)T_i$, and the C_i units of computation required for each invocation of τ_i have a deadline of $I_i+(j-1)T_i+D_i$. Liu and Layland assumed $D_i=T_i$. Such a task set is said to be *schedulable* (or feasibly scheduled) by a particular scheduling algorithm provided that all deadlines of all the tasks are met under all task phasings if that scheduling algorithm is used.

Liu and Layland proved three important results concerning static priority scheduling algorithms. Consider first the longest response time for any job of a task τ_i where the response time is the difference between the task instantiation time (I_i+kT_i) and the task completion time; that is, the time at which that invocation of τ_i completes its required C_i units of execution. If any static priority scheduling algorithm is used and tasks are ordered so that τ_i has higher priority than τ_j for $i<j$, then

Theorem 1. The longest response time for any invocation of τ_i occurs for the first invocation of τ_i when $I_1=I_2= \ldots =I_i=0$. □

The case with $I_1=I_2=\ldots=I_n=0$ is called a critical instant, because it results in the longest response time for the first job of each task. Consequently, this creates the worst case task set phasing and leads to a criterion for the schedulability of a task set. Theorem 1 is from Liu and Layland (1973).

Theorem 2. A periodic task set can be scheduled by a static priority scheduling algorithm provided the deadline of the first job of each task, starting from a critical instant, is met using that scheduling algorithm.

Liu and Layland went on to characterize the optimal static priority scheduling algorithm, the *rate monotonic* scheduling algorithm. The rate monotonic scheduling algorithm assigns priorities inversely to task periods. Hence, τ_i receives higher priority than τ_j if $T_i \leq T_j$. Ties are broken arbitrarily. Here the optimality of the rate monotonic scheduling algorithm means that if a periodic task set is schedulable using some static priority scheduling algorithm, then it is also schedulable using the rate monotonic scheduling algorithm. We summarize this as Theorem 3.

Theorem 3. The rate monotonic scheduling algorithm is optimal among all static priority scheduling algorithms for scheduling periodic task sets with $D_i = T_i$.

Interestingly, the rate monotonic scheduling algorithm considers only task periods, not task computation times or the relative importance of the task in the task set. Serlin and Liu and Layland (1973) went on to offer a worst case upper bound for the rate monotonic scheduling algorithm; that is, a threshold U_n^* such that if the utilization of a task set consisting of n tasks, $U = C_1/T_1 + \ldots + C_n/T_n$, is no greater than U_n^*, then the rate monotonic scheduling algorithm is guaranteed to meet all task deadlines. They accomplished this result by studying full utilization task sets. These are task sets which can be scheduled by the rate monotonic algorithm under critical instant phasing; however, if the processing requirement C_i of any single task τ_i, $1 \leq i \leq n$, were increased, a deadline of some task would be missed. They then identified the full utilization task set with smallest utilization, and this utilization became the worst case upper bound. The result is given by Theorem 4.

Theorem 4. A periodic task set $\tau_1, \tau_2, \ldots, \tau_n$ with $D_i = T_i$, $1 \leq i \leq n$, is schedulable by the rate monotonic scheduling algorithm if

$$U_1 + \ldots + U_n \leq U_n^* = n(2^{1/n} - 1), \; n = 1, 2, \ldots.$$

The sequence of scheduling thresholds is given by $U_1^* = 1$, $U_2^* = 0.828$, $U_3^* = 0.780$, $U_4^* = 0.756$, $\ldots$, $U_\infty^* = \ln 2 = 0.693$. Consequently, any periodic task set can be scheduled by the rate monotonic algorithm if its total utilization is no greater than 0.693. Theorem 4 is from Serlin (1972) and Liu and Layland (1973).

Extensions of the Liu and Layland Theory

The worst case bound of 0.693 given in Theorem 4 is respectably large; however, Theorem 4 is quite pessimistic. Randomly generated task sets are often schedulable by the rate monotonic algorithm at much higher utilization levels even assuming worst case phasing. It is also important to derive a more exact criterion for schedulability that can be used in more general circumstances. We first consider the situation in which the task deadlines need not be equal to the task periods. This problem was initially considered by Leung and Whitehead (1982). They introduced a new static priority scheduling algorithm, the *deadline monotonic* algorithm, in which task priorities are assigned inversely with respect to task deadlines, that is, τ_i has higher priority that τ_j if $D_i < D_j$. They proved the optimality of the deadline monotonic algorithm when $D_i \leq T_i$, $1 \leq i \leq n$.

Theorem 5. For a periodic task set $\tau_1, \ldots, \tau_n$ with $D_i \leq T_i$, $1 \leq i \leq n$, under assumptions A1, A2 and A3, the optimal static priority scheduling algorithm is the *deadline monotonic* scheduling algorithm. A task set is schedulable by this algorithm if the first invocation of each task after a critical instant meets its deadline (Leung and Whitehead, 1982).

Theorem 4 was generalized by Lehoczky and Sha (1986) and by Peng and Shin (1989) and Lehoczky (1990) for the case in which $D_i = \Delta T_i$, $1 \leq i \leq n$ and $0 < \Delta \leq 1$, and by Lehoczky (1990) for $\Delta > 1$. In this case, the rate monotonic and deadline monotonic scheduling algorithms give the same priority assignment. We have the following generalization of Theorem 4.

Theorem 6. A periodic task set with $D_i = \Delta T_i$, $1 \leq i \leq n$ and $0 \leq \Delta \leq 1$ is schedulable if

$$U_1 + \ldots + U_n \leq U_n^*(\Delta) = \begin{cases} n((2\Delta)^{1/n} - 1) + (1 - \Delta), & \frac{1}{2} \leq \Delta \leq 1 \\ \Delta & 0 \leq \Delta \leq \frac{1}{2} \end{cases}$$

An exact analysis of the schedulability of a task set using a static priority scheduling algorithm was first presented by Joseph and Pandya (1986). Lehoczky, Sha, and Ding (1989) used an exact analysis to determine the average case behavior of the rate monotonic scheduling algorithm. Lehoczky (1990) extended the exact analysis to the case of arbitrary deadlines. The exact methods are based on the following approach: under critical instant phasing,

$$\sum_{j=1}^{i} C_j \left\lceil \frac{t}{T_j} \right\rceil = W_i(t)$$

gives the cumulative demand for processing by tasks τ_j, $1 \leq j \leq i$ during $[0, t]$. Using assumption A4 and Theorem 2, task τ_i meets all its deadlines if its first invocation meets its deadline under critical instant phasing. This occurs if $W_i(t) = t$ at some time t, $0 \leq t \leq D_i$, the deadline of the first invocation of τ_i. Equivalently, this invocation will meet its deadline if and only if there is a t, $0 \leq t \leq D_i$, at which $W_i(t)/t \leq 1$. The smallest time t satisfying this inequality gives the longest possible completion time of any invocation of τ_i. Theorem 6 is from Lehoczky and Sha (1986) and Peng and Shin (1989). We summarize this in the following theorem.

Theorem 7. Let a periodic task set $\tau_1, \tau_2, \ldots, \tau_n$ be given in priority order and scheduled by a fixed priority scheduling algorithm using those priorities. If $D_i \leq T_i$, then τ_i will meet all its deadlines under all task phasings if and only if

$$\min_{0 \leq t \leq D_i} \sum_{j=1}^{i} \frac{C_j}{t} \left\lceil \frac{t}{T_j} \right\rceil \leq 1$$

The entire task set is schedulable under the worst case phasing if and only if

$$\max_{1\leq i\leq n} \min_{0\leq t\leq D_i} \sum_{j=1}^{i} \frac{C_j}{t} \left\lceil \frac{t}{T_j} \right\rceil \leq 1$$

The criterion given in Theorem 7 (Lehoczky, Sha and Ding, 1989) is not difficult to compute. The sum is a piecewise continuous decreasing function of t. Consequently, to find the minimum, only the points of discontinuity need be considered; namely, the values of t which are multiples of any of $T_1, T_2, \ldots T_{i-1}$ and D_i. Only a subset of these multiples needs to be checked. A more efficient approach is to create a sequence of times $S_0, S_1, \ldots$ with $S_0 = \sum_{j=1}^{i} C_j$, $S_{n+1} = W_i(S_n)$. If for some n, $S_n = S_{n+1} \leq D_i$, then task τ_i is schedulable. If, instead, $D_i \leq S_n$ for some n, the task τ_i is not schedulable.

The criterion given by Theorem 7 also provides a simple way of showing that the rate monotonic scheduling algorithm can schedule task sets up to 100% utilization when $D_i = T_i$ and the periods are harmonic. Suppose that T_i/T_j is an integer for $1\leq j\leq i$. Then, letting $t = T_i$,

$$\sum_{j=1}^{i} \frac{C_j}{T_i} \left\lceil \frac{T_i}{T_j} \right\rceil = \sum_{j=1}^{i} \frac{C_j}{T_i} \frac{T_i}{T_j} = \sum_{j=1}^{i} \frac{C_j}{T_j} = U_1 + \ldots + U_i$$

Consequently, τ_i will be schedulable if all higher priority tasks have periods which evenly divide T_i and $\sum_{j=1}^{i} U_j \leq 1$. If the periods are completely harmonic, that is if Ti/Tj is an integer, $1\leq j\leq i$, $1\leq i\leq n$, then all tasks are schedulable provided $U_1 + \ldots + U_n \leq 1$. We summarize this as Theorem 8.

Theorem 8. If a task set $\tau_1, \ldots, \tau_n$ is scheduled using the rate monotonic algorithm and T_j evenly divides T_i for $1\leq j\leq i$, then τ_i meets all its deadlines if and only if $U_1 + \ldots + U_i \leq 1$. If T_j evenly divides T_i for all $j\leq i$, $1\leq i\leq n$, then the task set is schedulable if and only if $U_1 + \ldots + U_n \leq 1$.

Theorem 7 can be used to obtain more detailed information about the ability of the rate monotonic algorithm to schedule periodic task sets. Since the earliest deadline algorithm can schedule all periodic task sets with utilization up to 100%, while the rate monotonic algorithm cannot in general. Also important is the need to characterize the loss in schedulability caused by using static priority instead of dynamic priority algorithms. A concept called *breakdown utilization* is particularly useful. Consider any periodic task set characterized by $(C_1, T_1), \ldots, (C_n, T_n)$. Suppose each of the computation times is scaled by a common factor and this factor is increased until a task deadline is first missed. The corresponding task set utilization is called the breakdown utilization and is given by the formula:

$$U_{BD}^{(n)} = \sum_{i=1}^{n} \frac{C_i}{T_i} \Big/ \max_{1\leq i\leq n} \min_{0\leq t\leq D_i} \sum_{j=1}^{i} \frac{C_j}{t} \left\lceil \frac{t}{T_j} \right\rceil$$

The breakdown utilization is a complicated function of the random variables $C_1, \ldots, C_n$ and $T_1, \ldots, T_n$; however, if n is large and all these random variables are independent, then $U_{BD}^{(n)}$ converges to a constant. This limiting value was characterized by Lehoczky, Sha, and Ding (1989). They showed that when periods are drawn from a uniform distribution with a sufficiently wide range of values, the breakdown utilization will generally be in the 88% to 92% range. Surprisingly, however, if periods are chosen according to a uniform (1, 2) distribution and n is large, then the breakdown utilization converges to the worst case upper bound of 0.693. This situation occurs because the full utilization task set having smallest utilization derived by Serlin and Liu and Layland consists of n tasks having equal utilization and periods nearly uniformly distributed over (1,2). Thus the random task set is very likely to be close to the worst case task set as n becomes large.

The worst case upper bound on utilization of 0.693 and the average case value of 0.88 are sufficiently large so that the rate monotonic scheduling algorithm has gained significant acceptance for its ability to provide predictable system behavior with high levels of schedulable processor utilization. There may, however, be cases in which higher processor utilization is required; for example, when an existing task set is modified. For such cases, several approaches are possible. The first and most radical approach is to change to a dynamic scheduling algorithm such as the earliest deadline algorithm. This approach is very unattractive, especially since some practical problems associated with dynamic scheduling algorithms have not been solved. Moreover, such a change might entail a total system redesign with full testing. A second approach would be to increase the deadline of the tasks for which timing faults occur, allowing them more time to complete their execution. Third, one might make modifications to the task priority structure. If one of the tasks is unable to always meet its deadline, it may be possible to divide the task into two serially executed subtasks. The first subtask would be given the ordinary rate monotonic priority, while the second subtask would be executed at an elevated priority, sufficiently high to ensure that it met its timing requirements. Both of these latter approaches have been addressed and schedulability criteria have been established for them.

The case in which task deadlines can be longer than task periods is different from the cases presented thus far. In particular, Theorems 2 and 3 are no longer valid, so a new characterization of the schedulability of a task set must be determined. The problem is more complicated than the case in which all task deadlines are shorter than the corresponding task periods, because an invocation of τ_i may have to wait for the completion of an earlier invocation of τ_i in addition to waiting for higher priority tasks.

This problem was studied by Lehoczky (1990), whereby he showed that neither the rate monotonic nor the deadline monotonic scheduling algorithms are optimal for scheduling periodic tasks when deadlines can exceed period lengths. In spite of this lack of optimality, it is straightforward to develop an exact schedulability criterion for any static priority scheduling algorithm in this case. The important concept is that of a *level-i busy period*.

Definition. A level-i busy period is a time interval $[a,b]$ within which invocations of tasks of priority i or higher are processed throughout $[a,b]$ but no invocations of tasks of level i or higher are processed in $(a-\varepsilon, a)$ and $(b, b+\varepsilon)$ for sufficiently small $\varepsilon>0$.

The exact schedulability condition is very similar to that presented in Theorem 7 except that checking only the first invocation of a task is no longer sufficient. A necessary and sufficient condition for schedulability of a task set is that for every i, $1 \le i \le n$, every invocation of τ_i during a level-i busy period initiated by a critical instant meets its deadline. Theorem 7 can also be generalized to provide an exact criterion for schedulability, and more general worst case upper bounds on schedulable utilization were derived by Lehoczky (1990).

Recently, Shih, Liu, and Liu (1990) considered the situation in which periodic deadlines are deferred. They defined the *modified rate monotonic algorithm* in which all task invocations which are not completed by the end of their period receive higher priority than all other task invocations. They were able to prove limited optimality properties for this algorithm and developed worst case upper bounds on utilization.

The situation in which tasks are divided into subtasks which are executed in serially order was treated by Gonzalez Harbour, Klein and Lehoczky (1991). This situation can arise in many practical circumstances; for example, when high priority tasks are blocked by the interrupts of low priority tasks (the interrupt portion of the low priority task would be considered an initial subtask that is executed at an elevated priority), when synchronization is required (and a task elevates its priority to enforce mutual exclusion) or when operating system activities (such as task swapping or scheduling) are included into the analysis. The static priority schedulability analysis of this problem is similar in nature to the usual case, except that care in determining all the task invocations whose deadlines must be checked and the worst case task phasings must be exercised. These conditions were fully spelled out by Gonzalez Harbour, Klein and Lehoczky (1991).

Rate Monotonic Scheduling and Task Synchronization

In the previous sections, the tasks being scheduled were assumed to be independent and to be completely preemptible. Consequently, there could never be a case in which priority inversion occurs; that is, when a high priority task is ready to execute but is blocked by the execution of a lower priority task. For example, if tasks require the use of nonpreemptible resources or access shared data, then a lower priority task's use of such a resource or such data can block a high priority task from executing. There are many well-known methods for task synchronization including semaphores, locks and monitors; however, a straightforward use of these synchronization primitives can lead to unbounded periods of priority inversion and even deadlock. Some care is needed to develop a task synchronization protocol which will prevent deadlock and which will still permit an associated schedulability analysis. To understand the problems that arise when tasks synchronize in a real-time systems with priority-based scheduling, consider the following example.

Example 1. Consider periodic tasks $\tau_1, \ldots, \tau_n$ arranged in descending order of priority. Suppose tasks τ_1 and τ_n share a data structure guarded by a semaphore S_1. Suppose that τ_n begins execution and enters a critical section using this data structure. Task τ_1 is next initiated, preempts τ_n and begins execution. During its execution, τ_1 attempts to use the shared data and is blocked on the semaphore S_1. Task τ_n now continues execution, but before it completes its critical section it is preempted by the arrival of one of tasks $\tau_2, \ldots, \tau_{n-1}$. Because none of these tasks require use of S_1, any of these tasks that arrive will execute to completion before τ_n is able to execute and unblock τ_1. This situation creates a period of *priority inversion.* Unless this period is of predictable duration, it is impossible to guarantee that τ_1 will meet its deadline.

The difficulty illustrated by Example 1 is that the lowest priority task is capable of blocking a high priority task, but it continues to execute at its original priority level. Consequently, the low priority task can be preempted for a prolonged period of time by an intermediate priority task, even when it is blocking a high priority task. Unlike the case of non-preemptive blocking mentioned earlier where a lower priority task can temporarily block all higher priority tasks, here the blocking can be selective. This selective blocking allows intermediate priority tasks to execute which creates a potentially unbounded duration of priority inversion with its consequent lack of predictability. The solution to this problem is to invoke *priority inheritance,* a task which blocks a high priority task and inherits the priority of the task it is blocking for the duration of the blocking period. In Example 1, priority inheritance would call for τ_n to elevate its priority to that of τ_1 from the time τ_1 blocks on S_1 until the blocking condition is removed. This technique would prevent any of $\tau_2, \ldots \tau_{n-1}$ from preempting τ_n and would bound the duration of the priority inversion to the length of time that τ_n holds S_1. However, being careful of deadlocks is a must, as the following example shows.

Example 2. Suppose two tasks, τ_1 and τ_2, both require shared access to two data structures guarded by semaphores S_1 and S_2, and τ_1 has higher priority than τ_2. Suppose τ_1 and τ_2 have the following sequence of operations:

$$\tau_1\text{: } \{\ldots P(S_1) \ldots P(S_2) \ldots V(S_2) \ldots V(S_1) \ldots\}$$
$$\tau_2\text{: } \{\ldots P(S_2) \ldots P(S_1) \ldots V(S_1) \ldots V(S_2) \ldots\}$$

If τ_2 executes $P(S_2)$, is preempted by τ_1 and then τ_1 executes $P(S_1)$, a deadlock is created. The only practical solution to this problem is to prevent τ_1 from executing $P(S_1)$ to prevent the deadlock.

One way of solving the potential deadlock problem illustrated by Example 2 is to define the *priority ceiling* of a semaphore.

Definition. The priority ceiling of a semaphore is defined as the priority of the highest priority task that may lock this semaphore. The priority ceiling of a semaphore S_j, denoted by $C(S_j)$, represents the highest priority that a critical section guarded by S_j can execute, either by normal or inherited priority.

The *priority ceiling protocol* was defined in Sha, Rajkumar, and Lehoczky (1990) and is given next. Job J refers to a particular invocation of an associated task.

Definition. This is the Priority Ceiling Protocol of Sha, Rajkumar, and Lehoczky, 1990, p. 1180).

1. Job J, which has the highest priority among the jobs ready to run, is assigned the processor, and let S^* be the semaphore with the highest priority ceiling of all semaphores currently locked by jobs other than job J. Before job J enters its critical section, it must first obtain the lock on the semaphore S guarding the shared data structure. Job J will be blocked and the lock on S will be denied, if the priority of job J is not higher than the priority ceiling of semaphore S^*. (Note that if S has been already locked, the priority ceiling of S will be at least equal to the priority of J. Because job J's priority is not higher than the priority ceiling of the semaphore S locked by another job, J will be blocked. Hence, this rule implies that if a job J attempts to lock a semaphore that has been already locked, J will be denied the lock and will be blocked instead.) In this case, job J is said to be blocked on semaphore S^* and to be blocked by the job which holds the lock on S^*. Otherwise, job J will obtain the lock on semaphore S and enter its critical section. When a job J exits its critical section, the binary semaphore associated with the critical section will be unblocked and the highest priority job, if any, blocked by job J will be awakened.
2. A job J uses its assigned priority, unless it is in its critical section and blocks higher priority jobs. If job J blocks higher priority jobs, J *inherits* P_H, the highest priority of the jobs blocked by J. When J exits a critical section, it resumes the priority it had at the point of entry into the critical section. That is, when J exits the part of a critical section, it resumes its previous priority. Priority inheritance is transitive. Finally, the operations of priority inheritance and of the resumption of previous priority must be indivisible.
3. A job J, when it does not attempt to enter a critical section, can preempt another job J_L if its priority is higher than the priority, inherited or assigned, at which job J_L is executing.

The priority ceiling protocol has many properties, but we single out the three most important for consideration.

Theorem 9. The priority ceiling protocol prevents deadlocks. (Sha, Rajkumar and Lehoczky, 1990).

Theorem 10. Under the priority ceiling protocol, a job J can experience priority inversion for at most the duration of one critical section (Sha, Rajkumar and Lehoczky, 1990).

To give a schedulability analysis using the rate monotonic scheduling algorithm in conjunction with the priority ceiling protocol, we define B_k, $1 \le k \le n$, the longest duration of blocking that can be experienced by τ_k. Note $B_n = 0$, because τ_n is assumed to have lowest priority and hence cannot experience a priority inversion. Once these blocking terms have been determined, they can be used to generalize Theorem 7.

Theorem 11. A set of n periodic tasks with $D_i = T_i$ using the priority ceiling protocol can be scheduled by the rate monotonic algorithm for all task phasings if the following conditions are satisfied (Sha, Rajkumar and Lehoczky, 1990):

$$\frac{C_1}{T_1} + \ldots + \frac{C_i}{T_i} + \frac{B_i}{T_i} \le i(2^{1/i} - 1),\ 1 \le i \le n$$

A more detailed condition is given by Theorem 12.

Theorem 12. A set of n periodic tasks with $D_i = T_i$ using the priority ceiling protocol can be scheduled by the rate monotonic algorithm for all task phasings if

$$\max_{1 \le i \le n} \ \min_{0 \le t \le T_i} \left(\sum_{j=1}^{i} \frac{C_j}{t} \left\lceil \frac{t}{T_j} \right\rceil + \frac{B_i}{t} \right) \le 1$$

Theorem 12 gives a sufficient condition for the schedulability of a task set in which task synchronization is done using the priority inheritance protocol. This procedure gives a fairly complete solution for the real-time task synchronization problem in uniprocessors. This problem becomes much more complicated in the multi-processor case. Rajkumar, Sha, and Lehoczky (1990) developed extended priority ceiling protocols for multi-processors using message passing architectures. Rajkumar (1991) has further generalized the priority ceiling protocol to be applicable in the shared memory multiprocessor case. The book by Rajkumar (1991) contains a wealth of information on real-time synchronization. Recently, Baker (1990) has developed an improvement on the priority ceiling protocol, the *stack based protocol*. This protocol is especially interesting because stack based protocol can be used with static priority scheduling algorithms such as the rate monotonic algorithm and dynamic algorithms such as the earliest deadline algorithm. Baker also provides a complete analysis of task set schedulability when this protocol is used.

Rate Monotonic Scheduling of Aperiodic Tasks

One of the practical problems encountered in real-time scheduling is handling mixtures of hard-deadline periodic tasks and soft-deadline aperiodic tasks. Any real-time scheduling algorithm must meet all of the hard deadlines of the periodic tasks to avoid timing faults; however, the response time of the aperiodic tasks must be as small as possible. There are two standard approaches to this problem: (1) treating the soft deadline tasks as background tasks and (2) creating a high priority polling task, the capacity of which is used to service the soft deadline tasks. The background approach, while simple to implement, results in the longest possible response times for the aperiodic tasks. The background approach does not take into account the fact that the hard-deadline tasks can be delayed because there is no advantage to having them completed before their deadline. Thus, treating all periodic tasks as having higher priority than all aperiodic tasks, disadvantages the aperiodic tasks unnecessarily. The polling approach is far superior to the background approach. The polling task creates a high priority resource which allows the soft deadline tasks to gain an advantage over the hard deadline tasks. Nevertheless, the polling approach also has disadvantages. The polling task is only ready periodically, and whenever there are soft deadline tasks ready, they must wait until the polling task is ready. Also, if the polling task is ready, but no aperiodic tasks are ready, then the polling capacity is temporarily lost. The difficulty lies in the mismatch between the periodic readiness of the polling task and the aperiodic arrival times of those tasks which use it.

Recently, this problem has been partially overcome with the introduction of aperiodic server algorithms such as the *deferrable server* (Strosnider, 1987) or the sporadic server (Sprunt, 1990). Both of these approaches create a periodic task having a given service capacity C and a period T. However, there are different rules for the server capacity replenishment. For the deferrable server, the capacity is held during the entire period, ready for use. For the sporadic server, any capacity used is replenished one period later. The sporadic server can be scheduled exactly as a typical periodic task, whereas a deferrable server can have a more invasive quality. Both of these algorithms are very compatible with rate monotonic scheduling, and both can offer up to an order of magnitude improvement in response time over background and polling, with the greatest improvements occurring for very short aperiodic tasks. As the aperiodic tasks lengthen with respect to the server capacity, the performance of any of the server algorithms degrades to that of a polling server.

The Deferrable Server Algorithm

The deferrable server (DS) algorithm creates a periodic server task τ_1 with C_1 units of execution and priority defined by the rate monotonic priority associated with the server's period T_1. The periodic server task, hereafter referred to as the DS task, is a special purpose task created to provide high priority execution time for aperiodic tasks. The DS task has the entire period, T_1, within which to use its C_1 units of execution time at priority P_1 to service aperiodic tasks. If at the end of the period T_1 any portion of the C_1 run-time has not been used, then it is discarded. The DS task's capacity, C_1, is renewed at the beginning of each server period. Assigning the DS task the highest priority (by giving it a period no longer than the shortest periodic task period) allows one to introduce guaranteed response times for high priority aperiodic tasks as well as enhancing the responsiveness of the soft deadline aperiodic class. Both of these capabilities are provided while maintaining guaranteed response time performance for periodic tasks. The possibility that the DS task execution can be deferred until the end of its period where the DS task execution could be immediately followed by a DS task execution from the next period, necessitates the development of a new schedulability analysis. This method is used to determine conditions on the size of the DS task which will ensure that all periodic tasks meet their deadlines. A full characterization of the bounds is provided by Strosnider (1988). The DS algorithm has successfully been applied to both processor scheduling (Lehoczky, Sha, and Strosnider, 1987) and local area network scheduling (Strosnider, Marchok, and Lehoczky, 1988; Strosnider and Marchok, 1989).

The Sporadic Server Algorithm

The use of a DS task to provide fast aperiodic response times results in lower levels of schedulable utilization than if an ordinary periodic task were used as a server. Furthermore, the analysis has been carried out only when the DS task has the highest priority. The sporadic server algorithm avoids the schedulable utilization penalty and can be implemented at any priority level. The sporadic server (SS) algorithm is similar to the DS algorithm in that it creates a relatively high priority task for servicing aperiodic tasks. This server preserves its execution capacity until an aperiodic request occurs. That request can receive immediate service by using some or all of the remaining SS execution capacity, so if there is sufficient capacity remaining, the aperiodic request can be serviced to completion, immediately. Unlike the DS algorithm, the SS algorithm has a more sophisticated replenishment policy because its total capacity may become divided into smaller execution allotments, each with a distinct replenishment time. Suppose the SS has period T and executes at priority level P. The replenishment time for an execution allotment is T plus the maximum of the time at which that execution allotment becomes available and the time at which priority level P becomes active. (A priority level P is active if a task with priority P or higher is being executed.) Execution allotments with equal replenishment times can be combined, and the replenishment times of very small allotments can be delayed to replenishment times of other allotments to reduce SS capacity fragmentation.

The important consequences of the SS algorithm replenishment policy are (1) the SS can be treated just like an ordinary periodic task in a schedulability analysis, and (2) several sporadic servers can be defined at different priority levels to handle different aperiodic streams. These consequences are summarized by the following theorems.

Theorem 13. A periodic task set that is schedulable with a task τ_i, is also schedulable if τ_i is replaced by a sporadic server with the same period and execution time (Sprunt, Sha and Lehoczky, 1989).

Theorem 14. A real-time system is composed of soft-deadline aperiodic tasks and hard deadline periodic tasks. Suppose the soft-deadline aperiodic tasks are serviced by a polling server that starts at full capacity and executes at the priority level of the highest priority periodic task. If the polling server is replaced by a SS having the same period, execution time and priority, the SS will provide high-priority aperiodic service at times earlier than or equal to the times the polling server would provide high priority aperiodic service (Sprunt, 1990).

Strosnider (1988) and Sprunt (1990) go on to study a wealth of issues related to aperiodic scheduling using the DS and SS algorithms including: processor and Local Area Network application studies; integrated hard-deadline aperiodic service; soft-deadline aperiodic response time prediction; incorporation of the priority ceiling protocol, and a comprehensive performance analysis.

Further Extensions of the Rate Monotonic Algorithm

There have been many extensions of the rate monotonic scheduling algorithm to address practical problems that arise with real-time systems. These extensions include

- Analyzing the loss in schedulable utilization due to a limit in the number of distinct priority levels; for example, in communication scheduling (Lehoczky and Sha, 1986).
- Ensuring that the most important tasks meet their timing requirements in cases of transient overload when not all deadlines can be met (Sha, Lehoczky, and Rajkumar, 1986).
- Providing the exact schedulability conditions for processor scheduling with operating system and hardware architecture details taken into explicit account (Katcher, Arakawa, and Strosnider, 1994).
- Giving the exact schedulability conditions for processor scheduling when the task phasing is taken into explicit account (Audsley and co-workers, 1992 and Tindell, 1992).
- Extending the processor scheduling theory to communication subsystems (Strosnider, 1988; Strosnider, Marchok, and Lehoczky, 1988; and Strosnider and Marchok, 1989).
- Developing a theory of predictable mode changes (Sha, Rajkumar, Lehoczky, and Ramamritham, 1989 and Tindell, Burns and Wellings, 1992).
- Incorporation of rate monotonic scheduling into Ada, POSIX and Futurebus+.
- Integration of processor scheduling and communication subsystem scheduling.

Some of these topics are addressed in the review article by Burns (1991). The interested reader should also consult the rate monotonic analysis handbook created by the RMARTS Project of the Software Engineering Institute (Klein and co-workers, 1993).

DYNAMIC SCHEDULING ALGORITHMS

There is a voluminous literature on the topic of dynamic scheduling algorithms. For real-time systems in which efficient scheduling algorithms and system predictability are mandatory, the earliest deadline algorithm represents a good basis upon which to build a practically implementable approach to scheduling. The earliest deadline algorithm is a fully preemptive algorithm in which the ready task with the closest deadline is accorded the highest priority. The algorithm is relatively simple to implement requiring only the need to enqueue ready tasks in a priority queue ordered according to earliest deadline. The earliest deadline algorithm has been shown to be optimal for uniprocessors. Indeed, Horn (1974) showed the optimality in the sense of finding a feasible schedule, if one exists, and in terms of minimizing the total tardiness. An important feasibility result was found by Liu and Layland (1973) in Theorem 15.

Theorem 15. Under assumptions A1, A2, A3 and A4, any periodic task set scheduled by the earliest deadline algorithm, will meet all task deadlines for all task set phasings, if and only if, the total task set utilizations is no greater than 100% (Liu and Layland, 1973).

This theorem is very useful and shows that the earliest deadline algorithm is fully efficient in scheduling periodic tasks. The major concern is that a number of important practical problems have not yet been solved for the earliest deadline algorithm including the problem of transient overload, efficient aperiodic scheduling and limited priority granularity in communication scheduling. Nevertheless, these problems are being addressed and advances are being made. For example, the stack-based protocol by Baker (1990) and the dynamic priority ceiling algorithm of Chen and Lin (1990) have effectively solved the synchronization problem for earliest deadline dynamic scheduling. The problem of non-preemptive scheduling of periodic task sets, using the earliest deadline algorithm, has been solved by Jeffay, Stanat, and Martel (1991). More recently, Jeffay (1992) presented an optimal on-line algorithm for sequencing a set of sporadic tasks on a uniprocessor, such that each invocation of each task meets its deadline and single unit software resource constraints are met. Given the activity in this area, it is reasonable to forecast that a comprehensive theory of dynamic scheduling algorithms for real-time systems will be developed.

Material for this article is drawn, in part, from J. P. Lehoczky, L. Sha, J. K. Strosnider, and H. Tokuda, "Fixed Priority Scheduling Theory for Hard Real-Time Systems," A. M. van Tilborg and G. M. Koob, eds., *Foundations of Real-Time Computing: Scheduling and Resource Management*, Kluwer Academic Publishers, 1991, pp. 1–30.

BIBLIOGRAPHY

N. Audsley, A. Burns, M. Richardson, K. Tindell, and A. Wellings, *Applying New Scheduling Theory to Static Priority Pre-emptive Scheduling*, Report RTRG/92/120, Department of Computer Science, York University, 1992.

T. P. Baker, "Stack-Based Scheduling of Real-Time Processes," in *Proceedings of the 11th IEEE Real-Time Systems Symposium*, Dec. 1990, pp. 191–200.

S. Baruah, G. Koren, B. Mao, A. Mishra, L. Raghunathan, L. Rosier, D. Shasha, and F. Wang, "On the Competitiveness of On-Line Task Real-Time Task Scheduling," *Real-Time Systems* **4,** 124–144 (1992).

A. Burns, "Scheduling Hard Real-Time Systems: A Review," *Software Engineering Journal,* 116–128 (May, 1991).

M. I. Chen and K. J. Lin, "Dynamic Priority Ceilings: A Concurrency Control Protocol for real-time systems," *Real-Time Systems* **2**(4), 325–346 (1990).

M. R. Garey, R. L. Graham, and D. S. Johnson, "Performance Guarantees for Scheduling Algorithms," *Operations Research* **26**(1), 1978, 3–21 (1978).

M. Gonzalez Harbour, M. H. Klein, and J. P. Lehoczky, "Fixed Priority Scheduling of Periodic Tasks with Varying Execution Priority," *Proceedings of the 12th IEEE Real-Time Systems Symposium,* 1991, pp. 116–128.

W. A. Horn, "Some simple scheduling algorithms," *Naval Research Logistics Quarterly,* **21,** 177–185 (1974).

K. Jeffay, D. F. Stanat, and C. U. Martel, "On Non-Preemptive Scheduling of Periodic and Sporadic Tasks," *Proceedings of the 12th IEEE Real-Time Systems Symposium,* 1991, pp. 129–139.

K. Jeffay, "Scheduling Sporadic Tasks with Shared Resources in Hard-Real-Time Systems," *Proceedings of the 13th IEEE Real-Time Systems Symposium,* 1992, pp. 89–99.

M. Joseph and P. Pandya, "Finding Response Times in a Real-Time System," *The Computer Journal,* **29**(5), 390–394 (1986).

D. I. Katcher, H. Arakawa and J. K. Strosnider, "Engineering and Analysis of Fixed Priority Schedulers," to appear *IEEE Transactions on Software Engineering,* in press 1994.

M. H. Klein, T. Ralya, B. Pollar, R. Obenza, and M. Gonzalez Harbour, *A Practitioner's Handbook for Real-Time Analysis,* Kluwer Academic Publishers, 1993.

G. Koren and D. Shasha, "D^OVER: An Optimal On-Line Scheduling Algorithm for Overloaded Real-Time Systems," *Proceedings of the 13th IEEE Real-Time Systems Symposium,* Dec. 1992, pp. 290–299.

J. P. Lehoczky, "Fixed Priority Scheduling of Periodic Task Sets with Arbitrary Deadlines," *Proceedings of the 11th IEEE Real-Time Systems Symposium,* Dec. 1990, pp. 201–209.

J. P. Lehoczky, L. Sha, and J. K. Strosnider, "Enhanced Aperiodic Responsiveness in Hard Real-Time Environments," *Proceedings of the 8th IEEE Real-Time Systems Symposium,* Dec. 1987, pp. 261–270.

J. P. Lehoczky and L. Sha, "Performance of Real-Time Bus Scheduling Algorithms," *ACM Performance Evaluation Review* **14,** 1986.

J. P. Lehoczky, L. Sha, and Y. Ding, "The Rate Monotonic Scheduling Algorithm: Exact Characterization and Average Case Behavior," *Proceedings of the 10th IEEE Real-Time Systems Symposium,* Dec. 1989, pp. 166–171.

J. Leung and J. Whitehead, "On the Complexity of Fixed-Priority Scheduling of Periodic, Real-Time Tasks," *Performance Evaluation* **2**, 237–250 (1982).

C. L. Liu and J. W. Layland, "Scheduling Algorithms for Multiprogramming in a Hard Real-Time Environment," *JACM* **20,** 46–61 (1973).

C. D. Locke, "Best Effort Scheduling of Real-Time Systems," Ph.D. Dissertation, School of Computer Science, Carnegie Mellon University, Pittsburgh, Pa., 1987.

A. K. Mok, "Fundamental Design Problems of Distributed Systems for Hard Real-Time Environments," Ph.D. Thesis, Laboratory for Computer Science, MIT, Boston, 1983.

D-T. Peng, and K. G. Shin, *A New Performance Measure for Scheduling Independent Real-Time Tasks,* Technical Report, Real-Time Computing Laboratory, University of Michigan, Ann Arbor, 1989.

R. Rajkumar, *Task Synchronization In Real-Time Systems,* Kluwer Academic Publishers, 1991.

R. Rajkumar, L. Sha, and J. P. Lehoczky, "On Countering the Effects of Cycle-Stealing in a Hard Real-Time Environment," *Proceedings of the 8th IEEE Real-Time Systems Symposium,* Dec. 1987, pp. 2–11.

R. Rajkumar, L. Sha, and J. P. Lehoczky, "Real-Time Synchronization for Multiprocessors," *Proceedings of the 9th IEEE Real-Time Systems Symposium,* Dec. 1988, pp. 259–269.

O. Serlin, "Scheduling of Time Critical Processes," *Proceedings of the Spring Joint Computer Conference,* 1972, pp. 925–932.

L. Sha, R. Rajkumar, and J. P. Lehoczky, "Priority Inheritance Protocols: An Approach to Real-Time Synchronization," *IEEE Transactions on Computers* **39,** 1175–1185 (1990).

L. Sha, and J. Goodenough, "Real-Time Scheduling Theory and Ada," *Computer* **23**(4), 53–62 (1990).

L. Sha, J. P. Lehoczky, and R. Rajkumar, "Solutions for Some Practical Problems in Prioritized Preemptive Scheduling," *Proceedings of the 7th IEEE Real-Time Systems Symposium,* Dec. 1986, pp. 181–191.

L. Sha, R. Rajkumar, J. P. Lehoczky, and K. Ramamritham, "Mode Change Protocols for Priority-Driven Preemptive Scheduling," *Real-Time Systems* **1,** 243–264 (1989).

W. K. Shih, J. W. S. Liu, and C. L. Liu, *Scheduling Periodic Jobs with Deferred Deadlines,* Report No. UIUCDCS-R-90-1593, University of Illinois, Urbana, Ill. 1990.

B. Sprunt, J. P. Lehoczky, and L. Sha, "Exploiting Unused Periodic Time for Aperiodic Service Using the Extended Priority Exchange Algorithm," *Proceedings of the 9th IEEE Real-Time Systems Symposium,* Dec. 1988, pp. 251–258.

B. Sprunt, L. Sha, and J. P. Lehoczky, "Aperiodic Task Scheduling for Hard Real-Time Systems," *Real-Time Systems* **1,** 27–60 (1989).

J. A. Stankovic and K. Ramamritham, *Tutorial: Hard Real-Time Systems,* IEEE Press, New York, 1988.

B. Sprunt, "Aperiodic Task Scheduling For Real-Time Systems," Ph.D. Dissertation, Department of Electrical and Computer Engineering, Carnegie Mellon University, Pittsburgh, Pa., Aug. 1990.

J. K. Strosnider, "Highly Responsive Real-Time Token Rings," Ph.D. Dissertation, Department of Electrical and Computer Engineering, Carnegie Mellon University, Pittsburgh, Pa., Aug. 1988.

J. K. Strosnider, T. Marchok, and J. P. Lehoczky, "Advanced Real-Time Scheduling Using the IEEE 802.5 Token Ring," *Proceedings of the 9th IEEE Real-Time Systems Symposium,* Dec. 1988, pp. 42–52.

J. K. Strosnider, and T. Marchok, "Responsive, Deterministic IEEE 802.5 Token Ring Scheduling," *Real-Time Systems* **1,** 1989, 133–158 (1989).

K. Tindell, *Using Offset Information to Analyse Static Priority Preemptively Scheduled Task Sets,* Report YCS-182, Department of Computer Science, York University, 1992.

K. W. Tindell, A. Burns, and A. J. Wellings, "Allocating Real-Time Tasks: An NP-Hard Problem Made Easy," *Real-Time Systems* **4,** 145–165 (1992).

K. W. Tindell, A. Burns, and A. J. Wellings, "Mode Changes in Priority Preemptively Scheduled Systems," *Proceedings of the 13th IEEE Real-Time Systems Symposium,* Dec. 1992, pp. 100–109.

JOHN P. LEHOCZKY
Carnegie Mellon University

REAL-TIME SYSTEM SPECIFICATION: META MODELS

INTRODUCTION

This article summarizes experiences from teaching and consulting for the last six years in the field of systems development. During this time, the author offered courses which apply the methods and tools found in the book *Strategies for Real Time System Specification.* When that book was written, both authors were from an avionics background. Since then, this author has been teaching methods courses, helping in their introduction and facilitating their usage on a wide variety of projects: ranging from communications systems to instrumentation systems and from 3 person projects to 50 person projects.

There are a number of underlying commonalties in all of these projects which form the basis for this article. First, the types of problems which have lead to further developing and integration of these methods will be identified. This identification can best be achieved by relating some typical telephone conversations with a number of clients from the past. Here are some examples:

- "We seem to be doing everything on the project, but we have a problem that is not quite tangible. We have read your book and feel that the architecture model that you talk about seems to address some of our concerns."
- "We have this problem where our Systems Engineers don't know how to talk with our hardware and software people."
- "I have a very large project which consists of many subsystems. My subsystem people don't seem to talk to each other; this lack of coordination leads to many problems."
- "Systems engineering or marketing or program office personnel write specifications which they throw over the wall to the systems developers. Once they do that, systems developers don't want anything to do with the realization."
- "The hardware developers seem to think their work is already done before the project begins. They seem to think that they have existing hardware that will fulfill the projects needs."

The usual response to all of these categories of calls with follow-up questions: "Do you now produce a system/hardware/software specification?" "If so, who prepares this set of documentation?" and: "Who has inputs into these specifications?"

The response is quite shocking. In many cases, a system specification does not exist. In others, a specification has been generated, but it addresses only the software with added boiler-plate materials for hardware, among other things. Also, in terms of who prepares the specification, the answers are quite disheartening. The software developers often have to interpret global requirements (derived from the customer specification)—guidelines which should also

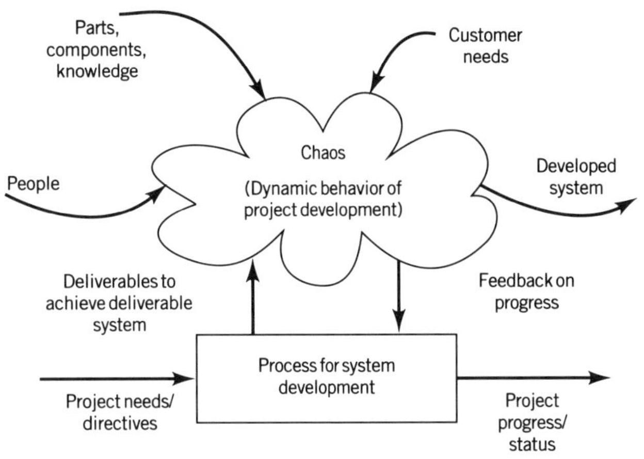

Figure 1. Project Chaos.

have been addressed by the hardware and systems engineers.

By global, these specifications have wider impact—those requirements which have an overlap with hardware or the user interface—not just the software. In essence, what seems to be lacking is a coherent framework for communication among all concerned parties. For all the difficulty being created, there must be a means of organization and out of all the chaos, there must be a means of coordinating all the activities to complement each other. Otherwise, there would be nothing but complete disorder.

These scenarios suggest looking beyond the software for solutions to problems. Also software people should not be blamed for things that are totally out of their realm of authority, or addressed too late in the program, or are under-specified or misunderstood. Software issues do need to be addressed. There is more to the system than just software, and so these other areas must be addressed as well.

WHAT IS A SYSTEMS APPROACH?

Many people often refer to "systems concepts." All people tend to use the word, "system" What, however, are the meanings of these terms and how can the terms help in specifying and developing systems? These questions will be answered in the following sections. First, the source of these concepts will be identified, and second, what these concepts might possibly have to offer to systems developers will be revealed.

You have probably heard the words "society as a whole is suffering from information overload." That concept may or may not be true in general, but it surely is true for projects and systems development. In any given project, there is so much information that one wonders how all that information gets sorted and through which sieve it has to pass before being considered meaningful information. The number of ways in which this information filters through over time tends to be overwhelming.

The best way to describe the interactions during any project can best be summarized by an analogy from a different field: Chaos Theory, as illustrated in Figure 1. There

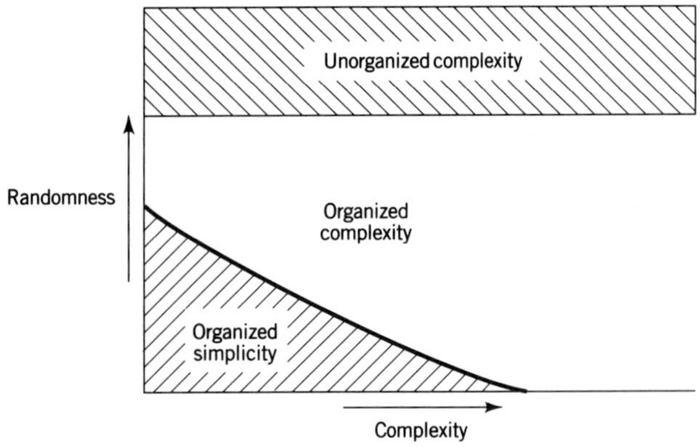

Figure 2. System categories.

are many factors which can give rise to chaos. One of the key reasons why chaos occurs on a given project is that there is simply too much information; that is to say, information needs meaning. The meaning of the information leads to its proper classification and its appropriate influence on the project. Interestingly enough, these assumptions have as their basis data gathered from the realm of physics.

By quantum mechanics no system can process information at a rate greater than 2×10^{47} bits per second per gram of its mass (LIVS). The earth (assuming an age of 10^{10} and mass of 6×10^{27}g) could process no more than 10^{93} bits of information in its age. These are big numbers. Compared to some facts from daily reality, however, these numbers seem small. The human eye can see a 100×100 matrix with 10^{3000} possible patterns; a single chess game has 10^{120} possible sequences. Unfortunately, numbers were not available for the amount of information associated with a given project. Nonetheless, something must be done about these large masses of (meaningful or irrelevant) information.

Filters need to be created to judge the importance, or lack thereof, about all the information associated with a project. This is where a systems approach can help. To show what needs to be done, we first need a classification of the types of systems that are addressed by a systems approach. Based on (IGST) we can classify our systems to fall into one of three categories, as illustrated in Figure 2. The three categories being:

- Unorganized Complexity: Systems that are so complex that they can only be studied by averages, aggregates, and statistical methods. Examples of these types of systems are the economy of a country, the stock market, or the country's political system. These types of systems have characteristics that are not totally independent of each other and often are not able to be isolated. Unless a stand is taken like most economics textbooks do by saying: "all other things being equal or all other things remaining stable," these types of systems would be impossible to analyze. They lack some inherent structure. They are difficult to organize, but predictions can be made about their behavior by studying trends and using other forecasting methods.
- Organized Complexity: These are the systems which are the focus of the Systems Approach. These systems lend themselves to organization. Organized complexity can be analyzed, synthesized, and investigated through the mechanisms provided by the systems approach. Examples of these types of systems are an airplane, an automobile, a computer system, a factory production line, or a communication system. These types of systems have an inherent structure, hierarchical or networked, or some mixture of the two, that lends itself to classification and arrangement. This organization allows a greater degree of understandability.
- Organized Simplicity: Those systems which are purely mechanistic, basically machines, where the total sum of what the system does can be attributed to the sum of what its parts do. Examples of these types of systems are a bicycle, a hand-driven egg beater, a lawn mower (the old-fashioned, human-propelled kind) or a door lock. These systems are simple, in that, their composite behavior is an aggregation of their distinguishable components.

The category of systems targeted using a systems approach are those which fall into the second category: organized complexity—a systems approach providing the point of view necessary to illuminate and illustrate different aspects of these systems. The key reason for requiring some sort of view-point in these systems is that "the whole is greater than the sum of its parts," meaning, as the components are assembled, their composite exhibits properties that are not visible at the lower (component) levels (as opposed to the third category where the whole is equal to the sum of its parts).

Finally, before exploring and defining a systems approach, it is important to recapitulate a phrase given in the previous paragraph: "a systems approach provides a point of view." This idea is necessary to remember because the systems point of view simply provides a perspective, like a map. A map provides the perspective. To use a map, both the origins and the destinations of the person using it must be known. The map has no way of knowing the location of the user. Hence, if someone is completely lost, a map will not help.

SYSTEMS CONCEPTS

What Is a System?

Before the problems and the ways to approach these problems can be understood, what constitutes a system needs to be understood. What do the often used words " system" and " systems approach" mean? Most of what follows refers to man-made systems, but it can also encompass systems in general. Before defining "system," then, it is necessary to establish the premises for all systems created or worked with.

- Every system exists for some purpose or a set of purposes.
- Every system consists of several components, which, through their interrelationships, fulfill the system's intended purpose.
- Every system interacts with the environment into which it is placed and exchanges information, material, or energy.
- Every system must fit into its operating environment. Usually the environment restricts the system's behavior.

There is no restriction on the purpose of a system. It could range, for example, from the entire set of avionics functions for an airplane to something as simple as an electrical switch. The components that constitute a system can include: laws of physics, software, hardware, mathematical algorithms, or any other conceptual or physical entities.

Every system is part of a larger system, from which we deduce: *Systems come in hierarchies.* Every system must find its place in this larger system. Communications between the system and its environment are via exchanges of information, material, or energy. The larger system is the operating environment, and the system's behavior is often restricted by, or must accommodate, the larger system in terms such as usage, maintainability, or extendibility. Thus, the communications between the system and its environment must be rigorously addressed.

Finally, another implication of the second premise is integration. These observations suggest a definition in answer to a question raised earlier: "What is a system?"

Definition: A system is a grouping of interrelated components that, together, form a unified whole that accomplishes a specific purpose or a set of purposes.

So, for a group of components to behave as a system, they must integrate together in purpose. An arbitrary grouping of sheet metal and rivets doesn't constitute an automobile, nor does a random grouping of hardware and software necessarily accomplish any desired purpose. Yet, this approach almost seems to be the norm. Very often, one of the first things that happens on a project is that a project team is split into separate hardware and software teams. How was the decision made to partition the hardware/software *a priori?*

A recent product advertisement included the following statements: "Hardware does very little without Software; Software does nothing without Hardware." To these statements can be added one more statement: "hardware and software exist to support people." These ideas may seem like truisms, but very often they are overlooked. When specifying systems the whole system must be looked at: hardware, software, and the role of and benefit to people. This last item constitutes the purpose of the system. If it is overlooked, the system will not be useful; further, it will not be developed or, if developed, will not be used. A system has been identified, but a specification for a specific system must identify what "the" system is, including its environment and interactions with people, as will be seen.

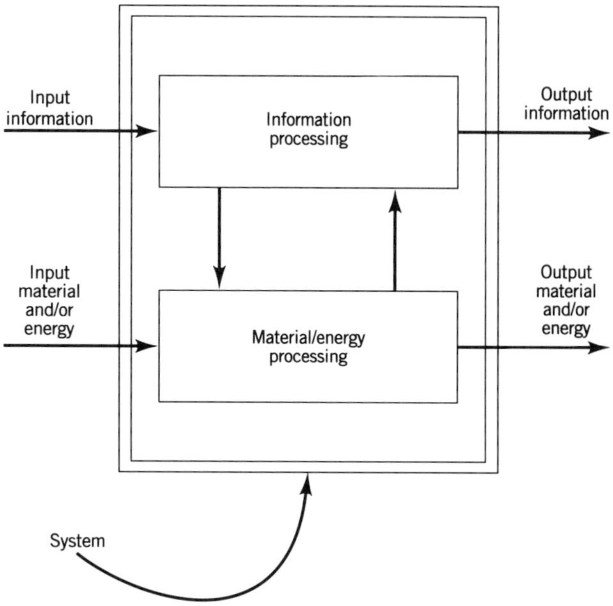

Figure 3. System processing.

System Processing

All systems are processors of information, materials, and/or energy, as illustrated in Figure 3. Systems consist of processors that fulfill its processing requirements. A word processor is not only simply hardware: CPU'S are being used; a processor being anything that is capable of taking inputs and transforming them to produce outputs. There are only three types of processors that are normally encountered in building systems: people, hardware, and software.

Types of hardware include mechanical, optical, and electrical components. Information processing can be performed by all three types of processors, whereas material and energy processing can only be performed by hardware or people. The fact that hardware can also process information may surprise a lot of software people. In any given system, not every kind of processor need be present. Remember, systems come in hierarchies.

Since people are such an integral part of the system and its environment, people must be carefully considered in all phases of the system specification. Automated and manual components of the system must be ensured to integrate well. This fact is often overlooked or is treated as an afterthought. Again, in any specific case, the question must be asked: "What is the System?"

Characteristics of Systems

Below are some more characteristics of systems, derived from the above discussions, and listed in no particular order.

- All (useful) systems exhibit cyclical (predictable) behavior.
- Systems come in hierarchies.

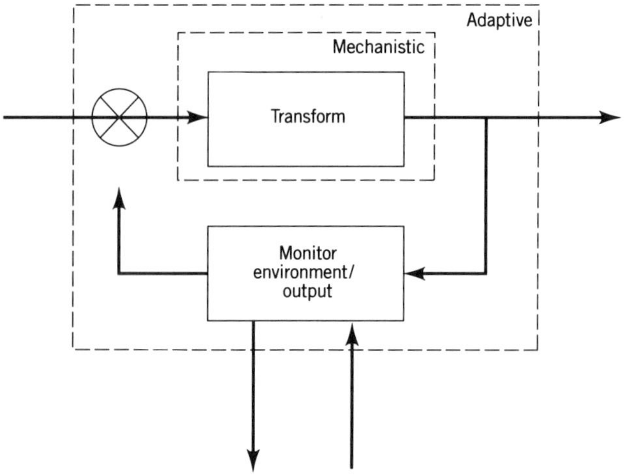

Figure 4. System classification.

- All systems at any one level of the hierarchy of systems exist as independent peers—forming a network.
- Systems can be classified as:

Mechanistic. Those systems that take a defined set of inputs, and through a predictable "transform process," produce a defined set of outputs, as illustrated in Figure 4.

Adaptive. Those systems that have a mechanistic component but, by either monitoring their output or interacting with the environment, change their behavior ("transform process").

Systems are cyclical by nature and this attribute allows for specifying and building them. The cyclical nature can occur *ad infinitum*, but this situation does not necessarily mean to imply an exact repetition of conditions. Rather it means that the system exhibits similar responses to repeated behavior in its environment, such as: the steps in a chemical process, or the take-off, cruise, and landing flight phases of an aircraft. In this sense, even the cycles are hierarchical. Major cycles are ordinarily associated with the system and subcycles within the system. These cycles can, in turn, be associated with either subsystems or subfunctions.

The fact that systems come in hierarchies (Fig. 5) is important. Instead of viewing a system as a random grouping of components, it is possible to focus attention on individual levels of systems and subsystems. A given level of a hierarchy can either control or be composed of the level below. There is no implication that the hierarchy represents a strict top-down control structure. The hierarchy represents a composition relationship, but usually software has been thought of as having only a control relationship hierarchically. The components at any one level can behave as a network interacting with each other as peers.

The hierarchical nature of systems leads to the often heard statement: "One person's requirement is another's design." For at every level of system specification, design decisions provide requirements for the level below (its component subsystems).

Finally, the fact that the system can be mechanistic (fixed), or adaptive, can help characterize systems into

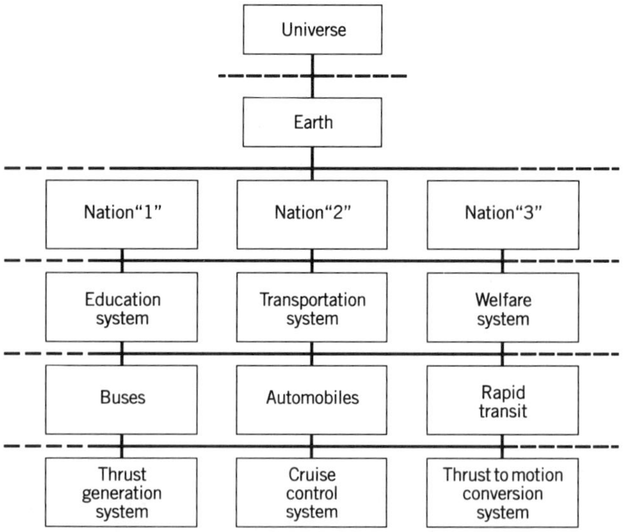

Figure 5. Universal hierarchy of systems.

these two types. In the case of adaptive systems, they require a means of monitoring the environment or themselves to change their own transform process. Most of the systems have both of these characteristics and by recognizing them further insight into our system can be gained.

What Is the System?

The general question, "What is a system?" has been discussed, but the question faced when a specific system is to be developed is: "What is the System?" Another important question to ask is "What is the context of the system?" Figure 6 shows that further questions need to be asked: "Which is the true system?" Is the system just the automated parts, or just the software, or is it the hardware, software, and people environment?

By not considering the system's hardware and software as a whole some important factors that affect both may be neglected. The hardware and software engineers tend to view their own areas as the system, but the best way to define the system is as the one the end user sees: the end product, including the automated and manual parts.

Every system exists to maintain or support its higher level system; development systems exist to develop systems; deliverable systems exist to support the development

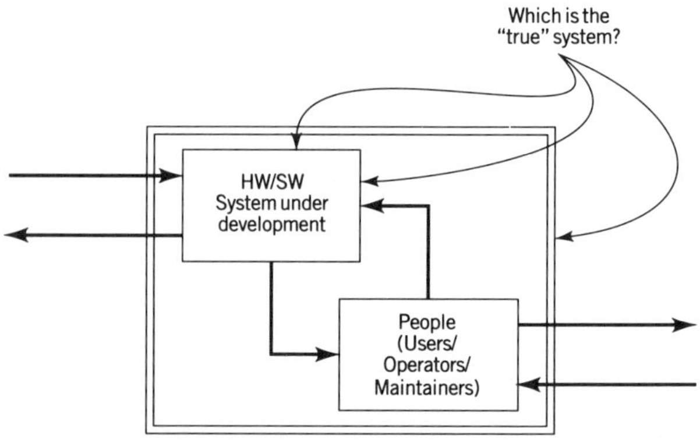

Figure 6. Would the Real System please stand up!

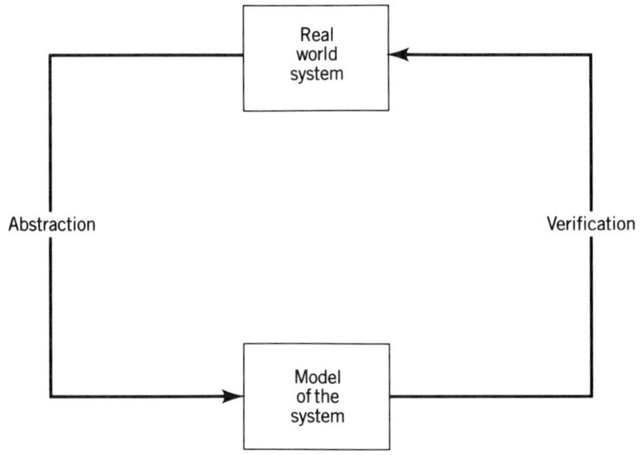

Figure 7. What is a model?

organization and the customer/user: the development organization exists to support the company, and similarly: the maintenance system exists to support the systems built.

A Systems Approach

This section so far has defined a system and its characteristics. One final element will complete the definition of the term: A Systems Approach. This final component is the use of models and modeling. As shown in Figure 7, a model represents an abstraction of something in the real world. The abstraction represented by the model is important because of real world complexity. In a model, abstraction replaces the real world system with a similar but simpler to understand representation. Models can be built to understand various aspects of the system. Why should systems be modeled?

Almost every industry, from architectural engineers to automobile engineers, uses models to determine the feasibility, manufacturability and overall requirements of an actual system. Only the hardware/software systems industry resists this approach. While models are used for some parts of software requirements and design, techniques for modeling the entire system are seldom even perceived as necessary and are rarely used.

But remember, a model, any model, is just a representation of the system (i.e., the real world). Every model is one thing hoped to be understood in terms of another that is

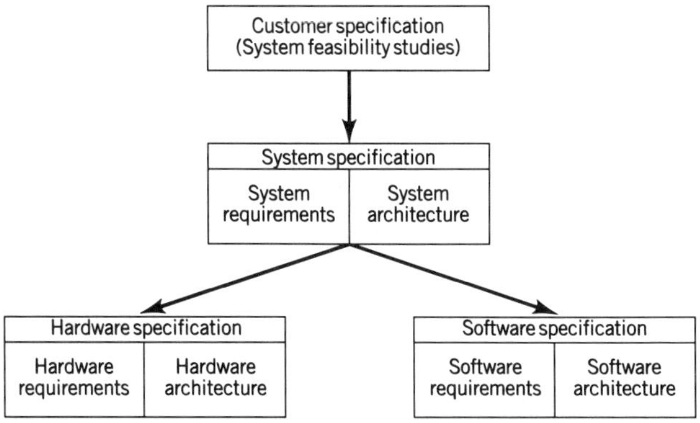

Figure 8. Hierarchal nature of system specification.

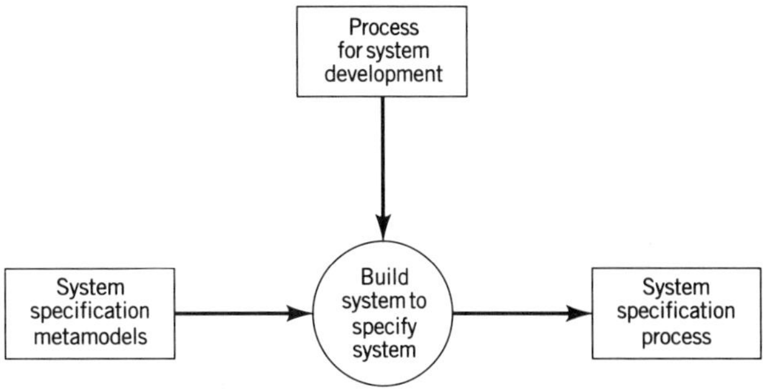

Figure 9. Meta model adaption.

thought to be understood. This concept is important. Any model is built to answer some questions about the system. Different types of models are built to answer many different types of questions about the system. But even if a hundred different models of the system are built, their aggregate would not be able to answer every possible question about the system. Only the final system can answer every possible question about the system.

This is a systems approach which exploits the various characteristics of systems. An integral part of this methodology is a modeling approach which allows users to understand, build, and work with systems. In the following sections, these concepts will be used to come up with a better means of specifying and understanding systems in general.

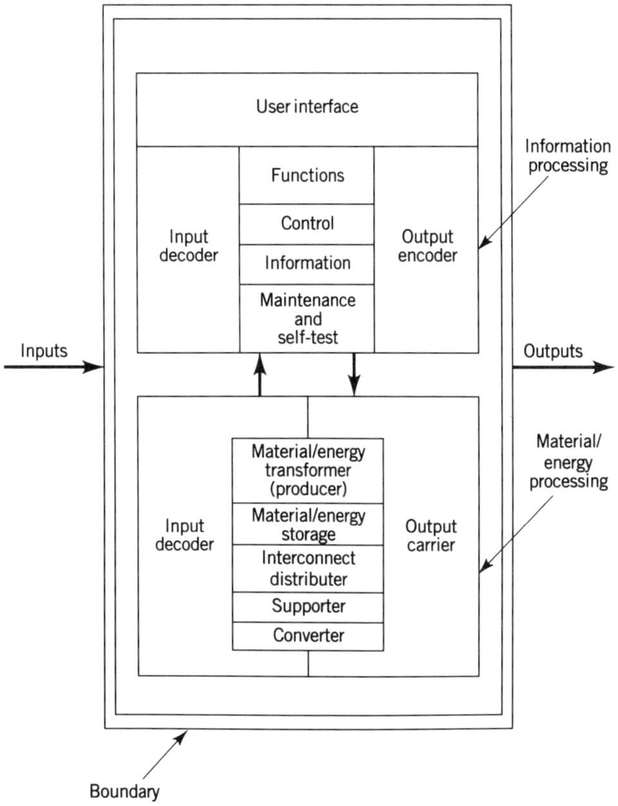

Figure 10. Subsystems of systems.

SYSTEM META MODELS

Exploiting the Hierarchical Nature of Systems

Integration is the key to developing the system. As the saying goes: "The whole is greater than the sum of its parts." As discussed, the systems to be developed require all of their components to integrate together: the software components must integrate together: the hardware components must integrate together: the hardware and software must integrate and, finally, the automated system must integrate with its operational environment. One way to insure this integration is to treat the specification of the system in levels. Figure 8 shows the levels of specification that are needed to ensure system integration and integrity.

This approach exploits the hierarchical nature of systems while ensuring integration: each level of specification providing the requirements of the next lower level of system. At every level the whole system is considered, and as the project proceeds to lower levels the requirements from the higher levels are used.

As illustrated in Figure 8:

- At the highest level, establish the place of the system in its environment and precisely define the objectives of the system and its communications with the environment.
- Using these objectives, proceed into the requirements and architecture of our system, remembering that it can be automated, manual, or both.
- Finally, take the system specification and partition it among the processors. At this stage proceed with the detailed hardware, software, and people architecture, corresponding to the hardware and software designs, and to the procedures by which people will use, operate, and maintain the system.

By proceeding in this manner a number of benefits can be reaped. Every level of system definition supplies the requirements for the next lower level. A firm link is established between the system and its environment. By stabilizing the upper level requirements and architecture first, the lower level design can proceed much more effectively. Resolution of the upper level requirements and architecture helps to identify risk areas and functions that might require prototyping. The system definition proceeds methodically in increasing degrees of detail, so that much detail is not gotten too fast.

System Specification Components: What and How

As noticed in Figure 8, every specification is to consist of two parts: the system requirements and the system architecture. Both of these parts consist of models. The system requirements model is a technology independent model of the problem the system is going to solve; and represents the "WHAT." The system architecture model is a technology dependent model of the solution to the problem and represents the "HOW." These two models are generated once for the entire system, then successively mapped through layers of specifications for subsystems. Finally, the same models are created for the hardware and software.

This separation of the "What" and "How" is extremely important. Below are some of the reasons listed in no particular order:

- A problem needs to be understood independent of any particular solution.
- Any given problem has many possible solutions, selection of a particular solution is a tradeoff process.
- The separation simplifies the considerations at a specific point and helps in the generation of clear and unambiguous specifications.
- "What" and "How" are considered at every level of the specification hierarchy. This process results in giving due consideration to the system and every component subsystem down to the hardware and software.
- Seldom are systems built totally from scratch. Most systems are built as either implementations using new technology or as the integration of several previous systems into a new system.

The separation of "What" and "How" basically provides the power to reimplement the "What" using new technology thereby gaining the advantages of not just software or hardware component reusability, but also requirements reusability.

Meta Models

The use of models as a part of the systems approach was mentioned in previous sections. An additional term which needs to be identified is meta model. A meta model is a higher level model of the modeling process. The systems approach can, in fact, be applied to itself. In this respect, two meta models will be employed. Both are used to specify systems, hardware, and software.

Before the detailed specification models can be adequately addressed, an examination of the role meta models play in applying the systems approach is necessary. The best way to think of meta models is to envision them as being tools within a tool box. The meta model tool box provides options for selecting, adapting, and/or adopting tools required for a particular project, as illustrated in Figure 9.

As implied by this illustration, meta models do not represent strict guidelines which must be adhered to blindly. Meta models provide a general framework which should be customized to fit any particular project.

SUBSYSTEMS OF A SYSTEM META MODEL

The first meta model under discussion is one that characterizes the subsystems of a system. This meta model is an adaptation of a large body of work done in the areas of biology and social sciences.

The best reference for the subsystems of systems meta model by Miller. In a wider context, this type of meta model can be applied to systems in general, but for this article the discussion will be in the vein of systems that are built and developed using hardware, software, and people.

Figure 10 shows the subsystems of systems meta model as applied to the system/hardware/software specification process. Can Figure 10 be related to any figure seen earlier in this paper? When system processing was introduced in an earlier section, systems were shown to be capable of processing information and material/energy. Figure 10 reflects this aspect.

This illustration represents a categorization of the information and material/energy processing into a finer degree of classification. These finer classifications are called subsystems of systems in this article. As indicated, subsystems exist which can perform the two different types of processing, but there is also one subsystem that can do both. In Table 1, various subsystems of systems is defined. In the subsequent section the applicability of the meta model will be discussed. For a fuller discussion on this meta model the reader is referred to *System Specification Case Studies: A Workbook*.

Applicability of the Subsystems of Systems Meta Model

In general, the meta model in Table 1 can be applied to any type of system. It is necessary to narrow our scope of discussion. The goal of this methodology is the application of the meta model to the development of hardware, software, and people systems. In the following subsections, the application of this meta model to automated systems and to people systems (organizations) will be described.

Why should the issues of people and people systems be addressed? First, it is necessary to realize that the organization which develops the system is the "system for developing systems." Second, by applying the same models and techniques to the deliverable system as well as the system to develop the deliverable system leverage can be provided. This is one of the reasons why biology and the social sciences were mentioned earlier. Automated systems are trying harder and harder to mimic "human systems." Automation, for example, has replaced many different types of labor intensive (mechanical) activities (Table 2).

It is impossible to predict whether or not automated systems will ever be able to achieve this goal completely. It is important, nonetheless, to recognize how the categorization of people activities can benefit systems methods. In the following subsections, definitions of the above meta model components are provided. Subsequently, the usages of two types of systems, people systems and automated systems, are explained (see Tables 3–5).

SYSTEM SPECIFICATION META MODEL

A meta model is proposed for system specification, as illustrated in Figure 11. The meta model describes an evolutionary and iterative approach to system specification. This meta model identifies the various types of models to be built in order to specify a system. As pointed out earlier,

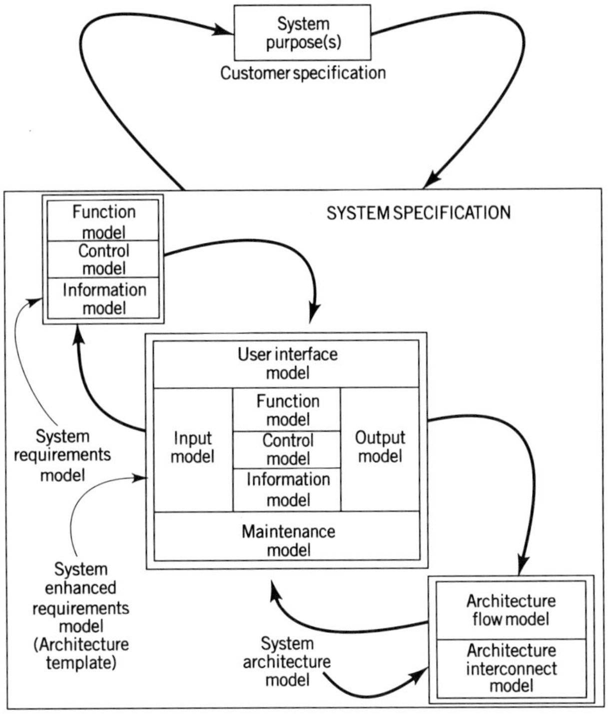

Figure 11. A meta model for system specification.

Table 1. Subsystems of System Definitions[a]

Material/Energy Processing Subsystems	Information Processing Subsystems
Input carrier: Transducer subsystem that brings matter/energy across boundary.	**Input decoder**: Subsystem to alter the coding for internal use.
Converter: Subsystem to transform from public to private material/energy forms.	**User interface**: Subsystem to allow external human interface.
Interconnect distributor: Subsystem that distributes external inputs or subsystem outputs.	**Maintenance adapter**: Subsystem for system monitoring and reconfiguration.
Producer: Subsystem to transform and associate matter/energy inputs to outputs.	**Functional transformer**: Subsystem to transform input information into input information.
Supporter: Subsystem to help in damage repair, accommodate growth reconfiguration.	**Decider**: Subsystem to help transformation take place in the system.
Storage: Subsystem to store matter/energy for later use or regulation.	**Memory**: Subsystem to retain information, and to show their relationships and organization.
Output carrier: Transducer subsystem to carry matter/energy across system boundary.	**Output encoder**: Subsystem to transform information coding from internal format.

[a]Subsystems that process both Information and Material/Energy.
Boundary: Subsystem that forms the protective barrier around systems, shielding it from the environment.

Table 2. Subsystems of Systems for a Deliverable System

Material/Energy Processing Subsystems	Information Processing Subsystems
Input carrier: Keyboards, switches, connectors, and pins by which the system receives incoming material/energy flows.	**Input decoder**: Protocol conversion algorithms, or any algorithm by which the information is converted from an external format into an internal standard.
Interconnect distributor: Any and all internal mechanisms for the transport of matter/energy, for example: or hardware buses that connect subsystems.	**User interface**: The processing required to interact with the users of the system.
Converter: Power supply and power generators.	**Functional transformer**: Any input to output transfer function such as algorithms, functions, math equations, string manipulation.
Producer: Computation devices such as CPUS, special purpose ICs, and components that transform material/energy.	**Decider**: The control algorithms by which processing and resources are scheduled and the exhibiting of the different states or modes of behavior of a system.
Storage: Battery for backup power.	**Memory**: A static view of information retained by the system.
Output carrier: Output connectors, display devices, and power supply heatsink.	**Output encoder**: Protocol conversion for outputs.
Supporter: Any specific devices to keep the system "together" and running, for example: a watch-dog timer or a fail-safe mechanism.	**Maintenance adapter**: The algorithms for information collection which perform fault isolation, error handling, system usage, system reconfiguration, and/or graceful degradation.

[a]Subsystems that process both information and material/energy
Boundary: The external housing, casing, or such other exterior that shelters the system from the environment.

decisions about adopting or adapting the meta model must be made prior to its use. The details of this model form the basis of the book by Hatley and Pirbhai. Readers who are interested in adapting or adopting meta models for use within their systems should consult the book by Pirbhai.

This meta model starts by defining the purpose of the system, then progresses into a technology-independent specification of requirements in terms of function, control, and information models. Then it proceeds to a technology non-specific model that captures technology dependent requirements. Finally, the total set of requirements is allocated to specific processors: hardware, software, and people.

This meta model is derived from the previous one. Accordingly, the first meta model captures *what* needs to be captured and the second shows you *how* this is accomplished.

Table 3. Example of Subsystems of Systems for a Deliverable System: Cruise Control System[a]

Material/Energy Processing Subsystems	Information Processing Subsystems
Input carrier: The shaft rotation sensor, the brake sensor, etc.	**Input decoder**: Interface to read the shaft rotation sensor.
Interconnect distributor: The wires that interconnect the various assemblies composing the Cruise Control System.	**User interface**: The keyboard interface or the switch interface to accept driver inputs.
Converter: The power source for the cruise control computer, the sensors, etc.	**Functional transformer**: The functions to capture and maintain speed.
Producer: The CPU and any other support chips.	**Decider**: The state machine that decides what state in which the cruise control is.
Storage: Backup battery.	**Memory**: The retaining of desired speed and the conversion factor.
Output carrier: The throttle linkage.	**Output encoder**: The computations for driving the throttle to the desired position.
Supporter: The fail-safe mechanism on the throttle linkage.	**Maintenance adapter**: Processing to change the conversion factors for shaft rotation.

[a]Subsystems that process both information and material/energy
Boundary: Box in which the Cruise Control Computer is housed, the entry switches, the assemblies for housing the shaft rotation sensor, brake sensor, etc.

System Purpose

Establishing the system purpose is the highest level of the specification process. The step could be documented in a number of ways; namely, as simple as a list of desired purposes for the end system: to a BLITZ (McMenamin and Palmer) model of the system's requirements and architecture, using the modeling components described in the following subsections.

System Functional Requirements Modeling

The purpose of system functional requirements modeling is to establish the core set of technology independent requirements: a set of three models that capture the essence of the system's purpose. Each of the three models has its own very specific role.

- Process Model: Captures the functional partitioning of the system and the interfaces between functions.
- Control Model: Captures the finite state aspects of the system and shows which functions are controlled by which system states.
- Information Model: Captures the memory, or information, storage aspects of the system.

The detailed contents of the process, control, and information models are shown in Figure 12. Figures 13 and 14 show a partial requirements model for a vending machine.

Table 4. Subsystems of Systems for a (People) System that Builds Deliverable Systems

Material/Energy Processing Subsystems	Information Processing Subsystems
Input carrier: Purchasing department, receiving department, secretarial staff.	**Input decoder:** Marketing and sales staff, program office, management in charge of market (customer) interface, legal department, language translators, cryptographers, technical and scientific researchers, and other interpreters of marketplace or technology.
Interconnect distributor: Organizational transport, supply room staff, elevator operators, tools distributor, delivery mechanisms, trucks, mail cart, equipment cart.	**User interface**: Management of responding to market needs, interface with potential customers providing the customer interface.
Converter: Power plant operator, packaging department, document reproduction, shredding machine.	**Functional transformer**: Engineers, factory production staff, project leaders, supervisors, managers, executives.
Producer: Managers, HW/SW engineers, nurse, computers, calculators.	**Decider**: Board of directors, company management committee, R & D board.
Storage: File cabinets, supply cabinets, equipment rooms, warehouse, holding areas, waiting areas.	**Memory**: Filing department, bookkeeping/accounting department, librarians, computers, file cabinets, secretaries.
Output carrier: Shipping department, delivery people, installers, facilities staff.	**Output encoder**: Marketing literature producers, document writers, users manual writers, publications department.
Supporter: Facilities, janitors, cafeteria cooks, accounting personnel.	**Maintenance adapter**: salary review committee, facilities design staff, payroll processing staff, project metrics measurement staff.

[a]Subsystems that process both information and material/energy
Boundary: Personnel Office, Receiving and Loading Dock Staff, Receptionist, Librarian, Mail-Room Employees, Security Guards, Buildings, Fences, Walls.

System Enhanced Requirements Model

The systems under discussion have much more imposed on them than just the technology independent process, control, and information storage requirements described so far. The technology dependent requirements need to be captured in order to complete realization of the specification. As indicated, the existing models define the what: requirements independent of any implementation technology. Earlier, the necessity of a system's integration with its operating environment was established. Interfacing requirements will therefore be the first category of technology dependent requirements that will be captured. They will define how our system is to transfer information, material and/or energy to and from the outside world.

Table 5. Example of Subsystems of Systems for a (People) System: A Garment Factory

Material/Energy Processing Subsystems	Information Processing Subsystems
Input carrier: The receiving trucks and the mail delivery.	**Input decoder**: The receivers of received goods. The people who order and buy production supplies and personnel department who acquires workers.
Interconnect distributor: The internal distribution system for supplies and finished products.	**User interface**: The people who negotiate the designs and contracts with the customers.
Converter: The power transformer, the conversion of raw materials into a usable form.	**Functional transformer**: The people who transform designs into garments to be produced.
Producer: The people to carry out the actual transformations such as cutting the fabrics, finishing products, sewing garments, etc.	**Decider**: The deciders of the production schedules, the factory plans, and the coordination of the factory floor.
Storage: The supply cabinets, the storage lockers, the stock room, etc.	**Memory**: The storing of the designs, accounting records, shipping records, the employee records, etc.
Output carrier: The shipping department, the delivery trucks, etc.	**Output encoder**: Invoicing of customers, the waste disposal coordination, etc.
Supporter: The facilities and maintenance crews who remove garbage, trash, and keep the factory in operating condition.	**Maintenance adapter**: Performers of customer accounting, the payroll department, etc.

[a]Subsystems that process both information and material/energy.
Boundary: The building that houses the factory and offices.

The Architecture Template resolves the interfaces by categorizing them into four groups. Its purpose is to identify the processing required to transform the external physical information into a logical form needed by the technology independent core of the system. In other words, it represents the encoding and decoding required for communications between our system and its environment, as illustrated in Figure 15.

The four architecture template buffers are the user interface, which specifies the mechanism which the user will interface with the system; the input and the output interfaces, which specify the interfaces with external automated systems: the maintenance/SE lf-test interface, which specifies a special user interface for maintenance.

Do we really need four buffers? It seems that the user and maintenance interfaces are just more input/output. The reasons for employing them are

- The user and maintenance interfaces require special consideration, such as human factors and ergonomics.
- The user interface technology (displays, keyboards, etc.) is very different from system to system interface technology (standard data bus, etc.).

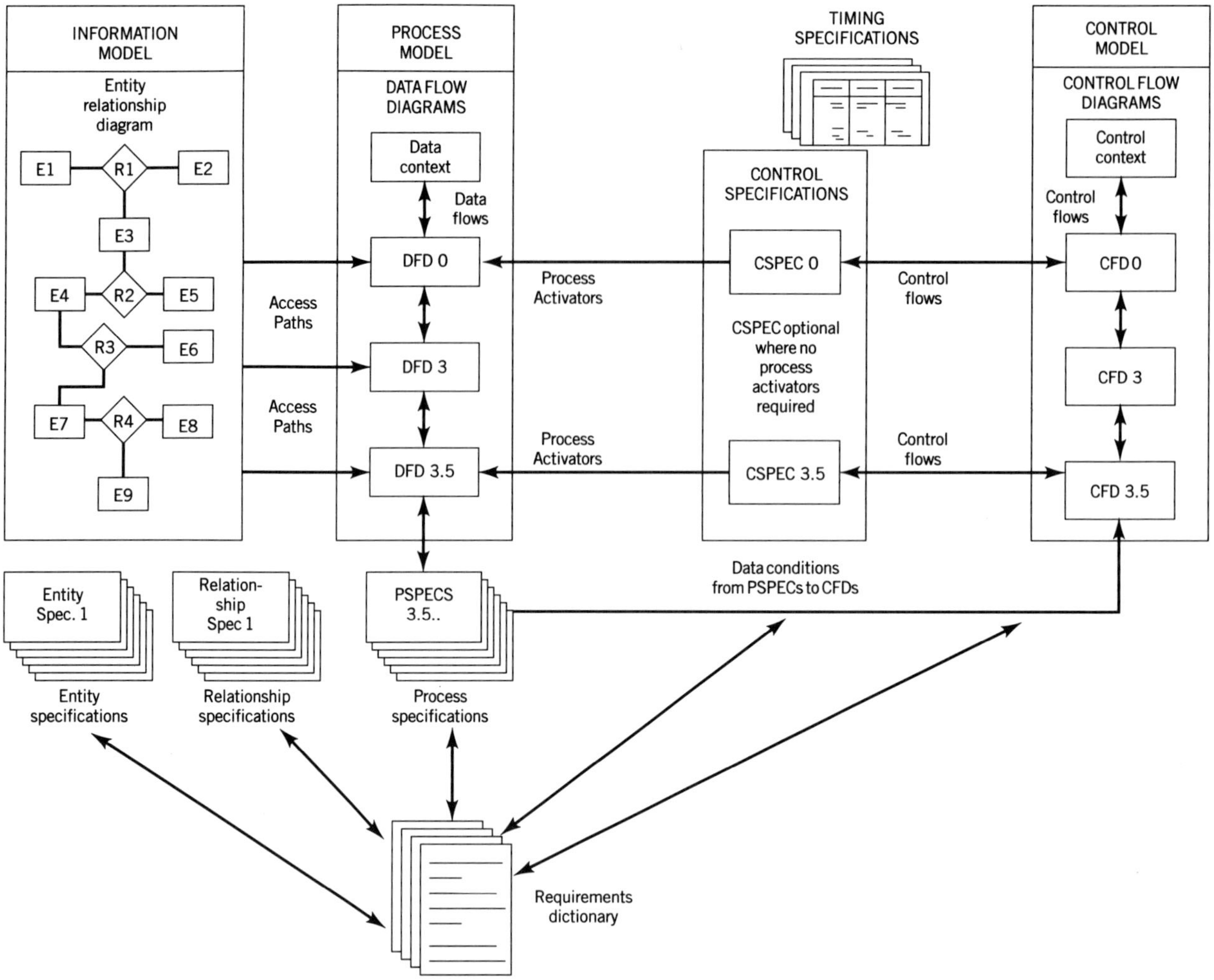

Figure 12. Requirements model components.

- The user and maintenance interfaces are historically the most misspecified and underspecified parts of the system and need special emphasis to counteract this.

Listed below are some benefits of using the architecture template:

- It allows all the different types of interfaces to be specified, yet allows for the creation of a cohesive, integrated model.
- It separates the different types of technology so that specialists in each type can easily identify their own territories.
- Subdividing the specification tasks allows them to be allocated more easily.
- It aids the identification of risk areas that might need prototyping, such as the user interface or the functional and control core, so that prototyping can proceed in parallel with the remainder of the specification.
- The resulting specification has information hiding built-in. That is, the requirements from the different buffers of the architecture template can be allocated to hardware or software modules or objects that hide the user interface, maintenance, input/output, functional, or control processing. This limits the effect of changes to these processing requirements to their own areas of design and reduces their ripple effect on the rest of the system.

In conclusion then, Figure 16 shows the enhanced DFD/CFD for the vending machine whose requirements model was shown in Figure 13 and 14. The components used in the requirements and enhanced requirements models are the same; that is, in the latter we add more DFDs, CFDs, PSPECs, CSPECs, and requirements dictionary elements, as described in (STRAT). These enhancements are the step in the evolutionary approach in which technology dependent processing and control requirements are added.

The additional processes, shown in Figure 16, which were added as a result of applying the architecture template may be primitives or may be decomposed into their own set of DFDS, CFDS, PSPECS, CSPECs, and requirements dictionary entries. The system's technology-inde-

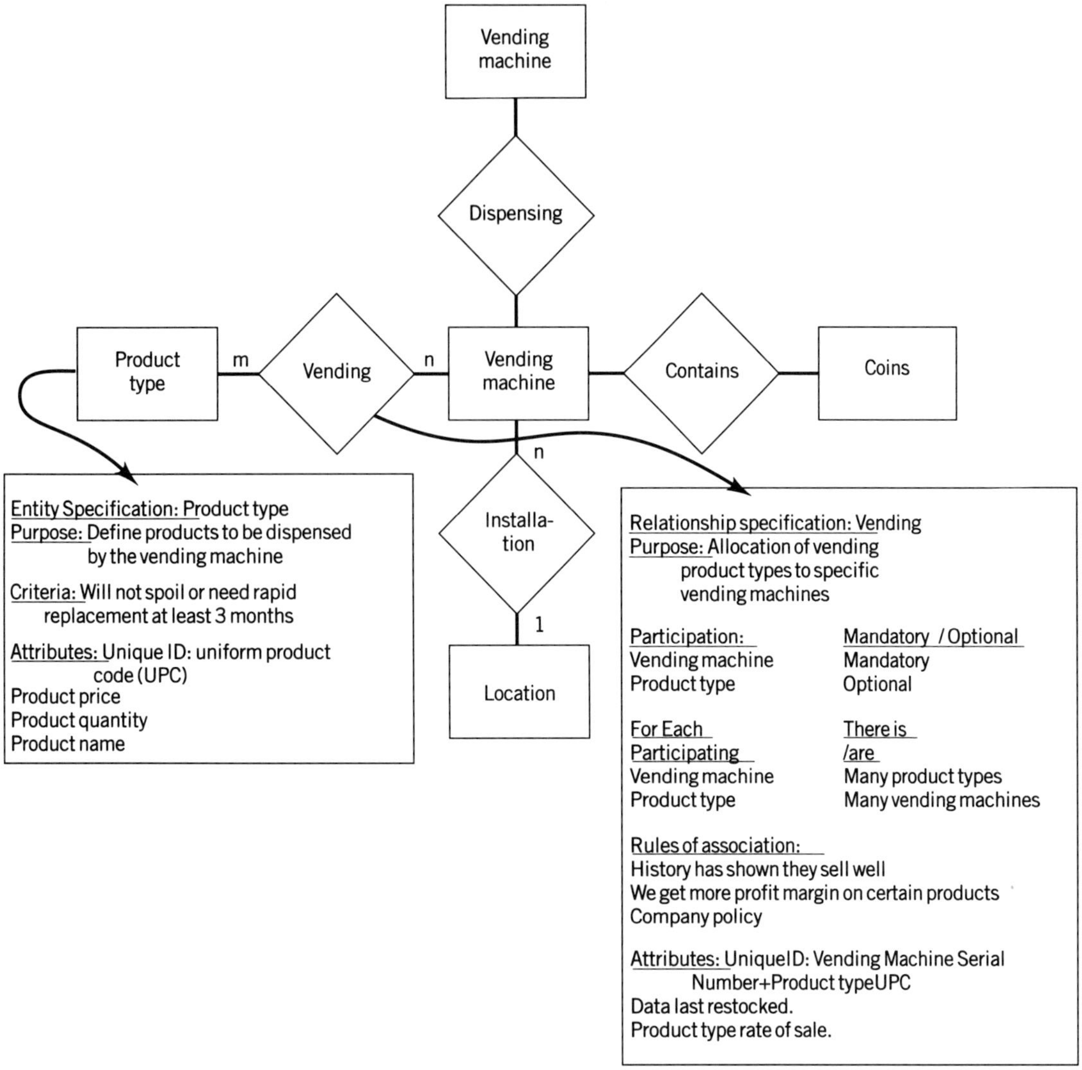

Figure 13. Vending machine information model.

pendent and interfacing requirements have now been specified; the latter requiring that interfacing technology is taken into account. The total model is, therefore, no longer technology independent.

However, any requirements to specific technology-dependent processors have not been allocated, so this is called the technology non-specific model.

System Architecture Model

The purpose of the architecture model is to document the allocation of both technology dependent and technology independent requirements to the processors that will be used in the implementation. At the system level, these processors could be just hardware, hardware and software, or people. But as the architecture development proceeds, the end goal will be to define the individual hardware and software implementation units, call them modules or objects or whatever.

In relationship to the adoption of methods by a design group, it is necessary to avoid following blindly any one architecture allocation or design scheme or principle available, such as: structured design, object-oriented design, or information hiding. All design schemes have only one end goal—the identification of implementation modules which show the allocation of requirements to them. The end goal here is to document the architecture and the allocation of requirements to it in order to yield a system that is technologically feasible (and that meets all the requirements, including any requirements for allocation, use of pre-existing hardware, processor grouping, maintainability, testability, reusability, and producability.) No matter what design criteria is best suited for the system, in the end, documentation of the system's modules or objects and the communications between them.

The architecture mapping scheme used (see STRAT) is shown in Figure 17. It consists of two graphical components: the Architecture Flow Diagram (AFD), which captures the system's architecture as a network of processors

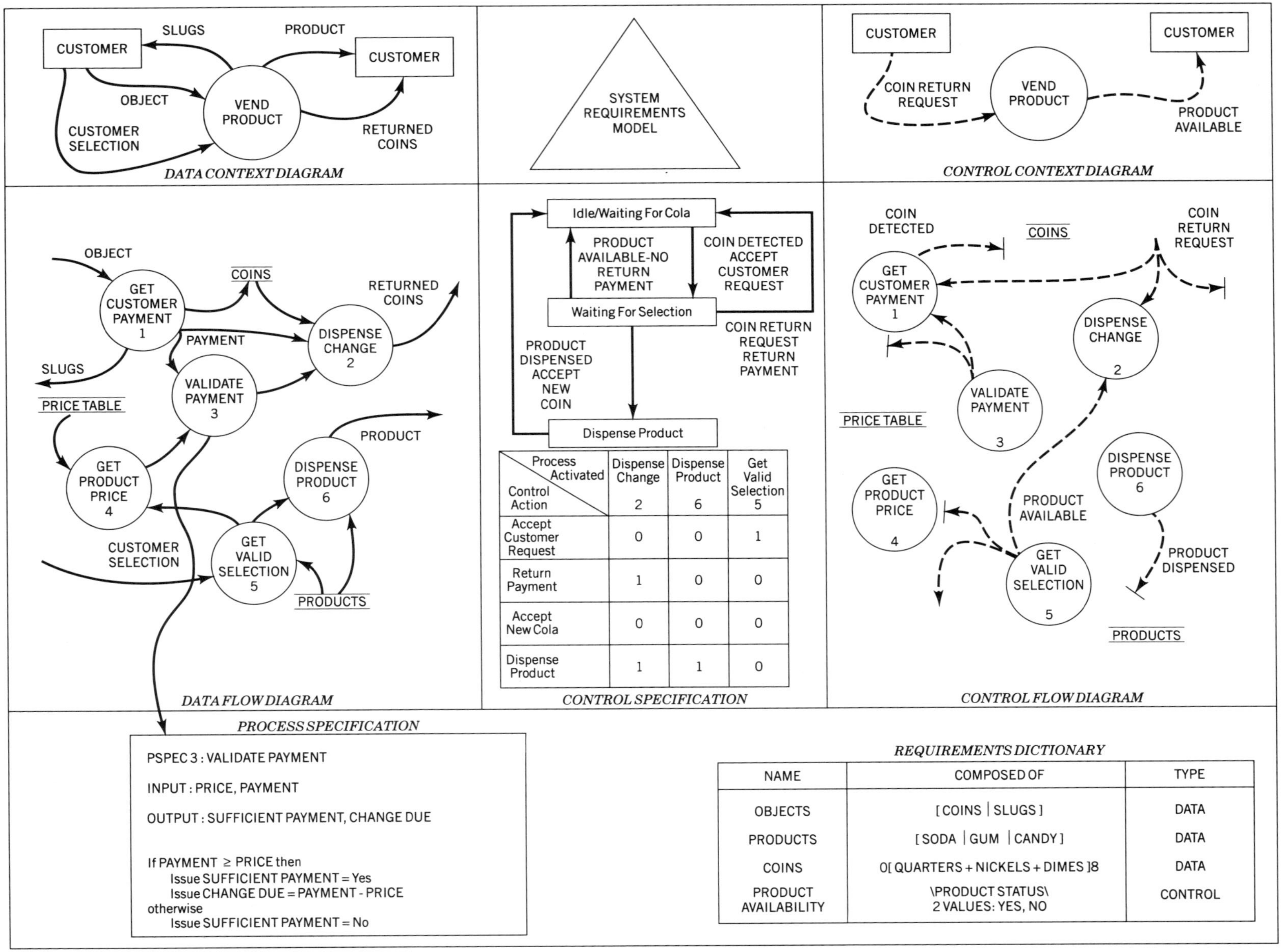

Figure 14. Vending machine requirements model composite. Copyright 1992 System Methods

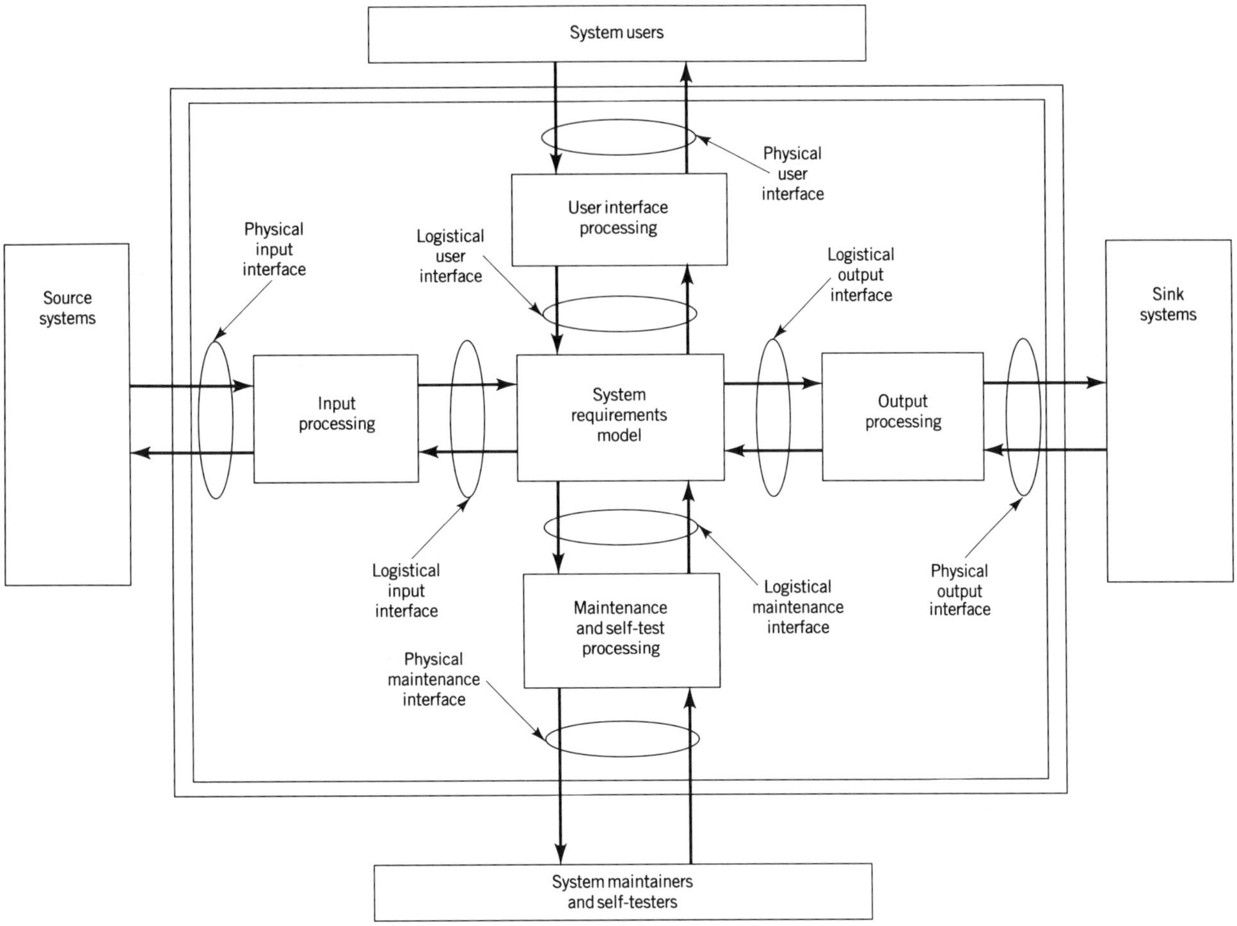

Figure 15. Architecture template processing.

with the information flow between them; and the Architecture Interconnect Diagram (AID), which shows the same processors interconnected by the channels on which the information flows. There are three supporting textual specifications: Architecture Module Specifications, which capture the allocation of requirements to specific processors: architecture interconnect specifications, which capture the physical characteristics of the channels, and the architecture dictionary, which captures the allocation of data and control flows from the enhanced requirements model to processors and their interconnections. Figure 18 shows a composite view of the vending machine's architecture model whose requirements and enhanced requirements models have been seen earlier.

This configuration completes another step in the evolutionary approach to system specification. The process has taken the reader from a concept definition of the system through several stages of processing. Finally, this processing has been allocated to specific processors. But this configuration is not the end of the system design. The process must proceed to the point where all the specific hardware, software, and manual modules or objects in the system have been designed.

In conclusion, any architecture packaging schemes result in the definition of the implementation modules connected in a hierarchy, a network, or a mixture of the two. Design schemes, such as structured design or object oriented design, allow the evaluation of this architecture in its various manifestations. It is desirable to keep the architecture and design evaluation scheme separate for the following reasons:

- No one design scheme is appropriate for all systems. A scheme that is appropriate for one system might be totally inappropriate for others.
- There are criteria for optimizing any particular system. (the word optimizing is used very cautiously, because it means something different for everyone.) By separating the architectural mapping from its evaluation scheme, a common thread for many systems is arrived at yet allows for their separate optimizations.
- As Weinberg correctly points out, "general systems engineers as well as specific systems engineers" are needed. By separating architecture and design evaluation, both are achieved.

System Specification Summary

The process outlined above is not a sequential process, although it has been covered in sequential steps. It is an iterative process, in that the execution of one step may

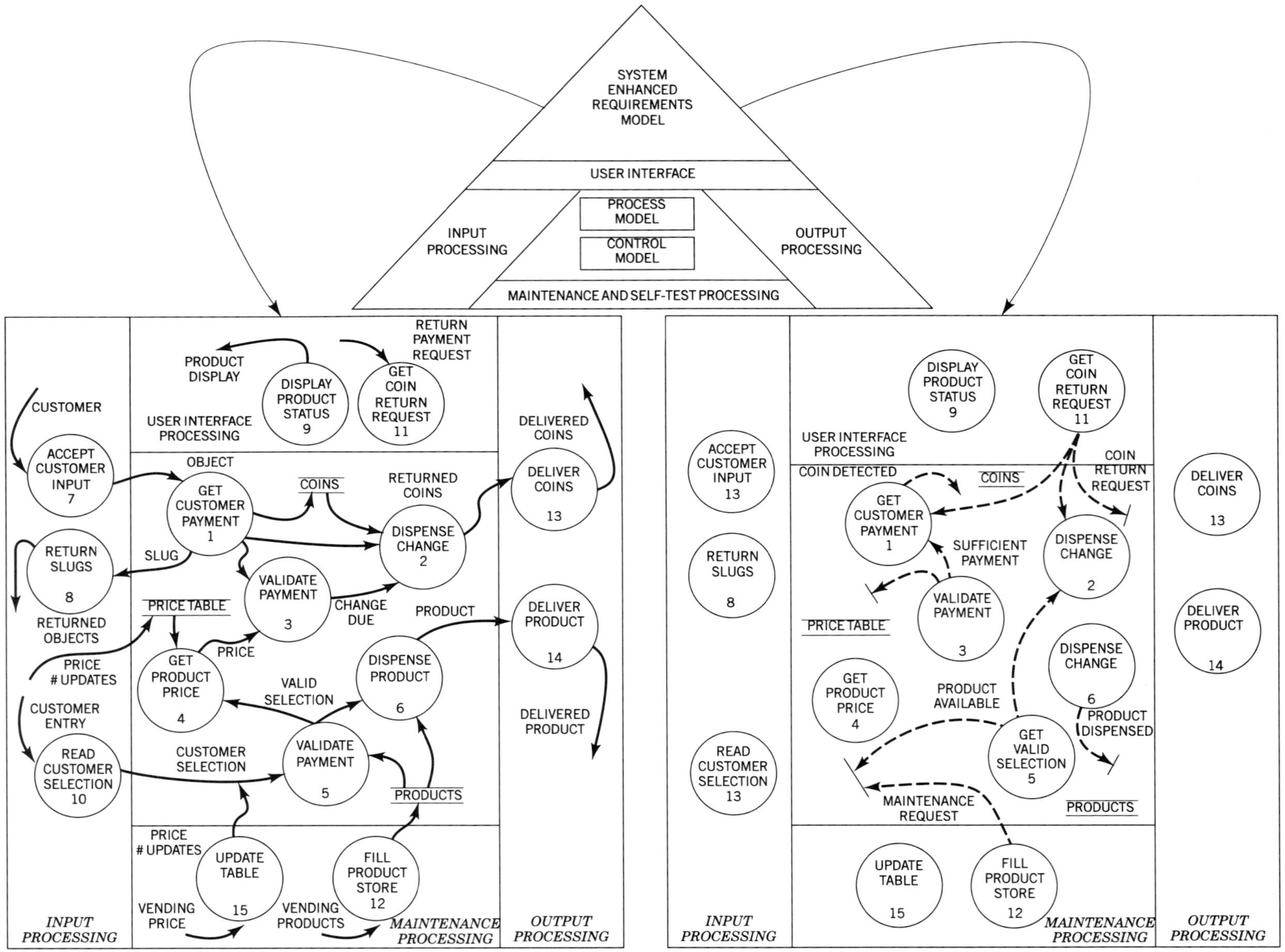

Figure 16. Vending Machine enhanced requirements model.

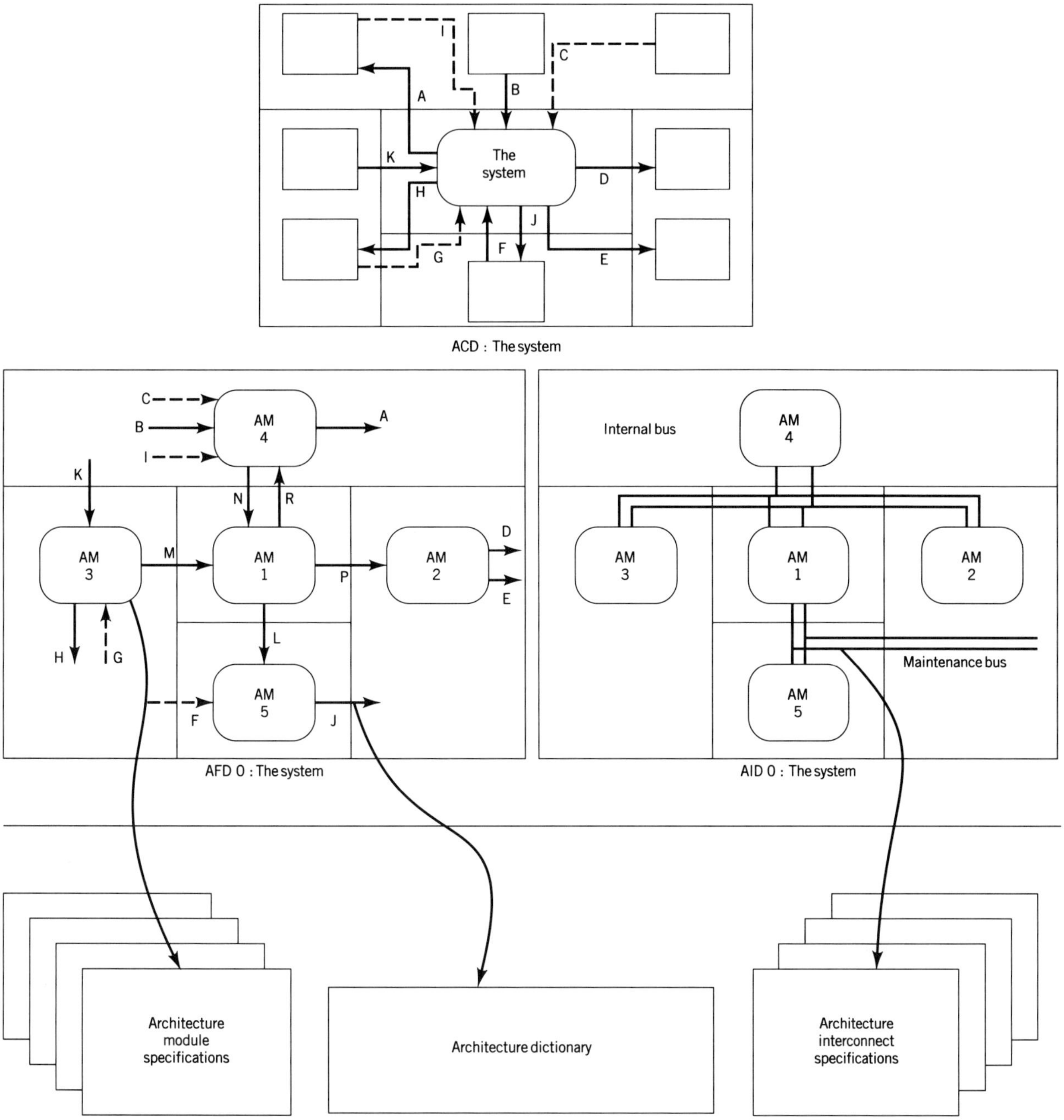

Figure 17. Architecture model components.

lead back to a previous one so that a portion of the previous step can be reevaluated or refined. This is the reason for the backward, as well as forward, paths between the requirements, enhanced requirements, and architecture models in the meta model, Figure 11. An iterative approach allows the higher levels of the specification to be stabilized before proceeding to the detailed levels.

A most important feature of the models and techniques described here is that, via the traceability matrix that resides in the architecture module specifications and the architecture dictionary that contains an allocation of the flows, there is a complete mapping between the requirements and architecture models. Thus, there is complete visibility into the impact of a change both in terms of identifying the parts of the implementation which are affected and in estimating the resources required to make the change.

Earlier it was pointed out that the modeling and specification processes are a system in themselves and must integrate together well like any other system. This is the situation. The requirements model and the architecture model components integrate with themselves and, via the traceability matrix, unite with each other to form a cohesive system specification.

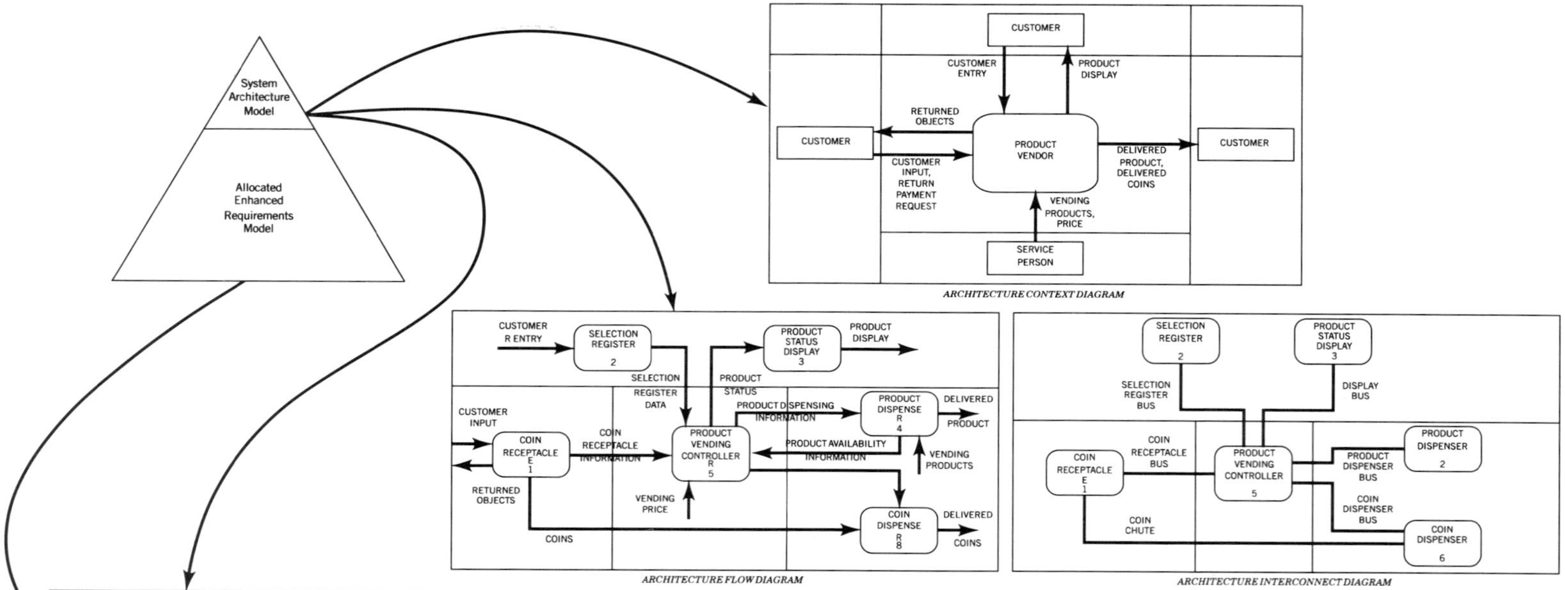

REQUIREMENTS MODEL COMPONENTS \ ARCHITECTURE MODEL COMPONENTS	COIN RECEP-TACLE 1	PRODUCT VENDING CONTROLLER 5	SELECTION REGISTER 2	COIN DISPEN-SER 6	PRODUCT STATUS DISPLAY 3	PRODUCT DISPENSER 4
VALIDATE COIN 1.1	x					
DISPENSE CHANGE 2				x		
VALIDATE PAYMENT 3		x				
GET PRODUCT PRICE 4		x				
GET VALID SELECT. EXCEPT 5.1		x				
DISPENSE PRODUCT 6						
ACCEPT CUSTOMER INPUT 7	x					x
RETURN SLUGS 8	x					
DISPLAY PRODUCT STATUS 9					x	
READ CUSTOMER SELECTION 10			x			
GET COIN RETURN REQUEST 11			x			
FILL PRODUCT STORE 12						x
DELIVER COINS 13				x		
DELIVER PRODUCT 14						x
CSPEC 0		x				
COIN STORE				x		
PRODUCT STORE						x
GET CUST. PMT. EXCEPT 1.1		x				
DETERMINE SELECT. 5.1			x			
UPDATE TABLE 15		x				

FLOW NAME	COMPOSED OF	TYPE	ORIGIN	DESTINATION	CHANNEL
OBJECTS	[COINS | SLUGS]	DATA	EXTERNAL	COIN RECEPTABLE	EXTERNAL
COINS	QUARTERS + NICKELS + DIMES	DATA	COIN RECEPTABLE	PRODUCT VENDING CONTROLLER	COIN RECEPTACLE BUS
PRODUCTS	{ SODA CANDY GUM }	DATA	PRODUCT DISPENSER	PRODUCT VENDING CONTROLLER	PRODUCT DISPENSER BUS

ARCHITECTURE DICTIONARY

AIS : PRODUCT DISPENSER BUS

The information on this bus will be sent as a discrete signal containing 8 serial bits. The product information will be encoded into 256 combinations
The characteristics of this bus will be

High = 5 +/- 0.2 Volts
Low = Ground

ARCHITECTURE INTERCONNECT SPECIFICATION

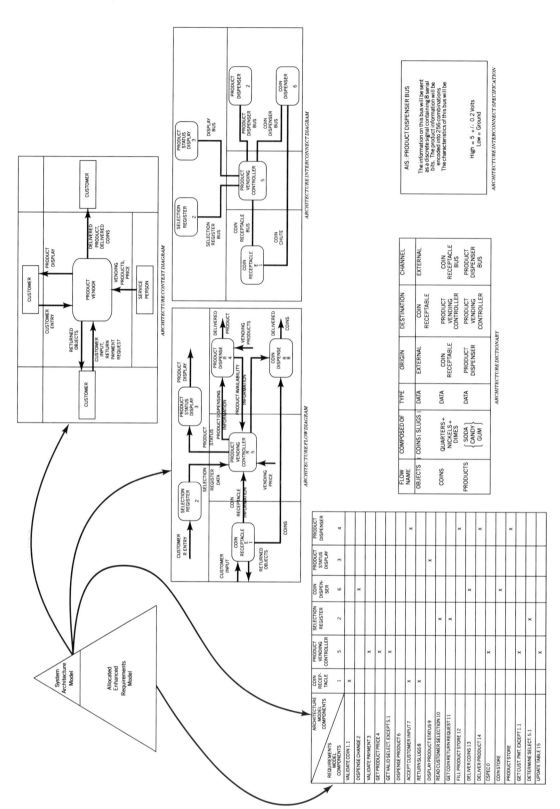

Figure 18. Architecture model vending machine.

CONCLUSIONS

In conclusion, the benefits which can be reaped from using the systems approach are summarized below:

- It is necessary to apply the systems approach to the whole system development process.
- Software development is not the only component of systems design. It is impossible to imagine software walking down the street executing itself! At the very least, software needs host hardware.
- Complexity manifests itself in many different ways. It is not restricted to the software.
- Communications need to be improved, not only between software developers and users, but between everyone involved in the project from its inception to its retirement.
- Just as the development life cycle is a process for developing systems, there needs to be a process embedded in it for specifying systems.
- The environment in which the system must fit and operate needs to be looked at, including user and maintenance interfaces.

Benefits of Using Meta Models

Two meta models representing the What and How of System Specification have been seen. Questions raised about meta models are often of the following sort: "Why should I care about meta models, aren't they just some academic abstraction?" and "How practical are they?" The benefits can be summarized as follows:

- At a very basic level, these meta models show the basic ingredients of a system. These tools provide a checklist to ensure that all pertinent issues arising during system development are addressed.
- These meta models are derived from *general systems thinking* and cover all aspects of the system to be developed or specified. Hence, they incline towards systems engineering. This means that the entire development of a system should be addressed to engineering and these meta models provide a platform for doing so.
- The meta models provide a common template which all project teams can use as a starting point—adapting and adopting them as appropriate. Herein lies the power of the meta models. They can be used on many different projects and still guarantee good intercommunication between those involved.
- Meta models offer systems developers a means of dealing with the complexity of systems. The integration of the models proposed by these methods allows the development of systems to proceed in an orderly fashion. They help in the management of overall systems design through the employment of incremental, step-by-step detailing.
- The meta models allow a high degree of reusability. People talk about software module reusability; the meta models provide system requirements reusability. For example, user interface specifications can be potentially reused on many different projects, the system specification meta model ensures its integration into different systems.

People Develop Systems

This article will conclude by pointing out some additional factors which need to be taken into account when specifying and developing systems. The systems approach which defines the specification process should also be applied to the development organization. People are also systems. The environment in which they work and the dynamics of an organization have far reaching effects on the productivity and product quality of the people involved in development. A total systems approach needs to be applied to the entire development process and environment. The methods described in this article should be treated as a set of meta methods. Remember, these meta models provide a framework to help people develop systems. They are not "hard and fast" guidelines for systems development or specification. They are just another set of tools in the system developer's tool box.

BIBLIOGRAPHY

D. J. Hatley and I. A. Pirbhai, *Strategies for Real Time System Specification*, Dorset House, New York.

S. McMenamin and J. Palmer, *Essential Systems Analysis*, Prentice Hall, Englewood Cliffs, N.J.

J. G. Miller, *Living Systems,* McGraw Hill Book Company, New York.

I. A. Pirbhai, *System Specification Case Studies: A Workbook*, Dorset House, New York.

G. Weinberg, *Rethinking Systems Analysis and Design*, John Wiley & Sons, Inc., New York, 1975.

G. Weinberg, *An Introduction to General Systems Thinking*, Dorset House, New York.

IMTIAZ A. PIRBHAI
Systems Methods

RECOVERY BLOCKS

It is normal to employ fault tolerance techniques for copying with the occurrence and the effects of anticipated hardware component faults, and mistakes by users and operators. In any computing system that is required to be highly reliable. However, particularly in complex systems whose failures could lead to loss of human life or great financial loss, the fault tolerance strategies used may well also include ones aimed at coping with residual design faults. The systems and applications software are typically of far greater logical complexity than the hardware on which they are running, so such design fault tolerance is usually aimed at software faults, and at complementing the verification and validation efforts that have been used to try to minimize the number of faults present when the software is deemed operational.

The recovery block scheme was developed with the aim of facilitating the provision of software fault tolerance. The provision of such fault tolerance requires the incorporation of useful redundant information into the design, for purposes of detecting and recovering from, or directly masking, the effects of residual design faults. However, since the principal cause of such faults is complexity, the use of appropriate structuring techniques is crucial if the addition of means of design fault tolerance to a system is not to increase its complexity to the point of being counter-productive.

To this end the recovery block scheme provides a single coherent error recovery strategy, while allowing use to be made of a variety of different error detection mechanisms. It is in fact a generalization of pre-existing error recovery techniques, and in its basic form applies simply to isolated sequential programs. Selected blocks of code in such programs are provided with one or more alternative ("standby-spare") blocks, which will be used temporarily in situations when the original ("primary") blocks fail. Such failures can be detected by conventional software of hardware checks, supplemented by final "acceptance tests". The syntax usually employ is

```
ensure        <acceptance test>
by            <primary block>
else by       <alternate block 1>
else by       <alternate block 2>
.....
else by       <alternate block n>
else error
```

The primary block is executed first, and if it fails, either through an internal check, or via the acceptance test, the system state is restored and the first alternate block is used instead. Similarly if this fails, the next is tried until either one succeeds (in which case any further alternate blocks are ignored) or the else error is reached. This represents a failure of the recovery block as a whole. Recovery blocks can be nested so such a failure could trigger further recovery, if the enclosing block is also part of a (higher level) recovery block. The fact that failure of a primary or alternative module causes state restoration (by some underlying mechanism) means that such modules could, and should, be designed quite separately, and their joint incorporation in a program will not add in any significant way to the overall complexity. All modules are subjected to the same acceptance test, such a test performs whatever checks are deemed adequately stringent, yet cost-effective, for the enclosing module to take responsibility for continuing the processing. The primary module is presumably the one that is expected to have the most complete functionality, and best performance. Successive alternates may be simpler and less efficient, or even less functional (albeit within the restrictions set by the acceptance test) so that the recovery block structure can be used to provide a form of "graceful degradation".

Since its introduction the recovery block scheme has been the subject of experimental evaluations and now, increasingly, industrial application. The above description is of just the original basic recovery block scheme Horning and co-workers, 1974; Randell, 1975. This scheme has however been greatly extended, so as to cope with programmer-defined data types and error recovery among sets of communicating processes, and to make combined use of recovery blocks and exception handlers. For further details see Randell, 1987.

BIBLIOGRAPHY

J. J. Horning, H. C. Lauer, P. M. Melliar-Smith, and B. Randell, "A Program Structure for Error Detection and Recovery," in *Proceedings Conference on Operating Systems, Theoretical and Practical Aspects,* IRIA, 1974, (reprinted in *Lecture Notes in Computer Science,* vol. 16, Springer, 1974, pp. 171–187.

B. Randell, "System Structure for Software Fault Tolerance," *IEEE Transactions on Software Engineering,* **SE-1** (2), 220–232 (1975).

B. Randell. "Design Fault Tolerance," in *The Evolution of Fault-Tolerant Computing,* Springer-Verlag, 1987, pp. 251–270.

B. Randell
University of Newcastle upon Tyne

REDWINE, SAMUEL T., JR. (1943–)

Samuel T. Redwine, Jr. has worked and published in a wide range of software engineering areas including software process software engineering environmental software dependability, software technology R&D management, quality, and technology transfer. He spent his early career working in business and government information systems—an experience that left him with a sense of the overriding importance of humans and organizations on one side and the power of rigor on the other. He also developed an ability to serve as a bridge between the differing communities of practitioners, technologists, and researchers as well as between engineers and managers.

From 1980 to 1987 he worked at Mitre and the Institute for Defense Analyses advising the Office of the Secretary of Defense on software technology R&D including planning for the Software Engineering Institute and the STARS Program. In 1987, he joined the Software Productivity Consortium, where he has worked in a number of positions including Assistant to the President/CEO. His activities since 1980 have often involved decisions on what software technology to research, develop, or transfer. He has been a consistent supporter of software measurement, application- or domain-specific reuse, relentlessly pursuit of quality, highly skilled teams, explicitness and rigor of software processes, automated support, interface standards, concern for systems and users, technology transfer methods, and use of what is known (mainly from other disciplines) about people and organizations.

Mr. Redwine is also somewhat known for his one-liners. Examples include, "I would rather try to do the right thing and fail than try to do the wrong thing and succeed," "Of all software products, the highest percentage of reuse is in the proposal," and "Software and cathedrals are much the same—first we build them, then we pray."

Mr. Redwine earned his BS and MS degrees in Management from MIT in 1971 and 1973. He is a member of ACM and IEEE. In the 1980s following his achievement of the highest scores on both their programmer and manager examinations, he was involved with the Institute for Certification of Computer Professionals, first on the Certificate in Computer Programming Certification Council as Member (1980–82) and Chair (1982–84) and second as a Member of its Board of Directors representing ACM (1984–88). He has been a member of the IEEE Computer Society Technical Committee on Software Engineering Executive Committee since 1987 serving for sustained periods as the TCSE Executive Vice Chair and Editor of the TCSE newsletter as well as being instrumental in the establishment of its Reuse and Technology Transfer subcommittees. He received the IEEE Award for meritorious service in 1993.

BIBLIOGRAPHY

S. T. Redwine with E. D. Siegel and G. R. Berglass, *Candidate R&D Thrusts for the Software Technology Initiative,* MITRE MTR-81W00160, (NTIS AD-A102180), May, 1981.

—"An Engineering Approach to Software Test Data Design," *IEEE Transactions on Software Engineering,* **SE-9**(2), 191–200 (March 1983).

—with L. Druffel and W. E. Riddle, "The STARS Program: Overview and Rationale," *Computer* **16**(11), 21–29 (Nov. 1983).

—with L. G. Becker, A. B. Marmor-Squires, R. J. Martin, S. H. Nash, and W. E. Riddle, *DoD Related Software Technology Requirements, Practices, and Prospects for the Future,* IDA Paper P-1788, June, 1984.

—with W. E. Riddle, "Software Technology Maturation," *Proceedings 8th International Conference on Software Engineering,* London, IEEE, Aug. 28–30, pp. 189–200, 1985.

—"The Software Development Process as a Fault-Tolerant System," *Proceedings of the 3rd International Software Process Workshop,* Breckenridge, Colorado, IEEE, Nov. 17–19, pp. 87–91, 1986.

—with C. DelFosse and W. F. Spencer, "1991 Technology Transfer at the Software Productivity Consortium," *American Programmer,* **5**(3) (March 1992).

REFINEMENT

See DESIGN.

REGRESSION TEST

See REGRESSION TESTING.

REGRESSION TESTING

INTRODUCTION

Regression testing is a testing process that is applied after a program is modified. It involves testing the modified program with test cases in order to re-establish our confidence that the program will perform according to the (possibly modified) specification. This is important in that a study by Hetzel (1984) indicates that for some instances of software maintenance, the probability of introducing an error while making a change is between 50 and 80%.

In the development phase, regression testing may begin after the detection and correction of errors in a tested program. Regression testing is a major component in the maintenance phase where the software system may be corrected, adapted to new environment, or enhanced to improve its performance. Modifying a program involves creating new logic to correct an error or to implement a change, and incorporating that logic into an existing program. The new logic may involve minor modifications such as adding, deleting, or rewriting a few lines of code, or it may involve major modifications such as adding, deleting, or replacing one or more modules or subsystems. Regression testing aims to check the correctness of the new logic, to ensure the continuous working of the unmodified portions of a program, and to validate that the modified program as a whole functions correctly.

Many modifications may occur during the maintenance phase where the software system is corrected, updated, and fine-tuned. Software maintenance is defined as the performance of those activities required to keep a software system operational and responsive after it is accepted and placed into production (FIPS, 1984). There are three types of modifications, each arising from different types of maintenance. According to Lientz and Swanson (1980), *corrective maintenance,* commonly called "fixes," involves correcting software failures, performance failures, and implementation failures in order to keep the system working properly. Adapting the system in response to changing data requirements or processing environments constitutes *adaptive maintenance.* For example, a change of the hardware platform is a common reason for adaptive maintenance. *Perfective Maintenance* covers any enhancements to the system, where the objective may be to provide additional functionality, increased processing efficiency, or improved maintainability.

During adaptive or perfective maintenance, new modules are usually introduced. The specification of the system is modified to reflect the required improvement or adaptation. However, in corrective maintenance, the specification is not likely to be changed, and no new modules are likely to be introduced. Most modifications involve adding, deleting, and modifying instructions. Many program modifications occurring during the development phase are similar to that of corrective maintenance, because the specification will not normally be modified due to a discovery of an error in the program.

TYPES OF REGRESSION TESTING

Two types of regression testing can be identified based on the possible modification of the specification. *Progressive regression testing* involves a modified specification. Whenever new enhancements or new data requirements are incorporated in a system, the specification will be modified to reflect these additions. In most cases, new modules will be added to the software system with the consequence that the regression testing process involves testing a modified program against a modified specification.

In *corrective regression testing,* the specification does not change. Only some instructions of the program and possibly some design decisions are modified. This has important implications because most test cases in the previous test plan are likely to be valid in the sense that they correctly specify the input-output relation. However, because of possible modifications to the control and data flow structures of the software, some existing test cases are no longer testing the previously targeted program constructs. Corrective regression testing is often done after corrective maintenance is performed on the software.

TESTING TOOLS

A number of testing tools exist to assist in software development; however, few of them can be applied directly to regression testing. Among those that claim to be useful for regression testing, most provide no more than the capability to store the previous tests and rerun them after every modification (Dogsa and Rozman, 1988; Raither and Osterweil, 1987; Steubing, 1980; Ziegler, Grasso, and Burgermeister, 1989). They do not provide any intelligent test selection capability or any estimation of the required testing effort. We will call this type of regression testing the *retest-all strategy*.

Recently, several strategies were introduced for regression testing at the unit level (Benedusi, Cimitile, and De Carlini, 1988; Harrold and Soffa, 1988; Leung and White, 1989; Ostrand and Weyuker, 1988; Yau and Kishimoto, 1987). These strategies all attempt to select a subset of the previous test for execution and do not repeat all the previous tests. Specific information is stored with the tests in order to identify the relevant tests with possible program changes. We will call this type of regression testing a *selective strategy*.

OVERVIEW OF SELECTIVE REGRESSION TEST STRATEGIES

Very few regression test tools have been described in the research literature. Most of the "known" regression test tools are either under development or in a prototype form. Few of them are of production quality. Also, most of them were introduced to aid in regression unit testing and cannot be used for regression integration or system testing.

Yau and Kishimoto (1987) recently introduced a regression testing tool that was based on the *input partition* testing strategy (Richardson and Clarke, 1985). This strategy divides the input domain of a module into different classes using both the program specification and code, and requires one test be selected from each input class. The objective of regression testing is to execute each new or changed input partition at least once. Symbolic execution is used to identify those input domains that are not modified, and to aid in test generation. This regression testing strategy selects a subset of the previous tests and adds new tests to exercise the modified code. Similar to most regression tools, this tool concentrates on unit regression testing.

A regression testing tool is an essential component of any software maintenance environment. A *post maintenance testing system* was described by Benedusi, Cimitile, and De Carlini (1988), and also deals with unit regression testing. It implements a path testing strategy by selecting tests to exercise a specific set of paths. The regression testing strategy uses the following two steps: (**1**) identify those paths that have been added, those deleted and those modified; (**2**) update and rerun the test cases that exercise the modified and new paths. Algebraic expressions are used to represent the program before and after the program modification. By comparing these expressions using elementary algebraic operations, it is possible to classify paths affected by the modification into new, deleted, modified and unmodified paths. By storing test cases and their associated program paths in a table, it is straightforward to identify those tests needed to be rerun based on the changed code.

Ostrand and Weyuker (1988) have proposed using data flow analysis for regression testing. They have modified their ASSET data flow testing tool to support this regressing testing. They allow regression tests to be selected in any of three ways based upon data flow:

- Choosing a subset of previously executed test cases
- Defining new test cases based upon newly established data flow associations
- Defining new test cases to satisfy a previously satisfied data flow criterion that is no longer satisfied by existing test cases

The method is primarily applicable at the unit testing level, although there is a brief description as to how this might be extended to interprocedural regression testing.

Harrold and Soffa have developed an incremental data flow tester that can be used for regression testing purposes (1988). This tool combines data flow testing with incremental data flow analysis to aid in unit and integration regression testing. During the initial testing, the system stores the previous data flow analysis results and test cases. After a module is modified, the system analyzes the effects of the changes on the *test history* and determines new and existing definition-use pairs for retesting. Existing test cases are reused whenever possible. The system identifies those definition-use pairs that have not been exercised. This tool does not help with test generation and uses only a white-box testing method (structural testing based on data flow coverage). Harrold and Soffa (1989; 1991) have recently extended their technique to include interprocedural testing. Data flow testing is performed across procedure boundaries to integrate those procedures.

Fischer, Raji, and Chruscicki (1981) use zero-one integer programming to find a minimum set of tests that can cover all the program segments (this is inherently white-box testing by assumption). Four tables are used to record the control flow relation between program segments, reachability between segments, test cases that cover the different segments, and variable use and define information within each segment, respectively. A series of inequality constraint expressions is created, one for each program segment, relating those tests that traverse the segment. An objective function relates the cost of running all the tests to individual tests. Given the program segments that have been modified, standard linear-programming techniques are used to solve for the minimum number of test cases that must be rerun to validate the modification. Recall that linear program problems may terminate with a noninteger solution. To arrive at a zero-one solution, additional constraints and iteration may be needed.

Another regression testing tool under development by Hartmann and Robson (1990) extends Fischer's method (Fisher, Raji, and Chruscicki, 1981) for test selection from the previous test set. It assumes that a test set that covers all program segments is available. The tool then takes this test set as input and produces a minimum test set that covers the same program segments. This tool also extends Fischer's method to include programs written in the C programming language, programs with several modules, and segments that have multiple use of variables. Because this tool also uses zero-one linear programming, it suffers from the same set of computational problems associated with other zero-one linear programming problems. This tool has the potential to aid in system regression testing by treating each module as a segment for test coverage purposes. Observe that this tool implicitly assumes that a white-box testing technique (segment cover) is used and cannot be generalized to include black-box testing.

Leung and White (1989; 1990) have conducted a fundamental study of regression testing. Regression strategies were developed at the unit, integration, and function testing levels that incorporated both functional and structural testing, but without specifying the specific testing methodology that would be applied at each level. Subsets of tests are selected at each level as regression tests.

One can view the issues of regression testing at the integration level or at higher levels of abstraction in terms of the *dependencies* that exist between modules in the program. For example, in the Korel and Laski study (1988) and in Leung and White (1989), the only dependency we considered was that imposed by the module call graph, which included parameters passed back and forth between calling and called modules. This can be defined as the *control-flow dependencies* between modules.

Another type of dependency that must be considered is that of *global variables,* where a variable is defined in one or more modules and then is referenced by many other modules. This can be viewed as a *data-flow dependency* between modules. Also there may be *resource dependencies* between modules, such as memory, where the resource is constrained between a number of modules.

In Leung and White (1990), the concept of *firewall* was introduced in order to deal with regression testing at the integration level. Given one or more modules that have been changed, the firewall encloses the set of modules that are affected and must be retested. As long as prescribed programming practices are observed, the effects of the change do not extend beyond the firewall. Leung and White (1990; 1992) have considered the regression testing of global variables, and have developed an alternative concept of *firewall* for data-flow module dependencies.

CONTROLLING THE SIZE OF A REGRESSION TEST SUITE

If new tests are always added to regression test suites (or "regression buckets"), but no tests are removed, these test suites can only grow. From Leung and White (1989), there are two categories of tests which can be removed from the regression test suite. One category is *obsolete tests,* where because of the changes to the software, these tests no longer perform the testing functionality for which they were designed. This observation illustrates how important it is to document the reason why tests have been designed and selected. The second category of tests that can be removed from the test suite is *redundant tests,* where although the tests still satisfy their intended functionality, new tests have now been added to the test suite, and the redundant tests can be removed from the test suite with that functionality still satisfied by other remaining tests. For example, suppose that a test T was originally added to the test suite in order to achieve a certain level of test coverage; later, after additional tests have been added to the test-suite, test T may no longer be needed to achieve that level of test coverage.

The methods of Fischer, Raji, and Chruscicki (1981) and of Hartmann and Robson (1990) proceed to find a minimum test suite by deleting as many obsolete and redundant tests as possible. However, these methods could potentially be very inefficient in achieving this minimum. Recently, Harrold, Gupta, and Soffa (1990) proposed a method to efficiently remove obsolete and redundant tests to obtain a substantially reduced test suite, although it is not guaranteed to be minimum.

PROGRAM SLICES AND REGRESSION TESTING

In unit regression testing, how can we systematically determine which statements in a module are affected by a change in that module? One technique for this has been *program slicing*, and thus has been closely associated with regression testing. Weiser (1984) introduced the concept of program slicing for debugging and program understanding, and provided algorithms based on data flow equations for slicing programs with static analysis of source code. A *(static) program slice* with respect to a variable v and a program location p contains all statements (including predicates) that *may* affect the value of variable v at location p. The potential problem with this concept is that too many statements may be included in the static slice, and yet during program execution only a small number of statements would actually affect variable v at location p of the program. For this reason, Korel and Laski (1988) defined *dynamic slicing.* Some reflection on program slices will indicate that a *forward slice* (Gupta, Harrold, and Soffa, 1992) would also be useful for regression testing: given a variable v defined at location p, a *forward slice* contains all statements that may be affected by the value of variable v at location p. A number of researchers have studied slicing recently (Gopal, 1991; Horowitz, Reps, and Binkeley, 1990; Podgurski and Clarke, 1990), and others (Agrawal, DeMillo, and Spafford, 1991; Jiang, Zhou, and Robson, 1991) have shown how unconstrained pointers can also be taken into account in obtaining program slices. Recently a paper by Gupta, Harrold, and Soffa (1992) has explicitly shown how program slices could modify the entire approach to regression testing in terms of what information needs to be maintained.

COST OF REGRESSION TESTING

There has been little work to show the cost-benefit analysis of regression testing, for it represents a large cost and effort in producing quality software. A beginning study was conducted by Leung and White (1991), where they proposed a cost model to compare regression testing strategies. Their specific objective was to compare the tradeoffs between retest-all strategies, where all available test data is used in regression testing, and selective strategies, which select a subset of this test data. There is a need to study and quantify the benefits of regression testing so that an overall cost-benefit analysis can be made.

REGRESSION TESTING OBJECT-ORIENTED PROGRAMS

Object-oriented design and programming represents a new paradigm, and we are just now beginning to learn how such systems can be maintained and what particular problems are presented in their maintenance. There are only a few research results for testing object-oriented programs, but a paper by Harrold, McGregor, and Fitzpatrick (1992) provides an initial analysis for incremental testing of class structures in the presence of change. Clearly more information of this type is needed for practitioners.

BIBLIOGRAPHY

H. Agrawal, R. DeMillo, and E. Spafford, "Dynamic Slicing in the Presence of Unconstrained Pointers," *Proceedings of the Symposium on Testing, Analysis and Verification (TAV4),* Victoria, British Columbia, Canada, 1991, pp. 60–73.

P. Benedusi, A. Cimitile, and U. De Carlini, "Post-Maintenance Testing Based on Path Change Analysis," *Proceedings of the Conference on Software Maintenance—88,* Phoenix, Ariz., 1988, pp. 352–361.

T. Dogsa and I. Rozman, "CAMOTE—Computer Aided Module Testing and Design Environment," *Proceedings of the Conference on Software Maintenance—88,* Phoenix, Ariz., 1988, pp. 404–408.

K. F. Fischer, F. Raji, and A. Chruscicki, "A Methodology for Retesting Modified Software," *Proceedings of the National Telecommunications Conference,* New Orleans, La., Nov. 1981, pp. B6.3.1–6.3.6.

R. Gopal, "Dynamic Program Slicing Based on Dependence Relations," *Proceedings on the Conference on Software Maintenance—91,* Sorrento, Italy, 1991, pp. 191–200.

FIPS PUB 106, Guideline on Software Maintenance, Federal Information Processing Standards, U.S. Department of Commerce/National Bureau of Standards, June 1984.

R. Gupta, M. J. Harrold, and M. L. Soffa, "An Approach to Regression Testing Using Slicing," *Conference on Software Maintenance—92,* Orlando, Fla., 1992, pp. 299–308.

M. J. Harrold, R. Gupta, and M. L. Soffa, "A Methodology for Controlling the Size of a Test Suite," *Proceedings of the Conference on Software Maintenance—90,* San Diego, Calif., 1990, pp. 302–310.

M. J. Harrold, J. McGregor, and K. Fitzpatrick, "Incremental Testing of Object-Oriented Class Structures," *15th International Conference on Software Engineering,* 1992, pp. 68–80.

M. J. Harrold and M. L. Soffa, "An Incremental Approach to Unit Testing During Maintenance," *Proceedings of the Conference Software Maintenance—88,* Phoenix, Ariz., 1988, pp. 362–367.

M. J. Harrold and M. L. Soffa, "Interprocedural Data Flow Testing," *Proceedings of the Third Symposium on Software Testing, Analysis and Verification,* Key West, Fla., 1989, pp. 158–167.

M. J. Harrold and M. L. Soffa, "Selecting and Using Data for Integration Testing," *Software,* 58–65 (Mar. 1991).

J. Hartmann and D. J. Robson, "Techniques for Selective Revalidation," *IEEE Software,* 31–38 (Jan. 1990).

W. Hetzel, *The Complete Guide to Software Testing,* QED Information Sciences, Wellesley, Mass., 1984.

S. Horwitz, T. Reps, and D. Binkeley, "Interprocedural Slicing Using Dependence Graphs," *ACM Transactions on Programming Languages and Systems* **12**(1), 26–60(Jan. 1990).

J. Jiang, X. Zhou, and D. Robson, "Program Slicing for C—The problems in Implementation," *Proceedings of the Conference on Software Maintenance—91,* Sorrento, Italy, 1991, pp. 182–190.

B. Korel and J. Laski, "Dynamic Program Slicing," *Information Processing Letters* **29,** 155–163(Oct. 1988).

H. K. N. Leung and L. White, "Insights into Regression Testing," *Proceedings of the Conference on Software Maintenance—89,* Miami, Fla., Oct. 1989, pp. 60–69.

H. K. N. Leung and L. White, "A Study of Integration Testing and Software Regression at the Integration Level," *Proceedings of the Conference Software Maintenance—90,* San Diego, Calif., 1990, pp. 290–301.

H. K. N. Leung and L. White, "Insights into Testing and Regression Testing Global Variables," *Journal of Software Maintenance* **2,** 209–222(Dec. 1990).

H. K. N. Leung and L. White, "A Cost Model to Compare Regression Test Strategies," *Proceedings of the Conference on Software Maintenance—91,* Sorrento, Italy, 1991, pp. 201–208.

B. P. Lientz and E. B. Swanson, *Software Maintenance Management,* Addison-Wesley Publishing Co., Inc., Reading, Mass., 1980.

T. Ostrand and E. Weyuker, "Using Data Flow Analysis for Regression Testing," *6th Annual Pacific Northwest Software Quality Conference,* Portland, Oreg., 1988, pp. 1–4.

A. Podgurski and L. Clarke, "A Formal Model of Program Dependencies and its Implications for Software Testing, Debugging, and Maintenance," *IEEE Transactions on Software Engineering* **SE-16**(9), 965–979(Sept. 1990).

B. Raither and I. Osterweil, "TRICS: a Testing Tool for C," *Proceedings of the First European Software Engineering Conference,* Strasbourg, France, 1987, pp. 254–262.

D. Richardson and L. Clarke, "Partition Analysis: A Method of Combining Testing and Verification," *IEEE Transactions on Software Engineering* **SE-11**(12), 1477–1490(1985).

H. G. Stuebing, "A Modern Facility for Software Production and Maintenance," *Proceedings of COMPSAC 80,* Chicago, Ill., 1980, pp. 407–418.

M. Weiser, "Program Slicing," *IEEE Transactions on Software Engineering* **SE-10**(4), 352–357(1984).

L. White and H. K. N. Leung, "A Firewall Concept for Both Control-Flow and Data-Flow in Regression Integration Testing, *Proceedings of the Conference on Software Maintenance—92,* Orlando, Fla., 1992, pp. 262–271.

S. Yau and Z. Kishimoto, "A Method for Revalidating Modified Programs in the Maintenance Phase," *Proceedings of COMPSAC 87,* Tokyo, Japan, 1987, pp. 272–277.

J. Ziegler, J. Grasso, L. Burgermeister, "An ADA Based Real-Time Closed-Loop Integration and Regression Test Tool," *Proceedings of the Conference on Software Maintenance—89,* Miami, Fla., pp 81–90.

LEE J. WHITE
Case Western Reserve University
HARETON K. N. LEUNG
Bell-Northern Research Ltd.

REIFER, DONALD J.

Donald J. Reifer is an internationally recognized expert in the fields of software engineering and management, with over 25 years of experience in both industry and government. He has successfully managed major projects, served on source selections, wrote winning proposals and led project recovery teams. While affiliated with TRW, Mr. Reifer was the Deputy Program Manager for Global Positioning Satellite (GPS) verification and validation projects. As a Software Director with the Aerospace Corporation, Mr. Reifer managed over major software contracts for the Space Transportation Systems (Space Shuttle). As a Project Leader at Hughes Aircraft, Mr. Reifer managed several weapons system developments. Currently as President of RCI, a software consulting firm, Mr. Reifer efforts are aimed at helping Fortune 500 firms (CAE-Link, Rockwell, Shell Oil, Texas Instruments, Westinghouse, etc.) and government agencies (DOD, NASA, etc.) to manage large software projects, organizations and technology introduction effectively.

Over the past ten years, Mr. Reifer has worked as a change agent to improve productivity and quality. He focuses on culture change as he builds teams and implements change using consensus approaches. His specialties are management, measurement, and people. Recently, Mr. Reifer has devoted his attention to developing strategies for systematic software reuse. Mr. Reifer serves as Chief Architect for DISA/JIEO/CIM on a DOD-wide reuse initiative which is trying to link together reuse to provide users with seamless access. He has developed reuse operational concepts for the JIAWG, OSS and RAASP projects.

Mr. Reifer is author of over 100 papers on software engineering and management topics. He is also the author of the popular ASSET-R size and SoftCost-Ada cost estimation models. Mr. Reifer holds a B.S. in Electrical Engineering from Newark College of Engineering (NCE), a M.S. in Operations Research from the University of Southern California (USC) and the Certificate in Business Management from the University of California at Los Angeles (UCLA).

RELIABILITY ALLOCATION

See SOFTWARE RELIABILITY ENGINEERING.

RELIABILITY TESTING

See CATEGORIES OF TESTING.

REPOSITORY

See REUSE LIBRARY.

REQUIREMENTS ENGINEERING

Requirements engineering is the systematic use of proven principles, techniques, languages, and tools for the cost-effective analysis, documentation, and ongoing evolution of user needs and the specification of the external behavior of a system to satisfy those user needs. Notice that like all engineering disciplines, requirements engineering is not conducted in a sporadic, random, or otherwise haphazard manner, but instead is the *systematic* use of *proven* approaches. Notice that like all engineering disciplines, requirements engineering applies *principles* (i.e., general rules or tenets), *techniques* (i.e., step-by-step procedures or recipes), *languages* (i.e., a syntax and semantics with which one can represent requirements, however formal or informal), and *tools* (i.e., pieces of software that aid in the enforcement or automation of the principles, techniques, or languages). Notice that requirements engineering entails *analysis* (i.e., the uncovering, discovery and elicitation of requirements), *documentation* (i.e., the specification or the recording of requirements on paper or on electronic media), and the *ongoing evolution* (i.e., requirements are in constant flux so that requirements engineering activity must transcend all life cycle phases). Notice that the domain of requirements engineering includes both *user needs* (i.e., the problem domain), and the *external behavior of a system to satisfy those user needs* (i.e., the solution domain).

Requirements engineering can be applied to a software system alone or to a system composed of hardware and software. In the former case, it is often termed *software requirements engineering* and in the latter case *system requirements engineering*. For software-only systems, software requirements engineering is the first activity of the software life cycle, as shown in Figure 1. For software-and-hardware systems, system requirements engineering is usually performed iteratively, alternating with system design. As shown in Figure 2, system requirements engineering is conducted initially to better understand the problem being tackled and to specify the desired external behavior of the solution system. Then system design decomposes the system into its constituent components (i.e., subsystems). Each of these is then analyzed and specified in a second system requirements engineering step. This process repeats until the subsystems are small enough to be considered manageable but large enough to be still

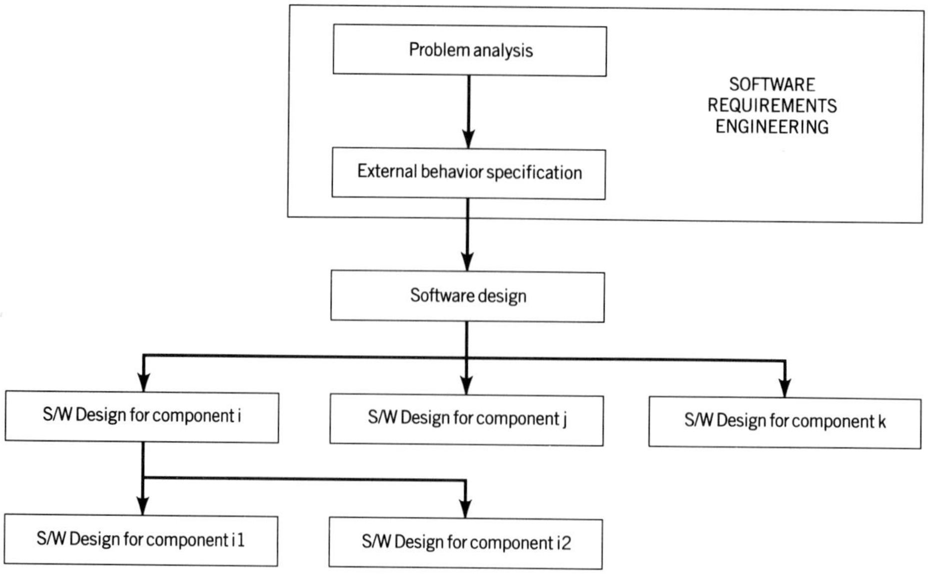

Figure 1. Software requirements engineering.

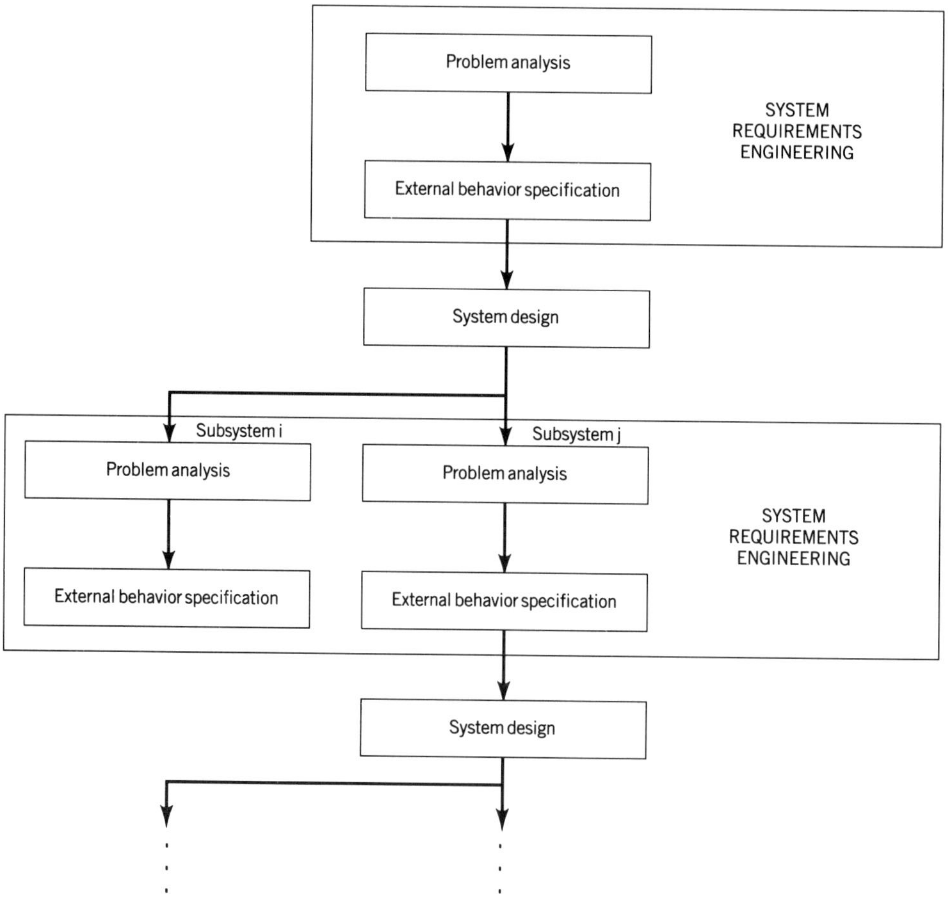

Figure 2. System requirements engineering.

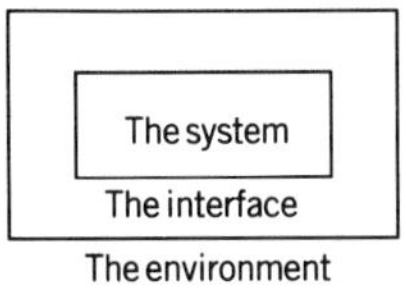

Figure 3. The end of the requirements phase.

considered (sub-)systems. Once these are defined at the last level of systems design, software requirements engineering takes over for the software subsystems and hardware systems engineering takes over for the hardware subsystems. See SOFTWARE REQUIREMENTS ENGINEERING METHODOLOGY for one approach for integrating system requirements and system design.

The remainder of this article will restrict the discussion to *software* requirements engineering only.

During the two sets of activities of software requirements engineering, i.e., problem analysis and external behavioral specification, very different types of activities are pursued. During problem analysis, analysts spend their time brainstorming, interviewing people who have the most knowledge about the problem at hand, building prototypes, and identifying all possible constraints on the problem's solution. At this time there is a considerable expansion of information and knowledge about the problem. The greatest difficulty during this time is finding ways of trading off constraints and organizing the plethora of information. Problem analysis must be performed until a complete understanding of the problem is reached. During product description it is time to take pen in hand, to make some difficult decisions about what is to be automated and prepare a document that describes the expected external behavior of the product to be built to solve the now-understood problem. This is a time to organize ideas, resolve conflicting views, and eliminate inconsistencies and ambiguities.

It must be pointed out, however, that these two do not represent two temporally sequential, mutually exclusive phases. There are two reasons for this. First, some product developments require little or no problem analysis. In particular, problem analysis is applicable to only new, difficult, or yet-unsolved problems. Why waste time analyzing a problem that is already well understood? Second, given a new, difficult, or yet-unsolved problem, we do not perform problem analysis and then when complete begin writing a software requirements specification (SRS). In reality what is done is something like this: Problem analysis is initiated; as parts of the problem become well understood, corresponding sections of the SRS are written; finally the last aspect of the problem is analyzed, and the SRS is finished.

Problem analysis is only occasionally documented. Most often it is a process that results in a keener understanding of the problem and thus what is learned is best utilized when writing the SRS.

The primary product of software requirements engineering is a *software requirements specification* (SRS). This specification contains a complete description of the external behavior of the software to be built. As shown in Figure 3, this includes a complete description of all interfaces between the software and its environment (e.g., host hardware, other hardware interfaced with, other software, humans).

When performing problem analysis or external behavioral specification, the types of information being discussed, analyzed, and documented tend to be some combination of objects, functions, and states. The following paragraphs discuss these three concepts.

From a requirements perspective, an *object* is any real-world entity, important to the discussion of the requirements, with a crisply defined boundary. The phrase *real-world* entity in the definition ensures that we remain in the requirements domain and helps to exclude such implementation-time objects such as stacks. The phrase *important to the discussion of requirements* helps to exclude real-world entities such as shoes from an analysis of an elevator control system. The phrase *crisply defined boundary* comes from Booch (1991) and helps to exclude verb phrases such as *going to the store* from being considered objects. Objects are often grouped into classes. A *class* of objects is a set of objects exhibiting common attributes and/or functions and/or states and/or common relationships with other objects. Objects that are members of a class *inherit* the attributes, functions, states, and relationships associated with the class. The system under specification is not an object. An object must be a real-world entity that is relevant to the problem being solved or to the system being specified to solve that problem.

From a requirements perspective, a *function* is a task, service, process, mathematical function, or activity that is either (1) now being performed in the real world, and/or (2) to be performed by the system being specified to solve the problem in the real world. Functions are often grouped hierarchically, where the root functions are the most abstract and the leaf functions are the most detailed. This hierarchy is purely a delineation of functionality, not a design of the software.

From a requirements perspective, a *state* is a condition of some thing that captures some history of that thing and is used by the thing to help determine how it is to behave in specific circumstances. The *thing* can be the system, an object, or a function. When the states are states of the system, they often represent the presence of a set of recognizable system responses, and are rarely specified explicitly in the SRS in practice. More usually their presence is implied by the specification of a function. Thus, for example, the requirement TO MAKE A LOCAL CALL, THE CALLER LIFTS THE PHONE, HEARS A DIAL TONE, THEN DIALS A LOCAL NUMBER implies a state of the system called *dial tone*. When the states are states of an object, they are occasionally specified explicitly, as in AN AIRCRAFT MAY BE ON THE GROUND, ON DEPARTURE, EN ROUTE, OR ON APPROACH.

PROBLEM ANALYSIS

Introduction

Problem analysis is the activity that encompasses learning about the problem to be solved (often through brainstorming and/or questioning and/or prototyping), understanding the needs of potential users, trying to find out who the user really is, and understanding all constraints on the solution. Assuming that the requirements stage ends with creating a document called the software requirements specification (SRS), which contains a complete description of the external behavior of the product to be built or purchased, problem analysis can be thought of as defining the product space, i.e., the range of all possible software solutions. The *product space* is that range of problem solutions that meets all known constraints. The sources of constraints may include users, customers, developers, technology, laws, and standards (Cronhjort and Gallmo, 1982).

For example, if the problem is that a currently manual process is inadequate in some way and needs to be upgraded, then the subjects investigated during problem analysis tend to include: (1) people and/or machines (including other systems) currently playing some role, (2) items produced, processed, or consumed by these people and machines, (3) functions performed by these people and machines, and (4) basic modes of operation that determine what functions are performed when. If the problem is that a particular function or set of functions is currently not performed, but needs to be, then the subjects investigated during problem analysis tend to include: (1) people and/or machines (including other systems) who have a need for some service to be performed or some item to be produced, (2) items that need to be produced to satisfy the need, (3) items that are necessary in order to produce the required new service or item, (4) functions (including intermediate functions) that need to be performed in order to generate the required new service or item and (5) basic modes of operation that determine what functions are performed when. In other words, regardless of the type of problem, analysis deals with the objects, functions, and states relating to the problem.

Objects, functions, and states can be described at multiple levels of detail. For example, objects can be described at any level from the very abstract (e.g., vehicle) to the very specific (e.g., 1993 BMW 750iL). Functions can be described at any level from the very abstract (e.g., provide voice communications) to the very specific (e.g., the local call shall be initiated by pressing the "X" button). States can be described at any level from the very abstract (e.g., phone busy) to the very specific (e.g., accessing directory assistance).

Yeh and Zave were the first to isolate partitioning, abstraction, and projection as three underlying principles of structuring used during problem analysis. *Partitioning* captures the "aggregation/part of" structural relation among objects, among functions, or among states in the problem domain. For example, let us look at the problem of defending a nation against enemy missiles. During analysis, it might be helpful to define the parts of an enemy missile: warhead, body, propulsion system. This hierarchy defines a partition relationship; it specifies that the warhead, body and propulsion system objects are *parts* of the missile object. It may be useful to show the partitioning of the functions to be performed. For example, the overall defense system problem can be partitioned into target detection, communication, intelligence gathering and resolution, defensive weapon launch, and defensive weapon guidance. Note that this is not a design. The problem analysis hierarchy simply defines a partition relationship; it specifies that target detection, communication, intelligence gathering and resolution, defensive weapon launch and defensive weapon guidance functions are *parts of* the functions of the entire system. It might be useful to recognize that the state of the defense system is composed of the state of the enemy forces, the state of the friendly forces, and the state of the war (e.g., conventional, cold, or limited). This hierarchy defines a partition relationship; it specifies that the enemy force, friendly force, and war states are *parts* of the state of the system.

Abstraction captures the "general/specific" or "example of" or "instance of" structural relationship among objects, among functions, or among states in the problem domain. For example, during the analysis of the same defense system problem, it might be helpful to define the various kinds of enemy missiles as conventional and nuclear; or ballistic and guided; or long-range and short-range. These three examples of abstraction show that the subordinate objects are *examples of* the missile object. It might be helpful to recognize that three kinds of threat identifications are required: identification of submarine threats, identification of surface threats, and identification of air threats. This hierarchy specifies that the three subordinate functions are *examples of* the threat identification function. It might also be helpful to differentiate between three major modes (or states) of the system: normal, wartime, and training. This hierarchy specifies that the three subordinate states are *examples of* the system state (see ABSTRACTION).

Projection captures the "view of" structural relationship among objects, among functions, or among states in the problem domain. For example, during the analysis of the same problem, it might be helpful to view the defensive missile from the perspectives of the missile system operator, the commander making the decisions, the intelligence analyst, and the enemy missile. This hierarchy shows that the operator, commander, intelligence analyst, and enemy missile are *views of* the defensive missile. In a telephone system, the call-waiting function can be most easily described in terms of its views, i.e., from the perspectives of the three involved parties. Projection can also be used to analyze states. For example, in a patient monitoring system, the state patient coded can be examined from the perspectives of the patient, the floor nurse, and the code team. This hierarchy shows these three subordinate items are *views of* the patient coded state.

In summary, partitioning, abstraction, and projection each define structural or hierarchical relationships among objects, among functions, or among states. Recording the fact that *A* is subordinate to *B* means different things when using the three techniques. In partitioning, it means *A* is a part of *B;* in abstraction, it means that *A* is an example of *B* and thus inherits all of *B*'s attributes; in projection, it means that *A* is one view of *B*.

Techniques

Many analysts analyze a problem randomly by asking key questions, writing down the answers, and asking other questions. The primary advantage of applying a more formal approach to problem analysis is that it simplifies the

Table 1. Similarities between Requirements and Design

Stage	Aspect	Primary Activity	Primary Goal
Software Only			
Requirements	Problem analysis Writing the SRS	Decomposition Behavior description	Understanding
Design	Preliminary design Detailed design	Decomposition Behavior description	Optimization
Software and Hardware			
System requirements	Problem analysis Writing the system requirements specification	Decomposition Behavior description	Understanding
System design	System design	Decomposition	Optimization
Software requirements	Problem analysis[a] Writing the SRS	Decomposition Behavior description	Understanding
Software design	Preliminary design Detailed design	Decomposition Behavior description	Optimization

[a] Relatively small effort.

task. But analysts do not need simplification of the easy parts of their job; they need simplification of the difficult parts. What is difficult about the job? The answer is organizing all the information, relating different people's perspectives, surfacing and resolving conflicts, and avoiding the internal design of the software.

Organizational aids are important because during the analysis of a nontrivial problem, reams of information about the problem are generated. During problem analysis, different people may have very different views of the problem. It is important to be able to track these different perspectives and relate them to each other. When these perspectives are in conflict, a good problem analysis technique will surface the conflict to aid in its resolution rather than bury it.

Perhaps the most difficult aspect of problem analysis is avoiding software design. If we examine the requirements and design stages of the software development life cycle, shown in Table 1 we see that the requirements stage consists of two parts—problem analysis and writing the SRS—and the design stage consists of two parts—preliminary design and detailed design. Problem analysis is primarily a decomposition process: decomposing problems into subproblems with the goal of understanding the entire problem at hand. Preliminary design is also primarily a decomposition process: decomposing software components into smaller software components with the goal of generating an optimal design that meets all requirements. From a technique or tool point of view, decomposition is decomposition regardless of the "stuff" being decomposed. As a result, most techniques and tools applicable to problem analysis are equally effective during preliminary design, and vice versa. There is very good reason for doing them both and not mixing the two. Remember that the goal of problem analysis is understanding, and the goal of preliminary design is optimization of performance or maintainability. For critical applications, preliminary design might consume 25 to 30 percent of total project resources. A project team certainly cannot afford to spend that kind of money during the requirements stage, especially not before project members even know what system they are going to build (i.e., there is no SRS yet). Since an analyst will obviously not be permitted to spend sufficient dollars during the requirements stage to do a thorough software design, including trade-off studies between competing design alternatives, such an analyst is forced to use criteria for creating the software design other than those that are appropriate. Too often analysts use the simple criteria, "that's how I've always designed such systems." And all this activity is taking place before we even write the SRS! It should be clear at this point why it is so crucial not to perform real design during the problem analysis stage and why it is so difficult to avoid.

The traits of a good problem analysis technique are:

1. Facilitate communication (probably via an easy-to-understand language).
2. Provide a means of defining the system boundary.
3. Provide a means of defining partitions, abstractions, and projections.
4. Encourage the analyst to think and document in terms of the problem (i.e., the application) as opposed to the solution (i.e., the software).
5. Allow for opposing alternatives but alert the analyst to their presence.
6. Make it easy for analysts to modify the knowledge .

As you read the rest of this section, keep in mind that different kinds of problems require different kinds of techniques. This means that to be a really effective analyst, you must keep a rich bag of tricks and know when and how to apply the right one at the right time. A famous but anonymous saying is, "If I gave a person nothing but a hammer to work with, he or she would start treating everything like a nail." It is unfortunate that when a software tool is used for the wrong purpose, users usually blame the tool. It is also unfortunate that many tool suppliers sell their tools as useful for any application. They get away with this because their tools *can* be used for many applications; they just are not optimal. For example, you *can* use a hand plane to smooth the hardwood floor of a ballroom, and you *can* use a jointer planer to sharpen toothpicks.

We will now discuss briefly two basic schools of problem analysis: object and structured. Each discussion includes refereces to other encyclopedia entries for more detailed information.

The concept of object orientation in software development has its roots in the language Smalltalk. Rentsch (1982) provides an excellent historic perspective of object oriented *programming*. Booch (1986) discusses the effect of object orientation on *design*. Finally, Booch and co-workers (1991), Borgida and co-workers (1983), Coad and Yourdon (1991), Rumbaugh and co-workers (1991), Shlaer and Mellor (1992) discuss the effect of object orientation on requirements.

Object oriented requirements (OOR) techniques have evolved from four different origins.

1. *From object oriented design (OOD).* A few of the OOR techniques evolved from OOD. At design time, an object is generally considered to be an abstract data type; thus an object is an encapsulation of protected data along with all the legal functions (also called processes or methods) that act upon that data. The biggest selling point of OOD is that systems designed using objects tend to be less error-prone and have structures that mimic structures in the real world. Since the purpose of problem analysis is to capture the real world as a model, it seems natural to use objects. Proponents of OOR from the OOD school usually do not differentiate between objects at requirements and objects at design. The only real difference appears to be a level of detail. The advantages are that (a) problem domain objects are often easier to define and stabilize than problem domain functions, and (b) the transition from requirements to design is relatively straightforward. The disadvantage is that the criteria for object selection at requirements time should be different than for design time. The criteria at requirements time must include some notion of a real world physical entity that is important to understanding the problem. It is irrelevant if it needs to be modeled at design time. For example, inclusion of a passenger object (with weight attribute) is essential for understanding an elevator control system, but is probably irrelevant at design time. On the other hand, a "floor requests" data abstraction (i.e., instance of an object) is essential for designing an elevator control system, but is probably unnecessary at requirements time.
2. *From database design.* Other object oriented requirements techniques evolved from entity relation (ER) modeling (Chen, 1976). ER diagrams have been used for years by database designers to capture the data about real world entities. ER diagrams record entities (which become records in a database), relations between entities (which become pointers between records), and often attributes of entities (which become fields within the records). Proponents of object oriented problem analysis from the ER school usually downplay, or completely ignore, functions or processes that act upon the entities. The advantages are that (a) problem domain objects are often easier to define and stabilize than problem domain functions, and (b) database design becomes relatively straightforward after requirements. The disadvantage is that there are many real world objects that need to be modeled in order to understand the problem but do not correspond to databases, e.g., passengers in the elevator control system.
3. *From the requirements analysis world.* Some object oriented problem analysis techniques evolved from standard requirements (systems) analysis. Their proponents have been analyzing problems using a variety of informal techniques. Their primary driver had been the understanding of the problem by analyzing entities in the real world. These OOR techniques emphasize the creation of objects that are exclusively in the problem domain. The advantages are (a) problem domain objects are often easier to define and stabilize than problem domain functions, (b) only real world problem-related objects are modeled, and (c) objects are encapsulated along with their attributes and services/functions/methods. The disadvantage over the previous two approaches is that the transformation to design may be non-trivial.
4. *From structured analysis (SA).* A number of recently published techniques claim to be object oriented simply because object orientation is *hot.* The proponents of these usually call their techniques something like "object oriented structured . . . ." All they have done is taken standard data flow diagrams changed the shapes of transforms from circles to rectangles, and declared themselves to be object oriented. The resulting units have no notion of information hiding, no notion of data protection/encapsulation, no notion of attributes. They are simply functions. The only advantage is that you can say you are using object orientation. The disadvantage is that you are not!

Most object-oriented approaches stress the definition and refinement of *objects* in the real world and classes of objects in the real world. A *class* of objects can be thought of as an abstraction that represents one or more objects or other classes of objects. Thus, if we have objects called manufacturers, wholesalers, and retailers, they might all be members of the class of objects called companies. Also in most object-oriented approaches, objects (and classes of objects) possess attributes, and objects *inherit* the attributes of the classes of which they are members. Since problem analysis is the analysis and description of the real world, its entities, attributes, and relationships, it makes sense to use object-oriented concepts in problem analysis. The primary motivation for object orientation is that as a system evolves, its functions tend to change, but its objects remain unchanged. Thus, a system built using object-oriented techniques may be inherently more maintainable than one built using more conventional functional approaches.

For the purposes of requirements, an object is defined as:

- A real world entity.
- Related to the problem domain.
- With crisply defined boundaries.
- Encapsulated along with its attributes and behavior.
- Whose behavior or attributes must be understood in order to understand the problem at hand.

See OBJECT-ORIENTED REQUIREMENTS ANALYSIS and JACKSON DEVELOPMENT METHODS for more details.

Structured Analysis was developed by Tom DeMarco (1979) and is an adaptation of the early requirements work of Ross (Ross and Schoman, 1977). Structured analysis is a pure top-down technique in which the analyst starts by representing the system in a context diagram showing all system inputs and outputs and repeatedly refines the system, representing each refinement as a more detailed diagram. These diagrams, called *data-flow diagrams* (DFD), consist usually of circles (representing functions), arrows (representing data-flowing between the functions), rectangles (representing sources and destinations of data external to the system being analyzed), and pairs of parallel lines (representing data bases, i.e., static stores of information).

As DFDs are iteratively refined, a hierarchy is developed with a large quantity of arrows, all with unique names. To help keep track of these, a *data dictionary* is created to store definitions, purposes and structure of all data given in the DFDs.

Structured analysis has its roots in the data processing world. In the mid to late 1980s, repeated attempts to apply it to real-time systems resulted in a number of useful extensions. Specifically, Ward and Mellor (1985) developed very useful extensions to DFDs that captured control flow, process activation, and process deactivation. Ward's methodological enhancements (based on McMenamin and Palmer's work 1984) helped the analyst stay out of the software design domain. Hatley and Pirbhai (1987) made other useful extensions to structured analysis. Specifically they added control flow diagrams to represent the desired behavior of its corresponding DFD. They also made methodological enhancements that capture the requirements-design iteration inherent in any complex system undertaking.

See also DATA FLOW ANALYSIS AND DESIGN.

THE SOFTWARE REQUIREMENTS SPECIFICATION

Introduction

A *Software Requirements Specification* is a document that describes the expected external behavior of the software system. An SRS may be written in two different scenarios. First the SRS could be written by a potential user (or customer) of a system. Second the SRS could be written by a developer of the system. The two scenarios create entirely different situations and establish entirely different purposes for the document. In the former case, the primary purpose of the SRS is to define the need. This document sometimes serves as a basis for a competitive bidding process among companies who desire to satisfy that need. In order to encourage competition (which potentially helps the customer receive the best product at the least cost), the SRS should be as general as possible. Let us say for example that a building owner wishes to buy an elevator control system. The SRS should be general enough to enable a number of elevator companies (each with a different dispatch algorithm and a different elevator flight path) to respond, but it should also be specific enough to eliminate clearly from the competition a company offering a series of ramps connecting the floors and a parade of elephants walking up and down the ramps transporting people on their backs. Ideally, the SRS should carve the universe of systems into two independent sets: a set containing all systems satisfying the users' real needs and one containing all those that would not.

On the other hand, an SRS written by a development organization as the first step of the software development process must be far more specific. This type of SRS is the subject of our discussion here, and it performs an entirely different set of functions from the so-called SRS described in the preceding paragraph. Its purpose is to provide a means of

- Communication among customers, users, analysts, and designers
- Supporting system-testing activities
- Controlling the evolution of the system

The first purpose of the SRS is to provide a means of communication on all parties. A well-written SRS reduces the probability of the customer being disappointed with the final product. The SRS defines the external behavior of the system to be built unambiguously, so there can be no misinterpretation. If there is a disagreement between customer and developer concerning external behavior, it is worked out during the requirements stage, not during acceptance testing, when it is much more costly to correct. Unfortunately many developers prefer to keep the SRS fairly ambiguous in order to provide themselves with more flexibility during design. However, this flexibility significantly increases the customer's risk. The SRS should be very specific about how the system will look externally to the system's environment (or the user). This does have a second-order effect on limiting possible designs, but it is not part of the design; in fact some designers claim such a specification is too constraining. If the SRS writer finds it impossible to specify external behavior without supplying a design, then the SRS should contain a note to the effect that:

WARNING: THE "DESIGN" CONTAINED HEREIN IS SUPPLIED AS AN AID IN UNDERSTANDING THE PRODUCT'S EXTERNAL BEHAVIOR ONLY. THE DESIGNERS MAY SE-

LECT ANY DESIGN THEY WISH PROVIDED IT BEHAVES EXTERNALLY IN A MANNER IDENTICAL TO THE EXTERNAL BEHAVIOR OF THE ABOVE SYSTEM.

Why should the "design" used in the SRS not be used as *the* design? The answer is simple: The "design" in the SRS was chosen because it helped make requirements more understandable. The real design is chosen to optimize such qualities as maintainability, performance, space, and modifiability.

The second purpose of the SRS is to serve as the basis for system testing and verification activities. The purpose of system testing is to stimulate the system with representative test scenarios in order to show that the as-built system meets requirements. If the SRS is ambiguous or inconsistent or some requirement stated is untestable, then such testing is impossible. The SRS is the primary input to the system test planning and generation process.

The third purpose of the SRS is to help control the evolution of the software system. Let us assume that a software product is either under development or has been deployed, and a customer says, "I want the software to do X." How does anyone know if that is a new requirement or an old one? The answer is to read the SRS and find out. If it is determined to be a new requirement, then the appropriate process to incorporate the customer's request is to (1) update the SRS, (2) update the design, (3) update the code, and so forth. The SRS serves as the definition and the only definition of what the software is supposed to do. Formal control of the contents of the SRS is precisely formal control of the evolution of the software system. This control process is part of the discipline of software configuration management (SCM) (Bersoff, 1980) which is outside the scope of this book. SCM works effectively during the maintenance and enhancement stages as well as during initial development stages.

What Should Be Included in an SRS?

Simply stated an SRS must include a complete yet concise description of the entire external interface of the system with its environment, including other software, communication ports, hardware, and human users. This includes two types of requirements: behavioral and nonbehavioral.

Behavioral requirements define what the system does. These describe all the inputs and outputs to and from the system as well as information concerning how the inputs and outputs interrelate. In other words, we must completely define the transform function of the system software being specified. These descriptions of how inputs map into outputs are typically called behavioral descriptions or operational specifications.

The nonbehavioral requirements define the attributes of the system as it performs its job. They include a complete description of the system's required levels of efficiency, reliability, security, maintainability, portability, visibility, capacity, and standards compliance, to name but a few.

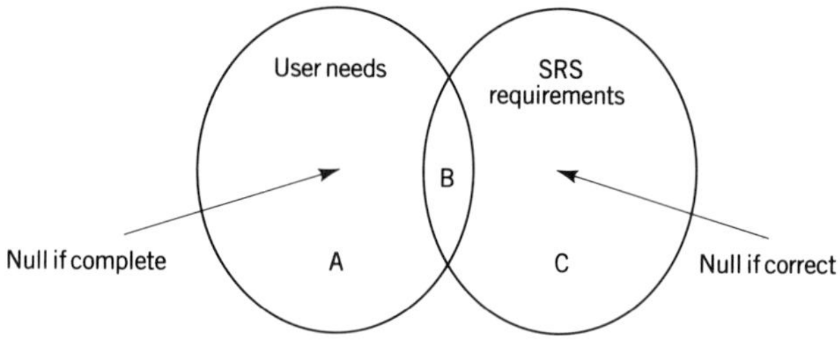

Figure 4. User's needs versus SRS requirements.

Attributes of a Well-Written SRS

If a perfect SRS could exist it would be (Davis and coworkers, 1993)

- Correct
- Unambiguous
- Complete
- Verifiable
- Consistent
- Understandable by customer
- Modifiable
- Traced
- Traceable
- Design independent
- Annotated

Each of these qualities is explained in the following paragraphs.

An SRS is *correct* if and only if every requirement stated represents something required of the system to be built. There is no real way of teaching this quality, since it depends totally on the application at hand. If the software must respond to all button presses within 5 seconds and the SRS states that "the software shall respond to all button presses within 10 seconds," that requirement is incorrect. The Venn diagram of Figure 4 helps to visualize this definition of correct. The left circle represents the users' real needs. The right circle represents the requirements as stated in the SRS. If the SRS is correct then region C has zero area, i.e., every requirement in the SRS helps to satisfy some need.

An SRS is *unambiguous* if and only if every requirement stated therein has only one interpretation (IEEE, 1984). Imagine that a sentence is extracted from an SRS, given to ten people who are asked for their interpretation. If there is more than one such interpretation, then that sentence is probably ambiguous. At a minimum all terms with multiple meanings must appear in a glossary. However, there is much more of a problem with ambiguity than can be solved with just a glossary. In particular using natural language invites ambiguity because natural language is inherently ambiguous.

An SRS is *complete* if it possesses the following four qualities:

1. Everything that the software is supposed to do is included in the SRS. In Figure 4 completeness implies that region A has zero area. Note that if an SRS is both complete and correct then regions A and C are null and the two circles of this figure are coincident. Completeness is the most difficult of the attributes to define or detect violations of. A violation is difficult to detect because it implies that something is not in the SRS; it is not simple to find something that is not present by examining what is present. The only people able to detect such an oversight or omission are those who own the problem to be solved by the software. One effective technique for locating a violation uses a prototype.
2. Definitions of the responses of the software to all realizable classes of input data in all realizable classes of situations is included. A thorough analysis of completeness of this type for finite state machines is given in (Jaffe and co-workers, 1991). Note that it is important to specify the responses to both valid and invalid inputs (IEEE, 1984). This implies that for every system input mentioned in the SRS, the SRS specifies what the appropriate output will be. However, the appropriate output may not be just a function of the input; it may also be a function of the current state of the system. For example, in a telephone switching system, the software's response to detection of the user dialing 9 is a function of the state of the system, which in turn is a function of what the user did previously. Thus, if the user's phone handset is in its cradle, no system output is generated (that is, the input 9 is ignored). If the user is listening to a dial tone, the system output might be a distinctive dial tone. If the user has already started dialing a phone number, the 9 is collected as one more digit of the phone number. In other words the SRS must establish a complete mapping from the cross product of the input domain (I) and state domain (S) into the cross product of the output domain (O) and the state domain (S), that is,

$$\text{SRS: } I \times S \rightarrow O \times S$$

3. All pages are numbered; all figures and tables are numbered, named, and referenced; all terms and units of measure are provided, and all referenced material and sections are present (IEEE, 1984). This is completeness from a word processing perspective.
4. No sections are marked "To Be Determined (TBD)." Inserting the three letters "TBD" in a section of an SRS should be avoided whenever possible. When included, the TBD should be appended with a notation of *who* has responsibility for determining the contents and *when* the section will be completed. This approach ensures that the TBD is not interpreted carte blanche as an excuse to delay completion of the SRS indefinitely as if the TBD meant "To Be Done Tomorrow," and of course tomorrow never occurs. By including the name of the responsible party and a date, we ensure that the TBD expires at some point.

An SRS is *verifiable* if, and only if, every requirement stated is verifiable. A requirement is *verifiable* if, and only if, there exists some finite cost effective process with which a person or machine can check that the actual as-built software product meets the requirement (IEEE, 1984). It is important to realize that verifiability is a function of the way the SRS is written. (Many people think it is purely a function of the product as-built.) There are a number of reasons why a requirement may be nonverifiable. First, any ambiguity would certainly lead to nonverifiability; obviously there is no way to verify that the software exhibits a trait if that trait is defined ambiguously. For example the statement "The product shall have an easy-to-use human interface" is ambiguous, that is, has multiple interpretations because opinions of what is easy to use varies greatly from individual to individual and cannot be verified to be an attribute of the final product. Second, using nonmeasurable quantities such as "usually" or "often," implies the absence of a finite test process and thus implies nonverifiability. For example, the statement that "The product shall usually ignite the red light when the button is pushed" is nonverifiable because if you try to verify compliance with the requirement by pushing the button a thousand times you may be tempted to declare the test successful if the red light ignited six hundred times. However it may be that if you pushed the button a thousand more times, the red light would never ignite again. In other other words the only way to test that "usually" is the case would be to push the button an infinite number of times. Third, any requirement that is equivalent to a statement of the halting problem cannot be verified (Turing, 1936). For example, it can be demonstrated that verification of the statement "the program shall not enter an infinite loop" is equivalent to the halting problem and thus is nonverifiable.

An SRS is *consistent* if, and only if, (1) no requirement stated therein is in conflict with other preceding documents, such as a system requirements specification or a statement of work, and (2) no subset of requirements stated therein conflict.

In an attempt to make an SRS less ambiguous, more verifiable, complete, and consistent, we might be tempted to resort to extremely formal notations. Unfortunately such notations often lose another important attribute: *For noncomputer specialists to understand the SRS.* Primary readers of the SRS in many cases are customers or users, who tend to be experts in an application area but are not necessarily trained in computer science. Perhaps one way of achieving the goal is to use formal notations but develop a tool to translate the resulting formal SRS into an equivalent easy-to-understand prose automatically. This is the approach taken by Balzer and co-workers on the GIST project (1982). If there exists a complete unambiguous mapping between the formal and informal representations, then the informal representation will satisfy all the required attributes, including understandability by the non-computer specialist.

While the six preceding paragraphs discussed attributes of the *content* of the SRS, the next five discuss attributes of SRS *format* and *style.*

An SRS is modifiable if its structure and style are such that any necessary changes to the requirements can be made easily, completely, and consistently (IEEE, 1984). Modifiability implies that there exists a table of contents, an index, and cross-references where necessary. Thus, if a requirement must be modified later, we can check and easily locate the section of the SRS that has to be modified. For example, if we want to change the required maximum response time of a dial tone in a telephone switching system from 5 seconds to 3 seconds, we would look in the index under "dial tone" to locate all the references to dial tone in the document in order to make the necessary changes. One technique that can be used to improve the readability of a SRS is to repeat selected requirements in different locations in the document. This attribute of a SRS is called *redundancy.* For example, in describing the external interface of a PABX we must define interactions between the user and the telephone switch. Thus, when describing the external view of a local call, the SRS may state that

> *Starting with an idle telephone, the user should lift the handset, the system shall respond with a dial tone, then the user should dial the seven-digit phone number of the party the user is trying to reach . . . .*

When describing the external view of a long-distance call, the SRS may state that

> *Starting with an idle telephone, the user should lift the handset, the system shall respond with a dial tone, then the user should dial a 1 followed by the ten-digit phone number of the party the user is trying to reach . . . .*

Note that the restatement of the first three steps makes the document considerably more readable. However, with the additional readability comes the potential for decreased modifiability because a later modification to only one occurrence would render the SRS inconsistent. To make redundancy acceptable, an index or cross-reference table is essential for locating multiple occurrences requirements.

An SRS is *traced* if the origin of each of its requirements is clear. That means that the SRS includes references to earlier supportive documents, as shown in Figure 5. Let us assume that an SRS contains the requirement

> *The system shall respond to any occurrence of request X within 20 seconds.*

Now the software has actually been built and when it undergoes its final test, response time is measured consistently at sixty seconds. There are two ways of correcting this problem: (1) Redesign or recode the software to make it more efficient, or (2) change the requirement from twenty to sixty seconds. If no reference is present in the SRS at this location to indicate that twenty seconds was anything

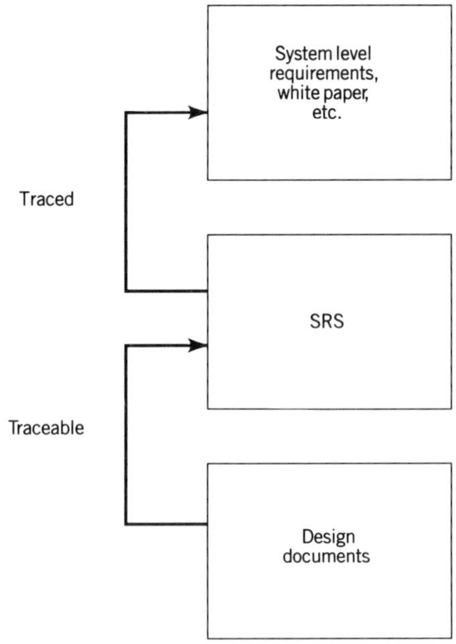

Figure 5. Traced and traceable SRS.

but a randomly selected timing constraint, we may be tempted to use solution 2 (and this *may* be perfectly satisfactory). However, if the application was a patient-monitoring system and the reason for the twenty-second response time was that an earlier white paper demonstrated conclusively that in the particular hospital environment in which this patient-monitoring system was to be installed and with the existing nurse to patient ratio, a nurse needed to make at least three queries of the system per minute in order to ensure the absence of emergency conditions with any patients. In such a case, traceability would insist on a reference being entered in the SRS at the site of the timing requirement back to the white paper. Then when solution 2 is considered, it is quickly dismissed after checking the white paper.

In order to design or test any component of the software, it is necessary to know which requirements are (perhaps in part) being satisfied by the component. Similarly, when testing the software system, it is necessary to understand which requirements are being validated by each test. An SRS is *traceable* if it is written in a manner that facilitates the referencing of each individual requirement stated therein, as shown in Figure 5. There are a variety of techniques to do this:

- Number every paragraph hierarchically. Then you can later refer to any requirement by a paragraph reference and a sentence number within that paragraph, e.g., requirement 2.3.2.4s3 refers to the requirement stated in sentence 3 of paragraph 2.3.2.4. This is very effective.
- Number every paragraph hierarchically and never include more than one requirement in any paragraph. Then you can later refer to any requirement by a paragraph number. This approach works but tends to create awkward hard-to-read documents.

- Number every requirement with a unique number in parentheses immediately after the requirement appears in the SRS.
- Use a convention for indicating a requirement, e.g., always use the word *shall* in the sentence containing a requirement; then use a simple *shall*-extraction tool to extract and unique number all sentence with a *shall*.

An SRS is *design independent* if it does not imply a specific software architecture or algorithm. Every requirement limits design alternatives; for example, stating that you want a system that transports people vertically in a building eliminates telephone switching system software as a possible design. No requirement in the SRS should limit the design to just one alternative. There are some exceptions to the need for design independence in an SRS. These tend to be specific to particular applications where the primary driver for building a new system is the use of a specific new architecture or algorithm. For example, an elevator control system SRS will undoubtedly include a dispatch algorithm. An integrated circuit layout program SRS will undoubtedly include placement and routing algorithms.

Annotating requirements in an SRS provides guidance to the development organization concerning the relative necessity of each requirement. Occasionally a development organization may spend an inordinate amount of time trying to satisfy a particular requirement, then discover afterward that the customer would have preferred the product on time without the requirement satisfied than six months late with the requirement satisfied. This scenario would have been avoided if the relative necessities of individual requirements had been stated initially. One way of doing this is to append to every individual requirement in the SRS with an *E*, *D*, or *O* in parentheses to indicate essential, desirable, or optional.

Achieving all of the preceding attributes in an SRS is impossible. For example, as we attempt to eliminate inconsistency and ambiguity (usually by reducing the natural language in the SRS), the SRS becomes less understandable to customers who are not computer specialists (one attempt to combine readability, unambiguity, and consistency is reported in (Davis, 1982)). As we attempt to be absolutely complete, cost of the SRS skyrockets and the document becomes extremely large and difficult to read. If we try to increase modifiability by eliminating all redundancy, the SRS becomes quite choppy, difficult to follow, and ambiguous. The only conclusion we can reach is that there is no such thing as a perfect SRS!

Organizing an SRS

There are many ways to organize an SRS for optimal understandability. A set of requirements can be grouped together because they:

1. Relate to the same external stimulus. For example, in an automatic helicopter landing system, we could group together all those requirements relating to gusts of wind, to sensing altitude, to fuel empty, and so on.

x. Detailed Requirements
x.1. Passenger
  x.1.1. Calling an Elevator
  x.1.2. Requesting a Floor
x.2. Maintenance Personnel
  x.2.1. Inspecting Shaft
  x.2.2. Inspecting Car Operation
  x.2.3. Taking Out of Service
  x.2.4. Placing Back in Service
x.3. Fire Person

Figure 6. Organizing an SRS Using Multiple Criteria.

2. Relate to the same system feature. For example, in a telephone switching system, we could group together all those requirements relating to local calls, to long distance calls, to call forwarding, and so on.
3. Relate to the same system response. For example, in a payroll system, we could group together all those requirements relating to generating paychecks, to generating a list of current employees, to generating a list of average salaries by labor category, and so on.
4. Relate to the same real world object. For example, in an automated library system, we could group together all those requirements relating to books, borrowers, publishers, and so on.
5. Relate to the same class of user. For example, in an elevator control system, we could group together all those requirements relating to passengers, maintenance personnel, firepeople, building owners, and so on.
6. Relate to the same class of function. This is the weakest of all the groupings, and corresponds to a typical stepwise decomposition of function into subfunction when using data flow diagrams without a technique. For example, in an ocean surveillance system, we could group together all those requirements relating to incoming data, user interface, report generation, maintaining the database of known ships, and so on.

In a typical complex application, the best way to organize requirements is probably a multi-level hierarchy where each level corresponds to a different grouping criteria. For example, in an elevator control system, we could organize first by class of user, then by feature, as shown below.

Although there are many valid ways of organizing requirements, one that is not valid is organizing by software or system component. An SRS is written for a single black box software system. If during a previously performed system design, we decided to construct the system out of three system components, each with hardware and software, then we should write three SRSs, one for each system component. If during the requirements phase, we decide to establish the software's architecture (i.e., by defining software components and their interfaces)—which is not healthy—then create a separate draft software design document which captures that architecture. We should still avoid that design in the SRS itself.

Techniques for Enhancing an SRS

Hundreds of techniques have been developed since the early 1970s to increase the quality of an SRS caused by the inherent ambiguity of natural language. One of the earliest attempts was done by Alford and Burns (1976) and Alford (1985). The basic tenet of this earlier work was to use finite state machines organized into units called R-Nets, each corresponding to the required system behavior in response to a single stimulus. Many dozens of techniques followed that were based on finite state machines. Similarly, there developed many techniques based on decision tables, Petri nets and cooperating asynchronous processes. See survey of all of these in Davis (1988, 1993).

In the early 1990s there developed a movement toward use of multiple representations for requirements, most of which combined analysis and specification techniques. These include some that were limited to a specific set of representations, e.g., Rumbaugh and co-workers (1991) and Embley and co-workers (1992) to those that allowed unlimited representations (e.g., Davis and co-workers, 1993a).

SUMMARY

The period 1965–1975 was the decade of programming breakthroughs. The period 1975–1985 was the decade of design breakthroughs. The period 1985–1995 is the decade of requirements breakthroughs. With the software industry's repeated attempts to find ways of producing quality software in a timely and cost effective manner, we are seeing a plethora of techniques now that allegedly enhance our ability to capture system and software requirements. If these prove to be effective, we will be more likely to build systems that solve the real needs of the users.

This entry is excerpted from A. Davis, *Software Requirements: Objects, Functions, and States,* Prentice Hall, Englewood Cliffs, N.J., 1993.

M. Alford and I. Burns, "R-Nets: A Graph Model for Real-Time Software Requirements," *Symposium on Computer Software Engineering,* Polytechnic Press, New York, 1976, pp. 97–108.

M. Alford, "SREM at the Age of Eight; the Distributed Computing Design System," *IEEE Computer* **18**(4) 36–46 (April 1985).

R. Balzer and co-workers, "Operational Specifications as the Basis for Rapid Prototyping," *ACM Software Engineering Notes,* **7**(5) 3–16 (Dec. 1982).

E. Berstoff and co-workers, *Software Configuration Management,* Prentice-Hall, Englewood Cliffs, N.J., 1980.

G. Booch, "Object-Oriented Development," *IEEE Transactions on Software Engineering,* **12**(2), 211–221 (Feb. 1986).

G. Booch, *Object-Oriented Design with Applications,* Benjamin/Cummings, Redwood City, Calif. 1991.

A. Borgida and co-workers, "Knowledge Representation as the Basis for Requirements Specification," *IEEE Computer,* **18**(4) 82–91 (April 1985).

P. Chen, "The Entity Relationship Model: Toward a Unifying View of Data," *ACM Transactions on Database Systems,* **1**(1) 9–36 (March 1977).

P. Coad and E. Yourdon, *OOA—Object-Oriented Analysis,* Prentice Hall, Englewood Cliffs, N.J. 1991.

B. Cronhjort and B. Gallmo, *A Model of the Industrial Product Development Process,* Ericsson Information Systems Report 1982-09-01 C TB BG 82010, Bromma, Sweden, 1982.

A. Davis, "The Design of a Family of Applications-Oriented Requirements Languages," *IEEE Computer* **15**(5) 21–28 (May 1982).

A. Davis, "A Comparison of Techniques for the Specification of External Behavior of Systems," *Communications of the ACM* **31**(9) 1098–1115 (Sept. 1988).

A. Davis, *Software Requirements: Objects, Functions, and States,* Prentice Hall, Englewood Cliffs, N.J., 1993.

A. Davis and co-workers, "Identifying and Measuring Quality in Software Requirements Specifications," *IEEE International Symposium on Software Metrics,* May 1993.

A. Davis and co-workers *A Canonical Representation for Requirements*, University of Colorado Department of Computer Science Technical Report, Colorado Springs, Colorado, 1993a.

T. DeMarco, *Structured Analysis and System Specification,* Prentice Hall, Englewood Cliffs, N.J., 1979.

D. Embley and co-workers, *Object-Oriented Systems Analysis,* Prentice Hall, Englewood Cliffs, N.J., 1991.

D. Hatley and I. Pirbhai, *Strategies for Real-Time System Specification,* Dorset House, New York, 1987.

Institute of Electrical and Electronics Engineers, *IEEE Guide to Software Requirements Specifications,* IEEE/ANSI Standard 830-1984, New York, 1984.

M. Jaffe and co-workers, "Software Requirements Analysis for Real-Time Control Systems," *IEEE Transactions on Software Engineering* **17**(3) 241–258 (March 1991).

S. McMenamin and J. Palmer, *Essential Systems Analysis,* Prentice Hall, Englewood Cliffs, N.J., 1984.

National Computer Centre, Ltd., *The STARTS Guide,* Manchester, UK, 1987.

T. Rentsch, "Object-Oriented Programming," *ACM SIGPLAN Notices,* **17**(9), 51–57 (Sept. 1982).

D. Ross and K. Schoman, Jr., "Structured Analysis for Requirements Definition," *IEEE Transactions on Software Engineering* **3**(1) 6–15 (Jan. 1977).

J. Rumbaugh and co-workers, *Object-Oriented Modeling and Design,* Prentice Hall, Englewood Cliffs, N.J., 1991.

S. Shlaer and S. Mellor, *Object-Oriented Systems Analysis: Modeling the World in Data,* Prentice Hall, Englewood Cliffs, N.J., 1988.

S. Shlaer and S. Mellor, *Object Lifecycles: Modeling the World in States*, Prentice Hall, Englewood Cliffs, N.J., 1992.

A. Turing, "On Computable Numbers, with an Application to the Entscheidungsproblem," *Proc. London Mathematical Society* **2**(42) 230–265 (1936).

P. Ward and S. Mellor, *Structured Development for Real-Time Systems,* Prentice Hall, Englewood Cliffs, N.J., 1985.

R. Yeh and P. Zave, "Specifying Software Requirements," *Proceedings of the IEEE* **68**(9), 1077–1085 (Sept. 1980).

E. Yourdon, *Modern Structured Analysis,* Yourdon Press, Englewood Cliffs, N.J., 1989.

ALAN MARK DAVIS
University of Colorado

REQUIREMENTS ENGINEERING VALIDATION SYSTEM (REVS)

See SOFTWARE REQUIREMENTS ENGINEERING METHODOLOGY.

REQUIREMENTS SPECIFICATION

See SOFTWARE REQUIREMENTS ENGINEERING METHODOLOGY.

RESPONSE NETS

See SOFTWARE REQUIREMENTS ENGINEERING METHODOLOGY.

REUSABILITY

The degree to which a software module or other work product can be used in more than one computer program or software system (IEEE).

REUSE

INTRODUCTION

Background

Software development costs are becoming a major factor in the world's economy. This situation is a result of systems becoming increasingly sophisticated (with software implementing most of the added functionality), while engineering salaries are rising and hardware costs are decreasing. Motivation to find more efficient and predictable ways to create software is growing annually.

Comparing the software and hardware industries is interesting. Hardware costs are going down not because hardware engineers are getting cheaper, but because of standardization on common parts, in other words, *reuse.* Is there a way to achieve the same benefits by practicing reuse in the software field? Hardware engineers today build systems from components that perform complex functions on a single chip, rather than depending on gate-level design and wiring. Can software be built from more complex software components, rather than from individual lines of code? As illustrated in Figure 1, this can be thought of as a "software components industry." (The term *megaprogramming* has been coined (see MEGAPROGRAMMING) to describe this concept.)

There are several advances in software engineering technologies that have encouraged this interest in reuse. One of these is the increasing prominence of *object-oriented* design and development. Object-oriented methods encourage software engineers to design components around invariant objects—objects that have meaning outside the system and therefore might be usable by multiple systems. An example of such an object might be a personnel record. If a software component is designed to provide all the capabilities associated with a personnel record, all systems in the company that are concerned with personnel (e.g., payroll, insurance, retirement) can use that package. Another factor is the emergence of programming languages, for example Ada and Modula 2, that support principles of packaging and abstraction. These languages allow development of components with the cohesiveness and parameterization needed to make software more reusable.

These technological enablers, coupled with a growing need to control software costs, have made software reuse a major field of research and development. Its promises are great, but there are many open issues and challenges. This article summarizes many of the major ideas and developments in this growing field; several key areas are treated in more depth in other articles.

Terminology

The following are definitions of some of the basic terms used by researchers and practitioners in the reuse field. There is no single accepted definition for most of these terms; terminology in the field is still evolving. These definitions are from Braun (1992a).

Reuse—the use of an existing software component in a new context, either elsewhere in the same system or in another system.

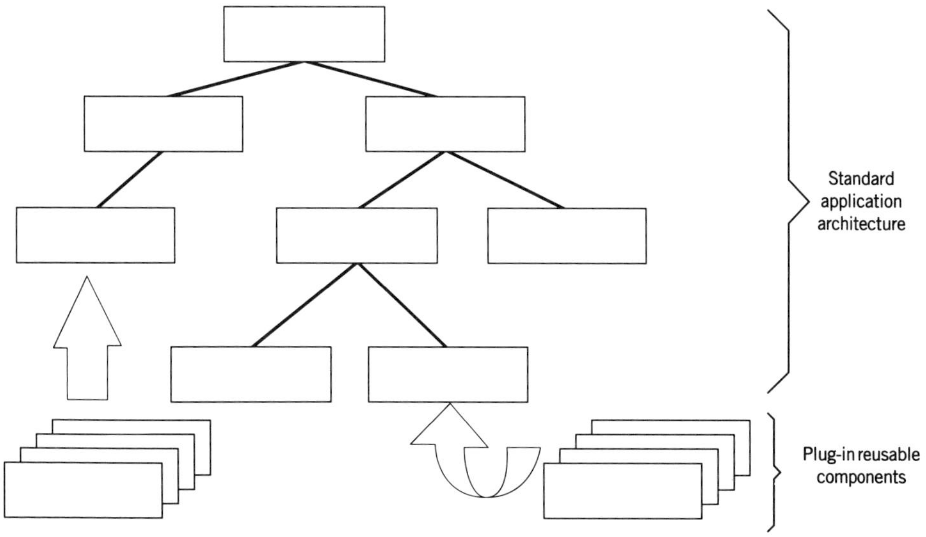

Figure 1. A software components industry, like the hardware industry today, will build software from plug-in reusable components based on a standard application architecture.

Reusability—the extent to which a software component is able to be reused. Conformance to certain design and coding standards increases a component's reusability.

Reusable software component—a software entity intended for reuse; may be design, code, or other product of the software development process. Reusable software components are sometimes called "software assets."

Reuser—an individual or organization that reuses a reusable software component.

Portability—the extent to which a software component originally developed on one computer and operating system can be used on another computer and/or operating system. A component's reusability potential is greater if it is easily portable.

Domain—a class of related software applications. Domains are sometimes described as "vertical"—addressing all levels of a single application area (e.g., personnel) and "horizontal"—addressing a particular kind of software processing (e.g., data structure manipulation) across applications. The potential for reuse is generally greater within a single domain.

Domain analysis—the analysis of a selected domain to identify common structures and functions, with the objective of increasing reuse opportunities.

Library—a collection of reusable software components, *together with* the procedures and support functions required to provide the components to users; may also be called a "reuse organization" or something similar (if "library" is used to refer only to an automated retrieval system).

Retrieval system—automated tool that supports classification and retrieval of reusable software components, also called a "repository" or "reuse library system."

Basic Concepts

Software reuse offers the very real potential of dramatically reducing software development and maintenance costs, while at the same time improving quality. Software reuse can be simply defined as "the use of a software component more than once." It can mean anything from informal reuse of an existing design to widespread use of a commercial software package. Some reuse researchers prefer a narrower definition (e.g., reuse of unchanged source code only), but a broad definition best allows for understanding and learning from past successes.

Reuse researchers generally classify approaches to reuse as either *compositional* or *generative.* Compositional approaches support the bottom-up development of systems from a library of available lower-level components. Much work has been devoted to classification and retrieval technology and to the development of *reuse library systems* (see REUSE LIBRARY) to support this process. Generative approaches are application area specific; they adopt a standard system structure (a *reference architecture* or *generic architecture*) and standard interfaces for the components. Their goal is to be able to *automatically* generate a new system from an appropriate specification of its parameters. (The Fourth Generation Languages used in business systems can be considered an example of generative reuse). Such systems can be immensely effective within particularly narrow application areas, but their scope is clearly limited. It is not realistic, at least with near-term technology, to imagine the completely automatic generation of most complex systems.

Many of today's reuse researchers and practitioners are exploring a combined approach; a frequently-used term for this is *domain-specific reuse.* A *domain* is simply an application area (e.g., insurance, personnel, avionics, network management). Domain-specific reuse takes advantage of the knowledge and experience of experts in the domain. Through the process of *domain analysis,* (see DOMAIN ANALYSIS ENGINEERING) this knowledge is used to define a standard software structure or *architecture* for systems in the domain. Reusable components that fit the architecture can then be identified and obtained. Application developers can then use the standard domain architecture as a starting point for system design, and can select reusable components that help build the system. Automated tools can help developers in this process.

Expected Benefits

The major and most obvious benefit of software reuse is improved productivity, resulting in cost savings. This productivity gain is not only in code development; costs are also saved in analysis, design, and testing phases. These cost savings allow businesses to price their products more attractively, leading to increased competitive advantage and market share, and to higher profits.

The benefits of reuse, in fact, go far beyond this:

- Reuse can lead to improved *quality, reliability,* and *performance.* As software components are used in systems, delivered and subjected to day-to-day use, they will evolve to a highly reliable state. This extensive use also means that effort can be invested in improving and optimizing the components.
- Reuse typically results in user-perceived *uniformity* among systems; for example, reusing the user interface software from a previous product when developing its replacement means that users will be able to transition to the new system much more easily.
- Reuse supports *interoperability*—the ability of two or more systems to work together. Both systems can use the same software components to implement key interfaces, assuring that these interfaces are implemented consistently.
- Reuse leads to greater *standardization.* System architectures will become more uniform, algorithms will become more consistent, and development processes will converge. Moving to more standard practice allows software engineers to become productive more quickly on a new project and provides a foundation for more effective quality management disciplines.
- Reuse supports *rapid prototyping*—putting together quick operational models of systems, typically, to get

customer or use feedback on the capability. A library of reusable components provides an extremely effective basis for quickly building application prototypes.

Reuse Inhibitors

If reuse is such an obviously good idea, why is it not more widely practiced? There are several reasons:

- Software cannot be reused unless it can be found. A programmer, tasked to implement a particular function, may feel sure someone in the company has written a program to do the same thing, but have no idea how to go about finding it.
- Even when a potentially reusable existing program can be found, it is usually not reusable as is. One programmer seldom writes the program just the way another programmer needs it. Modifying another person's program can quickly become more expensive than writing the program from scratch.
- The "not invented here" syndrome is an inhibitor. Programmers are creative people; they feel a pride of ownership in their own code. Using someone else's code can appear to be less satisfying. Managers are more comfortable when their project's success is fully under their own control. They often resist building in a dependency on an outside resource.
- Estimating projects that practice software reuse is even less well-understood than estimating traditional software projects.
- There are a number of legal and business issues that must be addressed, e.g., liabilities and data rights. In the government sector, there are additional issues concerning contracting practices that make reuse more difficult (see DATA RIGHTS).
- Reuse is still a research area. Many people have ideas for the best way(s) to institutionalize reuse; relatively few have any practical experience with their use. There is no consensus on what approaches work best, and no reason to assume that a single approach will be best for all application areas and all user groups.

Industry Examples

In spite of these challenges, a number of organizations have invested in establishing reuse programs and have demonstrated quantitative benefits:

- **Raytheon Missile Systems** recognized the redundancy in its business application systems and instituted a reuse program (Lanergan and Poynton, 1979). In an analysis of over 5000 production COBOL programs, three major classes were identified. Templates with standard architectures were designed for each class, and a library of parts developed by modifying existing modules to fit the architectures. Raytheon reports an average of 60% reuse and 50% net productivity increase in new developments.
- **NEC Software Engineering Laboratory** analyzed its business applications and identified 32 logic templates and 130 common algorithms (NEC, 1987). A reuse library was established to catalogue these templates and components. The library was automated and integrated into NEC's software development environment, which enforces reuse in all stages of development. NEC has reported a 6.7:1 productivity improvement and 2.8:1 quality improvement.
- **Fujitsu** analyzed its existing electronic switching systems and catalogued potential reusable parts in its Information Support Center—a library staffed with domain experts, software engineers, and reuse experts (Fujitsu, 1987). Use of the library has been compulsory; library staff members have been included in all design reviews. With this approach, Fujitsu has experienced an improvement from 20% of projects on schedule to 70% on schedule in electronic switching systems development
- **GTE Data Services** has established a corporate-wide reuse program. Its activities include identification of reusable assets and development of new assets, cataloguing of these assets in an automated library, asset maintenance, reuser support, and a management support group (Swanson and Curry, 1987). GTE reports first year reuse of 14% and savings of $1.5 million, and projected figures of 50% reuse and $10 million savings, in telephone management software development
- **SofTech, Inc.** employs a generic architecture approach in building Ada compiler products (SofTech, 1987). Compilers for new host and target systems can be developed by replacing only selected modules from the standard architecture. This approach has led to a productivity level of 50K lines of code per person-year (10–20 times the industry average). This productivity is typical of compiler developers, as this is a field in which reuse is accepted practice.
- **Universal Defence Systems (UDS),** in Perth, Australia, develops Ada command and control applications (Universal Defence Systems, 1991). The company began its work in this business with a reuse focus, and has developed a company-owned library of 396 Ada modules comprising 400–500 thousand LOC. With this base, UDS developed the Australian Maritime Intelligent Support Terminal with approximately 60% reuse, delivering a 700 thousand LOC system in 18 months. A recently begun new project anticipates 50% to 70% reuse based on the company's asset library.
- **Celsius Technology** in Sweden had a requirement to develop command, control, and communications systems for five ship classes (Rational, 1992). As each ship class is specific to a different country, there are significantly different requirements for each. In order to benefit from reuse, Celsius developed a single generic architecture and a set of large-scale reusable parts to fit that architecture. Because of a well-structured design, internal reuse, and a transition to Ada and modern CASE tools, Celsius experienced a productivity improvement even in building the first ship—from 1.3 lines of code (LOC) per hour previously to 3.28 LOC per hour. Improvements are much greater

for subsequent ships, with a projected productivity of 10.93 LOC per hour for the fifth ship, which is expected to obtain 65% of its code from reuse.

All of these efforts have achieved demonstrable benefits in software productivity and quality.

REUSE LIBRARIES

Component Classification

Much redundant software is written in the industry. Designers and programmers constantly find themselves writing functions they or their colleagues have written before. However, finding and retrieving such "software artifacts" is usually prohibitively difficult. A well-organized programmer *may* be able to find software that he wrote; hardly anyone can find software that other people wrote. They probably do not even refer to the function by the same name. The problem is analogous to trying to find a book in a cluttered junkyard rather than in an organized library. The answer to this problem is *component classification,* not unlike classification methods used by libraries. Collections of reusable software components are usually organized according to some *classification scheme.* (Collections without such classification are often called "software junkyards").

One approach to classification is a *hierarchical* scheme, analogous to the Library of Congress system. A set number of top-level categories is established; these are divided into sub-categories and sub-subcategories as appropriate. Such a scheme can be effective for classifying software, and some early reuse collections use such an approach, although this approach has shortcomings. For instance, it is somewhat inflexible and all categories must be identified initially; new topics can be added only at the lower level. Thus, in libraries books on new technology areas are often classified low in the hierarchy under a category that is only slightly appropriate. Card catalogs must provide extensive cross-referencing to make retrieval possible. Another difficulty is descriptive ambiguity. Does a book on medical computer systems belong under computers or under medicine? These shortcomings have led researchers to seek an alternative.

A commonly used alternative today in the reuse community is *faceted classification* (Prieto-Díaz and Freeman, 1987b). A *faceted classification* scheme consists of a set number of *facets* that can be used to describe the various characteristics of a software component. A set of facets might be, for example, *application area, function, object, programming language,* and *operating system.* A component is then classified by a specific descriptor, or *term,* for each relevant facet. For example, a component might be described by:

application area	=	billing systems
function	=	search
object	=	subscriber name
programming language	=	COBOL

Someone looking for a component could specify these exact term values and be directed to this component (and any others with all the same descriptors). Someone looking for a COBOL program to search for the subscriber name in an insurance system might not find any components with "*application area*=insurance," but might be directed to this component as a near match.

Component Retrieval Systems

Component retrieval systems (also called *library systems, software repositories,* etc.) are automated systems that search for components in response to a user's specification. They implement a classification scheme such as that described above. A retrieval system supports software librarians—the individuals who catalog software components and may be responsible for their maintenance—as well as designers and programmers.

Many additional capabilities can be offered:

- A *thesaurus,* or synonym list, can be used to help bridge the terminology gap. For example, "lookup" could be listed as a synonym for "search", so the individual who asks for a "lookup" component would be directed to a component classified as a "search".
- *Conceptual closeness* mechanisms allow the system to record knowledge about facet values that, while not synonymous, may be similar. For example, "sort" may be considered close to "search," because both operate on ordered lists. If no "sort" component is found, the user may be directed to "search."
- The system can record information about user's experiences, e.g., unfilled requests. If the librarian notices that many people are asking for a "sort" and not finding one, he or she can take steps to have one added to the library.
- The system can provide additional information about components to help the user make his choice. This information might include descriptive abstracts, metrics about the software, and recorded information about usage experiences by users who have previously "checked out" the component.
- The system can collect metrics about the use of the library, for example on frequency of particular kinds of requests and on usage of each component.
- The system can provide configuration management for the components–version management, archiving, etc.

Figure 2 is an example screen from a component retrieval system (Braun, 1992b).

There are a number of retrieval systems in development or in use today. One of the earliest was a system developed by GTE Data Services (Swanson and Carry, 1987), which implements a faceted scheme for classifying Management Information Systems (MIS) software. The U.S. Army has developed the Reusable Ada Products for Information Systems Development (RAPID) system for classifying reusable Ada components (Guerrieri, 1988). This system, which also employs a faceted scheme, has been adopted by the U.S. Department of Defense (DoD) Corporate Information Management (CIM) program, as the foundation for the Defense

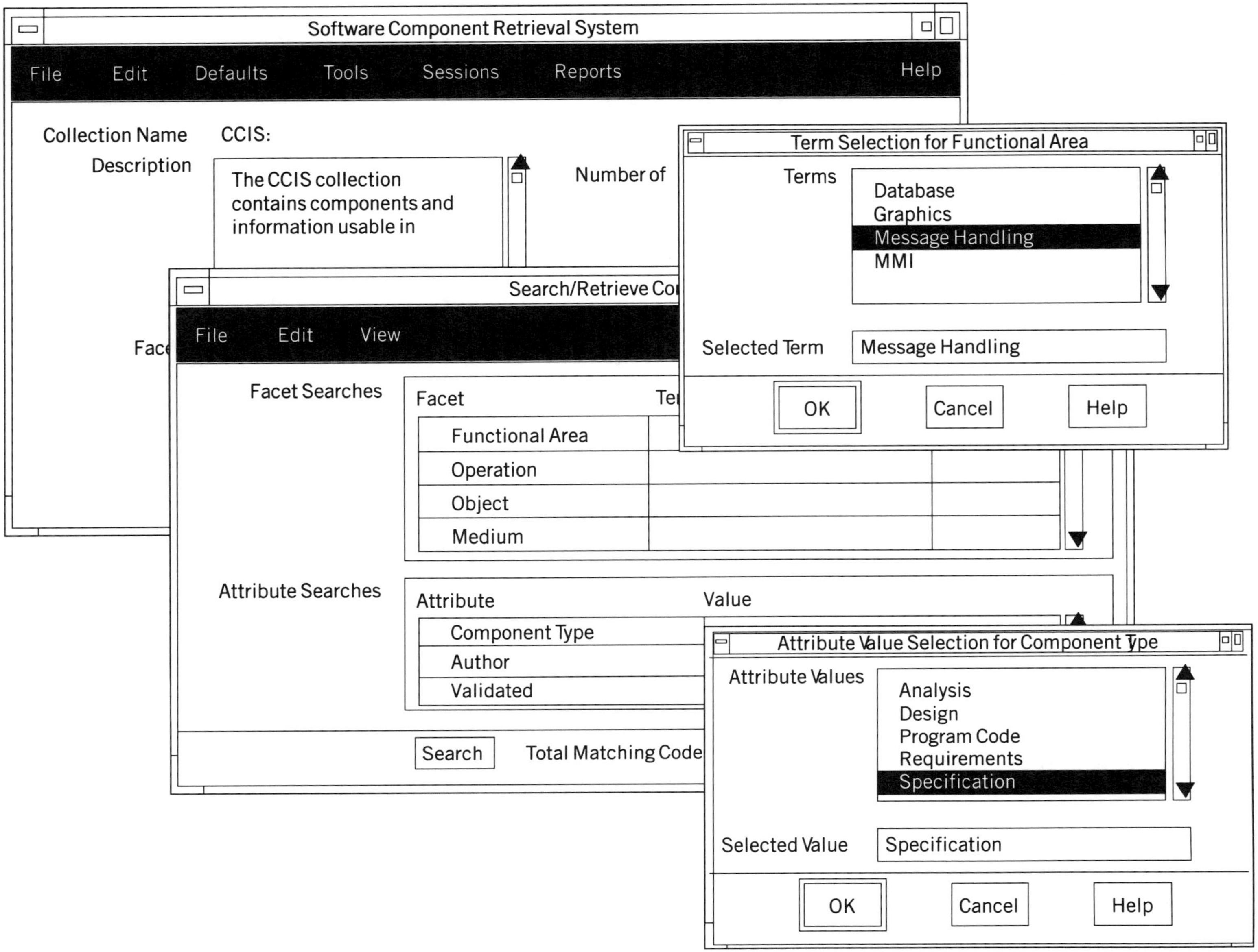

Figure 2. A component retrieval system allows a user to search a software component collection for reusable components that meet his/her criteria.

Software Repository System (DSRS). Systems that employ other classification methods include the Common Ada Missile Packages (CAMP) system (McNichol, 1985), a knowledge-based system developed by the U.S. Air Force; and the Reusable Ada Avionics Software Packages (RAASP) system (Westinghouse, 1992), a hypertext-based system also developed by the Air Force. Library systems are also beginning to be commercially available. T. Ruegsegger (1992) contains many helpful suggestions for establishing a software reuse library within an organization.

Public Libraries

Just as books are available at no cost at public libraries, there are beginning to be public sources of software components. (Of course, the software is copied rather than borrowed; it does not have to be returned like books do).

One source of potentially reusable software is "shareware"—software available free on communications networks. This is software to be used at one's own risk, and is typically not crafted to be particularly reusable. However, useful programs may be found.

There are increasing numbers of small components available for a nominal purchase price, often in conjunction with published books (which may include the software on a disk or provide a mailing address to obtain it). These components are usually collections of lower-level, frequently-performed functions such as mathematics routines or data structure manipulation routines. Collections of object packages implemented in object-oriented languages such as C++ and Objective C are also beginning to be available.

The U. S. government has purchased a great deal of software from contractors over the past few decades, most of which is in the public domain. While much of this software is difficult to find, some is beginning to be available in government-administered libraries, including the Defense Software Repository System (DISA/CIM, 1992), the Central Archives for the Reuse of Defense Software (Wallnau, 1992), and the Asset Source for Software Engineering Technology (Garr, 1992). These libraries vary in the extent to which software in them is crafted for reuse, vs. simply extracted from delivered systems.

DOMAIN-SPECIFIC REUSE

Domain Architectures

Reuse is an attractive concept, but efforts to increase reuse by providing large parts libraries like those noted above have been disappointing in their payback. In many cases, components that appear reusable simply do not quite fit the need. Further, the components are usually small; using them does almost nothing to decrease design complexity and results in only limited reduction in coding effort. Researchers have begun seeking a higher-payoff approach, looking for guidance at instances where reuse *has* been effective.

There is much real, effective reuse in practice today. Significant reuse (with significant savings) occurs:

- Every time a real-time system is built on top of an existing operating system
- Every time an information management system includes a Commercial-off-the-Shelf (COTS) Database Management System (DBMS)
- Every time a product vendor creates a new version of his product from parts of the old system
- Every time a compiler builder "retargets" a compiler rather than building a new one from scratch
- Every time a system designer draws on design knowledge from a previous similar system

What makes these cases of reuse successful? How can researchers learn from these successes and extend these benefits? Consider what they have in common. First, *each focuses on a particular application domain.* Each case reuses large entities that perform domain-specific functions. Second, *each case makes assumptions about the system architecture.* Systems can only make use of COTS operating systems, DBMSs, etc., if they are structured according to the model implemented by the COTS product. Product vendors must keep major architectures intact to allow reuse of existing parts when making product upgrades. Compiler front-ends are reused because the overall compiler architecture is the same from one compiler to the next. Design is constrained to fit these architectural assumptions. Finally, *each case is dependent on properly generalized and well-defined standard interfaces.* Many systems can use the same operating system or DBMS because the interfaces of these products are designed to accommodate a variety of needs and are well-understood and well-documented. Standard interfaces between compiler front-ends and back-ends allow reuse of these major components. Reuse researchers believe that these successes can be extended by following the same model—focusing on specific domains, developing standard (reference) architectures to direct and constrain designs toward the use of common components, and specifying standard interfaces to make reuse of these components possible. Such domain-specific, architecture-based approaches appear to have major promise for increasing the leverage obtainable through reuse. Figure 3 illustrates such an approach.

Domain Analysis

Domain-specific, architecture-based reuse programs depend on an in-depth understanding of the application domain. Domain analysis (Prieto-Díaz, 1987a) is the process of analyzing an application domain to discover the information necessary to support reuse. Specific outputs of the domain analysis activity are

- Identification of the *objects, operations,* and *relationships* that characterize applications in the domain
- Identification of *common* objects, operations, and relationships that are likely to occur in more than one application system within the domain (and are thus candidates for reusable entities)
- Identification of areas of variation in systems in the domain

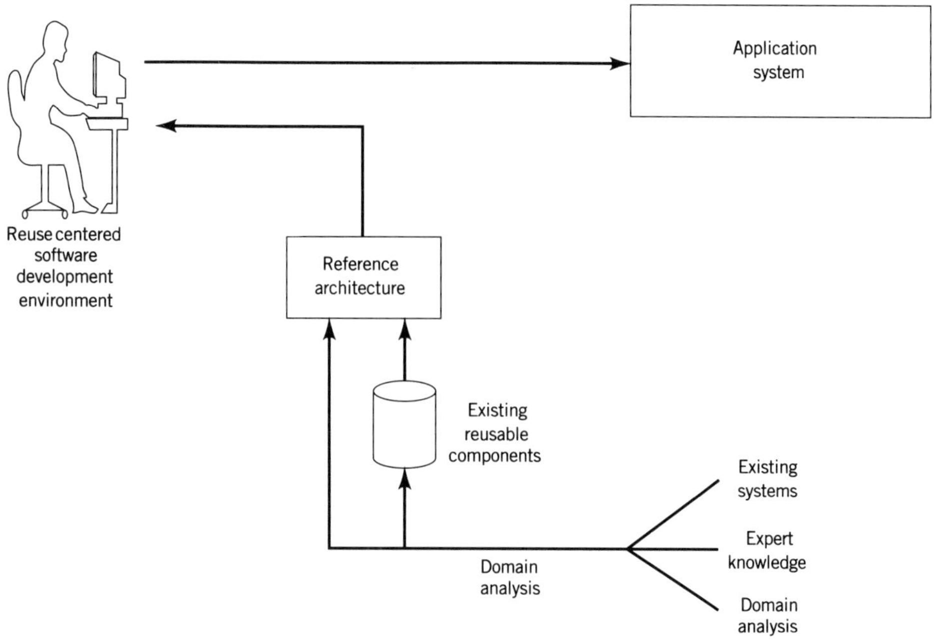

Figure 3. By using a reference architecture and a library of components that fit that architecture, an application developer can quickly construct applications that take advantage of existing software and of the understanding of experts in the domain.

- A common *vocabulary* for describing these objects, operations, and relationships (which forms the basis for the classification scheme)
- A *domain requirements model* that captures this common behavior
- A *reference architecture,* or common design framework that, at some level of abstraction, is applicable to all applications in the domain

Domain analysis—ways to do it effectively and how to best represent and use its results—is a major research area in the reuse field. In general, domain analysis is carried out by studying several representative systems within the domain and developing an initial view of the structure and functionality of each. The results of this analysis are expressed graphically using a selected analysis/top-level design notation (or perhaps combinations of notations). While no one approach is standard, the Structured Analysis and Design Technique (SADT) (Marca and McGowan, 1988), a graphical modeling technique, is widely used. Other modeling methods, for example Ascent Logic's RDD-100 (Ascent Logic Corporation, 1991), are also used. *Object-oriented* methods are increasing popular, as they promise to lead to a flexible, modular reference architecture.

Once representative systems are understood, commonality and variability analysis is performed. This analysis requires that the analyst be familiar enough with the domain to recognize functional commonality that is hidden behind variations in vocabulary and in selected solution. He or she must also understand ways to build generality into software through generalization/parameterization, so that common function is not obscured by differences in data. While there is little automated support available today for domain analysis (apart from tools supporting general requirements analysis notations), commonality analysis seems to be an area for which such tools could be useful. A domain requirements model is then built. This is, in essence, a common problem-space view of the domain; it describes the objects and functions of the domain, and their interrelationships.

Finally, the analyst must synthesize the understanding gained by analyzing the representative systems to develop the reference architecture—a design framework that applies to all systems in the domain, with well-understood interfaces between the design entities. Both the process for carrying out this synthesis and the way to best represent the result are open research issues. Currently, much individual skill and judgment are involved.

The domain analysis process is heavily dependent on domain experts—individuals who actually design systems in the application domain. Domain experts are a key source of information when initially analyzing representative applications and serve as reviewers of each step in the process. This involvement from the application side is critical to developing a reuse capability that is really usable by system developers.

An Approach to Domain-Specific Reuse

One of the major research programs currently investigating approaches to domain-specific reuse is the Advanced Research Project Agency (ARPA) Domain Specific Software Architectures (DSSA) program (Mettala and Graham, 1992). In this program, several domain teams are developing and demonstrating approaches to domain-specific reuse in their assigned domain. The tasks of each team include (a) modeling the assigned domain and developing a reference architecture, (b) defining a software development process that incorporates the concepts of domain-specific, architecture-based development, (c) constructing a tool set that supports this process, and (d) using these results in a demonstration development project.

DSSA is based on the concept of an accepted reference software architecture for the target domain. As defined by DSSA, a software architecture describes the topology of software components, specifies the component interfaces, and identifies computational models associated with those components. The architecture must apply to a wide range of systems in the chosen domain; thus it must be general and flexible. It must be established with the consensus of practitioners in the domain. Once an architecture is established, components that conform to the architecture—i.e., that implement elements of its functionality in conformance with its interfaces—will be acquired. They may be acquired by identifying and modifying (if required) existing components or by specifically creating them.

The existence of a domain-specific architecture and conformant component base will dictate a significantly different approach to software application development. The developer will not wait until detailed design or implementation to search for reuse opportunities; instead, he will be driven by the architecture throughout. The architecture and component base will help define requirements and allow construction of rapid prototypes. Design will use the architecture as a starting point. Design and development tools will be automated to "walk through" the architecture and assist the developer in the selection of appropriate components. The ultimate goal is to significantly automate the generation of applications.

Fundamental to the DSSA capability is the development of a reference architecture. This process starts with development of a multi-viewpoint domain model, created through interaction with domain experts. DSSA researchers are typically using a combination of modeling methods; for example, the Command and Control domain team (Braun and Alexander, 1993b) is using $IDEF_0$ (SofTech, 1981) for function modeling, RDD-100 (Ascent Logic Corporation, 1991) for dynamic modeling, and Object Modeling Technique (Rumbaugh and co-workers, 1991) for object modeling. From this set of models, an object-oriented software architecture is developed. The architecture ties back to the multi-viewpoint model so that mappings to different views of the domain functional decomposition are apparent. A base of components conforming to the architecture is then developed. Many of these will be existing components, perhaps modified to fit the architecture. Others might be automatically generated using application generator technology.

Figure 4 is a top-level view of the DSSA development process (Braun and co-workers, 1993a). It identifies the major four phases of the DSSA life cycle. These phases are briefly described in the following paragraphs:

Establish Domain-Specific Base. This is the set of activities performed by the person responsible for the overall domain—the "domain owner"—to establish a DSSA capability base for the domain. The domain is analyzed and a domain-specific software architecture (reference architecture) and development environment are provided.

The domain analysis must also look at future expansion and enhancement within the domain. As systems are developed using the domain architecture, information will be fed back to the domain owner. This information will be used to maintain and evolve the architecture.

The major products of this phase are the domain reference requirements model and reference architecture. The domain model is essentially a problem-space view—a representation of what systems in the domain actually do, and of the objects involved. The reference architecture is a mapping of that model to a solution-space view—a representation in terms of implementation entities (e.g., software modules).

Populate and Maintain Library. This is the set of activities that create and administer the collection of reusable components that implement the architecture. Components meeting the component class specifications in the reference architecture are collected, modified, and/or developed.

Components will be cataloged in a reuse library for access by developers building applications. The particular reuse library to be used can be selected by the organization carrying out the DSSA process. Ideally it will be a library that can maintain a close working relationship with the domain owner, so that its population can be enhanced and updated continuously as the domain architecture is improved and refined.

Build Applications. This is the set of activities required to build a specific application using the DSSA library and the domain-specific development environment. The DSSA environment will provide comprehensive support for this phase, partially automating each activity and supporting requirements traceability, prototyping, evaluation, and testing. Application development begins by expressing the application system requirements in terms of the domain reference requirements model, for example:

- Parameterized requirements, e.g., performance measures, are supplied with target system values
- Selections among alternative capabilities are made
- Unneeded capabilities are eliminated
- Additional detail is supplied as needed

The DSSA tools will support this requirements elicitation process, interacting with the designer to create the target system requirements. Rapid prototyping can easily and naturally be used to help clarify requirement distinctions.

The reference architecture is then instantiated and particulatized to establish a design architecture for the target system. This process is guided by the mapping from the domain reference requirements to the target system requirements, and in fact occurs concurrently with that activity. As each requirement is specialized for the target system, the corresponding element of the reference architecture is adapted to become a part of the target system architecture. Design components in the DSSA library are extracted to build the design.

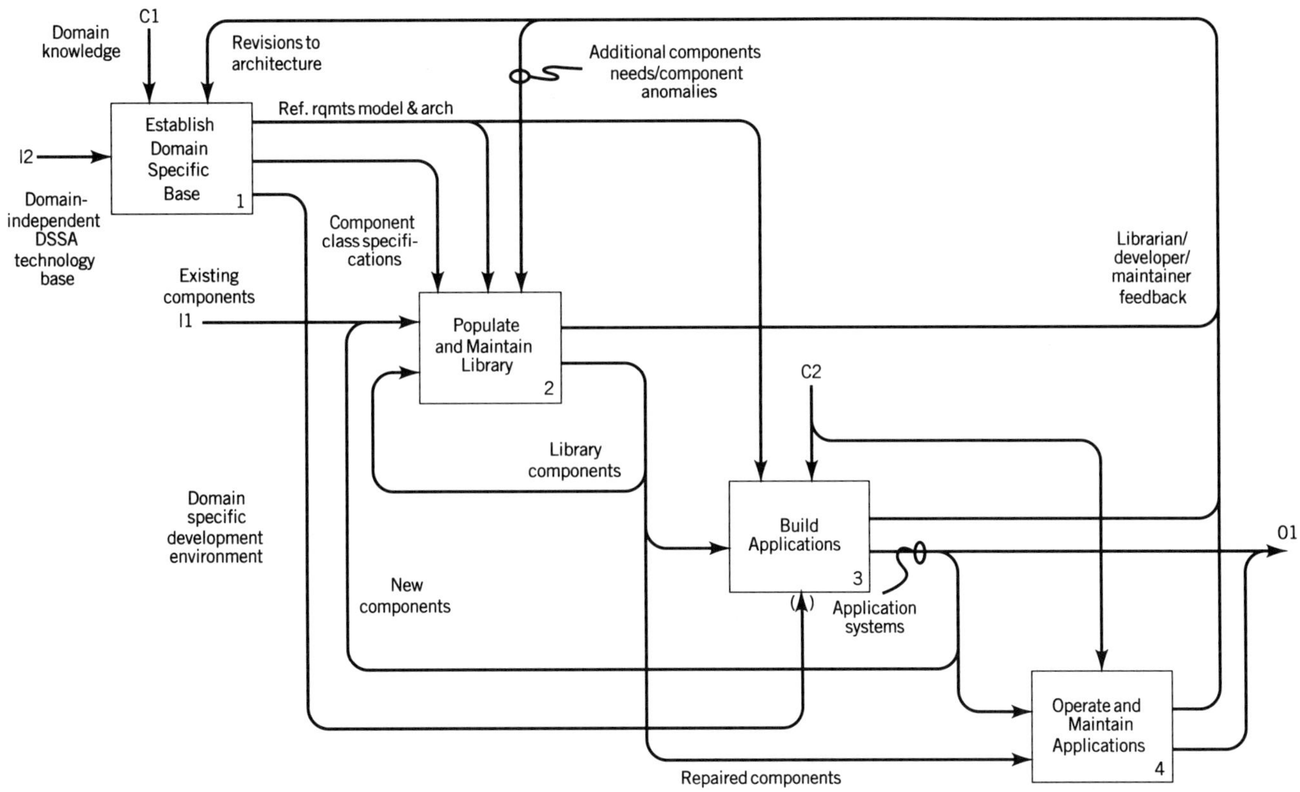

Figure 4. Domain-specific software development requires a new view of the software life-cycle, recognizing the roles of the domain owner and the software library.

Creation of the application system implementation (the actual code) follows naturally and automatically from the preceding steps. As each design element is chosen, a corresponding library code component is identified. Where the developer must provide adaptation or "glue" software to connect these components, DSSA tools identify this need and provide the needed interface specifications. If the toolset provides a component generator for the particular component class, the developer is automatically guided to its user interface, and it is designed to generate only components that conform to the architecture. When no library component meeting the application needs is available, the developer is provided with a specification from which to build one. Any such components developed when building applications can be placed in the reuse library for use by future developments.

At any step in the development process, any deficiencies or needed improvements in the domain model, architecture, or components are fed back to the responsible organizations (the domain owner or the library manager).

Operate and Maintain Applications. Once built, the application system is operated in the field and maintained by the maintenance center. As part of its normal operation, the effectiveness of the system is assessed against the needs of its continually changing mission. Needed changes and corrections are identified and reported to the maintenance center.

The maintenance center responds to all requests from users for changes or corrections to the system. This is their traditional role; however, the DSSA approach requires a much different strategy to system maintenance than when systems are built independently. An enhancement or correction may affect documentation, system requirements, library components, and eventually reference requirements and architecture. Some of these types of components may not be under maintenance control of the maintenance center. For example, library components may be maintained by the library organization, and the reference requirements and architecture may be maintained by the domain owner. Further, changes to these entities will potentially impact more than the one application system that requested the change. A close working relationship between the domain owner and the maintenance center is critical to the success of this activity.

Systems developed and in maintenance before the institution of DSSA practices will be one of the primary sources of domain knowledge and of components to populate the domain library. Components submitted to the domain library will undergo additional testing and could then be reinserted into the original system, increasing its reliability. The domain architecture can also be used to guide the evolution of pre-DSSA systems. Modifications and enhancements would be made with the domain architecture in mind and with new functionality implemented using components from the domain library.

New systems developed using DSSA techniques will be easier to maintain. Enhancements will be made at the domain library and the modified components can be rolled into the system before problems occur. The domain library will also be a source of components to implement new functionality as the system evolves and changes.

The DSSA process is described more fully in Armitage (1992).

DESIGNING AND IMPLEMENTING FOR REUSE

Preceding sections have dealt primarily with ways of encouraging the use of existing software. However, much existing software has little or no reuse value. Is reusable software different than other software? What software should be made reusable, and how is that done? The answers must address design, coding, and documentation considerations. A number of guidelines have been published for making software reusable (Braun and co-workers, 1985; The Software Productivity Consortium, 1989; Gautier and co-workers, 1990; SofTech, 1990; Braun, 1992a). The following subsections highlight some of the key issues addressed in these guidelines.

Design Considerations

Reusability is primarily a design issue. If a system is not designed with reusability in mind, component interrelationships will be such that reusability cannot be attained, no matter how rigorously coding or documentation rules are followed. A component with reuse potential is one that can be readily "extracted" from its surrounding application and "inserted" in another one. This means it must perform a single complete, *cohesive* function, and that its *coupling* to its surrounding application is minimal and well-defined. Accepted structured design principles—modular design, parameterization for change, low coupling and high cohesion—all support the design of reusable software.

The principle of *abstraction* also supports reusability. By recognizing that several apparently dissimilar functions are actually the same function with easily parameterized differences—by abstracting back to the underlying function—the software can be designed so that it can be reused to implement all functions in the class.

Interface standardization is another important consideration. The interfaces of a software component define the role of that component with respect to the "outside world." A component is specified by its interfaces. For the potential reuser of the component, the interface definition is a basis for determining whether reuse is possible and a guide for using it if it is. This view is analogous to considering a hardware chip to be specified by its pin connections and the functional descriptions of their roles. Often a reusable component's interfaces must be modified to fit into a new application; interface standardization makes the component reusable as is. In the absence of standardization, interfaces should be well-defined and documented to support such modification.

Another key concept in reuse is that of using an object-oriented design approach to build components around invariant objects. Basically, object-oriented design means that a system's design is expressed in terms of objects and the set of operations that can be performed on them. Each object and its operations are grouped into a single package. Any system that needs to deal with that object can then incorporate that package. An excellent example of such an object is a communications interface standard (e.g., X.25, TCP/IP). Packages that implement such interfaces have great reuse potential; they can potentially be reused by any application that needs to support the particular interface.

Software reuse is much simpler when systems are designed using a standard architecture model, as described in the earlier discussion of reference architectures. An example is the International Organization for Standards (ISO) Open Systems Interconnect (OSI) seven-layer model for communications systems. Such a model establishes a framework for expressing the needs of a planned system and the capabilities of existing software, and so increases the probability of matching needs and capabilities. It establishes a common vocabulary for describing functions and a basis for defining standard interfaces.

Coding Considerations

Many of the principles for coding reusable software are the same as the principles for coding "good" software. Reusable software should be modular and easy to understand, because it must be understandable to the reuser. The reuser will frequently have to modify the software, so it should conform to accepted "maintainability " standards.

An organization that intends to practice reuse should establish an organization-wide set of coding standards—standards for formatting, naming, in-line documentation, etc. This procedure supports the understandability of software across individual projects and reduces problems that can result when reusing software from one project in another one. If a programmer must rewrite much of the code to conform to his/her own project's coding standards, the programmer may not consider it worth reusing.

Naming conventions deserve particular mention. Depending on the programming language used, a reusable component can allocate and name data objects in such a way as to cause name space conflicts in the reusing system. Guidelines on the use of non-local names should be established.

Documentation

Good documentation is essential to software reusability. The software engineer seeking to reuse a software component has several needs not adequately met by "standard" software documentation:

- Identification—documentation should help identify components for potential reuse
- Functional Understanding—a clear, concise initial statement of the component's function aids initial selection; a full description is necessary for eventual use
- Resource Requirements—the potential reuser requires information on use of system resources such as memory, processor, and communications channels
- Limitations—any restrictions on use of the component—capacities, operating system dependencies, etc., must be made explicit

- Installation—documentation must explain how to adapt the component to a new application—how to modify interfaces, tailor functionality, select parameters
- Operation—use of the component's functions must be described in a form suitable for the developer and for incorporation in the new system's user documentation
- Support—documentation should provide a point of contact from which to get help, if needed, in adapting the component

To maximize the likelihood of reuse of a software component, such information must be included in its documentation or provided separately, perhaps online in a library system.

BUSINESS CONSIDERATIONS

There are many technical challenges in achieving software reuse, but there are perhaps even more non-technical challenges (Syms and Braun, 1991). Software reuse will require fundamental changes in business and contractual practices, organizational procedures, and the day-today activities of software engineers. Organizations naturally resist change; overcoming this resistance is a major consideration in moving toward an increased practice of reuse. The following subsections briefly identify some of the key management issues that impact reuse, and note possible approaches to resolving them.

Contractual Issues

When software is developed under contract, many issues arise concerning ownership of and rights to the developed software. Ordinarily, both the purchaser and the developer have some rights to the software, though the specific assignment of these rights should be delineated in the contract. When the purchaser pays for the full cost of software development, he or she typically expects to receive full rights to the software, including the right to resell it to others. If the purchaser is the government, the software, because it is paid for by taxpayers, is often placed in the public domain, and is thus made available to anyone who will pay a nominal reproduction cost. The developer typically retains some rights himself, for example to use the work to create other products. Normally, specific rights are delineated in the contract.

This model becomes more complicated in a reuse situation. If the developer wishes to build and take advantage of a library of reusable assets, he/she faces some questions. If he wishes to stock his library with components built on a government contract, what guarantee does the developer have that those same components will not be made available to the competitors, either directly by the purchaser or through the public domain? If he/she wishes to perform the contract using software that he/she already owns, must he/she abandon his/her rights to it when delivering it to the purchaser? The typical contracting model will answer both these questions to the developer's disadvantage, providing a disincentive to reuse.

Similarly, the purchaser who wishes to practice reuse also has concerns. If he/she wishes to obtain software that can be reused on other projects, how does he/she ensure that the software will in fact be reusable? Will it be adequately documented and comprehensible? Who should bear the responsibility if the software does not meet expectations? How will he/she arrange for its maintenance? The typical contracting model does not adequately address these concerns. In fact, it might be considered to provide an incentive to the developer to deliver software that *cannot* be easily reused.

However, the typical model is not the only possible one. Contract law (though it differs from country to country) is generally flexible enough to allow a contract that meets both parties' needs. However, both parties must be aware of the issues and explicitly address them. When issues are addressed up front, a satisfactory contract can usually be written (Joint Integrated Avionics Working Group, 1990; Steadman, 1988). While each case will differ, some of the options that might be considered are

- The developer who wishes to restrict the purchaser's right to distribute his/her software might negotiate a significantly reduced software development cost in return.
- The purchaser who wishes to reuse software that he already owns in a delivered system might restrict rights to only those components. (This is similar to a situation that arises frequently today, in which a delivered system includes a commercially-available software product such as an operating system or DBMS.)
- To address liability and maintenance issues, and to provide an incentive to the developer to deliver software that can be reused, the purchaser might arrange a continuing support contract of some kind. One possibility is to pay the developer a license fee for each "reuser" of the software, in return for support and maintenance.

Legal Issues

In addition to contract issues, a number of other legal considerations can impact the practice of software reuse. These considerations are significant not only in contract software development, but in the software products world at large. Software is protected legally as *intellectual property;* as such, a number of laws control its dissemination and use (Sookman, 1989). While these laws differ from country to country, in general there are three basic types of protection afforded to software—*trade secret* protection, *copyright* protection, and *patent* protection. A variety of rules and precedents determine whether a particular software entity can be protected in any one of these ways, and all have been the subject of court battles. In general, the most common form of protection for software is copyright protection.

Most commercial software products are protected by copyright. Developers of software under contract also often claim a software copyright, explicitly assigning a number of rights to the customer. Among the restricted rights usually held by the copyright owner are: the right to reproduce the software; the right to reuse the software; the right to maintain and adapt the software; the right to reverse engineer the software; the right to make backup copies of the software; and the right to authorize third parties to perform any of these restricted acts. This means that only the copyright holder and those to whom he/she specifically assigns such rights can perform any of these activities. (The particulars vary from country to country. For example, U.S. law permits a software purchaser to make a single backup copy, which must be destroyed if he/she ceases to be the owner of the software).

In writing contracts involving the reuse of software, it is important that both parties be aware of the legal implications of copyright law. Holding the copyright is often in the best interests of the developer. It limits the rights of the purchaser, but often the assigned rights can be defined so that the purchaser can in fact accomplish all of his objectives, while at the same time allowing the developer to retain some rights and thus providing more incentive for reuse. In this case, the purchaser must recognize his needs and negotiate for them.

When the developer uses software he/she already owns in performing a development contract, he/she is particularly likely to protect that software by copyright. In this case, the purchaser can usually negotiate the rights necessary to use the software as required. If he/she wishes to obtain full ownership of the delivered product, and the right to distribute it freely, he/she might be asked to pay for these rights, since he/she has not paid for development of the reused software.

Responsibilities and Liabilities

The increased practice of reuse introduces a number of interesting new problems concerning responsibilities and liabilities. When a developer considers reusing software developed by another organization or company, he/she will (or should) have a number of questions. Who guarantees the software will work? If it does not work, who will fix it? If the delivered system (with the reused software in it) malfunctions and causes harm, and the reused software was at fault, who is liable?

Today's usual model is "reuse at your own risk." The developer who decides to reuse software assumes full responsibility to his customer for the quality of the product he builds. This means he/she will want to test the reused software carefully along with software he develops. If he has paid for the software, he should have recourse to the original developer if a problem occurs. (Of course, support and liability issues should be addressed in the purchase agreement). If the reused software is "free" software from a public domain source, the developer typically has no recourse if the software does not work or causes a malfunction.

Sometimes a purchaser (for example, the government) directs a developer to reuse software that the purchaser supplies. Usually the purchaser assumes this arrangement will reduce cost and perhaps development time. However, unless he/she guarantees the software and accepts any consequences of its failure to perform as advertised, he/she must expect the developer to include in the price and schedule some allowance for such failure.

Cost/Economic Issues

As noted earlier, most people in the reuse field believe that reusable software is most useful when it is explicitly crafted for reuse by applying particular design, coding, and documentation standards. This is often more than simply good quality software; extra generality and flexibility are usually built into the design. This is in effect an additional requirement placed on the software developer, and it usually adds to the cost of development. Who pays this added cost?

The ideal answer to this question is that he/she who profits from reuse (since it presumably leads to reduced costs) should pay. However, this is not always what happens. A developer might be asked to make the software reusable with little recognition of the added cost required, so that he/she earns a lower profit. He/she may then be "rewarded" for this work by having his/her software given to a competitor to be reused, thus letting the competitor profit from the efforts. In an alternative worst case, the purchaser might pay an added cost for highly reusable software without realizing it, because the developer wants to reuse the software in future programs (and thus charges the purchaser for the added generality).

Even within a company there are such problems, because most budgets belong to particular projects or business groups. The project that originally develops a reusable component seldom has the opportunity to profit from its reuse; that opportunity comes to future projects. Why should the first project invest extra funds to make the component more reusable?

Generally, the best approach to such issues is to identify some point in the organization that is high enough up to have budget responsibility for both the developing activity and the reusing activities—the level that both pays and profits (Barnes and Bollinger, 1991). This level should pay any added costs required to make software reusable. (Ideally, the reuse program is managed at this level, so that this investment can be planned and tracked meaningfully).

Managing for Reuse

Reuse must be addressed when planning and defining the requirements for a software development effort. The anticipated development of software for reuse, or reuse of existing software, must be made explicit. Means of determining that these requirements are met must be established.

When a developer is expected to develop software that is reusable, there must be some definition of "reusable". A common way to do this is to specify standards or guidelines that, when followed, produce reusable software. (As noted earlier, several possible standards documents have been published; they might be tailored to project use). When software is developed under contract, the purchaser might have a set of such standards/guidelines that are referenced in the contract. Alteratively, the purchaser might ask the developer to document and then demonstrate compliance with his own standards. Within an organization, such standards should be common across all groups intending to reuse another group's software.

An alternative approach is to define "reusable software" as simply "software that is reused." Rather than relying on any standards or guidelines, the developer is considered to have delivered reusable software when it is reused successfully. This is hard to enforce as a contractual requirement as there is ample opportunity for the developer to blame the reuser. However, it may be a practical approach within a company, for example as a basis for an incentive program.

Similarly, program management practices must address the reuse of existing software. For example, it is usually not realistic to demand that reused software conform to all program standards, particularly in such details as coding style. If reused software must be reformatted and redocumented to meet a new standard, most of the cost saving may be lost. If a developer proposes to reuse software on a contract with established standards, it is ordinarily the responsibility of the developer to demonstrate to the customer that the software, documentation, etc., are sufficient. Customer flexibility regarding the use of a particular set of documentation standards can save significant cost. As long as documentation for reused components meets the customer's usability requirements, it is far more cost effective not to redo it to another standard. This may require a contractual modification, as the documentation standard is normally specified in the contract.

Another issue is the testing of reused software. Clearly, the software should be subjected to integration and system testing, but unit testing may not be required. This judgment is very situational and is based on the developer's familiarity with and confidence in the reused software.

SETTING UP A REUSE PROGRAM

How can an organization achieve the benefits of reuse? While the benefits seem apparent, the transition is not trivial and takes changes in priority, in investment, and in work practice. While some benefits can be realized even from a relatively casual approach, a focused plan of attack is necessary to achieve maximum payoff.

The following steps describe a rough overall approach to adding the practice of reuse to an organization:

- Understand the potential benefits of software reuse.
- Analyze the potential payoff and potential cost to the organization.
- Identify an initial reuse "experiment"—a first application of the practice—along with measurements and success criteria.
- Develop the needed resources.
- Carry out the experiment.
- Evaluate the results.
- Extend the practice.

The following subsections discuss the roles of corporate managers, business area managers, and project managers in making reuse happen.

Corporate Managers

The most important role of the corporate manager is to develop an understanding of the potential benefits of reuse and to decide on an organizational commitment. While most of the specifics of carrying out the transition described above are necessarily carried out by subordinate groups, support from above is essential. This support may take the form of financial investment; it certainly includes belief in and commitment to the change. Specific guidelines to the corporate manager are

- Understand enough about reuse to make an initial assessment of its benefits to the organization.
- Delegate to subordinate managers the task of carrying out a more detailed assessment of whether to invest in reuse. Acknowledge to them that reuse has a cost, and indicate a willingness to invest if the potential for payback seems to exist. Follow up with managers on their recommendations and decisions.
- Provide incentives (e.g., through a bonus program or other existing evaluative mechanism) for managers to carry out their plans.
- Continue to follow up. Ask for regular reports on activities and results.

Business Area Managers

Business areas are really the focal point for reuse. Reuse has most applicability and payoff when applied within a group of related applications—a business area. The business area manager, therefore, is the individual who must create the environment for reuse. The manager is also the one to profit most directly; reuse will make it possible to expand the business area through improved quality and more competitive prices.

Because the business area is the reuse focal point, this level usually carries out the preparatory activities to identify commonality, establish needed resources, and develop policies. Day-to-day engineering with reuse is the province of the project manager, as discussed in the next subsection. Some specific guidelines to the business area manager are

- Carry out an initial analysis to determine whether there is enough functional commonality across applications (present and future) in the business area to warrant a significant investment in reuse.
- Based on this analysis, decide on an appropriate level of investment in reuse. Possible conclusions might be:
  - There is significant commonality in overall software architectures as well as in specific functions. Proceed with a domain-specific approach, analyzing the domain for commonality, defining a reference architecture, and acquiring/developing appropriate assets.
  - There is little architectural commonality but significant lower-level functionality commonality. Consider establishing a software asset library,

preferably using a commercially available library system product. Identify assets to be acquired and an approach to acquiring them.
  - There is little commonality across projects. Do not invest in reuse at this time.
- Appoint someone in the organization to serve as a reuse focal point.
- Under this individual's leadership, carry out the recommendation from the preceding analysis, establishing appropriate resources and procedures within the organization. These resources and procedures might include:
  - A reference architecture for the domain
  - A collection of reusable assets
  - A component retrieval system to manage and provide access to the assets
  - A set of procedures for use and administration of the system
  - Design, coding, and documentation guidelines for the projects in the organization
- Identify an initial trial project for reuse—perhaps an ongoing project, perhaps a project to be proposed with a reuse approach. Devise criteria for measuring success, carrying out the trial, and assessing results. (This project should be short, or an initial part of a longer one, so that results are not delayed too long.)
- Recognize that project managers may incur additional cost through the practice of reuse because they will initially be more concerned with creating software for reuse by others than with taking advantage of a large store of available software. If required, provide support for effort above and beyond immediate project requirements.
- Establish a way to collect metrics on cost savings of reuse, in order to assess the benefits for future programs. Such metrics also support lower labor estimates on future development efforts, leading to more competitive pricing.

Project Managers

In a large project, reuse within the project is a significant goal and one that can be approached analogously to the discussion above for business area managers. However, the role of the individual project is as a member of a larger group practicing reuse across project boundaries. Thus, the project will function as a creator and a reuser of reusable software components. The project manager faces a challenge here—in that a reason must be provided for engineers to adopt a new practice. Some guidelines are

- Show commitment—real belief, not just acquiescence—to the success of reuse.
- Establish a focal point within the project for reuse.
- Provide incentives to engineers, both to build reusable software and to reuse existing software. Payoff should be rapid rather than once a year. (It need not be financial; recognition and special opportunities are other ways to encourage new practices.)
- Collect metrics on cost and schedule impact of reuse.
- Provide feedback to the business area manager on reuse resources and experiences.

More comprehensive guidelines may be found in S. Ruegsegger and Aubey (1992).

BIBLIOGRAPHY

J. Armitage, *Process Guide for the DSSA Process Life Cycle,* The Software Engineering Institute, Oct., 1992, PD-081 DSSA-PG-001 Rev. 0.1.

Ascent Logic Corporation, *RDD-100 Release 3.0 Users Documentation,* San Jose, Calif., 1991.

B. H. Barnes and T. B. Bollinger, "Making Reuse Cost-Effective," *IEEE Software* (Jan. 1991).

C. Braun, J. Goodenough, and R. S. Eanes, *Ada Reusability Guidelines,* Technical Report 3285-2-208/2, SofTech, Inc., Apr., 1985.

C. Braun, *NATO Standard for the Development of Reusable Software Components,* NATO Communications and Information Systems Agency, Apr., 1992a.

C. Braun, *Software Reuse,* ACM Professional Development Seminar, Nov., 1992b, p. 56.

C. Braun, R. Coutant, and J. Armitage, "Domain Specific Software Architectures: A Process for Architecture-Based Software Engineering," *Proceedings of the 11th Annual National Conference on Ada Technology,* Mar., 1993a.

C. Braun and L. Alexander, "Domain Specific Software Architectures—Command and Control," *Proceedings of the Fifth Annual Software Technology Conference,* Apr., 1993b.

C. L. Braun, D. F. Davis, W. L. Hatch, R. J. Might, T. B. Ruegsegger, and E. A. Vance, *Domain Specific Software Architectures Command and Control Domain Model Report,* CDRL CLIN 0006, ARPA Contract No. DAAB07-92-C-Q502, May, 1993c.

DISA/CIM Customer Support Branch, *Defense Software Repository System (DSRS) Programmer's User Guide for DSRS, Version 4.0 (VMS Character Based),* #1222-04-210/6.1C, Oct. 21, 1992.

J. Fitzgerald and R. Mathis, "Use of an Expert System in Software Component Reuse," *Proceedings of AIDA-88,* Nov., 1988.

Fujitsu, Inc., personal communication with R. Prieto-Díaz, 1987.

J. Gan, "ASSET: Asset Source for Software Engineering Technology," *Crosstalk—The Journal of Defense Software Engineering,* Mar. 1992.

R. U. Gautier and P. J. L. Wallis, eds., *Software Reuse with Ada,* Peter Peregrinus Ltd. on behalf of the Institution of Electrical Engineers, London, UK, 1990.

E. Guerrieri, "Searching for Reusable Software Components with the RAPID Center Library System," *Proceedings Sixth National Conference on Ada Technology,* Mar., 1988.

Joint Integrated Avionics Working Group, "Contract Elements for Software Reuse", J89-S8, Mar. 15, 1990.

R. G. Lanergan and B. A. Poynton, "Reusable Code: The Application Development Technique for the Future," *Proceedings of the IBM SHARE/GUIDE Software Symposium,* Oct., 1979.

D. A. Marca and C. L. McGowan, *SADT, Structured Analysis and Design Technique,* McGraw-Hill Book Co., Inc., New York, 1988.

D. McNichol, S. Cohen, and C. Palmer, *CAMP Final Technical Report*, AFATL-TR-85-93, U. S. Air Force, Sep. 1985.

E. Mettala and M. Graham, eds., *The Domain Specific Software Architectures Program,* CMU-SEI-92-SR-9, The Software Engineering Institute, June, 1992.

NEC, Inc., personal communication with R. Prieto-Díaz, June, 1987.

J. Nissen and P. J. L. Wallis, eds., *Portability and Style in Ada,* Cambridge University Press, Cambridge, UK, 1984.

E. Ostertag, J. Hendler, R. Prieto-Díaz, and C. Braun, "Computing Similarity in a Reuse Library System: An AI-Based Approach", *ACM Transactions on Software Engineering and Methodology,* July 1992.

R. Prieto-Díaz, "Domain Analysis for Reusability," *Proceedings of COMPSAC '87,* IEEE, Inc., 1987a.

R. Prieto-Díaz and P. Freeman, "Classifying Software for Reusability", *IEEE Software,* 6–17 (Jan., 1987b).

Rational, "Foundation for Competitiveness and Profitability:FS2000 System: Rational and Ada," copyright Rational, 1992.

S. Ruegsegger and K. Aubey, *NATO Standard for Software Reuse Procedures,* NATO Communications and Information Systems Agency, Apr., 1992.

T. Ruegsegger, *NATO Standard for Management of a Reusable Software Component Library,* NATO Communications and Information Systems Agency, Apr., 1992.

J. Rumbaugh, M. Blaha, W. Premerlani, F. Eddy, and W. Lorensen, *Object-Oriented Modeling and Design,* Prentice Hall, Inc., Englewood Cliffs, N.J., 1991.

SofTech, Inc., *Integrated Computer-Aided Manufacturing (ICAM) Architecture Part II, Volume IV—Function Modeling Manual (IDEF$_0$),* AFWAL-TR-81-4023, Materials Laboratory, Wright-Patterson Air Force Base, Ohio, 1981.

SofTech, Inc., personal communication with C. Braun, Jan., 1987.

SofTech, Inc., *RAPID Center Standards for Reusable Software,* document number 3451-4-012/6.4, 1990.

The Software Productivity Consortium, *Ada Quality and Style: Guidelines for Professional Programmers,* Van Nostrand Reinhold, Co., Inc., New York, 1989.

B. B. Sookman, "Intellectual Property Rights and Software Reuse: A Canadian and American Perspective," presented at SIGAda meeting, Ottawa, Ont., July, 1989.

A. L. Steadman, *A Study of the Air Force's Implementation of DOD Software Data Rights Policy for Reusable Software,* AFIT/GCM/LSL/88S-10, Air Force Institute of Technology, Sept., 1988.

M. Swanson and S. Curry, "Results of an Asset Engineering Program: Predicting the Impact of Software Reuse," *Proceedings of the National Conference on Software Reusability and Portability,* Sept., 1987.

T. Syms and C. Braun, "Software Reuse: Customer vs. Contractor Point-Counterpoint," *Proceedings of Ada-Europe '91,* Athens, Greece, May, 1991.

Universal Defence Systems, personal communication with C. Braun, Feb. 1991.

K. Wallnau, "An Introduction to CARDS," *Crosstalk—The Journal of Defense Software Engineering* (Sep. 1992).

Westinghouse Electronic Systems Group, *Software Design Document for the Radar Management Portion of the Radar Domain Library CSCI of the Reusable ADA Avionics Software Packages,* Contract Number F33615-90-C-1432, USAF Avionics Laboratory, Mar. 27, 1992.

CHRISTINE L. BRAUN
GTE Federal Systems Division

REUSE LIBRARY

OVERVIEW

A reuse library is a library which stores artifacts developed for computer systems for later reuse in other computer systems. A reuse library is typically automated, to provide convenient storage and retrieval of the reusable artifacts. The artifacts are of several types, including program source code, executable programs, designs, architectures, test suites, and documentation. Reusable artifacts are also called reusable assets. A reuse library may also be called a repository.

The reasons for building systems with reusable software artifacts, called software reuse, include achieving more robust systems by construction with robust, purpose-built standard parts, and avoiding the cost and delay of building completely new systems. A number of successes have been reported. Examples include the Raytheon COBOL experience and Japanese software factories, and Hewlett-Packard's software for just-in-time (JIT) manufacturing. Raytheon reported achieving 15–85% reuse in its COBOL systems (McClure, 1992, p. 230). The Japanese claim an order of magnitude increase in software productivity due to software reuse (McClure, 1992, p. 230). HP reported delivering about one million lines of code three months early with a ten percent cost savings (Reifer, p. 22).

Domain analysis is an important foundation for software reuse because it identifies what the appropriate reusable parts should be. Domain analysis is "an investigation of a specific application area that seeks to identify the operations, objects, and structures that commonly occur in software systems within this area" (Booch, 1987, p. 613).

To support software reuse, a reuse library must provide or arrange several functions for its users.

REUSE LIBRARY FUNCTIONS

Reuse library functions must include the storage, description, cataloging and retrieval mechanism of any library as well as identifying assets for inclusion (the "collection development" of any library), and may include evaluation of the reusable assets in its inventory. A reuse library operation may also be asked to estimate the value of the instances of reuse of its assets that occur. The work of describing assets in library format and constructing accompanying materials such as tests may be done by library staff, or by the donor who sends them to the library. For example, if donors who developed assets provide abstracts and test data, the library staff would not need to develop them.

Besides the above functions, a reuse library operation must be concerned with the legal status of assets. Commercial items must be specifically licensed for redistribution, and donors who offer assets as "freely redistributable" should be asked to state in writing that assets may be freely re-distributed. Also, a reuse library must exercise care in representing assets to reusers. For the library to offer a "guarantee" is far more serious than for the library to provide assets and descriptions as a best effort. Suitability for a re-user's task is particularly difficult for a library to define, because the library describes an asset for all users.

The Software Reuse Initiative of the United States Department of Defense is an example of an implementation of software reuse.

DEFENSE DEPARTMENT SOFTWARE REUSE

The Software Reuse Initiative of the U.S. Defense Department (DOD) has goals which include: improve the quality and reliability of software-intensive systems; shorten system development and maintenance time; and increase effective productivity through better utilization and leverage of the software industry. The Initiative has a concept which includes: ensure that reuse is treated as an inseparable part of software engineering; utilize an interconnected network of reuse libraries to drive the capture, storage and reuse of components within and across domains. The strategy of the initiative has ten elements which include define the types of products suitable for reuse and develop criteria to validate these components for new applications; define standards for various types of components which will permit their certification for reuse; and exploit near-term products and services which facilitate movement to a reuse-based paradigm.

The DOD Defense Information Systems Agency (DISA) operates a software reuse library as part of its Information Management mission. The library is operated by the DISA Software Reuse Program and located in Falls Church, Virginia. The library's operation is governed by DISA and DOD policies. The implementation of general reuse library functions at the DISA library is described below. The software engine used to automate the library is described below. In addition to the Falls Church site, a family of similar libraries using the same library software includes the Army, Air Force, Navy, Marines, and Defense Logistics Agency (DLA).

REUSE LIBRARY FUNCTIONS AT THE DISA SOFTWARE REUSE PROGRAM

The DISA library and others in its family perform collection development, description and cataloging, and installation. They also perform evaluation of assets as well as configuration management, quality assurance, and customer assistance. In the DSRS environment, collection development is called population, and description and cataloging are called classification and certification.

Classification is defined as selecting keywords to describe the assets to an automated retrieval engine, so that a user can later search the library. The DSRS uses a faceted description method. The eleven facets used include asset type, function, object, certification level, and language and environment.

Certification is defined as including determining what types of assets should be in the library, classifying those assets, evaluating and testing the assets, and making them available in a library. There are four levels of certification: Level 1 is as is. The asset is described with keywords and an abstract, and stored for automatic retrieval, but no tests are performed and its degree of completeness is unknown; For Level 2, source code assets must compile to be worthy. For languages with defined metrics, those metrics must also be determined for Level 2; Level 3 adds testing, test data and test results to level 2 requirements. When a user extracts a level 3 asset, test material is transmitted along with the asset. Level 4 adds a reusers manual to the Level 3 requirements.

Donors of assets are asked for written statements that the assets may be redistributed. The DISA libraries prepare reports to DISA and DOD management. The DISA libraries do not offer guarantees of correctness or of suitability for the reuser's purpose.

THE DEFENSE SOFTWARE REPOSITORY SYSTEM (DSRS)

The Defense Software Repository System is an example of software that automates a reuse library. DSRS was built for the U.S. Department of Defense Department of the Army by SOFTECH, Inc. It is built with a combination of Ada, the ORACLE relational data base and Pro-Ada embedded SQL products, and screen-management products. It was originally built for and run on the Digital Equipment Corp. (DEC) VAX computer and the DEC VMS operating system. It will be converted to the UNIX environment to increase its availability.

BIBLIOGRAPHY

G. Booch, *Software Components with Ada,* Benjamin/Cummings Publishing Company, 1987.

G. Booch, *Object-Oriented Design With Applications,* Benjamin/Cummings Publishing Company, 1991.

DISA, *Programmer's User Guide for DSRS Version 4.0,* Defense Information Systems Agency/Corporate Information Management Software Reuse Program, Oct. 21, 1992.

DISA, *Certification Framework for Reusable Software Components (Version 1.0),* Defense Information Systems Agency/Corporate Information Management Software Reuse Program, Feb. 26, 1993.

DISA, *Reusable Software Component Certification Guidelines for Ada Implementation Component Types (version 1.0),* Defense Information Systems Agency/Corporate Information Management Software Reuse Program, Feb. 26, 1993.

DOD, "Software Reuse Vision and Strategy," *Crosstalk, The Journal of Defense Software Engineering* (Oct. 1992).

C. McClure, *The Three Rs Of Software Automation: Re-Engineering, Repository, Reusability,* Prentice-Hall, 1992.

Reifer Consultants, Inc., *Software Reuse: A Report From The Field,* briefing prepared for Software AG User's Symposium by Reifer Consultants, Inc., Torrance, Calif.

W. Wong, *A Management Overview Of Software Reuse,* NBS Special Publication 500-142, National Bureau of Standards, Institute of Computer Science and Technology, 1986.

STEVEN MERRITT
DISA/CIM

REUSE—THE BUSINESS IMPLICATIONS

INTRODUCTION

Software reuse, as a standard element of software development practice, offers the potential to reduce the cost of developing and maintaining software significantly. Surely, if during a system development some portion of the software is reused from a previous application, less software is required to be developed for the new system. Developing less software should translate into reduced costs and schedule. The smaller number of engineers on the project would now be able to concentrate on the new aspects of the system rather than dilute their efforts reinventing the "wheel". Clearly, there is some benefit to be gained through software reuse.

The concept of software reuse has been gaining momentum over the past few years. The maturation of the programming language, Ada, has given additional impetus to software reuse through both Ada's wide adoption as a standard and its technical features that facilitate software reuse (see ADA). This popularity occurs at a time when the cost of developing and maintaining software is increasing dramatically and a severe shortage of software engineers is projected. Software reuse, with its powerful intuitive appeal, would appear to ameliorate the effects of both these problems.

However, to realize the potential benefits of software reuse many monumental technical problems must first be solved: Reuse domains must be identified and defined. Many different types of standards must be promulgated, such as for interfacing separately developed code, communicating internally among components of separately developed code, defining common programming practices, and for validating code for its reusability. Generic reusable architectures must be established so that when components are to be reused they will be compatible within the new environment. State-of-the-art libraries of reusable software components must be established, along with cataloging, retrieving, and validating mechanisms. The technical community is well aware of the technical problems and is working diligently on solutions.

A technical problem that has considerable business implications, is the inability to measure or quantify the reuse of software assets. Measurement of the reuse of software within each of the various levels of abstraction, including when the software asset is modified or only partially reused, must be possible. The inability to measure software reuse presents a serious impediment to the solution of many business related software reuse problems, especially in the case of validating contractual requirements, assessing liability, and determining remuneration. These issues will be discussed in greater detail later in this article.

The complex technical issues associated with software reuse are being pursued widely throughout government, industry, and academia. The intensity of this research and the effort expended have grown increasingly over the past three to four years. Conversely, the business aspects of software reuse, which can present major programmatic, contractual, and competitive considerations, are not being pursued as vigorously. This article, which is based on a study conducted by a National Security Industrial Association Software Reuse Subcommittee for the U.S. Army, will focus on the business issues associated with software reuse. The article will discuss the non-technical barriers to software reuse and identify the changes needed in the way that the software business is practiced, in order to facilitate and encourage software reuse.

SOFTWARE REUSE DEFINITION

Software reuse as used herein is defined as: The capability of a previously developed software asset to be used again or used repeatedly, in part or in its entirety, with or without modification. This definition points out many of the difficulties that must be overcome in order for the state-of-the-practice in software reuse to advance significantly. "Asset" is a key word in this definition, since it includes all levels of software abstraction. Software reuse at the code level of abstraction is the level most commonly discussed; however, it is necessary that all other levels be considered as well. There is a significant benefit to be realized from reusing software requirements specifications, software system architectures, designs, algorithms, test procedures, documentation, and even software engineers (and managers).

Further, the definition includes the qualification "in part or in its entirety, with or without modification." The inclusion of partial use and modification is important, since benefit can be realized in those ways as well.

FUNDING SOFTWARE REUSE

To capitalize on the potential benefits of software reuse, reuse must be more widely practiced. More software needs to be available for reuse, reuse needs greater acceptance as an engineering practice, and many cultural barriers need to be overcome. However, to accomplish these things costs money. There are many costs associated with software reuse. Software that is to be made available for reuse costs more to develop, document, and test. Capital investments must be made to establish software reuse repositories. To operate and maintain these repositories, to solve many of the technical software reuse problems, and so forth, will cost money. A major business impediment to the concept of software reuse is obtaining the required funds for these additional costs which are necessary to enable widespread software reuse.

The current success being enjoyed by Commercial-Off-The-Shelf (COTS) software has added to the confusion over the value of software reuse within application systems. COTS is often cited as an example of the virtues of reusable software, which, unfortunately, is not the case. The market for spread sheets, word processors, compilers, and the like, is orders of magnitude greater than the market for software that is very application specific, hardware dependent, or is based on algorithms that are evolving with the technology and the state-of-the-art. COTS shelf-life is also much greater due to their relatively stable and very specific applications. Consequently, the COTS return on investment model is not one that can be extrapolated to the enormous amounts of applications software that is developed for reuse.

In order to obtain the additional funding associated with software reuse, it must be shown that the costs associated with software reuse are justified by the expected benefits. In other words, is there sufficient return on investment? The answer to this question defies quantification. For example, we must first be able to answer the following:

How can the expected benefits be measured and priced?

How are the various abstract levels of software reuse measured?

What is the potential extent of reuse for a particular software asset?

What is the projected shelf-life for that asset?

How frequently will the requirements of that asset change?

Lacking the answers to those hard questions, direct funding for software reuse will be nearly impossible to obtain; particularly, in the amounts needed to make reuse a widespread practice in a reasonable time period. The solution appears to be that software reuse must pay its own way as it evolves over time.

A business approach is needed which encourages both the development and the use of reusable software. The incentives, financial or otherwise, need to be established that can be employed to encourage companies to create software that is reusable by other companies, and to utilize in their software developments software that has been developed by other companies. The legal and fiscal barriers to software reuse must additionally be minimized.

The following three sections, software engineering, contracting, and ownership, discuss the business issues related to software reuse.

SOFTWARE ENGINEERING

Evolution of the Practice

The basic notion of software reuse is that of drawing components from a repository of reusable software, along with an appropriate set of library tools, to use in the development of a new system. Ideally, such a repository would evolve into a powerful library populated with both original and modified parts. The evolution of this concept of software reuse has begun.

The NSIA study found that software reuse is occurring, but only within corporations. Currently, the software reuse practice depends largely on the expertise of a closed group of developers and their familiarity with previously developed software. Today's software reuse depends heavily on the intimate knowledge and judgment of these developers, their knowledge of the local practice concerning what parts or subsystems can be used, what modifications are necessary, and whether or not reuse is cost effective. Reuse of this nature is not a formalized practice.

To expand this notion beyond the corporation, considerably more work must be accomplished in a number of critical areas, especially standards, before a more widespread practice of software reuse can emerge.

The NSIA study did not identify a single initiative that could have a positive revolutionary impact on the evolution of software reuse. Attempts to impact the evolution of software reuse with premature or radical (revolutionary) initiatives, such as mandating its use, should be avoided. Actions of this type would result in a backlash that would seriously impede, if not destroy, the evolution of software reuse.

The concept of software reuse is currently evolving at a reasonable pace. Intervention must be limited to positive actions that stimulate its evolution. Success in software reuse will not likely result from efforts and ideas that immediately and drastically change the way that business is currently conducted. The practice of software reuse must evolve in a natural fashion. There is no "silver bullet".

Software Reuse Standards

Developers believe that the software currently in reuse libraries suffers from poor (or nonexistent) documentation and from poor software engineering practices. Most potential developers for a particular project have a very poor appreciation of existing third party software that might be available for reuse because that software was not developed according to any industry-accepted standards. None will choose to bid significant amounts of available reuse software because they lack confidence in its definition, applicability, quality, and reliability.

Developers are not convinced of the cost savings potential by using what is currently available in reuse libraries. The risks and costs of using library software cannot be determined quickly due to the lack of necessary standards and proper documentation. Today the basic premise is that unless a developer employs the individuals who created the software that is available for reuse the risk of miscalculating its utility or the cost of its modification is too great. Software developers simply lack confidence in the software assets available in reuse libraries.

Before software can be of utility for reuse, it must meet certain standards. These standards must be specific, easy to understand, and universally accepted. Industry standards for every phase of the life cycle are needed to enable software reuse. Some of the areas where standards are required include documentation, interface, design, and testing. Few of these standards exist today, others are just now being addressed.

If software reuse standards existed, there would be less risk to developers attempting to utilize appropriate reusable software assets for a specific new development effort. Reuse standards would also reduce risk, during the cost analysis of a software development, by aiding in estimating the effort needed to meet requirements specifications.

Large investments in software reuse libraries, at this time, are questionable because of the lack of industry and Government accepted standards. Building software reuse libraries without first establishing the standards that govern the software to be contained in those libraries is wasteful. Without the appropriate standards, a potential user of software from a reuse repository lacks confidence in that software's utility, quality, reliability, and performance. The availability of software reuse standards must precede the establishment of new software reuse repositories.

Standards related to reuse are vital to the concept of software reuse. Available software reuse resources should be invested in software engineering standards, particularly in standards specific to the concept of reuse. The software industry (Government, contractors, educators, professional organizations, and commercial businesses) must establish criteria for what constitutes good reusable software and the standards of practice for the software life cycle.

Discipline and Engineering Practices

"Will software reuse provide a significant increase in productivity?" There is general agreement that it should contribute, to some extent, to improving software productivity. The ultimate goal in software engineering is improved performance at reduced costs, i.e., increased productivity. Increased productivity is good for software developers because it makes them more competitive. Customers benefit since they can acquire more functionality with decreased budgets. Significant productivity gains can be achieved by utilizing a good, disciplined software development process.

Professional discipline is a prerequisite to having good software engineering practices. Unless software developers exercise the discipline to adhere to the standards of the practice, the only result can be inferior software, which will not be reused. The software engineering industry, especially its management, technical, and sales teams, must be convinced of the importance of good software engineering standards and of the need for disciplined adherence to the standards. Those who acquire software must also be convinced—they too must exercise the discipline to insist on delivery of products and services that conform to the standards of practice. With an enlightened professional industry, it then becomes an industry management responsibility (of both developers and users) to enforce the standards—this is discipline. Without this discipline, software engineering standards are useless. The net result is software developed with inadequate quality for reuse. Also, considerable progress in software reuse can be achieved through improving the practice of software engineering. (Implicit in good software engineering practices is the application of standards.) Improved software engineering practices and methods should result in higher quality of the software so developed: quality software is an obvious ingredient in software reuse. Assured of the quality of available software, system developers will be less hesitant to attempt to reuse it.

There are several major prerequisites to software reusability—strong discipline and good software engineering processes are the two most important. Management should increase attention being applied to the improvement of software engineering practices, procedures, and discipline. Once good software engineering practices are established and being followed with disciplined rigor, it is predicted that significant software reuse will result as a natural by-product.

CONTRACTING

Competition

The NSIA study had concluded that the competitive process offers the single, greatest potential for fostering software reuse. Competition is the dominant factor that motivates the industry. Winning the contract takes priority over all other business considerations. Incentives that help companies win new contracts are considered by the industry to be more critical than incentives which may incrementally increase profits earned on software development efforts.

Including appropriate reuse incentives in the process of selecting the winning contractor, appears to be the most effective current business incentive for software reuse. The inclusion of some software reuse considerations in the source selection process would have much greater potential for fostering reuse than any of the other business incentives that have been suggested. However, the relative immaturity of the practice of software reuse makes widely accepted objective measures of reuse for inclusion as source selection criteria difficult to find. Until the practice matures, the source selection process can and should rely on expert judgment for evaluation of software reuse.

The competitive process is such a powerful tool that it should be used in any reasonable way to foster the concept of software reuse.

Measurement

Incentives have been researched that could be incorporated into contract clauses to stimulate the evolution in the state-of-the-practice of software reuse. As a result of the research, unfortunately, the use of contract clauses to promote reuse is not yet practical. All of the clauses considered, in one way or another, have required quantification of software reuse in order to validate their compliance. For contracting purposes, there is not yet an acceptable method available for measuring the reuse of software.

Take as an example the contract clause phrase "X% of the software .... " The hard percentage approach introduces two interesting problems relating to quantification: one in proposals and the other in contract satisfaction. It is likely that if the solicitation requires X%, all proposals will offer X%. For evaluators to judge the veracity of the offeror's claims would be impossible. Admittedly, some offers may be more plausible than others, but the problem remains due to the absence of a way to quantify the amount of software reuse. Once the contract is awarded there are a number of techniques for obtaining relief from the claims of the proposal. But the contract requirement remains. At the end of the period of contract performance, compliance must be determined. The onus is on the customer to validate the contractor's satisfaction of X%. In order to do this analysis, the customer must somehow be able to measure the software reused.

There are a number of reasons why software reuse cannot be quantified. The definition of software reuse admits to several abstract levels of reuse. The consideration of the various levels of abstraction is prevalent throughout the software reuse community. These levels of software abstraction include: requirements, architecture, design, algorithms, documentation, knowledge/understanding, test, and lastly, code. How can the amount of software requirements or design that have been reused from some other application be measured? Clearly, only code stands a chance of its reuse being quantified, unless perhaps it is in the case of 100% reuse at one of the other levels. In the case of 100% reuse, while usually measurable, the occurrence is unlikely in non-trivial software developments. Some modification at any level of abstraction is most likely, compounding the problem of quantifying the higher abstract levels of software reuse.

This complexity points out another major reason software reuse measurement is difficult—the definition provides for modification. In the case of quantifying code reuse, lines of code can be counted, but once code is modified, measurement of how much of the original code is being reused is difficult.

Metrics are not yet available that permit the quantification of software reuse. There does not currently exist a method of quantifying software reuse that is sufficient for use in rigorous situations such as contracting, assessing liability, remuneration determination, and proposal evaluation (see also METRICS).

Contract Type

In fixed price contracting, if software reuse is a customer requirement, then it must be so stated and accounted for in the contract price. However, specifying this requirement in the contract is a form of direct payment for software reuse. The fixed price contractor is only required to satisfy his specific contractual requirements and is accountable for the price of his bid, with or without a software reuse requirement. Fixed price contracts that include software intensive developments, have rarely been practical because the requirements are so complex as to be nearly impossible to define adequately at the time of the contract solicitation. Fortunately, this fact is gaining recognition and the use of fixed price contracts for such developments is diminishing.

Under "Time and Materials" contracts the customer buys man hours, not software. The customer directs how these man hours are expended with the contractor having very little flexibility. If the customer requires software reuse, the customer simply directs the contractor accordingly. However, this too is a form of direct payment for software reuse.

Cost type contracts are the most effective for promoting software reuse without having to pay for it directly. Cost contracts provide the most flexibility on the part of both the customer and the contractor. Cost type contracts provide the customer with the visibility and flexibility needed to promote and monitor software reuse during the course of a contract. The forces of competition drive contractors to consider reusing some software, instead of developing it, as a means of reducing their proposal price. These are the only types of contracts wherein direct payment for software reuse can be avoided.

Only cost type contracts should be used when software reuse is to be an important factor unless management is willing to pay the extra cost associated with reuse.

Reusable Requirements

Software reuse at the lower levels of abstraction will be promoted by reuse at the higher levels of software abstraction. Management can make a significant contribution to the evolution of software reuse by developing system requirements and specifications that are themselves reusable. Reusable requirements foster reusable designs and algorithms, which in turn foster reusable code.

Standards for reusable requirements and specifications, followed by the development of reusable requirements and specifications that conform to such standards, would foster greater software asset reuse. This practice in the specification of hardware requirements for system developments is common. Management should identify the software equivalent of reusable hardware components and develop reusable specifications for their development. Then these specifications should be used, as appropriate, as a part of system requirements in contracts.

If the level of abstraction of the software assets was raised from the code level to the requirement and specification level, organizations could promote greater software asset reuse internally. Management should make an effort to develop techniques and tools for applying reuse at the requirements and specifications level and encourage developers to utilize and/or incorporate the results into their internal proprietary libraries.

Proprietary Corporate Reuse Libraries

Many companies, primarily the large prime contractors, are in the process of establishing internal proprietary software reuse libraries. These private libraries are typically organized along lines of business. Companies are already drawing from their libraries, whenever practical, to use in the development of proposals and, subsequently, the software development project. The development and use of these internal libraries on an individual company basis would be promoted by making such use a consideration in the competitive process, thus appealing to the strong competitive motivation within the contractor community. The NSIA study found there is evidence that, in some cases, software reuse has already made the difference in winning contracts.

Although contractors are actively establishing internal proprietary software reuse libraries for their competitive advantage, they have an exceptionally strong resistance to contributing useful software to a library accessible by others: since the contributing contractor fears a loss of some competitive advantage. Trying to promote libraries that are accessible across many companies would run counter to the competitive motivation within the contractor community. The Government is attempting to construct repositories for public domain software assets; however, contractors will not put their most useful software assets from their private libraries in the public repositories. Knowing this, contractors consider software developed by a competitor and placed in a public reuse library as generally being neither useful nor cost effective, and considerable risk would be associated with adapting the software for reuse.

Although cross-contractor reuse through public repositories is not considered practical, there are arguments that support adopting such a strategy for the future. From the Government standpoint, the potential cost savings from cross-contractor reuse is much greater than from internal reuse. The problem is, given the current state-of-the-practice, cross-contractor reuse requires cooperation between contractors. Currently, a contractor has little motivation to concede a competitive advantage to another contractor (or potential competitor).

Internal software reuse is making a very positive contribution to the evolution of software reuse. Software reuse is actively being pursued internally in corporate entities. The evolution of software reuse would be well served if the industry could find a way to stimulate developers to increase the reuse of software assets from their internal libraries to their new software developments.

Small Business Innovation Research (SBIR) Program

Some interest has been voiced in having the Government foster a reusable software component industry made up of small business entrepreneurs that would produce-these reusable software components. This would be analogous to many other industries, wherein products are developed utilizing components supplied by independent vendors. There is also some similarity to the COTS software industry currently supplying a wide variety of reusable components for business and management systems.

The Government's Small Business Innovation Research (SBIR) program already possesses many of the ingredients needed for the Government to stimulate the growth of a software component industry. The program is limited to participation by small businesses. The funding mechanisms for the program have already been established. The program's three phases of investigation, development, and commercialization are an extremely good fit. The program lends itself to small, well-defined statements of work. Finally, the program permits wide coverage of various interests of all Government agencies.

To adapt the SBIR program to yield software reuse components would obviously require several Government initiatives: the Government would need to coordinate its various SBIR programs in order to assure development of the proper mixture of components; technical standards would have to be developed and applied to the program; and funding for the program must be included in the budgeting process.

The reuse of commercially available software components is a promising approach to increase reuse, but the supply side of the market needs to be created in order to provide potential users with a practical selection of components. If the Government truly desires the emergence of a reusable software component industry, the SBIR program, or another similar program, appears to merit consideration.

OWNERSHIP

Legal Liability

Prime contractors and system integration contractors historically have reused hardware components produced by other vendors in developing systems for delivery to the customer. Integration of software, wherein some portion is being reused, is not very different from traditional hardware integration and so the liability considerations are the same. Considerations of legal liability are more of a management risk than a liability risk.

Crashes of commercial airliners and military aircraft provide an appropriate analogy. When these problems do arise, legal liability is decided in the civilian courts on a case-by-case basis. The liabilities associated with software reuse are not treated any differently from those of hardware reuse.

The many liabilities of ownership, especially legal, are often perceived as deterrents to the voluntary engagement in software reuse. However, they actually turn out not to be significant issues because when software is reused, either it is integrated into the new system unmodified, or some modification is needed for it to work properly in the new environment. Liability for reused software is somewhat different in those two situations. When software is used unmodified, the software's owner can be vulnerable to some of the liability for its use in the new system. This liability may be different for public domain and for proprietary software. On the other hand, once software is modified by someone other than its owner, the owner's exposure becomes almost nil. In developing non-trivial systems, the software being reused will almost certainly require some modification. Consequently, the system developer will bear the primary liability for the reused software just as he does for vendor supplied hardware.

The idea of sharing some of the liability when software reuse was involved, has been explored, but has been set aside as an unnecessary strategy (as well as an unaccomplishable strategy). There appears to be nothing that can or should be done to modify the risk of liability in order to foster software reuse.

The risks of liability due to reuse of software are important and deserve serious management attention. However, the liabilities associated with software reuse do not appear to offer a significant impediment to the concept.

Data Rights

Data rights(qv) associated with software reuse have been perceived as a potential impediment to the concept of software reuse. The data rights problems associated with software development and delivery under Government contracts have been studied extensively over the past several years and the issues although problematic, are well known. Several initiatives are underway to improve procurement regulations concerning data rights in the area of Government contracting.

Similarly, the data rights associated with COTS applications have become well defined over the past few years. Precedents in the judicial system have been established and many court cases tried and resolved. The Government and the industry have purchased tremendous amounts of COTS without experiencing serious problems in the area of data rights.

Many of the data rights issues have been studied for their impact on the concept of reuse. However, throughout this process no data rights issues have emerged that are uniquely associated with reusing software. The software reuse data rights issues turned out to be the same as for all other aspects of software use. Data rights are associated with protecting the owner of an item of software, whether its use or reuse is authorized or unauthorized.

Data rights issues associated with software reuse are very important and must be resolved; however, none of the software data rights issues are uniquely associated with reusable software. The set of problems associated with rights to reusable software is precisely the same set that has been and are currently being addressed by Government and industry for all software.

Related to data rights, nothing additional needs to be done by the Government in order to promote the concept of reuse, other than continue to vigorously support the ongoing software data rights initiatives already in progress.

Financial Incentives

Financial incentives, such as royalties, seem to offer great potential for stimulating the development of reusable software and reuse of previously developed software. Various forms of financial incentives have been explored, including royalties, contractual cost savings sharing, tax benefits, and elimination of reuse fiscal penalties. All these forms of incentives are handicapped by the common problem of not being able to quantify the reuse of software. At the same time, each form of incentive suffers unique problems that further limit their usefulness.

For example, royalties is the incentive most often suggested that could be used to promote wider software reuse. True, royalties for software reuse would be very powerful, if the following problems could be solved satisfactorily:

How to quantify and measure the reuse of software?

How to determine the appropriate royalty for reuse at each of the different abstract levels of software reuse?

How to obtain funding sources for software reuse royalties?

How to establish an organization to administer and adjudicate the payment of royalties?

How to establish guidelines to be used for royalties when code is modified, and then when that code is modified, and then when that code is modified? etc.

How to identify each time that a software asset is reused?

Each of the financial incentives most often suggested possesses a list of equally problematic issues to be resolved; for example, convincing the Internal Revenue Service to modify the tax codes in the interest of promoting software reuse. No financial incentive has been discovered that offers even the slightest potential of being implemented in a practical way. Consequently, there appears to be no financial incentive, other than direct payment, that can be utilized to encourage software reuse.

AREAS FOR ADDITIONAL STUDY

The following areas of software reuse are sufficiently complex as to require significant study prior to any attempt at their verbalization or implementation. The effects of an ill-advised resolution to any of these topics could cause serious detrimental consequences to the evolution of software reuse.

1. Study software reuse during the operational phase of the life cycle—some questions of interest are: What are the benefits to software enhancement and correction from software reuse during development? How can software reuse be practiced during this phase? Is the investment in software reuse during development returned during this phase?
2. There are many standards required before the concept of software reuse can advance significantly. A study should be conducted to identify the complete list of technical software reuse standards needed as well as the order of their development. This study should precede the study of reusable software components.
3. A study should be conducted to determine how to quantify software reuse at all levels of abstraction, taking into account modifications as well. This study should precede the studies on competition and cost type contracts.
4. A study should be conducted as to how management could stimulate increased discipline and improved software engineering practices on the part of software developers.
5. While competition possesses the most potential for fostering the concept of software reuse, it is also fraught with potential for serious adverse side effects. A study of how to integrate software reuse considerations into the competitive contracting process should be careful not to unfairly bias competition, be sensitive not to introduce hidden cost growths, and be concerned about the truth in proposals regarding software reuse.
6. Cost type contracts need to be investigated to determine how to incorporate the reuse requirement, how to incentivize the contractor to practice reuse, and how to prevent buy-ins and overruns in the name of software reuse.
7. In order to have software reuse at the lower levels of abstraction, reuse must also be practiced at the higher levels. A study needs to identify the tools and

techniques that would enable the customer to reuse system and software requirements and specifications in contracting for software development.

8. How software developers can be incentivized to reuse software from their internal proprietary libraries, should be investigated.
9. The Government needs to seriously study whether an industry of reusable software components is desirable, and if so, if it is feasible? This study should address how to identify the type and category of candidate reusable components. Having done this, then the SBIR program should be investigated for use in stimulating the evolution of such an industry.

CONCLUSION

The following is a summary of the most significant points presented above:

1. Competition is the dominant factor in motivating the industry and should be used to foster the concept of software reuse.
2. Software engineering standards are vital to the concept of software reuse. Management should invest their available software reuse resources in developing new software engineering standards, particularly those standards that are specific to software reuse.
3. Strong discipline and good software engineering processes are prerequisites to the concept of software reuse. Management should increase attention being applied to the improvement of software engineering practices, procedures, and discipline.
4. The legal liabilities associated with software reuse do not appear to offer a significant impediment to the concept.
5. There are no data rights issues uniquely associated with reusable software; however, the Government should continue to vigorously support on-going software data rights initiatives.
6. The current state of technology is not sufficiently mature to enable widespread software reuse.
7. Metrics are not yet available that permit the quantification of software reuse.
8. Financial incentives, such as royalties, for the purpose of fostering software reuse do not yet appear to be implementable.
9. The concept of software reuse is currently evolving at a reasonable pace. Management should avoid utilization of strategies (and requirements) to foster software reuse that employ revolutionary initiatives.
10. Software reuse is being pursued actively, internally, in many corporate entities. Management should investigate ways to promote increased utilization of their internal corporate software reuse libraries effectively.
11. Organizations should develop techniques and tools for reusing contract and system requirements and specifications, which will foster software reuse at the lower levels of abstraction.
12. For the present time only cost type software development contracts should be used wherein reuse is to be an important factor.
13. The Small Business Innovation Research (SBIR) program should be investigated by the Government as a vehicle for stimulating the development of reusable software components.

Software reuse is a very promising concept that is currently in its infancy. Major gains and improvements due to software reuse are not yet realizable. Evolution of the state-of-the-practice in software reuse will, in due time, enable the realization of the full benefits of the concept. Good software engineering will spawn software reuse. There are several initiatives that can be pursued to stimulate the evolution of the software reuse concept.

BIBLIOGRAPHY

National Security Industrial Association Software Reuse Subcommittee, *The Business Issues Associated with Software Reuse,* NSIA, Washington, D.C., Dec. 15, 1990.

JACK COOPER
Anchor Software Management

REVERSE ENGINEERING

Reverse Engineering is most recognized as the procedure for taking apart someone else's product to learn how it works. However, reverse engineering is a general term that refers to a process of analysis, supported by methods and tools to investigate an existing system, its components, and their interrelationships, regardless of the implementation and ownership of the system. In the context of software, reverse engineering is a set of techniques for the discovery of information about a software system, whether of your own or someone else's creation.

The term "reverse engineering" has had its origin in the analysis of hardware, particularly the hardware developed by a competitor. In a landmark 1985 paper on the topic, M. G. Rekoff defined reverse engineering as "the process of developing a set of specifications for a complex hardware system by an orderly examination of specimens of that system." Such a process is conducted by someone other than the developer "without the benefit of any of the original drawings ... for the purpose of making a clone of the original hardware system..." (Rekoff, 1985). Thus, this term has acquired a negative connotation of legal, if not ethical, concern.

Yet, reverse engineering is actually a very common analysis process. Every time a hardware engineer looks at an unfamiliar device or circuit, there occurs a natural and orderly process of investigation. That analysis process involves a conceptual, if not a physical, breakdown of the device into its subsystems and constituent parts. As the common expression states the engineer "takes it apart to see what makes it tick." Without thinking of the analysis as reverse engineering, the engineer analyzes the subject device and builds models of the device and how it operates. These models may be diagrams, notes, or just mental images and plans.

Reverse engineering is regularly applied to improve one's own products, as well as to analyze those of competitors. Even the developer of a device can learn more about it by applying a reverse engineering approach. In studying a completed product, a development team can discover flaws, hidden defects, and design issues that have been masked or overlooked in the development process. A developer who has been away from working on a device for an extended period can rediscover its secrets, and can perhaps gain new insight that can lead to improvements in later versions. A device for which the design drawings have been lost can be redocumented to enable further work.

In applying reverse engineering concepts to software systems, the emphasis is to gain a basic understanding of a subject system and its structure. While the hardware objective traditionally involves duplicating the system, the software objective is most often to gain a sufficient design-level understanding of the system in place. This understanding is then used to facilitate maintenance, to strengthen enhancement, to support replacement, or to improve quality assurance.

There is a clear and pressing need for Reverse Engineering technologies to help understand and maintain existing systems, often labeled "legacy systems." These systems are the lifeblood of business organizations which depend upon them for success. These systems pay bills and track credit. They schedule and monitor airplane flights; manage the climate of buildings; and detect daily changes in consumer behavior by region. Yet, most companies do not understand their existing systems. These systems have become more complicated over time and so dependence on them has grown. However, the complexity of such systems now frequently gets in the way of understanding them. As these systems evolve, it has become impossible to know these systems with certainty or to keep our knowledge current. In many organizations, the programmer is long gone and the documentation never was kept up to date. Some systems can be worked around, without change, because making a little fix can create big problems that can destroy a critical mechanism. As one IS manager commented, "There's no such thing as a small change."

Organizations have a critical need to change their information infrastructure hastily to meet rapidly changing needs. As the business climate changes, flexibility and response are key to meeting tactical opportunities or new strategic goals. Therefore, many organizations have embarked on reengineering projects to renovate and recast their information systems into more flexible forms. Such projects focus on change, yet they often do so without an understanding of what they are changing from. They throw out the old and build up the new without insight into what they had to begin with. Most IS organizations lack sufficient information about existing systems to cope with change effectively.

With the rapid shift in hardware and software economics toward dispersed and departmental computing, organizations are finding a greater need to regain an understanding of their existing software assets. Effective downsizing and distribution of computing resources and information access throughout an organization, utilizing the state-of-the-art in client-server computing technology, requires a greater understanding of the functional capability of the systems that companies are distributing access to or replacing.

Creating such an understanding of existing software assets is the principal objective of reverse engineering technology as applied to software systems. Reverse engineering is an analysis process intended to increase the overall comprehensibility of a system for both maintenance and new development. This objective has lead to a more comprehensive definition of reverse engineering: "the analysis of a subject system to identify the system's components and their interrelationships, and to create representations of the system in another form or at a higher level of abstraction" (Chikofsky and Cross, 1990). These representations may be documents or diagrams for understanding or databases for further computer analysis, such as the repository of a CASE tool.

KEY OBJECTIVES

There are seven key software objectives that reverse engineering helps to fulfill. Notably, reverse engineering shares many of these objectives and a sizable portion of its technology with other software engineering topic areas, including metrics, reuse, testing, and visualization.

Coping with Complexity

Reverse engineering helps companies deal with the sheer volume and complexity of software systems. As software systems have become more pervasive in society, the complexity of tasks they perform has increased. This, in turn, has meant a sizable increase in the complexity of the software systems themselves. Many software organizations are finding that even original principal designers of their products who are still hands-on day-today with the code, are no longer fully-cognizant of the intricacies and fine details of how their creations have evolved. This complexity introduces problems of cross-dependence between components that are hard to detect. Patches and quick fixes have compounded the complexity problem.

Reverse engineering tools, particularly when supported by CASE facilities, can provide road maps of the system for assistance. They provide a way to extract relevant information so decision makers can control the process and the product in systems evolution. Being able to query a database about the system and to use hypertext facilities to study related information, allows analysts to learn about and examine the system. Cleveland (1989) and Newcomb and Markosian (1993) illustrate kinds of information and presentations found useful in reverse engineering for program understanding.

Generate Alternate Views

Reverse engineering facilitates the generation of graphical representations of existing systems from different viewpoints. This capability is akin to recreating the blueprints of a building. A single blueprint provides only one perspective. To achieve a complete understanding, a contractor examines multiple views: floor plans for each level; front, side, and rear perspectives; overlay plans for electrical, heating; and plumbing systems. Often, by changing a viewpoint or perspective, the analyst can get a better understanding of the way the system works.

In software development, graphical representations have long been recofnized as comprehension aids (Peters, 1981; Martin, 1987; Martin and McClure, 1988; Stevens, 1991). However, graphical representations of software systems are difficult to create and cumbersome to maintain as the system changes. They easily become out-of-date with respect to the actual running system. Reverse engineering tools facilitate the generation and update of such graphical representations from the system itself. This method allows for the generation of different diagram types to provide multiple views, much like the blueprint set. While the designers may have worked from a single, primary perspective (e.g., data flow diagrams), reverse engineering tools can generate additional views from other perspectives (e.g., entity-relationship diagrams, control flow diagrams, structure charts, non-graphical documentation) to aid the review and verification process.

Recovering Lost Information

The continuous evolution of large, long-lived systems leads to lost information about the system design. Modifications are usually not reflected in documentation, particularly at higher levels than the code itself. While it is no substitute for preserving the initial design history in the first place, reverse engineering is a way to salvage working documents from the existing systems (Oman and Cook, 1990). The analyst can generate useful documentation where none may have existed before.

Detecting Side Effects and Analyzing Quality

Both haphazard initial design and successive modifications can lead to unintended and unexpected problems in the operational system. Reverse engineering can help detect anomalies and issues before users report them as defects. Analysis of the software system includes the use of metrics, such as the McCabe cyclomatic and essential complexity measures to assess structural quality. More complex modules and routines, where structural problems are more likely to hide defects and maintenance problems, can be targeted for further investigation. This strategy, in turn, allows for test case generation to examine program execution paths (McCabe, 1990; McCabe, 1976).

Facilitating Reuse

In building models of existing systems, reverse engineering can help detect candidates for reusable software components among present software assets. Reverse engineering techniques are being used to identify the objects, or structures that could become objects, that are hidden in non-object-oriented implementations.

Populating a Repository or Knowledgebase

Related to the reuse of software components is the ability to identify and reuse design artifacts. This ability requires a way of storing and retrieving design elements. Reverse engineering can be used to populate a repository or knowledgebase, often the database or encyclopedia of a CASE tool, with recovered information about an existing system. Derived knowledge of the present system can then be retained, analyzed, and communicated among many individuals in the organization.

Synthesizing Higher Abstractions

In the most basic form, reverse engineering techniques are used to generate documentation about the software ("code") of a system at a level of the code itself Here, a line of code or a module unit might be represented as a box in a diagram. Reverse engineering also allows the analyst to examine the system at more general levels. Higher-level abstractions can be synthesized from information collected at a detail level, particularly with the help of CASE tools. Within a single module, the use of known algorithm structures (called "plans") can be recognized, and the module can be represented in a more abstract form than the code as applications of plans (Rich and Wills, 1990). On a system level, from information collected on a module by module basis, the analyst can look at interaction, such as transaction data flow, across the system as a whole. Many kinds of design decisions inherent in the system can be deduced (Rugaber and co-workers, 1990).

For commercial systems, identifying the business rules enforced by the software is one of the key goals of reverse engineering. The business rules embodied in a legacy system can then be compared to the current needs of the business to determine how the system needs to be changed. Chikofsky (1990) illustrates how this form of high-level abstraction of business rules can be achieved by manual interpretation from reverse engineered data models. Comprehensive automation of such interpretation is, as yet a long way off.

There is debate in the community as to how completely the reverse engineering process can be automated. Clearly, expert system technology will play a major role in achieving the full potential of generating and interpreting high-level abstractions.

TAXONOMY

The concepts of directionality and levels of abstraction are fundamental in understanding the relationship between terms within the reverse engineering and reengineering vocabulary. The existence of a reasonably ordered life cycle model for the software development process is assumed. Such a model might be represented as the traditional waterfall, as a spiral, or in some other form that can generally be considered a directed graph. Recognizing that there will be iteration within and overlap between phases of the life

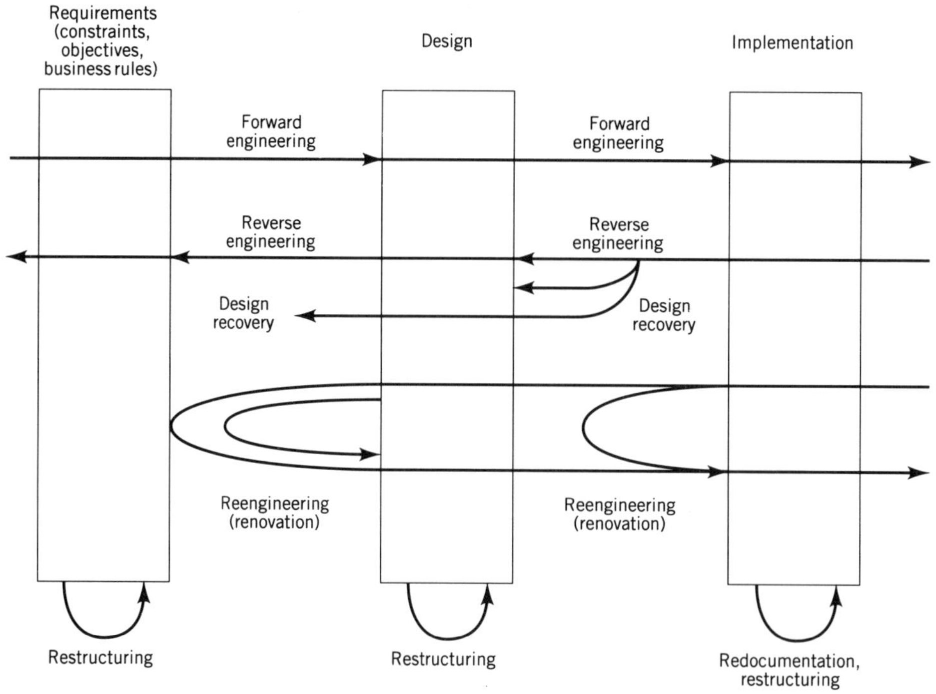

Figure 1. Relationship between terms. Adapted from Chikofsky and Cross, 1990 (IEEE Software).

cycle, the general directed nature allows sensible definition of forward (downward) and reverse (upward) activities.

The typical life cycle can be viewed as three fundamental activities or stages: requirements, design, and implementation, as illustrated in Figure 1. The requirements stage is defined by Sommerville (1992) as "establishing the services the system should provide and the constraints under which it must operate ...." It involves the capture and representation of business rules the system must satisfy or enforce. Design, the second major stage, is the specification of a solution with detailed plans for the software components needed to meet the requirements. The third stage, implementation, includes the coding of the solution, testing, debugging, and delivery of the operational system.

These activities described above can be considered as corresponding to different levels of abstraction. Viewed after the construction of the system, the implementation activity yields the most concrete or tangible representation of the system; namely, the system itself. The design of the system is a more abstract representation that hides implementation details and constraints. The requirements, representing the business rules inherent in the system, are a further (higher) abstraction from the design, without any details of the way the solution should appear. To be faithful to the term abstraction, the specifications can be referred from higher (earlier in the life cycle) phases as being summations, to some extent, of specifications from lower (later) phases.

Sommerville (1992) points out that the boundaries between levels of abstraction or degrees within levels can seem subjective and amorphous, especially when the artifacts of the various levels are similar. For instance, an Ada-like requirements specification, intended to describe system functions and how they might appear to the user, may look much like a design specification for the same system, even though the purposes for the two specifications have very different purposes at different levels. With this background, the relationship between terms, such as reverse engineering, reengineering, and restructuring can be considered. The definitions presented here were first presented in Chikofsky and Cross (1990) and subsequently maintained by the Taxonomy Project of the IEEE Computer Society TCSE's Subcommittee on Reverse Engineering.

Forward Engineering

Forward engineering is the traditional process of moving from high-level representations and logical, implementation independent designs to the physical implementation of a system. The adjective "forward" has come to be used where it is necessary to distinguish this process from reverse engineering. Forward engineering follows a sequence from the analysis of requirements through the design, and finally to an implementation. These activities have been fully described in Pressman (1992), Sommerville (1992) and many others.

Reverse Engineering

Reverse engineering is the process of analyzing a subject system in order to identify the system's components and their interrelationships, and to create representations of the system in another form or at a higher-level of abstraction. Reverse engineering generally involves extracting design artifacts and building or synthesizing representations that are less implementation-dependent.

While reverse engineering often involves an existing functional system as its subject, this is not a requirement.

Reverse engineering can start from most phases of the life cycle. In spanning the life cycle phases, reverse engineering covers a broad range starting from the existing implementation, recapturing or recreating the design, and deciphering the requirements actually implemented by the subject system. Pressman (1992) points out that "the reverse engineering process should be capable of deriving procedural design representations (a low level of abstraction), program and data structure information (a somewhat higher level of abstraction), data and control flow models (a relatively high level of abstraction), and entity relationship models (a high level of abstraction)."

Reverse engineering is an analysis process, not a change process. Reverse engineering in and of itself does not involve altering the subject system or creating a new system based on the reverse engineered subject system. Rather, it is a process of examination. Reverse engineering is often confused with reengineering, which is the change process.

Redocumentation

Redocumentation is the creation or revision of semantically-equivalent representations of a subject system within the same relative abstraction level. The redocumentation process creates its representations from information gathered from analysis of the subject system alone. The resulting forms of representation are considered alternate views, usually for a an audience, intended to improve the comprehensibility of the overall system. These alternate views include data flow, data structure, and control flow diagrams.

Redocumentation is the simplest and oldest form of reverse engineering, and is considered to be an unintrusive, weak form of restructuring. The "re-" prefix implies that the intent is to recover documentation about the subject system that once existed or should have existed. Redocumentation can be performed to create additional views that were not created during the original forward engineering process.

Redocumentation tools provide easier ways to visualize relationships among program components so that one can recognize and follow paths clearly. For example, pretty printers display a code listing in an improved form; diagram generators create charts from code directly reflecting the control flow, code structure or data structure of a program; cross-reference listing generators index the use of program variables. These tools present facts about the subject software in another form but without mitigating between life-cycle stages.

Design Recovery

Design recovery is a subset of reverse engineering in which domain knowledge, external information, and deduction or fuzzy reasoning are added to the observations of the subject system to identify meaningful higher-level abstractions beyond those obtainable directly by examining the system itself. Biggerstaff (1989) describes the ultimate goal of design recovery as recreating "design abstractions from a combination of code, existing design documentation (if available), personal experience, and general knowledge about problem and application domains .... In short, design recovery must reproduce all of the information required for a person to fully understand what a program does, how it does it, why it does it, and so forth. Thus, it deals with a far wider range of information than found in conventional software engineering representations or code."

Restructuring

Restructuring is the transformation of a software system from one representation form to another, usually at the same relative abstraction level, while preserving the subject system's external behavior, in particular its functionality and semantics. Restructuring usually involves some form of reverse engineering from the original representation to some intermediate form, which may or may not be made visible to the user. This intermediate form is then appropriately altered, with the restriction that the functionality be preserved.

A restructuring transformation is often one of appearance, such as altering code to improve its structure in the traditional sense of structured design. The term restructuring has come into popular use from the code-to-code transformations that recast a program from an unstructured form ("spaghetti code") to a structured (goto-less) form. However, the term has a broader meaning that recognizes the application of similar transformations and recasting techniques in reshaping data models, design plans, and requirements structures. Data normalization, for example, is a data-to-data restructuring transformation to improve a logical data model in the database design process. Redocumentation can be viewed as a form of restructuring because it provides an alternate if restructured" view of existing information, e.g., pretty-printing is a restructuring of the format of source code.

Many types of restructuring can be performed with knowledge of structural form but without an understanding of meaning. For example, one can convert a series of if statements into a case statement, or vice versa, without knowing the program's purpose or anything about its problem domain.

While restructuring creates new versions that implement or propose change to the subject system, it does not normally involve modifications to meet new requirements. However, it may lead to better observations, of the subject system, that suggest changes that would improve aspects of the system. Restructuring is often used as a form of preventive maintenance to improve the physical state of the subject system with respect to some preferred standard and may also involve adjusting the subject system to meet new environmental constraints that do not involve reassessment at functional requirement levels.

Restructuring tools are often used to attempt to bring order to apparently chaotic software for the purpose of greater understanding. However, it is not a universal cure. Restructuring breaks juxtaposition of code elements and other similar cues that programmers, experienced with a particular piece of software, may rely on. Useful comments in the source code can be rendered meaningless. A programmer who is well familiar with the original program may be lost in the restructured version. Corbi (1989) makes the case that while intramodule restructuring spaghetti-like code would have its benefits in the increase of order and understandability, the process will usually result in more voluminous code leading to higher compile times.

Reengineering

Reengineering is the examination and alteration of a subject system to reconstitute it in a new form and the subsequent implementation of the new form. Implied in this term is the possibility of change in essential requirements, rather than a mere change in form. Reengineering is a change process that generally includes some form of reverse engineering to achieve a more abstract description, followed by some form of forward engineering or restructuring. This process may include modifications with respect to new requirements not met by the original system. During the reengineering of information management systems, organizations generally reassess how the system implements high-level business rules and make modifications to conform to changes in the business.

When reengineering does not involve a change of function, it may look like a restructuring process. Automated program translation, as described by Waters (1988), is a reengineering process since it collects information about one program at a more abstract level and then reimplements the program in another language. While reengineering involves both forward engineering and reverse engineering, it is not their supertype. Reengineering uses available forward and reverse engineering technologies. Both forward and reverse engineering are evolving rapidly, independent of their application for reengineering.

TECHNOLOGY ELEMENTS

Reverse engineering is not a domain of primary invention. Rather, it is the application and expansion of techniques, from a number of software engineering technologies, to the problem of learning about and understanding existing systems.

Artifact Scanning

Reverse engineering draws upon compiler development for parsers and semantic analysis routines that allow source code to be scanned as implementation artifacts. Programs are often held for analysis in a standard intermediate form, such as an abstract syntax tree. The captured representations of programs can then be stored in a repository or database for later analysis.

Source code is not the only source of information. The object code (output of the compiler) can be an effective source of information about basic program structure. Various intermediate products of the compilation process, such as cross-reference tables, can be a rich resource.

System artifacts of all kinds are useful to the reverse engineering project. Job control information from batch JCL statements, Univ Make files, and various kinds of batch (.BAT) files, can provide system-level information that relates programs into execution streams. Data structures and database schemas can map the organization of information processed by programs in the system. Review of all of these artifacts can result in architectural information about the system to be reported or stored for later analysis.

Repository Browsing and Hypertext

Once artifacts about a legacy system are stored in a repository or database, standard database search techniques can be used to "walk around" the information structures and help the user derive new insight. Hypertext capability, such as the facilities described by Bigelow (1988), allow the analyst to gain new insights regarding the system and the way in which its components are interrelated.

A repository about a legacy system can become an organization's collective memory on the architecture of the system. When used in conjunction with CASE tools and metrics, the repository can be a focal point for detection of system problems and consideration of change strategies (Sayani and Svoboda, 1993).

Documentation and Diagram Generation

Document generation is probably the most common application of reverse engineering. Some forms of document and diagram generation, such as source code pretty printers and flow charters, have been refined over several decades. Contractors frequently use templates to generate contractually-required documents, conforming to standards for deliverables in government or military systems, from CASE tools. Selby and Basili (1988) illustrate the creation of hierarchical system descriptions from source code, as an aid to software maintenance.

Research is continuing on alternative ways of presenting information about a software system to achieve the best comprehension among the users of generated documents. For example, Oman and Cook (1990) propose using a book paradigm, generating documents that are cross-referenced topical "chapters" about the structure and features of program code. Their studies suggest a significant improvement in code understanding by using this approach instead of plainly formatted source code.

The generation of diagrams from recovered information is part of the research area becoming known as software visualization. To dump a lot of boxes and lines to a piece of paper is easy and is a hard problem to generate diagrams that are meaningful, readable, aesthetic to the user, and clearly shows the features intended. The state of layout and visualization work in reverse engineering is illustrated by (Brown and Gargiulo, 1992; Smart and Vemuri, 1992; Gansner and co-workers, 1992; Brown and Stafford, 1992).

Olshefski and Cole (1993), describing IBM Research's PUNDIT prototype, illustrate the use of diagram generation for both static and dynamic program information in an integrated tools environment. Cross (1993) describes the automatic generation of control structure diagrams from Ada PDL or source code.

Decomposition and Program Slicing

Various decomposition strategies are used in reverse engineering to learn more about the structure of the software. The foremost decomposition strategy is program slicing, introduced by Weiser (1974), whereby the program paths examined are restricted to those which use or change the value of a particular data item or structure. Beck and Eichmann (1993) illustrate how slicing techniques assist the comprehension of program function at both statement and module levels. The decomposition concept is carried further by Ning and co-workers, (1993) in their work on identifying potentially reusable components by program segmentation.

Recognition of Patterns/Plans

A major area of reverse engineering research is how to recognize understood structures in programs and systems. Letovsky (1988), as well as Letovsky and Soloway (1986), describe many of the issues involved in recognizing plans (known programming patterns, such as the bubble sort algorithm) in computer programs. Plan recognition has been, and continues to be, widely explored, particular in the intersection between the artificial intelligence and software engineering communities. For example, see the work of Rich and Waters (1988), Rich and Wills (1990), and Quilici (1993).

Integration of Tools/CASE

Reverse engineering on anything larger than toy examples requires a way to hold information about the subject system and multiple tools able to contribute to the capture and analysis of such information. Therefore, CASE and reverse engineering are well matched. CASE tools provide a repository for the storage of recovered and derived information, as well as a framework in which multiple tools can share the same information or knowledgebase. Reverse engineering provides CASE with access to existing systems, which, unlike all but the very late stages of new systems development, has sufficient complexity to fully utilize the analytical capabilities of CASE.

There are many commercial CASE systems that incorporate some reverse engineering capabilities, including products of Interactive Development Environments (IDE), Cadre Technologies, Knowledgeware, and ViaSoft. However, the kind and degree of reverse engineering varies widely. Any vendor whose tool can read some limited information from a Cobol program can promote the product as having reverse engineering, and many do so. But there are CASE vendors, such as CGI with its PAC/Reverse product, McCabe and Associates with its Battlemap and ACT toolkits, and the other vendors listed above, who have comprehensive reverse engineering offerings.

Perhaps the most robust set of reverse engineering tools is marketed by Bachman Information Systems in the area of database design. The Bachman system combines reverse engineering technology (capture, populate the repository, and derive more abstract presentations), code generation capability, and an expert system approach for the data analyst, data administrator, and database designer, based on specific expertise regarding analysis and migration of data structures and database architecture. The result is a comprehensive working environment for data engineering and database migration, incorporating reverse engineering as a natural part of the process.

The combination of CASE and reverse engineering creates new possibilities realigning existing systems with current business needs. See the article on CASE for a discussion of this realignment process.

BIBLIOGRAPHY

J. Beck, and D. Eichmann, "Program and Interface Slicing for Reverse Engineering," *Proceedings, Working Conf. on Reverse Engineering,* IEEE Computer Society Press, Los Alamitos, Calif., May, 1993.

J. Bigelow, "Hypertext and CASE," *IEEE Software,* 23–27 (Mar. 1988).

T. J. Biggerstaff, "Design Recovery for Maintenance and Reuse," *IEEE Computer* **22**(7), 36–49 (1989).

P. Brown, and T. Gargiulo, "An Object Oriented Layout for Directed Graphs," *Proceedings Assessment of Quality Software Development Tools,* IEEE Computer Society Press, Los Alamitos, Calif., 1992.

P. Brown and D. W. Stafford, "Graph Services for Program Understanding," *Proceedings, Assessment of Quality Software Development Tools,* IEEE Computer Society Press, Los Alamitos, Calif., 1992.

E. Byrne, "Software Reverse Engineering: A Case Study," *Software—Practice and Experience,* **21**(12), (Dec. 1991).

E. Chikofsky, "The Database as a Business Road Map—Reading Business Problems from the Database Structure," *Database Programming & Design* (May 1990).

E. Chikofsky and J. Cross, "Reverse Engineering and Design Recovery: A Taxonomy," *IEEE Software,* **7**(1), 13–17 (Jan. 1990).

E. Chikofsky, "Application of an Information Systems Analysis and Design Tool to the Maintenance Effort," *IFIP TC Working Conference on System Description Methodologies,* Kecskemet, Hungary, May, 1983, North-Holland, 1985.

L. Cleveland, "A Program Understanding Support Environment," *IBM Syst. J.* **28**(2), 324–344 (1989).

T. A. Corbi, "Program Understanding: Challenge for the 1990s," *IBM Syst. J.* **28**(2), 294–306 (1989).

J. Cross, "Reverse Engineering Control Structure Diagrams," *Proceedings Working Conf. on Reverse Engineering,* IEEE Computer Society Press, Los Alamitos, Calif., May 1993.

E. Gansner and co-workers, "Graph Visualization in Software Analysis," *Proceedings Assessment of Quality Software Development Tools,* IEEE Computer Society Press, Los Alamitos, Calif., 1992.

S. Letovsky and E. Soloway, "Delocalized Plans and Program Comprehension," *IEEE Software,* 41–49 (May 1986).

S. Letovsky, *Plan Analysis of Programs,* Yale University, New Haven, Conn., Dec. 1988, Ph.D. dissertation.

J. Martin, *Recommended Diagramming Standards for Analysts and Programmers,* Prentice-Hall, Inc., Englewood Cliffs, N.J., 1987.

J. Martin and C. McClure, *Structured Techniques: The Basis for CASE,* revised ed., Prentice-Hall, Inc., Englewood Cliffs, N.J., 1988.

T. J. McCabe, "A Complexity Measure," *IEEE Transactions on Software Engineering,* **2**(4), 308 (1976).

T. McCabe, Jr., "Battlemap, ACT Show Code Structure, Complexity," *IEEE Software* **7**(3), 62 (1990).

C. McClure, *The Three Rs of Software Automation,* Prentice-Hall, Inc., Englewood Cliffs, N.J., 1992.

P. Newcomb and L. Markosian, "Automating the Modularization of Large Cobol Programs: Application of an Enabling Technology for Reengineering," *Proceedings Working Conf. on Reverse Engineering,* IEEE Computer Society Press, Los Alamitos, Calif., May 1993.

J. Q. Ning, A. Engberts, and W. Kozaczynski, "Recovering Reusable Components from Legacy Systems by Program Segmentation," *Proceedings Working Conf. on Reverse Engineering,* IEEE Computer Society Press, Los Alamitos, Calif., May, 1993.

D. Olshefski and A. Cole, "A Prototype System for Static and Dynamic Program Understanding," *Proceedings Working Conf. on Reverse Engineering,* IEEE Computer Society Press, Los Alamitos, Calif., May, 1993.

P. W. Oman and C. R. Cook, "The Book Paradigm for Improved Maintenance," *IEEE Software* **7**(1), 39–45 (1990).

L. J. Peters, *Software Design: Methods & Techniques,* Yourdon Press, New York, 1981.

R. S. Pressman, *Software Engineering: A Practitioner's Approach,* 3rd ed., McGraw-Hill Book Co., Inc., New York, 1992.

A. Quilici, "A Hybrid Approach to Recognizing Programming Plans," *Proceedings Working Conf. on Reverse Engineering,* IEEE Computer Society Press, Los Alamitos, Calif., May, 1993.

M. G. Rekoff, "On Reverse Engineering," *IEEE Transactions on Systems Man and Cybernetics,* **SMC-15**(2), 244–252 (1985).

C. Rich and R. Waters, "The Programmer's Apprentice: A Research Overview," *Computer,* 10–25 (Nov. 1988).

C. Rich and L. M. Wills, "Recognizing a program's design: A graph-parsing approach," *IEEE Software,* **7**(1), 82–89 (1990).

S. Rugaber, S. B. Omburn, and R. J. LeBlanc, Jr., "Recognizing design decisions in programs," *IEEE Software,* **7**(1), 46–54 (1990).

H. Sayani and C. Svoboda, "Integrating CASE Using Existing Tools" in T. Bergin, *Computer-Aided Software Engineering: Issues & Trends for the 1990s and Beyond,* Idea Group Publishing, Harrisburg, Pa., 1993.

R. W. Selby and V. Basili, "Error Localization During Software Maintenance: Generating Hierarchical System Descriptions from the Source Code Alone," *Proc. Conf. on Software Maintenance 1988,* IEEE Computer Society Press, Los Alamitos, Calif., 1988, pp. 192–197.

J. Smart and V. Vemuri, "A-Vu: A Visualization Tool for Complex Software Systems," *Proceedings, Assessment of Quality Software Development Tools,* IEEE Computer Society Press, Los Alamitos, Calif., 1992.

I. Sommerville, *Software Engineering,* 4th ed., Addison-Wesley, Wokingham, UK., 1992.

W. Stevens, *Software Design: Concepts and Methods,* Prentice-Hall International, Hertfordshire UK., 1991.

R. Waters, "Program Translation Via Abstraction and Re-Implementation," *IEEE Transactions on Software Engineering,* **SE-14**(8), (Aug. 1988).

R. Waters and E. Chikofsky, eds., *Proceedings, Working Conf. on Reverse Engineering,* IEEE Computer Society Press, Los Alamitos, Calif., May, 1993.

M. Weiser, "Program Slicing," *IEEE Transactions on Software Engineering,* **SE-10**(4), 352–357 (July 1984).

ELLIOT CHIKOFSKY
Northeastern University

JAMES H. CROSS II
Auburn University

REVIEWS AND AUDITS

Reviews and audits are valuable tools used in software development projects. Reviews come in different forms and names. Some of these are formal reviews, inspections, audits, and walkthroughs. The most common characteristics that distinguish these forms are purpose, scope, and method. The purpose of this article is to introduce these forms, explain the basic differences between them, and provide insight into how they are applied in software development practice. Table 1 depicts these general characteristics which are detailed below.

The scope of a review may range from the entire project to a review of the design, or a single document such as a users guide. The purpose may range from an inspection of a product to a review of the completion of a development milestone. The method may vary from free form, or informal, to a specific methodology such as formal inspections.

DEFINITIONS

According to the IEEE Standard Glossary of Software Engineering Terminology (IEEE, 1990a) a review is

A process or meeting during which a work product, or a set of work products, is presented to project personnel, managers, users, customers, or other interested parties for comment or approval. Types include code review, design review, formal qualification review, requirements review, and test readiness review.

This definition is the most general form and is focused and customized depending on the specific purpose of the review.

Reviews are further classified according to formality. A formal review is typically one that is required by a contract commitment which is usually invoked through the application of a standard such as DOD-STD-2167A (DOD, 1988). The implication is that it is a contractual milestone witnessed by the customer, and denotes the completion of certain activities such as detailed design. Another view is that there is a certain obligation that needs to be met or satisfied. Freedman and Weinberg use the following criteria to classify a formal review (Freedman and Weinberg, 1990a).

1. A written report on the status of the product reviewed—a report that is available to everyone involved in the project, including management
2. Active and open participation of everyone in the review group, following some traditions, customs, and written rules as to how such a review is to be conducted
3. Full responsibility of all participants for the quality of the review—that is, for the quality of the information in the written report.

Informal reviews are those that are held which are not contractually required, such as technical interchange meetings, where the purpose is one of providing a periodic

Table 1. Review Characteristics

Type	Scope	Purpose	Method
Reviews	Usually broad	Project progress Assessment of milestone completion	*Ad Hoc*
Walk-through	Fairly narrow	Assess specific development products	Static analysis of products
Inspections	Narrow	Assess specific development products	Noninteractive, fairly procedural
Audits	Range from narrow to broad	Check processes and products of development	Formal, mechanical and procedure

interchange of information. There are other types of review classifications; for example, internal management reviews (Marciniak and Reifer, 1990). These types may be periodic reviews of the project by senior management within the developing organization to assess progress, or special reviews based on specific issues such as the impact of the development on other market areas. In the latter, management uses the review to provide general awareness of the direction of the project in order to take advantage of the resulting product in other market areas or to avoid conflict with other company projects.

Another major review classification, peer review, is usually walkthroughs, inspections, and round-robin reviews (Freedman and Weinberg, 1990b). The common characteristic of a peer review is that it is conducted by peers. These reviews are normally confined to a single product such as a segment of the design, or to a code unit or component. The definitions of these reviews follows: A walkthrough is

> *A static analysis technique in which a designer or programmer leads members of the development team and other interested parties through a segment of documentation or code, and the participants ask questions and make comments about possible errors, violation of development standards, and other problems (IEEE, 1990b).*

A walkthrough, normally a peer review, is conducted, in many cases, with participants who are non-peers. Walkthroughs are sometimes referred to as structured walkthroughs (not to be confused with formal inspections, see STRUCTURED WALKTHROUGHS; however, according to Freedman and Weinberg (1990c) they are one and the same. A walkthrough is a common review technique in a software project but the method will vary based on individual implementation.

A special form of a walkthrough, the Formal Inspection, was developed at IBM (Fagen, 1976) (also see Inspections) and is often referred to as Fagen Inspections. A principal distinguishing factor of a walkthrough and a formal inspection is that the formal inspection is always a peer review. It is led by a moderator whereas the walkthrough will be led by a reader or presenter, and the collection of anomalies is carefully structured to capture statistical evidence of the effort. A formal inspection should not be confused with an inspection. The choice of the term is perhaps unfortunate as the formal inspection is a type of walkthrough rather than an inspection. Hollocker discusses the procedures used for Formal Inspections; however, he chooses to use the words "Software Inspection" (Hollocker, 1990).

Inspection

An inspection is

> *a static analysis technique that relies on visual examination of development products to detect errors, violations of developing standards, and other problems. Types include code inspection; design inspections (IEEE, 1990c).*

Freedman and Weinberg define inspection as "a method of rapidly evaluating material by confining attention to a few selected aspects, one at a time" (Freedman and Weinberg, 1990d). The inspection, like an audit, is carried out in a noninteractive manner, usually by a party that is detached from the developer.

Audits

An audit is much like an inspection, however, tends to be more defined according to purpose and is usually conducted using defined criteria. An example is the physical configuration audit. In the general form an audit is

> *An independent examination of a work product or set of work products to assess compliance with specifications, standards, contractual agreements, or other criteria (IEEE, 1990d).*

The IEEE defines two specific forms of audits, the Functional Configuration Audit (FCA) and the Physical Configuration Audit (PCA). A functional configuration audit (FCA) is

> *an audit conducted to verify that the development of a configuration item has been completed satisfactorily, that the item has achieved the performance and functional characteristics specified in the functional or allocated configuration identification, and that its operational and support documents are complete and satisfactory (IEEE, 1990e).*

A physical configuration audit (PCA) is

> *an audit conducted to verify that a configuration item, as built, conforms to the technical documentation that defined it (IEEE, 1990f).*

These two audits are formal audits because they are required by the contractual instruments that govern the development project. If there were no contractual instrument, the eventual user would still conduct a form of the above to verify the product. A simple example is buying an automobile. When the automobile is ordered, a spec sheet or contract is normally filled out calling for items such as fog lights, radios, etc. A functional audit would verify that the radio performs, e.g., that it plays the bands specified, while a physical audit would verify that the type of radio ordered is the one that is actually delivered with the automobile.

There are other types of audits that are conducted during the development process. For example, there are quality assurance audits that audit a particular process of development such as the conduct of reviews and walkthroughs and there are configuration management audits that audit the processes of configuration management.

APPLICATION IN THE LIFE CYCLE

Reviews, audits, walkthroughs and inspections are used to provide assessment of the progress, processes used, and products of the project. The program management plan, or software development plan, will normally specify the types of reviews used and the methods that are applied in their use. Certain reviews, as mentioned above, will be dictated by contract requirements usually through the use of development standards such as DOD-STD-2167A (DOD, 1988). The 2167A life cycle with examples of system development reviews and audits is shown in ACQUISITION MANAGEMENT. In Figure 1, how other reviews are integrated into the life cycle model is shown.

The following examples of review procedures have been excised from Charles Hollocker's *Software Reviews and Audits,* John Wiley & Sons, New York, 1990.

Management Reviews

Objective. A *management review* is a formal management-team evaluation of a project-level plan or a project's status relative to such a plan. The review team communicates progress, coordinates the decision making within their span of control and provides recommendations for:

- Making activities progress according to plan, based on an evaluation of product development status
- Changing project direction or identifying the need for alternative planning
- Maintaining global control of the project through adequate allocation of resources

Moreover, to further tailor this review process for an individual project milestone, specific objectives are to be identified in a "Statement of Objectives" made available before the review meeting. The management review concept can be applied to new development or to maintenance activities. It can also be useful in managing process improvement projects.

People and Their Agendas. Roles for the management review include:

- Leader
- Reporter
- Team member

The review leader is responsible for the administrative tasks pertaining to the review, for assuring that the review is conducted in an orderly manner, and for issuing any minutes or reports. The reporter is responsible for having the project status and all supporting documentation available for distribution before the meeting. This individual is also responsible for documenting the findings, decisions, and recommendations of the review team.

When to Hold a Management Review. Typically, the project planning documents (for example, Software Quality Assurance Plan, Software Development Plan, or Software Verification and Validation Plan) establish the need for conducting specific management reviews. As stated in these plans, a management review can be initiated by the completion of a project phase or specific software deliverable (for example, a planning document, a requirements specification, or a design document). Moreover, management reviews not required by plan may occur, as needed, to deal with any unscheduled events or contingencies.

A selected review leader establishes or confirms a statement of objectives for the meeting and verifies that any appropriate software deliverables and any other documents or reports are available and sufficiently complete to support the review objectives. In addition to any applicable reference material supplied by project management, or requested by the review leader, these would include:

- A Statement of Objectives for the management review and its agenda
- Current project schedule, resource, and cost data
- Pertinent reports (for example, managerial review reports, technical review reports, or audit reports) from other reviews and/or audits already completed
- Software deliverable status or current disposition

Procedures. The review leader, having identified the team, schedules facilities for the meeting and distributes any materials needed by the review team for advanced preparation (for example, statement of objectives, agenda, or presentation requirements). In addition, the review leader might consider requesting that a project representative conduct an overview session for the review team. This overview can occur as part of the examination meeting or as a separate meeting. It is critical that each individual on the review team studies the material and prepares for the review meeting. The management review process is considered complete when all issues identified in the review "Statement of Objectives" have been addressed and the management review report has been issued. Project management typically tracks any action items through to resolution. If a re-review is required, it would provide confirmation of action item completion.

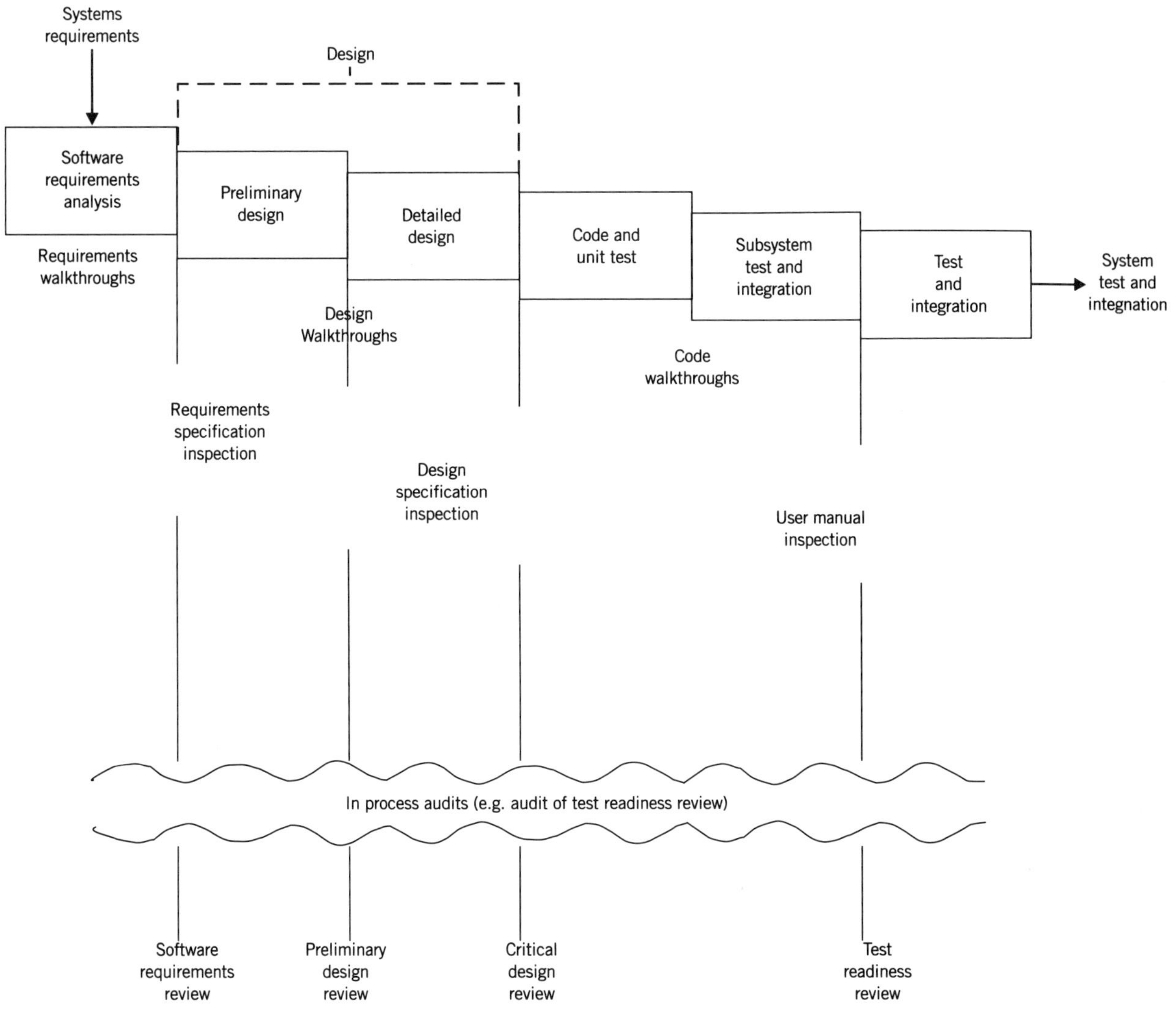

Figure 1. Reviews in the software life cycle.

Output. The Management Review Report identifies:

- The project being reviewed and the team that participated in that review
- Inputs to the review
- Review objectives
- Action item ownership, status, and tracking responsibility
- Project status and a list of issues that must be addressed for the project to meet its milestone
- Recommendations regarding any further reviews and audits, and a list of additional information and data that must be obtained before they can be executed

The Walkthrough

Objective. The walkthrough process has much in common with both the general technical review process and the inspection process. It, too, is used to evaluate a specific software element and provide evidence that the software element satisfies its specifications and conforms to applicable standards. Its statement of objectives includes software element specific objectives. They also exist in the form of a checklist that varies with the product being presented. Objectives typically do not pertain to any additional constraints on the walkthrough process.

Distinctions from other review processes, however, are established by unique objectives. The following always appear in the statement of objectives for the application of the walkthrough process:

- Detect, identify, and describe software element defects
- Examine alternatives and stylistic issues
- Provide a mechanism that enables the authors to collect valuable feedback on their work, yet allows them to retain the decision-making authority for any changes

People and Their Agendas. Roles for the walkthrough are similar to those for other review processes, with one important distinction. The leader responsible for conducting a specific walkthrough, handling the administrative tasks pertaining to the walkthrough, and ensuring that the walkthrough is conducted in an orderly manner is usually the author.

The scribe is responsible for writing down all comments made during the walkthrough that pertain to errors found, questions of style, omissions, contradictions, suggestions for improvement, or alternative approaches.

Each team member is responsible for reviewing any input material prior to the walkthrough and participating during the walkthrough to ensure that it meets its objective. Roles may be shared among the walkthrough members.

When to Hold the Walkthrough Meeting. The need for conducting walkthroughs, as with all product reviews, can be established either by local practice or in planning documents. Completion of a specific software element can trigger the walkthrough for that element. Additional walkthroughs can be conducted during development of the software element at the request of the author or management from various functional areas. A walkthrough is conducted when the author indicates readiness.

Procedures. *Planning.* During the planning phase the author:

- Identifies the walkthrough team
- Schedules the meeting and selects the meeting place
- Distributes all necessary input materials to the participants, allowing for adequate preparation time

Overview. An overview presentation is made by the author as part of the walkthrough meeting. Before that meeting, however, individual preparation is still required.

Preparation. During the preparation phase participants review the input material that was distributed to them and prepare a list of questions and issues to be brought up during the walkthrough.

Examination. During the walkthrough meeting:

- The author makes an overview presentation of the software element
- The author "walks through" the specific software element so that members of the walkthrough team may ask questions or raise issues about the software element, and/or make notes documenting their concerns
- The scribe writes down comments and decisions for inclusion in the walkthrough report

At the completion of the walkthrough, the team may recommend a follow-up walkthrough that follows the same process and would, at a minimum, cover areas changed by the author. The walkthrough process is complete when the entire software element has been walked through in detail and all deficiencies, omissions, efficiency issues, and suggestions for improvement have been noted. The walkthrough report is issued, as required by local standards.

Output. The walkthrough report contains:

- Identification of the walkthrough team
- Identification of the software element(s) being examined
- The statement of objectives that were to be handled during this walkthrough meeting
- A list of the noted deficiencies, omissions, contradictions, and suggestions for improvement
- Any recommendation made by the walkthrough team on how to dispose of deficiencies and unresolved issues. If follow-up walkthroughs are suggested, that should be mentioned in the report as well

Audits

Objective. Audits, performed in accordance with documented plans and procedures, provide an independent confirmation that product development and process execution adhere to standards, guidelines, specifications, and procedures. Audit personnel use objective audit criteria (for example, contracts and plans; standards, practices and conventions: or requirements and specifications) to evaluate:

- Software elements
- The processes for producing them
- Projects
- Entire quality programs

People and Their Agendas. It is the responsibility of the audit team leader to organize and direct the audit and to coordinate the preparation and issuance of the audit report. The audit team leader is ultimately responsible for the proper conduct of the audit and its reports, and makes sure that the audit team is prepared.

The entity initiating the audit is responsible for authorizing the audit. Management of the auditing organization assumes responsibility for the audit and the allocation of the necessary resources to perform the audit.

Those whose products and processes are being audited provide all relevant materials and resources and correct or resolve deficiencies cited by the audit team.

When to Audit. The need for an audit is established by one of the following events:

- A special project milestone, calendar date, or other criterion has been met and, as part of its charter, the auditing organization is to respond by initiating an audit.
- A special project milestone has been reached. The audit is initiated per earlier plans (for example, the Software Quality Assurance Plan, or Software Development Plan). This includes planned milestones for controlling supplier development.
- External parties (for example, regulatory agencies or end users) require an audit at a specific calendar date or project milestone. This may be in fulfillment of a

contract requirement or as a prerequisite to contractual agreement.

- A local organizational element(s) (for example, project management, functional management, systems engineering, or internal quality assurance/control) has requested the audit, establishing a clear and specific need.

Perhaps the most important inputs required to assure the success of the audit are the purpose and scope of the audit. Observations and evaluations performed as part of the audit require objective audit criteria, such as contracts requirements, plans, specifications, procedures, guidelines, and standards. The software elements and processes to be audited need to be made accessible, as do any pertinent histories. Background information about the organization responsible for the products and processes being audited (for example, organization charts) are critical for both planning and execution of the audit.

Procedures. The auditing organization develops and documents an audit plan for each audit. This plan should, in addition to restating the audit scope, identify the:

- Project processes to be examined (provided as input) and the time frame for audit team observations
- Software to be examined (provided as input) and their availability—where sampling is used, a statistically valid sampling methodology is used to establish selection criteria and sample size
- Reporting requirements (that is, results report, and optionally, the recommendations report with their general format and distribution defined)—whether recommendations are required or excluded should be explicitly stated
- Required follow-up activities
- Activities, elements, and procedures necessary to meet the scope of the audit
- Objective Audit Criteria that provide the basis for determining compliance (provided as input)
- Audit Procedures and Checklists
- Audit Personnel requirements (for example, number, skills, experience, and responsibilities)
- Organizations involved in the audit (for example, the organization whose products and processes are being audited)
- Date, time, place, agenda, and intended audience of "overview" session (optional)

The audit team leader prepares an audit team having the necessary background and (when allowed) notifies the involved organizations, giving them a reasonable amount of advance warning before the audit is performed. The notification should be written to include audit scope, the identification of processes and products to be audited, and the auditors' identity.

An optional overview meeting with the audited organization is recommended to "kick-off" the examination phase of the audit. The overview meeting, led by the audit team leader, provides:

- Overview of existing agents (for example, audit scope, plan, and related contracts)
- Overview of production and processes being audited
- Overview of the audit process, its objectives, and outputs
- Expected contributions of the audited organization to the audit process (that is, the number of people to be interviewed, meeting facilities, et cetera)
- Specific audit schedule

The following preparations are required by the audit team:

- Understand the organization: It is essential to identify functions and activities performed by the audited organization and to identify functional responsibility
- Understand the products and processes: It is a prerequisite for the team to learn about the products and processes being audited through readings and briefing
- Understand the Objective Audit Criteria: It is important that the audit team become familiar with the objective and criteria to be used in the audit
- Prepare for the Audit Report: It is important to choose the administrative reporting mechanism that will be used throughout the audit to develop the report that follows the layout identified in the audit plan
- Detail the audit plan: Choose appropriate methods for each step in the audit program

In addition, the audit team leader makes the necessary arrangements for:

- Team orientation and training
- Facilities for audit interviews
- Materials, documents, and tools required by the audit procedures
- The software elements to be audited (for example, documents, computer files, personnel to be interviewed)
- Scheduling interviews

Elements that have been selected for audit are evaluated against the Objective Audit Criteria. Evidence is examined to the depth necessary to determine if these elements comply with specified criteria.

An audit is considered complete when:

- Each element(s) within the scope of the audit has been examined
- Findings have been presented to be audited organization
- Response to draft findings have been received and evaluated

- Final findings have been formally presented to the audited organization and initiating entity
- The audit report has been prepared and submitted to recipients designated in the audit plan
- The recommendation report, if required by plan, has been prepared and submitted to recipients designated in the audit plan
- All of the auditing organization's follow-up actions included in the scope (or contract) of the audit have been performed.

Output. Following a standard framework for audit reports, the draft and final audit reports contain:

- Audit Identification: Report title, audited organization, auditing organization, and date of the audit
- Scope: Scope of the audit, including an enumeration of the standards, specifications, practices, and procedures constituting the Objective Audit Criteria against which the audit of the software elements and processes was conducted
- Conclusions: A summary and interpretation of the audit findings, including the key items of non-conformance
- Synopsis: A listing of all the audited software elements and processes, and associated findings
- Follow-up: The type and timing of audit follow-up activities

Additionally, when stipulated by the audit plan, recommendations are provided to the audited organization, or the entity that initiated the audit. Recommendations are reported separately from results.

Comments and issues raised by the audited organization must be resolved. The final audit report should then be prepared, approved, and issued by the audit team leader to the organizations specified in the audit plan.

SUMMARY

There are many different types of reviews used in a software development process ranging from informal technical reviews to formal reviews such as the FCA. The types and number of reviews are largely determined by the complexity and size of the project. In a project that is internal to an organization the reviews tend to be more informal compared to a project that is under contract to a customer. They are just as important, however, and must not be ignored in an internal project. Normally the number and types of reviews will be detailed in management plans with specific methods left to a procedures and standards handbook.

There are different reasons for conducting reviews. The principal purpose is to assess the progress or integrity of a process or product. Reviews are also important for gathering data. The systematic collection of data is essential for assessing the process in order to support process improvement programs as well as developing experiential data for application with new projects. These data can support the prediction of various activities such as the quality of products through comparisons of previous data collected on prior projects.

Thus, reviews, of all sorts, provide a basic performance and assessment technique that bridges the individual project, and even organization. They are the essential performance technique in software development practice.

Portions of this article have been excised from Charles Hollocker, *Software Reviews and Audits,* John Wiley and Sons, Inc., New York, 1990.

BIBLIOGRAPHY

Department of Defense Standard 2167A, Defense System Software Development, Feb. 29, 1988.

M. Fagen, "Design And Code Inspection to Reduce Errors in Program Development" *IBM Systems Journal* **15**(3) (1976).

D. Freedman and G. M. Weinberg, *Walkthroughs, Inspections, and Technical Reviews,* 3rd ed., Dorset House, New York, 1990a, pp. 10–11; 1990b, p. 243–249; 1990c, p. 232; 1990d, pp. 239–242.

C. Hollocker, *Software Reviews and Audits,* John Wiley & Sons, Inc., New York, 1990, pp. 44–48.

IEEE Std 610.12-1990, Standard Glossary of Software Engineering Terminology, IEEE, New York, 1990a, p. 64; 1990b, p. 81; 1990c, p. 40; 1990d, p. 11; 1990e, p. 35; 1990f. p. 55.

J. J. Marciniak and D. J. Reifer, *Software Acquisition Management,* John Wiley & Sons Inc., 1990, p. 26.

John J. Marciniak
CTA INCORPORATED

REVS

See Software requirements engineering methodology.

RISC

RISC, or Reduced Instruction Set Computer, implies a computer with an instruction set that is reduced in number and complexity of instructions from typical third generation computers. (Contrast with Complex Instruction Set Computer, see CISC.) A RISC machine typically has less than 100 instructions as contrasted with a CISC machine which could have up to 300 instructions. As the evolution of computers progressed, advanced instruction sets became more complex for a variety of reasons: (1) to decrease the semantic distance between the machine and the programmer, thus, increase the efficiency of High Order Language (HOL) implementation; (2) the ease at which new instructions and features could be implemented in microcode chip implementations, and (3) achieving upward compatibility in new machines through the super-setting of instruction set functions and features. It was found, however, that many of these complex instructions were never used or executed, yet there implementation in hardware was costly in terms of chip architecture. Clearly, the simpler the chip, the lower chip manufacturing costs. The concept of reducing the instruction set to lower chip cost resulted in the creation of the RISC chip. In their paper "Instruction Sets and Beyond: Computer, Complexity, and Controversy," Colwell and colleagues propose the following six criteria for RISC classification:

1. Single-cycle operation.
2. Load/store design.
3. Hardwired control.
4. Relatively few instructions and addressing modes.
5. Fixed instruction format.
6. More compile-time efforts.

There is controversy over the execution efficiency of RISC machines versus CISC machines. However, there are a number of RISC machines that are offered on the market today.

BIBLIOGRAPHY

R. P. Colwell and co-workers, "Instruction Sets and Beyond: Computer, Complexity, and Controversy," *IEEE Computer,* Vol. **18**(9), 8–19 (Sept. 1985).

RISK MANAGEMENT

The art of management has been defined as the distribution of current resources to shape a more desirable future state (Glickman, 1990). However, the future is not always as envisioned, because the path to the future is neither immutable nor totally predictable. How well one manages the risks, as well as the opportunities, that materialize along the way will determine whether a more desirable state is achieved. Thus risk management can be described as the continuous analysis of the current situation to realign current resources and management policies against current and future threats, or to maximize the opportunities that are present, thus helping to ensure that the state originally envisioned or one that is better occurs. The basic questions that risk management attempts to answer are (Charette, 1989):

- What risks confront the current situation?
- What is the probability of loss from them?
- How much are the losses likely to cost?
- What might be the losses if the worst happened?
- What alternative choices exist to avert the risks?
- How can the potential losses be reduced or eliminated?
- Will the alternatives produce other risks?

Risk management has been applied for many years in the financial, petrochemical, and insurance communities, but the application of formalized risk management is a relatively new phenomenon in the software engineering community. Although the evaluation and management of risk in software-intensive projects have been recognized as an important issue for some time, especially in the defense community (DMSC, 1983), the first full length treatments of the subject relating to software engineering appeared in 1989 (Boehm; Charette). The prime motivation for the currently rising interest in risk management and software engineering can be directly traced to two overriding business, as opposed to technology, considerations. The first is the ever increasing complexity and cost of developing software-intensive systems, coupled with the intensifying negative impact on businesses and individuals when they go awry (Neumann, 1991). The second is that software-intensive systems have finally achieved the long promised state of becoming the paramount strategic element in an organization's short-term and long-term competitive success equation (Porter, 1985).

The ability to apply computing effectively and efficiently has now become the most important element in the majority of businesses' operations, and this ability is strongly linked to the organization's software engineering capability. However, it has been demonstrated convincingly that there is no direct link between corporate profitability and the degree to which money is spent upon computing systems and related technology such as software engineering (Strassman, 1990). This surprising and, to many, distressing result has caused many businesses to rethink the value they are receiving from their computing operations. For many businesses the question is increasing becoming not only what computing will do for the organization, but what will computing do *to* the organization. Thus, by necessity, the concepts of risk management and software engineering are becoming very tightly coupled to one another.

Due to its early historical use, the term "risk management" possesses different meanings to different parts of the software engineering community (Charette, 1990). To some members of the community the term risk management implies involvement primarily with security concerns such as privacy, unauthorized access, viruses, etc., while to others risk management involves principally software safety issues. Still to others risk management chiefly involves software operational and disaster recovery concerns. The trend that is emerging, however, is to consider risk management as including not only each of these specific topics, but to include them within a framework that also encompasses the analysis and management of the risks involved in the acquisition, systems engineering, software engineering, and operations of software-intensive systems. The terms, "risk engineering" or "total risk management" invoke this wider meaning, as well as take into account the creation of business opportunities that risk taking implies (Charette, 1990; Haimes, 1991).

The risk management field as it applies specifically to software engineering is currently experiencing a period of rapid growth and increased stature, with many governmental and commercial initiatives being pursued to codify the many diverse aspects of the subject into a unified whole. Current research and applicative efforts undertaken in software engineering related risk management have been concentrated in three overlapping provinces: theory, mechanics, and practice.

RISK MANAGEMENT THEORY

The theory of the management of risk usually begins with the definition of the term "risk." This is not necessarily such an easy task, since risk is a "portmanteau word." For example, in some cases, the term risk will be used to denote an action, such as "to risk success," while in others it will be used to denote a thing, such as "the risk of losing." To muddy the waters still further, the term "hazard" is often used interchangeably with the term risk, and is has been defined in the risk management literature as meaning "to risk the occurrence of something happening" as well as a "source of risk" (Moore, 1983; Cohrssen, 1989).

Because of its multiple, and often subtle, meanings, full agreement on the definition of a risk is often accomplished neither quickly nor easily in practice. For instance, risk is often defined as, "the potential for realization of unwanted, negative consequences of an event" (Rowe, 1988). A careful study of the definition, however, demonstrates the difficulty in attempting to determine what constitutes a risk. One needs to look no further than investigate the use of the term "unwanted" in the definition above, as the use of this term implies that two different properties may simultaneously coexist. The first is that a risk does not represent an absolute quantity that can be measured in the scientific sense, but is in actuality a perceived quantity. What is wanted or unwanted can vary from situation to situation, and what is once wanted may quickly become unwanted as circumstances change. It is an old aphorism, but one person's risk is often another person's opportunity.

The other property implied by the use of the term "unwanted" is that there may or may not be some choice involved in being a party to the event at risk. It is this second property, especially when coupled with the word "potential," where most often trouble erupts in the practical application of risk management. For example, consider the risk (i.e., the chance or likelihood) of a person's home being struck by some random celestial body penetrating the earth's atmosphere. This situation is typically christened a probabilistic exposure to risk (Rowe, 1988). Now, if the collision was with say, a meteorite weighing 1 ton, as the one that fell in Kansas in 1948, one could reasonably be sure that the house would be destroyed in the collision's aftermath. On the other hand, if the object were a typically sized meteorite, the likelihood of the house being struck and destroyed is infinitesimally small. Thus the effects or consequences of a random celestial body causing damage to a house may be said to be deterministic in nature, as in the case of a collision with a 1-ton meteorite, or probabilistic, as in the case of a typical meteorite. Similarly, there are the cases of (**1**) deterministic exposure to risk, such as getting a vaccination, with a probabilistic effect, e.g., health effects from an allergic reaction to the vaccine, and (**2**) deterministic exposure and deterministic effects, e.g., jumping out of a plane without a parachute. These four possibilities are depicted in Figure 1.

The cases of probabilistic vs. deterministic events and consequences seem straightforward in the examples above, but in practice, situations are not that clear (Glickman, 1990). The main difficulty lies in the area of perspective. For example, one can choose oneself to be placed at risk (i.e., deterministic exposure) or be placed at risk by "acts of God" (i.e., probabilistic exposure). Acts of God are usually thought of as earthquakes, hurricanes, floods, plagues, etc. (Rowe, 1988). We are using the term to indicate anything that is probabilistic in nature. But what about the case of being placed at risk by another? For instance, many engineers would argue that a catastrophic failure of an airliner's automatic landing control system would constitute an example of a certain deterministic exposure (choosing to use the landing control system) possessing probabilistic effects (stemming from unpredictable hardware or software failure). A lawyer for a family member killed in an airplane crash that experienced such a catastrophic failure occurring during approach, on the other hand, might categorize this same situation as a case of probabilistic exposure (the same system would have been built differently by other engineers) possessing deterministic effects (the engineers used poor systems or software engineering practice with the result being the failure of the system).

	Probabilistic exposure	Deterministic exposure
Probabilistic consequence	Having allergic reactions after being stung by a bee	Health effects after getting a vaccination
Deterministic consequence	Being hit by a large meteorite while standing in a field	Jumping out of a plane without a parachute

Figure 1. Different methods of exposure and consequences.

As a practical manner in the software engineering domain, one usually views all situations as falling into the deterministic exposure category (Charette, 1989). This is not to say that probabilistic exposure situations are not recognized, such as the probability of hardware wearing out, but that there is assumed to exist some explicit (i.e., deterministic) choice made in accepting that possibility, and furthermore, that a choice has been explicitly made for either dealing with it (e.g., through redundancy) or ignoring it. This requires the assumption that everything about a system is known and/or can be accounted for in some way. Although admittedly not realistic, it is the most conservative approach that can be taken to the management of risk, and it does force one to examine and detail very carefully every source of risk and the perspective(s) from which they are viewed. In cases where the failure of a software-intensive system may threaten life or property, taking a conservative approach is of paramount importance (Roland, 1983).

Given this understanding, one can now state that a risk is composed of three elemental ingredients (Rowe, 1988). First, some decision or choice must be involved in the situation under examination. Without a choice being available, what one is faced with can be described as being in a "certainty" situation. In the software engineering domain, the choice can involve a number of issues, such as what particular Computer Aided Software Engineering (CASE) tool should be selected, what systems architecture is most feasible, or what return on investment the utilization of a particular software-intensive system will bring to the organization. The second ingredient is that some uncertainty or chance must be associated with each choice. Otherwise, one is faced once again with a certainty situation, not a risky one. This implies that the choices faced must be "real." Leaving the planet to avoid a possible meteorite strike is not a real choice, for example. Finally, some potential loss must exist among one or more of the choices available for selection. One can have both gains (or opportunities) and losses present in a risky situation. The only criterion is that there must be some (perceived or actual) loss associated with at least one of the choices.

When risk is viewed in this manner, it is possible to quantify the risk involved in a choice to some degree. Typically, risk is defined as the probability or likelihood of its occurrence multiplied by its consequence (Rescher, 1983). Mathematically, this is often written as:

$$\text{Risk} = P_f \times C_f \quad (1)$$

where P_f is the probability of the risk occurring (i.e., the probability of failure), and C_f is the resulting consequence of the risk if it does occur (i.e., the consequence of failure). If the probability of the risk represents the average or mean of the probability distribution, then one says that equation 1 above describes the expected value of the risk. Often in practice, however, the probability of failure is left out of the equation, with the result that the risk is seen simply as the absolute cost that one is willing to pay if the risk indeed does occur (Thornhill, 1990).

The expected value approach is the one most favored by risk analysts, whereas the second approach is most favored by decision makers (Rescher, 1983). The reason for this discrepancy lies in the essence of risk. When one uses an expected value approach, one is asserting that the value of the risk's likelihood can be calculated, quantified, or measured to within some (known) degree of accuracy. Furthermore, when faced with more than one choice to make, the expected value approach is straightforward and mathematically simple. However, in reality, the probability distribution of most risks' likelihood of occurrence cannot be determined, or cannot be determined with any acceptable degree of accuracy. (Technically, when the risk's probability distribution is not known, one is faced with uncertainty, rather than risk. In fact, a wide body of literature exists describing this specific situation, and is termed decision making under uncertainty (Baird, 1989). For convenience, we will make no such distinction here.) For example, it is difficult to determine with any degree of accuracy the likelihood of occurrence that a new financial software program will cause catastrophic operational failure in a bank's transaction system. One may know that in the past, such events have occurred in similarly built systems, but the question remains, does that knowledge provide a good indicator of future events, and if so, what should be done about it (Schwartz, 1991)? The fact that little accurate quantitative data exists makes the risk calculation in equation 1 qualitative by default, and therefore, has more inherent error associated with it.

If one were to possess perfect information, one would not have a risky situation since one would know exactly what choice to make. Thus the lack of information about the likelihood and or consequence surrounding a risk is an important cause of risk. Two other fundamental causes of risk also have been identified in conjunction with the lack of information (MacCrimmon, 1986). These are the lack of control and/or the lack of time. If there is a lack of control present in the situation under analysis, such as being placed at risk by another, then one again has difficulty in describing the possible likelihood of a risk's occurrence or its consequences. Not having sufficient time also affects the degree to which a full understanding of the situation can be gained. The occurrence of other events in the meantime also results in changing the basic risk parameters. One can say that a severe risk is one where all three causes or risks (i.e., a lack of time, control, and information) are present simultaneously.

When faced with a situation where only qualitative data is present, decision makers tend to focus more upon the consequences of risk than upon their likelihoods (MacCrimmon, 1986). One reason is that consequences of risk are usually easier to determine with accuracy, another reason is the psychology of decision makers faced with making risky decisions. Decision makers will gravitate towards those things they feel can be understood. Like most people, since they find probability theory difficult, they will shy away from it. Classifying a risk as either high, medium, or low based upon its potential consequences is more intuitively satisfying and contains less perceived uncertainty. For example, this can be seen by applying equation (1) to a situation where one can choose between: (**1**) a risk having a probability of occurrence of 0.2 but a consequential loss of $400, or (**2**) a risk having a probability of occurrence of 0.8 but a loss of only $100. Mathematically, it can be easily shown that they have the identical expected value of $80. Few, however, would perceive the risks as being identical (Rescher, 1983).

How one would choose between the two situations above depends upon how one perceives the acceptability of risk, and that in turn depends upon the psychology of the decision maker. The psychology of decision makers is extremely important in understanding how a risk is perceived and what actions will be undertaken to manage it (Dixon, 1979). Decision makers can be categorized as either being risk seekers, risk takers, risk neutral, or risk averse. Risk neutral is an economist's term meaning that given a fair bet (50–50 odds), no attention is paid by the decision maker to the degree of dispersion possible in the outcomes. In other words, a risk-neutral decision maker will take a risk only if the odds are favorable, but he or she will continue to take the risk if it yields a profit on average, even after a string of losses. A risk averse person will refuse a fair bet, and will take risks only if the odds are very favorable. On the other hand, if one is a risk taker, then there is an inclination to accept situations possessing less favorable odds, as well as having uncertain information and or little direct control associated with them. Risk takers tend to look for the best-case scenarios, whereas risk averse decision makers focus on down-side analysis, with probabilities of risk occurrences being biased upwards, and over emphasis placed upon the consequences of risk. Risk takers accept higher losses and higher likelihoods of risk than do risk averters. Risk averters tend to devote much effort in reducing and monitoring risk, while risk takers devote much less time to both regards. If one is a risk seeker, one will take a risky decision regardless of the consequences or the likelihood. As the name implies, one will seek out risky situations.

The perception and acceptability of risk are ultimately based upon value judgments made by the decision maker. These judgments are colored by many diverse factors such as organizational function, position in the hierarchy, or corporate politics. For example, a technical or marketing person will most often perceive situations in degrees of cost–benefit (i.e., as long as the benefit is greater than the cost, it is worthwhile proceeding), whereas to a finance director or senior manager the same situations will likely be perceived in terms of cost alone (i.e., if the cost is above a certain set amount, one cannot proceed, regardless of the benefit) (MacCrimmon, 1986). Perception and acceptability of risk are also heavily influenced by societal factors. For example, the risks found in driving an automobile are perceived as being more acceptable than those found in flying, even though flying is much safer statistically than driving (Kandel, 1986). The degree to which the definition of risk can be articulated will determine greatly the ability to understand it and to manage it.

Before moving on to discuss the mechanics of risk management, one needs to discuss for a moment the aspect of risk management that is often overlooked, namely that of opportunity creation (Drucker, 1964). Opportunity and risk are closely intertwined, and it is impossible to have one without the other being present as well. Every decision leads to other decisions, each having more courses of action with yet other risks and other opportunities. It is a mistake, however, to believe that risk and opportunity are always commensurate. High risk does not necessarily imply high gain, nor does low risk imply low gain. Risk and opportunity are not static items, but change as the context in which they are viewed changes. This is what makes it so difficult to come to grips with them in any meaningful way. The rule is to avoid high risk, low gain situations whenever possible.

Today's risks are often yesterday's opportunities, and tomorrow's success is constrained by how well today's risks are managed. This can be seen very clearly in Figure 2, which illustrates the Risk–Opportunity:Opportunity–Risk (RO:OR) cycle (Charette, 1991). For example, assume that a software-intensive system development project perceives that it has a productivity risk, i.e., the project has not been able to produce the amounts of software code required to meet the projected schedule. At the project level this can be viewed as a very large risk, one that is not easily managed. The typical way to handle this situation is either to hire more programmers, reduce the scope of the project, lengthen the schedule, invest in productivity-enhancing software engineering tools, or possibly some combination of all of these. Whatever the tactic taken requires more investment in resources than was originally planned.

However, this risk, when viewed at a higher organizational plateau, (i.e., the left side of Fig. 2), for example the program level, may be seen as an opportunity. For example, it may turn out that there are many projects possessing the same risk, and let us say by a prudent organization-wide investment in productivity tools, the risk could be greatly reduced. Note that for an individual project this investment may be seen as too great a risk to undertake, since the cost (and resulting benefit) may not be justifiable in that specific context. However, by expanding the environments of interest, the investment risk may now be seen as acceptable at this higher level. This shifting of risk and opportunity is one of the primary strategies used in risk management. In other words, when a risk may be too great to handle locally, the pooling together of many parties with the same risk can often lead to the opportunity for a more appropriate and cost effective method for risk aversion (Thornhill, 1990). This case also points out the importance and need to search out endemic risks that may exist across many projects, rather than the prevalent approach of viewing risk management as useful in only isolated contexts (Charette, 1991).

As one moves up the organization hierarchy, one continues to see this risk–opportunity transformation. The risks that move up the organization tend to take on the characteristic of performance risks, while risks that move down the organization tend to be in the shape of capitalization risks (Charette, 1990). This can be seen most clearly at the top of the diagram in Figure 2. What most organizations consider as business opportunities are actually risks that another organization cannot manage on its own. A prime example of this can be found in the computer facilities' management business, where an organization cannot afford either the cost, time, and/or internal personnel to manage or operate their own computer systems, and therefore contract these operations out to third parties. These third parties view the situation as an opportunity, while the contracting organization views the same situation as a risk that has been successfully managed.

The opportunities flowing to a company, however, transform into risks that must also be managed at each level of the organizational hierarchy. These opportunities/risks flow down throughout the organization, and how well they are managed constrains how well the organization can pursue future opportunities (i.e., the right side of Fig. 2). If the risks are not managed effectively, then opportunity costs are incurred (i.e., capital that could be spent on pursuing new opportunities is being spent trying to handle old ones), and the future is constrained by the ongoing efforts to reduce yesterday's risks. Moreover, the resulting organizational risk will be seen by competitors as an opportunity to pursue at the organization's expense.

In summary, one can begin to see a number of themes that will recur during the discussions on risk management mechanics and practice. First, risk is concerned with making choices, including making choices among differing alternatives that may have many different negative consequences. Second, a risk is caused by one or more critical factors involved in the choices, either a lack of information, a lack of time, or a lack of control. Third, an individual or organization may be placed into risk by itself, by another,

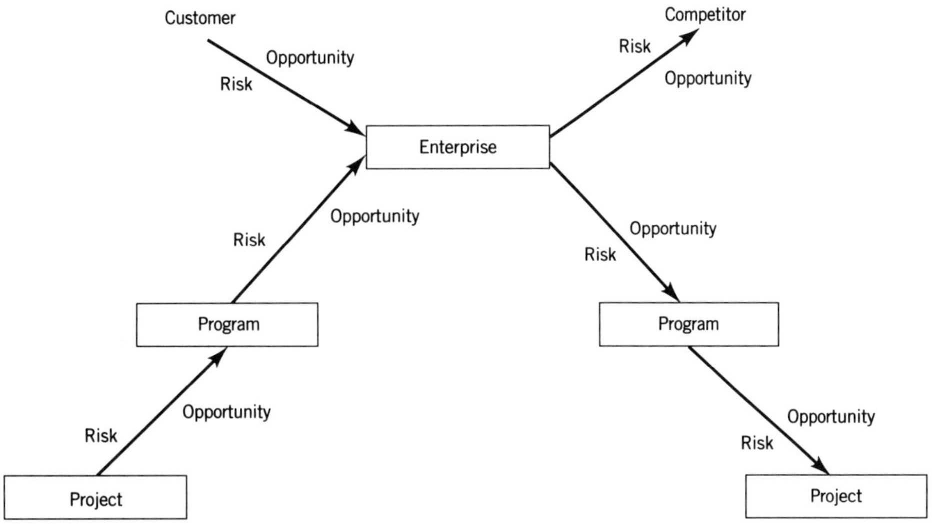

Figure 2. Risk-opportunity; opportunity-risk cycle. Courtesy of ITABHI Corp.

or by acts of God. Fourth, a risk can be a combination of deterministic or probabilistic exposures and consequences. The exact combination will often be a matter of dispute, as it depends upon one's perception. This leads to the fifth and last recurring theme, that a risk's acceptability is dependent upon context and its perception. Not everyone sees risk in the same way, and it is this articulation of what constitutes a risk that is crucial. These underlying theories and more will be explored in greater depth in the next section on risk management mechanics.

RISK MANAGEMENT MECHANICS

The mechanics of risk management embody the functions of risk management theory into practical procedures and techniques. Classically, the mechanics of risk management have been divided into two segments involving first, the investigation and assessment of risks (termed risk analysis), followed by their aversion and ongoing supervision (termed risk management). Although often portrayed as distinct entities, in practice each overlaps and interacts with the other greatly.

The process of risk analysis, as in risk management, has a number of sub-activities associated with it. Risk analysis has at least three major activities: risk identification, risk estimation, and risk evaluation, as depicted in Figure 3. Risk identification is concerned with identifying sources of risk to the endeavor under consideration, and classifying them as to their causes. Risk estimation is concerned with attempting to understand and provide a succinct valuation of the likelihood and potential consequence of the risks identified, as well as the degree of certainty attached to the valuation made. Risk evaluation is concerned with assessing and prioritizing the risks, considering the tradeoffs necessary to recommending a desirable course of action given the risks, and determining what aversion strategies (if any) are applicable. Although each aspect of risk analysis occurs generally in the above sequence, each activity also interacts with the others in a systemic manner. Risk evaluation may identify new sources of risk that were not previously recognized as existing, or risk identification may indicate how a risk can be best managed, for example.

Risk management consists of the five basic aspects of traditional management, i.e., planning, controlling, monitoring, directing, and staffing, as shown in Figure 3, but with these activities aimed primarily at the selection and implementation of the aversion recommendations resulting from the risk analysis. The planning activity is concerned with determining which risk analysis recommendations are feasible, and once that is accomplished, to reassign resources necessary for the implementation of the recommendations within the organization. Controlling is concerned with embedding into the organization the primary management and organizational mechanisms required to avert the risks identified and deemed of greatest importance. Monitoring is concerned with at least three issues. First, monitoring is meant to ensure that the selected risk analysis recommendations are being followed. Second, it is tasked with observing the effectiveness of the risk aversion strategies. Third, it is concerned with recommending changes in aversion strategies as required. Directing is concerned with guiding the total risk management effort, integrating it into the overall organizational process, and determining when to conduct supplemental

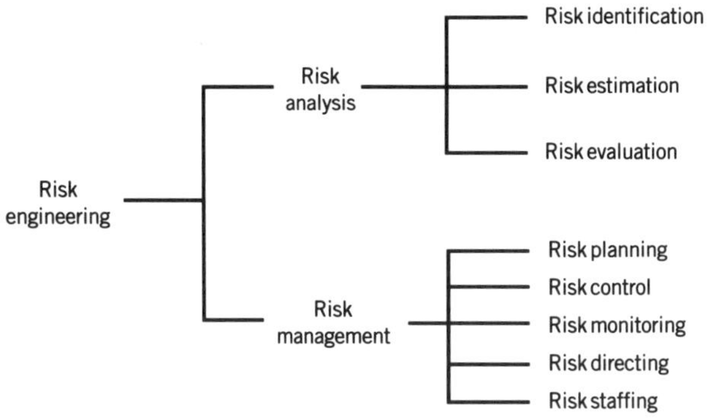

Figure 3. Risk engineering taxonomy.

risk analysis. Staffing is concerned with ensuring the hiring and or positioning of the right personnel to implement the risk analysis aversion recommendations. As with risk analysis, the boundaries between each activity are not well defined, may overlap, and may be implemented concurrently.

Often, it is more useful to think of the risk management process in terms of a general medical paradigm (Charette, 1991). In the risk analysis phase, one is concerned with examining the symptoms of risk, diagnosing their possible causes, and then evaluating and recommending different treatments. These treatments may be in the forms of cures (i.e., one can eliminate the risk completely) or therapies (i.e., the risk cannot be eliminated, but it can be controlled). Risk management examines the recommended treatments postulated, evaluates any known side effects the treatments may have, selects the treatment required, plans how to implement treatment, sets up evaluation criteria from which to monitor the effectiveness of the treatment, and directs and modifies the treatment on a day-to-day basis.

Risk Analysis

When performing a risk analysis, and before starting the specific risk identification activities, the first item that is required to be accomplished is to determine whether a risk analysis is required, while the second item is to define the scope of the analysis, i.e., its terms of reference. In establishing the first item, the degree to which software costs dominate total system costs, or software is essential to the successful performance of the system's function, or whether software integrates or interfaces with a number of other systems, needs to be considered. Also, financial, competitiveness, productivity, and other organizational issues should be considered for risk (Charette, 1990; Strassman, 1990). If the risks present appear significant, or, just as importantly, this fact cannot be determined, then an analysis is required.

The risk analysis' terms of reference are critical to the analysis' future success and ultimate relevance. Often, for example, a risk analysis is targeted at the examination of the risks involved in a predetermined course of action, as opposed to a situation that allows for choice among alternative courses of action. The differences in the approach to the analysis in these two cases involve not only the amount of detailed information the subsequent analysis requires, but also the environments of interest to be considered and the possible aversion strategies that can be recommended. For instance, if the analysis is concerned with analyzing only one course of action, then there are usually fewer strategies from which to choose to avert risks than if multiple alternative courses of action are available. This situation can severely constrain the aversion approaches and heighten the degree of risk experienced. The ideal situation is one that has as many options open as possible at the time of the analysis, as this means there is less possibility that one of the root causes of risk (i.e., the lack of time, control, and/or information) will be exacerbated later. However, this situation is not always practical.

Bounding the risk analysis' environments of interest is often very difficult and is the single greatest source of error in any analysis (Rescher, 1983). Selecting too few environments may mean missing important sources of risk, while selecting too many makes the analysis difficult and expensive. Regardless of which are chosen, it is important to realize that selecting the environment of interest means making a certain set of assumptions. These assumptions are risks that are accepted.

In selecting the risk analysis' environment of interest, a few more items need to be taken into account. First, the organizational perspective of analysis must be selected. In other words, is the analysis going to provide coverage of a single project, multiple projects, a program, etc., and is it going to be from a software or system developer's point of view, a marketing person's point of view, a project manager's point of view, etc.? Each perspective implies a different set of objectives that the consequences of the risk are going to be measured against (Charette, 1989). An analysis supporting a project-level developer's perspective usually primarily concerns technical objectives and, therefore, technical risks, whereas a project-level project manager's perspective concerns cost and schedule objectives in addition to those relating to technical ones. Moving up the organizational hierarchy expands the environments of interests even more to include returns on investment, image, politics, etc. (Charette, 1990). Software engineering-related risk analysis has primarily concerned itself with project-level objectives involved in doing the right task, and doing the task correctly. This means that the question of whether the project should be undertaken in the first place is often considered (unfortunately) to be an unquestionable assumption at this organizational level. This view is being vigorously challenged (Charette, 1989; 1990). However, once the risk analysis' environment of interest and terms of reference are decided, one can then proceed with the specific risk identification activities. For discussion purposes we will assume that the context of the risk analysis involves determining the risks in a software-intensive system development under consideration.

Risk Identification

Risk identification is concerned with identifying sources of risk to the endeavor under consideration, and classifying them as to their causes or symptoms. In other words, risk identification attempts to answer the questions: what are the risks, and how can they be categorized?

In software engineering risk identification, three primary types of risk are considered at a minimum. These are process risks, product risks, and organizational risks. Process risks concern the risks involved with the processes used in the development, operation, and support of the software-intensive system, such as what life-cycle model is utilized, how well the software engineering methodologies support the development process and are integrated into the life-cycle model, and how well automation supports both the life-cycle models and methodologies proposed to be used. A complete analysis will consider the identification of risks across the whole life-cycle of the system, from its conceptual design to its operational use to its eventual retirement, and include phase dependent risks (e.g., risks in the requirements' analysis phase) as well as phase independent risks (e.g., risks in project management). Product risks concern the risks found in the software-intensive system's architecture and subsequent implementation. Architectural issues involve the logical aspects of the system as defined by the system requirements. These include such matters as the requirements for fault tolerance or fault avoidance, the degree of centralization or decentralization of the processors, threads of control, and/or database; the space and time complexity of the software design and/or its algorithms, etc. Whereas the architectural risks concern logical issues, implementation risks concern the physical system that results from the architectural creation and evaluation process. This includes risks related to such issues as hardware reliability, software error rates, human factors, operational performance, etc. Organizational risks concern the risks found in the business unit developing and operating the software-intensive system. These risks include the organization capability required to produce a software-intensive system, the organizational politics involved, the organizational structure used, the individual capability required to develop and/or operate the system, etc.

Information concerning each of the different risk types can be found from one or more of the following six sources: tradition or folklore, analogies, commonsense, results of experiments or tests, reviews of inadvertent exposure, and epidemiological surveys. In software engineering-related risk analysis, the most common source of risk data is obtained from commonsense assessments and folklore. Very little experimental data or general survey information is readily available from which to identify risks. This means that often the risks are misidentified, in other words, they are only symptoms of risk rather than the risks themselves. For example, a commonly identified risk is cost risk, but cost is not by itself a risk (Charette, 1990). On the other hand, being *over* a budgeted cost can be considered a risk, not only to the current system under development but to future projects as well, because extra funding may not be available to cover any cost overruns. As a reminder, risks that affect the future are termed *opportunity costs.* These can be seen explicitly in the R-O:O-R cycle in Figure 2. The fact is that being over a budget target is only a symptom of one or more unplanned events occurring, and therefore these should be considered as sources of risk that force a budget to overrun.

Risks such as being over budget are said to be compound risks, i.e., the overall risk is composed of many separate component risks grouped together, often with synergistic effects. These component risks are sometimes said to be risk drivers, i.e., they account for much of the fluctuation in the overall risk. Alongside compound risks exist risks that are said to be coupled. These are individual risks (often unseen) that are linked in some direct or indirect way. For example, crashes involving motorcyclists not wearing helmets often resulted in the motorcyclist receiving severe skull injuries. Helmet laws were passed in many states to avoid this particular source of risk. Now, instead of skull injuries, motorcyclists involved in crashes are experiencing severe neck injuries resulting from use of the helmet.

Separating risks into their constituent parts is a difficult but extremely important facet of risk identification. By classifying a risk into its underlying causes or characteristics, one can begin to identify: (**1**) the general location of the major project risks, (**2**) the general timing of such risks, (**3**) the occurrence of system risks within a project, and (**4**) the overall aversion strategies that one will be able to apply later. This separation is normally accomplished by means of a risk taxonomy.

We have previously given examples of simple taxonomies when by dividing risk management into different distinct parts, as in Figure 3, as well as classifying software engineering risks into process, product, and organizational risks. One common taxonomy used to classify risks uses the likelihood of occurrence over time as the partitioning guideline, e.g., known, predictable, or unpredictable risks (Charette, 1989). Known risks are those that are known with great certainty to exist currently. Predictable risks are those that one can reasonably expect to occur in the future, such as the risk caused by personnel leaving. Unpredictable risks are those that are possible in the far future and generally have a high degree of uncertainty associated with them. The risks resulting from a change in government is an example. The U.S. Department of Defense categorizes risks into two major groups: acquisition risks (i.e., risks that occur during the procurement of a system) and decision risks (i.e., risk that occurs after the system is fielded) (AFSC, 1988). Each group has been further divided into the sub-categories of cost, schedule, and technical risks, and operational and support risks respectively. Yet another way to categorize risk is to classify them as to whether they are caused by a lack of time, a lack of information, and/or a lack of control (MacCrimmon, 1986). In practice, some combination of the different classification schemes above is generally used.

Risk Estimation

Not every risk is likely to be disclosed or classified in the initial pass through the risk identification stage. Additionally, even for the risks that have been identified, their likelihood of occurrence and the severity of impact have not yet been fully established. The further identification of risks, the determination of a succinct valuation of the likelihood and potential consequence of the risks identified, as well as the degree of certainty attached to the valuation made, are the three main objectives of risk estimation.

Placing a value on the likelihood and severity of a risk is dependent on a number of different factors. As was mentioned earlier, descriptions of risks can come from such disparate sources as folklore or tradition to epidemiological surveys, with the confidence in the accuracy and precision of the description ascribed to each ranging from none at all to very exact. The reason for this wide range is that in many cases the descriptions of risk are nothing more than narratives, describing risks in loose, qualitative terms. Thus the difficulty most often confronted in conducting software engineering risk estimation is that likelihood or consequences of risks are frequently not able to be described either precisely or accurately. This is not really surprising because in many situations new technology and/or development procedures are being used. Since no previous objective information is available on which to base a risk estimate, common sense assessments are usually made. The lack of available data is one that is currently crippling software engineering risk management, since the field as a whole has not kept accurate records of software-related failures and their causes.

Another reason for estimation inaccuracy and imprecision is that the language used to describe risk is itself very imprecise. For example, it is not uncommon to find the words likely, probably, and possible, simultaneously being used to describe the situation where the likelihood of risk is great (MacCrimmon, 1986). These identical words are also often found being used to describe the situation where the severity of the risk is also great. Exactly what the difference in meaning exists between likely and probably or likely and possible is frequently not clear, as one individual using the word likely, for instance, may have something entirely different in mind from another. This again highlights the fact that risk, like quality, is a subjective quantity and depends greatly on the analyst's beliefs.

The problem of defining an accurate risk estimation measurement system is one that plagues risk analysis in general, and leads to vociferous debates concerning the validity of using quantitative vs. qualitative estimates of risk (Thompson, 1990). A related issue is in trying to come up with a uniform measure of risk that is useful against all the various risks encountered. For example, how does one measure the risk of an inadequate life-cycle model in relation to a poor organizational model or an organization's software engineering expertise? Additionally, how does one come up with a total risk number that is meaningful given each of these individual risks? Work in the area of software engineering productivity metrics provide some clues (Boehm, 1981; Jones, 1986; 1991), but no satisfactory approach has yet emerged. Complicating the situation even further is the problem of individual estimation bias, which can cause the risk estimates to be highly skewed (MacCrimmon, 1986).

There is no easy answer to overcoming these problems of subjective valuation, but one can use a number of different criteria against which to judge the value of the estimates provided (Lowrance, 1976). The first criterion is the consistency of association, i.e., is the estimate in agreement with information from other sources? The second is the strength of association, or the degree to which the associations formed with other information sources hold. A third value criterion is the temporal relationship of association, or the degree to which time influences, positively or negatively, the association. The fourth is the specificity of association, or the uniqueness of the relationship that exists with other information sources. The last is coherence of association, or the degree to which all the above parameters hold and experience matches or calibrates the results. By reviewing the risk estimate against as many other sources of information as possible, and judging against the five criteria listed above, it is possible to reduce the error in the overall risk estimate.

Another approach to reduce estimation error is to buy back certainty. In other words, expend resources to increase the accuracy and precision of the risk estimates. This can be done in numerous ways, but the two most popular approaches are to develop prototypes of the system under development, or to apply a delphi technique to the estimates (Boehm, 1981; Baird, 1989). Prototypes are just models of the system that range from paper- or computer-based simulations to partial physical implementations that exercise operational items. By creating prototypes of the system, one can calibrate the amount of uncertainty that exists in the process, product, and organization risk estimates, as well as achieve an added benefit of possibly eliminating some sources of risk early in the development. The delphi technique takes the slightly different approach in that instead of creating models of the system, a group of experts with an understanding of the system and/or development processes to be used are asked to evaluate the risks involved. This approach is meant to reduce the biases that may be in the risk estimates. The estimates of the likelihood and consequence of each risk identified are obtained from each expert and are passed to each of the others, and the group is again asked to re-estimate the risks given this new data. This process continues until the group has reached a consensus or the experts no longer change their views, at which point the exercise is complete. The delphi technique is typically faster and less expensive than the prototyping approach, but its accuracy can vary widely. Regardless of which approach is applied, the information gleaned should be evaluated against the five criteria listed earlier to judge its value.

Previously, it was stated that decision makers tend to focus not on the likelihood of a risk occurring, but its actual consequences. Therefore, a key to estimating a risk in practice is to describe as much as possible three core risk attributes: the character of the risk, its extent, and its timing (Rescher, 1983). The character of the risk is its "spectrum of unpleasantness," i.e., is the loss due to the risk physical, economic, political, or some combination in nature? The extent of the risk refers to its severity and coverage. This means both the amount of the potential loss and who or what is affected. Is the loss severe or trivial, and is it an individual, a group, a business, etc., that is affected? Finally, one needs to understand the chronology of the loss, such as is the loss immediately felt, felt later, or is the loss spread out over time? How these three attributes interact creates tremendous variation that often cannot be totally understood until the risk evaluation stage.

Risk Evaluation

After each risk has been given an estimate for its likelihood of occurrence and its consequence, an evaluation of how the various risks interact with one another and form the total development exposure to risk is conducted. In general, risk evaluation is concerned with assessing and prioritizing the risks, considering the tradeoffs necessary to recommending a desirable course of action given the risks, and determining what aversion strategies (if any) are applicable.

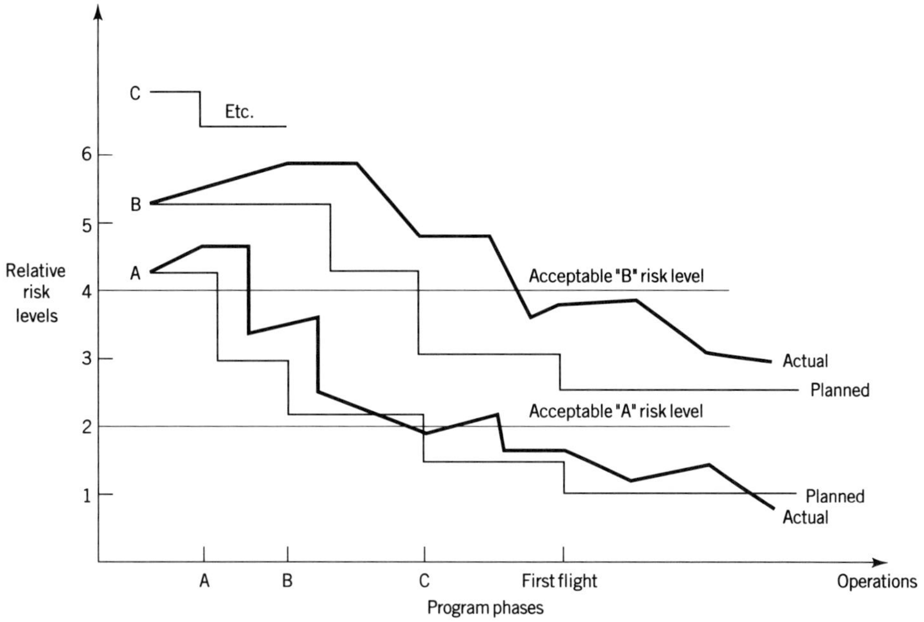

Figure 4. Shuttle risk referents. A, loss of life risk; B, loss of vehicle risk; C=etc.

The first step in conducting a risk evaluation is to select for each risk, and the system development as a whole, a risk referent. A risk referent is a measurement criterion against which a risk is to be judged as being acceptable or not. The risk referent is usually defined as one or more of the objectives of the overall project, and can be related to operational, developmental, or organizational goals. For example, a referent may be to meet developmental timescales, or that the system is safe to operate, or it may be to maximize yearly profit. A risk referent can also be related to less quantitative goals, such as increasing an organization's image or prestige, although these referents are harder to state and evaluate. Risk referents may be static, in that they do not change over the lifetime of the system, or they may instead be dynamic, changing over a period of time. For example, as shown in Figure 4, in developing the Space Shuttle, NASA set increasingly more stringent risk referents (e.g., loss of vehicle, loss of life, etc.) as the development progressed to reflect the need for increased reliability and safety (NAP, 1988). The referents also become part of the metrics used later in the monitoring activities within the risk management process.

Figure 4 illustrates one of the most difficult issues in risk analysis, and that is where to set the risk referents (Crockford, 1980). If the referents are set too stringently, then it is unlikely that the system development will be seen as an acceptable risk. If the referents are set too loosely, then dangerous risks may be missed. Furthermore, how does one combine all the different referents into one that illustrates the total referent for the system? There are no easy answers (Moore, 1983). The answer will in fact often depend upon selecting one system-wide referent or a select few that signal the worse case and assessing all the evaluation results against them. One will not often know what precise approach to take until well into selecting the risk referents in the risk evaluation stage. Much will depend upon what techniques are available for evaluating the risks as well. There are many different types of risk evaluation techniques that are available that deal in both the qualitative and quantitative analysis domains. Common types are those that focus on analyzing alternative risk decisions (Rescher, 1983).

Decision analysis techniques are those that try to map out each of the various alternatives under consideration and then evaluate each alternative until the one that meets the desired referent (e.g., least loss, most gain, etc.) is discovered. This can be done by creating decision trees such as shown in Figure 5, where the initial decision is modeled as a root node from which a number of alternatives spring. Each branch has a probability of occurrence (the sum of the branch probabilities must sum to one) and the consequence (called a leaf) if that alternative is selected. Each consequence has a value associated with it. One then computes the expected value of each branch and makes a decision based upon the result. In more complicated cases, as illustrated in Figure 6, a branch can connect to another node with its own set of payoffs. One must then compute the expected values of each alternative from the leaves backwards to each node, then through the various alternatives, until the root node is reached.

Decision trees are useful when the alternatives are clearly defined and the probabilities of occurrence and value of consequences are understood. When this is not the case, the usual approach is to define the likelihood and consequence values as probability distributions, and compute a range of possible values, frequently by the use of Monte Carlo techniques (Crockford, 1980). Other forms of decision analysis techniques may also be used to analyze different types of decision questions, such as those resolved by PERT charts (e.g., to analyze schedules and resource conflicts), queueing models (e.g., to analyze system performance issues), or game theory decision matrices (e.g., to determine best decision strategy) (Dixit, 1991). Other risk evaluation techniques that also exist are not based upon

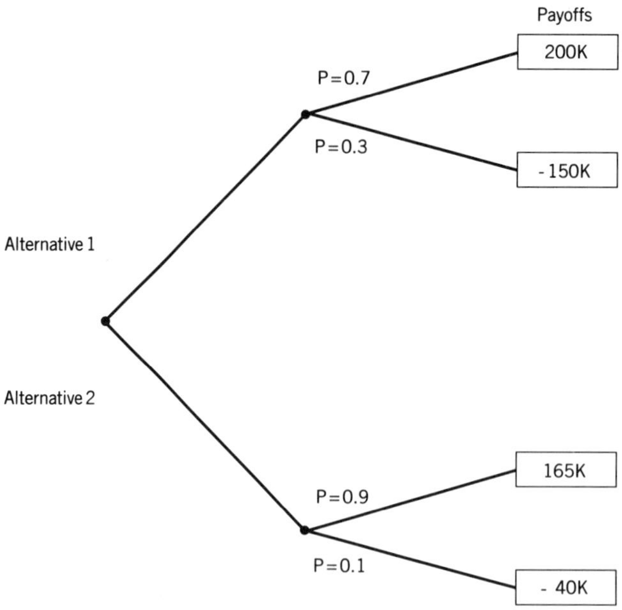

Figure 5. Decision tree.

formal decision approaches. These cover a range of specific topic areas that relate back to the specific risks identified and categorized by the risk taxonomy, i.e., process, product, and organizational risks. Some of the more commonly used evaluation techniques include financial cost–benefit analysis (Strassman, 1990), process model applicability analysis (Davis, 1988), application evaluation (AFSC, 1987) and organizational capability assessment (SEI, 1991).

Which evaluation technique to use will depend largely upon how the risk referents are selected, which risks were originally identified and categorized, and the general evaluation approach formulated, i.e., is it decision-oriented, cost-oriented, etc. Many times multiple evaluation techniques or very specialized techniques will be required to gain a greater understanding of the risks and their consequences (Baird, 1989; Morgan, 1990). Any evaluation approach is valid if it helps one better understand the risks. An important guideline, however, is not to preselect an evaluation technique before the risk estimation phase is complete and the precision and accuracy of both the likeli-

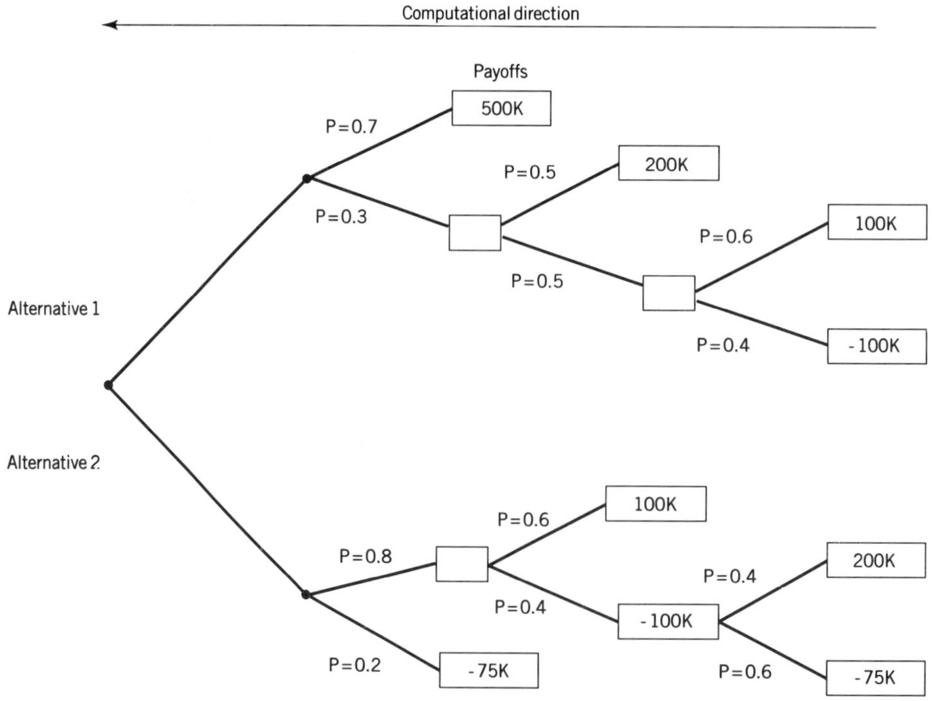

Figure 6. Multiple branch decision tree.

hood of a risk occurring and its consequence are completely understood. Preselection can lead to force fitting a quantitative analysis where only a qualitative analysis is practical. It is an accepted practice that as the evaluation process continues, the risk estimates and/or risk categories made earlier are revised as it becomes clear that certain estimates were too high or too low in relation to other risks, that an individual risk was a compound risk, or that a so-called risk was only the symptom of a risk, etc. The process of identification, estimation, and evaluation is very iterative, and it may take multiple passes through each of the stages to complete an analysis.

As the evaluation progresses, certain risks will begin to emerge as having a higher priority of concern than others. This prioritization will necessarily be specific to the system development context, but it will generally be driven by the overall objectives of the development, the degree of risk found, the time a risk is projected to occur, and the amount of funding available for the management of the risks (Lifson, 1982). As the prioritization becomes clear, the evaluation process will then be concentrated on a reduced number of risks with the intent of investigating which risk aversion strategies are most useful in lowering specific risks, as well as the overall system development risk level.

If the passive acceptance of a risk as it exists is not an option, there are four basic strategies that can help avert a risk: reduction, protection, transference, and pecuniary (Charette, 89). These strategies are used to change either the consequences of a risk, its likelihood, or both. Each has a slightly different emphasis: reduction emphasizes direct approaches to lowering of the likelihood or the impact of the consequences; protection also emphasizes reduction of likelihood and consequences, but at a system level; transference emphasizes the acceptance of risk, but reducing the consequences by sharing the risk with others; and pecuniary emphasizes financial means to avert risk. Which, or how many, aversion strategies are used frequently depends upon the unique risk circumstances of the development. Each of the strategies have specific instantiations that can be used to avert product, process, and organizational risks. It is useful to note again, however, that certain aversion strategies may reduce one set of risks at the expense of increasing others. This is especially true where the reduction of one specific risk may increase the total risk of the development. Care should be taken to ensure that risks are not directly or indirectly coupled before recommending any specific risk aversion approach. Additionally, not every risk necessarily can be prevented or eliminated, and therefore a strategy for dealing with a risk that does occur needs to be considered.

Selecting the proper aversion strategy will frequently take some trial and error, although different decision strategies such as min-max, satisficing, etc., are available as guides (Baird, 1989). More often the selection of an aversion strategy will be dictated by strict cost–benefit assessments. One common way that can be used to reflect the cost–benefit considerations in prioritizing risk aversion tasks is by determining the optimal level of risk. This is the point that minimizes the sum of all undesirable outcomes, as illustrated in Figure 7. The optimal point is

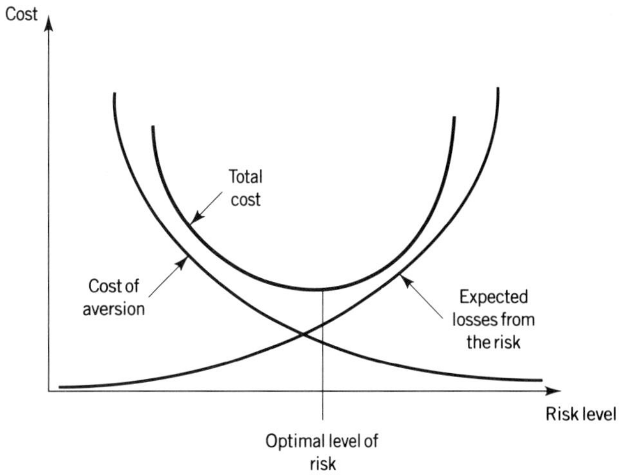

Figure 7. Optimal level of risk.

usually very difficult to pinpoint, thus the second most common way to select an aversion strategy is through determining an acceptable level of risk. This implies that there is some threshold at which risk will be tolerated. One approach to finding this threshold is by means of risk leveraging (Boehm, 1988). Risk leveraging is computed as follows:

$$(\text{Risk Exposure}_{[\text{Before}]} - \text{Risk Exposure}_{[\text{After}]})/\text{Risk AversionCost} \quad (2)$$

where Risk Exposure=(Risk Probability) (Loss of Utility).The loss of utility is the same as consequence of failure, but in practice also accounts for the "unquantifiables" that often need to be given consideration but that do not show up as a concrete value. Notice that the greater the ratio, the greater the leveraging obtained.

Once the risks have been placed in priority order and risk aversion recommendations (where feasible) have been made for the highest priority risks, the risk analysis phase is considered complete. The results of the analysis, both with aversion recommendations in force and without, are presented to the management team responsible for the system development. The degree of certainty in each evaluation outcome is also provided. Providing evaluations without certainty estimates attached can produce unwarranted decisions being made (Charette, 1991b). Notice that the result of the evaluation process is to provide management with a full understanding of the risks and different proposals for their aversion. It is not the role of the risk analyst to make any decisions as to what final courses of action to take. That is the prerogative of management.

Risk Management

At the end of the analysis, indications of answers to the following questions should be achieved (Charette, 1989):

- What can go wrong?
- How and when will it likely go wrong?
- What are the options for preventing it from going wrong?
- What will be done if a risk occurs?

It is the objective of risk management to ensure that each of the questions above can be fully answered for every highest priority risk identified, with a rating of the degree of certainty attached to each answer.

At the end of the evaluation stage, each of the risks have been listed in priority order, along with their individual likelihoods and consequences. They are also shown with and without recommended aversion strategies, as well as their costs. Each risk will be shown either to be over, below, or at its referent, and will also show its contribution to the total risk of the system development. This will give the appropriate decision makers all the information they require. The management team responsible for the project must now decide the exact course of action to follow. The first course of action is to examine the risk to the development as a whole. If the total system development risk referent is exceeded, management must decide to either: (**1**) proceed with the development as stated, and accept the risk; (**2**) if possible, accept some of the aversion recommendations that can bring the total risk into acceptable range (**3**) change some of the development objectives that fixed the project risk referent at the current level, or (**4**) not proceed with the development because the risk is unacceptable. If situation (**3**) holds true, then another risk analysis will be required to re-calibrate the findings, and to determine if the overall risk remains unacceptable.

Once the overall risk to the system development is deemed acceptable, attention is shifted to examining whether any (more) individual aversion recommendations are feasible. It is not likely that every recommendation will be found to be qualified for implementation, as aversion funding is likely to be at a premium. Once the general aversion approaches are selected, then formal risk management procedures can be applied to secure their implementation. Risk management has five overlapping aspects: planning, controlling, monitoring, directing, and staffing.

Risk management planning is primarily concerned with reassigning the resources necessary for the implementation of the aversion recommendations within the organization. This means making changes to the relevant system development plans as well as creating a risk management plan to ensure that the aversion recommendations are carried out in full. The exact details of the risk management plan will depend highly upon how the organizational culture encourages risks to be managed.

There are seven basic organizational approaches to managing of risk (Charette, 1991a), as shown in Figure 8. These seven approaches can be divided into two general types. The first type involves the reactive management of risk, while the second involves the proactive management of risk. There is also a transitional type, which is called prevention. Prevention is the change point between reactive and proactive approaches to managing risk. For example, prevention occurs when one is planning for a new project. In other words, an organization attempts by way of the planning process to take actions that prevent risks from occurring. Once the plan is complete, one has a choice of either reacting only to the consequences of an identified risk or proactively trying to influence the likelihood and or potential consequence of the risk. This distinction will become clearer in a moment.

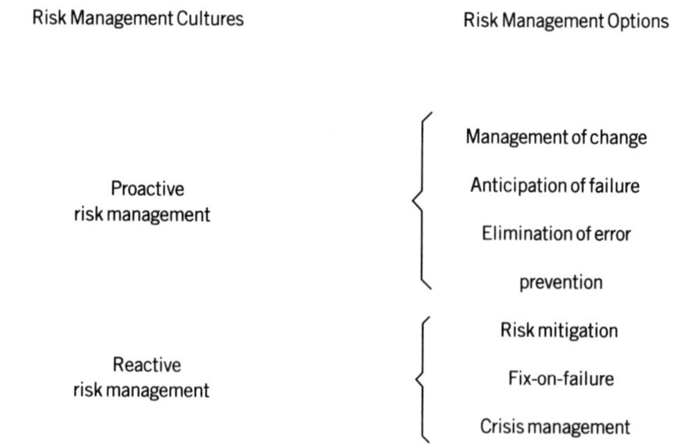

Figure 8. Risk management aversion recommendations.

Reactive risk management is as its name implies, i.e., the organization reacts to the consequences of risks as they occur. (Reactive risk management can be considered a form of problem management.) Reactive risk management consists of three kinds of strategies: mitigation, fix-on-failure, and crisis management. Mitigation is the "best of the worst," i.e., of the three types of reactive management strategies, an organization would in most circumstances like to choose to implement a risk mitigation strategy initially. Mitigation can be thought of as providing for a resource contingency to cover the potential consequences of a risk's occurrence. If an organization does not possess the resources for mitigation efforts, or decides that mitigation is not required, then it must fix the consequences of risk as they occur, i.e., fix-on-failure. This is a step lower in the management of risk hierarchy, and is more reactive in nature than risk mitigation. It is also where most organizations operate as standard procedure. If the failures cannot be fixed quickly enough, the organization slips to the stage of crisis management. In this case, there is a total lack of information, time, and control present in the situation, or in other words, maximal risk exists. Organizations that are applying crisis management as a means to manage risk usually are the ones that are fighting for survival, and are the ones that are most vulnerable to competition.

For a long period in traditional risk management planning, mitigation approaches were considered the best form of managing an organization's risk. However, it was soon recognized that the prevention of risk was even better. Furthermore, prevention is still only a reactive type of strategy, and is usually very context sensitive. It is not a cure for risk. Only by being proactive can an organization really begin to manage risk.

This is done by starting with the first proactive strategy of the management of risk. This is termed the elimination of root causes, or in other contexts, total quality management (Ross, 1988). For this situation to occur, an organization requires: (**1**) an environment of interest that has a visible process, (**2**) a process is measurable, and (**3**) a process that it is repeatable. If these conditions exist, an organization can discover many of the root causes of risk, as well as the means to eliminate them efficiently and effectively. Once these are understood, an organization can also begin to exploit the risk-opportunity cycle mentioned earlier.

By understanding and eliminating the root causes of risk in the environment of interest, an organization can stabilize the process, make it predictable, and minimize the uncertainty involved. The organization can then begin to accomplish the same thing for more environments of interest. By casting the net wider, an organization can begin to anticipate where risks will spring from in the future and can then place itself into a position to manage them effectively.

If an organization becomes very successful at anticipating risk, it can then move to the highest stage, that being the management of change. By continuously increasing the environments of interest that are understood, an organization can place itself into a position to manage change to its own advantage.

Every organization is in one or more of these different stages of managing risk. Which one is primary will depend upon the risk management control exercised throughout the organization. Control is concerned with embedding into the organization the primary management and organizational mechanisms required to avert the risks identified and deemed to be of greatest importance. Controlling focuses both on the total risk to the system development as well as the individual risks. Control can be exercised in a variety of means, such as by periodic risk reviews, the maintenance of a top-10 risk list, audits, and inspections (Boehm, 1988).

The monitoring of the risks provides another means for implementing the control mechanisms and is one of the most important aspects of risk management. Monitoring ensures that: (**1**) the selected risk aversion recommendations are indeed being followed, (**2**) the recommendations are having the effects predicted, (**3**) any new risks are quickly identified and evaluated, and (**4**) risks that have been identified, but were not perceived as immediate threats, do not become surprise threats. Monitoring is also concerned with making new aversion recommendations if the current ones are deemed to be ineffective. In implementing the monitoring process, a number of different approaches can be followed. The prevailing approach is to apply a number of different software engineering metrics that can track different risk-related parameters. The IEEE in its *Dictionary of Measures to Produce Reliable Software* has over thirty different metrics that can be used to monitor both process- and product-oriented risks, including fault density, design structure, test accuracy, and software maturity (IEEE, 1988). The U.S. Air Force in conjunction with the MITRE Corporation has also developed some organizational risk metrics (AFSC, 1987), as has the Software Engineering Institute (Paulk, 1993).

In conjunction with monitoring are the risk management functions of directing and staffing. Directing is concerned with the guiding the day-to-day risk management efforts and integrating them into the overall development process. It is also concerned with determining when to conduct supplemental risk analysis. The specific organizational structure will determine who is responsible for the directing function, but in small system developments this is usually given to the project manager, while in larger developments, a separate team may be given the responsibility for directing the risk management efforts (Charette, 1990). In the latter case, the risk management team leader reports to and coordinates with the development manager.

Staffing is concerned with ensuring the hiring and/or positioning of the right personnel to implement the risk analysis aversion recommendations. Personnel might be assigned a specific risk management position or be assigned on a temporary basis as the need arises. The staffing function also concerns making sure that properly qualified analysts are found and put into place.

In the next section the final aspect of risk management, namely what is the state of the current practice, is discussed.

RISK MANAGEMENT PRACTICE

As was noted at the beginning of this article, the application of risk management in the software engineering community is still in its infancy. Current practice revolves around the utilization of ad hoc approaches that are rooted in common project management approaches. These typically deal with general technical, cost, and schedule issues where risk is a consideration, but not in any formal sense. Part of the reason for the current ad hoc nature of risk management is that at the project level, as depicted in Figure 2, risk management and project management are perceived by many as being indistinct from one another. Unfortunately, the fact is that risk management has been given more lip service than actual use in project management (GAO, 1986). At the project level, risk management should be seen as akin to performing quality control, i.e., ensuring that the project is being done in accordance to prescribed standards. At this level, risk management provides a means to come to grips with locally controllable risks. At the program level, risk management is similar to quality assurance, i.e., ensuring the project is using the most effective standards. Risk management at this level starts to distinguish itself from quality. It takes a more holistic view, reviewing not only the risks to the project, but also the risks in relation to other projects to see if there are any existing endemic risks. At the enterprise level, risk management is similar to, but distinct from, quality management. Risk management at this level asks the question, is the project the correct one for the business today, and are similar projects good for the business tomorrow? There are few formal risk management organizations that exist within any software development organizations as of yet, and where they do exist, they tend to fall under the quality management organization.

There are a number of risk management specializations that have created their own cultures and specialized techniques that are treated elsewhere. The three major specialization areas include software safety (Levenson, 1986; Roland, 1983), software security (Turn, 1981), and operational disaster recovery (QED, 1985). A new specialization area that deals specifically with software technical risks is beginning to form (SEI, 1993), but this effort is still a number of years away from reaching the maturity level of either of the other three.

A trend that is appearing not only in software engineering-related risk management, but risk management as a

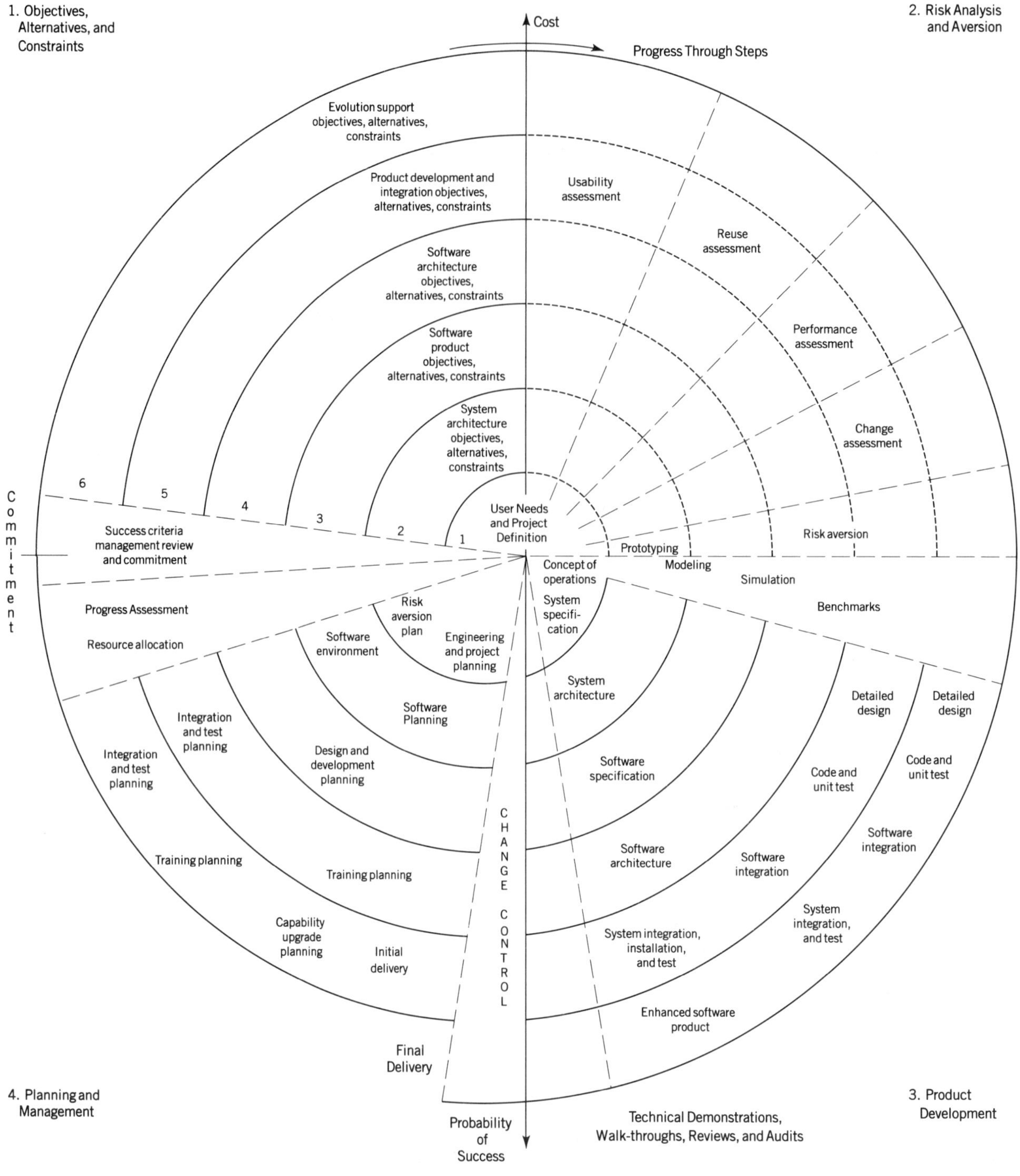

Figure 9. SPCI evolutionary spiral model. Courtesy of Software Productivity Consortium.

discipline, is to try to provide a more integrated approach (Haimes, 1989, Kloman, 1990). There has been a general feeling among the risk management community that as practiced, risk management has become too fractured and specialized, and that this is diluting its overall value. One attempt to bring a more integrated approach to software engineering-related risk management is found in the Spiral model approach postulated by Boehm (1988) and extended by the Software Productivity Consortium (SPC, 1991), as shown in Figure 9.

The Spiral model is a software meta-life cycle process model, meant specifically to support large, government-type software-intensive system developments. It is an evolutionary approach to developing software-intensive systems that encompass other life cycle models such as the waterfall model and rapid prototyping model as subsets within it. The Spiral model's objective is to create a risk-driven management process for software development where the risks that confront a development can be eliminated or averted early in the development cycle. A development only proceeds around the spiral shown when the risks have been analyzed, aversion strategies determined, and a decision has been taken to accept the remaining existing risks. Prototyping or similar approaches such as software reuse to buy-back certainty is generally advocated as central to each stage's risk analysis.

The various aspects included in risk identification, estimation, and evaluation, along with the management of each of the identified risks, are performed during each of the circuits. These are incorporated within the specific activities that take place in each of the four quadrants shown in Figure 9. In general, there are eight activities to a circuit. These are

1. Identify the technical and management objectives for each circuit
2. Identify any constraints that might affect the objectives
3. Identify alternative means of meeting the objectives
4. Identify and evaluate risks and areas of uncertainty for each alternative
5. Select and apply risk aversion approaches
6. Evaluate the risk aversion results
7. Plan for the next circuit
8. Review the plan and commit to the next circuit

The greatest benefit of the Spiral model is that it brings risk to the forefront as a concern in developing software-intensive systems. Although the Spiral model has not yet developed a long history of use, where it has been used significant gains are reported in software productivity and quality.

Another integrated risk management approach developed by Charette is called the CYNIC Risk Engineering Framework Methodology (Charette, 1990). In the CYNIC approach, the emphasis is on creating a systemic risk engineering framework to support opportunity and risk analysis and management across a variety of enterprise, systems engineering, and software engineering domains. The framework also simultaneously supports multiple organizational perspectives such as development, marketing, finance, and operations as well as a wide variety of evaluation techniques including security, safety, and operational recovery specific techniques.

CYNIC is driven by a set of standard risk engineering guidelines that prescribe how an analysis should be conducted (i.e, the techniques to be used, the information required, estimation data from which to compare results of the evaluation, etc.), based upon the particular analytical context (i.e., enterprise, program, and/or project). When the analysis is completed, a range of management strategies based upon the seven-level model of risk management and the risk–opportunity cycle described earlier are applied. These are then documented within a standard risk management plan that can be used to help direct the enterprise, program, and/or project. The CYNIC approach allows for risk to become a common currency to be traded off against opportunity across a business rather than just in one specialized area of concern. Users of CYNIC have reported substantial increases in project revenue and reduced operational costs.

Risk management, when it is properly used, can greatly improve the likelihood of developmental success and/or reduce the negative consequences of risk if it does occur. Regardless of what risk management approach is taken, however, there are a number of issues that must be resolved before risk management will find its way as a standard practice when performing software engineering. First, there needs to be a standard taxonomy of risks. Currently the definition of what constitutes a software engineering risk is confusing, with risks and symptoms of risks being perceived as the same. This makes for a poor understanding of risks as well as the proper means to avert risk. This is the same state in which medicine found itself in the 18th century, and, until solved, will provide the same inhibitions to good risk analysis practice. Second, there are no universally accepted software engineering-related risk referents or even metrics against which to set referents. There is a requirement for developmental and operational referents that are linked to some measurable indicator of risk. Finally, there is a requirement for a forensic database of software engineering data for risk estimation purposes. Currently, one cannot state whether a specific risk is actual or illusory since there is little data to compare it with. Until a repository of historical data is provided, the practice of software engineering risk management will not reach its full potential.

BIBLIOGRAPHY

AFSC, Management Quality Insight, Air Force Systems Command Pamphlet 800-43, Jan. 20, 1987.

AFSC, Software Risk Abatement, Air Force System Command Pamphlet 800-45, Sept. 30, 1988.

B. F. Baird, *Managing Decisions Under Uncertainty,* John Wiley & Sons, Inc., New York, 1989.

B. W. Boehm, *Software Engineering Economics,* Prentice-Hall, Inc., Englewood Cliffs, N.J., 1981.

B. W. Boehm, "A Spiral Model of Development and Enhancement," *IEEE Computer* **21,** 61–72 (May 1988).

B. W. Boehm, *Tutorial: Software Risk Management,* IEEE Computer Society Press, Washington, D.C., 1989.

R. N. Charette, *Software Engineering Risk Analysis and Management,* McGraw-Hill, Inc., New York, 1989.

R. N. Charette, *Application Strategies for Risk Analysis,* McGraw-Hill, Inc., New York, 1990.

R. N. Charette, "Risk Management to Maximise Commercial Opportunity," *Proceeding of the Software Tools Conference,* Blenheim Online, Middlesex, England, 1991b.

R. N. Charette, "The Risks With Risk Analysis," *CACM* **34,** 106 (June 1991b).

J. J. Cohrssen and V. T. Covello, *Risk Analysis: A Guide to Principles and Methods for Analyzing Health and Environmental Risks,* Department of Commerce, Washington, D.C., 1989.

N. Crockford, *An Introduction to Risk Management,* Woodhead-Faulkner, Cambridge, UK, 1980.

A. Davis and co-workers, "A Strategy for Comparing Alternative Software Development Life Cycle Models," *IEEE Trans. on Software Engineering* **14,** 1453–1461 (Oct. 1988).

A. Dixit and B. Nalebuff, *Thinking Strategically: The Competitive Edge in Business, Politics, and Everyday Life,* W. W. Norton, New York, 1991.

N. F. Dixon, *On the Psychology of Military Incompetence,* Jonathan Cape Ltd., London, UK, 1979.

DMSC, Defense Systems Management Handbook, Defense Management Systems College, Ft. Belvoir, Va., 1983.

P. F. Drucker, *Managing for Results,* Harper & Row, New York, 1964.

IEEE Standard Dictionary of Measures to Produce Reliable Software, IEEE, Std 982.1-1988, New York, 1987.

GAO, Technical Risk Assessment: The Current Status of DoD Efforts, Government Accounting Office, Report GAO/PEMD-86-5, Apr. 1986.

T. S. Glickman and M. Gough, eds., *Readings in Risk,* Resources for the Future, Washington, D.C., 1990.

Y. Y. Haimes, "Towards a Holistic Approach to Risk Assessment and Management," *Risk Analysis* **9**, 169–171 (June 1989).

Y. Y. Haimes, "Total Risk Management," *Risk Analysis* **11,** 147–150 (June 1991).

M. C. Paulk, B. Curtis, and co-workers, *Capability Maturity Model For Software*, Software Engineering Institute, Technical Report CMU/SEI-93-TR-24 and ESC/TR-93-177, Feb. 1993.

C. Jones, *Programming Productivity,* McGraw-Hill, Inc., New York, 1986.

C. Jones, *Applied Software Measurement*, McGraw-Hill, Inc., New York, 1991.

A. Kandel and E. Avni, eds., *Engineering Risk and Hazard Assessment,* Vol. 1, CRC Press, Boca Raton, Fla., 1986.

H. F. Kloman, "Risk Management Agonistes," *Risk Analysis* **10,** 201–205 (June 1990).

N. G. Levenson, "Software Safety," *ACM Computing Surveys* **18,** 125–164 (June 1986).

M. W. Lifson and E. F. Shaifer, *Decision and Risk Management for Construction Management,* John Wiley & Sons, Inc., New York, 1982.

W. W. Lowrance, *Of Acceptable Risk: Science and Determination of Safety,* William Kaufman, Los Altos, Calif., 1976.

K. R. MacCrimmon and D. A. Wehrung, *Taking Risks,* The Free Press, New York, 1986.

P. G. Moore, *The Business of Risk,* University Press, Cambridge, UK, 1983.

M. G. Morgan and M. Henrion, *Uncertainty: A Guide to Dealing With Uncertainty in Quantitative Risk and Policy Analysis,* Cambridge University Press, New York, 1990.

NAP, Post-Challenger Evaluation of Space Shuttle Risk Assessment and Management, National Academy Press, Washington, D.C., 1988, 35.

P. G. Neumann, "Illustrative Risks to the Public in the Use of Computer Systems and Related Technology," *SEN* **16,** 1–9 (Jan. 1991).

M. E. Porter, *Competitive Advantage,* The Free Press, New York, 1985.

N. Rescher, *Risk,* University Press of America, Lanham, Md., 1983.

R. Roland and B. Moriarty, *System Safety Engineering and Management,* John Wiley & Sons, Inc., New York, 1983.

P. J. Ross, *Taguchi Techniques For Quality Engineering,* McGraw-Hill, Inc., New York, 1988.

W. D. Rowe, *An Anatomy of Risk,* Robert E. Krieger Publishing Co., Malabar, Fla., 1988.

Proceedings of the SEI 2nd Annual Conference on Risk Management, Carnegie Mellon University, Pittsburgh, Pa., 1993.

SPC, "Consortium Prepares Evolutionary Spiral Process Deliverables," *SPC Quarterly* **5,** 4–6 (Spring 1991).

P. A. Strassman, *The Business Value of Computers,* The Information Economics Press, New Canaan, Conn., 1990.

P. Schwartz, *The Art of the Long View,* Doubleday, New York, 1991.

P. B. Thompson, "Risk Objectivism and Risk Subjectivism: When are Risks Real?, *Risk: Issues in Health & Safety* **1,** 3–22 Rolling Meadows, Ill. (Winter 1990).

W. T. Thornhill, *Risk Management For Financial Institutions,* Bankers Publishing Co., 1990.

R. Turn, ed., *Advances in Computing Security,* Vol. 1, Artech House, Inc., Dedham, Massachusetts, 1981.

Ibid, Vol. 2, 1984.

Ibid, Vol. 3, 1988.

QED, Disaster Recovery: Contingency Planning and Program Evaluation, QED Information Sciences, Inc., Wellesley, Mass., 1985.

ROBERT N. CHARETTE
ITABHI Corp.

ROUTINE

A subprogram that is called by other programs and subprograms. Note: The terms "routine," "subprogram," and "subroutine" are defined and used differently in different programming languages; the preceding definition is advanced as a proposed standard (IEEE).

ROYCE, WINSTON W. (1929–)

Dr. Royce received a BS in Physics and MS and Ph.D in Aeronautical Engineering from the California Institute of Technology.

He is Director of Software Development Technology for the Systems Integration Group at TRW. Besides being the founding Director of Lockheed's Software Technology Center, Dr. Royce has had a series of industrial positions at Lockheed, Space Applications Corporation, McDonnell Douglas, and TRW. In these assignments he has contributed to the development of large, complex software systems for spacecraft, C3I and avionics applications. At Caltech he was an Assistant Professor of Aeronautical Engineering.

In 1970 he published a paper which first introduced the waterfall methodology for software development. In 1985 he received the Information Sciences Award from the American Institute of Aeronautics and Astronauts (AIAA). He is currently a guest lecturer at the Defense Systems Management College at Ft. Belvoir, Virginia and a member of the Air Force Scientific Advisory Board. Dr. Royce is a member of the Industrial Advisory Board of *IEEE Software* magazine, a periodical in which he also writes a column. He is a member of the Carnegie Mellon University Computer Science Department Advisory Group.

RUN

(1) In software engineering, a single, usually continuous, execution of a computer program. (2) To execute a computer program (IEEE).

S

SAFETY

INTRODUCTION

Until recently, a natural reluctance to introduce unknown and complex factors has kept digital computers out of safety-critical control loops for high risk processes. Nevertheless, computers are increasingly being used to monitor and control complex, time-critical physical processes or mechanical devices, where a runtime error or failure could result in death, injury, loss of property, or environmental harm. The potential advantages of using computers are so great that digital computers are being given more and more control functions previously performed only by human operators or proven analog methods. (The word *computer* is used in this article to denote digital computers only.) Examples can be found in transportation, energy, aerospace, basic industry, medicine, and defense systems. For instance, only 10% of weapon systems required computer software in 1955, whereas today the figure is over 80% (Griggs, 1981). Both computer scientists and system engineers are finding themselves faced with difficult and unsolved problems regarding the safety of the software used in these systems.

Some of these issues and problems along with a survey of some currently suggested solutions are presented in this article. Unfortunately, there are many more problems than solutions. Most of the problems are not new but are only of a greater magnitude. Some techniques that have not been cost effective suddenly become more viable. Some issues call for unique and original research and procedures.

IS THERE A PROBLEM?

There are a variety of reasons for introducing computers into safety-critical environments. Digital computers have the potential to provide increased versatility and power, improved performance, greater efficiency, and decreased cost. It has been suggested that introducing computers will also improve safety (Rouse, 1981), yet there is some question about this. Safety-critical systems tend to have reliability requirements ranging from 10^{-5} to 10^{-9} over a given time period. For example, NASA has a requirement of 10^{-9} chance of failure over a 10-hr. flight (Dunham and Knight, 1981). British requirements for reactor safety systems mandate that no single fault shall cause a reactor trip and that there be a 10^{-7} average probability, over 5000 h, of failure to meet a demand to trip (Wellbourne, 1974). Federal Aviation Authority (FAA) rules require that any failure condition that could be catastrophic must be extremely improbable. The phrase *extremely improbable* is defined by the FAA as 10^{-9} per hour or per flight, as appropriate, or to quote, "is not expected to occur within the total life span of the whole fleet of the model" (Waterman, 1978). There is no way that these levels of reliability can be guaranteed (or even measured) for software with the techniques existing today. In fact, it has been suggested that we are orders of magnitude below these requirements (Dunham and Knights, 1981). When computers are used to replace electromechanical devices that can achieve higher reliability levels, then safety may even be impaired.

Even when computers *can* improve safety, it is not clear that the end result is actually an *increase* in system safety. Perrow (1984) argues, e.g., that although technological improvements reduce the possibility of aircraft accidents substantially, they also allow those making the decisions to run greater risks in search of increased performance. As the technology improves, the increased safety potential is not fully realized because the demand for speed, fuel economy, altitude, maneuverability, and all-weather operations increases.

Despite potential problems, however, computers are being introduced to control some hazardous systems. There are just too many good reasons for using them and too few practical alternatives. Decisions will have to be made as to whether the use of computers provides more potential improvements than problems, i.e., computer use will need to be evaluated in terms of benefits and risks. There have been suggestions that certain types of systems provide too much risk to justify their existence (or to justify using computers to control them) (Borning, 1985; Perrow, 1984). More information is needed to make these decisions.

One important trend is the building of systems in which manual intervention is no longer a feasible backup measure (Anderson and Lee, 1981). The Space Shuttle is totally dependent on the proper operation of its computers; a mission cannot even be aborted if the computers fail (Anderson and Lee, 1981). The new unstable, fuel-efficient aircraft require computer control to provide the fine degree of control surface actuation required to maintain stability. The Grumman X-29, for example, is flown by digital computers. If the digital computers fail, there is a backup analog system, but the switch to the backup system must be made at a speed that precludes human control.

Direct monitoring or control of hazardous processes by computers is not the only source of problems. Some computers provide indirect control or data for critical processes, such as the attack warning system at NORAD, where errors can lead to erroneous decisions by the human operators or companion systems. As an example of what can happen, in 1979 an error was discovered in a program used to design nuclear reactors and their supporting cooling systems (Neumann, 1979). The erroneous part of the program dealt with the strength and structural support of pipes and values in the cooling system. The program had supposedly guaranteed the attainment of earthquake safety precautions in operating reactors. The discovery of the program error resulted in the Nuclear Regulatory Commission shutting down five nuclear power plants.

Space, military, and aerospace systems have been the largest users of safety-critical software, and software faults are believed to account for many operational failures of these systems (Bonnett, 1984; Hauptmann, 1981). Some incidents are cited throughout this article. For those who are interested in finding out more about actual incidents, many examples have been collected by Neumann (1985). Frola and Miller (1984) describe aircraft accidents and near accidents caused by software faults. Bassen and coworkers (1985) cite examples of serious problems in medical devices. Reiner (1979) reports pilot concerns about computer malfunctions, unexpected mode changes, loss of data, and other anomalies of flight guidance systems.

SYSTEM SAFETY: AN OVERVIEW

Understanding the techniques and approaches used in building safety-critical electromechanical devices will aid the design of new techniques for software and ensure that these techniques will interface with the hardware approaches and tools. Ideally, global integrated techniques and tools can be developed that apply systemwide.

System safety became a concern in the late 1940s and was defined as a separate discipline in the late 1950s (Rodgers, 1971; Roland and Moriarty, 1983). A major impetus was that the missile systems developed in the 1950s and early 1960s required a new approach to controlling hazards associated with weapon systems (Roland and Moriarty, 1983). The Minuteman ICBM was one of the first systems to have a formal, disciplined system safety program associated with it. NASA soon recognized the need for system safety and has made extensive system safety programs a part of space activities. Eventually, the programs pioneered by the military and NASA were adopted by industry in such areas as nuclear power, refining, mass transportation, and chemicals.

System safety is a subdiscipline of systems engineering that applies scientific, management, and engineering principles to ensure adequate safety, throughout the system life cycle, within the constraints of operational effectiveness, time, and cost. Safety here is regarded as a relative term. Although safety has been defined as "freedom from those conditions that can cause death, injury, occupational illness, or damage to or loss of equipment or property" (MIL-STD-882B, 1984), it is generally recognized that this is unrealistic (Gloss and Wardle, 1984); by this definition *any* system that presents an element of risk is unsafe. But almost any system that produces personal, social, or industrial benefits contains an indispensable element of risk (Browning, 1980): Safety razors and safety matches, for example, are not *safe,* only *safer* than their alternatives; they present an acceptable level of risk while preserving the benefits of the devices they replace. No aircraft could fly, no automobile move, and no ship put out to see if all hazards had to be eliminated first (Hammer, 1972).

This problem is complicated by the fact that attempts to eliminate risk often result in risk displacement rather than risk elimination (Malasky, 1982). Consider nitrates in food, which may cause cancer but prevent deaths from botulism. Benefits and risks often have trade-offs, such as trading off the benefits of improved medical diagnosis capabilities against the risks of exposure to diagnostic x-rays. Unfortunately, the question "How safe is safe enough?" has no simple answer (Morgan, 1981a, 1981b).

Safety is also relative in that nothing is completely safe under all conditions. There is always some case in which a relatively safe material or piece of equipment becomes hazardous. The act of drinking water, if done to excess, can cause kidney failure (Gloss and Wardle, 1984). Thus safety is a function of the situation in which it is measured. One definition might be that safety is a measure of the degree of freedom from risk in any environment.

To understand the relationship between computers and safety, it is helpful to consider the nature of accidents in general. An *accident* is traditionally defined by safety engineers as an unwanted and unexpected release of energy (Johnson, 1973). However, a release of energy is not involved in some hazards associated with new technologies (e.g., recombinant DNA) and potentially lethal chemicals. Therefore the term *mishap* is often used to denote an unplanned event or series of events that result in death, injury, occupational illness, damage to or loss of equipment or property, or environmental harm. The term *mishap* includes both accidents and harmful exposures.

Mishaps are almost always caused by multiple factors, and the relative contribution of each factor is usually not clear (Frola and Miller, 1984; Hammer, 1972; Hope and coworkers, 1983; Johnson, 1973; Perrow, 1984; Petersen, 1981; Ridley, 1983). A mishap can be thought of as a set of events combining in random fashion (Peterson, 1971) or, alternatively, as a dynamic mechanism that begins with the activation of a hazard and flows through the system as a series of sequential and concurrent events in a logical sequence until the system is out of control and a loss is produced (the domino theory) (Malasky, 1982). Either way, major incidents often have more than one cause, which makes it difficult to blame any specific event or component of the system. The high frequency of complex, multifactorial mishaps may arise from the fact that the simpler potentials have been anticipated and handled. However, the very complexity of the events leading up to a mishap implies that there may be many opportunities to interrupt the sequences (Johnson, 1973). Three Mile Island is a good example.

The mishap at Three Mile Island (Perrow, 1984) involved four independent hardware failures (Fig. 1). It started in the secondary cooling system, where water leaked out of the condensate polisher system through a leaky seal. The moisture got into the instrument air system, interrupting the air pressure applied to two feedwater pumps. This interruption erroneously signaled the pumps that something was wrong and that they should stop. Ordinarily, when the cold water flow is interrupted, the turbine shuts down automatically (a safety device), and the emergency feedwater pumps come on to remove the heat from the core. Unfortunately, two pipes were blocked; a valve in each pipe had been accidentally left in a closed position after maintenance two days before. The emergency pumps came on, which was verified by the operator, who did not know that they were pumping water into a closed pipe. Two indicators on the control panel showed that the valves were closed instead of open; one was obscured by a repair tag hanging on the switch above it. At this point the operators were unaware of the problem with emergency feedwater and had no occasion to make sure that those valves, which are always open during tests, were indeed open.

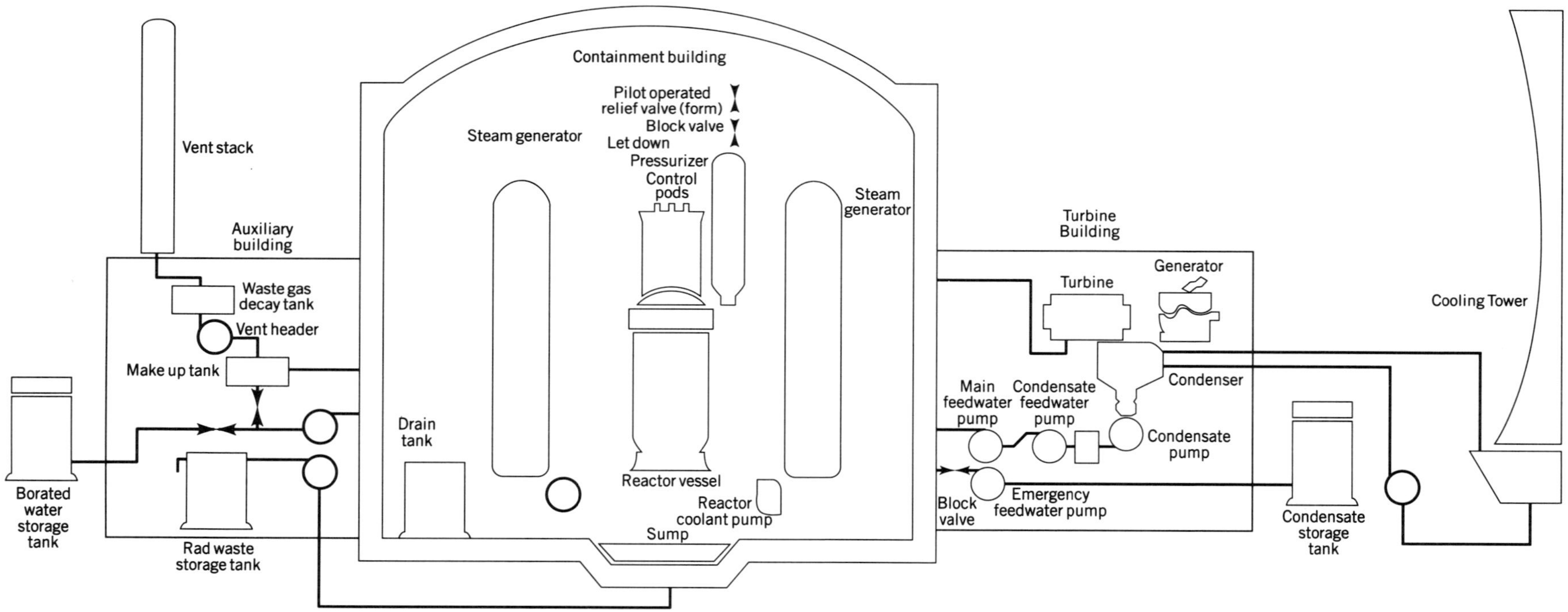

Figure 1. Three Mile Island Unit 2, March 28, 1978. From Kemey and co-workers (1979): and Perrow (1984). (*Continued on next page*).

Failure 1	Clogged condensate polisher line Moisture in instrument air line False signal to turbine
ASD	Turbine stops
(ASD)	Automatic safety device
ASD	Feedwater pumps stop
ASD	Emergency feedwater pumps start
Failure 2	Flow blocked; valves closed instead of open
	No heat removal from primary coolant
	Rise in core temperature and pressure
ASD	Reactor scrams
	Reactor continues to heat, "decay heat"
	Pressure and temperature rise
ASD	Pilot-operated relief valve (PORV) opens
ASD	PORV told to close
Failure 3	PORV sticks open
Failure 4	PORV position indicator signifies that it has shut
ASD	Reactor coolant pumps come on
	Primary coolant pressure down, temperature up
	Steam voids form in coolant pipes and core, restricting flow forced by coolant pumps, creating uneven pressures in system
ASD	High-pressure injection (HPI) starts, to reduce temperature
	Pressurizer fills with coolant as it seeks outlet through PORV
"Operator error"	Operators reduce HPI to save pressurizer, per procedures
	Temperature and pressure in core continue to rise because of lack of heat removal, decay heat generation, steam voids, hydrogen generation from the zirconium–water reaction, and uncovering of core. Reactor coolant pumps cavitate and must be shut off, further restricting circulation

Figure 1. *Continued.*

Eight minutes later they discovered it, but by then much of the initial damage had been done. It is interesting that some experts thought that the closed valves constituted an important operator error, whereas others held that it did not make much difference whether the valves were closed or not, because the supply of emergency feedwater is limited and worse problems were happening anyway.

With no heat being removed from the core, the reactor "scrammed" (a process that stops the chain reaction). Normally there are thousands of gallons of water in the primary and secondary cooling systems to draw off the intense heat of the reactor core, but the cooling system was not working. An automatic safety device, called a pilot-operated relief valve (PORV), is supposed to relieve the pressure. Unfortunately, it just so happened that with the block valves closed, one indicator hidden, and the condensate pumps out of order, the PORV failed to close after the core had relieved itself sufficiently of pressure. Because there had been problems with this relief valve before, an indicator had recently been added to the valve to warn operators if it did not reseat. This time however, the indicator itself failed, probably because of a faulty solenoid.

Note that at this point in the mishap there had been a false signal causing the condensate pumps to fail, two valves for emergency cooling out of position and the indicator obscured, a PORV that failed to reseat, and a failed indicator of its position. Perrow claims that the operators could have been aware of none of these. From that point on, there is considerable debate about whether the following events in the mishap were the result of operator errors or events beyond what the operators could have been reasonably expected to be able to handle. The point of all this is that the mishap was caused by many factors.

It is interesting to note that some of the events contributing to this mishap involved failures of safety devices. In fact, safety devices have more than once been blamed for causing losses or increasing the chances of mishaps (Perrow, 1984). For example, in Ranger 6 (designed to survey the moon) redundant power supplies and triggering circuits were used to ensure that the television cameras would come on to take pictures of the moon's surface, but a short in a safety device (a testing circuit) depleted the power supplies by the time Ranger 6 reached the moon. It has been noted that the more redundancy is used to promote safety, the more chance for spurious actuation; thus "redundancy is not always the correct design option to use" (Weaver, 1981). Another example of a safety device causing a mishap can be found in the core meltdown at the Fermi breeder reactor near Detroit (Fuller, 1977), where a triangular piece of zirconium, installed at the insistence of an independent safety advisory group, broke off and blocked the flow of sodium coolant. An example of software error occurred with a French meteorological satellite (Blown Balloons, 1971); the computer was supposed to issue a "read" instruction to some high-altitude weather balloons but instead ordered an "emergency self-destruct." The self-destruct instruction had been included to ensure that no mishaps would occur from out-of-control balloons. As a result of the software error, 72 of the 141 weather balloons were destroyed.

Finally, mishaps often involve problems in subsystem interfaces (Frola and Miller, 1984; Hammer, 1972). It appears to be easier to deal with failures of components than failures in the interfaces between components. This should not come as any surprise to software engineers. Consider the large number of operational software faults that can be traced back to requirements problems (Boehm and coworkers, 1975; Endres, 1975). The software requirements are the specific representation of the interface between the software and the processes or devices being controlled. Another important interface is that between the software and the underlying computer hardware. Iyer and Velardi (1985) examined software errors in a production operating system and found that 11% of all software errors and 40% of all software failures were computer hardware related.

How do engineers deal with safety problems? The earliest approach to safety, called *operational* or *industrial safety,* involves examining the system during its operational life and correcting what are deemed to be unacceptable hazards. In this approach, accidents are examined, the causes determined, and corrective action initiated. In some complex systems, however, a single accident can involve such a great loss as to be unacceptable. The goal of *system safety* is to design an acceptable safety level into the system before actual production or operation.

System safety engineering attempts to optimize safety by applying scientific and engineering principles to identify and control hazards through analysis, design, and management procedures. Hazard analysis involves identifying and assessing the criticality level of the hazards and the risk involved in the system design. The next step is to eliminate from the design the identified hazards that pose an unacceptable level of risk, or, if that is not possible, to reduce the associated risk to an acceptable level. Procedures for accomplishing these analysis and design objectives are described in separate sections of this article.

Poor management procedures are often the root cause of mishaps (Petersen, 1971). Similarly, the degree of safety achieved in a system depends directly on management emphasis. Safety engineers have carefully defined such requirements for management of safety-critical programs as setting policy and defining goals, defining responsibility, granting authority, documenting and tracking hazards and their resolution (audit trails), and fixing accountability. Specific programs have been outlined and procedures developed, as, e.g., MORT (Management Oversight and Risk Tree) (Johnson, 1973), which is a system safety program originally developed for the U.S. Nuclear Regulatory Commission. The application of safety management techniques to the management of software development has been explored by Trauboth and Frey (1979). This is an important area that deserves more investigation.

WHY IS THERE A PROBLEM?

Many of the system safety techniques that have been developed to aid in building electromechanical systems with minimal risk do not seem to apply when computers are introduced. The major reasons appear to stem from the differences between hardware and software and from the lack of system-level approaches to building software-controlled systems. By examining why adding computers seems to complicate the problem and perhaps increase risk, researchers may be able to determine how to change or augment the current techniques.

Before software was used in safety-critical systems, they were often controlled by conventional (nonprogrammable) mechanical and electronic devices. System safety techniques are designed to cope primarily with random failures in these systems. Human design errors are not considered because it is assumed that all faults caused by human errors can be avoided completely or located and removed before delivery and operation (Lauber, 1980). This assumption, which is based on the use of a systematic approach to design and validation as well as on the use of hardware modules proved through extensive prior use, is justified because of the relatively low complexity of the hardware.

The advent of microprocessors and powerful automation procedures have dramatically increased the complexity of software and hardware, causing a nonlinear increase in human-error–induced design faults. Because of this complexity, it appears to be impossible to demonstrate that the design of the computer hardware or software of a realistic control system is correct and that failure mechanisms are completely eliminated (Lauber, 1980). Perrow (1984) has examined the factors involved in "system accidents" and has concluded that they are intimately intertwined with complexity and coupling. By using computers to control processes, engineers are increasing both of these factors and, therefore, if Perrow is right, increasing the potential for problems.

An important difference between conventional hardware control systems and computer-based control systems is that hardware has historical usage information, whereas control software usually does not (Gloe, 1979). Hardware is generally produced in greater quantities than software, and standard components are reused frequently. Therefore reliability can be measured and improved through experience in other applications. Software, on the other hand, is almost always specially constructed for each application. Although research is being conducted, extensive reuse of software (outside of mathematical sub-routine libraries or operating system facilities) or reuse of software design is unlikely to occur soon in these special-purpose systems.

But lack of reuse is only part of the explanation for the added problems with software. An excellent discussion of why software is unreliable can be found in Parnas (1985). He argues that continuous or analog systems are built of components that, within a broad operating range, have an infinite number of stable states, and their behavior can be described by continuous functions. Most traditional safety systems are analog, and their mathematics is well understood. The mathematical models can be analyzed to understand the system's behavior. Discrete state or digital systems consist of components with a finite number of stable states. If digital subsystems have a relatively small number of states or a repetitive structure, then exhaustive analysis and exhaustive testing is possible. Software, however, has a large number of discrete states without the repetitive structure found in computer circuitry. Although mathematical logic can be used to deal with functions that are not continuous, the large number of states and lack of regularity in the software results in extremely complex mathematical expressions. Progress is being made, but researchers are far from able to analyze most realistic control-system software.

Not only are exhaustive testing and analysis impossible for most nontrivial software but it is difficult to provide realistic test conditions. Operating conditions often differ from test conditions, because testing in a real setting (e.g., actually controlling a nuclear power plant or an aircraft that has not been built yet) is impossible. Most testing must be done in a simulation mode, and there is no way to guarantee that the simulation is accurate. Assumptions must always be made about the controlled process and its environment. For example, the limits on the range of control ("travel") imposed by the software for the F18 aircraft are based on assumptions about the ability of the aircraft to get into certain attitudes, but unfortunately, a mishap occurred because an intentionally excluded attitude was in fact attainable (Neumann, 1981). Again, a wing-mounted missile on the F18 failed to separate from the launcher after ignition because a computer program signaled the missile-retaining mechanism to close before the rocket had built up sufficient thrust to clear the missile from the wing (Frola and Miller, 1984). An erroneous assumption had been made about the length of time that this would take. The aircraft went violently out of control. As another example, it has been reported that aviation software written in the Northern Hemisphere often has problems when used in the Southern Hemisphere (Bonnett, 1984). Finally, software designed to bring aircraft to the altitude and speed for best fuel economy has been blamed for flying the aircraft into dangerous icing conditions (Sliwa, 1984).

These types of problems are not caught by the usual simulation process because they either have been considered and discarded as unreasonable or involve a misunderstanding about the actual operation of the process being controlled by the computer. After studying serious mishaps related to computers, system safety engineers have concluded that inadequate design foresight and specification errors are the greatest cause of software safety problems (Ericson, 1981; Griggs, 1981). Testing can show consistency only with the requirements. These can be specified; it cannot identify misunderstanding about the requirements. These can be identified only by use of the software in the actual system, which can, of course, lead to mishap. Also, accurate live testing of computer responses to catastrophic situations is, of course, difficult in the absence of catastrophes.

Furthermore, the point in time or environmental conditions under which the computer fault occurs may determine the seriousness of the result. Software faults may not be detectable except under just the right combination of circumstances, and it is difficult, if not impossible, to consider and account for all environmental factors and all conditions under which the software may be operating. The operating conditions may even change in systems that move or in which the environment can change. In one instance, a computer issued a "close weapons bay door" command on a B-1A aircraft at a time when a mechanical inhibit had been put in place in order to perform maintenance on the door. The "close" command was generated when someone in the cockpit punched the close switch on the control panel during a test. Two hours later, when the maintenance was completed and the inhibit removed, the door unexpectedly closed. Luckily, nobody was injured (Frola and Miller, 1984). The software was altered to discard any commands not completed within a certain time frame, but this situation had never been considered during testing.

To complicate things even further, most verification and validation techniques for software assume "perfect" execution environments. However, software failures may be caused by such undetected hardware errors as transient faults causing mutilation of data, security violations, human mistakes during operation and maintenance, errors in underlying or supporting software, or interfacing problems with other parts of the system such as timing errors. As an example of what can happen, a mechanical malfunction in a fly-by-wire flight control system set up an accelerated environment for which the flight control computer was not programmed. The aircraft went out of control and crashed (Frola and Miller, 1984). It is difficult, if not impossible, to test the software under all failure modes of the system. Trying to include all of these factors in the analysis or testing procedures makes the problem truly impossible to solve, given today's technology.

It appears that the removal of all faults and perfect execution environments cannot be guaranteed at this point in time (and perhaps never will be). Because of this, there have been attempts to make software fault tolerant, that is, able to function correctly despite the presence of errors.

For hardware, redundancy can be used to provide fault tolerance, because either the individual components can be shown to fail independently, or common-mode analysis techniques can detail dependent failure modes and minimize them. A similar application of redundancy has been proposed for software (Anderson and Lee, 1981; Avizienis, 1985). However, independence in failure behavior between independently produced software versions has not been found in empirical studies (Knight and Leveson, 1986a). Although in theory reliability may still be increased without this assumption (Knight and Leveson, 1986b), there are not yet enough data to show that the amount of increase will justify the added cost of producing multiple versions of the software, and there is no evidence that the *ultrahigh* reliability required in safety-critical software can be achieved using these techniques. In fact, the added complexity of providing fault tolerance may itself cause run-time failures (e.g., the synchronization problems caused by the backup redundancy procedures on the first Space Shuttle flight (Garman, 1981). Perhaps the most important consideration is that most fault-tolerance methods do not solve the problem of erroneous requirements.

The greatest cause of the problems experienced when computers are used to control complex processes may be a lack of system-level methods and viewpoints. Many hardware-oriented system engineers do not understand software because of the newness of software engineering and the significant differences between software and hardware (Ericson, 1981). The same is true, in reverse, for software engineers. This has led system engineers to consider the computer as a black box (Griggs, 1981; Kletz, 1983), whereas the software engineer has treated the computer as merely a stimulus–response system (e.g., Alford, 1985; and Davis, 1982). This lack of communication has been blamed for several mishaps.

An illustrative incident involved a chemical reactor (Kletz, 1983). The programmers were told that if a fault occurred in the plant, they were to leave all controlled variables as they were and to sound an alarm. On one occasion, the computer received a signal telling it that there was a low oil level in a gearbox (Fig. 2). The computer reacted as the requirements specified: it sounded an alarm and left the controls as they were. By coincidence, a catalyst had just been added to the reactor, and the computer had just started to increase the cooling-water flow to the reflux condenser. The flow was therefore kept at a low value. The reactor overheated, the relief valve lifted, and the contents

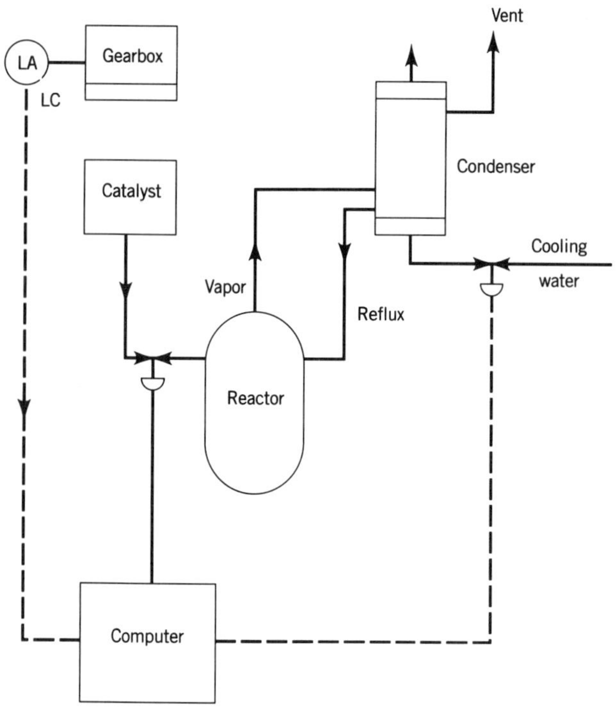

Figure 2. A computer-controlled batch reactor. From Kletz (1983).

of the reactor were discharged into the atmosphere. The operators responded to the alarm by looking for the cause of the low oil level. They established that the level was normal and that the low level signal was false, but by this time the reactor had overheated.

Later study of the causes of the mishap (Kletz, 1983) determined that the system engineers had performed a hazard and operability study on the plant, but that those concerned had not understood what went on inside the computer. It is also apparent that there was a misunderstanding by the programmer about what was meant by the requirement that all controlled variables be left as they were when a fault occurred: did this mean that the cooling-water valve should remain steady or that the temperature should remain steady? A lack of understanding of the process being controlled may have contributed to the programmer's confusion. Unfortunately, such situations are not uncommon.

An obvious conclusion is that system-level approaches are necessary (Boebert, 1980; Lauber, 1980; Leveson, 1984a, 1984b). Note that the software itself is not "unsafe." Only the software that it controls can do damage. Treating the computer as a stimulus–response allows verifying only that the computer software itself is correct or safe; there is no way to verify system correctness or system safety. To do the latter, it must be possible to verify the correctness of the relationship between the input and the system behavior (not just the computer output).

In fact, it is difficult to define a software "fault" without considering the system. If the problem stems from an error in the requirements, then the software may be "correct" with respect to the stated software requirements but wrong from a system standpoint. It is the interaction between the computer and the controlled process that is often the source of serious problems. For example, a particular software fault may cause a mishap only if there is a simultaneous human or hardware failure. Also, a failure of a component of the system external to the computer may cause a software fault to manifest itself. Software engineering techniques that do not consider the system as a whole, including the interactions between the hardware (computer and noncomputer), software, and human operators, will have limited usefulness for real-time control software.

IMPLICATIONS AND CHALLENGES FOR SOFTWARE ENGINEERING

How does all this affect the software engineering practitioner and researcher? Most major safety-critical system purchasers are becoming concerned with software risk and are incorporating requirements for software-safety analysis and verification in their contracts (Ericson, 1981). In many countries, a formal validation and demonstration of the safety of the computers controlling safety-critical process is required by an official licensing authority. Standards for building safety-critical systems (e.g., MIL-STD-882B, 1984; MIL-STD-1574A; 1979; MIL-STD-SNS, 1986) often already include, or are being updated to include, software-related requirements, such as software-hazard analysis and verification of software safety.

Standards and licensing requirements are pushing researchers to find strategies for designing and building computer hardware and software that satisfy these standards and that can be certified by safety licensing authorities. Several national and international working groups are studying these problems and attempting to promote and evaluate current practice and research.

The problem is complicated by the fact that safety involves many areas of traditional software research, and where it fits in exactly has been a matter of some controversy. Neumann (1984) suggests that safety requires a merging of a wide range of concepts, including reliable hardware, reliable (although not necessarily totally correct) software, fault tolerance, security, privacy, and integrity. He adds that not only is the running software of concern but also its use, administration, and maintenance.

Safety has most frequently been argued to be a part of either reliability or security. But although these areas of traditional software research are related to safety, changes or differences in emphasis may be required to apply them to safety problems, and there are some aspects of software safety that are unique with respect to current software engineering concerns.

Reliability versus Safety

Safety and reliability are often equated, especially with respect to software, but there is a growing trend to separate the two concepts. Reliability is usually defined as the probability that a system will perform its intended function for a specified period of time under a set of specified environmental conditions. Although a more precise definition in given in a later section, safety is the probability that conditions that can lead to a mishap (*hazards*) do not occur, whether or not the intended function is performed (Ericson, 1981; Konakovsky, 1978; Leveson, 1984a). In general, reliability requirements are concerned with making a system *failure* free, whereas safety requirements are concerned with making it *mishap* free. These are not synonymous. Failures of differing consequences, from minor annoyance up to death or injury, are possible in any complex system. Reliability is concerned with every possible software error, whereas safety is only concerned with those that result in actual system hazards. Not all software errors cause safety problems, and not all software that functions according to specification is safe (Ericson, 1981). Severe mishaps have occurred while something was operating exactly as intended, ie, without failure (Roland and Moriarty, 1983.)

System requirements can be separated into those related to the *mission* and those related to safety while the mission is being accomplished. There are some systems in which safety is the mission, but these are rare. Generally, some requirements are not safety related at all, some are related to the mission and can result in a mishap if they are not satisfied, and others are concerned only with preventing hazards. If the probability of safety-related requirements being satisfied increases, then safety increases. However, reliability can also be increased by increasing the satisfaction of the nonsafety-related requirements. Unfortunately, in many complex systems, safety and reliability may imply conflicting requirements, and thus the system cannot be built to maximize both.

Consider the hydraulic system of an aircraft. The reliability of that system is more or less complementary to safety as reliability increases, safety increases (Roland and Moriarty, 1983) i.e., the probability of a mishap resulting from hydraulic system failure decreases. The risk of a mishap increases as a result of the inability of the system to perform its mission. For munitions, the opposite is true: since reliability is the probability of detonation or functioning of the munition at the desired time and place, while safety is related to inadvertent functioning, there is no direct relationship. However, one would expect that as the reliability of a munition is increased, the safety would decrease. Procedures to increase the ability of the weapon to fire when desired may increase the likelihood of accidental detonation, unless the design of the munition is modified to improve the safety as the reliability increases (Roland and Moriarty, 1983). In fact, the safest system is sometimes one that does not work at all. These same types of conflicts can be found when comparing software design techniques (Knight and Leveson, 1986b).

Another aspect of reliability that has been equated with safety is availability. However, like reliability, a system may be safe but not available and may also be available but unsafe (eg, operating incorrectly).

For the most part, reliability models have merely counted failures, which is tantamount to treating all failures equally. Recently there have been suggestions that the relative severity of the consequences of failures be considered (Cheung, 1980; Dunham, 1984; Laprie and Costes, 1982: Leveson 1981; Littlewood, 1980).

Leveson (1984a) has argued that there is a need for a completely different approach to safety problems, i.e., for an approach that is complementary to standard reliability techniques and focus on the failures that have the most drastic consequences. Even if all failures cannot be prevented, it may be possible to ensure that the failures that do occur are of minor consequence or that, even if a potentially serious failure does occur, the system will fail safe. *Fail-safe,* or fail passive, procedures attempt to limit the amount of damage cause by a failure; there is no attempt to satisfy the functional specifications except when necessary to ensure safety. This contrasts with *fail-operational* behavior, which provides full functionality in the face of a fault. A *fail-soft* system continues operation but provides only degraded performance or reduced functional capabilities until the fault is removed or the runtime conditions change.

This approach is useful when not all failures are of equal consequence and there is a relatively small number of failures that can lead to catastrophic events. Under these circumstances, it is possible to augment traditional reliability techniques that attempt to eliminate *all* failures with techniques that concentrate on the high cost failures. These new techniques often involve a "backward" approach that starts with determining what are unacceptable or high cost failures and then ensures that these particular failures do not occur or at least minimizes the probability of their occurrence. This now approach and the, traditional reliability approach are complementary, but their goals and appropriate techniques are different.

Security versus Safety

Safety and security are closely related. Both deal with threats or risks, one with threats to life or property and the other with threats to privacy or national security. Both often involve negative requirements that may conflict with some important functional or mission requirements. Both involve global system requirements that are difficult to deal with outside of a system context. Both involve requirements that are considered of supreme importance (in relation to other requirements) in deciding whether the system can and should be used; that is, particularly high levels of assurance may be needed, and testing alone is insufficient to establish the required level of confidence (Landwehr, 1984). Both involve aspects of a system that are regulated by government agencies or licensing bureaus (e.g., National Security Agency and Nuclear Regulatory Commission), where approval is based on factors other than whether the system does anything useful or is economically profitable.

These shared characteristics lead to other similarities. Both may benefit from using techniques that are too costly to be applied to the system as a whole, e.g., formal verification, but that may be cost effective for these limited subsets of the requirements. Both also involve problems and techniques that apply specifically to them and not to other more general functional requirements.

There are differences, however, between safety and traditional security research. Security has focused on malicious actions, whereas safety is also concerned with inadvertent actions. Furthermore, the primary emphasis in security research has been on preventing unauthorized access to classified information, as opposed to preventing more general malicious actions.

Safety as a Separate Research Topic

Including safety with either reliability or security, or vice versa would require major changes in the way that these two more traditional topics are defined and handled. Nonetheless, much work highly applicable to software safety has been accomplished in the areas of software reliability and security, and all three obviously have a close relationship. Laprie and Costes (1982) have suggested that the three be differentiated but that all be considered under the general rubric of "dependability."

Leveson (1984a) has argued that it would be beneficial to consider safety as a separate research topic for several reasons. First, separation of concerns allows the safety aspects of systems to be considered together in a smaller realm, making solutions easier to generate. Divide and conquer is a time-honored approach to handling complexity.

Separate consideration of safety also allows special emphasis and separation of concerns when decisions are being made. The construction of any large, complex system requires weighing alternative and conflicting goals. In automobiles, e.g., safety and fuel economy may vary inversely as design parameters such as weight are changed. The quality and usefulness of the resulting system will depend on how the trade-offs are made. To ensure that the final system is safe, it is necessary to make explicit any trade-offs that involve safety. Resolution of conflicts in a consistent and well-reasoned manner (rather than by default or by the whim of some individual programmer) requires that safety requirements be separated and identified and that responsibilities be assigned.

In systems engineering, reliability and safety are usually distinguished. This distinction has arisen from actual experiences in building safety-critical systems. To cite one example, an early major antiballistic missle system had to be replaced because of serious mishaps caused by previously unnoticed interface problems (Rodgers, 1971). Later analysis suggested that the mishaps stemmed from a lack of specific identification and assignment of responsibility for safety. Instead, safety had been regarded as every designer's and engineer's responsibility. Since that time, system safety has received more and more attention with strict standards being issued and enforced. When software constitutes an important part of a safety-critical system, software safety needs to be given the same attention.

Software engineers may find these distinctions and issues forced on them soon. As mentioned earlier, government regulations and liability laws are beginning to require that the builders of safety-critical systems establish safety standards and programs to verify the safety of the software involved. Current software reliability enhancing techniques and software reliability assessment models do not satisfy these requirements. New techniques and approaches are needed, along with new perspectives and emphases.

In the rest of this article a starting point is established for those interested in this new research area. Some preliminary definitions are advanced, and a survey of some of the currently available techniques is presented. In each section basic system safety concepts are followed by their implications for software. The emphasis is on describing open research questions. As the reader will see, there are many interesting and important questions to be answered. General references are included at the end to provide some guidance for further search. For completeness, papers that have not been directly referenced in this survey have been included there.

DEFINITIONS

Definitions tend to be controversial in a relatively new area of research, and as more is learned, they often change. However, to have a place to start, some preliminary working definitions are given. To further communication and the exchange of ideas, an attempt has been made to make these definitions as consistent as possible with those of system safety. A more formal definition of software safety may be found in Leveson (1983a).

It has been argued that there is no such thing as software safety because software cannot, by itself, be unsafe. However, since software by itself is of little value to anyone other than a programmer, a broader system view is that software can have various unexpected and undesired effects when used in a complex system (Dean, 1981). The same argument can be made about correctness (when correctness is considered in a larger sense than just consistency with the specified requirements). Software is correct or incorrect only with respect to some larger stem in which it is functioning.

A *system* is the sum total of all its component parts working together within a given environment to achieve a given purpose or mission within a given time over a given life span (Ridley, 1983). If safety is defined in terms of a mishap or catastrophic event, then difficulties arise from the fact that mishaps are often multifactorial and may involve conditions in the environment (i.e., not part of the system being considered or evaluated) over which the designer has no control. In fact, a near miss is usually considered a safety problem: The software in an air traffic control system would be considered unsafe if it caused two aircraft to violate minimum separation distances whether a collision actually resulted or not (which may depend on pilot and air traffic controller alertness and perhaps luck).

Safety must be defined in terms of *hazards* or states of the system that when combined with certain environmental conditions *could* lead to a mishap. *Risk* is a function of the probability of the hazardous state occurring, the probability of the hazard leading to a mishap, and the perceived severity of the worst potential mishap that could result from the hazard. Thus there are two aspects of risk: (1) the probability of the system getting into a hazardous state (e.g., the probability of the air traffic control software giving information to the air traffic controller that could lead to two aircraft violating minimum separation assurance) and (2) the probability of the hazard leading to a mishap (e.g., the probability of the two aircraft actually colliding) combined with the severity of the resulting mishap. The question of how to combine probability and severity is a key problem in the area of risk analysis. How does one compare and event that is catastrophic but very unlikely with another event that is much more likely but less serious? Although ad hoc methods exist to accomplish this (MIL-STD-882B, 1984), in the end the process must necessarily involve qualitative judgment and personal values.

The former aspect is sometimes referred to as the *hazard probability,* whereas the latter is sometimes called the *danger* or *hazard criticality.* System hazards may be caused by hardware component failure, design faults in the hardware or software, interfacing (communication and timing) problems between components of the system, human error in operation or maintenance, or environmental stress.

The state of the system is made up of the states of the components of the system, one of which is the computer. Often the computer functions as a controller of the system and thus has a direct effect on the current state. Therefore, it makes sense to talk about "software safety" because the software usually has at least partial control over whether the system is in a hazardous state or not. That is, system safety involves the entire hazardous state of the system, whereas component safety involves just the part of the hazardous state that the component comprises or controls. Each component may make a contribution to the safety or unsafety of the system state, and that contribution constitutes the safety (or risk) of the component.

Software safety then involves ensuring that the software will execute within a system context without resulting in unacceptable risk. What risk is acceptable or unacceptable must be defined for each system and often involves political, economic, and moral decisions outside the decision-making realm of the software engineer. As with "hardware safety," software safety is achieved by identifying potential hazards early in the development process and then establishing requirements and design features to eliminate or control these hazards (Ericson, 1981). *Safety-critical software functions* are those that can directly or indirectly cause or allow a hazardous system state to exist. *Safety-critical software* is software that contains safety-critical functions.

Starting from these definitions, attention is now turned to some aspects of software safety that are of particular concern to the software engineer: requirements analysis, verification, assessment, and design of safety-critical software. The goal is not to provide a complete description of all related work but instead to examine the status of the field and the important research issues.

ANALYSIS AND MODELING

System safety analysis begins when the project is conceived and continues throughout the life cycle of the system. Among the various analyses performed at different stages are preliminary hazard analysis (PHA), subsystem hazard analysis (SSHA), system hazard analysis (SHA), and operating and support hazard analysis (OSHA); these are described briefly in a later section. Recently the need for software hazard analysis has been recognized. In this section, after a brief introduction to hazard analysis in general, software hazard analysis is defined and proposed techniques to accomplish it are described.

The purpose of system safety modeling and analysis is to show that the system is safe both if it operates an intended and in the presence of faults. To prove the safety of a complex system in the presence of faults, it is necessary to show that no single fault can cause a hazardous effect and that hazards resulting from sequences of failures are sufficiently remote. The latter approaches the impossible if an attempt is made to combine all possible failures in all possible sequences and to analyze the output. Instead, system safety analysis procedures often start by defining what is hazardous and then work backward to find all combinations of faults that produce the event. The probability of occurrence of the event can then be calculated and the result evaluated as to acceptability.

The first step in any safety program is thus to identify hazards and categorize them with respect to criticality and probability (i.e., risk); this is called a preliminary hazard analysis. Potential hazards that need to be considered include normal operating modes, maintenance modes, system failure modes, failures or unusual incidents in the environment, and errors in human performance. Hazards for some particular types of systems are identified by law or government standards. To illustrate, the U.S. Department of Defense (DOD) requires that the following be considered in any hazard analysis for nuclear weapon systems (MIL-STD-SNS, 1986):

- Inadvertent nuclear detonation.
- Inadvertent prearming, arming, launching, firing, or releasing of any nuclear weapon in all normal or credible abnormal environments.
- Deliberate prearming, arming, launching, firing, or releasing of any nuclear weapon, except upon execution of emergency war orders or when directed by a competent authority.

Note the inclusion of what are usually considered security issues within the safety standards.

Once hazards are identified, they are assigned a severity and probability. Hazard severity involves a qualitative measure of the worst credible mishap that could result from the hazard; a later section shows some typical hazard categorization strategies. Identification and categorization of hazards by severity may be adequate during the early design phase of a system. Later on, qualitative or quantitative probability ratings can be assigned to the hazards.

Typical qualitative probability categories might include frequent (likely to occur often), occasional (will occur several times in life of system), reasonably remote (likely to occur sometime in life of item), remote (unlikely to occur but possible), extremely remote (probability of occurrence cannot be distinguished from zero), and physically impossible. Quantitative probability assessment is often stated in terms of likelihood of occurrence of the hazard, for example, 10^{-7} over a given time period.

Once the primary hazard analysis is completed, software hazard analysis can begin. Software safety modeling and analysis techniques identify software hazards and safety-critical single- and multiple-failure sequences; determine software safety requirements, including timing requirements, and analyze and measure software for safety. As mentioned previously, software safety analysis and verification are starting to be required by contractors of safety-critical systems. For example, at least three DOD standards include related tasks; one general safety standard (MIL-STD-882B, 1984) includes tasks for software hazard analysis and verification of software safety; an Air Force standard for missile and weapon systems (MIL-STD-1574A, 1979) requires a software safety analysis and integrated software safety analysis (which includes the analysis of the interfaces of the software to the rest of the system ie, the assembled system); and the U.S. Navy has a draft standard for nuclear weapon systems (MIL-STD-SNS, 1986) that requires software nuclear safety analysis (SNSA). All of these analyses are not meant to substitute for regular verification and validation but instead involve special analysis procedures to verify that the software is safe. It is not clear, however, that procedures exist to satisfy these requirements.

It has been stressed repeatedly in this article that software must be analyzed within the context of the entire system, including the computer hardware, the other components of the system (especially those that are being monitored and/or controlled), and the environment. In the next three sections three particular aspects of the software analysis and modeling activity, i.e., requirements analysis, verification, and validation, and measurement, are discussed.

Software Safety Requirements Analysis

Determining the requirements for software has proved difficult. This is a major source of software problems and may be the most important with respect to safety. Many of the mishaps cited in this article can be traced back to a fundamental misunderstanding regarding the desired operation of the software. These examples are not unusual; as noted earlier, after studying mishaps in which computers were involved, safety engineers have concluded that inadequate design foresight and specification errors are the greatest cause of software safety problems (Ericson, 1981, Griggs, 1981). The problems arise from many possible causes, including the intrinsic difficulty of requirements analysis, a lack of emphasis on it in software engineering research (which has tended to concentrate on avoiding or removing implementation faults), and a certain cubbyhole attitude that has led computer scientists to concentrate on the computer aspects of the system and engineers to concentrate on the physical and mechanical parts of the system, with few people dealing with the interaction between the two (Ericson, 1981).

While functional requirements often focus on what the system shall do, safety requirements must also include what the system shall *not* do, including means of eliminating and controlling system hazards and of limiting damage in case of a mishap. An important part of the safety requirements is the specification of the ways in which the software and the system can fail safely and to what extent failure is tolerable.

Some requirements specification procedures have noted the need for special safety requirements. The specifications for the A-7E aircraft include both specification of undesired events and the appropriate response to these events (Heninger, 1980). SREM (Alford, 1982, 1985) treats safety-related requirements as a special type of nonfunctional requirement that must be systematically translated into functions that are to be implemented by a combination of hardware and software.

Taylor (1982b) has suggested that goal specifications, rather than the more common input–output specifications, may have advantages for error and safety analysis. Input–output specifications state the required relationship between inputs and outputs of the software at different points in time or as a function of time. A goal specification states the conditions to be maintained (regulated) and the conditions or changes to be achieved in the process that the software is controlling. The goal specification can be compared and tested with respect to a model of the environment, and faults can be detected.

An important question is how to identify and analyze software safety requirements. Several techniques have been proposed and used in limited contexts, including fault tree analysis, real time logic, and time Petri nets.

Fault tree analysis (FTA) (Vesely and co-workers, 1981) is an analytical technique used in the safety analysis of electromechanical systems. An undesired system state is specified, and the system is then analyzed in the context of its environment and operation to find credible sequences of events that can lead to the undesired state. The fault tree is a graphic model of various parallel and sequential combinations of faults (or system states) that will result in the occurrence of the predefined undesired event. The faults can be events that are associated with component hardware failures, human errors, or any other pertinent events. A fault tree thus depicts the logical interrelationships of basic events that lead to the hazardous event.

The success of the technique is highly dependent on the ability of the analyst, who must thoroughly understand the system being analyzed and its underlying scientific principles. However, it has the advantage that all the system components (including humans) can be considered. This is extremely important because a particular software fault may cause a mishap only if there is a simultaneous human or hardware failure. Alternatively, the environmental failure may cause the software fault to manifest itself. Like the mishap at Three Mile Island, many mishaps are the result of a sequence of interrelated failures in different parts of the system.

The analysis starts with the categorized list of system hazards that have been identified by the preliminary hazard analysis (PHA). A separate fault tree must be constructed for each hazardous event. The basic procedure is to assume that the hazard has occurred and then to work backward to determine the set of possible causes. The root of the tree is the hazardous event to be analyzed, called the *loss event.* Necessary preconditions are described at the next level of the tree with either an AND or an OR relationship. Each subnode is expanded in a similar fash-

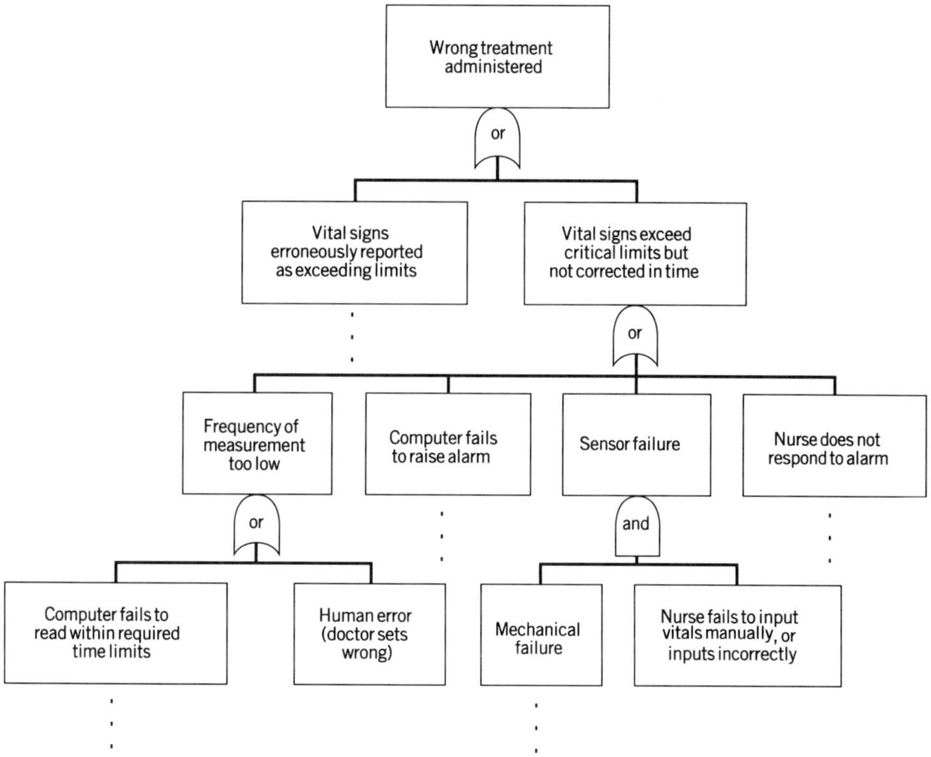

Figure 3. Top levels of patient-monitoring system fault tree.

ion until all leaves describe events of calculable probability or are unable to be analyzed for some reason. Figure 3 shows part of a fault tree for a hospital patient-monitoring system.

Once the fault tree has been built down to the software interface (as in Fig. 3), the high level requirements for software safety can be delineated in terms of software faults and failures that could adversely affect system safety. Software control faults may involve

- Failure to perform a required function, i.e., the function is never executed or no answer is produced.
- Performing a function not required, i.e., getting the wrong answer, issuing the wrong control instruction, or doing the right thing but under inappropriate conditions (e.g., activating an actuator inadvertently, too early, too late, or failing to cease an operation at a prescribed time.
- Timing or sequencing problems, e.g., failing to ensure that two things happen at the same time, at different times, or in a particular order.
- Failure to recognize a hazardous condition requiring corrective action.
- Producing the wrong response to a hazardous condition.

As the development of the software proceeds, fault tree analysis can be performed on the design and finally the actual code.

Jahanian and Mok (1986) have shown how to formalize the safety analysis of timing properties in real-time systems using a formal logic RTL (real-time logic). The system designer first specifies a model of the system in terms of events and actions. The event–action model describes the data dependency and temporal ordering of the computational actions that must be taken in response to events in a real-time application. This model can be mechanically translated into RTL formulas. While the event–action model captures the timing requirements of a real-time system, RTL is more amenable to mechanical manipulation by a computer in a formal analysis. In contrast to other forms of temporal logic specification, RTL allows specification of the absolute timing of events (not only their relative ordering) and provides a uniform way of incorporating different scheduling disciplines in the inference mechanism.

To analyze the system design, the RTL formulas are transformed into predicates of Presburger arithmetic with uninterpreted integer functions. Decision procedures are then used to determine whether a given safety assertion is a theorem derivable from the system specification. If so, the system is safe with respect to the timing behavior denoted by that assertion as long as the implementation satisfies the requirements specification. If the safety assertion is unsatisfiable with respect to the specification, then the system is inherently unsafe because successful implementation of the requirements will cause the safety assertion to be violated. Finally, if the negation of the safety assertion is satisfiable under certain conditions, then additional constraints must be imposed on the system to ensure its safety. Although a full Presburger arithmetic is inherently computationally expensive, a restricted set of Presburger formulas that allows for a more efficient decision procedure is used. Jahanian and Mok also describe ways of restricting the design complexity to ease the job of design verification.

Time Petri net models have also been proposed for software hazard analysis. Petri nets (Peterson, 1981) allow mathematical modeling of discrete-event systems in terms of conditions and events and the relationship between them. Analysis and simulation procedures have been developed to determine desirable and undesirable properties of the design, especially with respect to concurrent or parallel events. Leveson and Stolzy (1985, 1986) have developed analysis procedures to determine software safety requirements (including timing requirements) directly from the system design; to analyze a design for safety, recoverability, and fault tolerance; and to guide in the use of failure detection and recovery procedures. For most cases the analysis procedures require construction of only a small part of the reachability graph. Procedures are also being developed to measure the risk of individual hazards.

Faults and failures can be incorporated into the Petri net model to determine their effects on the system (Leveson and Stolzy, 1986). Backward analysis procedures can be used to determine which failures and faults are potentially the most hazardous and therefore which parts of the system need to be augmented with fault-tolerance and fail-safe mechanisms. Early in the design of the system it is possible to treat the software parts of the design at a high level of abstraction and consider only failures at the interfaces of the software and nonsoftware components. By working backward to this software interface, it is possible to determine the software safety requirements and identify the most critical functions. One possible drawback to this approach is that building the Petri net model of the system is nontrivial. Some of the effort may be justified by the use of the model for other objectives, e.g., performance analysis. Petri net safety analysis techniques have yet to be tried on a realistic system, so there is no information available on the practicality of the approach.

The whole area of requirements analysis needs more attention. Systemwide techniques that allow consideration of the controlled system, rather than just of the software in isolation, are in short supply.

Verification and Validation of Safety

A proof of safety involves a choice (or combination) of the following:

1. Showing that a fault cannot occur, i.e., the software cannot get into an unsafe state and cannot direct the system into an unsafe state.
2. Showing that if a software fault occurs, it is not dangerous.

Boebort (1980) has argued eloquently that verification systems that prove the correspondence of source code to concrete specifications are only fragments of verification systems. They do not go high enough (to an inspectable statement of system behavior), and they do not go low enough (to the object code). The verification system must also capture the semantics of the hardware.

Anderson and Witty (1978) have provided an early attempt to specify what is meant by a proof of safety. Instead of attempting to prove the correctness of a program with respect to its original specification, a weaker criterion of acceptable behavior is selected. That is, if the original specification is denoted by *P*, then a specification *Q* is chosen such that (1) any program that conforms to *P* will also conform to *Q*, and (2) *Q* prescribes acceptable behavior of the program.

The program is then designed and constructed in an attempt to conform to *P*, but so as to facilitate the provision of much simpler proof of correctness with respect to *Q* than would be possible using *P*. They identify a special case of adequacy termed *safeness*. This weaker specification takes *Q* to be *P or error*, meaning that the program should either behave as was originally intended or should terminate with an explicit indication of the reason for failure. A proof of safeness, in these terms, can rely on *assert* statements holding when the program is executed, because otherwise a failure indication would be generated. Of course, a complete proof of safety would require that the recovery procedures involved when an *assert* statement failed be verified to ensure safe recovery.

Another verification methodology for safety involves the use of *software fault tree analysis* (SFTA) (Leveson and Harvey, 1983; Taylor, 1982a). Once the detailed design or code is completed, software fault tree analysis procedure can be used to work backward from the critical control faults determined by the top levels of the fault tree through the program to verify whether the program can cause the top-level event or mishap. The basic technique used is the same backward reasoning (weakest precondition) approach that has been used in formal axiomatic verification (Dijkstra, 1976), but applied slightly differently than is common in "proofs of correctness."

The set of states or results of a program can be divided into two sets: correct and incorrect. Formal proofs of correctness attempt to verify that given a precondition that is true for the state before the program begins to execute, then the program halts and a postcondition (representing the desired result) is true. That is, the program results in correct states. For continuous, purposely nonhalting (cyclic) programs, intermediate states involving output may need to be considered. The basic goal of safety verification is more limited. It is assumed that, by definition, the correct states are safe (ie, the designers did not intend for the system to have mishaps). The incorrect states can then be divided into two sets: those that are considered safe and those that are considered unsafe. Software fault tree analysis attempts to verify that the program will never allow an unsafe state to be reached (although it says nothing about incorrect but safe states).

Because the goal in safety verification is to prove that something will not happen, it is helpful to use proof by contradiction. That is, it is assumed that the software has produced an unsafe control action, and it is shown that this could not happen because it leads to a logical contradiction. Although a proof of correctness should theoretically be able to show that software is safe, it is often impractical to accomplish this because of the sheer magnitude of the proof effort involved and because of the difficulty of completely specifying correct behavior. In the few SFTA proofs that have been performed, the proof appears to involve much less work than a proof of correctness (especially since the proof procedure can stop as soon as a contradiction is reached on a software path). Also, it is often easier to specify safety than complete correctness, especially because the requirements may be actually mandated by law or government authority, as with nuclear weapon safety requirements in the United States. Like correctness proofs, the analysis may be partially automated, but highly skilled human help is required.

Details on how to construct the trees may be found in Leveson and Harvey (1983) and Taylor (1982a). Software fault tree procedures for analyzing concurrency and synchronization are described in Leveson and Stolzy (1983). Introducing timing information into the fault tree causes serious problems. Fault tree analysis is essentially a static analysis technique, whereas timing analysis involves dynamic aspects of the program. Taylor (1982a) has added timing information to fault trees by assuming that information about the minimum and maximum execution time for sections of code is known. Each node in the fault tree then has an added component of execution time for that node. In view of the nondeterminism inherent in a multitasking environment, it may not be practical to verify that timing problems cannot occur in all cases. However, information pined from the fault tree can be used to insert runtime checks, including deadline mechanisms, into the application program and the scheduler (Leveson and Shimeall, 1983).

Fault trees can also be applied at the assembly language level to identify computer hardware fault modes (such erroneous bits in the program counter, registers, or memory) that will cause the software to act in an undesired manner. McIntee (1983) has used this process to examine the effect of single bit failures on the software of a missile. The procedure identified credible hardware failures that could result in the inadvertent early arming of the weapon. This information was used to redesign the software so that the failure could be detected and a "DUD" (fail-safe) routine called.

Finally, fault trees may be applied to the software design before the actual code is produced. The purpose is to enhance the safety of the design while reducing the amount of formal safety verification that is needed. Safe software design techniques are discussed in a later section of this article.

Experimental evidence of the practicality of SFTA is lacking. Examples of two small systems (approximately 1000 lines of code) can be found in the literature (Leveson and Harvey, 1983; McIntee, 1983). There is no information available on how large a system can be to be analyzed with a realistic amount of effort and time. However, even if the software is so large that complete generation of the software trees is not possible, partial trees may still be useful. Partial analysis may still find faults, and partially complete software fault trees may be used to identify critical modules and critical functions, which can then be augmented with software fault-tolerance procedures (Hecht and Hecht 1982). Partial trees may also be used to determine appropriate runtime acceptance and safety tests (Leveson and Shimeall, 1983).

In summary, software fault tree analysis can be used to determine software safety requirements, detect software logic errors, identify multiple failure sequences involving different parts of the system (hardware, human, and software) that can lead to hazards, and guide in the selection of critical runtime checks. It can also be used to guide testing. The interfaces of the software parts of the fault tree can be examined to determine appropriate test input data and appropriate simulation states and events.

Other analysis methods have been developed or are currently being developed. *Nuclear safety cross check analysis* (NSCCA) (Middleton, 1983) is a methodology developed to satisfy U.S. Air Force requirements for nuclear systems. The method employs a large selection of techniques to attempt to show, with a high degree of confidence, that the software will not contribute to a nuclear mishap. The NSCCA process has two components: technical and procedural The technical component evaluates the software by multiple analyze and test procedures to ensure that it satisfies the system's nuclear safety requirements. The procedural component implements security and control measures to protect against sabotage, collusion, compromise, or alteration of critical software components, tools, and NSCCA results.

NSCCA starts with a two-step criticality analysis: (1) identification of specific requirements that are the minimum positive measures necessary to demonstrate that the nuclear weapon system software is predictably safe according to the general DOD standards for nuclear systems, and (2) analysis of each software function to determine the degree to which it controls or influences a nuclear critical event (e.g., prearming or arming). Qualitative judgment is used to give each function an influence rating (high, medium, low), and suggestions are made for the best methods to measure the software functions. The program manager uses the criticality assessment to decide where to allocate resources to meet the requirements, and an NSCCA plan is written. The program plan establishes the tools and facilities requirements, test requirements, test planning, and test procedures. These documents establish in advance the evaluation criteria, purpose, objectives, and expected results for specific NSCCA analysis and tests to promote the independence of the NSCCA and to avoid rubber stamping.

NSCCA has the advantage of being independent of the software developers. It spans the entire development cycle of the system and thus is not just a *post facto* analysis. Whether NSCCA is effective, however, depends on the particular analyses and test procedures that are selected.

A more specialized technique, called software common mode analysis, is derived from hardware common mode analysis techniques (Noble, 1984). Redundant, independent hardware components are often used to provide fault tolerance. A hardware failure that affects multiple redundant components is called a common mode failure. For example, if a power supply is shared by redundant channels, then a single failure in the power supply will cause the failure of more than one channel. Hardware common mode failure analysis examines each connection between redundant hardware components to determine whether the connection provides a path for failure propagation. If there are shared critical components or if the connection is not suitably buffered, then the design must be changed to satisfy the independence requirement.

Noble argues that there is a potential for a hardware failure to affect more than one redundant component through a software path as well as through a hardware path. For example, a processor could fail in such a way that it sends out illegal results that cause a supposedly independent processor to fail. Software common mode analysis, which examines the potential for a single failure to propagate across hardware boundaries via a software path (usually a serial or parallel data link or shared memory), essentially involves a structured walkthrough. All hardware interconnections identified in the hardware common mode analysis are examined to identify those with connections to software. Then all software processes that receive input from the connection are examined to determine whether any data items or combinations of data items can come through this interface and cause the process to fail. In some cases the analyst must examine a path through several modules before it can be determined whether there is an undesired effect. Software common mode analysis has been used by Noble as part of the safety analysis of a commercial system, and it did identify areas of common mode exposure in the design.

Sneak software analysis (Tuma, 1983) is derived from hardware sneak circuit analysis, and it has been claimed that it is useful for verfication of software safety. The software is translated into flow diagrams using electrical symbols (i.e., into a circuit diagram) and examined to detect certain control anomalies such an unreachable code and unreferenced variables. It is basically just a standard static software flow analysis. Much of this type of information is provided by a good compiler. There are several problems with the technique. First, it attempts to find all faults and therefore is more a reliability than a safety technique. More important, it is unlikely that many serious faults will be found this way. An analogy might be trying to find the errors in a book by checking the grammar. Compared with other software safety verification and analysis techniques that have been proposed, this appears to be the least useful.

This section has outlined the approaches that are known or suggested to date for analyzing safety. A few of the methods have been tested and used extensively, while others are still in the development stage; none of them are sufficient to completely verify safety. For example, most of the methods assume that the program does not change while running, yet subtle faults can occur because hardware failures alter a program or its flow of control. A program may also be altered as a result of overwriting itself. Furthermore, all of the methods are complex and error prone themselves.

Many open questions remain, such as

- For what size and how complex a system are these techniques practical and useful?
- How can they be extended to provide more information?
- How can they be used most effectively in software development projects?
- What other approaches to software hazard analysis are possible?

Important work remains to be done in extending and testing these proposed techniques and in developing new ones.

Assessment of Safety

Safety may not be as amenable to quantitative treatment as reliability and availability (Frola and Miller, 1984). As previously noted, mishaps are almost always caused by multiple factors. Furthermore, the probabilities tend to be so small that assessment is extremely difficult. For example, the frequency of mishaps for any particular model of aircraft and cause or group of causes (such as those that might be attributable to design or production deficiencies) is probably not great enough to provide statistically precise assessments of whether or not the aircraft has met a specified mishap rate (Frola and Miller, 1984). But despite this, attempts at measurement are being made.

There are three forms of quantitative risk analysis: single-valued best estimate, probabilistic, and bounding (Morgan, 1981a, 1981b). Single-valued best estimate is useful when a particular risk problem is well understood and enough information is available to build determinate models and use best estimate values for the model's parameters. If the science of the problem is reasonably well understood but only limited information is available about some important parameters, probabilistic analysis can give an explicit indication of the level of uncertainty in the answers. In this case, the single-valued best estimates of parameters are replaced by a probability distribution over the range of values that the parameters are expected to take. If there is uncertainty about the functional form of the model that should be used, this uncertainty may also be incorporated into the model. Finally, some problems are so little understood that a probabilistic analysis is not appropriate. However, it is sometimes possible to use what little is known to at least bound the answer.

There are pros and cons in using any of these assessment techniques. Quantitative risk assessment can provide insight and understanding and allow alternatives to be compared. The need to calculate very low probability numbers forces the analyst to study the system in great detail. However, there is also the danger of placing implicit belief in the accuracy of a calculated number. It is easy to overemphasize the models and forget the many assumptions that are implied. Most important, these approaches can never capture all the factors, such as quality of life, that are important in a problem and should not substitute for careful human judgment (Morgan, 1981a, 1981b).

One of the most complex probabilistic risk analyses that has been attempted is a United States reactor study WASH-1400 (Levine, 1984; USAEC, 1975). This was an enormously complex undertaking because of the many possible failures that could lead to a mishap. This study has been criticized (MacKenzie, 1984) for using elementary data that were incomplete or uncertain and for making many unrealistic assumptions. For example, independence of failures was assumed; that is, common mode failures were largely ignored. It was also assumed that nuclear power plants are built to plan and properly operated; recent events suggest that this may not be the case. Critics also maintain that the uncertainties are very large, and therefore the calculated risk numbers are not very accurate.

Another problem associated with formal safety assessment is the "*Titanic* effect." The *Titanic* was thought to be so safe that some normal safety procedures were neglected, resulting in the loss of many more lives than may have been necessary. Unfortunately, assumptions were made in the analysis that did not hold in practice. For example, the ship was built to stay afloat if four or fewer of the sixteen watertight compartments (spaces below the waterline) were flooded. There had never been an incident in which more than four compartments of a ship were damaged, so this assumption was considered reasonable. Unfortunately, the iceberg ruptured five compartments. It can be argued that the assumptions were the best possible, given the state of knowledge at that time. The mistake was in placing too much faith in the assumptions and the models and in not taking measures in case they were incorrect. Effort is frequently diverted to proving theoretically that a system meets a stipulated level of risk when that effort could much more profitably be applied to eliminating, minimizing, and controlling hazards (Hammer, 1972). This seems especially true when the system contains software. Considering the inaccuracy of present models for assessing software reliability, some of the resources applied to assessment might be more effectively utilized if applied to sophisticated software engineering and software safety techniques. Models are important, but care and judgment must be exercised in their use.

Since safety is a system quality, models that assess it must consider all components of the system. Few currently do so when the system contains programmable subsystems. In general the expected probability with which a given mishap will occur (M) is

$$M = \text{Pr(hazard occurs)} * \text{Pr(hazard leads to a mishap)}.$$

For example, if a computer has a control function, such as controlling the movement of a robot, a simple model (Daniels and co-workers, 1983) is

M=Pr(computer causes a spurious or unexpected machine movement) * Pr(human in field of movement) * Pr(human has no time to move or will fail to diagnose the robot failure).

Given that the computer has a continuous protective or monitoring function, along with a requirement to initiate some safety function on detection of a potentially hazardous condition; another example is

M= f (Pr(dangerous plant condition arising), Pr(failure of computer to detect it), Pr(failure of computer to initiate safety function), Pr(failure of safety function to prevent hazard), Pr(conditions occurring that will cause hazard to lead to a mishap)).

Note that the mishap probability or risk will be overstated if all computer failures are included and not just those that may lead to hazards. Furthermore, the analysis is an oversimplification, since it assumes that the factors involved in the mishap are statistically independent. However, the probability of a hazard leading to an accident may not be independent of the probability of a hazard occurring, e.g., the probability of a person being in the field of movement of a robot may be higher if the robot is behaving strangely, because the operator may have approached in order to investigate. A more sophisticated model would also include such factors as the exposure time of the hazard (the amount of time that the hazard exists, i.e., the average time to detection and repair). The longer the exposure time, the more likely it is that other events or conditions will occur to cause the hazard to lead to a mishap. If an event sequence is involved, exposure time for the first fault must be short or the fault must be rare in order to minimize the probability of a mishap (Mineck and co-workers, 1972).

Complex fault sequences are often analyzed by using fault trees. Probabilities can be attached to the nodes of the tree, and the probability of system and minimal cut set failures can be calculated. Minimal cut sets are composed of all the unique combinations of component events that can cause the top-level event. To determine the minimal cut sets of a fault tree, the tree is first translated into its Boolean equations, and then Boolean algebra is used to simplify the expressions and remove redundancies.

The question of how to assess software safety is still very much unsolved. High software reliability figures do not necessarily mean that the software is acceptable from the safety standpoint. Several researchers (Brown and Buchanan, 1973; Cheung, 1980; Dunham, 1984; Frey, 1974, 1979; Friedman, 1986; Konakovsky, 1978) have attempted to assess the safety of software using software reliability models either by applying the model only to the critical functions or modules or by adding penalty cost or severity to the model. Arlat and Laprie (1985) have defined measures of safety and reliability using homogeneous Markov processes.

This is an area of research that poses many interesting questions, including when and how safety assessment should be used and how it can be accomplished. There also needs to be some way of combining software and hardware assessments to provide system measurements.

DESIGN FOR SAFETY

Once the hazardous system states have been identified and the software safety requirements determined, the system must be built to minimize risk and to satisfy these requirements. It is not possible to ensure the safety of a system by analysis and verification alone, because these techniques are so complex as to be error prone themselves. Furthermore, the cost may be prohibitive, and elimination of all hazards may require too severe a performance penalty. Therefore hazards will need to be controlled during the operation of the software, and this has important implications for design.

System safety has an accepted order of precedence for applying safety design techniques. At the highest level, a system is intrinsically safe if it is incapable of generating or releasing sufficient energy or causing harmful exposures under normal or abnormal conditions (including outside forces and environmental failures) to create a hazardous occurrence, given the equipment and personnel in their most vulnerable condition (Malasky, 1982).

If an intrinsically safe design is not possible or practical, the preferred alternative is a design that prevents or minimizes the occurrence of hazards. This can be accomplished in hardware through such techniques as monitoring and automatic control (e.g., automatic pressure relief valves, speed governors, limit-level sensing controls), lockouts, locking, and interlocks (Hammer, 1972). A lockout device prevents an event from occurring or someone from entering a dangerous zone. A lockin is provided to maintain an event or condition. An interlock ensures that a sequence of operations occurs in the correct order, i.e., it ensures that event A does not occur (1) inadvertently (e.g., a preliminary, intentional action B is required before A can occur), (2) while condition C exists (e.g., an access door is placed on high voltage equipment so that when the door is opened, then the circuit is opened), and (3) before event D (e.g., the tank will fill only if the vent valve has been opened first).

The next, less desirable choice is a design that controls the hazard, if it occurs, using automatic safety devices. This includes detection of hazards and fail-safe designs as well as damage control, containment, and isolation of hazards. The lowest precedence design option is to provide warning devices, procedures, and training to help personnel react to the hazard.

Many of these system safety design principles are applicable to software. Note that software safety is not an afterthought to software design; it needs to be designed in from the beginning. There are two general design principles: (1) the design should provide leverage for the certification effort by minimizing the amount of verification required and simplifying the certification procedure, and (2) design features to increase safety must be carefully evaluated in terms of any complexity that might be added. An increase in complexity may have a negative effect on safety (as well as reliability).

A safe software design includes not only standard software engineering and fault-tolerance techniques to enhance reliability but also special safety features. The emphasis here is on those design features directly related to safety. Risk can be reduced by reducing hazard likelihood or severity, or both. Two approaches are possible: Hazards can be prevented, or they can be detected and treated. Both have drawbacks; prevention of hazards tends to involve reducing functionality or inhibiting design freedom, whereas detection of hazards is difficult and unreliable.

Preventing Hazards through Software Design

Preventing hazards through design involves designing the software so that faults and failures cannot cause hazards; either the software design is made intrinsically safe or the number of software hazards is minimized.

Software can create hazards through omission (failing to do something required) or commission (doing something that should not be done or doing it at the wrong time or in the wrong sequence). Software is usually tested extensively to try to ensure that it does what it is specified to do. Owing to its complexity, however, it may be able to do a lot more than the software designers specified (or intended). Design features can used to limit the actions of the software.

As an example, it may be possible to use modularization and data access limitation to separate noncritical functions from critical functions and to ensure that failures of noncritical modules cannot put the system into a hazardous state, i.e., they cannot impede the operation of the safety-critical functions. The goal is to reduce the amount of software that affects safety (and thus reduce the verification effort involved) and to change as many potentially critical faults into noncritical faults as possible. The separation of critical and noncritical functions may be difficult, however. In any certification arguments that are based on this approach, it will be necessary to provide supporting analyses that prove that there is no way that the safety of the system can be compromised by faults in the noncritical software.

Often in a safety-critical software there are a few modules or data items that must be carefully protected because their execution (or, in the case of data, their destruction or change) at the wrong time can be catastrophic: For example, an insulin pump administers insulin when the blood sugar is low or a missile launch routine is inadvertently activated. It has been suggested (Landwehr, 1984) that security techniques involving authority limitation may be useful in protecting safety-critical functions and data. Security techniques devised to protect against malicious actions can be used sometimes to protect against inadvertent but dangerous actions: the safety-critical parts of the software are separated, and an attempt is made to limit the authority of the rest of the software to do anything safety critical. The safety-critical routines can then be carefully protected. For instance, the ability of the software to arm and detonate a weapon might be severely limited and carefully controlled by requiring multiple confirmations. Note that this is another example of safety possibly conflicting with reliability. To maximize reliability, it is desirable that faults be unable to disrupt the operation of the weapon; however, for safety, faults should lead to nonoperation. Put another way, for reliability the goal is a multipoint failure mode, whereas safety is enhanced by a single-point failure mode.

Authority limitation with regard to inadvertent activation can also be implemented by retaining a person in the loop, ie, a positive input by a human controller is required before execution of certain commands. Obviously, the human will require some independent source of information on which to base the decision besides the information provided by the computer.

In some systems, it is impossible always to avoid hazardous states. In fact, they may be required for the system to accomplish its function. A general software design goal is to minimize the amount of time a potentially hazardous state exists. One simple way this can be accomplished is to start out in a safe state and require a change to a higher risk state. Also, critical flags and conditions should be set or checked as close to the code that they protect as possible.

Finally, critical conditions should not be complementary (e.g., absence of the arm condition should not mean safe).

Often the sequence of events is critical, as when a valve needs to be opened before filling a tank to relieve pressure. In electromechanical systems an interlock is used to ensure sequencing or to isolate two events in time. An example is a guard gate at a railroad crossing that keeps people from crowing the track until the train has passed. Equivalent design features often need to be included in software. Programming language concurrency and synchronization features are used to order events but do not necessarily protect against inadvertent branches caused by either a software fault (in fact, they are often so complex as to be error prone themselves) or a hardware fault (a serious problem, for example, in aerospace systems where hardware is subject to unusual environmental stress such as cosmic ray bombardment). Some protection can be afforded by the use of batons (a variable that is chocked before the function is executed to ensure that the previously required routines have entered their signature) and handshaking. Another example of designing to protect against hardware failure is to ensure that bit patterns used to satisfy a conditional branch to a safety-critical function do not use common failure patterns (i.e., all zeros).

Neumann (1986) has suggested the application of hierarchical design to attain simultaneously a variety of important requirements such as reliability, availability, security, privacy, integrity, timely responsiveness, long-term evolvability, and safety. By accommodating all of these requirements within a unified hierarchy, he claims that it is possible to achieve a sensible ordering of degrees of criticality that is directly and naturally related to the design structure.

Detection and Treatment at Run Time

Along with attempts to prevent hazards, it may be necessary to attempt to detect and treat them during execution. The latter techniques can be divided into those concerned with detection of unsafe states and those that involve response to unsafe states once they have been detected.

Ad hoc tests for unsafe conditions can be programmed into any software, but some general mechanisms have been proposed and implemented, including assertions, exception handling, external monitors, and watchdog timers. Surveys of runtime fault-detection techniques can be found in Anderson and Lee (1981), Yau and Cheung (1975), and Allworth (1981).

Monitors or checks may be in line or external, and they may be at the same or a higher level of the hierarchy. In general it is important (1) to detect unsafe states as quickly as possible to minimize exposure time, (2) to have monitors that are independent from the application software so that faults in one cannot disable the other, and (3) to have the monitor add as little complexity to the system as possible. A general design for a safety monitor facility is proposed in Leveson and co-workers (1983).

Although many mechanisms have been proposed to help implement fault detection, little assistance is provided for the more difficult problem of formulating the content of the checks. It has been suggested that the information contained in the software safety analysis can be used to guide the content and placement of runtime checks (Hecht and Hecht, 1982; Leveson and Shimeall 1983).

Recovery routines are needed (from a safety standpoint) when an unsafe state is detected externally, when it is determined that the software cannot provide a required output within a prescribed time limit, or when continuation of a regular routine would lead to a catastrophic system state if there is no intercession. Recovery techniques can, in general, be divided into two types: backward and forward.

Backward recovery techniques basically involve returning the system to a prior state (it is hoped one that precedes the fault) and then going forward again with an alternative piece of code. There is no attempt to diagnose the particular fault that caused the error or to assess the extent of any other damage the fault may have caused (Anderson and Lee, 1981). Note the assumption that the alternative code will work better than the original code. To try to ensure this, different algorithms may be used (e.g., algorithms that, for efficiency or other reasons, were not chosen originally). There is, of course, a possibility that the alternative algorithms will work no better than the original code, particularly if the error originated from flawed specifications and misunderstandings about the required operation of the software.

Backward recovery is adequate if it can be guaranteed that software faults will be detected and successful recovery completed before the faults affect the external state. However, this usually cannot be guaranteed. Fault-tolerance facilities may fail, or it may be determined that a correct output cannot be produced within prescribed time limits. Control actions that depend on the incremental state of the system, such as torquing a gyro or using a stepping motor, cannot be recovered by checkpoint and rollback (Rose, 1982). A software error may not necessarily be readily or immediately apparent. A small error may require hours to build up to a value that exceeds a prescribed safety tolerance limit. Even if backward application software recovery is attempted, it may be necessary to take concurrent action in parallel with the recovery procedures. For example, it may be necessary to ensure containment of any possible radiation or chemical leakage while attempting software recovery. In such instances forward recovery to repair any damage or minimize hazards will be required (Leveson, 1983b).

Forward recovery techniques attempt to repair the faulty state, which may be an internal state of the computer or the state of the controlled process. Forward recovery may return the system to a correct state or, if that is not possible, contain or minimize the effects of the failure. Examples of forward recovery techniques include using robust data structures (Taylor and co-workers, 1980), dynamically altering the flow of control, ignoring single cycle errors that will be corrected on the next iteration, and changing to a reduced function or fail-safe mode.

Most safety-critical systems are designed to have a safe side, i.e., a state that is reachable from any other state and that is always safe. Often this safe side has penalties from a performance standpoint, e.g., the system may be shut down or switched to a subsystem that can provide fewer services. Besides shutting down, it may be necessary to take some action to avoid harm, such as blowing up a rocket in midair. Note that these types of safety systems may themselves cause harm as in the case of the emergency destruct facility that accidentally blew up 72 French weather balloons.

In more complex designs, there may be intermediate safe states with limited functionality, especially in those systems for which a shutdown would be hazardous itself. A failed traffic light, for instance, is often switched to a state with the light blinking red in all directions. The X-29 is an experimental, unstable aircraft that cannot be flown safely by human control alone. If the digital computers fail, control is switched to an analogue device that provides less functionality than the digital computers but allows the plane to land safely. The new U.S. Air Traffic Control system has a requirement to provide for several levels of service including full service, reduced capability, and emergency mode. Keeping a person in the loop is another simple design for a backup system.

In general, the nonnormal control modes for a process-control system might include

- *Partial Shutdown.* The system has partial or degraded functionality.
- *Hold.* No functionality is provided, but steps are taken to maintain safety or limit the amount of damage.
- *Emergency Shutdown.* The system is shut down completely.
- *Manual or Externally Controlled.* The system continues to function, but control is switched to a source external to the computer; the computer may be responsible for a smooth transition.
- *Restart.* The system is in a transitional state from nonnormal to normal.

Reconfiguration or dynamic alteration of the control flow is a form of partial shutdown. In real-time systems the criticality of tasks often change during processing and may depend on runtime environmental conditions. If peak system overload is increasing the response time above some critical value, runtime reconfiguration of the system may be achieved by delaying or temporarily eliminating noncritical functions. Note that system overload may be caused or increased by internal conditions, such as excessive attempts to perform backward recovery. Some aspects of deadline scheduling have been explored by Campbell and co-workers (1979).

Higgs (1983) describes the design of software to control a turbine generator. It provides an example of the use of several of the techniques described above, including a very simple hierarchy, self-test, and reduction of complexity. The safety requirements for the system include the requirements that (1) the governor always be able to close the steam valves within a few hundred milliseconds if overstressing or even catastrophic destruction of the turbine is to be avoided and (2) under no circumstances can the steam valves open spuriously, whatever the nature of the internal or external fault.

The software is designed as a two-level structure with the top level responsible for the less important governing functions and for the supervisory, coordination, and management functions. Loss of the upper level cannot endanger the turbine and does not cause it to shut down. The upper control level uses conventional hardware and software and resides on a separate processor from the base-level software.

The base level is a secure software core that can detect significant failures of the hardware that surrounds it. It includes self-checks to decide whether incoming signals are sensible and whether the processor itself is functioning correctly. A failure of a self-check causes reversion of the output to a safe state through the action of fail-safe hardware. There are two potential software safety problems: (1) the code responsible for self-checking, validating incoming and outgoing signals, and promoting the fail-safe shutdown must be effectively error free; (2) spurious corruption of this vital code must not cause a dangerous condition or allow a dormant fault to be manifested.

Base-level software is held as firmware and written in assembler for speed. No interrupts are used in this code other than the one, nonmaskable interrupt used to stop the processor in event of a fatal store fault. The avoidance of interrupts means that the timing and sequencing of operation of the processor can be defined for any particular state at any time, allowing more rigorous and exhaustive testing. It also means that polling must be used. A simple design in which all messages are unidirectional and no contention or recovery protocols are required is also aimed at ensuring a higher level of predictability in the operation of the base software.

The organization of the base-level functional tasks is under the control of a comprehensive state table that, in addition to defining the scheduling of tasks, determines the various self-check criteria that are appropriate under particular conditions. The ability to predict the scheduling of the processes accurately means that very precise timing criteria can be applied to the execution time of certain sections of the most important code, such as the self-check and watchdog routines. Finally, the store is continuously checked for faults.

Many more techniques for enhancing safety could be invented beyond those briefly described here. Although much has been written about how to design software, there needs to be a sorting out of which techniques are actually the most effective for systems in which safety is important.

HUMAN FACTORS ISSUES

As computers take over more and more monitoring and control functions in systems in which they are required to interact with humans, software engineers will need to consider human factors issues, especially with respect to software requirement specifications. Several issues arise with regard to safety.

When designing a system that humans and computers will interact to control, one of the basic problems is the allocation of tasks between the human and computer. The goal is to optimize with respect to such criteria as speed of response, deviations of important variables, availability, and safety. It may not be possible to optimize all the variables because of conflicts, and therefore trade-offs must be considered.

An essential ingredient in solving the task allocation problem is knowledge of the ways in which multiple tasks may interact and subsequently degrade or enhance the performance of the human or computer. Two or more tasks may be complementary in that having responsibility for all of them leads to improved performance on each because they provide important information about each other. On the other hand, tasks can be mutually incompatible in that having responsibility for all of them degrades performance on each (Rouse, 1981).

Rouse (1981) notes that there are two possible approaches to task allocation: (1) partition the tasks into two subsets, giving one to the computer and one to the human, or (2) dynamically allocate a particular task to the human or computer controller that has at the moment the most resources available for performing the task.

Air traffic control (ATC) provides an interesting and timely example of the difficulty in solving the task-allocation problem. The long-term plan of the FAA is to increase automation of the controller function; the human role changes from controlling every aircraft to being an ATC manager who handles exceptions while the computer takes care of routine ATC commands. There has been some concern voiced about this goal in Europe (Voysey, 1977) and the United States (Lerner, 1982). The European approach involves more of a partnership between the computer and the human that, it is hoped, will be superior to either of them working alone. Questions have been raised in Europe as to whether the controller who has to intervene in an exceptional case will be properly placed and able to do so. The lack of experience in talking to aircraft individually over a long period of time may lead either to mistakes in instructions or to a generally increasing reluctance to intervene in the system at all (Voysey, 1977).

There is little experimental evidence to support or negate these hypotheses, but a study of an automated steel plant in The Netherlands (Voysey, 1977) found serious productivity problems resulting from the changed role of the human operators. The operators found that they did not know when to take over from the computer, and they became unsure of themselves. They were hampered from observing the process by a lack of visual contact and had difficulty in assessing when the computer was failing to control the operation effectively. The operators also failed to understand fully the control programs used by the computer, and this reinforced their attitude of "standing well back" from the operation except when things were clearly going awry. Therefore, they tended to intervene too late.

A Rand report (Wesson and co-workers, 1980) has proposed a concept for air traffic control called shared control in which primary responsibility for traffic control would rest with human controllers, but the automated system would assist them by continually checking and monitoring their work and proposing alternative plans. In high traffic periods, the controllers could turn increasing portions of the planning over to the automated system. They could thus keep their own workloads relatively constant. The most routine functions, requiring the least intellectual abilities, such as monitoring plans for deviations from agreed flight paths, would be the only functions fully automated.

The question of whether the best results are achieved by automating the human operator's tasks or by providing aids to help the operator perform has not yet been answered. The current trend is to have the human become more of a monitor and supervisor, and less of a continuous controller. As this happens, one of his or her primary responsibilities may be to detect system failures and diagnose their source. A particularly important issue in the area of failure detection concerns how the human's performance is affected by simultaneously having other tasks to do in addition to failure detection. Experimental data are conflicting (Ephrath and Young, 1981; Rouse 1981; Shirley, 1982). Rouse (1981) suggests that having to control while monitoring for failures is beneficial if performing the control task provides cues that directly help to detect failures and if the work load is low enough to allow the human to utilize the cues. Otherwise, controlling simply increase the work load and decreases the amount of attention that can be devoted to failure detection.

The problem of human complacency and keeping the operator's attention appears to be a serious one. There is evidence that complacency and Lock of situational awareness has become a problem for pilots of aircraft with sophisticated computer controls (Frola and Miller, 1984; Hoagland, 1982; Oliver and co-workers, 1982; Perrow, 1984; Ternhem, 1981). For example, Perrow (1984) reports that a government study of thousands of near mishaps reported voluntarily by aircraft crews and group support personnel concluded that the altitude alert system (an aural signal) had resulted in decreased altitude awareness by the flight crews. The study recommended that the device be disabled for all but a few long-distance flights. Ternhem (1981) reports many examples of pilots relying on automatic flight control systems to such a degree that they become lax in their attention to the primary flight instructions or even revise their priorities. Complacency and inattention appeared to cause them to react to failures and errors in the automatic controls much more slowly than they should have. Experiments have shown that the reliability of an operator taking over successfully when the automated system fails increases an the operator's subjective assessment of the probability of equipment failure increases (Venda and Lomov, 1980). Perrow (1984) contends that when a pilot suddenly and unexpectedly is brought into the control loop (i.e., must start participating in decision making) as a result of equipment failure, he or she is disoriented; long periods of passive monitoring make one unprepared to act in emergencies.

Another aspect of complacency has been noted with regard to robots. For example, Park (1978) suggests that warning signals that a robot arm is moving should not be present continuously because humans quickly become insensitive to constant stimuli. Humans also commonly make mistaken assumptions about robot movements. For example, if the arm is not moving, they assume that it is not going to move; if the arm is repeating one pattern of motion, they assume that it will continue to repeat that pattern; if the arm is moving slowly, they assume that it will continue to move slowly; and if they tell the arm to move, they assume that it will move the way they want it to.

There are other interesting issues with respect to safety and human factors. One is selecting the amount, type, and structure of information presented to the human under both normal and emergency conditions to optimize the human's performance. Another is maintaining human confidence in the automated system. For example, unless the pilot has confidence in an aircraft autolanding system, he or she is likely to disconnect it instead of allowing the landing to be completed automatically (Mineck and coworkers, 1972). Below certain altitudes, however, safe manual go-arounds cannot be assured when the system is disconnected. The autolanding system, therefore, must consistently fly the aircraft in a manner that the pilot considers desirable. Data should also be provided to allow the pilot to monitor the system progress and dynamic performance. When the pilot is able to observe on the flight displays that the proper altitude corrections are being made by the autopilot, then the pilot is more likely to leave it engaged even in the presence of disturbances that cause large control actions.

A final issue is that of spurious shutdowns. Although it is important that the computer provide fail-safe facilities, evidence shows that, if the rate of spurious shutdowns or spurious warnings is too high, operators can be tempted to ignore them or to make unauthorized modifications in relevant devices to avoid them (Chamoux and Schmid, 1983).

For many reasons, some of which involve liability and other issues that have little to do with safety, operators have unfairly been blamed for mishaps that really resulted from equipment failures. Some of the reasons for this are examined by Perrow (1984). One result has been the suggestion that humans be removed from the loop. The current evidence appears to be that, although humans do make mistakes, computers also make mistakes, and removing humans from the loop in favor of so-called expert systems or total computer control is probably not desirable.

A mishap at the Crystal River nuclear reactor plant in February 1980 (Marshall, 1980) provides just one example of an incident that would have been much more serious if the operator had not intervened to counteract erroneous computer commands. For unknown reasons, a short circuit occurred in some of the controls in the control room. The utility said that it could have resulted from a bent connecting pin in the control panel or some maintenance work being done on an adjacent panel. The short circuit distorted some of the readings in the system, in particular the coolant temperature. The computer "thought" that the coolant was growing too cold, and so it speeded up the reaction in the core. The reactor overheated, the pressure in the core went up to the danger level and then the reactor automatically shut down. The computer correctly ordered the pressure relief valve to open, but incorrectly ordered it to remain open until things settled down. Pressure dropped so quickly that it caused the automatic high pressure injection to come on, which flooded the primary coolant loop. A valve stuck, and 43,000 gallons of radioactive water were dumped on the floor of the reactor building. The operator noticed the computer's error in keeping the relief valve open and closed the valve manually. Had the operator followed the dictum that the computer is always right and hesitated to step in, the incident would have been much more serious.

Considering the much-repeated statement in this article that mishaps often result from unanticipated events and conditions, it is doubtful that computers will be able to cope with emergencies as well as humans can. The emphasis should be on providing the human operator with an operational environment and appropriate information that will allow intervention in a timely and correct manner. Because this involves software requirements and design, it is important that (1) software engineers become more familiar with human factors issues and (2) requirement specification procedures and fault-tolerance techniques consider human–computer interaction.

HAZARD CATEGORIZATION EXAMPLES

Hazard severity categories are defined to provide a qualitative measure of the worse potential consequences resulting from personnel error, environmental conditions, design inadequacies, procedural deficiencies, and system, subsystem, or component failure or malfunction. Some examples follow.

MIL-STD-882B: System Safety Program Requirements

Category I. Catastrophic; may cause death or system loss.

Category II. Critical; may cause severe injury, severe occupational illness, or major system damage.

Category III. Marginal; may cause minor injury, minor occupational illness, or minor system damage.

Category IV. Negligible; will not result in injury, occupational illness, or system damage.

NHB 5300.4 (1.D.1): A NASA Document

Category 1. Loss of life or vehicle (includes loss or injury to public).

Category 2. Loss of mission (includes both postlaunch abort and launch delay sufficient to cause mission scrub).

Category 3. All others.

DOE 5481.1 (nuclear)

Low. Hazards that present minor on-site and negligible off-site impacts to people or the environment.

Moderate. Hazards that present considerable potential on-site impacts to people or environment, but at most only minor off-site impacts.

High. Hazards with potential for major on-site or off-site impacts to people or the environment.

HAZARD ANALYSES

There are many different types of hazard analyses and multiple techniques for accomplishing them. The following is a brief description of some typical types of hazard analyses. More information can be found in system safety textbooks (e.g., Marshall, 1980; and Ridley, 1983).

Preliminary Hazard Analysis (PHA). PHA involves an initial risk assessment. The purpose is to identify safety critical areas and functions, identify and evaluate hazards, and identify the safety design criteria to be used. It is started early during the concept exploration phase or the earliest life-cycle phases of the program so that safety considerations are included in tradeoff studies and design alternatives. The results may be used in developing system safety requirements and in preparing performance and design specifications.

Subsystem Hazard Analysis (SSHA). SSHA is started as soon as the subsystems are designed in sufficient detail, and it is updated as the design matures. Design changes are also evaluated to determine whether system safety is affected. The purpose of SSHA is to identify hazards associated with the design of the subsystems, including component failure models, critical human error inputs, and hazards resulting from functional relationships between the components and equipment comprising each subsystem. This analysis looks at each subsystem or component and identifies hazards associated with operating or failure modes, including performance, performance degradation, functional failure, or inadvertent functioning. SSHA is especially intended to determine how failure of components affects the overall safety of the system. It includes identifying necessary actions to determine how to eliminate or reduce the risk of identified hazards and also evaluates design response to the safety requirements of the subsystem specification.

System Hazard Analysis (SHA). SHA begins as the design matures (around preliminary design review) and continues as the design is updated until it is complete. Design changes need to be evaluated also. SHA involves detailed studies of possible hazards created by interfaces between subsystems or by the system operating as a whole, including potential safety-critical human errors. Specifically, SHA examines ad subsystem interfaces for (1) compliance with safety criteria in system requirements specifications; (2) possible combinations of independent, dependent, and simultaneous hazardous events or failures, including failures of controls and safety devices, that could cause hazards; and (3) degradation of the safety of the system from the normal operation of the systems and subsystems. The purpose is to recommend changes and controls and evaluate design responses to safety requirements. It is accomplished in the same way as SSHA. However, SSHA examines how component operation or failure affects the system, whereas SHA determines how system operation and failure modes can affect the safety of the system and its subsystems.

Operating and Support Hazard Analysis (OSHA). OSHA identifies hazards and risk reduction procedures during all phases of system use and maintenance. It especially examines hazards created by the human–machine interface.

Several techniques are used to perform these analyses. These include

- Design reviews and walkthroughs.
- Checklists.
- Fault tree analysis: Construction of a logic diagram containing credible event sequences, mechanical and human, that could lead to a specified hazard. Probabilities can be assigned to each event, and thus an overall probability for the hazard can be calculated (Vesely and co-workers, 1981).
- Event tree analysis (or incident sequence analysis): Tracing a primary event forward to define its consequences. It differs from a fault tree in that the fault tree traces an undesired event back to its causes. The two trees together comprise a cause–consequence diagram.
- Hazard and operability studies (HAZOP): A qualitative procedure that involves a systematic search for hazards by generating questions considering the effects of deviations in normal parameters.
- Random number simulation analysis (RNSA): Use of a fault tree or similar logical model as a basis for the analysis. However, instead of the probability of each individual contributing failure event being expressed as a single number, it is expressed as a range of values over which the failure event can occur. It results in a probability distribution curve of the hazard instead of a single numerical value.
- Failure modes and effects analysis (FMEA): Basically a reliability technique sometimes used in safety studies. It examines the effects of all failure modes of the system or subsystems. The advantages of FMEA are that it can be used without first identifying the possible mishaps and can therefore help in revealing unforeseen hazards, but it is very time consuming and expensive since all failures, including nonhazardous failures, are considered. It is good at identifying potentially hazardous single failures, but normally does not consider multiple failures. Failure mode, effect, and criticality analysis (FMECA) extends FMEA by categorizing each component failure according to the seriousness of its effect and its probability and frequency of occurrence.

CONCLUSIONS

This article has attempted to survey software safety in terms of why, what, and how. A fair conclusion might be that *why* is well understood, *what* is still subject to debate, and *how* is completely up in the air. There are software safety techniques that have been widely used and validated. Some techniques that are touted as useful for software safety are probably a waste of resources. The best that builders of these types of systems can do is to (1) select a suite of techniques and tools spanning the entire software development process that appear to be coherent and useful and (2) apply them in a conscientious and thorough manner. Dependence on any one approach is unwise at the current state of knowledge.

Although this article has focused on the technological aspects of the problem, there are also larger social issues that must be considered by us as humans who also happen to be technologists. Perrow (1984) and others (Borning, 1985) have asked whether these systems should be built at all. Perrow suggests partitioning high risk systems into three categories. The first are those systems with either low catastrophic potential or high cost alternatives. Examples include chemical plants, aircraft, air traffic control, dams, mining, fossil-fuel power plants, highways, and automobiles. These systems are self-correcting to some degree and could be further improved with quite modest efforts. Systems in this category can be tolerated, but should be improved. The second category includes those technologies with moderate catastrophic potential and moderate-cost alternatives. These are systems that could be made less risky with considerable effort and that either are unlikely to be able to do without (e.g., marine transpose) or where the expected benefits are so substantial that some risks should be run (e.g., recombinant DNA). The final category includes systems with high catastrophic potential and relatively low cost alternatives. Perrow argues that systems in this final category should be abandoned and replaced because the inevitable risks outweigh any reasonable benefits. He places nuclear weapons and nuclear power in this group. This is just one view, but addresses a question that needs to be raised and considered by us all.

Another issue is that of regulation and the government's right to regulate. Does the government have the right to impose a small involuntary cost on many or most of its citizens (in the form of a tax or higher prices) to make a few or even most people a little safer (Morgan, 1981a, 1981b)? Alternative forms of regulation include tort law, insurance, and voluntary standards-setting organizations. The decision to rely on any of these forms of regulation involves ethical and political issues on which not everybody would agree.

Morgan (1981a, 1981b) argues that managing risk involves using resources that might otherwise be devoted to advancing science and technology, improving productivity, or enriching culture. If we become overly concerned about risk, we are likely to build a society that is stagnant and has little freedom. Yet no reasonable person would argue that society should forget about risk. There is a need for a continual balancing act.

It is apparent that there are more questions than answers with regard to software safety. Many important research problems are waiting for creative and innovative ideas. Just as the developing missile and space programs of the 1950s and 1960s forced the development of system safety, it has been suggested that because of the increasing use of computers in safety-critical systems, we must force the development of software safety before major disasters occur (Bonnett, 1984).

This article is reprinted from Computer Surveys, 18(2) 125-163 (June 1986). Printed with permission of the Association of Computing Machinery.

BIBLIOGRAPHY

M. Alford, "Summary of presentation of Validation and Verification pane," in *Proceedings of the Second International Workshop on Safety and Reliability of Industrial Computer Systems* Pergamon, Elmsford, N.Y., 1982.

M. Alford, "SREM at the Age of Eight; The Distributed Computing Design System," *IEEE Comput.* **18**(4), 36–46 (Apr. 1985).

S. T. Allworth, *Introduction to Real-Time Software Design,* Springer-Verlag, New York, 1981.

T. Anderson and P. A. Lee, *Fault Tolerance: Principles and Practice.* Prentice-Hall, Inc., Englewood Cliffs, N.J., 1981.

T. Anderson and R. W. Witty, "Safe Programming," *BIT* **18,** 1–8 (1978).

J. Arlat and J. C. Laprie, "On the Dependability Evaluation of High Safety Systems," in *Proceedings of the Fifteenth International Symposium on Fault Tolerant Computing* IEEE, New York, 1985, pp. 318–323.

A. Avizienis, "The N-Version Approach to Fault-Tolerant Software." *IEEE Trans. Software Eng.* **SE-11**(12), 1491–1501 (Dec. 1985).

H. Bassen and co-workers, "Computerized Medical Devices: Usage Trends, Problems, and Safety Technology," in *Proceedings of the Seventh Annual Conference of IEEE Engineering in Medicine and Biology Society,* IEEE, New York, 1985, pp. 180–185.

"Blown Balloons," *Aviat. Week Space Technol.,* 17 (Sept. 20, 1971).

W. E. Boebert, "Formal Verification of Embedded Software," *ACM Software Eng. Notes* **5**(3), 41–42 (1980).

B. W. Boehm, R. L. McClean, and D. B. Urfig, "Some Experiences with Automated Aids to the Design of Large-Scale Reliable Software," *IEEE Trans. Software Eng.* **SE-1**(2), 125–133 (1975).

B. J. Bonnett, "Position Paper on Software Safety and Security Critical Systems," in *Proceedings of Compcon '84* IEEE, New York, 1984, p. 191.

A. Borning, *Computer Systems Reliability and Nuclear War,* Technical Report, University of Washington, Computer Science Department, Seattle, Wash.

J. R. Brown and H. N. Buchanan, *The Quantitative Measurement of Software Safety and Reliability.* TRW, Redondo Beach, Calif., Aug. 1973.

R. L. Browning, *The Loss Rate Concept in Safety Engineering,* Marcel Dekker, Inc., New York, 1980.

R. H. Campbell, K. H. Horton, and G. G. Belford, "Simulations of a Fault Tolerant Dead-Line Mechanism," in *Proceedings of the Ninth International Conference on Fault Tolerant Computing* IEEE, New York, 1979, pp. 95–101.

P. Chamoux and O. Schmid, "PLC's in Off-shore Shut-down Systems," in *Proceedings of the Third International Workshop on Safety and Reliability of Industrial Computer Systems,* Pergamon, Elmsford, N.Y., 1983, pp. 201–205.

R. C. Cheung, "A User-Oriented Software Reliability Model," *IEEE Trans. Software Eng.* **SE-6**(2), 118–125 (1980).

B. K. Daniels, R. Bell, and R. I. Wright, "Safety Integrity Assessment of Programmable Electronic Systems," in *Proceedings of IFAC SAFECOMP '83.* Pergamon, Elmsford, N.Y., 1983, pp. 1–12.

A. M. Davis, "The Design of a Family of Application-Oriented Languages," *IEEE Comput.,* 21–28 (May, 1982).

E. S. Dean, "Software System Safety," in *Proceedings of the Fifth International System Safety Conference,* Vol. 1, Part 1, System Safety Society, Newport Beach, Calif., 1981, pp. III-A-1–III-A-8.

E. Dijkstra, *A Discipline of Programming,* Prentice-Hall, Inc., Englewood Cliffs, N.J., 1976.

J. R. Dunham "Measuring Software Safety," in *Proceedings of Compcon '84* IEEE, New York, 1984, pp. 192–193.

J. R. Dunham and J. C. Knight, eds., "Production of Reliable Flight-Crucial Software," in *Proceedings of Validation Methods Research for Fault-Tolerant Avionics and Control Systems Sub-Working-Group Meeting,* NASA Conference Publication 2222, NASA, Langley, Va., 1981.

A. B. Endres, "An Analysis of Errors and Their Causes in Software Systems," *IEEE Trans. Software Eng.* **SE-1**(2), 140–149 (1975).

C. A. Ericson, "Software and System Safety," in *Proceedings of the Fifth International System Safety Conference,* Vol. 1, Part 1, System Safety Society, Newport Beach, Calif., 1981, pp. III-B-1–III-B-11.

H. H. Frey, "Safety Evaluation of Mass Transit Systems by Reliability Analysis," *IEEE Trans. Reliability* **R-23**(3), 161–169 (Aug. 1974).

H. H. Frey, "Safety and Reliability—Their Terms and Models of Complex Systems," in *Proceedings of IFAC SAFECOMP [79,* Pergamon, Elmsford, N.Y., 1979, pp. 3–10.

M. Friedman, *Modeling the Penalty Costs of Software Failure,* Ph.D. dissertation University of California, Irvine, Department of Information and Computer Science, Mar. 1986.

F. R. Frola and C. O. Miller, *System Safety in Aircraft Management,* Logistics Management Institute, Washington, D.C., Jan. 1984.

J. G. Fuller, "We Almost Lost Detroit," in P. Faulkner, ed., *The Silent Bomb,* Random House, New York, 1984, pp. 46–59.

J. G. Fuller, "Death by Robot," *Omni* **6**(6), 45–46, 97–102 (Mar. 1984).

J. R. Garman, "The Bug Heard 'Round the World," *ACM Software Eng. Notes* **6**(5), 3–10 (Oct. 1984).

G. Gloe, "Inspection of Process Computers for Nuclear Power Plants," in *Proceedings of IFAC SAFECOMP '79.* Pergamon, Elmsford, N.Y., 1979, pp. 213–218.

D. S. Gloss and M. G. Wardle, *Introduction to Safety Engineering,* John Wiley & Sons, Inc., New York, 1984.

J. G. Griggs, "A Method of Software Safety Analysis," in *Proceedings of the Safety Conference,* Vol. 1, Part 1, System Safety Society, Newport Beach, Calif., 1981, pp. III-D-1–III-D-18.

W. Hammer, *Handbook of System and Product Safety.* Prentice-Hall, Inc., Englewood Cliffs, N.J., 1972.

D. L. Hauptmann, "A Systems Approach to Software Safety Analysis," in *Proceedings of the Fifth International System Safety Conference,* Systems Safety Society, Newport Beach, Calif., 1981.

H. Hecht and M. Hecht, "Use of Fault Trees for the Design of Recovery Blocks," in *Proceedings of the Twelfth International Conference on Fault Tolerant Computing,* IEEE, New York, 1982, pp. 134–139.

K. L. Heninger, "Specifying Software Requirements for Complex Systems: New Techniques and Their Application," *IEEE Trans. Software Eng.* **SE-6**(1), 2–12 (Jan. 1980).

J. C. Higgs, "A High Integrity Software Based Turbine Governing System," in *Proceedings of IFAC SAFECOMP '83,* Pergamon, Elmsford, N.Y., 1983, pp. 207–218.

M. Hoagland, "The Pilot's Role in Automation," in *Proceedings of the ALPA Air Safety Workshop.* Airline Pilots Assoc., Washington, D. C., 1982.

S. Hope and co-workers, "Methodologies for Hazard Analysis and Risk Assessment in the Petroleum Refining and Storage Industry," *Hazard Prevention,* 24–32 (July–Aug. 1983).

R. K. Iyer and P. Velardi, "Hardware Related Software Errors: Measurement and Analysis, *IEEE Trans. Software Eng.* **SE-11**(2), 223–231 (Feb. 1985).

F. Jahanian and A. K. Mok, "Safety Analysis of Timing Properties in Real-Time Systems," *IEEE Trans. Software Eng.* **SE-12**(9), 890–904 (Sept. 1986).

W. G. Johnson, *The Management Oversight and Risk Tree,* MORT, U.S. Atomic Energy Commission, Washington, D.C., SAN 821-2, UC-41, 1973.

J. Kemeny and co-workers, *Report of the President's Commission on the Accident at Three Mile Island,* U.S. Government Printing Office, Washington, D.C., 1979.

T. Kletz, "Human Problems with Computer Control," *Hazard Prevention 24–26 (Mar.–Apr. 1983).*

J. C. Knight and N. G. Leveson, "An Experimental Evaluation of the Assumption of Independence in Multi-Version Programming," *IEEE Trans. Software Eng.* **SE-12**(1), 96–109 (Jan. 1986a).

J. C. Knight and N. G. Leveson, "An Empirical Study of Failure Probabilities in Multiversion Software," in *Proceedings of the Sixteenth International Symposium on Fault-Tolerant Computing,* IEEE, New York, 1986b, pp. 165–170.

R. Konakovsky, "Safety Evaluation of Computer Hardware and Software," in *Proceedings of Compsac '78.* IEEE, New York, 1978, pp. 559–564.

C. Landwehr, "Software Safety Is Redundance," in *Proceedings of Compcon '84* IEEE, New York, 1984, p. 195.

J. C. Laprie, *Dependable Computing and Fault Tolerance: Concepts and Terminology.* Research Report No. 84.035, LAAS, Toulouse, France, June 1984.

J. C. Laprie and A. Costes, "Dependability: A Unifying Concept for Reliable Computing," in *Proceedings of the Twelfth International Symposium on Fault Tolerant Computing,* IEEE, New York, 1982, pp. 18–21.

R. Lauber, "Strategies for the Design and Validation of Safety-Related Computer-Controlled Systems," in G. Meyer, ed., *Real-Time Data Handling and Process Control,* North-Holland Publishers, Amsterdam, 1980, pp. 305–310.

E. J. Lerner, "Automating U.S. Air Lanes: A Review," *IEEE Spectrum,* 46–51 (Nov. 1982).

N. G. Leveson, *Software Safety: A Definition and Some Preliminary Ideas,* Technical Report 174, University of California, Computer Science Department, Irvine, Apr. 1981.

N. G. Leveson, "Verification of Safety," in *Proceedings of IFAC SAFECOMP '83* Pergamon, Elmsford, N.Y., 1983a, pp. 167–174.

N. G. Leveson, "Software Fault Tolerance: The Case for Forward Recovery," in *Proceedings of the American Institute for Astronautics and Aeronautics (AIAA) Conference on Computers in Aerospace,* AIAA, New York, 1983b.

N. G. Leveson, "Software Safety in Computer-Controlled Systems," *IEEE Comput.,* 48–55 (Feb. 1984a).

N. G. Leveson, "Murphy: Expecting the Worst and Preparing for It," in *Proceedings of the IEEE Compcon '84* IEEE, New York, 1984b, pp. 294–300.

N. G. Leveson, *The Use of Fault Trees in Software Development,* n.d.

N. G. Leveson and P. R. Harvey, "Analyzing Software Safety," *IEEE Trans. Software Eng.* **SE-9**(5) 569–579 (Sept. 1983).

N. G. Leveson and T. Shimeall, "Safety Assertions for Process Control Systems," in *Proceedings of the Thirteenth International Conference on Fault Tolerant Computing,* IEEE, New York, 1983.

N. G. Leveson and J. L. Stolzy, "Safety Analysis of Ada Programs Using Fault Trees," *IEEE Trans. Reliability* **R-32**(5) 479–484 (Dec. 1983).

N. G. Leveson and J. L. Stolzy, "Analyzing Safety and Fault Tolerance Using Time Petri Nets," in *TAPSOFT: Joint Conference on Theory and Practice of Software Development* Springer-Verlag, New York, 1985.

N. G. Leveson and J. L. Stolzy, "Safety Analysis Using Petri Nets," *IEEE Trans. Software Eng.* 1986.

N. G. Leveson, T. J. Shimeall, J. L. Stolzy, and J. Thomas, "Design for Safe Software," in *Proceedings of the American Institute for Astronautics and Aeronautics (AIAA) Space Sciences Meeting,* AIAA, New York, 1983.

S. Levine, "Probabilistic Risk Assessment: Identifying the Real Risks of Nuclear Power," *Tech. Rev., 41–44 (Feb.–Mar. 1984).*

B. Littlewood, "Theories of Software Reliability: How Good Are They and How Can They Be Improved?" *IEEE Trans. Software Eng.* **SE-6,** 489–500 (Sept. 1980).

J. J. MacKenzie, "Finessing the Risks of Nuclear Power," *Technol. Rev.,* 34–39 (Feb.–Mar. 1984).

S. W. Malasky, *System / Safety Technology and Application,* Garland STPM Press, New York, 1982.

E. Marshall, "NRC Takes a Second Look at Reactor Design," *Science* **207,** 1445–1448 (1980).

J. W. McIntee, *Fault Tree Technique as Applied to Software (SOFT TREE),* BMO/AWS, Norton Air Force Base, Calif., 1983.

P. Middleton, "Nuclear Safety Cross Check Analysis," *Minutes of the First Software System Safety Working Group Meeting,* Andrews Air Force Base, June, Norton Air Force Base, Calif., 1983.

MIL-STD-1574A (USAF), *System Safety Program for Space and Missile Systems (15 Aug.).* Department of Air Force, U.S. Government Printing Office, Washington, D.C., 1979.

MIL-STD-882B, *System Safety Program Requirements (30 March),* U.S. Department of Defense, U.S. Government Printing Office, Washington, D.C., 1984.

MIL-STD-SNS (Navy), *Software Nuclear Safety (Draft) Feb. 25,* U.S. Navy, Kirtland Airforce Base, N. Mex., 1986.

D. W. Mineck, R. E. Derr, L. O. Lykken, and J. C. Hall, "Avionic Flight Control System for the Lockheed L-1011 Tristar," *SAE Aerospace Control and Guidance Systems Meeting No. 30* San Diego, Calif., Sept. 1972, pp. 27–29.

M. G. Morgan, "Probing the Question of Technology-Induced Risk," *IEEE Spectrum,* 58–64 (Nov. 1981a).

M. G. Morgan, "Choosing and Managing Technology-Induced Risk," *IEEE Spectrum,* 53–60 (Dec. 1981b).

P. G. Neumann, "Letter from the Editor," *ACM Software Eng. Notes* **4,** 2 (1979).

P. G. Neumann, "Letter from the Editor," *ACM Software Eng. Notes* **6,** 2 (1981).

P. G. Neumann, "Letter from the Editor," *ACM Software Eng. Notes* **9**(5), 2–7 (1984).

P. G. Neumann, "Some Computer-Related Disasters and Other Egregious Horrors," *ACM Software Eng. Notes* **10**(1), 6–7 (1985).

P. G. Neumann, "On Hierarchical Designs of Computer Systems for Critical Applications," *IEEE Trans. Software Eng.* **SE-12**(9), 905–920 (Sept. 1986).

W. B. Noble, "Developing Safe Software for Critical Airborne Applications," in *Proceedings of the IEEE Sixth Digital Avionics Systems Conference,* IEEE, New York, 1984, pp. 1–5.

J. G. Oliver, M. R. Hoagland, and G. J. Terhune, "Automation of the Flight Path—The Pilot's Role," in *Proceedings of the 1982 SAE Aerospace Congress and Exhibition,* SAE, New York, 1982.

W. T. Park, *Robot Safety Suggestions,* Technical Note No. 159, SRI International, Palo Alto, Calif., Apr. 29, 1978.

D. Parnas, "Software Aspects of Strategic Defense Systems," *Commun. ACM* **28**(12), 1326–1335 (1985).

C. Perrow, *Normal Accidents: Living with High Risk Technologies,* Basic Books, New York, 1984.

D. Petersen, *Techniques of Safety Management,* McGraw-Hill Book Co., Inc., New York, 1971.

J. L. Peterson, *Petri Net Theory and the Modeling of Systems.* Prentice-Hall, Inc., Englewood Cliffs, N.J., 1981.

A. Reiner, "Preventing Navigation Errors During Ocean Crossings," *Flight Crew* (Fall 1979).

J. Ridley, *Safety at Work,* Butterworth & Co., London, 1983.

W. P. Rodgers, *Introduction to System Safety Engineering,* John Wiley & Sons, Inc., New York, 1971.

H. E. Roland and B. Moriarty, *System Safety Engineering and Management,* John Wiley & Sons, Inc., New York, 1983.

C. W. Rose, "The Contribution of Operating Systems to Reliability and Safety in Real-Time Systems," in *Proceedings of IFAC SAFECOMP '82,* Pergamon, Elmsford, N.Y., 1982.

W. B. Rouse, "Human-Computer Interaction in the Control of Dynamic Systems," *ACM Comput. Surv.* **13**(1), 99 (Mar. 1981).

R. S. Shirley, "Four Views of the Human–Process Interface," in *Proceedings of IFAC SAFECOMP '82,* Pergamon, Elmsford, N.Y., 1982.

A. F. Sliwa, "Panel Proceedings Software in Safety and Security-Critical Systems," in *Proceedings of Compcon '84,* IEEE, New York, 1984.

D. J. Taylor, D. E. Morgan, and J. P. Black, "Redundancy in Data Structures: Improving Software Fault Tolerance," *IEEE Trans. Software Eng.* **SE-6**(6), 585–594 (Nov. 1980).

J. R. Taylor, *Logical Validation of Safety Control System Specifications Against Plant Models,* RISO-M-2292, Riso National Laboratory, Roskilde, Denmark, May 1981.

J. R. Taylor, *Fault Tree and Cause Consequence Analysis for Control Software Validation,* RISO-M-2326, Riso National Laboratory, Roskilde, Denmark, Jan. 1982a.

J. R. Taylor, "An Integrated Approach to the Treatment of Design and Specification Errors in Electronic Systems and Software," in E. Lauger and J. Motoft, eds., *Electronic Components and Systems,* North-Holland, Amsterdam, 1982b.

K. E. Ternhem, "Automatic Complacency," *Flight Crew,* 34–35 (Winter 1981).

H. Trauboth and H. Frey, "Safety Considerations in Project Management of Computerized Automation Systems," in *Proceedings of IFAC SAFECOMP '79,* Pergamon, Elmsford, N.Y., 1979, pp. 41–50.

F. Tuma, "Sneak Software Analysis," in *Minutes of the First Software System Safety Working Group Meeting* Norton Air Force Base, Calif., 1983.

USAEC, *Reactor Safety Study: An Assessment of Accident Risks in the U.S. Commercial Nuclear Power Plants Report,* WASH 1400 1975, U.S. Atomic Energy Commission, Washington D.C., 1975.

V. F. Venda and B. F. Lomov, "Human Factors Leading to Engineering Safety Systems," *Hazard Prevention,* 6–13 (Mar.–Apr. 1980).

W. E. Vesely, F. F. Goldberg, N. H. Roberts, and D. F. Haasl, *Fault Tree Handbook,* NUREG-0492, U.S. Nuclear Regulatory Commission, Jan. 1981.

H. Voysey, "Problems of Mingling Men and Machines," *New Sci.* **18** 416–417 (Aug. 1977).

H. E. Waterman, "FAA's Certification Position on Advanced Avionics," *AIAA Astronaut, Aeronaut.,* 49–51 (May 1978).

W. W. Weaver, "Pitfalls in Current Design Requirements," *Nucl. Safety* **22**(3) (May–June 1981).

D. Wellbourne, "Computers for Reactor Safety Systems, " *Nucl. Eng. Int.,* 945–950 (Nov. 1974).

R. Wesson and co-workers, *Scenarios for Evolution of Air Traffic Control,* Rand Corporation Report, Rand Corp., Santa Monica, Calif., 1980.

S. S. Yau and R. C. Cheung, "Design of Self-Checking Software, " in *Proceedings of the 1975 International Conference on Reliable Software,* ACM, New York, 1975, pp. 450–457.

General References

B. Andrews, "Using Executable Assertions for Testing and Fault Tolerance," in *Proceedings of the 9th International Symposium on Fault Tolerant Computing,* IEEE, New York, 1979, pp. 102–105.

S. Bologna and co-workers, "An Experiment in Design and Validation of Software for a Reactor Protection System," in *Proceedings of the International Workshop on Safety and Reliability of Industrial Computer Systems,* Pergamon, Elmsford, N.Y., 1979, pp. 103–115.

D. B. Brown, *Systems Analysis and Design for Safety,* Prentice-Hall, Inc., Englewood Cliffs, N.J., 1976.

M. L. Brown, "Software Safety for Complex Systems," in *Proceedings of the Seventh Annual Conference of IEEE Engineering in Medicine and Biology Society,* IEEE, New York, 1985.

C. W. Bruch and co-workers, *Report by the Task Force on Computers and Software as Medical Devices,* Bureau of Medical Devices, Food and Drug Administration, Washington, D.C., Jan. 1982.

G. Dahll and J. Lahti, "An Investigation of Methods for Production and Verification of Highly Reliable Software," in *Proceedings of IFAC SAFECOMP '79,* Pergamon, Elmsford, N.Y., 1979, pp. 89–94.

B. K. Daniels, A. Aitken, and L. C. Smith, "Experience with Computers in Some U.K. Power Plants," in *Proceedings of IFAC SAFECOMP '79,* Pergamon, Elmsford, N.Y., 1979, pp. 11–32.

W. D. Ehrenberger, "Aspects of Development and Verification of Reliable Process Computer Software," in *Proceedings of the Sixth IFAC / IFIP Conference on Digital Computer Applications to Process Control,* Pergamon, Elmsford, N.Y., 1980.

W. D. Ehrenberger and S. Bologna, "Safety Program Validation by Means of Control Checking," in *Proceedings of IFAC SAFECOMP '79,* Pergamon, Elmsford, N.Y., 1979, pp. 120–137.

P. D. Griem, "Reliability and Safety Considerations in Operating Systems for Process Control," in *Proceedings of IFAC SAFECOMP '82,* Pergamon, Elmsford, N.Y., 1982.

B. Gusmann, O. F. Nielsen, and R. Hansen, "Safety-Critical Fast-Real-Time Systems," in *Software for Avionics,* AGARD Conference Proceedings No. 330, NATO, 1983.

J. Jorgens, C. W. Bruch, and F. Houston, "FDA Regulation of Computerized Medical Devices, *Byte* (Sept. 1982).

J. Kronlund, "Organising for Safety," *New Sci.* **82** (1159), 899–901 (July 14, 1979).

A. A. Levene, "Guidelines for the Documentation of Safety Related Computer Systems," in *Proceedings of IFAC SAFECOMP '79,* Pergamon, Elmsford, N.Y., 1979, pp. 33–39.

G. Marshall, *Safety Engineering,* Brooks/Cole Engineering Division, Monterey, Calif., 1982.

P. M. Melliar-Smith and R. L. Schwartz, "Formal Specification and Mechanical Verification of SIFT: A Fault-Tolerant Flight Control System," *IEEE Trans. Comput. C-31,* **7,** 616–630 (July 1982).

M. Mulazzani, "Reliability Versus Safety," in *Proceedings of SAFECOMP '85,* Pergamon, Elmsford, N.Y., 1985.

NAVORD, *NAVORD OD 44942,* Chapter 7, *Hazard Analysis Techniques,* U.S. Navy. U.S. Government Printing Office, Washington, D.C.

C. V. Ramamoorthy, G. S. Ho, and Y. W. Han, "Fault Tree Analysis of Computer Systems," in *Proceedings of the National Computer Conference,* IEEE, New York, 1977, pp. 13–17.

J. Rasmussen and W. B. Rouse, *Human Detection and Diagnosis of System Failures.* Plenum Press, New York, 1981.

R. J. Rogers and W. J. McKenzie, *Software Fault Tree Analysis of OMS Purge Ascent and Entry Critical Function,* Interim Technical Report 78:2511.1-101, TRW, Redondo Beach, Calif., Dec. 1978.

N. C. Thomas and E. A. Straker, "Experiences in Verification and Validation of Digital Systems Used in Nuclear Applications," in *Proceedings of IFAC SAFECOMP '82,* Pergamon, Elmsford, N.Y., 1982.

A. Y. Wei and co-workers, "Application of the Fault-Tolerant Deadline Mechanism to a Satellite Onboard Computer System," in *Proceedings of the 10th International Symposium on Fault Tolerant Computing,* IEEE, New York, 1980, pp. 107–109.

E. L. Weiner, "Beyond the Sterile Cockpit," *Human Factors* **27**(1), 75–90 (1985).

D. Woods, "Comments on Man/Machine Interface Session," in *Proceedings of IFAC SAFECOMP '82,* Pergamon, Elmsford, N.Y., 1982.

S. S. Yau, F. C. Chen, and K. H. Yau, "An Approach to Real-Time Control Flow Checking," in *Proceedings of Compsac '78,* IEEE, New York, 1978, pp. 163–168.

A. G. Zellweger, "FAA Perspective on Software Safety and Security," in *Proceedings of Compcon '84,* IEEE, New York, 1984, pp. 200–201.

Nancy G. Leveson
University of California at Irvine

SCACCHI, WALT

Walt Scacchi received a B.A. in Mathematics, a B.S. in Computer Science, in 1974 at California State University, Fullerton, and a Ph.D. in Information and Computer Science at University of California, Irvine in 1981. He is currently an associate research professor in the Decision Systems Dept. at USC.

Since joining the faculty at USC in 1981, he created and continues to direct the USC System Factory Project. This was the first software factory research project in a U.S. university. Dr. Scacchi's research interests include CASE technologies for developing and reengineering large software systems, business process reengineering, process-driven software engineering environments, software technology transfer and transition, and organizational analysis of system development projects.

Dr. Scacchi is an active researcher with more than 70 research publications in national and international journals, periodicals, and conference proceedings. He has held numerous consulting and visiting scientist positions with firms including AT&T Bell Laboratories, BellCore, Hewlett-Packard, IBM, Microelectronics and Computer Technology Corporation (MCC), Pacific Bell, Perceptronics, Software Engineering Institute at Carnegie Mellon University, and SUN Microsystems. His consulting assignments have included reporting to senior executives on corporate strategies for software technology and software production organizations, briefings on potential applications emerging software technologies in current/new software products and product families. Current consulting engagements include work in new software product developments and strategies targeted to distributed and geographically dispersed CASE and CAE (computer-aided engineering) frameworks for UNIX workstation environments.

Dr. Scacchi also directs a number of contracted research projects at USC which prototype or empirically assesses a variety of advanced CASE or knowledge-based software engineering technologies for both industrial firms and government centers.

Finally, Dr. Scacchi is a member of ACM, IEEE, AAAI, Computing Professionals for Social Responsibility (CPSR), and Society for the History of Technology (SHOT).

SCCS

The Source Code Control System, a suite of UNIX operating system programs for tracking and control of versions of text files (see M. J. Rochkind, "The Source Code Control System," *IEEE Transactions on Software Engineering* **SE-1** (4), 225–265 (April 1975).

SECOND GENERATION LANGUAGE

See ASSEMBLY LANGUAGE.

SECURITY KERNEL

THE BASIC CONCEPT

Information is a valuable and vital asset that requires security against unwanted modification and disclosure. The security kernel concept provides highly effective controls, internal to a computer system, to mediate access of people to information, thereby preventing unwanted modification and disclosure. The need for such internal security controls has grown with the need to share computing resources and information. The security kernel concept was introduced by Schell in 1972 in response to the inability of contemporary computers and their operating systems to protect effectively against illicit modification or disclosure of information. Such illicit information accessibility may result from accidental errors in the system or from flaws maliciously introduced through subversion (e.g., by a virus or more directly) by a designer, programmer, distributor or others with the opportunity. Without use of the security kernel, a determined user or other attacker can usually circumvent the internal security controls and access any computerized information.

Employing a security kernel is the only proven way to build a highly secure computer system. Security kernel technology provides a theoretical foundation and a set of engineering principles that can be applied to the design of computer systems to effectively protect against internal attacks, including those that the designers of the system have never considered. A security kernel provides an effective security perimeter (Gasser, 1988), inside which the information is protected, no matter what is happening outside. In fact, an implicit assumption in the design of a security kernel is that the attackers may build the remainder of the system, and yet the kernel will remain effective in prohibiting unauthorized access.

A security kernel (Ames, Gasser, and Schell, 1983) is a small, basic subset of the system software and supporting hardware that is applicable to all types of systems, wherever the highly reliable protection of information in shared-resource computer systems is required—from general-purpose multiuser operating systems to special-purpose systems such as communication processors. The security kernel is designed to meet three engineering principles: **(1)** completeness—all accesses to information must go through the kernel; **(2)** isolation—the kernel must be protected from unauthorized alteration; and **(3)** verifiability—the kernel must be small, well-structured, and understandable enough to be completely analyzed and verified to perform its functions properly. A security kernel is defined as the hardware and software which implements the reference monitor (Anderson, 1972). The reference monitor provides a framework for conceptualizing the idea of information protection-extending the protection common for people accessing sensitive documents to processors accessing memory. The abstract models of Lampson (1971) were adapted to form the reference monitor concept, which is illustrated in Figure 1.

THE NEED

Security of information inside a computer is fundamentally very difficult to ensure. This is true because, in this unbalanced "game of wits," an attacker bent on modification or disclosure has a substantial advantage. The fundamental problem of security is that the designer must anticipate

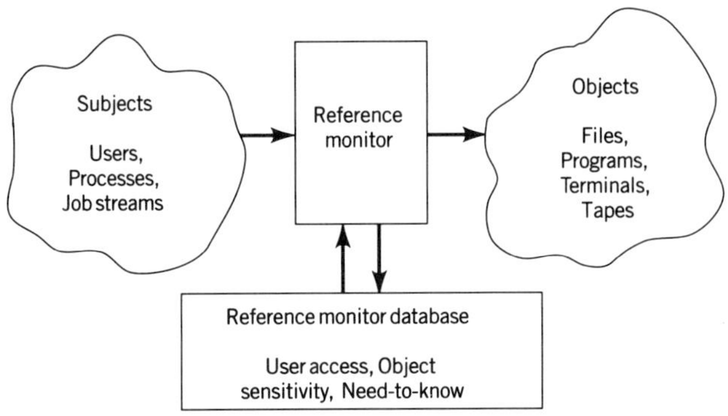

Figure 1. Reference monitor.

every way to circumvent security and correct them all; the attacker is really only interested in finding and using *one*.

Numerous efforts to design reliable internal security controls by various ad hoc means have proven unsuccessful. Furthermore, technology investigations (Anderson, 1972; Schell, 1979) have consistently concluded that it is impractical to ensure that traditional internal controls contain no security flaws. Not only is it impractical, but, in fact, Harrison (1976) showed that it is in general theoretically *impossible* (i.e., mathematically "undecidable") to determine whether an arbitrary protection system can prevent a (perhaps malicious) process from gaining unwanted access to information. The security kernel, however, constitutes a very special case—it is the only type of protection system that can be proven through a structured analysis. This is in sharp contrast to relying on testing to demonstrate the presence of avenues of security control circumvention, since testing is not a reliable means of demonstrating a system to be secure: testing can only prove the presence of flaws and not their absence. Similarly, depending on an audit log of accesses to secure a computer system is futile, because the attacker can likely eliminate or mask any record of the attack on the security controls (Karger and Schell, 1974).

THE WAY TO BUILD A SECURITY KERNEL

A given system is secure only with respect to some specific security policy. The security policy is the set of rules that prescribe what information each person can access. It is conceptualized in a way that is independent of (i.e., external to) computers. As the first step in building a security kernel, the external security policy must be interpreted (Lunt and co-workers, 1988) in a way that allows it to apply to the internal entities of the computer system. A security policy is interpreted in terms of the permissible modes of access (read or write) between the active entities, or subjects (typically surrogates for users), and the passive entities, or objects (repositories for information).

It is essential to have a security policy that is precisely defined and interpreted in order to build a security kernel. In practice, there are two classes of security policies: nondiscretionary and discretionary. A nondiscretionary policy (Saltzer, 1975) contains mandatory security rules that are imposed on all users. This class of security policy can always be represented as a (partially ordered) set of sensitivity labels relating all subjects and objects. A discretionary policy, on the other hand, contains security access control rules that can be specified at the option of individual users. The security policy enforced by a security kernel must be encapsulated in a set of mathematical rules that constitute a formal security policy model. It must be formally proven that these rules are sufficient to preserve security for all possible implementations of the rules.

The model enforced by most security kernels is derived from work performed at the Mitre Corporation, which, in 1974, in work directed by Steven Lipner, completed a mathematical model, design, and prototype implementation for the DEC PDP-11/45 (Schiller, 1974). Commonly referred to as the "Bell and LaPadula Model" (1975), this model provides rules that are provably sufficient for preventing unauthorized observation and modification of information. By representing the security kernel as a finite state machine, these rules define allowable transitions from one "secure" state to the next. What this means in practice is that there exists no software—even malicious software never considered by the designer—that can force the system into an nonsecure state.

The mathematical model aids in identifying the abstract functions that a kernel can include and still be proven secure. It does not, however, specify the precise design for the interface to a kernel. To bridge the gap between model and implementation, the development process must be broken into smaller steps. One common technique is to apply a hierarchy of abstract specifications to the design of the security kernel (Parnas, 1972a; b). The top level specification can be written in a formal specification language enabling automated tools to be used to prove that it corresponds to the model (Levin, Padilla, and Schell, 1989). Below this top-level specification, each layer in the hierarchy is shown to be sufficient to provide the services needed to meet the requirements of the next higher layer. Ideally, this sufficiency would be shown through mathematically formal means if the technology allowed; however, such formal methods are currently beyond the state of verification technology. Therefore, informal arguments are used for establishing the correspondence between the top-level specification and the implementing code. These techniques for building a security kernel permit a third party to effectively evaluate its security (DOD, 1985).

THE PRACTICAL EXPERIENCE

Today, the security kernel remains the only available technology for demonstrably secure, practical computer systems. During the past two decades, the maturation of this technology and the improvements in software engineering and microelectronics have made the use of a security kernel practical and affordable. Several organizations have successfully developed security kernels (Shockley and co-workers, 1988; Fraim, 1983; Schnackenberg, 1985; Karger and co-workers, 1991; Weissman, 1992), but they are not yet in mass market use.

BIBLIOGRAPHY

S. R. Ames, Jr. M. Gasser, and R. R. Schell, "Security Kernel Design and Implementation: An Introduction," *Computer,* **16**(7), 14–22 (July 1983).

J. P. Anderson, *Computer Security Technology Planning Study, ESD-TR-73-51,* Vol. 1, Hanscom Air Force Base, Mass., 1972.

D. E. Bell and L. J. LaPadula, *Computer Security Model: Unified Exposition and Multics Interpretation, ESD-TR-75-306,* Hanscom Air Force Base, Mass., 1975.

DOD 5200.28-STD, DoD Trusted Computer System Evaluation Criteria, Department of Defense, 1985.

L. Fraim, "Scomp: A Solution to the Multilevel Security Problem," *Computer* **16**(7), 26–34 (July 1983).

M. Gasser, *Building a Secure Computer System,* Van Nostrand Reinhold Company, Inc., New York, 1988.

M. A. Harrison, W. L. Ruzzo, and J. D. Ullman, "Protection in Operating Systems," *Communications of the ACM* **19**(8), 461–471 (Aug. 1976).

P. A. Karger and R. R. Schell, *Multics Security Evaluation: Vulnerability Analysis, ESD-TR-74-193,* Vol. 2, Hanscom Air Force Base, Mass., 1974.

P. A. Karger and co-workers, "A Retrospective of the VAX VMM Security Kernel," *IEEE Transactions on Software Engineering* **17**(11), 1147–1165 (Nov. 1991).

B. W. Lampson, "Protection," *Proceedings of the Fifth Princeton Symposium on Information Sciences and Systems,* Princeton University, Mar. 1971, pp. 437–443, reprinted in *Operating Systems Review* **8**(1), 18–24 (Jan. 1974).

T. E. Levin, S. J. Padilla, and R. R. Schell, "Engineering Results from the A1 Formal Verification Process," *Proceedings of the 12th National Computer Security Conference,* National Institute of Standards and Technology/National Computer Security Center, Oct. 1989.

T. F. Lunt and co-workers, *Secure Distribution Data Views: Security Policy and Interpretation for Database Management System for a Class A1 DBMS, RADC-TR-89-313,* Vol. 1, Rome Labs, Griffiss Air Force Base, Rome, N.Y., Aug. 1988.

D. L. Parnas, "A Technique for Software Module Specification with Examples," *Communications of the ACM* **15**(5), 330–336 (May 1972).

D. L. Parnas, "On the Criteria to be used in Decomposing Systems into Modules," *Communications of the ACM* **15**(12), 1053–1058 (Dec. 1972).

J. H. Saltzer and M. D. Schroeder, "The Protection of Information in Computer Systems," *Proceedings of the IEEE* **63**(9), 1278–1308 (Sept. 1975).

R. R. Schell, "Computer Security: The Achilles' Heel of the Electronic Air Force," *Air University Review,* US Air Force, Jan.—Feb., 1979, pp. 16–33.

W. L. Schiller, *The Design and Specification of a Security Kernel for the PDP-11/45, ESD-TR-75-69,* Hanscom Air Force Base, Mass., May 1975.

D. D. Schnackenberg, "Development of a Multilevel Secure Local Area Network," *Proceedings of the 8th National Computer Security Conference,* National Bureau of Standards/National Computer Security Center, Oct. 1985, pp. 97–101.

W. R. Shockley, T. F. Tao, and M. F. Thompson, "An Overview of the GEMSOS Class A1 Technology and Application Experience," *Proceedings of the 11th National Computer Security Conference,* National Institute of Standards and Technology/National Computer Security Center, Oct. 1988, pp. 238–245.

C. Weissman, "Blacker: Security for the DDN," Examples of A1 Security Engineering Trades, *Proceedings of the 1992 IEEE Computer Society Symposium on Security and Privacy,* 1992, p. 286–292.

Roger R. Schell
Gemini Computers, Inc.
Donald L. Brinkley
Sybase, Inc.

SECURITY MODELS

INTRODUCTION

The term *security model* has been used to describe any formal statement of a system's confidentiality, availability, or integrity requirements. In this article the focus is on the primary use of security models, which has been to describe general confidentiality requirements. Pointers are given to security model work in other areas.

MODELS OF CONFIDENTIALITY

Even if discussion is limited to models of confidentiality, there are two related, but distinct, senses of the term *security model* in the computer security literature (McLean, 1990b). In the more limited use of the term, a security model specifies a particular mechanism for enforcing confidentiality, called access control, which was brought over into computer security from the world of documents and safes. In the more general use of the term, security models are specifications of a system's confidentiality requirements and are not "models" at all in that they specify security requirements without describing any particular mechanism for implementing those requirements. These models specify restrictions on a system's interface (usually its input–output relation) that are sufficient to ensure that any implementation that satisfies these restrictions will enforce confidentiality. In this section, access control models and interface models are considered in turn.

ACCESS CONTROL MODELS FOR CONFIDENTIALTY

The access control model for confidentiality was first formulated by Lampson (1971) and later refined by Graham and Denning (1972). The structure of the model is that of a state machine for which each state is a triple (S, O, M), where S is a set of subjects, and O is a set of objects (which has S has a subset). M is an access matrix that has one row for each subject and one column for each object and is such that cell $M[s,o]$ contains the access rights subject s has for object o. These access rights are taken from a finite set of access rights, A. States are changed by requests for altering the access matrix, M. An individual machine in the model is called a system. Despite its simplicity, the model has had a long, useful life in computer security, based primarily on the work of Harrison, Ruzzo, and Ullman and the work of Bell and LaPadula.

The HRU Model and Its Derivatives. Harrison, Ruzzo, and Ullman (1976) used Lampson's concept of an access control model to analyze the complexity of determining the effects of a particular access control policy. To make the problem precise they considered a particular access control model, called the HRU model, which is similar to Lampson's but contains requests only of the following form:

if

a_1 in $M[s_1, o_1]$ and
a_2 in $M[s_2, o_2]$ and
. . .
a_m in $M[s_m, o_m]$ and

then

op_1
. . .
op_n

where each a_i is in A, and each op_i is one of the following primitive operations:

enter a into (s,o),
delete a from (s,o),
create subject s,
create object o,
destroy subject s,
destroy object o.

The semantics of the primitive operations are exactly as would be expected.

Given a system, an initial configuration Q_0, and a right a, we say that Q_0 is safe for a if there is no sequence of system requests that, when executed starting in state Q_0, will write a into a cell of the access matrix that did not already contain it. Harrison, Ruzzo, and Ullman proved two fundamental theorems about the complexity of determining whether or not a system is safe. The first is that the safety problem is decidable for monooperational systems, ie, systems in which every request has only one operation, and the second is that the safety problem is undecidable in general.

Theorem. There is an algorithm for determining whether or not a given monooperational system and initial configuration of that system is safe for a given right a (Harrison, Ruzzo, and Ullman, 1976).

Proof. The proof depends on the fact that for every sequence of requests $r_1, r_2, \ldots, r_n$ that leaks a from an initial configuration (S_0, O_0, M_0), there is a sequence of requests from that configuration that also leaks a but that contains only enter requests except for an initial create subject request. To form this new sequence first insert an initial create subject request to the beginning of $r_1, r_2, \ldots, r_n$ that creates a new subject, call it s_{init}, and then drop all delete and destroy requests from $r_1, r_2, \ldots, r_n$. This new sequence will still leak a because the conditional part of a request can test only for the presence of rights and not for the absence of either rights or objects. Next, consider the right-most create subject request. Remove this request from the sequence, and simply replace all references to the new subject in future requests by references to s_{init}. Continue with this procedure until the initial create subject request is reached, which is left intact. Finally, remove the create object requests, right-most first, again replacing all references to the new object in future requests by references to s_{init}. Finally, drop any enter requests that enter a right a_i into a cell that already contains it.

The resulting sequence will still leak a but can be at most $l = (|A| \times (|S_0| + 1) \times (|O_0| + 1)) + 1$ requests long, because each request, except the initial create subject request, must enter a new symbol from A into an access matrix cell and the number of cells in the matrix cannot be greater than $(|S_0| + 1) \times (|O_0| + 1)$. Hence, it is possible to decide whether or not a system is safe by looking at all possible sequences of enter requests (preceded by an initial create subject request) of length less than or equal to l.

Theorem. The general problem of determining whether or not a given configuration of a given system is safe for a given right a is undecidable (Harrison, Ruzzo, Ullman, 1976).

Proof. The proof depends on the fact that the access control model is expressive enough to model any given Turing machine. As an example, consider a Turing machine that is in state q and reading position 3 of its tape. Furthermore, assume that so far, the machine has written the symbols c_1, c_2, c_3, and c_4 on tape positions 1, 2, 3, and 4, respectively, and that the machine has proceeded no further than the fourth position of the tape. Such a machine can be represented by a state machine whose access rights are the machine's states and tape symbols, plus the two additional rights own and end. The particular state of the machine would correspond to a state that had four subjects s_1, s_2, s_3, and s_4 corresponding to tape positions 1, 2, 3, and 4, respectively. $M[s_i, s_2]$, $M[s_2, s_3]$, and $M[s_3, s_4]$ would each contain the symbol own, representing the fact that for $1 \le i \le 3$, position i is to the immediate left of position $i + 1$ on the tape. For $1 \le i \le 4$, $M[s_i, s_i]$ would contain c_i, representing the fact that position i contains the symbol c_i. Finally, $M[s_3, s_3]$ would also contain the symbol q, and $M[s_3, s_4]$ would also contain the symbol end, representing the facts that the machine is currently in state q reading tape position 3 and that it has not proceeded beyond tape position 4. Moves of the machine correspond to the requests that keep the system's state in correspondence with the machine's. The problem of determining whether a right is leaked now corresponds to the problem of determining whether a machine enters a certain state. If that right is equated with the machine's final state, the safety problem has been reduced to the halting problem.

The two theorems force on modelers the following dilemma: on one hand, the general HRU model can express a wide variety of policies, but there is no general, computationally feasible way to determine the effects of these policies; on the other hand, there is a general, computationally feasible way to determine the effects of policies modeled via monooperational HRU, but the model is too weak to express many policies of interest. For example, monooperational systems cannot express policies that give subjects special rights to objects they create, because there is no single operation that both creates an object and flags it as belonging to the creating subject.

Harrison, Ruzzo, and Ullman (1976) proved that the safety problem is decidable (although PSPACE complete) for systems that have no create requests and that it is decidable for systems that are both monotonic, i.e., contain no destroy or delete requests, and monoconditional, i.e., have only requests the condition parts of which have, at most, one clause (Harrison and Ruzzo, 1978). However, such systems are still very limited as far as expressing useful properties, and safety for even monotonic systems becomes undecidable if biconditional requests are allowed (requests whose condition parts have two clauses) (Harrison and Ruzzo, 1978). Lipton and Snyder (1978) have shown that the safety problem for systems with a finite set of subjects is decidable, but it is computationally intractable.

Taking another tack, the take-grant model, introduced by Jones, Lipton, and Snyder (1976) and extended by Snyder (1981) and others (Bishop and Snyder, 1979; Biskup, 1984), has a linear time algorithm for safety, yet falls outside the known decidable cases of HRU. Closer to the HRU model is the schematic protection model (SPM) developed by Sandhu (1988). SPM, which contains security types, has a decidable subset that is more expressive than the take-grant model. An extension by Ammann and Sandhu (1990) yields a model that is formally equivalent to monotonic HRU, but maintains positive safety results. More recently, Sandhu (1991) has had success with the typed access matrix model (TAM), which introduces strong typing into HRU. Like HRU, monotonic TAM is undecidable. However, if all commands are limited to three parameters and cyclic creates are avoided, the resulting model is decidable in polynomial time yet expressive enough to capture a wide variety of policies. This model is the current state of the art with respect to models for generalized access control policies.

The Bell and LaPadula Model and Its Derivatives. The HRU results show that it is often difficult to predict how access rights can propagate in a given access control model, even with complete knowledge of the programs that propagate those rights. A related, but distinct, problem arises from the fact that users are often unaware of everything a program operating on their behalf is doing. For example, consider a user who accepts the right to execute another user's program. The first user may be unaware that executing the program will pass to the second user some entirely unrelated set of rights possessed by the first user. Programs such as these, which on the surface perform one function, e.g., provide editing capability for a file, but clandestinely perform another, e.g., distribute read rights for the same file, are known as Trojan Horses.

The Trojan Horse problem has led to a distinction between two types of access control policies: discretionary access control (DAC) and mandatory access control (MAC). Whereas DAC allows users to pass rights they possess to other users without constraint, MAC restricts how users can pass rights to other users. The existence of Trojan Horses that pass a user's rights without the user's knowledge is generally viewed as making DAC an insufficient method of access control in high assurance environments.

The best known example of MAC policies are in the military with its well-known lattice of security levels that range from top secret, perhaps with various compartments, down through secret and confidential to unclassified. Rights to read a top secret file, e.g., cannot be passed by any mechanism to an unclassified user. However, other examples of MAC policies pervade everyday life. For example, although an employee may grant an employer rights to view his or her salary, the employee would not want the employer to be able to pass these rights on to another employee. More generally, people are often willing to grant to a second party (perhaps a doctor or loan officer) the right to gather information about themselves, but only on the condition that the right to gather this information is not passed on to arbitrary third parties.

The best known security model for MAC is that of Bell and LaPadula (1975). Like the HRU model, the Bell and LaPadula model (BLP) employs subject, objects, rights, and an access control matrix. However, BLP differs from HRU in that the sets S and O do not change from state to state and the set A contains only two rights: read and write. (In Bell and LaPadula's formulation (1975), A also contains the rights append and execute, but their existence makes no difference in what follows. Other similar liberties were taken to simplify the model when the simplifications do not affect the discussion.) BLP also introduces an unchanging lattice of security levels L and a function $F{:}S \cup O \rightarrow L$, which when applied to a subject or object in a state yields the security level of its argument in that state. The set of states, V, in the model is a set of ordered pairs (F, M), where, as in HRU, M is the access matrix. A system consists of an initial state v_0, a particular set of requests R, and a transition function $T{:}\ (V \times R) \rightarrow V$ that transforms the system from one state to another when a request is executed. However, the most important difference between BLP and HRU is the introduction of a series of definitions that culminate in necessary and sufficient criteria for a system to be secure.

Definition. A state (F, M) is read secure (called simple security in Bell and LaPadula, 1975) if and only if for every $s \varepsilon S$ and every $o \varepsilon O$, read$\varepsilon M[s,o] \rightarrow F(s) \geq F(o)$.

Definition. A state (F, M) is write secure (called the *-property in Bell and Lapadula, 1975) if and only if for every $s \varepsilon S$, $o \varepsilon O$, *write* $\varepsilon M[s,o] \rightarrow F(o) \geq F(s)$.

Definition. A state is state secure if and only if it is read secure and write secure.

Definition. A system (v_0, R, T) is secure if and only if v_0 is state secure and every state reachable from v_0 by executing a finite sequence of one or more requests from R is state secure.

Read security prohibits low level users from gaining read access to high level files. Write security prevents high level Trojan Horses from copying the contents of high level files to files to which low level users can gain read access. Bell and LaPadula go on to prove the following theorem about secure systems, known as the basic security theorem (*BST*).

Theorem. A system (v_0, R, T) is secure if and only if (**1**) v_0 is a secure state and (**2**) T is such that for every state v reachable from v_0 by executing a finite sequence of one or more requests from R, if $T(v,c) = v^*$, where $v^* = (F,M)$ and $v^* = (F^*,M^*)$, then for each $s \in S$ and $o \in O$:

- if *read* $\in M^*[s,o]$ and *read* $\notin M[s,o]$ then $F^*(s) \geq F^*(o)$.
- if *read* $\in M[s,o]$ and $F^*(s) \not\geq F^*(o)$, then *read* $\notin M^*[s,o]$.
- if *write* $\in M^*[s,o]$ and *write* $\notin M[s,o]$ then $F^*(o) \geq F^*(s)$.
- if *write* $\in M[s,o]$ and $F^*(o) \not\geq F(s)$, then *write* $\notin M^*[s,o]$.

Proof. Going from left to right, if the system is secure, then v_0 must be a secure state by definition. If there were some state v reachable from v_0 by executing a finite sequence of one or more requests from R such that $T(v,c) = v^*$ yet v^* does not satisfy one of the first two restrictions on T, then v^* would be a reachable state that failed to be read secure. If v^* failed to satisfy one of the second two restrictions on T, then v^* would be a reachable state that failed to be write secure. In either case, the system would not be secure.

Going the other direction, assume that the system is not secure. In that case, either v_0 must be a nonsecure state or there must be a nonsecure state reachable from v_0 by executing a finite sequence of one or more requests from R. If v_0 is not a secure state, the proof is done. If v_0 is a secure state, let v^* be the first state in the request sequence that is not secure. This means there is a reachable, secure state v such that $T(v,c) = v^*$ where v^* is not secure. However, this is ruled out by the four restrictions on T.

Many have taken the BST as a justification for the definition of security offered by BLP. Although the argument is seldom made explicit, the belief is probably based on the fact that the BST seems to show that there is a natural notion of a secure transition (ie, a transition that satisfies the four restrictions placed on T by the BST) that yields the same class of systems as the state restrictions of BLP yield. The fact that there are two natural definitions of security that yield the same class of systems gives credence to the belief that they are correct.

The trouble with this interpretation of the BST is that it is transparent with respect to the definition of secure state. An analogous theorem would hold no matter how a secure state is defined (McLean, 1985). A truly secure transition must ensure not only that every state reachable from a secure state is secure, but also that the new state must be reachable in an intuitively secure manner. To see that BST fails to do this, consider the system Z whose initial state is state secure and has only one type of transition: when a subject s requests any type of access to an object o, every subject and object in the system are downgraded to the lowest security level and access is granted. System Z satisfies BLP's notion of security, but it is obviously not secure in any meaningful sense (McLean, 1990b).

To address the problem raised by System Z, McLean (1990b) defines a framework of security models that contain transition restrictions. A framework is a quadruple (S,O,L,A), where each element of the quadruple keeps the same meaning it has in BLP. As in BLP, a model within the framework is a set of state machines whose states are of the form (F,M) where F and M are as before. However, the framework contains a new function, $C: S \cup O \rightarrow P(S)$, which returns the set of subjects that are allowed to change the security level of its argument. As before, a system consists of an initial state v_0, a particular set of requests R, and a transition function T, but T is now the function $T: (S \times V \times R) \rightarrow V$, which gives the new state that results from a subject executing a request in a current state. Given this framework, a secure system can be defined as follows.

Definition. A transition function T is transition secure if and only if $T(s,v,r) = v^*$, where $v = (f,m)$ and $v^* = (f^*,m^*)$, implies that for an $x \in S \cup O$ if $f(x) \neq f^*(x)$ then $s \in C(x)$.

Definition. A system (v_0, R, T) is secure only if (**1**) v_0 and all states reachable from v_0 by a finite sequence of one or more requests from R are (BLP) state secure, and (**2**) T is transition secure.

This framework forms a Boolean algebra of models whose bottom (most restrictive) element is BLP with tranquility, the transition restriction that no security level can change, and whose top element (least restrictive element) is BLP with no restrictions on security level changes whatsoever (McLean, 1990b). Because it gives only necessary conditions for a system to be secure, the policies in the framework do not contradict each other, and hence, sense can be made of the Boolean meet, join, and complement of policies. McLean also considers the framework that results when S is replaced by $P(S)$ and shows that the resulting framework forms a lattice of models that can be used to model multiperson rules such as the restriction that it takes two people to launch a missile or that payment for a shipment requires approval from both a receiving official, who vouches that the shipment was received, and an accounting official, who vouches that the charge is correct and has not previously been paid. These two frameworks constitute the current state of the art with respect to models for mandatory access control.

Problems with Access Control Models. An advantage of access control models is that they are intuitive and can be implemented with high assurance. One provides a tamperproof, nonbypassable reference monitor that controls all subjects' accesses to objects and is small enough to be susceptible to rigorous verification methods. However, it should be emphasized that determining a system's subjects, objects, read accesses, and write accesses is not as trivial as it first may seem. For example, consider a program that opens a high level file for reading, reads a bit from the file, and then branches to one of two internal subroutines, write-one or write-zero, depending on what the high level bit is. If write-one (write-zero) closes the high level file, downgrades the program of which it is a subroutine, opens a low-level file for writing, and then writes 1 (0) to the low level file, the result is a nonsecure information flow that violates BLP only if the program counter itself is regarded as an object (McLean, 1990b).

However, it is not the case that all such channels are so easy to detect and eliminate. Consider, eg, a reference monitor's response to a subject that attempts to write to a nonexistent file. If the reference monitor informs the subject of the mistake, it will allow a channel in which a low level subject attempts to write to a high level file that a high level Trojan Horse systematically creates and removes. If the subject is not informed of the mistake or if a file is automatically created when a subject attempts to write to a nonexistent file, then the subject will not be made aware of legitimate attempts to write that were thwarted through a minor typing error.

Channels such as these, called covert channels (Lampson, 1973), are caused by the difficulty of mapping an access control model's primitives to a computer system. The problem is exacerbated in distributed systems in which a program must first write to a subsystem to read a file located on that subsystem. It is not surprising that such a problem is inherent in access control models if the origin of the model is considered. The concept of access control did not originate with computers but rather was brought over to computers from the paper-and-safe world. In that world, papers are kept in safes and access to safes by individuals are moderated by a security official. Covert channels are possible in such a scheme. For example, a high level user can pass information to a low level user by either approaching or not approaching a safe. However, such channels are not troublesome for three reasons. First, high level users are trusted not to exercise such channels. This is partly because they have been subject to background checks, but primarily because if a high level user wanted to communicate with a low level user, he or she could do so in a much more efficient manner after hours. Second, any such channel would be extremely slow. Third, the monitoring security official could detect something funny if such a channel were often exploited.

Turning to computers, note that covert channels become a real problem. First, users may be trusted not to divulge information they are cleared to see, but given the existence of Trojan Horses, all programs cannot be trusted. Second, the speed of a computer raises the capacity of covert channels to a unacceptable level. Third, seldom is there a human who can determine that such a channel is being exploited in real time.

For this reason, covert channel analysis goes hand in hand with the implementation of access control models. It assures users that a system's interpretation of the model's primitives is not too weak. Such analysis is usually based on tracing the information-flow paths of programs (Denning, 1976, 1982), checking programs for shared resources that can be used to transfer information (Kemmerer, 1983), or checking systems for clocks that can be used for timing channels (Wray, 1991). However, although such channels can often be detected, their detection comes at the end of the system development process when system changes are much more expensive to correct (Boehm, 1976). It would be cheaper to rule out such channels from the beginning and make sure that they were never introduced into the system in the first place.

Interface Models of Confidentiality

Rather than specifying a particular method for enforcing security, interface models specify restrictions on a system's input–output relation that are sufficient for ruling out nonsecure implementations. It is up to the implementer to determine a method for satisfying the specification. Such an approach allows implementors more flexibility in designing and building systems, is more natural for dealing with networks, and in general, does better with respect to covert storage channels. However, although the interface approach is relatively straight forward with respect to deterministic systems, it becomes rather subtle when extended to nondeterministic systems.

The Noninterference Model for Deterministic Systems. Most interface models for confidentiality are based on noninterference, the restriction that high level user input cannot interfere with low level user output. The original formulation of noninterference (Goguen and Meseguer, 1982), is based directly on the work of Feiertag (1980) and indirectly on earlier work by Cohen (1977) and Popek and Farber (1978). Goguen and Meseguer consider a deterministic system whose output to user u is given by the function *out(u, hist.read(u))* where *hist.read(u)* is an input history (trace) of the system whose last input is *read(u)*, a read command executed by user u. (In Goguen and Meseguer (1982), *out* actually takes three arguments: *u, read,* and the state *s* reached by executing the commands in *hist.* The formulation is identical for purposes of exposition and more in keeping with other interface models discussed.) Security is defined in terms of purges of input histories, where a purge removes commands executed by a user whose security level is not dominated by u.

Definition. Let *cl* be a function from users to security levels such that *cl(u)* is the clearance of u. Furthermore, let *purge* be a function from *users* × *traces* to *traces* such that

- *purge(u,* <>*)* =<>, where <> is the empty trace.
- *purge(u,hist.command(w))* = *purge(u,hist)* • *command (w)* if *command(w)* is an input executed by user w and $cl(u) \geqq cl(w)$.
- *purge(u, hist.command(w))* = *purge(u, hist)* if *command (w)* is an input executed by user w and $cl(u) \ngeqq cl(w)$.

A system satisfies noninterference if and only if for all users u, all histories T, and all output commands *c*, *out(u,T.c(u))* = *out(u,purge(u,T)•c(u))*.

To help verify that a system satisfies noninterference, Goguen and Meseguer (1984) developed a set of unwinding conditions that are sufficient for establishing noninterference in state machines. Although these conditions are relatively straightforward to verify, their application depends on the development of a state machine model of the system under consideration. More recently, McLean (1992) has shown how to sidestep the development of such a state machine and verify noninterference directly. These verification techniques help make noninterference as useful in practice as BLP. Although verifying noninterference, in general, may be harder than verifying BLP, there is no covert storage channel analysis remaining to do after the verification.

Because the primitives of BLP lack a precise semantics, it is not possible to compare the two models precisely

(McLean, 1990a). However, it can be noted that (**1**) in general BLP is weaker than noninterference in that the latter prohibits many of the covert channels that the former would allow under the standard interpretation of its primitives and (**2**) noninterference is weaker than BLP in that it allows low level users to copy one high level file to another high level file, which BLP would normally disallow as a high level read by the low level user. In both cases noninterference seems to be closer to the intuitive notion of security than BLP.

In fact, Millen (1987) has shown in that for deterministic systems, noninterference is practically perfect in that if input sequence X is noninterfering with output sequence Y and X is independent of the input from other users, then $I(X,Y) = 0$, where $I(X,Y)$ is the mutual information between X and Y and represents the information flow over the system from X to Y (Jones, 1979). Of course, for noninterference to rule out timing channels, time must be considered as part of the input and output alphabet.

The reason why noninterference is only "practically perfect" is that, as shown originally by Sutherland (1986), it can be too strong. Consider, eg, a system in which user X and user V are each independently given an opportunity to give an input from the alphabet {0,1} and in which Y receives as output $x \oplus v$, where x (v) is the input from X (V), if there is one, else 0. Clearly, X interferes with Y. For example, if $x = 1$ and $v = 1$, then $y = 1 \oplus 0 = 0$, but if X's input is eliminated, $y = 0 \oplus 0 = 1$. In general, such a system should not be allowed if X and V were high level users and Y were a low level user because there are input sequences from V that would allow X to communicate with Y. (Remember that V could be a Trojan Horse using the system or a user whose interface to the system was under the control of a Trojan Horse.) However, if V's inputs were randomly distributed over 0, 1, then V would, in effect, be providing perfect encryption for X's input, and $I(X, Y)$ would be 0. In such a case, X would be interfering with Y, but no information could flow because Y cannot detect X's interference. In this sense, noninterference is possibly too strong in that it makes a worse-case assumption about the behavior of other users on the system. As such, it rules out cryptographic systems as being nonsecure.

Despite this limitation, noninterference constitutes the current state of the art with respect to interface models for deterministic systems. However, it would be nice if it were possible to apply noninterference to nondeterministic systems as well. Although, ultimately, all systems may be (ontologically) deterministic, it is unreasonable to require that all system specifications (the system descriptions that will, in fact, be analyzed for security flaws) be (epistemically) deterministic. Furthermore, the limitation to deterministic systems rules out probabilistic algorithms. In the next two sections, ways of generalizing noninterference to nondeterministic systems are examined.

Possibilistic Models for Nondeterministic Systems. Before giving a nondeterministic version of noninterference, a framework for describing nondeterministic systems is needed. It is possible simply to generalize the language in which noninterference was presented and consider *out* to be a relation instead of a function, i.e., allow the same input to generate different output. However, to catch channels through which information is passed by the order in which output is transmitted by the system, it is necessary instead to include outputs in the history itself. The resulting traces represent acceptable input–output behaviors, and a system is a set of acceptable traces, e.g., a system in which a user can give as input either 0 or 1 and immediately receives that input as output is specified by the following set of traces: {<>,*in*(0), *in*(1), *in*(0). *out*(0), *in*(1).*out*(1),*in*(0).*out*(0).*in*(1), . . .}. For simplicity, assume that any prefix of an acceptable trace must also be an acceptable trace and that a user can give input at any time (although the system may choose to ignore it).

The obvious way to generalize noninterference is to require that the purge of an acceptable trace be an acceptable trace, where the purge of a trace is formed by removing all high level inputs from the trace. The problem with this definition is that the purged trace may not be unacceptable due to any security violations but due to other system requirements. For example, consider the system described in the previous paragraph and assume that all input and output is high level. Because the system generates no low level output, it is trivially secure. Remember that *in*(0).*out*(0) is an acceptable trace of the system. However, the purge of this trace, *viz. out*(0), is not an acceptable trace because it contains an unsolicited output, which the system is not supposed to give.

At this point, the obvious approach is to keep the requirement that the purge of an acceptable trace be an acceptable trace but redefine the purge operator so that it removes, not simply all high level input, but all high level output as well. This approach, however, also has problems. First, it is too strong in that it rules out any system in which low level input must generate high level output. As a result, it would be necessary to regard as nonsecure a system that secretly monitors low level usage and sends its audit records as high level output to some other system for analysis. A more severe problem is that it allows nonsecure systems. Consider a system in which the following traces are acceptable: {<>, *highin*(0), *highin*(1),*lowout*(0), *lowout*(1), *highin*(0). *lowout*(0), *highin*(1).*lowout*(1)}. This system satisfies the security property, because if all the high level events are removed from an acceptable trace, the result is an acceptable trace. However, it is not hard to come up with a scenario in which a Trojan Horse acting on behalf of a high level user can pass information to a low level user using such a system. For example, if it is assumed that the high level user always has the option of giving input before the next low level output is generated, then information can be passed noiselessly. If the Trojan Horse wants to send a 0 or 1 to the low level user, it simply gives the appropriate bit as input before the next low level output is generated.

The problem with the approaches so far is that when the same input is allowed to issue a variety of outputs to the low level user, the requirement that the purge of an acceptable trace be an acceptable trace is too weak. The requirement that high level events can be introduced into an acceptable trace without rendering the resulting trace unacceptable to the system is also needed. For the last system to meet this stronger requirement, it would also have to regard the traces *highin*(0).*lowout*(1) and *highin*

(1).*lowout*(0) as being acceptable, which would close the nonsecure channel. Such a requirement was not necessary when only deterministic systems were considered, because if the insertion of a high level input altered the low level output of a trace, then it would not be possible to satisfy the requirement that the trace that would be the purge of both traces have the same output as the original traces.

Of course, it would be too strong to require that any arbitrary insertion of high level events into an acceptable trace must be acceptable. The high level events themselves must be acceptable to the system, and it is necessary to take into account the fact that these new events (possibly in conjunction with existing low level events) can alter the values of high level outputs. These considerations lead to the requirement that for any two acceptable traces, T and S, there is an acceptable trace R consisting of T's low level events (in their respective order), S's high level inputs (in their respective order), and possibly some other events that are neither low level events from T nor high level inputs from S. This property, known as nondeducibility, was first put forward by Sutherland (1986) to capture the requirement that whatever the low level user sees is compatible with any acceptable high level input.

Although nondeducibility is more general than noninterference in that it does not assume determinism, it is equivalent to noninterference for deterministic systems with only two users. However, nondeducibility is strictly weaker than noninterference if deterministic systems with more than two users are considered. For example, consider the system described earlier in which user Y receives as output the $X \oplus V$, where x and v are inputs from users X and V, respectively. It was seen that in such a system user X interferes with Y's output, although Y may not be able to detect this. As such, this system fails to satisfy noninterference with respect to X and Y. It does satisfy nondeducibility, however, because any acceptable input sequence from X and any acceptable output sequence to Y can be combined into an acceptable trace by inserting suitable inputs from V. In fact, there is a problem with our formulation since Y's output trace must be long enough to account for all of X's and V's inputs. This is an artifact of the formulation, however, and is not a problem for the original statement of the model. Although it is possible to avoid this problem, nondeducibility has other problems that render any solution to this problem otiose.

The trouble with nondeducibility is that it is too weak. For example, consider a system in which a high level user H gives arbitrary high level input (presumably a secret messages of some sort) and some low level user L gives the low level input, *look.* When L issues *look,* he or she receives as low level output the encryption of H's input up to that time, if there is any, or else a randomly generated string. Such a system models an encryption system in which low level users can observe encrypted messages leaving the system, but to prevent traffic flow analysis, random strings are generated when there is no encrypted output. This system satisfies nondeducibility because low level users can learn nothing about high level input. The problem arises when it is realized it would still satisfy nondeducibility even if the encryption requirement were removed. For example, given the high level input *highin (Attack at dawn),* and the low level trace *lowin(look).lowout(xxx),* the legal system trace *lowin (look).lowout(xxx).highin(Attack at dawn)* can be constructed. Similarly, given the acceptable traces <> and *highin (Attack at dawn).lowin(look).lowout(Attack at dawn),* a legal trace from the high-events of the former and the low-events from the latter can be constructed, *viz. lowin (look).lowout(Attack at dawn),* because it is possible that the string *Attack at dawn* was randomly generated. This problem was first noticed by McCullough (1987).

A second problem with nondeducibility is that it is not composable. Composability is the second-order property that holds of a first-order property if and only if any composite system formed by connecting two subsystems that satisfy the first-order property in an appropriate way satisfies the first-order property as well. McCullough (1990) showed that nondeducibility is not preserved by secure composition (i.e., composition in which outputs from one subsystem are connected to inputs of another subsystem only if the outputs and inputs have the same security level).

Referring back to the definition of nondeducibility, it can be seen that the cause of these problems is that it allows too much freedom in constructing an acceptable trace R from the high level inputs of an acceptable trace T and the low level events from an acceptable trace S. It should be required that event order be maintained within T and S, and limitations should be imposed on how events from the two different traces can be interspersed. In effect, it should be required not simply that there is some place in an acceptable trace to insert a high level event and still obtain an acceptable trace, but that an acceptable trace can be constructed no matter where a high level event is inserted. This observation is the motivation for the following security property, known as generalized noninterference: given any acceptable system trace T and an alteration T_1 formed by inserting or deleting a high level input to or from T, there is an acceptable trace T_2 formed by inserting or deleting high level outputs to or from T_1 after the occurrence of the alteration in T made to form T_1 (McCullough, 1987). For example, consider the system described above in which a low level user monitors high level output. As noted, a possible trace for that system is *lowin(look).lowout(xxx).* Altering this trace to obtain *highin(Attack at dawn).lowin(look).lowout(xxx),* yields an unacceptable trace that cannot be made acceptable by inserting or deleting high level outputs after the occurrence of the inserted high level input. Hence, the system fails to satisfy generalized noninterference.

Unfortunately, although generalized noninterference solves the first problem with nondeducibility, it does not solve the second. Generalized noninterference is not composable either (McCullough, 1987). To create a composable security property, it is necessary to be even more restrictive about how T_2 is formed. This leads us to the following definition, known as restrictiveness: given any acceptable trace T and alteration T_1, formed by inserting or deleting a high level input to or from T, there is an acceptable trace T_2 formed by inserting high level outputs to or from T_1 after the occurrence of the alteration in T made to form T_1 and any sequence of low level inputs that immediately follow the alteration to T (McCullough, 1987). For example, consider the acceptable trace $wxyz$ where z is a high level output and both x and y are low level inputs. Now consider the alteration obtained by inserting a high level input h after w to form $whxyz$. Generalized noninterference would allow one to form an acceptable trace from this alteration either by removing z or by inserting a high level output anywhere in the trace after h. Restrictiveness limits one to forming an acceptable trace either by removing z or by inserting a high level output somewhere after y. McCullough (1990) showed that this restriction to generalized noninterference yields a composable security property.

Although restrictiveness goes a long way toward providing a nondeterministic version of noninterference, it is not problem free. One problem is that it is not preserved by many standard views of refinement (Jacob, 1989). For example, consider a system in which a high level user can either input 0 or 1, and a low level user can receive as output either 0 or 1. In other words, assume that the following set of traces are all acceptable {*highin*(0),*highin*(1), *lowout*(0), *lowout*(1), *highin*(0). *lowout*(0), *highin*(0). *lowout*(1), *highin*(1). *lowout*(0), *highin*(1).*lowout*(1)}. Because low level output is compatible with any high level input, the system is obviously restrictive. If the notion of refinement used in a number of software engineering paradigms is considered, however, a perfectly correct implementation of this program could eliminate the nondeterminism contained in the specification and produce a program that accepted, eg, only the following traces: {*highin*(0). *lowout*(0), *highin*(1). *lowout*(1)}. Such a program is not restrictive. Because it is possible to have functionally correct implementations of restrictive specifications that are not themselves restrictive, it is necessary to check for restrictiveness at each level of the software development process. This leads to a major increase in the cost of software engineering.

This problem is caused by the fact that most of these methodologies view properties as sets of traces and view a program as satisfying a property if its acceptable traces are a subset of the property. The rub is that security properties such as noninterference are not sets of traces but rather properties of sets of traces, ie, metaproperties. Properties such as this, including average response time, are not preserved by subsetting. Although there are specification–refinement methodologies that do a better job of preserving security under refinement, they have so far been applied only to relatively simple generalizations of noninterference (McLean, 1992; Meadows, 1992).

A second problem with restrictiveness is that it addresses only noise-free channels. For example, consider the system described above, but assume that the traces *lowout*(0), *lowout*(1),*highin*(0).*lowout*(1), and *highin*(1). *lowout*(0), although possible, occur with only a small probability, say .0001. Assume further, that whenever a high level input occurs, a low level output immediately occurs with a high probability. Although this system is restrictive, it passes high level information to low level users at an extremely high rate. If a low level user sees an output, he or she can be almost certain that the output was given as a high level input, and whenever a high level user gives an input, it is almost certain that the low level user will soon receive it as a low level output. Such noisy or probabilistic channels are beyond the scope of the possibilistic approach to modeling so far considered here.

Probabilistic Models for Nondeterministic Systems. The first models formulated explicitly to deal with probabilistic channels were put forward in 1990. They were the flow model (FM), (McLean, 1990a) and P-restrictiveness (Gray, 1990). FM is an extremely general model that Gray (1991) applied to a specific system description, calling the system-specific interpretation AFM. Gray (1991) also introduced a new security model, probabilistic noninterference (PNI), which he compared with AFM. Gray and Syverson (1992) produced a verification logic that supports the formal verification of systems implementing probabilistic models.

Both AFM and PNI regard a system as a 4-tuple $<S,I,C,O>$. S is a set of information sources, ie, entities that introduce probabilistic behavior into the system. S normally consists of all system input channels and any internal random number generators. C is the set of system output channels. I and O are the alphabets of S and C, respectively. For simplicity, assume that S consists of two input channels: *highin* (input from the high level user) and *lowin*(input from the low level user), and that O consists of two output channels: *highout*(output to the high level user) and *lowout*(output to the low level user). At any time, the low level user knows the history of the two low channels, and the high level user knows the history of all the system channels.

At any given time t the input to the system consists of the ordered pair $<highin_t, lowin_t>$, which is denoted by in_t, and the output from the system consists of the ordered pair $<highout_t, lowout_t>$, which is denoted by out_t. Denote the history of inputs and outputs up to and including t by $<in_1, in_2, \ldots, in_t>$ and $<out_1, out_2, \ldots, out_t>$, respectively.

Assume that there is a function $\hat{O}$ which intuitively gives the probability of a certain output occurring at time $t + 1$ given the input and output histories up to time t, ie, $\hat{O}(out_{t+1} \mid <in_1, in_2, \ldots, in_t>, <out_1, out_2, \ldots, out_t>)$ is the probability that the system will produce out_{t+1} as output at time $t + 1$ given input history $<in_1, in_2, \ldots, in_t>$ and output history $<out_1, out_2, \ldots, out_t>$. Assume that there is an analogous function $\hat{I}$ that intuitively gives the probability of a certain input occurring at time $t + 1$ given the input and output histories up to time t. Although it is unrealistic, in general, to assume that a particular $\hat{I}$ correctly models a user's input, in the security properties that follow quantification is made over all such functions so it is never necessary to assume that a particular $\hat{I}$ models any individual user. The reason for introducing $\hat{I}$ is to prevent high level Trojan Horses from communicating information to low level users via game theoretic strategies (Wittbold and Johnson, 1990) and, more important, to define a probability measure on system events. Given $<S,I,C,O>$, $\hat{O}$, and $\hat{I}$, a probability measure P can be constructed that gives the probability of any event in which the system can engage.

To limit the discussion to systems in which high level users do not pass information to low level users outside the system (because if they do, computer security becomes moot), it is required that low level input at time t can depend only on previous low level events and that conditioned on previous history the low level input at time t must be statistically independent of high level input at time t. This requirement can be formalized by requiring that there are two probability measures H and L, called the high environment behavior and low environment behavior, respectively, such that (**1**) $H(highin_{t+1} | <in_1, \ldots, in_t>, <out_1, \ldots, out_t>)$ gives the probability of $highin_{t+1}$ being the high level input at time $t + 1$; (**2**) $L(lowin_{t+1} | <lowin_1, \ldots, lowin_t>, <lowout_1, \ldots, lowout_t>)$ gives the probability of $lowin_{t+1}$ being the low level input at time $t + 1$; and (**3**) $I(in_{t+1} | <in_1, \ldots, in_t>, <out_1, \ldots, out_t>) = H(highin_{t+1} | <in_1, \ldots, in_t>, <out_1, \ldots, out_t>) \times L(lowin_{t+1} | <lowin_1, \ldots, lowin_t>, <lowout_1, \ldots, lowout_t>)$.

AFM, Gray's formalization of FM within this framework, is the requirement that given $<S,I,C,O>$ and O, for any I that satisfies the secure environment criteria, $P(lowout_{t+1} | <in_1, \ldots, in_t> \cap <out_1, \ldots, out_t>) = P(lowout_{t+1} | <lowin_1, \ldots, lowin_t> \cap <lowout_1, \ldots, lowout_t>)$. Hence, AFM intuitively says that conditioned on low level history, low level output at time t is statistically independent of previous high level events.

To formalize PNI, note that because P is determined by $<S,I,C,O>$, O, and I, whereas I is determined by H and L, it follows that P is determined by $<S,I,C,O>$, O, H, and L. Given $<S,I,C,O>$ and O, Gray defines PNI as the requirement that for any two high environment behaviors $H1$ and $H2$, any low environment behavior L, and any low level event e, $P_{H1,L}(e) = P_{H2,L}(e)$, ie, the probability measure constructed from $<S,I,C,O>$, O, $H1$, and L assigns the same probability measure to e as the one constructed from $<S,I,C,O>$, O, $H2$, and L. Hence PNI intuitively says that the probability of a low level event occurring is independent of any high level user behavior.

Gray has shown that PNI is sufficient for guaranteeing that there is no information flow from high level users to low level users and that (A)FM is strictly stronger than PNI. In other words, both models are sufficient to guarantee confidentiality, but there are systems that satisfy PNI, but fail to satisfy (A)FM. For example, consider a system in which low level data are randomly generated. If such data appear as high level output and then as low level output at a later time, the system will satisfy PNI, but not (A)FM. Whether such systems show that (A)FM is too strong is debatable, because it is unclear why low level data should be regarded as high level output. The real strength in (A)FM, however, is that it is easier to verify than PNI and can be used as a verification condition for PNI (Gray and Syverson, 1992). Whether it is possible to build systems that conform to either model and, if not, it is possible to weaken the models to be more generally applicable are open research issues. If the answer to both questions is negative, users may be forced to abandon general interface models for computer security and retreat to access control, relying on covert channel analysis to detect probabilistic channels (Moskowitz and Miller, 1992). For the time being, (A)FM and PNI constitute the current state of the art with respect to such models.

OTHER TYPES OF MODELS

Not all security models address general confidentiality concerns. Although space does not permit a thorough discussion of other types of security models, here are some pointers for where to look. Whereas confidentiality prohibits the unauthorized reading of information, availability prohibits the unauthorized withholding of information. Its concern is not that low level users can read high level files, but that they can prevent high level users from accessing these files. There has been a fair amount of formal work in this area, first by Gligor (1983), and then by Yu and Gligor (1990) and by Millen (1992). The latter two models present resource allocators. The model of Yu and Gligor uses temporal logic to specify constraints on such an allocator, and the one by Millen uses a finite state machine framework.

When one turns to integrity, which prohibits the unauthorized modification of information, less progress has been made. The most famous integrity model to date was formulated by Clark and Wilson (1987). The basis of the Clark-Wilson model is that controlled data items can be altered only by certain transactions and that such transactions may require collaboration from other people. The disadvantages of the model are that it is far from formal and it is unclear how to formalize it in a general setting (although the framework described in McLean 1990b can be used to formalize the multiperson rule part of the model). Part of the problem is that although there seems to be a clear formal concept of confidentiality (via information theory), there is yet to be developed a general concept for integrity.

A different approach to dealing with these problems is to move from general models to application-specific models. The first model to try this approach was the secure military message system model of Landwehr, Heitmeyer, and McLean (1984). The constraints expressed in this model are not general security constraints on subjects and objects, but specific security constraints that a message system must meet in its handling of messages. Since then, the application-specific approach has been applied in a number of areas, most notably in the area of database security (Denning and co-workers, 1988).

BIBLIOGRAPHY

P. Ammann and R. Sandhu, "Extending the Creation Operation in the Schematic Protection Model," in *Proceedings of the 1990 IEEE Symposium on Research in Security and Privacy,* IEEE Computer Society Press, 1990.

D. Bell and L. LaPadula, *Secure Computer Systems: Unified Exposition and Multics Interpretation,* Technical report MTR-2997, MITRE, Bedford, Mass., 1975.

J. Biskup, "Some Variants of the Take-Grant Protection Model," *Info. Pro. Lett.,* **19**(3) (1984).

M. Bishop and L. Snyder, "The Transfer of Information and Authority in a Protection System," in *Proc. Seventh ACM Symposium on Operating Systems Principles,* 1979.

B. Boehm, "Software Engineering," *IEEE Trans. on Comput.* **C-25**(12), 1226–1241 (Dec. 1976).

D. Clark and D. Wilson, "A Comparison of Commercial and Military Computer Security Policies," in *Proceedings of the 1987 IEEE Symposium on Research in Security and Privacy,* IEEE Computer Society Press, 1987.

E. Cohen, "Information Transmission in Computational Systems," *ACM SIGOPS Operating Sys. Rev.* **11**(5), 133–139 (Nov. 1977).

D. Denning, "A Lattice Model of Secure Information Flow," *Commun. ACM* **19**(5), 236–243 (May 1976).

D. Denning, *Cryptography and Data Security,* Addison-Wesley Publishing Co., Inc., Reading, Mass., 1982.

D. Denning, T. Lunt, R. Schell, W. Shockley, and M. Heckman, "The Sea View Security Model," in *Proceedings of the 1988 IEEE Symposium on Research in Security and Privacy,* IEEE Computer Society Press, 1988.

R. Feiertag, *A Technique for Proving Specifications are Multilevel Secure,* Technical report CSL-109, SRI, Menlo Park, Calif. 1980.

V. Gligor, "A Note on the Denial-of-Service Problem," in *Proceedings of the 1983 IEEE Symposium on Research in Security and Privacy,* IEEE Computer Society Press, 1983.

J. Goguen and J. Meseguer, "Security Policies and Security Models," in *Proceedings of the 1982 IEEE Symposium on Research in Security and Privacy,* IEEE Computer Society Press, 1982.

J. Goguen and J. Meseguer, "Unwinding and Inference Control," in *Proceedings of the 1984 IEEE Symposium on Research in Security and Privacy,* IEEE Computer Society Press, 1984.

G. Graham and P. Denning, "Protection—Principles and Practice," in *Proceedings of the Spring Joint Computer Conference,* AFIPS Press, 1972.

J. Gray, "Probabilistic Interference," in *Proceedings of the 1990 IEEE Symposium on Research in Security and Privacy,* IEEE Computer Society Press, 1990.

J. Gray, "Toward a Mathematical Foundation for Information Flow Security," in *Proceedings of the 1991 IEEE Symposium on Research in Security and Privacy,* IEEE Computer Society Press, 1991.

J. Gray and P. Syverson, "A Logical Approach to Multilevel Security of Probabilistic Systems," in *Proceedings of the 1992 IEEE Symposium on Research in Security and Privacy,* IEEE Computer Society Press, 1992.

M. Harrison and W. Ruzzo, "Monotonic Protection Systems," in R. DeMillo, D. Dobkin, A. Jones, and R. Lipton, eds., *Foundations of Secure Computation,* Academic Press, Inc., New York, 1978, pp. 337–365.

M. Harrison, W. Ruzzo, and J. Ullman, "Protection in Operating Systems," *Commun. ACM* **19**(8), 461–471 (Aug. 1976).

J. Jacob, "On the Derivation of Secure Components," in *Proceedings of the 1989 IEEE Symposium on Research in Security and Privacy,* IEEE Computer Society Press, 1989.

A. Jones, R. Lipton, and L. Snyder, "A Linear Time Algorithm for Deciding Security," in *Proc. 17th Annual Symp. on Found. of Comp. Sci.,* 1976.

D. S. Jones, *Elementary Information Theory,* Oxford University Press, Oxford, UK, 1979.

R. Kemmerer, "Share Resource Matrix Methodology: An Approach to Identifying Storage and Timing Channels," *ACM Trans. on Comput. Sys.* **1**(3), 256–277 (Aug. 1983).

B. Lampson, "Protection," in *Proc. Fifth Princeton Symposium on Information Sciences and Systems,* Mar. 1971.

B. Lampson, "A Note on the Confinement Problem," *Commun. ACM* **16**(10), 613–615 (Oct. 1973).

C. Landwehr, C. Heitmeyer, and J. McLean, "A Security Model for Military Message Systems," *ACM Trans. of Comput. Sys.* **2**(3), 198–222 (Aug. 1984).

R. Lipton and L. Snyder, "On Synchronization and Security," in R. DeMillo, D. Dobkin, A. Jones, and R. Lipton, eds., *Foundations of Secure Computation,* Academic Press, Inc., New York, 1978, pp. 367–385.

D. McCullough, "Specifications for Multi-Level Security and a Hook-Up Property," in *Proceedings of the 1987 IEEE Symposium on Research in Security and Privacy,* IEEE Computer Society Press, 1987.

D. McCullough, "A Hookup Theorem for Multilevel Security," *IEEE Trans. Software Eng.* **16**(6), 563–568 (June 1990).

J. McLean, "A Comment on the 'Basic Security Theorem' of Bell and LaPadula," *Inf. Proc. Lett.* **20**(2), 67–70 (Feb. 1985).

J. McLean, "Security Models and Information Flow," in *Proceedings of the 1990 IEEE Symposium on Research in Security and Privacy,* IEEE Computer Society Press, 1990a.

J. McLean, "The Specification and Modeling of Computer Security," *Computer* **23**(1), 9–16 (Jan. 1990).

J. McLean, "Proving Noninterference and Functional Correctness Using Traces," *J. Comput. Security* **1**(1), 37–57 (Jan. 1992).

C. Meadows, "Using Traces Based on Procedure Calls to Reason About Composability," in *Proceedings of the 1992 IEEE Symposium on Research in Security and Privacy,* IEEE Computer Society Press, 1992.

J. Millen, "Covert Channel Capacity," in *Proceedings of the 1987 IEEE Symposium on Research in Security and Privacy,* IEEE Computer Society Press, 1987.

J. Millen, "A Resource Allocation Model for Denial of Service," in *Proceedings of the 1992 IEEE Symposium on Research in Security and Privacy,* IEEE Computer Society Press, 1992.

I. Moskowitz and A. Miller, "The Channel Capacity of a Certain Noisy Timing Channel," *IEEE Transactions on Information Theory* **38**(4), 1339–1344 (July 1992).

G. Popek and D. Farber, "A Model for Verification of Data Security in Operating Systems," *Commun. ACM* **21**(9), 237–249 (Sept. 1978).

R. Sandhu, "The Schematic Protection Model: Its Definition and Analysis for Acyclic Attenuating Schemes," *J. ACM* **35**(2), 404–432 (1988).

R. Sandhu, "The Typed Access Matrix Model," in *Proceedings of the 1991 IEEE Symposium on Research in Security and Privacy,* IEEE Computer Society Press, 1991.

L. Snyder, "Theft and Conspiracy in the Take-Grant Model," *J. of Comp. Sys. Sci.* **23**(3), 333–347 (1981).

D. Sutherland, "A Model of Information," in *Ninth National Computer Security Conference,* National Bureau of Standards/National Computer Security Center, 1986.

T. Wittbold and D. Johnson, "Information Flow in Nondeterministic Systems," in *Proceedings of the 1990 IEEE Symposium on Research in Security and Privacy,* IEEE Computer Society Press, 1990.

J. Wray, "An Analysis of Covert Timing Channels," in *Proceedings of the 1991 IEEE Symposium on Research in Security and Privacy,* IEEE Computer Society Press, 1991.

C.-F. Yu and V. Gligor, "A Specification and Verification Method for Preventing Denial of Service," *IEEE Trans. Software Eng.* **16**(6), 581–592, (June 1990).

JOHN MCLEAN
Naval Research Laboratory

SECURITY TESTING

OVERVIEW

Security testing is conducted to verify the trustworthiness of systems requiring a high degree of reliability. It not only involves comprehensive application of developmental testing methodologies at the unit, interface, integration, and system levels, but also extension to functional security testing methodologies *in situ* to the environment in which the system has been installed. The need for testing within the target environment is illustrated by an example which occurred on a large heterogeneous peer-level network. Extensive work was done to modify a supercomputer's TCP/IP network server protocol, activating the packet security label field. The modifications were tested extensively during development and, using a developmental model of the overall network, "bugs" were corrected where found. The modification performed as expected, until placed into full service on the entire network. Then every Sun workstation on the network crashed. The modification was disabled immediately, whereupon every Macintosh system on the network crashed. Subsequent analyses revealed that a complex interaction of routers had combined with vendor-specific implementations to cause the anomalous behavior. The effect of this interaction was dramatic. However, serious but less dramatic anomalous behaviors are also potentially present in modern complex environments, requiring application of testing at the environment level.

Governmental or commercial activities of the 1980s saw a dramatic increase in awareness on the part of management to the fact that information is a valuable resource (Schweitzer, 1986; Turn, 1981). Managers recognized computer systems as much more than electronic warehouses in which to store information until needed, but, rather, as constituting dynamic resource facilities that support a wide range of data processing activities (Baker, 1985). Protection of these resources implies requirements for threat identification and risk reduction methodologies, including testing. Security testing involves many of the same topics as the general category of software testing but with a somewhat greater emphasis toward more explicitly defining the testing scope, nature, and results which the testing must achieve. Much of the earlier and continuing security testing emphasis arose from U.S. Federal Governmental concerns with protecting critical information stored and processed by computer systems. However, some aspects of the security testing arena, such as computer virus detection, are being applied to other non-Federal governmental activities as well as to the private sector. It may be noted that, as of the early 1990s, overall guidelines for the entire arena of software product assurance and risk reduction methodologies were still maturing (Hankinson, 1989). Thus completely definitive guidelines regarding what is both necessary and sufficient within the security testing area were also maturing. This article examines the scope of security testing, the U.S. Federal security testing environment, and some general security testing approaches and considerations.

ESTABLISHING THE TESTING SCOPE

Although many people often associate security testing with the protection of information considered vital to the government, a more accurate view could be that of threat identification and risk reduction in terms of any vital assets needing high reliability and/or protection. As with other forms, security testing is conducted to reduce system-anomalous behavior and involves a significant resource expenditure during the software production life cycle. A number of

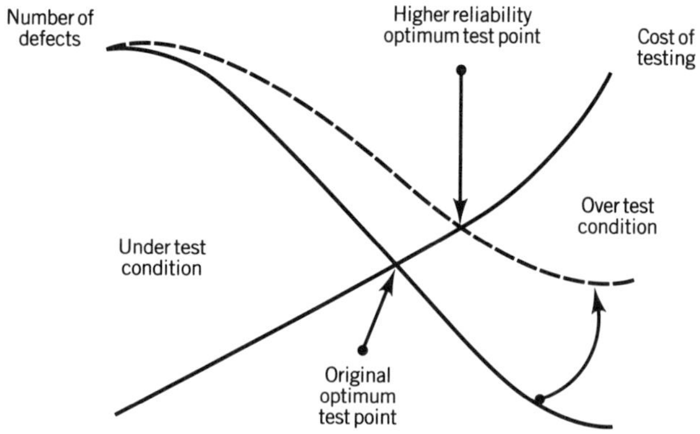

Figure 1. Security testing modifies the cost curve; -routine/commercial reliability level, - - higher security/reliability level.

studies (for example, Boehm, 1975 and Radatz, 1981) have provided data that 25 to 50 percent of the total effort involved to yield a production program can be consumed by general testing. Since the 1950s, academia touted various methodologies as offering the "answer" to developing bug-free software. For example, structured programming techniques were proposed (Linger, 1979) to provide a "new reality" in which programs could be "correct from the beginning" and "error free in their testing and subsequent use." However, others have pointed out (Beizer, 1990) that testing is also done to detect bugs, for no methodology does more than reduce the total potential which computer software evinces toward anomalous behavior.

Security testing, particularly of larger and more complex systems, cannot be entirely exhaustive in scope and application. Figure 1 is a general testing cost-effectiveness curve derived from Perry (1988) that illustrates an applicable model for security testing cost-effectiveness. Perry's original model illustrated that, as the cost to accomplish testing increases, the number of undetected anomalies decreases. The left side reflected an "under test" condition, in which the investment in testing is less than the loss incurred from system anomalies, while the right side showed the inverse, "over test," condition. The difference between routine, commercially based software testing and that involved for high reliability software security testing would be the slopes of the two curves. The dotted curve shows that higher reliability requirements will change the slope of the number of defects curve causing it to intersect the test cost curve at a higher value point. This revised point indicates that fewer defects are acceptable as reliability requirements increase. In short, when higher reliability is a requirement, then a higher cost of testing is expected and acceptable.

Defining Threat and Risk

Companies must spend large resources to evolve reliable production software via large testing efforts. Security testing is accomplished with the goal of assuring a very high degree of reliability in order to reduce risk. It involves significant resource costs over the system life cycle. A key element to risk reduction and avoidance is an accurate identification and analysis of the threats against the given system and of the risks associated with those threats. The single most difficult task of threat analysis is accomplishing the identification of all significant threats (Parker, 1981). Past efforts to accomplish comprehensive, threat identification often have resulted in long lists of threats, which analysis found to be both duplicative and overlapping, while also being discontinuous and not covering all potential concerns. Some efforts propose approaching threat identification from a modeling perspective. One (Clever, 1988) models threats as actually composed of three elements: a threat agent, an implementing method, and a potential impact, This particular model provides for the application of countermeasures to reduce the risk at any of the three elements, Once the threat posture has been modeled, the risk analysis can be accomplished to determine the points at which managers can cost-effectively apply countermeasures.

For example, a threat agent might be characterized as the system programmer, the implementation method characterized as the program anomalies, and the potential impact(s) the adverse effects such as system crashes. Follow-on analysis might indicate the number of bugs to be higher than the company average because the programmer was not using structured methodologies. Certainly the programmer could spend large amounts of effort debugging the code. However, in determining appropriate application of costly testing resources, the programmer's management might well wish to review the programmer environment and consider other potentially less costly countermeasures to reduce the overall risk, such as increased methodology training for the programmer, code inspections, etc. Once the risk had been reduced through non-testing means, one would expect the resulting code to retain a reduced level of bugs for which testing would be an appropriate activity.

Threat analysis directly assists in the determination of the optimum test point and general scope of testing. For example, if the system will operate in a friendly user environment in which all accounts have a "common need-to-know" to the data within the system, then the threats are reduced compared to those encountered when one is concerned with an "insider threat" and hostile environment. In the latter instance, the level of protection and number of countermeasures afforded by the system's security apparatus would be greater to counter a higher level of threat. The security testing environment also would be extended to validate a higher level of reliability. This type of consideration is reflected in the National Computer Security Center specifications for trusted computer systems, which are summarized below.

Security Models

Higher level trust and reliability systems require the development of a security model. Depending on the level of trust, the modeling may range from an informal, descriptive level to a formal, mathematically based specification level.

The Bell and LaPadula Model. During the early 1970s, Bell and LaPadula (1976) published work of particular interest because of its relation to Anderson's "reference monitor" concepts (Anderson, 1972), which were adopted in later Department of Defense documentation.

This particular model had three major facets: a descriptive capability referred to as "the elements," general mechanisms represented as the limiting theorems, and specific solutions referred to as "the rules." The Bell and LaPadula model has the ability to provide abstract representation of a computer system as well as of the security environment for that system. In the model, active entities (subjects) affect passive entities (objects) via actions with certain constraints between the subjects and objects. The model addresses access attributes, system state descriptions, and security properties, Object access can have two effects, either information insertion or extraction, which combine to result in four possible states or access modes:

- *e:* access involving neither observation nor alteration;
- *r:* access involving observation with no alteration;
- *a:* access involving alteration with no observation;
- *w:* access involving both observation and alteration.

This allows the system state description triple:

(subject, object, access-attribute)

interpreted as subject having some current access-attribute to object for the given state. Using this triple, the model supports assignment of a hierarchical structure to object relations, object access permissions, and classification/clearance levels. Bell and LaPadula continued their model with the development of the simple security property ideal. This stipulated that if some specific (subject, object, access-attribute) for an observe-only attribute represents a current access, then the subject clearance or right of access level must dominate. In other words, it must be greater than or equal to the object classification or restriction to access level. They also articulated another property called the **-property* (star-property), which provided the rules for simultaneous access to two objects of potentially differing levels. Although not exhaustive, the following examples indicate the nature of the overall model:

- Subjects of higher level may read (observation/no alteration) lower level objects, so long as of "no control mechanisms" are required to affect the read.
- Subjects of a higher level may execute (no observation/no alteration) lower level objects, so long as no control mechanisms are required to affect the execution.
- Subjects of lower level append (no observation/alteration) information to higher level objects, so long as no control mechanisms are required to affect the operation.
- Subjects on an equal level with objects may write (observation/alteration) to those objects.

The requirement of no control mechanisms for the read, execute, and append operations recognizes that various system control mechanisms such as locking devices can be used covertly to communicate information between levels, violating the security integrity.

Other Models. Other security models exist and have utility in the software production and testing cycle. For example, Denning noted that many access control mechanisms were designed to control immediate access to objects without necessarily examining the issue of the information flows implied by a collection of access rights. She developed an information flow model to provide constraints on the flow (1976). As another example, Cornwell suggested that the use of proof-driven, formal modeling techniques have several potential benefits including: (*1*) allowing the security design to proceed in an orderly fashion, (*2*) providing a system with a high security assurance, and (*3*) exposing security flaws early in the design cycle (1989). He derived a software module using a security model and suggested that security proofs using formal techniques would increase the level of confidence with which some specific design is viewed as actually meeting the security requirements. Heaney proposed methodologies which furnish an environment of interactive tool suites supporting a systems engineering and integration approach to security models (1990).

FEDERAL SECURITY TESTING

With the move to place ever greater amounts of federal information into computer systems came an increasing awareness of the need to protect that information. Although the U.S. Department of Defense interest in secure military information caused early security assurance emphasis, other federal agencies have also promulgated policy documentation which specifies various security considerations including those to be applied to computer systems.

U.S. Department of Defense (DOD)

The Department of Defense (DOD) recognized the need to acquire secure computer systems to support sensitive military applications, leading to the early-1980s formation of the National Computer Security Center (NCSC) at the National Security Agency in Fort George G. Meade, Maryland. Over the next decade, the NCSC developed and published a wide range of computer security guidance manuals, colloquially known as the "Rainbow Series" because of their varying colorful covers. One of the first NCSC publications, the "Orange Book," was the *DOD Trusted Computer System Evaluation Criteria.* It presented the concept of a trusted computing base (TCB) and provided for four evaluation divisions of criteria, from *D* (the least level of trust) through *A* (the highest level of trust). Division *D*— Minimal Protection had only a single class and was reserved for evaluated systems that failed to meet any higher level. Division *C*—Discretionary Protection consisted of two classes (*C1*and *C2*) which provided for discretionary (need-to-know) protection and audit capabilities. To meet *C1* security testing requirements, the system security mechanisms were to be tested and found to work as specified in the system documentation, and also tested to assure that there were no obvious means by which an unauthorized user could bypass/defeat the security mechanisms. To meet *C2*, the more stringent class, the security testing also was required to search for apparent flaws that would allow resource isolation violation and/or permit unauthorized access to audit or authentication information. Division *B*—Mandatory Protection consisted of three classes (*B1* to *B3*). Systems in Division *B* are required to have all of the protections of Division *C*. Additionally, Division *B* introduced the concept of a trusted computing base that maintained the integrity of sensitivity labels, which enforce mandatory access control rules. This division also introduced the concept of security models to serve as a foundation for the trusted computing base.

At the *B1* class (Labeled Security Protection), security testing and assurance was significantly increased to deal with a number of issues, including the mandatory access control environment. At *B1* the system must be tested and shown to work as claimed in its documentation. Further, a team of persons who fully understand the specific implementation of the trusted computing base must undertake to examine in detail the design documentation, source code, and object code. The examination has the objective of uncovering both design and implementation system vulnerabilities of the system that would allow penetration to achieve unauthorized access, modification, or deletion of data. The testing also must be designed to show that an unauthorized person cannot cause the system to enter a state denying the system to authorized users. The testing for *B1* is iterative, with discovered flaws being corrected, removed, or otherwise neutralized and retested to assure that the effort was successful without introducing additional bugs.

To meet the *B2* class, testing must demonstrate that the system was "relatively" resistant to penetration and consistent with the top-level specification model, introduced as a requirement for this class, For the *B2* class, the system developer additionally must search the system for covert channels and arrive at the finding that the system was resistant to penetration. At the *B3* class, "no design flaws and no more than a few correctable implementation flaws" were allowed to be found as a result of the testing, and "there shall be reasonable confidence that few remain." Division *A*—Verified Protection was characterized by the use of formal security verification methods to assure that both the mandatory and discretionary system security controls were able to effectively protect information stored/processed by the system. Division *A* had only a single class (*A1*) and emphasized formal security verification methods (DOD, 1985).

Other National Computer Security Center (NCSC) Guidance

The NCSC has published several additional documents to assist in implementing the information in *DOD 5200.28-STD.* However, the guidance tends to be somewhat general in nature, For example, the NCSC has published guidelines that "formal verification systems" are those which have the capability of formally specifying and verifying the design of a trusted system to meet the *A1* Design Specification and Verification (NCSC, 1989b). Required testing for such products involve two levels of testing: functional and stress. Functional tests are to be conducted in a manner which will "demonstrate that the verification system operates as advertised" and are to be maintained over the system life cycle. Functional tests are to be done at both the module level "to demonstrate compliance with design documentation" and at the system level "to demonstrate that software accurately generates assertions, correctly implements the logic, and correctly responds to user commands."

As another example, the NCSC has defined a program (NCSC, 1989a) known as the Rating Maintenance Phase (RAMP) to allow vendors to continue certification of systems over the system life cycle. Necessarily stressing configuration control, the guidance provides only general guidance for change testing, noting that testing and test development are to be independent activities and implying some level of "functional security tests."

Other Federal Agency Guidance

Other agencies have been concerned with assuring that computer systems operate in a manner which allows them to be trusted to some level. However, although the various documents tend to have significant amounts of information about how the system must act, including such specific protection mechanisms as passwords, guidance concerning verification through testing tends to be much more general. For example, the U.S. Department of Energy (DOE, 1988) addresses a number of requirements for systems which process classified information. However, "assurance testing" guidance is quite general, specifying only that the Security Plan must provide a basis for determining that the system has correctly implemented the requirements, including specific functional testing of security features of the system, and that, if uncleared personnel are used to produce hardware or software, such systems must be examined before being placed into use.

General Guidance Affect on Security Testing

The general nature of most federal security testing guidance may result in a compliance implementation problem. When examining a system, some necessary functional tests which demonstrate that given feature performs as expected are often apparent. What is perhaps not so clear is whether a given security test suite also is sufficient in its coverage. This issue of suite sufficiency applies to both the software developer and to the user, and is addressed in greater detail in the discussion of functional testing below.

LIFE CYCLE SECURITY TESTING CONSIDERATIONS

Regardless of the general nature of system security test guidance, testing has been accomplished to a point that some empirical information exists, For example, research has reported efforts in the nuclear power industry, which clearly needs highly reliable, tested software that performs exactly as expected, This research suggests that testing alone is not sufficient in developing highly reliable software, but, rather, is only one necessary part of an overall software life cycle program based on sound software engineering principles.

Requirements, Specifications, Configuration Control, and Inspections

The overall environment within which the system is developed has importance to system reliability. Reports indicated the need for highly detailed formal specifications, structured design techniques, dual programming, strong configuration control methods, and design/code inspections in order to assure that ambiguities are avoided and anomalies reduced (Geiger, 1979; Ford Aerospace and Communications Corporation, 1977). One study attributed "a significant percentage" of all errors detected to specification errors and ambiguities, which could be minimized through the use of formal specification techniques (Ramamoorthy, 1979). Design and code inspections reduce overall errors (Fagan, 1976).

Security Testing during Developmental Phases

It was noted as late as 1978 that, although "security testing is the single most common technique for gaining assurance that a system operates within the constraints of a given set of policies and mechanisms," little research had been done to determine effective testing methods specifically tailored to the security area (Gligor, 1978). However, some security testing information has been reported for the development phases.

Security Testing and Models. Formal modeling specification increases the reliability of software systems by guaranteeing the "correctness" of the system. In this approach to system development, the analyst prepares the formal model with mathematical statements, providing a precise mathematical description of the behavior of the system while omitting all implementation details. Next, the analyst reduces the model to some less abstract representations, which are in turn coded into a high order language (HOL). The HOL code must then be shown to be consistent with the original formal model. Commonly, holding verification until the HOL phase of development can increase the overall difficulty level. Kemmerer discussed the common verification technique of using a state machine approach, which requires demonstration of the fact that the initial state satisfies the formal model, as well as the fact that every operation preserves the model. This demonstration must then proceed through the various subordinate levels of specification. A problem with this approach is that there may exist no implementation consistent with the specification, a fact that is often discovered after several refinements of the design and that causes redesign from the model downward. Kemmerer suggests early tests of the formal specifications to determine whether they provide the required functionality, particularly for special cases. Many specification languages are not procedural. To cope, Kremmerer suggests two approaches: (*1*) conversion of the specifications to procedures for rapid prototype testing, and (*2*) symbolic execution of the sequence of operations to check the resultant symbolic values and determine whether they define the proper states at the proper times (Kemmerer, 1985).

Kernel Validation. A security kernel can be considered a software and/or hardware construct that will enforce some specified security constraints upon a system. An early example of such a kernel's developmental life cycle and validation was reported by Millen (1976) for a PDP-11/45 system, in which the kernel was based on a Bell-LaPadula type of access control model. The approach involved Parnas software module specification techniques (Parnas, 1972) and provided a methodology for testing the formal model axioms. If the axioms were found to be satisfied, then the virtual environment described by the specification was deemed secure. Millen also noted that the verification approach did not produce sufficient coverage for "time problems," in which two cooperating users could signal each other by establishing a covert channel through the system clock. In a more recent application to security testing, Gligor and associates described the advantages and disadvantages of monolithic functional testing and of functional synthesis-based testing directed to verification of a secure XENIX kernel (Gligor, 1987), both of which are examined below.

Functional Security Testing

The end user of a system often may need to verify that a system does or does not evince particular security features and capabilities. This arises from two general conditions. First, the relatively high costs associated with obtaining NCSC certification have led several system vendors to claim that their products are compliant with trusted computer base criteria without actually having been submitted to the certification process. In essence, the vendor claims are that if their system were to be submitted for certification, it would be found to have the features necessary to allow certification at the level claimed. Secondly, as already noted, anomalous behavior is a given for systems, although the level and frequency may be greatly reduced for highly reliable systems. Thus even when systems have undergone the certification process, bugs can and will occur.

A major security testing difficulty which exists for the end user of a system is that many security testing methodologies are targeted to the development cycle, requiring resources which are not readily available after the system is in production. However, functional testing methodologies are more amenable to application by the end user. To functionally test, several things must be determined. First, the function must be accurately and explicitly described. Next, that description must be examined to determine whether it is in whole or part amenable to testing. If testing is feasible, then the specific test suite, (rules, constraints, data, etc.) must be prepared and reviewed with respect to whether it will provide the level of coverage desired. Gligor and associates (1987) examined functional testing with respect to two generic approaches: monolithic testing and functional-synthesis-based testing. Although they examined these testing methodologies in terms of the security kernel, much of their comments can be said to have general application. Both approaches expect the test environment to be conducted with respect to the security model, whether it be formal or informal, explicitly stated or implied, for the system under consideration.

Monolithic Functional Testing. Monolithic functional testing has been described as a black box approach, in which the security model is used to derive the functions to be tested on a system to which the end user may have no additional information. Thus the approach treats the security kernel and related implementing structures as a black box, for which certain inputs will cause some expected outputs. It is usually possible to develop tests which demonstrate two factors (*1*) that the specific function performs as expected when a within-bounds test is conducted, and (*2*) that the function fails when the test is conducted using data exceeding the boundaries. Thus tests tend to direct themselves to boundary values, examining conditions at, above, below, and at extremes to the bounds for some function (Haley, 1985). A clear advantage to this form of testing is the fact that there is no need for the tester to have access to the internal structure, code, and related technical elements of the system under test, allowing the technique to be used by any party with access to the system product. The shortfalls to this form of testing include the essential impossiblity often to determine the true extent of coverage, even when the test is designed in an attempt to be functionally exhaustive. For example, password authentication is a common mechanism used to provide system-level access controls. Assume that a password subsystem is given with one of the common implementations, which is documented to allow any alphabetic, numeric, or special character in construction of the password, with some specifiable minimum number of characters. Often such a description as this has been implemented to mean printable characters between 30H (30 hexadecimal) and 7FH. What may not be clear in preparing to test would be the impact of nonprinting control characters and/or special characters with a bit mask greater than 7FH. In addition to examining the length boundaries, questions arise concerning whether the password subsystem is capable of coping with control and special characters above 7FH, including considerations of position dependencies within the password set. If the internal password algorithm is not known, then one could argue that testing the extended character set would be needed combinatorially for all positions, and retesting should occur as the password length is extended. Without knowing how the internal algorithm handles these conditions, the potential functional suite could be considered effectively unlimited. In this example, functional security testing could demonstrate that the subsystem worked as expected; that is, it allowed establishment of minimum lengths, allowed access when a proper password was entered, and did not allow access when at least some improper passwords were entered. However, testing to determine the subsystem's susceptibility to accidental or deliberate attack involving an extended character set may not be practical for exhaustive verification. Statistical coverage methodologies reduce but may not eliminate the chance that some untested combination(s) of character(s) and position(s) may adversely effect a given function to produce unwanted anomalous behaviors.

Functional-Synthesis-Based Testing. This form of security testing examines the full system and also each internal function implemented to achieve that system. It has been referred to as white box testing. Testing procedures used vary based on the various types of functional synthesis. Control synthesis addresses the control decomposition of functions into sequences of other functions, which then individually transform into an input state and an output state. A possible set of state transitions is known, and the control synthesis graph exists prior to testing. Tests are selected to be able to detect missing functions within a sequence, to determine unexpected functional sequences, and to identify faulty functions within a sequence. Of the various types of functional synthesis-based testing, some deem that only the control synthesis method is suitable for security kernel testing (Gligor, 1987).

OTHER SECURITY TESTING ENVIRONMENTS

Much of the foregoing has addressed some of both generalized and stand-alone operating system security testing considerations. It should be noted that additional security considerations are encountered when various specialized environments are involved. Two examples of this would be some specialized applications software which acts within the purview of a given stand-alone operating system and network systems in which two more separate computer systems interact over some data link.

Specialized Application Software: Trusted Database Management System Example

Some specialized application software environments tend to create or extend security-related problems and considerations. One example of this would be that of complex commercial database management systems (DBMS). Criteria for conditions attendant to a trusted DBMS emerged within the federal sphere with the 1991 National Computer Security Center (NCSC) publication of the *Trusted Database Management System Interpretation of the Trusted Computer System Criteria* (NCSC, 1991). In this document the NCSC examines and extends the use of the reference monitor concept to subsets of the overall trusted computing base. The subset can be any combination of software, firmware, and/or hardware which allows regulation of the access of some set of subjects to some other set of objects, based on a specifically stated access control policy and properties. The evaluation of a single subset is generally a direct evaluation against the *DOD-5200.28-STD* stand-alone system criteria. However, this becomes more complicated when two or more subsets are involved, such that one subset uses abstractions of another subset when dealing with its own abstractions. The NCSC guide examines conditions under which verification of the individual subsets will or will not be required, For example, if there is a direct dependency relation of one subset to another, then verification of the latter subset is a necessary condition to verification of the first. As another example, if two subsets operate in a well-defined manner, essentially in near isolation from each other through domain boundaries, it may be possible to clearly delineate the nature, scope, and other considerations of their interactions with each other such that independent verifications are appropriate.

In the case of a DBMS, several general conditions of verification are of concern. An example of one consideration would be the verification that the DBMS achieves some given level of trust through inherent features. Thus if the DBMS supports *B*-level mandatory access controls with labeling at the individual variable-node-attribute level, then this must be verified. As another consideration, if the DBMS consists of major subsystems, such as occurs with a front-end/back-end/Servers architecture, then the subset considerations indicated above will generally apply the verification and testing. For example, if a relational DBMS supports individually labeled attributes, a security test concern might well be inter-server label integrity, that is, whether the label is maintained when accessed by a DBMS back-end server, passed to a separate communications server, etc.

The Network Environment

As with the considerations attendant to subelements generally more complex than those of a stand-alone system, so also are the network considerations for security verification and testing a more complex superset of those associated with the stand-alone system environment. This arises from the need to extend single-entity system considerations into a larger surroundings of interactions among the network components. The NCSC has published initial guidance for network security considerations (NCSC, 1987). This recognizes that there exist at least two views of "network security." In one involving interconnected accredited systems, the view is operational in nature, recognizing that network components may be created, managed, tested, and accredited separately and independently. In this view the various systems are assigned operational sensitivity ranges, with each range consisting of the highest and lowest sensitivity levels which the given system may process. Two interconnected systems are allowed to exchange data within some established boundary that may not exceed the intersection of their range sets. As the structure of a network increases in complexity, rate of change, etc., so too does the difficulty with separate component verification, testing, and accreditation, including combinatorial interactions. In a different view it is possible to examine the network security environment by modeling as a single, overall trusted system. In this model, every trusted component of the network must enforce, at its level, the security policy of the overall network. Then the sum of all of the individual component policy enforcements must be shown to achieve network-wide policy enforcement.

In the federal guidance, the minimum *C*-level approach to network security testing requires a test bed which will exercise individual component interfaces and protocols, and which also uses an integrated test of all components involved with a given network-trusted computing base (NTCB) partition. Integrated testing is a necessary criteria above any individual component testing and is accomplished for some allowable configuration(s) of the network. At the higher *B*-levels of trust, the guidance includes the need to introduce unfriendly subjects from outside the NTCB, which then attempt to accomplish some denied data access, modification, or deletion action. *B*-level mandatory access control testing also should address label integrity during data element and aggregate importation, manipulation, and exportation activities. Test documentation is required at each level.

Network security testing issues and considerations parallel many of those found in individual software system testing. By analogy, just as branch and inter-module coverage considerations exist within individual software module and system testing, so also exist similar considerations in dealing with the network software and hardware components which act together as a system.

RELATED TOPICS

The interested reader may want to read other related articles, including COMPUTER SECURITY, DATABASE SECURITY, SECURITY KERNEL, SECURITY MODELS, and SOFTWARE TESTING.

BIBLIOGRAPHY

J. P. Anderson, *ESD-TR-73-51, Computer Security Technology Planning Study,* (AD-758206), J. P. Anderson Company, Oct. 1972.

R. H. Baker, *The Computer Security Handbook,* TAB Professional and Reference Books, Blue Ridge Summit, Pa., 1985.

B. Beizer, *Software Testing Techniques,* ed., Van Nostrand Reinhold, New York, 1990.

D. E. Bell and L. J. LaPadula, *ESD-TR-75-306, Secure Computer Systems: Unified Exposition and MULTICS Interpretation,* Defense Technical Information Center (DTIC), (originally MITRE Corporation Report MTR-2997 rev. 1), Mar. 1976.

B. W. Boehm, "The High Cost of Software," in Ellis Horowitz, ed., *Practical Strategies for Developing Large Software Systems,* Addison-Wesley Publishing Company, Reading, Mass., 1975.

J. J. Clever, "Computer Site Threat Identification and Analysis," *Proceedings of the Digital Equipment Computer Users Society: Atlanta, Georgia-Spring, 1989,* Digital Equipment Computer Users Society, Marlboro, Mass., 1989.

M. R. Cornwell, "A Software Engineering Approach to Designing Trustworthy Software," *Proceedings 1989 IEEE Symposium on Security and Privacy,* IEEE Computer Society Press, Washington, D.C., 1981.

D. E. Denning, "A Lattice Model of Secure Information Flow," *Communications of the ACM* **19,** 5, Association for Computing Machinery, (May 1976).

DOD 5200.28-STD, Department of Defense Trusted Computer System Evaluation Criteria, Library Number S-225711, Department of Defense, Washington, D.C., 1985.

DOE Order 5637.1, Classified Computer Security Program, U.S. Department of Energy, Washington, D.C., Jan. 29, 1988.

M. E. Fagan, "Design and Code Inspections to Reduce Errors in Program Development," *IBM Systems Journal* **3,** (1976).

Ford Aerospace and Communications Corporation, *A Secure Minicomputer Operating System (KSOS): Secure UNIX Implementation Plan,* Ford Aerospace and Communications Corporation, Western Development Laboratories Division, DTIC File ADA111567, Palo Alto, Calif., 1977.

W. Geiger. L. Gmeiner, H. Trauboth, and U. Voges, "Program Testing Techniques for Nuclear Reactor Protection Systems,"*IEEE Computer Magazine* **12,** (1979).

V. D. Gligor, C. S. Chandersekaran, W. Jiang, A. Johri, G. L. Lukenbaugh, and L. E. Reich, "A New Security Testing Method and its Application to the Secure Xenix Kernel," *IEEE Transactions on Software Engineering* **SE-13,** 2, (Feb. 1987).

C. J. Haley and F. L. Mayer, "Issues on the Development of Security Related Functional Tests," *Proceedings of the DoD-NBS Conference on Computer Systems Security,* Gaithersburg, Md., Sept. 1985.

A. L. Hankinson, "Computer Assurance: Security, Safety and Economics," *COMPASS '89: Proceedings of the Fourth Annual Conference on Computer Assurance, Systems Integrity, Software Safety and Process Security,* IEEE Service Center, Piscataway, N.J., 1989.

J. Heaney, M. Adkins, G. Dolsen, and J. Page, "Security Model Development Environment," *Proceedings of the first International Colnference on Systems Integration -ICSI '90,* IEEE, Piscataway, N.J. (IEEE Catalog 90-TH0309-5), 1990.

R. A. Kemmerer, "Testing Formal Specifications to Detect Design Errors," *IEEE Transactions on Software Engineering* **SE-11,** 1, (Jan. 1985).

R. C. Linger, H. D. Mills, and B. I. Witt, *Structured Programming: Theory and Practice,* Addison-Wesley Publishing Company, Reading, Mass., 1979.

J. K. Millen, "Security Kernel Validation in Practice," *Communications of the ACM* **19,** 5, (May 1976).

NCSC-TG-005, Trusted Network Interpretation of the Trusted Computer System Evaluation Criteria, Version 1, National Computer Security Center, Library Number S-228526, Washington, D.C., July 31, 1987

NCSC-TG-013, Rating Maintenance Phase: Program Document, Version 1, National Computer Security Center, Library Number S-232468, Washington, D.C., June 23, 1989a.

NCSC-TG-014, Guidelines for Formal Verification Systems, Version 1, National Computer Security Center, Library Number S-231308, Washington, D.C., April 1, 1989.

NCSC-TG-021, Trusted Database Management System Interpretation of the Trusted Computer System Criteria, Version 1, National Computer Security Center, Library Number S-235625, Washington, D.C., April 1991.

D. B. Parker, *Managers Guide to Computer Security,* Reston Publishing Company Inc., Reston, Va., 1981.

D. L. Parnas, "A Technique for Software Module Specification with Examples, *Communications of the ACM* **15**(5), (May 1972).

W. E. Perry, *A Structured Approach to Systems Testing,* ed., QED Information Sciences Inc., Wellesley, Mass., 1988.

J. W. Radatz, *RADC-TR-81-145, Analysis of IV&V Data,* Logicon, Inc., Rome Air Development Center Report Griffis AFB, N.Y. June 1981.

C. V. Ramamoorthy, F. B. Bastani, J. M. Favaro, Y. R. Mok, C. W. Nam, and K. Suzuki, "A Systemataic Approach to the Development and Validation of Critical Software for Nuclear Power Plants," *Proceedings: 4th International Conference on Software Engineering, September 17–19, 1979, Munich, Germany,* IEEE Computer Society, IEEE Catalog Number 79CH1479-5C, Long Beach, Calif., 1979.

J. A. Schweitzer, *Computer Crime and Business Information: A Practical Guide for Managers,* Elsevier Science Publishing Company, New York, 1986.

R. Turn, *R-2811-DR&E, Trusted Computer Systems: Needs and Incentives for Use in Government and the Private Sector,* The Rand Corporation, June 1981.

JOHN J. CLEVER
Sandia National Laboratories

SECURITY, COMPUTER

INTRODUCTION

Computer security is an area that is growing in importance as more business applications are being automated and more vital and sensitive information is being stored in computers. Almost daily one can read newspaper accounts of computer abuse. Stealing information from a computer (e.g., a competitor's bid on a lucrative contract) is just liking stealing goods from a warehouse, for information is a commodity. The primary difference is that the loss of information often goes unnoticed.

The term *computer security* means the protection of resources (including data and programs) from accidental or malicious disclosure, modification or destruction. In addition, the system resources must also be protected (i.e., system services should not be denied). These computer security properties are usually referred to as confidentiality, integrity, and availability. More precisely:

Confidentiality ensures that sensitive information is not disclosed to unauthorized recipients.

Integrity ensures that data and programs are modified or destroyed only in a specified and authorized manner.

Availability ensures that the resources of the system will be usable whenever they are needed by an authorized user.

The degree to which each of these three properties is needed varies from application to application. For instance, the defense industry is primarily interested in confidentiality. In contrast, the banking industry is primarily interested in integrity, and the telephone industry may value availability most. The exact requirements that are needed for a particular system or application are expressed in the security policy for that system or application.

BACKGROUND

In the early days of computing when stand alone systems were used by one user at a time, computer security consisted primarily of physical security. That is, the computer and its peripherals were locked in a secure area with a guard at the door that checked each user's identification before allowing them to enter the room.

As time sharing systems emerged in the mid to late 1960s and multiple jobs and users were able to run at the same time, controlling the access to the data on the system became a major point of concern. One solution that was used was to process classified data one level at a time and then "sanitizing" the system after the jobs from one level were run and before the jobs for the next level were run. This procedural approach to computer security was known as *periods processing* because the jobs for each level were all run in their particular period of the day. This approach was an inefficient way to use the system, and an effort was made to find more efficient software solutions to the multilevel security problem.

The initial interest in computer security was spearheaded by the Department of Defense (DOD). The "Ware Report, (Ware, 1970), pointed out the needs for computer security and highlighted the difficulties in evaluating a system to determine if it provided the necessary security for particular applications. This report was the final report of the Defense Science Board Study, and was named after Willis Ware, of the RAND Corporation, who chaired the advisory group.

In 1972 the Air Force Electronics System Division sponsored the Computer Technology Planning Study. The intent of this study was to define the Research and Development paths required to make secure computers a reality in the USAF. The final report from this study was called the "Anderson Report" (Anderson and co-workers, 1972). The major contribution from this study was the *reference monitor* concept, which led to security kernel architectures.

In the mid to late 1970s a number of systems were designed and implemented using a security kernel architecture. These were built to run on PDP-11s (Millen, 1976; McCauley and co-workers, 1979; Walker and co-workers, 1980), MULTICS (Schroeder, 1977), Honeywell Level 6 (Fraim 1983), and IBM 370s (Gold and co-workers, 1979). The systems were all sponsored by the defense establishment, and as a result, they were concerned primarily with confidentiality.

Another effort that occurred in the mid to late 1970s was the use of "tiger teams" to test the security of a system. These teams attempted to obtain unauthorized access to the system by exploiting design and implementation errors (Linde, 1975; Hebbard and co-workers, 1980). The tiger team studies showed further the difficulty of providing secure software; virtually every system that was attacked by a tiger team was penetrated.

In 1977 the DOD Computer Security Initiative began. This initiative was an effort to consolidate the results of the work of the last decade and to focus on the computer security issues that had been raised. One of the results of the initiative was a number of workshops and conferences on computer security topics. An effort was also made to interest the vendor community in building secure systems.

In 1981 the DOD Computer Security Center (CSC) was established. Its charter was to evaluate commercially developed computer systems with regard to computer security, to set standards for the evaluations, and to conduct computer security Research and Development. The center was established at the National Security Agency and it dealt primarily with the security problems of the defense community.

In 1983 the DOD Computer Security Center released its first official evaluation criteria, titled the "Department of Defense Trusted Computer System Evaluation Criteria" (DOD 1983). This book, which has an orange cover, is usually called the "orange book" or the "TCSEC." This effort was the first attempt to provide a set of criteria for evaluating the effectiveness of the security controls of a computer system. In 1985, after some minor revisions, the orange book was made a DOD standard. In 1985 the CSC was renamed the National Computer Security Center (NCSC) although it still dealt primarily with defense problems.

In 1987 the Computer Security Act partitioned computer security in the Federal Government into two distinct branches. The National Computer Security Center at NSA was to deal with classified information, and the National Computer Systems Laboratory (NCSL) at NIST was to deal with unclassified information. In addition, NIST was tasked to support the civil government and unclassified defense communities. This act of Congress clearly pointed out the need for computer security in the non-defense communities.

The Canadian government also recognized the need for an evaluation capability and formed the Canadian System Security Centre (CSSC) in 1988. In May 1989 the first version of the Canadian Trusted Computer Product Evaluation Criteria (CTCPEC or Canadian Criteria) was released. The most recent version of the Canadian Criteria (version 3.0e) was released in January 1993 [CSSC 93].

The need for computer security in the non-defense community was also realized by European nations. In 1989 the West German Information Security Agency published a criteria for the evaluation of the trustworthiness of information technology systems (ZSI, 1989). Unlike the TCSEC, which dealt primarily with confidentiality, the German criteria also addressed the issues of integrity and availability and of network security. At the same time the British Commercial Computer Security Center (CCSC), which was established by the Department of Trade and Industry and the Ministry of Defense, also released a computer security criteria (DTI, 1989). A notable feature of the British criteria has been that it provides a "claims language" that allows vendors to construct security-worthiness statements about their products.

In 1990 the countries of France, Germany, the Netherlands, and the United Kingdom made a joint effort to produce an international set of computer security evaluation criteria. The document is called the "Information Technology Security Evaluation Criteria" (ITSEC) (ITS, 1990). This "harmonized" effort is primarily a combination of the evaluation classes contained in the German criteria and the claims language from the British criteria.

In 1990 a National Research Council study group, the System Security Study Committee, pointed out the need for computer security in the commercial sector. The final report from this committee—"Computers at Risk: Safe Computing in the Information Age"—alerted the public to the risks posed by inadequate security and proposed actions to be taken to solve the problem (NRC, 1991). Most noteworthy of their proposals was the establishment of an Information Security Foundation (ISF), which would be a private, not-for-profit organization. One of the tasks proposed for the ISF was to produce a comprehensive set of Generally Accepted System Security Principles (GSSP) that would be a basic set of principles for designing, using and managing secure systems. The ISF would also be responsible for certifying commercial security systems, much like the Underwriters Laboratory certifies electrical systems. The NRC committee also recommended that attempts be made to harmonize with the international criteria efforts.

In an attempt to broaden the scope of the TCSEC, the federal government has started a joint program between NIST and NSA called the Federal Criteria (FC) project. In December of 1992 the first draft of the FC (FC, 1992) was circulated for review. The final FC document was originally intended to be a Federal Information Processing Standard (FIPS) for use by the U.S. Federal government, which would replace the TCSEC.

In June 1993, at the start of a joint NIST/NSA workshop that was held to discuss the draft FC, the participants were informed that NIST and NSA had decided to work with the Canadians and the Europeans to develop a "Common Information Technology Security Criteria " (CC).

COMPUTER SECURITY TODAY

Computer security consists largely of defensive methods used to detect and thwart would-be intruders. The principles of computer security thus arise from the kinds of threats intruders can impose. This section presents four approaches to achieving secure computing and discusses the various national and international evaluation criteria. Finally, today's approaches to developing secure systems are compared and contrasted with standard software development techniques.

Approaches to Secure Computing

There are four general approaches to achieving a secure computing environment. They are: the use of special procedures for working with the system; the inclusion of additional functions or mechanisms in the system; the use of assurance techniques to increase one's confidence in the security of the system; and the use of intrusion detection systems. Each of these approaches is discussed in the following subsections.

Some security requirements can either be achieved by requiring procedures to be followed or by using system mechanisms or functions to enforce the requirement. Also, in some cases system users need to follow specific procedures in order to make security mechanisms effective. It is also possible to trade off assurance techniques for less mechanism. For instance, one can use assurance techniques, like formal proofs, to assure that the system can not get into a particular state; thus, alleviating the need for the software mechanism that would deal with that state.

Procedural Approaches

Procedural approaches prescribe the appropriate behavior for the user to follow when using the system. The periods processing approach for processing jobs at different security levels is an example of a procedural solution to satisfy a security requirement.

Many successful penetrations are initiated by an intruder guessing a user's password. With the advent of personal computers and dial-up modems, this hazard has become much more of a problem. In addition, the availability of online dictionaries also makes the process of guessing easier. Would-be penetrators also have lists of commonly used passwords that they can try automatically with the aid of their personal computer, and if passwords are short they are easily found by an exhaustive search. In a study carried out at Bell Labs in 1979 (Morris and Thompson, 1979) it was shown that by using the available computer power of the day an exhaustive search could be used to try all 4 letter lower case passwords in 7 minutes. If the characters were mixed case and numeric characters the search took 5 hours, and if the characters of the password were chosen from all printable characters, the search took 28 hours. For six character passwords the respective search times were 107 hours, 2.2 years and 29 years. Using the desktop workstations that are readily available today, such as a DEC 3100, these times can be reduced by a factor of 15. Thus, a four letter lower case only password could be exhaustively searched in less than a minute and a six letter lower case only password in less than an hour. Another vulnerability with passwords is that computer vendors deliver systems with standard accounts that have default passwords, and these passwords often are not changed by the system administrators.

User guidelines for the appropriate choice of a password is the most prevalent example of using procedural approaches to achieve a security requirement. For example, to deter password guessing by a potential intruder, one should choose a long password (at least eight characters) that is not obvious and not easily guessable (e.g., not a spouse's first name, a middle name, a login name, or any of these spelled backwards). Passwords should also use both upper and lower case letters, numerics and possibly special symbols. In addition, a password should not be written down, or if it is it should not be written in an obvious place. Furthermore, users should be trained to change their passwords at appropriate intervals. Many of these restrictions can be enforced by the system when a user chooses a new password.

Another example of a procedural approach is a set of rules for the appropriate handling of removable storage devices. Oftentimes data that is perfectly safe while in a protected system is compromised by a penetrator getting access to removable storage, such as a dump tape, and analyzing it on an unprotected system. For this reason most security conscious organizations have explicit rules for handling removable media, such as requiring them to be stored in an approved vault.

Functions and Mechanism

Including additional functions or mechanisms in a computer system is another way of enhancing computer security. The mechanisms presented in this section are grouped into authentication mechanisms, access control, and inference control.

Authentication Mechanisms. Authentication mechanisms are used to assure that a particular user is who he/she claims to be. The first mechanism discussed is the *secure attention key*. This key, when hit by a user at a terminal, kills any process running at the terminal except the true system listener and thus guarantees a trusted path to the system. This strategy will foil attempts at "spoofing," which is the process of fooling a user into believing that he/she is talking to the system, resulting in information being revealed. For instance, the spoofer may display what looks like the system login prompt on a terminal to make the terminal appear to be idle. Then when an unsuspecting user begins to use the terminal, the spoofer retrieves the login name and asks for the user's password. After obtaining this information, the spoofer displays a message to try again and returns ownership of the terminal to the system. If a secure attention key is used, it is important that users make a habit of always hitting the key to begin a dialogue with the system. One way of ensuring this is for the system to only display the login prompt after the key is depressed. This strategy is an example of procedures and mechanism working together to achieve a security property.

Most of the password guidelines that were discussed above as a procedural approach can be enforced by the system. For instance, the password program can require long passwords and it can check the password chosen against an online dictionary or against a list of obvious passwords. The login program can also inform the user that it is time to change passwords and not allow further logins if the password is not changed in time. Finally, the system can generate secure passwords for the users using a secure password generator.

Password files stored in the system may be compromised like any other file. Therefore, it is not good practice to store passwords in the clear. Instead, a *one-way function* (i.e., a function whose inverse is computationally infeasible to determine) is used to encipher passwords and the result is stored in the password file. When a user's password is presented at login time it is enciphered and compared to the stored value. By using one-way functions to encipher passwords the login file can be made public.

Access Control. Assuming that by using authentication mechanisms and good password practice, the system can guarantee that users are who they claim to be, the next step is to provide a means of limiting a user's access to only those files that policy determines should be accessed. These controls are referred to as *access control*. Different applications and systems have different security requirements, and these requirements are expressed in the *access control policy* for the application or system. Access control policies are enforced by the access control mechanisms.

When describing access control policies and mechanisms it is necessary to consider the *subjects* and *objects* of the system. Subjects are the users of the system along with any active entities that act on behalf of the user or the system (e.g., user processes). Objects are the resources or passive entities of the system (e.g., files, programs, memory, devices). Subjects may also be objects (e.g., procedures). The *access control mechanism* determines for each

	OBJECTS				
SUBJECTS	O1	O2	O3	O4	O5
S1	R		W	RW	W
S2		E		R	
S3		RW	E		
S4	RE		RW		RE

Figure 1. Example access matrix.

subject what *access modes* (sometimes called access rights), such as read, write, or execute, it has for each object.

There are two types of access control: *discretionary access control* (DAC) and *mandatory access control* (MAC). More precisely:

Discretionary access control—the owner of an object specifies what type of access the other users can have to the object. Thus, access is at the discretion of the owner.

Mandatory access control—the system determines whether a user can access a resource based on the security attributes (e.g., labels or markings) of both the user and the object.

Mandatory access control is often called non-discretionary access control.

One of the earliest forms of discretionary access control, which is still being used on some mainframe and PC systems, is the use of passwords for file access. That is, the owner selects a password for each file and distributes the password to those users to whom he wants to give access to the file. A major problem with this approach is that one user may pass a password onto another user without the consent of the owner of the file. A second major problem is that the owner cannot revoke access from one user without revoking access from all users and then selecting a new password for the file. Another problem with this approach is that the passwords tend to get embedded in other files and are vulnerable to browsing.

Another form of DAC, which is used on UNIX systems, is the *owner/group/other* approach. With this approach the owner of a file assigns the types of access that are allowed for the owner, for all users in the group associated with the file, and for all users on the system. The problem with this approach is that if an owner wants to give access to a single user, he either has to set up a group with only that user in it or else give access to everyone on the system. That is, because each user is allowed to be a member of only a finite number of groups (usually 16) there is often no group that contains only the specified user(s) to which access should be given. As a result the owner needs to give access to more individuals than is desired.

A convenient way of describing access rights is with an *access matrix* (see Fig. 1). In the access matrix rows correspond to subjects and columns correspond to objects. Each entry in the matrix is a set of access rights that indicate the access that the subject associated with the row has for the object associated with the column. From this matrix one can determine that subject S3 has read and write access to object O2 and execute access to object O3.

Although an access matrix is a convenient way of describing the allowable accesses, it is not an efficient way of representing these accesses in a computer, because the matrix is usually sparse. There are 2 commonly used and more efficient ways of representing an access matrix in a computer system: *access control lists* (sometimes called authorization lists) and *capability lists* (often called c-lists). With the access control list approach each object has an access list associated with it. This list contains the name of each subject that has access to the object along with the modes of access allowed. In contrast, the capability list approach associates a list with each subject. The elements of the list are *capabilities* which can be thought of as tickets that contain an object name and the modes of access allowed to the object. A subject's capability list defines the environment or domain that the subject may directly access. The reader should note that an access list corresponds to a column in the access matrix and a capability list corresponds to a row.

An important aspect of either approach is that both the capabilities and the elements of access lists must be unforgeable or else the entire protection mechanism breaks down. One way of guaranteeing the unforgeability of these elements is by restricting access to them through an intermediary trusted piece of code. The reference monitor introduced in the Anderson report (Anderson and co-workers, 1972) is one such mechanism.

Access control policies often incorporate *access hierarchies.* That is, subjects may have different ranks ranging from the most to the least privileged, where the more privileged user automatically gets the rights of the less privileged user. For instance, in a UNIX system a subject with "superuser" privilege can access any object in the system. Multics systems provide eight hierarchical rings that separate the operating system from system utilities and users, and different level users from each other.

As an example of an access control policy that incorporates access hierarchies, consider the following mandatory control policy. In this model every subject and every object has an access class made up of a level (e.g., unclassified, confidential, and secret) and a (possibly empty) set of categories (e.g., crypto, nuclear, and intelligence). Levels are ordered and categories are not. When comparing access classes the result can be equal, less than, greater than, or not comparable. For instance, the access class with level secret and category set containing only crypto is greater than the access class with level unclassified and an empty category set. Furthermore, secret/{crypto} is less than secret/{crypto,nuclear}, and secret/{crypto} is not comparable to confidential/{nuclear}. The access rules for this policy are as follows: A subject may obtain read permission to an object if its access class is greater than or equal to the access class of the object. This property is known as the *simple security property.* In addition, a subject may write an object if the subject's access class is less than or equal to the access class of the object. This is a simplified version of the **-property* (pronounced star property).

To assure that all access control policies are enforced, a means of mediating each access of an object by a subject is needed. The *reference monitor* (Anderson and co-workers, 1972) provides this mediation. A reference monitor is defined by three basic properties:

1. It must be tamperproof; that is, isolated from modification by system entities.
2. It must always be invoked; that is, must mediate every access.
3. It must be small enough to be subjected to analysis and tests, the completeness of which can be assured.

A *security kernel* is defined as the hardware and software that realize the reference monitor. The idea is to keep the security kernel small and to have it contain the security relevant parts of the system.

Inference Controls. The last class of security mechanisms discussed in this section is inference controls. These controls attempt to restrict database access to sensitive information about individuals while providing access to statistics about groups of individuals. The ideal is a statistical database that discloses no sensitive data.

As an example of the type of threat that is addressed by inference control mechanisms consider a database that contains enrollment and grade statistics for a university class. If Morgan is the only economics major in a particular class one could deduce Morgan's grade by retrieving the average grade for the course, the average grade of all non-economics majors in the class, and the number of students in the class.

Two approaches to solving the inference problem are to restrict queries that reveal certain types of statistics and to add "noise" to the results returned. To foil small and large query set attacks, such as the Morgan example above, a technique called *query-set-size control* is introduced. This technique forbids the release of any statistics pertaining to a group less than some predetermined size n or greater than $N-n$, where N is the total number of records in the database. Other techniques restrict queries with more than some predetermined number of records in common or with too many attributes specified.

Among the techniques that add noise to the statistical results returned are *systematic rounding, random rounding,* and *controlled rounding.* The third alternative requires the sum of rounded statistics to equal their rounded sum. The idea is that it is all right if the user posing the queries knows the exact answer about a large sample, but nothing should be released about a small sample. *Random sample query control* is another promising approach to solving the inference problem. With this approach each statistic is computed using 80–90 of the total number of records and a different sample is used to compute each statistic. For an excellent presentation of these techniques see (Denning 1982).

Assurance Techniques

The third approach to enhancing the security of a system is to subject the system to rigorous assurance techniques that will raise one's confidence that the system will perform as desired. Among these techniques are penetration analysis, formal specification and verification, and covert channel analysis. None of these methods guarantee a secure system. They only increase one's confidence in the security of the system.

Penetration Analysis. One approach to locating security flaws in computer systems is *penetration analysis.* This approach uses a collection of known flaws, generalizes these flaws, and tries to apply them to the system being analyzed. Usually a team of penetrators called a *tiger team,* is given the task of trying to enter the system. Flaws in many major systems have been located by using this approach (Hebbard and co-workers, 1980; Linde 1975).

The problem with the tiger team approach is that, like testing, "penetration teams prove the presence, not absence of protection failures" (Popek, 1974). This observation has led to the use of *formal specification and verification techniques* to increase one's confidence in the reliability and security of a computer system.

Formal Verification. Formal verification demonstrates that an implementation is consistent with its requirements. This task is approached by decomposing it into a number of easier problems. The critical requirements, which are usually a natural language statement of what is desired, are first stated in precise mathematical terms. These requirements are known as the *formal model* or *criteria* for the system. For example, the formal model for a secure system could be that information at one security level does not flow to another security level. Next, a high level formal specification of the system is stated. This specification gives a precise mathematical description of the behavior of the system omitting all implementation details, such as resource limitations. This step is followed by a series of less abstract specifications each of which implements the next higher level specification, but with more detail. Finally, the system is coded in a high order language (HOL). This HOL implementation must be shown to be consistent with the original requirements.

It should be emphasized that demonstrating that HOL code is consistent with security requirements is a difficult process. The process is made tractable by verifying the design at every step. The first step of the verification process is to informally verify that the formal model properly reflects the security requirements. This is the only informal step in the process. Since the formal model is at a high level of abstraction and should contain no unnecessary details, it is usually a simple task to review the formal model with the customer who generated the requirements and determine whether the model properly reflects the critical requirements. Next, it is necessary to prove that the highest level specifications are consistent with the formal model. Both a state machine approach (Hoare, 1972) and an algebraic approach (Guttag and co-workers, 1978) are possible.

After the highest level formal specification has been shown to be consistent with the formal model, it is necessary to show that the next lower level specification, if one exists, is consistent with the level above it. This process continues from level to level until the lowest level specification is shown to be consistent with the level above it. Finally, it is necessary to show that the HOL implementation is consistent with the lowest level specification. By transitivity, the implementation is thus shown to be consistent with the formal model. For a detailed description of the formal specification and verification process for a secure system see Kemmerer (1990).

The advent of the security kernel as a means of encapsulating all security relevant aspects of the system makes formal verification feasible. That is, by developing kernel architectures that minimize the amount and complexity of software involved in security decisions and enforcement, the chances of successfully verifying that the system meets its security requirements are greatly increased. Because the remainder of the system is written using the facilities provided by the kernel, only the kernel code must be verified. Examples of work in this area are (McCauley and Drognowski, 1979; Walker and co-workers, 1980; Silverman, 1983).

Covert Channel Analysis. Secure computer systems use both mandatory and discretionary access controls to restrict the flow of information through legitimate communication channels such as files, shared memory and process signals. Unfortunately, in practice one finds that computer systems are built such that users are not limited to communicating only through the intended communication channels. As a result, a well-founded concern of security-conscious system designers is the potential exploitation of system storage locations and timing facilities to provide unforeseen communication channels to users. These illegitimate channels are known as covert storage and timing channels (Lampson, 1973; Lipner, 1975, Millen, 1976; Kemmerer, 1983).

Covert channels signal information through system facilities not intended for data transfer, and they support this communication using methods not detected or regulated by the access control mechanisms. *Storage channels* transfer information using the manipulation of storage locations for their coding scheme. That is, the sending process alters some system attribute and the receiving process monitors the alteration. *Timing channels* transfer information using the passing of time for their coding scheme; the sending process modulates the receiver's response time to detect a change in some shared entity.

Although there is concern that a user at a high security level may use a covert channel to signal information to a user at a lower level, the major threat from a covert channel is its potential to be employed by a Trojan horse. A *Trojan horse* is a program that gives the appearance of providing normal functionality, but whose execution results in undesired side effects.

The severity of a covert channel threat has been traditionally measured in terms of the channel's bandwidth, i.e., the number of bits signaled per second. The higher the bandwidth, the greater the potential for serious compromise. An alarming possibility regarding covert channels is that as operating systems are ported to faster hardware architectures, the bandwidths of their covert channels may increase significantly. In fact, timing channels with estimated bandwidths in the megabits per second range have been demonstrated on symmetric multi-processing architectures (COV, 1990).

In addressing the threat of covert channels two major challenges have been identified. The first challenge is in developing techniques to identify covert channels in a comprehensive, systematic manner. Several covert channel analysis techniques have been proposed and utilized in recent years. Usually these techniques base their analysis either on code inspection or on inspection of the high-level specification. Among these techniques are the Non-Interference approach (Goguen and Mesequer, 1982), the Shared Resource Matrix (SRM) methodology (Kemmerer, 1983), and Information Flow analysis (Denning, 1976). The second, and more difficult challenge, is in removing the channels, or at least lowering their bandwidths, without rendering the system unacceptably slow or restrictive. Hu (1991) and Karger and Wray (1991) provide excellent examples of how this second covert channel challenge is being met.

Prior to the 1980s the covert channel analysis that took place was mostly *ad hoc.* The SRM approach, which was introduced in the early 1980s did not aid in the analysis of covert channels, but rather gave a form for describing what attributes might be used for signaling information. More importantly, it identified those attributes that could not be used. This gave the analyst more time to concentrate on those that could be used.

In the mid 1980s some researchers began applying the non-interference approach to systems. With this approach the failed proofs of the unwinding theorems should have lead the analyst to the flows to consider, but like the SRM it too did not aid the analyst in the actual analysis. With both the SRM and the non-interference approaches the analyst had to come up with the signaling sequences and determine whether they could be used as covert channels (Haigh and co-workers, 1987).

A more recent approach called the Covert Flow Tree (CFT) approach (Kemmerer and Porras, 1991) uses tree data structures to model the flow of information from one shared attribute to another. The CFTs are then used to perform systematic searches for operation sequences that allow information to be relayed through attributes and eventually detected by a listening process. When traversed, the paths of a CFT yield a comprehensive list of operation sequences that support communication via a particular resource attribute. These operation sequences are then analyzed and either discharged as benign or determined to be covert communication channels. That is, the analyst with his/her experience is still the one that makes the determination.

Intrusion Detection and Prevention

Over the past decade, significant progress has been made toward the improvement of computer system security. Unfortunately, the undeniable reality remains that all computers are vulnerable to compromise. Even the most secure systems built today are vulnerable to authorized users who abuse their privileges. Given this reality, the need for user accountability is very important. Accountability is key, both as a deterrent and for terminating abusive computer usage once it is discovered. In addition, the need to maintain a record of the transactions that have occurred on a system is crucial for performing damage assessment. In recognition of these needs and in recognition that security violations are a fact of life for computers, many systems implement a form of transaction record-keeping called *audit collection.* The data collected is called an *audit log.*

Although the audit logs normally contain enough information to determine that a computer abuse has occurred, the amount of data collected is so voluminous that manual audit data analysis is impractical. By introducing automated audit data analysis tools, referred to as *intrusion detection systems,* security violations that might have once gone unnoticed can be identified. In addition, when intrusion detection is performed in real-time it can use the audit data to track a user's behavior and to determine if the user's current actions represent a threat to security. If they do, the system can halt the user's actions.

Within the past five years, there has been a steadily growing interest in the research and development of intrusion detection systems. Surveys of implemented intrusion detection systems, many of which are in operation today, can be found in (Lunt (1988), McAuliffe and co-workers (1990) and Neumann (1990). This section briefly reviews the current approaches to intrusion detection.

Statistical Anomaly Detection. One of the most prevalent approaches used in the development of intrusion detection systems involves the use of statistical analyses to measure variations in the volume and type of audit data produced on a system. The statistical analysis of audit data can be applied to individual user audit trails or applied to all of the target system's audit records as a whole. There are 2 techniques for intrusion detection involving statistical anomaly detection: *threshold detection* and *profile-based anomaly detection.*

The idea of threshold detection is to record each occurrence of a specific event and, as the name implies, detect when the number of occurrences of that event surpass a reasonable amount that one might expect to occur during normal system operation. The event is such that an unnaturally high number of occurrences within a short period of time may indicate the presence of an intruder.

Profile-based anomaly detection uses statistical measures to identify intrusions by monitoring a system's audit logs for usage that deviates from established patterns of usage. These can be applied at the user, group, remote host and target system levels. The main advantage of anomaly detection is that it provides a means of detecting intrusions, without *a priori* knowledge of the security flaws in the target system. The IDES system uses a profile-based anomaly detection component and a rule-based component for identifying known penetrations (Lunt, 1990).

Rule-Based Anomaly Detection. Rule-based anomaly detection is like statistical anomaly detection except that rather than using statistical formulas to identify usage patterns in audit data, rule-based anomaly detectors use sets of rules to represent and store suspect usage patterns. "These rules are then used to pattern match sequences of audit records to the expected audit trails of known penetrations. An example intrusion detection implementation that employs rule-based anomaly detection is Wisdom and Sense (W&S) (Vaccaro and Liepins, 1989).

Rule-Based Penetration Identification. A rule-based penetration identification system is an expert system whose rules fire when audit records are parsed that appear to indicate suspicious, if not illegal, user activity. The rules may recognize single audited events that represent significant danger to the system by themselves, or they may recognize sequences of events that represent an entire penetration scenario.

Rule-based penetration identifiers have become a common supplemental component of intrusion detection systems that employ other approaches. For example, intrusion detection systems that employ anomaly detectors often supplement their detection capabilities with expert rules for identifying known penetration. The expert rules offer the additional capability of identifying dubious behavior, even when the behavior appears to conform with established patterns of use. Examples of intrusion detection implementations that supplement their anomaly detection components with expert penetration rules include IDES and W&S. Unlike anomaly detection systems, the rulebase of a penetration identifier is very machine specific.

Intrusion Prevention. Efforts to develop practical tools for preventing intrusions are also available. One notable prevention tool is the Computer Oracle Password and Security System (COPS), developed by Farmer and Spafford (1990). COPS is designed to aid UNIX system administrators in testing their configurations for common weaknesses often exploited by intruders. COPS is a collection of shell scripts and programs that search out and identify a myriad of security holes (e.g., writable system files) commonly present on UNIX systems.

Essentially, no intrusion detection approach stands alone as a catch-all for computer penetrations. Instead, each approach is technically suited to identify a subset of the security violations to which a computer system is subject. Accordingly, intrusion detection system designers often implement multiple approaches within a single intrusion detection system.

Evaluation Criteria

This section presents the various national and international efforts to develop computer security evaluation criteria.

United States. The National Computer Security Center's "Department of Defense Trusted Computer System Evaluation Criteria," which was released in 1983, was the first national computer security evaluation criteria. This criteria is usually referred to as the "orange book" or the "TCSEC." The TCSEC was intended for evaluating operating systems, and it deals primarily with nondisclosure. The TCSEC is based on 6 fundamental security requirements (DoD, 1983). They are

Security Policy—There must be an explicit and well-defined security policy enforced by the system.

Marking—Access control labels must be associated with objects.

Identification—Individual subjects must be identified.

Accountability—Audit information must be selectively kept and protected so that actions affecting security can be traced to the responsible party.

Assurance—The computer system must contain hardware/software mechanisms that can be independently evaluated to provide sufficient assurance that the system enforces the four requirements above.

Continuous Protection—The trusted mechanisms that enforce these basic requirements must be continuously protected against tampering and/or unauthorized changes.

The TCSEC is structured into 4 divisions, each representing a major improvement in the overall confidence that one can have in the system. Sometimes this improvement is the result of additional functionality and sometimes it is the result of more assurance. The 4 divisions are A, B, C, and D, with A being the most secure. Some of the divisions are further divided into classes. Each higher class has the function and assurance requirements of all of the classes below it.

The lowest division is division D. Systems that have been evaluated to be in this division fail to meet even the minimum requirements of the higher classes. Note that this is different than not having been evaluated. These systems have been evaluated and it has been determined that they provide virtually no security.

Division C provides discretionary access control and is intended for systems that are dealing with a single level of sensitivity. This division contains 2 classes, C1 and C2. Systems that meet the C1 requirements have user authentication and have been functionally tested for assurance. For class C2, a login procedure, auditing of security-relevant events and resource isolation are required.

Division B deals with multilevel security and provides mandatory protection. There are three classes in this division, B1, B2, and B3. Class B1 requires an informal statement of the security policy, internal labels for data, and mandatory access control. In addition, there needs to be an identifiable security perimeter and the capability to label exported data. Penetration tests are required at this level. For class B2 one needs a formal security policy, labels for everything, and a trusted path for authentication. In addition, the system must be structured into protection critical and protection non-critical components. For assurance, configuration management and covert channel identification are required at this level. Class B3 requires a reference monitor architecture, a security administrator and recovery procedures.

Division A contains a single class, A1. This class is functionally equivalent to class B3, but requires a higher level of assurance. For a system to be rated at A1 there needs to be a formal model, a formal top level specification (FTLS), and formal model to FTLS consistency proofs must be carried out. In addition, an informal FTLS to code consistency proof and formal covert channel analysis are required. A "beyond A1" class, which would require formal FTLS to code consistency proofs is sometimes discussed.

A perceived problem with the TCSEC is the tight coupling between functionality and assurance. That is, to get a system evaluated for increased functionality the system also needs to undergo increased assurance. Thus, one can not get a system with lots of functionality and minimal assurance evaluated. Similarly, a system with minimum functionality, but with a high degree of assurance can not be evaluated. Another problem with the TCSEC is that it deals almost exclusively with confidentiality; integrity and availability are not addressed in depth. A third problem with the TCSEC is that because it was developed for standalone operating systems, it does not deal with distributed systems or communication security.

The National Computer Security Center noted the shortcomings of the TCSEC and, in response, produced a number of additional documents for extending the TCSEC to deal with systems other than standalone operating systems. Most notable of these are the Trusted Network Interpretation (NCS, 1987) and the Trusted Database Management System Interpretation (NCS, 1991).

More recently, a joint program between NIST and NSA, called the Federal Criteria (FC) project, is attempting to broaden the scope of the TCSEC. The first draft of the FC (FC, 1992) was circulated for review in December of 1992. The final FC document, which was supposed to replace the TCSEC, was to be a Federal Information Processing Standard (FIPS) intended primarily for use by the U.S. Federal government. However, while the FC was still in its first draft NIST and NSA decided to work on a Common Criteria with the Europeans and Canadians.

Germany. The West German criteria, "Criteria for the Evaluation of Trustworthiness of Information Technology (IT) Systems," was released in 1989 by the German Information Security Agency (ZSI, 1989). This criteria considered 8 basic security functions: identification and authentication, administration of rights, verification of rights, audit, object reuse, error recovery, continuity of service, and data communication security.

The German criteria unbundled function and assurance, and also considered integrity and availability, and communication security. There are 10 functional classes, F1 through F10. F1 through F5 are roughly equivalent to the functionality required for classes C1 through B3 of the TCSEC. The additional functions are

F6—System and data integrity
F7—Availability
F8—Communication data integrity
F9—Communication functionality
F10—Network security.

There are also 8 assurance levels Q0 through Q7. These assurance levels are roughly equivalent to the assurance required for classes D through A1 of the TCSEC. With this approach a vendor can develop a system with differing levels of functionality and assurance, such as a system that is rated F2Q7 or F5678Q1. That is, the assurance and functionality are completely independent.

British. The criteria of the British Commercial Computer Security Centre (CCSC) was also released in 1989 and also separates functionality and assurance (DTI, 1989). This criteria distinguished between security controls and security objectives. *Security controls* have been identified as prerequisites that are enforceable. The criteria defined six security controls:

X1—Accountability
X2—Authentication
X3—Permission
X4—Object protection
X5—Object reuse
X6—No repudiation

The *security objectives,* in contrast, are prerequisites that are not enforceable, and five are identified:

Y1—No addition
Y2—No loss
Y3—Confinement
Y4—Timeliness
Y5—No denial of resources

The most interesting part of the British criteria is the "claims language," which consists of action phrases and target phrases. A vendor can combine the action and target phrases to make claims, which must be validated, about the product to be evaluated. As an example consider the following action phrase:

This *product* can (not) determine ... (using the mechanism described in paragraph *n* of this document).

and the following target phrase:

...the identity of an *object* to which *access-type* was requested.

which can yield the following claim:

This *add-in security board* can determine the identity of *any file* to which *write* or *delete permission* was requested.

The British criteria has six evaluation levels:

L1—Product is treated as a black box
L2—High level design is examined
L3—Module specifications are examined
L4—Module designs and source code are examined
L5—Module interrelationships are examined
L6—Formal methods are required

The evaluation process proceeds as follows. The vendor identifies a product and defines claims about the product using the claims language. The vendor next selects a commercially licensed evaluation facility (CLEF) and the CLEF evaluates the product against its claims. The vendor then applies to the certification body for certification of the product. The certification body considers the evaluation report, and if it is satisfactory a certificate and license for the product are issued.

Harmonized Effort

France, Germany, the Netherlands, and the United Kingdom joined together to produce an international set of computer security evaluation criteria, which was released in 1990 (ITS, 1990). This document, called the "Information Technology Security Evaluation Criteria" (ITSEC), is a "harmonized" effort between the countries involved. The ITSEC is primarily a combination of the evaluation classes contained in the German criteria and the claims language from the British criteria.

Common Criteria

In 1993 the governments of North America and European nations agreed to develop a common criteria to be called the "Common Information Technology Security Criteria" (CC). A Common Criteria Editorial Board (CCEB) was also created with members from Canada, France, Germany, the United Kingdom and the United States. The CCEB was tasked with aligning the TCSEC, ITSEC and the CTCPEC.

Computer Security and Software Engineering

The key difference between secure software and other high quality software is that secure systems have to be able to withstand active attacks by potential penetrators. When developing any reliable software one must try to minimize the faults in the system and assure that accidental abnormal user actions or abnormal external events do not result in undesired events. When developing a secure system the developers must also assure that intentional abnormal actions cannot compromise the system. That is, secure systems must be able to avoid problems caused by malicious users with unlimited resources.

Because security is a system requirement just like performance, capability, and cost, it must be designed in from the beginning and must not be added on after-the-fact. In addition, because security is only one of many goals for a system, it may be necessary to trade off certain security requirements to achieve other goals.

When designers first start thinking about developing secure systems they often think that it would be beneficial to keep the system design secret. However, the security community had realized many years ago that the benefits of an open design far outweigh any advantages of keeping the design hidden from would be intruders. The *open design principle* (Saltzer and Schroeder, 1975) states that "the mechanism should not depend on the ignorance of potential attackers..." By having peer reviews of the design of a secure system, security weaknesses in the system are often discovered during the design phase. It is always better to have a colleague find a weakness during the design phase rather than having it discovered through a compromise after the system has been fielded.

The main difference between secure systems and other high quality systems is that secure systems are subject to malicious attack; therefore, it should be no surprise that a primary difference in developing secure systems is the need for additional testing and for a somewhat different form of testing. Penetration analysis is a form of testing. However, unlike standard testing techniques where a tester's primary task is to demonstrate that the program gives the correct result when presented with varying inputs, with penetration analysis the system is either given input that is not expected to give a good result or given operations that are executed in an unexpected sequence. Thus, instead of concentrating on showing that the system gives the expected result when used properly, the testing concentrates on demonstrating that the system gives an undesired result when used improperly. Thus, the test cases concentrate more on trying the unusual or the unexpected.

Finally, because the need for a high level of assurance was recognized by the security community many years ago, the use of formal methods is more prevalent in the design and analysis of secure systems than in most other software development areas. All of the national and international evaluation criteria specify the need for the use of formal methods to achieve added assurance.

FUTURE TRENDS

Advances in computer security in the next decade will be in the areas of computer networks, privacy issues, trusted systems, and education. As computers are becoming more prevalent and are linked together on world-wide networks, there is more concern about network security. In addition, as more personal data is being kept in databases, there is a growing concern about the security of that data. Also, with the increased use of computers in life-critical systems there is the broadening of the concerns of security to include safety and dependability. Finally, there are not enough qualified computer security personnel to handle the technical problems that arise. Each of these issues is discussed in more detail in the following paragraphs.

Network Security. As more applications are distributed and the use of networking increases, there is also an increased need for network security. Because networks can be viewed as systems, they have most of the same problems that have been discussed for computer security, such as authentication, access control, and availability. However, these problems become more complex as the application becomes distributed. For instance, spoofing across the network is harder to foil, because it deals with "mutually suspicious subsystems." That is, the remote system or server needs to authenticate that the user that is logging on or requesting resources is who he/she claims to be. However, the user also needs to verify that he/she is connected to the correct system, even though that system may be thousands of miles away. With networked systems there is also an increase in the number of points of attack. In 1988 a National Research Council study raised concern about the present state of network security (NRC, 1989).

Currently most messages on networks, like the Internet, are unencrypted. However, in the future, as more sensitive data is transmitted over these networks, more encryption will be needed. When considering a secure network that uses encryption to achieve its security, one must consider both encryption algorithms and encryption protocols. An *encryption algorithm,* such as DES or RSA, is used to convert clear text into cipher text or cipher text into clear text. That is, the unencrypted message (clear text) is enciphered using a particular encryption algorithm to produce the unreadable cipher text. Similarly, the same or a symmetric algorithm is used to recover the original clear text message from the encrypted cipher text. An *encryption protocol* is a set of rules or procedures for using the encryption algorithm to send and receive messages in a secure manner over a network. Recently there has been an interest in encryption protocols, and a number of protocols have been shown to be insecure. This interest is expected to increase in the next decade.

NCSC's Trusted Network Interpretation (TNI) extended the TCSEC to deal with networks (NCS, 1987). The TNI introduces two ways of viewing a secure network. The first view is the *Interconnected Accredited AIS View.* The assumption is that it is not practical to accredit the total system using the TCSEC, and the approach of accrediting individual parts for specific operational sensitivity ranges is adopted. When using this approach two accredited AIS devices may communicate at a range no greater than the intersection of their respective ranges. The second view is the *Single Trusted System View.* A common level of trust is exhibited throughout a single trusted system. "It is accredited as a single entity by a single accrediting authority." The single trusted system implements a reference monitor and has a trusted computing base (referred to as the Network Trusted Computer Base or NTCB). When using this approach, the sum of the component security policies must be shown to enforce the overall network security policy. Therefore, the network design must completely and unambiguously define the security functionality of components as well as between components. In addition, for accreditation the network architecture must demonstrate the linkage between the "connection-oriented abstraction" and its realization in the individual components. The problem is that the TNI is devoted almost exclusively to the single system view, while most secure networks are not built as a single system, but rather as interconnected components. In the coming decade more attention will be given to the interconnected trusted component approach.

Privacy Concerns

As computers and particularly databases are being used by most large corporations and government agencies to store and retrieve information on individuals, there is an increasing need to protect that data. Because these systems contain sensitive information on individuals, such as medical and financial records, if one of these systems is compromised, an individual may be harmed even though it is not that individual's computer. As a result, there is likely to be an increased concern for the privacy rights of individuals in the next decade.

In the coming decade one can also expect to see new legislation for the handling of data sensitive to an individual's privacy. The trend of computer security, which has moved from exclusively defense oriented into a defense and commercial domain, is likely to concentrate more on privacy issues than has been the case in the past.

Trusted Systems

As computers are being embedded in more safety critical systems, such as nuclear reactors, power control plants, aircraft auto-pilots, aircraft collision avoidance systems, and medical instruments, there is a need to expand the purview of computer security to a broader "trusted systems" view. This broadening is already taking place and the trend will continue. The new view of trusted systems will be systems that are secure, safe, and dependable.

Another concern with the use of computers in safety-critical systems is that terrorists may start attacking these systems. The AT&T long distance network failure in 1989 is evidence of the vulnerability of some of these supposedly dependable systems.

Computer Security Education

Currently there is a shortage of individuals who are trained in designing, building, and managing secure systems. The National Research Council's System Security Study Committee also identified the lack of university-based research in their 1991 report (NRC, 1991). Although activity in this area has increased in the last few years, more is still needed, and the need will increase over the next decade.

One suggestion is to introduce security awareness training as part of the initial introduction to computers. Computer security should be introduced in the elementary schools where students are currently learning how to use computers. The security awareness at this level is likely to be more successful if introduced as an awareness of the possibility of accidental loss of data or programs. Students should realize that they may lose their data due to a hardware failure or another student inadvertently destroying their data. The students should also be made aware of the ethics of the situation. They should know that destroying someone else's data is not a joke, but should be taken seriously. In the more advanced grades (e.g., middle school and high school) computer modules should include the possibility of malicious destruction of data. The students again should be made aware of the possibility and should know that doing this is unethical. They should also be made aware that copying someone else's programs, etc., without their permission, is like plagiarizing their work or like cheating on a test.

At the college level, modules to be included in the undergraduate courses already exist although they may not be taught due to the lack of qualified instructors. In June 1987, the NCSC had a workshop to create modules for this purpose. The result was the design of computer security modules for the following courses: basic concepts course, operating systems, database, software engineering (formal specification and verification and risk analysis), and networks. These modules are available as Institute of Defense Analysis Reports (IDA, 1987). The SEI also has a document on computer security modules. These modules should be included in all undergraduate computer science curriculum.

Finally, as a short-term solution, government and industry need to invest in training their personnel in computer security. As these organizations are made aware of the vulnerabilities of their systems they will be more willing to educate project members in the techniques needed for building, maintaining and managing secure systems. Eventually funding for this training will begin to show up as line items in project budgets.

BIBLIOGRAPHY

J. P. Anderson and co-workers, "Computer Security Technology Planning Study," *Deputy for Command and Management Systems, HQ Electronic Systems Division (AFSC),* Vol. 1, 1972, ESD-TR-73-51.

The Canadian Trusted Computer Products Evaluation Criteria, Version 3.0e, Canadian System Secutiry Centre, Jan. 1993.

D. E. Denning, "A Lattice Model of Secure Information Flow," *Communications of the ACM,* **19**(5), 236–243 (May 1976).

D. E. Denning, *Cryptography and Data Security,* Addison-Wesley Publishing Co., Inc., Reading, Mass., 1982.

Department of Defense Trusted Computer System Evaluation Criteria, Computer Security Center Standard, CSC-STD-001-83, Dec., 1983, released as a DoD standard, DOD 5200.28-STD.

DTI Commercial Computer Security Centre, *Overview of Documentation,* Vol. 1, version 3.0, Feb. 1989.

D. Farmer and E. H. Spafford, "The COPS Security Checker System," *Proceedings of the Summer 1990 Usenix Conference,* Anaheim, Calif., June, 1990.

Federal Criteria for Information Technology Security, Draft, **1,** National Institute of Standards and Technology and the National Security Agency, Dec. 1992.

L. Fraim, "Scomp: A Solution to the Multilevel Security Problem," *Computer,* **16**(7), 26–34 (July 1983).

B. D. Gold, R. R. Linde, R. J. Peeler, M. Schaefer, J. F. Scheid, and P. D. Ward, "A Security Retrofit of VM/370," *Proceedings of the National Computer Conference,* Vol. 48, AFIPS Press, Montvale, N.J., 1979.

J. Goguen, J. and J. Meseguer, "Security Policies and Security Models," *Proceedings 1982 Symp. Security and Privacy,* Oakland, Calif., IEEE, New York, pp. 11–20, April 1982.

J. Guttag, E. Horowitz, and D. Musser, "Abstract Data Types and Software Validation," *Communications of the ACM,* **21**(12), 1048–1064 (Dec. 1978).

J. T. Haigh, R. A. Kemmerer, J. McHugh, and W. D. Young, "An Experience Using Two Covert Channel Analysis Techniques on a Real System Design," *IEEE Transactions on Software Engineering,* **SE-13**(2) (Feb. 1987).

B. Hebbard and co-workers, "A Penetration Analysis of the Michigan Terminal System," *ACM Operating Systems Review,* **14**(1) (Jan. 1980).

C. A. R. Hoare, "Proof of Correctness of Data Representations," *Acta Informatica,* **1,** 271–281 (1972).

W. M. Hu, "Reducing Timing Channels with Fuzzy Time," *Proceedings of the 1991 Symposium on Research in Security and Privacy,* Oakland, Calif., May, 1991.

Minutes of the First Workshop on Covert Channel Analysis, *IEEE Cipher,* Los Angeles, Calif., July, 1990.

Institute for Defense Analysis memorandum reports, M-379 through M-384, IDA, Alexandria, Va., Oct. 1987.

Information Technology Security Evaluation Criteria" (ITSEC), Netherlands National Comsec Agency, Hague, The Netherlands, May, 1990.

P. A. Karger and J. C. Wray, "Storage Channels in Disk Arm Optimization," *Proceedings of the 1991 Symposium on Research in Security and Privacy,* Oakland, Calif., May, 1991.

R. A. Kemmerer, "Shared Resource Matrix Methodology: An Approach to Identifying Storage and Timing Channels," *ACM Transactions on Computer Systems,* **1**(3), (Aug. 1983).

R. A. Kemmerer, "Integrating Formal Methods into the Development Process," *IEEE Software,* 37–50 (Sept., 1990).

R. A. Kemmerer and P. A. Porras, "Covert Flow Trees: A Visual Approach to Analyzing Covert Storage Channels," *IEEE Transactions on Software Engineering,* **17**(11), 1166–1185 (Nov. 1991).

B. W. Lampson, "A Note on the Confinement Problem," *Communications of the ACM,* **16,** 613–615 (Oct. 1973).

R. R. Linde, "Operating System Penetration," *Proceedings of National Computer Conference,* Vol 44, AFIPS Press, Montvale, N.J., 1975.

S. B. Lipner, "A Comment on the Confinement Problem," *Proceedings of the Fifth Symposium on Operating Systems Principles,* The University of Texas at Austin, Nov., 1975.

T. F. Lunt, "Automated Audit Trail Analysis and Intrusion Detection: A Survey," *Proceedings of the 11th National Computer Security Conference,* Baltimore, Md., Oct. 1988.

T. F. Lunt, A. Tamaru, F. Gilham, R. Jagannathan, C. Jalai, H. S. Javitz, A. Valdes, and P. G. Neumann, "A Real-Time Intrusion Detection Expert System," June 1990, *SRI CSL Technical Report, SRI-CSL-90-05.*

N. J. McAuliffe, L. J. Schaefer, D. M. Wolcott, T. K. Haley, N. L. Kelem and B. S. Hubbard, "Is Your Computer Being Misused? A Survey of Current Intrusion Detection System Technology," *Proceeding of the Sixth Computer Security Applications Conference,* Dec. 1990.

E. McCauley and P. Drognowski, "KSOS: The Design of a Secure Operating System," *Proceedings of the National Computer Conference,* AFIPS Press, June 1979.

J. K. Millen, "Security Kernel Validation in Practice," *Communications of the ACM,* **19,** 243–250 (May 1976).

R. Morris and K. Thompson, "Password Security: A Case History," *Communications of the ACM,* **22**(11), (Nov. 1979).

National Computer Security Center, *Trusted Network Interpretation of the Trusted Systems Evaluation Criteria,* NCSC-TG-005, Version 1, July, 1987.

National Computer Security Center, *Trusted Database Management System Interpretation of the Trusted Systems Evaluation Criteria,* NCSC-TG-021, Version 1, April, 1991.

National Research Council, *Growing Vulnerabilty of the Public Switched Networks: Implications for National Security Emergency Preparedness,* National Academy Press, Washington, D.C., 1989.

National Research Council, *Computers at Risk: Safe Computing in the Information Age,* National Academy Press, Washington, D.C., 1991.

P. G. Neumann, "A Comparative Anatomy of Computer System/Network Anomaly Detection Systems," assembled by Peter G. Neumann, CSL, SRI BN-168, Menlo Park, Calif., May, 1990.

G. J. Popek, "Protection Structures," *Computer* (June 1974).

J. H. Saltzer and M. D. Schroeder, "The Protection of Information in Computer Systems," *Proceedings of the IEEE,* **63**(9), 1278–1308 (Sept. 1975).

M. D. Schroeder, D. Clark, J. H. Saltzer, "The MULTICS Kernel Design Project," *Proceedings of the 6th Symposium on Operating Systems Principles,* 1977.

J. M. Silverman, "Reflections on the Verification of the Security of an Operating System Kernel," *Communications of the ACM,* 1983.

H. S. Vaccaro and G. E. Liepins, "Detection of Anomalous Computer Session Activity," *Proceeding of the IEEE Symposium on Research in Security and Privacy,* Oakland, Calif., May 1989.

B. W. Walker, R. A. Kemmerer, and G. J. Popek, "Specification and Verification of the UCLA Unix Security Kernel," *Communications of the ACM,* **23,** 118–131 (Feb. 1980).

W. H. Ware, "Security Controls for Computer Systems," The Rand Corporation, classified document, Feb., 1970 reissued as an unclassified document R-609-1, Oct., 1979.

Zentralstefle fur Sicherheit in der Informationstecknik, *IT-Security Criteria: Criteria for the Evaluation of Trustworthiness of Information Technology (IT) Systems,* Koln, West Germany, 1989.

RICHARD A. KEMMERER
University of California, Santa Barbara

SEI

See SOFTWARE ENGINEERING INSTITUTE.

SHAW, MARY (1943–)

Mary Shaw has been a member of the software systems faculty at Carnegie Mellon University since 1972. From 1984 to 1987 she served as Chief Scientist of CMU's Software Engineering Institute. She was educated at Rice University and Carnegie Mellon University and previously worked in systems programming at the Research Analysis Corporation and Rice University.

Shaw works in the area of programming systems and software engineering with the objective of establishing an engineering discipline of software engineering. She has made major research contributions to software architectures (Vitruvius), abstraction techniques for software engineering (abstract data types, generic definitions), programming languages (Alphard), and software organization for human interfaces (Descartes). This work helps to establish a well-founded technical basis for software engineering. She has also innovated in software engineering and computer science education.

Shaw received the 1993 Warnier prize for contributions to software engineering. She is a Fellow of the IEEE and of the American Association for the Advancement of Science.

BIBLIOGRAPHY

M. Shaw, "The Impact of Abstraction Concerns on Modern Programming Languages," *Proceedings of the IEEE* **68**(9), 1119–1130 (Sept. 1980).

—, ed., *Alphard: Form and Content,* Springer-Verlag, 1981.

—, ed., *The Carnegie-Mellon Curriculum for Undergraduate Computer Science*, Springer-Verlag, 1985.

—"Prospects for an Engineering Discipline of Software," *IEEE Software* **7**(6), 15–24 (Nov. 1990).

—with W. A. Wulf, P. N. Hilfinger, and L. Flon, *Fundamental Structures of Computer Science,* Addison-Wesley, Reading, Mass., 1981.

SHELL

A user selectable operating system command interpreter. Usually a shell is also usable as an operating system programming language interpreter (see UNIX).

SHEN, VINCENT Y. (1945–)

Vincent Y. Shen taught at the Computer Sciences Department of Purdue University from 1969 to 1985. He also held visiting positions at National Tsing Hua University and IBM's Santa Teresa Laboratory during that period. He joined the Microelectronics and Computer Technology Corp. (MCC), a research consortium supported by 20 major computer companies, in 1985. Before he joined the Hong Kong University of Science & Technology (HKUST) as Professor and Founding Head of the Computer Science Department in 1990, he directed MCC's Software Technology Program involving about 60 staff. He is also Director of HKUST's Sino Software Research Centre.

Shen has published over 50 research papers and is coauthor of the book, *Software Engineering Metrics and Models,* published in 1986. He has served on the editorial boards of *IEEE Software, IEEE Computer,* and *IEEE Transactions on Software Engineering.*

SIMULA

Simula is a general-purpose programming language based on Algol60 to which it added the class concept providing inheritance and support for concurrency. It was designed and originally implemented at the Norwegian Computing Center in Oslo (Norway) in the mid 1960s by Ole-Johan Dahl and Kristen Nygaard. For many years the language was known as Simula67 after the year of its first definition and implementation. Both by its language features and by the approach to programming that was often taught for it, Simula introduced the currently fashionable techniques of Object-Oriented Programming. All of the so-called Object-oriented Programming languages are direct or indirect descendents of Simula. The most prominent of these are C++ and Smalltalk. Simula is generally acknowledged to have been 10 or even 20 years ahead of its time; it is one of the most innovative and influential programming languages ever.

Simula is, with one minor exception, a superset of Algol60 and on many systems Simula67 provided the best Algol60 compiler. Like Algol60, Simula provides what is now called strong static type checking; that is, no object can be used in a way inconsistent with its declaration. This is a noticeable advantage to programmers but the absence of loopholes made Simula less suitable for systems work where direct access to hardware resources was essential.

Because of its name, Simula was often unfairly characterized as a special purpose language. Lack of run-time performance for tasks that did not require Simula's sophistication also hurt it in competition with less elegant but more efficient languages such as Fortran and C. Other significant practical barriers to the spread of Simula was the high cost of its implementations (for years all implementations were supplied by or under license from the Norwegian Computing Center) and the relative large amount of work needed to port early Simula implementations to new systems.

To provide greater flexibility than is possible exclusively with static type checking, Simula also provided convenient mechanisms for run-time type identification (the QUA operator and the INSPECT statement). Unfortunately, this was widely misunderstood and misused by programmers who was not in direct contact with the core Simula community and not taught along the lines intended by its creators. Reliance on garbage collection added further convenience, at a cost that was often difficult for people to afford on the hardware of the day.

Simula was for years unique among general purpose languages in its direct support for concurrency in the form of a quasi-parallel sequencing mechanism. The Simula concurrency mechanisms supports the running of several processes within a single address space based on non-preemptive scheduling. Simula itself uses this feature for implementing its discrete-event simulation facility. The key concept of the discrete-event simulation paradigm in SIMULA is the process.

Simula comes with standard libraries for text input and output, event-driven simulation, and simple mathematics. It is an excellent language for implementing and using libraries. Because Simula was the first major language supporting user-defined types (classes) and inheritance directly, it is the first language for which this can reasonably be claimed.

Simula saw wide use in academia especially in its native Scandinavia and in Eastern Europe, but failed to come into significant use in industry and in the United States. There are still thousands of Simula users scattered across the world and no widely available programming language can rightfully claim to be better than Simula in every way. The definition of Simula is "The Simula Common Base Standard" (SS636114 Databehandling Programsprok-SIMULA) from the Swedish Standards Institute, the standard textbook for Simula was Birtwistle, Dahl, Myrhaug, and Nygaard: "SIMULA BEGIN" Studentlitteratur, Lund, Sweden, 1979, and the best source to the history of Simula is the SIMULA chapter of R. Wexelblat, ed., *History of Programming Languages*, Academic Press, 1981.

Bjarne Stroustrup
AT&T Bell Labs

SIMULATOR

A device, computer program, or system that behaves or operates like a given system when provided a set of controlled inputs (IEEE).

SMALLTALK

SOME HISTORY

The Smalltalk programming language currently available in the commercial and educational marketplace is the outcome of research dating from 1971. The original research project, carried out at the Xerox Palo Alto Research Center, was founded on the belief that computer technologies represented the key with which we could improve technology-mediated communication among people. The goal was to support both business and personal information exchange and processing needs. Project activities focused on finding new ways in which to organize information stored in a computer, and to allow end users more direct access and manipulation of this information. A number of tantalizing articles were written about Smalltalk, prior to 1981 (including the software requirements for a new programming language, the development environment in which the language would be used, and the numerous applications written by the research team). The formal details were basically unknown until the August 1981 edition of *Byte* was dedicated to Smalltalk. This issue introduced the Smalltalk approach to managing the complex information world of modern applications, to taking full advantage of new graphics and distributed computing, and to improving the ability for experts (business and personal experts) to describe their world models.

A series of books that described Smalltalk in technical detail were published in 1983–1984 (Goldberg and Robson, 1983; Goldberg, 1983; Krasner, 1984). This fully published version of the language was named Smalltalk-80, indicating the primary design date to be 1980. Smalltalk-80 was actually the third major revision of the language, having been preceded by Smalltalk-72 (Goldberg and Kay, 1976) and Smalltalk-76 (Ingalls, 1978). As part of the effort to move Smalltalk off its proprietary Xerox hardware and software base and onto commercially available microprocessors, operating systems, and window systems, a small number of changes to the language and a significant set of changes to the implementation technology and the library of reusable software components were made. These changes were aimed at creating a credible, concrete, and robust realization of the ideas that could only be presented in sheltered research form in 1981.

There are a number of commercial products that deliver programming tools and libraries for the Smalltalk-80 language. This paper documents the language and basic system components that are the *de facto* standard; it also identifies additional aspects of the commercial offering provided by the original researchers from Xerox. Notably, the approach taken by this group aimed to provide applications developers with portability across multiple industrial standards. This was accomplished by identifying usefully reusable interfaces in the following areas:

- Between Smalltalk applications and an underlying set of graphics facilities
- Between Smalltalk applications and an underlying window system
- Between the Smalltalk run-time support library and the underlying processor and operating system
- Between the Smalltalk library of classes to support user interaction and platform mechanisms, such as clipboards and dynamic data exchange.

The result of all this is that the Smalltalk-80 systems today that resulted from the original Xerox work are not bound to a single proprietary hardware and software base. Rather, they provide the applications developer with the most portability of any programming environment of comparable power.

BASIC SEMANTICS

Smalltalk (and here we will use the term "Smalltalk" to refer to the Smalltalk-80 language) is a uniformly object-oriented language. Smalltalk terminology has become synonymous with object-oriented technology. Its heritage dates to the 1960s, with the introduction of Simula-67 (Dahl and Nygaard, 1966), which first introduced the notion of classes of objects. Its heritage is also linked to that of Sketchpad (Sutherland, 1963), and other visual programming efforts, where the notion of concrete objects, manipulable on a display screen, was first introduced.

All components of the Smalltalk-80 system are represented as objects. An *object* consists of some private memory and a set of operations. The nature of an object's operations depends on the type of component it represents. Objects representing numbers compute arithmetic functions. Objects representing data structures store and retrieve information. Objects representing positions and areas answer inquiries about their relation to other positions and areas.

All processing in the language is stated in terms of sending messages to objects. A *message* is a request for an object to carry out one of its operations. A message specifies which operation is desired, but not how that operation should be carried out. Note that other object-oriented languages might refer to a message as a function call.

The *receiver*, the object to which the message is sent, determines how to carry out the requested operation. For example, addition is performed by sending a message to an object representing a number. The message specifies what number should be added to the receiver. The message does not specify how the addition will be performed; the receiver determines how to accomplish the addition. Computing is viewed as an intrinsic capability of objects that can be uniformly invoked by sending messages.

The set of messages to which an object can respond is called its *interface with the rest of the system.* The only way to interact with an object is through its interface. A crucial property of an object is that its private memory can be manipulated only by its own operations. A crucial property of messages is that they are the only way to invoke an object's operations. These properties ensure that the implementation of one object cannot depend on the internal details of other objects, only on the messages to which they respond.

Messages ensure the modularity of the system because they specify the type of operation desired, but not how that operation should be accomplished. For example, there are several representations of numerical values in the Smalltalk-80 system. Fractions, small integers, large integers, and floating point numbers are represented in different ways. They all understand the same message requesting the computation of their sum with another number, but each representation implies a different way to compute that sum. To interact with a number or any object, one need only know to what messages it responds, not how it is represented.

A *class* describes the implementation of a set of objects that all represent the same kind of component. Each class has a name that describes the type of component its instances represent. The individual objects described by a class are called its *instances.* A class describes the form of its instances' private memories and it describes how they carry out their operations. All instances of a class have the same message interface since they represent the same kind of component. The messages represent the object's public properties. An object's private properties are a set of *instance variables* that make up its private memory and a set of *methods* that describe how to carry out its operations. Each instance variable refers to one object, called its *value.* The instance variables and methods are not directly available to other objects. The instances of a class all use the same set of methods to describe their operations.

This simple explanation of the basic information representation and processing in Smalltalk highlights the basic idea of object-oriented software organization: software should be designed in units that are as autonomous as possible, should correspond to identifiable entities in the problem domain whenever possible, and should communicate through identified interfaces. This idea grows out of work on modular software design, dating back to the 1960s. What object-oriented terminology adds is the emphasis on direct mapping of problem domain concepts to software units, the idea of shared behavior and multiply instantiated state, and the focus on the interfaces between the units. The latter of these in particular makes it easy to think about systems that are configured or that grow dynamically. Smalltalk has no monopoly even on the newer concepts, but it has been a leader in the public relations necessary to get them out into the computing mainstream.

Object-oriented software organization has a natural relation to two important trends in software construction today: combinable applications and open systems. Our interpretation of the term "open systems" is simply that in order for systems to be able to grow, evolve, and combine gracefully, they should be constructed out of software with published interfaces. Functional software should be designed to be used as a component by other software, as opposed to being monolithically united with a particular interface designed for human users at a terminal.

BASIC SYNTAX

The expression syntax for describing objects and messages is quite simple, taking the form *receiver message.*

Literals describe constant objects.

numbers	42 3.14159
individual characters	$g
strings of characters	'this is a string'
symbols	#boo
arrays of other literals	#($a 'this' 435 $b)

Variable names describe accessible variables. They consist of a sequence of alphanumeric characters.

```
index, house, Model, ref12, Frog
```

Assignment of a value to a variable takes the form

```
var :=value
```

Message expressions describe messages to receivers. A unary message is a message without an argument. A keyword message is a message with one or more arguments, each argument preceded by an identifier with a trailing colon. Binary messages also have one argument, but the message name is one of a special set, consisting of one or two nonalphanumeric characters.

binary	3+4. index >=limit
unary	mouse move. frog jump. frame center
keyword	frame intersect: clippingBox. ages at: 'Joe' put: 30

Message expressions are separated by periods. Unary message expressions are parsed left to right; parentheses set precedence. For example, frame center black is understood as first sending the message center to frame, and then sending the message black to the object resulting from the first message.

Blocks represent deferred sequences of actions. A block expression consists of a sequence of expressions separated by periods and delimited by square brackets. For example,

```
[index :=index +1.
array at: index put: 0]
```

A *control structure* determines the order of some activities. The fundamental control structure in Smalltalk provides that a sequence of expressions will be evaluated sequentially. Nonsequential control structures can be implemented with blocks, and then invoked either by sending a message to a block or by sending a message with one or more blocks as arguments. The following are examples of conditionals and conditional repetitions.

Conditionals are expressed as keyword messages to objects representing true and false (instances of the class True and False respectively).

```
(number  2) =0
      ifTrue: [parity :=0]
      ifFalse: [parity :=1]
```

Repetition is expressed by a unary message to a numeric value, with a block expression as the argument.

```
4 timesRepeat: [amount :=amount+amount]
```

Conditional repetition is expressed using a unary message to a block, either whileTrue: or whileFalse:, each of which takes a block as an argument.

```
[index <=list size
   whileTrue:
      [list at: index put: 0.
      index :=index+1]
```

Blocks can have arguments and locally declared temporary variables whose scope is the block expression. A block without arguments can be evaluated by sending the unary message value. For example, the message expression

```
[i :=i+1] value
```

increments the value of i, where i is a variable known outside the block. A block with arguments is evaluated by sending the keyword message value: or value:value: (etc., depending on the number of arguments). The syntax for declaring the arguments is shown in the example, with a vertical bar separating the declaration from the sequence of message expressions.

```
[:arg1 :arg2 |
arg1 <=arg2
   ifTrue: [arg1+1]
   ifFalse: [arg2−1]] value: 10 value: 15
```

In the example, two block arguments, arg1 and arg2 , are declared. Values 10 and 15 are assigned to these block arguments as arguments of the message value:value:. The single statement within the block tests to see if arg1 is less than or equal to arg2. If so, the block returns the value of arg1+1; otherwise the block returns arg2 −1. In this case, arg1 is less than arg2 (10<15), and the block returns 11.

A *subclass* specifies that its instances will be the same as instances of another class, called its *superclass*, except for the differences that are explicitly stated. A system class named Object describes the similarities of all objects in the system, so every class will at least be a subclass of Object. A subclass inherits both the variable declaration and methods of its superclass. New variables may be declared and new methods may be added by the subclass.

classname	Frog
superclass	Object
instance variable names	frogName, ground
instance methods	

initialization
  name: aString
    frogName := aString
  pond: aStream
    ground := aStream

movement
  jump
    frogName printOn: ground
    'hop hop' printOn: ground
    ground endEntry

Figure 1. Class example.

An example class and subclass are shown in Figures 1 and 2. The example is of a Frog, a subclass of Object, and then of Toad, a subclass of Frog. Instances of Frog have two instance variables, frogName and ground; instances of Toad have three instance variables, the additional one being size. In the figure, the message interfaces are shown in bold font.

Suppose we create an instance of Frog called hopper,

```
hopper :=Frog new
```

and set the values for the two instance variables

```
hopper name: 'Mr. Hopper': hopper output: Transcript.
```

where Transcript is an object by means of which textual information may be printed on a graphical display.
Now ask the frog to jump

```
hopper jump
```

classname	Toad
superclass	Frog
instance variable names	size
instance methods	

initialization
  size: aNumber
    size := aNumber

movement
  jump
    frogName printOn: ground.
    size timesRpeat: ['jump high' printOn: aStream].
    ground endEntry

Figure 2. Subclass example.

Basic System Classes

Object

- Behavior
  - ClassDescription
    - Class
    - Metaclass
- BlockClosure
- Boolian
  - True
  - False
- ClassOrganizer
  - SystemOrganizer
- Delay
- Exception
- Message
  - MessageSend
- ProcessorScheduler
- RemoteString
- SharedQueue
- Signal
- UndefinedObject
- UninterpretedBytes

Operating System Classes

- DisplaySurface
  - UnmappableSurface
    - Mask
    - Pixmap
  - Window
    - ScheduledWindow
- ExternalConnection
  - FileConnection
- Filename
- InputState
- KeyboardEvent
- MemoryPolicy
- NameAccessor
- OSErrorHolder
  - OSHandle
    - Cursor
    - IOAccessor

Data Structure Classes--Collections

- Collection
  - Bag
  - MappedCollection
  - SequenceableCollection
    - ArrayedCollection
      - Array
        - ScannerTable
      - CharacterArray
        - String
          - GapString
          - Symbol
        - Text
      - IntegerArray
        - ByteArray
        - WordArray
      - RunArray
      - WeakArray
    - Interval
    - LinkedList
      - Semaphore
    - OrderedCollection
      - HandlerCollection
      - SortedCollection
  - Set
    - Dictionary
      - CacheDictionary
      - IdentityDictionary
        - MethodrDictionary
        - WeakDictionary
          - HandleRegistry
      - SystemDictionary
    - IdentitySet
      - SignalCollection
- Link
  - Process
- Stream
  - Random
  - PeekableStream
    - PositionableStream
      - ExternalStream
        - BufferedExternalStream
          - ExternalReadStream
            - ExternalReadAppendStream
            - ExternalReadWriteStream
          - ExternalWriteStream
      - InternalStream
        - ReadStream
        - WriteStream
          - ReadWriteStream
          - TextStream

Data Structure Classes--Magnitude

- Magnitude
  - ArithmeticValue
    - Number
      - Fraction
      - Integer
        - LargeNegativeInteger
        - LargePositiveInteger
        - SmallInteger
      - LimitedPrecisionReal
      - Double
      - Float
      - Point
  - Character
  - Date
  - LookupKey
    - Association
  - Time
  - TimeZone

Figure 3. Classes available in one commercial implementation of the system Objectworks/Smalltalk.

The result will be that the following text will print on the screen.

Mr. Hopper hop hop

Now let us create an instance of Toad called prince.

prince :=Toad new

and set the values for the two instance variables

prince name: 'His Highness'.
prince output: Transcript.
prince size: 4

All three instance variables are set with values. The methods for the first two are found in the class description for Frog, the superclass of Toad. If we send the toad the message jump, the method is found in the class description for Toad. When a message is sent, the methods in the receiver's class are searched for one with a matching message name. If none is found, the methods in that class's superclass are searched next. The search continues up the superclass chain until a matching method is found. So in the case of sending prince the unary message jump, the match is found in the class description for Toad, and the resulting screen is

His Highness jump high jump high jump high jump high

(that is, the name is printed, followed by jump high printed four times because the value of size is 4).

In the case of sending prince the initialization message name:, the search fails to find the matching messages in Toad; the search moves Frog where the search succeeds.

Graphics Classes

- CharacterAttributes
- <Collection>
  - Palette
    - ColorPalette
      - FixedPalette
      - MappedPalette
        - MonoMappedPalette
    - CoveragePalette
- DispatchTable
- DitherUpTo4
- FontDescription
- Graphic
- ImageRenderer
  - ErrorDiffusion
  - PaintRenderer
    - NearestPaint
    - OrderedDither
- Paint
  - Pattern
  - SimplePaint
    - ColorValue
    - CoverageValue
- PaintPolicy
  - LuminanceBasedColorPolicy
- RasterOp
- Rectangle
- Screen
- TextAttributes
- TextMeasurer
  - CharacterScanner
    - CharacterBlockScanner
    - CompositionScanner
    - DisplayScanner

Interface/Tools Classes

- VisualComponent
  - CachedImage
  - Icon
  - Image
  - OpaqueImage
  - TextLines
    - ComposedText
    - TextList
  - VisualPart
    - CompositePart
      - DependentComposite
        - BrowserView
        - CompositeView
          - DialogView
      - InspectorView
    - DependentPart
      - View
        - BooleanWidgetView
          - LabeledBooleanView
        - FractionalWidgetView
        - LauncherView
        - NotifierView
        - ScrollerView
          - ScrollingLinesView
            - ComposedTextView
              - StringHolderView
                - TextCollectorView
              - TextView
                - CodeView
            - ListView
              - ChangeListView
              - SelectionInListView
    - Wrapper
      - TranslatingWrapper
        - BoundedWrapper
          - BorderedWrapper
            - EdgeWidgetWrapper

- Border
- Controller
  - ControllerWithMenu
    - ListController
      - ChangeListController
      - SelectionInListController
    - NotifierController
    - ParagraphEditor
      - StringHolderContr
      - TextController
        - CodeController
        - TextItemEditor
    - StandardSystemController
      - DialogController
  - DialogCompositeController
  - LauncherController
  - NoController
  - WidgetController
- ControlManager
- InputSensor
  - TranslatingSensor
  - WindowSensor
- LayoutFrame
- LookPreferences
- MenuTracker
- Model
  - Browser
    - Debugger
    - MethodListBrowse
  - Explainer
  - FileBrowser
  - Inspector
    - ContextInspector
    - DictionaryInspector
    - SequenceableCollectionInspector
      - OrderedCollectionInspector
  - PopUpMenu
    - ActionMenu
  - StringHolder
    - ChangeList
    - Project
    - TextCollector
    - TextHolder
  - SyntaxError
  - ValueModel
    - PluggableAdaptor
      - ValueHolder

Figure 3. *(Continued).*

THE SMALLTALK DEVELOPMENT ENVIRONMENT: SYSTEM CLASSES AND TOOLS

The Smalltalk-80 system includes a set of classes that provides the standard functionality of a programming language and environment: arithmetic, data structures, control structures, and input/output facilities. Figure 3 lists the classes available in one commercial implementation of the system, Objectworks/Smalltalk, as an illustration of a rich library of reusable components. The class names in this figure are shown in an indented list form to indicate a hierarchical relationship.

A comprehensive programming environment for an object-oriented language like Smalltalk consists of a wide range of software tools. The editors for quick change and extension of existing capability include source code browsers, flexible system cross-referencing and annotation tools, and a history/change management tool. A source language debugger supports the programmer in analyzing and modifying the runtime behavior of an object, while inspectors permit analysis and change of an object's static state. As part of the analysis, it is possible to ask for a semantic explanation for any part of a message expression (i.e., for any token) and to find uses and implementations for any object referenced in a message expression. The capability of a source code browser includes the ability to obtain a view of the class hierarchy for any class, to locate any class or message implemented in the class, and to request access to all methods that refer to a particular class or message and to all implementations and uses for any message.

In addition to the tools directly associated with the creation, modification, and testing of class definitions, the programming environment supports workspaces for simple text editing and graphical drawing, and tools to access the underlying file system and to edit, read, and write files. Using modern workstations with graphical display screens, the typical Smalltalk programming environment makes extensive use of mouse-driven input techniques. These include windows in which the different tools appear, menus or lists of items from which the user selects tool options, scroll bars, and other iconic approaches by which the human user sends messages to the system.

SOFTWARE ENGINEERING IMPACT

The Smalltalk object model described here, with its emphasis on modularity in terms of defining objects, and on programming by refining existing class descriptions, has encouraged a growth in studies on object-oriented analysis and design (Booch, 1991; Meyer, 1988; Rumbaugh, 1991), object-oriented project management, and a renewed interest in the economics of reusing software components or objects. In an object-oriented environment where inheritance is supported, it is not only individual components that are combined. The design of interfaces between objects is often more important than the implementation of functions within objects.

Many people expect that this emphasis on specifying clear software interfaces will encourage a market for software componentry, much like the one that exists for hardware parts (Cox, 1988). However, from our experience with many developers and users of Smalltalk systems in many different environments, we think the key economic shift will be in a different area. A public market is a very loosely organized environment. Objects placed in a market will face a very wide variety of different demands, and even well-designed object definitions, with minimally constrained interfaces, will have trouble attracting a critical mass of customers. On the other hand, within a single organization, reusable objects can be developed and redesigned within a context that can span a large fraction of their intended uses. In this way, the accumulation of reusable code can become an important business asset, and can be treated (as we believe is appropriate) as an investment and a capital good, rather than (as at present) simply a cost.

BIBLIOGRAPHY

G. Booch, *Object-Oriented Design,* Benjamin-Cummings, Redwood City, Calif., 1991.

B. Cox, *Object-Oriented Programming,* Addison-Wesley Publishing Co., Reading, Mass., 1986.

O.-J. Dahl and K. Nygaard, "SIMULA—an ALGOL-Based Simulation Language," *CACM* **IX,** 671–678 (1966).

A. Goldberg, *Smalltalk-80: The Interactive Programming Environment,* Addison-Wesley Publishing Co., Reading, Mass., 1983.

A. Goldberg and A. Kay, eds., *Smalltalk-72 Instruction Manual,* Technical Report #SSL-76, Xerox Palo Alto Research Center, Calif., 1976.

A. Goldberg and D. Robson, *Smalltalk-80: The Language,* Addison-Wesley Publishing Co., Reading, Mass., 1989.

D. H. H. Ingalls, "The Smalltalk-76 Programming System: Design and Implementation," *Proceedings of the 5th ACM Symposium on the Principles of Programming Languages,* 1978, pp. 9–16.

G. Krasner, ed., *Smalltalk-80: Bits of History, Words of Advice,* Addison-Wesley Publishing Co., Reading, Mass., 1984.

B. Meyer, *Object-Oriented Software Construction,* Prentice-Hall, Hertfordshire, UK, 1988.

J. Rumbaugh, M. Blaha, W. Premerlani, F. Eddy, and W. Lorensen, *Object-Oriented Modeling and Design,* Prentice-Hall Publishers, Englewood Cliffs, N. J., 1991.

I. Sutherland, "Sketchpad, a Man-Machine Graphical Communication System," *Proceedings of the AFIPS Conference,* 1963, pp. 329–346.

Adele Goldberg
L. Peter Deutsch
ParcPlace Systems

SOFTWARE DEVELOPMENT ENVIRONMENT

See CASE; Software engineering environments.

SOFTWARE DEVELOPMENT FILE

INTRODUCTION

The software development file is an outgrowth of the software development folder concept (see Software development folder). It is a more generic descriptor for the software development folder.

HISTORICAL PERSPECTIVE

The term software development file was introduced with the advent of DOD-STD-2167. The practice employed by many companies at that time was to implement the software development folder concept as a "paper and pencil" exercise, utilizing three-ring borders to maintain its contents. Some of the larger companies had developed their own automated software development folder tools, using, file management techniques combined with a library management tool.

Some of the earlier review drafts of DOD-STD-2167, identified as DOD-STD-SDS, had referred to the practice as the use of software development folders. To many of the reviewers of these review drafts, software development folder sounded too much like a requirement for a three-ring binder, and they felt that the requirement could be interpreted as precluding the use of automated means for generating and maintaining the content. Consequently, the term *software development file* was coined.

Commercially available software development file tools are quite scarce. For the most part, those tools that have been developed were produced by various defense contractors for their own in-house use. Virtually none of these companies have attempted to market these tools commercially. With the advent of the F-22 fighter aircraft program, however, there was a necessity to establish a common aerospace software development environment. More than 200 different Computer Software Configuration Items (CSCIs) comprise the software to be developed (a CSCI is, effectively, an application program). With three major airframe manufacturers teamed together as the prime team, and a much greater number of second-tier contractors supporting the effort, all of whom are developing the software for the aircraft, the problem of system integration becomes more acute. The necessity became accordingly greater for a common development environment to be utilized by all the contractors developing software. Digital Equipment Corporation was given the contract to develop the common environment (known as the ASD/SEE), and produced a tool for automating the production of the software development file. Both the environment and the software development file tool are being marketed commercially (Dec, 1992).

CURRENT PRACTICES

Software development files are not in general use within the industry. By and large, this practice is implemented almost exclusively by defense contractors. This practice has become wide-spread throughout the defense industry because of the requirements specified by DOD-STD-2167 and DOD-STD-2167A (DOD, 1985, 1988).

Very few organizations developing software for nondefense applications utilize the practice. In fact, very few such organizations are even aware of the practice or how it might be of help to them.

FUTURE DIRECTIONS

The use of software development files will continue to grow within the defense industry. With the file management and library management tools available today, the means for creating customized automated software development files exists. The trend toward the automated software development folder (software development file) will continue.

The use of software development files within the nondefense community should also start to grow. This concept has been presented at a number of public seminars. The attendees, many of whom are professionals in the nondefense software development community, frequently comment on the utility and importance of the concept. If this is any indication, the use of the software development file will grow in the nondefense community.

BIBLIOGRAPHY

DEC ASD/SEE Toolkit for VMS, Version 2.0, Software Product Description 37.09.03, Digital Equipment Corporation, Feb. 1992.

DOD-STD-2167A, Defense System Software Development, U.S. Department of Defense, Washington, D.C., Feb. 1988.

DOD-STD-2167, Defense System Software Development, U.S. Department of Defense, Washington, D.C., June 4, 1985.

EMANUEL BAKER
Software Engineering Consultants, Inc.

SOFTWARE DEVELOPMENT FOLDER

HISTORICAL PERSPECTIVE

The use of software development folders began at TRW in the early 1970s on a project known as the Site Defense Program. This program began as a development effort for a tactical anti-ballistic missile system. The system was effectively an unmanned one and relied quite heavily on software for all the mission functions. Development of the software for the system involved a staff of several hundred people. With such a major software development effort, management of that effort became an important consideration. There were considerations of management visibility into the effort, support for the production of massive amounts of design documentation, and support for the maintenance of the software that entered into the picture. Many innovations in managing software development were introduced during this effort. One of these innovations was the Unit Development Folder (UDF), which is a particular form of a development notebook.

The UDF concept was applied because of what was commonly referred to as "the 90% complete syndrome" (Ingrassia, 1978). Any time a developer was asked about the development status of the unit of software that he or she was responsible for, the answer was, generally, "I am about 90% done." This answer was often based on pure supposition (or a desire to have the questioner simply go away), and typically referred only to the coding effort. Related activities, such as unit test planning or documenting the design, generally did not enter into the estimate. What was needed was a method for tying together unit development schedules, milestones, and the products of that effort in a highly visible form. The UDF was such a device.

The UDF was intended as an informal document, i.e., it was not intended to be a deliverable document to the customer. The intent was for it to be a tool that the developer could use to maintain a current status of the development of a unit of software. A UDF was generally organized around a single compilable or assembleable unit of software (a unit was typically limited in size in a range from 50 to 300 lines of executable source code). Groundrules were also established to permit more than one unit per UDF; for example, the units had to be logically related, developed by the same developer, etc. The content of the UDF was organized in a way that it provided all the information necessary to evolve the design for the unit from the requirements allocated to it, to code it, and to test it (Ingrassia, 1976). The format for the content of the design section was structured such that it and the source code listings contained in the UDF could migrate in toto into the deliverable design documentation for the entire application under development. The cover pages included a schedule for each section showing the due date and the actual completion date, as well as the date that the content of that section was reviewed for technical adequacy. Consequently, the actual status of the development effort for the unit could be ascertained.

The contents of the UDF included:

- A cover sheet, which also contained the schedule for the development of the unit and, for multiple units, a composite schedule.
- A change log, which recorded all changes to each UDF section after signoff.
- A statement of the requirements allocated to the unit.
- The design description; for example, flow charts, PDL, algorithms, etc.
- A functional capabilities list, which listed each testable function and conditional execution (this was used as the basis for developing the unit-level test plan and procedures).
- The listing for the current version and the immediately previous version of the source code for the unit.

- The unit-level test plan and detailed procedures for performing the test.
- Unit-level test results.
- Copies of problem reports initiated against the contents of any section that was also included in a document entered into a project baseline, or initiated against the code itself after it entered a project baseline.
- Notes that the developer felt might be of use at a later date to him/her or to a maintainer of the code.
- Comments that the reviewer of a section of the UDF might have made about the contents of any section.

As implemented by TRW, UDF audits were performed by the Software Quality Assurance group to ensure that the developers were keeping the content current and to ensure that the right kind of content was being entered. As might be inferred, the UDF was also a valuable tool for maintenance of the code as well as for ensuring that the deliverable design documentation was being produced in a timely manner. The UDF audits facilitated the utilization of the UDF for those purposes.

The UDF concept spread within TRW from the Site Defense Program to become a standard practice for the entire Systems Engineering and Integration Division. It also spread from TRW to other defense contractors and began to have wide-spread acceptance. In its incarnation in other companies, generally only minor modifications to the content were made. Many companies referred to the tool as a "software development folder" (SDF), rather than a UDF. Logicon, which played a major role in the development of DOD-STD-2167 and DOD-STD-2168, used the terminology "SDF" in its implementation of the concept. Consequently, Logicon greatly influenced the reference in these standards to the tool as an SDF rather than as a UDF or some other name.

Because of the great utility of the development folder concept, a requirement for defense contractors to implement it was specified in DOD-STD-2167. As defined in DOD-STD-2167A (DOD, 1988), the content requirements are effectively the same as originally adopted by TRW. In DOD-STD-2167A, however, the SDF is referred to as a "software development file" (see SOFTWARE DEVELOPMENT FILE). To many of the reviewers of early DOD-STD-2167 review drafts, "software development folder" sounded too much like a requirement for a three-ring binder, and they felt that the requirement could be interpreted as precluding the use of automated means for generating and maintaining the content. Consequently, the term "software development file" was coined.

CURRENT PRACTICES

By and large, this practice is implemented almost exclusively by defense contractors. Very few organizations developing software for non-defense applications use the practice. In fact, very few such organizations are even aware of the practice or how it might be of help to them.

There are trade-offs to consider in determining the utility of the concept for any organization (McManus, 1992). These include considerations such as the time and effort involved in generating and maintaining the SDF; complications resulting when some of the data that would go into the SDF is classified; and high visibility of the contents when the information is preliminary, sketchy, and not well-developed. The generation and maintenance of SDFs are very time consuming if the SDF is maintained as a three-ring binder. Under this condition, it may become necessary, when populating the SDF, to produce hard copy of the products of the development effort that are very often contained in computer files. On the other hand, if the SDF is produced by automated means, the generation and maintenance of the SDF are virtually transparent to the developer, and they greatly aid in generating design documentation. They also greatly facilitate maintenance of the software.

FUTURE DIRECTIONS

The SDF concept is well-established within the defense community and will continue to be used. Its implementation within the commercial sector should begin to grow. Utilization of the SDF concept within both the defense and commercial sectors should be facilitated by the advent of automated software development files, whether developed by companies as proprietary tools or purchased as items of commercial off-the-shelf software. (See SOFTWARE DEVELOPMENT FILE.)

BIBLIOGRAPHY

F. S. Ingrassia, *The Unit Development Folder (UDF): An Effective Tool for Software Development,* TRW SS-76-11, Oct. 1976.

F. S. Ingrassia, "Combating the '90% Complete' Syndrome", *Datamation,* (Jan. 1978).

DOD-STD-2167A, Defense System Software Development, U.S. Department of Defense, Washington, D.C., Feb. 29, 1988.

J. I. McManus, "SQA Management: Negotiation, Compliance, Regression," in J. I. McManus and G. G. Schulmeyer, eds., *Handbook of Software Quality Assurance,* 2 ed., Van Nostrand Reinhold, New York, 1992.

EMANUEL BAKER
Software Engineering Consultants, Inc.

SOFTWARE DEVELOPMENT LIBRARY

INTRODUCTION

The software development library concept is defined as "a software library containing computer readable and human readable information relevant to a software development effort" (ANSI IEEE, 1990). It is closely linked with the practice of configuration management, but is not usually considered to be a part of the configuration management process (see SOFTWARE CONFIGURATION MANAGMENT). Many of the items contained in the software development library are under configuration control, but not all. In many respects, the software development library can be used as an arm of the configuration management function as an adjunct to the release process. The definition of the software development library contained in DOD-STD-2167A alludes to that by noting (in part) that it "provides storage and controlled access to software and documentation in human-readable form, machine-readable form, or both" (DOD, 1988).

HISTORICAL PERSPECTIVE

Over the years, most companies have implemented various forms of engineering libraries, especially for hardware systems. For hardware systems, the engineering library was generally an outgrowth of the drafting room practices: it was a repository for the masters of drawings and specifications, and the distribution focal point for the copies used on the factory floor. Configuration management as is currently practiced, especially as practiced in the defense industry, was unknown, although many of the principles embodied in today's configuration management practices were implemented. It was clear to these companies, particularly in a mass production environment, that maintaining some form of version control over the specifications and drawings was necessary in order to maintain sanity in the manufacturing and maintenance processes. Furthermore, some form of release control was also necessary.

The necessity of implementing configuration management practices for software, and for maintaining a software development library, was not readily apparent in the early years of the software industry. Software was developed primarily for use in highly specialized, customized applications. A programmer would be assigned to assist a user in developing the program he or she wanted. The programmer would be responsible for the development of the program and maintaining the card deck for it. Typically, the contents of the program were completely unintelligible to the user, and the correctness of the program could only be determined by reviewing the results of any runs executed with the program. If the results of the run appeared to be incorrect, the problem was communicated directly with the programmer, who was responsible for working it out. Documentation of the program, when it existed, generally consisted of notes compiled by the programmer, which were contained in a programmer's notebook.

With the advent of mass storage devices, and the recognition that many of the programs (such as statistical packages or bookkeeping programs) could have applicability to wider audiences, master libraries of programs started to be kept on magnetic or punched tape. When disk drives began to have widespread utilization, magnetic tape became relegated to being the medium for backing up copies of the master libraries rather than actually being the master. These master copies were generally stored in the computer room. Enlightened software organizations recognized the need for duplicating these master copies and storing them off-site as a hedge against a disaster, such as a fire in the computer room. They may have also sent obsolete versions of current production software to be stored elsewhere, in the event that some unforeseen event necessitated recreating an old version of the software.

These master copies, the back-up "disaster" copies, and the archived copies all became the contents of the first software libraries.

In the defense industry, more rigorous practices were needed. Documentation of the requirements for and design of the software became crucial, as did the production of manuals for the use and maintenance of the software. Requirements and design documents were essential for providing visibility into the technical adequacy of the delivered software, and for ensuring that the software could be maintained after it was delivered. It was necessary for contractors to place the evolving software under configuration control so as to provide an audit trail of changes during formal qualification testing. It was necessary to know if the changes to the software that occurred during qualification testing invalidated the results of test cases that were run prior to the change being incorporated. Some mechanism had to be put into place to ensure that all the disparate pieces (i.e., the software, formal documentation, or informal project correspondence documenting the rationale for design decisions) were all collected together under a single control process. Thus a more formalized software development library was born.

Criteria for the software development library varied from project to project. No standard existed which specified requirements for a software development library. The statement of work would invoke a data management task, and often there would be a requirement for a deliverable data accession list which identified *all* documentation, formal or informal, produced on the project. DOD-STD-2167 (DOD, 1985) was the first standard to formalize a requirement for a software development library and to identify specifically what should be included in it.

CURRENT PRACTICES

Software development libraries are fairly common among defense contractors. As implemented by them, the functions are often distributed. For instance, a data management library may exist which is the focal point for the distribution of hard copies of project documentation. Generation and updating of master source and object libraries, however, may be the responsibility of a librarian who reports to the configuration management organization, or perhaps the development organization. A single point of control will generally exist, however. It may be in the form of a single manager who is responsible for all aspects of operating the software development library, or it may be in the form of a set of standards and procedures that cover all such aspects. The use of on-line documentation, documentation templates, word processors, and library management tools facilitate the process of generating and controlling document masters as well as providing for timely distribution of copies.

Configuration management for software is an idea that has been slow to get a foothold outside of the defense industry. The necessity for configuration management of software for weapons systems became apparent back in the

1970s, but the importance of it for software developed for the commercial sector of the economy has not been as rapidly acknowledged. Most commercial organizations maintain version control of one form or another for their software; however, for the most part, practices such as formalized change control boards or configuration auditing are virtually unheard of in the commercial sector. Likewise, the concept of the software development library is not well-developed in the commercial sector. As practiced by such organizations, the software development library is primarily a "code" library—a place where master copies of current and archived versions of software important to the organization are maintained.

FUTURE DIRECTIONS

Software development libraries will become a more widely utilized practice. Within the defense and aerospace community, the requirements of DOD-STD-2167A will continue to cause companies within this sector of the economy to apply this concept and follow very rigorous practices. The implementation of software development libraries within software development organizations not associated with the defense industry will grow more slowly. Applying such practices increases overhead, and commercial organizations are reluctant to expend resources on non-revenue-producing activities. Nonetheless, they will begin to apply more rigorous practices as well. This results from several considerations:

- A greater recognition of and a greater emphasis on the importance of documentation (of some form) to capture planning, requirements, and design information for the development and maintenance of commercial applications and software developed for in-house use, such as MIS applications.
- A greater appreciation for the need for version control.
- A recognition that the implementation of processes that facilitate the orderly development and maintenance of software reduces life cycle costs, and increases overall profitability.

The implementation of software development libraries for all software development organizations will become easier, as software tools to facilitate the activity become more sophisticated. As end-to-end CASE tools, object-oriented data base management systems, object-oriented development support and integration environments, and configuration management tools become more readily available, the capability will improve to implement a software development library in a way that is virtually transparent to the organization.

BIBLIOGRAPHY

ANSI IEEE Std. 610-12-1990, IEEE Standard Glossary of Software Engineering Terminology, The Institute of Electrical and Electronics Engineers, Inc., New York, 1990.

DOD-STD-2167, Defense System Software Development, U.S. Department of Defense, Washington, D.C., June 4, 1985.

DOD-STD-2167A, Defense System Software Development, U.S. Department of Defense, Washington, D.C., Feb. 29, 1988.

EMANUEL BAKER
Software Engineering Consultants, Inc.

SOFTWARE DEVELOPMENT PLAN

The Software Development Plan (SDP) is a document that describes the plan for the development of software products. The purpose of the document is to demonstrate that sufficient planning has been performed before proceeding into development, and that the expectations of the user, the criteria for completion of the product, and the risks associated with the development are understood before a significant commitment of resources is made.

The SDP may be a requirement levied by the customer for products that are to be built to customer specifications. In this case the SDP is often prepared during the generation of a proposal as a prerequisite for authorization to proceed with a development contract. Also, the SDP is sometimes used as a basis for a company's authorization of internal software activity, for example, to support the development of a commercial product or for internal computing needs. When prepared as part of a government contract, the preparation, delivery, and approval of the SDP by the government may be a contractual requirement. For example, in the case of contracts with the Department of Defense, the SDP is often part of a larger set of documentation required by the government. The SDP may be required to be written by the contractor as the result of a government standard, such as *DOD-STD-2167A, Military Standard for Defense System Software Development.* In cases like this, the government may also specify the content and format. Parts of the SDP may be prepared as separate plans that include more detailed procedures for specific areas. For example, the methods to be used for the control and change of product versions are often documented separately.

The SDP is usually intended to provide a complete guide for the development of the software product. The emphasis of the SDP is on the proper management of the technical development effort rather than on the particular architecture and design approach for the software product. Management issues addressed by the SDP include the organizational approach to be used during software development and the relationship of the development organization to other organizations, companies, subcontractors, and agents of the customer or project sponsor. The SDP includes budgets, schedules, a description of the management methods for cost and schedule control, personnel and staffing needs, and the risk management approach.

The SDP also addresses the need for computing security, development standards, test approaches, and quality evaluations, and it identifies the processes to be used to develop the product. The SDP includes the requirements for the configuration control of the product and the associated software libraries as well as the methods for the reporting and resolution of problems.

In addition to serving as a basis for authorizing software development work, the SDP may be a useful tool for training new employees, for serving as a basis for assessing development progress, and for helping to communicate the software development approach to other organizations.

In cases where the software product is a part of a larger system of hardware and software elements, the SDP includes an overview of the larger system and identifies the relationship and interactions of the product with the larger system. The system descriptions also include the identification of the "target" processor that the software will operate on, as well as the identification of other software or hardware that the product must be compatible with. The description of resources in the SDP includes the identification of the computing equipment needed to develop the software, such as workstations, printers, mass storage devices, simulators, and special-purpose equipment for the troubleshooting, evaluation, and verification of proper operation of the software. Other software needed for the development of the software product is identified. An essential part of the SDP is the listing of any resources that must be available to the development organization in order to perform the tasks outlined in the plan. This list of dependencies is one of the most critical elements of planning the software development activity and is sometimes not given sufficient attention because it involves resources that are not directly under the control of the development organization. The listing includes the identification of the item, the source, the method of acquisition, and the date needed.

The SDP identifies how the development organization relates to other organizations, including the methods by which development personnel will participate in the communication process with external organizations, and the methods to be used to obtain agreements and commitments from those organizations. External organizations include as appropriate, the project sponsors, associate organizations, and subcontractors. The number of personnel needed for the development activity is identified, including their skill and experience requirements. Areas typically addressed are the personnel needs for management, requirements development, design and code, evaluation, test, and software configuration management. The product release approach is reflected in the identification of the schedules and milestones associated with the development. For example, an iterative or incremental build approach may be used to produce certain capabilities needed first, or to reduce development risk.

Schedules and milestones include the reviews desired by the customer or project sponsor during the development activity. In addition to cost and schedule reviews, technical reviews may be appropriate to address the concept of operation, the system and software requirements, the architecture and design, the test program, and overall completion status.

Another essential part of the SDP is the description of the risk management approach to be used and the identification of development risks in order of importance. An underlying element for risk management is the appropriate use of metrics to measure and assess performance against the SDP. The measurements selected address the broad aspects of the development effort and may be applied to processor memory, throughput, input/output allocations, development status, and the skill and experience levels of the development team. The methods proposed to reduce development risk are listed and may include the prototyping of high risk designs or the development of alternative design approaches in parallel with the selected design approach, or the reuse of software.

The SDP describes the purpose and method of operation of the library for the software development products. The library includes the documentation, source (human readable) code, and executable (machine-readable) code. Procedures for the access and security of the library are described. The method of controlling change to the product is identified for errors and product enhancements. The method for identifying and reporting problems with the software and its documentation is identified including the procedures for initiating corrective actions.

Proprietary rights to the software and the associated data are described, including those incorporated into the product as a result of the reuse of previously developed software.

The SDP addresses the plans for "maintaining" (updating) the software after the product has been made available for use. This part of the plan shows the responsibility for software maintenance and the resources needed for the maintenance activity.

J. R. ELSTON
Boeing Defense & Space Group

SOFTWARE ENGINEERING, A HISTORICAL PERSPECTIVE

INTRODUCTION

Software engineering is a relatively young discipline which is evolving at a rapid pace. This pace is advanced by two phenomena: one, the performance capability of computer hardware is advancing rapidly, and two, applications are becoming more complex as the opportunity presented by the attractive performance/price ratio of hardware enables the creation of more diverse and complex applications. In this environment we see several predominant activities:

- Software engineering curricula evolving.
- The movement towards more powerful programming paradigms such as object-oriented.
- CASE tools continue to evolve both in capability and scope of application.
- Standards such as the European ISO 9000 series being implemented.
- Methodologies such as object-oriented becoming adopted in more segments of the computer industry.
- National thrusts with the objective of creating advanced "software factory" types of environments.

DEFINITIONS

The term "software engineering" was coined at the NATO conference in Garmisch-Partenkirchen in 1968. Since that time, there has been considerable discussion over whether software development is an engineering discipline, and the nature of software engineering itself. Mary Shaw suggests that it "is not yet a true engineering discipline, but it has the potential to become one" (Shaw, 1990). While most of the discussion has been in academia, we have seen a steady acceptance of results by industry from the research community (e.g., formal methods, advanced design and programming languages). These results have contributed to the advances made in and the discipline of software engineering.

The word engineering is an accepted word in today's practice. In Webster's *New World Dictionary,* engineering is described as follows:

> *(a) the science concerned with putting scientific knowledge to practical uses, divided into different branches, as civil, electrical, mechanical, or chemical engineering (b) the planning, designing, construction, or management of machinery, roads, bridges, buildings, etc. (Webster, 1982).*

The *IEEE Standard Glossary of Software Engineering Terminology* defines software engineering as:

> *The application of a systematic, disciplined, quantifiable approach to the development, operation, and maintenance of software; that is, the application of engineering to software (IEEE, 1990).*

We can obtain insight into how the field has advanced by comparing this definition with the 1983 version:

> *the systematic approach to the development, operation, maintenance, and retirement of software (Charette, 1986).*

Notice the introduction of the words "quantifiable", implying measurement, and "disciplined", implying process control. Also, the deletion of "retirement" implies that software continually evolves, and perhaps just fades away in the same context as old soldiers as General Douglas MacArthur described the process to a joint session of Congress in 1951.

Thus, software engineers are those who apply engineering principles in the cooperative development and production of systems where software is an intrinsic or dominant part of the overall system. The software engineer brings engineering skills; in terms of software management, selected methods, and the application of tools to the solution of the engineering problem. Others may help in this endeavor: the analyst who may be engaged in analyzing requirements; the programmer, who is engaged in writing the code that implements the design; the tester who is responsible for planning and conducting a test program to determine if the system meets its intended requirements, as well as others. Each of these specialization's apply unique software engineering practices. The skill partitioning and organization can assume several dimensions, for example, engineering development, engineering support, and management. In engineering development we have roles of application domain understanding, architecting, design, coding, and testing. In the support role we have quality assurance, configuration management and tool development and support. In the management role we have cost estimation, planning, control or performance management, and risk mitigation. The important point is that software engineering, like other engineering disciplines, is a discipline that is devoted to the construction of software systems employing the skills practiced by a variety of people.

Current Practice

To understand current practice it is useful to examine the evolution of software development practice. In order to do this we employ the concept of characterizing software production environments which dominated over selected epochs. Figure 1 depicts this evolution relative to practices that were introduced or popularized over some period of time.

Early Practice

Early computer programming started, in the 1940s with the development of the Mark I and ENAIC computers (World Book, 1970). Through the early 1960s, software development was typified by a small programming team environment. Essentially, software was developed by a single programmer, or by a small group of programmers. Programming practice was more or less dictated by the tools available on the computer being programmed. Thus, the availability of the assembler and basic support tools such as a link editor were the tools that were employed and formed the foundation of software development practice. Methods were virtually nonexistent. Flow diagrams were used to construct an overall picture of what the program was intended to accomplish and the programmer coded directly from the flow chart. Cards had to be punched in order to convert the source code to machine readable form. Programs were run in a batch computer environment, where jobs were fed to the machine and executed in sequence, the output fed back in a computer print out (see Fig. 2).

Management practices were virtually nonexistent, largely a carryover from other management areas. Process was not a concept at all that was evident. Thus, this era was basically defined by the individual programmer.

Since many programmers were operating in an environment where their managers had little understanding of what they were doing, and management practices for managing software development were minimal or nonexistent, programming was viewed as a cult with highly individualistic practitioners. Even today, this cult perspective carries over, and sometimes software development is described as more of an art than a science.

The allocation of effort for software engineering in the early years can be characterized as in Figure 3.

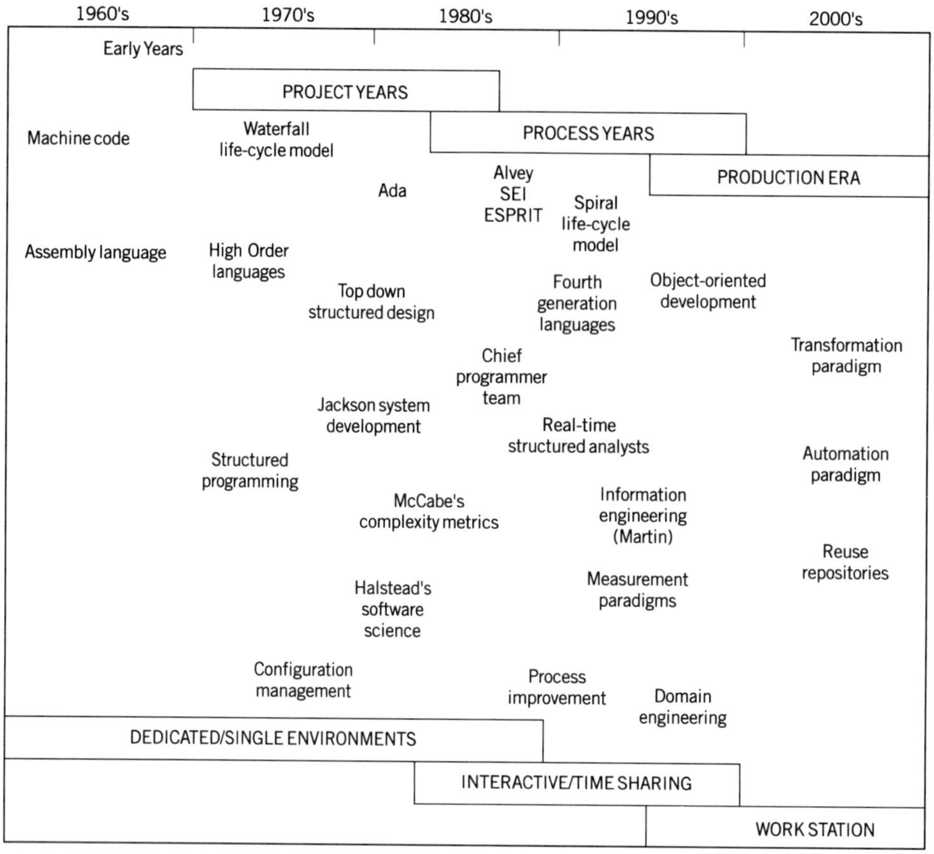

Figure 1. Software engineering genealogy.

The Project Years

The concept of programming evolved from a programming-in-the-small team environment, to programming in the many. With this larger scale development came an emphasis on project management of software development (see Fig. 2).

As software systems became more complex, for example, the development of early military systems such as the Semi-Automated Ground Environment (SAGE), developed by the United States (U.S.) Department of Defense (DOD) to monitor the airspace surrounding its borders, it became clear that developing systems in a single programmer environment of this first generation was inadequate. SAGE involved an application program of 100,000 instructions with a support system of over 100 million instructions and was implemented on a computer with 58,000 vacuum tubes. (Augustine, 1983) It was this increasingly wider use of software in complex and critical areas that provided the impetus for better management and engineering (or programming techniques depending on the personal point of view at the time) for developing software.

From a product development, or production point of view, programming was advanced through the use of high order languages (HOLs), the most common of which were FORTRAN and COBOL, at least in the United States. Abstraction techniques such as "top-down" structured design were introduced in an attempt to provide, to the programmer, methods that allowed better analysis of require-

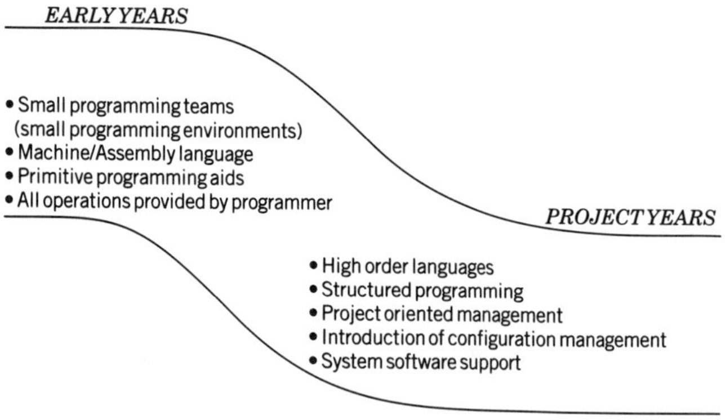

Figure 2. Software development through circa 1980.

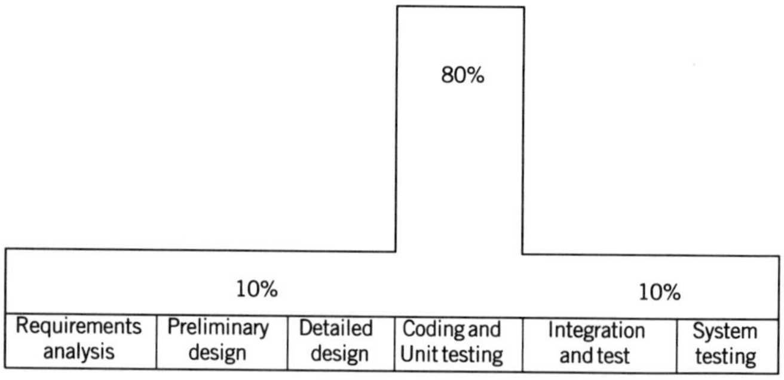

Figure 3. Allocation of effort, early years.

ments and formulations of design. Programmer tools were still pretty basic, relegated to debuggers and other tools found in the programmer toolbox. Testing was largely an art that more often than not was forgotten until late in the development, and then mostly a functional demonstration that the system worked so the client would accept it.

Project management was now seen as a necessity to develop software systems properly. The programmer was no longer a single person or small group operating entirely on their own. Management methods, although still basic, were emerging. Cost estimation and tracking was virtually nonexistent. Tracking of development was accomplished principally by line of code projection and reporting of actual lines of code that were written. Management of the evolution of several cooperating components required configuration management (qv). Managed development of many related activities demanded planning tools where techniques such as PERT (Marciniak, 1990) were adapted for use.

If the early part of this era was best known for programming techniques, the latter part is best known for an emphasis on quality (see QUALITY ASSURANCE). Project management practices were dramatically changing. There were many reasons for this depending on one's point of view. In a commercial environment, the opportunity to develop and sell programming services for financial services such as payroll production was a motivation. In the U.S. DOD the amount of software was growing, and for the first time, was appearing in weapons systems such as missiles and aircraft. In the National Aeronautics and Space Agency (NASA), the software dramatically jumped in the development of the Space Shuttle, where initial estimates paled compared to the resulting 25 million lines of code (Schlender, 1989).

In the U.S. the most important initiative was the development of the Ada language (see ADA). While still somewhat controversial, this development focused enormous attention and resource to software engineering issues such as the use of strong typing in HOLs and information hiding. Ada created an international following, and today still has a strong advocacy lobby and following. As the importance of software grew, both in the government and commercial sectors, national efforts were organized to focus resources on unproving the productivity and quality of software production.

The Process Years

The Japanese, in 1982, described the fifth generation computer project. This project, had as its intention the development of a computing environment based on knowledge-based systems and computers that directly executed advanced or fifth generation languages such as Prolog. (Cusumano, 1991a) The Japanese, however, are best known for their implementation of the "Software Factory". This term, initially conceptualized in the U.S. at the Systems Development Corporation (now part of Unisys), was implemented in Japan during the 1980s and set the standard for producing software in a highly disciplined environment (Cusumano, 1991b). The Japanese Software Factory is grounded in two characteristics: the use of highly trained and concentrated development teams, and the application of metrics to measure process improvement and product quality and to improve the factory based on these measures. While software metrics had an early beginning in the late 1970s the Japanese made it a cornerstone of the software factory concept (see Fig. 4).

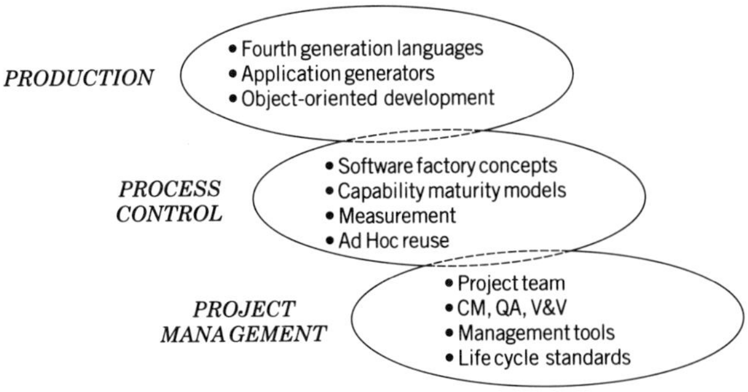

Figure 4. The process years.

In 1982 the ALVEY project was organized in the UK when the ALVEY committee recommended a broad program in research in Information Technology. The program was spurred by the Japanese initiative. The five year program involved major IT firms such as BT, and was funded on a fifty/fifty cost sharing basis. In the five years 198 projects were carried out involving 2500 researchers (see ALVEY).

The European community formed the European Strategic Program for Research and Development (ESPRIT) in 1984 to develop software technology to cope with this expanding commercial base in Information Technology, as well as in microelectronics, Advanced Information Processing, and Computer Integrated Manufacturing. Thirty-eight projects were launched in the pilot phase. As of mid-1992 a total of 721 distinctive results have been achieved. Examples of ESPRIT programs are the Portable Common Tool Environment (PCTE), RAISE, an enhancement to the VDM method, BOOTSTRAP, which helped map the Software Engineering Institute (SEI) Capability Maturity Model (CMM) onto the International Organization for Standardization (ISO) 9000 series quality standards, and MUSIC, focusing on the development of metrics. ESPRIT continues today with a viable program of projects (qv).

The U.S. DOD organized the Software Engineering Institute (SEI) in 1984, hosted at the Carnegie Mellon University. The objective of this Federally Funded Research and Development Center (FFRDC) is to advance software engineering practice and improve quality. The SEI program has five thrust areas: Software Engineering Process, Software Engineering Techniques, Real-Time Distributed Systems, Software Engineering Education, and Software Risk Management (See SOFTWARE ENGINEERING INSTITUTE).

The advent of the software factory brought new practice and attention to the infrastructure of software development, and set the stage for the focus on the process of software development. With measurement other practices began to emerge. In order to measure productivity, the basic unit of work needed definition. Many attempts were made to define a "line of code" so that the basis for comparison between systems was clear. Productivity data that was available provided the early means to develop and implement cost estimation practices. Error data provided the means for implementing reliability mechanisms that had been under development, but had not been introduced into practice.

Perhaps the most significant happening in this time was the concentration on process improvement programs. Initially conceived in the United States by Watts Humphrey while at IBM, then later at the SEI, its impetus can be attributed to the gains that the Japanese were making in managing the software development process in their software factories. Now codified by method and practice by the SEI, the process improvement program is an extension of the principles of Total Quality Management (TQM) customized for software development. The goals of the program are to instill a process improvement program in industrial practice and to establish the means to quantify and assess the attainment of the program (Humphrey, 1989).

The quality emphasis of this generation saw the development and implementation of new standards of practice. The first management process/life cycle standard was Federal Information Processing Standard (FIPS) 38, Guidelines for Documentation of Computer Programs & Automated Data Systems. Published in 1976 it is now obsolete, however, it provided the basis for other management and development standards. In 1988 the US published DOD-STD-2167A, Standard for Defense System Software Development. [(It was preceded by DOD-STD-2167 which was quickly revised) DOD, 1988)]. It provided a common life-cycle management process for the development of software in systems. While it has received criticism, mainly in implementation issues and the reliance on a waterfall life cycle model, it did provide a basis for standard development practice for U.S. DOD weapon systems. The IEEE has an active standards program with examples such as the Standard for Software Life Cycle Processes. (ANSI, 1991) The International Organization for Standardization has been active, the most notable example, perhaps, is the quality standard, ISO 9000.

Methods. Perhaps the most important method that emerged in the last decade was object-oriented development. We will continue to see that method on a wider use throughout the next decade. Originally supported by the object-oriented language and environment Smalltalk, it is joined by Eiffel and C++ and soon Ada 9X, the upgrade to current Ada (Ada '83).

Tools. We have seen a number of tool or Computer-Aided Software Engineering (CASE) companies arise with new offerings. Examples are CADRE which makes a product called Teamwork, Interactive Development Environments (IDE), which makes Software through Pictures, and Mark V, which makes Object-maker. The explosion in tools matches the capabilities of lower cost, higher performance workstations that allow even more sophisticated tools. Ascent Logic Corporation offers a tool capability called RDD-100, which is based on the technology and method of SYSREM (see SOFTWARE REQUIREMENTS ENGINEERING METHODOLOGY). Virtual Software factory makes a meta tool called VSF which affords the rapid development and automation of methods to create custom tools. In the testing area companies such as Software Research Inc. builds a number of general testing tools based on coverage and management of the testing environment. McCabe Associates markets a number of code analyzers, based on techniques such as complexity analysis, that help in the testing process.

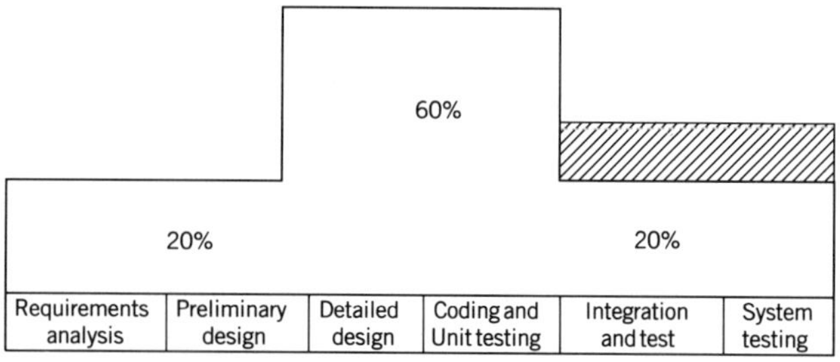

Figure 5. Allocation of effort, process years.

Early software engineers were trained as programmers. Since there were no academic curricula for software engineering, their training was characterized as "on-the-job" supplemented by industrial and commercial programming courses. Programmers stemmed from a variety of educational backgrounds. In 1976 Peter Freeman, then with the University of California at Irvine, and Anthony Wasserman, then with the University of California at San Francisco, organized a workshop on software engineering education (see EDUCATION AND CURRICULA IN SOFTWARE ENGINEERING). As the era proceeded, computer science programs were organized in many academic institutions. These were mainly found in the mathematics departments of universities and colleges. The first software engineering curriculum was offered by Texas Christian University, in 1978. By the end of the seventies this curriculum was taking hold in a number of institutions and became the nominal source for software engineers. Since the curriculum was a graduate one, the major source for software engineers was drawn from a variety of computer science, engineering, and mathematics programs.

The allocation of software engineering effort in the Process era is depicted in Figure 5 (Boehm, 1981). The shaded area shown in the testing phases pays homage to the fact that sufficient resources were not allocated to testing, however, in typical developments the testing phase increased in resource requirements.

This process era, then, is best characterized by the following salient points:

- Definition and organization of national initiatives to promote the use and development of software.
- Development of process improvement programs: e.g., SEI CMM.
- Codification of management practice in standards: e.g., DOD-STD-2167A.
- Definition and implementation of software engineering curricula.

The Production Era

While it would be presumptuous to state what will happen in the future it is possible to discuss directions that seem to be emerging in third generation computing environ-

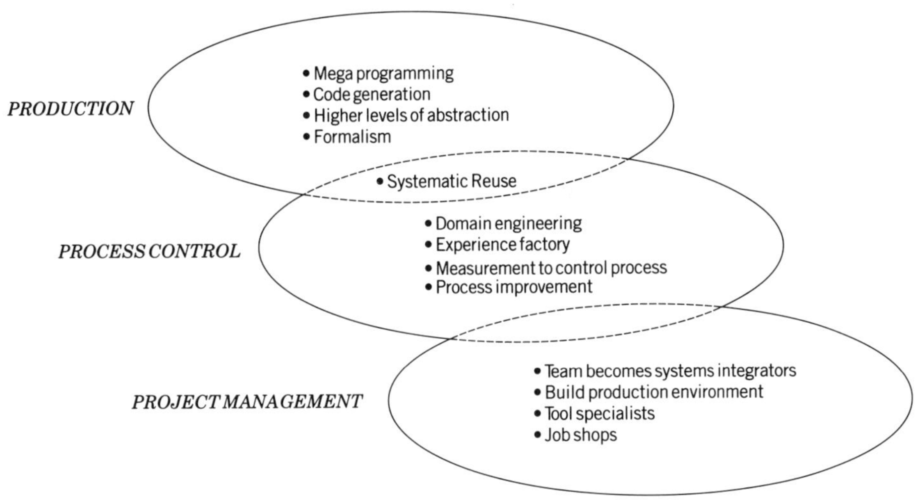

Figure 6. The production era.

ments. As Anita Jones suggested in her keynote address at the 15th International Conference on Software Engineering, we are moving from an emphasis on process (management) to product (development). That is not to say that the importance of process management is waning, or will dissolve, but that new programming paradigms will create more emphasis on the product, or production of software (see Fig. 6).

In the product area there are two significant and closely related thrusts: a move towards a mega programming (qv) environment, and the move to a more abstract programming environment. From a mega programming environment we see the availability of more powerful user oriented languages, coupled with robust reuse repositories. Mega languages will allow users to rapidly build new applications, where the implementation details have already been worked out in a generic way. From an abstract programming view we see emphasis on moving towards the construction of programs at a higher level of abstraction in the development process through the use of formalisms such as formal specifications, which can then be directly implemented through code generation. This allows the implementer to operate at a higher level of abstraction with more robust capabilities to produce systems. We now examine some of the most important thrusts.

Reuse. From a repository view there are a number of initiatives to build large, general purpose repositories such as the Defense Software Repository Systems (DSRS) organized and developed by the DOD Defense Information Systems Agency (DISA) (see REUSE LIBRARY). Software artifacts, placed into the library, and described in some suitable manner, would be available to a wide set of users at some cost. On a more localized aspect, commercial repositories will range from those built to support a contractor's business interests, i.e., the building of customized software systems, to those that are productized for release to the open market. Examples of the latter are the SNAP product built by Template Software, Inc. and UNAS, built by TRW (Royce, 1991). Both of these offer an object-oriented prototyping capability that allows a user to get applications up and running in a very short period of time.

New Programming Paradigms. The impact of knowledge-based systems will reach some level of acceptance and impact as this new "programming paradigm" begins to take some interest in the real world. In the US the best known example of this work is that of the Knowledge-Based Software Assistant (KBSA) project carried out by the United States Air Force's Rome Laboratory (White, 1991). The project has two powerful concepts: the capture of knowledge during the development process so that that knowledge can be reused, and the use of formal methods to specify requirements and design, and automate the generation of code. Thus, as new requirements are elicited, or changes are required due to maintenance requirements, the changes are described through a high level formalism and "transformed" from this high level abstraction to a new instantiation. One manifestation of this direction is the use of code generators commonly available with many commercial CASE products.

From a Process view we can expect to see continued emphasis on the use of process improvement programs such as that of the SEI based on the Capability Maturity Model. In the European community, a version of this model has been developed in the ESPRIT BOOTSTRAP project and integrated into the ISO 9000 quality standard. We can expect to see the models evolve as they are refined and increased in use through, for example, the use of measures.

One of the most significant developments in this generation could be the employment of the so-called experience factory (qv). The purpose of the experience factory is to build a disciplined environment through the establishment of an infrastructure that is experience based. That is, it will capture life cycle experiences and reuse those experiences along with reused products. The experience factory is both a physical and logical organization. The principal method of the factory is the Quality Improvement Paradigm. Developed by Basili and co-workers at the University of Maryland and the NASA Goddard Space Flight Center (GSFC), it is based on the Shewart-Deming cycle Plan/Do/Check/ Act paradigm (Deming, 1986). Examples of experiences are histograms of data, lessons learned from previous projects, and models of processes. An experience factory exists at NASA GSFC, where it originated.

High Integrity Software. The continued motivation for quality systems will see increased emphasis on techniques to achieve higher quality. During the late 1980s and early 1990s we have seen both the need, and the means to achieve higher quality and integrity in systems. The need arises from systems with human critical safety requirements. Examples are in transportation systems, with ever increasing reliance on computer software, medical treatment systems such as linear accelerators which are controlled and monitored by software, and the obvious aircraft systems where the number of computational devices has dramatically increased in flight control systems as well as maintenance monitoring.

To meet the requirements in these areas a number of techniques are being employed to include increased and more disciplined verification and validation, formal methods, and safety analysis. Formal methods have been under development for some time, however, it was only in the late 1980s that they were being used in real systems. The National Institute of Standards and Technology (NIST), in collaboration with the U.S. Navy's Naval Research Laboratory (NRL) and the Canadian Atomic Energy Control Board, sponsored a survey of practice that described method and tools usage in a number of international industrial projects (Craigen, 1993). A newer field, albeit one that is receiving more attention and interest, is software safety. The field has been largely popularized by Nancy Leveson of the University of California at Irvine (see SAFETY). Verification and validation is becoming a more described discipline with the publication of the FIPS/IEEE/ANSI standards (NBS, 1987, IEEE, 1986).

We can expect to see changes in the way projects are managed based on the changes in the product environment and process improvement programs. For example, as the emphasis on process improvement programs increases, there will be commensurate increases in program management techniques. Better visibility into project status should result from measurement programs established as a means to achieve higher maturity levels.

The production capabilities, along with continued emphasis on process improvement will present new challenges to management. The concept of a project organization, with its organic resources, could give way to a team that is more attuned to building systems from "parts" based on repositories and using advanced methods and tools, and programming paradigms such as the KBSA. Management will have to understand how documentation requirements will change to accommodate advanced methods. Reviews may take on more of an electronic flavor as the products themselves become housed inside the machine.

In Figure 7 we project what may be expected in the allocation of resources in the future. As one can see, the move towards mega programming and transformation paradigms of development will afford more rigorous techniques in the early part of the life cycle. This will result in more efficient specifications which, with code generation and automated testing techniques, will result in decreased resource expenditure in the latter part of the life cycle. This reduction is expected to result in lower maintenance costs as well. The overall expectation is that development and total life cycle costs will be lowered.

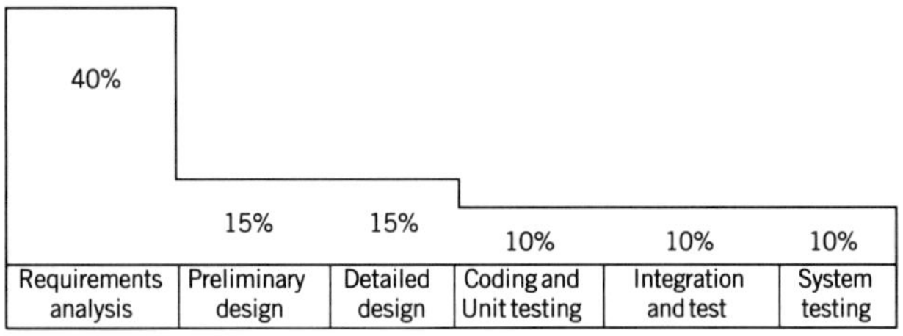

Figure 7. Allocation of effort, production era.

SUMMARY

Software development, and software engineering, have evolved dramatically over the last twenty-five years. To a large extent the pace of development has mirrored programming or automation capability as machines have progressed from batch oriented standalone computers to individual workstations with contained development environments. There are highly active international efforts underway to develop advanced development environments such as the Eureka Software Factory (qv). Process improvement programs are in full swing across the globe. Methods are evolving, with CASE companies supporting a number of them. The introduction of disciplines such as performance engineering (qv), software safety (qv), mega programming, and the Experience Factory all contribute to a robust software engineering environment. In the 1990s, we can expect to see dramatic changes, and hopefully improvement to both the management and production of software systems.

I wish to express my appreciation to Dolores Wallace of the National Institute of Standards and Technology and George Heyliger of CTA Inc. for their review and useful comments of this article.

BIBLIOGRAPHY

ANSI/IEEE Standard 1012-1986, Standard for Software Verification and Validation Plans, IEEE, New York, 1986.

ANSI/IEEE Std. 1074-1991, Standard for Software Life Cycle Processes, IEEE, New York, 1991.

N. R. Augustine, *Augustine Laws,* American Institute for Aeronautics & Astronautics, 1983, New York.

B. W. Boehm, "Software Engineering Economics," Prentice-Hall, New Jersey, 1981, Chaps. 6 and 7.

R. N. Charette, *Software Engineering Environments,* McGraw Hill, New York, NY, 1986, p. 7.

D. Craigen, S. Gerhart, and T. Ralston, "An International Survey of Industrial Applications of Formal Methods," *NIST GCR 93/626,* two volumes, National Institute of Standards and Technology, Gaithersburg, Md., 1993.

M. A. Cusumano, *Japan's Software Factories,* Oxford University Press, New York, 1991a, pp. 410–416.

M. A. Cusumano, *Japan's Software Factories,* Oxford University Press, New York, 1991b, p. 7.

E. Deming, *Out of the Crisis,* MIT Center for Advanced Engineering Study, MIT Press, Cambridge, Mass., 1986.

Department of Defense Standard 2167A, Standard for Defense System Software Development, 1988.

IEEE Std 610.12-1990, Standard Glossary of Software Engineering Terminology, IEEE, New York, 1990.

W. S. Humphrey, *Managing the Software Process,* Addison-Wesley, 1989.

J. J Marciniak and D. J. Reifer, *Software Acquisition Management,* John Wiley & Sons, New York, 1990, p. 99.

NBS, *Guideline for Software Verification and Validation Plans,* FIPSPUB132, National Bureau of Standards (US), Gaithersburg, Md., 1987.

W. Royce, P. Blankenship, E. Rusis, and B. Willis, "Universal Network Architecture Services: A Portability Case Study," *Proceedings of Ninth Annual National Conference on Ada Technology,* ANCOST, Inc., U.S. Army Communications-Electronics Command, New Jersey, Washington, D.C., 1991.

B. R. Schlender, "How to Break the Software Logjam," *Fortune,* **120,** 100–112 (Sept. 25, 1989).

M. Shaw, "Prospects for an Engineering Discipline of Software," *IEEE Software,* 15–24 (Nov. 1990).

Webster's, *New World Dictionary,* second college edition, Simon & Schuster, New York, 1982.

D. A. White, "The Knowledge-Based Software Assistant: A Program Summary," *Proceedings of the 6th Knowledge-Based Software Engineering Conference (KBSE-91),* IEEE Press, Los Alamitos, Calif., 1991, pp. 2–6.

The World Book Encyclopedia, *Computer,* World Book, Chicago, 1970, Vol. 4, p. 744.

JOHN J. MARCINIAK
CTA INCORPORATED

SOFTWARE ENGINEERING ENVIRONMENTS

INTRODUCTION

A Software Factory is meant to be capable of providing computer support for the coordinated work of software developers in large software development projects. The term Software Factory hence denotes a number of things: people and their respective roles in software development; computer supported tools and their combined use in software development; and a co-ordination process model to guide people in their proper use of tools and in their proper joined work integration as depicted below (see Fig. 1).

Recent developments have led from closed environments, comprising fixed sets of tightly coupled tools for specific phases, to open environments that enable the plugging of new tools as the requirements evolve (see also SOFTWARE FACTORY).

To cope with this new dimension in CASE technology, standards organizations intend to support the effort with reference models; for example, the Information Systems Engineering Reference Model (ISE/RM) of the ISO; the Standards Manual of the Object Management Group (OMG), ECMA's Reference Model for Computer Assisted Software Engineering Environment Frameworks; ECMA's Support Environment for Open Distributed Processing (SE/OPD); and OSF's Distributed Computing Environment (OSF/DCE).

The concepts presented in this article have been primarily developed in the Eureka Software Factory (ESF) project. This article hence carries the flavor of that project in the way it introduces software factory concepts and in the way it explains these concepts in the larger context of computer-aided software development (see also EUREKA SOFTWARE FACTORY).

Computer support in a software factory will be provided by a software system that is called *factory support environment* (FSE). In order to support software development in the manner outlined above, the FSE is needed to provide a number of integration services. FSE integration services will be explained first by introducing a conceptual view of a software factory and later on as an architectural view. The conceptual view, called the software factory core, introduces a number of integration stages: interworking, interaction, interoperation, and interconnection. The architectural view introduces the mechanisms that support integration at the respective stages.

THE SOFTWARE FACTORY CORE

What the ESF CoRe Contains

The ESF CoRe is a road map of the Software Factory domain. As such, it embodies a view of what industrial software production means: what sorts of entities and events ought to be distinguished in software factories, and how these relate to each other. Concretely, the CoRe consists of a set of *definitions,* some *arguments* as to what those definitions imply, and some *pictures* showing how the definitions are interrelated.

The structure of the CoRe derives from a strategic decision to view industrial software production as supported by layered communication processes. Two views result:

- A *conceptual* view, using an extended OSI layer model to distinguish levels of factory communication and the kinds of work that can be conducted at each level.
- An *architectural* view, which categorizes the entities that communicate through and across each of the layers, and places them in an evolutionary context.

The conceptual view hence introduces an extended reference model for factory communication and the architectural view the essential ingredients of a software factory support environment.

Why Another Reference Model?

Major international effort has already been invested in reference models for software engineering, the most important being the ECMA(TC33)/NIST work which produced the "toaster" model, and the several integrating programs/visions being marketed by the major manufacturers (e.g., IBM's AD/Cycle and DEC's Cohesion). Why does not ESF make use of what is already available?

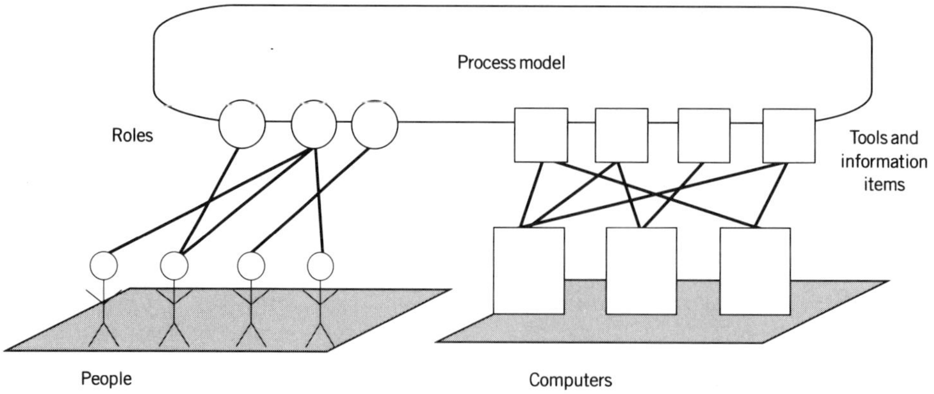

Figure 1. Software factory model.

The problem is that existing reference models are either incomplete or inconsistent. None can support the wide spectrum of uses envisioned for the ESF CoRe. There is a great need for an integrating framework that can assimilate the various approaches currently available, so that the user can move from one to the next without getting conceptually lost. In particular, there is a need for a model that includes:

The Factory Context. ESF is aimed specifically at software efforts characterized by:

- *industrial-scale* operations (programming in-the-many), with
- tightly constrained *budgets* and *schedules,* which puts
- a high priority on effective *management control,* and thus provides
- powerful economic incentives to *standardize parts* and *processes*

Existing technical reference models tend to focus *either* on system architecture *or* on project methodology; such mundane matters as network administration, contract renegotiation, or resource procurement are often ignored.

The Evolutionary Context. Factory administration and production process (re)design happen outside the project time-scale. Software factories are capital assets subject to long-term corporate investment. Our model must include the work whereby successful processes and results are identified, reused, maintained and developed. This means being able to represent streams of factory events with very different granularities (months, milliseconds), and forces the issues of synchrony and parallelism, tool evolution and configuration control (i.e., the management of evolutionary chances in the factory itself).

The Human Context. Uncomfortable, most tools have far more power than their users know how to apply. Worse—it has been persuasively argued (in particular by Watts Humphrey) that the present state of software project management is so deficient that better tools will only make things worse. The central challenge in software engineering is to make special-purpose technology effectively support human expertise. Existing reference models based on tool integration offer no sensible place to put these matters.

The Theoretical Context. The ECMA reference model (by far the most complete available) describes itself as a "collection of services" drawn from current experience and research. Its catalog is structured only by a rough grouping of services into major categories and a template for service descriptions. This arrangement makes it easy to add new material (just extend the list, or at most, define a new category), but hard to judge whether the result is complete or redundant or even internally contradictory. Two examples of the cost of building as you go, without a firm theoretical foundation: the lack of effective means for evaluating trade-offs between tools and training, and the difficulty of distinguishing, different time-threads of factory process.

The ESF CoRe is an attempt to fill these gaps. Our goal is to complement the work so well begun by ECMA/NIST and other teams.

First Principles

The basic structure of the CoRe is governed by two "axioms:"

1. Work on software consists to a large extend of *coordinating communication;*
2. *People* and *machines* communicate in fundamentally different ways.

Axioms are by definition not subject to proof, but it is worth indicating, at least briefly, why these two should be accepted as given.

The arrangement of walls and spaces, desks and utilities in an office building tells little about how the building works. Much more informative are the traffic patterns determined by the flow of people, papers, water and electricity which the building supports. Once the static support structures are shifted into the background, questions of use and purpose can come into focus.

Consequently, software production consists largely of communication. The development of software systems consists of teams of engineers negotiating and codifying agreements as to how data are to be represented and manipulated. (Remember: industrial software engineering, not programming as a personal learning activity or as a vehicle for individual entrepreneurship is the subject.) Software system quality is assured by monitoring the negotiation and codification processes and then communicating back to the development team any inconsistencies discovered in the records of its results. Things that happen during software production, which are not communicated either to a colleague or to the system itself, do not become part of the product, nor even a (replicable) part of the production process. Note the emphasis on coordinating communication. This circumstance reads two ways:

Communication in support of coordination.
Coordinating the flow of communication.

Industrial software production has been characterized as "programming in-the-many" ("many people using many tools to make many versions of many modules for use in many configurations at many sites by many users over many years...") *Coordination* is the discipline for coping with "many"; *communication* is the only means of exercising that discipline.

Thus, support for software factory production means support for coordinating communication among the people who manage and develop software assets and the machines that support them in that work.

Axiom #2 is given special emphasis by the observation that factory work is accomplished by the coordinated work of people supported by machines. Just what does this imply for a production process consisting largely of communication? The answer is that software factory coordination is constrained by the fundamentally different kinds of communication of which people and machines are capable.

Only people can interpet unexpected events in terms of ambiguous and conflicting purposes, and make—or break—commitments as a result. Only machines can reliably evaluate rapidly changing information in terms of complexly structured constraints, and communicate the results without ambiguity. Designing a work package for delegation to a person is quite different from designing a program for execution by machines. People must/can be managed; machines must/can be configured. Managers who ignore the difference soon regret the results.

Whether these differences are ontological or merely reflect the current state of technological advance (a question on which "much ink has been spilt") does not matter here. No one denies that for now, and for the forseeable future, the difference remains a fact. We must therefore distinguish clearly between communications in which:

- Two mechanisms exchange information.
- One person exchanges information with one or more mechanisms.
- Two people exchange information via one or more mechanisms.

A realistic reference model for software factories must identify the defining characteristics of each of these basic classes of communication, and what it takes to support each of them with appropriate technology.

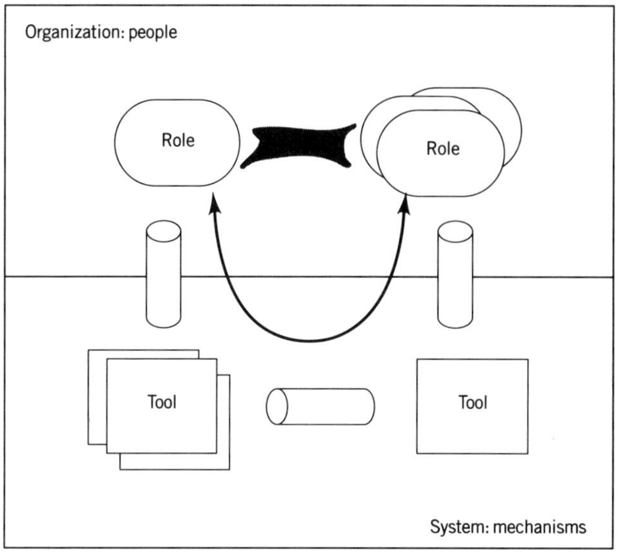

Figure 2. Factory fundamentals.

ESF CoRe Image #1: The "Smile". The ESF CoRe model is represented by a set of three "Core Images" and a glossary of terms used to label those images. The images form a series, each building on what has come before, each adding a new dimension to the analysis.

ESF CoRe Image #1 does *not* represent a component architecture analogous to the ECMA "toaster" or IBM's building-block logo for AD/Cycle. Rather, it shows the basic factory *communication structure* implied by the argument so far.

Image #1 suggests that a software factory (like any factory) consists of an Organization of people whose work is managed to achieve various goals, and a System of machines whose operations are configured to serve various support functions. The organization's human resources appear as functional sets called roles, much as the system's mechanical resources are grouped functionally into tools.

Since the work of a software factory can (by axiom #1) be defined as a set of communication processes, the primary requirement on the System is that it provide efficient, effective and reliable *communication channels.* These are shown in Figure 2 as pipes that connect bits of the system to each other, and reach out from the system into the human world. The arrow shows the flow of information carried from one part of the Organization to another by the supporting System; the "cloud" reminds us that an important communication channel exists outside the technical system boundary.

The total flow of factory communication is thus decomposed according to the different capabilities of people and machines. In a deliberate analogue to the ISO model of Open Systems Interconnection, the three flows are called:

InterWorking — Communication among *people* that enables and ensures effective integration of the *organization*.

InterAction — Communication between individual *users* and their *tools* that enables and ensures effective integration of *actions* taken in different *contexts*.

InterOperation — Communication among *mechanisms* that enables and ensures effective integration of the *system*.

In these terms, the goal of software factory engineering is to make the interworking of software factory organizations more effective, by providing better interaction contexts based on more effective system interoperation.

What Kind of CoRe? Setting our basic observations in the context defined by our two "axioms," the picture of a software factory as a complex communications network emerges. The elements of the network may be either people or machines. The communication channels that bind the elements together into a network may also be either human or mechanical. The work of the nodes is to negotiate and codify a complex of messages: descriptions of information and its manipulation (i.e., software). By "a complex" is meant:

- A large number of "message packets" is involved (typically 10,000s of documents and programs).
- An even larger number of links exists among these message packets (typically at least 10s of links per packet), such that changes made to any one packet is likely to produce a "chain reaction" of changes in other packets.

The complex defined by these sets of messages and links is relatively long-lived: the definition of any message or any link is likely to change many times in the life of the complex. It is also likely that the capabilities of both the communicating elements and the communication channels of the factory network that creates the complex, will change during the long life of the software complex.

Question — If a software factory is a complex communications network for creating and manipulating long-lived message-complexes, what is the appropriate structure of a software factory reference model?

Answer — One which classifies the communicating *elements* of the factory by the kinds of message they exchange, and which classifies the messages by their semantic relationship to each other.

A conceptual reference model for software factories thus requires two dimensions:

- A view of the *information flow* as defined by the nature of its contributors, and
- A view of the *contributors* in terms of their role in the information flow.

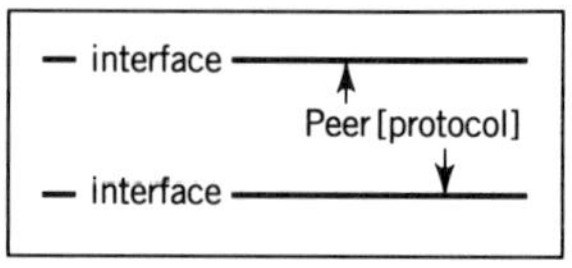

Figure 3. The OSI metamodel.

Because the latter (architectural) view is easily mistaken for a conventional list-of-components of the sort embodied in the ECMA "toaster" model, the discussion begins with the conceptual view: a model for representing a software factory's information flow.

Factory Communication Semantics

The three Inters are not accidentally named. The conceptual view of a software factory offered by the CoRe is an extension and refinement of the ISO Reference Model for Open Systems Interconnection (OSI).

The OSI designers were faced with a similar, conceptual problem. The designers needed a unified vocabulary that could be applied to both existing and future communication technologies operating at very different levels of abstraction (e.g., electrical potentials vs application procedures) and based on wholly different physical principles (e.g., telephone vs microwave links). In much the same way, ESF needs a common integration framework that can span three wholly different classes of information exchange.

The 7-layer OSI Reference Model was invented specifically to map this kind of terrain. The strategic solution was to decode communication flows into semantically separate *layers*. The strategy is based on a distinction between *protocols* (known only within a single layer) and *interfaces* published for use by unknown clients calling from a higher layer. It is represented by Figure 3.

The function of communication in each layer is to construct, from the services offered to it by the layer below, new services to enable a more abstract exchange of information at the next higher layer. Seen from the other direction, peers at each layer decompose service requests received at their "upward" interface into (legal, effective) sequences of lower level service requests.

A set of (rules for constructing) such sequences is called a protocol. The concept of a protocol allows peers to define conventions to support particular purposes. The concept of an interface defined as a set of services allows these conventions to be effectively hidden from clients interested only in the facilities published outside the layer.

On the basis of this metamodel, the OSI Reference Model defines seven semantically independent layers of machine–machine interconnection. The power of this approach is shown by the success at providing a common interpretive framework for descriptions of an enormous variety of pre-existing communication facilities. In the area of LANs, for example, this dual effect can be seen in the competitive coexistence of NetWare and TCP/IP, both making use of the same physical network services.

The relevance for the ESF CoRe is the independence of each layer from the others means that the model still holds if the "implementation" of a layer consists of "John telling

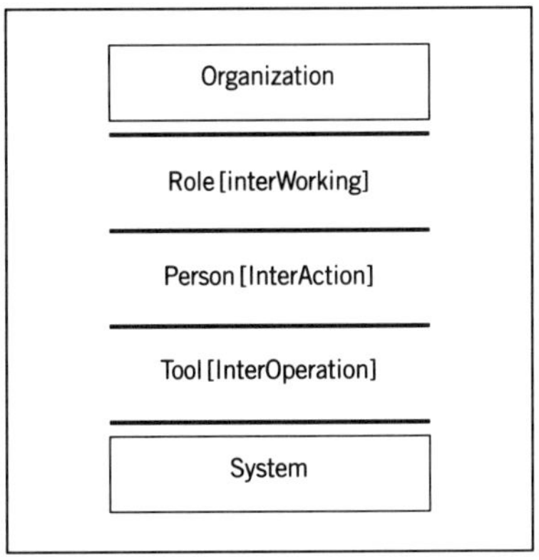

Figure 4. Factory communication layers.

Mary something over a cup of coffee." OSI gives us a framework that can include both people *and* machines.

The Value of Following the OSI Approach. The OSI framework provides a valuable foundation for the ESF CoRe because:

- It is the established standard for discourse about communication.
- The OSI principle of composition (i.e., protocols, services) is powerful enough to generalize beyond its original domain, to cover the whole factory.

There is more. The OSI metamodel of layers separated by interfaces has the effect of making any set of adjacent layer a ear to those above (and below) it as a single layer. Conversely, the seven-layer model can be taken as one instance of a general approach to analyzing the function of any single layer.

CoRe Image #2: The "Ladder". The differences in the way people and machines communicate oblige us to distinguish the three fundamental classes of communication which we have called InterWorking, InterAction and InterOperation. The central assertion embodied in the ESF CoRe is that these three communication classes are best understood as layers in the sense of the Open Systems Interconnection reference model.

If the general concepts sketched in Figure 2 as a formal OSI-style model of software factory communications is redrawn, Figure 4 represents the new configuration:

Organizational effectiveness depends on coordinating work done by many people. *System* effectiveness depends on coordinating the operation of many mechanisms. *Personal* effectiveness depends on coordinating actions taken by people in various organizational and system context. Coordination is achieved by communication. Therefore, total factory effectiveness is a function of the quality of communication maintained among the people and machines of which it consists.

The Limits of the OSI Model. The most obvious limitation of the OSI model as a basis for talking about software factories is that it says nothing at all about what is communicated. On the other hand, the argument just made above implies that the relative weight given to different layers is subject to the needs of the designer. There is nothing to forbid us from collapsing layers 1–7 into something we take for granted as the Platform, and expanding level 7 by as many further layers as we need to map the semantics of software factory information flow— which is precisely what the ESF CoRe does.

But it is not simply a matter of adding extra layers. The problem is to cope with the information explosion *within* layers. The OSI model provides no principles for *layer construction*—nor does it need to. OSI has a clearly circumscribed job: to get a data stream from point A to point B. The *content* of the data stream is largely irrelevant. In the software factory, the concern is precisely with the complexly interwoven meanings of specification and object code, design review and test protocol. Principles are needed for defining and classifying (sub)sets of both interfaces and protocols, and principles for assembling such sets into (re-)usable compositions.

FACTORY CONSTRUCTION AND EVALUATION

As with any technology, software engineering concepts and especially software engineering environments for software factories, can be introduced into their industrial use only in a gradual fashion. This rationale is due to a number of reasons.

New technologies will be tested before their widespread use for their practicability. Practicability in turn depends on factors like:

1. The understandability of a new technology for the practising professional.
2. The total cost of introducing the new technology in terms of the needed initial investments, the expected permanent costs etc.
3. The "compatibility" between existing and new technologies.

In addition to those rational factors, the introduction of new technologies depends even more on a number of psychological factors like:

1. The general retarding momentum towards chance as it may be observed for individuals and for organizations.
2. The desire to minimize risks that may come along with change.
3. The desire to secure a large step in changes by subdividing it into successfully accomplishable small steps.

These factors play an important role in all kinds of evolutions and are by no means specific to the introduction of new software technologies. But unfortunately enough they are all too often forgotten in the domain of software. To bear these factors in mind, however, may be even more important for software technology than for many other technologies since the surrounding hardware and network-

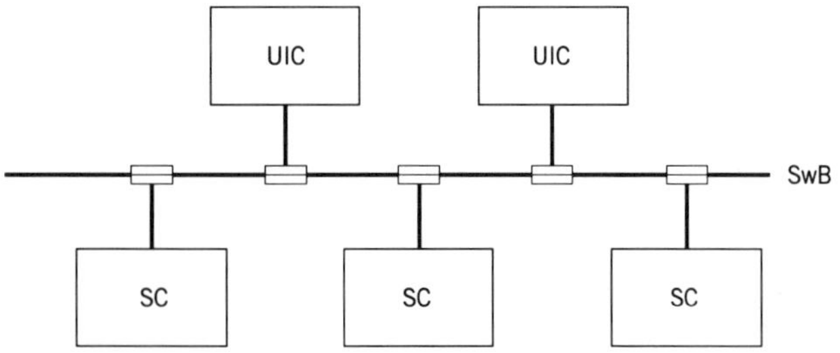

Figure 5. The FSE architecture: a set of service components of user interaction components connected to a Software Bus.

ing technologies change with an extremely fast pace. The rapid change, in turn, accounts for continuously developing new software demands and hence for better software production capabilities. Computer supported software technology, thus, has to cope with both the general problem of resistance towards chance and with a strong demand for change.

As indicated above, technological change always depends on both a proper psychological/organizational setting and on the appropriateness of the technology to accommodate its gradual move into industrial practice. Computer supported software production within a software factory is meant to enable the gradual introduction of this technology into industrial practices by making "extensibility" of the support environment one of the prime principles applied in the development of a factory architecture.

The notion of extensibility will be introduced here with a number of scenarios that are useful to depict the possible upgrading of a support environment to enable the gradual introduction of computer supported software production into industrial use. Extensibility is meant to be an orderly extension of something that exists. It is not left to a trial and error procedure to develop a software factory but is meant to be a preplanned approach. The preplanning however is meant to leave at least some degrees of freedom to accommodate different needs. ESF proposes therefore a minimal software factory reference architecture that represents the essential invariants of a software factory. A software factory support environment (FSE) is then constructed according to that software factory reference architecture. The essential ingredients of the software factory reference architecture are chosen to enable extensibility by the plugging and removing of components into and from the FSE.

According to the software factory reference architecture an FSE consists of two sets of components connected to a Software Bus (SwB) (ESF trademark). The one kind of components are user interaction components, the others are service components (see Fig. 5).

The components are pieces of software which can be "plugged into" the SwB, and thus have the following characteristics:

- The FSE is meaningful without the component,
- A component can be added to the FSE without changing any surrounding.
- A component can be purchased independently by an end user.

A minimum amount of functionality must be present in every FSE: the *kernel mechanisms.* These are provided partly by the SwB, partly by user interaction components and by service components. Components that implement such compulsory functions are called *kernel components.*

This architecture has been *chosen* to accommodate the extensibility mentioned above that may be needed to cope with the situations described in the following scenarios.

Scenario 1. A "minimal" instance of a software factory support environment must provide only the essential parts in order to satisfy a client's desire to limit costs, disturbances of the current operation, and the involved risk altogether. On the other hand it must be attractive enough to demonstrate the potential benefits of the FSE.

According to the ESF reference architecture, such a minimal instance must provide the following essential components: at least one user interaction component, at least one service component and the Software Bus. The user interaction component provides in this scenario the only interface to the software factory that enables accesses to and invocations of all service components. The interconnection and interoperation between the user interaction component and service components or between different service components will be enabled by the Software Bus.

Both the user interaction component and the service components may reside on the same host computer. The Software Bus then serves as a local interconnection and interoperation facility providing primarily the extensibility of the software factory by enabling the plug-in of additional service components. An instance of that nature shall be called software factory workstation.

Scenario 2. The division of labor among software developers and the proper use of their special skills for the development of larger software systems will lead to the clients desire to employ a number of software factory workstations at a minimal cost. To arrive at that minimal cost will be possible by tailoring each software factory workstation to the individual needs. As a consequence, software factory workstations that belong to one FSE may differ in both their user interaction component and in the set of services they encompass. Then they altogether constitute a minimal configuration for a software factory support environment.

A minimal configuration of a software factory support environment may—according to the reference architecture—consist: of a number of user interaction components that do not necessarily reside on the same host computer; of a number of service components that also do not necessarily reside on the same host; of a possible distributed Software Bus that enables the interconnection and interoperation of the possible distributed user interaction components and service components.

Scenario 3. A second kind of division of labor among software developers may be accommodated by providing a "complete" software factory workstation to every software developer or a small group of software developers who are endowed with the responsibility for the development of a component of a system. The component development by a number of developers in this mode may then be integrated to form the complete system. The configuration of the resulting software factory instance may now not be necessarily minimal any more than in the sense as defined above. It may however provide some other advantages that relate to the homogeneity across the entire configuration, like manageability and maintenance of the configuration.

Under this scenario an FSE consists once again of a number of software factory workstations. Thus each host has the same or almost the same set of user interaction components and service components that get interconnected and interoperate over the distributed Software Bus.

Obviously this kind of a configuration will only be installed after a period of gradual extension to make it really conform to the needs. After development over an extended period of time, it represents an FSE supporting a certain software development style or even software development culture, that is based on the specific skills and organizational setting in a specific software development enterprise.

The extensibility concept, rather vaguely introduced with the three scenarios above, will be given a more technical foundation in the sequel. It should however be emphasized again that the concept is meant to introduce a FSE, not as a monolithic system but as a concept that allows for incremental upgrading. As such this configuration enables an inaugeration with low investments and low costs for its initial use, as well as a gradual extension and test for acceptance. It represents a low threshold into computer supported software production.

The FSE Architecture introduced above has been acclaimed for being able to support its evolutionary extension. This extension will be further explained now with its refined description.

The refined architecture now introduces evaluation stages for an FSE:

1. FSE kernel components.
2. FSE support components.
3. FSE application components as depicted in Figure 6.

The FSE kernel is the run-time system for a basic set of languages developed to allow for the description of interworking, interaction, and interoperation in a software factory. The FSE kernel consists of three components: the interworking process engine (IWPE), the software bus (SwB), and multiple instantiations of the interaction process engine (IAPE):

- A process is defined in a process model described in the process modeling language, PML. The IWPE component in the FSE Kernel is the executant for that part of the process model that defines the *interworking*.
- The IAPE is the executant of the interaction part of the process model. It hence implements the "local part," part of the process model. Since there may be numerous factory users, there are multiple instantiations of the IAPE.
- The backbone of the FSE is the SwB. It implements the *interoperation* and *interconnection* of components within the factory. The purpose of the SwB is twofold. At factory-building-time the SwB is the mechanism to integrate components. At factory-operating-time the SwB has the responsibility to process and forward requests issued by a client to a server and to return the results. The interoperation description language is used to describe the interplay of FSE components.

The FSE support consists of two parts: the kernel support which provides generic support for the executants IWPE, SwB, and IAPE, and the general support which, for instance, provides central data management facilities for the entire FSE, editors, compilers, linkers, etc.

An application oriented part of the FSE, the FSE application components, accounts for the application domain and customer specifics. For example, the software development in the world of finance and banking imposes tight security regulations on people and machines (hardware and software) and these restrictions may only apply in the domain "Banking".

KERNEL $K/2_R$

The $K/2_R$ is one of two kernel developments in ESF. While Kernel/1 is an industrial product development, $K/2_R$ is a research project, aiming at developing advanced integration concepts for a possible later incorporation into the ESF product development.

$K/2_R$ Interworking Support

Many of the existing approaches tackle the problem of software process management by defining an executable process modeling language and by building an interworking process engine that is able to enact the process models. Thus, the focus of these approaches lies only on process model enaction.

The $K/2_R$ takes a broader view of software process management. It aims at addressing the:

- Process model development/software process understanding.
- Process model analysis (validation/verification/post-evaluation).
- Process model enaction.

As process model development and analysis are considered to be integral parts of the process management, the process modeling language that is being used in $K/2_R$ must give support to all three process management phases that have been listed above.

Process Model Development/Software Process Understanding. The development of process models is a complex task that can only be performed in a coordinated effort between the process designer (as a representative of the factory builder) who is responsible for developing the process model and the project manager (as a representative of the

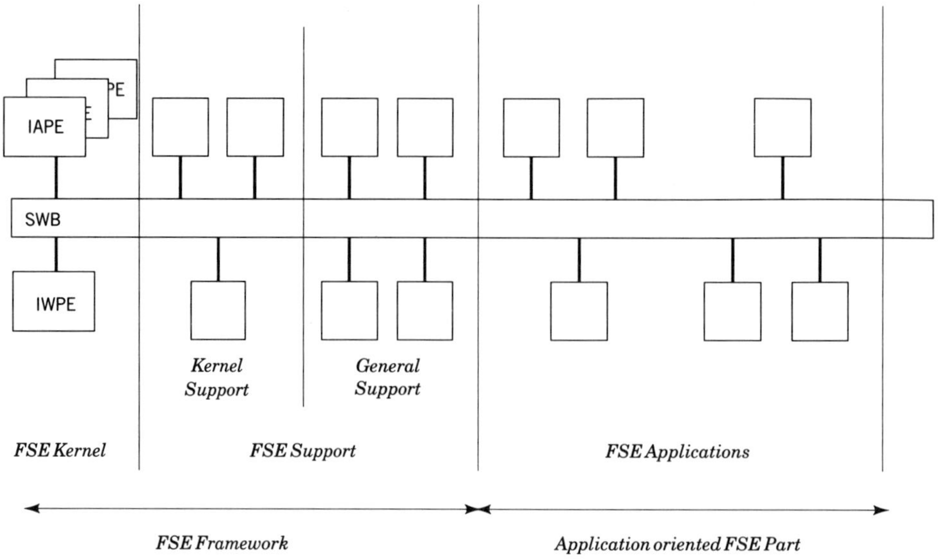

Figure 6. Refined architectural view of an FSE.

factory user) who knows the guidelines, procedures, and policies of the company or the project that is to be captured in the process model. The process designer gets the information the user needs in discussions and interviews with the project manager. A language is provided to represent the information about the software process.

Process Model Analysis. Process models that have been developed must be intensively tested before being enacted. The testing of process models is called process model analysis. Analyzing process models should be done for detecting: (1) errors in the process model (i.e. the model does not reflect what it was intended to reflect) and (2) detecting errors in the software process (i.e., the model reflects what it was intended to reflect but it shows that processes derived from the models are erroneous or run ineffectively). Furthermore, process model analysis can detect inefficient process models.

Process Model Enaction. Process models that have been developed and analyzed can be used for process model enaction. Enacting a process model means guiding software developers in their work and taking routine tasks off them. As it is the purpose of process management to make different people co-operate effectively, the interworking process engine must guide the work of many software developers acting in different roles, concurrently.

One important issue that has to be managed when enacting process models, is the issue of software process adaptation. Adapting a process model that has been enacted is necessary since it is literally impossible to model a software process completely in advance. Thus, adapting process models means on the one hand, adding information into the process model that has not been available during process model development, and to change/adapt the process model due to changed needs, on the other hand. Of course, it must be possible to perform the process model adaptations during the software process, i.e., *on the fly*. An interruption of the whole software process for performing the adaptation would unbearably delay the software production process.

The Process Modelling Language FUNSOFT. The language that has been defined to match the requirements discussed above is called FUNSOFT nets (Gruhn, 1991).

The FUNSOFT nets language is a graphical high level Petri net language. The nets comprise three different graphical elements. Channels are containers for software objects. Agencies represent software process activities. They can either be composed or simple. Composed agencies represent complex activities (addressed as tasks in the following), simple agencies represent basic software process activities (addressed as actions in the following). Edges connect channels and agencies defining which objects are input for, and which objects are output of activities.

A refinement of agencies enables the breaking down of complex process models into smaller models that are easier to grasp. Thus, a hierarchical structuring of process models is supported. A process model can be produced by stepwise refining agencies and by incrementally adding information to the process model.

Figure 7 depicts a sample of a FUNSOFT net. The sample net shows a fraction of a process model that describes the adaptation of a software system due to implementation change requests.

The integration of existing tools and services into the process model is realized in FUNSOFT nets by associating "jobs" with agencies. Jobs implement activities. A job consists of a name, a parameterization, an informal description, a firing behavior description, a formal description of its input/output behavior, and an execution description.

In addition to the definition of necessary input objects by specifying channels, the definition of start conditions for activities is supported by using the mechanism of predicates in FUNSOFT. The firing of an agency depends on conditions and not only on the fact that all channels are

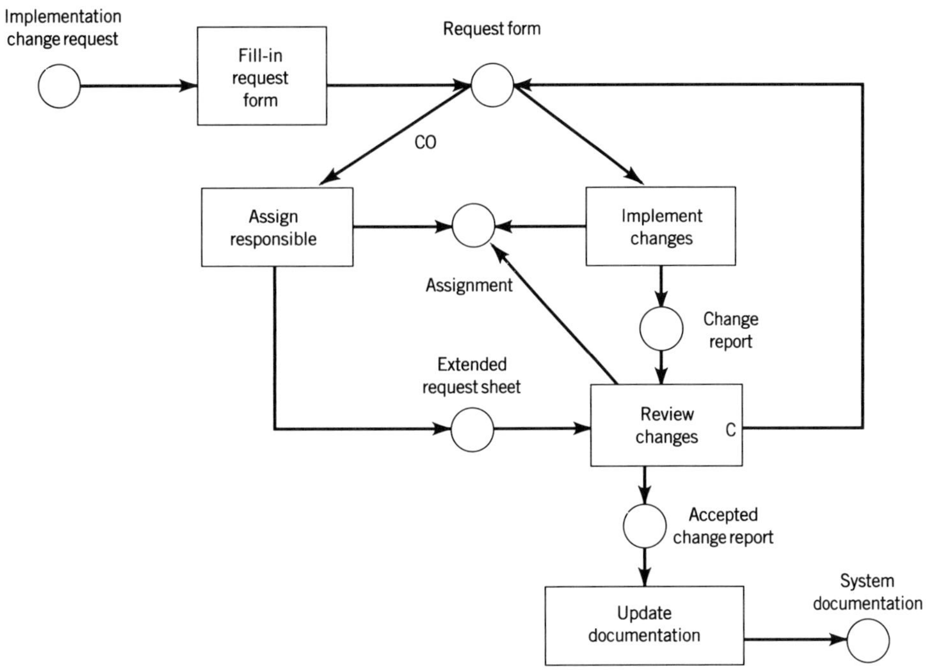

Figure 7. Example of FUNSOFT net.

marked. Predicates define conditions on the names and values of objects which will be read within a firing.

Furthermore, it is possible to define a set of postconditions for each activity as a set of channels which are connected to the corresponding agency through edges. The token in these channels may again be start conditions for other activities.

A model specified in FUNSOFT nets is open to extension and modification. Details about how to modify FUNSOFT nets can be found in Deiters and Gruhn (1990).

FUNSOFT nets have a formally defined semantic. Thus process models described by FUNSOFT nets can be formally analyzed (Deiters and Gruhn, 1991), Analysis can be performed by verification, validation, and post evaluation. Using verification techniques, properties of the process model (such as e.g., the existence or absence of deadlocks) can be proved. During process model validation, the behavior of software processes can be tested by applying simulation techniques. Software process post evaluation means to test software processes that have been performed already. The knowledge that has been gained during the software process can be used for improving the process model.

Because of the execution model of Petri nets, process models expressed in terms of FUNSOFT nets may be used for guiding the software process. Activities that do not need human intervention can be started automatically by the interworking process engine, human activities that can be performed are provided to the software developer by putting the respective tools into the software developer's working context that is under the control of the user's interaction process engine (IAPE). Hence the software developers are assisted during their development work.

MELMAC: Components for Software Process Management in K/2$_R$. MELMAC (Deiters and Gruhn, 1990) provides support for developing, analyzing and enacting process models that are described using FUNSOFT nets. The following figure represents the architectural view of the K/2$_R$ Process Management Components (Fig. 8).

K/2$_R$: Interaction Support

Interaction is concerned with the interactive work of a single person involved in the software development process by governing the use of interactive tools and/or services that can be requested.

The organization of the interactive work is described in an interaction model. Logically, the interaction model forms a part of the global software process model (qv). From the runtime perspective, the global process model is, however, decomposed into one or more interworking model parts, many interaction and interoperation model parts. The enaction of these models is performed by means of specific process engines. In particular, interaction models are enacted by interaction process engines.

Interaction is supported by providing a user with multiple views on the tasks to be performed (e.g., role-oriented, project-oriented, deadline-oriented). A set of actions to be performed and a set of services that can be requested by the same user, acting in some role, are presented on a screen which is generated specifically for the user and, subsequently, automatically updated according to the work progress. Of course, the same user can act in different roles.

Users working under the control of the IAPE perform actions (as constituents of a task) by using interactive tools that are accessible through their desktop. This results in

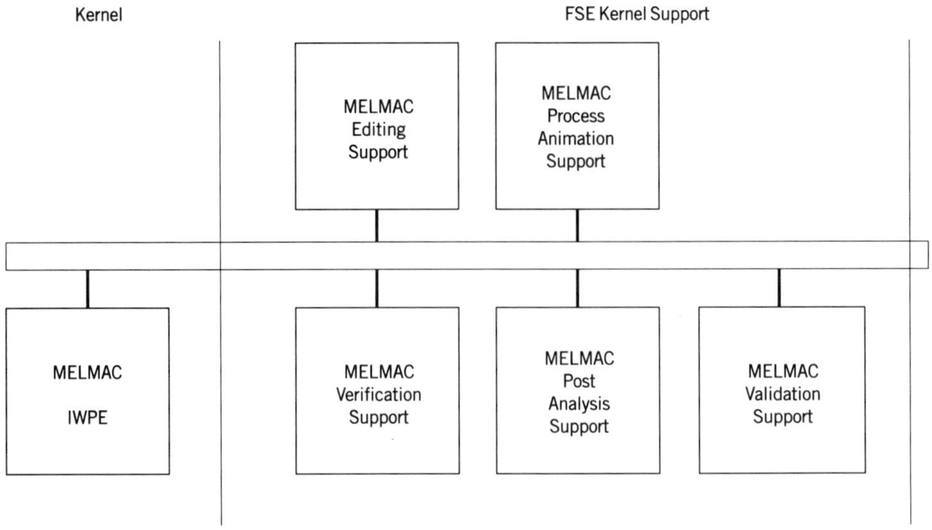

Figure 8. The MELMAC process management environment.

a modified working context as a modified set of tasks/actions to be performed by the user.

Figure 9 shows an example of an IAPE screen at the runtime of the execution of an interaction model which refines the interworking model example presented in Figure 6 towards the interaction level. In this example the IAPE presents a user acting in the role "Programmer" and the actions to be done in the context of the task "implement changes" as defined on the interworking level.

At each point where the work of a single person requires cooperation with other persons involved in the process of software development, a switch from interaction to interworking is performed by transferring control from the IAPE to the IWPE.

A switch from interaction to interoperation is actively performed by transferring control from the IAPE to the Software Bus and from there to a Service Component or a set of interoperating Service Components.

The $K/2_R$ project supports interaction as described above by providing:

- An interaction modeling language
- An interaction modeling language executant
- Tools for interaction support.

The $K/2_R$ uses the FUNSOFT net language to express interaction models in order to be in conceptual coherence with the language used for modeling on the interworking level.

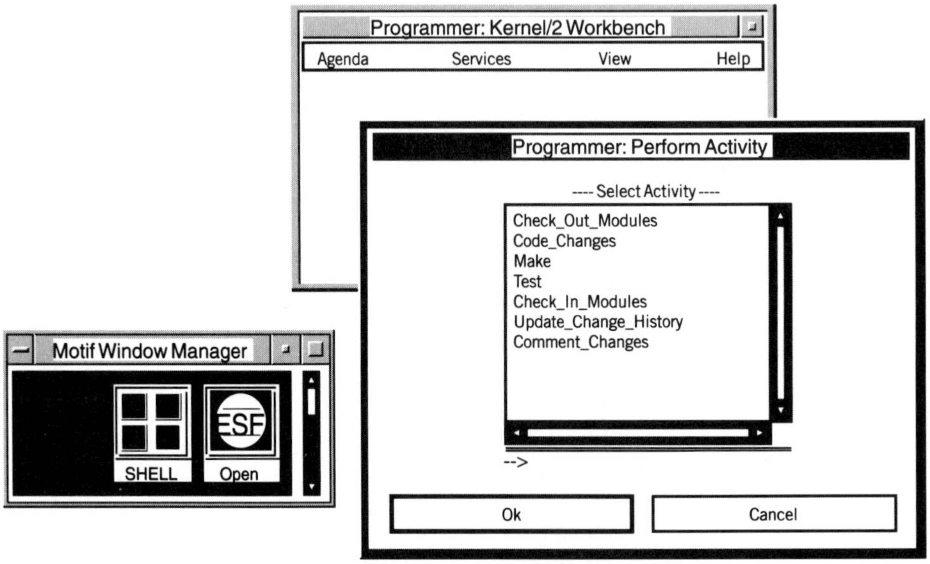

Figure 9. Example of IAPE screen.

$K/2_R$: Interoperation Support

The $K/2_R$ supports distribution transparency and interoperation between factory components by providing for:

- An interoperation description language
- An interoperation description language executant
- Standards-based name and location services.

Interoperation Description Language. The $K/2_R$ Interoperation Description Language has been tailored towards the needs of administrative autonomy of components and the concept of transaction-based interoperation. The problem of transaction processing in the context of cooperating autonomous sites has been tackled by a variety of transaction concepts (Elmagarmid 1992). They are all based on the nested transactions concept (Moss 1982).

For $K/2_R$ the S-transaction concept has been chosen as a representative for an autonomous transaction concept. In the following an informal definition of S-transactions is given. For a detailed discussion of the S-transaction concept, refer to Eliassen (1992).

The concept of S-transactions has been developed in order to describe the cooperation of autonomous components, located at geographically dispersed sites, in an integrated, cooperative system like the $K/2_R$ FSE. The underlying system model is that of a set of cooperating peer components. The interrelationships between these components are dynamically defined within S-transaction type definitions. Basically, the S-transaction type definition contains an execution plan indicating what requests are to be processed where, i.e. local or at remote sites. The execution plan of the S-transaction is predefined and expressed in terms of STDL, the S-Transaction Definition Language.

An S-transaction is recursively defined. A top-level S-transaction is composed of a set of subordinate S-transactions and/or local transactions (LTs). The local transactions interface to the SCs that are allocated to the local FSE sites. Hence, by definition, S-transactions are multi-level transactions. A top-level S-transaction is the parent node for a set of subordinate S-transactions which are initiated at logically different FSE sites. Normally, these sites are geographically dispersed. Any S-transaction can request services from SCs encapsulated at the site that it is allocated to (referred to as local site). These services are provided by the local site as transactions, hence called local transactions. Local transactions are self-contained, conventional transactions, i.e., they are executed as transactions providing atomicity, consistency, isolation, and durability. As a consequence they commit prior to the termination of their parent S-transactions.

The local FSE sites are responsible for the implementation of local transactions (due to their autonomy). Hence, implementations of the same local transaction may differ from site to site. Its semantics, however, must be the same at each site. A local transaction is executed under the control of the local site and the site is responsible for the recovery of the failing transaction. Thus, the local site's execution autonomy is preserved as the local transaction execution control is beyond the scope of the S-transaction that requests the local transaction. In general, recovery from failure during the execution of a local transaction is performed by means of conventional UNDO recovery techniques, i.e., backward recovery. Recovery of S-transactions is based on compensation. For any component S-transaction ST and for any local transaction LT the existence of compensating transactions -STs and -LTs, respectively, is required.

The STDL-scripts are defined at installation time and stored in a S-transaction repository at all participating sites. An S-transaction handler takes these scripts and processes the S-transaction by initiating the required local and remote transactions. Hence, the S-transactions represent "canned transactions" in the sense of predefined execution descriptions.

In STDL an S-transaction is described by its name and a set of different sections. Figure 10 shows the syntactic framework for the definition of S-transactions. We roughly distinguish between a data definition part (i.e. STDL/DDL) and an operations part (i.e., STDL/DML).

STDL/DDL. As STDL is aimed at being used for the specification of transactions in a dedicated decentralized system, the structure of the data being exchanged between two interacting sites must be known to both sites. Hence, in the request data section, the data types and data structures are defined that form a part of the parameter list a request to a remote site consists of. The input data section contains the data type definitions for the input parameters that have to be filled in when invoking an S-transaction. Furthermore, local results and intermediate results of an S-transaction must be manageable. Finally, data structures are needed that are shared by different parts (continuation points) of a single S-transaction at the same site. For these purposes STDL provides the local data section.

The data definition features of STDL correspond to those of modern high-level programming languages. STDL provides the primitive data types INTEGER, BOOLEAN, REAL, and STRING. By means of the operators union, intersection, enumeration, and cartesian product, more complex data types can be constructed.

```
s_transaction <name>
    input_data
        <set of input data>
    end
    request_data
        <set of request data>
    end
    local_data
        <set of local data>
    end
    continuation_points
        <set of continuation points>
    end
end /* of s-transaction <name>*/
```

Figure 10. Basic STDL components for an S-transaction definition.

STDL/DML. A sub-S-transaction provides a service and might request services from remote sites. Therefore, an S-transaction is divided into different parts that can be invoked via continuation points. The set of continuation points constitutes the execution plan for the entire transaction. The continuation points denote the entries at which a superior or sub-S-transaction may be activated or may receive results. The special continuation point "init_cp" is activated at the root S-transaction initiation time if the initiation is requested from a user. The other continuation points can be activated either from remote sites by requesting a service, provided by that S-transaction type the continuation point belongs to, or by submitting results that were requested from another continuation point of the already active S-transaction.

A continuation point consists of a unique identification within an S-transaction, an input parameter list, and a path. The path describes the execution plan for that continuation point. The path consists of calls to built-in functions and/or requests to other continuation points of remote S-transactions. For these activities an execution order has to be defined and execution constraints may be specified. The order is defined by means of operators indicating sequential, parallel, or conditional execution. Execution means calling a built-in or local transaction and waiting for a result (like a procedure call) or sending a request to another continuation point. In the latter case the originating transaction has no control over the execution. It is not possible to wait within the initiating path for a result of another continuation point executed at a different site. This result is sent to another continuation point of the requesting transaction. It is, however, possible to use local data for synchronization.

For the execution of the operations within a path, constraints in terms of time conditions or conditions on expected results, can be specified. In addition to these conditions STDL also provides facilities for formulating conditions on communication level. Delivery notification of messages, successful execution of S-transactions, transaction aborts, etc., can be indicated if they are specified within a path.

Interoperation Description Language Executant. The interoperation language executant of K/2_R is MUSE, a system that has been implemented for managing the interoperation of components in a distributed environment by means of autonomous transaction processing. MUSE supports the execution of S-transactions (Eliassen, 1992) that coordinate the interoperation of autonomous, geographically dispersed FSE components. (The first version of MUSE has been developed in the framework of the Multi-Annual Program (MAP 761B), a pre-ESPRIT program funded by the CEC. STDL has been redefined and MUSE has been redesigned in the course of the K/2_R development.)

A MUSE instance consists of an S-transaction repository, an S-transaction Handler, interpreting STDL-scripts, a sophisticated application interface, and an interface to the SCs encapsulated. Communication between MUSE instances is based on the interconnection mechanisms of K/2_R. The S-transaction handler employs dedicated "send" and "receive" modules to interface with the K/2_R interconnection support. Local communication with encapsulated SCs though, is customized corresponding to the needs of the SC interface.

The K/2_R Interoperation Language Executant MUSE is the nucleus of the K/2_R SwB. The interface between the MELMAC K/2_R IWPE and the MUSE K/2_R SwB is defined through sets of STDL scripts which realize the jobs associated with the instances of the FUNSOFT net. In general, a job is characterized by its parameterization, the precondition, the action, and the postcondition. The action is expressed in terms of STDL and may consist of one or more service requests, utilizing all features STDL provides for. After checking the preconditions, the interworking process engine only needs to request the initiation of the corresponding S-transaction and then awaits the results that may or may not fulfil the postconditions.

Distribution Transparency Support. Within an FSE a lot of entities or objects have to be managed; for example, there are persons, components, services, development objects and many more. These objects are widely spread allover the distributed environment. In adherence with the demand for configuration and execution dynamics, inherent to complex and extensible environments like the FSE, there is a need for distribution transparency (ECMA 1990).

In order to support overall distribution transparency, the K/2_R FSE provides for name and location services that access an information base containing data about locations of objects in the K/2_R software factory. This information base is called the K/2_R data dictionary (DD). The data dictionary serves as the basis for the K/2_R name and location services. In the aggregate, the K/2_R data dictionary and the K/2_R name and location services support the following aspects of distribution transparency:

- *Location transparency* ensures that bindings between objects are independent of the routes that connect them. This configuration requires name services for logical addressing, i.e., addressing-by-naming.
- *Replication transparency* allows for multiple instances of objects to be used in order to increase availability and performance. The name and location services support the selection of a particular object and thus facilitate execution dynamics.
- *Migration transparency* enables the movement of an object in a distributed environment. This feature lays the foundation for dynamic system configurations.
- *Naming transparency* means the identification of an object by an arbitrary key independent from its logical name. This key consists of a description of the characteristics (properties) of the object. This kind of logical naming is also called naming-by-criteria.

Additionally, there are other aspects of distribution transparency that are embedded in the K/2_R interoperation description language, respectively its executant:

- *Access transparency* is concerned with the means of hiding the mechanisms employed to achieve interoperation between components. Obviously, the K/2_R inter-

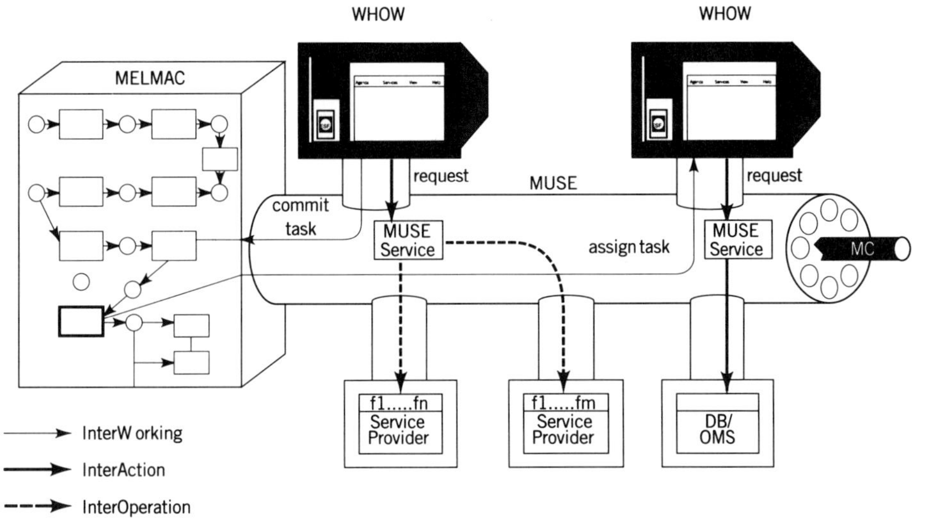

Figure 11. Functioning of K/2_R.

operation description language STDL provides for access transparency, since it allows service requests irrespective of how services are accessed and irrespective of whether services components are local or remote.

- *Concurrency transparency* hides the effects of parallel use of shared resources (SCs) without permitting inconsistent use of the resource. In K/2_R concurrency transparency is achieved by employing an autonomous transaction concept, namely S-transactions.
- *Failure transparency* enables the concealment of faults despite the failure of SCs. In the K/2_R this concealment is accomplished by ensuring that service requests reach the SC (store and forward), respecting the SCs autonomy, and conventional local recovery techniques as well as global compensation-based recovery.

Besides the different facets of distribution transparency the data dictionary is the foundation for a general information retrieval system on objects and their locations within the software factory. For this purpose the data dictionary may be accessed both in an interactive and non-interactive manner; for example, by human FSE users and by kernel components.

K/2_R: Interconnection Support

The interconnection stage of the software factory reference framework deals with different means for the integration of different computer sites in a computer network. In general, the Interconnection stage is covered by the ISO/OSI Reference Model. Of course, the K/2_R interconnection support adheres to this accepted standard.

Within the ESF community so far, the concept of "pluggability" was restricted to component plug-in, i.e. attaching SCs to the SwB in order to make their services accessible for all SwB clients. Conveying the idea of "plug-in" to the Interconnection level means that a set of communication carriers is made available and communication carriers may be added and removed at any time. As the requirements of the ESF partners suggest, a full coverage of communications means ranging from IPC mechanisms to WAN support is indispensable for the SwB. Therefore, K/2_R proposes and implements a universal multi-communication system (MCS) that enables access to a diversity of encapsulated communication carriers. Each communication carrier is considered to be a message handling system (MHS) and the set of integrated MHSs are collected under a uniform K/2_R MHS interface, the MCS.

A MHS is an entity of the seventh (application) OSI layer which provides reliable message transfer between heterogeneous systems. In consideration of the requirements imposed on the K/2_R interconnection support, the implementation of a presentation layer is not required since the data exchange is restricted to MUSE sites. The session layer is not necessary either. Moreover, an arbitrary number of sub-S-transaction implies an arbitrary number of sessions which may be blocking the whole system. Hence, the K/2_R MHS may be based directly on the ISO-transport layer or DOD TCP protocol. For local area communication it is conceivable to move even further down. The IEEE 802 LLC protocols or dedicated IPC primitives may also be used as a basis for the MHS.

The central concept of the K/2_R interconnection support is to provide a universal MHS which enables access to a variety of communication carriers. Each communication carrier is considered to be internal to the MHS which adheres to the defined $K/2_R$ service standard. This concept enables the MCS to exhibit gateway functionality. An MCS gateway manages different protocols within a single network and between different networks. For this purpose the MCS has to be able to integrate a number of communication carriers which, of course, results in a considerable overhead. Therefore, an MCS gateway is able to interconnect the ISO and DoD standards in the WAN domain merge wide area communication, local area communication, and inter process communication.

$K/2_R$ at a Glance

Figure 11 aims at explaining the functioning of $K/2_R$. Activities, initiated at one of the WHOW stations (We Help you Organize your Work), will first be guided by the IAPE associated with the respective WHOW. In order to enable guidance the IAPE receives task assignments from the IWPE, provided by the MELMAC system. For that purpose messages of the type "offer task" or "assign task" are transferred between the IWPE and an IAPE via the MUSE software bus. Upon task offering, the IAPE may have to check back with the IWPE. The IWPE decides as to whether the offering is turned into an assignment or not. If granted the IWPE sends an "assign task" message. An IAPE signals the completion of a task to the IWPE by means of a "commit task" message. Any IAPE may simultaneously issue requests for MUSE software bus services which will in turn result into requests for services from service components. The proper coordination between all components takes place as modeled in the FUNSOFT process model.

CONCLUSION

This article aims at motivating the need for process-oriented software development and presents a solution in terms of an open and extensible integration framework for a process-controlled software factory. The first part of the article introduces the ESF software factory reference framework as a means of defining and describing the scope of a software factory support environment. The demand for openness and extensibility motivates the partitioning of the entire integration task into integration stages (i.e. interworking, interaction, interoperation, and interconnection in contrast to presentation integration, data integration and control integration). The second part describes the implementation of the concepts with a kernel for a factory support environment.

The discussion encompasses an introduction of the MELMAC process modeling, analysis, and enaction components as a means to support interworking, the IAPE to support interaction processes, the MUSE system as a Software Bus instance in support of interoperation, and the MCS multicommunication system for interconnection support.

These components have been developed and are running on SUN/4 under Unix. For the time being, component integration is under way and will be finished within the next three months. The running kernel $K/2_R$ and initial factory support environment was demonstrated in the summer of 1992.

BIBLIOGRAPHY

H. Achkar and co-workers, *Software Factory Reference Framework,* Version 1.3, ESF, Report of the Reference Model Working Group, May 1991.

M. R. Cagan, "The HP SoftBench Environment: An Architecture for a New Generation of Software Tools," *HP Journal* (June 1990).

W. Deiters and V. Gruhn, "Managing Software Processes in the Environment MELMAC," *ACM SIGSOFT'90: Fourth Symposium on Software Development Environments (SDE4),* Irvine, Calif. Dec. 3–6 1990.

W. Deiters and V. Gruhn, *Software Process Model Analysis Based on FUNSOFT Nets,* Mathematical Modelling and Simulation, Berlin, FRG, No. 8, May 1991.

ECMA TC32-TG2; *Support Environment for Open Distributed Processing (SE-ODP)*; ECMA Technical Report 49, Jan. 1990.

F. Eliassen, J. Veijalainen, and B. Holtkamp, "The S-transaction Model", in A. K. Elmagarmid, ed., *Database Transaction Models for Advanced Applications,* Morgan Kaufmann Publishers Inc., 1992.

A. K. Elmagarmid, ed., *Database Transaction Models for Advanced Applications,* Morgan Kaufmann Publishers Inc., 1992.

V. Gruhn, *Validation and Verification of Software Process Models,* Ph.D. Thesis, University of Dortmund, Dortmund, Germany, May 1991.

J. S. Hurwitz and J. R. Rymer, "NCR Cooperation-Strategy for Open Integration", *Patricia Seybold's Office Computing Report* **14**(1) (Jan. 1991).

International Organization for Standardization and International Electrotechnical Committee, *Information Processing Systems-Open Systems Interconnection—The Directory; Overview of Concepts, Models, and Service,* International Standard 9594-1 Dec. 1988.

International Telegraph and Telephone Consultative Committee, *The Directory-Overview of Concepts, Models, and Service,* Recommendation X.500, Dec. 1988.

V. J. Mercurio, B. F. Meyers, A. M. Nisbet, and G. Radin, "AD/Cycle Strategy and Architecture," *IBM Systems Journal* **29**(2) (1990).

J. E. B. Moss, "Nested Transactions and Reliable Distributed Computing," *Proceedings of the 2nd Symposium on Reliability Software and Database Systems,* 1982.

A. S. Tanenbaum, *Computer Networks,* 2nd ed., Prentice Hall, N.J. 1989.

TRG (TAT), Technical Reference Guide, version 1.1, July 6, 1989.

Reinhard Adomeit
Wolfgang Deiters
Frank Schülke
Herbert Weber
University of Dortmund
Bernhard Holtkamp
Fraunhofer Institute for Software Engineering and Systems Engineering (ISST)
Robert Rockwell
Softlab GmbH

SOFTWARE ENGINEERING ETHICS

OVERVIEW

Software engineering is a developing profession. One of the key elements in any profession is the recognition of its ethical and moral responsibilities to its clients, to society, and to the profession itself. Many professions, such as engineering and medicine, declare these responsibilities publicly in a code of ethics and then later require training in professional ethics in order to enter the profession.

Early concepts of *software engineering* such as "the establishment and use of sound engineering principles [methods] in order to obtain economically software that is reliable and works on real machines" (Bauer, 1972) do not explicitly point out the existence of ethical issues. As the discipline matured toward a profession and the impact of its product enlarged, the descriptions of the discipline begin explicitly to mention places where ethical issues might arise. When software engineering is described as a discipline that "requires understanding and application of engineering principles, design skills, good management practice, computer science, and mathematical formalism" (BCS, 1989), some areas of ethical concern such as good management practices begin to emerge. These early descriptions do not give prominence to ethical issues. Bauer's definition does not mention satisfaction of the clients needs or satisfying the standards of the profession, yet these are implied in terms such as *reliable, economical,* and *works.* The British Computer Society's (BCS) complete definition does include some reference to the software engineer's responsibility to the profession.

The professionalization of any discipline involves the realization that being a professional involves more than the rigid application of formal principles to the artifacts of that discipline. The practice of medicine is more than the application of drugs to the human body. Physicians are concerned with the well-being of their patients. The professional architect does not merely apply principles of structural stress when designing a building but is concerned with the effect of the design on the people who will be using the building. In the professionalization of a discipline there is a realization of the impact on society of the application of the special skills and knowledge of the practitioner of that profession and a realization of the responsibility that comes with the privilege of being allowed to apply those principles. This kind of realization in software engineering is seen in the definition offered by the Software Engineering Institute. It defines software engineering as a "form of engineering that applies the principles of computer science and mathematics to achieving cost-effective solutions to software problems" (Ford, 1990). But software engineering, as a subset of engineering, is the creating and building of "cost-effective solutions to practical problems in the service of mankind" (Ford, 1990). Ford goes on to explicitly point out that cost-effective does not mean making something of marginal quality to minimize time and resources, rather "cost-effective . . . implies getting good value for the resources invested; this value includes quality."

SOFTWARE ENGINEERING ETHICS

Software engineering has been described as "the disciplined application of engineering, scientific, and mathematical principles, methods, and tools to the economical production of quality software" (Humphrey, 1989). As a software engineer applies these principles, human values become intertwined with technical decisions. Software engineering ethics studies the interactions of human values and technical decisions involving computing. This engineering-like discipline has a direct connection to ethics.

Software engineering is an applied science. Every product of software engineering involves people, and so at any stage of product development the users of the intermediate and final products must be kept in mind. Software engineers have obligations to the users of their products, which include not only the implemented system but also other products such as requirements, software project management plans, specifications, designs, documentation, test suites, and programs.

In developing software engineering artifacts, each decision is a compromise that is affected by such constraints as available budget, clients needs, available software, reliability requirements, environmental considerations, societal effects, and even political realities. All of these make the job of the professional software engineer more difficult and more subjective.

Software engineering ethics establishes principles of conduct that members of the profession are expected to observe in the practice of software engineering. Software engineering ethics are related to two basic aspects of the software engineer's status. On the one hand, the engineer is employed by clients to serve their interests; on the other, the engineer is participating in an important social function. He or she represents the clients' interests but cannot act in a way that endangers society or is contrary to the principles of good software engineering. Sometimes the interests of the clients and society conflict, and the technical principles of software engineering do not address these conflicts. For example, suppose, a software engineer's work on a vote-tabulating program has not been completely tested, and it is the day before elections. The choice between releasing an uncertified product and continuing testing while it is being used and failing to release the product and thereby disenfranchising people is not a purely technical decision. To deliver the system will meet the clients' deadlines but delivering it might not be in the best interests of society. There are sets of competing values that must be adjudicated. Sometimes these decisions are resolved based on technical knowledge. In this case, the quality and coverage of the completed testing is significant.

Software engineering ethics covers a wide ethical spectrum. It participates in general, professional, and technical ethics. This involvement in such a wide spectrum has led to a misconception about software engineering ethics. A brief discussion of this misconception is followed by a taxonomy of software engineering ethics, which includes some applied examples. This is followed by a brief discussion of future trends in software engineering ethics.

THE TOO BROAD VIEW

The concepts of software engineering ethics and computer ethics have been broadly interpreted to include any misuse of computer technology, any mistake made in the development of software artifacts, and many significant social issues involving computers. The imprecision of this broad view does not help the software engineer make ethical decisions. Moreover, this broad view is based on the mistaken assumption that the tool used in an unethical act determines the appropriate ethical category for that action. Fraud committed with a fountain pen is not a case of "fountain pen" ethics, nor is beating someone to death with a law book a case of legal ethics. *A fortiori,* committing a crime with a computer does not make something a case of computer ethics.

New applications of computer technology generate a set of ethical puzzles. For example, sociologists are concerned about computer monitoring of employees. The use of computers in this monitoring does not make it an issue of computer ethics. The ethical questions of computer monitoring are the same ethical questions involved in monitoring employees through one-way mirrors. Most of these so-called issues in software engineering ethics and computer ethics have analogies with general ethical issues and are resolved when one finds an appropriate analogous situation (Johnson, 1985). Fraud committed with the aid of a computer is fraud and nothing more. This broad view continues the confusion about computer ethics, a confusion that ties the concept of computer ethics to the machine or tool rather than to the practices and behaviors of individuals.

A MODEL FOR SOFTWARE ENGINEERING ETHICS

A consistent and manageable view of software engineering ethics is derived from a concept of ethics as "a public system applying to all rational persons governing behavior which affects others and which has the minimization of evil as its end" (Gert, 1988). The behavior of professional software engineers, in so far as it affects others, is guided by a set of principles that is designed to minimize evil. This definition ties software engineering ethics to the individual rather than to machines. Furthermore, using some elements of professional ethics as a model has the advantage of bringing software engineering ethics within the horizon of action of the practice of the individual *moral* software engineer. Software engineering ethics is a type of professional ethics. The relation between software engineering ethics and other professional ethics can be understood by developing a partial taxonomy of ethics.

ETHICS AND PROFESSIONAL ETHICS

General Ethics

In the first category of the taxonomy of ethics, software engineering ethics participates in a very general sense of ethics, which includes most human interaction. This is the concept of ethics as a means to facilitate the interactions of people living in a society by placing obligations of action and avoidance of action on them. In any given society ethics regulates individual behavior in those circumstances in which it cannot be or as yet has not been regulated by law. Ethics depends entirely on voluntary acceptance of established rules and is not enforced by the state. In this category, ethics has human well-being as one of its primary goals. Some principles in this category include hurt no one, be honest, and keep your promises. These are the moral foundations for the obligation to complete a contract and the obligation to be concerned with the user of software engineering artifacts.

Professional Ethics and General Ethics

The second category is a the category of professional ethics that has elements in common with the first category of general ethics. Some occupations, which have a significant impact on human well-being, require a high degree of special knowledge to produce a product or service. People in these occupations are called professionals.

Professional ethics is a category of ethics that is required of all professionals, regardless of their particular profession. Architects, doctors, engineers, and lawyers are all bound by professional ethics. This broad sense of professional ethics is derived from the concept of a profession. There are several marks of a professional. They generally include a special skill or knowledge to produce a product or service, a commitment to public service, a commitment to cause no harm, membership in a representative organization, adherence to a code of ethics, being licensed by a representative organization, and autonomous judgment based on this specialized knowledge (Johnson, 1985). A profession is permitted by society to lay exclusive claim to a body of knowledge because through the use of the knowledge, society as a whole gains. This claim to exclusive knowledge is only justified if indeed society does gain. In exchange for this exclusive claim, a profession assumes an obligation to serve society (Bayles, 1981). These obligations are generally articulated in professional codes of ethics.

The principle of responsibility to one's profession and to one's client does not change across professions. This category of ethics is common to all of the technical professions. In some professional codes the role of the professional is defined in terms of a relationship between consultant and client and the primary concerns are obligations to clients and to the profession as a whole. This emphasis directs ethical concerns toward issues of group loyalty (do not criticize another engineer), paternalism (the doctor will decide what is best for the patient), and advertising (do not compete with a fellow professional by advertising) (Martin and Schinzinger, 1989).

There has been an new importance given to the social consequences of professional decisions in the professions. Many codes of ethics now include commitments to strive for a level of excellence in the practice of the profession. The codes of ethics for civil engineers, the IEEE, and the various computing societies emphasize "the dignity and worth of other people, . . . personal integrity and honesty, . . . responsibility for work, . . . public safety, health, and welfare" (Martin and Schinzinger, 1989). A mixture of loyalties can cause ethical difficulties for the software engineer. A software engineer designed a system to ensure adequate testing, but the client wants the system redesigned in a way that the software engineer knows is impossible to test. The only way to achieve a quality product is to go against the client's wishes.

Although software engineering does not meet all of the marks of a profession mentioned above, it does meet those marks that are significant for understanding how ethics is related to software engineering. There is a special skill and training used to develop products that directly affect many lives and affects the way software artifacts are used in society, and by virtue of that training one gains the power to have a significant effect on society. The responsible application of software engineering principles has a direct effect on the public's well-being. These two fundamental facts identify software engineering ethics as a professional ethics. Like other engineering fields, software engineering ethics are tied closely to commercial products. Like medical professionals, software engineers are privy to knowledge that is generally inaccessible to people outside the profession. Like lawyers, software engineers have special obligations to clients, obligations that may conflict with obligations to society at large. Software engineering ethics, although uniquely tied to the technical details of computing, shares common ground with other professional ethics.

Technical and Professional Ethics

The third category in this taxonomy of ethics, technical professional ethics, is different in each of the professions. Although medical ethics and engineering ethics are examples of the same professional ethics, these two professions are quite different in the way that they implement professional ethics. Each profession operates in a different context with different tools and addresses different problems. Although there are some principles such as "cause no harm" that are true across the professions, in this category different professions employ different ethical principles and give these principles different priorities. The physician has a significant obligation to patient confidentiality, but this has little relevance for the mechanical engineer. The technical requirements and skills of the professional have a direct connection to ethics at this level. The standards and methods to achieve the best medical therapies, the safest bridges, the most reliable software designs are determined within each profession. The intentional failure to follow these standards gives rise to some ethical issues within a profession.

These technical standards and values are determined by consensus within a profession (Gotterbarn, 1991; Miller, 1992). Society trusts that the educated professionals are best equipped to determine these principles because of their special knowledge. This is the basis for self-regulation of the professions.

Software professionals have a set of standards they can follow, and recent work has shown that there is significant agreement about these technical and ethical standards among software professionals. Within the realm of professional ethics there is a surprising degree of agreement (Leventhal et. al., 1992).

Technical Ethics and Values

Although there are technical standards, there are a variety of solutions available for most software engineering problems. The choice of which solution to use is based on professional values. Consequently, professional values have a direct impact on the way one develops applications and the quality of those artifacts.

Software engineering ethics consists of two major elements. One element, called technical ethics, consists of doing a technically competent job at all phases of the software development process. The other element is the use of a set of moral values to guide the technical decisions.

In the professions, technical skill guides processes: processes of building bridges, of healing patients, and of building software artifacts. The performance of these processes involves numerous ethical issues. The physician's choice of which medicine to dispense involves a technical judgment about its curative powers, but it also involves questions about the side effects of the medicine. Is it too expensive for the patient to purchase? Is it addictive? Is it likely to cause other problems? Technical decisions in software engineering are analogous to this. The choice of which life cycle to use will lead to radically different products, although they both might satisfy the requirements.

In general, all professional ethics (engineering ethics, legal ethics, and medical ethics) are only distinguished by the context to which they apply moral rules. There are, of course, differences in the professional ethics. The contexts bring out different ethical problems. Because different contexts raise different ethical concerns, the order in which the moral rules are applied varies for each application domain. Even within the software engineering process, moral rules are given different significance at different stages of a development life cycle. Consider the different ways informed consent is treated. During the requirements phase of life-critical software, informed consent (understanding agreement) is an important rule. During testing, principles about not deceiving and not cheating are important, but informed consent is not a major concern.

Although technical responsibility involves a strong sense of individual responsibility, this sense of professional ethics should not be confused with merely following the law. Professionals are aware of many technical solutions to problems. These solutions vary in their adequacy to solve a particular problem. Even if a developed product does not meet the ideological technical goals of the profession there is no cause for legal action until some damage has occurred. There are three basic "requirements for a tort law suit: (1) a duty is owed; (2) the duty is breached; and (3) damages are caused by the breach of duty" (West, 1991). Attempts to define technical professional responsibility legally have been unsuccessful.

Different values and rules apply to different phases of the software development life cycle and the application of these values in making decisions involves no violation of the law. In the testing phase, if funds are exhausted before the testing is satisfactorily completed, and there is no possibility of further funds, there are several options. Whichever option is taken it must be conditioned by moral rules such as "don't deceive," "keep promises," and "act professionally." Depending on the type of software being tested, rules like "don't cause pain" and "don't kill" might also come into play.

In the design phase, other moral rules might get applied first. Consider designing a journal file for a library checkout system to determine the popularity of books and the number of additional copies that should be ordered, if any. The association of the patron's name with the book checked out has a potential for the violation of several moral rules, e.g. the violation of privacy, the deprivation of pleasure because one does not feel free to read what one wants, and possibly causing psychological pain. Notice that there are no laws violated by this design.

In the design phase, the choice of a language for a life-critical system can have moral implications. If the language is hard to debug, write, or modify, then one puts people at risk and violates principles of good system design in the choice of that language (Gotterbarn, 1990). The ethical issues can come from two directions here. If the designers were ignorant and did not know a better language, they are morally culpable for undertaking a project that was beyond their skill. If on the other hand, they were well aware of these significant differences in languages but decided to stick with the more dangerous language for other reasons such as profit, then they have violated professional ethics. It is unlikely that they would lose a tort suit.

Software engineering has many of the marks of a profession and the responsibility of professional ethics. In this sense it is like all other professional ethics. Because the context of software engineering is different from other engineering disciplines, its technical professional ethics is unique. Technical responsibility is concerned with the approach taken by professionals while they are solving technical problems. Sometimes this is subsumed under terms like *quality* and *professionalism.* This involves the consequences of knowing and following good professional standards.

The senses of responsibility that need to be discussed in software engineering include both societal and technical responsibility. Technical responsibility involves moral commitments to standards of software production and to the process. Societal responsibility involves commitment to using these special skills in the service of society. Software engineers have an obligation to consider the safety, health, and welfare of those who interact with their product. The society that interacts with their products also includes all others participating in the software development process. Software development is a social process, and the software engineer has a twofold obligation to strive for excellence. One source of the obligation is based on technical standards, and the other source of the obligation is social responsibility to those who will have to work with the product. Both of these approaches to ethics give positive guidance for the engineer's behavior as a software practitioner.

FUTURE TRENDS

The movement toward professionalization of the computer industry and software engineering is continuing. There has been renewed attention to ethical issues within the engineering and computing professions with special attention given to the well-being of the client and the user of software engineering artifacts. In November 1991 the IEEE significantly strengthened its code of ethics. Adherence to the new code of ethics requires that, in addition to not causing harm, engineers must do what they can to prevent harm. This means that an engineer is expected to report another engineer's faulty work. In May 1992 the ACM published its proposed code of ethics (Anderson, 1992). Adherence to this code requires reporting any signs of danger from computer systems, whether or not the individual reporting the risk designed the system. Both of these codes now require the practicing professional to be concerned with the well-being of the users of their artifacts. Concurrently, there is an interest in establishing licensing standards for the computer industry. Several state legislatures are considering bills to license software professionals. Although these bills are meeting resistance from some software developers, some large corporations like IBM and federal government agencies like the U.S. Air Force have already established standards and tests that must be passed in order for someone to be considered a software engineer in these organizations. Historically, the next step in most professions is the establishment of a code of ethics.

BIBLIOGRAPHY

R. R. Anderson, and co-workers, "ACM Proposed Code of Ethics and Professional Conduct," *Communications of the ACM* May 1992.

B. H. Bauer, "Software Engineering," in *Information Processing,* North Holland, Amsterdam, 1972, V. 71.

BCS, *A Report on Undergraduate Curricula for Software Engineering Curricula,* the British Computer Society and the Institution for Electrical Engineers, London, June 1989.

M. D. Bayles, *Professional Ethics,* Wadsworth Publishing Co., Belmont, Calif., 1981.

G. Ford, *1990 SEI Report on Undergraduate Software Engineering Education,* Technical Report CMU/SEI-90-TR-3, Carnegie Mellon University, Pittsburgh, Pa., 1990.

B. Gert, *Morality, Oxford University Press, New York, 1988.*

D. W. Gotterbarn, "Software Engineering Ethics Workshop," *J. Sys. Software,* (Mar. 1990).

D. W. Gotterbarn, "Computer Ethics: Responsibility Regained," *Nat. Forum,* (Summer 1991).

W. S. Humphrey, *Managing the Software Process,* Addison Weseley Publishing Co., Inc., Reading, Mass., 1989.

L. M. Leventhal, K. E. Instone, and D. W. Chilson, "Another View of Computer Science Ethics," *J. Sys. Software,* (1992).

M. W. Martin and R. Schinzinger, *Ethics in Engineering,* McGraw-Hill Book Co., Inc., New York, 1989.

K. Miller, "Paramedic Method For Computer Professionals," *J. Sys. Software,* (Jan. 1992).

L. B. West "Professional Civil Engineering: Responsibility," *J. Prof. Issues Eng. Educ. Pract.* **117,** 4 (Oct. 1991).

DONALD GOTTERBARN
East Tennessee State University

THE SOFTWARE ENGINEERING INSTITUTE

Software has become an increasingly critical component of U.S. defense systems, and the demand for quality software produced on schedule and within budget exceeds the supply. To address these needs, the U.S. Department of Defense (DOD) competitively awarded the Software Engineering Institute (SEI) to Carnegie Mellon University in Pittsburgh, Pennsylvania, in 1984.

The SEI, under contract to the DOD through the Advanced Research Projects Agency (ARPA), is a federally funded research and development center with a mission to advance the state of the practice of software engineering to improve the quality of systems that depend on software. The SEI expects to accomplish this mission by promoting the evolution of software engineering from an *ad hoc,* labor-intensive activity to a discipline that is well managed and supported by technology. The best means for carrying out the mission is to transfer new software engineering principles and technology to practitioners. The SEI staff of approximately 250 technical and support people from industry, academia, and government achieve this transfer through constant interaction with the creators, users, and customers of new software technology.

The SEI addresses the following aspects of software development:

Quality. Defense systems, because of their demanding operational conditions, require software of the highest quality in terms of correctness, reliability, and performance.

Management. Managing the software engineering process to control schedule, budget, and quality is particularly important when the software is part of a large and complex mission-critical computer resource system.

Productivity. Increasing productivity helps solve two fundamental problems related to the capacity of the defense industry to produce software: (1) the overall shortage of highly qualified software professionals, and (2) the high cost of software production.

The SEI focuses on five technical areas of software development.

SOFTWARE ENGINEERING PROCESS

Process activities are concerned with making lasting improvements in software engineering practice to enable production of high-quality software within budget and schedule constraints.

The SEI assists organizations in improving their software process, develops and transitions improved acquisition techniques to the DOD, and develops and introduces improved software management methods.

The goals in the process area are to: be the leading center of competence in software process management; establish the standard of software process excellence; provide leadership to DOD organizations in enhancing software source selection and improving software contract management; and motivate the rapid improvement of U.S. industrial software capability.

SOFTWARE ENGINEERING TECHNIQUES

The Software Engineering Techniques area of the SEI accelerates the development, introduction, and reduction to practice of methods, tools, and environments that improve software productivity and enhance quality. Its goals are to conduct research in software architecture and models; improve the requirements analysis process; transition simulation design methodology; identify critical parts of software domain analysis; develop a model for tool adoption; and produce a state-of-the-practice view of software configuration management (see CONFIGURATION MANAGEMENT).

REAL-TIME DISTRIBUTED SYSTEMS

A major concern for the DOD is the development of systems that must deal with real-time constraints, often in a distributed or parallel-processing context. In the Real-Time Distributed Systems area, the SEI helps ensure that all major DOD systems involving real-time distributed or parallel processors are developed in a systematic way.

SOFTWARE ENGINEERING EDUCATION

The SEI is advancing the state of software engineering practice by increasing the number of highly qualified software engineers throughout the education communities of academia, government, and industry. To accomplish this, the SEI focuses on accelerating the development of software engineering programs in academia, enhancing opportunities for the continuing education of practitioners, and producing more and improved educational materials for all members of the software engineering community.

SOFTWARE RISK MANAGEMENT

The SEI seeks to improve the management of risks that arise in the development of software-intensive systems. In this context, "risk" refers to the uncertainty and impact associated with an event and "management" to the identification and resolution of the risk. Managing risk, then, entails identifying those things that can go wrong and assessing their likelihood and impact. A premise of the Risk area is that confronting risk in a systematic way is fundamental to controlling the quality, cost, and schedule of software products.

OTHER AREAS

The SEI also maintains CERT—the Computer Emergency Response Team. The CERT Coordination Center supplements existing mechanisms by which informally organized experts deal with and prevent computer emergencies. The CERT/CC supports two different communities: Internet users, and developers of network technology such as UNIX (qv). CERT provides a reliable, trusted, 24-hour point of contact for security issues and allows for rapid communication during emergencies. It also raises constituents' awareness of security issues and assists individual organizations in improving the security of their systems. Finally, the CERT/CC maintains a highly secure repository of information for team members and cultivates close ties with researchers in the area of trusted systems.

AFFILIATES

Technology flows to and from the SEI through affiliate relationships with government, industry, and academia. These relationships can be at one of three levels: information exchange, technology exchange, and in-house residence. Information on new technologies and methods is disseminated to affiliates through mailings, telephone contact, special meetings, and an annual Affiliates Symposium. In addition, with the cooperation of the SEI Joint Program Office, Affiliate Relations matches the interests and needs of affiliates with specific SEI projects and sponsors resident affiliates on those projects.

FUTURE

On December 19, 1989, the Air Force Systems Command (Electronic Systems Division) renewed the SEI contract for another five years. The SEI will continue its efforts to contribute to a better understanding of technology transition and to the software needs of the defense community.

This work is sponsored by the U.S. Department of Defense.

LARRY DRUFFEL
Software Engineering Institute

SOFTWARE EVOLUTION

EVOLUTION

The term *evolution* is used to describe a phenomenon observed in a variety of entity classes, each in its own context. Natural species, societies, cities, artifacts, concepts, theories, ideas are all said to evolve. The term conveys a meaning of continuing positive change, in some sense, in the properties or characteristics of some material or abstract entity or sequence of entities. It describes a process of progressive change in the attributes of the entity(ies). Such change may include, for example, improvement in some sense, adaptation to a changing environment, loss of not-required or undesired properties or the emergence of new ones.

A full study of the evolutionary properties of entities demonstrating such behavior indicates that these vary widely. To distinguish between them one may start by classifying the entities according to their evolutionary characteristics. By studying the common factors and distinctions between classes one learns more about each class and obtains clues to the relationship between their evolutionary and other properties and how individual evolutionary patterns may be directed, controlled, or predicted. Something may undoubtedly be learned about software evolution by studying evolution in general. For the purpose of this article, however, the discussion is limited to evolution as it is relevant in software technology.

EVOLUTION IN SOFTWARE TECHNOLOGY

It is, by now, generally accepted that software must be continually adapted and changed if it is to remain satisfactory in use. Concern about this universal experience was first expressed publicly at the Garmisch Conference in 1968 (Naur, 1969); a conference which also first advanced the concept of software development as an engineering technology. At about the same time the present author studied the programming process within IBM (Lehman, 1969) though his report did not become generally available till much later (Lehman, 1985). *Inter alia,* the report examined and modeled the continuing change process being applied to IBM's OS/360 operating system. The investigation derived models of that system's evolution from measures of software release characteristics and used them as tools to support planning and management of sequences of such releases (Belady, 1972; Lehman, 1980). Subsequent collaboration with Belady postulated and investigated a phenomenon initially termed Program Growth Dynamics and later renamed Program Evolution Dynamics. It was, probably, this study that first applied the term *evolution* to a phenomenon in the field of software technology. In addition to providing tools for release management, models of the release process data collected for OS/360 and other large software systems (Lehman, 1980; 1985) yielded valuable insight into the nature and properties of software and the software process. In particular, it led to a classification scheme that defined three types of programs including the E-type (Lehman, 1982; 1985), a program solving a problem or implementing an application in a *real-world* domain. The others are the P- and S-type. The latter is defined later. The former overlaps the other two, displaying S- or P-type characteristics according to circumstances (Lehman, 1985, 1991). The referenced works showed that evolution is intrinsic to E-type software, intrinsic indeed to all real world computer application (Lehman, 1991). Continuing change cannot be avoided if software is to be maintained satisfactory; but it can be managed and directed. The data also provided strong evidence that software evolution is a feedback phenomenon (Lehman, 1980) though the full implications of that observation have only recently been recognized (Lehman, 1993). Figure 1 provides such evidence displaying the classical feedback ripple in the OS/360 growth curve. Similar responses were also observed for other software systems (Lehman, 1980). Moreover, the instability following release serial number 20 is symptomatic of a feedback system with excessive positive feedback. The evolution phenomenon in software technology is not confined to sequences of program releases or even to program material in general. Other entities involved in software engineering also evolve. The different evolution processes impact and affect one another. All must be understood and mastered if software evolution is to be directed, planned, and controlled. The following entity classes must be considered.

- A sequence of versions or *releases* of a program or software system that implement changes in system quality, performance, function etc. and make them available to users.
- A *program* or *software system* in its evolution from first statement of an application concept or of a change required to an existing system to the final, released, installed and operational program text with its documentation.
- An *E-type application* comprising both the source concept and its implementation as a computer supported activity in some operational domain.
- The *process* of software evolution (commonly considered as two phases termed *development* and *maintenance* respectively)—software process for short.
- *Models* of that process.

EVOLUTION OVER SYSTEM RELEASES

As already mentioned the mid-seventies evolution study concentrated on evolution over releases. Comparable phenomena were observed for the software of several manufacturers (Lehman, 1980; Chong, 1981). The study generated a view of the evolution process as one that produced a sequence of releases, each constituting a stable state in a forever changing body of program text. Such changes were needed to correct errors and faults, provide support for new hardware, improve performance and cost-effectiveness, increase functionality and so on. It was shown that evolution was intrinsic to *E*-type systems, that the process was statistically normal in certain attributes and, in that sense, disciplined and predictable at some level. Most immediately it led to the formulation of Laws of Program Evolution (Lehman, 1974; 1978; 1980; 1985; 1991).

The observations and insights on which the laws were based strengthened the view that the release process is feedback driven (Lehman, 1985, chapt. 16; 1991), though advances in technology also play a role. Fault *reports* from the field demand correction. Domain changes due to installation, operation and use of the system change user needs and provide new opportunities. These, if implemented, create a need for changes to previously formulated requirements and specifications. Above all, *experience* changes user *perception* and *understanding,* and hence underlying application and system concepts, abstractions and assumptions. All these combine to produce pressure for software change. Relevant information is fed back to suppliers and demands action on their part. The information propagates along paths involving human interpretation and significant delays. In this feedback the people involved have a direct impact on the information, that is on feedback characteristics. Nor is the source of feedback confined to developers and the user community as they exploit insight gained from experience, learning, concept evolution and advances in technology. Many others contribute to the change process. But in all cases information feedback is the principal driver, with the nature of the path determining its significance. Process internal feedback paths are relatively short and involve people who are experts in the application, the development process and the target system. Their feedback is based on expert interpretation. In control theoretic terms it represents a low level of amplification, delay and distortion. It is the long external user and business based loops that are primarily responsible for the characteristics of *release* dynamics.

A preliminary classification of the attributes of software release sequences is indicated in Table 1. It suggests that such sequences are both *adaptive* and *developmental, in vitro* (Minsky, 1985) evolution of a *many-bodied* entity in *discrete* steps over many *generations* driven *primarily* by multi-loop *external feedback.* It may be termed *macro-evolution.*

Note that the assignments of Table 1 are tentative. Classes must still be precisely defined and specific characteristics determined. Only when this has been systematically achieved will it be possible to relate evolution patterns to identified characteristics precisely and consistently.

SOFTWARE SYSTEM EVOLUTION

As a program is developed (unless otherwise stated, from here onwards the term *develop* and its derivatives refer to both initial program development of an application concept and its subsequent maintenance, where the term includes adaptation and enhancement) from a raw application concept or problem statement to final code with support documentation or as a change is implemented, it evolves in a step by step process of *successive refinement* (Wirth, 1971). Models such as the Waterfall (Boehm, 1976), LST (Lehman, 1984), and process programs (Osterweil, 1987), reflect the discrete, sequential but often overlapping steps executed by interacting humans and machines whose joint activity leads to the final implementation. The program evolves through a series of transformations that abstract away from the original concept in its domain and reify towards the final solution system.

S-type programs (Lehman, 1982; 1985) are programs for which, by definition, the *sole* criterion for successful implementation is that the program satisfies a prestated specification. As a consequence of incomplete understanding of how the solution is to be obtained, feedback driven iteration may be necessary during development. It may also be stimulated by developing insight. *S*-type programs may, therefore, experience some degree of *developmental* evolution. But since the specification is fixed before the start of implementation, step wise evolution of the program, is basically a linear process. Global evolution, driven by feedback from unsatisfactory output which indicate changes to the specification, is ruled out by definition.

Where a specification cannot be fixed initially because of incomplete understanding of the problem, the absence of a complete theory covering the problem and its solution, for example, Turski (1981), one cannot be certain of the properties required to make the solution acceptable. One converges to an implicit specification during development. Its finalization must await program execution since absence of a complete theory implies some degree of ignorance

Table 1. Comparative Evolution Attributes

Attribute Pairs	Release	System	Application	Process	Process Models
Developmental	✓	✓		✓	✓
Adaptive	✓		✓	✓	✓
One body		✓	✓		✓
Many body	✓		✓	✓	
Individual		✓	✓		✓
Generational	✓			✓	
Discrete	✓		✓	✓	✓
Continuous		✓			
Durable	✓	✓	✓		✓
Ephemeral				✓	
Internal feedback		✓		✓	✓
External feedback	✓		✓		
Local feedback dominant		✓		✓	✓
Global feedback dominant	✓		✓		
In vitro	✓	✓			✓
In vivo			✓	✓	
Micro-evolution		✓	✓	✓	✓
Macro-evolution	✓				

about both the properties of the solution in execution and the properties required. Acceptance is a matter of judgment under a variety of constraints. Even if it does not involve real-world phenomena the program will behave like an E-type program and must be treated as such.

E-type programs and systems are the objects of ultimate concern of software technology. Their development and

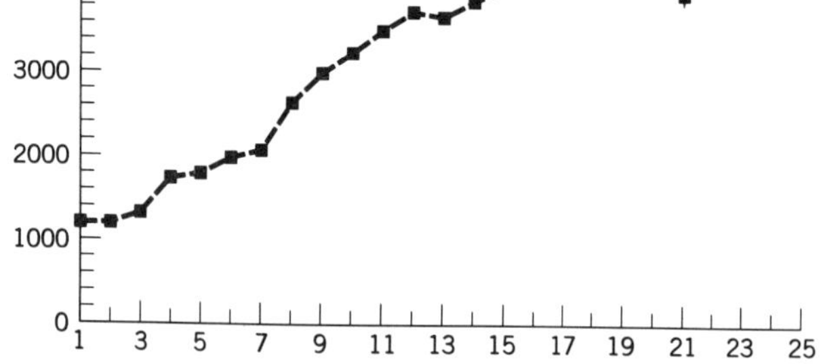

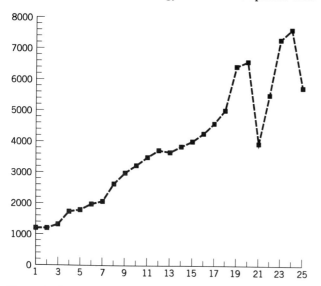

Figure 1. Size of OS/360 in modules as a function of release serial number.

adaptation cannot be covered by a complete theory if only because of human involvement in the applications, the non-absolute nature of procedures such as business or manufacturing processes, for example, and the potential or actual unboundedness of the domain (Turski, 1981). Properties such as these make development and use of the systems a learning experience. The system is intrinsically evolutionary. Moreover, the system is a bounded and discrete model of an unbounded and effectively continuous application domain. Its boundaries and other attributes are fuzzy, not absolute. They are determined during development by operational, economic, time, and technology considerations; some explicitly in processes such as requirements analysis and specification, others as a result of explicit or implicit assumptions adopted and embedded in the system during the evolution process. Fixing the detailed properties of human/system interfaces or interactions between people and the operational system, for example, must include trial and error. The fine design detail cannot be finalized on intuition, conjecture or statistics alone. It arises from continuing human experience, judgment and decision by development staff and users. Development changes perception and understanding of the application itself, of facilities that may be offered, of how incompatibilities may be resolved, what requirements should be satisfied by the solution, possible solutions and so on. In combination such considerations drive the process onwards to its final goal, a satisfactory operational system, by experience and learning based feedback. The joint characteristics of many long feedback paths determine the evolutionary characteristics of software development and the precise characteristics of the final system.

Preliminary analysis suggests that for direct (as distinct from release) software development the main feedback paths are internal to the process. They serve as much as process controllers as they do as evolution drivers. There will be fewer, more localized, paths with lower levels of interpretation, distortion and time delay than those that are critical in release evolution and involve users, system support and sales staff. A complete investigation remains to be conducted but the characteristics of direct system evolution appear to follow the pattern listed in Table 1. It identifies system development as *developmental, in-vitro* evolution of a *one body, individual,* entity in a *continuous forward* driven process controlled by multiple short or medium delay internal feedback paths. The process may be termed *micro*-evolution. A complete analysis of the feedback attributes of software development and software release sequences, respectively, should explain why their evolution patterns differ.

One final and important observation must be added. Real world interest in the attributes of any program or software system will relate to the manner in which some activity or domain is supported, guided, and controlled. The concern will be the application domain, how its attributes are affected by computer installation, the behavior of the system in execution, changes to system and domain, how they evolve. Software (code and documentation) determine the impact of execution and user satisfaction with the behavior of the total system in which the software is embedded. Its evolution is of real interest only to the extent that it impacts evolution of the application in its operational domain. The computing system and the domain form a closed loop. The software, moderated by human interaction, is the primary determinant of real world behavior. Its evolution drives that of the integrated system and, hence, evolution of the application; which is what really matters.

EVOLUTION OF THE APPLICATION IN ITS DOMAIN

The preceding sections have focused on the evolution of the software itself. But as indicated the real value of software lies in the application that it implements in some domain. The term *application* is to be taken in a broad sense to imply the solution of a problem or the monitoring, guidance and/or control of some activity or process that may involve people. The application is grounded in a concept that for *S*-type applications is completely defined before implementation begins. For *E*-type applications the definition of both the application itself and the domain to which it applies is initially fuzzy. They are, in general, broadly defined during definition and feasibility studies over the early phases of the development process. They are refined during the entire process and subsequently as operational experience is gained and the system evolves.

The initial fuzziness involves two separate and distinct aspects each of great significance in the context of software evolution. The first relates to the unbounded nature of *E*-type applications which constitute the class of general concern. The domain over which the application is to be valid or supported is generally unbounded both in extent and in level of detail. This double unboundedness must be limited, abstracted and defined so as to identify a manageable domain over which the software system is to be implemented (or adapted) to provide satisfactory service at acceptable cost in some defined time frame. Once the system is in operation the need or desire to extend its use to regions of the domain or to levels of detail previously excluded will inevitably arise. The system must be evolved to satisfy this newly recognized or emerging need. This is achieved by feeding back to the development organization the information that permits evolution of the system in order to modify or extend its domain of applicability as required. Note that this aspect of fuzziness relates to the range of applicability of the system, its operational domain. Some parts of the multi-dimensional domain boundary may be well defined, establishing conditions, circumstances or states for which execution is legitimate. Others are clearly out of bounds. Still others will be vague, uncertain or undecidable, a situation that may be explicitly known or remain unrecognized until exposed by chance or during system operation. The operational domain can be depicted as a cloud with undefined and fluctuating boundaries.

The second aspect is concerned with the boundaries of the system to be implemented. As anyone with experience in systems analysis, specification and design knows any list of properties and function that could be included in a system is potentially unbounded. It is always in excess of what can be accommodated within the resources and time allocated for system implementation. Hence, from the point of view of potential coverage the boundaries of the final system are arbitrary. But once developed and installed the system boundaries, unlike those of the domain, are solid. At any one time they are determined by the installed software and hardware. In diagrammatic form the system may be represented by a box with a solid but open boundary to suggest a potential for the addition of further hardware units. A user requiring a facility not included within this boundary will have to exploit additional, stand alone, software. It may be possible to couple such software tightly to the system for greater convenience in cooperative execution. But a need for capabilities excluded from the system leads to additional execution overhead, time delays, performance and reliability penalties and so on. The omission become onerous, a source of user irritation and soon leads to a request for system extension. The history of the evolution of computation is rich with examples of function first developed and exploited as a stand alone application program, migrated inwards to become, at least conceptually, a part of an operating or run time system and ultimately becoming an integral part of some larger application system. In some instances the migration continues until the function is implemented in the hardware itself. The evolving system is an *expanding universe* with an inward drift of function from the domain to the core of the system. The process is driven by feedback about the strengths, weaknesses, effectiveness and potential of the system at each moment and from every execution.

Table 1 characterizes the evolution of the application in its domain. But E-type software, once installed, becomes an integral part of the operational application domain. As already observed, the application, its domain and the system comprise a multi-loop, stochastic, non-linear feedback system whose evolution is the consequence of the individual but interacting evolutionary behavior of its constituents. The study, direction and control of overall system evolution through management of the evolution of its constituents lies at the core of software engineering. It depends critically on the design and management of the *process* of software development and adaptation.

PROCESS EVOLUTION

The software development process also evolves. In part this is due to the fact that the technology is relatively new, different in principal to other engineering technologies and without a comprehensive scientific base or framework. The process has, therefore, had to be gradually improved by means of a process based on experience, insight, and inventiveness. Inputs to drive its evolution derive from observation, measurement and analysis of the process in execution, from its product and from process models. Its evolution is also a direct consequence of the complex linkages and interdependencies between the software and its operational environment. These make progress in following the overall process to achieve a satisfactory, quality, product, dependent on the application area, on the application itself, on a variety of special circumstances and on earlier steps of the process. However derived, process changes, may be exploited in future processes as can premeditated changes. Each process instance is a descendant of earlier processes. It is very unlikely that any two instances will be identical. All instances are adapted to the needs of the objective, to circumstances, to the judgment, taste, experience or whim of implementors and to constraints applying before and during execution.

Any instance of the process is transient and ephemeral. Once executed it is gone for ever. It will normally have been preplanned in outline with details filled in as progress is made. Unanticipated circumstances and unexpected conditions are the norm and lead to process adjustments, adaptations and changes *on the fly*. Such changes may be initiated by observing the results or consequences of past activity or by perception of what lies ahead. The consequence may be a change to the planned upcoming process activity or a need to backtrack or iterate. In any event there is a complex mixture of feedback and *feed forward* based on individual and collective interpretation, intellectual judgment and decision by humans that will determine how to proceed. Whenever people are involved some degree of freedom exists; otherwise their activity could be mechanized. That freedom relates to what is done, what is not done and how the former is done. Hence the process can sensibly only be preplanned and defined to a limited extend and to some arbitrary level of detail. It can only be enforced at a comparatively high level. Any expectation that it will be carried out in detail as planned is naive in the extreme. The process will inevitably evolve.

Since any process instance is transient, its evolution must be classified as *discrete* and *generational*. Since it is *ephemeral* it is also *many body*. Evolution of the process is both *adaptive* and *developmental* being driven by needs of the moment, the need to cope with up coming tasks, evaluation of completed activity and a desire for process improvement. It is dominated by *internal feedback* with *global* feedback restricted, primarily, to analysis of the product and the product that produced it. Process evolution is also essentially *in vivo*. Process improvements can be developed or evaluated on process models, but the realization and fine tuning can only be achieved in actual execution. Process models are crucial for achieving and communicating process understanding.

THE EVOLUTION OF PROCESS MODELS

Together with the process as such, process models in general and process programs in particular have been a major focus of software technology research in recent years. Interest in the former went public with the first International Process Workshop (Potts, 1984). The latter was triggered by a keynote paper (Osterweil, 1987) and a response to it (Lehman, 1987). It is generally agreed that process models, of whatever form, facilitate understanding processes and communication about them. Models, preferably formal, are, indeed, essential as vehicles for communication and reasoning. They provide means for systematic and disciplined examination, evaluation, comparison, and improvement of processes and, through process enactment and simulation, preliminary measurement, exploration, and evaluation of proposed changes (Tully, 1989). Formal models such as process programs may also find application in guiding processes at some relatively high level of detail. But they cannot control them, cannot provide instant to instant guidance. If any model could, it would constitute a tool. If the process it described represented a significant portion of the life cycle the authors of the model would have achieved Automatic Programming since the model can then be considered a tool. The evolutionary nature of software development implies that this is not possible for E-type software.

Inevitably, process models also evolve. If such a model is to serve a useful purpose it must continually reflect the process as it evolves. The evolution of a process and its model must be linked. What is the nature of that linkage? Where impetus for change comes from a need to adapt a process to specific conditions or circumstances model evolution is basically a consequence of process evolution. This is so even though the change may be evaluated by implementing, exploring, and comparing potential change in the model by enactment or otherwise before incorporating the selected change in the process itself. Where this is not done changes made to the process, whether premeditated or on the fly (something that should rarely, if ever, be done) must be reflected in a change to the model if the latter is to retain its value. If, on the other hand, the pressure for evolution comes from recognition of a need for improvement the process model can play a seminal role being used to design and evaluate the change before implementation. However exploited, the information that drives improvement is garnered from observation and previous experience. Model evolution is also feedback. The flow will be from within the organization, from other software developers and from process experts, software engineers (Lehman, 1991). Disciplined, and directed effort in process improvement is typified by the work of the Software Engineering Institute at Carnegie Mellon University (Humphrey, 1989). Their work does not explicitly focus on process models or feedback direction and control. But those, in essence, are among the issues addressed.

This preliminary analysis indicates that process model evolution is both *adaptive* and *developmental.* It is also characterized as *one body, individual, discrete* and *durable, in vitro micro-evolution* involving a moderate degree of short delay *internal feedback.*

THE SOFTWARE/PROCESS/PROCESS MODEL CONTRAST

Preliminary comparison of the evolutionary attributes of the various entities considered indicates that software process evolution differs significantly from that of software itself. This follows, in the first place, from the fact that the relationship between the software process and its models differs fundamentally from that between E-type software and the application processes that such software models drive, support and/or monitor.

Wherein lies the difference? When software development processes and the models that describe them are considered, the focus of immediate and continuing concern is the process. The source of evolutionary change may sometimes arise from a study of a model in general and a process program in particular. Equally, and as already discussed, the design of a proposed change and its consequences may be explored by use of such a model and be evaluated by its enactment. Even where a model driven support environment is used to directly guide a process (Taylor, 1989) the center of concern remains with the process *in execution;* the consequences of humans interpreting specifications, processing directives, choosing directions, taking decisions, following methods, and applying tools. The proof of the pudding lies in the eating. Any instance of the process depends on the specific action of individuals. The models are incomplete; at best a high level guide to the process. They can never provide a precise and complete representation of actuality, of the process actually followed. This must be contrasted with software which must provide a precise, detailed and complete representation of the actuality required or desired. *Software defines a process, process models reflect one.*

Process change must, therefore, ultimately focus on the process. Changes to the model are incidental, a description of process changes implemented or proposed, the expression of a concept to be translated into reality by people. Even where a process change is first conceived and incorporated in a model, the acid test comes with its execution in an instance of the process. In general, process evolution is the principal driver of model changes.

The ultimate concern with E-type software is also with a process, the application process, and the consequences of program execution in the real world (Lehman, 1991). In program design, however, one deals with systems to be used by a changing population of anonymous people with different degrees of understanding, skill and experience. The concern must, in general, be with user community behavior. Only in exceptional instances can code make provision for individual misuse. An essential ingredient of successful software design is insulation of the system from user behavior. For software, therefore, the direction of interaction is reversed. Computer application processes evolve as a result of changes to the software and any system in which it is embedded. This even though such changes may have been inspired by observation of real world processes themselves influenced or controlled by execution of that software. Model changes are the immediate drivers of (application) process changes.

There are also other significant differences. For example, process evolution is *in vivo* whereas software evolution occurs, primarily, *in vitro.* Moreover, in the case of process quality, productivity and cost concerns relate to the process not the model. For software the reverse is the case. Quality, productivity, and cost concerns relate to the software as a model of the application in its domain, not to the process. Finally, consider the time relationship between model changes and process changes and the nature of the feedback loops that convey the interactions. For the development process the key word is immediacy whereas for software there is, in general, significant relative delay in feedback. One could go on listing the differences. The analysis given suffices to demonstrate that *software processes are not and must not be regarded as software.*

CONCLUSIONS

The objective of this discussion has been to expose the crucial role of evolution and feedback in software technology. Only recently has serious thought been given to this topic (*Proceedings of International Workshop on Process Evolution*) and firm conclusions must await future directed and intensive study. The analysis presented here must be considered preliminary and exploratory. Its principal conclusions stem from the conjecture that evolution in software technology is primarily feedback-driven, that the characteristics of individual phenomena are functions of the properties of the feed back loops and that process evolution is fundamentally different to the other instances of evolution in software technology. Serious questions have also been raised about the wisdom of viewing software processes as software (Osterweil, 1987). Evolution in software technology must become a major focus of future academic and industrial research and development.

BIBLIOGRAPHY

L. A. Belady and M. M. Lehman, "An Introduction to Program Growth Dynamics," in W. Freiburger, ed., *Statistical Computer Performance Evaluation,* Academic Press, New York, 1977, pp. 503–511.

B. W. Boehm, "Software Engineering," *IEEE Trans. on Comp.* **C-5**(12), 1226–1241 (Dec. 1976).

C. K. S. Chong Hok Yuen, *Phenomenology of Program Maintenance and Evolution,* PhD thesis, Department of Computing, Imperial College, 1981.

D. Gries, *Programming Methodology—A Collection of Articles by Members of IFIP WG23,* Springer Verlag, New York, 1978, p. 437.

W. S. Humphrey, *Managing the Software Process,* Addison-Wesley, Reading, Mass., 1989.

M. M. Lehman, *The Programming Process, IBM Research Report RC2722M,* IBM Research Center, Yorktown Heights, New York, Sept. 1969; also in Lehman, 1985, pp. 39–84.

M. M. Lehman, *Programs, Cities, Students—Limits to Growth,* Imperial College Inaugural Lecture Series, Vol. 9, 1970–1974; also in Gries, 1978.

M. M. Lehman, "Laws of Program Evolution-Rules and Tools for Programming Management," *Proceedings of the Infotech State of the Art Conference, Why Software Projects Fail,* April 9–11, 1978, pp. 11/1–11/25.

M. M. Lehman, "Program Life Cycles and Laws of Software Evolution," *Proceedings IEEE Special Issue on Software Engineering,* Sept. 1980, pp. 1060–1076.

M. M. Lehman, "Program Evolution," *Symposium on Empirical Foundations of Computer and Information Sciences,* Georgia Institute of Technology, in *Journal of Information Proc. and Management,* **19**(1), 19, 38 (Jan. 1984).

M. M. Lehman, "Process Models, Process Programs, Programming Support," Invited Response to a Keynote Address by Lee Osterweil, *Proceedings of the 9th International Conference on Software Engineering,* Monterey, Calif., March 30–April 2, 1987, IEEE Computer Society Pub no. 767, pp. 14–16.

M. M. Lehman, "Software Engineering, the Software Process and Their Support," *IEE Software Engineering J.,* Special Issue on Software Environments and Factories, **6**(5), 243–258 (Sept. 1991).

M. M. Lehman, *Perspectives on Software Engineering, Overseas Speaker Series,* Washington, D. C., ACM Professional Development Seminar, University of Maryland, May 17, 1993.

M. M. Lehman and L. A. Belady, *Program Evolution—Processes of Software Change,* Academic Press, London, 1985.

N. Minsky, "Controlling the Evolution of Large Scale Software Systems," *Proceedings of the Conference on Software Maintenance,* 1985, pp. 50–58.

P. Naur and B. Randell, Software Engineering—Report on a Conference Sponsored by the NATO Science Committee, Garmisch, 1968, Scientific Affairs Division, NATO, Brussels, 1969, p. 164.

L. Osterweil, "Software Processes are Software Too," *Proceedings of the 9th International Conference on Software Engineering,* Monterey, Calif., March 30–April 2, 1987, IEEE Comp. Soc. Pub. 767, pp. 2–13.

C. Potts, ed., *Proceedings of the Software Process Workshop,* Egham, Surrey, UK, Feb. 1984, Washington, D. C., IEEE order no. 587.

R. N. Taylor and coworkers, "Foundations for the Arcadia Environment Architecture," *SIGPLAN Notices* **24**(2) (1989); "Software Engineering Symposium on Practical Software Development Environments," special issue of *Proceedings of ASCM SIGSOFT/SIGPLAN,* Feb. 1989.

C. Tully, ed., "Representing and Enacting the Software Process," *Proceedings of the 4th International Workshop,* Jan. 1989, *ACM SIGSOFT Software Engineering Notes,* June 1989, ACM Press, 1989.

W. M. Turski, "Specification as a Theory with Models in the Computer World and in the Real World," *Infotech State of the Art Report* **9**(6), 363–377 (1981).

N. Wirth, "Program Development by Stepwise Refinement," *ACM* **14**(4), 221–222 (April 1971).

M. M. Lehman
Imperial College, London

SOFTWARE FACTORY

INTRODUCTION

The story of the "software factory" within the field of software engineering is about how companies have attempted to push forward the state of programming practice in order to move beyond loosely organized craft or job-shop modes of operation that treated each project as unique, to a more structured process and organization for multiple projects. Factorylike approaches have tended to emphasize standardization of development methods and tools, systematic reuse of program components or designs, some divisions of labor and functional departments, and disciplined project management, as well as product quality control. Many firms, led by IBM in the United States, have introduced these and other concepts for large-scale programming operations but in varying degrees. This discussion focuses on the specific origins of the term "factory" as used in software and the histories of several companies that have explicitly used this term to describe their approaches to managing software development: System Development Corporation (SDC) in the United States, and Hitachi, Toshiba, NEC, and Fujitsu in Japan. (For a fuller treatment of the material discussed in this article, see Cusumano, 1991.) The latter part of this article also includes a brief discussion of other factorylike efforts in the United States and Europe.

EARLY FACTORY CONCEPTS

The earliest public proposals for the introduction of factory-type methods, tools, and organizations to software development appeared in the late 1960s, as outgrowths of comparisons of programming with established engineering and manufacturing processes. An engineer at General Electric, R. W. Bemer, made numerous suggestions that culminated in a 1968 paper encouraging GE to develop a "software factory" to reduce variability in programmer productivity through standardized tools, a computer-based interface, and an historical database for financial and management control. GE's exit from the computer business in 1970 ended the company's commitment to commercial hardware and software production, although Bemer provided the industry's first working definition of what might constitute a software factory:

> *[A] software factory should be a programming environment residing upon and controlled by a computer. Program construc-*

tion, checkout and usage should be done entirely within this environment, and by using the tools contained in the environment. . . . A factory . . . has measures and controls for productivity and quality. Financial records are kept for costing and scheduling. Thus management is able to estimate from previous data . . . . Among the tools to be available in the environment should be: compilers for machine-independent languages; simulators, instrumentation devices, and test cases as accumulated; documentation tools—automatic flow-charters, text editors, indexers; accounting function devices; linkage and interface verifiers; code filters (and many others). (Bemer, 1969, pp. 1626–1627)

While Bemer focused on standardized tools and controls, M. D. McIlroy of AT&T emphasized another factory-like concept—systematic reusability of code when constructing new programs. In an address at a 1968 NATO Science Conference on software engineering, McIlroy argued that the division of software programs into modules offered opportunities for "mass production" methods. He then used the term factory in the context of facilities dedicated to producing parameterized families of software parts or routines that would serve as building blocks for tailored programs reusable across different computers (McIlroy, 1969). But reception to McIlroy's ideas was mixed: It seemed too difficult to create program modules that would be efficient and reliable for all types of systems and which did not constrain the user; software was also heavily dependent on the specific characteristics of hardware. Nor did anyone know how to catalog program modules so they could be easily found and reused (Horowitz and Munson, 1984). Nonetheless, by the late 1960s, the term factory had arrived in software and was being associated with computer-aided tools and management-control systems, as well as modularization and reusability.

THE U.S. FACTORY PIONEER: SDC

One of the U.S. leaders in the custom software field, System Development Corporation (SDC), formerly a part of the Rand Corporation and in 1991 a Unisys division, established the first U.S. software facility called a factory in 1975–1976. SDC had been separated from Rand in the 1950s to develop the SAGE missile control system for the U.S. Department of Defense. It later took on other real-time programming tasks as a special government-sponsored corporation, but went public in 1970. Top management then had to control software costs and launched a process-oriented R&D effort in 1972 to tackle five problems SDC programmers continued to encounter project after project:

1. Lack of discipline and repeatability or standardized approaches to the development process;
2. Lack of an effective way to visualize and control the production process, as well as to measure before a project was completed how well code implemented a design;
3. Difficulty in accurately specifying performance requirements before detailed design and coding, and recurrence of disagreements on the meaning of certain requirements, or changes demanded by the customer;
4. Lack of standardized design, management, and verification tools, making it necessary to reinvent these from project to project;
5. Little capability to reuse components, despite the fact that many application areas used similar logic and managers believed that extensive use of off-the-shelf software modules would significantly shorten the time required for software development (Bratman and Court, 1975, 1977).

After several years of R&D work, a team of SDC engineers, led by John B. "Jack" Munson, constructed a detailed factory plan that consisted of three elements: an integrated set of tools (program library, project databases, on-line interfaces between tools and databases, and automated support systems for verification, documentation, etc.); standardized procedures and management policies for program design and implementation; and a matrix organization, separating high-level system design (at customer sites) from program development (at the software factory). The first site to utilize the factory system, which SDC copyrighted under the name "The Software Factory," was a facility of about 200 programmers in Santa Monica, California. SDC thus continued to have "program offices" at each customer site, with program managers that maintained responsibility throughout the life cycle for project management, customer relations, requirements and performance specifications, systems engineering, and quality control and assurance. To build the actual software and test it, however, program managers that wanted to use the factory (its usage was not mandatory) had to transfer system specifications to what was essentially an assembly line of three groups within the new software factory, which served SDC's System Division: Computer Program Design, Computer Program Development, and System Test and Verification (Figure 1).

SDC gave the name Factory Support System to the "basic structural and control components" designed to facilitate the factory methodology. This tool set, written in a high-level language to ease portability, ran on an IBM 370 mainframe computer and used the facilities of IBM's operating system to automate procedures for keeping track of program development and collecting data (Fig. 2). Tools included compilers and other basic programs that worked with the operating system, as well as Top-Down System Developer (TOPS), a modeling tool that helped outline and verify designs as well as describe much of the control and data interface logic in the actual coding language; Program Analysis and Test Host (PATH), which analyzed a source program and inserted calls to a recording program at appropriate locations, helping developers find information about the structure of the program to aid in testing; Integrated Management, Project Analysis, and Control Techniques (IMPACT), which utilized production information on milestones, tasks, resources, system components, and their relationships to provide schedule, resource computation, and status reports at the individual components level or summarized at any module or task hierarchy level.

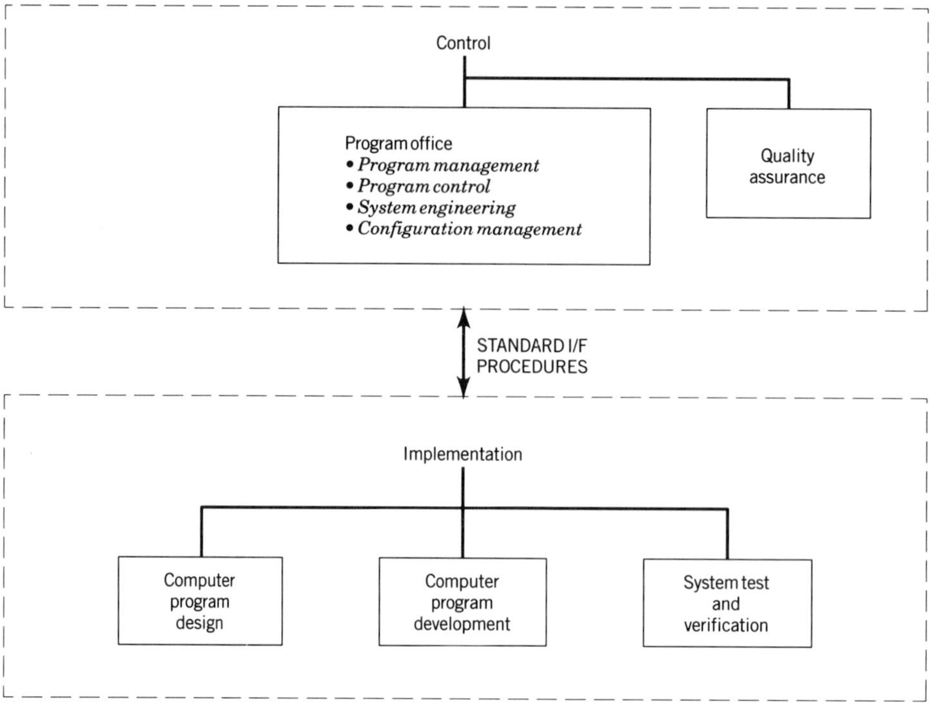

Figure 1. Software factory organizational principles. From Bratman and Court, 1977, copyright ©1977, System Development Corporation (Unisys Corporation). Reproduced with permission.

It took a year and a half during 1975–1976 for the R&D team to identify standards and procedures—general rules and specific guidelines—that might be applied to a variety of software projects. They based their process around a life cycle model of software development covering the major activities, events, and product components common to all projects. The methodology, codified in what SDC called the *Software Development Manual* or *SDM,* called for structured design and coding, top-down program development, and program production libraries. In addition, *SDM* outlined a management and control process, providing guidelines for planning, project control, review and

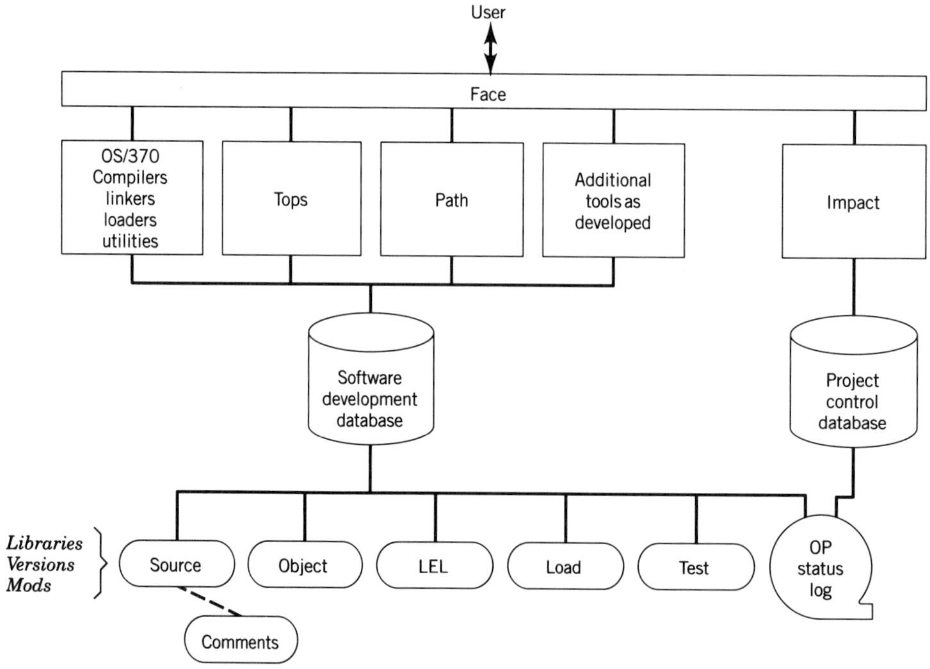

Figure 2. SDC software factory architecture. From Bratman and Court, 1977, copyright © 1977, System Development Corporation (Unisys Corporation). Reproduced with permission.

evaluation procedures, and quality assurance. The R&D team in part borrowed from existing U.S. military standards, but established most of the *SDM* methodology by examining previous projects SDC had done through written records and interviewing personnel to determine what had worked well and appeared to represent "best practice" within the company. According to two of the key factory architects, Harvey Bratman and Terry Court, this effort was critical to creating a common language and methodology that made the factory more than just a building with programmers working from a common pile of tools.

Approximately 10 projects went through the SDC Software Factory between 1976 and 1978, including systems for weather satellite control, air defense, and communications for the Los Angeles Police Department. SDC managers claim that all the projects, with the exception of the system for the L. A. Police, came in on time and within budget and with fewer defects and problems than SDC usually experienced with large systems. The company history even described the factory projects as, for the most part, "accurate, timely, and on budget," and models of "optimum software development" (Baum, 1981, pp. 205, 224). In fact, the factory worked so well that SDC's chief executive, George Mueller, directed all divisions to adopt the methodology as a corporate standard, and in 1978 he promoted Munson to oversee this transfer.

After Munson left, however, the factory fell gradually into disuse. Tools were not very portable among different projects; program managers preferred to build their own software, rather than hand over specifications to the factory; and specifying the L.A. Police system, which was an unfamiliar application for SDC engineers, took a year or more longer than scheduled, leaving factory programmers idle as the number of other new projects coming into the facility declined. Future jobs also went back to the project system, rather than using the factory structure for program development. The factory methodology remained in the *SDM* manual, although SDC dispersed the factory personnel among different projects and sites. SDC also updated the manual every few years and continued to use it through the late 1980s, while concepts from the factory methodology spread to other firms after the U.S. Department of Defense contracted with SDC in 1976 to devise guidelines for military-use software procurement. SDC completed a first set in 1979, with the help of the U.S. Department of Defense and an off shoot of MIT's Lincoln Laboratories, Mitre Corporation. The government subsequently published these procedures as a 16-volume set of guidebooks on software acquisition and management (Baum, 1981). SDC also influenced factory initiatives underway or soon to appear in Japan.

JAPANESE FACTORY EFFORTS

Hitachi

Hitachi boasted the oldest and largest software factories in Japan (Table 1). Its Software Development Center (formerly the Software Works), established in 1969, had approximately 4000 employees in 1991, including approximately 2000 assigned from Hitachi subsidiaries and subcontractors. This work force built a range of basic software for Hitachi mainframes, including operating systems, language compilers, and data base systems. The Information Systems Development Center (formerly called the Omori Works and then the System Design Works), separated from the original factory in 1985, housed 7000 software developers (including at least 4000 employees from subsidiaries and subcontractors) in two 31-story towers. This facility, unlike some other Japanese applications software factories, combined systems engineers (those who designed the systems) with programmers who built the actual software (did the module design, coding, and testing). It concentrated on customized business applications such as for financial institutions, securities firms, inventory control, management information, accounting, and personnel management.

By founding its Software Works in 1969, Hitachi was the first company in the world to apply the term factory (actually, its Japanese equivalent, *kojo,* translated either as "factory" or "works") to an actual software facility (Hitachi, 1979). A history of independent factories for each major product area prompted executives in the computer division to create a separate facility for software when this became a major activity. The factory represented a deliberate attempt to transform software from an unstructured "service" to a "product" with a guaranteed level of cost and quality, using a centralized organization to achieve productivity and reliability improvements through process standardization and control. Management saw a need to offset a severe shortage of skilled programmers in Japan and deal with numerous complaints from customers regarding defects in the software Hitachi was providing (most of which, along with the hardware, Hitachi imported from RCA until 1970). It was also important that all Hitachi factories had to adopt corporate accounting and administrative standards; this forced software managers to analyze the software development process in great detail and experiment with a series of work standards and controls that led to the current factory organization.

Managers concentrated initially on determining standards for productivity and costs in all phases of development, based on data collected for project management and quality control. Hitachi then standardized design around structured programming techniques in the early 1970s and reinforced these with training programs for new employees and managers. This approach reflected an attempt to improve average skills through a standard process rather than specify every procedure to be performed in each project and phase of development.

Yet Hitachi managers underestimated how difficult implementing factory concepts such as reusability and process standardization would be. Two examples illustrate this. First, their attempt in the early 1970s to introduce a "components control system" for reusability failed because of the lack of knowledge about how to produce reusable modules. Managers changed their priorities and decided to find a way to standardize product designs and then worry about components. A survey of the programming field suggested that structured design and programming techniques would help standardize software design and coding. A committee then spent several years studying

Table 1. Major Japanese Software Factories[a]

Year Estimated	Company	Facility/organization	1991 Estimated[b]
1969	Hitachi	Software Development Center (Hitachi Software Works)	4000 BS[c]
1976	NEC	Software Strategy Project	
		Fuchu Works	3000 BS[c]
		Mita Works	3000 APP[d]
		Mita Works	2000 RT[e]
		Abiko Works	2000 Tel[f]
		Tamagawa Works	2000 Tel[f]
1977	Toshiba	Fuchu Software Factory	2500 App[d]
1979	Fujitsu	Systems Engineering Group	5000 App[d]
		(Kamata Software Factory	2000 App[d]
1983	Fujitsu	Numazu Software Division (Numazu Works est. 1974)	4000 BS[c]
1985	Hitachi	Information Systems	7000 App[d]

[a] Cusumano, 1991. All facilities develop software for mainframes or minicomputers.
[b] Employee figures refer to 1988 or 1989 estimates.
[c] BS=Operating systems, Database management systems, Language utilities, and Related basic software
[d] App=General business applications
[e] RT=Industrial real-time control applications
[f] Tel=Telecommunications software (switching, transmission)

these techniques (as they were evolving) and analyzing programs Hitachi had already written. This was truly a pioneering move, because it would be several years before articles in industry journals began discussing structured design and programming widely and companies such as IBM adopted these practices for their internal standards.

Second, Hitachi failed to introduce one standardized process for both basic software and custom applications software. At the start of the factory, a committee for work standards took on the task of establishing procedures for all activities, based on a life cycle model of development. They met almost weekly, studying available materials on software development and examining practices within Hitachi and completed a first cut set of standards by the end of 1970, referred to as the Hitachi Software Standards (HSS). These covered product planning, design and coding methodology, documentation and manuals, testing, and any other activities necessary to complete a software product. However, Hitachi managers clearly recognized these procedures and standards would have to evolve as personnel and technology changed and they made provisions to revise performance standards annually, drawing up the procedures helped them identify best practices within the company and within the industry for dissemination to all projects and departments.

Struggling with work standards also helped the committee recognize the need to distinguish between basic systems and applications software rather than continue trying to impose similar controls and expectations on all types of software development. Hitachi started developing separate standards for applications during 1971–1972 and completed an initial set by 1975 now termed HIPACE (Hitachi Phased Approach for High Productive Computer System Engineering). HIPACE standardized formats for proposals, designs, and program construction, as well as aided in developing tools for design automation.

By the late 1970s, Hitachi had succeeded in organizing its software factory around a combination of manual engineering and factory techniques—structured design and coding coordinated with data collection and standard times for each activity, detailed documentation, design reviews independent of project personnel, rigorous defect analysis, and other elements. Only at this point, after spending years studying and standardizing the development process, was Hitachi management ready to invest heavily in computer-aided tools, relying on engineers mainly from the Software Works and the Systems Development Laboratory, part of the central laboratories.

The tools Hitachi devised supported major functions and activities. For basic software, during the late 1970s Hitachi introduced Computer-Aided Software Development System (CASD) to facilitate design, coding, documentation, and testing, and then Computer-Aided Production Control System for Software (CAPS) for manpower estimation, process flow control, and quality control (Shibata and Yokoyama, 1980; Kataoka et al., 1980). Both have been continually evolving. For custom applications, in the late 1970s Hitachi began developing another set of tools called Integrated Computer-Aided Software Engineering System (ICAS) (Kobayashi and co-workers, 1983). The most important consisted of the Software-Engineering Workbench (SEWB), which supported both system design and programming on advanced work stations, and Effective Approach to Achieving High Level Software Productivity (EAGLE), which ran on Hitachi mainframes and helped programmers build software from reusable modules as well as structure new designs and code for reuse. HIPACE continued to serve as the basic methodology used with these tools.

Performance improvements were impressive. Although direct productivity data is unavailable, sales per employee at the Software Works, combining systems and applications programs, doubled after the first year of founding the factory in 1969 and overall rose 12-fold between 1969 and 1984. The percentage of projects delivered late to the Quality Assurance Department dropped from over 72% in 1970 to a low of 6.9% in 1974 and averaged about 12% between 1975 and 1985. Defects reported by users per month for each computer in the field also dropped from an index of 100 in 1978 to 13 in 1983–1984 (Cusumano, 1991).

Toshiba

Toshiba created a highly disciplined factory around focused product lines, using a centralized software facility to develop real-time process control software for industrial applications (Matsumoto 1981, 1984, 1987). The decision to establish a software factory stemmed from rapid increases in actual and projected demand, beginning around 1975, for industrial control systems relying on a new generation of relatively inexpensive minicomputers. Typical of the changing demands Toshiba faced as sales of its control minicomputers rose were orders from Japanese utility companies to develop automated thermal power generating stations. These used enormous amounts of software; the typical power-generation control system rose from a few hundred thousand lines of code in the mid-1970s to two million by the early 1980s, necessitating years of development and hundreds of new programmers. Furthermore, to achieve safe and untended operation, the hardware and software for these and many other control systems had to be nearly free of defects or at least highly tolerant of system faults.

An R&D group responsible for industrial systems software in Toshiba, led by Yoshihiro Matsumoto, introduced an organization and process in 1977 integrating tools, methods, management and personnel systems with a physical layout for work stations (Table 2). The strategy for utilizing this infrastructure centered around four policies:

1. Standardize the development process to reduce variations among individuals and individual projects;
2. Reuse existing designs and code when building new systems to reduce redundant work and maximize productivity;
3. Introduce standardized and integrated tools to raise the performance levels of the average programmer; and
4. Provide extensive training and career-development tracks for programmers, to relieve the shortage of skilled engineers.

Table 2. Elements of the Toshiba Software Factory[a]

Combined tool, methodology, and management systems

Project progress management system
Cost management system
Productivity management system
Quality assurance system with standardized quality metrics
A standardized, baseline management system for design review, inspection and configuration management
Software tools, user interfaces and tool maintenance facilities
Existing software library and maintenance support
Technical data library
Standardized technical methodologies and disciplines
Documentation support system

Personnel systems

Quality circle activities
Education programs
Career development system

Physical infrastructure

Specially designed work spaces

[a] Matsumoto, 1987.

Perhaps the most delicate feature of Toshiba's factory was its organizational structure, a matrix imposed over product departments from several operating groups and divisions, all located on one site, Toshiba's Fuchu Works. Established in 1940 and set on 198 acres in the western outskirts of Tokyo, the Fuchu Works in 1991 had at least 8,000 employees working primarily in four areas: Information Processing and Control Systems, Energy Systems, Industrial Equipment, and Semiconductors (Printed Circuit Board Division). Operating departments within the divisions corresponded roughly to 19 product lines, including systems for information and control in public utilities, factories, power-generation plants, and various industrial and transportation equipment. Each department contained sections for hardware and software design as well as for manufacturing, testing, quality assurance, and product control.

Similarities in the type of software the Fuchu Works built from project to project allowed Toshiba to deliver "semicustomized" programs that combined reusable designs and code with newly written modules rather than writing all software from scratch. Toshiba also relied heavily on a standardized tool and methodology set, the Software Engineering Workbench (SWB), developed gradually after 1976 and modeled after AT&T's UNIX Programmers Workbench. Toshiba utilized its customized version of the UNIX operating system as well as a full complement of tools for design-support, reusable module identification, code generation, documentation and maintenance, testing, and project management. Important features of the Toshiba methodology were the design of new program modules (ideally limited to 50 lines) for reusability, the requirement that programmers deposit a certain number of reusable modules in a library each month, and the factoring in of reuse objectives into project schedules and budgets (Matsumura and co-workers, 1987).

Software productivity at the Toshiba Software Factory rose from 1,390 delivered equivalent-assembler source lines (EASL) per person per month in 1976 to over 3,100 in 1985, while reuse levels (lines of delivered code taken from existing software) increased from 13% in 1979 to 48% in 1985. The 3,130 lines of EASL source code per month per employee translate into approximately 1,000 lines of Fortran, the most common language Toshiba used in 1985—considerably more than the 300 lines or so of new code per month commonly cited for U.S. programmers making similar real-time applications. Quality levels (defined as the number of major faults detected after final testing) also improved dramatically after the opening of the factory, ranging from 7 to 20 per 1,000 lines of delivered code converted to EASL to .2 to .05 in 1985 (the range depended on quality control practices as well as the reliability requirements and the amount of testing customers contracted for) (Cusumano, 1991).

Toshiba data indicated that reusability was the major reason for productivity and quality improvements. The organization Toshiba created to promote reuse and overcome short-term concerns of project managers and development personnel (such as the longer time required to write and document reusable software) relied on Software Reusing Parts Steering Committees and a Software Reusing Parts Manufacturing Department and Software Reusing Parts Center. The factory formed a steering committee for different areas (with different members, depending on the application) to determine if customers had a common set of needs suitable for a package, and then allocated funds from the Fuchu Works' budget for these special projects. Some packages were usable in different departments, although most served specific applications. The Reusing Parts Manufacturing Department and Parts Center evaluated new software (and documentation) to make certain it met factory standards; after certification, engineers registered the software in department or factory reuse databases (libraries). Registered items required a key word phrase to represent the functionality of the part or correspond to a specific object, as well as reuse documentation that explained the part's basic characteristics.

Management also relied on an integrated set of incentives and controls to encourage project managers and personnel to take the time to write reusable software parts and reuse them frequently. At the start of each project, managers agreed to productivity targets that they could not meet without reusing a certain percentage of specifications, designs, or code. Design review meetings held at the end of each phase in the development cycle then checked how well projects met reuse targets, in addition to schedules and customer requirements. At the programmer level, when building new software, management *required* project members to register a certain number of components in the reuse databases, for other projects. Personnel received awards for registering particularly valuable or frequently reused modules, and they received formal evaluations from superiors on whether they met their reuse targets. The SWB system, meanwhile, monitored reuse as well as deviations from targets at the project and individual levels, and sent regular reports to managers.

NEC

The first step toward a factory structure for software development at NEC consisted of founding the Basic Software Development Division at its Fuchu Works in 1974, thereby separating organizationally operating-systems development from hardware development. NEC subsequently established other organizations at Mita, Tamagawa, and Abiko, all within the Tokyo metropolis or suburbs, for its other software needs. It also dispersed programming work throughout Japan through numerous subsidiaries and satellite offices (Fujino, 1984). However, the separation and separate histories of these facilities gradually presented greater problems for managers pursuing standardization and common goals such as quality improvement throughout the NEC group. Table 3 and the discussion below summarize the key initiatives NEC managers adopted to create a more effective multiproduct, multiprocess factory network.

The Software Strategy Project, started in 1976, attempted to integrate programming operations on a groupwide basis (including all in-house divisions and subsidiaries, rather than just the computer division). The objective was to introduce standards for tools, procedures, and methodologies for all phases of development and all aspects of management. Yet it took several years of trial and error to accomplish this while allowing individuals, projects, and divisions sufficient flexibility to tailor standards to the needs of their products and customers. When the Software Strategy Project ended, managers who worked on the effort, led by Dr. Yukio Mizuno, noticed another weakness in NEC's structure for managing software development: the lack of permanent staff to explore and follow through on key issues or technologies. Thus, to insure continuity and proceed beyond the Software Strategy Project, NEC in 1980 established the Software Product Engineering Laboratory to lead the company's efforts in software engineering R&D, making this organization part of NEC's central research laboratories. The Software Factory Design Project, started in 1986 under the auspices of the laboratory, developed guidelines for designing actual software factories, from higher-level concepts, such as tool and methodology standardization, to smaller details, such as how to arrange programmers' work spaces or recreation areas.

NEC's Software Quality Control (SWQC) Program dates back to 1978, when a handful of NEC managers established a software quality control study group. Several specific conclusions came out of their reviews. First, research in software development indicated a strong correlation between quality and productivity, reflecting the manpower needed to fix defects. Hence they concluded that any revolution in software productivity would require correspondingly dramatic improvements in quality control practices. Surveys of NEC projects also supported the observation that "human factors," that is, differences in programmer skills and experience, seemed to be the most important elements influencing individual performance, and that NEC had to address training more seriously if it were to make major advances in productivity or quality (Mizuno, 1983). NEC management then set up a quality control program that focused on motivation, teamwork methodologies, training, and other factors affecting individual performance. Since evidence from manufacturing departments indicated that bringing employees together in small groups helped solve quality problems, NEC imported the concept of quality circles. Next, in 1981 NEC created a formal, companywide organization covering all aspects of software production, management, services, sales, and training, under the SWQC Program.

The Software Problem Strategy Project, another three-year effort launched in 1982, attempted to encourage more standardization in development and quality control practices, explore various productivity-improvement measures, and establish or formally designate a series of software factories to serve NEC's different product divisions. Under

Table 3. NEC Software Factory Implementation[a]

Year	Initiative	Focus/Outcomes
1974	Basic Software Development Division	Organizational separation of software from hardware development
1976-1979	Software Strategy Project	Standardization of data collection, tool and structured-programming methodology for basic and applications software throughout the NEC group, with the objectives of raising productivity and quality
1980	Software Product Engineering Laboratory	Centralization of process and tool R&D for dissemination to divisions and subsidiaries
1981	Software Quality Control (SWQC)	Establishment of a groupwide methodology, training program, and control measures for improving software quality, including quality circle activities
1982-1985	Software Problem Strategy Project	1."Mapping" of software development activities 2. Subcontracting management 3. Software productivity improvement
1986	Software-Factory Design Project	Establishment of Hokuriku Software Development Center, based on ergonomic principles and other software-factory concepts
1987	C&C Software Development Group	Reorganization of the Software Product Engineering Laboratory and expansion of applied research

[a] Cusumano, 1991.

this project, NEC executives decided to act in three areas. First, they carried out a "software production mapping" that consisted of constructing a logistical and organizational layout of programming operations within NEC by product (basic software, industrial systems, business applications, transmission systems, switching software, and microcomputer software), to determine which software houses NEC's product divisions were using to assist in development and whether divisions needed more help, such as new subsidiaries that might serve as additional software factories. Second, they formalized and systematized procedures for managing software subcontractors. Third, they launched another effort to improve and link software productivity and quality assurance measures by establishing a Software Productivity Committee to study documentation control, quality control, software productivity and quality measurements, cost estimation, personnel education, project management, support tools, and production environments.

Although NEC has not released as much performance data as Hitachi or Toshiba, NEC did report major improvements in productivity through reusability in business applications programming as well as significant gains in quality (Matsumoto and co-workers, 1987). The SWQC Program, for example, claimed to have achieved declines in defects reported for transmission control software from an average of 1.37 faults per 1000 lines of code to 0.41. In minicomputer operating-system software, the decline in defects was from 0.35 per 1000 lines to 0.20 (Mizuno, 1983).

On the other hand, the centralized laboratory for software-engineering process R&D did not work quite as well as NEC managers had hoped. Some laboratory researchers had become too "academic" in orientation while engineers and SWQC teams in the product divisions seemed to be doing more useful applied studies. To encourage more practical research that better met the needs of divisions but without eliminating all basic research, a 1987 reorganization moved the basic researchers to NEC's Central Research Laboratories. This involved no organizational change, since the Software Product Engineering Laboratory had been a part of the central labs. However, physically removing the more academic researchers left a group more concerned with applications of new methods and tools. Management then expanded the number of applied researchers and divided them into four areas under the umbrella of a newly created C&C (Computers and Communications) Software Development Group.

The Software Planning Office took charge of running the companywide software quality control effort. The Software Engineering Development Laboratory conducted research on tools and integrated development environments, as well as software engineering management and established a consulting department to help transfer technology or assist operating divisions and subsidiaries. The C&C Common Software Development Laboratory developed basic software packages for microcomputers, while the C&C Systems Interface Laboratory worked on compatibility and network technology.

Fujitsu

Fujitsu established a basic software division within its hardware factory in the mid-1970s that closely resembled Hitachi's Software Works in practices and organization except that Fujitsu kept basic hardware development on the same site as basic software development. An important characteristic of Fujitsu's development approach and organization was the gradual integration of controls for product, process, and quality. Direction of Fujitsu's efforts in these areas, as at NEC, came from the Quality Assurance Department in the Numazu Works's Software Division.

According to a chronology the department prepared, these efforts fell into three main phases: prior to 1970, when Fujitsu had no set procedures and managers allowed programmers to test software at their own discretion; 1970–1978, when Fujitsu set up its first product and process standards and formal systems for inspection and quality control; and after 1978, when Fujitsu began placing more emphasis on structured design and programming techniques and established the procedures that formed the basis of its current practices. Distinguishing the last phase was a broadening of the Quality Assurance Department's concerns to include not only testing and documentation conformance, or product evaluation, but analysis of the development process itself. As with Hitachi, Toshiba, and NEC, these practices brought Fujitsu major improvements in quality as well as productivity, with, for example, the number of defects in all outstanding basic software code supported by Fujitsu dropping from 0.19 per 1,000 lines in 1977 to 0.01 in 1985 (Yoshida, 1985).

In applications, Fujitsu's decision to create a software factory stemmed from the same need SDC as well as Hitachi, Toshiba, and NEC had encountered: to produce a variety of nominally different programs more efficiently, primarily sold with the company's own hardware and basic software. Management began cautiously. First, it experimented with a centralized organization by setting up a Software Conversion Factory Department in 1977, with approximately 100 employees. Customers wanted to run these modified programs on new machines, which were not compatible with Fujitsu's previous architectures, as well as software originally written for other companies' machines for operation with Fujitsu hardware. Managers believed conversion work was fairly straightforward and that centralization of personnel and equipment would foster standardization and thus dissemination of good methods and tools, making tasks easier to manage and resulting in higher productivity and quality. This seemed feasible, especially since in coordination with the factory establishment, a team of Fujitsu engineers defined a set of structured design and programming techniques as well as detailed procedures for project management, called Software Development Engineering Methodology (SDEM), and introduced support tools for programming in Fortran, called Software Development Support System (SDSS), which Fujitsu quickly replaced with tools for COBOL programming (Murakami and co-workers, 1981).

The conversion factory worked well enough to expand the facility to include program construction by adding another 200 employees and charging them with turning requirements specifications received from systems engineers into code. Prior to this, Fujitsu had managed systems engineering and program construction in integrated projects, with no separation of these two functions. But the process for new development did not work smoothly for all projects. Much like SDC had experienced a few years earlier (but without publicizing this), Fujitsu managers found that many projects depended on close interactions with customers and knowledge of very different requirements, or that writing the application program required access to proprietary information that customers, for security reasons, preferred not to give Fujitsu personnel unless they worked at the customers' own sites. On other occasions, Fujitsu needed to provide programming services at locations around Japan, again departing from the centralized factory model. In addition, as Fujitsu improved the tools and reuse data bases available in the factory, less experienced programmers became better able to build complete systems on their own, making separation of work and use of more skilled engineers unnecessary.

Rather than abandoning the objective of streamlining software development through a factory approach, Fujitsu improved its system gradually, recognizing that different projects had different optimal processes. The major change consisted of expanding the scope of work in the factory departments to let factory personnel do detailed design and eventually systems design for projects where it was difficult or unnecessary to separate these tasks, either for logistical reasons or because factory engineers had the expertise to design and build systems on their own.

Fujitsu introduced other changes. One encouraged systems engineers outside the factory, who initially did surveys and project planning, systems design, and a program's structural design, to leverage their expertise more widely, not only by letting the factory personnel do more work, but by writing software packages to cover the needs of many users—with a single design effort. Any packages or pieces of them that Fujitsu could deploy for custom jobs, as is or modified, reduced the need to write new software. In addition, to spread the burden of programming more widely Fujitsu management established or engaged more subsidiaries and subcontractors, as well as leased methods, tools, and training services to customers of Fujitsu hardware, beginning with SDEM in 1980. Fujitsu also continued to refine the factory's methods and tools as the technology and customer needs evolved.

The Systems Engineering Group consisted of three main areas, with several divisions, departments, and subsidiaries, as well as a research institute. One area, the Common Technology Divisions, included the Systems Engineering (SE) Technical Support Center, the Applications Software Planning Division, and the Office Computer Systems Support Division. The SE Technical Support Center housed the Software Factory Department and a portion of its 1,500 to 2,000 associated programmers, as well as other departments for Systems Development Engineering (technology planning and transfer), Information Support (product information for customers), Systems Engineering Support Services (tools and methods), and the Japanese Sigma project, (a joint company and government effort started in 1985 by Japan's Ministry of International Trade and Industry in an attempt to disseminate, through a national communications network and standardization around Unix as a programming environment, the same type of work stations, support tools, and reusable software techniques that factories such as Toshiba's relied on). The factory built about 20% of new applications done in the Systems Engineering Group as well as handled about 75% of all program conversion work (modifying software to run on new Fujitsu machines). Most of the remaining jobs, approximately 800 small projects per year in the late 1980s, went to approximately three dozen subsidiaries as well as subcontractors outside the factory. A second area consisted of departments with systems engineers specializing in particular industry applications (finance, insurance, securities, manufacturing, distribution, NTT, scientific, technical, government), so that they had adequate knowledge to specify customer requirements and accurate system designs. The third area, functionally specialized departments of systems engineers, designed management information systems, "value added networks" for different on-line services, personal computer systems, and software for new telecommunication firms (the new common carriers, or NCCs).

RECENT EUROPEAN AND U.S. EFFORTS

Except for the SDC episode, most software producers in Europe and the United States did not specifically set up "software factories," although many were attempting to incorporate factorylike approaches or tools into their development organizations. Andersen Consulting in the United States was perhaps the most prominent example of an applications producer that closely resembled Japanese software factories in terms of methods, tools, and process emphases, although there were other examples of facilities that were trying to become more structured and predictable in their operations. In addition, several cooperative projects in the European community during the 1980s and early 1990s were aimed explicitly at developing software factory tool sets and programming environments, while similar efforts under way in the United States also supported the dissemination of common tools and structured management concepts.

With regard to government support or cooperative R&D related to factorylike approaches in Japan, it is true that several research projects during the 1970s and 1980s promoted the development of tools that made their way into or at least resembled systems used at Hitachi, Toshiba, Fujitsu, and NEC. Nonetheless, the Japanese software factories resulted primarily from initiatives at individual firms. Two other cooperative projects have drawn considerable attention but have had little practical results. Japan's Software Industrialized Generator and Maintenance Aids SIGMA) Project, begun in 1985, has attempted to build and disseminate factorylike tools and reusable packages that ran in a Unix environment and were accessible through a national on-line network. Although Sigma helped to familiarize Japanese developers with Unix, the project has had difficulty diffusing its work stations and getting firms to contribute useful tools and applications packages. The Fifth Generation Computer project, begun in 1982, has greatly improved Japanese research capabilities in parallel processing and artificial intelligence but has not produced much in the way of commercial products or technologies that aid software development.

In contrast, the European Strategic Program for Research and Development in Information Technologies (ESPRIT) (qv), begun in 1984, has attracted considerable attention in Europe, spending $1.5 billion on more than 200 projects. The research included approximately 50 projects devoted to software technologies—knowledge engineering and expert systems, advanced computer architectures, and improved user-machine interfaces, similar to Japan's Fifth Generation Computer Project; as well as applied tool and methodology development, similar to Japan's Sigma Project. Several groups worked on method and tool integration as well as reuse technology for a software factory environment, with the Portable Common Tools Environment (PCTE) based on UNIX V. The main firm behind this initiative, Bull of France, offered PCTE on its work stations. Other firms followed, including GEC and ICL in the United Kingdom, Nixdorf and Siemens in Germany, Olivetti in Italy, and Sun Microsystems in the United States (see also UNIX).

Another cooperative program, the European Research Coordination Agency (EUREKA) Software Factory Project (ESF), worked on developing a tool set and integrated environment resembling PCTE but tailored for specific applications such as real-time software development and complex business programming (see also *Eureka Software Factory*). The development group consisted of Nixdorf, AEG, ICL, and several other firms in Germany, the United Kingdom, Norway, and Sweden. Individual countries made other efforts to explore similar tools and techniques, with perhaps the largest consisting of Britain's Alvey program, modeled after the Fifth Generation Project in objectives but resembling ESPRIT in organization, with 2,000 researchers from universities and companies working on 200 separate projects (Toole, 1989).

In the United States, the most prominent example of a cooperative effort was the Microelectronics and Computer Corporation (MCC) (qv), founded in 1983 by several U.S. firms and located in Austin, Texas (Peck, 1986). In 1992, this had approximately 400 researchers and a budget of $55 million per year. With regard to software production technology, R&D conducted at MCC resembled work done in Japanese and European cooperative projects as well as many corporate laboratories, ranging from artificial intelligence applications to more conventional but advanced software tools, methods, and concepts that facilitated reusability and group programming within an integrated environment. MCC had difficulty getting member firms to use its software support tools, however, and was shifting its research emphases away from this area.

The U.S. Department of Defense had a longer history of promoting research on computer hardware and software. Many of the results have benefited the world industry—the Multics time-sharing system, the Ada language, very large scale integrated circuits, and various other tools and techniques, as well as basic research. In contrast to the European and Japanese projects or to MCC, a common theme in defense research has been the focus on military applications, thus limiting the total impact of cooperative ventures on the U.S. commercial sector. Nonetheless, in the 1980s, the Department of Defense shifted somewhat and exhibited more interest in basic problems in software engineering and potentially general solutions, in response to the growing complexity and expense of software for modern weaponry and other defense as well as information systems.

For example, the Department of Defense in 1982 initiated Software Technology for Adaptable, Reliable Systems (STARS) as a multiyear industry, government, and university effort, with annual an budget of around $60 million. This included the establishment of a Software Engineering Institute (SEI) at Carnegie Mellon University in 1985, where a staff of 250 researched software tools and methods, made recommendations for process management, as well as evaluated development practices at individual firms, primarily in the United States. The concepts promulgated by SEI (see Humphrey, 1989) closely resembled the style of management in Japanese software factories, although this is not surprising. The SEI work was based mainly on management practices for software programming devised at IBM, which also had a major influence on Hitachi, Fujitsu, and other Japanese firms.

In addition, the U.S. Department of Defense Advanced Research Projects Agency (DARPA) directly sponsored several projects that overlapped with the technical themes being explored in Japanese and European projects, besides making grants to U.S. universities for research in every major area of computer hardware and software technology. Of particular prominence among the DARPA projects was the Strategic Computing Initiative, a $600-million, 5-year effort begun in 1983–1984. This brought together university, government, and industry researchers to study parallel architectures for symbolic computing, advanced microelectronics, and new hardware; with the objective, to an extent inspired by the Japanese Fifth Generation Project, of integrating vision, speech recognition and production, natural-language understanding, and expert systems, especially but not exclusively for military applications (Flamm, 1987).

CONCLUSION: EVOLUTION TOWARD FACTORY PRACTICE

This review of factorylike efforts at major software producers in Japan as well as in the United States and Europe demonstrates that, whether or not companies adopted the factory label for particular facilities, industry participants clearly attempted to move beyond craft practices that treated each software project as unique. They succeeded in introducing more systematic engineering and manufacturinglike processes that included recycling reusable components as well as standardizing methods and tools. The result has been the ability to rely less on highly skilled people and ad hoc practices, at least for similar projects; and to rely more on common methods and tools, reuse of designs and code, as well as accumulations of process knowledge over time such as for project scheduling and budgeting or predicting defect levels. The transition to a more structured management style and organization required years of effort and passage through overlapping phases comparable to what firms in other industries encountered as they grew and formalized operations.

The initial motivation to make this transition required an unusual conviction on the part of key engineers, division managers, and top executives that software was not an unmanageable technology. This led to an initial phase of creating formal organizations and control systems for managing software development rather than continuing to treat programming as a loosely organized service provided more or less free to customers primarily to facilitate hardware sales. Imposing greater structure on the development process while effectively accommodating different types of software also demanded a product focus for facilities or departments to limit the range of problems managers and programmers faced. IBM and Hitachi led in these efforts during the 1960s, whereas SDC's factory encountered problems in managing a variety of projects and ultimately ceased operating.

Subsequent phases of evolution in facilities that continued to structure the development process were comparable at Hitachi, Toshiba, NEC, and Fujitsu (as well as at IBM, which did not use the factory label), as summarized in Table 4. All moved through periods of tailoring methods, tools, control systems, and standards to different product families; developing tools to mechanize or automate aspects of project management, code generation, testing, documentation generation; refining their development tools and techniques as well as extending them to subsidiaries, subcontractors, and customers; pursuing greater levels of integration among tools through engineering workbenches as well as adding new functions, such as to support reuse, design, and requirements analysis; and gradually increasing the types of products under development as well as paying more attention to issues such as product functionality and ease of use. Throughout, software factories and factorylike organizations reflected long-term management commitments and integrated efforts—above the level of individuals or individual projects—to standardize, structure, and support software development along the lines suggested by software engineering literature since the late 1960s and early 1970s.

As for the future of Japanese-style factories as a way of systematizing software development, it remained possible that large centralized factory organizations represented a transitional stage even in Japan. Between the late 1960s and the early 1990s, factory concepts provided a useful mechanism to centralize, study, and manage a series of projects more efficiently than treating each effort as separate, with scale economies restricted to individual jobs and no scope economies systematically exploited. With improvements in electronic communications technology, it was no longer essential to concentrate large numbers of people in single locations, as seen in the NEC and Fujitsu cases, although Hitachi and Toshiba managers clearly preferred to bring people together, and it seemed more likely that factorylike organizations would continue to coexist with job shops, depending on the kind of software being built as well as company objectives.

In general, factory strategies appeared best suited for software systems that could rely on reusable designs and components as well as common development tools and techniques. For totally new or innovative design efforts, Japanese software producers tended to utilize less structured organizational forms, such as special projects, laboratories, or subsidiaries and subcontractors, that gave individual engineers more freedom to invent and innovate. To the extent that Japanese firms wished to place more emphasis on individual creativity, they were likely to build more software in nonfactory environments as well as emphasize the design and engineering roles of personnel in internal projects, especially since new engineering recruits in Japan seemed to prefer labels other than "factory" to describe their places of work.

On the other hand, software programs continued to grow in size and complexity along with computer processing capabilities, demanding more rather than fewer skills in coordination and management. Computing as well as programming demands also appeared to change more in an incremental rather than radical fashion, with progress constrained to some extent by enormous existing investments in current software and hardware systems. While

Table 4. Phases of Factory Structuring in Software

Phase I:	*Formalized Organization and Management Structure*
(Mid-1960s to early 1970s)	Factory objectives established Product focus determined Process data collection and analysis begun Initial control systems introduced
Phase II:	*Technology Tailoring and Standardization*
(Early 1970s to early 1980s)	Control systems and objectives expanded Standard methods adopted for design, coding, testing, Documentation, maintenance On-line development through terminals Program libraries introduced Integrated methodology and tool development begun Employee training programs to standardize skills
Phase III:	*Process Mechanization and Support*
(Late 1970s)	Introduction of tools supporting project control Introduction of tools to generate code, test cases, and documentation Integration of tools with On-line data bases and engineering work benches begun
Phase IV:	*Process Refinement and Extension*
(Early 1980s)	Revisions of standards Introduction of new methods and tools Establishment of quality control and quality circle programs Transfer of methods and tools to subsidiaries, subcontractors, hardware customers
Phase V:	*Integrated and Flexible Automation*
(Mid-1980s)	Increase in capabilities of existing tools Introduction of reuse-support tools Introduction of design-automation tools Introduction of requirements analysis tools Further integration of tools through engineering work benches
Phase VI:	*Incremental Product / Variety Improvement*
(Late 1980s)	Process and reliability control, followed by: better functionality & ease of use more types of products

some new design and programming techniques, such as object orientation, made it possible to break up designs and projects more easily into small pieces and facilitated reusability, this methodology still required extensive product and project coordination. The diffusion of packaged software products as well as improvements in computer-aided tools made it increasingly easy for computer users, even those without software training, to buy, make, or modify their own programs, although Japanese firms were also developing packages as well as conducting extensive research on new tools and techniques and then introducing them gradually into their development operations. Thus it seemed likely that software producers in Japan and elsewhere who wished to balance efficiency (productivity and quality control, project and budget control) with flexibility or creativity (some, but not all, innovative or fully customized features) over a series of similar projects would continue to refine the kind of organizational approaches and process technologies found in software factories, whatever labels they used for their facilities.

BIBLIOGRAPHY

C. Baum, *The System Builders: The Story of SDC*, System Development Corporation, Santa Monica, Calif., 1981.

R. W. Bemer, "Position Papers for Panel Discussion—The Economics of Program Production," *Information Processing 68,* North-Holland, Amsterdam, 1626–1627, 1969.

H. Bratman and T. Court, "The Software Factory," *IEEE Computer,* 28–37 (May 1975).

H. Bratman and T. Court, "Elements of the Software Factory: Standards, Procedures, and Tools," in Infotech International Ltd., *Software Engineering Techniques,* Berkshire, England, Infotech International Ltd., 1977, pp. 117–143.

M. Cusumano, *Japan's Software Factories: A Challenge to U.S. Management,* Oxford University Press, New York, 1991.

K. Flamm, Targeting the Computer: *Government Support and International Competition,* Brookings Institute, Washington, D.C., 1987.

K. Fujino, "Software Development for Computers and Communications at NEC," *IEEE Computer,* 57–62 (Nov. 1984).

Hitachi Ltd., *Sofutouea Kojo 10 nen no ayumi* (A 10-year History of the Software Works), Hitachi Ltd., Yokohama, 1979.

E. Horowitz and J. B. Munson, "An Expansive View of Reusable Software," *IEEE Transactions on Software Engineering* SE-10, **5,** 477–487 (1984).

W. S. Humphrey, *Managing the Software Process,* Addison-Wesley Publishing Company and Software Engineering Institute, Reading, Mass., 1989.

M. Kataoka and co-workers "Sofutouea kaihatsu shien shisutemu (CASD shisutemu)" [Computer-aided Software Development System [CASD System], *Hitachi hyoron* **62**(12), 37–42 (Dec. 1980).

M. Kobayashi and co-workers, "ICAS: An Integrated Computer Aided Software Engineering System," *IEEE Digest of Papers-—Spring '83 COMPCON,* 238–244 (1983).

M. Matsumoto and co-workers "Joho shisutemu-kei sofutouea togo seisan shisutemu" (Integrated Software Life Cycle System for Information Systems), *NEC giho* **40**(1), 19–24 (1987).

Y. Matsumoto, "SWB System: A Software Factory," in H. Hunke, ed., *Software Engineering Environments,* North-Holland, Amsterdam, 1981, pp. 305–318.

Y. Matsumoto, "Management of Industrial Software Production," *IEEE Computer,* 59–71, (Feb. 1984).

Y. Matsumoto, "A Software Factory: An Overall Approach to Software Production," in Peter Freeman, ed., *Tutorial: Software Reusability,* IEEE Computer Society Press, Washington, D.C., 1987, pp. 155–178.

K. Matsumura and co-workers, "Trend Toward Reusable Module Component: Design and Coding Technique 50SM," *Proceedings of the Eleventh Annual International Computer Software and Applications Conference—COMPSAC,* IEEE Computer Society Press, Oct. 1987, pp 7–9, 1987.

M. D. McIlroy, "Mass Produced Software Components," in P. Naur and B. Randell, eds., *Software Engineering: Report on a Conference Sponsored by the NATO Science Committee,* Brussels, Scientific Affairs Division, NATO, 1969, pp. 151–155.

Y. Mizuno, "Software Quality Improvement," *IEEE Computer,* 66–72 (March 1983).

Y. Murakami and co-workers, "SDEM and SDSS: Overall Approach to Improvement of the Software Development Process," in H. Hunke, ed., *Software Engineering Environments,* North-Holland, Amsterdam, 1981, pp. 281–293.

M. J. Peck, "Joint R&D: The Case of Microelectronics and Computer Technology Corporation," *Research Policy* **15,** 219–231 (May 1986).

K. Shibata and Y. Yokoyama, "Sogo sofutouea seisan kanri shisutemu 'CAPS'" (Computer-aided Production Control System for Software 'CAPS'), *Hitachi hyoron* **62**(12), 37–42 (Dec. 1980).

G. Toole, "ESPRIT and European Software Capability," unpublished Master's Thesis, M.I.T. Sloan School of Management, Cambridge, Mass., May 1989.

T. Yoshida, "Sofutouea no keiryo-ka" (Quantifying software), *Joho shori* **26**(1), 48–51 (1985).

MICHAEL A. CUSUMANO
Massachusetts Institute of Technology

SOFTWARE LIFE CYCLE PROCESS MODEL

See PROCESS MODELS IN SOFTWARE ENGINEERING.

SOFTWARE MAINTENANCE

See MAINTENANCE.

SOFTWARE MANAGEMENT

See PROJECT MANAGEMENT.

THE SOFTWARE PRODUCTIVITY CONSORTIUM

The Software Productivity Consortium was founded in 1985 by a group of the United States' leading companies in the aerospace, defense, electronics, and systems integration industries. In both its original charter and its accomplishments to date, the Consortium represents a unique national resource for organizations facing the many challenges of designing and deploying large, software-intensive systems.

Current Consortium member companies include Boeing, Grumman, Lockheed, Martin Marietta, Rockwell International, United Technologies, Aerojet, GDE Systems Inc, SYSCON, Vitro, BTG, and SEMA, Inc. These companies, and other customers within the Federal government, are using Consortium products in dozens of critical programs.

Located in Virginia's Center for Innovative Technology (CIT) complex, adjacent to Dulles International Airport near Washington, D.C., the Consortium offers U.S. industry and government a means of leveraging the strategic investments required to improve U.S. software engineering practices. In close partnership with member companies and government customers, and in alliance with the commercial software industry, academic institutions, government organizations, and trade associations, the Consortium provides validated processes, methods, tools, and services to help its customers reduce the time and risks of building high-quality systems.

The Consortium technical program provides members with four critical benefits in their systems development efforts: increased productivity; higher quality; lower risk; and reduced time-to-market. Consortium products are focused on advancing the fundamental *processes and methods* required to build large, complex systems competitively. This focus is timely, as industry experience increasingly demonstrates that organizations without such software engineering processes and methods can expect only marginal productivity rains through the use of automation (i.e., CASE) technologies.

Sharing a common focus on continuous risk mitigation and advanced reuse maturity, the Consortium's suite of integrated technical capabilities builds on successful achievements in areas of critical interest to its customers. These areas include evolutionary systems and software development; software and systems requirements engineering and design; software reuse and measurement; continuous process improvement; and technology insertion.

SERVING ARPA, OTHER FEDERAL AGENCIES

The Consortium is also a co-founder (with Virginia's Center for Innovative Technology) of the Virginia Center of Excellence (VCOE) for Software Reuse and Technology Transfer. Under an award from the U.S. Defense Department's Advanced Research Projects Agency (ARPA), the VCOE is delivering a series of Consortium-developed technologies addressing reuse adoption, domain engineering, software measurement, requirements engineering, and technology insertion.

As a licensed provider of software process assessments authorized by the DOD Software Engineering Institute (SEI), the Consortium can help any organization to assess its software maturity— an increasingly strategic asset. In addition, Consortium process improvement specialists perform a variety of post-assessment activities for members and government customers. Such work is currently underway at the U.S. Patent and Trademark Office, the Internal Revenue Service, the Federal Aviation Administration, and other agencies.

BUILDING CUSTOMER SATISFACTION

Through its technical program and support activities, the Consortium helps to increase the effectiveness and competitiveness of each of its customers. The Consortium seks to build customer satisfaction by helping its members and clients to:

- *Work smarter,* through software process assessments, continuous process improvement, and systematic risk management activities.
- *Work faster,* using efficient and integrated methods, tools, and environments.
- *Avoid re-work,* through the *reuse* of software components (requirements, designs, test results, and code), ongoing measurement of software projects, and early identification and correction of software errors.

Without initiating such improvements, many organizations will find it impossible to meet competitive requirements for improved software processes, much less the threats posed by ever-escalating demands for software, leaner budgets, and a continuing shortage of qualified software engineers.

TECHNICAL PROGRAM BASED ON MEMBER NEEDS

The Consortium bases its technical program on the idea that fundamental process improvements are the first step toward improved competitiveness. Consortium technologies combine improved processes with the methods, tools, and services needed to implement them. Ongoing feedback from customers is gathered through a variety of technical and executive-level advisory boards, customer surveys, and other communication mechanisms. This feedback has confirmed a common need for improvements to address the most critical aspects of the software development process. These include:

- Specifying and evaluating the true *requirements* of complex systems, which are often poorly defined, misunderstood, and continuously change.
- *Integrating* the processes, methods, and tools used by an organization throughout the development life cycle.
- *Verifying* software systems, to detect errors early in the life cycle and throughout development and implementation.
- *Measuring* and predicting, on an ongoing basis, program performance and costs.
- *Reusing* software components (requirements, designs, and test procedures, as well as code) whenever possible.

The Consortium offers a suite of integrated capabilities to address these needs. These capabilities include process, method, and tool support in areas such as requirements engineering, systems and software design and programming, reuse maturity, measurement, and technology insertion. Collectively, these capabilities allow line engineers, project managers, business area managers, and technologists to achieve immediate improvements throughout the entire software development life cycle and to plan the longer-term software activities of their organizations.

HIGH-LEVEL SOFTWARE SYNTHESIS (HLSS)

While continuing to evolve these existing technologies, the Consortium also continues its progress toward the larger increases in productivity and quality needed to address the complexity of tomorrow's systems. Toward this end, the Consortium's 1993–1995 Strategic Technical Plan introduced a new paradigm for software engineering that fully addresses the need for dramatic increases in productivity.

This paradigm, High-Level Software Synthesis (HLSS), will allow for the production of software with significantly less attention required to maintenance and testing activities, and further transform software design into an engineering discipline. It will be as applicable to *systems* development as it is to *software* engineering.

Most of the technological foundations for HLSS already exist, but have not been matured and integrated. The Consortium will integrate these technologies, filling in the holes necessary to support the application of HLSS in its customers' environments.

SUPPORTING PRODUCTS AND SERVICES

Each Consortium technical capability is supported by at least one major deliverable (usually a guidebook), and by one or more supporting deliverables (courses, workshops, videos, consulting services, etc.), all integrated within a cohesive technology transfer program to facilitate wide adoption and use. The Consortium bases its selection of supporting products, tools, and support services on the capability being provided and on the needs of its customers. All such supporting products and services are packaged to provide customers with a comprehensive solution to a given problem in the software life cycle. Commercial-strength software tools, developed by vendors participating in the Consortium's Strategic Alliance program, also support key Consortium technologies.

The Consortium validates each technology by internal review, and by extensive testing programs (case studies, verification exercises, pilot projects) conducted at customer sites or in partnership with other sponsoring organizations. All Consortium technical staff dedicate time to work with customer personnel, helping them apply Consortium technologies in pilot or line projects. This type of "hands-on" consulting serves as an effective technology transfer mechanism, greatly broadening customer understanding and use of Consortium products while enhancing Consortium knowledge of the actual environmental constraints and needs of each customer.

PROCESS IMPROVEMENT SPECIALISTS

The Consortium is nationally recognized for its work in the process improvement area. In addition to providing SEI-authorized software process assessments, the Consortium offers post-assessment consulting services to help its customers design and implement plans for continuous software process improvements. All key Consortium technologies focus on enhancing software processes, and provide an integrated, "how-to" approach to implementing improved software engineering practices throughout the software development life cycle.

The Consortium is also widely known for its expertise in Ada, the DOD-mandated programming language for all defense software systems. The Consortium's *Ada Quality and Style: Guidelines for Professional Programmers* is recommended by the DOD Ada Joint Program Office (AJPO) as the "suggested Ada style guide for DOD usage," and has become a standard reference for project managers, software engineers, and programmers at many organizations. Additionally, the Consortium's Ada-based Design Approach for Real-Time Systems (ADARTS℠) (service trademark of the Software Productivity Consortium Limited Partnership) is a standard design method for several of its member companies and is being widely applied in mission-critical systems and major avionics programs (e.g., the F-22, RAH-66 Comanche, and EF-111A programs).

Many of the work products resulting from the use of Consortium technologies can be integrated within an innovative, comprehensive approach to complete life cycle development: the Evolutionary Spiral Process (ESP). A variant of the spiral model developed by Dr. Barry Boehm in the mid-1980s, the Evolutionary Spiral Process formalizes and validates the application of spiral development theory through continuous risk identification and management, rigorous definitions, extensive guidelines for all activities within the life cycle, and descriptions of the functionality and correct usage of a wide range of supporting methods and tools.

Centrally focused on risk reduction, the ESP can be tailored to the current environments and software maturity levels of any Consortium customer. The Consortium has designed ESP with flexibility to allow partial adoption of standalone methods, as desired. ESP combines both process and reuse maturity guidelines and technologies, and is designed to provide Consortium customers with systematic, optimized levels of process and reuse maturity.

ACTIVE TECHNOLOGY TRANSFER

The Consortium maintains an aggressive, proactive technology transfer philosophy designed to move new technologies into active and institutional use at the line-project and divisional levels of its client organizations. As appropriate, the Consortium uses the following technology transfer mechanisms to empower each customer in the use of its products and to generate feedback from them for future product improvements:

- *Pilot projects,* involving extensive collaboration between Consortium staff and customer engineers in targeted software efforts. Usually applied in "live," real-time systems development, pilot projects allow the early implementation of new technologies and provide the customer with a means of influencing the Consortium's technical activities in critical areas.
- *Workshops, seminars, and training courses,* held at the Consortium or at regional sites convenient to members, are designed to benefit software engineers, project managers, and executives. Increasingly, satellite teleconferences and facilitated video courses are used to provide training in key technologies to a growing number of member participants. The Consortium provided more than 3000 training days in 1992 and estimates it will provide more than 5,000 training days in 1993.
- *Video/audio training cassette library,* comprising over 50 distinct titles, has enjoyed wide usage. More than 3,000 videotapes have been shipped to customer distribution sites, and have been viewed by tens of thousands of software developers and managers.
- *On-site technical support,* in addition to the support provided for pilot projects. Consortium technical and technology transfer staff members engage in a variety of advisory and consultative activities to help customers apply new or existing technologies more effectively.
- *Communication and collaborative channels,* including several communication mechanisms that help to ensure technical development activities truly meet customer needs. These interactive and collaborative mechanisms include a Board of Directors, a Technical Advisory Board, several Technical Advisory Groups, and ongoing customer surveys.
- *Strategic alliances,* through agreements with selected vendors for the development of "commercial-strength" products that support its technologies. In this way, the Consortium further extends the growth and usage of its methods and processes through advanced CASE software tools.

Such ambitious technology transfer programs are necessary to ensure that customers can successfully implement Consortium advances in software engineering processes and methods in the development of large, software-intensive systems. As a result of this proactive technology transfer approach, member companies have applied Consortium technologies in hundreds of applications. Many of these are considered by Consortium members to be "key uses," of critical importance to the success of a program. Expanding this list of "key uses" is the primary goal of the Consortium's technology transfer program.

Greg Friedmann
Software Productivity Consortium

SOFTWARE RELIABILITY

See SOFTWARE RELIABILITY ENGINEERING.

SOFTWARE RELIABILITY ENGINEERING

DEFINITION

Software reliability engineering (SRE) is the quantitative study of how well the operational behavior of software-based systems meets user requirements. It also includes consideration of the product and development process factors that affect this behavior, and the application of this knowledge to specify and guide software development, acquisition, and use. The purpose is to maximize customer satisfaction. SRE uses prediction, measurement, and statistical estimation and modeling. Software product reliability is highly dependent on how the software is used; consequently, the quantitative characterization of use is an integral part of SRE.

Software reliability is the probability of failure-free operation of a program for a specified time under a specified set of operating conditions. This definition is consistent with the definition of hardware reliability. With this definition of software reliability, the reliabilities of the hardware and software components of a system can be combined to yield a reliability figure for the system as a whole.

In measuring and analyzing software reliability, software reliability engineering must deal with failures and the rate at which failures occur, since this is how the customer views reliability. Failures are departures of operational behavior from customer expectations. However, since faults (the defects in code that cause failures) affect reliability, software reliability engineering also must be concerned with how and where faults are introduced into the software product during development. In addition, software reliability engineering encompasses the study of ways of reducing the number of faults introduced in each development stage and minimizing the number of faults that propagate from one development stage to another.

Software reliability engineering is a subdiscipline of software engineering. The broader discipline of software engineering is concerned with the techniques, tools, and all other aspects of designing, implementing, and managing the development of software. It is also concerned with the economics of developing software, with the interfaces between software systems and humans, and with practices for ensuring that the other attributes required for "quality" software are achieved. SRE is employed by system test designers, system engineers and analysts, quality and reliability engineers, and project and product managers responsible for products and services that depend on software.

SRE provides the technology for more efficiently accomplishing software quality assurance (SQA). The goal of SQA is to improve software quality by monitoring the software and the development process that produces it for conformance with requirements and established standards and procedures. SQA ensures that any inadequacies in the product or the process are brought to management's attention so that they can be fixed. The responsibility for producing quality products or for making quality plans rests with the development organization.

SRE has been used by a wide variety of projects worldwide, and there are no known theoretical or practical limits on its application except project size. Very small software systems (under 1000 source lines and possibly up to as high as 5000 source lines) may experience small numbers of failures, resulting in larger confidence intervals in statistical estimates of reliability. However, reliability estimation is only a part of SRE technology, and other parts such as determining the operational profile and using it to guide development and test may still be useful for very small programs.

RATIONALE

As mentioned above, SRE is a subdiscipline of software engineering. Since it is one of the newest disciplines in this field, this section describes why it is needed and the special perspective it brings to software engineering.

Software is a sequence of instructions that are executed by a computing machine to perform some specified task. Given this definition, software has the following properties that are pertinent to this discussion:

1. The sequence of instructions is finite, that is, it has a beginning instruction and an ending one.
2. A computer program has a large set of possible sequences of instructions that can be executed.
3. The exact sequence of instructions executed in any particular instance of a program's operation depends on the particular values that occur in designated input registers and when these values occur.
4. As software executes, it changes the values of designated output registers. Changes in output register values often result in actions in the physical world, for example, a train stops, a missile fires, a pacemaker stimulates a human heartbeat, a pixel changes color, and so forth.

One of the fundamental tasks of software engineering is to specify the set of possible instruction sequences and to relate each to the values of the input variables, so that the outputs produced are the right ones at the right times. Thus one deals with the proper mapping of input space to output space. In addition, the program must have certain properties such as correct syntax, maximum size, understandability, maintainability, etc. Abstractly, this is not a difficult task. For example, the task of specifying a sequence of instructions which, when given an input register x of so many bits that are interpreted as the value of a positive integer n, will produce a value a in the output register y such that a is the largest positive integer for which $a^2 \leqq n$ is not unduly difficult. The traditional techniques and processes of mathematics (often called "formal methods") can be applied to demonstrate that if the memory and logic of the executing computing machine operate correctly, the sequence of instructions developed will always produce the right result at the right time.

Practically, however, for a program of useful size this is an enormously difficult task. The result is that *every* computer program of practical interest contains faults! And even if by some miracle it does not contain faults, there is no practical way to be absolutely certain of this!

The result is that as the use of computers proliferates and invades every aspect of everyday life, every member of society is exposed to the risk of physical, financial, and social harm caused, in the final analysis, by a fault in a computer program. This risk is not large, and like most of the risks of advancing technology, it has been accepted, although the potential for large scale catastrophic damage is as great for software as for any previous technology, including nuclear power. Much of the discipline of software engineering is directed toward containing and ameliorating the risk of damage from software failures. Many techniques, including traditional mathematics, have been successfully applied, and new ones are being continually devised and put into practice, but except for software reliability engineering, they all fall into three broad classes: (1) those that prevent the introduction of faults, (2) those that discover and correct faults, and (3) those that counteract faults. The techniques that attempt to prevent the introduction of faults are based on reducing complexity by structuring the software specification process in some way that allows mathematical techniques to be applied, as hypothesized for the simple square root problem discussed above. The techniques that discover and correct faults include inspections and testing. The techniques that counteract faults include fault tolerant approaches such as audits, reinitializations, and recovery programs. Much has been done and much more will be done with such techniques to keep the risk of software failure within socially acceptable bounds. But none of these techniques can guarantee that the instructions that are loaded into a nuclear power plant control circuit, or a heart pacemaker, or an automatic pilot will perform flawlessly for all possible input conditions. Hence the necessity for software reliability engineering.

Fundamentally, software reliability engineering uses the enormously large numbers associated with software (number of possible execution sequences, number of possible real-time input combinations, number of instructions executed per second, etc.) to apply a statistical approach to measuring, managing, and containing the risk of software failure, which never goes to zero. Software reliability engineering, then, serves an absolutely essential function within software engineering. Without it, the risk of software failure cannot be measured and hence cannot be managed. Without it, software engineering is hardly engineering, and is certainly socially irresponsible.

BENEFITS

The benefits derived from the use of SRE include:

1. Gaining a competitive edge by more precisely specifying and satisfying the quality attributes desired by the customer. This means determining and achieving the optimum trade-off for the customer among reliability, delivery date, and cost.
2. Increasing productivity and hence reducing cost by focusing development resources on those functions most frequently executed by the customer (weighted by *criticality* or importance of the function to the overall system), based on quantitative measures.
3. Reducing development and test time by sequencing development and test of operations with respect to relative usage, again weighted by criticality.
4. Cost effectively guiding software development process improvement.
5. Conveying requirements with respect to quality attributes more precisely to suppliers and being able to test to see that they are met.
6. Controlling more precisely the operational reliability of systems receiving software changes.
7. Planning field maintenance operations more accurately.

Many project users have observed that SRE adds a quantitative discipline to the software development process. They note that it greatly stimulates communication with customers and focuses it on their real needs, tending to push identification of and resolution of issues up front in the development process. Users indicate that these benefits, although difficult to quantify, have a solid financial impact that cannot be ignored.

Experience has indicated that the application of software reliability engineering, including the necessary training, the collection and processing of data, and the execution of studies, typically adds about $25,000 to the overall project cost. The direct financial benefits alone usually are an order of magnitude greater. Training requires a three-day course for the project SRE specialist. Development of the operational profile requires about one person-month of effort for the "average" project (it may be somewhat more for very large projects). Processing and analysis of failure data averages about 4 person-hours per week during test. The project may also want to invest in some basic orientation training for other members of the project team.

The benefits noted derive from the employment of customer-oriented reliability and usage measures and software reliability models that incorporate delivery date and cost. The models can be related to various factors, many of which can be controlled by the project.

HISTORY

The history of SRE can be characterized by the interplay of need, theory, and practice.

Need

The need for SRE can best be appreciated by looking at the evolution of software development practice (Musa and Everett, 1990). This has involved a shifting emphasis from function to schedule to cost, and now, to reliability. Successes in the earlier stages made the need for this latest stage possible. The need derives from the increasingly total operational dependence of most users on their information systems.

It is not acceptable to achieve reliability without regard to functionality, schedule, and cost. In fact, these four characteristics of a system are the principal attributes of quality, as viewed by users. Suppliers and users must contend with the reality that improvements in one attribute are generally achieved at the expense of the others. If a supplier ignores this situation, a competitor can capture a market by trading off an attribute regarded as unimportant by users in that market for an attribute(s) that is. Thus quality can be viewed as the closeness of the match between quality attributes desired by the customer and the quality attributes achieved.

Quantitative technologies had previously been developed for hardware and software schedules and costs and hardware reliability. But there was a vital missing link—-software reliability technology—that prevented the development of a quantitative technology for quality of total systems. The absence of this link may well explain the poor reputation for reliability that has been associated with much software. Rewards and penalties for managers tend to be allocated on the basis of objective, measurable results. Since concrete measures exist for delivery date and cost, it is natural that managers will direct their projects in a way to satisfy these measures. But something had to give—and again, what was more natural than the unmeasured reliability?

Theory

Fortunately, this vital need was met by a developing body of theory (see SOFTWARE RELIABILITY THEORY in this encyclopedia for that history). It may be appropriate at this point to note that some projects count the faults that are removed as a result of system test, compute a fault density (faults per thousand lines of delivered executable source code), and use this number as a reliability figure. This is *wrong* and misleading. Although faults *remaining* has some correlation with reliability on the average, faults removed does *not.* Removal of a large number of faults can indicate *either* high quality testing or very low quality software.

Fault-based measures have been useful as developer-oriented measures of the quality of software development processes, and they are likely to continue to play an important role. However, the current trend is to measure the quality of products from the customer's perspective, which requires customer-oriented measures of quality. Users of software products experience failures, not faults. They are not so much concerned with how many faults there are in a product, but rather with how often the product will fail to meet their needs. Specifically, they are concerned with the cost of failures (in terms of additional work or lost business), based partly on how often these failures will occur. Evaluating the reliability of software from the customer's perspective requires measures related to failures and the rates at which failures occur.

The precise definition of the term "failure" was an important problem in the late 1970s and early 1980s. Confusion between failures and faults and related terms caused much difficulty (see SOFTWARE RELIABILITY THEORY), remnants of which exist to this day. The generally accepted definition of *failure* is a departure of operation from user expectations. A *fault* is the defect in the code that is causing the failure. A fault can result from incorrect code or missing code. A failure is observable by the customer. It can occur only when code is executed. Thus the mere existence of a fault does not result in a reliability effect until the code containing the fault is *used.*

Collecting failure data and estimating failure intensities in terms of execution time was the important development that made software reliability estimates useful (Musa, 1975). Execution time is the processor time for which the program is executing, usually measured in CPU hours. It is a major factor in the failure-inducing stress placed on software. In reality, the stress and thus the reliability depend on the number of instructions executed. Although instructions executed has the advantage of being processor-independent, execution time is chosen because of its greater convenience when combining software with hardware components. Originally, software reliability, in an extension of hardware reliability theory, was represented as a function of calendar time. The large variations in execution with relation to calendar time proved to be a serious confounding factor in arriving at accurate reliability measures.

Failure intensity is the number of failures experienced per unit execution time (typically, per thousand CPU hours). For example, the failure intensity for a particular software product might be 8 failures per 1000 CPU hours. Reliability may be expressed in terms of failure intensity or, more formally, as the probability that the software will function without failure for some specified period of execution. In the case above, an alternative expression would be a reliability of 0.92 for 10 hours of execution. The two alternatives are related by a simple formula when there is no fault correction (Musa, Iannino, and Okumoto, 1987).

Useful software reliability models require both execution and calendar time components. The modeling of failure occurrences is first performed in terms of execution time. Then many of the results expressed in terms of execution time must be converted to calendar time to be useful for managing the development process. For example, the time required to reach the failure intensity objective during test is initially calculated in execution time. It is necessary to convert this to calendar time to determine the expected date on which the objective will be reached. A number of execution time components and three principal approaches to statistical inference (maximum likelihood, least squares, and Bayesian), but essentially only one calendar time component, have been developed (see SOFTWARE RELIABILITY THEORY for a discussion).

Practice

SRE theory has been applied, and this has resulted in rapidly expanding practice. Practice has evolved through a number of stages, and of course is still evolving. The initial applications of SRE were motivated by the need to follow the progress of software reliability during system test and to have a rational means for determining when this test could be terminated and a program released to the field. As system test proceeds, failures are experienced. Developers search for the faults that are causing these failures and correct them. In the process, some faults may not be found, some may not be properly corrected, and additional faults may be introduced. However, the trend over time in the number of faults remaining in the software, and hence the failure intensity experienced, is generally downward.

In applying SRE, testers collect data on the execution times of occurrence of the failures or the number of failures experienced in a period of execution time. Using maximum likelihood estimation, these data are used to estimate the current failure intensity. This failure intensity can then be compared to a failure intensity objective to determine when release is feasible. The model most commonly used in initial applications of SRE was the basic execution time model (Musa, 1975). Researchers sometimes applied other models to the published data (Musa, 1979) after the projects were completed, but their results were not used to make real time decisions.

As practice progressed, there were many questions concerning specific aspects of the term "failure" in particular applications. For example, if repeated failures of the same type occur because the causative fault has not yet been removed, should they be counted? How should failure be interpreted for fault tolerant systems? Are there important differences between failures, especially in relation to their consequences, that pose a need for classification schemes? Most of these questions have been answered, based on practical needs and project experience.

Practitioners also had to deal with problems related to the determination of the execution time at which failure occurred. Sometimes this could only be established within a range. There were also cases where it was considered, for various practical reasons, difficult or costly to measure execution (CPU) time directly. In these situations, suitable alternatives or even approximations were needed. Again, these problems have generally been solved.

Another important problem was how to handle the estimation of reliability for software that is evolving (increasing in size with time). Different approaches have been developed, based on the nature of the evolution.

Correct estimates of reliability depend on executing software in a manner that is representative of the way in which it will be used. This is because usage determines the execution paths followed in the software and the values of various variables processed. This in turn determines when an execution path will be followed that contains a fault and when the values of the variables are such that the failure will occur. The *operational profile,* which is the set of operations performed by the software, along with the probabilities of their occurrences in operational use, was defined to meet this need. An example operational profile is shown in Figure 1. Practice has now progressed to the point where many projects use the operational profile to guide test planning and selection of test cases.

Thus, the evolution of software reliability practice has involved the development of a rich lore of definitions, concepts, and methods for solving problems that has been organized and integrated as a body of knowledge (Musa, Iannino, and Okumoto, 1987).

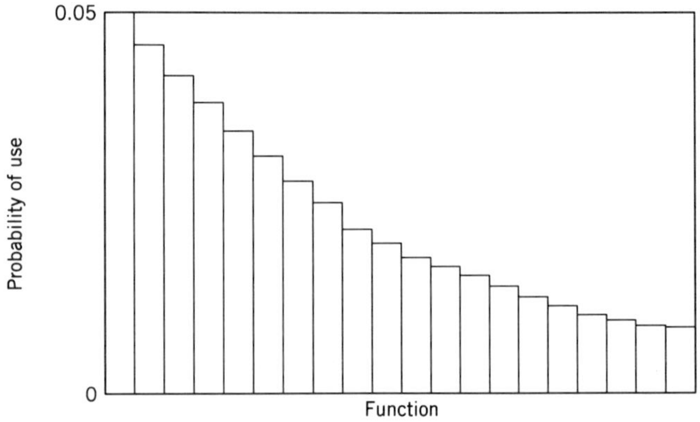

Figure 1. Example operational profile.

The most commonly used (in real time) models have been the basic and logarithmic Poisson execution time models, with maximum likelihood estimation and the calendar time component mentioned. Note that the basic execution time model essentially incorporates the Jelinski-Moranda (Jelinski and Moranda, 1972), Shooman (Shooman, 1972) and Goel-Okumoto (Goel and Okumoto, 1979) models. The Littlewood-Verrall (Littlewood and Verrall, 1973) model and S-shaped models (Yamada, Ohba and Osaki, 1983) have been employed in some cases, but they do not have a calendar time component.

Tools have been developed to perform the calculations required by the statistical inference process and to compute and plot various useful quantities. The tools include SRE TOOLKIT (UNIX and MS/DOS versions bundled with training, available from AT&T, telephone 800-327-9503, 908-949-5045 outside continental U.S.), SMERFS (available from W. Farr, Naval Surface Weapons Laboratory, Dahlgren, VA), SQMS (available from SQT Corp., 2000 West Park Drive, Suite 200, Westborough, MA 01581), and a program from RSC Ltd. (Richmond, Surrey, England).

APPLICATIONS

Many different applications have been documented in the literature. Iannino and Musa (1991) provide a summary of applications at AT&T through 1989. The International DEFINITY telecommunications switching system (Abramson, Jensen, Juhlin, and Spudic, 1992) employed SRE as one of several key improvements in their development process. As a result of these improvements, they experienced a decrease by a factor of 10 in customer-reported problems and program maintenance costs, a reduction of 50% in the system test interval, and a reduction of 30% in the time to market. There were no serious service-affecting outages in the first two years after release. Customer satisfaction improved significantly, with the result that sales were 10 times those of the previous version.

Ejzak (1987) used a software reliability model to continually monitor status and predict completion of system test of a software development environment program for UNIX System V. The criterion for completion was to attain a specified level of reliability. After a sufficient sample of failure data was available (this occurred after 20% of a system test period of about 2½ months), the model consistently predicted the date when a reliability goal would be attained with an error of one week or less.

Christenson (1988) applied a software reliability model to the AT&T 5ESS telephone switching system, making predictions of field failures for different releases and hundreds of installations. In this case, the predictions were based on early field experience rather than system test. After periods ranging up to two full years in the field, predictions differed from actual experience by values of from 5% to 13%.

Drake and Wolting (1987) employed a software reliability model fitted to failure data acquired during testing for estimating the failure intensity anticipated for firmware in Hewlett-Packard HP2394A terminals after release to the field. Actual results were within 12% of predictions. This information can be used to predict the amount and cost of firmware field maintenance. Such data are obviously useful in planning the size of the field engineering force and determining the PROM production rate required.

Stark (1987) reports the use of software reliability monitoring for the Space Shuttle Mission Simulator. The monitoring is used for identifying changes in system reliability due to the addition of new features in the software. It has also been used to identify software reliability trends and software problem areas. As a result of the benefits obtained, Stark notes that software reliability engineering will be used for the Space Station Training Facility.

Ehrlich, Stampfel, and Wu (1990) presented data on reliability measurements taken on a project at AT&T that showed that availability of an accurate operational profile to guide testing would have reduced field failures by a factor of five.

SRE was applied to a system for remote testing of telecommunication circuits (Ehrlich, Lee, and Molisani, 1990). The basic (exponential NHPP) execution time model was used. They found that the model had good predictive validity of failure intensity for this project after about 60% of system test.

Hewlett-Packard's Lake Stevens Instrument Division has successfully applied SRE to a range of projects from 6,000 to 150,000 source lines in size (Kruger, 1989). Functions varied from instrument firmware to application software. SRE was used to estimate the duration of system testing, to assist in the release decision, and to estimate field reliability. The HP Medical Products Group (Rapp, 1990) found that SRE was easily implemented and effective, provided that a stable test process has been established.

Software reliability predictions are made for the space shuttle onboard software to determine the probability of encountering a serious software failure on the next mission (Keller, 1990).

The French space agency CNES has applied NHPP models to their applications, and finds them accurate enough to justify using them in onboard systems (Vallée, 1991).

Bell Northern Research (a subsidiary of Northern Telecom) has applied SRE to a digital switching system of over 8 million source lines (Jones, 1991). They noted that software reliability methods were very applicable. They found that the logarithmic Poisson execution time model performed best in this environment.

CURRENT RECOMMENDED PRACTICE

Software reliability engineering should be applied in each phase of the life cycle: definition, design and implementation, validation, and operation and maintenance (some projects may use variants of these names). The definition phase focuses on developing a requirements specification for a product that can profitably meet a set of needs for a group of customers. System and software engineers develop product designs from the product requirements. Software engineers implement them in code in the design and implementation phase. Test teams, normally independent of the design and implementation teams, operate the product in the validation phase to see if it meets the requirements. The product is delivered to and used by the customer in the operation and maintenance phase. The maintenance staff responds to customer requests for new features and to reported problems by developing and delivering software changes. In this section the software reliability engineering activities that occur in each phase will be outlined. For further details, see Musa, Iannino, and Okumoto (1987), Everett and co-workers (1989), and Everett (1990).

Definition Phase

Good product definition is necessary for success in the marketplace. The primary output of the definition phase is a product requirements specification. The product's failure intensity objective should be explicitly included.

The first step in setting the failure intensity objective is to work with the customer (or customers) to define what a failure is from the customer's perspective. The determination of who the customers are is valuable and not trivial; it includes market analysis, which should be part of the planning for any product. Even in the case of a single contract customer, one may have to resolve competing needs among different constituencies within the customer organization. Next, failures are categorized by severity, or the effect they have on the customer. The customer's tolerance to failures of different severities and willingness to pay for reduced failure intensities in each failure-severity category should be determined. Severity can be measured in terms of cost, service degradation, or safety. For example, a categorization for telecommunication systems based on service degradation might be:

1. Catastrophic—entire system has failed, with little or no functionality remaining;
2. Severe—the majority of shared resources are not available or a high priority customer feature is not working;
3. Significant—impact is noticeable by the customers and requires that they change how they use the system;

4. Minor—impact is noticeable by customers but requires little change in how they use the system;

Examining customers' experiences with both past and existing products will help determine the value they place on reliability. Software production costs almost always increase less than linearly with the number of copies sold. Thus a larger market reduces the per copy cost of reliability, making higher reliability more feasible. Another consideration is assessing the reliability of competitors' products. In considering relative reliabilities among competitors, relative delivery dates must also be factored in.

Frequently, not only the reliability but also the availability of a system is important to a customer. Availability is up-time divided by total time. Thus it is strongly influenced by both failure intensity and mean time for recovery after each failure. Sometimes a failure is only transient in nature, and recovery only involves restoring some data and restarting the program. In other cases, customers may recover from a failure through a "work-around."

"Work-around" refers to the customer/user being able to accomplish a task performed by the failed software function by some other means. There are two times involved in accomplishing the work-around: the time to determine the work-around needed, and the time to perform the work-around. For example, the first time might be the time for a user to contact a "support hot line" or to contact his or her computer system administrator. If the particular software failure happens often enough so that the user does not forget the "work-around," this time will be short for subsequent failures. The second time actually depends on what is involved in performing the work-around, which often includes restoral. The information developed in each of these steps can then be used to establish failure-intensity objectives, trading off product reliability, cost, and delivery date.

Two types of trade-off studies that can support development planning are balancing product feature set size with reliability level, and balancing life cycle cost (or delivery date) with reliability level. These studies center on the cost of doing reliability-oriented testing and the cost of failures in the field after the product is released. Testing costs are significant for many products. They sometimes account for more than half the development costs. Doing a lot of testing is costly but it reduces the risks (such as loss of market share) and costs arising from field failures after the product is released. Doing only a little testing may significantly reduce development costs but may result in significant costs associated with field failures.

In the first type of trade-off study, increasing (reducing) the feature set size of the product results in increasing (reducing) the number of lines of code developed for the product. Increasing (decreasing) the number of lines of code developed increases (decreases) the total number of faults introduced that increases (decreases) the failure intensity of the product when reliability testing begins. More features also increase the difficulty of problems due to feature interactions. The cost in terms of resources and time needed to complete reliability testing depends on the ratio of the failure intensity at the start of test to the failure intensity objective for the product. Hence changing

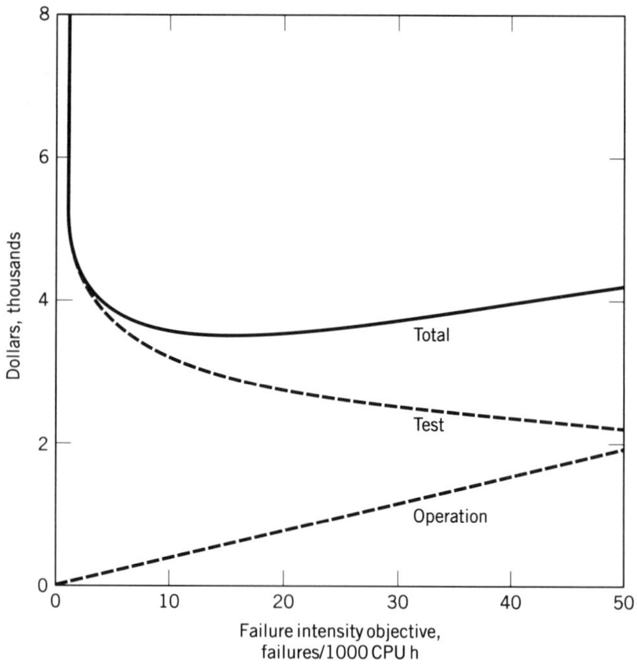

Figure 2. Cost as a function of failure intensity objective.

feature set size can change the amount of resources and time needed to do reliability testing. These changes can be quantified using existing models when the right data are available.

In the second type of trade-off study, increasing the failure intensity objective (and hence reducing reliability) will reduce the resources and time needed to complete reliability testing but increase the costs associated with field failures. If the total life cycle cost (defined here to be the sum of the cost of doing reliability testing and field failure cost) is plotted versus failure intensity objective, there is an optimum value of failure intensity objective for which the life cycle cost is minimum (see Fig. 2). Similarly, delivery date can be plotted versus failure intensity objective to determine what delivery date would correspond to a specified objective (see Fig. 3).

The reliability objective can also be used in planning necessary field support. The expected failure intensity will determine the number of field personnel required. In the case of firmware, where failures may be serviced by replacing faulty memory chips, chip production rates may be affected. The foregoing information will help estimate maintenance costs for the product. Business planning must, of course, consider the entire life cycle, including costs that will be incurred by the customer. Such costs have an important impact on the marketability of the product.

Customers generally view the communication with them inherent in trade-off studies very favorably. It greatly improves the match between product characteristics and customer needs, and it markedly increases the customer's trust in the supplier.

Now, two other items are needed

1. The operational profile, as the product's reliability may depend on how the product will be used.

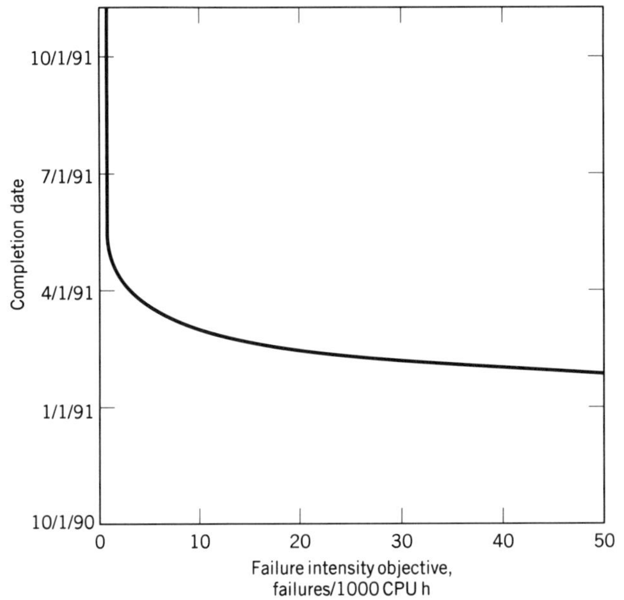

Figure 3. Completion date as a function of failure intensity objective.

2. Information relating calendar time to execution time, in order that failure intensity objectives expressed in terms of calendar time (the form customers can relate to) can be translated into failure intensity objectives expressed in terms of execution time (the form relevant to software).

In addition, program features for obtaining operational profile data and automatic failure identification and reporting should also be considered during the definition phase. Operational profile data can be obtained by using a small number of counter variables. These need not be present in standard production versions if their inclusion is deemed intrusive. System generation procedures can be established so that this feature is only present in versions used for special studies.

In most cases it is possible for the software itself to determine that internal verification conditions are not met and to note a log entry whenever this occurs. Such anomalies may not result in user-observable failures, but if a ratio between these "anomalies" and user-observable failures is established during reliability growth testing, then field reports on the number of these anomalies can be used to estimate operational reliability even when observable failures are very rare, which is the desired situation.

Two questions frequently asked about application of models during the definition phase are

1. How accurate are the reliability predictions made at this time?
2. Is the effort to model reliability at this point worth it?

The first question cannot be answered definitively at present, although there are some indications that the accuracy may be within a factor of three or four. Prediction accuracy is likely to be determined and to improve as the field progresses and appropriate data are collected.

In response to the second question, the effort would probably not be worthwhile if the modeling were carried no further than merely predicting software reliability. However, the modeling should continue throughout the design and implementation, validation, and operation and maintenance phases. Particularly during the validation and the operation and maintenance phases, you can use modeling with collected data to track whether reliability objectives are being met. Also, the results can be used to refine the prediction process for the future. The real utility of modeling becomes evident when applying this cycle of model, measure, and refine. Furthermore, applying models during the definition phase forces project teams to focus very early on reliability issues and to baseline assumptions about the product's reliability *before* design and implementation begins.

Design and Implementation Phase

The first step in the design and implementation phase is to develop the design specifications for the product and the development process. The latter specifications are currently known as the project plan, but "development process design specification" is used here to emphasize the quantitative nature and process focus of this activity when guided by software reliability engineering. The second step is to implement the designs.

Allocating the system-reliability objective among the components is an early activity of this phase. In some cases, different architectural options may be considered. It is important to analyze whether the reliability objective can be attained with the proposed design.

In addition to the physical nature of the system itself, other important factors need to be considered when dividing a system for reliability analysis. If the system has more than one significant system mode or way of operating (for example, prelaunch and flight for a space vehicle), components will need to be associated with the system mode(s) in which they operate, and the overall reliability objective for each particular mode will need to be allocated across the associated components. Other considerations for dividing the system into components include:

1. Will the system evolve in stages? If so, the nature of the stages may suggest the best way to divide the system.
2. Is there a special need to track the reliabilities of certain components? This could happen when certain components are considered critical from a cost, schedule, or development risk point of view. For example, it may be desired to track the reliability separately for component(s) being acquired from an outside supplier.
3. What are the complexity and difficulty involved in collecting failure data? The collection of data for many independent components, or for multiple system modes, will increase the cost and effort, as well as dividing the failure sample so that accuracy is reduced.

In general, overall reliability objectives for individual failure categories and for multiple system modes are allocated to functional components. The first consideration is that the allocation to components be done so that the overall reliability objective is satisfied. In addition, component reliability objectives should be "well balanced" among themselves. Well balanced usually refers to an approximate equality of development time, difficulty, or risk or to the minimization of overall system development cost.

When the reliabilities of hardware and software components are combined, it is important to remember that these reliabilities be stated with respect to a common time basis. Hardware reliabilities are expressed in terms of calendar time, but software reliabilities are expressed in terms of execution time. Before the combinatorial relationships can be applied to component reliabilities, conversion is required so that all components are on a common time basis. This conversion usually entails translating software reliabilities so that they are expressed in terms of calendar time.

Allocation of overall reliability to individual components defines, in effect, a reliability "budget." As each trial allocation is made, an analysis must be conducted to ascertain whether the reliability budget can be achieved within the proposed design.

Critical functions are identified for which failure may cause catastrophic effects. The components whose satisfactory operation is essential to the functions should then be determined, using techniques like failure modes and effects analysis and fault tree analysis. These critical components may require special fault avoidance or fault removal activities. Fault tolerant techniques such as periodic auditing of key variables during program execution and recovery blocks may also be employed in the design of these components.

The design of the development process consists of determining the development activities to be performed, along with their associated time and resource requirements. The development activities are selected from a relatively small, relatively standard set, but there can be differences in allocation of time and resources and differences in tools employed. Usually, more than one development process plan can meet the product requirements, but some plans are faster, less expensive, or less risky than others.

The software reliability engineering part of the development process design involves examining and understanding the controllable and uncontrollable factors that influence reliability. Controllable factors include variables such as use or nonuse of requirements and design inspections, thoroughness of such inspections, and time and resources devoted to unit test and system test. Uncontrollable (or perhaps minimally controllable) factors are generally related to the product or the work environment; for example, program size, volatility of requirements, and average experience of staff.

The values anticipated for the uncontrollable factors are used to predict the failure intensity that would occur without any attempt to influence it. Choose suitable values of the controllable factors to achieve the failure intensity objective desired within acceptable cost and schedule limits. Techniques now exist to predict the effects of some of the factors, and appropriate studies should be able to determine the effects of the others. The relationships between these factors and reliability must be expressed in simple terms that software engineers can intuitively understand and readily apply.

Construct a reliability time line to indicate reliability objectives at various points in the life cycle such as start of system test, start of acceptance test, release to beta test, and release for general availability. This time line will be used to evaluate progress. If progress is not satisfactory, several actions are possible:

1. Reallocate project resources (for example, from test team to debugging team or from low usage to high usage functions).
2. Redesign the development process (for example, lengthening the system test phase).
3. Redesign subsystems that have low reliability.
4. Respecify the requirements in negotiation with the customers (they might accept lower reliability for on-time delivery).

Reliability cannot currently be directly measured in the design and coding stages. However, there is a good chance that indirect methods will be developed based on trends in finding design errors and later trends in discovering code faults by inspection. Syntactic faults are usually found by compilers or perhaps syntax-directed editors. Consequently, concentrate on *semantic* faults to predict reliability. In unit test, it is anticipated that methods will be developed to estimate reliability from failure trends.

Another important activity is certifying the reliability of both acquired software and reused software (not only application software but also system software like operating system and communication interface software). The reliability of such components should be established through testing with the operational profile expected for the new product.

The operational profile (weighted by criticality where appropriate) can help increase productivity and reduce cost during the design and implementation phase by helping to guide where design resources should be focused. It can also be used to help prioritize the different work activities. Developers can use information on the frequency of use of different features to weigh design alternatives. For example, a designer might opt for a simpler manual recovery design for an operating condition that occurs very infrequently rather than a more complex automated recovery design. In general, simpler designs lead to a more reliable product.

Verification activities like inspections, unit test, and subsystem test are commonly conducted during the design and implementation phase. Inspections can be applied to requirements, design, code, test plans, and other work products.

So that one can readily determine failure intensity in testing and in the field, one should consider building automatic failure identification and reporting into the system.

Validation Phase

The primary thrust of validation is to certify that the product meets customer requirements and is suitable for customer use. Product validation for software generally includes system tests and field trials. The *effectiveness* of testing can be conveniently stated in software reliability terms; it is the ratio of failure intensity before testing to failure intensity after testing.

Software reliability measurements are particularly useful in combination with reliability growth testing. During reliability growth testing, functions are executed with relative frequencies that match what is specified in the operational profile. This not only provides the best representation of field conditions, but it generally results in optimum testing *efficiency* in that the testing effectiveness ratio per unit execution time is the largest (the decrease in failure intensity per unit execution time is the most rapid). Tests are generally selected randomly to prevent the influence of external factors. When failures are experienced, developers start a failure resolution process to identify and correct the faults causing them.

Multiple operational profiles may be used, each relating to a different application with its associated market segment. It is expected that it will be possible in the future to test using strategies with function-occurrence frequencies that depart from the operational profile. Compensation for this departure from the profile would be made by adjusting the measured failure intensities.

Reliability growth testing can be performed at different times during system test as a replacement for regression testing. Since the testing is in accordance with the operational profile, it is very efficient per unit test time in uncovering the undesirable effects of program changes with the greatest impact on reliability.

Reliability growth testing can also often be combined with performance or load testing, since it is desirable for the latter to reflect actual usage. However, some care must be exercised. Performance testing may focus on heavy traffic conditions and hence not represent true usage accurately.

To obtain the desired reliability quantities during testing, first record failures and the corresponding execution times (from the start of test). Then run a software reliability estimation program such as SRE Toolkit (see History section) with the recorded failure data. This program uses statistical techniques to estimate the parameters of the software reliability model's execution time component, based on the recorded failure data. Applying the execution time component with the estimated parameters, it determines such useful quantities as current failure intensity and the remaining execution time needed to meet the failure intensity objective. It also uses the calendar time component to estimate remaining calendar time needed for testing to achieve the failure-intensity objective (Musa and Ackerman, 1989).

Using such a program, managers and engineers can track reliability status during reliability growth test, as Figure 4 shows. The graph shows failure intensity derived from real project data and plotted against calendar time. The downward trend is clear despite real world perturba-

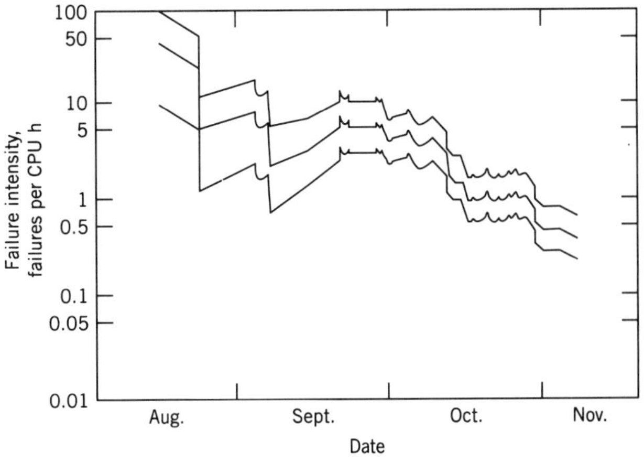

Figure 4. Tracking reliability status in system test. The center curve indicates the most likely value of failure intensity. The two outer curves represent the interval within which the true failure intensity lies with 75% confidence. The *y* axis is logarithmic so the data can fit the graph.

tions resulting from statistical noise and departures of the project from underlying model assumptions. The improvement in failure intensity is about 70 to 1, a fact deemphasized by the need to use a logarithmic scale to accommodate the large changes in failure intensity common during reliability growth testing.

Problems are highlighted early when the downward trend in failure intensity does not progress as expected. Cray Research is one company that applies reliability tracking for this purpose as standard practice in its compiler development. For example, note the upward swing in the failure intensity trend at one point. This is a strong warning for the test manager to investigate. The most probable causes are

1. The testers have not been following a uniform testing strategy. Instead of selecting from the entire set of operations for the program, they have been selecting from a subset associated with part of the program. When they expand this subset to include operations associated with other parts of the program, they reach untested areas and failure intensity rises.
2. Additional code is being added to the program. It contains new faults and this causes an increase in failure intensity.

Figure 5 shows a sample printout produced by SRE Toolkit. The central ("Most Likely") column represents the maximum likelihood estimate for the quantity specified for the row. The columns sandwiched around it represent lower and upper confidence limits. It is easy to observe current failure intensity in relation to the failure intensity objective. By requiring that the failure intensity objective be met as a criterion for release, one can be confident that customer needs are satisfied before shipping. There have been several demonstrations of the value of software reliability as a release criterion, including applications at AT&T (Harrington, 1989) and Hewlett-Packard (Drake

SOFTWARE RELIABILITY ESTIMATION
EXPONENTIAL (BASIC) MODEL
TST DATA SET

BASED ON SAMPLE OF	136 TEST FAILURES
TEST EXECUTION TIME IS	25.3356 CPU-HR
FAILURE INTENSITY OBJECTIVE IS	2.4 FAILURES/1000-CPU-HR
CURRENT DATE IN TEST	861109
TIME FROM START OF TEST IS	96 DAYS

	CONF. LIMITS				MOST	CONF. LIMITS			
	95%	90%	75%	50%	LIKELY	50%	75%	90%	95%
TOTAL FAILURES	139	139	140	141	142	144	145	147	149
******FAILURE INTENSITIES (FAILURES/1000-CPU-HR)******									
INITIAL	953.0	988.1	1044	1099	1178	1258	1316	1376	1415
PRESENT	28.64	31.30	35.94	40.99	49.24	58.95	66.80	75.93	82.29
ADDITIONAL REQUIREMENTS TO MEET FAILURE INTENSITY OBJECTIVE									
FAILURES	3	3	4	4	6	7	9	11	12
TEST EXEC. TIME	16.11	17.20	19.04	21.00	24.11	27.72	30.65	34.11	36.56
WORK DAYS	3.80	4.10	4.61	5.17	6.14	7.40	8.50	9.88	10.92
COMPLETION DATE	861113	861114	861114	861117	861118	861119	861120	861121	861124

Figure 5. Sample printout from SRE Toolkit. The present failure intensity lets one determine whether the failure-intensity objective has been met.

and Wolting, 1987). Cray Research (Zinnel, 1990) uses such a release criterion as standard practice.

If different classes of failures must be distinguished, the recommended procedure is to collect failure data without regard to class, compute the total failure intensity for all failures, and then distribute this total in proportion to the percentage of failures in each class to obtain a *class failure intensity* in each case.

For example, if 100 failures are observed in four classes (10 in class A, 20 in class B, 40 in class C, and 30 in class D) and the overall failure intensity is 0.1 failure per CPU hour, then the class failure intensity for class B would be 0.02 failures per CPU hour.

Failure intensity can also be weighted by cost in a continuous fashion to obtain a failure cost intensity (cost of failure per CPU hour). A risk analysis of a commercial loan system has been performed (Sherer, 1991) to illustrate this concept.

Sometimes it is difficult to directly measure execution time for the software component of interest. For example, the component of interest might be part of a much larger system in which the processor switches dynamically between a number of active components. In such a case, other measures may be used if they are correlated to execution time.

For example, suppose the component of interest is the usage data collection package on a time sharing system. Assume that this component is only executed each time a user's CPU usage exceeds 10 minutes, and also when a user logs off. Then, knowing the average number of log-offs each day, the average number of CPU minutes used for each user connect period, and the average execution time for this component each time it is invoked, the average amount of CPU time this component executes each day can be calculated. Examples of other approximations to execution time are transactions processed, calls processed by a switch, and copies generated.

If a program runs on different computers with different average instruction execution rates, then failure data from the different computers must be adjusted by the ratios of these rates to a common reference computer.

In this article programs have been implicitly discussed as being of constant size (except for fault correction) and functionality throughout their life. Often this is not so. For example, in system test three common cases can be distinguished:

1. Components are tested separately and then together as a system.
2. Testing begins with a basic system, but small changes are added throughout the test period.
3. Testing begins with a piece of the system, but major parts are added at distinct intervals during the test period.

The first case can be handled by combining component reliabilities. The second case can be handled by letting the model adapt as testing proceeds, that is, model parameters are continually recalculated, based on observed failure behavior. A different approach is required for the third case.

Assume that a piece of software is under test, with the fault responsible for each failure type being removed as the failure occurs. The times between failures are recorded. In general, as faults are removed, reliability will improve. That is, the average time between failures will be getting longer. Now suppose a major new piece of software is added to the program being tested. There will be two effects: the time to run the program will be longer (since there is now more of it) and the number of faults will increase. The first effect can be expected to lengthen the time between failures; the second effect can be expected to shorten the time between failures. In either case, if the original observations are not adjusted to account for the effect of suddenly adding this new piece of software, the model is likely to give invalid estimates. However, if the basic execution time model is used, the necessary adjustments can be made by adjusting the original failure time observations (Musa, Iannino, and Okumoto, 1987).

If the basic execution time model is applied to the adjusted failure times, valid estimates of such quantities as current failure intensity and the number of additional failures needed to reach failure intensity objective will be obtained.

Operation and Maintenance Phase

The primary thrust of the operation and maintenance phase is to move the product into the customers' day-to-day operations, support customers in their use of the product, develop new features needed by customers, and fix faults in the software that affect the customers' use of the product.

Failure data collected in the customer's operating environment can be used to compare the customer's perceived level of reliability to the measured reliability of the product at release. Various items could contribute to differences in the customer's perceived level of reliability and the measured reliability of the product:

1. The definition of what the customer perceives as failures is different from the definition used in testing the product.
2. The operational profile for the customer environment is significantly different from the operational profile used in testing the product.
3. The original reliability objectives set for the product do not reflect what the customer originally desired, or the customer's desires have changed.

The determination of what factors contribute to the differences and feeding this information back to the appropriate development phase are important tasks.

The users of software can apply SRE to insure that delivered or purchased software meets their specified requirements. Alternatively, they may rely on third parties employing SRE in centralized test for widely distributed packages.

A verification procedure can be applied (Musa, Iannino, and Okumoto, 1987) that is based on sequential sampling theory. The procedure involves:

1. Selecting the discrimination ratio δ with which the test will be performed;
2. Selecting the risk α of falsely deciding the objective is not met; and
3. Selecting the risk β of falsely deciding the objective is met.

The discrimination ratio δ determines the alternative against which the desired failure intensity objective λ_{obj} will be tested. For example, if $\delta=3$, the alternative is $3\lambda_{obj}$. To be 95% certain of *not accepting* the software if the actual value is at or above this value, and also 95% certain of

Failure number	Failure time	Normalized failure time	Decision
1	8 CPU h	0.8 CPU h	Continue
2	19 CPU h	1.9 CPU h	Continue
3	60 CPU h	6.0 CPU h	λ_{obj} met

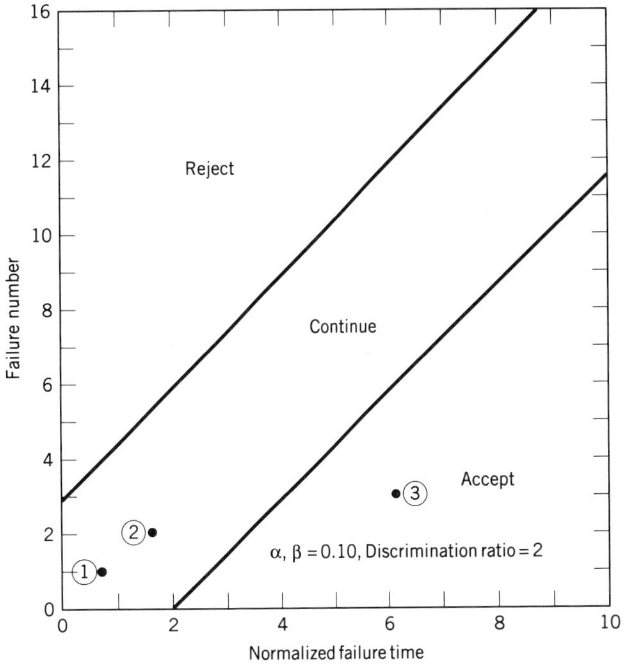

Figure 6. Use of a reliability demonstration chart.

accepting it if the actual value is at or below λ_{obj}, set both α and β to 0.05.

When δ, α, and β have been selected, it is possible to construct a simple demonstration chart for the verification procedure. Such a chart would be used in the following way: As each failure is encountered, plot it on the chart. If the plotted point falls within the accept region, stop testing and accept the software. If it falls within the reject region, reject it. Otherwise, continue testing. This procedure is very efficient; it requires only the testing necessary to reach a decision. An example of such a chart is shown in Figure 6. This is the chart for $\delta=2$, and $\alpha=\beta=0.1$. That is, the selected demonstration will verify whether the failure intensity objective has been met, with a 10% risk of falsely stating it has when actually the failure intensity is $2\lambda_{obj}$ or greater, and a 10% risk of falsely stating it has not when actually the failure intensity is λ_{obj} or less.

The use of this chart to verify $\lambda_{obj}=0.1$ failure per CPU hour is shown in the top part of Figure 6. If the demonstration runs, with inputs selected at random according to the given operational profile, have consumed a total of 8 CPU hours of execution time at the first failure, we will be at point (1) on the chart. If a total of 19 CPU hours of execution time have been experienced at the time of the second failure, we will be at point (2), and if we have experienced 60 CPU hours of execution time at the time of the third failure, we will be at point (3). At this point it has been verified, within the precision selected, that the delivered software meets its failure intensity requirement.

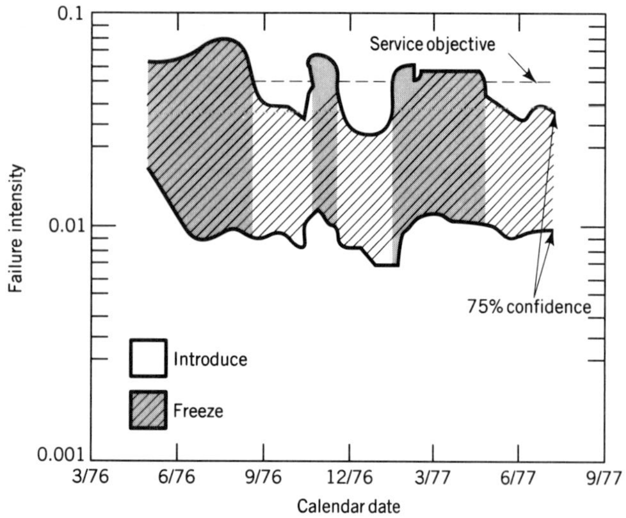

Figure 7. Managing the introduction of new features.

For those organizations that have operational responsibility for software products, reliability measurement can help monitor the operating software's reliability. The results can be used to determine if there is any degradation in reliability over time (for example, degradation caused by the introduction of additional faults when new software features are installed). The supplier will also want to monitor the reliability of software delivered if possible. It appears to be feasible to include automatic recording and reporting of failures in many cases. If not, random sampling of the installations in the field can be used to make data collection manageable.

Software reliability measurement can help time the addition of new software features so reliability is not reduced below a tolerable level for the user. The manager of a large computer facility is often caught between two opposing forces. On the one hand, customers constantly demand that new capabilities be added to the facility or that existing components be upgraded to provide new functionality or improved performance. On the other hand, the same customers constantly demand proven, reliable service. The two demands are usually incompatible, since the upgrade or new components are generally less reliable than the old ones, which have been shaken down by use. This situation can arise even when software reliability measurement is being used by the supplier to control releases if the facility in question has a unique hardware environment or a unique operational profile.

Software reliability measurement can provide a way out of this conflict. The manager need only work with the customers to quantify what they mean by reliable service in terms of a threshold failure intensity level. With such an agreement, the manager will install new or upgraded components only when the observed failure intensity falls below this threshold service objective. Otherwise, all effort will be focused on reducing the failure intensity to the service objective by identifying and eliminating the failures. This concept is illustrated in Figure 7. The acceptable service objective was set at 50 failures per 1000 CPU hours. Whenever the 75 percent confidence interval of the observed failure intensity rises above this level system enhancements are not permitted.

Software reliability engineering can also be applied by maintenance staff managers. One example is using the frequency and severity of failures to rank the order for repairing underlying faults. In addition to other considerations, users usually consider failures in old functions more severe than those in new functions because their operations are likely to be more heavily affected by the old functions they depend on. Another example is the sizing of maintenance staff needed to repair faults reported from field sites. Software reliability engineering methods can be used to estimate PROM production rates for firmware. Also, they can help estimate warranty costs. A potential use is to determine the optimum mix of fault removal and new feature activities in releases.

SRE principles have been applied to studying field service of software (Baker, 1988) by investigating the effects of characteristics of the service organization. The reliability experienced by the average user can be enhanced or degraded, depending on the values of these characteristics.

Obtaining failure data from field operations requires some extra considerations. In field operations, there are more systems to monitor and more people will be involved in data collection. There is a tendency for some users not to report failures. They may not be certain whether a failure occurred. Also, they often want to recover from the situation quickly and get back to work. Consequently, more motivation must be provided, and more feedback is necessary to maintain motivation.

After being told that a given problem is "known" and receiving a "work-around," the customer at a particular site is not likely to report the problem again. In practice, then, instead of indicating the total number of failures occurring in the field, the number of reports will be between the first-occurrence failure rate and the total failure rate.

Although they may not continue to report all the failures that occur, the operations staff at a local site may very well have a complete local record of failures in their logs. If it is necessary for the development organization to have an indication of the total failures occurring in the field, direct discussions with the customers and examination of the site failure logs may provide the information required to develop a relationship between the number of reported failures and the actual number of failures taking place. Direct discussion with customers at the sites can also clear up misleading situations, when, for example, the number of failure reports is very low yet the customer voices dissatisfaction with the system. Such a situation can result if a project organization has been unresponsive to field problems reported in the past.

Process Improvement

SRE can be applied along with "root cause analysis" (RCA) to develop a cycle of continuous improvement of a software development process. SRE is used to identify and prioritize failures in terms of how frequently they are experienced by customers and the impact they have on the customers. This information in turn can be used to prioritize the list of underlying faults causing failures. RCA is used to identify what processes need to be modified to prevent similar faults from being delivered with future products. The priorities developed from failure impact can be used along with costs for improving particular development processes to select which processes to change first.

Also, if one has used a new technique, tool, or other "improvement" for the software-engineering process, he or she should try to evaluate its effect on reliability. A fair comparison requires that all product and process variables be held constant except the one whose effect is being checked. One may compare with a similar project or between subsystems of the same project. For example, suppose one is trying to determine whether or not software inspections are cost effective. One finds that a project without software inspections has a failure intensity at 100 CPU hours of system test of 60 failures per thousand CPU hours. A similar project at the same point in time that uses software inspections has a failure intensity of 30 failures per thousand CPU hours. One can now weigh the failure intensity improvement against the cost of doing these inspections.

FUTURE PRACTICE

In most cases the applications of SRE described below have been based on existing capabilities. In some instances, the applications have already been made on a pilot basis. However, some depend on extensions requiring studies, usually based on actual project data. The structure of this research appears reasonably clear, and in many cases it is well under way. There is, of course, some risk that all the extensions might not come to fruition.

Predicting Reliability

The largest and most significant area of potential advance is the prediction of reliability before program execution from characteristics of the software product and the development process. Initial work (Musa, Iannino, and Okumoto, 1987) indicates that failure intensity is related to the number of faults remaining in the software at the start of system test, the size of the program in object instructions, the average processing speed of the computer running the software, and the fault-exposure ratio.

The fault-exposure ratio represents the proportion of time that a hypothetical encounter with a fault would result in failure. Some evidence indicates that the fault-exposure ratio may be a constant. This needs to be verified over a range of projects. If not constant, it may vary with a few factors like some measures of program "branchiness" and "loopiness." These relationships would need to be developed.

The number of faults remaining at the start of system test is clearly related to program size. One can approximate it by the number of faults detected in system test and operation, provided the operating period totaled over all installations is large and the rate of detection of faults is approaching zero. Studies indicate that it depends (to a lesser degree) on the number of specification changes, thoroughness of design documentation, average programmer skill level, percent of reviews accomplished, and percent of code read. It is possible that adding more factors would further improve such predictions; finding out requires a study of multiple projects. The selection of appropriate factors might be aided by insight gained from root-cause analysis of why faults get introduced. The experience of the authors indicates that the factors are most likely related to characteristics of the development process rather than the product itself. Interestingly, complexity from sources other than size seems to average out for programs above the module level. Thus, it is not an operative factor. This fact appears to support the conjecture that the fault-exposure ratio may be constant.

With better reliability prediction, one can expect the product definition phase to become much more quantitative than it is at present. This will lead to more precise trade-offs, and these will yield substantial economic benefit. Scheduling will also improve, and this should allow better planning. Managers will use software reliability engineering to help evaluate whether a proposed software-based product is feasible, and to help compare competing proposed products. There will probably be a move to a more quantitatively designed software development process, where tools and technologies will be chosen to realize the precise quality attributes that are required.

Estimating Before Test

An area of challenge is to find a way to estimate the number of remaining faults based on patterns of data taken on design errors detected in design inspections and coding faults detected in desk-checking or code walkthroughs.

This estimate of remaining faults is needed to estimate software reliability before test for comparison with a reliability time line. One possibility would be to apply an analog of software-reliability-modeling and -estimation procedures to the values of inspection or walkthrough "execution" times at which one experiences the design errors or code faults. If good fault estimation proves feasible, reliability monitoring can be expected to be seen through almost all of the development cycle, with identification of reliability problems much earlier than at present. The costs of resolving these problems, as well as the disruptive impacts on schedules, can be expected to lessen.

Estimating During Test

Work is needed to develop ways of applying software reliability theory to estimating failure intensity during unit test. There are two problems to deal with:

- The possibility of small sample sizes of failures if units are small; and
- Efficiently determining the operational profiles for units from the system's operational profile.

Estimating reliability from failure data in system test works fairly well, but improvements could be made in reducing the bias that occurs in estimating parameters and hence predicted quantities. Adaptive prediction, which feeds back the prediction results to improve the model, is showing considerable promise.

Other Opportunities

Current work on developing algorithms to compensate for testing with run profiles that are different from the operational profile may open up a substantially expanded range of application for SRE.

As software reliability engineering is used on more and more projects, special problems may turn up, as is the case with any new technology. These offer excellent opportunities for those who can closely couple research and practice and communicate their results.

SUMMARY

Software reliability engineering, although not yet completely developed, is a discipline that is advancing at a rapid pace. Its benefits are clear. It is being practically applied in industry. And research is proceeding to answer many of the problems that have been raised. It is likely to advance further in the near future. This will put the practice of software engineering on a more quantitative basis.

BIBLIOGRAPHY

S. R. Abramson, B. D. Jensen, B. D. Juhlin, and C. L. Spudic, "Customer Satisfaction-Based Product Development, *Proceedings International Switching Symposium*, Yokohama, Japan, Oct. 25–30, 1992, vol. 2, 65–69.

C. T. Baker, "Effects of Field Service on Software Reliability, *IEEE Trans. on Soft. Eng.*, **SE-14**(2), 254–258, (1988).

D. Christenson, "Using Software Reliability Models to Predict Field Failure Rates in Electronic Switching Systems,"*Proceedings Fourth Annual National Conference on Software Quality and Productivity,* Washington, D.C., March 1–3, 1988.

H. D. Drake and D. E. Wolting, "Reliability Theory Applied to Software Testing," *Hewlett-Packard Journal,* 35–59, (April 1987).

W. K. Ehrlich, S. K. Lee, and R. H. Molisani, "Applying Reliability Measurement: A Case Study," *IEEE Software,* 56–64, (March 1990).

W. K. Ehrlich, J. P. Stampfel, and J. R. Wu, "Application of Software-Reliability Modeling to Product Quality and Test Process," *Proceedings 12th International Conference Software Engineering,* CS Press, Los Alamitos, Calif., 1990, 108–116.

R. P. Ejzak, "On the Successful Application of Software Reliability Modeling,"*Proceedings Fall Joint Computer Conference,* Dallas, Texas, Oct. 26–29, 1987, p. 119.

W. W. Everett, "Software Reliability Applied to Computer-Based Network Operation Systems,"*Proceedings Fall Joint Computer Conference,* Dallas, Texas, Oct. 26–29, 1987, p. 120.

W. W. Everett, "Software Reliability Measurement," *IEEE Journal on Selected Areas in Communications,* **8**(2), 247–254.

W. W. Everett, R. J. Furlong, Jr., D. J. Klinger, R. V. León, M. Tortorella, and K. S. Vanderbei, *Reliability by Design,* AT&T, 1989, 75–93.

A. L. Goel and K. Okumoto, "Time-Dependent Error Detection Rate Model for Software Reliability and Other Performance Measures," *IEEE Trans. on Rel.,* **R-28**(3), 206–211, (1979).

P. Harrington, "Applying Customer-Oriented Quality Metrics," *IEEE Software,* 71, 74, (Nov. 1989).

A. Iannino and J. D. Musa, "Software Reliability Engineering at AT&T," in G. Apostolakis, ed., *Probabilistic Safety Assessment and Management,* Elsevier, New York, 1991, pp. 485–491.

Z. Jelinski and P. B. Moranda, "Software Reliability Research," in W. Freidberger, ed., *Statistical Computer Performance Evaluation,* Academic Press, New York, 1972, pp. 465–484.

W. D. Jones, "Reliability Models for Very Large Software Systems in Industry" *Proc. 1st International Symposium on Software Reliability Engineering,* IEEE Computer Society Press, 1991, pp. 35–42.

T. W. Keller, "Space Shuttle Primary Onboard Software Reliability Approach," *Proceedings IEEE Subcommittee on Software Reliability Engineering Conference,* 1990, available from the authors.

G. A. Kruger, "Validation and Further Application of Software Reliability Growth Models," *Hewlett-Packard Journal,* 75–79, (April 1989).

B. Littlewood and J. L. Verrall, "A Bayesian Reliability Growth Model for Computer Software," *J. Royal Stat. Soc.-Series C,* **23**(3), 332–346, (1973).

J. D. Musa and A. F. Ackerman, "Quantifying Software Validation: When to Stop Testing?" *IEEE Software,* 19–27, (May 1989).

J. D. Musa and W. W. Everett, "Software Reliability Engineering: Technology for the 1990s," *IEEE Software, 36–43, (Nov. 1990).*

J. D. Musa, A. Iannino, K. Okumoto, *Software Reliability: Measurement, Prediction, Application,* McGraw-Hill, New York, 1987.

J. D. Musa, *Software Reliability Data,* 1979, report available from Data and Analysis Center for Software, Rome Air Development Center, Rome, N.Y.

J. D. Musa, "A Theory of Software Reliability and its Application" *IEEE Trans. Soft. Eng.,* **SE-1**(3), 312–327 (1975).

W. Rapp, "Application of Software Reliability Models in Medical Imaging Systems," *Proceedings IEEE Subcommittee on Software Reliability Engineering Conference,* 1990, available from the authors.

S. A. Sherer, "A Cost-Effective Approach to Testing," *IEEE Software,* 34–40, March 1991.

M. L. Shooman, "Probabilistic Models for Software Reliability Prediction," W. Freidberger, ed., *Statistical Computer Performance Evaluation,* Academic Press, New York, 1972, pp. 485–502.

G. E. Stark, "Monitoring Software Reliability in the Shuttle Mission Simulator," *Proceedings Fall Joint Computer Conference,* Dallas, Texas, Oct. 26–29, 1987, p. 123.

F. M. Vallée, "Reliability Evaluation Using NHPP Models,"*Proc. 1st International Symposium on Software Reliability Engineering,* IEEE Computer Society Press, 1991, pp. 157–162.

S. Yamada, M. Ohba, and S. Osaki, "S-Shaped Reliability Growth Modeling for Software Error Detection," *IEEE Trans. on Rel.,* **R-32**(5), 475–478, (1983).

K. C. Zinnel, "Using Software-Reliability Growth Models to Guide Release Decisions," *Proceedings IEEE Subcommittee Software Reliability Engineering Conference,* 1990, available from the authors.

JOHN D. MUSA
WILLIAM W. EVERETT
AT&T Bell Laboratories
A. FRANK ACKERMAN
Octel Communications Corporation
GEOFFREY A. WILSON
Software Reliability Engineering Associates

SOFTWARE RELIABILITY MODEL

See SOFTWARE RELIABILITY ENGINEERING.

SOFTWARE RELIABILITY THEORY

HISTORICAL PERSPECTIVE

The generally available software engineering literature abounds with between 50 and 100 models for the reliability of software (Stalhane, 1988; Mazzuchi and Singpurwalla, 1988; Barlow and Singpurwalla, 1985). Indeed, interest in this area is growing. During the 1970s an average of about $2^1/_2$ new software reliability models were being proposed each year. This increased to nearly $4^1/_2$ proposed new models per year during the 1980s. Since the first significant study on software reliability (Hudson, 1967), several important themes, developments, and issues are apparent from reviewing the literature. These include the following.

1. The clarification of the relationship between hardware reliability and software reliability.
2. The discovery that measuring software reliability with respect to execution time substantially simplifies modeling and results in improved reliability estimates and predictions.
3. The clarification of the terms "error," "fault," and "failure."
4. The comparison of different software reliability models in an attempt to recommend the best one or ones.
5. The classification and unification of software reliability models.
6. The realization that the exponential model for software failure times plays a central role in software reliability modeling.
7. The problems of estimating model parameters and of improving their predictions.
8. The split between the classical and Bayesian approaches.

This section briefly discusses these items in a general way, rather than attempting to discuss a long list of models. For an interesting perspective by one of the pioneers, see Shooman (1984).

Relationship between Hardware and Software Reliability

Hardware reliability is a generally understood and accepted concept with a long history. Early during the much shorter history of software reliability it became apparent to researchers that a division (often perceived to be large) exists between hardware reliability and software reliability. Three important and often cited differences accounting for most of the division are the inherent nature of the failure process, the replication process, and the affects of the failure resolution or repair process on reliability.

The failure process for hardware is usually thought of as being the result of a myriad of random physical changes operating on a microscopic level over time. That is, hardware components simply deteriorate and wear out. Within normal stress or operating limits they are not subject to failure from their inputs. Software, on the other hand, has no wear out phenomena, and failures are caused by specific conditions determined from the input data being processed, including operator inputs.

The replication process for software and hardware is different. No matter how well a hardware component is designed or how "clean" the manufacturing process is that produces it, the component can fail because of imperfections in the manufacturing process when operated for a long enough period. Software can usually be replicated to very high standards of quality because of highly reliable error detection and correction methods applied to internal data transmission.

Correcting a hardware failure typically involves replacing one or more failed components with new ones and restoring the system to more or less the same level of reliability. Thus hardware failure rate has a tendency toward a constant value (except during the burn-in and end of useful life periods). Software reliability usually changes (hopefully improves) after a failure correction. Assuming a perfect repair, that is, no new design faults are injected into the software, the cause of the failure is removed forever. Thus software reliability tends to increase after a failure repair.

At first these differences raised the question of whether reliability theory can be applied to software at all. It was discovered that the distinction between hardware and software is somewhat artificial. Both may be defined in the same way, so that hardware and software component reliabilities can be combined to get system reliability. Traditionally, hardware reliability focused on physical phenomena because failures resulting from these factors are much more likely to occur than design-related failures. It was possible to keep hardware design failures low because hardware was generally less complex logically than software. Besides, hardware design failures had to be kept low because of the large expense involved in retrofitting of manufactured items in the field. However, when hardware tests show that reliability is not within specified design limits because of problems or faults in the original design, a sequence of engineering changes may be necessary to improve reliability. Thus hardware reliability can and has been modeled like software reliability when the failures are the result of design faults.

Perhaps the first hardware reliability model that can also be used as a model of reliability for software was developed in 1956 by Northrop Aircraft (Weiss, 1956). This model considers complex systems where engineering changes are made to improve system reliability. It was used to determine the level of system reliability, how rapidly reliability was improving, and the expected reliability at the end of the projected development program. Two other early hardware reliability models along similar lines consider the problem of estimating reliability of a system undergoing development testing and changes to correct design deficiencies (Corcoran, Weingarten, and Zehna, 1964; Barlow and Scheuer, 1966).

It is now also generally accepted that the software failure process is random. This randomness is introduced in many ways. The location of design faults within the software is random because the overall system design is extremely complex. The programmers who introduce the design faults are human, and human failure behavior is so complex that it can best be modeled using a random process. Also, the occurrence of failures is dependent on the operational profile, which is defined by input states. It is usually not known which input state will occur next, and sometimes an input state will occur unexpectedly. These events make it impossible to predict where a fault is located or when it will be evoked to cause a failure.

All in all, software reliability theory has generally been developed in a way that is compatible with hardware reliability theory, so that system reliability figures may be computed using standard hardware combinatorial techniques (Shooman, 1990; Lloyd and Lipow, 1984).

Execution Time as a Simplifying Factor

Three kinds of time are relevant to software reliability: execution time, calendar time, and clock time. Execution time is the time used by a central processing unit to execute the instructions of a program. Calendar time is the "regular" time that everyone is familiar with. Clock time, used only occasionally, represents the elapsed time from start to end of program execution on a running computer. It includes wait time and the execution time of other programs. Periods during which the computer is shut down are not counted. If computer utilization, the fraction of time the processor is executing a program, is constant, clock time will be proportional to execution time.

In 1972 Shooman published a study where the behavior of a key parameter in his model was related to how the project personnel profile varied over time (Shooman, 1972). Several different mathematical forms were proposed for the project personnel profile, with the choice of the best one depending on the particular project. Similarly, Schneidewind approached software reliability modeling from an empirical viewpoint (Schneidewind, 1972). He recommended the investigation of different reliability functions and selection of the one that best fit the particular project in question. He found that the best distribution varied from project to project.

Up to 1975, the time domain being used in software reliability modeling was exclusively calendar time. The lack of modeling universality resulting from using calendar time caused Musa to question the suitability of this time domain (1975). He postulated that execution time was the best practical measure for characterizing failure-inducing stress being placed on a program. Calendar time, used by Shooman and Schneidewind, did not account for varying usage of a program in a straightforward way. It turned out that the removal of this confounding factor greatly simplified modeling and yielded better model predictions.

There is now substantial evidence showing the superiority of execution time over calendar time for software reliability growth models (Trachtenberg, 1985; Musa and Okumoto, 1984a; Hecht, 1981). Despite this, many published models continue to use calendar time or do not explicitly specify the type of time being used. Some models, originally developed as calendar-time models or without regard to the type of time, are now being interpreted as execution-time models. In such cases, it becomes necessary to develop a modeling component that converts execution time into calendar time, if possible. This component characterizes and predicts the passage of calendar time with execution time. With it, projections of when failure intensity objectives will be met can be made in terms of calendar dates rather than execution time and therefore are much more valuable to managers and engineers. Thus it is seen that software reliability models based on execution time and having a calendar-time component are the most desirable and useful.

An interesting development concerning calendar-time-based models has taken place during the mid-1980s. In Japan, primary focus has been on the time-dependent behavior of testing resources over the testing period and its resulting affect on software reliability models (Yamada, Ohba, and Osaki, 1984; Yamada and Osaki, 1985). Indeed, many Japanese software houses use what are referred to as S-shaped software reliability models. It seems that these models are generally applicable to modeling failure processes in calendar time, which has apparently been more readily available than execution time in Japan. Sometimes an S-shaped model is obtained using execution time. This may result if one or more of the following occurs (This is not necessarily an exhaustive list).

1. System testers record but do not report failures at the start of system testing. This will cause a rush of failures shortly after the start of system testing and an S-shaped curve if the time of failure occurrence is taken to be the time a failure is reported.
2. System testers are too busy planning and thereby missing failures at the start of system testing.
3. The program being tested is evolving (integrated in phases) and the testing resource levels (number of debuggers and testers) are increasing until system integration is complete.

A common theme in these is "start up" effects; that is, it takes some time for system testing to get up to full speed.

The friendly controversy between execution-time models and S-shaped calendar-time models is likely to continue for some time to come. However, most researchers agree that execution time is the most fundamental and simplying time domain to use.

Clarification of Errors, Faults, and Failures

The clarification of the terms errors, faults, and failures and its resulting importance for understanding and modeling software reliability became clear in the mid to late 1980s after a long period of evolution. Prior to that time these terms, as well as terms like bugs, defects, maintenance reports, change reports, trouble reports, etc., were used interchangeably. Naturally, this caused confusion and made it practically impossible to compare or judge the results that were obtained from different studies, and even made it questionable whether the results were generally useful.

Many of the early (and present) studies were based on the developer-oriented counting of faults or defects found in a program. In reality, what was usually counted were either failures (software did not do what it was suppose to do) or repairs (for example, maintenance reports), neither of which are equivalent to faults. It is now known that counting the number of repairs does not yield a stable approximation of the number of faults inherent in the software until execution time becomes very large. This is so because the full nature and extent of a fault are often not known until several related failures have been experienced, and this can require a large amount of execution time (testing).

There is still some controversy as to what an error is. For example, the IEEE has four different definitions for error (1990). One of these defines error as a human action that produces an incorrect result, also the definition advocated in Musa, Iannino, and Okumoto (1987).

The clarification of these terms increased the scope or meaning of software reliability. The IEEE now accepts the meanings of fault, failure, and software reliability as standards. This allows a common basis for data collection, reporting of results, and comparison studies and with it the potential to advance the state of the art.

Comparison of Different Software Reliability Models

The large number of proposed models tend to give quite different predictions for the same set of failure data. It should be noted that this kind of behavior is not unique to software reliability modeling but is typical of models that are used to project values in time and not merely represent current values. Even a particular model may give reasonable predictions on one set of failure data and unreasonable predictions on another. All this has left potential users confused and adrift with little guidance as to which models may be best for their application.

The search for the best software reliability model(s) started in the late 1970s and early 1980s and still continues today. Initial efforts at comparison by Schick and Wolverton (1978) and Sukert (1979) suffered from a lack of good failure data and a lack of agreement on the criteria to be used in making the comparisons. The former deficiency was remedied to some degree in 1979 when over 20 reasonably good-quality sets of failure data were published (Musa). The data sets were collected under careful supervision and control and represent a wide variety of applications including real time command and control, commercial, military, and space systems and they ranged in size from about 6K object instructions to 2.4M object instructions.

The latter deficiency was remedied when Iannino and co-workers (1984) worked out a consensus from many experts in the field on the comparison criteria to be employed. The proposed criteria include the following.

1. The capability of a model to predict future failure behavior from known or assumed characteristics of the software; for example, estimated lines of code, language planned to be used, and present and past failure behavior (that is, failure data). This is significant principally when the failure behavior is changing, as occurs during system testing.
2. The ability of a model to estimate with satisfactory accuracy the quantities needed for planning and managing software development projects or for running operational software systems. These quantities include the present failure intensity, the expected date of reaching the failure intensity objective, and resource and cost requirements related to achieving the failure intensity objective.
3. The quality of modeling assumptions (for example, support by data, plausibility, clarity, and explicitness).
4. The degree of model applicability across software products that vary in size, structure, and function, different development environments, different operational environments, and different life cycle phases. Common situations encountered in practice that must be dealt with include programs being integrated in phases, system testing driven by a strategy to test one system feature at a time, the use of varying performance computers, and the need to handle different failure severity classes.
5. The degree of model simplicity (for example, simple and inexpensive data collection, concepts, and computer implementation).

An interesting development in recent years is the proposal by some researchers to sidestep the issue of selecting the best model by using a (large) subset of models at the same time on a given set of failure data and then picking the one that is working best (Keiller and co-workers, 1983). It is interesting to observe that the best model for a particular project may change as the size of the set of failure data increases. This seems unsatisfactory both from a practical and theoretical point of view.

Model Classification

A significant side benefit from the model comparison efforts has been the advances made in model classification and unification. Kremer (1983) unified many software reliability models using a nonhomogeneous birth-death Markov process. A couple of years later Langberg and Singpurawalla (1985) illustrated that many well-known models can be obtained by specifying prior distributions for the parameter of the Jelinski-Moranda model. Miller (1986) developed the idea of exponential order statistic models that provides another important viewpoint on the different models. A similar unification and classification to that of Kremer's occurred in Musa, Iannino, and Okumoto (1987).

The latter approach is based on Markov processes that are characterized by the distribution of the number of failures over time. The two most important distributions are the Poisson and binomial. Models based on the binomial distribution are finite failures models, that is, they postulate that a finite number of failures will be experienced in infinite time. Models based on the Poisson distribution can

Table 1. Markov Software Reliability Models

Poisson-type	Binomial-type	Other types
Crow, 1974	Jelinski and Moranda, 1972	Shooman and Trivedi, 1975
Musa, 1975	Shooman, 1972	Kim and co-workers, 1982
Moranda, 1975	Schick and Wolverton, 1973	Kremer, 1983
Schneidewind, 1975	Wagoner, 1973	Laprie, 1984
Goel and Okumoto, 1979	Goel, 1977	Shanthikumar and Sumita, 1986
Brooks and Motley, 1980	Schick and Wolverton, 1978	
Angus and co-workers, 1980	Shanthikumar, 1981	
Yamada and co-workers, 1983	Littlewood, 1981	
Yamada and Osaki, 1984		
Ohba, 1984		
Yamada and co-workers, 1984		

be either finite-failures or infinite-failures models, depending on how they are specified. Table 1 shows how some of the published models are classified using this approach. The Bayesian model of Littlewood and Verrall (1973) and the geometric de-eutrophication model of Moranda (1975) are among the few published models that are not Markov.

These unifications highlight relationships among the models and suggest new models where gaps occur in the classification scheme. Furthermore, they greatly reduce the task of model comparison.

Central Role of the Exponential Model

The first software reliability model was independently developed by researchers in 1972 (Jelinski and Moranda, 1972; Shooman, 1972). This model, henceforth referred to as the exponential model, makes three basic assumptions.

1. All faults in the program contribute the same amount to the overall failure intensity of the program. Thus at any time the program failure intensity is proportional to the number of remaining faults.
2. The successive times between failures are independent exponentially distributed random variables.
3. A fault is immediately and perfectly fixed after each failure. Actually, this assumption is not completely necessary since reoccurrences of the same failure can be ignored in the data analysis.

Figure 1 shows the characteristic step curve for the variation of program failure intensity with execution time for the exponential model.

Several other models that are either identical to the exponential model except for notational differences or are very close approximations were developed by Musa (1975), Schneidewind (1975), and Goel and Okumoto (1979). The latter is a continuous approximation to the original exponential model and is described in terms of a nonhomogeneous Poisson process with a failure intensity function that is exponentially decaying. Figure 1 also shows this curve and how closely it approximates the exponential model curve. For all practical purposes the Goel-Okumoto and the other models are indistinguishable from the exponential model.

The parameter estimation of the exponential model (and, therefore, the other closely related or equivalent models) has been often criticized. Forman and Singpurwalla (1977 and 1979), Littlewood and Verrall (1981), and Joe and Reid (1984), to name a few, have shown that parameter estimation for the model suffers from two unfortunate tendencies. Sometimes there is a tendency for estimates of the total failures expected to come out nearly equal to the number of failures experienced. This leads to overly optimistic conclusions. Sometimes there is a tendency for these same estimates to be nonfinite. Meinhold and Singpurwalla (1983) suggested that when nonfinite parameter estimates are obtained it is the method of inference that needs to be questioned not the model.

Nevertheless, the exponential model plays a key role in software reliability theory. Shock models and renewal theoretic arguments were used by Stefanski (1982) and Langberg and Singpurwalla (1985), respectively, to provide alternative motivations for and alluded to the centrality of the exponential model. In the former reference, it was also illustrated that many other well-known models,

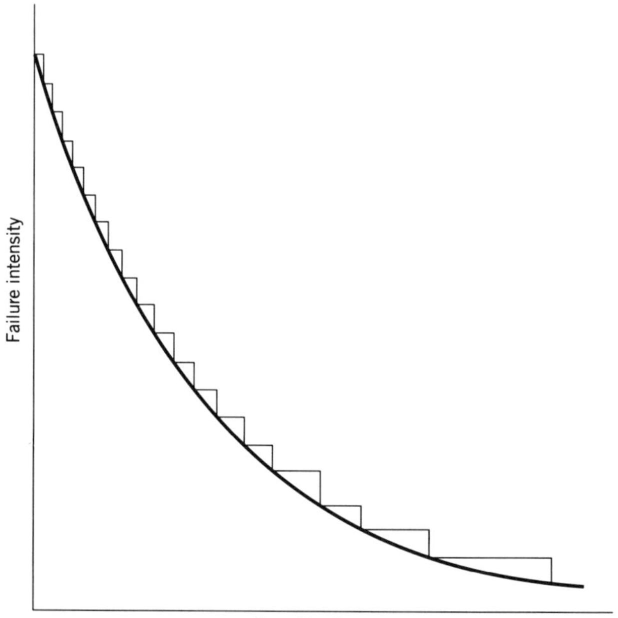

Figure 1. Characteristic step curve and continuous approximation for variation of program failure intensity with execution time for the exponential model.

including Littlewood and Verrall (1973), can be obtained by specifying specific distributions for the parameters of the exponential model. The following sections on execution time modeling provide further justification for the equivalent exponential nonhomogeneous Poisson process model.

Parameter Estimation and Model Predictions

The quality of parameter estimation and of model predictions has been and continues to be a major research area in software reliability modeling. As alluded to in the preceding discussion on the exponential model, some problems exist. These or related problems are shared to some degree or other by many of the current models (Musa, Iannino, and Okumoto, 1987). Predictions from many models frequently tend to be biased. There appear to be consistent patterns among models of predicting values of failure intensity that are either too pessimistic or too optimistic, and there is also a fair amount of dispersion in predictions.

The most promising development to date for improving model predictions is adaptive prediction (Littlewood, Ghaly, and Chan, 1986). Adaptive prediction is a statistical procedure that allows a model to "learn" from its past mistakes and produce improved predictions. Preliminary results show that adaptive prediction removes a substantial amount of the prediction bias experienced with models. It may also greatly reduce the difference in predictive validity experienced between models. Recently, techniques for assessing the quality of adapted predictions, relative to the unadapted or raw predictions, have also been developed (Brocklehurst and co-workers, 1989).

Classical and Bayesian Approaches

Very early in the history of software reliability modeling two distinct and important modeling approaches that are also prevalent in hardware reliability appeared: classical and Bayesian. The Bayesian approach essentially challenges some of the deterministic assumptions made in the classical approach. For example, the exponential model assumes that each fault contributes equally to the overall program failure intensity. The Bayesian approach argues that each fault's contribution to the overall failure intensity is unknown and can be modeled as originating from a given random distribution (with unknown parameters) of values (Littlewood, 1981). The analysis then proceeds along traditional Bayesian techniques. The resulting model leads to the intuitive notion that earlier failure corrections have a greater effect than later ones on the program failure intensity. However, it should be noted that many classical models also share this property.

Any of the classical models can be made Bayesian by specifying appropriate distributions for one or more of their parameters. Surprisingly, most of the Bayesian models use the exponential model as a starting point (for example, Littlewood and Verrall, 1974; Goel, 1977; Littlewood, 1980; Jewell, 1985) or are completely new models (for example, Littlewood and Verrall, 1973; Kyparisi and Singpurwalla 1985). It seems that the Bayesian approach suffers from its complexity and from the difficulty in choosing appropriate distributions for the parameters. Added to this is the fact that most software engineers do not have the required statistical background to completely understand and appreciate Bayesian models. The latter is perhaps the main reason why these models have not enjoyed the same attention as the classical models (there are almost five times as many classical models as Bayesian models, and they are used in a great majority of the practical applications).

EXECUTION TIME MODELING

Software reliability models generally fall into two categories depending on the domain they operate in. By far the largest and most popular category of models is based on time. Their central feature is that reliability measures, such as failure intensity, are derived as a function of time. The second category of software reliability models provides a contrasting approach by using operational inputs as their central feature. These models measure reliability as the ratio of successful runs to total number of runs. However, this approach has some problems, including the fact that many systems have runs of widely varying lengths (so that the proportion may give inaccurate estimates) and that the resulting measures are incompatible with the time-based measures used for hardware. Because of this and the amount of research currently being devoted to time-based models, the second model category will not be considered further here.

Two approaches for modeling software reliability in execution time are particularly instructive. The first approach is based on random point processes and draws upon a large body of results found in the general literature on stochastic processes. The second approach is based on exponential order statistics and provides an intuitive representation of the failure process.

Random Point Processes

The reliability of software is mainly influenced or determined by three factors: fault introduction, fault removal, and the operational profile (relative frequency of occurrence of each input state or system function). Fault introduction depends primarily on the characteristics of the developed code (code written or modified for the program) and the development process. The code characteristic with the greatest effect is size. Development process characteristics include the software engineering technologies and tools employed and the average level of experience of programmers. Note that code is developed when adding features or removing faults. Fault removal is affected by time, the operational profile, and the quality of the repair activity. Since most of the foregoing factors are probabilistic in nature and operate over time, the behavior of software failures with execution time is usually modeled using some kind of random point process. The upper portion of Figure 2 shows an example of such a process where each failure epoch is represented by an X. A counting process giving the number of failures experienced by execution time τ is associated with every point process. Figure 2 also shows a typical counting process, denoted by $M(\tau)$, having a unit jump at each failure epoch.

At this point it is appropriate to remark that the counting process being considered here is strictly nondecreasing

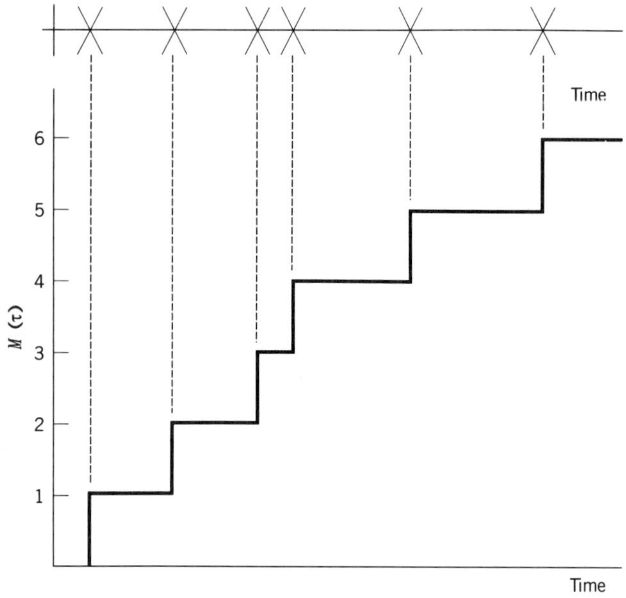

Figure 2. A random point process and its associated counting process.

because failures are being modeled. A counting process based on faults is a different story. When a failure occurs, an attempt is made to identify and remove the fault that caused the failure. However, because of possible imperfect debugging, the fault may not be removed with certainty. Furthermore, the repair activity may introduce a new fault. Goel and Okumoto (1978; 1979), Shanthikumar (1981), and Kremer (1983) studied this counting process and provided valuable insights; however, expressions for reliability and other quantities of interest are complex, and it is difficult to apply this approach in practice. Also, the fault-based counting process cannot be clearly observed as argued in Musa, Iannino, and Okumoto (1987).

There are many different kinds of random point processes; however, the Markov process is a good place to start. As previously noted, these processes play a key role in the unification and classification of many published models, and there are some central theoretical results that come into consideration. Necessary and sufficient conditions for a counting (failure) process to be a Markov process with a continuous failure intensity function $\lambda(\tau)$, derivative with respect to τ of the expected number of failures at time τ, are

1. The probability of a failure occurring in the interval $(\tau, \tau+\Delta\tau)$ given that $M(\tau)=m$ is $\lambda_m(\tau)\Delta(\tau)$. Note that the probability of failure (failure intensity) depends on time τ and the number of past failures m.
2. Failures do not occur simultaneously.
3. Failures do not occur at preassigned times.
4. There is no finite interval in $[\tau, \infty]$ where failures occur with certainty.
5. $Pr[M(0)=0]=1$.

Figure 3 shows a transition diagram describing a Markov birth process (appropriate for counting failures) where

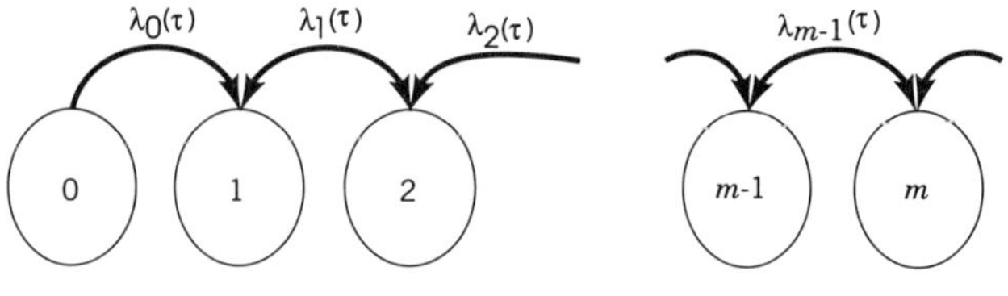

Figure 3. Markov birth process transition diagram.

$\lambda_m(\tau)$ is the time variation of the failure intensity in state m. With the preceding assumptions the probability that $M(\tau)$ equals m is given by

$$Pr[M(\tau) = m] = P_m(\tau) = e^{-\lambda_m\tau}\left[\lambda_{m-1}\int_0^\tau P_{m-1}(x)e^{\lambda_m x}dx\right], \quad m = 0, 1, \ldots, \tag{1}$$

where $P_0=e^{-\lambda_0\tau}$. Details leading to equation 1 are omitted here but can generally be found in most textbooks on queueing theory (Kleinrock, 1975). The specific type of model given by equation 1 is determined by the form of distribution of m, that is, $P_m(\tau)$.

The following cases show the origins of the Poisson-type and binomial-type models mentioned earlier (Table 1).

1. The failure intensity is constant, that is, $\lambda_m(\tau)=\lambda$. Here equation 1 reduces to the Poisson distribution characteristic of a homogeneous Poisson process.

$$P_m(\tau) = \frac{(\lambda\tau)^m e^{-\lambda\tau}}{m!}, \tag{2}$$

2. The failure intensity depends on time but is independent of past events, that is, $\lambda_m(\tau)=\lambda(\tau)$. This leads to the Poisson distribution

$$P_m(\tau) = \frac{[\mu(\tau)]^m e^{-\mu(\tau)}}{m!} \tag{3}$$

where $\mu(\tau)=\int_0^\tau \lambda(x)dx$. Equation 3 is characteristic of a nonhomogeneous Poisson process.

3. The failure intensity depends on the number of remaining faults and the per-fault hazard rate $z_a(\tau)$ that is, $\lambda_m(\tau)=(u_0-m)z_a(\tau)$, where u_0 is the initial number of faults in the software. (An assumption being made is that there is a one-to-one correspondence between faults and failures.) This leads to the binomial distribution

$$P_m(\tau) = \binom{u_0}{m}[F_a(\tau)]^m[1 - F_a(\tau)]^{u_0-m}, \tag{4}$$

where $z_a(\tau)=f_a(\tau)/[1-F_a(\tau)]$, $f_a(\tau)=dF_a(\tau)/d\tau$, and $F_a(\tau)$ is the per-fault cumulative failure probability function. This represents a binomial-type model. It is instructive to note that as $u_0 \rightarrow \infty$ and $u_0 F_a(\tau) \rightarrow \mu(\tau)$ equation 4 becomes equation 3.

Thus many of the Poisson-type and binomial-type models discussed extensively in the literature, are special cases of the Markov birth process with specific forms for $\lambda_m(\tau)$. Other forms for $\lambda_m(\tau)$ can be used and lead to different kinds of models, but usually not to ones that have simple expressions for $P_m(\tau)$.

It is well-worth discussing the preceding conditions for a Markov process here because this will help determine the plausibility of the entire modeling approach. Some of the affects of altering the first condition were already investigated when the origin of the Poisson-type models and binomial-type models was clarified. If this condition is relaxed so that the failure intensity may depend on τ, $M(\tau)$, and the occurrence times for all failures before τ, a self-exciting random point process is obtained. In this type of process, since $M(\tau)$ is a random variable, the failure intensity itself is a random process. Other types of point processes can be obtained if an "outside" process affects the failure intensity. These processes are beyond the scope of this discussion. A general self-exciting point process can be conceived of as a modified nonhomogeneous Poisson process in which the future evolution of failures is not only a function of time but can also be influenced by all past occurrences of failures. Of course, when the evolution depends only on time and the total number of past failures, a Markov birth process results.

It seems that by relaxing this condition the number of possible models, and with it the complexity of determining which of them is best in some sense has been greatly increased. A useful result about the pooling of independent self-exciting point processes is found in Franken (1963) and Grigelionis (1963). They showed that if independent component processes are such that almost every one contributes no more than a single failure to the pooled or overall process, then the pooled process is approximately a Poisson process. Indeed, under weak conditions, pooling the failures of independent self-exciting processes converges to a Poisson process. If a component process is viewed as arising from a single software fault and assuming faults are causing failures to occur independently, the pooled process is approximately a Poisson process. This helps to explain, in part, why the Poisson process is often found to be a reasonable model in applications (Iannino and Musa, 1991).

Further support for this observation can be found in Miller (1986) where it was shown that a single realization or observation of a reliability growth process, that is, one sequence of failure times, is not sufficient to discriminate between processes. Snyder (1975) also showed that maximum likelihood estimation between the different processes of the type discussed lead to identical results, thus making it impossible to distinguish between the processes. This was also verified in Musa, Iannino, and Okumoto (1987).

Thus it seems theoretically and practically justified to restrict software reliability modeling to the nonhomogeneous Poisson process. It is important to consider the first condition for a Markov process in light of this conclusion. For a nonhomogeneous Poisson process this condition is the realization of failures during the interval $[\tau, \infty]$ does not depend in any way on the sequence of failures that have happened in the interval $[0, \tau]$. The validity of this condition is sometimes questioned by some researchers in the field who may not be familiar with the preceding theoretical results or who just question the failure independence this condition implies. In most cases, failures are independent because they are the result of two processes: the introduction of faults and the activation of faults through the selection of input states. Both of these processes are random, and hence the chance that one failure would affect another is small. The independence conclusion is supported by a study of correlograms of failure data from 15 projects (Musa, 1979) which found no significant correlation.

Independence is sometimes disputed because the two process situation is not well known. Some argue that programmers tend to have patterns of errors (that is, one error may influence the next one). Related faults may indeed be produced, but this does not imply the existence of related failures. Similarly, it is sometimes stated that one failure can prevent access to certain code and thus prevent another failure that is associated with that code from occurring. This prevention may occur occasionally in unit testing, but it is much less common during system testing or in the operational phase. In any case, it is even rarer to have the fault causing the first failure to cause the introduction of a second fault into the "hidden" code.

The remaining four conditions for a Markov process also apply to a Poisson process and are generally well accepted by researchers in the field, but they can also be easily relaxed, especially for a nonhomogeneous Poisson process. For example, the condition that requires that the process starts out with no failures can be easily changed to one that assumes that the process starts out with a known or random number of failures simply by treating this as a separate term in the model formulations. As another example, the condition that no failures occur simultaneously can be relaxed, leading to what is called a compound Poisson process (Sahinoglu, 1990). Many other powerful and useful generalizations are possible and can be found in Synder (1975).

Reliability estimates for nonhomogeneous Poisson process models come directly from equation 3 and by noting that the event $M(\tau) \geq i$ is equivalent to the event $T_i \leq \tau$, where T_i is a random variable for the ith failure time. In addition, unknown model parameters are usually determined using the maximum likelihood principle, least squares, or Bayesian techniques. Again, specific derivations are omitted, however, Table 2 provides a summary of some important relationships for these models (Musa, Iannino, and Okumoto, 1987). These can be used for a particular model, that is, for a particular mean value function.

Exponential Order Statistics

The exponential order statistics approach to modeling software reliability, studied by Downs (1985; 1986), Miller (1986), and Ross (1985a; b) is essentially equivalent to the preceding approach except that it provides a more intuitive feeling for the actual failure process. Figure 4 shows the

Table 2. Some Derived Relationships for a General Poisson process

Quantity	Formula
Failures experienced	$Pr[M(\tau) = m] = \frac{[\mu(\tau)]^m}{m!} e^{-\mu(\tau)}$ Expected value $= \mu(\tau)$ Variance $= \mu(\tau)$
Failure time	$Pr[T_i \leq \tau] = F(\tau_i) = \sum_{j=i}^{\infty} \frac{[\mu(\tau)]^j}{j!} e^{-\mu(\tau)}$
Reliability	$R(\tau_i' \mid \tau_{i-1}) = Pr[T_i' > \tau_i' \mid T_{i-1} = \tau_{i-1}] = e^{-[\mu(\tau_{i-1} + \tau_i') - \mu(\tau_{i-1})]}$
Conditional failure time	$f(\tau_i' \mid \tau_{i-1}) = \lambda(\tau_{i-1} + \tau_i')e^{-[\mu(\tau_{i-1} + \tau_i') - \mu(\tau_{i-1})]}$
Failure intensity	$\lambda(\tau) = \frac{d\mu(\tau)}{d\tau}$
Unconditional failure time	$f(\tau_i) = \frac{dF(\tau_i)}{d\tau_i} = \frac{\lambda(\tau_i)[\mu(\tau_i)]^{i-1}e^{-\mu(\tau_i)}}{(i-1)!}$
Maximum likelihood equations	$-\frac{\partial\mu(\tau_e)}{\partial \hat{\beta}_k} = \sum_{i=1}^{m_e} \frac{1}{\lambda(\tau_i)} \frac{\partial\lambda(\tau_i)}{\partial\hat{\beta}_k}; \quad k = 1, 2, \ldots n$ $\hat{\beta}_0 = \frac{m_e}{\mu_l(\tau_e; \hat{\beta}_1, \hat{\beta}_2, \ldots, \hat{\beta}_n)}$

τ_i = i th failure time
τ_i' = time interval between($i-1$)th and i failure
$\mu(\tau) = \beta_0\mu_1(\tau; \beta_1, \beta_2, \ldots, \beta_n)$
$\beta_j(j = 0, \ldots, n)$ are unknown model parameters
$\hat{\beta}_j$ is estimated value of β_j
m_e observed failures at time t_e
t_e = total time of observation or testing

modeling environment. A piece of software initially containing an unknown number of faults ω_0 is subjected to testing where input states A, B, C, etc are chosen at random according to some operational profile. Most input states result in successful execution (correct program results). Some input states exercise a collection of instructions containing a fault and cause a failure to occur. Still others exercise a collection of instructions containing a fault but do not cause a failure to occur because the data state or specific conditions are not right. For example, input state C in Figure 4 does not encounter a fault and causes no failure, whereas input states A and B both encounter fault a (Bug) with only input state A causing a failure. Therefore, the only input states of consequence as far as fault a causing a failure are the ones like input state A in the example. The collection of these input states is called fault a's fail set.

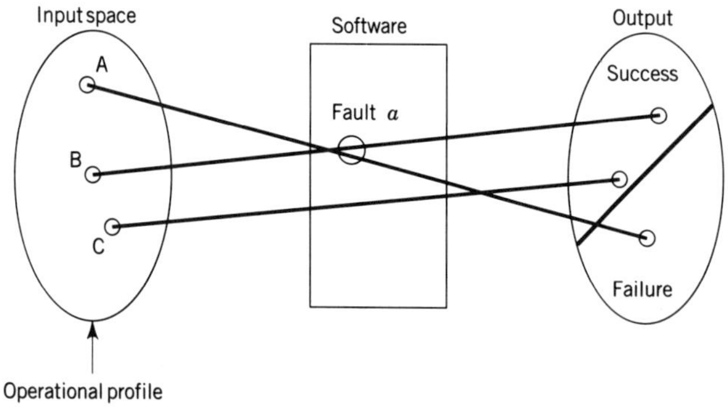

Figure 4. Software reliability modeling environment.

Two factors determine the failure-causing potential of a fault. They are the size or number of input states in the fault's fail set and the frequency with which these states are chosen for execution. Clearly, if the operational profile were to change, so also would the importance or contribution of the input states in the fail set to the failure-causing potential of the fault.

Let p_k be the probability that input state k is picked for execution, τ_k the execution time of input state k, and Y_a the fail set for fault a. Then the failure intensity for fault a, denoted by λ_a, is

$$\lambda_a = \frac{\sum_{k \varepsilon Ya} p_k}{\sum_{all k} \tau_k p_k} = \frac{1}{\tau} \sum_{k \varepsilon Y_a} p_k \tag{5}$$

where τ is the average execution time over all input states and the value of the sum on the far right is defined as the fault exposure.

Equation 5 ignores several potential issues. The first issue that may come up is the matter of input state dependencies; for example, a specific input state may always be executed after a given input state. This can be incorporated into the model, but the increase in accuracy, if any, is probably outweighed by the added complexity. The second issue is that a fault may prevent access to code containing one or more faults. This issue is less common during system testing or operational use than it is during unit testing and is considered to be a secondary effect and is therefore ignored. Finally, another issue concerns multiple failures resulting from an execution of a given input state. This is usually considered to be secondary or not worth the effort to explicitly model.

The failure intensity for the program depends on whether faults are being removed or not. Assume for the moment that they are not being removed. This is typical of a program in production use. The program failure intensity λ is determined by summing the contributions of the individual faults, that is,

$$\lambda = \frac{1}{\tau} \sum_{a=1}^{\omega_0} \sum_{k \varepsilon Y_a} p_k = \sum_{a=1}^{\omega_0} \lambda_a \tag{6}$$

Equation 6 implicitly assumes that the failures from different faults are independent.

Now suppose that faults are being repaired. The program is exercised for a period of time τ and each time a failure occurs the software is debugged and the fault responsible for the failure is removed. Let $I_a(\tau)$ be a function that takes on a value of 1 if fault a has not caused a failure by τ and 0 otherwise. As before, the program failure intensity at time τ, denoted by $\Lambda(\tau)$ since this time it is a random variable, is determined by summing the contributions of the individual faults still remaining in the program. Thus

$$\Lambda(\tau) = \sum_{a=1}^{\omega_0} \lambda_a I_a(\tau) \tag{7}$$

Note that λ_a contributes to the sum only if fault a has not been removed yet. Implicit assumptions being made here are that failures from different faults are independent and that a fault causing an observed failure is immediately resolved. The latter assumption, however, need not be the case. Subsequent occurrences of the same failure can be ignored in the analysis if necessary.

To move on, an assumption concerning the failure process itself must be made. The usual assumption is that faults cause failures to occur in accordance with independent homogeneous Poisson processes with unknown failure intensities given by equation 5. A natural result of this is that failure times for a fault are exponentially distributed. Miller (1986) provides several justifications for the exponential distribution, and these will not be repeated here.

Given the preceding assumption about the failure process, the probability of fault a not causing a failure by time τ is $e^{-\lambda_a \tau}$. Therefore, the expected failure intensity for the program, $\lambda(\tau)$, is given by

$$E[\Lambda(\tau)] = \lambda(\tau) = \sum_{a=1}^{\omega_0} \lambda_a E[I_a(\tau)] = \sum_{a=1}^{\omega_0} \lambda_a e^{-\lambda_a \tau} \tag{8}$$

Equation 8 is sufficient to completely describe the overall failure process for the program. The integral of this equation gives the mean value function $\mu(\tau)$ or the expected number of failures at time τ; that is,

$$\mu(\tau) = \sum_{a=1}^{\omega_0} (1 - e^{-\lambda_a \tau}) \tag{9}$$

Equations 8 and 9 show how $\lambda(\tau)$ and $\mu(\tau)$, respectively, depend on the failure intensity of the individual faults.

Many possibilities exist for the form of $\lambda(\tau)$ depending on the form of the λ_a s. The latter can be treated in several ways. One such way is deterministically; that is, following a known pattern. Two examples include constant failure intensities ($\lambda_a = \lambda_0$ for all a) and geometric failure intensities ($\lambda_a = \alpha\beta^a, 0 < \beta < 1$ for all a). The failure intensities can also be treated as a finite collection of independent and identically distributed random variables drawn from some distribution; for example, the gamma distribution. Finally, the failure intensities can be treated as a realization of a random point process such as the nonhomogeneous Poisson process. It is also mathematically possible to permit an infinite value for ω_0 and treat finite ω_0 as a special subcase. Doing this, it is possible to simultaneously deal with infinite failures and finite failures models and to unify a great many models. Miller (1986) gives a complete discussion on the types of models resulting from these and other patterns of failure intensities and gives some rather significant results. One result, concerning the inability to distinguish between the different types of models for the λ_a s, based on a single observation of the failure process, has already been mentioned. Another closely linked idea is that the mean value function is the primary characteristic of a model and the particular type of model is a secondary characteristic. For example, a model based on deterministic λ_as and a model based on λ_as drawn from a probability distribution are close to each other if their mean value functions are close. An example of an application of this idea is in Musa and Okumoto (1984b) where the Littlewood-Verrall model was analyzed using a nonhomogeneous Poisson process with appropriate mean value function.

Keeping in the spirit of this, the natural step that arises is to determine what equation 9 reveals about the kinds of mean value functions likely to be good candidates for models. Let $\bar{\lambda}$ represent the average per-fault failure intensity of the inherent faults, that is

$$\bar{\lambda} = \frac{1}{\omega_0} \sum_{a=1}^{\omega_0} \lambda_a$$

Also, let σ^2 be a measure of the variation in the inherent per-fault failure intensities, that is

$$\sigma^2 - \sum_{a=1}^{\omega_0} (\lambda_a - \bar{\lambda})^2.$$

Then, expanding equation 9 in a Taylor series about λ keeping τ fixed yields

$$\mu(\tau) = \omega_0(1 - e^{-\bar{\lambda}\tau}) + \sum_{a=1}^{\omega_0} \tau e^{-\tau\bar{\lambda}}(\lambda_a - \bar{\lambda}) - \frac{\tau^2 e^{-\bar{\lambda}\tau}}{2} \tag{10}$$

$$\sum_{a=1}^{\omega_0} (\lambda_a - \bar{\lambda})^2 \ldots = \omega_0(1 - e^{-\bar{\lambda}\tau}) - \frac{\tau^2 e^{-\bar{\lambda}\tau}\sigma^2}{2} \ldots$$

where higher-order terms are not explicitly shown. The significant point about equation 10 is the first term which represents an exponential mean value function characteristic of many popular and useful models (Musa, 1975; Goel and Okumoto, 1979). The conclusion to be drawn is that the exponential mean value function is a first-order approximation of all possible mean value functions based on a finite number of initial faults. This explains, in part, why the exponential nonhomogeneous Poisson process model enjoys such success in many applications (Zinnel, 1990; Erhlich and co-workers, 1991; Iannino and Musa, 1991).

As can be seen, the exponential nonhomogeneous Poisson process model is exact if all per-fault failure intensities are the same. Note that this does not imply a uniform operational profile as is sometimes claimed in the literature. It does imply that the joint effect of the operational profile and of the fail set size, the fault exposure, is the same for all faults. Thus a fault will a large fail set size and small individual operation usage proabilities may be the same, in terms of failure intensity, as a fault with small fail set size and large individual operation usage proabilities.

The nature of the higher order terms in equation 10 is also important since it gives an idea of the error that can result in using just the first order term (or exponential mean value function). Here we consider only the second order term for simplicity. The maximum contribution of the second order term to the overall mean value function occurs at $\tau = 2/\lambda$ and has a value of

$$2e^{-2}\frac{\sigma^2}{\lambda^2} = 2e^{-2}C^2 \tag{11}$$

where C is defined as the coefficient of variation of the inherent per-fault failure intensities. The relative contribution of the second order term (that is, the ratio of the second order term to the first order term) when this term is at it's maximum is

$$0.31C^2/\omega_0 \tag{12}$$

Equation 12 gives some idea why the exponential nonhomogeneous Poisson process model is robust to departures from equal per-fault failure intensities requirement. For example, alternatives for the per-fault failure intensities that are sometimes used incorporate gamma distributions that usually have $C^2 \leq 1$. If $C = 1$ (exponential distribution), then the maximum contribution of the second order term is about 0.27 failures and the relative contribution is about $0.31/\omega_0$. Since ω_0 is usually large, the relative contribution is small. Another argument is to consider the uncertainty in the collected failure data. Suppose, there is a 10 percent error on average in the failure data. This equates to C^2 slightly greater than 30 for a program containing 100 faults. That is to say, a 10 percent uncertainty in the failure data is equivalent to nonequal per-fault failure intensities with $C^2 = 30$ and exact future data.

The case for the exponential mean value function can be further strengthed by relaxing the homogeneous Poisson process assumption underlying each fault's failure process. It turns out that any per-fault failure process whose first time to failure is exponentially distributed will lead to the same conclusions, provided that subsequent occurrences of the same failure are ignored. This is an important observation especially when dealing with failures that tend to cluster as described in Ehrlich and co-workers (1991).

Summary

The nonhomogeneous Poisson process is emerging as the most practical and useful choice for modeling software reliability. This is based on many theoretical results. The process is fully specified by its mean value function, and an emerging choice here, both in theory and in practice, is the exponential mean value function. This function was shown to play a central role in modeling and to be quite robust from departures in its assumptions.

CALENDAR TIME MODELING

The relationship between the accumulation of execution time during system testing and the passage of calendar time has received relatively little attention compared to modeling software reliability in execution time, despite its obvious importance to software managers and engineers. The earliest, best known, and perhaps most validated calendar time model was developed in 1975 (Musa). Though not formulated as such, this model can and will be viewed here as a queueing network model. Queueing network models tend to capture the most important features of what they are modeling, and their application to computer systems show that they are much more sensitive to parameters like mean service time at a resource service center than they are to many of the details of policies and mechanisms being employed (Graham, 1978). The same also seems to be true for the queueing network model for system testing.

To understand calendar-time modeling fully, it is necessary to know what major activities affecting the passage of calendar time typically take place during system testing. A common scenario begins with the start of system testing where a large number of failures separated by short time intervals are usually experienced. Testing must be stopped from time to time to let the debuggers working on the failures keep up with the load. As testing progresses, the intervals between failures become longer and longer. The debuggers are now able to keep up with the lighter load; however, the testing team is fully occupied in the effort required to run tests and analyze the results. Finally, as the intervals between failures become even longer, the capacity of the computing facilities is pushed to its limits. Thus it is not unusual to see three phases or periods occurring during system testing while a different resource is used to its maximum capacity. The resource that is fully utilized at any time is called the limiting resource and governs how much calendar time is being spent with respect to execution time. This is the key concept in calendar time modeling.

A queueing network model for the system testing phase must include the interaction of three resource centers: failure identification, failure resolution, and computing. It is sometimes useful to consider a queueing network model as comprising two subcomponents. One component, called the configuration component, specifies the characteristics of the servers, such as their number, at each resource center. The other component, called the workload component, specifies the characteristics of the resource demands placed on the resource centers. Figure 5 shows such a model. Note that failure identification (testing) and failure resolution are usually performed by different people, so they are considered as separate resources. To simplify the modeling process, the quantities of the available resources are assumed to be constant (from the point of view of the model) through the period of prediction. It is possible to handle more complex patterns of resource availability; however, it does not seem to be worth the effort primarily because constant, or nearly constant, resources are a common condition or at least a reasonable first approximation to reality. Naturally, the development that follows can be generalized in a straightforward fashion to include more resource centers, if necessary. The two components of the queueing network model are described in the following sections.

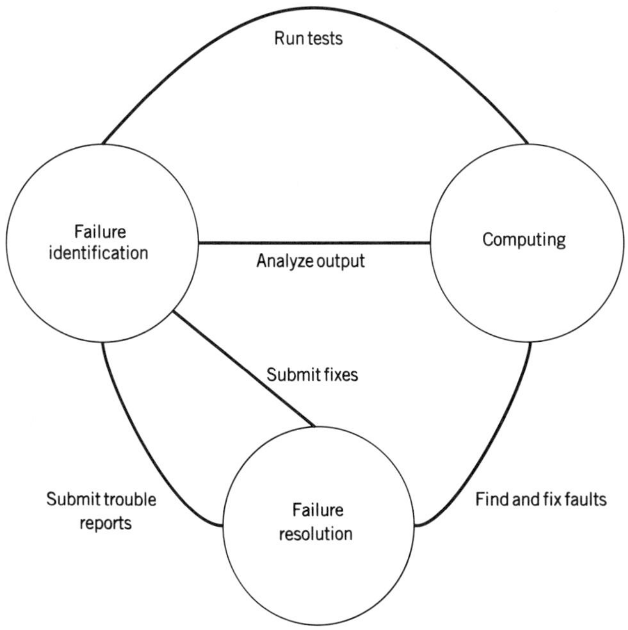

Figure 5. Queueing network model for system testing.

Configuration Component

The configuration component basically specifies the effective amount of each resource available during system testing, especially during the period each resource is limiting. Each of the three resource centers previously identified will be briefly discussed in the following.

Failure-Identification Personnel. The failure-identification personnel are the members of the test team. They run test cases and compare the results against program requirements to establish what failures have occurred, if any. They also generate a trouble or failure report for each failure identified, giving all the pertinent facts. They do not search for the fault causing a failure. The work of test planning and test case development is usually completed before testing, thus not ordinarily burdening the failure-identification personnel when that resource governs the pace of testing. The number of available failure-identification personnel, denoted by P_I, do not necessarily work full time on testing. "Available" only means that they be able to do so given sufficient notice.

The maximum utilization of the failure-identification personnel, ρ_I, is equal to 1 since utilization of this resource is not restricted by any queueing constraints. That is, there is no reason for available failure-identification personnel not being fully used.

Failure-Resolution Personnel. The failure-resolution personnel are the debuggers or developers available to remove faults from the software. They determine the fault that caused a failure, remove it, and prove that the failure no longer occurs. Resolution includes preparing change documentation during (not after) the testing period. The number of available failure-resolution personnel is denoted by P_F. "Available" is used with the same meaning as for the failure-identification personnel.

Unfortunately, available failure-resolution personnel cannot be fully used during the early period of system testing (if they are the limiting resource) because of the unpredictable identification times of failures and the inequality in load among the debuggers. Projects appear to naturally prevent an excessive backlog of failures awaiting resolution from building up in any area of code by limiting utilization of failure-resolution personnel. Such a backlog could hamper further testing in that area. In measuring backlog, failures whose resolution is deferred for reasons other than availability of personnel to fix them are not counted. Note that the area of code is generally associated with one responsible person.

The queueing constraints on each debugger are modeled as a classical queueing system with random arrivals and random service. Both identification and resolution of failures are considered to be time-invariant Poisson processes in calendar time. Use of the Poisson process to represent the resolution of failures has two implications. First, the resolution of each failure is independent of the resolution of other failures. Second, the probability that a fault is removed during any time period of debugging effort is equal to the probability that it is removed in any other such time period. The latter is a good assumption, although it may overestimate the proportion of failures with short fix times.

The Poisson failure-resolution process also implies that the failure-resolution effort (in person hours) is exponentially distributed. Musa, Iannino, and Okumoto (1987) present data taken from the unit debugging phase of a project involving eight programmers that is consistent with this implication. In system testing, a constant component will probably be added to the distribution of time given for unit testing. This component represents administrative overhead and retest requirements and is usually smaller than the mean time for the variable component (Herndon and Keenan, 1978). It is not likely to have any appreciable effect on the relationship between utilization and queue length.

For failure identification, the Poisson process implies a constant arrival rate in calendar time for failures needing to be fixed. It also requires a random assignment of failures among the failure-resolution personnel.

The random assignment assumption is reasonable since usually no section of code (and the programmer responsible for it) is favored during testing. If an evolving (being integrated piecemeal) program is under test, random assignment can still occur as long as each debugger has some code in the part of the system being tested. If not, this case can still be handled by applying an appropriate correction based on the debuggers who are involved. For example, the number of debuggers can be equated to the average number to whom failures can be assigned.

A theoretical demonstration that the arrival of failures with respect to calendar time is constant during the period when the failure-resolution personnel are limiting was given in Musa, Iannino, and Okumoto (1987) and independently verified by Ehrlich and Ejzak (1988). The arrival rate λ has a value of $P_F\rho_F/\mu_F$, where ρ_F is the utilization of each debugger and is defined (in queueing theory) as the ratio of the arrival rate to the service rate. The arrival rate of failures needing resolution to each debugger is λ/P_F and the service rate of each debugger is $1/\mu_F$. Thus

$$\rho_F = \frac{\lambda\mu_F}{P_F} \tag{13}$$

The probability that a debugger has a queue of m_Q or more failures awaiting resolution or being corrected is $\rho_F^{m_Q}$ in the steady state (Kleinrock, 1975). The probability P_{m_Q} that no debugger has m_Q or more failures queued is

$$P_{m_Q} = (1 - \rho_F^{m_Q})^{P_F} \tag{14}$$

Hence, no debugger has m_Q or more failures to work on at any given time with probability P_{m_Q} if ρ_F is limited to

$$\rho_F = (1 - P_{m_Q}^{1/P_F})^{1/m_Q} \tag{15}$$

If ρ_F is controlled at the preceding value, then the effective manpower, under the constraint of preventing excessive backlogs, is maximized. The topic of what queue length is most commonly encountered is a matter for further research. Musa, Iannino, and Okumoto (1987) suggest using 5 until more data are available.

Using the steady-state value of probability for queue length results in slightly overestimating the time expended, as queues are shorter during the buildup transient. However, the identification and resolution of failures were also assumed to be parallel processes. Since resolution always follows identification, there are intervals at the start and the end of the testing phase during which only one process is occurring. This assumption results in a small underestimate of calendar time expended. The two preceding factors are assumed to approximately cancel. (See also Debugging in distributed systems.)

Computer Time. Computer time represents the computer facilities necessary for the failure-identification and failure-resolution personnel to do their jobs. Available computer time is denoted by P_C and is measured in terms of prescribed work periods to put it on the same basis as personnel. The prescribed work period is the standard work week for which personnel are normally available. It can be greater than 40 hours if overtime is standard.

The method for determining the computer utilization factor ρ_C depends on whether turnaround time or response time can be controlled or not. In the case of a small project using a general-purpose computation facility, it usually cannot. Here ρ_C should be set to its measured value. If wait time is much greater than usual and it cannot be profitably used in other activities, then μ_F should be increased by the ratio of correction work time plus excess wait time to correction work time. In the case of larger project that uses a major portion of the computer's load, ρ_C may be controllable. If so, then its value should be set to obtain good turnaround or response. Response is probably most important, since almost all failure-identification and resolution activity is interactive. Frequently, utilization is controlled by providing sufficient hardware to maintain it at an economic optimum. The sum of computing costs and wait time (for response) costs of software is minimized. When utilization is high, response is poor and salary costs (due to waiting) are high, although direct computing costs are low. When utilization is low, response is excellent and salary costs are low, but direct computing costs are high. Minimum overall cost occurs at some intermediate value of utilization.

Workload Component

Relating calendar time to execution time requires knowledge of how resource requirements are related to execution time. These requirements are approximated by a model of the form

$$\chi_r = \theta_r\tau + \mu_r\mu(\tau) \tag{16}$$

where r denotes a resource ($r=C$, F, or I for computer time, failure-identification personnel, or failure-resolution personnel, respectively), χ_r is the resource requirement, θ_r

is the average resource usage rate with execution time, μ_r is the average resource usage per failure, τ is the execution time, and $\mu(\tau)$ is the mean-value function. Resource usage represents a resource applied for a time period; for example, one person hour.

Consider a test team that is working with a particular piece of software. If they conduct two hours of testing rather than one, they will have twice the amount of work to do. There will be about twice the amount of output to examine, and they will spend twice as much time conducting tests. The work effort related to failures experienced will be dependent on the number. A failure report must be written whenever a failure occurs. Some time is needed to check the requirements to determine whether each suspected failure really is one. The test team may have to record some information and perhaps make a couple of runs to get all the pertinent facts about the particular failure. Note that mean failures is used to estimate effort, so that mean resource requirements are obtained.

For failure resolution, required resources depend only on the mean failures experienced. However, computer time is expended for both identification and resolution of failures. Thus computer time used depends on the amount of execution time and the number of failures.

These arguments certainly make equation 16 plausible; and indeed, it was validated in Musa, Iannino, and Okumoto (1987) using data from various projects. During that validation a statistical analysis showed that the θ_F term for failure-resolution work is 0. The invariance of failure-resolution work with execution time is also supported by data taken by Shooman and Bolsky (1975). One might believe that failures occurring late in a test phase are more complex and hence require more effort to correct. Apparently this hypothesis is false or there is a countervailing factor, such as increasing programmer experience.

Calendar-Time Relationship to Execution-Time. The rate of passage of calendar time with respect to execution time is related to the rate of resource usage with respect to execution time for a given limiting resource through the relation

$$\frac{dt_r}{d\tau} = \frac{1}{P_r\rho_r}\,\frac{\partial x_r}{\partial \tau}, \tag{17}$$

where $dt_r/d\tau$ represents the instantaneous ratio of calendar time to execution time. At any point in execution time one resource is used at its limit and gives the largest value for the preceding ratio. Thus the passage of calendar time is determined by the equation

$$\frac{dt}{d\tau} = \max_r \left(\frac{dt_r}{d\tau}\right) \tag{18}$$

Substituting equations 16 and 17 into 18 yields

$$\frac{dt}{d\tau} = \max_r \left\{\frac{1}{P_r\rho_r}\,[\theta_r + \mu_r\lambda(\tau)]\right\} \tag{19}$$

The point, in terms of failure intensity, where a potential transition occurs from one limiting resource r to s, may be determined by equating $dt_r/d\tau$ and $dt_s/d\tau$. The potential transition points are given by

$$\lambda_{rs} = \frac{P_s\rho_s\theta_r - P_r\rho_r\theta_s}{P_r\rho_r\mu_s - P_s\rho_s\mu_r}, \quad r \neq s \tag{20}$$

The term potential transition is used because an actual transition does not occur, unless one of the resources of equation 20 is limiting.

It can be readily shown that the increment of calendar time over a segment made up of one limiting resource is given by

$$\Delta t_r = \int_{\tau_1}^{\tau_2} \frac{\theta_r + \mu_r\lambda(\tau)}{P_r\rho_r}\, d\tau \tag{21}$$

where τ_1 and τ_2 define the boundaries of the region for which the resource is limiting. For practical cases increments of caledar time may have to be summed over as many as three segments of limiting resources.

The equations in this section were derived in a way to allow the use of any mean value function. Thus they are quite general and in a sense provide a calendar time component for many of the published execution time models.

FUTURE DIRECTIONS

Since the beginnings of software reliability, the application of software reliability models has generated considerable interest and substantial advances in the fundamental theory have been made. Coupled with this is a huge accumulation of practical experience. Yet some important issues requiring further research still remain.

The major emphasis of software reliability research has been and continues to be the development of models based on a variety of assumptions and techniques. The sheer number of models is often used by some to argue that the research effort has not been as successful as one would have wished, and that adequate models do not exist. An alternate view is that there has been an overemphasis on elegance and complexity (with the resulting lack of practicality) to model software reliability at very detailed levels; indeed, at levels of detail unlikely to be obtained in practice. Practical users of potential models are generally quite satisfied with an accuracy of 10 percent or so (keeping in mind the noisy failure data that is typically used). Some models consistently give this type of accuracy provided that good-quality failure data is used. A similar phenomena, of sorts, occurred in the field of queueing theory where simple models with assumptions generally known to be suspect yield quite useful and accurate results. Despite this, many researchers continued to develop more and more sophisticated models to try to explain what was happening in greater detail. During the next decade, the most fruitful research efforts are likely to be directed away from model building towards more neglected areas (see following).

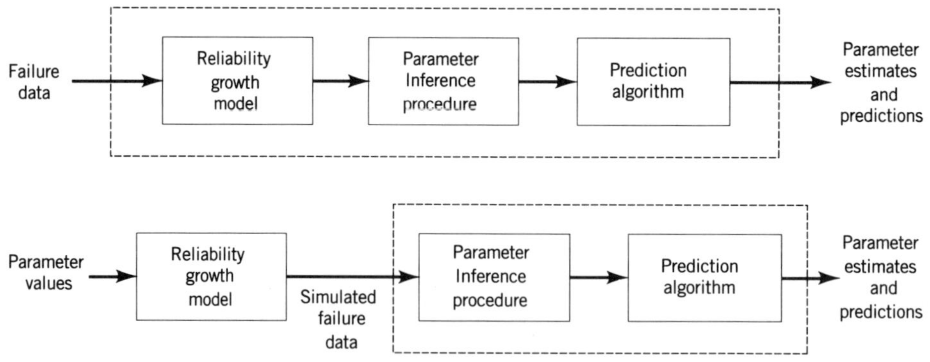

Figure 6. Software reliability model prediction scheme.

Major research effort is likely to be devoted to the area of improving model predictions by improving parameter inference procedures, providing advanced prediction algorithms, or a combination of both. All too often a model's reputation is linked to the quality or lack of quality of its predictions, not realizing that the parameter inference procedure or prediction algorithm used by the model may not be operating well. The combination of reliability model, parameter inference procedure, and prediction algorithm is called a prediction scheme. Littlewood (1987) considers three stages in making predictions: stochastic model, statistical inferences, and prediction procedure. Typically, the prediction algorithm is nothing more than a collection of simple formulas based on estimates made of the model parameters using the parameter inference procedure.

Figure 6 shows the normal way a model is used and evaluated. All parts of the prediction scheme are critical to the success of the model. In reality, what is being evaluated is the prediction scheme as a whole and not the model itself. A poor result is not necessarily a bad reflection on the model, since a change in the parameter inference procedure or prediction algorithm may result in a much improved result. In a sense, all model comparisons to date have been flawed to some degree because the model has not been unlinked from the prediction scheme. That is, judgments have been correctly made about the prediction scheme in total but not about each component separately.

To judge the quality of the parameter inference procedure or prediction algorithm, it is necessary to unlink them from the model and perhaps from each other. The following diagram shows one way of doing this. Rather than use failure data, the model is presented with assumed parameter values and it generates simulated failure data. The parameter inference procedure is then used to estimate the parameter values. A comparison between the estimated and assumed parameter values can be made to judge the effectiveness of the parameter inference procedure. If the procedure is not adequate, improvements or a new procedure should be sought. Similarly, rather than comparing estimated parameter values with known values, one can compare predictions made by the prediction algorithm with the known values. This sort of investigation is advocated by Littlewood (1987). In this way one can be sure that the results depend solely on the performance of the parameter inference procedure or prediction algorithm. It is essential to find the best or optimal estimation and prediction technique for the leading models (for example, the exponential nonhomogeneous Poisson process). Some promising work has been done, but much more is needed.

A variety of techniques can be used to test software (Myers, 1979); however, most of them exercise the software in a manner that is necessarily different than the way the eventual customer of the software will actually use the system. For example, one common technique is to test each software feature separately until the entire system has been tested. At times there may be significant practical difficulty testing large and extremely complex software systems under realistic operational profiles. There may be times when multiple operational profiles make it prohibitively costly to test the software separately for each profile. The relationship between failure intensity and usage is intimately tied together, and any nonrepresentative usage pattern runs the risk of poor or inaccurate predictions from a software reliability model.

There are two main problems requiring attention here. The first is the difficult challenge of defining a proper operational profile, both from a theory and management point of view. The second problem is to develop theoretically sound techniques permitting failure data collected when using one profile to be adjusted or transformed so that reliability predictions can be made for another profile without having to rerun or retest the software. Almost no research effort has been devoted to this area. A recent statistics paper (Beckman and McKay, 1987) provides the beginnings of a promising approach; however, much more work and research are needed before practical methods become available.

The execution time approach to software reliability modeling is generally accepted as best; however, the use of S-shaped models in Japan presents an inconsistency problem. These latter models are generally applicable using calendar time so that it may be possible to unify the two approaches using the calendar time modeling technique described in the preceding section. That is, the conditions necessary for a non-S-shaped execution time model given by $\mu(\tau)$ to be transformed into a S-shaped curve in calendar time given by $\mu(t)$ using the calendar time component $dt/d\tau$ should be sought. It may turn out that the calendar time model, based on the steady state behavior of a queueing network needs modification to incorporate the initial transient behavior that is probably characteristic of the S-shaped models. Research is needed to clear up this loose end.

In summary, the near-term future is likely to see, at a minimum, the following:

1. Fewer models being developed.
2. Improved estimates and predictions from the better models.
3. The ability of models to handle varying testing environments.
4. The grand unification of execution-time models and S-shaped calendar-time models.

BIBLIOGRAPHY

R. E. Barlow and E. M. Scheuer, "Reliability Growth During a Development Testing Program," *Technometrics* **8**(1), 1966.

R. E. Barlow and N. D. Singpurwalla, "Assessing the Reliability of Computer Software and Computer Networks: An Opportunity for Partnership with Computer Scientists," *Amer. Statist.* **39,** (1985).

R. J. Beckman and M. D. McKay, "Monte Carlo Estimation Under Different Distributions Using the Same Simulation," *Technometrics* **29**(2), 1987.

S. Brocklehurst, P. Y. Chan, B. Littlewood, and J. Snell, "Adaptive Software Reliability Modeling," in B. A. Kitchenham and B. Littlewood, eds., *Measurement for Software Control and Assurance,* Elsevier Science Publishing Co., Inc., New York, 1989.

W. J. Corcoran, H. Weingarten, and P. W. Zehna, "Reliability After Corrective Action," *Management Science* **10,** (1964).

T. Downs, "An Approach to the Modeling of Software Testing with Some Applications," *IEEE Trans. on Soft. Eng.* **SE-11**(4), (1985).

T. Downs, "Extensions to an Approach to the Modeling of Software Testing with Some Performance Comparisons," *IEEE Trans. on Soft. Eng.* **SE-12**(9), (1986).

W. K. Ehrlich and R. Ejzak, "Approximating Program Execution Time for the Purpose of Software Reliability Modeling," *Proceedings of the 4th Annual National Conference for Software Quality and Production,* 1988.

W. K. Ehrlich, A. Iannino, B. S. Prasanna, J. P. Stampfel, and J. R. Wu, "How Faults Cause Software Failures: Implications for Software Reliability Engineering," *International Symposium on Software Reliability Engineering,* Austin, Tex., 1991.

E. H. Forman and N. D. Singpurwalla, "An Empirical Stopping Rule for Debugging and Testing Computer Software," *JASA* **72,** (1977).

E. H. Forman and N. D. Singpurwalla, "Optimal Time Intervals for Testing Hypotheses on Computer Software Errors," *IEEE Trans. on Rel.* **28,** (1979).

P. Franken, "A Refinement of the Limit Theorem for the Superposition of Independent Renewal Processes," *Teor. Veroyatnost. i Primen.* **8,** (1963).

A. L. Goel, *Summary of Technical Progress on Bayesian Software Prediction Models, RADC-TR-77-112,* Rome Air Development Center, Rome, N.Y., 1977.

A. L. Goel and K. Okumoto, "An Analysis of Recurrent Software Errors in a Real-time Control System," *Proceedings of the ACM Conference,* 1978.

A. L. Goel and K. Okumoto, "Time-Dependent Error-Detection Rate Model for Software Reliability and Other Performance Measures," *IEEE Trans. on Rel.* **R-28**(3), (1979).

G. S. Graham, "Queueing Network Models of Computer System Performance," *ACM Computing Surveys* **10**(3), (1978).

B. Grigelionis, "On the Convergence of Sums of Random Step Processes to a Poisson Process," *Teor. Veroyatnost. i Primen.* **8,** (1963).

H. Hecht, "Allocation of Resources for Software Reliability," *Proceedings COMPCON Fall 1981,* Washington, D.C., 1981.

M. A. Herdon and N. T. Keenan, "Analysis of Error Remediation Expenditures During Validation," *Proceedings of the 3rd International Conference on Software Engineering,* 1978.

G. R. Hudson, "Program Errors as a Birth and Death Process," Systm Development Corporation *Report SP-3011,* Santa Monica, Calif., 1967.

A. Iannino and J. D. Musa, "Software Reliability Engineering at AT&T," *Proceedings of PSAM,* Beverly Hills, Calif., 1991.

A. Iannino, J. D. Musa, K. Okumoto, and B. Littlewood, "Criteria for Software Reliability Model Comparisons," *IEEE Trans. on Soft. Eng.* **SE-10**(6), (1984).

IEEE, "Glossary of Software Engineering Terms," *IEEE Std. 610.12-1990,* 1990.

Z. Jelinski and P. B. Moranda, "Software Reliability Research," in W. Freiberger, ed., *Statistical Computer Performance Evaluation,* Academic Press, New York, 1972.

W. S. Jewell, "Bayesian Extensions to a Basic Model of Software Reliability," *IEEE Trans. on Soft. Eng.* **SE-11**(12), (1985).

H. Joe and N. Reid, "Estimating the Number of Faults in a System," *JASA,* 1984.

P. A. Keiller, B. Littlewood, D. R. Miller, and A. Sofer, "Comparison of Software Reliability Predictions," *13th Annual International Symposium on Fault Tolerance Comparisons,* 1983.

L. Kleinrock, *Queueing System, Volume I: Theory,* John Wiley & Sons, Inc., New York, 1975.

W. Kremer, "Birth-Death and Bug Counting," *IEEE Trans. on Rel.* **R-32**(1), 1983.

J. Kyparisis and N. D. Singpurwalla, "Bayesian Inference for the Weibull Process with Applications to Assessing Software Reliability Growth and Predicting Software Failure," *Computer Science and Statistics: The Interface,* Elsevier Science Publishers B.V. North Holland, 1985.

N. Langberg and N. D. Singpurwalla, "Unification of Some Software Reliability Models Via the Bayesian Approach," *SIAM J. Sci. Stat. Comp.* **6,** (1985).

B. Littlewood, "A Bayesian Differential Debuggung Model for Software Reliability," *Proceedings of COMPSAC,* 1980.

B. Littlewood, "Stochastic Reliability-Growth: A Model for Fault-Removal in Computer Programs and Hardware-Design," *IEEE Trans. on Rel.* **R-30**(4), 1981.

B. Littlewood, "How Good are Software Reliability Predictions," in B. Littlewood, ed., *Software Reliability: Achievement and Assessment,* Blackwell Scientific Publications, Boston, 1987.

B. Littlewood and J. L. Verrall, "A Bayesian Reliability Growth Model for Computer Software," *J. Royal Stat. Soc. Series C* **23**(3), (1973).

B. Littlewood and J. L. Verrall, "A Bayesian Reliability Model with a Stochastically Monotone Failure Rate," *IEEE Trans. on Rel.* **R-22**(2), (1974).

B. Littlewood and J. L. Verrall, "Likelihood Function of a Debugging Model for Computer Software Reliability," *IEEE Trans. on Rel.* **R-30,** (1981).

B. Littlewood, A. A. Ghaly, and P. Y. Chan, "Tools for the Analysis of the Accuracy of Software Reliability Predictions," in J. K.

Skwerzynski, ed., *Software System Design Methods, NATO ASI Series* **F-22,** Springer-Verlag, Heidelberg, (1986).

D. K. Lloyd and M. Lipow, *Reliability: Management, Methods, and Mathematics,* 2nd ed., ASQC, Milwaukee, Wis., 1984.

T. A. Mazzuchi and N. D. Singpurwalla, "Software Reliability Models," in P. R. Krishnaiah and C. R. Rao, eds., *Handbook of Statistics,* Vol. 7, Elsevier Science Publishers B.V., North Holland, 1988.

R. J. Meinhold and N. D. Singpurwalla, "Bayesian Analysis of a Commonly Used Model for Describing Software Failures," *The American Statistician* **32,** (1983).

D. R. Miller, "Exponential Order Statistic Models of Software Reliability Growth," *IEEE Trans. on Soft. Eng.* **SE-12**(1) (1986).

P. B. Moranda, "Predictions of Software Reliability During Debugging," *Proceedings of the Annual Reliability and Maintenance Symposium,* Washington, D.C., 1975.

J. D. Musa, "A Theory of Software Reliability and Its Application," *IEEE Trans. on Soft. Eng.* **SE-1**(3), (1975).

J. D. Musa, *Software Reliability Data,* report available from Data and Analysis Center for Software, Rome Air Development Center, Rome, N.Y., 1979.

J. D. Musa and K. Okumoto, "A Comparison of Time Domains for Software Reliability Models," *J. Sys. Soft.* **4**(4) (1984a).

J. D. Musa and K. Okumoto, "A Logarithmic Poisson Execution Time Model for Software Reliability Measurement," *Proceedings of the 7th International Conference on Software Engineering,* Washington, D.C., IEEE Computer Society Press, 1984b.

J. D. Musa, A. Iannino, and K. Okumoto, *Software Reliability: Measurement, Prediction, Application,* McGraw-Hill Book Co., Inc., New York, 1987.

G. J. Myers, *The Art of Software Testing,* John Wiley & Sons, New York, 1979.

S. M. Ross, "Software Reliability: The Stopping Rule Problem," *IEEE Trans. on Soft. Eng.* **SE-11**(12) (1985a).

S. M. Ross, "Statistical Estimation of Software Reliability," *IEEE Trans. on Soft. Eng.* **SE-11**(5) (1985b).

M. Sahinoglu, "Compound Poisson Density Estimation of the Number of Software Failures," *IEEE / TCSE Subcommittee on Software Reliability Engineering Meeting,* Washington, D.C., 1990.

G. J. Schick and R. W. Wolverton, "Assessment of Software Reliability," *Proc. Oper. Res.,* Physica-Verlag, Wurzburg-Wein, 1973.

G. J. Schick and R. W. Wolverton, "An Analysis of Competing Software Reliability Models," *IEEE Trans. on Soft. Eng.* **SE-4**(2) (1978).

N. F. Schneidewind, "An Approach to Software Reliability Prediction and Quality Control," *1972 Fall Joint Computer Conference* Vol. 41, AFIP Press, Montvale, N.J., 1972.

N. F. Schneidewind, "Analysis of Error Processes in Computer Software," *Proceedings of the 1975 International Conference on Reliabile Software,* Los Angeles, 1975.

J. G. Shanthikumar, "A State- and Time-Dependent Error Occurrence-Rate Software Reliability Model with Imperfect Debugging," *Proceedings of the National Computer Conference,* 1981.

M. L. Shooman, *Probabilistic Reliability: An Engineering Approach,* 2nd ed., Krieger, New York, 1990.

M. L. Shooman, "Software Reliability: A Historical Perspective," *IEEE Trans. on Reliability* **R-33**(1), (1984).

M. L. Shooman, "Probabilistic Models for Software Reliability Prediction," in W. Freidberger, ed., *Statistical Computer Performance Evaluation,* Academic Press, New York, 1972.

M. L. Shooman and M. I. Bolsky, "Types, Distribution, and Test and Correction Times for Programming Errors," *Proceedings of the 1975 International Conference on Reliable Software,* Los Angeles, 1975.

M. L. Shooman and A. K. Trivedi, "A Many-State Markov Model for the Estimation and Prediction of Computer Software Performance Parameters," *Proceedings of the 1975 International Conference on Reliabile Software, 1975.*

D. L. Snyder, *Random Point Processes,* John Wiley & Sons, Inc., New York, 1975.

T. Stalhane, "Software Reliability-A Summary of State of the Art," The Computing Center at the University of Trindheim, SINTEF, *Report No. STF14 A88034,* National Technical Information Service, Springfield, Va., 1988.

L. A. Stefanski, "An Application of Renewal Theory to Software Reliability," *Proceedings of the 27th Conference on the Design of Experiments in Army Research Development Testing,* ARO Report **82-2,** 1982.

A. N. Sukert, "Empirical Validation of Three Software Error Prediction Models," *IEEE Trans. on Rel.* **R-28**(3) (1979).

M. Trachtenberg, "The Linear Software Reliability Model and Uniform Testing," *IEEE Trans. on Rel.* **R-34**(1) (1985).

H. K. Weiss, "Estimation of Reliability Growth in a Complex System with a Poisson-type Failure," *Operations Research* **4** (1956).

S. Yamada and S. Osaki, "An Error Detection Rate Theory for Software Reliability Growth Models," *Trans. of IECE of Japan* **E68**(5) (1985).

S. Yamada, M. Ohba, and S. Osaki, "s-Shaped Software Reliability Growth Models and Their Applications," *IEEE Trans. on Rel.* **R-33**(4) (1984).

K. C. Zinnel, "Using Software Reliability Growth Models to Guide Release Decisions," *IEEE / TCSE Subcommittee on Software Reliability Engineering Meeting,* Washington, D.C., 1990.

General References

J. E. Angus, R. E. Schafer, and A. Sukert, "Software Reliability Model Validation," *Proceedings of the 1980 Annual Reliability and Maintenance Symposium,* 1980.

W. D. Brooks and R. W. Motley, *Analysis of Discrete Software Reliability Models, RADC-TR-80-84,* Rome Air Development Center, Rome, N.Y., 1980.

L. H. Crow, "Reliability Analysis for Complex Repairable Systems," in F. Proshan and R. J. Serfling, eds., *Reliability and Biometry,* SIAM, Philadelphia, Pa., 1974.

J. H. Kim, Y. H. Kim, and C. J. Park, "A Modified Markov Model for the Estimation of Computer Software Performance," *Operations Research Letters* **1** (1982).

J-C. Laprie, "Dependability Evaluation of Software Systems in Operation," *IEEE Trans. on Soft. Eng.* **SE-10** (6) (1984).

M. Ohba, "Software Reliability Analysis Models," *IBM Jour. of Res. and Dev.* **28** (4), (1984).

J. G. Shanthikumar and U. Sumita, "A Software Reliability Model with Multiple-Error Introduction and Removal," *IEEE Transactions on Reliability* **R-35** (4) (1986).

W. L. Wagoner, *The Final Report on a Software Reliability Measurement Study, Report TOR-0074 (4112)-1,* Aerospace Corporation, 1973.

S. Yamada and S. Osaki, "Non-homogeneous Error Detection Rate for Software Reliability Growth," in *Stochastic Models in Reliability Theory,* Springer-Verlag, New York 1984.

S. Yamada, M. Ohba, and S. Osaki, "S-Shaped Software Reliability Growth Modeling for Software Error Detection," *IEEE Trans. on Rel.* **R-32** (5) (1983).

ANTHONY IANNINO
Pipeline Associates, Inc.

SOFTWARE REPOSITORY

See REUSE LIBRARY.

SOFTWARE REQUIREMENTS ENGINEERING METHOD

SREM is an acronym for software requirements engineering methodology and is also a shorthand name for the technology for specifying and designing systems resulting from a series of research efforts that started with SREM. The SREM approach is characterized by the following features:

1. The use of an executable graphic notation to describe system and software behavior (e.g., RNETs and FNETs).
2. The use of a user-extensible element-relation-attribute (ERA) language to describe the various system requirements and design characteristics, including traceability and decisions.
3. The use of automated tools to accept the above information, perform static and dynamic consistency–completeness checking, validate the specifications by executing them, and generate required specification documents.
4. The definition of a method for using the language and tools described as a sequence of steps, each of which adds a specific subset of the ERA and executable information and then uses the tools to check a subset of the consistency–completeness conditions.
5. An intent to provide a smooth transition from system requirements and design through software requirements and design and testing.

OVERVIEW

The SREM technology evolved over a 20-yr period to specify requirements and designs of ballistic missile defense systems, with alternating periods of research and application. It was primarily developed at TRW Huntsville under sponsorship of the U.S. Army, with some funding by the U.S. Air Force, and more recently, as a commercial product by Ascent Logic Corp. The development of the SREM technology has taken place in a series of phases:

1968–1973: Development and use of engagement logic.
1973–1977: Development of SREM (software requirements).
1977–1981: Development of SYSREM (system requirements).
1981–1986: Development of DCDS (system and software requirements, distributed and module design, and test planning).
1986–1993: Use of DCDS, Development and use of RDD-100.

Each of these phases is discussed below.

The Starting Point: Engagement Logic

The concepts of engagement logic were developed to provide a better way to understand the relationship between the desired behavior of the SAFEGUARD ballistic missile defense system when engaging hostile ballistic missiles and the distributed design of its hardware and software. The computer hardware consisted of 10 1 MIP processors, with multiple units of code scheduled in each processor. Because of the complexity of the design, new approaches were sought for linking requirements to designs. A contract was made with TRW to address this problem, and the resulting engagement logic was characterized by the following approach:

- The system-level behavior was described using time lines of functions for each incoming object.
- The function communications were described using *N*-squared charts as shown in Figure 1.
- The software requirements were described using graphs that described how input messages, arriving from an external subsystem or another system function, were processed using decision blocks and algorithms that accessed data files of state information; a fragment of such a graph is shown in Figure 2. Although the graphs were not formally executable, they were used as the basis for simulation of the computer system behavior.
- Each system function was associated with specific subsets of active stimulus–response paths of the software requirements.
- Each portion of the stimulus–response paths was traced to a specific task allocated to one of the processors, and each data file of the requirements was traced to a data structure, thus defining the software design.
- The software requirements were simulated to estimate the required execution time and memory, and the software design was simulated to predict response times.

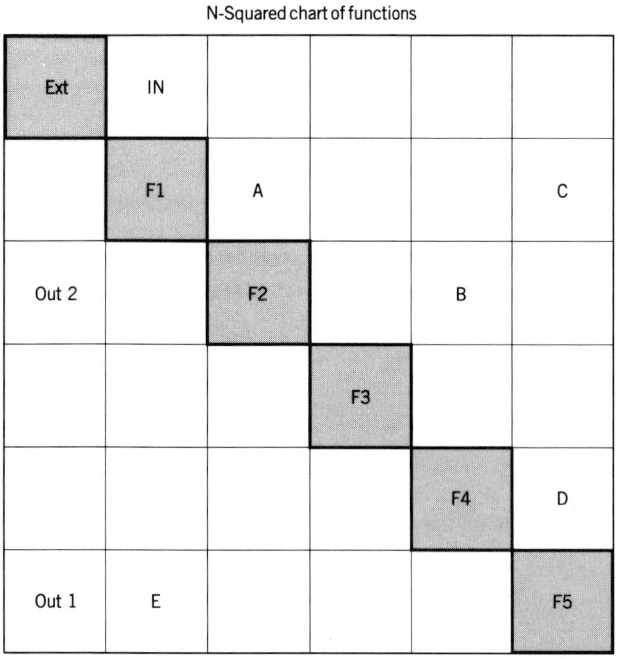

Figure 1. Example of an N-squared chart.

This approach was next applied by MDAC and TRW to what became known as the systems technology project (STP), which designed and developed a terminal defense system to defend fixed assets against ballistic missile attack. The engagement logic approach was used successfully to develop system and software requirements and a software design for two to three processors. The software was delivered significantly under budget and on time.

SREM

The success of STP led the U.S. Army to initiate research to formalize the engagement logic approach and to determine if it was feasible to use computerized tools to perform consistency and completeness checking. The research initially focused on two problems: formalizing the stimulus–response descriptions and capturing this information in a structured form. The research then moved on to the prototyping of automated tools to accept and analyze the information.

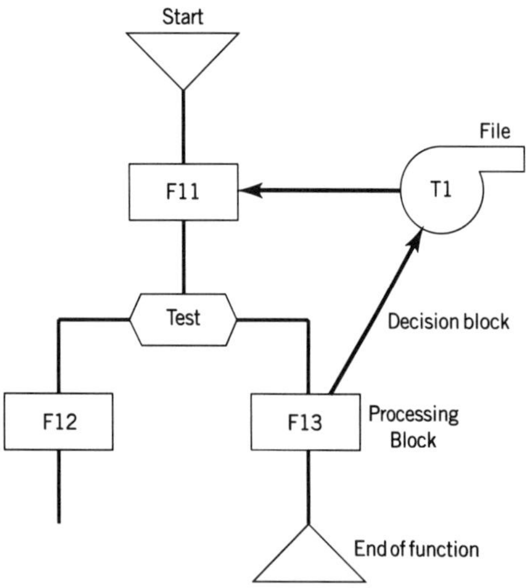

Figure 2. Example of an engagement logic diagram.

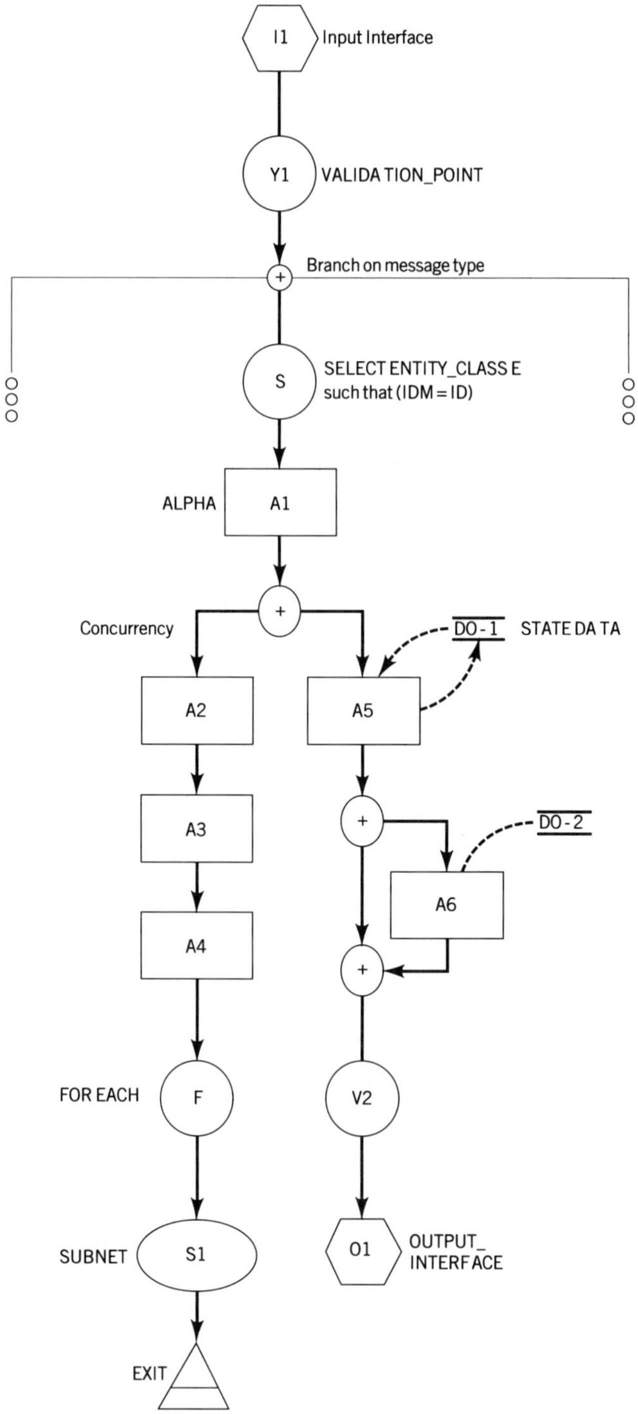

Figure 3. Example of an R-Net.

R-Nets

The heuristic engagement logic graphs were formalized into a set of response nets (R-Nets), as shown in Figure 3, that provide a precondition–postcondition specification of an extended state machine. The state consists of named global DATA plus the DATA ASSOCIATED with instances of an ENTITY_CLASS that is of a specific ENTITY_TYPE. When an input MESSAGE (consisting of a structure of DATA) arrives, it will be accepted by the INPUT-INTERFACE of exactly one R_NET; the R_NET then specifies the required processing, including accesses to state information, state updates, transformations, and output messages for different conditions. Each path of processing on the R_NET can be defined to be accomplished with a specified accuracy and minimum–maximum response time. These graphs contain the following nodes of the following kinds:

- An INPUT_INTERFACE node accepts an enumerated list of MESSAGE; only one arrives at a time and hence constitutes a stimulus to the R-Net. An R-Net without an INPUT_INTERFACE can be enabled at a regular time interval.
- A SELECT node, which specifies the condition for selecting an instance of an ENTITY_CLASS, makes its ASSOCIATED DATA available for processing and update.
- An OR node indicates the condition under which one of its branches is to be taken.
- An AND node specifies all branches of processing are to be taken.
- An ALPHA node indicates a specific transformation of input data to output data; it can also CREATE or DESTROY an instance of an ENTITY_CLASS, change its TYPE, or CREATE a MESSAGE.
- A FOR_EACH node iterates the next node a specified number of times.
- A SUBNET contains another net of processing that contains exactly one output branch.
- A VALIDATION POINT node indicates the beginning or ending of a PATH of processing, to which response times and accuracy can be specified. It could also be specified to RECORD DATA for use by an accuracy pass–fail test.
- An EXIT node terminates processing on the branch.

When the R_NET is activated (either by time or the arrival of a message), processing continues until all branches terminate, yielding outputs and state updates. The associated paths of processing then must occur within specified response times and accuracies.

Structuring Requirements Information Using Elements-Relations-Attributes

After the R-Net approach to requirements specification was worked out, attention turned to the search for a technique for capturing the remainder of the specification information. Some project members knew about the PSL/PSA project at the University of Michigan, which captured software design information using an element-relation-attribute approach. After some consultation with Teichroew, this approach was adopted. The remainder of the requirements information was captured using elements with attributes and relationships ιo other elements. This was used to capture descriptions as well as traceability and design decisions. For example, the ALPHA on an R-NET would be specified as follows:

```
ALPHA: TRACKING_UPDATE.
DESCRIPTION: "This block transforms old state plus a new
measurement into a new state which is saved."
INPUTS: DATA OBJECT_STATE,
    DATA RADAR_MEASUREMENT.
OUPUTS: DATA OBJECT_STATE.
TRACED_FROM
    ORIGINATING_REQUIREMENT TRACK_ACCURACY.
CREATES ENTITY_CLASS
DESTROY ENTITY_CLASS
SET ENTITY_TYPE
COMPOSE MESSAGE
```

This form of information capture uses a different template for each element, thus prompting the user to enter information previously found to be necessary for a complete software requirements description. This turned out to be ideal for the engineers working on software requirements. This also served as the basis for consistency–completeness checking. For example, an ALPHA that does not have a target of the INPUTS relationship suggests that the information is incomplete. Part of the research was then to identify the consistency–completeness conditions that should be satisfied by the ERA information base. This approach proved to be elegant (both simple and powerful) and was accepted by the engineers who had to do the work.

Prototype Tools: Requirements Engineering Validation System (REVS)

The key issue of the SREM project was whether automated tools could be used to evaluate consistency–completeness. The REVS tools were originally written in Pascal, a new language at the time. For a while, REVS was the largest Pascal program in the world. REVS performed the following functions:

- *Input.* Processed the ERA and text representation of the R-Nets into computer memory, and identified syntax errors (e.g., missing keywords and periods).
- *ERA Analysis.* Identified sets of elements that failed to satisfy specific properties (e.g., set of ALPHA without description, ALPHA without INPUTS). These were user extensible.
- *Graph Analysis.* When directed, REVS would walk the R-Net graphs and evaluate the completeness and consistency of the processing definitions (e.g., an ALPHA should not output DATA that was INPUT by another ALPHA located on a parallel branch of processing; all DATA containing in an input MESSAGE should be input by some ALPHA; all DATA contained in an output MESSAGE should be OUTPUT by some ALPHA).
- *Output.* On user command, the element attributes and relationships for lists of elements could be output. Also, REVS would drive a plotter to plot the R-Net graphs. A set of analysis and output commands would

be used to yield information that could be included in software requirements specification documents.

- *Execution.* When each ALPHA was replaced by either a BETA (containing code to simulate its execution) or GAMMA (containing code that actually performed its specified transformation), REVS would generate a Pascal program that executed the specified processing.
- *ERA Extension.* Almost every user liked the structuring of information but wanted to tailor the ERA language to include additional information. An extender was supplied for users to do this. The extender and extensible ERA analysis capabilities became the key for the later prototyping and implementation of the remainder of the DCDS languages.

REVS was developed on the Texas Instruments Advanced Scientific Computer and later transported to the CDC 7600, both providing approximately 15 MIPS and costing approximately $15 million. Early versions of REVS required many hours of computer time to perform input and analysis on these machines, thus making REVS unavailable to most software requirements practitioners and, if available, subject to high cost (although, even then, REVS could perform consistency–completeness analysis more cheaply and effectively than an army of users).

SRE Method

The SRE method was defined as a sequence of phases for entering and checking the requirements information for specific consistency–completeness properties. For example:

- *Phase 1.* Establish initial database of requirements, interfaces, messages and contents, and initial set of ENTITY-CLASS and ENTITY-TYPE.
- *Phase 2.* Develop initial R-Nets, enabled by arrival of messages.
- *Phase 3.* Define ALPHA inputs–outputs, establish data flow consistency and completeness.
- *Phase 4.* Complete traceability and ensure both traceability and design decision completeness.
- *Phase 5.* Establish performance requirements (response times and accuracies for each path of processing).
- *Phase 6.* Generate software specification.

Discussion

The software specification resulting from the application of the SREM ensures certain qualities that are often still lacking from other methods:

- Internal consistency, which is difficult to attain using less formal techniques.
- Explicitness, which requires clear, complete descriptions of what is to be done, when, and with what kind of data.
- Testability, which ensures that all requirements are directly testable.
- Traceability, including design decision traceability, which allows easier assessment of the impact of a proposed originating requirement change.

SYSREM

In 1977, research attention turned to the problem of specifying system requirements, defining a system design, and providing a smooth transition to software requirements. The result was an ERA-based system specification language (SSL), which included graphic language to express decomposition of functions, a new set of consistency checks, and a systems requirements method for using the above.

The goal of the research was to introduce rigor into the systems engineering design approach developed in the 1960s. Systems engineers are responsible for translating customer goals, desires, and requirements into an integrated functional description of the black box behavior of a system and associated performance. This behavior is reviewed with the customer to gain concurrence, and then these functions and their performance are decomposed and allocated to components, thus providing a systematic method of exploring the design space. Each design is evaluated by component developers for feasibility, cost-effectiveness, schedule, and risk: the process is iterated until an optimized (or at least acceptable) design is found. In addition, the designs are evaluated by the engineering specialties (e.g., reliability, availability, logistics, human interface, training, and manufacturability) to ensure that these aspects of the design are acceptable as well. When there is consensus on feasibility, acceptability, and cost-effectiveness of a design by all players (including the customer), this design becomes the baseline description.

The mechanism for defining the system behavior originally promulgated in the 1960s was to use the functional flow block diagrams (FFBDs). These provided a hierarchical approach for the definition of the time lines of function execution. The original applications of the approach was the design of a missile and its launch time line, so there was a significant bias toward representation of sequences and concurrencies of functions. The objective of the system requirements research was to enhance this modeling notation to make it executable and to provide a bridge to software requirements notations, using the concepts of decomposition, allocation, interface design, and fault tolerance, yielding black box descriptions of the computer system component (Fig. 4).

Function Nets (F-Nets)

Whereas SREM provides a stimulus–response definition of a single extended finite state machine, SYSREM used F-Nets to describe the decomposition of a function into a graph representing sequences and concurrencies of lower level functions. This yields an executable definition of system behavior in terms of a hierarchy of concurrent, interactive, extended, terminating, finite state machines.

The fundamental building block of the F-Nets is the discrete function, which inputs and outputs items that are

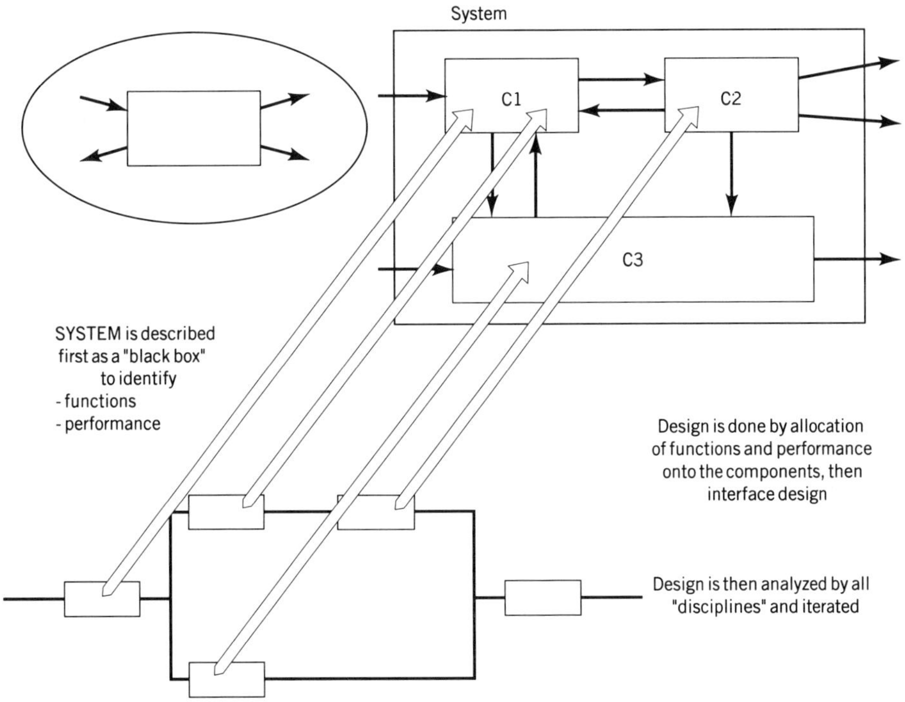

Figure 4. Fundamental concepts of systems engineering.

discrete and hence observable. In the Figure 5, a function F inputs a state item (leftover from previous processing) and one of items A, B, or C; after some interval of time, it outputs some combination of items X, Y, and Z; and exits with condition C1 or C2 (which enables a subsequent function).

Sequences of functions are described with a Function Net, or F-Net, containing functions, as shown in Figure 5. Time flows from top to bottom (indicating arrival of items to be processed) and left to right (reflecting inputs transformed into outputs). Looking at the black box boundary of Figure 6, note that first a peach arrives, then a can; that first a peach skin, then a pit, and then canned slices exit the boundary: these are all explicitly observable. The processing is described as a sequence of three functions. Note that state items pass from "Skin a peach" to "Slice a peach" and from "Slice a peach" to "Can a peach," and because they are inside the box, they are not observable.

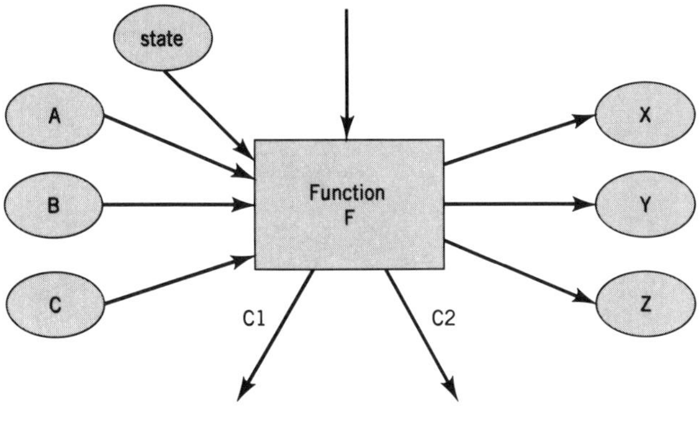

Figure 5. Example of a discrete function.

The function "Can a peach" cannot execute until the can arrives.

This notation is executable, i.e., it can be executed to yield the times of the outputs from the times of the inputs and the durations of the functions. Figure 7 presents a sample time line. Note that the empty bar indicates a period of time during which a function is enabled but waiting for an input, and a dark filled bar indicates the time required for the execution of the function. Outputs are available when the function completes. When incorporated into DCDS, the SSL was translated into an Ada simulator, which provided a direct execution of the processing, yielding estimates of time lines and resource use.

The functions can be placed into graphs containing not just sequences but selections, iterations, loops, concurrencies, and replications as well. The notation for these graphic constructs appears in Figure 8.

The replication construct requires a special word of explanation. One defines the domain of replication (e.g., for each aircraft in track, for each user of the system) and then defines one function per replicate. In this way, users do not have to deal explicitly with indices of functions to define them. Finally, a coordination function is defined, which accepts status from the replicates and generates controls back to them. The coordination function is responsible for detecting and resolving all conflicts between the replicates (e.g., two aircraft collide or priority is given to certain users if there are insufficient resources to service all).

To deal with large models, a graph of functions can be aggregated into a higher level constructed called a Time Function, i.e., a function that inputs and outputs specified sequences of items called Time Items. In Figure 9, a graph

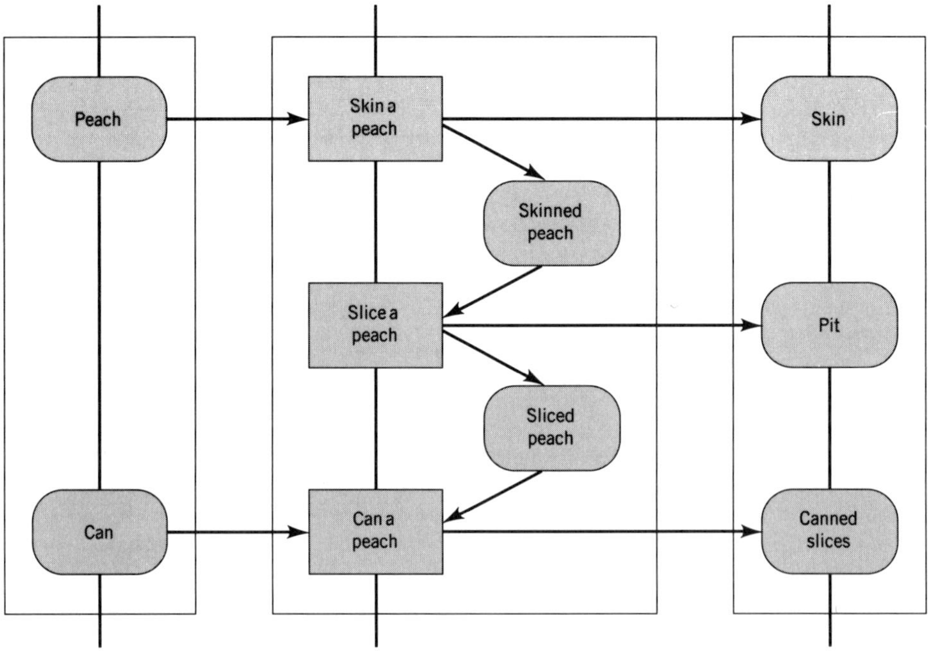

Figure 6. Example sequence.

of functions is defined in which F1 inputs A and outputs S and then, depending on the conditions of the input, either enables F2 (which inputs B) or F3 (which inputs C and outputs D). The whole graph of functions exits by the completion of condition E1 or E2. When these functions are aggregated into the higher level function F123 and the inputs to the graph of functions are aggregated into the higher level item ABC, it is defined as the graph of lower level items (i.e., first A, then either B or C). Similarly, the output of F123 is defined to be the graph of items. Thus function F123 inputs ABC and outputs DE, when all are decomposed, the original is graph is returned.

Functional decomposition reverses the aggregation process, defining a graph of functions, which preserve specific properties of the original function (i.e., input–output content and sequence, number and kinds of exits, and ability to calculate the performance of the parent function from the performance indices of the functions on the graph). The aggregation or decomposition procedure can be recursive to organize a graph of arbitrary size and complexity into a hierarchy of functions and their decompositions to support understandability.

When the desired behavior of a system is defined, functions are allocated to the system components. Figure 10 illustrates this process. The black box behavior of the system is decomposed to the level that functions can be partitioned and allocated to the components of a postulated architecture (e.g., C1, C2 and C3, shown in the upper right). Note that the allocation yields the requirements for a new interface function labeled IF, which is decomposed and allocated between sender and receiver (and possibly a communications component). This process can be recursively applied to yield layers of interface design. The resulting allocated functions, including those implementing the interface design, then are extracted to yield the black box behavior of a component. The extraction process can be implemented by projection operators.

This notation thus provides the system designer with the ability to define an executable description of the desired behavior and its allocation to components. It supports separation of concerns (e.g., separation of normal from exceptional behavior, single object behavior from behavior to coordinate concurrent functionality, and normal from interface behavior).

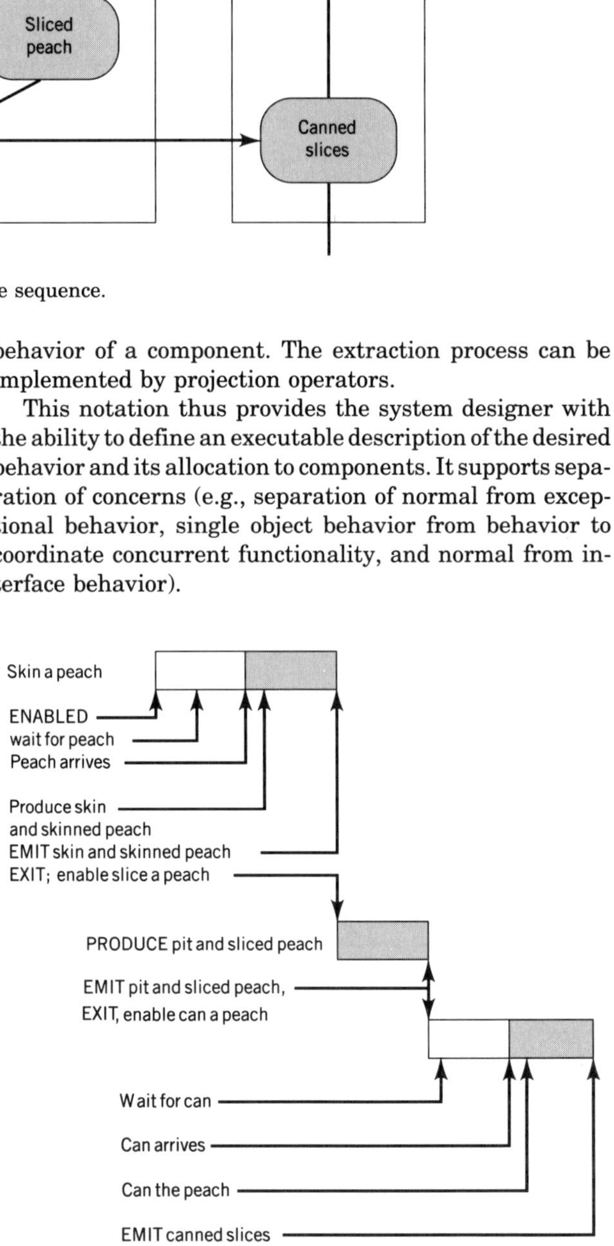

Figure 7. Sample time line.

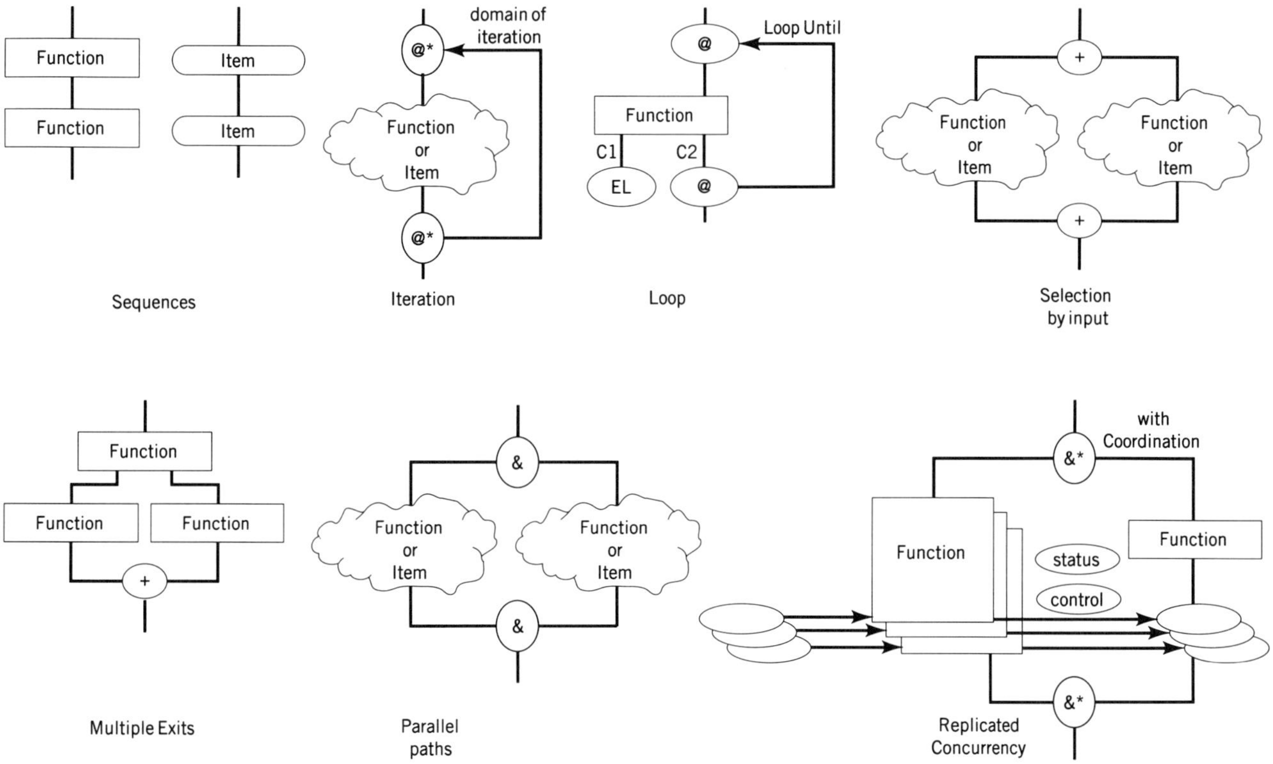

Figure 8. Behavior graph constructs.

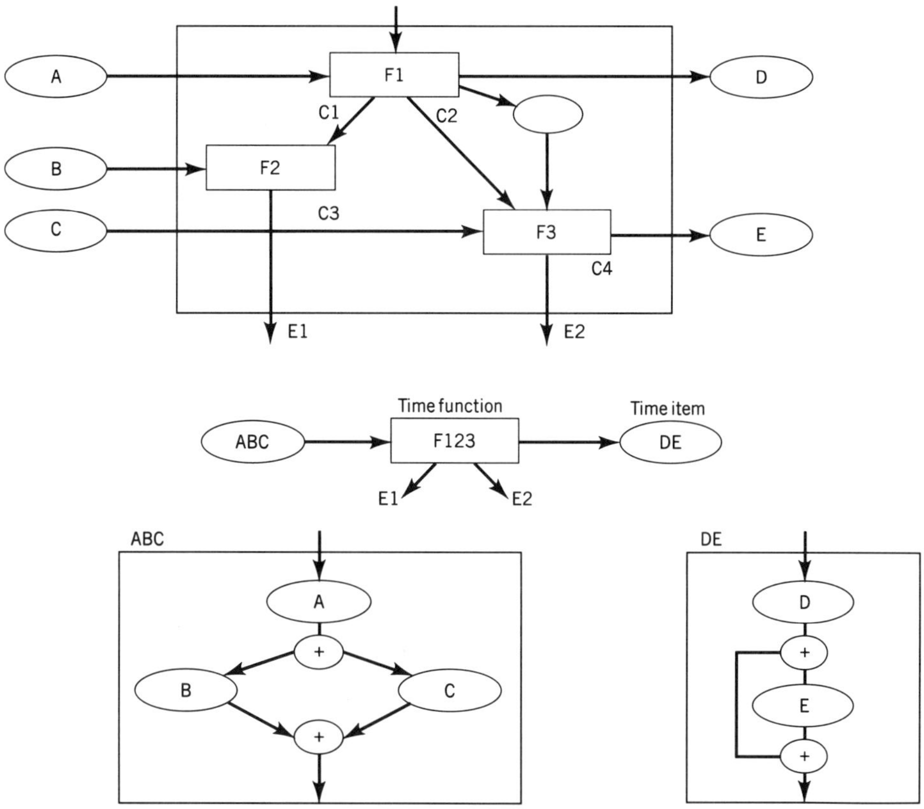

Figure 9. Example of aggregation.

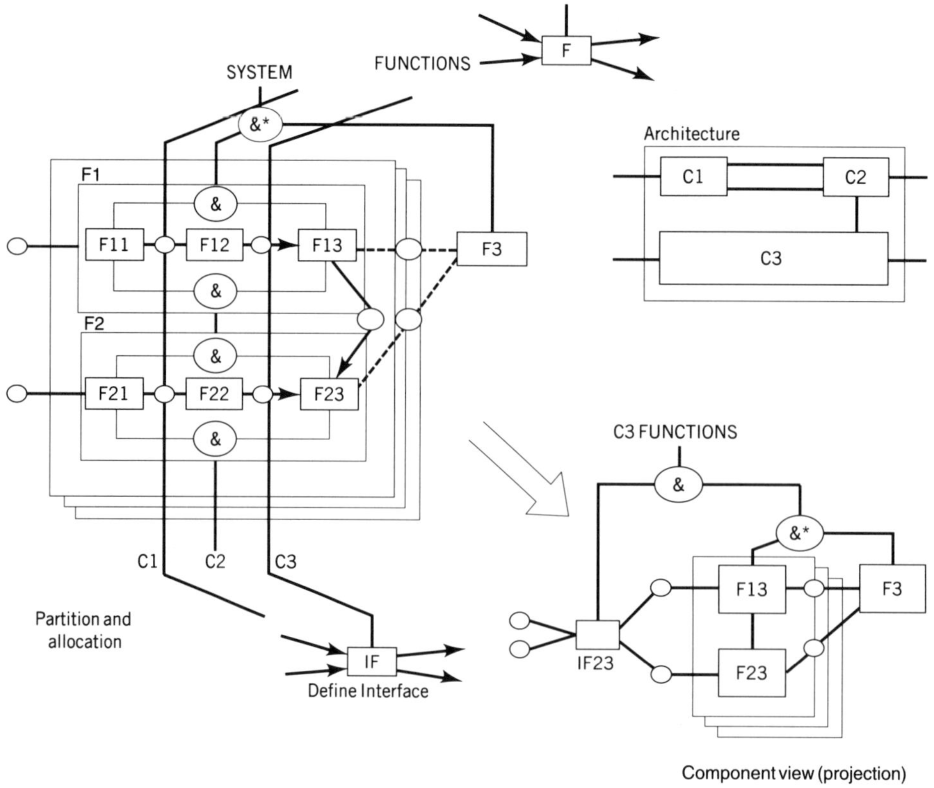

Figure 10. Allocation of functions to components.

System Requirements Method

The SYSREM approach to using the above concepts to perform a system design that establishes a requirements baseline, defines the black box system, postulates an architecture of components, defines observable behavior (first with scenarios, then integrated, then adding detection and recovery from environment anomalies), allocates functions to components, defines interfaces, estimates feasibility (including cost, schedule, and risk), adds functionality to detect and recover from component faults, repeats all for multiple designs, performs trade-offs, selects the final design, and publishes a specification. The link to SREM is as follows: each discrete function allocated to the computer system is decomposed into a SUBNET of an R_NET; each discrete item entering the computer system is defined as a MESSAGE; the interface functions are decomposed to yield the R_NETs that accept the messages and invoke the subnets of processing of the functions. Each discrete function that inputs a state item is mapped onto an ENTITY_TYPE which associates the state DATA. This provides a smooth transition between the system and software or processing requirements.

DISTRIBUTED COMPUTING DESIGN SYSTEM (DCDS)

The next phase of research addressed the problem of designing the distributed computing system and defining both hardware and software architectures and their relationships. The approach selected was to use the decompose–allocate–interface design approach, described above, to define three kinds of mappings:

- Mapping required processing onto modules, described by a module design language (MDL).
- Packaging the required processing onto tasks and files (or data objects) that are allocated onto the the distributed processors, described by the distributed design language (DDL).
- Mapping required processing onto integration test cases, defined by a test support language (TSL).

In its original form, the tasks, files, and modules were to be implemented by program and procedure constructs of a real-time Pascal: the languages were later augmented to describe designs implemented in Ada (e.g., tasks, packages, and procedures). MDL and DDL provide a separation of concerns between packaging for reusability and packaging of software for distribution onto processors, yet were tightly coupled. MDM must know whether an algorithm needs to be designed to minimize processing time or memory, whereas the DDM must know how big the modules are (memory and execution time) to know how to package them to fit into the processors and not exceed processing time, memory, or communication rates.

The SREM REVS tools were extended to accept these languages, perform consistency–completeness checking, and generate required documentation. Each of these languages and their associated methodologies are described below.

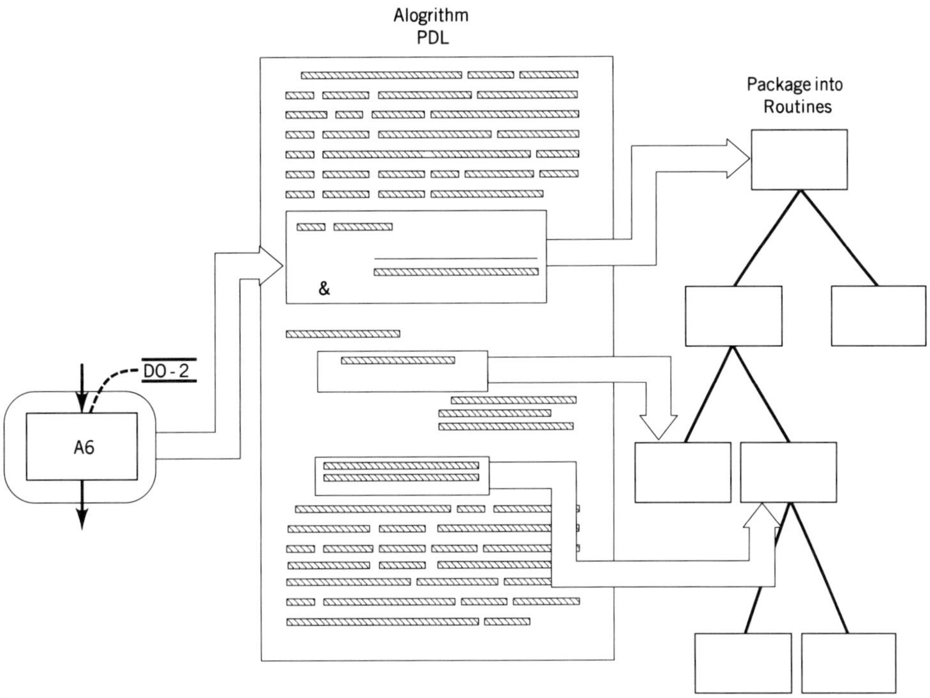

Figure 11. Mapping requirements of modules.

MDL and MDM

The primary goals of MDM are to support critical algorithm investigation and develop and support software reusability. It does this by rigorously differentiating among

- A required transformation (defined in the ALPHA).
- An algorithm (i.e., a sequence of steps to carry out a transformation).
- A module (i.e., a reusability element of code in a specific language that performs an algorithm).
- A routine (i.e., the lowest level architecture element of code).

These are tied together as shown in Figure 11. The ALPHA, representing a unit of processing at the requirements level, is mapped onto an algorithm (note, this is nonunique, as more than one algorithm can solve a problem), which is then mapped onto a hierarchy of routines to take advantage of reusability. The data defined as inputs and outputs at the requirements level are similarly mapped onto variables and variable constructs at the programming language level. This provides one way to implement the "Families of Modules" concept of Parnas.

Each module is then associated with estimates of execution time and memory utilization for use in the distributed design. These are then provided for feasibility analyses at the system and software requirements level and later to the distributed design methodology for their allocation to processors.

Phase 1 identifies the different algorithmic approaches for performing a transformation (more than one can be considered), and selection proceeds, depending on the expected environment assumed for the processing (i.e., the DDM phase should identify whether the processor onto which the module will be allocated will be tight for memory, processing time, both, or neither). Potential reusable units of code are identified that are to support different algorithms. The phase is complete when there is a recommended algorithm for each ALPHA.

Phase 2 identifies and defines reusable modules. Included in this step is the definition of their interfaces, identifying the variables input to and output from the module.

Phase 3 accomplishes the design of each of the routines. An automated unit development folder (AUDF) approach is recommended (and supported by the DCDS tools), which provides a systematic method of performing and reviewing the module and routine design, code, and test. Note that this step may result in the identification of additional routines, which results in repeating the above steps for each of these additional units of code. Phase 4 develops the unit level test plans, which also reside in the AUDF.

Phase 5 performs coding and unit tests. The completed code is then made available for mating with the distributed design and integration testing.

DDM and DDL

The purpose of the distributed design methodology is to produce distributed real-time software and hardware design at four levels of distributed processing: geographical distribution, local area network distribution, computer system distribution, and the software units residing in a single processor. Each of these levels address a separate set of concerns, and designs are typically performed top-down and then the entire design is evaluated for feasibility, cost, schedule, risk, etc. Note that any of these phases may be skipped when not applicable.

Phase 1 accomplishes the geographical design and addresses the problem of allocating processing identified in the software requirements onto a postulated architecture of geographically dispersed nodes. The issues addressed here include the transport delay for geographically separated processors (i.e., measured in the range of seconds), the unreliability of communication links, and problems of failing geographic nodes. This is the level that addresses the problem of allocation between space and ground. This may be done for several designs to perform trade-offs and select a best one. Note also that the geographic design cannot be completed without an estimate of feasibility and cost of the nodes.

Phase 2 accomplishes the local node design, addressing the problem of postulating a local area network of processors (communication delays on the order of milliseconds) and allocating node processing onto the processors without overloading local communications capacity or processor capacity. A central problem here is the design or selection of the interface design mechanisms between software in different hardware locations (ie, layers of communications protocols). Again, many designs are possible, with different estimates of cost, schedule, and risk, and the node design is not complete until feasibility is established for each of the computer systems.

Phase 3 accomplishes the design of each computer system. For each postulated multiprocessor architecture, by which communication may take place through shared memory, processing is allocated to the processors, and processor loading is evaluated. This may also address the problem of allocation of processing between hardware and software at the chip level.

Phase 4 accomplishes the "process design" of each of the computer systems. The primary problem of software design is to divide the processing into components (i.e., tasks that are the scheduled units of code and data objects or files that encapsulate the state information and provide specific methods for access) that define the required operating system services needed to support the design (e.g., intertask communication, scheduling, and computer fault detection).

The key issue is that, given the estimates of the execution times of modules, tasks, data objects, operating system services, and communications at all levels, the response times of the entire black box computer system must be estimated and compared with the required response times of the software requirements. Until response times can be ensured, the design is not feasible.

At each level of design, starting with the stimulus–response processing defining in the software requirements, an architecture is postulated, and the previous level requirements are strictly allocated to the design components (this preserves the overall stimulus–response processing rigorously). When necessary, processing is decomposed and allocated to the components, interfaces are designed (e.g., at the geographic node level, communication protocols are defined), and additional functions are added to support fault detection–recovery.

Because the MDM provides estimates of processing and memory size per module (and hence per ALPHA), the mapping of processing onto tasks takes place as shown in Figure 12. Note that if the allocation to software units is accomplished before allocation to hardware, the design is "location transparent," and locations can later be changed without changing any code. On the other hand, if the software units are too big, they may not be able to be allocated to meet response times without their subdivision into smaller units. The allocation approach to design is independent of implementation language and is equally applicable to function as well as object-oriented languages.

In Figure 12, the tasks are represented as parallelograms, and queues are shown as storing outputs from one task to become inputs to the next. Data objects (or files) are shown as encapsulating state data. Note that the sequences of processing through the tasks preserves the paths of processing in the requirements, so there is strict traceability and, in fact, preservation of behavior between requirements and design. Of course, the design will have additional fault detection–recovery behavior not specified in the requirements, but the original behavior will be preserved. Note also that the validation points become requirements for points at which information is to be measured to test the software.

It is noted that the design shown in Figure 12 (tasks, data objects, and buffers) is implementable in any programming language, whether functional or object oriented. This provides a uniform design approach for real-time embedded software independent of the implementation language.

Phase 5 performs the detailed design of the task control routine, and starts the development process. The detailed design is, of course, programming language specific is recommended to. The use of automated unit develop folders systematically to create and inspect the evolving design.

Phase 6 constructs an executable model of the software. In general, the first version will have all modules stubbed off so that they eat up the required execution time but perform no computations. A process construction system is used to read the DCDS database, access source files, combine them into compiler input files, and then download the resulting code into the processors for test. Phase 7 produces the required design specifications in the project mandated format and keeps it up to date as the project proceeds.

Test Support Language and Test Support Methodology

The key concept of the testing approach is that each stimulus–response path in the requirements must correspond to a specific path through the tasks and modules and hence can be used to define systematic integration testing. Accuracy can be analyzed by executing the paths of processing and capturing the required data at the points in the design corresponding to the validation points on the R-Nets. Response times are also keyed to these paths of processing at full load (hence accuracy and response-time testing can be separated).

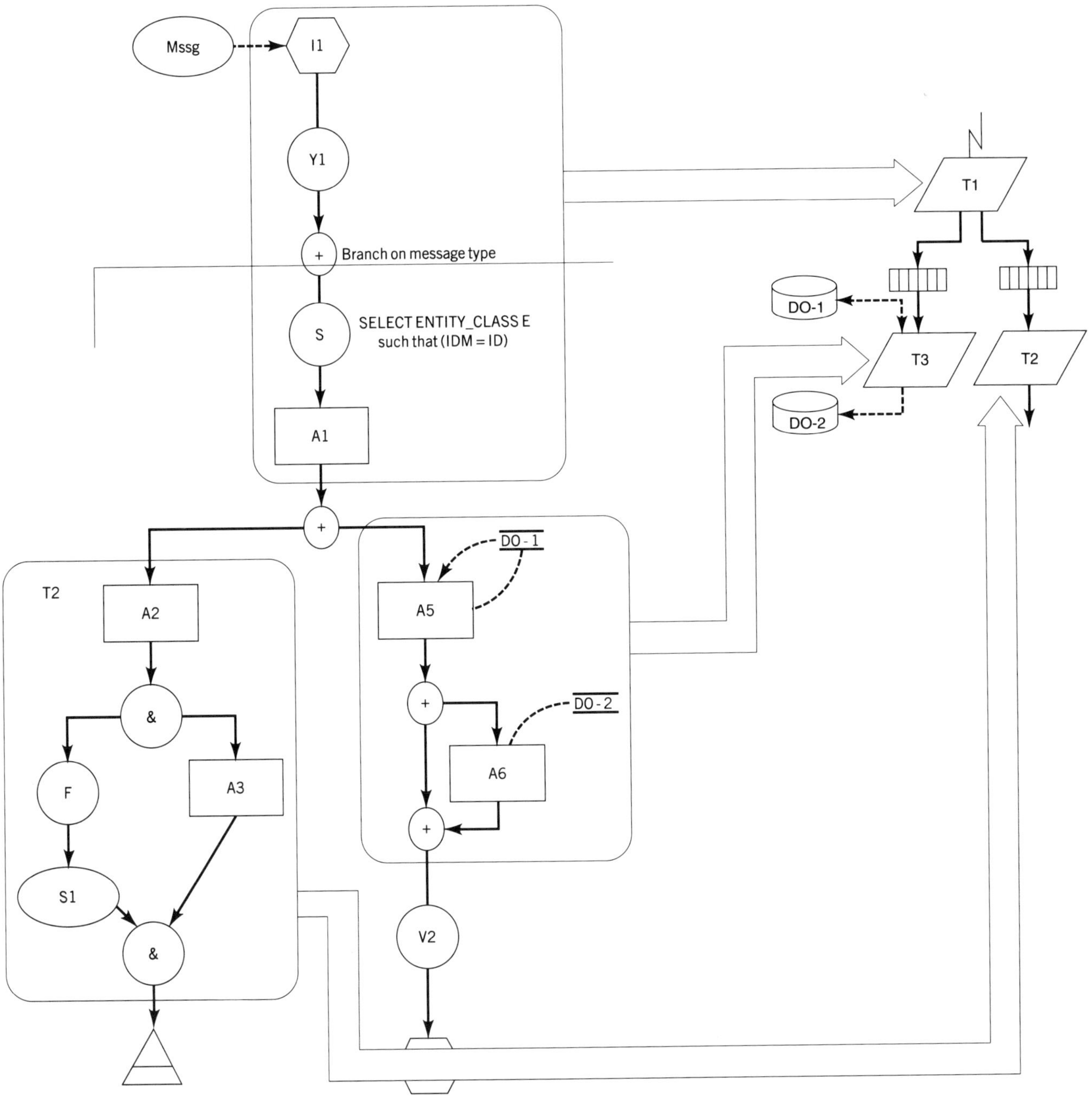

Figure 12. Allocation of processing to process designs.

Phase 1 prepares the initial test approach by extracting the appropriate information from the SSL, RSL, and DDL databases. This provides traceability from system through requirements and design to test. A software end or product acceptance plan and requirements verification matrix is established. This also starts the process of software configuration identification.

Phase 2 develops the test plans and test environment. Each test is associated with a software configuration, specific functions to be tested, a specific hardware configuration, specific test tools, and a schedule. This results in the definition of the program BUILDs. Note that this planning must be tightly integrated with the schedules for both DDM and MDM (obviously, one cannot test code that has not yet been built). In fact, this provides a mechanism for the test planning to drive the development schedules (a form of just-in-time manufacture).

Testing can be performed on a host processor (with lots of good debug available), a target processor (e.g., to ensure accuracy), or a test bed (to ensure timing at peak load). A total of 13 levels of integration testing were identified, ranging from testing of communication between tasks to full-scale testing of the black box computer system in its simulated system level environment of threat, sensors, and controlled subsystems. This is required to support the software preliminary design review.

In Phase 3, test procedures are developed for each of the tests. TESTCASEs are identified for all tests. This supports the software critical design review.

Phase 4 performs the integration testing according to the plan previously developed, using the code delivered by the MDM and DDM.

DCDS USAGE

At the time of this writing, the SREM–DCDS research has been essentially completed, after an expenditure of approximately twenty million dollars over a duration of more than 20 yr. Concepts of SREM, SYSREM, and DCDS were first used together in 1981 to specify and develop software to process data from an optical sensor. Since that time, over a dozen projects have been successfully completed using DCDS methods and tools, thus validating its concepts over a variety of projects and personnel. Because of this record of success, the Army Strategic Defense Command (the army portion of SDI) now requires all software to be delivered in a DCDS format (see SSS Conference).

Discussion

The primary strength of DCDS is that by 1985 it provided the first comprehensive environment for the development of real-time embedded system and software development, from systems engineering through integration testing. At each level of description, an ERA-based language provides for the structuring of the information and an executable model of behavior. Tools provide for incremental consistency–completeness checking, model execution, and documentation.

DCDS has three primary weaknesses:

- DCDS is currently primarily batch oriented, having been developed first on supercomputers (i.e., TI ASC, CDC 7600, which were 15 MIP fifteen million processors) and later transferred to smaller processors (i.e., VAX 11/780 with a nonstandard graphics work station). This was mitigated in the mid-1980s by rewriting the DCDS software into Ada and retargeting the SSL portion to UNIX work stations.
- These tools used substantial computer time (e.g., full consistency checking of a 600-function SSL model required approximately 72 hr of computer time on a VAX 11/78). This inhibited use by cost-conscious projects.
- Although the documentation of the methods and tools were and are available through the Defense Technical Information Agency, the DCDS software was by and large reserved for use by U.S. military contractors.

The combination of these factors severely inhibited widespread technical transfer of the concepts and tools into the software engineering community.

REQUIREMENTS-DRIVEN DESIGN

In 1987, Ascent Logic Corp. announced the availability of RDD-100 System Designer on engineering work stations to provide interactive implementation of the SYSREM concepts. The language was slightly revised to reflect knowledge gained since SSL was defined, but the basic concepts of a user-extensible ERA language supporting an executable system behavior description was retained. The interactive interface provides the following user-oriented features:

- The extensible ERA language was inplemented as a set of interactive "forms," and the user could literally fill in the blanks.
- Considerable user navigation features were added (e.g., any time a function or item name is visible, a separate window of the information can be opened, and users navigate information by selecting an initial element and specifying relationships to traverse, yielding a custom hierarchy diagram).
- Graphics editors provide user-interactive viewing and graph editing.
- Additional interactive graphics notations views of the behavior were added to enhance communication. Some views were fully productized (e.g., FFBDs, IDEFO, and function hierarchy), some were prototyped (e.g., VHDL and PDL), and many others were analyzed.
- Consistency checking was made interactive, reducing execution time from hours to seconds, with elements disappearing from the list as defects were corrected.
- An organic execution capability was added, thus providing near-instantaneous model modification and re-execution, and reducing debug time by several orders of magnitude.
- Document production capabilities were added, with interfaces to interleaf for more formal document preparation.

The RDD-100 system designer is fully supported with documentation, training courses, and hot line support. This has provided the necessary ingredients for the widespread dissemination of the technology into the systems engineering community in the early 1990s, with applications from SDI to the space station (see Hartley, 1991). RDD-100 users have extended its application to process modeling, enterprise modeling, manufacturing process modeling, etc. This suggests that the DCDS–RDD concepts have far wider applicability than their origins might imply. The remainder of the DCDS concepts have been implemented in an RDD prototype, but at the time of this writing, they have not yet been fully productized.

TECHNOLOGY ASSESSMENT

As indicated above, the SREM technology was developed over a 25-yr period, with alternate periods of research, development, and prototype application to validate the concepts. Its research results were at the edge of the state of the art for more than 15 yr. It is unique in its breadth of coverage, and focuses on providing a smooth transition between the different phases of system design. It has demonstrated that

- Executable specifications not only are possible but have become the state of the practice for practicing engineers on real projects. This provides an unanticipated challenge for software engineering, i.e., to develop design techniques that preserve the executable black box behavior allocated to the computer system.
- Information for each project phase of development can be captured in an ERA-based language and consistency–completness checks can be used to define and check each step for completeness.
- There is a feasible approach for design of embedded real-time distributed computer hardware and software architectures that has been validated on a number of projects. Commercial tools to support this approach are becoming available.
- The applicability of these concepts is not limited to software but to the definition of processes as well.

BIBLIOGRAPHY

Hartley, Application of RDD-100 to Space Station, 1991.

SSS Conference, 1991.

The SREM–DCDS research was performed primarily by the TRW Huntsville Laboratory, under funding by a series of U.S. Army contracts, the last of which was DASG60-85-C-0047.

MACK ALFORD
Ascent Logic

SOFTWARE SUPPORT ENVIRONMENT

See CASE; SOFTWARE ENGINEERING ENVIRONMENTS.

SPACE SYSTEMS

INTRODUCTION TO THE SPACE ENVIRONMENT

Humanity has grown up in a world which shrinks in comparison with the wide expanse of sky sprawling before them every evening. Even this view seems to shrink as the human race learns in school that the visible expanse is replicated innumerable times, in what Dr. Carl Sagan describes as "billions and billions of stars." Thus, space is forever linked in people's mind with the idea of something that is limitless or unconstrained. Contrary to this awareness, however, the development and fielding of space systems have been faced with multitudinous constraints from inception. In exploring the seeming contradiction between such a constrained entity in such an unconstrained medium, a definition of what is meant by "space system" is in order.

A space system is created to operate in the environment of outerspace as opposed to a system which operates near the earth in the presence of the atmosphere. Compared to most places on Earth, the space environment is extremely hostile to humans and to the systems humans build and use. This hostility is caused by the lack of an atmosphere, which would otherwise moderate the extremes of radiation, heat, and cold. Normal means of system support, such as ambient air-cooling, are no longer viable and so more difficult, costly methods must be used. An additional problem is the fact that even escaping the earth's atmosphere is not an easy thing to do. To ensure that a system remains in space for a reasonable time, it must either attain orbit or escape velocity. Very expensive launch systems must be developed to achieve the speeds necessary to attain orbit or escape velocity. Thus, a fundamental problem is encountered: the cost of launching each pound of a system into space is very high; therefore, components of space systems have always remained small and lightweight. Power on-board is either supplied by heavy solar panels or electricity generators. The size and weight of these elements can be reduced by minimizing the power consumption of the space systems they support. Because space systems must operate in a remote environment where modifications are not easily made, space systems must be extremely reliable, to reduce the need for repair, and modular to make unavoidable repairs manageable. Safe operation is also required of these systems to protect humans and expensive hardware. These requirements and constraints combine to offer a daunting challenge to the space systems developer who must skillfully balance them against the needs of the user.

Other articles have thoroughly addressed the general problems facing software engineers and the practices established to solve those problems. The purpose of this article is to survey these unique problems applying to data-processing systems designed to operate in the space environment. This discussion will also include current engineering solutions to those problems and will provide actual examples. An introductory overview of the history of space data-processing systems will be followed by a discussion of space-system design considerations including: hardware constraints, compilers and languages, communications and interfaces, software complexity and functionality, environmental factors, and remote maintenance. A discussion of quality assurance processes to "space qualify" data processing systems will then be followed by sections addressing unique aspects of: testing and simulation, autonomy, and problem diagnosis. The article will be completed with a perspective on future challenges facing the engineers of software systems for space applications.

INITIAL SPACE SYSTEMS

The first computers to fly aboard rockets were tiny analog flight control systems designed by a German engineer, Helmut Hoelzer in 1935. These devices were first used in 1944 by the German military to guide the dreaded V-2 rockets launched against England in World War II. For his scientific research which led to these "computing devices," the Technical University at Darmstadt, Germany, awarded Hoelzer the first doctorate ever received for research in Computer Science in 1946 (*Space,* 1987). Although these early rockets only passed above the atmosphere briefly on ballistic trajectories with a ground range of approximately 200 miles, early rockets do represent the genesis of data processing systems designed for space applications.

The first general-purpose digital computer aboard a spacecraft for guidance, navigation, and flight control was constructed by IBM for NASA's Project Gemini (*Space,* 1987). The first manned Gemini mission in 1965 contained on-board software consisting of a few hundred instructions. The software used in the Apollo Program to send man to the moon, required approximately 16,000 lines of code, while the on-board software required to fly the Space Shuttle has exceeded half-a-million lines of code.

DESIGN CONSIDERATIONS

As on-board software for space systems is designed to operate in these uniquely constrained data processing environments, software engineering activities must be modified in order to accommodate these imposed constraints. Virtually every design decision involves complex and tedious tradeoff analyses to converge to an overall optimum compromise among many factors. Significant areas for consideration include the following.

Hardware Lead-Time Effects

"Space qualification" of on-board computer hardware involves extensive testing to demonstrate radiation, acceleration, sterilization, thermal, and reliability requirement compliance. Safety certification of "life-critical" computer systems for manned space flight, typically requires multiple years. As a result of these long lead times, space-borne computers usually represent relatively old technology by the time they are actually launched (Hanaway, 1989). For example, the Space Shuttle on-board computers which were in use between 1981 and 1991, represent mid-1970s technology. In 1991 the Shuttle computers were upgraded to a newer, more powerful version which had been under space qualification for more than seven years (*Space News,* 1991). The effect of long technology lead-times, combined with the inherent size and weight constraints on space-based computers, have had a unique influence on software engineering efforts. The following paragraphs discuss examples of these influences related to the areas of programming languages, electronic and human interfaces, software architectures and designs, and maintenance.

Compilers and Higher-Order Languages

Data processing within highly automated spacecraft typically involves extremely complex functions, often required in real-time. Unlike large mainframe computers, employed for functionally equivalent ground-based data processing, space-based computers are restricted to relatively small memory and processing capacities. Therefore, software engineers responsible for space-borne software frequently have not had the freedom or flexibility to employ higher productivity programming languages or computer-aided software engineering technologies which produce object code more appropriate for larger, less constrained systems. Thus, programming efficiency often has, by necessity, been traded for memory and instruction minimization. For larger space-based platforms, such as the Space Station Freedom, these constraints have diminished sufficiently to enable ADA and C languages to be employed in the on-board software development. As new computer technologies evolve and achieve sufficient maturity for space application, these limitations will also lessen for smaller space-borne computer systems.

Communications and Interfaces

Design decisions with respect to the communications between spacecraft computers and other internal or external computer systems, can create special on-board software requirements. Interfaces between the computers and humans, sensors, and peripheral devices may have unusual attributes in the space environment. Data acquisition, on-board data storage, and data transmission activities for the Voyager interplanetary spacecraft, have placed unique software architectural challenges before software engineers (Jones, 1985). Because of the extreme distances involved and the large magnitude of data to be acquired, tradeoffs have had to be considered between antenna size, on-board data processing capability, and radio transmission power, which inherently involved heat dissipation and weight as well as electrical requirements. The optimum solution has involved on-board storage of the large amounts of data acquired in real-time. That information then has been later transmitted to earth at a much slower data rate than originally obtained.

Distributed workstation networks, such as those being developed for use aboard the Space Station Freedom, represent an altogether different set of design considerations dealing with: conformity of software applications to system requirements; network-operating system fault-tolerance; hardware and software configuration management; and processing dynamics across the network. Some satellite-assisted navigation systems even involve networked software systems aboard individual spacecraft within arrays of multiple free-flying spacecraft in different orbits.

Manned space flight has introduced new human-interface issues for software engineers to resolve. There are times during launch or atmospheric entry that computer input or monitoring devices are inaccessible to crew members due to acceleration or safety-derived constraints. Spacesuit gloves and helmets can further restrict human interfaces. The solutions to these problems have required additional automation and have resulted in innovative user input and monitoring techniques which uniquely complicate software and system designs for manned spacecraft.

Complexity and Functionality

Even though the size of space-borne computer programs are generally dwarfed by typical mainframe data processing and system control software, the program complexity of spacecraft software can exceed that of functionally equivalent earthbound systems by an order of magnitude. This high program complexity, related to the number of mathematical operations and decisions per program line, results from the combined requirements for sophisticated levels of autonomy, automation, redundancy, and fault-tolerance, with real-time response, performed by such compact software packages. Special software engineering activities are employed to provide the necessary quality and reliability of spacecraft software possessing these unique characteristics (AIAA, 1992). Also, existing Department of Defense standards are frequently used in the development and quality assurance of this special type of software (DOD-STD-2167A and DOD-STD-2168).

Environmental Effects

Software engineers must take into account additional space system architecture features as well as constraints on memory and speed. For example, the Space Shuttle General Purpose Computers currently use a memory technology which was known to be susceptible to upsets caused by cosmic-ray impacts. A cosmic ray has sufficient energy to neutralize an electrical charge within a memory chip, thereby altering a single bit of stored binary data.

In order to avoid any deterioration of the data processing function due to cosmic ray exposure, engineers have designed the Shuttle data processing system to include an error correction mechanism. This defensive design takes advantage of standard Error Detection And Correction Hardware which cycles through the entire memory, reading each memory location and checking for single-bit errors using a special algorithm and correcting any errors that are found. This precaution is accomplished by appending each 16-bit word in memory with six additional bits of encoded information which can be used to reconstruct the correct bit pattern of the original 16-bit word. If the reconstructed bit pattern differs from the actual existing pattern of the original 16 bits by a single bit, then the error correction function assumes that a cosmic-ray upset has occurred and replaces the current 16 bit pattern with the reconstructed bit pattern. This feature is very valuable since typical Shuttle missions in low earth orbit experience several cosmic-ray upsets of single memory data bits each day.

Depending on the hardware and software architectures for a given spacecraft computer, the software design can include a variety of autonomous monitoring and recovery functions which complement hardware functions such as memory-upset correction. In the case of a critical space based computer which is susceptible to frequent memory upsets, special load-balancing may be required and processing margins must be carefully managed by the operating system to allow sufficient opportunity for the memory to be checked and corrected in the background of applications processing. For example, the Space Shuttle computers complete this function for each of the redundant memories every 1.7 seconds to maintain full functionality for applications processing.

Maintenance

Space-borne software systems are expected to operate in the remote environment of space for extended periods of time usually ranging between weeks and years. The on-board software for space systems must be designed to be modified remotely as system performance changes or environmental changes are experienced. In some situations new technologies or innovations for improved functionality of a spacecraft may occur long after it has been launched.

All of these situations occurred in the case of the Voyager 2 spacecraft launched in 1977 on a spectacular twelve-year photographic mission through the solar system. During the mission, a number of system design assumptions changed or were circumstantially redefined. For example, several important sensors and on-board systems failed. This caused engineers to consider alternative and expanded applications for the remaining operational sensors and systems to minimize data loss and recover mission objectives. Also, in the years following launch, innovations by engineers on earth resulted in new applications for the on-board instruments, and enhanced techniques for telemetry data compression were developed. Expanded mission objectives were defined as it became obvious that the spacecraft was going to exceed its design lifetime. Additionally, a more accurate understanding of the operational behavior of the on-board systems was obtained as the mission continued. As a result of these combined factors, the Voyager 2 spacecraft computer software was substantially modified remotely from millions of miles away after eight years in space (Jones, 1985). The success of the final four years of the mission was made possible by the original design features which allowed this type of remote software redesign.

SPACE QUALIFICATION OF SOFTWARE

Because of the extreme cost of developing and launching spacecraft, and where national security, human life, physical assets, or valuable research are involved, proper on-board software operation is critical. The difficulty in developing and assuring quality software for space applications has significantly influenced software engineering methodologies and approaches for improving and demonstrating software reliability. Taking advantage of methodologies for providing higher quality software has had the effect of increasing the cost and effort of software development for space systems. However, when compared to the potential cost of a software failure on a space mission, increased software development costs have been generally accepted by space projects. A discussion of typical quality assurance practices for space systems follows.

In order for software to be considered sufficiently reliable for a specified type of space application, it usually must be "space qualified." This pedigree for a software product is typically achieved for a particular project only after strictly following a prescribed process, completing specific quality assurance activities, and meeting prerequisite safety and reliability qualifications. Required processes typically involve: exceptionally rigorous configuration control activities and documentation; formal structured design, code, and test case inspections; extensive testing; formal resolution of all problem reports; independent verification and validation; and a formal certification review (Macina, 1980). Development of software using this type of process may require significantly more time and can increase cost by as much as an order of magnitude (Rone, 1990). This decreased productivity effect has been offset significantly by implementing process improvements derived from the quality control programs to eliminate defects and the causes of those defects. One return on the investment in these activities has been a significant reduction in overall software defect insertion rates (Ryan, 1987). Reduced error detection and correction activities throughout the life-cycle and minimal maintenance during operational use are a direct result of minimizing defect insertion rates (Kolkhorst, 1988). This modification is extremely important, because the potential effects of errors in space-borne software generally preclude the more common earthbound approach of achieving a finite quality level and then providing appropriate maintenance resources to service subsequent software failures.

Total Quality Management concepts, based on the types of approaches successfully applied to critical space systems, have subsequently gained industry-wide acceptance and credibility (Scott, 1989). Quality Assurance activities may include: process compliance audits; code element criticality and risk assessments; and software defect analyses in which software failure modes are identified and errors categorized according to the severity of the resultant effect of such a failure.

Software Reliability Engineering is the process of actively managing software quality improvement and continuously evaluating failure history to determine when a desired reliability has been or will be achieved. This approach is finding increased application in "Space Qualification" efforts (Everett, 1990). In order to employ these methodologies the software engineer needs to institutionalize a procedure of archiving historical data describing every software fault and failure encountered throughout the software development and operational life-cycle. As methods for determining the trustworthiness and reliability of software intended for space applications continue to evolve, software engineers have the opportunity to use this data to evaluate multiple approaches and determine which ones best apply to their products, processes and environments (Kwan, 1990). Only after this type of empirical validation, are new approaches or techniques inserted into processes for critical space systems.

Developing "space qualified" software continues to present a series of unique challenges to the software engineering profession. An interesting illustration of the difficulty and potential impacts of these challenges is apparent from the experience of the former Soviet Union in the development of the Buran Space Shuttle. One of the major factors involved in the delays of the first Buran launch was the development of the necessary "Space Qualified" on-board software. The flight was delayed from 1985 until November 1988 partly because only three of the required fifteen "software packages" had been completed. By the end of 1991 the operational software was still incomplete (Covault, 1992).

TESTING AND SIMULATION

Perhaps the most unique aspect of space-borne software is the difficulty in simulating its intended operational environment. Based on concurrent design schedules, complete hardware and software systems typically are not integrated into the operational configuration until just before launch or deployment. To expect to execute an extensive set of development and performance test cases in the actual proximity to a distant planet or in the target earth orbit with all the expected environmental conditions the system has been designed to encounter is impractical. While the software is, after all, an abstract entity inherently impervious to physical conditions, software performance is totally dependent on the hardware in which it is executing and on the inputs and responses of the external physical systems with which it interfaces. Therefore, it is essential to create as realistic an external environment as possible for software testing.

Because of the expense and difficulty of actually duplicating flight hardware and environmental conditions, many engineering disciplines have jointly developed elaborate simulation facilities to allow software and hardware testing of space systems. In most programs, to reduce cost and schedules, only a limited set of all software tests are performed in actual flight hardware configurations inside physical environmental test chambers. The majority of the software testing for space systems is conducted in simulation facilities where a virtual environment can be created and controlled through computer simulations.

Many space projects have developed high-fidelity digital simulation facilities in which celestial mechanics, hardware sensors, flight control effecters, and other systems with data or electronic interfaces are represented or modelled mathematically. In simulation facilities of this type actual on-board software can be integrated with a computer-emulated spacecraft and external environment for testing purposes. For example, NASA developed three separate simulation facilities for the Space Shuttle on-board software. One facility was designed primarily for man-in-the-loop simulations, another combined actual avionics hardware and software for integration testing, and the third was created for software development and mission data verification (Macina, 1980).

Additional advantages of testing software in simulators, rather than testing the software in actual space hardware, include enhanced capabilities to: manipulate and control inputs to the software; closely monitor and extract outputs from software functions; and examine internal or intermediate results within processing operations. Automation of testing activities is facilitated in a simulator of this type so that test cases can be executed in minimum time. A simulation capability also becomes essential in attempts to recreate anomalies encountered in space when there is insufficient data to readily determine problem causes or effects (See the section Software Problem Diagnosis).

One disadvantage, which must be taken into consideration in simulation test planning, is the difficulty in modeling the actual timing of individual hardware system elements. Realistic hardware failure signatures are also extremely difficult to simulate for every possible failure scenario.

Tradeoffs must be performed between simulator costs, simulator development schedules, and operational environment requirements. Technical advantages and disadvantages of various simulation options must be addressed in the conceptual and planning stages of projects to provide resource planning. If existing simulators are unavailable, then development and verification costs for new simulation software and associated tools must be factored into project sizing activities. Simulation software quality requirements must be established based on the projected influences of simulation defects on the quality of flight software being tested. Simulation and other support software can exceed the size and cost of the on-board software significantly, depending on the system requirements.

AUTONOMY

With a few exceptions, most spacecraft have been nonserviceable in space. Future space stations may provide opportunities to maintain spacecraft, but in general, software engineers must assume that spacecraft are not retrievable or serviceable. Even if a spacecraft is originally required to be serviceable, future programmatic decisions, in-flight failures, or other situations may subsequently negate those intentions. Most spacecraft are designed to operate with as much autonomy as possible within budget and design constraints (Hanaway, 1989). Software is usually a less expensive mechanism for in-flight fault identification, isolation, and reconfiguration of hardware systems than designing those same functions into the actual hardware. Nonetheless, both hardware and software redundancy, at some level, is a standard spacecraft design feature.

In the case of the Space Shuttle, three and four levels of redundancy are used for many critical systems, including the on-board computers (Killingbeck, 1979). Software redundancy management can be very complex depending on the fault detection algorithms used and the combinations of failure scenarios the on-board data processing system must accommodate. Multi-computer synchronization for the Space Shuttle combined with the tremendous number of other redundancy management functions and extensive automatic system reconfiguration logic make the Shuttle onboard software system the most complex flight computer program ever developed through the end of the 1980s (Carlow, 1984). Timing requirements associated with the software corrective action may add complexity to space-borne software. This situation is often the case where extreme distances make ground intervention impractical or where a spacecraft can be destroyed if appropriate responses are not performed within milliseconds (Hanaway, 1989). Requirements to perform these types of functions significantly influence simulation and testing requirements as well as onboard software system architectures.

Software itself must be fault-tolerant. Designs must be unusually robust by reducing the probability of system lockups or loss of program control. Safe default processing modes for error conditions, restart capabilities, and processing overload handling are examples of fault tolerance requirements which may be much more extreme for autonomous space-borne software than equivalent ground based or airborne software where elaborate back-up control systems are feasible.

SOFTWARE PROBLEM DIAGNOSIS

Unlike a conventional aircraft, which has a flight recorder intended to preserve diagnostic data, spacecraft typically cannot accommodate the weight and power consumption of a nonessential element such as a dedicated recorder, which would have a very low probability of ever being recovered. Instead, spacecraft transmit internal status and system monitoring data to ground stations for recording and processing. The majority of the data in spacecraft telemetry streams are scientific data from on-board payloads or instruments. The remaining telemetry information is primarily dedicated for monitoring the health of sensors and instruments and providing sufficient insight for limited hardware failure analysis. Since software is expected to operate without failure during space missions, the proportion of the limited telemetry data available for internal software health and failure diagnosis is usually minimal.

Software engineers attempt to maximize their chances of diagnosing software and other system anomalies having subtle or obscure causes, by considering the need for such diagnosis in the software design. Within memory and processing limitations, coding techniques have been devised to log key software execution signatures and to store or trap critical diagnostic information that can be remotely retrieved from specified memory locations after an anomaly has been observed (Horne, 1982). Data of this type in the hands of highly trained "detective-like" software analysts can represent the only "clues" available in unraveling the sequence of software and hardware events which explain an anomaly or malfunction. For example, remote analysis of software processing events are greatly facilitated by capturing and retaining, on-board, a history of appropriate computation steps, parameter values, and program control state changes. Such data often includes an identification of the sub-program in execution at the time of the event of interest, and the modes or states of a series of control flags and error logging registers within the computer memory.

Because memory is at such a premium in space systems, arrays of diagnostic data are reduced by saving only the data from the most recent processing events. This procedure, of course, assumes that the data processing system is still sufficiently operative following the malfunction or anomaly to allow access and retrieval of the diagnostic data. Some computer systems have been designed with auxiliary hardware functions that can read memory locations and copy them to backup systems which can be used to transmit the needed information to analysts on earth. There is always the need to receive a minimum set of this diagnostic data "live" in case the data is actually lost or destroyed on-board by the failure event itself. Clever software designing, with this type of requirement in mind, and optimized packing of diagnostic information are some of the unique challenges faced by software engineers who develop space systems.

FUTURE OF SPACE SYSTEMS

As new space systems evolve, more and more functions such as fault detection and computer synchronization, are being designed into computer chips, thereby eliminating the need for software dedicated to these activities. Computer processor chip technology is advancing at a much faster pace than the space qualification processes for entire computer systems. Although this development is not unique to space systems, software engineers must design software that does not depend on the speed or other characteristics of a specific computer processor. During the lengthy space qualification process, improved processor chips will become available and it will be possible to upgrade the computer system by a simple replacement of individual chips. This process must be accommodated by future space software designs, not only to ensure compatibility for upgrading, but to take full advantage of the additional capabilities provided by the upgrade.

Requirements for increased autonomy, terabyte data-transmission rates, and longer operational lifetimes are certainties for space systems in the near future. Technological advances, including increased computer memory capacity, expanded chip speed and functionality, enhanced parallel processing, and artificial intelligence, are expected to be more fully exploited to meet these needs. Breakthroughs in increasing software development productivity and proof of program correctness are also among the challenges facing software engineers in their critical role for future space systems.

BIBLIOGRAPHY

AIAA Recommended Practice for Software Reliability, American Institute of Aeronautics and Astronautics Space Based Observations Systems Committee On Standards, R-013-92, 1992.

G. D. Carlow, "Architecture of the Space Shuttle Primary Avionics Software System," *Communications of the ACM* **27**(9), 926–936 (Sept. 1984).

C. Covault, "Russians Reveal Secrets of Mir, Buran, Lunar Landing Craft," *Aviation Week & Space Technology* **136**(6), 38–39 (Feb. 10, 1992).

Defense System Software Development, DOD-STD-2167A, Apr. 29, 1988.

Defense System Software Quality Program, DOD-STD-2168, Apr. 29, 1988.

W. W. Everett and J. D. Musa, "Software-Reliability Engineering: Technology for the 1990s," *IEEE Software* **7**(6), 36–54 (Nov. 1990).

J. F. Hanaway and R. W. Moorehead, *Space Shuttle Avionics System,* U.S. Government Printing Office, Washington D.C., 1989, pp. 3–6, 47.

C. G. Horne and T. W. Keller, "The Problem Diagnosis & Resolution Techniques Applied to the Primary On-Board GN&C Software Developed for the NASA Space Shuttle," *Proceedings of the American Astronomical Society Guidance and Control Conference,* Jan. 30–Feb. 3, 1982.

C. P. Jones, "Engineering Challenges of In-Flight Spacecraft-Voyager: A Case History," *Mission Systems—Journal of the British Interplanetary Society* **38**(10), 465–471 (Oct. 1985).

L. Killingbeck, "Space Shuttle On-Board Data Processing System," *Software Engineering Exchange* **1**(4), 1–15 (July 1979).

B. G. Kolkhorst and A. J. Macina, "Developing Error-Free Software," *IEEE AES Magazine* **3**(11), 25–31 (Nov. 1988).

S. P. Kwan, D. L. Parnas, and A. J. van Schouwen, "Evaluation of Safety-Critical Software," *Communications of the ACM* **33**(6), 636–648 (June 1990).

A. J. Macina, "Independent Verification and Validation Testing of the Space Shuttle Primary Flight Software System," paper presented at the *NSIA / AIA / SD / NASA Mission Assurance Conference,* Apr. 28, 1980.

K. Y. Rone, "Cost and Quality Planning for Large NASA Programs," *Proceedings of the Fifth Annual Software Engineering Workshop,* NASA Goddard Space Flight Center, Nov., 1990, SEL-90-006.

J. Ryan, "This Company Hates Surprises," *Quality Progress* **20**(9), 12–16 (Sept. 1987) American Society for Quality Control.

W. B. Scott, "TQM Expected to Boost Productivity, Ensure Survival of U.S. Industry," *Aviation Week & Space Technology* **131**(23), 64–69 (Dec. 4, 1989).

"Shuttle Computer System Upgraded," *Space News,* 8 (June 3–9, 1991).

Space (Understanding Computers), Time-Life Books, Inc., Chicago, Ill., 1987, pp. 9–13, 33.

General References

IEEE Computer **23**(7), 15–88 (July 1990).

T. W. Keller and N. F. Schneidewind, "Applying Reliability Models to the Space Shuttle," *IEEE Software* **9**(24), 28–33 (July 1992).

K. Y. Rone and W. A. Madden, "Design and Development of Space Shuttle Primary Flight Software System," *Communications of the ACM* **27**(9), 926–936 (Sept. 1984).

Space (Understanding Computers), Time-Life Books, Inc., Chicago, Ill., 1987.

T. W. KELLER
KYLE Y. RONE
IBM Federal Sector Services Corporation

SPECIFICATION DRIVEN TOOLS AND TECHNIQUES

Specification Driven Tools (SDTs) translate specifications to products such as programs, documentation, tables, and test scripts. SDTs represent a large class of techniques that have independently evolved under a variety of names including application generators, program generators, 4GLs (Fourth Generation Languages), automatic programming, lower CASE tools, and application-oriented languages. SDTs increase productivity and quality and are most successful in programming areas that are well understood and repetitive such as databases, user interfaces, and translators. SDTs are an effective way to reuse soft-

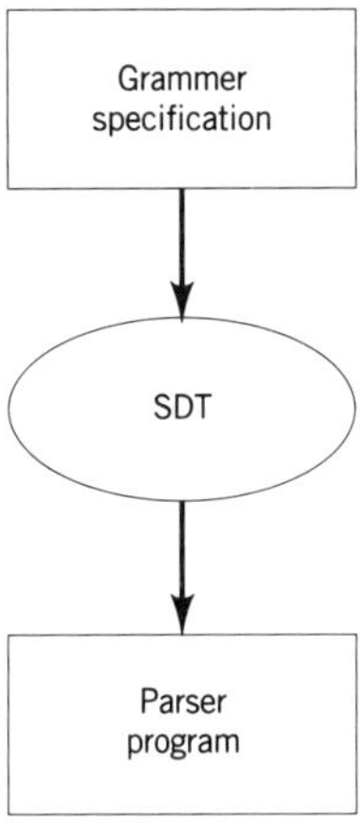

Figure 1. A typical parser SDT.

ware code and design (Krueger, 1992). Unlike code reuse libraries, SDTs generate customized software that is not modified by the user.

Figure 1 shows a typical SDT for building parsers from grammar descriptions. The input is a textual specification of a language expressed with a formal grammar. The output is a program that implements the parser. The grammar describes *what* language is desired; the program describes *how* to parse the language. The SDT separates the what from the how. The grammar description is much shorter and abstract than the parser implementation. The grammar is much easier to understand and requires little or no knowledge about parsing techniques or parsing algorithms. Someone using this SDT can produce a parser in perhaps one tenth of the time it would take someone implementing the parser by hand. A person using this SDT writes and debugs the grammar; he or she does not design, write, or debug the code. Subsequent changes are always made at the specification level, not at the code level. This means that maintenance is also significantly cheaper using an SDT. The SDT "captures" domain expertise in parser implementation and such expertise is reused each time the SDT is used. Productivity increases of 10 to 1 are not uncommon with such an approach across a large variety of problem domains. Quality is also increased because the reliability of code produced by a well-tested SDT does not have the accidental mistakes and errors that accompany code written manually.

The productivity and quality of SDTs is achieved by two major factors: narrow domains and understandable specification languages. A "domain" is the area of applicability. General purpose programing languages are useful for very large problem domains. In contrast, a grammar description language cannot be used to solve problems outside the domain of grammars. A parser generator is useful only for generating parsers. By looking at a narrow domain such as parsers, specific domain knowledge can be incorporated into the SDT to translate grammar descriptions to efficient parser programs using well-established parsing techniques. Thus while an SDT provides tremendous increases in productivity and quality, they can be used only in narrow well-defined problem domains.

The second major factor for increased productivity and quality of SDTs is the specification language. It must be significantly easier to understand than the generated code. It should be much shorter, should not contain unnecessary implementation details, and it should be understandable to nonprogrammers—ideally, the customer. However, specification languages are not necessarily simple. A grammar specification must still be able to describe all of the complexity of a language. The power of an SDT will increase in direct proportion to to the ease of reading, writing, and debugging specifications.

EXAMPLE PROBLEM DOMAINS

Before describing methods or tools for building SDTs, a series of example problem domains where SDTs have been very successful are briefly described.

Databases

Databases and information management systems have been using application generators and 4GLs effectively for many years (Martin, 1985, Martin and Leben, 1986). Such systems include various combinations of user-interface generators, report generators, and business data processing generators. Such systems avoid the excessive amounts of COBOL coding that would otherwise be required. SQL and other query languages make it increasingly easy to perform database searches (Jarke and Vassiliou, 1985). Although most such systems are interpretive, they could just as easily be translated to low-level languages and compiled (sometimes called "program generators") (Belanger and Kintala, 1985). Entity-relationship schemas and modeling of databases provides an ideal language (textual or graphical) for specifying database systems (Kim, 1986). Vendor independence can be achieved by SDTs by specifying a data base system in a generic language that is then translated to the various vendor languages and systems. Entire database management systems can be customized for specific application areas (including query processing algorithms, storage system) by such systems as EXODUS (Carey and co-workers, 1989) and GENESIS (Bartory, 1986).

User Interfaces

SDTs have been used to generate user interfaces for many years. Textual descriptions of user dialogues (that includes information such as prompt string, help information, expected range of responses) are among the simplest tools in this area. With the advent of complex graphical window applications, the use of SDTs is necessary to limit the expensive nature of user-interface programming; such code can be as much as half the application. Along with this increased complexity, user-interface tools have also increased in complexity by incorporating graphical descriptions and WYSIWYG-style (What You See Is What You Get) interactions (Myers, 1989). The use of such tools also promotes standardized user interfaces. There are also many user-interface toolkits that have been combined with specific problem domains. ObjectVision (trademark of Borland) uses decision trees and spreadsheet as actions to guide a user-process through a series of forms. ProKappa (trademark of Intellicorp) combines logic programming with data extraction for the analysis and display of data.

Translators

A traditional use of SDTs is in the area of building translators. Lexical analysis and parsers are particularly good candidates because of the tedious and error prone nature of building lexer and parser tables by hand. Compilers also have well understood optimization and code generator phases that can be automated with SDTs (Aho, Sethi, and Ullman, 1986). Interface Description Language (IDL) can be used to automate the production of a suite of useful subroutines and programs that read and write interfaces between program segments (SIGPLAN, 1987). IDL has been used to specify Descriptive Intermediate Attributed Notation for Ada (DIANA), an intermediate representation for ADA compilers. SDTs themselves can be built with SDTs (see Tools for Building SDTs below).

Editors and Environments

Syntax-directed editors use knowledge of a language to aid a user in editing programs or documents. Editor generators can use a grammar as a specification language to automatically create language-specific editors (Reps and Teitelbaum, 1984). An extension of this is the creation of entire environments, where a language specification (along with additional specifications) can be used to generate a suite of objects and tools including editors, translators, software processes, and project data bases; examples include Gandalf (Habermam and Notkin, 1986) and ALMA (van Lamsweerde and co-workers, 1988). Computer-Aided Software Engineering (CASE) tools can also be generated by such systems; Metaview (Sorenson and co-workers, 1988) and the Virtual Software Factory (trademark of Systematica Ltd.) are two such examples of CASE tool generators.

Real-Time Systems

Many parts of a real-time system can take advantage of SDTs. In many cases the behavior of a real-time system can be expressed by using some variation on finite-state machines. Such finite-state machine descriptions might use some standard such as Specification and Description Language (SDL) (Rockstrom, 1982), Statemate (Harel, 1990), Paisley (Zave and Schell, 1986) or a more customized domain-specific approach. Protocols can be expressed at a high level, validated (Holzman, 1992), and then translated to low-level target code. Other areas of interest include communication interfaces to other systems, interprocessor communications, hardware device abstractions, and diagnostics.

METHODS FOR BUILDING SDTS

Not every domain has off-the-shelf SDTs ready to use. Even in well-established areas such as user interfaces, new SDTs are developed all the time to take advantage of project-specific domains. Building new SDTs is a nontrivial undertaking. A large part of the task includes what is called *domain analysis* and *domain engineering*. Domain analysis consists of understanding the problem domain and solutions. Domain engineering refers to the activities of turning the results of domain analysis into methods and tools usable by software engineers (Prieto-Diaz and Arango, 1991). The Synthesis project (Campbell and co-workers, 1990) uses the idea of program families and exploits the similarities found within domains. Using layers of domains and transformations between domains, the DRACO approach attempts to construct software from reusable components (Freeman, 1987). All of these approaches have the same goal of automating the generation of code from high level specifications within a narrow domain.

The domain engineer specifies the SDT. The domain engineer must know the needs of a wide range of customers to understand the generic problem. The domain engineer must be aware of the potential range of current and future applications and must know what things are and are not likely to change. The domain engineer must decide the best form of specification input (e.g., textual, dialogues, or diagrams). The domain engineer must know the language and conventions used by customers in the domain and be able to formalize descriptions of customers' needs into a specification language. Such language design work requires an understanding of well-crafted language constructs, parsing requirements, conventional terms and expressions in the domain area, and human factors.

The domain engineer must also consider what set of products should be generated (that is, whether documentation, analysis reports, or test cases should be generated along with the application program). The domain engineer must know how different products should interface with other system tools or other SDTs. For example, documentation products may be input to text formatters. The domain engineer must also have a good understanding of the common design techniques and strategies used to build applications in the domain area and devise generic designs for an entire range of applications. In summary, the domain engineer has a challenging job, and must have considerable knowledge about a variety of customers, design techniques, products, and specification languages.

What follows in the next seven sections is a step-by-step process for building SDTs (Cleaveland, 1988). In practice, these steps are blurred and merged into a more chaotic design process. But for the purpose of explanation it is easier to focus on each step separately.

Recognizing Domains

A successful SDT quickly becomes part of the natural way of developing software. It seems obvious, but recognizing a potential domain for SDTs is one of the most difficult steps toward building one. The basic trick is to recognize patterns. Patterns may occur at the code level in the form of tables, large case statements, repetitive code, or many similar looking routines. Patterns also occur at higher levels in the form of similar programs, designs, or software architectures. Although pattern recognition is the most important way of recognizing potential domains, there are a number of other important clues that sometimes point out the need for SDTs.

Sometimes recognition occurs when there is a need to separate the *what* from the *how*. This separation is a fundamental design principle and is the basis of procedural and data abstractions. In both cases, the what is the functional behavior of the procedure or data type. The how is the implementation. SDTs achieve this separation by putting what information into the specifications, and the how information into the SDT. Sometimes the recognition occurs when one is working in a formal or informal notation that is then translated to code. Then the thought occurs, "Can this translation be automated?" Sometimes the recognition occurs when one needs to consolidate scattered information. An analogy at the programming language level is shown below:

```
int t [100];
for (j = 0; j < = 99; j++) {
    if (t [j] ==100)
        ++ perfect;
  . . .
}
printf ("100 test cases");
```

The above program segment has certain information scattered throughout the program, which makes it difficult to change. To change the number of test cases from 100 to 200 requires looking throughout the program for constants. Not all 100s refer to the number of test cases (100 might also be a perfect score), and some of the 100s are disguised or transformed to other constants, such as 99, which equals 100−1. Most languages provide a mechanism for consolidating this scattered information, such as the #define construct in C.

```
#define NUMTESTS 100
#define PERFECT 100

int t [NUMTESTS];
for (j=0; j<=NUMTESTS-1; j++) {
    if (t [j]==PERFECT)
        ++perfect;
    . . .
}
printf("%d test cases",NUMTESTS);
```

This problem also occurs at higher levels and in more complex ways. High-level information is scattered throughout design documents, user documents, software code, and regression test systems. This information is often transformed in complicated ways and is hard to follow through such a diversity of forms. This makes it difficult to change software systems in a consistent and complete manner. One method to solve this problem is to consolidate the information in a specification and use SDTs to transform the information to program, documentation, and tests. An example is the information about command line options used to execute software programs. The information is transformed to data declarations for programs, embedded in user documentation, and permuted in various combinations for testing purposes.

Defining Domain Boundaries

The next major step is determining domain boundaries. This step determines the "scope" or "range" of the SDT. What features should be included or excluded? Frequently, an SDT is a small part of a larger system, so interfaces between automatically generated code and the rest of the system become important. What and where should the interfaces be? What should the interfaces include or exclude?

In determining the domain boundaries, it is also important to look ahead and anticipate future directions. It may be best to adopt an evolutionary approach to building SDTs to test feasibility. Evolutionary growth requires that the features and the specification language be extensible. New SDT products sometimes require additional information in the specification, and this also expands the specification language. Designing for this potential future growth is important.

Defining the domain boundaries essentially defines the domain width of the SDT. It is important to realize the various trade-offs between domain width, domain leverage, cost, and efficiency. Given a fixed cost and efficiency for the SDT, there is a trade-off between domain width and domain leverage. If one makes the domain width too broad, the SDT will not be able to do much application-specific work, thus decreasing the domain leverage. The domain leverage can be increased by making assumptions about the problem domain, but this narrows the domain width.

Defining an Underlying Model

An SDT is more likely to be comprehensible, consistent, and complete if it is based on some underlying mathematical model. The specification expresses information in terms of the underlying model, and products are designed based on the model. Common and simple underlying models include sets, directed graphs, temporal logic, formal logic systems, and computation models such as finite state machines. In other cases, a model may be object-oriented, consisting of a set of object types, operations, and properties. A model provides a base for defining domain semantics in a consistent way. Each feature of the SDT can be explained in terms of the model. Each product can be verified or validated with respect to the model. Enhancements are more easily evaluated in terms of compatibility and implications become more obvious when a mathematical model is used.

Defining the Variant and Invariant Parts

A *variant* part is something under the control of the application builder, and an *invariant* part is something that remains the same for every use of the SDT (that is, a part that cannot be changed). Deciding what is variant and what is invariant corresponds to making a software module reusable by deciding what to parameterize. The difference is that parameterizing a software module is limited by what the programming language allows, whereas determining variant parts of an SDT is limited only by general language constraints.

The variant parts of an SDT usually correspond to the specification part of a system (the what), and the invariant parts are usually fixed assumptions about the domain or implementation and design details (the how) that users would rather not worry about. The variant parts are expressed in a specification language (or equivalent) that is used by the SDT to build a customized program. SDTs have two significant advantages over simple parameterized programs:

1. The ability to express variant information in whatever language is appropriate (rather than restricted to function parameters, manifest constants, or tables).
2. The ability to freely construct a program that is customized to the specific need expressed by the user (including optimization details).

The constructed program is not a generic program that attempts to solve many problems; it solves only the problem described by the user. This means that the program can be optimized for the particular application of the user. Thus this method partly reconciles the conflict between the need for customized software and reusable software.

An *escape* is a specification language construct that allows something to be expressed in an underlying implementation language. An analogy in programming languages is the ability to insert assembly language statements in a program. An example of an escape in most parser generators is a clause that expresses what to do after a grammar rule has been reduced. In the parser generator *yacc,* the escape is to the underlying implementation language C. An escape can be considered a "super" variant. It adds flexibility and power. Unfortunately, there is a high price for such benefits.

- Escapes degrade the readability of the specification language because escapes require understanding the underlying implementation language.
- Escapes degrade the testability and reliability of the SDT because one must now test at both the specification level and the programming language level.
- Escapes degrade the analysis capabilities and predictability of the SDT because run-time behavior of programs is difficult to statically analyze.

Escapes are so useful, however, that they appear in many SDTs. Arbitrary actions can be inserted at prespecified points in the generated program. Escapes can be used to meet a wide variety of unanticipated needs of future users. Escapes dramatically increase the domain width of an SDT while leaving the domain leverage nearly unchanged. At the same time, the SDT builder has control over what escapes are to be allowed and exactly where in the generated program they are permitted. If the specification language is designed so that escapes are seldom needed, and application builders resort to escapes only when necessary, then the disadvantages of escapes are minimized.

Defining the Specification Input

Input to SDTs may take the form of textual languages, dialogues, or diagrams (and possibly other sources such as data bases and expert systems). All these methods are useful depending on the circumstances and the application area. In some cases, a combination of methods is used, particularly when a window system is used. Briefly, the specification can take the following forms:

Textual Languages. This is the traditional approach. A language or notation is devised to express all the needed information. The SDT parses the input to obtain the information for program construction. This method is useful when there is a large amount of information or when specifications include complex expressions or escapes. However, language design is difficult because of issues such as human factors and parsing constraints.

Dialogues. Many commercial SDTs use an interactive approach such as menus and other queries to obtain information for generating programs. Changing the application means invoking the dialogue again with the assumption that the SDT "remembers" the previous dialogue. This method is useful when most of the application information can be chosen from menus of alternatives.

Diagrams. Many specifications are naturally expressed as graphs containing different types of nodes and links. Entity-relationship diagrams, finite state machines, dialogue graphs, networks, dataflow diagrams, are just a few examples. Some specifications, such as SDL (Rockstrom and Saracco, 1982), have both a textual representation and a graphical representation. Much of the power and appeal of CASE tools comes from the ability to express designs as diagrams. Visual formalisms, rather than just text, can have a spectacular effect on engineers (Harel, 1988, 1992).

Defining Products

The product outputs of an SDT can range from programs to documentation and test scripts. Generally, the SDT formats the specification information to a form that can be used by other tools such as text formatters, compilers, and even other SDTs. But often the product of most interest is code in some programming language. Typically, a generic software design must be developed that will meet the needs of applications in the domain. The SDT must tailor the generic design for each application.

There are two basic approaches to generating program code. The *code-driven* approach generates code with embedded data. For example, if the specification was "one, two, three" and the generated program is supposed to print out these words. A code-driven approach generates:

```
printf ("one\n") ;
printf ("two\n") ;
printf ("three\n");
```

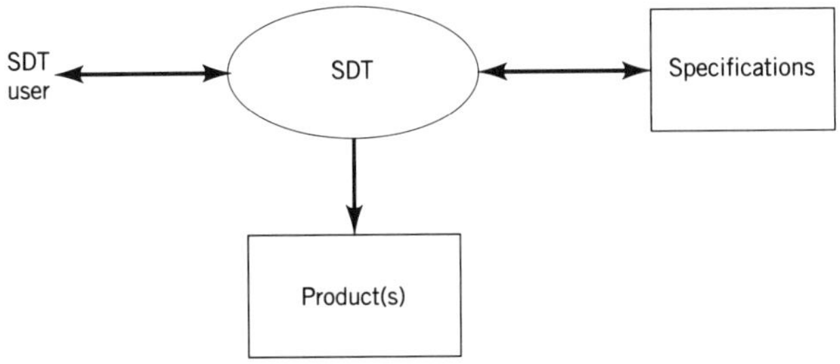

Figure 2. An interactive SDT.

The second approach, termed *table-driven,* generates code that places data in data structures and code that accesses the data through the data structures:

```
#define num_data 3
char *data [] = {
   "one",
   "two",
   "three",
   };

for (j=0; j<num_data; ++j)
   printf ("%s\n",data [j]);
```

If code is made and maintained manually by humans, there is a clear motivation for favoring table-driven approaches, since tables are easier to change correctly than statements. Which approach is better in an SDT context depends on the specific situation. The code-driven approach is much easier to implement and the code is more time efficient However, the code-driven approach may generate excessive amounts of code; in such instances a table-driven approach is preferred. Other issues to consider in this step include potential use of optimization techniques to reduce time or space requirements of the generated program. For example, Huffman encoding could be used to reduce the storage needed for help messages.

Implementing the SDT

The last and easiest step of all, if all the prior steps have been carefully analyzed and completed, is the construction of the SDT. The domain engineer determines how to implement the SDT from the requirements provided by the result of all the previous steps. An SDT may be a purely textual batch-oriented tool (as shown in Figure 1), in which case the job is to write a program that will translate the specification language to the desired products. The basic parts of the SDT (like most translators) will include a lexer and parser that generate a parse tree (or equivalent data structure), a semantic analyzer that will check for semantic errors or compute attributes, and product generator(s) that produce the output(s). The design of these parts of the SDT are conventional and repetitive. Thus it is appropriate to build SDT generators for automating most of the process.

An alternative architecture to the standard batch-oriented SDTs, is the interactive-editor approach (shown in Figure 2). Instead of using a text editor, the user executes the SDT to view, modify, and generate products. The user interface is typically window-oriented, which allows multiple views of all or selected portions of the specification. Specifications could be stored in a textual file or a data base.

Compilers and SDTs are both translators and share many common parts, but there are some significant differences that motivate different approaches to the design of these tools. Compilers must be high performance tools because they are used often by many people. SDTs need not be as efficient because they are used less often and by fewer people. Specification languages are usually simpler in both syntax and semantics than programming languages. The output of compilers is typically assembly language that may require specialized analysis and optimization techniques. The output of SDTs is typically a program that requires little or no analysis or optimization techniques, and if needed, the techniques would probably be quite different from what is found in compilers. Testing and debugging automatically generated programs can be frustrating because the standard programming tools, such as debuggers, work at the code level, not the specification level.

TOOLS FOR BUILDING SDTS

Very simple SDTs can be built with batch editors or macroprocessors. An extension of these ideas is the Frame-based system, which allows macrolike expansions to customize reusable software components (Bassett, 1987). These tools, however, have limited language recognition capabilities. SDTs built with these tools are not likely to be much better than simple parameterized software modules that are expanded at compile-time or run-time.

Awk is a software tool that is principally used for extracting information from files and reformatting it. It is also an excellent tool for building SDTs (Van Wyk, 1986). Unfortunately, awk provides only limited language recognition capabilities (regular expressions).

Perhaps the best known tools for building SDTs are lex and yacc (or bison). These tools are themselves SDTs used to build lexers and parsers. Beyond lexer and parser generators, a new class of tools is being developed to build SDTs, such as Draco (Neighbors, 1989), SSAGS (Payton, 1982), PG2 and Stage. Stage is now known as MetaTool Specification-Driven Tool Builder. MetaTool is a trademark of AT&T. (Cleaveland and Kintala, 1988). These tools use SDT technology to help develop SDTs. Stage has been used to build a wide variety of SDTs. The input to Stage consists of two parts: a *source description* that describes the input to the SDT and one or more *product descriptions* that describe the output of the SDT (see Figure 3).

The source description is a grammatical description of the specification language that is simultaneously used for building the parser and constructing a parse tree representation. The product description uses a templatelike approach to describing products and allows a wide variety of parse tree traversals and navigation. From these specifications, Stage produces an SDT built from automatically produced pieces such as a lexer (using lex), a parser (using yacc), data structure definitions, parse tree construction

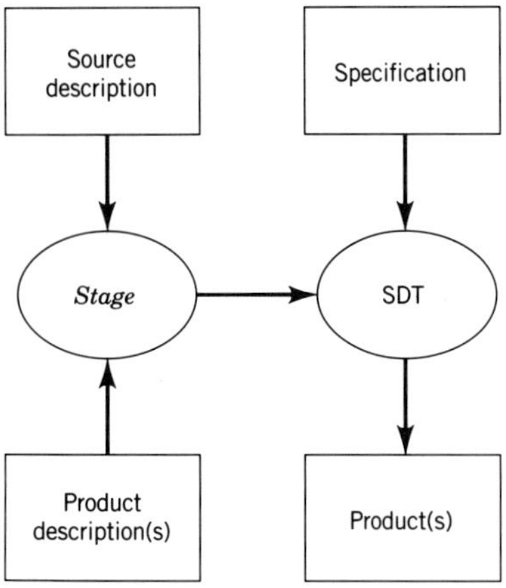

Figure 3. Building an SDT with Stage.

routines, traversal routines, and product generation routines. Stage is easier to use than tools such as lex and yacc because Stage does a more complete job of automating the translation process. Stage was designed so that SDTs could be built rapidly, at the expense of space (large parse trees) or time (excessive number of parse tree traversals). However, in practice the performance bottleneck is in the compilation phase, and not the generation phase.

The use of such tools reduces the effort needed to build SDTs. This is an essential ingredient in encouraging the development and use of SDTs. When an SDT is available off-the-shelf the only question to consider is whether it will meet the project's needs. When no SDT is available the much harder question becomes whether to develop one for the project or not. This decision is based on some economic analysis that weighs the short-term costs of building an SDT and the long-term benefits derived from using the SDT (Levy, 1986). Projects are often driven by short-term project-specific goals rather than long range companywide goals. Thus an SDT development must usually be justified in terms of a single project. This narrow vision limits innovative approaches and software reuse.

BIBLIOGRAPHY

A. Aho, R. Sethi, and J. Ullman, *Compilers: Principles, Techniques, and Tools,* Addison-Wesley, Reading, Mass., 1986.

D. Bartory, "GENESIS: A Project to Develop an Extensible Database Management System," *Proceedings of 1986 International Workshop on Object-Oriented Database Systems,* Asilomar, Sept. 1986.

P. G. Bassett, "Frame-Based Software Engineering," *IEEE Software* **4**(4), 9–16 (July 1987).

D. G. Belanger and C. M. R. Kintala, "Data-Extraction Tools," *AT&T Technical Journal,* 2025–2035 (Nov. 1985).

G. Campell Jr., S. Faulk, and D. Weiss, "Introduction to Synthesis," *Software Productivity Consortium Report 90019-N,* Herndon, Va., June 1990.

M. Carey and co-workers, "The EXODUS extensible DMBS project: An overview," S. Zdonik and D. Maier, eds., *Readings in Object-Oriented Databases,* Morgan-Kaufman, 1989.

J. C. Cleaveland, "Tools for Building Application Generators," *IEEE Software* **5**(4), 25–33 (July 1988).

J. C. Cleaveland and C. M. R. Kintala, "Building Application Generators," *AT&T Technical Journal* **67**(4), 46–58, (Aug. 1988).

P. Freeman, "A Conceptual Analysis of the Draco Approach to Constructing Software Systems," *IEEE Trans. Software Eng.* **13**(7) 830–844, (July, 1987).

A. Habermann and D. Notkin, "Gandalf: Software Development Environments," *IEEE Trans. Software Eng.* **SE-12,** 1117–1127 (Dec. 1986).

D. Harel, "On Visual Formalisms," *Comm. ACM* **31**(5), 514–530 (May, 1988).

D. Harel, "Biting the Silver Bullet," *IEEE Computer* **25**(1), 8–24 (Jan. 1992).

D. Harel and co-workers, "Stalemate: A Working Environment for the Development of Complex Reactive Systems," *IEEE Trans. Software Eng.* **16**(4), 403–414 (Apr. 1990).

G. Holzman, "Protocol Design: Redefining the State of the Art," *IEEE Software* **9**(1), 17–22, (Jan. 1992).

C. W. Krueger, "Software Reuse," *ACM Computing Surveys* **24**(2), 131–183 (June 1992).

M. Jarke and Y. Vassiliou, "A Framework for Choosing a Database Query Language," *ACM Computing Surveys* **17**(3), 313–340 (Sept. 1985).

H. J. Kim, "Graphical Interfaces for Database Systems: A Survey," *Proc. ACM Mountain Regional Conf.,* Santa Fe, N.M., Apr. 1986).

L. S. Levy, "A Metaprogramming Method and Its Economic Justification," *IEEE Trans. Software Eng.,* 272–277 (Feb. 1986).

J. Martin, *Fourth-Generation Languages,* Vol. 1, Prentice-Hall, Englewood Cliffs, N.J., 1985.

J. Martin and J. Leban, *Fourth-Generation Languages,* Vol 2., Prentice-Hall, Englewood Cliffs, N.J., 1986.

B. A. Myers, "User-Interface Tools: Introduction and Survey," *IEEE Software* **6**(1), 15–23 (Jan. 1989).

J. M. Neighbors, "DRACO: A Method for Engineering Reusable Software Systems," *Software Reliability,* Vol. 1, ACM Press, 1989, pp. 259–320.

T. F. Payton and co-workers, "SSAGS: A Syntax and Semantics Analysis and Generation System," *Proc. Computer Software and Applications Conf.,* CS Press, Los Alamitos, Calif., 1982, pp. 424–433.

R. Prieto-Diaz and G. Arango, eds., *Domain Analysis and Software System Modeling,* IEEE Computer Society Press, Los Alamitos, Calif., 1991.

T. Reps and T. Teitelbaum, "The Synthesizer Generator," Proc. 1st ACM Sigsoft/Sigplan Symp. Practical Software Development Environments in *SIGPLAN Notices* **19**(5), 42–48 (May, 1984).

A. Rockstrom and R. Saracco, "SDL—CCITT Specification and Description Language," *IEEE Trans. Comm.,* 1310–1318 (June 1982).

SIGPLAN Notices, Special issue on IDL **22**(11) (Nov. 1987).

P. G. Sorenson, J. Tremblay, and A. J. McAllister, "The Metaview System for Many Specification Environments," *IEEE Software* **5**(2), 30–38 (March 1988).

A. van Lamsweerde, B. Delcourt, E. Delor, M. Schayes, and R. Champagne, "Generic Lifecycle Support in the ALMA Environment," *IEEE Trans. Software Eng.* **14**(6), 720–741 (June 1988).

C. J. Van Wyk, "Awk as Glue for Programs," *Software Practice and Experience,* 369–388 (Apr. 1986).

P. Zave and W. Schell, "Salient Features of an Executable Specification Language and Its Environment," *IEEE Trans. Software Eng.* **12**(2), 312–325 (Feb. 1986).

J. CRAIG CLEAVELAND
AT&T Bell Laboratories

SPIRAL MODEL

See DESIGN; PROCESS MODELS IN SOFTWARE ENGINEERING; RISK MANAGEMENT.

SREM

See SOFTWARE REQUIREMENTS ENGINEERING METHODOLOGY.

STAGE

Period of execution during which total code and developed code for a program remain constant, J. D. Musa, A. Iannino, and K. Okumoto, *Software Reliability: Measurement Prediction, Application,* McGraw-Hill, New York, 1987.

STAMP COUPLING

See STRUCTURED ANALYSIS/STRUCTURED DESIGN.

STARS

HISTORY/DOD SOFTWARE INITIATIVE

Studies conducted in the 1970s and early 1980s established that computer software problems in U.S. Department of Defense (DOD) mission critical systems were pervasive and severe. Indeed, none of the problems was unique to any individual component; in fact, all of the Military Services had been experiencing the same type of problems. By 1982, the DOD decided that resolution of these long festering problems required a strong, focused initiative to attack the problems on a broad front, and began a series of DOD-wide task force efforts to address the issues.

In June 1983, the Department of Defense endorsed the DOD Software Initiative which had been proposed to offset growing manpower shortfalls and to improve capabilities for supporting software development and maintenance. This new initiative came to contain three components. One component was the Ada Joint Program Office (AJPO), and a second component was a Federally Funded Research and Development Center (FFRDC), later to be called the Software Engineering Institute (SEI). The third component was designated as a program in software technology. This program, which was prescribed to have a fixed life time, became known as Software Technology for Adaptable, Reliable Systems (STARS).

STARS was established as a tri-Service program, managed in the DOD. The DOD envisioned that STARS progress and its organization, by working closely with the Components, industry, and the software research community, would create the technology and establish the practices to improve the ability of the Defense community to manage the complexity of software, to develop and support software more quickly, and to improve the quality, adaptability, and reliability of software across the defense communities (services contractors and Defense Agencies). In November 1984, the Under Secretary of Defense for Research and Engineering (USDRE) summarized STARS requirements and goals and promulgated them in a Charter which established STARS as a DOD Program.

EARLY PROGRAM ACTIVITIES

During the first two years of STARS (1984 and 1985), the program was focused in seven areas teams:

1. Program management
2. Methodology team
3. Business practices team
4. Application team
5. Software engineering environment team
6. Human resources team
7. Measurements team

By the end of 1985, the STARS program had met with limited success. DOD responded by reorganizing the program.

STARS FOUNDATION EFFORTS

In 1986, under new management, STARS contracted to industry to develop 33 basic foundation technology products to support Ada applications development. These foundation efforts which addressed such things as operating systems, database management systems, user interfaces, command language graphics and communications protocols and were completed in 1987, and the resulting products were made available outside STARS to stimulate commercial off-the-shelf (COTS) offerings.

ENLARGED PROGRAM VISION

In April 1988, the Director of Defense Research and Engineering (DDR&E) transferred the STARS Program and the SEI to the Defense Advanced Research Projects Agency (DARPA). During the period 1988–1989, STARS activities fell into four major areas:

- Software Engineering Environments (SEEs)
- Technology development
- Fundamental research.
- "Shadow" projects/demonstrations

The STARS SEEs, focused on specific problem domains, were to provide the framework, controls, tools, techniques, methods and documentation to:

1. Deal with the complexities inherent in the creation and maintenance of software.
2. Improve software quality, including reliability, adaptability, and performance.
3. Improve the management and control of the complex and varied activities required to develop, field, and support MCCR software.

In the area of technology development, STARS strategy was to develop the tools and processes to demonstrate and support a software-first approach to systems engineering. In the fundamental research area, STARS was to pioneer a new approach to resolving high-risk MCCR acquisition issues. Experience STARS gained in MCCR applications, environment products, and technology developments were to provide the basis for several annual briefings to industry at which fundamental research issues were to be described for creative proposals called technolgy "breakthroughs". Lastly, demonstration projects called Shadow would use Ada and other subsequent STARS technologies and products on segments of operational weapons, command and control, or intelligence systems.

STARS PRIME CONTRACTS

In August 1988, the STARS Prime program was awarded to three leading defense systems integrators: Boeing Aerospace Company, IBM Federal Systems Integration Division (now called Federal Systems Company), and Unisys Defense Systems. Three prime contractors were selected in order to reduce risk, accelerate acceptance of changing technology and perform cooperative development work from a very broad experience base.

Prime Accomplishments (1988–1990)

Some of the accomplishments during this period were the development of an editor, AdaPEERmacs that supports the review of Ada source code; DBFORMGEN, a generator/manager for relational database forms; the definition of Software First Life Cycle (SFLC) data item descriptions; Ada Command Environment (ACE), continued development an interactive Ada environment, an interactive environment which allows the user to rapidly prototype general Ada applications, and in which Ada becomes the command language as well as the programming language.

CURRENT STARS (1990–1993)

In December 1989 (FY90), based on an assessment of the program, new DARPA management directed a slight change in emphasis/direction in STARS which emphasized leveraging and influencing commercially available solutions to the DOD problems. This change was motivated by the growing realization of the costs incurred by DOD maintaining, and distributing DOD-specific tools. Greater emphasis was to be placed on frameworks for software engineering environments, working with standards bodies and commercial vendors and on software reuse and software process as technology areas.

The current STARS program is a technology development, integration, and transition program to demonstrate a process-driven, domain specific, reuse-based approach to software engineering that is supported by appropriate tool and environment technology. This approach is often referred to as "megaprogramming".

Megaprogramming is a product line (family of systems) approach to the creation and maintenance of software intensive systems. Megaprogramming is characterized by the reuse of software life-cycle assets within a product line to include common architecture and components. Megaprogramming also includes the definition and enactment of disciplined processes for development of applications within the product line and for the development and evolution of the product line itself.

The product line approach involves two separate and distinct life cycles. The first is development and maintenance of product line assets, and the second is creation of individual applications using these assets. The processes applied to development and maintenance of the product line and its family of applications continuously evolve and improve through measurement and evaluation to meet new and better understood application and product line needs. The process-driven approach to product line development is supported by tools and integrated software engineering environment technology. Megaprogramming, therefore, combines a product line approach, process-driven discipline, and integrated support environments to provide a new way to develop and maintain software-intensive systems.

Each of the STARS prime contractors is required to have an active partnership with a leading commercial vendor (referred to as a commercial counterpart) in order to bring technologies developed by STARS to the commercial marketplace. Commercial counterparts are as follows: IBM with IBM commercial, Unisys with HP and SUN, and Boeing with Digital.

Recent Achievements

In support of a process-driven, domain-specific, reuse-based approach to software engineering, major STARS achievments during 1990–1993 include:

- Successfully transitioned the STARS developed technologies based on the Cleanroom Software Engineering Process to the Mortar Ballistic Computer reengineering effort at the Picatinny Arsenal Life Cycle Support Center.
- Process Asset Library jointly created with SEI. This library contains detailed definitions/models of various

processes to include Cleanroom, TRW Ada process model and others. This is a significant milestone in understanding the effort necessary to define a software engineering process.

- Definition and trial usage of domain analysis processes [Domain Analysis Process Model (DAPM) and Organization Domain Modeling (ODM)] to support selection of high-leverage domains and analysis and modeling of the commonality/variability within these domains.
- Development of concepts of operation for software reuse to include the CFRP (conceptual framework for reuse processes) document and Version 1 of the Reuse Strategy Model (RSM).
- A knowledge-based Reusable Library Framework (RLF) for a new generation of storage and retrieval systems, especially applicable to the graphical/architectural display and manipulation of reuse libraries.
- Development of open architecture standards to facilitate the interoperability of reuse libraries, and client/server prototype demonstrations of these standards.
- Establishment of the Reuse Library Interoperability Group (RIG) to define a common software reuse library interface such that disparate libraries can exchange information. RIG is composed of representatives from Government, industry and academia active in reuse library technology.
- Establishment in Morgantown, West Virginia of the Asset Source for Software Engineering Technology (ASSET), the central node for a network of software reuse libraries.
- Reuse library interoperability: During FY 93, two-way interoperability between two reuse libraries, ASSET and the Central Archive for Reusable Defense Software (CARDS), became operational, and three-way interoperability was demonstrated across three reuse libraries, ASSET, CARDS and the Defense Software Repository System (DSRS). Not only does this capability allow access to software assets in other libraries through one account, the technology is extensible and moves us toward a large 'virtual' reuse library system.
- Development of an Ada semantic interface specification (ASIS) that has been incorporated into two Ada compiler vendors' products.
- Major contributions to existing knowledge regarding the PCTE and ATIS integration frameworks, as well as influence on commercial framework suppliers and standards activities.
- Sponsoring the definition and development of an IEEE software testing standard based on Ada and a software system to support this standard.
- Integrated three instances of SEEs, built on commercial frameworks, that directly incorporate support for process-driven, reuse-based software engineering.
- Creation of Technology transition programs to transfer emerging technologies actively to early adopter organizations.

Demonstration Projects

STARS technology is being demonstrated on real DOD programs in each of the three services. These demonstration projects are on the order of 100,000 lines of code and will cover the period 1993–1995. summary information about the demonstration projects follows:

- Army: A subsystem of the Improved Guardrail V software will be re-engineered at the Lifecycle Support Center at CECOM, Ft. Monmouth. The application domain of this project is electronic warfare (EW). Significant emphasis will be placed on domain analysis/engineering for the entire EW domain.
- Air Force: A subsystem of the Space and Warning software will be re-engineered at Air Force/AFSPACECOM, Colorado Springs. The application domain of this project is command and control. Significant emphasis will be placed on software architecture definition and implementation, integration of commercial tools, and definition of software processes.
- Navy: A T-34C Flight Instrument Trainer will be developed at Navy Training and Simulation Center (NTSC), Orlando. The application domain of this project is flight trainers. Significant emphasis will be placed on domain analysis, SEE and process integration, and additional support for developing a training devices software product line.

Joel Trimble
STARS Technology Center

STATEMENT COVERAGE

See Testing.

STATEMENT TESTING

Testing designed to execute each statement of a computer program (IEEE).

STATIC ANALYSIS

The process of evaluating a system or component based on its form, structure, content or documentation (IEEE).

STEPWISE REFINEMENT

A software development technique in which data and processing steps are defined broadly at first and then further defined with increasing detail (IEEE).

STRESS TESTING

See CATEGORIES OF TESTING.

STRUCTURAL TESTING

See TESTING.

STRUCTURED ANALYSIS/ STRUCTURED DESIGN

OVERVIEW

The Concepts and Evolution

The techniques of structured analysis and structured design are outgrowths of structured programming concepts and techniques, and of the early ideas about modular design. Collectively they are referred to as structured methods or structured techniques. Structured techniques apply structured programming constructs to process and data definitions, and build on ideas, about modularity offered by David Parnas (1972), that suggest "good" ways to partition a system. Parnas has proposed that independence which allows for graceful change should be a goal of a well-designed system. This is a strong theme in both structured analysis and design, although the terminology and application of this idea in the two techniques diverge. Inherent in a structured approach are guidelines for recognizing independence and simplicity of function. In contrast to coding techniques, structured analysis and design explore systems and software at a higher conceptual level and with a more expansive view than code to identify elements that are critical to success.

The "structured" aspect of this higher and broader view of systems is the disciplined use of a limited set of logical constructs and the planned hierarchical organization of information. Structured analysis uses this approach to investigate the problem domain which is the application or system subject matter. Structured design uses this approach to precisely define and organize detail about the planned implementation of both the system and the software design. Also, structured design and analysis have been developed in the reverse order of their logical relationship in the development process, meaning that the definition and practical application of the design model and technique predates that of the analysis technique Further, practice of both structured analysis and design has emphasized the need to clearly understand that boundary between them and the traversal from analysis to design, which in this article is called architecture.

The Goals of Structured Analysis and Design

These models and techniques have evolved out of a need to improve software quality and reduce risk of failure. Accordingly, quality in this context is usually defined as a measurable increase in software reliability, flexibility, maintainability, and effectiveness. Failure in this context is either loss of face due to delivery of an inferior or inadequate product or financial loss because a project has been cancelled when the specification and, therefore, project completion was elusive and funds already expended were wasted. Failure can mean both. Behind the primary goals lies a need to obtain a more clear and more complete specification, as well as documentation for systems. Structured analysis and structured design tackle these goals by making visible and precise models which show analysis and design information. A benefit of these models has been that they are relatively simple notations which make the developers' ideas observable and therefore easy to discuss with others for verification and for consensus. The formality of the models is in rules for completeness and consistency of specifications, to replace arbitrary rules of completeness from system and software development organizations.

Quality is improved through the emphasis on analysis and design activities which encourage project team members to be more thoughtful about a system's underlying purpose and about the specific detail which is needed to make a system successful both from the system user's view and from a technological view. Another benefit of the techniques has been that the project team develops software documentation as they go. The models stand as maps of the system domain and of the system and software design and can be used as formal documents for traceability, as well as useful guides in maintenance or enhancement activities.

Innovative Aspects

Larry Constantine's work (Yourdon, 1975) marks a formal beginning to structured analysis and design methods; with his coauthors he has written about hierarchical design and has introduced data flow analysis. This collection of research, observations, and suggested notation comprise a foundation of guidelines and of pattern development and recognition much of which has remained relevant for nearly twenty years both for design and for analysis. This research has described a territory distinctly different than code, and this distinction represents a major shift in thinking that has been a product of what Ed Yourdon called the "Structured Revolution" (Yourdon, 1982).

In structured analysis and in structured design, models are used by the system analyst, system architect, or software designer to express and organize his or her ideas. Each activity requires different levels of thinking which reflect corresponding logical levels of abstraction in the resultant document. This method has initiated a clear separation and definition of the activities of analysis, architecture (system design), detailed design (software design) and code. Also, terminology has evolved, such as Tom DeMarco's "logical" and "physical" models, and has served to highlight the distinctions between activities and models, emphasizing both intent and difference.

STRUCTURED ANALYSIS

The Model

This section refers to DeMarco's notation (DeMarco, 1978), as it is by far the most well known and most used; variations are discussed separately. Four components are discussed in this section: Data Flow Diagrams, The Data Dictionary, Mini-specifications, and the Data Structure Diagram. The Data Flow Diagram (DFD) is the most recognizable component of a structured analysis model. A DFD is a graphic view of transform processes and their interfaces called flows and it is shown in its simplest form as labeled circles and arrows. Also, a DFD may show that a process requires memory to complete its job. The symbol is called a data store and is represented by a single or double line with an identifying label. DFDs are only one component and not a complete structured analysis model.

The Data Dictionary and Mini-specifications complete the model and provide detail used to verify that the graphic view is correct, complete and consistent. The Data Dictionary defines, in an unambiguous and concise way, the structure of all flows and data stores which are referenced by the transform processes. The definitions are constructed using data composition notation which mirrors the structured programming constructs of sequence, selection and iteration as introduced by Bohm and Jacopini (1966), plus notation to highlight comments, optional parameters, and elements which are unique identifiers for a set. These definitions allow for declaration of quantity-values or range-continuous values, for logic values or any type of range-discrete values, and for values which are composites of any or all types. The Mini-specification is a textual definition of requirements for the correct operation of a transform process in terms of policies and/or of formulas.

In general, the separation of information and its allocation into the three components is an attempt to place the information in its most appropriate place and not repeat that same detail in any other component. Since all processes, flow and data store objects are named, the object name serves as a key to cross-reference information from one component to another. A fourth component that DeMarco proposed, but is often overlooked, is a graphic model of memory structure called a Data Structure Diagram (DSD). The DSD has been mapped to the data stores on the DFD, but was rarely built in practice, and eventually information models provided a better data analysis tool. Data models have been part of the structured analysis model from the start, although not often stressed, and not strongly integrated with the Data Flow Diagrams.

A characteristic of the entire structured analysis model is that there are multiple levels of DFDs, in addition to multiple Data Dictionary entries and multiple Mini-specifications. The multiple DFDs depict various levels of detail in the problem domain or application area. The top level is a simple scoping document called a context diagram, which declares the boundary separating the system of interest to the analysis effort from the environment the system is placed in. Items of interest which lie immediately outside the system boundary and with which the system communicates are illustrated on the context diagram as rectangles or squares and are known as terminators, external entities or sources and sinks. The flow of information between each external entity and the system is also specified on the context diagram in order to declare the major system interfaces. At levels below the context diagram, DFDs describe interior views of system functioning. A process that can be simply and unambiguously described in a textual mini-specification is called a "primitive". A mini-specification for the higher level processes would summarize the lower levels and therefore be redundant, and so, is not part of a structured analysis model. The mini-specifications for the primitives collectively define the transformational requirements for the problem domain. The DFDs show upper and middle level views which allow the users of models to focus on the top, middle or more detailed views of processes and their interfaces.

The Technique

Structured analysis has been long associated with top-down thinking as the main strategy for model building. In fact, the original analysis technique of functional decomposition was an evolution of the step-wise refinement techniques of modular design (Wirth, 1971) and of the top-down development of structured design hierarchies. The basic idea was to take the whole and break it into pieces, test the validity of the pieces and refine the boundaries for the pieces. The pieces in turn could be given the same treatment. Later techniques, which will be discussed under Significant Refinements, replaced functional decomposition. However, even though functional decomposition as an overriding strategy was replaced, the model has retained its top-down structure, which has allowed for iterative development and refinement and for selective review by different audiences, both of which have been valuable aspects of the overall analysis technique.

A desirable characteristic of the analysis model is having the model components be orthogonal, meaning that they do not overlap and are a minimally redundant model. How to arrive at that outcome has been a key part of the technique. DeMarco (1978) has recognized that the technology used to build systems and that the operational structures an organization uses to accomplish the delivery of its product or service, will employ redundancy as a strategy to gain efficiency, robustness, integrity, safety or security. If all of this could be stripped away, then perhaps an understanding of the fundamental information and behavior required could be comprehended as well as the raw material that managers, system architects and software designers need to create effective systems. DeMarco has used the term "logical" to label a model that defines a problem domain or a system which has been fully independent of all technological and operational consideration and the term "physical" to describe a model which has incorporated operational and technological considerations (DeMarco, 1978). The logical model, then, has been one that theoretically could be reused to create new system architectures or software designs when technology and operation changed. This concept contains the seed of Parnas' idea of minimizing the effect of change (Parnas, 1972).

An approach that DeMarco has recommended is to start with a current physical model of the system; then strip away the technological and organizational artifacts to reveal the current logical model; then add in the new logical requirements; and finally integrate new physical requirements into a repartitioned model to reflect an effective, working system. In the nineties, as DeMarco has looked back on the effect of this particular recommendation, he admits that this four-part process has been a counterproductive contribution (DeMarco, 1992), since modelers ended up wasting time modeling an existing system, rather than getting on with the real analysis work of defining the logical requirements for the new system. DeMarco claims that he had only "limited experience with the four-model sequence at the time of his book's publication, and he has admitted that its treatment of the topic was a "mistake" (Ward, 1992).

However, the importance of the logical versus physical view and the emphasis on its usefulness is a significant contribution to system development techniques and to systems and software methodology. Later refinements to structured analysis remedy the problems associated with the four-part process. A companion technique for deriving logical data structures from physical data structures was also presented by DeMarco (1978). The construction of the DSD was an eight step process of "logicalizing" the information found in the data stores. In more steps, it derived third normal-form data.

Additional aspects of the structured analysis technique cover rules and guidelines for checking the integrity of the model and include heuristics for testing and refining the partitioned pieces of the problem to improve the model. The former addresses the grammar and the syntax of the complete model and of its individual components: the DFD graphic and the supporting detail components. The latter encompasses a set of guidelines which act as reasonability checks, keeping the modeler focused on the model content and on the model objective of communicating information to the rest of the people involved in the project. The grammar is defined by "balancing" rules, which are used to ensure completeness and consistency among the three model components. Balancing ensures that:

- All graphic objects on the DFD are shown correctly according to their rules of usage. For instance, a transform process must have both inputs and outputs.
- Each flow and data store has a definition in the data dictionary, which will contain definitions for all entries down to the elemental level.
- Definitions in the data dictionary contain legal data composition notation.
- In the case that a process is not detailed on a child DFD, it must be defined with a mini-specification.
- Flow definitions for flows in and out of a parent or upper level process are totally consistent with flows definitions for flows in and out of any child DFD. No new interfaces may be introduced and none may be dropped.
- Mini-specifications are consistent with the graphic representation on the DFD. For example, inbound flows should be referenced in the mini-specification as to how they are used, outbound flows as to how they are created or selected and references to data stores as to how that memory is selected, used or altered.
- Mini-specifications refer to the use of all information defined for the inbound flows and refer to the production of all information on the outbound flows.

Interestingly, the DSD has only simplistic consistency checking, which was reference to data store names. This emphasized its weak relationship to the rest of the model.

The development of a useful analysis model is dependent on how useful the content, names and visuals are to the others on the project. A useful analysis model is one which communicates well, clearly describes functionally independent pieces of the problem, uses language understandable to anyone who has a stake in the system product and is visually simple so that reviewers can absorb a lot of information quickly and understand immediately what is or appears to be wrong. In his seminars DeMarco has emphasized the importance of developing strong communication skills and non-linear thinking skills by discussing with students and demonstrating to them writing style, visual presentation, philosophy and cognitive sciences (DeMarco, 1979). Much of the guidelines for readable models center around language and visual complexity analysis. Some of the guidelines are to control complexity, such as:

- Limiting the number of objects on a diagram to roughly 72 to facilitate human comprehension (Miller, 1956)
- Examining the number of interfaces around each process and looking for other possible partitions which might reduce interface complexity (Sometimes whether a process has too many flows in and out is relative to the other processes depicted on the same diagram and to the level of abstraction shown).
- Analyzing data content to determine if all of the inbound information was required to produce the outbound information [This technique is referred to as "conservation of data" (DeMarco, 1978). Conversely, all information produced by a process should be derivable from the information that went into the process (Gane, 1977)].

Some guidelines to keep the model content meaningful are:

- Use the language of the system user and not the language or jargon of software and systems people. This included a recommendation to use English or natural language for mini-specifications.
- Keep mini-specifications concise and precise by restricting the mini-specification constructs to a limited set, including verbs, nouns (sentence subjects and objects), prepositions, some conjunctions, numbers, and known formulas. The limited set of English constructs DeMarco has called "structured English" and

it has excluded adverbs and adjective, except those formally declared as part of a flow or data store name.

Pioneers and Contributors

Although Tom DeMarco's simple set of notations for a structured analysis model are the most well known, he was not the first to publish on structured analysis, nor were the bulk of the ideas his alone. The credit to the early recognition of a structured analysis technique goes to Douglas Ross, (Ross and Shoman, 1977) who developed with coauthors, a technique called SADT. This technique had involved building a leveled set of DFDs to define behavior and also had some distinction between a requirements model and an implementation model. However the latter distinction was not as clearly drawn as DeMarco's logical and physical. SADT notation has used rectangles to represent processes and has formalized the placement of inbound and outbound flows left to right for data flow and top to bottom for control flow. Also, the rectangles and arrows have been used for a data modeling notation.

The early SADT model did not include a Data Dictionary nor did it include any formal specification for the processes. However, it did include control annotation to show process activation. This distinguishing characteristic has been significant, as it would take another decade for the notion of process control, activation and deactivation to be formalized. (DeMarco's processes are activated by the arrival of data). The idea of process control had reappeared in the real-time extensions to structured analysis. Probably, the reason that Ross' work did not have the impact of DeMarco's work and the reason that these two characteristics were overlooked for so long, was due to the fact that SADT was considered a proprietary method by SofTech, the company which Ross co-founded (Ward. 1992). The first release of SADT to the public domain took place in 1981 when a subset of SADT, known as IDEF0, was released as part of the Integrated Computer-Aided Manufacturing (ICAM) project. DeMarco has admitted to using SADT and being influenced by it. He used SADT's concepts, added the detail documents, and integrated some ideas on notation offered by Ed Yourdon which simplified the model graphics and made it less formidable looking and more accessible to a broad audience (DeMarco, 1992). These notational changes included discarding flow placement rules and using a circle to depict processes. These changes allowed a diagram to be drawn freehand quite easily.

Other early works on structured analysis were written by Chris Gane and Trish Sarson (1977) and by Victor Weinberg (1978). Gane and Sarson's published notation and technique used SADT conventions and introduced two new notations: the data store and the terminator. Weinberg's book has represented the earliest work on project management considerations which references structured methods and uses notation that are the circles seen in DeMarco's work. Interestingly, these authors and DeMarco all met in an organization called Yourdon, Inc. founded by Ed Yourdon in 1974 to promote the education and use of structured methods through seminars and through publications. Ed Yourdon is well-known as a popularizer of the structured methods. His contribution to structured analysis has been in the skillful refinement and presentation of the ideas of others, as described above. Yourdon has had the ability to absorb and synthesize information and to communicate his ideas effectively, as seen in his numerous books, articles and presentations. This natural style of communication characterized many of the books which came from Yourdon Press, including those of DeMarco, whose style seems to have been a fortuitous match to Yourdon's.

An indirect contribution to structured analysis worth noting has been that of information modeling. As noted, data models in some form had always been part of structured analysis techniques, but not wholly embraced by the practitioners of structured analysis. This situation was likely due to the weakly defined techniques by both SADT and DeMarco for building data models. As an information modeling discipline matured, the information model began to be used by those who were already using structured analysis and were looking for a better tool and technique for "logicalizing" data. Probably the person whose technique most influenced structured analysis users has been that of Peter Chen (1976). His notation appealed to modelers because of the formal recognition of a relationship as a legitimate object with its own symbol and statement of policy and as a natural intersection of two or more data sets or entities. Other techniques forced a modeler to define all relationships as binary, which was perceived as arbitrary and constraining. Other data modeling approaches were considered either too implementation-oriented in nature or lacking rigor in their associated technique. Matt Flavin, already quite familiar with structured analysis, added more precise definitions and processes to Chen's technique and also related the information model to behavioral aspects of a system (Flavin, 1981). What Chen called entities, Flavin called "objects." Flavin described objects as having associated states and processing suggesting the beginnings of object-oriented methods (Flavin, 1981).

Significant Refinements

Since the popularization of structured analysis several refinements have been made to both the notation and the technique. McMenamin and Palmer (1984) refined DeMarco's basic technique by the recognition of events as key to uncovering true problem domain requirements. They reasoned that systems that are candidates for automation provide planned responses to some specific stimulus. The event was defined as that stimulus to the system. Part of their contribution was new terminology to better define DeMarco's often misunderstood "logical". That term was "essential" and reflected the analysis goal of striving for the essence of a system, stripped of the trappings of its incarnation. Their technique involved building lists of events and responses which were used to derive a first-cut essential model. This technique was easier to verify, faster to build and less-error prone than the preceding functional decomposition and stands as an important analysis modeling tool (McMenamin and Palmer, 1984). McMenamin and Palmer were also the first to advocate in print the use of Entity-Relationship Models to organize the "essential" memory of a system.

A large body of work which refines structured analysis has been the integration of new model components to accommodate of the needs of real-time and embedded systems development. The specific need that has been addressed in real-time extensions was that of formally modeling control logic. But despite the name, formal timing models have not been integrated with structured analysis. Two dominant approaches to real-time model extensions were developed by Paul Ward and Steve Mellor (1985, 1986), and by Derek Hatley and Imtiaz Pirbhai (1987). Both approaches have employed a Mealey-based State Transition Diagram (STD) in which an action that was associated with a transition condition was assumed to occur during the transition between states.

Ward and Mellor adopted the McMenamin and Palmer notion of an event and used it to drive the transitions from state to state. Every essential state could be related back to a system event. Model construction was based on event modelling. Since events are easily associated with time and timing is an important aspect of real-time systems, Ward and Mellor extended the flow notation to highlight events and timing. Flows that represented the occurrence of events (known as "event flows") have been shown as a dashed line, time-discrete flows as solid lines with a single-headed arrow, and time-continuous flows as solid lines with a double-headed arrow. In addition, they introduced a control transform process to formally link the STD to the DFD. Process activation as a possible action during state transition was shown in a special flow symbol with a small circle at the end instead of an arrowhead. Within the circle process enabling, disabling, pausing, restarting or triggering was indicated by the initial letter (Ward and Mellor, 1985–1986).

Hatley and Pirbhai (1987) represented control as finite state machines that dovetail with DFDs. The STD is just one of several finite state models, other formal control models offered by Hatley and Pirbhai are state event tables, decision tables and process activation tables. Hatley and Pirbhai's finite state machines operate on information that may take on a finite number of discrete values (states) while primitive processes operate on continuous inputs. This circumstance has led to the distinction between control and data flows by the continuity of their domains; Hatley and Pirbhai partition flows into control flows, defined as range-discrete, and data flows, defined as range-continuous. Control flows are depicted with dashed lines and data flows with solid lines. Each finite state machine is considered to be primitive, and is called a Control Specification (Cspec). Hatley and Pirbhai's symbol for a control process on a DFD is a bar, which is a single vertical line and can represent any number of Cspecs.

Hatley and Pirbhai have started with functional decomposition and created a parallel technique of control decomposition which is significant as a general technique to manage complexity. Ward and Mellor employ event modelling in place of functional decomposition. This difference in technique between the modellers is reflected in their notational extensions. The distinction between the various types of flows in a Ward and Mellor Model is based upon timing and events, while the distinction between control and data flow in a Hatley-Pirbhai Model is based on the range continuity of the information along a flow path. An extension of partitioning and separating control from data was that Hatley and Pirbhai also have recommended the use of a Control Flow Diagram (CFD) which was separate from the DFD (Hatley and Pirbhai, 1987). The CFD showed only control flows and the DFD showed only data flows, but in all other symbols they were identical. In both the Ward and Mellor and Hatley and Pirbhai techniques, the balancing rules have been extended to account for event flows and control flows, respectively, in both the Data Dictionary and from the DFD to the STD or from the CFD to Cspecs the STD and the Cspecs.

A third approach to modeling control is demonstrated by Dave Harel (Harel and co-workers, 1988). Harel models are event-based (as are Ward and Mellor models), and Harel models embody a strict separation of data and control (as do the Hatley and Pirbhai models). Harel's visual language for control departs from the languages of Ward and Mellor and Hatley and Pirbhai by using nested state machines as a means to level control algorithms. Both the Hatley and Pirbhai and the Ward and Mellor models assume that control is flat or "unleveled". For those two approaches it is possible to level control by chunking primitive control algorithms into summary processes on data flow diagrams. Harel allows the modeller to level control without data flow diagram notation, thereby retaining the separation of control and data. Special events, conditions and actions are defined in Harel's notation to tie the control of nested state machines at different levels together and simplify the representation of information flow between control algorithms at several levels. Harel's notation is well-suited for applications that are commonly expressed in terms of nested state machines, such as communications protocols and process control systems.

CASE Treatments

In the early 1980s software vendors emerged who sold automated support for structured analysis methods. Some would argue that the earliest CASE tool was the inception of PSL/PSA in the 1970s at the University of Michigan (Teichroew and Hershey, 1977). At that time, however. PSL/PSA as an analysis tool did not incorporate any graphics and, so, was missing the most recognizable document associated with structured analysis. PSL/PSA caught up with the other CASE tools in the 1980s. As the CASE industry emerged it focused primarily on supporting the drafting and syntax-checking of structured analysis models. Many of the heuristics have been hard to incorporate into the tools, since they have been applied with judgement and not as a rule.

CASE products have included many of the notational extensions and their corresponding syntax rules. Some products provide simulation features for structured analysis model using events and real-time extensions. Some CASE products tie prototyping facilities to the Data Dictionary component of the model. Much of the usefulness of CASE tools depends on the user's understanding and skill in doing structured analysis. Analysis is not an automated process. However, there remains opportunity in the future to provide further automated support. For example, the technique of event modeling could be better integrated into CASE products. Other automated support could simplify the mechanics of drafting and with expert system analysis of model patterns, the construction of models could be greatly simplified reducing the learning curve currently required for CASE users.

ARCHITECTURE MODELS

Background

The roots of architecture are fully recognizable in the published work on structured analysis and design, but are not very completely addressed in the general literature on structured methods. While architecture is derived from structured analysis, it is a design activity which deals with what DeMarco called the "physical" aspects of systems (DeMarco, 1978). In many system and software development projects there are two design activities, typically called architectural and detailed design. Architectural design, also known as conceptual or high-level design, is concerned with the identification of the system and software components (such as tasks, software subsystems and system subsystems) and their interrelationships. Detailed or low-level design is a discipline which organizes blocks of code to effectively execute system component functions. Complete system functional requirements include both essential and implementation requirements. During the analysis phase of a project, the architecture of a system may be partially modeled in order to define the implementation requirements requested by the customer, and explore possible configurations of components to arrive at an effective system solution. In the design phase of a project, system functions are assigned to system components, and the architectural model is refined and expanded to reflect the functions allocated to software tasks and physical processors.

Pioneers and Contributors

Architecture has grown from the notion of DeMarco's new physical model. This evolution has usually been overlooked because the effort of introducing structured analysis, focuses on getting system and software professionals to think in logical or essential ways and specifically not in design-oriented ways. DeMarco established the role of architecture as an expansion and repackaging of the analysis model. The two teams of McMenamin and Palmer and of Ward and Mellor contributed more along the same lines, but provided some clear definition lacking in DeMarco's coverage of the topic. McMenamin and Palmer added specific observations about architectural patterns and packaging strategies. Ward and Mellor provide a clear framework for architecture models, which they call an implementation DFD. Their framework consisted of levels of processor views and task views. Hatley and Pirbhai (1987) probably explored the subject of architecture more extensively than the other methodologists. They elevated the architecture model to a status of its own. They developed formal notations, suggested a means of overall model organization with a template and recognized the need for some systems to address the hardware architecture's inter-relationship with the function and information which had been defined in analysis.

The Models and Techniques

The two predominant types of architecture models used are based on DeMarco's models and on those of Hatley and Pirbhai. The models and techniques described in this section cover the innovations of all of the contributors noted above. Architecture models are generally constructed with the tools or based on the tools of structured analysis, as opposed to the primary tool of structured design: the code structure chart. The benefits of using a DFD for design become evident when considering the unwieldiness of a structure chart used to describe in detail anything that is large and when the need to show independent and asynchronous or even parallel tasks is required. The naturally asynchronous and layered DFD is a natural choice.

DeMarco's technique for physical modelling has centered around identifying the domain of change and the scope of automation, adding implementation-dependent features, and revising interfaces to reflect the new technology boundary. This process, done iteratively, should produce several alternative designs (DeMarco, 1978). These individual design options can then be evaluated in a cost-benefit study. Much of DeMarco's technique, although theoretically useful, has been tedious to perform without automated support, so the benefit of developing alternate options for evaluation become impractical. In the rush to bring new systems to market, many organizations just can't or won't find the time to build two or more architectural views. Unfortunately, the benefits of this technique, which is an open-minded evaluation of two or more viable designs, are then lost.

In their technique of essential systems analysis McMenamin and Palmer bring out some strong design patterns while describing how to avoid an implementation-bias. They define an anatomy of physical systems, showing how the shape of a system is affected by various requirements for communication and administration (McMenamin and Palmer, 1984). In their technique they discuss specifically the kinds of functions to be considered for implementation and specific strategies for packaging memory and system services. This discussion is useful as it makes the evaluation of design options a more conscious process. Ward and Mellor also address architecture packaging, which they refer to as an implementation DFD, and propose a particular method of mapping functions to an implementation view. The process symbol is used to represent physical processors at the highest level. Functions are allocated to a specific processor or processor group and required functions for the infrastructure are added. Then, functions are allocated to software tasks or task groups with consideration of added functionality for robust and reliable operation. Ward and Mellor provide clear definitions of processor and task: A processor is defined as a person or device that can store data and perform transactions. A task is defined as a set of instructions that is manipulated as a unit within the processor. (Ward and Mellor, 1985-1986). In their treatment of implementation views, they also propose separate models for system services and transportation mechanisms when their complexity warrants detailed modelling. Otherwise, if trivial, they could be left to detailed design. In practice, non-real-time systems have had, on occasion, these same issues, and the architecture definition provided by methodologists concerned with embedded and process control systems have provided some generally applicable strategies and frameworks.

Possibly the most extensive discussion of architecture within the context of structured methods is found in the Hatley and Pirbhai (1987) text. They address the expansion of the analysis model in a similar fashion to other authors, but offer a different framework for the architecture model. This framework stresses the separation of physical or hardware-related considerations from the logical or software-related considerations and is a significant part of their approach. They introduce two new notations caged Architecture Flow Diagrams (AFDs) and Architecture Interconnect Diagrams (AIDs) which are notationally derivative of DFDs. Differences with the DFD are the use of rectangles to represent system "modules" instead of circles. On the AID is the introduction of interface notation to represent different physical types of interconnects, such as mechanical linkage, an optical connection and an electronic bus (Hatley and Pirbhai, 1987). The technique used to derive the architecture models emphasizes a system engineering point of view, mapping the traceability of requirements in a matrix and showing allocation for three sets of architecture models: a system architecture, a software architecture and a hardware architecture. For easy reference to all of this information, they suggest a template which categorizes different sub-systems and related functions by using formal placement for everything in those categories. All user interface processing is positioned at the top of the diagram, device input processing to the left, device output processing to the right, and maintenance, redundancy and self-test processing at the bottom. In the center are the sub-systems which implement the essential requirements of the system. As might be imagined, this modeling approach is difficult without automation to help create, store and retrieve the various views.

Refinements

Where refinements exist for architecture, they are generally found in the literature published at conferences, by periodicals, or in discussions with seasoned practitioners. Many of the ideas about architecture refinements to structured models address timing criticality and performance issues. These issues have been addressed through the extended use of event lists and the integration of informal timing diagrams. Architecture tasks are evaluated with regard to event-response pairs and event frequency to assess potential problems with performance.

Gomaa (1986) has formally related event modeling to architectural design with the Event Sequence Diagram. An Event Sequence Diagram shows the set of tasks involved in processing a single external event and the sequence of actions expected to take place when the event occurs. An Event Sequence Diagram is constructed for every external event, and may be used during the design process to partition the system into groups of tasks and during the integration process as the basis for specifying test cases. Gomaa has also introduced notational extensions to structured models that emphasize task interface mechanisms. Three mechanisms for task interfacing are provided: message communication modules, information hiding modules, and synchronization modules. The advantage of Gomaa's notation over the others discussed so far is that both the information flow between tasks as well as the mechanism for information flow is visible on each data flow diagram. Gomma's ideas on task modeling is a subset of the formal method known as DARTS (Design Approach for Real-Time Systems) and its Ada extension ADARTS (Gomaa, 1986).

CASE Treatment

Most CASE tools do not explicitly support an architecture DFD as something different than an analysis DFD. The patterns that uniquely distinguish an implementation view in some tools may show up as notational errors or in a warning, since the CASE tools implement guidelines for analysis whose goals are different than design. Hatley and Pirbhai's notations have not yet been supported in any of the larger CASE products, which are typically used in larger embedded system development.

STRUCTURED DESIGN

The Model

The Yourdon and Constantine (1975) notation and technique for structured design is described in this section, as it is the most widely used design model and frequent companion to DeMarco's structured analysis. Other structured design models and approaches are discussed under the topic, Variations. The structured design model is called a structured chart and bears a striking resemblance to a corporate organization chart. The similarities correlate with physical representation, as well as with distribution of function in a hierarchy. In a structure chart the boxes represent a functional unit, called a "module". The structure chart has managing modules at the top and upper levels and simpler, specialized functions at the bottom. The structured chart differs from an organization chart in many of the additional notations that are used to represent interfaces, iteration, and module types and relationships. The basic notation is the hierarchy of modules and the interfaces, called couples, traveling between modules. Managing modules, dependent on their internal logic, may invoke any number of subordinates. A subordinate module may be invoked by more than one manager, supporting the design practice of isolating reusable routines. The couples may represent data or control and are shown with an open circle at the end of an arrow or a solid circle at the end of an arrow, respectively. They may travel along any hierarchical connection and represent the information passed from a manager to a subordinate and from the subordinate back to its manager upon completion of its work. The model that Constantine and his coauthors wrote about has little mention of formal support documents to declare data definitions and little notion of a formal module specification.

Those additions to structured design models have come later and reflect the influence that structured analysis models have had on design.

An interesting observation is that design notation has a far richer set of representations for ideas than does the analysis notation. Analysis stays within a limited set of notations. This idea is consistent with the different goals of the two activities. Design by its nature needs to be precise about plans for construction and needs to have correspondence to the medium of construction. Analysis uses a restricted model vocabulary to avoid encumbrance. Some of the construction specifics that may be annotated on a structure chart are recursion, iterative invocation, information hiding structures, shared parameters, hidden references from one module to another, asynchronous links, macros, library routines and transaction centers which invoke subordinate modules based on mutually exclusive conditions.

The Technique

An important part of structured design is its provision of extensive guidelines to determine the quality of a design. Most of the Yourdon-Constantine book, in fact, discusses methods for deriving and refining structure charts through classification of patterns and observations about independence. A key concept has been the treatment of a module as a black-box, which could be understood by its external characteristics: its name, inputs and outputs. In using black-boxes, designers could keep their thinking at a higher level of detail and avoid getting caught up in the internals of specific conditional logic, algorithms and procedural steps.

Most notable among the structured design guidelines is the classification of interfaces and of module partitioning called coupling and cohesion, respectively. Coupling is the degree of interdependence of two or more modules. Cohesion is the strength of association of the elements inside of a single module. Coupling and cohesion work hand in hand; weak coupling of a module to other modules is almost always an indication that the module has poor cohesion. Strongly cohesive modules tend to be loosely coupled to other modules. Structured Design furnishes objective yardsticks for the measurement of inter-module coupling and cohesion. The five categories of coupling, data, stamp, control, common, and content coupling, are listed in decreasing order of quality:

- Data coupling is the simplest form of coupling. Atomic data elements are passed to and from a module through module parameter passing.
- Stamp coupling is where at least one parameter passed along an interface contains an internal structure. Examples of stamp coupling are: strings or records.
- Control coupling is where a flag is passed along an interface. The flow of control in the receiving module can be altered by testing the flag.
- Common coupling is where two or more modules share a common data area. An example of common coupling is any global information.
- The weakest form of coupling is content coupling, where one module needs to know data structures or program statements that exist in another module. Examples of content coupling are: branches from one module into another, a module that changes program statements in other modules (self-modifying code) and a module that reads and writes a static memory area scoped for use within another module.

Cohesion reflects the thought process of the designer creating and maintaining a module. The criteria used to determine whether an activity belongs inside of the module governs which cohesion category best fits it. Designers tend to think in the following seven categories of cohesion, functional, sequential, communicational, procedural, temporal, logical and coincidental, listed in decreasing order of quality:

- Functional cohesion is the strongest; activities within the module form one natural group of processing. It would be difficult to imagine any circumstance within the life of the system where it would be necessary to relocate any of the activities in the module.
- (Sequential or communicational cohesion refers to a module whose activities are related by data and is often a result of good analysis using data flow diagrams).
- Sequential cohesion is characterized by a sequence of processing where the output of one activity is the input to the next.
- Communicational cohesion occurs when the module elements operate on the same input data set or produce the same output data, without any restrictions on the sequence of processing. The result of each activity would be the same regardless of the order in which it was performed.

(Procedural and Temporal Cohesion refer to a module whose activities are related by flow of control and are not related by data, and is often a result of thinking with flowcharts. Procedural and Temporal Cohesion often cut across functional lines because fragments of unrelated functions that share a common control algorithm are grouped together).

- Procedural cohesion occurs when the designer packages a branch of a flow chart into a single module. The activities will be executed in the order reflected in the original flowchart.
- Temporal cohesion is where all of the activities in the module are required or permitted to take place within a specific time period. Examples of temporal cohesion are Start-up and Wrap-up modules.

The remaining two categories classify modules that are not related by data or by control flow. The criteria for including activities within the module is weaker.

- Logical cohesion implies the elements fall into the same logical class of similar or related functions. Examples of logical cohesion are: Input modules, where all system inputs are managed by this module; and Validation modules, where all incoming data is validated regardless of source, type or use. The problem with logical cohesion is that an entire class of activities has been squeezed into one module, and control is used to select only one of the activities. Often the control logic is complex and the activities hopelessly interlocked.

- Coincidental cohesion is where there is little or no constructive relationship among the activities of a module. Coincidental cohesion is most often the result of years of maintenance on a module that was originally designed with a stronger cohesion.

Structured design strives for the best coupling and cohesion possible. Coupling may often be improved by reorganizing the placement of modules in the hierarchy or re-partitioning the structure chart. Common coupling may be improved by encapsulating the common data in an information cluster. Information clusters, also known as information-hiding modules, are based on the concepts of information hiding introduced by Parnas (1972). Interface functions are provided as the sole means of access to the shared information contained in the cluster, so that the actual data structure is hidden from all other modules. This method minimizes the amount of rework required to other modules when either the structure or the meaning of the shared information changes. There will be times when a designer must create a module with a relatively low category of coupling or cohesion. For example, many systems require a start-up module. The designer may be able to minimize the size of the start-up module by factoring out functionally cohesive sets of start-up activities into independent modules to be called by the start-up module. When settling for a lower category of coupling or cohesion, the designer is able to anticipate maintenance problems and plan accordingly.

Another important aspect of design is system morphology or shape, which is the placement of modules in a hierarchy. A hierarchy is an imposition of control, where higher level modules determine when lower level modules will be invoked. In Structured Design, decision making logic is placed closer to the top of a hierarchy and modules that carry out the work related to the decisions, are placed closer to the bottom of a hierarchy. Decision-making logic is the most complex to write and test, so it is beneficial to isolate decision makers from the modules that perform work. Another perspective on system shape is the impact a change to a single module can have on other modules in its hierarchy. Generally, the higher the module is placed in the hierarchy, the more modules could be affected by the change. A guideline of Structured Design is to place modules that are likely to change closer to the bottom of the hierarchy to limit impact of change, while placing modules that are stable closer to the top. As an example, I/O functions tend to be placed near the bottom of the structure chart to minimize the impact of environmental changes to the design.

In addition to guidelines for determining the quality of a design, Structured Design provides strategies for design. It is important to recall that Structured Design Techniques predate Structured Analysis and Architecture. Early design practice has been to "restate the design problem as a data flow diagram", then convert the data flow diagram into an initial structure chart using Transform and Transaction Analysis techniques (Constantine and co-workers, 1974). Multiple tasks and operating system interventions were explicitly shown on a single structure chart. As Structured Analysis and Structured Architecture have evolved, the strength of Constantine's Transform and Transaction Analysis techniques have been tested. In practice, they are not reliable, although the patterns associated with the techniques can be used when refining or evaluating an existing design.

The strength of Transform Analysis is its ability to produce an initial design with a desirable system shape- interfaces to the the physical environment are placed low in the hierarchy, while essential system functionality is placed high in the hierarchy. As modern application development is supported by system services, and by layered design concepts, the isolation and placement of physical interfaces is addressed at the architectural design phase, instead of the detailed design phase, and so the need for Transform Analysis is reduced. In addition, the success of Transaction and Transform Analysis depends on the modellers' ability to spot patterns in Data Flow Diagrams which for new modelers is nearly impossible.

Text book examples of small systems never have reflected the large, leveled DFDs that practitioners are faced with. The application of Transform and Transaction Analysis to large systems is non-trivial. Most practitioners construct a set of structure charts, one per software task defined on the Architectural Model. First cut designs are based on a simple top-down conversion algorithm, where the levels of hierarchy on the initial structure chart matches the levels of organization of the task's architecture. This is then refined to accommodate the designers needs relative to maintenance, flexibility, and efficiency. Top-down conversion is easier for new modelers and for large systems.

Pioneers, Contributors, and Model Variations

The design methods of the seventies was really divided into two camps: process-driven approaches and data-driven approaches. Larry Constantine laid the foundation for process-driven approaches. Wayne Stevens, Glenford Myers, and Edward Yourdon all contributed to Structured Design. Myers and Stevens were colleagues interested in the extensive research that Constantine had already done on software design. They added new ideas and refined the existing ideas of Constantine. Yourdon added his own research and practical experience on program and software design and also the considerable effort that his company, Yourdon, Inc. had on the popularization of the methods. Meilir Page-Jones' book *The Practical Guide to Structured System Design* (1979) was a significant text in that it synthesized many good ideas of all of the existent design techniques, in addition to integrating the good ideas from structured analysis. It is in the Page-Jones book that formalizations of module specifications and data dictionaries are brought together with structure charts in a methodology.

An opposing camp in software program design was the data-driven approach of Michael Jackson and Jean-Dominique Warnier. Their methods received more use in their own countries (England and France), but were recognized in the United States due to their claim to be easier than the process-driven design approaches of Constantine and co-workers (1974). Data-driven techniques base the hierarchical structure of a program on the hierarchical structure of the information in files and transactions used by the program. Data-driven techniques uses the same basic notation to represent program and data structures. This breakdown of data structures and program structures are based on the structured programming constructs of sequence, selection and iteration. For example, a file containing a header and a set of records would be represented as a sequence consisting of one header, and iterations of records. The corresponding program to read the file would consist of the invocation of a sequence of two modules. The first module will read the header, and the second module will iteratively read records from the file. This match of the program structure to the data structure is at the core of data-driven design. Warnier contributed the original ideas of data-driven design (Warnier, 1974). Jackson extended the scope of data-driven design to address multitasking and system design, and introduced techniques for dealing with input and output data structures that don't combine well to form a neat program structure (Jackson, 1975).

Ken Orr has been responsible for the popularization of data-driven design in the U.S. Orr used Warnier's notation to express software design, which was the only hierarchical model that didn't use boxes, but used successive brackets, "{", to show the breakdown of processes that were subsets of other processes, keeping in mind that Warnier's technique, like Jackson's, was data-driven. Orr extended the Warnier's notation to the representation of systems design and even analysis (Orr, 1977).

CASE Treatment

Most CASE treatments cover only notation, and many do not cover all of it. Links to a Data Dictionary and module specifications may or may not be provided. Some CASE tools don't fully incorporate coupling. Technique guidelines such as coupling and cohesion are provided with tools that have a Data Dictionary link. The CASE industry focused on SA as an initial product offering. Only with the rise in interest in reverse engineering has Structured Design reemerged in importance. However, reverse engineering may produce a very weakly annotated model. Practitioners would like to see CASE tools provide a Data Dictionary, module specifications containing the source code, and coupling and cohesion analysis on reverse engineered code. Practitioners would also like the ability to seamlessly perform forward and reverse engineering of code from structure charts. CASE tools have the potential to automate the creation of a first-cut structure chart from a data flow diagram by employing the top-down conversion technique. Few CASE tools support any automated generation of structure charts from Data Flow Diagrams.

BIBLIOGRAPHY

C. Bohm, and G. Jacopini, "Flow Diagrams, Turing Machines, and Languages with Only Two Formation Rules," *Communications of the ACM* **9**(5), 366–371 (May 1966), reprinted in Yourdon (1979).

P. Chen, "The Entity-Relationship Model: Toward a Unified View of Data," *ACM Transactions on Database Systems,* **1**(1), 9–36 (Mar. 1976).

L. Constantine, G. Myers, and W. Stevens, "Structured Design," *IBM Systems Journal,* **13**(2), 115–139 (May 1974), reprinted in Yourdon (1979).

T. DeMarco, *Structured Analysis and Systems Specification,* Yourdon Press, Englewood Cliffs, N.J., 1978.

T. DeMarco, *Structured Analysis and System Specification,* Yourdon, Inc., seminar, ed. 6.1, 1979.

T. DeMarco, "Structured Analysis: The Beginnings of a New Discipline," *Proceedings of The First National Conference on Software Methods,* Orlando, Fla., Mar. 30–Apr. 1, 1992.

T. DeMarco, and T. Lister, *Software State of the Art: Selected Papers,* Dorset House, New York, 1990.

M. Flavin, *Fundamentals Concepts of Information Modeling,* Yourdon Press, New York, 1981.

C. Gane, and T. Sarson, *Structured Systems Analysis: Tools and Techniques,* Improved System Technologies, Inc., New York, 1977.

H. Gomaa, "Software Development of Real-Time Systems," *Communications of the ACM,* **29**(7), 657–658 (July, 1986).

D. Harel, H. Lachover, A. Naamad, A. Pnueli, M. Politi, R. Sherman, and A. Shtul-Trauring, "Stalemate: A Working Environment for the Development of Complex Reactive Systems," *Proceedings of the IEEE Tenth International Conference on Software Engineering,* Singapore, Apr. 11–15, 1988, pp. 396–406, reprinted in (DeMarco and Lister, 1990).

D. J. Hatley, and I. Pirbhai, *Strategies for Real-Time System Specification,* Dorset House Publishing, New York, 1987.

M. Jackson, *Principles of Program Design,* Academic Press, London, 1975.

D. A. Marca, and C. L. McGowan, *SADT: Structured Analysis and Design Technique,* McGraw-Hill Book Co., Inc., New York, 1988.

S. McMenamin, and J. Palmer, *Essential Systems Analysis,* Yourdon Press, New York, 1984.

G. A. Miller, "The Magic Number Seven, Plus or Minus Two: Some Limits on our Capacity for Processing Information," *Psychological Review,* **63,** 81–97 (Mar. 1956), reprinted in Yourdon (1982).

G. J. Myers, *Reliable Software Through Composite Design,* Petrocelli/Charter, New York, 1975.

K. Orr, *Structured Systems Development,* Yourdon Press, New York, 1977.

M. Page-Jones, *A Practical Guide to Structured Systems Design,* Yourdon Press, Englewood Cliffs, N.J., 1979; 2nd ed., 1988.

D. L. Parnas, "On the Criteria to Be Used in Decomposing Systems into Modules," *Communications of the ACM,* **15**(12), 1053–1058, (Dec. 1972), reprinted in Yourdon (1979).

D. Ross, and K. E. Shoman, Jr., "Structured Analysis for Requirements Definition," *IEEE Transactions on Software Engineering,* **SE-3**(1) (Jan. 1977).

D. Teichroew, and E. A. Hershey, III, "PSL/PSA: A Computer-Aided Technique for Structured Documentation and Analysis of Information Processing Systems," *IEEE Transactions on Software Engineering,* **SE-3**(1), 41–48 (Jan. 1977), reprinted in Yourdon, 1979).

P. Ward, and S. Mellor, *Structured Specifications for Real-time Systems,* vols. 1–3, Yourdon Press, Englewood Cliffs, N.J., 1985–1986.

P. Ward, "The Evolution of Structured Analysis, Part II: Maturity and its Problems," *The American Programmer,* **5**(4) (Apr. 1992).

J. D. Warnier, *Logical Construction of Programs,* Van Nostrand Reinhold Co., Inc., New York, 1974.

V. Weinberg, *Structured Analysis,* Yourdon Press, New York, 1978.

N. Wirth, "Program Development by Stepwise Refinement," *Communications of the ACM,* **14**(4), 221–227 (Apr. 1971).

E. Yourdon, and L. Constantine, *Structured Design,* Yourdon Press, New York, 1975; 2nd ed., 1979.

E. Yourdon, *Classics in Software Engineering,* Yourdon Press, New York, 1979.

E. Yourdon, *Writings of the Revolution,* Yourdon Press, Englewood Cliffs, N.J., 1982.

IRA WEINSTEIN
REBECCA WINANT
Esprit Systems Consulting, Inc.

STRUCTURED PROGRAM

A computer program constructed of a basic set of control structures, each having one entry and one exit. The set of control structures typically includes: sequence of two or more instructions, conditional selection of one or more sequences of instructions, and repetition of a sequence of instructions (IEEE).

STRUCTURED PROGRAMMING

Any software development technique that includes structured design and results in the development of structured programs.

STRUCTURED WALKTHROUGH

A Structured Walkthrough is sometimes referred to as a variant form of a Walkthrough. Freedman classifies a Structured Walkthrough as a Walkthrough. In the vernacular it is sometimes used to connote procedure to a Walkthrough, as opposed to what may be a more unstructured peer review. However, in the accepted use of the term "Walkthrough" a definite procedure is followed calling for a presenter, the review leader, a recorder, the developer, and other reviewers. Thus, the use of the term has no real meaning except to place emphasis on the discipline of the procedure that is dictated (see REVIEWS AND AUDITS.) [D. P. Freedman and G. M. Weinberg, *Walkthroughs, Inspections, and Technical Reviews,* 3rd ed., Dorset House, New York, 1990, p. 232.]

SYMBOLIC DEBUGGERS

See SYSTEM DEBUGGING.

SYMBOLIC LANGUAGE

A programming language that expresses operations and addresses in symbols convenient to humans rather in machine language. Examples are Assembly language; high order language (IEEE).

SYNTAX TESTING

See TESTING.

SYSREM

See SYSTEM REQUIREMENTS ENGINEERING METHODOLOGY.

SYSTEM BUILDS

INTRODUCTION

Software build is the process used to construct an executable software program from it components. Inputs and outputs of the process normally consist of the following:

Inputs	Outputs
Source Code	Executable Program
Object Code	Listings, Memory Maps and Other Documentation
Compiler/Assembler or Translator	
Linker	
Computer Control Language Directives	

There can be a variety of inputs to the build process depending upon the source code language chosen for the program; however, the output is always an executable program with some documentation. A software build takes source and/or object code and produces an executable representation of the code. Languages such as C, C++, and

Ada require a compiler to produce object code from source and then a linker to produce executable code from object code. Some high-level languages, such as FoxPro, FOCUS, and CLIPPER are able to create an executable program directly from the source code. The programmer is required to instruct the development computer on how to create the executable program through the use of computer control language directives. These instructions vary according to the source language and/or the computer system that will execute the program.

Using the above stated inputs, the typical software build process consists of the following steps:

1. Computer control language directives are prepared; these will tell the development computer the proper compiler/assembler or translator and associated user options to use, where to find the source code, and where to put resultant intermediate and final outputs.
2. The compiler/assembler or translator is executed with source code provided as input, and associated listings, objects, or final executable output is produced and placed in storage files as directed by the computer language directives.
3. If intermediate object is produced, for instance COBOL or FORTRAN, then a linker tool may be necessary to complete the build process and produce the executable representation of the code. A linker will take object code created by a compiler or assembler and produce an executable representation of the code which, along with the listings, memory maps, and other documentation.

The build process assists the software developer in many evaluation and delivery preparation activities. Builds of prototype or temporary code are performed during the development process to produce executable programs that aid in validation of software requirements and designs. One of the last steps in the development process is to perform a build of all the components producing the final executable program for delivery to the user. Depending on the software development model chosen, software builds may occur very early in the requirements definition phase and continue until the final executable is produced. In some models, builds of deliverable code may only occur after coding is complete for one or more components. Let's examine how software builds may be utilized during typical software development phases. The reader is referred to other sections of this encyclopedia for discussions on software life cycles and development models. A generic and rather simple model will be used here to demonstrate the flexibility and usefulness of software builds as a tool to assist the developer in producing high-quality products.

REQUIREMENTS DEFINITION

A build may be used very early in the development process to produce an executable prototype of the software program. In such a case, the developer may code a small portion of the program and provide nonfunctional components (stubs) for the remainder of the program. The resultant build is a prototype and is very limited functionally, but it is intended to only provide enough functionality to validate one or more requirements. Normally, the prototype is shown to a user or user representative who will verify that the functionality is or is not properly represented by the build. Many requirements are easily verified by using prototypes and builds. For example, the location of information on a display; the results of an algorithm; and response times to certain inputs all may be verified in this manner. The developer can utilize an iterative process of modification and demonstration to refine the builds functionality until the requirement is clearly understood and demonstrated. When the developer has successfully captured a requirement in this manner, it may then be documented succinctly in a requirements specification. Code produced for such a prototype purposes may or may not be used in the final software product. The resultant requirements specification forms the functional baseline for the product.

DESIGN

During the design phase, the developer will use the functional baseline to establish the architecture of the software product. Functionality will be allocated to a module or group of modules. The developer can utilize prototyping and builds to determine the optimum allocation of requirements to modules to meet functional and performance requirements. The resulting software structure, algorithms, and user interfaces becomes the detailed design. This information is normally documented in detail design documents and/or software development folders and will establish the allocated baseline for code development and test.

CODE AND A UNIT TESTING

Once the developer begins to write code, the software build process takes on an added dimension of importance. The developer will normally plan ahead to determine when each module or collection of coded modules is needed in order to be able to test certain functionality. This planning activity normally involves others besides the developer. Quality assurance, configuration management, project management, and the customer may play roles in determining the schedule for module coding and unit test activities. This overall plan is termed a software build plan, and its preparation is normally part of the code and unit test phase activities. It will define module content and schedule for many builds that will be constructed over time and will lead to a final build of all modules representing the complete software product. Planning and scheduling the coding efforts to produce modules that enable builds and subsequent testing early in this phase minimize the time needed to complete the coding phase. As modules are demonstrated to satisfy their intended functionality, they should be put under a change control process to ensure that no unauthorized changes are made. This will also ensure repeatability of the completed testing and the integrity of the code.

Logically, a software program requires a minimum number (as few as one) of individual modules to be coded before the first build can be performed. For this reason, it is important to analyze and plan the coding activity so that an orderly flow of coded modules is produced. The modules can be built and unit-tested as coding continues. This collection or configuration of modules is usually given a name (identification) and is normally placed under change control following unit testing. Once coded, the developer will compile or assemble the modules to remove syntax errors as the first step of the the build process. The compiler outputs may be used to conduct code inspections to evaluate the quality and completeness of the code and documentation on a module-by-module basis. When a sufficient number of modules have been coded, the developer will create the first build and perform tests to demonstrate the functionality of each module. As each new module or collection of modules is coded, the developer will incorporate them with previously tested modules and perform another build for further testing. This process continues until all modules are coded and tested.

INTEGRATION AND SYSTEM TESTING

The process of integrating configurations of software modules for testing system functionality is accomplished by creating a software build using selected unit tested modules and by testing the resultant executable. Normally this level of testing also requires a schedule and plan, relying on software builds, in order to ensure that system testing objectives are met. The build plan used for this phase may be an extension of the build plan used during the code and unit test phase above, or it may be a separate plan. If the integration and system test activities are conducted in parallel with code and unit test activities, then the schedule and plan for integration and system test builds will be closely coordinated with the code and unit test build plan. Otherwise, system integration and test activities will begin after all modules have been coded and unit tested.

The software build process is one of the principle tools used to conduct integration and system test. The tester will have prepared a test plan and procedure for the system. These test plans and procedures are normally dependent on having selected configurations of functionality available in the executable being tested. The tester will use software builds to produce selected configurations of modules, hence functionality, for testing. When system testing is completed, the configuration of modules built and tested becomes the product baseline.

MAINTENANCE

Software maintenance activities normally begin after the product has completed development and has been accepted by the customer(s). Typical activities that occur during this phase include correction of problems, addition of new features, or adaptation of the software to function with other products. Software builds assist the developer in performing these activities.

In isolating and correcting problems, software builds assist the developer in creating executable configurations consisting of reduced functionality that may simplify problem isolation. Also, the developer may use builds to incorporate special debug tools into the software that will help in detection and isolation of faults. Builds may be used to verify the completeness and accuracy of the code to correct a problem. The developer will rebuild the software by replacing the original code with changed code and perform on to demonstrate that the problem has been corrected.

Adding increased functionality involves repeating the development steps outlined above except that a product baseline of coded and tested modules already exists that the developer will add to and/or replace with new modules. Software builds will be utilized in much the same way as during initial development to verify new requirements, proposed design, verify coded modules, and perform integration and system test.

CHARLES R. FREDERICK
Consultant

SYSTEM DEBUGGING: A BROAD PERSPECTIVE

INTRODUCTION

System debugging is the diagnostic and repair work that begins after a system fails, and it concludes with successful repair and testing of the product. The knowledge and skills of system debuggers are varied. Accordingly, this article will cover a diversity of topics, both psychological and technological, including traits of expert debuggers, mental representations used by experts for understanding systems, strategies used in debugging, social factors impacting debugging effectiveness, the management of debugging expertise, and debugging technologies and tools.

This article is organized in the following manner. After a brief discussion of the history of debugging, a five-stage model of debugging is described, consisting of familiarization, stabilization, localization, correction, and validation. Several of these stages are used to organize the two following sections of this article, which concern the psychology and technology of debugging. This article concludes with a discussion of management issues relevant to system debugging.

History and Recent Trends

In the early years of commercial computing, debugging was characterized by several attributes. Debugging, like programming, was generally conducted in batch mode. At best, this may have elicited meticulous reasoning and planning among debuggers; at worst, it was inefficient and frustrating in the extreme. Tools for detecting and representing malfunctions were relatively simple and few. For example, Greenwald and Kane (1959) noted that, "The most generally used debugging technique is the post-mortem (static) dump" (Parenthesis by the original authors). This technology required programmers to debug code offline in a lower level language than that in which the source code was written. Greenwald and Kane noted that an alternative technique, run-time tracing (using print statements embedded in source code, for example) was often prohibitively costly in machine time and programmer time during the era about which they reported.

Advances in computing hardware, operating systems, and programming environments and techniques have revolutionized debugging. Among the most influential factors has been the rise of interactive computing in place of the batch environment. This advance makes it practical to debug programs by altering their data values and execution paths during execution. Modern symbolic debuggers also enable a programmer to debug code in the high-level language in which it is written and to insert sophisticated conditional debugging commands that reduce the attention the programmer must devote to monitoring the system during diagnosis (Serberger, 1985). Advances in computer graphics have provided new ways of visualizing the flow of control and data during execution. The availability of vast storage has made it practical to record execution histories through which advanced debuggers can backtrack (Agrawal and co-workers, 1991), or with which serial representations of parallel execution can be created. Artificial intelligence techniques have made it possible to process the same historical databases in ways that facilitate hypothesis testing (Tsai, Fang, and Chen, 1989) and to build intelligent, domain-specific debugging tools (Akao, Imai, and Tsuchida, 1989).

Have these advances made debugging a trivial task? They have not. Studies indicate that software engineers spend upward of 50% of their time engaged in one form of debugging or another, and this proportion has not changed significantly over at least two decades (Boehm, 1977). Several technical and institutional factors account for the constant enormity of the debugging burden.

While the development and debugging tools and techniques have improved substantially, the size and complexity of systems has increased at the same time. With regard to complexity, it is known that a major source of failures in systems lies in the interfaces between functional modules (Jones, 1988). Larger and more complex systems are composed of more modules and thus, correspondingly, more interfaces between modules. This greater number of interfaces increases the opportunity for defects and errors to be incorporated into the systems.

In addition, many of the systems developed and deployed over the past decade are now manifesting failures attributable to changes in execution environments (including processing load, data characteristics, user activities, and associated hardware and software). These changes violate assumptions originally made in the design and implementation of these systems. Thus subtle and difficult-to-define problems are arising with increasing frequency in systems long in the field.

Another cause of failure, both for these systems and for those that have not undergone significant environmental changes, is the emergence of bugs on rarely exercised execution paths. Though such events decrease in frequency over time, they increase in subtlety as "easy" bugs are eliminated, leaving the "hard" bugs for last. Such problems pose a special challenge to maintenance personnel. Regrettably, the people who are assigned to do maintenance work are often the most inexperienced and the least trained.

Information concerning debugging procedures and strategies is scarce. Texts on the topic are rare (Koenig, 1989; Ward, 1986). Debugging is not taught in most undergraduate or graduate curricula, nor has the Joint ACM/IEEE-Computer Science Curriculum Task Force recommended that it be integrated into these curricula in the near future (Tucker, 1991). Debugging is rarely taught in industry, where it is generally assumed that new hires will pick up the necessary skills as they study and practice professionally. This assumption is rarely made with respect to other costly, complex, and time-consuming tasks. The lack of texts and training is important because debugging involves skills that differ from those acquired in design and programming courses. For example, the dominant methodological model for system construction is engineering, but the model employed in debugging is the scientific method. Some of the heuristics of debugging are unique to that discipline, among them stack tracebacks. Design heuristics, such as tossing out the first draft or fitting every module on a page, are an anathema to debugging, just as debugging heuristics like suspecting pointers and tests involving "=" are foreign to design. In the long run, lack of debugging training leads to costly delays in diagnosing and correcting defects. This article discusses a number of important areas that training, to be effective, should include, such as strategy and teamwork.

These issues are compounded by a right-minded emphasis in industry on preventing bugs through disciplined design as well as an unfortunate, related view of debugging as a diminishing and minor activity. This belief, however inaccurate, has resulted in industry giving relatively little time, attention, or resource to developing the debugging skills of developers (as discussed above). Academics have not conducted as much research in the field as is warranted given the immensity of the debugging burden. Extant academic research is generally restricted to nonrepresentative problems, or it focuses on advanced technologies not yet in use in industry.

Given that developers have, for decades, spent a significant proportion of their time debugging, coupled with the growing complexity of systems, the changing environments of older ones, the staffing preferences of management, and a general lack of focus on debugging research and education, it stands to reason that debugging will continue to constitute a major part of programmer activity.

We now turn to the stages of debugging, the strategies of expert debuggers, debugging tools, and factors involved in managing debuggers. Much of this discussion will concern system maintenance, since that often involves the most difficult debugging. Many of the examples used here concern software systems, but the principles can be employed on systems of all types.

STAGES OF THE DEBUGGING PROCESS

The debugging process has five stages: familiarization, stabilization, localization, correction, and validation:

Familiarization. The programmer studies the system in order to build an understanding, a foundation, on which to frame hypotheses about the bug.

Stabilization. This phase is devoted to acquiring adequate experimental control over the system in the debugging environment. The debugger attempts to recreate the symptom and to experiment with inputs and environmental parameters to determine the range or generality of conditions that produce the behavior.

Localization. The debugger begins actively searching for the bug. The debugger uses the knowledge gained during stabilization to formulate a hypothesis about the location of the bug, to construct an experiment to test the hypothesis, and to use the results to refine the hypothesis or build a new one.

Correction. Having identified a likely cause for the system failure, the debugger corrects the code or replaces the faulty component.

Validation. During validation, the debugger exercises the corrected code to confirm that the change behaves as expected and that the changes have not wrought new damage. Depending on the subtlety of the bug, this step is as simple as a demonstration run using the test input developed during stabilization, or it can be as extensive as a full set of regression tests employing both the data used for acceptance testing and the data generated during stabilization and localization.

While debuggers can and often do proceed through these stages in sequence, their insights sometimes shorten the path, and their confusion or technical difficulties can twist the linear sequence of complex cycles. Nonetheless, it is helpful for individuals interested in improving their debugging expertise to approach debugging as a scientific enterprise involving the stages just described.

This article principally concerns the first three stages of debugging: familiarization, stabilization, and localization. Correction and validation correspond to the design, programming, and system testing procedures used during development and modification. They are not addressed below. However, see the articles, DESIGN; TESTING; VERIFICATION AND VALIDATION.

THE PSYCHOLOGY OF SYSTEM DEBUGGING

Strategies for Several Stages of Debugging

Familiarization. Expert debuggers have two advantages that empower them to use the five-stage model better than novices: their knowledge is broader, deeper, and better organized; and their strategies are superior. Readers of this article undoubtedly appreciate the importance of expert knowledge in debugging: experienced debuggers simply recognize situations that others struggle to understand. Psychological research verifies that experts more quickly and accurately perceive important patterns in source code (KcKeithen and co-workers, 1981; Ehrlich and Soloway, 1984; Adelson, 1981) and in abstract representations of system structure and dynamics, such as data-flow diagrams (Pennington, 1987a). However, experts also leverage their knowledge further than novices by using the familiarization strategies discussed here.

Study Longer. A principle tactic of expert debuggers during familiarization is simply to spend a great deal of time studying the buggy system, more time than novices invest on average. Experts work longer at this phase despite their ability to comprehend code and documentation more quickly than novices (Nanja and Cook, 1987; Vessey, 1985; Oman, Cook, and Nanja, 1989).

By spending more time in the familiarization stage, experts gain at least two benefits. One is a better memory for code. This enables them to recall and locate relevant parts of a program easily (Jeffries, 1982). The second benefit is a richer understanding of the code. With deeper knowledge, the debugger can quickly construct different representations of the system as strategy and circumstances demand. For example, the expert can shift between control flow and data flow descriptions rapidly and as needed (Littman and co-workers, 1986; Pennington, 1987a). Finally, the additional preparation time may help experienced practicioners to discard poor hypotheses more quickly. Because less experienced debuggers do not familiarize themselves as thoroughly with the system, they more easily become disoriented when reading, have fewer strategies for representing and thinking about the system, and may generate and test hypotheses prematurely and, thus, futilely.

Study Better

Study Actively. Experienced debuggers not only study systems longer, but better, according to in-depth interviews by Riedl and co-workers, (1991). Like good students generally, they are active readers. Experts select what they do and do not read, a strategy that is expressed in the heuristic, "Don't read source code until you have to." They often rely heavily on other experts and system specifications to help them select key modules for study. When they do read complex documents, such as source code, expert debuggers, like good readers, attend to their assumptions and their insights by hunting for evidence that verifies them. Finally, better debuggers do more than ask themselves how a system works; they ask why it was designed to work in the way that it does. Thus they are more likely to perceive changes in the operating environment of older, putatively stable systems that violate the assumptions made by the original designers.

To implement these strategies when reviewing code, experienced debuggers apply at least two distinct methods of reading. Loose reading, a form of scanning, is used to generate a rough sense of implementation and to gather cues concerning code quality that help the debugger predict classes of errors. Close reading involves examining the details of implementation and simulating execution at relevant levels of detail. In short, loose reading is done to determine the "what" of a program (the author's intentions), while close reading is done to determine the "how" of implementation. Expert programmers commonly assert that their juniors become caught in detailed code inspection too early in debugging, or they fail to inspect key procedures with adequate rigor. They advise novices to attend to the need to shift between loose and close reading strategically. Not coincidentally, this is the same recommendation that instructors of general study skills courses offer to their students.

When experienced debuggers study systems, they are peculiarly perceptive to what we will call *differences* and *cues to quality*. Differences are changes in environmental factors that force a historically well behaved system to fail. Those factors, and sources of information about them, can be categorized as follows:

- Recent changes to software or hardware. Information concerning such changes is often recorded through software management systems, noted in code comments, or carried by gossip within the development team.
- Recent changes in data quantity or quality. Data-related information is often captured by system accounting or monitoring functions, or can be garnered from interviews with users and field personnel.
- Recent changes in users or use patterns. Users and their supervisors, as well as monitoring subsystems, can provide cues to shifts in use. Changes in use and data are particularly relevant when a system fails unexpectedly after years of reliable use.
- Differences between the development, testing, and field environments that may explain why bugs arise in the field but not the lab. Hardware configuration, processing load, concurrent processes, and user practices are often among these.

Attention to these factors can help narrow the scope of a debugging venture.

Expert debuggers also look for a variety of peculiar cues to quality in code that point to misconceptions by the original developers. Experienced debuggers note nonstandard styles of structuring and writing code. These often connote problems. They read code comments for evidence of inaccuracy, incompleteness, or incomprehensibility that may indicate sloppy coding or undocumented revisions. Finally, experts concern themselves with the number of changes a given-piece of code has undergone and the number of authors involved. Numerous changes sometimes indicate a perennially troublesome procedure. The greater the number of authors who have worked on the code, the more likely it is that the code is problematic. The history of code changes and authorship are easily traced if the developers and maintenance staff use a formal change control system (such as the Source Code Control System (SCCS) or Revision Control System (RCS) available under Unix).

Thus the familiarization stage involves learning about technical aspects of a system as well as attending to subtle cues concerning the quality of authorship. These cues help to eliminate or generate debugging hypotheses.

This review of strategies for system familiarization has focused on expert practices such as investing heavily in studying the system at the outset of an assignment, studying strategically, and capitalizing on the knowledge of colleagues. Strategies for the stabilization phase are discussed next.

Stabilization. During the stabilization phase, the debugger manipulates the environment until the symptoms arise consistently, then continues this work to learn the range of conditions that generate the failure. Replicating a failure involves simultaneously manipulating at least four classes of factors: hardware, operating environment, data quantity, and data quality.

Hardware. The debugger must attempt to reproduce the hardware platform involved. This can be simple if the target system is a kitchen blender, difficult but manageable if it is a microcomputer, or prohibitively complex and expensive if it is a large-scale customized device such as a telephone switching system. In the last case, the debugger may have to do much of the work on a device that simulates the performance of the target system, and run some complex or hardware-specific tests on the field system or a shared, laboratory-based unit. Under such conditions, experts place a premium on understanding the differences between the field and laboratory platforms (for example, differences in word length between the simulator and the field unit), interviewing observers for the details of failure scenarios, studying error reports in depth, and designing tests that are as simple, quick, and conclusive as possible.

Operating Environment. The debugger must experimentally manipulate environmental parameters for each test run. While system configuration is often easy to replicate from start-up files, the same cannot be said of the initial state of system memory and the events associated with interactive use and concurrent processes. For example, when debugging a database application, the debugger will probably not go to the trouble of replicating an automated, daily, field audit of database integrity. However, audits have been known to inject errors into otherwise stable systems. The matter of replicating environmental parameters is ripe with judgement calls, and debuggers are well-advised to consult liberally with users, field personnel, and system authors concerning salient events.

Data Quantity. The amount of system traffic or processing load must also be experimentally controlled, particularly in cases where race conditions and memory allocation errors are suspected. Unfortunately, the quantity of data processed over time is difficult to replicate if it has not been monitored in the field.

Data Quality. The quality of system data—by which is meant the specific data values encountered at run-time—is best replicated by using the data involved in a field failure. When this isn't available, as is often the case, the debugger must use some approximation of the data. The importance of communicating well with field technicians and users is at a premium in this situation.

Testing the Range of Failure Conditions. If the debugger can replicate hardware, environment, data quantity, and data quality, then the failure should reoccur reliably. If these factors cannot be replicated because of the complexity or expense of doing so, or because the failure scenario was not documented, then the debugger must form hypothyses which are the most culpable characteristics and test whether they produce the failure. This process involves the hypothesis generation and testing strategies discussed in the following section on localization.

The final stage of stabilization is to expand the boundaries of the failure conditions experimentally, that is, to identify the broadest range of conditions that produce the symptom. For example, the literature on software testing suggests a number of data "boundary values" that can be worth testing. These include values that trigger important control constructs, extreme conditions for data structures (such as empty arrays), and arithmetic boundaries, including those that generate faults (division by zero), those that cause overflow, and those that probe conceptually difficult number schemes such as hexadecimal or modulus operations.

Localization. Successful debuggers are concerned, during the localization stage, with generating insightful hypotheses and testing them rigorously.

Generating Hypotheses. Hypothesis generation is fundamentally a creative act. It is difficult to specify how to go about conceiving of clever hypotheses, even in a specific domain, like debugging. However, psychological research on human problem solving has identified several domain-independent strategies on which debuggers rely. The following list is arranged roughly in order from the most to least economical and effective methods for debuggers.

Backward Analysis. The optimal method of investigating system failures is often to trace backward from a failure message, such as a core dump or assert, through the sequence of events to the causal action. Ironically, tools that support this strategy, such as backward-stepping debuggers, are only now becoming widely available. Many debuggers must still conduct backward analysis by reasoning with a pencil and code printout in hand.

Means-Ends Analysis. Means-ends analysis is a heuristic approach in which the debugger applies knowledge of the system to identify the functional componenents (the means) required to produce the failure (the ends). The deeper the knowledge of the system, the more efficient is means-ends analysis. Teams can apply means-ends analysis productively by pooling their knowledge to debug mammoth software systems.

Subgoaling. Subgoaling is the process of segmenting the system into relatively independent, functional components and testing each against its performance specifications. The goal is to validate the performance of the largest number of components with as few tests as possible, leaving only the suspect components for detailed study. It is useful when means-ends analysis fails or is inefficient because the debugger does not understand the system well.

Analogy. Analogical reasoning involves recalling a similar problem, adjusting for differences from the current situation, and formulating a hypothesis accordingly (Weitzenfeld, 1983). This strategy is limited in part by the range of experience of the debugger. That experience can be acquired first- or second-hand, through debugging stories told informally in the workplace or described formally in reports of post mortem analysis sessions. Management that encourages analysis of debugging episodes and documents those analyses for their staff helps them to apply analogical reasoning to debugging assignments. A group method for analogical problem solving is implemented in the synectics method of directing meetings (Hogarth, 1987).

Forward Analysis. Among the most complex and costly debugging strategies is to reason from known a input and system state forward along all or many possible branches in search of the failure point. Rather than apply-forward analysis, it is often preferable to insert more precise error reporting functions into the code, reintroduce the system to the field, and apply a more efficient analytic strategy when the failure reoccurs.

Generate and Test. The generate and test strategy amounts to indiscriminately testing every hypothesis that comes to mind. Experts assert that this is so inefficient a strategy that its use should be interpreted as a signal to abandon the localization phase entirely and return to familiarization or stabilization. Particularly effective strategies at this juncture are to discuss the problem with a colleague, attempt to adopt a radically different view of the system (a discussion of alternative system representations can be found, below), or switch to an entirely different task.

Selecting among Hypotheses. The debugger who is fortunate enough to produce several plausible hypotheses using these strategies must apply some rules for prioritizing or choosing among the ideas. The heuristics for doing so are underspecified, but offer some leverage. They are, to choose hypotheses that:

- Explain present symptoms
- Do not predict absent symptoms and, if possible
- Rule out other hypotheses

Testing Hypotheses. Several heuristics facilitate the process of selecting tests to evaluate hypotheses.

If several tests are feasible, experts tend to run easy or inexpensive tests first (Gould, 1975), even if those tests are almost certain to disprove a weak hypothesis (Riedl and co-workers, 1991). To illustrate this strategy, we point to two tests recommended by Koenig (1991) for every software debugging assignment. He suggests that the debugger confirm that the bug reported by the field is a bug and not a feature. Similarly, he recommends that the debugger insert a "Hello world" statement into the suspect source code to ensure that the executable file corresponds to the source code being debugged, and not to a different source version in another directory. These are tests of highly unlikely hypotheses, but they are easy to run, satisfying to complete, and they offer insurance against massive mistakes at the outset of debugging.

In extremely complex systems, there often are no easy tests to run. In such circumstances, the expert turns to the tests that seem most likely to reveal the bug. Alternatively, the debugger may test the part of the system most recently studied. This strategy capitalizes on relatively unstable knowledge before it is lost.

Empirical research indicates that successful testers are those who more often design tests to disprove hypotheses or evaluate them at the margins (as is done in boundary testing). Less successful individuals tend to avoid tests that threaten their hypotheses in favor of simple confirmatory tests (Wason, 1960; Klayman and Ha, 1969; Leventhal, 1991). This strategy can blind the novice to errors that include but are not limited to the specific instance that is tested.

In selecting a testing methodology, the skilled debugger considers the "probe effect," the manner in which tools distort system operation. For example, tracing disrupts both timing and the stack. This makes tracing a poor tool in highly active parts of real time systems unless the side effects are themselves informative. When tracing changes an otherwise stable symptom, tracing's changes to the stack may be responsible; the debugger should consider that a pointer error may be responsible for the original, stabilized symptom.

Having selected a test, the expert debugger more often than the nonexpert attempts to predict the variety of possible test results. This practice screens out tests that may be inconclusive or impractical. In addition, it sets up expectations that, if violated by unexpected results, may indicate that the debugger needs to return to the familiarization stage.

Summary. In sum, expert debuggers employ a range of strategies that simplify three key stages of debugging: familiarization, stabilization, and localization. This section concerning debugging psychology will conclude with a discussion of issues that span the stages of debugging, including meta-strategies, representations of systems, and social strategies for debugging.

Expertise and Self-Monitoring

Expert performance involves some strategies for monitoring the state of the debugging process and selecting tactics. These are called metastrategies, and they span all phases of debugging.

Experts monitor their progress and comprehension more frequently and more accurately than do less experienced debuggers (Riedl and co-workers, 1991). In particular, they frequently test their confidence in the accuracy and completeness of their knowledge of:

- The target system—its features, functionality, design and architecture, code, hardware, etc.
- The history of the software—what, when, and how changes were made
- The developers involved in creating and maintaining the software—their experience and style
- The development environment—the host system, methodologies, tools available, etc.
- The documentation—its quality and accuracy

Veteran debuggers employ two strategies that facilitate such self-monitoring. One is to cycle from detailed reading and testing up to an overview of the problem. Experts frequently use metaphors such as "taking a step back and looking at what you know," that signal the use of this tactic (Weitzenfeld and co-workers, 1993). This maneuver has two benefits: it draws the programmer out of focused working session periodically to assess his or her progress, and it offers the opportunity to assess the global importance of local discoveries.

A second technique to enhance self-monitoring is to use a lab notebook. The format can be as primitive as the back of used data processing paper, or as sophisticated as a bound volume with a heading for system and symptom, followed by columns for date and time, hypothesis, a description of the test conducted, predicted test outcome, and actual outcome. Recording procedures, findings, and ideas on paper in this way offloads data from working memory, freeing the individual to take a broad view. The notebook also allows the individual to scan the steps taken to solve the problem, and plan new paths. Finally, the very act of writing and drawing formalizes ideas in ways that can bring insight.

Better debuggers also employ a form of metacognition that resembles cost/benefit analysis. In so doing, they apply their knowledge of the time, resources, and effort of proceeding along specific paths, and weigh this against the value and likelihood of the benefit. As noted above, they also consider the confidence they have regarding their own knowledge of these factors. Knowing, for example, that one cannot estimate the cost of using a protocol analyzer is a clue that doing so may be fruitless—at least without expert aid.

Mental Representations: How Programmers Understand Systems

Psychological studies indicate that success in problem solving is largely a function of the manner in which one frames or represents a problem—whether mentally, with paper and pencil, or with other media (Newell and Simon, 1972). Accordingly, success in debugging hinges on the debugger's ability to select and construct a representation of the system (Pennington, 1987b; Gilmore, 1991). Expert debuggers often choose among a variety of system representations during debugging. Each view reveals certain classes of bugs better than others. One particularly comprehensive scheme for classifying debugging representations is the proximity model (Ward, 1986; 1989).

The Proximity Model. In this model, every event in a program is viewed as occuring simultaneously in three independent spaces: lexical, temporal, and referential. All system events occur at some measurable distance from each other in these spaces. Two events are lexically adjacent if they are generated by neighboring lines of source code. The events are temporally adjacent if one occurs immediately after the other. Finally, two events that refer to the same variable are referentially adjacent if no intervening events refer to that variable.

The earliest appearance of a bug symptom is, by definition, immediately adjacent to its cause in at least one of these three spaces. Thus the debugger can identify any bug by tracing backward through events in the appropriate proximity space until the first appearance of the symptom is encountered. The bug's cause will be immediately adjacent, either lexically, temporally, or referentially. While only type-safe environments can guarantee this characteristic at the logical program level, all sequential environments guarantee these properties at least at the machine level. Non-safe environments, such as C, cannot guarantee these properties because these environments don't safeguard the integrity of the underlying virtual machine. However, even in non-safe environments, lexical, temporal, and referential proximity will exist until the virtual machine is first damaged, and that damage will always be adjacent, in temporal space, to its cause. Thus proximities can be exploited even in unsafe environments as long as the debugger is equipped to look for bug symptoms in virtual machine resources as well as in logical program resources.

Each tool available to debuggers is specifically suited to exploring one or more types of proximity. For example, simple printouts are most useful for studying lexical proximity. Tracing tools exploit temporal proximity. Watchpointing tools (which monitor memory addresses). are used to explore referential space (a broader discussion of tools follows).

Many of the traditional, graphical methods of representing system organization and activities are implementations of the proximity spaces. Data flow diagram, for example, represent referential space. Similarly, control flow diagrams depict temporal space.

Other Models. There are some representations of the system that do not fit neatly into the proximity model, however. One is the conception of the system's function in the world, sometimes referred to as the designers' intention. For example, a program that computes the diameter of cable conduits and their placement in a building's walls can be conceived of at the implementation level as a collection of general algorithms, or at the intentional level as a machine that, in some sense, "handles" cables and conduits. Experienced and inexperienced debuggers can employ either view, but only successful debuggers employ both, shifting rapidly between intentional (or functional) and implementational representations as needed. Poorer debuggers focus on one or the other (Pennington, 1987b).

Another intriguing and prominent mental model of systems is anthropomorphic. Expert programmers often refer to a system in the first person (Weitzenfeld and co-workers, 1993), as in the expression "I have been called by function X but never return to it." This type of metaphor highlights attributes of code that are similar to human characteristics, and it uses those attributes to make predictions about the system in the same ways that people predict the actions of their friends. Specifically, anthropomorphic descriptions of a system component allude to the task that component performs, what "knowledge" it has, the resources it needs, and the assumptions it makes about its operating environment. All of these are important characteristics of a system during debugging.

Shifting between Representations Strategically. Expert debuggers exhibit three advantages over non-experts with respect to representations. The first is that they construct representations more accurately and more quickly than non-experts (Pennington, 1987a; 1987b). This is partly a function of longstanding knowledge and partly a product of better use of familiarization strategies. Second, experts appear to select the most appropriate form of representation more often. Finally, experts shift between representations more fluidly (Weitzenfeld and co-workers, 1993), which allows them to take new perspectives on problems more easily and avoid entrapment in dark, but bug-free alleys of a system.

Social Aspects of Debugging

The preceding discussion has treated debugging largely as a solitary activity. This is in line with the conventional view that debugging is an inherently technical undertaking and that it requires, above all else, knowledge of the components, language, tools, and functional specifications of the system. With such strong emphasis placed on the technical aspects of the work, social skills are often neglected. However, such skills can be critical during any one assignment, and they facilitate acquiring technical skills over the long term.

The prominence of social skills in program development is evident in the daily work of individual software developers, which consists overwhelmingly of social activities, not solitary cogitation and keypunching (Krasner, Curtis, and Iscoe, 1987). Social skills are obviously important in group debugging sessions, such as code review. There the activities that consume 90% of meeting time capitalize on group attributes, such group memory for previous decisions, the ability of a group to critique code from varied perspectives, and division of labor when cross-checking documents (Letovsky and co-workers, 1987; Flor and Hutchins, 1991). Similar social skills are key to the work of individual debuggers. In interviews at AT&T Bell Labs (Riedl and co-workers, 1991), veteran debuggers indicated that less experienced professionals (as well as management) often overlook the social nature of software development, and this accounts for many of the difficulties they encounter in the course of debugging systems.

It is characteristic of better performing debuggers that they know when they need help from their colleagues, and they know how to get it. The following is a list of "social strategies" used by experts for getting help in their discussions with other experts.

At the beginning of the interaction:

- Approach people strategically. Some people like to socialize before addressing problems. Some like to address only "important" technical problems. Others find interest in almost any juicy technical mystery.
- Estimate the amount of time the assistance will take. Tell it to your informant.
- Tell your informant what the priority of your problem is and why. Let the informant determine the appropriate time to talk or to work together.

- Tell your source why you chose him or her. At best, this is a compliment; at worst, it gives them the opportunity to point you to a better source.

During the interaction:

- Unless the informant already respects your expertise, do not expect him or her to trust your reports. Bring all the relevant evidence with you, such as error reports, relevant code, lists of observations, lists of recent changes, and configuration data. This helps the expert evaluate the situation and your level of understanding of it.
- Be an egoless interviewer. Let the informant talk. Paraphrase what you have heard to let informant check your understanding. When you do not understand, say so. Do not try to impress the informant. (If you know so much, there is no need to tell you anything.)

At the end of the interaction:

- Adhere to your time estimates. If your session runs too long, allow the informant to decide whether to continue then or to resume later.
- Review out loud what you plan to do next; get the informant's response.
- Thank your informant.

After the interaction:

- Review your notes right after leaving the interview.
- Let your informant know how things turned out. Keep him/her involved to build a long-term relationship.
- Be available to help others. You need to make deposits to the favor bank periodically in order to make withdrawals.

In general:

- Keep track of who gives good advice and who knows system internals—they are not always the same people.
- Recognize when you need help from others. Learn the symptoms of "thrashing" that you exhibit when you are stuck. Condition yourself to ask for advice when those symptoms arise.

This review of the psychology of debugging has addressed strategies for system familiarization, stabilization, and localization, as well as meta strategies, system representation, and social aspects of debugging. The remaining sections describe debugging tools and issues in managing the debugging process.

TECHNOLOGY FOR SYSTEM DEBUGGING

Introduction

Most modern development environments are rich in debugging resources. In the following catalogue of tools and techniques, we group the items according to the debugging stage (familiarization, stabilization, or localization) with which they are most clearly associated. This grouping is somewhat arbitrary. For example, the techniques of program instrumentation during localization can also be used to explore the program during familiarization. Modern debuggers include features that are useful in all stages of the process. Even so, we find this process-oriented structure to be valuable because it relates each tool to its principle use and suggests how some tools have evolved from others.

Familiarization: Aids to Understanding the Program

Tools in this group facilitate static analysis, that is building an understanding of the source code without executing it. During familiarization, expert debuggers exhibit a marked preference for these tools over those described later.

Pencil and Paper. The same techniques that help manage complexity during the design phase also organize program information, and thus simplify familiarization, while debugging. Multiple analyses, especially analyses that draw from multiple design methodologies or that operate at different levels of abstraction, can help to build a rich knowledge base that supports alternate representations of the program's operation and structure. Pictorial and schematic representations can be used to capture and clarify program structures and key relationships. Depending upon the nature of the problem, expert programmers may create drawings of key data structures and record layouts, memory maps, flow charts, structure charts, hierarchy charts, timing diagrams, communications graphs, etc.

Source code also may be abstracted into pseudo code, separated into related families of functions, or partitioned into major subsystems. The code may be annotated with "critiques" of the style or comments. Idiosyncracies indicative of multiple authors may be highlighted, along with changes attributable to prior maintenance efforts.

Hand simulation remains one of the most important of the paper and pencil techniques. Manually tracing through the instructions and states can do much to explain the operation of an unfamiliar or arcane section of code. While hand simulation is most often applied to understanding the dynamic behavior of the program, some programmers will hand simulate a parser to better understand unusual syntax errors.

Various Listings. Various utilities and translator options will generate listings that describe the program from a selected view. Cross-reference generators help the programmer understand the referential structure of the program, and to locate objects within specific modules. In many environments, special utilities will generate text-based or diagrammatic representations of the programs calling structure. Most compilers can be forced to output assembly listings, with the high-level source contained in comments. Linkers can usually be forced to generate a link map that will help the programmer understand how the translator and operating system are managing the program's memory space. Software metric systems can identify the most complex portions of the program and in some cases can identify differences in style that might reflect differences in authorship.

Some static analysis tools go beyond describing the program and actually comment on or restructure the code. Expert programmers often use a custom tuned "pretty printer" to reformat code. Reformatting code to the expert's preferred style not only improves its accessibility, but also often reveals significant structural aspects that may have been obscured in the original presentation. Delimiter checkers clarify the nesting structure of various syntactic structures. Sophisticated syntax analysis tools like Unix's lint can not only locate many bugs, they may even go so far as to critique the portability and readability of the original code.

Sophisticated Editors. A powerful multiwindow, multifile program editor is sometimes preferable to utilities that summarize aspects of the code, such as cross-reference tools. Multifile search commands can quickly locate, all occurrences of a given identifier or expression. Multiple windows allow the programmer to compare the calling code, subordinate function definitions, and relevant declarations. Minimized windows can be used as placeholders, giving instant access to related information, such as system specifications. Some editors even allow the programmer to attach annotations (which are kept in a separate file) to specific lines in the source file. Such notes can be useful when repairing the code and describing the fix in technical reports.

Browsers. Unlike the tools discussed so far, browsers are designed to provide a few, specific, coordinated representations of the program. Early browsers were simply graphical interfaces to a collection of traditional source manipulation utilities (like cross-reference generators). In a modern integrated development environment, the browser is a query interface into a comprehensive database of information about the source code. Sophisticated browsers can generate views of historic and dynamic information as well as static information. Thus the programmer can view revision history, calling hierarchies, object hierarchies, data dictionaries, and even execution histories and object instances through a single user interface.

Stabilization

Input Control. In simple programs, the programmer can make repeatable, reliable input by redirecting input from a file containing the test cases. In more complex environments, the programmer can either modify low-level routines to retrieve input from files during testing, or use a package that exploits operating system hooks to provide simulated input. Such packages are often available as part of commercial regression testing systems and sometimes available from the operating system vendor as an add-on or development utility (for example, Microsoft Test for Windows).

Interpreters. An interpreter provides a particularly efficient environment in which to debug programs. Because interpreted environments tend to be "safer" than compiled environments, many unstable bugs can be identified or stabilized immediately, merely by executing the program with an interpreter.

Localization. Once the programmer has formed an understanding of the program, developed a hypothesis about the bug, and conceived an experiment to test that hypothesis, it remains to install instrumentation that will reliably and accurately measure the results of the experiment and report them. Tools and techniques for program instrumentation are discussed in this section.

Code-Based Tracing. By code-based tracing, we mean instrumentation that is installed by making additions or changes to the source code. Code-based tracing has the disadvantage of being intrusive: it changes the program being observed, and thus may change the program's behavior in ways that change or mask the bug. This tendency of a bug to change when it is to measured is called the *probe effect.*

Code-based tracing also requires repeated compilation of the source, a disadvantage in that it slows the test cycle. Even so, code-based techniques are widely used, in large part because they are extremely portable.

Print Statements. The simplest and oldest trace technique, print statements embedded directly in the source code, is still the most widely used debugging tool. The simplest usage merely prints a message saying "the program reached line . . ." or gives the value of some critical variable. In some cases, the trace code may output the current value of a variable and then give the programmer a chance to replace that value (perhaps with a correct value to allow continued testing of subsequent code).

Snapshots. To monitor complex data structures, the programmer will add a snapshot function, a programmer-supplied function that prints or displays the contents of the structure in an appropriate format. To monitor the state of the structure, the programmer inserts calls to the snapshot function at appropriate points in the code.

Assertions. Instead of displaying state, sometimes code-based instrumentation simply checks to confirm that constraints intrinsic to the problem have not been violated. For example, a function that squares integers should never return negative results. Assertions test for results that violate such constraints, and can abort a process and return source code line numbers or other useful debugging information. Some languages provide built-in provision for coding such constraints.

Allocation Logging. Dynamic memory operations can be monitored by attaching logging code to the system allocation and deallocation routines. In some languages (C for example), macros can be used to insert the logging code before or after each call to an allocation or deallocation routine. In other languages, the programmer must link to a special debugging library. Adding a "serial number" field to each dynamically allocated data structure makes this technique more useful (Ward, 1991). This type of logging can be adapted and applied to any use of any major program service, whether supplied by the operating system or by a subsystem of the application.

Integrity Checks. In "unsafe" environments—environments where an errant program can damage supporting system resources—the instrumentation must monitor the virtual machine resources as well as the logical program resources. For example, by misusing pointers, a C programmer can unintentionally overwrite the run-time stack, the heap, and, in many single user systems, even overwrite the operating system. To identify the source of such damage, the programmer needs instrumentation that monitors and reports the state of these normally hidden resources. Common integrity checks include stack sanity tests, heap walk functions, and memory checksums.

Like assertions, integrity checks rely on natural constraints. Unlike assertions, integrity checks test constraints unrelated to the application program. Instead, these tests rely upon constraints intrinsic to the development environment. A stack sanity test, for example, walks through the context frames saved on the stack, checking to see that frame pointers and return addresses have reasonable (or at least possible) values. Similarly, a heap walk function will examine the heap manager's internal data structures. Memory checksums can be used to check for an unwarranted change in any block of memory, whether it be code or data. In single user operating systems, a checksum of the code may be the only practical method for detecting a pointer that overwrites code.

Trace Macros or Libraries. Well-designed debugging packages, implemented as macros or library routines, can incorporate all of the above tools. They can make source-based debugging more efficient by adding dynamic trace controls with which the programmer can activate or deactivate selected instrumentation points without recompiling the source, or even restarting the program. Such debugging tools can also systematize coding by automating the insertion of trace code. The elaborate macros of Sherlock (Ream, 1992), the breakpoint-style debugger of Ward (1986), and Unix's ctrace (Steffen, 1984) illustrate the wide range of implementations possible using this implementation strategy.

Profilers. Profilers report how execution activity is distributed over the body of the code. While normally considered performance tuning tools, profilers that count each instruction execution (as opposed to sampling them) can be used to report loop iterations and other execution patterns.

Breakpoint Debuggers. After code-based trace statements, breakpoint debuggers are probably the most widely used debugging tool: Breakpoint debuggers provide interactive control of program execution and support dynamic investigation and modification of memory.

These debuggers control execution by allowing the programmer to associate a point in the source code at which to break (that is, suspend) the run, thus the name "breakpoint." When the program halts under breakpoint control, its internal state is saved and control is returned to the programmer.

In the most straight-forward implementation, the debugger effects the breakpoint by substituting a different instruction for the instruction that would normally reside at the breakpoint address. By installing a fault or interrupt causing instruction at the breakpoint address, the debugger can force a transfer of control, should the program ever attempt to execute the instruction at the breakpoint address. In some implementations, finding a suitable "break" instruction requires some ingenuity. Intentional errors (e.g., divide by zero), traps, specialized subroutine call, jump, and interrupt instructions are used in various systems. In multi-user systems, the memory protect hardware can sometimes be used to generate an access fault on the breakpoint address.

Debugger implementations also differ in their degree of intrusiveness. For example, some debuggers require that the application be compiled using options that cause debugging information to be inserted into the object module. Even debuggers that do not require modified object code still change execution timing enough to create a probe effect when used to debug real-time and parallel applications.

For purposes of the following discussion, we will divide breakpoint debuggers into three functional classes—monitors, symbolic debuggers, and source level debuggers.

Monitors. The simplest of all breakpoint debuggers, monitors seldom provide much functionality beyond absolute breakpoints, display and edit of raw memory, and primitive execution control (i.e., step, run, continue, restart). Monitors are usually intended as tools for manipulating the hardware, especially memory, and thus may be ignorant even of the machine's instruction set. Monitors often allow only a very small set of simultaneously set breakpoints (perhaps three to ten). Memory is referenced by address, not by symbolic identifier. Typically monitors supply only a cryptic, command-oriented user interface. Monitors are often ROM-resident, and thus historically have been kept very small to preserve precious ROM space.

(The term *monitor* also refers to much more sophisticated debuggers, in which context it usually indicates that the tool has limited program control facilities, but perhaps extensive capabilities for manipulating system resources.)

Symbolic Debuggers. This class of debuggers features conditional breakpoints, symbolic memory references, and instruction disassembly. Symbolic debuggers are usually intended to be used as assembly language tools. While more sophisticated symbolic debuggers feature multiwindow information displays, the user interface for these debuggers is usually command-oriented.

Symbolic debuggers break execution at a conditional breakpoint if a specified condition is true. In different implementations, supported conditions can range from a simple passcount (e.g., break if this instruction has been executed three times) to full logical and arithmetic expressions involving variable references and function evaluations.

Debuggers in this class often allow programmers to associate breakpoints (often called *watchpoints*) with data addresses as well as instructions. A watchpoint will cause a break anytime the associated address is accessed or modified. Conditional watchpoints are a common, more elaborate version of the tool. Watchpoints are particularly effective tools for locating pointer errors.

In single-step mode, these debuggers may include options for controlling the depth and detail of the execution trace. Commands that treat a function call and execution as a single "step" allow the programmer to more easily examine the high-level behavior of a program.

To allow the programmer to reference memory locations by symbolic name, these debuggers import the compiler's symbol table and linker information. Depending on the implementation, the debugger may also import type information, allowing it to appropriately display and access data objects. When type information isn't available, the programmer usually controls access and display by attaching type modifiers to symbols or commands.

Symbolic debuggers will usually allow the programmer to associate an action with each breakpoint. When the breakpoint is reached, the attached action will be executed, and program execution will automatically resume. Depending on the implementation, the actions can be specified by simple keystroke macros or complex routines in a small programming language.

Attached actions are obviously useful for building trace instrumentation. Not so obvious (and perhaps not even anticipated by their inventor), is their use as a code patching mechanism. Attached actions can be used to replace faulty return values (or supply non-existent return values), to jump to small code patches stored elsewhere in memory, and to invoke various consistency checks, for example.

Source Level Debuggers. This class of debuggers provides all the capabilities of symbolic debuggers, but adds the ability to connect compiled object code to it's high-level source form. Source level debuggers virtually always sport a sophisticated user interface and at least a limited form of browser. Attached actions can usually be expressed in terms of the relevant high-level language. The debugger may also allow the programmer to execute a large class of code fragments "on the fly," in the style of an interpreter. Debuggers with interactive execution capabilities can often be used as test harnesses, allowing individual modules to be tested and debugged as they are written.

To be used effectively as instrumentation platforms, the source level debugger must include the ability to save the debugger's state in a named session file. This allows the programmer to save different instrumentation configurations for later reuse. Instrumentation is easier to build and install if the debugger also includes commands that automatically place breakpoints and attached actions systematically throughout the code or sections of the code, for example, at the beginning of each function, or on every tenth line in a module.

Researchers are experimenting with a tool quite different from breakpointing but potentially as useful for examining referential proximity. It extracts from a larger program an executable sub-program (called a *slice*), which consists of all statements that explicitly reference a specified variable (Venkatesh, 1991; Weiser, 1984; Korel and Laski, 1988). However, the value of this tool is, so far, minimal for debugging complex systems, errors involving intricate interactions, and pointer errors (Weiser and Lyle, 1986).

Logic Analyzers. Unlike the instrumentation above, which is implemented primarily in software, logical analyzers are implemented primarily in hardware. (Note that some breakpoint debuggers employ hardware assists.) In its simplest form, the logic analyzer is a multichannel digital logging device. When properly attached to the computer bus, the logic analyzer can be used to record bus transactions, including instruction fetches and data transfers. Modern logic analyzers can capture several thousand samples or transactions at speeds well over 100 MHZ. By specifying logical qualifiers, the user can select only certain transactions for logging, greatly reducing the amount of irrelevant information. For example, the logic analyzer can be configured to capture only instructions within a certain address range, only references to a particular memory cell, or the only the sixteen addresses preceding the execution of a certain instruction code (perhaps to discover what part of the program is generating a particular interrupt).

Also unlike all the other techniques discussed so far, logic analyzers are virtually free of the "probe effect" (except for the inept user who shorts the bus by misplacing the physical probes). This, plus the fact that most logic analyzers can be driven from an internal clock in a high speed sampling mode, make them extremely useful in analyzing timing problems.

Modern logic analyzers include substantial off-line data analysis capabilities. Some are knowledgeable about target machines' instruction sets. Many include convenient tools for filtering and searching the trace log.

Shadow Registers. Another form of hardware support for debugging is built into some computers. "Shadow registers" are designed to dynamically capture and log the contents of specified CPU registers for later inspection.

Test Evaluation/Management

Many of the tools discussed above, especially breakpoint debuggers and regression testers, are also useful for managing and evaluating experimental data. However, a few simpler tools are particularly well-suited for this work.

Whenever an experiment generates large amounts of trace data or program output, the programmer should consider automating the search for significant items. Standard file comparison tools, like Unix's diff, can be used to highlight differences from prior runs. A good macro editor can easily be configured to look for certain kinds of patterns in data. In some cases, patterns that are too complex to find with an editor may become easy to identify if the file is first undergoes a little preprocessing. For example, the tens of thousands of lines produced by a complete trace of all dynamic memory allocations can be sorted, then processed by a simple filter before the programmer reads them (Ward, 1991).

Special Problem

Special capabilities are required of instrumentation for embedded systems, real-time systems, and parallel machines. These environments pose some formidable challenges to the debugger—so formidable that in some cases the solution is still an open research question.

Embedded Systems. Because the target environment in most embedded systems work is not a suitable development host, embedded systems programmers usually practice cross-development. The program is developed and compiled on a development host, using a cross-compiler. The resulting object code is then downloaded to the target machine for execution and testing.

Debugging support in this environment can consists of a tiny custom monitor built into the application, a logic analyzer attached to the target machine, a remote debugger running on the host that communicates with a debugging kernel on the target, or an in-circuit emulator (ICE). The remote debugger and ICE are usually the most convenient alternatives, but the remote debuggers are far less expensive.

Some situations, however, require an ICE, costly or not. A remote debugger, for example, cannot set breakpoints in code that resides in ROM. (This is an issue only when "probe effects" or hardware limitations prevent the system from emulating the ROM in RAM.) And, while a logic analyzer can eliminate probe effects, it cannot capture the contents of internal CPU registers.

An ICE replaces the target CPU and provides hardware control and monitoring of CPU functions. Like a logic analyzer, an ICE includes hardware support for trace logging. The ICE, however, often has far more computing power than a logic analyzer and is always knowledgeable about the target machine's instruction set. The workstation attached to an ICE will often provide the software debugging capabilities of source-level debuggers as well as ability to simulate the target CPU and various I/O activities. Such high-end development and testing platforms can significantly shorten the development cycle by allowing programmers to test software before the target hardware is completed.

Real Time Systems. Because real time systems may have demanding response time requirements or demanding input/output timing constraints, real-time instrumentation must record the timing as well as the sequence of events. A logic analyzer used in high-speed sampling mode may do the job if there is hardware to generate properly timed inputs. When inputs are difficult to generate, an ICE with simulation capabilities is indicated.

Parallel Environments. Programs running on multiple processors are inherently difficult to instrument. First, the debugger must manage a more complex environment; the command set must be expanded to recognize multiple processors and multiple processes. Second, existing debuggers, which are premised on the assumption that execution can be frozen so that the machine's global state can be examined, don't adapt well to the parallel environment where there may be no meaningful global state. For example, because of unpredictable communication delays between processors, when a breakpoint is encountered in one process, the other processes can usually not be stopped instantly, and in fact will each stop only after some short, but apparently random interval of time. Third, parallel environments are non-deterministic and very sensitive to the "probe effect." Even without the interference of a probe, the probability that a certain sequence of parallel events will repeat may be vanishingly small. Certainly, if a bug depends upon the timing of competing accesses to shared memory, any timing change introduced by the instrumentation will change the behavior of the bug.

Despite these difficulties (or, more accurately, because of these difficulties) most existing commercial parallel debuggers are implemented by launching a separate sequential debugger for each execution thread. For the standard sequential debugger to be used meaningfully in a parallel environment, it must at least be able to monitor and modify interprocess communications and monitor and control the clock used for timeouts.

At present "event-based" debuggers are the most promising line of parallel debugging research. These debuggers work by logging "events," which are points in the execution stream where one process performs an operation that might affect another process. Accessing shared memory or sending an IPC message are examples of such operations. The event log can then be used to "replay" and debug each thread of the execution. Some researchers are even experimenting with using the event log to create an animated presentation of all execution threads. Provided that event histories can be continuously recorded, the replay will be deterministic.

Researchers are also working to improve static analysis tools for parallel environments. Using data flow techniques, static analysis tools could potentially identify errors, such as deadlock and mutual exclusion failures, that are difficult to find with current dynamic techniques. Unfortunately, in the worst case, these techniques often exhibit exponential computational complexity (McDowell and Helmbold, 1989).

MANAGEMENT AND DEBUGGING

The Need for Better Debuggers: Selection vs. Training

Finding and training professionals who can do the difficult job of debugging systems are significant problems. The least expensive option for industry is to hire individuals who will mature into superior debuggers by virtue of superior traits, and some of these traits correlate at least modestly with diagnostic skills. The ability to restructure problems (Moran, 1986; Henneman and Rouse, 1984), particularly in combination with problem-solving skills (Foreman, 1988), correlates with machine diagnosis and programming ability. The tendency to be methodical or reflective rather than impulsive is an attribute of better machine diagnosticians (Rouse and Rouse, 1982; Henneman and Rouse, 1984; Morris and Rouse, 1985; Morrison and Duncan, 1988). Finally, spatial ability appears to benefit debugging specifically (Foreman, 1988), perhaps by enabling programmers to orient themselves while reading large bodies of code. However, studies of machine diagnosis indicate that the most recognized and easily measured trait, intelligence, does not differentiate good diagnosticians from bad within a restricted population of bright, highly educated individuals, such as those who apply for programming jobs (Henneman and Rouse, 1984). There are no standardized tests that employ these traits to predict potential debugging or programming potential.

The few standardized tests available to managers focus on programming aptitude. For example, the measures used in the Programmer Aptitude Test, developed at IBM, are skills with numbers and analogical reasoning; the Wolfe tests assess ability to follow instructions; and the Berger Aptitude for Programming Test (published by Psychometrics, Inc.) requires the subject to learn and use a small procedural language (Curtis, 1988). However, at least one of these tests has a history of low reliability (Weinberg, 1971). Furthermore, these tests are designed to evaluate programming, not debugging aptitude. Debugging skills and heuristics are unlike those employed by designers and programmers, as are the methods. For example, debugging typically involves investigating the intent and implementation of other peoples' designs and programs. It is a fallacy to say that one who is a good programmer is necessarily a good debugger. The disciplines and skills needed are, to a large extent, distinct.

The complement of good hiring is good training, to which there are two approaches. The prevalent one is that people should learn debugging on their own. In academia, this orientation is reflected in a paucity of courses concerning debugging, as previously noted. In industry, formal training in debugging is generally eschewed in favor of assigning junior programmers to maintenance projects in the belief that they will learn the same skills. However, debugging is, in many ways, more intellectually demanding than other duties. The cleverness that professionals often employ when they conceive and implement systems dictates that even greater cleverness be used to debug them. Novices may need a more gradual and structured education to debugging than maintenance assignments provide.

The alternative strategy for developing debugging skills is to train people. Surveys done at AT&T Bell Laboratories regarding the need for training in debugging, indicated that a large audience exists (Riedl and co-workers, 1991). A course that was developed and offered there experienced strong demand among software engineers. This attests further to the need for training in debugging. Unfortunately, few courses in the topic are available in industry as of this writing, and those that exist focus heavily on tools. The field is open to research and course development that brings strategic training in debugging to students and professionals.

Issues of Management

As important as finding and developing debugging talent is managing its use. Managing debugging assignments is often left to the individual debugger. However, one study of managers and debugging experts at AT&T Bell Laboratories, (Riedl and co-workers, 1991) produced explicit recommendations for managing the process to obtain higher quality products and more efficient performance are sought. Those recommendations are

- Train professionals how to find and use the expertise of others during debugging.
- Ensure that the reward system permits and encourages sharing of expertise within and across group boundaries. Debuggers often have great difficulty getting the time of project experts. Rewarding experts for aiding less experienced personnel helps to solve specific debugging problems more quickly, and perpetuates the corporate knowledge base over the long term.
- Encourage developers to debrief themselves after debugging episodes (preferably on the record or in the company of others). This preserves individual knowledge and can help build the corporate knowledge base. Do not give them other assignments until after they have done the debriefing.
- Preserve and document the best tools that debuggers build while fixing code, particularly sophisticated tracing and memory inspection schemes that they construct in the source code itself.
- Provide those doing debugging with networking opportunities. Enable them to make social contact with experts before they need their help.
- Track the expertise generated during project development, or at least its repositories. Make that resource available to team members doing maintenance and debugging.
- Build plans to develop expertise. Encourage planning processes that focus on growing expertise. Provide the resources to carry out these plans.
- Introduce new members of the group to the high-level organization of both the system and the human organization of which it is a product.

CONCLUSION

System debugging involves a broad variety of knowledge, skill, and activity. Managers and debuggers themselves often overlook this and focus only on technical issues. Partly as a result, the debugging of ever more complex systems consumes a large fraction of programmers' time. This dictates improvements in debugging expertise. As industry and academia commit more resources to training and research in debugging, system producers, purchasers, and users will realize benefits in reliability, reduced time, and lower cost. The first steps have been taken, and many steps lie ahead.

BIBLIOGRAPHY

B. Adelson, "Problem Solving and the Development of Abstract Categories in Programming Languages," *Memory and Cognition* **9**(4), 422–433(1981).

H. Agrawal, R. A. De Millo, and E. H. Spafford, "An Execution-Backtracking Approach to Debugging," *IEEE Software* **9**(3), 21–26(1991).

C. Y. Akao, K. Imai, and K. Tsuchida, "Debug Expert System for Switching Systems Software," *NEC Research & Development* (95), 107–115(Oct. 1989).

B. W. Boehm, "The High Cost of Software," in *Proceedings of COMPSAC 1977— Program Testing Techniques,* Chicago, 1977.

B. Curtis, "Five Paradigms in the Psychology of Programming," in M. Helander, ed., *Handbook of Human-Computer Interaction,* North Holland, 1988.

K. Ehrlich and E. Soloway, "Empirical Studies of Programming Knowledge," *IEEE Transactions on Software Engineering* **SE-10,** 595–609(1984).

N. V. Flor and E. L. Hutchins, "Analyzing Distributed Cognition in Software Teams: A Case Study of Team Programming During Perfective Software Maintenance," in J. Koenemann-Belliveau, T. G. Moher, and S. Robertson, eds., *Empirical Studies of Programmers: Fourth Workshop,* Ablex Publishing Corp., Norwood, N.J., 1991.

K. H. Foreman, *Cognitive Style, Cognitive Ability, and the Acquisition of Initial Computer Programming Competence,* ERIC Document Reproduction Center, Alexandria, Va., 1988.

D. J. Gilmore, "Models of Debugging," *Acta Psychologica* **78,** 151–172(1991).

J. D. Gould, "Some Psychological Evidence on How People Debug Computer Programs," *International Journal of Man-Machine Studies* **7,** 151–182(1975).

I. D. Greenwald and M. Kane, "The SHARE 709 System: Programming and Modification," *ACM Journal* **6,** 128–133(1959).

R. Henneman and W. B. Rouse, "Measures of Human Problem Solving Performance in Fault Diagnosis Tasks.," *IEEE Transactions on Systems, Man, and Cybernetics* **14**(1), 99–112(1984).

R. M. Hogarth, *Judgement and Choice,* John Wiley & Sons, Inc., New York, 1987.

R. Jeffries, "A Comparison of the Debugging Behavior of Expert and Novice Programmers," paper presented at the 1982 annual Conference of the American Educational Research Association, 1982.

T. C. Jones, ESP Research Group Seminar, Software Productivity Research Group, Cambridge, Mass., 1988.

J. Klayman and Y. W. Ha, "Hypothesis Testing in Rule Discovery: Strategy, Structure, and Content," *Journal of Experimental Psychology: Learning, Memory, and Cognition* **15**(4), 596–604(1989).

A. Koenig, *C Traps and Pitfalls,* Addison-Wesley Publishing Co., Inc., New York, 1989.

A. Koenig, personal communication, 1991.

B. Korel and J. Laski, "Dynamic Program Slicing," *Information Processing Letter* **29**(3), 155–163(1988).

H. Krasner, B. Curtis, and N. Iscoe, Communication Breakdowns and Boundary Spanning Activities on Large Programming Projects," in G. M. Olson, S. Sheppard, and E. Soloway, eds. , 1987.

S. Letovsky and co-workers, "A Cognitive Analysis of a Code Inspection," in G. M. Olson, S. Sheppard, and E. Soloway, eds., 1987.

L. M. Leventhal, *Hypothesis Testing During Debugging,* poster presented at Empirical Studies of Programmers: Fourth Workshop, Rutgers, N.J., 1991.

D. C. Littman and co-workers, "Mental Models and Software Maintenance," in E. Soloway and S. Iyengar, eds., *Empirical Studies of Programmers,* Ablex Publishing Corp., Norwood, N.J., 1986.

C. E. McDowell and D. P. Helmbold, "Debugging Concurrent Programs," *ACM Computing Surveys* **21**(4), 593(1989).

K. B. McKeithen and co-workers, "Knowledge Organization and Skill Differences in Computer Programmers," *Cognitive Psychology* **13,** 307–325 (1981).

A. P. Moran, "Field Independence and Proficiency in Electrical Fault Diagnosis," *IEEE Transactions on Systems, Man, and Cybernetics* **16**(1), 162–165(1986).

N. M. Morris and W. B. Rouse, "Review and Evaluation of Empirical Research on Troubleshooting," *Human Factors* **27**(5), 503–530(1985).

D. L. Morrison and K. D. Duncan, "Strategies and Tactics in Fault Diagnosis," *Ergonomics* **31**(5), 761–784(1988).

M. Nanja and C. R. Cook, "An Analysis of the On-Line Debugging Process," in G. M. Olson, S. Sheppard, and E. Soloway, eds., 1987.

A. Newell and H. A. Simon, *The Theory of Human Problem Solving,* Prentice-Hall, Inc., Englewood Cliffs, N.J., 1972.

G. M. Olson, S. Sheppard, and E. Soloway, eds., *Empirical Studies of Programmers: Second Workshop,* Ablex Publishing Corp., Norwood, N.J., 1987.

P. W. Oman, C. R. Cook, and M. Nanja, "Effects of Programming Experience in Debugging Semantic Errors," *Journal of Systems and Software* **9**(3), 197–207(1989).

N. Pennington, "Stimulus Structures and Mental Representation in Expert Comprehension of Computer Programs," *Cognitive Psychology* **19,** 295–341(1987a).

N. Pennington, "Comprehension Strategies in Programming," in G. M. Olson, S. Sheppard, and E. Soloway, eds., 1987b.

E. K. Ream, "Debugging With Sherlock," *C Users Journal* **10**(6), 121(1992).

T. R. Riedl and co-workers, "What We Have Learned About Software Engineering Expertise," in J. E. Tomayko, ed., *Software Engineering Education: SEI Conference 1991,* Springer-Verlag, New York, 1991.

S. H. Rouse and W. B. Rouse, "Cognitive Style as a Correlate of Human Problem Solving Performance in Fault Diagnosis Tasks," *IEEE Transactions on Systems, Man, and Cybernetics* **12**(5), 649–652(1982).

D. Serberger, *DDT: LRLTRAN Dynamic Symbolic Debugging Tool,* NTILS Document #DE86057756/HDM, 1985.

J. L. Steffen, "Experience With a Portable Debugging Tool," *Software Practice and Experience* **14**(4), 323–334(1984).

J. J. L. Tsai, K-Y. Fang, and H-Y. Chen, "A Knowledge-Based Debugger for Real-Time Software Systems Based on a Non-Interference Testing Architecture," *Proceedings of the 13th Annual International Computer Software & Applications Conference,* Orlando, Fla., 1989.

A. B. Tucker, ed., "Computing Curricula 1991," *Communications of the ACM* **34**(6), 68–84(1991).

G. A. Venkatesh, "The Semantic Approach to Program Slicing," *Proceedings of the ACM SIGPLAN 91 Conference on Programming Language Design and Implementation,* Toronto, Ontario, Canada, June 26–28, 1991.

I. Vessey, "Expertise in Debugging Computer Systems: A Process Analysis," *International Journal of Man Machine Studies* **23**(5), 459–494(1985).

R. Ward, *Debugging C,* Que Corp., Indianapolis, Ind., 1986.

R. Ward, *A Programmer's Introduction to Debugging C,* R & D Publications, Lawrence, Kan., 1989.

P. C. Wason, "On The Failure to Eliminate Hypotheses in a Conceptual Task," *Quarterly Journal of Experimental Psychology* **12,** 129–140(1960).

G. M. Weinberg, *The Psychology of Computer Programming,* Van Nostrand Reinhold Co. New York, 1971.

M. Weiser, "Program Slicing," *IEEE Transactions on Software Engineering* **10**(4), 352–357(1984).

M. Weiser and J. Lyle, "Experiments on Slicing-Based Debugging Aids," in E. Soloway and S. Iyengar, eds., *Empirical Studies of Programmers,* Ablex Publishing Corp., Norwood, N.J., 1986.

J. S. Weitzenfeld and co-workers, "Cross-Domain Language Among Expert Software Developers," *Metaphor and Symbolic Activity* **7**(3,4), 185–196(1993).

J. S. Weitzenfeld, "Valid Reasoning by Analogy," *Philosophy of Science* **51**(1),(1983).

Jared T. Freeman
Columbia University
Thomas R. Riedl
Software Quality Services
Robert Ward
R&D Publications

SYSTEM DYNAMICS MODELS

WHAT IS SYSTEM DYNAMICS?

System dynamics is the application of feedback control systems principles and techniques to model, analyze, and understand the dynamic behavior of complex systems; that is, the behavioral patterns they generate over time. Its origins trace back to the pioneering work of Jay W. Forrester into industrial dynamics (Forrester, 1961).

In the 30 years since the publication of Forrester's *Industrial Dynamics,* the scope of application of the method has widened to include R&D management, urban stagnation and decay, commodity cycles, economic fluctuations, community drug policy, energy life cycles and transitions, dynamics and management of ecosystems, and *software engineering.* As the field "grew up," the name evolved from "industrial dynamics" to "system dynamics" to indicate its perceived generality. Today,

> *. . . the field has academic and applied practitioners worldwide, degree-granting programs at a few major universities, newsletters and journals, an international society, and a large and growing body of literature. [For extensive bibliographies see Lebel (1981); Legasto, Forrester, and Lyneis (1980). For current publications see issues of Dynamica,* the *System Dynamics Newsletter* (MIT), and the *System Dynamics Review].* (Richardson, 1991, p. 296)

The system dynamics philosophy is based on several premises:

1. The behavior (or time history) of an organizational entity is principally caused by its structure. The structure includes, not only the physical aspects, but more importantly the policies and procedures, both tangible and intangible, that dominate decision making in the organizational entity.
2. Organizational decision making takes place in a framework that belongs to the general class known as information-feedback systems.
3. Intuitive judgment is unreliable about how these systems will change with time, even with good knowledge of the individual parts of the system.
4. Model experimentation with computer simulation now fills the gap where judgment and knowledge are weakest—by showing the way in which the known separate system parts can interact to produce unexpected and troublesome overall system results.

Based on these philosophical beliefs, two principal foundations for operationalizing the system dynamics technique were established:

1. The use of information-feedback systems to model and understand system structure (premises 1 and 2).
2. The use of computer simulation to understand system behavior (premises 3 and 4).

In the remaining sections these two foundations of the system dynamics approach are discussed in more detail. A model developed to study the dynamics of software project management will then be presented as a sample application of the system dynamics technique to the software engineering domain.

THE CONCEPT OF FEEDBACK

The system dynamics approach views organizations, economies, societies—in fact, all human systems—as feedback systems. Feedback processes are thus, seen to hold the key for structuring and clarifying relationships within such systems and, indeed, in understanding their dynamic behavior (Forrester, 1968).

Feedback is the process in which an action taken by a person or thing will eventually affect that person or thing. A feedback loop is the closed sequence of causes and effects from an initial cause, its series of ripples through an entire chain of causes and effects, until the initial cause eventually becomes an indirect effect of itself.

> *The consequences [of an initial action] may be quick and directly apparent in results produced: as when one prospective buyer's bid at an auction influences a second bidder's price, which in turn feeds back to affect the first bidder's next decision. Or the consequences may be delayed though directly apparent in results produced; as when a farmer's decision as to how much to water his crops affects the later growth rate of the crops, which in turn influences the farmer's later watering decisions. Or the consequences may be both delayed and quite indirect in perceived results; as when a decision to increase the R&D budget leads to the hiring of more scientists, which may produce improved products and processes several years later, which may enhance the company's competitive position, in turn increasing*

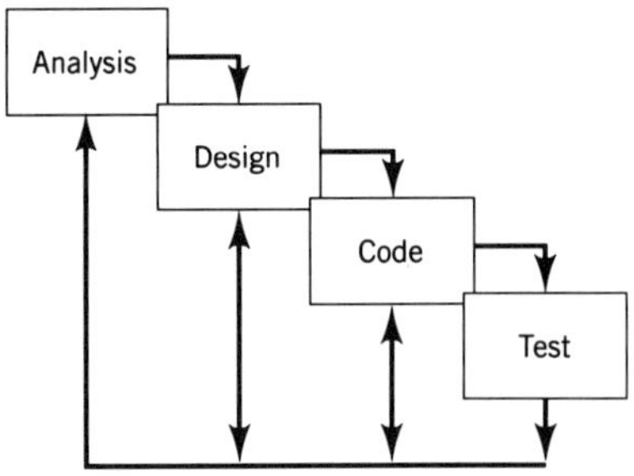

Figure 1. The waterfall life cycle model.

sales and/or profits, which may then influence the decision on the R&D budget. In all these cases a "closing the loop" occurs; in all cases a delay, whether short or long, intervenes between initial action and fed-back results. Closed loops and time delays in consequences are characteristic of all feedback processes. (Roberts, 1981)

Insight into the behavior of feedback systems begins with the observation that feedback processes divide naturally into two categories, positive and negative. "A thermostat-heating system is a goal-seeking system. . . . These loops are called *negative feedback loops* because each attempts to negate any deviation from some equilibrium or goal state. . . . In contrast, *positive feedback loops* amplify deviations or disturbances around the loop. . . . Their common characteristic is a tendency to reinforce, rather than negate, a change in an element in the loop" (Richardson and Pugh, 1981, pp. 7–10).

FEEDBACK IN THE SOFTWARE ENGINEERING DOMAIN

The significance and applicability of the information-feedback concept to software engineering is perhaps most vividly captured by the classic waterfall model of the software development life cycle, illustrated in Figure 1. The model clearly portrays how work units (whether analysis, design, or coding) typically recirculate several times before leaving as a finished product. The primary reason for this feeding back of work units to prior phases is to rework them. "For example, it is clear that if any tests uncover defects in the system, we have to go back at least to the coding phase and perhaps to the design phase to correct some mistakes. In general, any phase may uncover problems in the previous phases; this will necessitate going back to the previous phases and redoing some earlier work" (Ghezzi, Jazayeri, and Mandrioli, 1991, p. 8).

The waterfall model of Figure 1 is intended to capture the engineering and production activities of software development. In addition, the development of software involves management-type activities to plan, control, and staff these engineering/production processes. An integrated software development model is presented in Abdel-Hamid and Madnick (1991), (Figure 2) that integrates these two aspects of the software development process, that is the management-type functions (e.g., planning, control, and staffing) as well as the software production-type activities

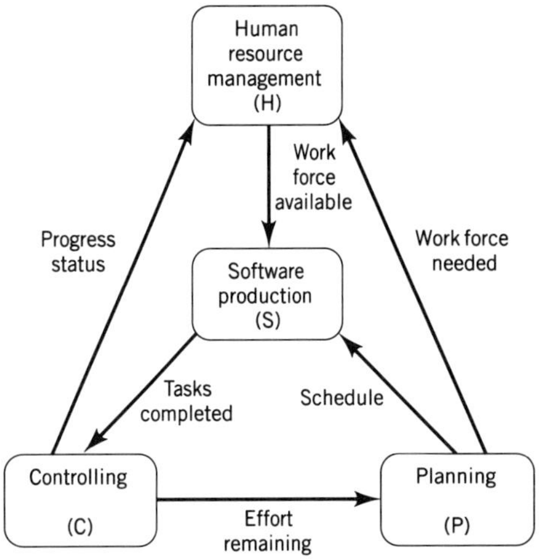

Figure 2. Integrated model of software development.

(e.g., the design, coding, and testing activities of the waterfall model).

The software development process, like most organizational systems, is characterized by a complex conglomerate of interconnected feedback loops. The rework feedback loops of Figure 1 (which are incorporated within the Software Production Subsystem of Figure 2) are, thus only a small subset of the feedback processes that underlie the software development process. Figure 3 illustrates a high-level feedback loop that couples the four management/engineering building blocks of Figure 2; it shows how schedule estimates (in the Planning Subsystem of the model) influence work force hiring and firing (in the Human Resource Management Subsystem). A tighter schedule leads to a higher work force and vice versa. The work-force level acquired determines the communication and training overheads incurred on the project, which in turn affects the team's productivity and, thus the effort expenditures on the project (in the Software Production Subsystem). As work is accomplished on the project it is reported through the project control system (the Controlling Subsystem). Such reports accumulate and are processed to create the project's forecast completion time. The feedback loop is completed (closed) as the difference, if any,

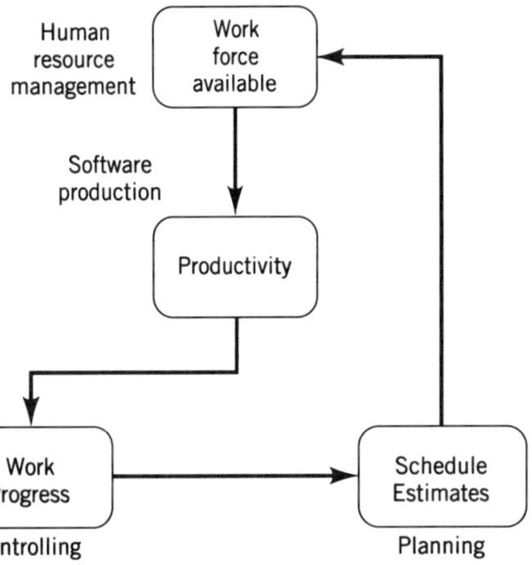

Figure 3. The feedback impact of schedule estimates.

between the scheduled completion date and the forecast completion date causes adjustments in the magnitude or allocation of the project's resources.

SIMULATION: THE SECOND FOUNDATION OF THE SYSTEM DYNAMICS APPROACH

Perhaps the most visible feature of the system dynamics approach is its use of computer simulation. Computer simulation is utilized for two reasons. The first is to handle *dynamic complexity*.

Dynamic Complexity

> *The behavior of systems of interconnected feedback loops often confounds common intuition and analysis, even though the dynamic implications of isolated loops may be reasonably obvious. The feedback structures of real problems are often so complex that the behavior they generate over time can usually be traced only by simulation (Richardson and Pugh, 1981, pp. 6–7)*

The experience of managers working in many environments indicates that they are generally able to specify the detailed relationships and interactions among managerial policies, resources, and performance. However, managers are usually unable to determine accurately the dynamic behavior implied by these relationships. Studies have shown that human intuition is ill-suited for calculating the consequences of a large number of interactions over time, especially when cause and effect are distant in time and space. Unlike a mental model, a system dynamics simulator can reliably and efficiently trace the implications of a messy maze of interactions through time. And it can do so without stumbling over phraseology, emotional bias, or gaps in intuition (Richardson and Pugh, 1981).

By utilizing computer simulation techniques, system dynamicists purport to combine the strengths of the manager with the strengths of the computer. The manager aids by specifying relationships within his or her organizational environment; the computer then calculates the dynamic consequences of these relationships.

Experimentation

The second reason for constructing computer-based simulation models is to use them as laboratory tools for *experimentation*. Engineers turn to laboratory experiments to learn about the behavior of complex engineering systems. Social systems are far more complex and harder to understand than many technological systems. Why then not use the same approach of making computer models of social systems, such as a software development organization, and conduct laboratory experiments on these models?

> *The answer is often stated that our knowledge of social systems is insufficient for constructing useful models. But what justification can there be for the apparent assumption that we do not know enough to construct models but believe we do know enough to directly design new social systems? . . . I am suggesting that we now do know enough to make useful models of social systems. Conversely, we do not know enough to design the most effective social systems directly without first going through a model-building experimental phase (Forrester, 1971)*

Indeed, over the last three decades the work of Forrester and others in the system dynamics field has demonstrated both the feasibility and utility of constructing computer-based models to study complex social systems.

Most systems dynamics models are implemented using DYNAMO, a special-purpose simulation language developed in the late 1950s at MIT by Forrester's research team. In recent years other modeling languages have been developed, for example, DYSMAP2 (Dangerfield and Vapenikova, 1987) for the IBM PC and STELLA (Richmond and co-workers, 1987) for the Apple Macintosh family of computers.

EXAMPLE SOFTWARE ENGINEERING APPLICATION

Recently, the system dynamics approach has been successfully applied to the software project domain (Abdel-Hamid, 1984; Abdel-Hamid and Madnick, 1991; and Lin and Levary, 1989). Using the modeling technique of system dynamics and desktop computers, the software manager, like the engineer, can have a laboratory in which he or she can simulate project behavior and learn quickly and at low cost the answers that would seldom be obtainable from trials on real projects.

Figure 4 shows a high-level view of the four subsystems in the Abdel-hamid and Madnick (1991) model, namely, human-resource management, software production, control, and planning (the same subsystems of Figure 2). The actual model is very detailed and contains more than 100 causal links; a full description of the model's structure, its mathematical formulation, and its validation is published in their book.

Human-Resource Management. This subsystem captures the hiring, assimilation, and transfer of people. The project's work force is segregated into employee types (newly hired and experienced). This distinction is made because new team members are usually less productive than veterans. This segregation also allows the capture of the training process to assimilate new members. The veterans usually train the newcomers, both technically and socially. This is important because the training can significantly affect a project's progress by reducing the veteran's productivity.

In deciding how big a work force is needed, project managers typically consider several factors. One, of course, is the project's scheduled completion date. Another is the work force's stability; so managers try to predict project employment time for new members before they are hired. Generally, the relative weight managers give to stability versus completion date changes as the project progresses.

Software Production. This subsystem models development; it does not include the operation and maintenance phases. The development phases included are designing, coding, and testing.

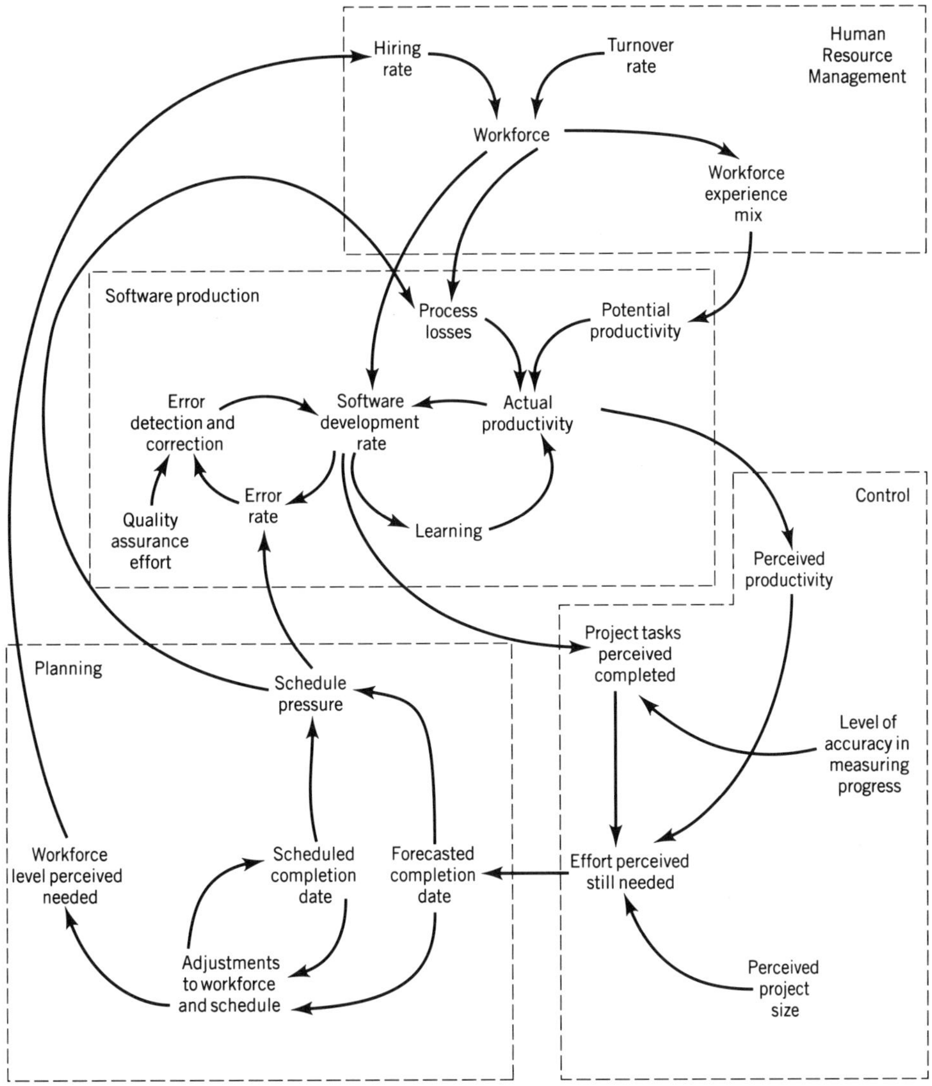

Figure 4. Overview of model structure.

As software is developed it is reviewed for errors using quality assurance activities such as structured walk-throughs; errors detected through such activities are reworked. Not all software errors are detected during development, however; some escape detection until the testing phase.

The software-production subsystem models productivity and its determinants in great detail. Productivity is defined as potential productivity minus the loss from faulty processes. Potential productivity is the maximum level of productivity that can occur when an individual or group makes the best possible use of its resources, and is a function of the nature of the task and the group's resources. Loss from faulty processes include losses due to communication and coordination overhead and low motivation.

Control Subsystem. Progress is reported as it is made. A comparison of the degree of project progress to the planned schedule is captured within the control subsystem. In all organizations, decisions are based on the information available to the decision maker. Often this information is inaccurate. Apparent conditions may be far removed from those actually encountered, depending on information flow, time lag, and distortion.

Progress rate is a good example of a variable that is difficult to assess during the project. Because software is basically an intangible product during most of its development, it is difficult to measure things such as programming performance and intermediate work. In the earlier phases of development, progress is typically measured by the rate of resource expenditure rather than accomplishments. As the project advances toward its final stages, though, work accomplishments become relatively more visible and project members better perceive how productive the work force has actually been.

Planning Subsystem. In the Planning Subsystem, project estimates are initially made and later revised as the project progresses. For example, when a project is behind schedule, the plan may be revised to hire more workers, extend the schedule, or both.

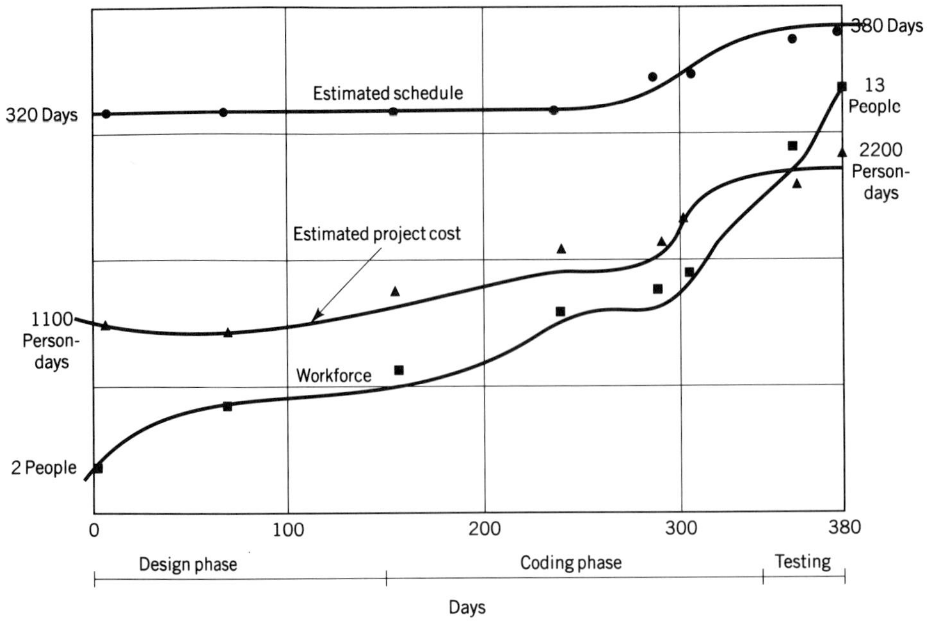

Figure 5. Simulation run output. ●, Actual estimated schedule in days; ▲, actual estimated project cost in man-days; ■, actual workforce (full-time equivalent people).

By dividing the value of person-days remaining at any point in the project by the time remaining, a manager can determine the indicated work force level, which is the work force needed to complete the project on time. However, hiring decisions are not made solely on the basis of scheduling requirements. Managers must also consider the training requirements and the work force's stability. Thus, before adding new project members, management assesses the project employment time for the new members. In general, the weighing between the desire for work-force stability and the desire to complete the project on time is not static; it changes throughout the project's life.

Although management determines the work-force level needed to complete the project, this level does not necessarily translate into the actual hiring goal. The hiring goal is constrained by the ceiling on new hires. This ceiling represents the highest work-force level management believes can be adequately handled by its experienced project members.

Thus three factors—scheduled completion time, work-force stability, and training requirements—affect the work-force level.

Sample Model Output

A sample model output is shown in Figure 5. It is a simulation of a real software project conducted at one of NASA's flight centers. Initially, this project was estimated to be 16,000 delivered source instructions (DSI) in size, and its cost and schedule were estimated to be 1,100 person-days and 320 working days, respectively. The actual results were: 24,400 DSI 2,200 person-days, and 380 days.

As shown, the model's results conformed quite accurately to the project's actual behavior. Notice how the project's management was inclined not to adjust the project's scheduled completion date during most of the development phase of the project. Adjustments in the earlier phases of the project were instead made to the project's work-force level. This behavior is not atypical. It arises, according to DeMarco because of political reasons:

> *Once an original estimate is made, it's all too tempting to pass up subsequent opportunities to estimate by simply sticking with your previous numbers. This often happens even when you know your old estimates are substantially off. There are a few different possible explanations for this effect: It's too early to show slip. . . . If I re-estimate now, I risk having to do it again later (and looking bad twice). . . . As you can see, all such reasons are political in nature. (DeMarco, 1982)*

The work-force pattern, on the other hand, is quite atypical. In the literature, work-force buildups tend to follow a concave type curve that rises, peaks, and then drops back to lower levels as the project proceeds toward the system testing phase (Boehm, 1981). Because of NASA's particular requirements, serious schedule slippages were not tolerated. As the completion date approached, pressures developed that overrode normal work-force stability considerations. That is, project management became increasingly willing to "pay any price" necessary to avoid a serious schedule slippage. This translated, as the figure indicates, into a management that was increasingly willing to add more workers. Abdel-Hamid (1989) investigates whether such a staffing policy did or did not in fact contribute to the project's late completion.

MODEL EXPERIMENTATION

In Abdel-Hamid and Madnick (1991), the above model serves as an experimentation vehicle to study the dynamic implications of an array of managerial policies and procedures. Four areas are studied: scheduling, quality assurance, control, and staffing. The exercise uncovers dysfunctional consequences of some currently adopted policies (e.g., in the scheduling area), provides guidelines for managerial policy (e.g., on the allocation of quality assurance effort), and provides new insights into software project phenomena (e.g., "90% syndrome"). In the remainder of this section one of the studies will be discussed in some detail in order to give the reader a better feel for model experimentation.

The purpose of the scheduling study was to investigate the scheduling practices within a major U.S. minicomputer manufacturer. In the particular organization, project managers were rewarded, in part, on how closely their project results matched their initial cost and schedule estimates. To "rationalize" the estimation process, a quantitative estimation model [TRW's COCOMO model (Boehm, 1981)] was institutionalized (see also COCOMO). However, quantitative estimation models are known to be nonportable, that is, they need to be recalibrated to each organization's unique project environment. Lacking the historical data base (as most organizations do) to recalibrated COCOMO and the time and resources to build one, they improvised the following estimation "strategy": The project managers would use the COCOMO model to determine "base" estimates, and then adjust the estimates upwards using a judgmental "safety factor."

The rationale for using a safety factor (commonplace in many organizations) is based on the following assumptions:

1. Past experience indicates a strong bias to underestimate the scope of software projects.
2. One might think biases are the easiest of estimating problems to correct since they involve errors moving always in the same direction. But as DeMarco (1982) suggests, biases are almost by definition invisible; the same psychological mechanism that creates the bias (for example, the optimism of software developers) works to conceal it.
3. To rectify the bias, a safety factor is used.

In other words, when project managers add contingency factors (ranging, say, from 25% to 100%), the assumption is that a safety factor is a simple mechanism to bring initial person-day estimates closer to true project cost in person-days as shown in Figure 6.

The above mental model has one critical flaw: A project's final cost and duration are not only a function of the product's characteristics (e.g., size and complexity), the development environment (e.g., programming tools), and the project team (e.g., experience), but in addition, is very much affected by the project's *initial estimates* themselves. The causal loop diagram in Figure 3 can help explain why. As was discussed earlier, it shows how initial estimates influence decision-making behavior throughout the project's life cycle. For example, schedule estimates directly influence work force hiring and firing, which affect the communication and training overheads incurred on the project, which, in turn, affects the team's productivity and,

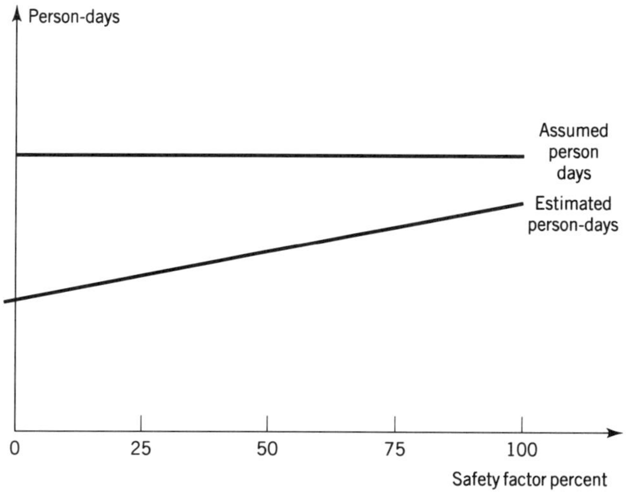

Figure 6. A comparison of assumed person-days and estimated person-days.

thus the ultimate cost of the project. In addition, schedule estimates can influence project behavior through more subtle and less direct means. For example, if a project is overestimated, "Parkinson's law indicates that people will use extra time for . . . personal activities, catching up on the mail, etc." (Boehm, 1981). This means, of course, that they become less productive, leading to a higher project cost. (The reader may want to sketch the *feedback* process that underlies Parkinson's law onto Figure 3.)

Thus, in a real sense, different estimates create different projects. In this particular organization, the researchers found that as higher safety factors were used, leading to increasingly generous initial estimates of effort and duration, the actual amount of person-days consumed did not remain at some inherently defined value as Figure 6 suggests; rather, it rose as shown in Figure 7.

The managerial lesson learned from these results is that managerial actions can have *indirect* (often unintended) consequences, and that such second-order effects may well influence project performance in significant ways. The safety factor policy did reduce the average estimation error

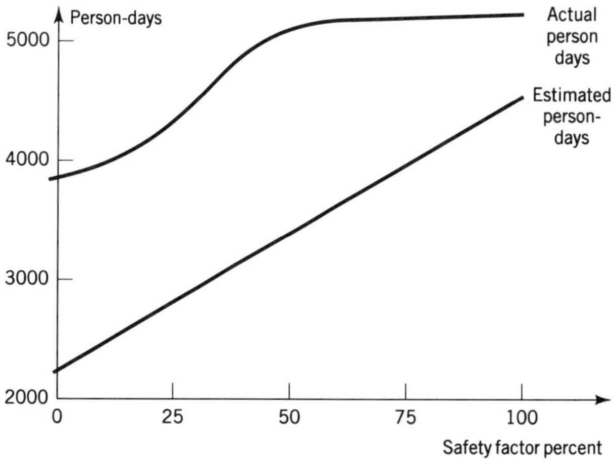

Figure 7. A comparison of actual person-days and estimated person-days.

from 38% to 9%. From the point of view of the individual project managers, the safety factor policy did work. The managers looked better. But the price the organization paid was a steep one: a 43% increase in the average project cost!

Management also learned that more accurate estimates are not necessarily "better" estimates. An estimation "strategy" should not be judged only on how accurate it is; it should also be judged on how costly the projects it creates are.

SUMMARY

The software development environment, like most organizational systems, is characterized by a complex conglomerate of interdependent functions. Action taken in one functional area (e.g., human resource management) can be traced throughout the entire system (e.g., software production, planning, and control). Furthermore, the behavior of an individual subsystem in isolation may be very different from its behavior when it interacts with other subsystems.

The information feedback perspective of the system dynamics approach provides a powerful lens to view and understand the structure and behavior of such systems. A sample application of the system dynamics approach to software project management was presented. The model integrates knowledge of the individual components of the software engineering environment to provide an integrated dynamic view. Such models are viable tools to support managerial decision making (e.g., on the allocation of quality assurance effort), provide new insights into software project phenomena (e.g., "90% syndrome"), and uncover dysfunctional consequences of adopted policies (e.g., in the scheduling area).

BIBLIOGRAPHY

T. K. Abdel-Hamid, "The Dynamics of Software Development Project Management: An Integrative System Dynamics Perspective," Ph.D. dissertation, Sloan School of Management, MIT, Jan., 1984.

T. K. Abdel-Hamid, "The Dynamics of Software Project Staffing: A System Dynamics Based Simulation Approach," *IEEE Transactions on Software Engineering,* **15**(2), 109–119, Feb. 1989.

T. K. Abdel-Hamid and S. E. Madnick, *Software Project Dynamics: An Integrated Approach,* Prentice-Hall, Inc., Englewood Cliffs, N.J., 1991.

B. W. Boehm, *Software Engineering Economics,* Prentice-Hall, Inc., Englewood Cliffs, N.J., 1981.

B. Dangerfield and O. Vapenikova, *DYSMAP2 User Manual,* University of Salford, 1987.

T. DeMarco, *Controlling Software Projects,* Yourdon Press, Inc., New York, 1982.

J. W. Forrester, *Industrial Dynamics,* The MIT Press, Cambridge, Mass., 1961.

J. W. Forrester, *Principles of Systems,* The MIT Press, Cambridge, Mass., 1968.

J. W. Forrester, "Counterintuitive Behavior of Social Systems," *Technolo Review,* **73**(3), Jan. 1971.

C. Ghezzi, M. Jazayeri, and D. Mandrioli, *Fundamentals of Software Engineering,* Prentice-Hall, Inc., Englewood Cliffs, N.J., 1991.

R. L. Glass, *Modern Programming Practices: A Report from Industry,* Prentice-Hall, Inc., Englewood Cliffs, N.J., 1982.

J. D. Lebel, "System Dynamics," *Dynamica* **7**(1), 7–31, (1981).

A. A. Legasto, J. W. Forrester, J. M. Lyneis, eds., *System Dynamics: TIMS studies in Management Science,* North-Holland, Amsterdam, 1980.

C. Y. Lin and R. R. Levary, "Computer-Aided Software Development Process Design," *IEEE Transactions on Software Engineering* **15**(9), 1025–1037, (Sept. 1989).

G. P. Richardson, *Feedback Thought in Social Science and Systems Theory,* University of Pennsylvania Press, Philadelphia, 1991.

G. P. Richardson and G. L. Pugh, III, *Introduction to System Dynamics Modeling with Dynamo,* The MIT Press, Cambridge, Mass., 1981.

B. M. Richmond, P. Vescuso, and S. Peterson, *STELLA for Business,* High Performance Systems Publications, Lyme, New Hampshire, 1987.

E. B. Roberts, "System Dynamics: An Introduction," in *Managerial Application of System Dynamics,* The MIT Press, ed., E. B. Roberts, Cambridge, Mass., 1981.

TAREK K. ABDEL-HAMID
Naval Postgraduate School

SYSTEMS ENGINEERING SCIENCES

INTRODUCTION

Systems Engineering Defined

Systems engineering is an integrated set of engineering disciplines that support the design, development, and operation of large-scale systems. It may be more formally defined as "an iterative process of top-down synthesis, development, and operation of a real-world system that satisfies, in a near-optimal manner, the full range of requirements for the system" (Eisner, 1988). By way of further definition, systems engineering may be viewed in terms of its basic elements, as listed here in Table 1. Each of these elements is carried out as part of the systems engineering process in as integrated a manner as possible, meaning that each element must be executed with due regard for its compatibility with all other appropriate elements. Thus the interfaces and interactions between elements is important as practitioners seek an integrated and wholistic systems engineering approach and process.

Systems engineering is supported by both engineering and scientific disciplines. As an example, the disciplines of electrical engineering, mechanical engineering, civil engineering, and chemical engineering serve as a partial base for systems engineering, depending upon the nature of the system that is under consideration. In a similar manner, the science disciplines of physics, chemistry, astronomy, aerodynamics, fluid mechanics, meteorology, and others may be needed to contribute to the individual and systems engineering disciplines and elements.

Table 1. Elements of Systems Engineering

Definition of needs/goals/objectives
Requirements definition
Requirements and functional analysis
Specification development
Formulation of systems architectures
Requirements/specifications allocation
Trade-off/alternatives evaluation
Subsystem design
Subsystem analysis
Software design and development
Interface definition
Schedule development
Life-cycle costing
Technical performance measurement
Program and decision analysis
Risk analysis
Integrated logistics support (ILS)
Pre-planned product improvement (P3I)
Reliability–maintainability–availability (RMA)
Specialty engineering
Integration
Test and evaluation
Configuration management
Quality assurance
Training Documentation
Production
Installation
Operations and maintenance (O&M)
Operations evaluation/modification

Illustrative Application Areas

Systems engineering is normally applied when considering the construction of such large-scale systems as:

- Space stations, satellites, and space probes
- Rapid transit (subway) systems
- Energy-generating systems such as nuclear reactors and power plants
- Military defense command and control systems
- The national telecommunications system
- The national air transportation system

The latter, the national air transportation system, may itself be viewed in terms of its subordinate parts—airports, airways, air vehicles, air-traffic control, access, and egress—each of which constitutes a large-scale system in its own right. The air traffic control component, for example, consists of a large assortment of radar, communications, control, navigation, and automation systems which the U. S. Federal Aviation Administration develops, operates, and manages (FAA, 1990). The systems engineering process and elements are especially useful and applicable when dealing with these types of very large and complex systems.

Related Areas

Some areas related to systems engineering which are acknowledged and utilized by builders of large-scale systems include:

- Software engineering
- Systems integration (SI)
- Systems engineering, integration and test (SEIT)
- Systems engineering management (SEM)
- Systems engineering and technical assistance (SETA)
- Computer-aided systems engineering
- Computer-aided software engineering

Software engineering is normally regarded as a subset of systems engineering and is essentially the same as the software design and development element listed in Table 1. Systems integration relates most directly to the integration element of systems engineering, and focuses on ways and means of effectively constructing an integrated system when its subsystems are relatively well-defined. Systems engineering, integration, and test is largely a set of activities that emphasizes the integration as well as the test and evaluation elements of systems engineering. In a similar sense, systems engineering management is oriented toward the program and decision analysis as well as the specialty engineering aspects of systems engineering (DOD, 1974), as shown in Table 1. Computer-aided systems and software engineering represent the systematic application of automated tools to facilitate the execution of the various elements of systems and software engineering, respectively (Eisner, 1988).

HISTORICAL PERSPECTIVES

The beginnings of the formal definition of the field of systems engineering and its related engineering and scientific bases are largely traceable to 1957 and the publishing of a book entitled *System Engineering: An Introduction to the Design of Large-Scale Systems* (Goode and Machol, 1957). These authors recognized the need for a large-scale system design theory and focused on probability theory and computers as the "basic tools" of exterior system design and interior system design, respectively. Some of the other specific areas presented included statistics, analog and digital techniques, logic, queuing theory, linear programming, game theory, group dynamics, information theory, cybernetics, servomechanism theory, simulation, and human engineering. This fundamental text articulated some of the engineering and scientific bases for systems engineering and set the stage for further developments.

In the 1960s several researchers and authors continued to investigate and define the nature of systems engineering. These included a book and articles by A. D. Hall (1962; 1965; 1969), two books by H. Chestnut (1965; 1967), and another book edited and compiled by R. E. Machol (1965). The latter was a substantial system engineering handbook that dealt with the methodology of systems engineering and a collection of papers organized by the topics of system environments, system components, system theory, system techniques, and related useful mathematics. This handbook gave further structure to the technical and scientific bases for systems engineering and included subject areas not previously considered, such as communication systems, sensors, satellites, guidance, propulsion, energy-conversion, radio telemetry, reliability, testing, and economics. The two articles by A. D. Hall (1965; 1969) focused on establishing the formal dimensions of systems engineering. The earlier article addressed some objectives of systems engineering as well as eight perspectives regarding the definition of systems engineering. In the second paper a three-dimensional approach is set forth based upon morphological precepts (Zwicky, 1967; 1969). Hall's three dimensions of systems engineering represented:

- A definition of seven phases, defined in a time sequence
- The seven steps of a problem solving or logic procedure
- The body of facts that define a discipline, profession or technology, constituting a knowledge dimension

The Department of Defense (DOD) issued a military standard (DOD, 1974) that defined three aspects of systems engineering management (SEM):

- Technical program planning and control
- The systems engineering process
- Engineering specialties

This standard had a significant influence upon how systems engineering was performed for the government, and it called for the execution of the standard under a systems engineering management plan (SEMP). In 1977 A. P. Sage gave further impetus to systems engineering with two books (Sage, 1977a; 1977b), the latter providing an overview of systems engineering methodologies and applications through a series of significant papers. Application areas of systems engineering included energy, resource and land use, medicine and health, technology assessment, and policy analysis. In 1978 systems engineering was placed in the context of industrial engineering (Turner, Mize, and Case, 1978).

In 1981 systems engineering was articulated in terms of the tools for systems analysis, the system design process, designing from several points of view, management, and a series of four case studies (Blanchard and Fabrycky, 1981). In 1983 the Defense Systems Management College published a guidebook dealing with systems engineering management (Defense Systems Management Guide, 1983). An update, published by the college seven years later (Defense Systems Management Guide, 1990), discusses in some detail several of the elements in Table 1. Related companion guidebooks from the College deal with the subjects of:

- Integrated logistics support
- Mission-critical computer resources management
- Test and evaluation management
- Risk management concepts and guidance
- Manufacturing management
- Subcontracting management

By 1988 the systems engineering elements were organized approximately as shown in Table 1 and were examined as well in terms of supporting computer-based tools and the introduction of computer-aided systems engineering (Eisner, 1988). Subsequent expositions dealt with systems engineering from an architecture and design point of view (Beam, 1990) as well as advanced technology for command and control (Andriole, 1990). The latter explored command and control and related subjects of information systems engineering, modeling and simulation, intelligent systems, decision aids and communications technology. Many subjects related to systems engineering are also cited in a concise encyclopedia of information processing (Sage, 1990).

THE ELEMENTS OF SYSTEMS ENGINEERING

The elements of systems engineering, cited in Table 1, are discussed here in greater detail. The order listed does not necessarily represent their time sequence. Each element may properly be the subject of a text in its own right.

Definition of Needs/Goals/Objectives

The design and development of a real-world system normally begins with an articulation of needs, goals, and objectives by the party responsible for procuring the system and satisfying the user. Such a party may be the user or an agent working on behalf of the user. As an example, the military is generally considered to be both the user as well as the party responsible for procuring the system. In the case of an urban rapid-transit system, the user is the general public, and a legal government or other authority may be responsible for both procuring and operating the system. In any case, it is ultimately the needs, goals, and objectives of the user that are to be satisfied. Definition and documentation of these needs, goals, and objectives are normally the initial steps in the systems engineering process. All subsequent systems engineering activities must attempt to assure that user needs, goals, and objectives are met.

Requirements Definition

The definition of user requirements flows directly from the statements of needs, goals, and objectives, and it represents a further step in documenting what the user desires. As such, a good requirements document is specific, detailed, complete, consistent, and quantitative to the maximum degree possible. Requirements reflect user wants and should not be constructed in such a way as to constrain or infringe upon the design architecture of the system itself. Failure to develop a good set of requirements has been a significant cause of the ultimate failure to design and build effective systems. Often during the design process inadequate requirements have been uncovered and attempts made to repair such deficiencies. Inflexibility in terms of changing requirements has also been a contributor to system development failures.

Requirements and Functional Analysis

After the requirements have been defined and documented, they are generally, but not necessarily, turned over to the system designer and developer. An initial step is to both analyze these requirements and place them in the context of the functions that are ultimately to be incorporated into the system. Analysis of requirements involves such activities as checking for completeness and consistency as well as defining interrelationships. Functional analysis relates to the precise definition of the functions and subfunctions to be performed by the system, as implied or made explicit by the requirements. As an example, functions of a city's rapid transit system include providing the capabilities for people movement, access, egress, fare collection, traffic signalling and control, power generation and conversion, etc. Functional definition likewise must be complete, and requirements are generally sorted by the functions to which they are related. If the analysis shows the presence of problems in any of these two areas, it is usual to go back and solve such problems by formal change processes. This systems engineering element may at times be referred to also as requirements and functions verification and validation.

Specification Development

In general, requirements and their related functions, after they have been analyzed, verified, and validated, are converted into a specification for the system. Organization of specifications by system functions is usual, as is the definition of specifications by increasing levels of detail. Some government agencies have provided guidance as to the desired format of a set of specifications (DOD, 1972). These specifications should represent precise statements as to all required performance and operating characteristics of the system.

Formulation of System Architectures

An architecture is a top-down, high level, and fundamental design choice for the system. For example, for a communications system such a choice might involve the selection of a frequency division vs. a time division multiplexing approach, and the top-level implications of that approach. One or more architectures may be formulated under this element, which is also sometimes called top-level systems engineering. As a minimum, each architecture is likewise described by function, sub-functions, and performance attributes.

Requirements/Specifications Allocation

Given the architecture(s) and the sets of requirements and specifications, it is then possible under this element to formally allocate requirements and specifications to functions and sub-functions for each of the architectures. This step gives further precision to the necessary performance attributes of all functions and sub-functions.

Trade-off/Alternatives Evaluation

This element involves trade-offs among and between the functions constituting each of the system architectures. In such a process, the above two elements are likely to be modified in an attempt to optimize the architectural design of the system as well as its functional components. If more than one architecture has been defined, the completion of this element usually leads to the selection of one preferred-system architecture. Such an architecture must satisfy, at a systems level, all requirements and specifications and related performance, cost, and schedule constraints. A formal set of system-level evaluation criteria is normally developed as a basis for assessing alternative architectures and selecting the one preferred architecture. Multi-attribute decision analysis tools may be used in order to support this type of assessment and selection process.

Subsystem Design

This element involves the conversion from functional definitions and descriptions to the specific subsystems that are needed in order to carry out each of the prescribed functions and sub-functions for the preferred system architecture. This is fundamentally a synthesis process, utilizing the systems engineer's talents for creating a potentially new set of subsystems that will satisfy all requirements and specifications.

Subsystem Analysis

This element goes hand in hand with the subsystem design in an iterative design–analysis process. The trade-off/alternatives evaluation element is also an integral part of this process, at this stage operating at the subsystem and lower levels of indenture of the system. Special tools such as modeling and simulation are often brought to bear in order to converge to the best possible subsystem design.

Software Design and Development

This element is emphasized here due to the orientation of this text as well as the fact that software has become the most difficult aspect of the design and development of most, if not all, large-scale systems. As herein defined, this element may be viewed as subsuming all features of software engineering, including all that is necessary to have the software interoperate with the hardware and human components of the system. Managing the software design, development, and acquisition process is viewed as a significant subject in its own right (Marciniak and Reifer, 1990). Further definitions of several aspects of software design and development are found in other sections of this overall text.

Interface Definition

Systems engineering necessarily involves the deliberate decomposition of the overall system in both the functional and subsystem dimensions. Further levels of decomposition into subfunctions and of subsystems into components, etc., is a natural part of such processes. The decomposed functions and subsystems, however, interact and interoperate with one another. The nature of such interaction and interoperation is normally made explicit and more precise in this interface definition element. Indeed, if the interfaces are too complex and unwieldy, it may be necessary to go back to earlier elements and modify them so as to both clarify and minimize undesired interfaces. Such interfaces are usually defined in many dimensions (e.g., electrical/power, electrical/signal, mechanical, thermal, etc.).

Schedule Development

The execution of all the elements of systems engineering in terms of start and completion dates, as well as important interim milestones, is usually set forth in a master schedule. Typically, schedule formats can be represented by a Gantt Chart (Frame, 1987) or a PERT (Program Evaluation and Review Technique) Chart (Frame, 1987) or some combination of the two. Schedules are updated as necessary and are utilized at detailed levels of the various systems engineering elements, often tracking due dates on a weekly basis. Automated commercial tools have become commonplace in the overall area of scheduling.

Life-Cycle Costing

The set of procedures used to estimate the total cost of the system that is being developed is called life-cycle costing. The three major cost categories for life-cycle costing are

- Research, development, test and evaluation (RDT&E)
- Procurement (or acquisition)
- Operations and maintenance (O&M)

Additional dimensions for cost estimation include:

- Hardware, software and personnel
- Function and sub-function
- Subsystem and component
- Calendar and fiscal year

Often, formal cost-estimating relationships (CERs) are employed in order to develop system cost profiles, as, for example, in the estimation of the effort and cost associated with the development of software as a function of the number of delivered source instructions. Profiles of system cost, by year, can be compared against budgeted costs for the system as well as projected revenues for the system, if appropriate, to assure economic viability of the system. This might be done, for example, with a rapid-transit system in an attempt to verify financial cash flow and profitability over a thirty-year time period. The effects of inflation are also normally accounted for in life cycle costing. The overall structure of life cycle costing can be embedded in what is called a life cycle cost model (LCCM).

Technical Performance Measurement

Technical performance measurement (TPM) is normally associated with the detailed assessment and monitoring of key performance variables and parameters of the system. These variables and parameters are sometimes also called measures of merit or measures of effectiveness. The purpose of technical performance measurement is to assure that all performance-related requirements and specifications for the system are being met. Prior to system construction, all such measurement is normally carried out by estimation and prediction procedures, which themselves are supported by a variety of modeling and simulation activities and tools. As subsystems are built, they can be formally tested as a means of technical performance measurement and monitoring. Technical performance measurement as a mechanism for guiding the design process and verifying performance envelopes and attributes is viewed as an exceedingly critical and challenging part of the systems engineering process.

Program and Decision Analysis

This element is sometimes referred to as program or project management and is defined to include all programmatic analyses and decision-making in relation to a large-scale system. Typical functions to be carried out include planning, organizing, directing, controlling, and staffing of a project or program (Archibald, 1976). Planning is viewed as a key activity which, at a summary level, deals with such areas as (Kezsbom, Schilling, and Edward, 1989):

- A set of objectives
- The statement of work (SOW)
- The milestone schedule
- The master budget
- The work breakdown structure (WBS)
- A task responsibility matrix

Monitoring of all cost, schedule, and performance activities and results vs. plan is a major orientation of this element.

Risk Analysis

The construction and operation of large-scale systems may involve two types of risks: development risk and societal risk. The former is concerned with risks associated with satisfying requirements with respect to cost, schedule, and performance. Societal risk usually deals with potential hazards to living organisms as a result of system operation, as in the case of systems that contain nuclear materials. Risk analyses are often probabilistic (Henley and Kumamoto, 1981) in nature and are intended to both estimate and minimize the above two aspects of risk.

Integrated Logistics Support (ILS)

Integrated logistics support may be defined as "a composite of all considerations necessary to assure the effective and economical support of a system for its life cycle" (Blanchard, 1986). Its focus is to assure that systems are logistically supported so as to optimally satisfy readiness requirements at minimum cost. ILS involves the consideration of such factors as corrective maintenance, periodic maintenance, spare parts provisioning, built-in testing, maintenance engineering, the nature and location of repair facilities, etc.

The significance of logistics engineering is underscored by the Department of Defense sponsored computer-aided acquisition and logistics support (CALS) initiative and program (Goodstein, 1990). The intent of CALS is to automate, to the maximum extent possible, the system acquisition and logistics support processes, thereby improving operational effectiveness and reducing cost.

Pre-Planned Product Improvement (P3I)

This element formalizes the notion of planning, in advance, for potential improvements in various subsystems and components. The motivation for such planning is often that the current system is cost-constrained, thereby necessarily limiting the system's performance envelope. As technology improves and additional funds become available, it may be desirable to extend and expand this performance envelope. By preplanning areas of improvement, "hooks" may be placed in the system to which improvements in capability may be attached. This avoids major redesign and facilitates system upgrades, incorporating new technologies at affordable costs.

Reliability–Maintainability–Availability (RMA)

RMA activities are designed to assure that readiness reliability (availability) and operational reliability meet requirements and specifications, consistent with the maintenance engineering design that is derived from the ILS element. Availability and reliability parameters are estimated and confirmed throughout the system's life cycle, utilizing formal prediction techniques and testing procedures. Redundancy is often employed in order to satisfy extremely high reliability and availability requirements.

Specialty Engineering

This element of systems engineering brings a variety of system-specific engineering disciplines into consideration, such as:

- Safety
- Security
- Value engineering
- Environmental engineering
- Nuclear engineering
- Electromagnetic effects and interference

Such specialty engineering activities, while not normally a part of the generic systems engineering process, may be critical to a particular system. For example, safety considerations are extremely significant in matters of civil aviation and air traffic control. Security may also be important in aviation and is important in another context when dealing with computer or communications security. Electromagnetic interference does not affect all systems, but represents a potential problem in a shipboard environment with a large number of radiating and receiving antennas.

A relatively new discipline known as "concurrent engineering" (DICE, 1990) may be considered at this time to be a part of the specialty engineering element. In time it may evolve to be a discrete element of systems engineering in its own right. Concurrent engineering principles suggest the complementary use of all system or product capabilities at all points along the life cycle. This implies, for example, that even during preliminary system/product design, personnel from manufacturing, quality control and assurance, testing, marketing/sales, finance/accounting, etc., should be involved in and contribute to the design process, thus adding value represented by their area of individual expertise.

Integration

Integration occurs for both hardware and software as components are connected to produce subsystems and as units are combined to yield computer system components and configuration items. Integration involves the piecing together of smaller parts into larger parts in a planned and systematic manner. Progressive integration steps eventually lead to a full system for which hardware, software, and human capabilities interoperate in a harmonious manner so as to meet or exceed system requirements.

Test and Evaluation

Under most circumstances, each integration activity is followed by a test activity whose purpose is to verify the performance characteristics of the integrated unit or component. For this reason, at times, integration and test is viewed as a singular element of systems engineering. Testing is clearly critical in order to assure system integrity and interoperation, and it implies rework and retest when and if test results lead to failure at any level of testing. Large-scale major subsystem or system testing in a development or operational context is called development test and evaluation (DT&E) and operational test and evaluation (OT&E), respectively. Test and evaluation activities are usually documented in a formal Test and Evaluation Master Plan (TEMP) (Eisner, 1988).

A systems engineering activity known as verification and validation (V&V) is sometimes included within the test and evaluation element, often viewed as more important in the software development aspect of systems engineering. V&V is intended to be a formal and additional check on the correctness of the system design and its implementation. Some system acquisition agents insist that V&V be carried out by a third party in an independent manner.

Configuration Management

In order to effectively engineer a large-scale system, configuration items must be well-defined, and changes to these items tightly controlled and managed. These needs have led to a systems engineering element known as configuration management, which generally incorporates the following five features (Bersoff, Henderson, and Segal, 1980):

- Identification
- Control
- Auditing

- Status accounting
- Traceability

Configuration management in the software arena has become particularly important, since software changes can be made with relative ease. Automated tools have become available commercially to support the configuration management element.

Quality Assurance

Quality assurance, sometimes including quality control, is a set of activities whose purpose is to verify that the system conforms to specifications. Especially in the 1980s, quality assurance has undergone a type of reformation as it has evolved into a broader concept known as Total Quality Management (TQM) (DOD, 1989). There is a growing body of knowledge regarding TQM whose major principles may be articulated as follows:

- Continuous improvement of process
- Focused attention on customer requirements
- Cross-functional development (concurrent engineering)
- Use of the plan–do–check–act (PDCA) cycle
- Assured conformance to specifications

Such principles are drawn from both United States (Deming, 1982; Juran, 1989; Crosby, 1984) and Japanese (Ishikawa, 1985; Imai, 1986; Roy, 1990) initiatives and perspectives. Classical tools of quality assurance and TQM include statistical process control (SPC), quality function deployment (QFD), sampling theory, design of experiments, and various types of process control charting.

Training

Training is often critical to the success of a system and normally occurs in three distinct domains: with users, operators, and maintainers of the system. Users may not need a great deal of training, as is the case when a long distance call is placed using our national telecommunications system. Operators and maintainers usually require extensive training and retraining when system upgrades are introduced. Computer-based training (CBT) has been increasing in popularity as computer tools have become more prevalent and cost-effective.

Documentation

Documentation is clearly required to support all elements of systems engineering. The extensive availability of automated word processors and desktop publishing software has greatly enhanced the overall productivity of this element.

Production

After a system has been built, tested, and accepted in terms of meeting all requirements, it moves into the production phase, if production quantities are called for. A variety of production engineering tasks support this element which seeks to replicate the system at minimum cost and maximum quality.

Installation

System production units are installed at their operational locations and checked out to assure that no system degradation has occurred during transit and the installation process itself.

Operations and Maintenance (O&M)

This systems engineering element refers to the steady-state operation of the system in its intended operational environment.

Operations Evaluation/Modification

Most systems undergo continuous evaluations of their performance while in operation. Where cost-effective enhancements can be made, the system is modified on a continuing basis in order to improve performance. Engineering change proposals (ECPS) and the results of preplanned product improvement analyses can be the vehicles for consideration of such enhancements.

SCIENCE BASE FOR SYSTEMS ENGINEERING

Systems engineering is supported by an extensive science knowledge base whose use depends largely upon the type of system that is under development. For example, space systems and missions depend strongly upon physics and the disciplines of orbital mechanics, trajectory analysis, thermodynamics, and others. Medical engineering likewise can depend upon the sciences of chemistry and biology. Essentially all large-scale systems require some amount of software, which itself has as a basis what is known as computer science. Thus, we may summarize some of disciplines that form a science base for systems engineering as:

- Natural sciences (e.g., physics, chemistry, biology, astronomy, etc.)
- Mathematics and computer science (e.g., calculus, optimization theory, data structures, programming, etc.)
- Engineering (electrical, mechanical, chemical, nuclear, etc.)
- Applied engineering/technology (communications, propulsion, materials science, aerodynamics, etc.)

Some of the subdisciplines that have been of special importance in systems engineering have included such areas as:

- Control systems theory
- Diagramming
- Forecasting
- Linear programming
- Linear systems theory
- Network analysis

- Nonlinear systems theory
- Probability theory and statistics
- Search theory
- Urban dynamics

In addition, several of the above can be decomposed into subsets of disciplines that have contributed to the development and practice of systems engineering. As an example, various types of diagramming techniques have been widely applied to systems engineering and its software development element. Such diagramming procedures have included (Martin and McClure, 1985; Eisner, 1988):

- Action diagrams
- Decision network diagrams
- Decision trees
- Decomposition diagrams
- Dependency diagrams
- Data flow diagrams
- Entity-relationship diagrams
- Functional flow diagrams and descriptions
- Hierarchical input-process-output (HIPO) diagrams
- Logic flow charts
- Michael Jackson diagrams
- N2 diagrams
- Nassi-Shneiderman diagrams
- Parameter dependency diagrams
- Process flow charts
- Programming flowcharts
- Sequence and timing diagrams
- Signal flow diagrams
- Warnier-Orr diagrams

COMPUTER-AIDED SYSTEMS ENGINEERING

A special discipline that supports systems engineering is computer-aided systems engineering. This subject is to systems engineering what computer-aided design (CAD) and computer-aided manufacturing (CAM) are to engineering design and manufacturing, respectively. In addition, the subsidiary subject of software engineering is supported as well by computer-aided software engineering.

Computer-aided systems engineering is the systematic development and application of computer tools to the various elements of systems engineering (Table 1). With the advent of powerful desktop personal computers and workstations, a great amount of attention has been given to bringing computer tools directly to the lead systems engineer and the systems engineering team. Table 2 provides a list of some categories of tools that support systems engineering (Eisner, 1988).

Since all of the tools are available in an automated environment, it may be said that computer science forms a basis for all of the broad subject of computer-aided systems engineering. In that sense, as well as the fact that software is a part of essentially all large-scale systems, computer science and engineering are ubiquitous in carrying out the tasks and activities of systems engineering.

Table 2. Categories of Computer Tools that Support Systems Engineering

Spreadsheets
Database management systems (DBMSs)
Word processors
Graphics packages
Integrated software
Multi-task applications managers
Project management software
Alternatives and preference evaluators
Decision support systems (DSSs)
Executive information systems (EISs)
Toolchests/desk managers
Idea processors
Management evaluators/aids
Statistical tools
Mathematical tools
Engineering tools (CAE)
Reliability tools
Mathematical programming
Simulation software
Computer-aided design packages (CAD)
Computer-aided manufacturing packages (CAM)
Structured analysis/design tools
Languages
Utilities
Configuration management tools
Imaging systems
Forecasting tools
Expert and artificial intelligence systems
Communications and networking tools
Desktop publishers

Among the elements of systems engineering cited in Table 1, several stand out as rather advanced in terms of the development and application of supporting computer tools. These include:

- Requirements and functional analysis
- Subsystem design and analysis
- Software design and development
- Schedule development
- Life cycle costing
- Technical performance measurement
- Program and decision analysis
- Risk analysis
- ILS and RMA
- Configuration management
- Training
- Documentation

Requirements and Functional Analysis

A variety of requirements analyzers and languages provide traceability, sorting, checking, and general analysis capabilities. Several tools explicitly allow for functional decomposition and matching of requirements under functional areas. Examples are the Input-Output Requirements Language (IORL), the Problem Statement Language/Problem

Statement Analyzer (PSL/PSA) and the Software Requirements Engineering Methodology (SREM).

Subsystem Design and Analysis

Design tools exist at the level of detailed electrical circuit analysis (e.g., SPICE) and higher-level simulators of performance (e.g., General Purpose System Simulation [GPSS] and Simscript II.5).

Software Design and Development

Tools that support software design and development are numerous and can be identified under the overall subject of computer-aided software engineering (CASE). Some of the broad categories of such tools are listed in Table 3. In general, one seeks computer aids that are integrated and cover as much of the software development life cycle as possible. Examples of well-known tools are the Information Engineering Facility (IEF), Information Engineering Workbench (IEW), Excelerator, and Teamwork.

Schedule Development

Commercial project management software is available that allows for the automated generation of Gantt and PERT charts. Popular low-price examples are Timeline, Project Scheduler, and Microsoft Project.

Table 3. Categories of Software Development Computer Tools

Requirements languages and traceability tools
Report generators
Database Management Systems (DBMSs)
Project management software
Spreadsheets/integrated packages
Graphics tools
Effort/cost/productivity estimators
Desktop managers
Workbenches/structured analysis tools
High level/order languages
Coding languages
Code generators
Code analyzers
Compilers
Performance simulators/predictors
Emulators
Performance monitors/probes
Operating systems
Cross development tools
Scheduling/Sequencing tools
Support tool libraries
Benchmark systems
Utilities
Integration and test tools
Quality assurance/V & V tools
Configuration management software
Training/CAI/CBT tools
Editors
AI support tools
Real-time processing tools

Life Cycle Costing

Although the DOD has sponsored the development of automated life cycle cost models (LCCMs), as for example a system known as FLEX, such tools can be constructed by using spreadsheet software (e.g., Lotus 1-2-3, Excel, and Quattro Pro).

Technical Performance Measurement

Measuring the performance of large-scale systems is often addressed by utilizing commercial simulation software such as the Simulation Language for Alternative Modeling (SLAM), DYNAmic MOdel (DYNAMO) and those cited above under subsystem design. Particularly specialized performance analysis problems may be solved with similarly specialized aids (e.g., linear programming software packages) or building a simulator using any one of several available programming languages (e.g., Fortran, C, Pascal).

Program and Decision Analysis

Program analysis capabilities are normally embedded in project management software, as cited above. Consideration of alternative decisions can be supported by a wide variety of available generic decision support systems (DSSs) and executive information systems (EISs).

Risk Analysis

Many risk analysis tools utilize decision tree structures and therefore can be constructed from a basic decision support system. Others are more specialized and are represented directly as risk analysis software (e.g., @ Risk) and simulation packages (e.g., Q-GERT).

ILS and RMA

Many tools are being developed under the DOD CALS program previously cited. Other software focuses on the computation of both hardware and software reliability measures.

Configuration Management

As this area has become more important, commercial tools have become available that are basically specialized applications of a database management system (e.g., Change and Configuration Control (CCC), Configuration Management Automation System (CMAS)).

Training

Automated packages for training first appeared under the general categories of computer-aided instruction (CAI) and computer-based training (CBT). As the computer and software state of the art has improved, this software has expanded in scope and capability to include multimedia training systems.

Documentation

Two broad categories of software tools that support this area are word processors and desktop publishers, the latter including extensive graphics capabilities. Most other software packages have report generators as an integral part, thus providing their results in documented form.

FUTURE DIRECTIONS

Expansions in systems engineering sciences and related information technologies are expected both in scope and in basic capabilities (Eisner, 1990). Six areas of particular significance include:

- Rapid evolution of workstation technology
- Extensive networking
- Integrated environments
- Standardization
- Recognition by academic community
- Meta-systems engineering

The focus of computer manufacturers on very capable and inexpensive workstation technology (Kaplan, 1991) is expected to spur the future expansion of systems engineering sciences and the application thereto of automated tools. These workstations are being installed in networked configurations that allow for massive sharing of information between members of systems engineering teams. Further, it is expected that additional force will be directed toward establishing fully integrated environments in which to carry out the tasks and activities of systems engineering, including software engineering. These environments will accommodate data exchange between tools through transparent interfaces as well as very user-friendly graphics capabilities and full life cycle system support.

Trends toward increased levels of standardization are expected to continue, which in turn will help to facilitate both networking and the evolution of integrated environments. At the same time, it may be assumed that systems engineering as a discipline will find its way more and more into engineering school curricula, alongside of the more conventional fields of electrical, mechanical, civil, nuclear, and similar long-standing engineering areas. Finally, as systems become larger and more complex, new structures for systems engineering sciences may be expected that will explicitly account for size, interoperability, and interface concerns along with a host of related management issues.

BIBLIOGRAPHY

S. J. Andriole, ed., *Advanced Technology for Command and Control Systems Engineering,* AFCEA International Press, Fairfax, Va., 1990.

R. D. Archibald, *Managing High-Technology Programs and Projects,* John Wiley & Sons, Inc., New York, 1976.

W. R. Beam, *Systems Engineering, Architecture and Design,* McGraw-Hill Book Co., Inc., New York, 1990.

E. H. Bersoff, V. D. Henderson, and S. G. Segal, *Software Configuration Management: An Investment in Product Integrity,* Prentice-Hall, Inc., Englewood Cliffs, N.J., 1980.

B. S. Blanchard, *Logistics Engineering and Management,* Prentice-Hall, Inc., Englewood Cliffs, N.J., 1986.

B. S. Blanchard and W. J. Fabrycky, *Systems Engineering and Analysis,* Prentice-Hall, Inc., Englewood Cliffs, N.J., 1981.

H. Chestnut, *Systems Engineering Tools,* John Wiley & Sons, Inc., New York, 1965.

H. Chestnut, *Systems Engineering Methods,* John Wiley & Sons, Inc., New York, 1967.

P. B. Crosby, *Quality Without Tears,* New American Library, New York, 1984.

Defense Systems Management Guide, *System Engineering Management Guide,* Defense Systems Management College, Fort Belvoir, Va., Oct. 3, 1983.

Defense Systems Management Guide, *Systems Engineering Management Guide,* Defense Systems Management College, Fort Belvoir, Va., Jan. 1990.

W. E. Deming, *Quality, Productivity, and Competitive Position,* MIT, Center for Advanced Engineering Study, Cambridge, Mass., 1982.

Department of Defense (DOD), *Specification Practices,* Military Standard 490, U. S. Government, Washington, D.C., May 18, 1972.

Department of Defense (DOD), *Systems Engineering Management,* Military Standard 499A, U. S. Government, Washington, D.C., May 1, 1974.

Department of Defense (DOD), *DOD 5000.51-G, Total Quality Management Guide,* U. S. Government, Washington, D.C., Aug. 23, 1989.

DICE: DARPA Initiative in Concurrent Engineering, Concurrent Engineering Research Center (CERC), West Virginia University, Drawer 2000, Morgantown, W.V., Feb. 1990.

H. Eisner, *Computer-Aided Systems Engineering,* Prentice-Hall, Inc., Englewood Cliffs, N.J., 1988.

H. Eisner, "Information and Decision Technologies: Nine Needs and Niches for the Nineties," *Information and Decision Technologies* **16,** Elsevier Science Publishers B. V. (North-Holland), New York, 1990, pp. 101–106.

Federal Aviation Administration (FAA), *Capital Investment Plan,* U. S. Department of Transportation, Washington, D.C., Dec. 1990.

J. D. Frame, *Managing Projects in Organizations,* Jossey-Bass Publishers, San Francisco, Calif., 1987.

H. H. Goode and R. E. Machol, *System Engineering,* McGraw-Hill Book Co., Inc., New York, 1957.

D. H. Goodstein, *CALS: Creating the Electronic Information Ecology,* Business and Technology Consultant, May 1990.

A. D. Hall, *A Methodology For Systems Engineering,* Van Nostrand Reinhold Co., Princeton, N.J., 1962.

A. D. Hall, "Systems Engineering from an Engineering Viewpoint," IEEE Transactions on Systems Science and Cybernetics, IEEE, New York, Nov. 1965; also in A. P. Sage, *Systems Engineering: Methodology and Applications,* IEEE Press, New York, 1977.

A. D. Hall, "Three-Dimensional Morphology of Systems Engineering," IEEE Transactions on Systems Science and Cybernetics, IEEE, New York, Apr. 1969; also in A. P. Sage, *Systems Engineering: Methodology and Applications,* IEEE Press, New York, 1977.

E. J. Henley and H. Kumamoto, *Reliability Engineering and Risk Assessment,* Prentice-Hall, Inc., Englewood Cliffs, N.J., 1981.

M. Imai, *Kaizen, The Key to Japan's Competitive Success,* McGraw-Hill Book Co., Inc., New York, 1986.

K. Ishikawa, *What Is Total Quality Control? The Japanese Way,* Prentice-Hall, Inc., Englewood Cliffs, N.J., 1985.

J. M. Juran, *Juran on Leadership for Quality,* The Free Press, a Division of Macmillan, Inc., New York, 1989.

G. Kaplan, *A Special Guide to Engineering Workstations,* IEEE Spectrum, IEEE Press, New York, Apr. 1991.

D. S. Kezsbom, D. L. Schilling, and K. A. Edward, *Dynamic Project Management,* John Wiley and Sons, Inc., New York, 1989.

R. E. Machol, ed., *System Engineering Handbook,* McGraw-Hill Book Co., Inc., New York, 1965.

J. J. Marciniak and D. J. Reifer, *Software Acquisition Management,* John Wiley & Sons, Inc., New York, 1990.

J. Martin and C. McClure, *Diagramming Techniques for Analysts and Programmers,* Prentice-Hall, Inc., Englewood Cliffs, N.J., 1985.

R. Roy, *A Primer on the Taguchi Method,* Van Nostrand Reinhold Co., Inc., New York, 1990.

A. P. Sage, *Methodology for Large Scale Systems,* McGraw-Hill Book Co., Inc., New York, 1977a.

A. P. Sage, *Systems Engineering: Methodology and Applications,* IEEE Press, New York, 1977b.

A. P. Sage, ed., *Concise Encyclopedia of Information Processing in Systems and Organizations,* Pergamon Press, Inc., New York, 1990.

W. C. Turner, J. H. Mize, and K. E. Case, *Introduction to Industrial and Systems Engineering,* Prentice-Hall, Inc., Englewood Cliffs, N.J., 1978.

F. Zwicky and H. G. Wilson, eds., *New Methods of Thought and Procedure,* Springer-Verlag, New York, 1967.

F. Zwicky, *Discovery, Invention, Research—Through the Morphological Approach,* Macmillan, New York, 1969.

HOWARD EISNER
The George Washington University

T

TCI/IP

Transmission Control Protocol and Internet Protocol are networking standards developed by the Defense Advanced Research Projects Agency (DARPA), originally for use in the ARPANET. These Protocols have been adopted worldwide and form the basis of the global Internet (see D. Comer, *Internetworking with TCP/IP,* Prentice-Hall, Englewood Cliffs, N.J., 1988).

TCSE

TCSE is the acronym for the Technical Committee on Software Engineering of the IEEE Computer Society. With over 7000 members, it is the IEEE-CS' largest technical activity. Founded in 1973, TCSE provides a forum for exchange of ideas among interested practitioners, researchers, developers, maintainers, users, and students in the software engineering field.

TCSE sponsors many conferences and technical meetings to advance both the state-of-the-art and the state-of-the-practice of software engineering. It sponsors the annual International Conference on Software Engineering (ICSE), flagship conference of the field. It also sponsors or co-sponsors the International Workshop on CASE (CASE), the Conference on Software Maintenance (CSM), the International Software Metrics Symposium (Metrics), the Working Conference on Reverse Engineering (WCRE), the International Symposium on Requirements Engineering, the International Workshop on Software Reusability, and the International Symposium on Software Reliability Engineering (ISSRE). Besides meetings sponsored or co-sponsored directly, TCSE joins as a cooperating society in many other software engineering meetings throughout the world.

IEEE's development work in software engineering standards is under the auspices of TCSE's Software Engineering Standards Subcommittee (SESS). TCSE also has active topical subcommittees on software reliability engineering, reverse engineering, software reuse, quantitative methods, technology transfer, and software engineering education.

Many notable software engineering researchers and practitioners have served as chair of TCSE, including Barry Boehm, Marvin Zelkowitz, Lorraine Duvall, Peter Freeman, Annelise von Maryhauser, and Elliot Chikofsky.

TCSE is a well-spring of new and innovative projects for the advancement of the software engineering field, as well as a home for many grassroots projects. It provides projects with structure, support, encouragement, and access to a diverse and interested membership.

TECHNOLOGY TRANSFER

INTRODUCTION

What is software technology transfer (STT) and how is it facilitated? This issue is a basic concern to most people who develop new software technologies. This article examines the diffusion and adoption of software as a way to understand STT. As such, the focus is on empirical research that examines the process of STT, rather than on popular treatments or ad hoc suggestions for how to transfer software from producers to consumers.

The next sections examine studies which look into how software applications and tools are diffused into the community of potential adopters for their subsequent use. A brief research agenda for understanding and affecting software technology transfer concludes the article.

THE DIFFUSION OF SOFTWARE

When a new software application or tool is developed, it represents a technological innovation that is ready to be diffused into a marketplace or user community. As such, we can ask, What is known about the diffusion of innovations, such as new software technologies? The diffusion of innovations, in general, is one of the most researched topics in the social sciences, with nearly 4000 cited studies appearing in the literature (Rogers, 1983). However, in computer science or software engineering, diffusion of innovations is one of the least researched.

Historically, most studies of software innovations maintain a tight coupling between their diffusion and adoption. Not surprisingly, diffusion represents where "technology push" is most apparent, and where "technology pull" from users prepared to adopt, must be identified and engaged (Abernathy, 1979). Thus, the diffusion and adoption of software innovations are interrelated, as is this review of published studies.

The focus in this article is on empirical studies of STT. However, attention will be directed to the findings reported in these studies, rather than upon the various kinds of empirical research methods (e.g., case studies, field studies, and surveys) employed. Interested readers can consult the original studies cited in the references for more information on the methods employed.

Kling and Gerson (1977) argue that the computing world emerged around "structural interests" that direct the flow of hardware and software innovations from technology stimulators (e.g., funding agencies such as ARPA, NSF) and academic and industrial developers toward organizational users and public consumers. Stimulators and developers collectively represent the dominant structural interest, while organizational users, the contending interest, and general public consumers, the repressed interest. As such, for the computing world as a social institution to survive and grow, new software technologies will be stimulated and developed whether or not there is demand from organizational users or consumers for these technologies. But as this might then result in a large, diverse volume of new software technologies, then some adventuresome organizational users will find potential opportunity or competitive advantage from these new technologies. In turn, their successful or troublesome experiences will be communicated through both informal and professional channels to other prospective adopters. Thus, some organizational users will act to adopt select new technologies and provide sufficient reinforcement for the stimulators and developers to continue.

Perry and Kraemer (1979) argue that attributes of new versus in-place software applications strongly determine what will be adopted where. Using data collected from a nationwide survey of software applications in public agencies (as did the Kling and Gerson study above), they sought to isolate which innovation attributes would be most critical to facilitating diffusion and adoption in different settings. They considered the following attributes:

- Task complexity—the number, interdependence, and functional specialization of organizational information processing tasks brought together by an innovation
- Pervasiveness—degree to which an innovation relates to or requires adjustments to other elements in the organization
- Communicability—degree to which an innovation is visible to others as indicated by the extent of an innovation's documentation, or by the existence of multiple interpersonal communication channels where information pertaining to the innovation appears (cf. Brancheau and Wetherbe, 1990)
- Specificity of evaluation—degree to which an innovation's output or payoff can be objectively measured
- Departure from current technology—the relative differences between innovative technology and technology in place
- Relative cost—the cost of implementing an innovative system as either low, medium or high.

Perry and Kraemer also analyzed whether policies such as (a) locus of an innovation's development, (b) number of published reports in professional literature, and (c) availability of subsidized assistance, had significant effects in facilitating software innovation, diffusion and adoption. Their analysis indicates that a software innovation's pervasiveness most strongly determines what new applications will be successfully transferred. The other attributes showed much weaker or insignificant associations. Similarly, they found some evidence indicating that the availability of subsidies did encourage the adoption of innovative software applications.

Lieblein (1986) cites several mechanisms that should facilitate the diffusion and adoption of new software technologies. In particular, he suggests the following set:

- Technically astute managers, supportive executives, and technology champions responsible to affect technology transition (cf. Maidique 1979)
- High-quality prototypes, scaled-up demonstrations, and a successful real application that can be measured and evaluated
- Personnel rotation through development organizations
- Newsletters, courses, seminars, and conferences that communicate the capabilities and potential benefits of new technology and
- Readily available assistance.

Lieblein further observes that STT will be easier if the new technology is relatively easy to use, causes minimal disruption of existing business practices, and represents an incremental extension of existing technology.

Lieblein's prescriptions utilize the data and analyze various sources including those reported by Redwine and Riddle (1985), and by Manley and others as reported in the IEEE Workshop on Software Engineering Technology Transfer (1983). Subsequently, the second IEEE workshop on STT includes a number of additional informal studies of the diffusion and adoption of software innovations to specific organizations which further examine these issues (Przyblynski, 1988).

ADOPTION AND ACQUISITION OF SOFTWARE INNOVATIONS

The adoption of innovations is the most commonly studied aspect of STT. In general, these studies seek to answer the question: Why do people in organizations choose to adopt a particular software innovation?

Adopting a new software application, tool, or technique implies an organization's commitment of budget, schedule, and staff skill resources to acquire and install the innovation. Accordingly, the focus on innovation adoption clusters into three concerns: (a) decision to adopt, (b) rate of adoption, (c) organizational innovativeness. As this selection is a well-studied facet of technology transfer, research has also begun to address problems arising in adoption research as well as software acquisition dilemmas and strategies. Each in turn will be examined.

Decision to Adopt

Downs and Mohr (1976, 1979) were among the first to recognize that the adoption of a innovation is not a simple decision-making process. They have argued that it may be possible to (re)construct the decision to adopt an innovation in terms of cost-benefit trade-offs. But as King and Schrems (1978) found, cost-benefit analyses for software systems tend to underestimate the total costs, and overestimate the benefits actually realized. Accordingly, Downs and Mohr add that attention should instead be directed to the shifting incentives and constraints that mitigate the participants, innovation adoption decision.

Perry and Danziger (1980) took a different view of the adoption decision. They were concerned with an innovations "adoptability;" that is, the probability that a new software application will be adopted by an organization. Based on a nationwide study, they found that a higher probability of adoption of certain software innovations is strongly associated with: (a) greater visibility of the software system within the organization, (b) less uncertainty about the cost and evaluation of the innovation's adoption, (c) greater availability of technical staff competence to implement the innovation, and (d) higher level of objective need for the innovation. Thus, senior managers or other new technology champions in a consuming organization could be expected to adopt new software technologies when such conditions exist.

Tornatzky and Klein (1982) examined 75 studies of the adoption and implementation of various technological innovations. Through their meta-analysis of the 30 different innovation characteristics appearing in these studies, they found 3 characteristics that had the most consistent significant relationship to an innovation's adoption; namely, the innovation's compatibility, relative advantage, and complexity (Rogers, 1983). Compatibility refers to the degree to which an innovation is perceived as being consistent with the existing values, past experiences, and the needs of the adopters. This notion of compatibility is similar to the concept of an innovation's pervasiveness as used by Perry and Kraemer (1978). Relative advantage refers to the degree to which an innovation is perceived to be better than the technology it replaces. Complexity refers to the relative difficulty of understanding and using an innovation. In this regard, a software system that is (upward) compatible, provides additional new functional capabilities, and is easy to use in routine work situations, is more likely to be adopted and implemented than software technologies that lack these characteristics. However, Tornatzky does caution that the evidence for such inferences is only weakly supported, with fault lying in the quality of the studies examined.

One other aspect of software system adoption concerns the decision to build versus buy the desired system (Scacchi, 1984). In deciding to adopt a new system: Which system will do the job? Should the system be developed with in-house staff or should it be purchased from an outside vendor? Going with in-house staff facilitates the development of local product and production knowledge, which is useful in system maintenance. Similarly, in-house staff more readily enables the development of customized systems fitted to local, idiosyncratic organizational arrangements. But if the system represents an unfamiliar or unproven technology, uncertainty over completing the system development project within resource constraints may point to a lack of incentives for an in-house effort. On the other hand, buying a new system from an outside vendor means trying to figure out the strength of the system's signal from the promotional noise. What criteria can be used to filter promotional information on the new system? The choices include: (a) vendor reputation, (b) prior experience of similar users, (c) performance characteristics, (d) quality of available documentation, and (e) ease of fit into local computing arrangements. In any case, uncertainty over what to consider in selecting and from whom to get the system, is present. Thus, it is very likely that system selection will be influenced either by the mobilization of participants favoring one product, or by the participants whose input is trusted most by those making the selection decision.

Rate of Adoption

Rate of adoption refers to the relative speed by which a specific new software technology is adopted throughout the software community (Rogers, 1983). This is the kind of data reported by Redwine and Riddle (1985). They report that software innovations such as Unix, object-oriented languages and techniques, and expert systems, take as much as 15 years or more to move from their initial development to widespread adoption and use. Such a finding is a dismal prospect for new technology developers hoping to change industry software practices in less than a decade. Why is the rate of adopting such popular software innovations so low? To answer such a question, Danziger and Dutton (1977) a decade earlier, conducted a nationwide study to find out.

In their study, Danziger and Dutton sought to identify what might explain differences among municipal government agencies in the rate they adopt new software applications across the U.S. The researchers report that there are 4 factors that primarily determine how quickly new software applications will be adopted: (a) functional capabilities of the particular innovation, (b) a high-pull oriented user environment, (c) people whose interests and values within the organization are primarily served through the innovation's adoption, and (d) who controls the decision to adopt the innovation. They point out that these last two reasons indicate that political conditions within the adopting organizations are clearly associated with an innovation's adoption. Kling (1978) and Gerwin's case studies report similar findings regarding the organizational politics that underlie the adoption of major software innovations.

Organizational Innovativeness

Innovativeness simply reflects the fact that one organization is earlier in adopting some new software technology than other comparable organizations (Rogers, 1983). As described above, existing organizational conditions that affect the decision to adopt and the rate of adoption would seemingly be associated with an organization's innovativeness. However, in the case of software technologies, no direct studies of organizational innovativeness could be found. Instead, there are empirical studies that identify barriers to adopting new software applications that mitigate innovativeness.

Gross and Ginzberg (1984) identified 30 potential obstacles to the acquisition and implementation of new software packages. On close observation, they report that the primary obstacles include: (a) uncertainty in estimating the amount of effort required to make a package fit; (b) uncertainty in evaluating the utility of documentation provided with a package to reduce the uncertainty of (a); (c) uncertainty in the developer's ability to accommodate or sustain the package's fit within the organization; and (d) uncertainty about precise user needs and the package's ability to fulfill those needs. Accordingly, more innovative or early adopter organizations will be those organizations who can most easily avoid or resolve these uncertainties.

Software Acquisition

In contrast to the preceding studies of the adoption of software innovations, there is a dearth of studies of software acquisition practices. Software acquisition is a form of adoption primarily practiced by large government agencies restricted by law or policy to adoption practices that are loaded with contractual regulations and obligations. Since system acquisitions can cost upwards of a billion dollars, and thousands of acquisitions are made each year, acquisition practices seem to differ from traditional adoption concerns primarily by the scale of investment, public accountability, and legislative oversight. Thus, studies of software acquisition practices by federal agencies seem to be within the exclusive purview of the U.S. Congress General Accounting Office. However, there is one notable exception in the comparative case studies of Glaseman (1982). In his monograph, Glaseman examines the practices of acquiring embedded software systems by the U.S. Air Force. Based upon his studies of the acquisition process, its management, and incentives and impediments within it, he recommends the following strategies to better realize the Air Force's acquisition goals:

- In formulating a plan to adopt some new software technology, institute an organizational unit responsible for developing and communicating alternative concepts for the role of the focal technology.
- Require a formal and competitive system definition dealing explicitly with computing resource requirements before full-scale system development is sent out to bid.
- Require the collection, maintenance, and delivery of software development data.
- Identify and make better use of multiple sources of software expertise.
- Take steps to institute a formal sanctioned career path in software management.

Summary on Adoption and Acquisition Research

Summarizing the various studies of the adoption of software innovations reveals the following: Adoption of new software technologies will not occur unless: (a) there is a mobilization of people who favor adoption of certain software innovations that are aligned with their incentives and constraints, (b) these people will attempt to influence adoption decisions since they expect to realize some of the benefits, and (c) they will act to reduce the potential for non-adoption by promoting software technologies that are compatible with preferred technological work arrangements in order to increase their visibility and control over evaluation. In the eyes of some analysts, this situation amounts to informally organized political action within the adopting organizing. To others, it might just simply be, "business as usual." Either way, there is no evidence that indicates that improved or superior technology alone is a sufficient condition to facilitate its adoption.

Also, shortcomings across these studies of new software adoption can be seen. First, there is an apparent bias to study software innovations that succeed, rather than also including those that fail to be adopted. Should an assumption be made that those technologies that fail to be adopted only fail due to poor promotion or marketing? Second, there is another bias in studying only large system or application innovations, rather than small incremental innovations as well. In addition, should the assumption be made that small-size software innovations require the same level of organizational mobilization and political action reported above? Warner (1974) argues that this bias toward big departure innovations ignores the critical incremental enhancements and maintenance modifications that keep in-place systems viable. In short, there is still a need for new software adoption research that mitigates these biases in study selection.

CONCLUSIONS

The starting point was to ask what software technology transfer has been all about and how it can be facilitated. What this chapter reveals is that a myriad of social, organizational, and technological variables determine the idiosyncratic trajectory through the STT process. No simple or well-defined set of theoretical axioms of STT processes can yet be formulated, if at all.

If an assumption is made that our interest is to develop selected new software technologies for transfer and transition within targeted organizational settings, then how do we engineer software innovations for successful transfer, use, and evolution?

There are at least two directions that can be pursued to articulate, use, and evolve understanding of the processes of software technology transfer. The first is synthetic, while the second is empirical.

The synthetic approach is easiest to start with. Simply put, it is possible to take the results of studies and reviews such as those noted above, and deductively construct a model for how to engineer particular software innovations to facilitate STT. Since the blueprint to particular software innovations might be vague, then analytical mechanisms such as comparative analysis across multiple perspectives might be employed (cf. Kling and Scacchi, 1980, 1982). The purpose of applying such mechanisms is to help broaden the analyst's sensitivity to developing alternative accounts for how the STT process might work in practice. Further, recent developments with software process modelling technologies may suggest that the STT process is a prime candidate for computational representation, analysis, and simulation (Scacchi, 1991) (see also SOFTWARE LIFE CYCLE AND PROCESS MODEL).

The second approach is to conduct a systematic empirical study of specific software technologies as they move through the STT process. The studies reviewed in this chapter suggest a variety of variables and complex interrelationships need to be examined over a period of time. This suggests that a long-term, comparative research design combining field studies and survey research is needed. The survey could then be followed by carefully selected in-depth comparative field studies focused on acquiring a deep base of knowledge of current software work arrangements and transfer practices, as well as identifying what alternative interventions should be considered in different kinds of organizational settings.

Overall, each of these approaches to understanding how to engineer the life cycle of software innovations to facilitate STT represent current research problems. However, it seems likely that progress in each direction will lead to the most useful results. Research in software technology transfer is still in its infancy, and many more questions need to be explored through systematic empirical means.

BIBLIOGRAPHY

W. Abernathy and B. Chakravathy, "Government Intervention and Innovation in Industry: A Policy Framework," *Sloan Management Review,* 3–18 (Spring 1979).

J. Brancheau and J. C. Wetherbe, "The Adoption of Spreadsheet Software: Testing Innovation Diffusion Theory in the Context of End User Computing," *Information Systems Research* **1**(2), 115–143 (June 1990).

J. Danziger and W. Dutton, "Computers as an Innovation in American Local Governments," *Communications ACM,* **20**(12), 945–956 (1977).

G. Downs and L. Mohr, "Conceptual Issues in the Study of Innovation," *Administrative Science Quarterly* **21,** 700–714 (1976).

G. Downs and L. Mohr, "Toward a Theory of Innovation," *Administration and Society,* **10**(4), 379–408 (1979).

S. Glaseman, *Comparative Studies in Software Acquisition,* Lexington Books, Lexington, Mass., 1982.

P. Gross and M. Ginzberg, "Barriers to the Adoption of Application Software Packages," *Systems, Objectives, and Solutions,* **4,** 211–226 (1984).

IEEE Computer Society, *Workshop on Software Engineering Technology Transfer,* **4,** 211–226 (1983).

J. L. King and E. Schrems, "Cost-Benefit Analysis for Information System Development and Operation," *Computing Surveys* **10**(1), 19–34 (1978).

R. Kling, "Automated Welfare Client Tracking and Service Integration: The Political Economy of Computing," *Communications ACM* **21**(6), 484–493 (1978).

R. Kling and E. Gerson, "The Social Dynamics of Technical Innovation in the Computing World," *Symbolic Interaction* **1,** 132–146 (1977).

R. Kling and W. Scacchi, "Computing as Social Action: The Social Dynamics of Computing in Complex Organizations," *Advances in Computers* **19,** 249–327 (1980).

R. Kling and W. Scacchi, "The Web of Computing: Computing Technology as Social Organization," *Advances in Computers* **21,** 1–87 (1982).

E. Leiblein, "The Department of Defense Software Initiative—A Status Report," *Communications ACM* **29**(8), 734–743 (1986).

J. Perry and J. Danziger, "The Adoptability of Innovations," *Administration and Society,* **11**(4), 461–492, (1980).

J. Perry and K. Kraemer, "Innovation Attributes, Policy Intervention, and the Diffusion of Computer Applications Among Local Governments," *Policy Sciences,* **9**(2), 179–205 (1979).

S. Przyblynski and P. J. Fowler, eds., *Transferring Software Tool Technology Transfer,* IEEE Computer Society Press, 1988.

S. Redwine and W. Riddle, "Software Technology Maturation," *Proceedings 8th. International Conference Software Engineering,* 1985, pp. 189–200.

E. M. Rogers, *Diffusion of Innovations,* 3rd ed., Free Press, New York, 1983. (1st ed., 1962)

W. Scacchi, "Managing Software Engineering Projects: A Social Analysis," *IEEE Trans. Soft. Engr.* **SE-10**(1), 49–59 (1984).

W. Scacchi, "Understanding Software Productivity: Towards a Knowledge-based Approach," *Intern. J. Soft. Engr. and Know. Engr.* **1**(3), 293–321 (1991).

L. Tornatzky and K. Klein, "Innovation Characteristics and Innovation Adoption-Implementation: A Meta-Analysis of Findings," *IEEE Trans. Engineering Management* **EM-29**(1), 28–45 (1982).

K. Warner, "The Need for Some Innovation Concepts of Innovation: An Examination of Research on the Diffusion of Innovations," *Policy Sciences* **5,** 433–451 (1974).

WALT SCACCHI
University of Southern California

TEST GENERATORS

INTRODUCTION

Many people think of automated software testing as executing or running test cases. Actually software testing involves three technical activities: creating, executing, and evaluating test cases. Creating test cases is the most essential activity in software testing, because all other testing activities depend on having test cases to run or evaluate.

WHAT IS A TEST CASE?

Tools called test case generators can create test cases automatically. However, to do so, a test case generator needs a precise definition of a test case as follows.

A test case is a set of information that contains

1. A unique identifier: a name that distinguishes this test case from all others
2. A list of actions (functions, processes, services, etc.) that this test case will exercise
3. A list of names and values for inputs to actions that this test case will exercise
4. A list of outputs that will result when this test case exercises actions

Item 3 is particularly important. A test case is hard to use unless it includes both names and values for all inputs (also called causes or stimuli). For example, if a test case provides the name of an input such as "valid telephone number" but does not include a value such as 911, the test case is incomplete. The tester must finish the test case by adding the telephone number—a simple enough job for one input. But suppose the input to the software under test is a file containing thousands of telephone numbers. Then the tester is confronted with creating and managing huge numbers of input values.

Test case generators can produce test cases, as just defined, at rates exceeding 300 test cases per minute (Programming Environments, Inc., 1992). Considering that the average tester in the U.S. creates 30 to 300 test cases by hand in one month (Jones, 1992), automated test case generators offer compelling productivity gains.

WHAT IS A TEST CASE GENERATOR?

A test case generator is an automated software tool that creates test cases from one of three inputs: specifications, software programs, or test design languages. The most

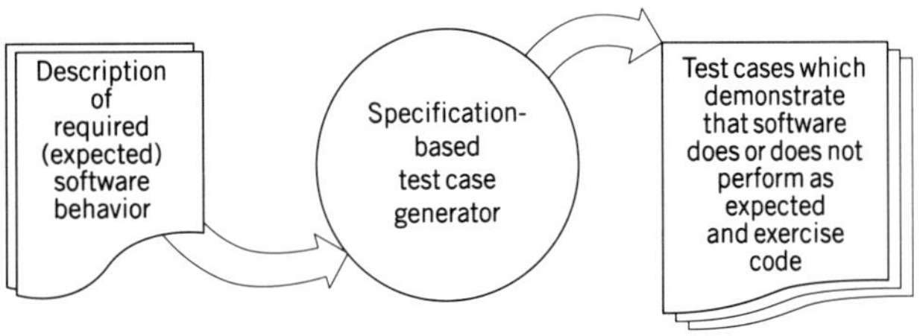

Figure 1. Specification-based test case generator.

widely employed generators use specifications or software programs as their inputs. Test case generators driven by test design languages were once popular as well. However, test design language-based generators are fading from use rapidly, because they require testers to write more documentation than other generators.

SPECIFICATION-BASED TEST CASE GENERATOR

This generator reads requirements for the software product and creates test cases that show that the product does or does not perform as specified. See Figure 1. For this generator to read requirements, the requirements must be written in a language the generator can parse and verify. Common formal specification languages include LOTOS, Estelle, Specification Description Language (SDL), and Z (or ZED) (Moriconi, 1990).

A language called the Semantic Transfer Language (STL) described in IEEE Standard 1175, *A Standard Reference Model for Computing System Tool Interconnections* (IEEE, 1991), is a superset of other specification languages. Because the STL allows people to describe software behavior thoroughly, it is particularly useful in specification-based test case generation.

Just as compiler reads and analyzes source code, a specification-based test case generator reads and analyzes specification information. Just as a compiler uses rules or algorithms to produce object code, this generator uses rules called test design techniques to create test cases. These techniques are the key to understanding specification-based test case generation.

Functional Testing. The rules that a generator uses to create a functional test case are simple. For every specified function (action, operation, service, etc.), the generator must create one test case. The test cases must contain at least one value for every input as well as the name of at least one expected result.

To a tester, functional testing is so obvious and elementary that is seems trivial. However, a specification-based test case generator must incorporate the rules of functional testing to guarantee that every function gets exercised at least once. Functional test cases are very good at discovering missing functions. However, as its name implies, functional testing addresses functions only. It provides no guidance for selecting the input values to use. Input value selection is governed by the rules of the test design techniques discussed next.

Boundary Value Analysis. History shows that most software failures are detected by a tester or an end user applying an input at its highest or lowest valid values (boundaries). Consider these classic boundary problems. Communication systems are most likely to fail when message queues are empty or full. Accounting systems frequently crash at the beginning or end of a fiscal time period. Data base systems often fail the first time disk capacity is exceeded.

To detect boundary value failures, a specification-based test case generator creates a test case for each input at its highest and lowest allowed value. Some generators go beyond simple boundary value analysis to create test cases that will probe just above and just below each boundary. These "adjacent" test cases speed debugging by helping a test pinpoint where a failure occurred.

Equivalence Class Partitioning. Every input to software under test has a set of possible values called a domain. The domain is divided into a valid and an invalid subdomain. Sometimes subdomains are further divided into smaller groups called equivalence classes. In equivalence class partitioning, the software under test should process every value or member in a class in the same or equivalent manner. Every class is treated a little differently by the code, so each class represents a "functional variation." A specification-based test case generator should produce test cases that will probe every input at least once for every subdomain and every equivalence class.

Cause-Effect Graphing. This testing technique is also called logic, predicate, or condition testing. In cause-effect graphing, every condition is probed for a true and a false value. Since conditions can have only true and false values, cause-effect graphing is an efficient way to test Boolean logic. A specification-based test case generator should create test cases to probe every condition for a true and a false value.

State-Directed Testing. Testers often deal with states as screens or menus and test the many sequences of transitions among screens or menus. Most programmers have difficulty keeping functions in the right order, so testers are likely to find many state transition errors in software. Frequently state transition errors involve incorrect initializing and re-initializing of variables in error recovery routines. A generator that produces state-directed test cases selects input values to exercise transitions in prescribed valid and invalid sequences.

Event-Directed Testing. States and events are closely related, so a specification-based tool that generates state-directed test cases probably will create event-directed test cases also. An event is an occurrence in the outside world that causes an action, such as a state transition, to take place in the software world. A computer operator hits a backup key. That event causes the software to respond by making a backup copy. A test case generator creates event-directed test cases which exercise every event at least once. A test case that exercises one event is not likely to find a failure. However, a set of test cases that exercises many

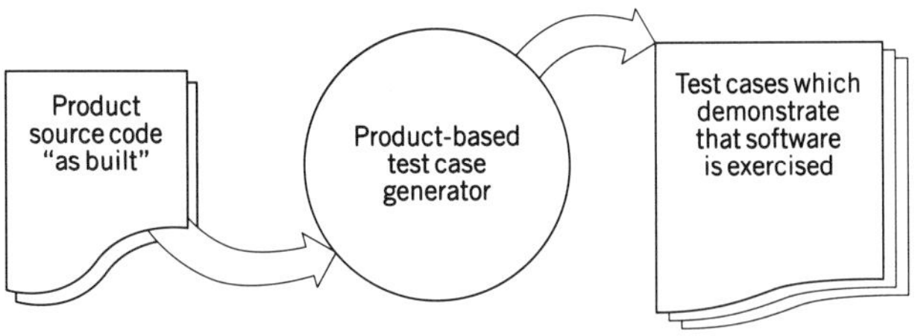

Figure 2. Product-based test case generator.

different events in valid and invalid sequences is very likely to find a failure.

Other Test Design Techniques. The techniques just discussed are considered primary techniques, because each addresses a frequently-occurring class of software failures. Besides the primary techniques, several secondary test design techniques may be incorporated into specification-based test case generators. For example, some tools create test cases by the rules of random, reliability, or fault-directed testing. However, test cases created by the rules of such secondary techniques are redundant with some test cases created with primary techniques. Therefore, a test case generator that uses both primary and secondary techniques must include additional rules that help prevent or eliminate redundant test cases.

Primary and secondary test design techniques are easy to apply when the software under test has only a few functions with a few inputs. But most software does not remain simple. Instead, functions and inputs are quickly added, as are conditions, events, and states. Not only do things get added to software, but they get rearranged within the software to become nested hierarchical structures. Sooner or later a specification-based test case generator must be able to handle complex recursive structures of data, conditions, and states.

Product-Based Test Case Generator

A product-based test case generator is a software tool that analyzes source code to derive test cases that will exercise the code (see Figure 2). A large body of work has been published about product- or program-based test case generation (Mathur and Horgan, 1992; Clark and co-workers, 1989; Rapps and Weyuker, 1985). In the early years of software development and testing, specifications were poorly written or not written at all. Without specifications, practitioners and researchers had to create test cases directly from code.

Unfortunately, product-based testing is fundamentally flawed, because it attempts to test code against its actual or "as implemented" behavior without knowledge of its specified behavior. The code represents what a software product does, not what it should do. Code can have missing or wrong functions, but the product-based generator will not know that. Since the generator cannot distinguish good code from bad, it will try to produce test cases to exercise every part of any code.

Product-based testing shifts the problem of determining if test cases pass or fail back to the tester. Even if test cases exercise every statement, branch, and path in code, the tester still does not know that the software product performs as it should.

Today Computer-Aided Software Engineering (CASE) tools, prototyping tools, and formal language tools help software developers produce specifications efficiently. Testers with written specifications have the reference they need to complete software testing; they have no need to test software against itself and no need for a product-based test case generator.

Product-based test case generators often are confused with code coverage tools. These tools are significantly different, however. A product-based test case generator creates test cases from code, while a code coverage tool measures the effects of running tests.

THE FUTURE OF TEST CASE GENERATORS

Increasing competition means that the software industry will push for higher development productivity and product quality. The only way to know that quality or productivity has been improved is to test (see Figure 3). Software testing depends on having test cases. Therefore, the interest in

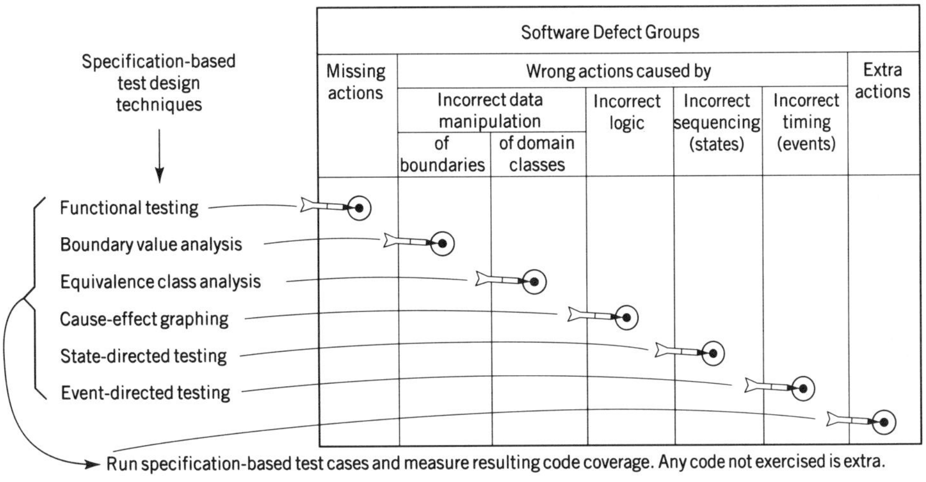

Figure 3. Software defects found by test design techniques.

and demand for automated test case generators is bound to grow.

BIBLIOGRAPHY

C. Clark and co-workers, "A Formal Evaluation of Data Flow Path Selection Criteria," *IEEE Transactions on Software Engineering* **15**(11), 1318–1332 (Nov. 1989).

"Generating Test Cases Automatically," *The Letter T* **6**(1), Programming Environments Inc., Tinton Falls, N.J., 1992.

IEEE, *IEEE Standard 1175, A Standard Reference Model for Computing System Tool Interconnections,* New York, 1991.

C. Jones, *Applied Software Measurement,* McGraw-Hill, Inc., New York, 1992, pp. 253–307.

A. Mathur and J. Horgan, "Assessing Testing Tools in Research and Education," *IEEE Software* **9**(3), 61–69 (May 1992).

M. Moriconi, "Proceedings of the ACM SIGSOFT International Workshop of Formal Methods in Software Development," *Software Engineering Notes* **15**(4), ACM Press, New York, 1990.

S. Rapps and E. Weyuker, "Selecting Software Test Data Using Data-Flow Information," *IEEE Transactions on Software Engineering* **11**(4), 367–375 (Apr. 1985).

ROBERT M. POSTON
Programming Environments, Inc.

TESTING

INTRODUCTION

The word "test" derives from the Latin word "testum" meaning a pottery vessel used to measure or assess weight. The testing of software is a means of measuring or assessing the software to determine its quality. It is often taken to mean dynamic assessment, i.e., the running of sample input through software programs, and comparing actual outcome with expected outcome, but static analysis is also considered to be part of software testing. Debugging, the removal of defects in software, is closely associated with testing, but debugging is a correction process, not an assessment process. Testing typically consumes 40–50% of development effort (Beizer, 1988).

The current discipline of software testing embraces a wide range of activities which support the assessment of quality; testing activities also help to achieve and preserve software quality.

There are two basic views of testing techniques, referred to as "black-box" and "white box". Academic work in testing has tended to emphasize white box approaches; most practitioners have found black box approaches to be more useful.

This article is intended for software development practitioners and managers. It does not attempt to summarize research in this field, but to lay a foundation for the basic principles and well-established techniques in software testing.

The History of Software Testing

Software has been tested from as early as software has been written. A historical perspective given in Hetzel (1988) traces references back to the 1950s: "Testing is what programmers do to find bugs in their programs".

In the 1970s, it was thought that software could be tested "exhaustively," with "exhaustive testing defined either in terms of program paths or a program's input domain" (Goodenough and Gerhart, 1975). This is now realized as impractical for any reasonably sized program, but the phrase is still (mis-)used in testing, generally to imply that the testing should be thorough or complete.

Early definitions of testing tended to stress that the purpose of testing is to demonstrate correctness. "An ideal test, therefore, succeeds only when a program contains no errors" (Goodenough and Gerhart, 1975). "The test plan specifies the objectives of testing (e.g., to achieve error-free operation under stated conditions for a stated period of time.).." (Fairly, 1985) The first conference in software testing, organized in 1972, defined testing as "the process of establishing confidence that a program or system does what it is supposed to" (Hetzel, 1973).

The book which laid the foundation for more effective test case design was *The Art of Software Testing* by Glenford Myers in 1979. His definition of testing is "Testing is the process of executing a program with the intent of finding errors." Myers makes the point that the value of a test case is much greater if an error is found, so error-seeking tests give greater return on investment in testing.

Two other significant books on testing appeared in the 1980s. Boris Beizer's *Software Testing Techniques* is the most complete catalogue of testing techniques, although with an academic slant. He extends the definition of testing to bug prevention as well its bug detection activities. "The act of designing tests is one of the most effective bug preventers known." Beizer, (1983) is a classic insight into the power of early testing. Beizer also gives us the Pesticide Paradox: "Every method you use to prevent or find bugs leaves a residue of subtler bugs against which those methods are ineffectual".

Bill Hetzel's *The Complete Guide to Software Testing* (Hetzel, 1983) extends the definition of testing to: "Testing is any activity aimed at evaluating an attribute or capability of a program or system and determining that it meets its required results." Testing includes reviews, and should be a planned and managed process. The book describes a testing methodology which includes early test design, and gives guidance for the management of testing. An important aspect of this book for practitioners is the recognition of economic reality and a risk-driven approach to limiting the amount of testing.

The 1990s view of testing emphasizes the importance of early test design. A 1991 definition by Hetzel was "Testing is planning, designing, building, maintaining and executing tests and test environments." (Hetzel, 1991) Beizer gives four stages of thinking about testing: 1: to make software work, 2: to break the software, 3: to reduce risk, and 4: a state of mind, i.e., a total life-cycle concern with testability (Beizer, 1990).

The most significant development in testing in the late 1980s and early 1990s was the emergence of tool support for testing. Reports such as *The Testing Tools Reference Guide* (Durant, 1988), *The CAST Report* (Graham, 1991), and *Dynamic Testing Tools* (Norman, 1992) provided timely information on the growing marketplace for testing tools.

There are a number of testing conferences which meet regularly, and various publications specialize in or carry articles on software testing. Details of these and other books on software testing are given in the bibliography at the end of this entry.

Organization of This Article

Tests are run to *assess* the quality of software, but test design activities, applied early in the development life cycle, also help to *achieve* quality software, in parallel with other quality achievement techniques such as requirements validation. Testing also helps to *preserve* quality, by enabling tests to be re-used whenever changes are made to the system, particularly in maintenance and when tests are automated.

First testing to assess quality is discussed, then, testing to achieve quality, including life-cycle issues. The next section will discuss the management of testing. Other sections will give an overview of standard testing techniques. Testing to preserve quality and maintenance testing is followed by an outline of software tool support for testing, followed by a discussion of the future of testing and the bibliography.

SOFTWARE TESTING TO ASSESS SOFTWARE QUALITY

The Importance of Testing

Testing is essential in the development of any software system. Testing is needed in order to assess what the system actually does, and how well it does it, in its final environment. A system without testing is merely a paper exercise; it may work or it may not, but without testing, there is no way of knowing this before live use.

As a rule of thumb, software developers tend to spend approximately 40% of development cost and time in testing, in order to achieve reasonable quality levels. (Software Management Survey, 1991) In real-time systems this may be much higher. In maintenance, it may be far higher if extensive testing of systems after changes is performed (called REGRESSION TESTING). In Fourth generation language development, where the software production process is speeded up, testing is a proportionately greater percentage of total development time. Testing, therefore, is a significant proportion of software development and maintenance.

A later section discusses the full scope of testing activities. This section will start by looking at the fundamentals of the testing activity, that of test execution. We give a descriptive definition of test execution, and a prescriptive definition of testing in terms of why tests are performed. This section ends by looking at the fundamental limitation of testing.

Descriptive Definition Test Execution

There are a number of conditions which must be met in order for a dynamic execution of software code to be considered a test, based on an extension of Goodenough's definition (Goodenough, 1980).

- A controlled/observed environment. The environment must be strictly controlled (or observed if control is not possible). This is essential for the test to be reproducible. Tests must be exactly reproducible in order to ensure that a software bug has been correctly removed. If an initial test reveals a defect and the only change is the software modification, then the same test reproduced in exactly the same environment and under the same conditions give confidence that the software change is what has caused the defect to disappear.
- Sample input. A test uses only a (small) sample of all possible inputs to the software. See the limitations of testing below.
- Predicted results. The results of the test should ideally be predicted in advance of the test being run. The expected outcome for each input should be defined, so that the actual outcome from the test run can be compared with it in order to assess whether the software has performed correctly on that input. If the expected outcome is not predicted in advance of the test being run, there is a danger of the computer outcome being accepted without objective evaluation, which would make the test of less value. However, it is not worth expending a great deal of effort in predicting outcomes which are very difficult to do manually, since the result-prediction activity may be significantly more error-prone than the checking process; then running and checking the result is better.
- Analysed Outcome. The actual outcome of the test must be examined and compared with the expected outcome in each instance. Although this is the obvious purpose of running a test, this activity can be skimped particularly when tests are rerun many times. If no analysis of actual outcome against expected outcome, will be performed, there is no point in running the test (unless expected outcome is not required for a particular type of test, e.g., performance).

The results of test execution are used to arrive at conclusions about the properties of the program tested, i.e. about the quality of the software. The idea behind testing is that one can infer attributes of the software being tested from the results of the tests.

The Purpose of Testing

Testing is a measuring instrument for software quality, with the unit of measurement being the number of defects found in testing. But testing actually has two aspects which may appear to be contradictory; the purpose of testing is two-fold, leading to the testing paradox.

Why Test Software? To Gain Confidence The reason why untested software is not released to general use is because software is notoriously difficult to produce in an error-free form. The software supplier or developer needs to have some knowledge about the quality of the software, even if that knowledge is not perfect. Since software testing is used to assess the quality of the software, if no errors are found, then the quality is assumed to be good. The overall purpose of testing is to give confidence that the system is working well.

Correctness Demonstration is Ineffective Testing. However this approach to testing is not effective for test case construction. As Myers points out (Myers, 1979) if the goal of testing is to show that the software is working, a "successful" test is one where the software does what it should. Under time pressure to deliver systems, however, the fastest way to achieve the goal of "showing that the system works" is to use only the easiest test cases, the ones that have already passed. However, this will not find any of the errors which are still lurking in the software. The result of this approach to testing, during software development, is that errors will be left in the software. Showing that something works, when you already know it works, is a demonstration, not a test. This is why deadline pressure, combined with inadequate test planning, gives poor quality software.

Of course, there is a place for demonstration in software testing: for example in product acceptance. But this definition of testing is not effective for testers during software development.

Testing to Find Errors is Effective. A better approach for testing in development is to try to break the software. The goal of testing is to find errors, and a successful test is one that finds an error, i.e., a good test is one where the system does not work correctly. One such error-revealing test gives far more useful information to software developers than 100 tests which just run through correctly.

The result of this approach to testing is that there are fewer errors left in the software. Note that the result is not that there are no errors, only fewer errors. In fact, nothing can ever guarantee that there are no errors in software. A test can only show that an error has been found, or that no error has been found by this test (a better test might have found one).

The Testing Paradox. Finding defects destroys confidence; obviously you cannot have confidence that something is working when it has just been proved otherwise. Therefore is the purpose of testing to destroy confidence, rather than to build it? This is a paradox because both are true: the best way to build confidence is to try and destroy it.

The units of measurement, defects found, is dependent not only on the quality of the software, but also on the quality of the testing: better tests find more defects in the same software. Therefore, you cannot justifiably conclude anything about the quality of the software tested without some knowledge of the quality of the testing.

Fundamental Limitation of Testing

Testing can only show the presence of an error; testing can never prove the absence of all errors (usually attributed to Dijkstra). There are always more test cases that can be tried, so testing is never finished, only abandoned. No matter how much testing is done, it can never ensure that all defects have been found.

A test is analogous to a counter-example in mathematics. In order to prove a mathematical theorem, there are two alternatives: prove it correct by rigorous logical reasoning from axioms, or disprove it, i.e., prove it incorrect by one simple concrete case where the theorem does not hold: a counter-example. A large number of examples for which the theorem appears to be true has no mathematical validity whatsoever (although it may increase one's confidence that it is true). In software testing, a test case which shows that the software works can increase the confidence felt that the program is correct, but it does not prove it correct. One test case which causes the program to fail, however, does disprove program correctness.

Because it is not possible to test everything, testers need to be as effective as possible within the limitations of testing. As Myers (1979) points out, the "counter-example" attribute of testing can be turned to advantage by consciously devising tests with the intent of causing the software to fail. The cost of running 100 tests is the same whether all the tests work correctly or whether they reveal defects. The value of a defect-revealing test case is greater than for a test which works correctly because the defect can then be fixed, which improves the quality of the software being tested.

In Practice

In practice, a mixture of defect-revealing and correct-operation tests are used. Once a defect is corrected, then the same test which was formerly defect-revealing now shows correctness. Sometimes tests which are designed to reveal defects do not, because the defects are not there. But designing tests which should reveal defects if there are any is good testing practice.

TESTING IN THE SOFTWARE DEVELOPMENT LIFE CYCLE

Software Development Life Cycle Models

Test Design and Test Execution. Testing is often considered something which is done after software has been written; after all, the argument runs, you cannot test something which does not exist, can you? This idea makes the assumption that testing is merely test execution, the running of tests. Of course, tests cannot be *executed* without software (although static analysis, a nonexecuting form of testing can be carried out, see later). But testing activities include more than running tests, because before they can be run, the tests themselves need to be written and designed. As Beizer points out, the act of designing a test is one of the most effective ways of finding defects (Beizer, 1990). If tests need to be designed, when in the life cycle should the test design activities happen?

The discussion below, on the timing of the test design activities, applies no matter what software life cycle model is used during development or maintenance. Many descriptions of life cycles do not make the proper placing of test design activities clear. For example, many development methods advocate early test planning, (which is good), but it is the actual construction of concrete individual test inputs and expected outcomes which is most effective at revealing errors in the specification, and this aspect is often not explicit.

When Are Tests Designed: As Late as Possible? A common misconception is that tests should be designed as late as possible in the life cycle, i.e., only just before they are needed. The reason for this is supposedly to save time and effort, and to make progress as quickly as possible. But this is progress only from a deadline point of view, not progress from a quality point of view, and the quality problems, whose seeds are sown here, will come back to haunt the product later on.

No test can be designed without a specification, since the specification is the source of what the correct results of the test should be, even if that specification is not formally written down or fully completed, but the test design activity will reveal defects in whatever specification is used to base the tests on. This applies to code, a part of the system, the system as a whole, or the user's view of the system.

If test design is left until the last possible moment, then the errors are found too late, when they are most expensive to fix. An example using a simple model is given by Boehm. (Boehm, 1981) If the cost of detecting and correcting an error in the requirements analysis phase is $10, typical conservative figures give a cost of $100 for detecting and correcting the same error during test execution, and $1000 when the software is operational.

In addition, the errors in the highest levels, the requirements specification, are found last; these are also the most critical and most important errors. The actual effect of this approach is the most costly and time-consuming approach to testing and software development. Leaving the test design until the last possible moment is like the ostrich who buries its head in the sand; the problems will not disappear simply because we refuse to look at them.

When are Tests Designed: As Early as Possible. If tests are going to be designed anyway, there is no additional effort required to move a scheduled task to a different place in the schedule.

If tests are designed as early as possible, the inevitable effect of finding errors in the specification comes early, when those errors are cheapest to fix. In addition, the most significant errors are found first. This means that those errors are not built in to the next stage, e.g., major requirements errors are not designed in, so errors are prevented.

An argument against this approach is that if the tests are already designed, they will need to be maintained when the inevitable changes due to subsequent life cycle development stages affects the earlier stages. This is correct, but the cost of maintaining tests must be compared with the cost of the late testing approach, not simply be accepted as negating the good points. In fact, the extent of the test design detail should be determined in part by the maintenance costs, so that less detail (but always some detail) should be designed if extensive changes are anticipated.

One of the frequent headaches late in software development is a rash of requirement change requests which come from users very late in the life cycle; a cause for this is the user acceptance test design process. When the users only begin to think about their tests just before the acceptance tests are about to start, they realize the errors in the requirements specification, and request changes to it. If they had designed their tests at the same time as they were specifying those requirements, the very mental activity of test design would have identified those errors before the system had built them.

The way in which the system will be tested also serves to provide another dimension to the development; the tests form part of the specification. If you know how it will be tested, you are much more likely to build something which will pass those tests. Thus the acceptance criteria become the completion criteria for what is built at every stage of development (Quentin, 1992).

The end result of designing tests as early as possible is that quality is built in, costs are reduced, and time is saved in test running because fewer errors are found, giving an overall reduction in cost and effort. This is how testing activities help to build quality into the software development process.

This can be taken one stage further as recommended by a number of experts (Beizer, 1990; Hetzel, 1991; Quentin, 1992), by designing tests before specifying what is to be tested. The tests then act as a requirement for what will be built.

Levels of Testing in Software Development

Testing is applied at different levels of software development in the life cycle, but the testing done is different in nature and has different objectives at each level. The focus of all of development testing is to find errors, but different types of error are looked for at each level.

Unit Testing. At the lowest level, the function of the basic unit of software is tested in isolation (under the control of any necessary test harnesses). This is where the most detailed investigation of the internal workings of the individual unit is carried out. Unit testing is often performed by the programmer who wrote the code, although this is not necessarily the most effective alternative. (See Management of testing below.) The purpose of unit testing is to find errors in the individual units, in either data or logic. Tests can be derived from the detailed logic of the unit (the detailed design specification), with any additional structural tests derived from the physical design, as a result of coverage measurement.

The term "unit", "module" and "component" are often used interchangeably in practice. Beizer defines a unit as the smallest testable piece of software, and a component as an integrated aggregate of one or more units (Beizer, 1990).

Component Integration Testing. When two or more tested components are combined into a larger structure, the tests should look for errors in two ways: in the interfaces between the components, and in the functions which can be performed by the new group which was not assessable for the individual components or units forming the group. (Beizer distinguishes these two respectively as integration testing and component testing of the new combined component.)

The decision as to which components to combine will usually be related to an identifiable function which is performed by the group. Components are combined according to an integration or link test strategy, which is related to the hierarchy of the system design (e.g., the call tree). Alternatives include top-down, bottom-up, minimum capability, or timing thread. Tests are derived from the logical design or architecture of the system. Detail on Integration Testing strategies is found in the separate article in this encyclopedia.

The term "integration testing" is often used in a different way to that described above, for the integration not of low-level units, but of high level systems, for example the integration of batch processes, or the integration of hardware and software elements of a system. Other terms for component integration testing include "link testing" or "sub-system testing"

System Testing. After integration testing is completed, the entire system is tested as whole. The functional specification or requirements specification is used to derive the test case selection at this level. System testing looks for errors in the end-to-end functionality of the system, and also for errors in nonfunctional quality attributes, such as performance, reliability, volume, stress tolerance, usability, maintainability, security, etc. System testing can be carried out by independent testers.

Acceptance Testing. After system testing is completed, the system is handed over to the customer or users, and acceptance testing marks the transition from ownership by the developers to ownership by the users. The acceptance test is different in nature to the development testing in three ways: first, it is the responsibility of the accepting organization rather than the developing organization. Secondly, the purpose of acceptance testing is to give confidence that the system is working, rather than trying to find errors. The acceptance test is actually a demonstration rather than a test. Thirdly, acceptance testing also includes the testing of the user organization's working practices, to ensure that the computer system will fit with clerical and administrative procedures. The acceptance test gives confidence to the users that the system is ready for operational use.

Other Testing Levels. Different systems or different organizations may have a different number of test levels or may give them different names. Each test level corresponds to a development level, and tests what is developed at that level. In addition, alpha testing (use by real users at the developer's site) and beta testing (use at user sites) are often used before a general release to a large number of users, for example for testing commercial packages such as word processors. Other aspects may be included in system or large-scale integration tests, such as parallel running, where a new system is run in parallel with the system it is replacing, and the outcomes are compared. (This generally finds a few errors which have been in the old system for years.)

THE MANAGEMENT OF TESTING

The management issues within software development and maintenance which are specific to testing will be covered in this section. The general management tasks such as drawing up plans, scheduling, assigning resources, measuring progress, etc. are all relevant to testing as well, but these general management concerns are covered elsewhere in this encyclopedia.

However, there are additional concerns of particular importance for testing, such as how to assign resources to achieve independence, how much testing to plan for, and how to plan and monitor a process which is often iterative and apparently unpredictable.

This section will be concerned mainly with the management of testing in development. The management of testing in maintenance is similar for significant enhancements; the other differences for maintenance testing are outlined later.

Testing Policy and Management Responsibilities

Management Responsibilities in Testing. There are management responsibilities at a high level which would apply to all software development projects, and there are detailed responsibilities at the project level which apply to a specific project. At the project level, testing may be the responsibility of the development manager, the quality manager, or a test manager. The important thing is that someone is responsible for testing.

The high-level responsibilities for testing (for a company or large work group) include resource allocation and the monitoring of test metrics. Resource allocation includes:

- Set the testing policy, strategy and objectives for the company and for individual projects.
- Ensure that metrics for test effort and results are collected, analyzed and used.
- Invest in tool support.
- Improve the whole [development and] test process.

Test management responsibilities at the project level include resource allocation and the monitoring of test metrics. Resource allocation includes:

- Assignment and organization of resources;
- Test planning (before development)
- Reviews and/or Inspections (throughout)
- Test design (in parallel with development)
- Test execution (end of development)
- Debugging (whenever needed)

The following test metrics should be monitored:

- Error rates; in design and test design, in test execution (at each level), and in operation or field use (i.e., post-test)
- Error severity and rework costs for errors of defined severity at defined stages of development and use
- Time/cost in test design
- Time/cost in debugging tests
- Time/cost in test running
- Time/cost in bug fixing
- Time/cost in Inspections or reviews

Testing Policy. A policy for software testing is normally set at the highest levels of the organization, in order to achieve consistent quality of testing. The policy should include the following:

- Objectives of testing
- Economic constraints for testing
- The planning and resourcing of testing activities such as who makes pass/fail decisions for systems under test; who decides what tests not to do, and on what basis; training of staff in testing techniques and tool use;
- Documentation of tests
- Quality and acceptance criteria for test documentation, and means of ensuring quality (e.g., review of test plans)
- What tools will be available to support testing, and the training and support in their use
- Monitoring aid evaluation of test effectiveness (errors not caught in testing which cause problems in operational use of the software)

A sample test policy is included as an appendix in Hetzel (1988).

Economic Constraints

Trying to reduce the cost of testing may be one of the most counter-productive things which a software development manager can do, because the cost of testing can only be realistically assessed by comparing that cost with the alternatives. The only way to gain control of the testing process is to assess the balance of a number of costs:

- The cost of testing (test design, debugging tests, test execution)
- The cost of other quality techniques, such as reviews
- The cost of error detection
- The cost of error correction
- The cost of customer service and support
- The cost of lost opportunity and lost business as a result of poor quality

The Cost of Testing. The costs involved in testing software are due to effort, machine usage, and additional hardware and/or software. Hardware and machine usage are straightforward and covered elsewhere in this encyclopedia. Testing tools are covered in a later section.

The resource effort costs are spent in the following areas:

- Preparing test scripts
- Setting up test data
- Debugging tests
- Running tests
- Debugging software: investigating problems found and correcting errors
- Re-testing the changed software
- Regression tests (of things which should not have changed)

Strictly speaking, the last three activities should be counted as debugging activities rather than testing activities; if no errors had been found, then no debugging or retesting would need to be done! These are the costs of producing "nonquality" software. Typically, the test phase is composed of at least half debugging activities rather than planned test activities.

Once the software is released, there are likely to be still more errors found in operation, and these will also have to be fixed.

Why Testing is Often Neglected. Because defects are not inserted into software intentionally, testing often seems to be regarded as something which should not be needed. There is also a very reasonable argument that emphasis should be on software "front-end" activities, such as requirements analysis and design, because errors removed early are cheapest to fix.

Even with the best analysis and design methods available, errors still do occur in software. This is inevitable, given the complex nature of the task, the incompatibility between people and computers, and the intolerance of the computer environment. The choice is not between having errors and not having them; the choice is when to find them.

Therefore, test activities should also be "front-end" activities, for exactly the same reason: they detect errors early. The actual technique used to detect the error in an early life cycle phase could be a review such as Inspection, or it could be the writing of the test documentation such as the test plan, test designs or test cases.

The Costs of Not Testing. The total effect of correcting errors later, errors which should have been caught in testing, is increased cost of repair. The greater the lag between the error being introduced and detected, the higher the correction cost will be.

The priorities of different types of errors also need to be taken into account, as this can have a dramatic effect on the cost of correcting the error. Normally, the cost of fixing an error immediately is higher than if it could be scheduled in a batch or the next build.

However, these additional technical costs are not the only additional costs incurred. The users or customers may also incur costs to their business due to the faulty software. This may entail:

- Lost information (lost customer records, lost invoices)
- Inability to retrieve information
- An incorrect picture of the true state of the business
- Business decisions based on inaccurate information leading to market loss
- Failure to use the system for the purposes intended, due to loss of confidence in the system
- Increased difficulty in gaining acceptance of the system after the errors have been fixed, due to previous experience of errors

Even this is not the end of the matter. An unhappy customer typically tells ten other people about their experience, so there is a significant effect on your own business from the policy of letting customers find the software errors for you. Consider the following:

- Market reputation is detrimentally affected by a customer's bad experiences.
- Time spent in fixing bugs in maintenance is time not spent in developing new products for the marketplace, leading to loss of market position.
- Customers will tend to seek out the competition when considering their next system, decreasing repeat sales.
- Certification to recognized quality management standards, such as ISO 9001 may be a requirement for eligibility to tender for certain work.
- Legislation makes you responsible for any effect of faulty software, whether the fault was due to your negligence or not. Failure to test software would be very likely to be considered negligent in a court of law.
- Confidence in a product and supplier is built up slowly over a long period of time. But one serious software fault can destroy that confidence at once. Once lost, confidence is built up much more slowly a second time, if at all.
- The effects of software errors vary depending on the system in which they occur, but can include inconvenience, annoyance, misinformation, loss of information, loss of money, personal injury and even death.

This means that the true cost of not testing is in the region of two orders of magnitude (100 times) greater than the cost of testing in development.

Balancing the Cost of Testing with the Risk of Not Testing. The main problem in budgeting for testing is that often there is no clearly defined end point. It is not possibly to put a fixed cost on an activity of unknown duration. Testing is seen as a "black hole" of development, which can absorb an infinite amount of resource.

It is easy to spend too much on testing; if testing is not effective, this money is wasted. However, it is also easy to spend too little on testing (e.g. by not doing any) which is also wasteful. The key to cost-effective testing is to get the balance right between the risk of not testing enough and spending too much on testing.

In order to achieve the most effective balancing of costs with benefits, it is essential to know what the actual costs are within your own organization, including the cost of testing, the cost of other quality techniques, and the cost of defects missed by testing and other techniques. Some quality improvement techniques already include the collection of cost metrics, in particular Inspection (Fagan, 1976; 1986; Gilb, 1988; Buckle, 1990; Gilb and Graham, 1993).

The management decision about how much testing should be planned and carried out can only be made on the basis of balancing these risks. The manager's main task is to ensure that testing is effective within time and budgetary constraints.

Keys to Effective Testing. Testing does not have to be uniformly distributed over the system being tested; in fact this is wasteful. In order to be cost-effective, testing should concentrate on the areas where it will be most effective.

It is most important to test the most *critical* parts of the system, but this means the parts which are most critical to the system users, not the parts that the developers consider to be most critical to the users. It is only the users who have the background knowledge needed to identify these areas correctly.

Concentrate the testing on the most difficult and *complex* parts of the system, the parts which were the hardest to write, at the edges of the human design envelope.

If software is developed by more than one group of people, misunderstandings are much more likely between groups than within groups, and this leads to errors in the interfaces of the software developed by different groups ("*inter-groupware*") (Price, 1991).

Software which is *difficult to use* is more likely to lead to misuse and therefore is more likely to suffer from "human error." These areas should receive special attention from testers.

The software which is *least liked* is often also the least well-written and the most error-prone.

Errors are social creatures. The most likely place to find more errors is where you have found the most errors already (DeMarco, 1982), in *error-prone* software.

The *most important principle* is to plan the testing so that whenever testing is stopped, the *most effective testing* which could have been done in the time available has already been done.

How Much Testing is Enough: Test Stopping Criteria. Hetzel gives the classic guideline for how much testing is enough: the absolutely definitive answer is "it depends" (on risk). (Hetzel, 1988)

In order to be manageable, the amount of testing to be done should be planned at the beginning of software development. These plans are made on certain assumptions about the quality of the software to be tested. The manager must plan the criteria for deciding when testing should be stopped, which will either confirm or disprove those assumptions. The assumptions should be based on past history, not uninformed optimism.

The most commonly used test-stopping criterion is when the time scheduled for testing has run out (Myers, 1979—and still true). This has no relationship to either software quality or test quality.

Another common test stopping criterion is when no errors are found with existing tests, or when the number of errors found per test hour is below an acceptable threshold. This may be related to software quality, but only if the quality of the tests is known independently. This is a good criterion to use in combination with a test quality evaluation technique, such as coverage measurement.

Other test-stopping criteria given by Myers are

- When the required test case selection techniques have been used. This is useful for unit testing, and may help to ensure test quality.
- When "enough" errors have been found

Myers bases this on his philosophy of "the only good test finds an error" which works best for very poor quality software. The fundamental drawback is that the total number of errors cannot be known, so the actual number of findable errors can only be estimated roughly.

Other test criteria which have been developed since the publication of Myers' book include:

- Coverage measurement

Software tools (Graham, 1991) can give a percentage figure for the structural elements of software which are exercised by a set of tests. This can be used to assess to some extent the quality of the tests derived by functional techniques. Coverage measurement can be used in conjunction with the number of errors found to provide reasonable test stopping criteria in practice.

- Reliability growth models

A method which is based on probability theory predicts the time to the next failure, based on continuous and varied user-profile testing over a long period of time. (Littlewood, 1988) See also separate entries in this encyclopedia by Musa and co-workers.

Limitations of Testing. Testing is a sampling technique. The skill in devising test cases is to devise the most cost-effective test cases, i.e. those which are most likely to reveal an error, so that error can be removed. The scheduling of tests should aim for the maximum variety and diversity of testing, so that errors are found as quickly as possible.

Testing can never find all errors. No matter how well the testing has been designed and carried out, it can never guarantee that all errors have been found. After extensive testing, it is not uncommon for a novice user to find a "new" error when they first encounter the software.

The testing process is just as error-prone as software development, and may contain errors in test cases, evaluation procedures, documentation, etc.

Measuring the structural coverage of the tests gives an idea of whether you have tested every part of the software at least once. However, it gives you no idea about how well you tested those parts, or about missing functions which were therefore not tested.

The Oracle Assumption. Fundamental to testing is the assumption that it is routinely possible to determine what the executed outcome should be, i.e. whether the outcome which is produced is correct. This is known as the "oracle" assumption (Weyuker, 1982).

Normally, the oracle assumption is true, but not for all programs. Examples are programs which are written specifically to compute a result, programs which produce a very large volume of output where it is impractical to check every outcome, or when the tester is under a misapprehension about the existence of an oracle, e.g, the tester thinks there is an oracle but there is not. This can lead to the certifying as correct a program which is incorrect, or the attempt to find errors in a program which is actually correct.

In other cases, there is a partial oracle: you cannot know whether the outcome is exactly correct, but you would know if it was wildly wrong.

Programs without an oracle are called "nontestable" programs. In order to test nontestable programs, the following approaches are used:

- Use simple data for which there is an oracle, and assume the results will scale up
- Use a pseudo-oracle, e.g. dual coding and comparison (two ways of calculating it)
- Accept results which are plausible, and assume they are correct

Staffing of Testing Activities

Who Makes the Best Tester? It is important that testing (and review) take an independent view of the software to be tested. This is virtually impossible for the person who developed the software to do, for two important psychological reasons:

- No-one can adequately *see* the errors in their own work. We tend to see what we think is there, what we intended to write, not what is actually there. You can only find 25–30% of your own errors (Beizer, 1988). If you have no independent testing, you are guaranteed to leave in at least 70% of the errors.
- Motivating yourself to test destructively, i.e., to look for errors, is very difficult to do. If you have just produced what you consider your best work, you do not immediately want to destroy it.

It is a well-known phenomenon that as soon as the users start to use a new system, they have a knack of finding a large number of errors which are a complete surprise to the developers. "Who would have thought they would do that?" is a typical response. The reason why users have this (very valuable) skill is because they are independent. They do not suffer from the psychological drawbacks of developers trying to test their own work (Graham, 1992). They are therefore much more capable of finding many types of errors than developers are (although there are other areas of testing where developers are more capable).

In order to be a good test designer, it helps to have a devious mind, as well as being a first-class diplomat. The ideal tester, according to Kaner is "bright, articulate, attentive to detail but able to appreciate a larger picture, assertive without being obnoxious, creative, with a blend of management and technical skills" (Kaner, 1988). Five qualities are given by Hetzel: "controlled, competent, critical, comprehensive, and considerate" (Hetzel, 1988).

Independent Test Team? Setting up an independent test team is a popular choice, particularly for system testing. The advantages are that a separate team has true independence, and expertise in testing can be developed; the test team can act as internal consultants in testing for other staff involved in testing (Hall, 1990).

There are a number of problems to be avoided in setting up an independent test team, however. Because the main focus of the testers is to find errors in software produced by someone else, the reporting of those errors must be done in a tactful manner in order to establish a good working relationship. The test team has a good relationship with developers when they are thanked for finding bugs.

There is a danger of developers thinking that they have no responsibility for producing good quality software or testing their own work. They simply throw it "over the wall" for the test team to test it. However, it is very demoralizing to the test team to be given very poor quality obviously untested software. They quickly throw it back over the wall, and antagonism can easily build up.

Test Documentation

A full set of documentation for testing includes a number of different types of documents, to record different aspects of testing, and to separate out the levels of detail of testing. The types of documents listed below are taken from the IEEE Standard for Software Test Documentation (IEEE 829-1983):

- Test Plan (management of test activities)
- Test Design Specification (approach to testing features)
- Test Case Specification (detailed input and expected outcome)
- Test Procedures Specification (how to perform the test)
- Test Item Transmittal Report (what is being tested)
- Test Log Specification (what happened when the test was run)
- Test Incident Report (which may indicate a bug)
- Test Summary Report (management summary of all tests)

The test documents may be combined (e.g., test procedures included in test case specifications) or broken down into further levels of detail (e.g. overall test design and detailed test design) as required for each particular situation. The detailed contents of each of these documents as specified in IEEE 829-1983 is described below.

The principles of test documentation in this standard apply whether test documentation is stored on paper or in automated form. Automated forms may include a word-processed version of the manual document, or a test script which can automatically be run by a software testing tool. In this case, the script may contain elements from several of the documents listed below, such as test procedures, test cases, test log, etc. The important thing with test documentation is not what medium it is kept in, but that all the important items of information are recorded somewhere so that the testing process is visible and controllable. The elements which should be documented are well described in the standard, and are outlined below.

Test Plan

- Test Plan (ID)
- Introduction: summary of software items and features to be tested, with references to external authorization, plans, policies and standards
- Test Items: logical and physical requirements to assemble software to be tested, including versions, references to software documentation, e.g. requirements, design, user manuals
- Features to be tested, with reference to Test Design Specification
- Features not be tested, with reasons
- Test Approach: how it will ensure adequate testing, detailed enough for test task estimation, testing techniques to use, any constraints
- Item Pass/Fail Criteria: how to tell if the item has passed or failed the test
- Suspension and Resumption: when tests should be suspended, when they can be resumed
- Test Deliverables: all documents described in this section, plus input and output data and testing tools
- Testing Tasks: with interdependencies and special skills required
- Test Environment: hardware, system software, communications, special purpose devices, security, office space, testing tools
- Responsibilities: who is responsible for test activities
- Staffing and Training Needs
- Schedule, including test milestones, what resources are needed when
- Risks and Contingencies
- Approvals: space for signature of designated approvers of the test plan

Test Design Specification

- Test Design ID
- Features to be tested, with reference to requirements and design documentation
- Approach: test techniques, how results will be analyzed, rationale for test-case selection, common attributes of test cases
- Test Identification for each Test Case designed, with brief description
- Pass-Fail Criteria for the feature being tested

Test Case Specification

- Test Case ID
- Test Items and features to be tested, with references to requirements, design, user manual, operation or installation manuals.
- Input specification for the test case
- Expected Outcome, including non-functional qualities, e.g., response time
- Environmental Needs: hardware, system and other software, other facilities or personnel
- Any special procedural requirements, e.g., set-up
- Intercase dependencies

Test Procedure Specification

- Test Procedure ID
- Purpose of the procedure, with references to relevant test cases
- Special requirements for the procedure
- Procedure steps: Logging, Set-Up, Start, actions needed during execution of the procedure, how measurements will be taken, Shut-Down, Restart, Stop, Wrap-up, and Contingencies

Test Item Transmittal Report

- Transmittal Report ID
- Transmitted Items, including version, references, and those responsible for the items transmitted
- Location, media, labeling
- Current Status, outstanding modifications, deviations from documentation
- Approvals: space for signature of designated approvers of the transmittal report

Test Log Specification

- Test log ID
- Description of items being tested, environment
- Activities and Events, date, time and author
- Execution Description: identify test procedure, personnel present and their responsibilities
- Procedure Results, visually observable, location of output, success or failure of the test
- Environmental information, e.g., substituted hardware
- Anomalous Events., i.e. circumstances surrounding unexpected happenings, e.g. power failure, unusually long response time
- Incident Report Identifiers: reference to each logged incident

Test Incident Report

- Test Incident Report ID
- Summary, including test items, version, references to procedures, test cases, and test logs
- Incident Description: inputs, expected results, actual results, anomalies, date and time, procedure step, environment, attempts to repeat, testers, observers, and any related information (e.g., similar previous incidents)
- Impact of the incident on test plans, designs, procedures or test cases
- Incident Resolution (not in the standard) (recommendation, action, date cleared, source of incident, e.g., test, field, etc.)

Test Summary Report

- Test Summary Report ID
- Summary of evaluation of test items, with versions, environment, references to other test documentation
- Variances from test plans, procedures or designs, with reasons
- Comprehensiveness of Testing Assessment, against that specified in the Test Plan, with features which were not sufficiently tested and reasons
- Summary of Results, with resolved and unresolved incidents
- Evaluation of test items, including limitations
- Summary of major testing activities and events: resource usage, staffing levels, elapsed time
- Approvals: space for signature of designated approvers of the Test Summary Report

Test Effectiveness Analysis

Testing Effectiveness. In order to know whether testing is cost-effective, the manager must know first whether testing has been effective. The only true measure of effective testing is that no or very few errors are passed on to the next stage, either a further testing stage or into final operational use. It is essential to keep records of errors found in field use, and relate these errors back to development including testing.

Reducing Costs of Effective Testing. If testing is effective, then ways to achieve the same quality of testing at less costs can be explored. For example, if it is found that inspections are more effective at finding defects in detailed design and coding than unit testing is, then the unit testing may be able to be reduced. However, if different types of errors are found by the two approaches, then even the less effective methods should not be eliminated.

If a large number of errors are found during system testing which were detectible in unit tests but were not found at that stage, then the unit testing should not be reduced but increased, or made more effective. For example, if programmers test their own programs and are not effective, alternative solutions include: training programmers in testing techniques, having code reviewed or Inspected, having a different programmer write the tests from the programmer who wrote the code, writing the tests before the code is written.

If testing is well controlled and effective but uses a large amount of human resource, the use of software testing tools to automate parts of the testing process can be very cost-effective (see Testing Tools below).

The purpose of evaluating the effectiveness of testing is to improve the quality of the testing for future developments, and thereby also to improve quality of software.

Test Management Pitfalls And How To Avoid Them. High-level management pitfalls:

- Absence of testing policy or strategy
- Failing to plan the testing
- Spending too much time, effort or budget on testing (i.e., ineffective testing)
- Running out of time for testing

The way to overcome the high-level management pitfalls is to ensure that there is a testing policy and strategy, and the testing is thought about before beginning to develop software. The effect of an inadequate or nonexistent high-level test policy will be that too much will be spent on testing or there may not be enough time for testing, or both.

Test data pitfalls:

- Inadequate and inefficient test data
- Too much test data

At the project level, the testing also must be planned, and this includes planning what data will be needed when. Doing the test design activities early in the development process will highlight what is needed both in test data, test "scaffolding" (harnesses, stubs and drivers), and test input, as well as testing tools which may be useful. To overcome test data pitfalls, plan the testing early and design tests early.

Uneven testing:

- Omitting to test an important major functionality area
- Testing at too detailed a level in some areas, and not enough in others

Uneven testing is usually the result of an unplanned approach with no regard to testing priorities. Priorities for all testing should be decided before any testing activities are begun, and priorities for running tests should be set before any tests are executed. Different priorities may apply for different levels of testing. For example, for integration testing, the priority may be to focus on those test cases that best help to create a viable test engine. For system level testing, the most important operational tests may be more important. It is easy for testers to become side-tracked into mechanical repetition of tests in one area; testers should be encouraged to go for diversity of test approaches, test cases and test design ideas. The most important principle is to order the tests so that the most important testing is always done first.

Tool support:

- Lack of testing tools
- Over-reliance on testing tools

There are two pitfalls with regard to testing tools. Not using tools when it would be much more cost-effective to use them is wasteful of resources. However, expecting too much of a tool is another trap; be aware of the limitations of tools, and use them to do what they do best, while the human resources freed up from more tedious tasks can be directed to becoming more effective in testing in general. See a later section for more detail on tools.

Test quality:

- Errors made in testing
- Unknown quality of testing, poor quality testing

Confidence in the quality of the software cannot be justified without knowledge of the quality of the testing; if the test quality is unknown, it is likely to be poor, and this will lead to the multiplication of costs as outlined above. However, errors are likely to occur in tests and test documentation as in software, so reviews or inspections of test documentation are very effective at improving test quality. One of the earliest reports on inspection success included the inspection of test documents (Fagan, 1976).

Software quality:

- Some areas difficult to test, not designed for testability
- Large number of errors found, stopping test progress, producing a debug bottleneck
- No errors found in testing, leading to questioning the effectiveness of testing or the value of testing

The quality of the software being tested has a direct bearing on the management of the testing process. If the software is very difficult to test (regardless of whether it is basically correct or not), the tester's job will be much more difficult than it need be. This is where early test design helps to identify and ensure testability. If the software is of very poor quality, the test execution will soon grind to a halt because so many errors are found that the tests cannot be continued. It is important that this is recognized as a software quality problem and not a testing problem. If the software is extremely good, so that no or very few errors are found in testing, then the test execution is either not effective at finding errors, or if there really are no or few errors, testing may be seen as having little or no value. In fact, if confidence in software quality is gained in other ways, then fewer tests need to be executed, but some tests should always be run in order to confirm software quality. In this case, a selection of high priority tests may be sufficient to execute.

TECHNIQUES

This section on techniques is intended as an overview of the more established techniques which should give an idea of the range and variety of testing techniques available. More in-depth and academically up-to-date material can be found in additional entries in this encyclopedia, in technical journals, and in books. A good source is Beizer (1990). See also DATA FLOW TESTING; DOMAIN TESTING; INTEGRATION TESTING; RANDOM TESTING; and REGRESSION TESTING.

Static and Dynamic Testing

Static Analysis. Testing evaluates the quality of software. Testing is sometimes distinguished into static and dynamic analysis. Static techniques do not exercise the software, they only examine it, but they are considered part of testing because they do evaluate software quality. Dynamic testing techniques exercise the software using sample input values.

Static analysis techniques grew out of compiler technology, and many compilers have static analysis features available (surprisingly often unused). Commercial tools are also available which can carry out extensive static analysis on software code without executing it. A significant number of programming errors are statically detectable (Hatton, 1993). Static analysis examines control flow and data flow, and can discover "dead code", infinite loops, uninitialized variables, unused data values, standards violations, etc. Various complexity metrics can also be computed.

Static analysis does not replace dynamic analysis, but is a very useful quality check normally carried out before dynamic test execution begins.

Dynamic Analysis. Dynamic test techniques are generally classified into Functional or Black Box techniques and Structural or White Box techniques. There is no one "best" test technique; rather the best testing makes use of as many techniques as are relevant and useful.

Black Box: Functional Test Case Selection Techniques

Functional techniques are based on the function of the software. Tests are derived from a specification, either a requirements specification for system level tests, a design specification for integration tests, or a detailed module specification for unit tests. The structure of the code or system is not taken into account when designing functional tests. They are called "black box" to indicate that the internal structure of the code is not looked at, i.e., the inside of the box is not relevant.

The black box techniques are concerned with selecting test cases to exercise the software in a thorough and systematic way, where a test case consists of a sample input value, the expected result (what the software should do), and the actual result (what the software did do), together with any other necessary information (procedure for executing the test, environment needed, etc.).

Equivalence Partitioning. The idea behind equivalence partitioning is that testing is more effective if the tests are distributed over all the different possibilities rather than all testing the same thing.

Input values which are treated the same way by the software can be regarded as being in some sense equivalent (they probably follow the same execution path for example). To choose good test cases, it is better to chose one from each equivalence partition than to choose all from one partition. This basic philosophy can be applied at different levels of testing; it is probably better to exercise each menu option once than to leave some unused and concentrate all testing on only a few. (This must be taken with a "grain of salt", because in some cases it may be better to do the reverse, for example if only a few options are critical to users and testing time is severely limited.)

For example, if the numbers 0 to 99 are valid, then any of those 99 numbers should be handled in exactly the same way by the software. If the program works correctly for the value of 7, for example, it will probably also work correctly for 2, 35, 50, etc. All of the values 0 to 99 are within the same equivalence class or equivalence partition.

The values less than 0 form another equivalence partition, that of the invalid values below the valid partition. The values 100 and above form a third invalid partition above the valid partition. Choosing the three test values of −25, 50, and 150 is more likely to reveal an error than the values of 49, 50, and 51. (But see Boundary Value Analysis below.)

−1	0 99	100
Invalid partition	Valid partition	Invalid partition

This is an over-simplification to illustrate the basic principle, and makes the assumption that an input variable is independent of other variables, which is rarely the case in practice. Equivalence partitions may also be dependent on previous input or data values stored, or on some other context factor. For example, an order quantity of 0 to 99 might be valid in isolation, but if it were referring to items packed in sets of six, not all values would be valid.

Boundary Value Analysis. The values which lie at the edge of an equivalence partition are called boundary values. One of the most common types of coding error is for the boundary of the equivalence partition to be "out by one". In addition to choosing one value from each partition, chose values on each side of each partition boundary.

The boundaries in the example above are where the invalid partitions meet the valid partition: one boundary is between −1 and 0, the other is between 99 and 100. Those boundary values, −1, 0, 99, and 100 can determine whether the processing is correct for the boundaries. If the loop control is out by one, then for example, 99 might be regarded as invalid, or 100 as valid.

Again, this is an oversimplification, assuming that a variable is linearly independent from any other variables. Domain Testing is the formalization of this type of partitioning strategy (see DOMAIN TESTING).

Boundary Value Analysis is more prescriptive than Equivalence Partitioning, since any value in a partition is regarded as equally valid as a test case for equivalence partitioning, but the particular values for the boundaries are determined by those boundary values.

Equivalence partitions and boundary conditions can exist on output values, as well as on input values. Test cases should be devised to attempt to achieve both valid and invalid output values, and to test at the output partition boundaries.

There can also be "hidden" boundaries, which should also be tested for, since they often result in unexpected failures. Hidden boundaries are related to internal structure, for example, the disc block transfer size. If 256 characters fill a block, test with 256 and 257 characters.

For real rather than integer values, the boundary values would include the boundary value and small ranges on each side of that value. For integer values, the boundary can be thought of as being between two values, or on one of the values. Some variants of boundary value analysis would result in three values, on, above and below the boundary.

Cause-Effect Graphing. Cause-effect graphing is a systematic way of organizing combinations of inputs (causes) and outcomes (effects) into test cases.

There are different variations of this technique; some involve constructing a "logic diagram" using logical operators such as And and Or, and then constructing a decision table from the diagram (Myers, 1979; Bender, 1992). Other variants omit the logic diagram and go directly to the decision table (Hetzel, 1983).

The cause-effect analysis involves examining a specification, optionally constructing a Boolean network to express the effects as related to the combinations of causes, eliminating any redundant combinations, and constructing a decision table summarizing the conditions and actions. Test cases are then derived from the decision table, and can also take boundary conditions into account. The cause-effect graph can often be simplified by eliminating different inputs which result in the same output, and then combining for "don't care" entries.

Logic-Based Testing. Beizer describes a method of deriving test cases from and validating a specification expressed as a decision table (Beizer, 1990). The reader is referred to this reference for detailed information.

Finite-State-Machine Testing. Many computer systems are finite state machines, because they can be in a limited (i.e. finite) number of different internal conditions (i.e., states), and the rules which determine when they change from one state to another are specified in terms of inputs to the system. For example, an automated bank teller system ("hole in the wall") is a finite state machine, with states such as Waiting for card, Card Inserted, Correct PIN (Personal Identification Number) entered, etc. Tests derived to exercise finite state machines seek to exercise sufficient states and transition paths between states.

Random Testing. One of the perennial arguments in testing is the relative worth of finding and removing defects which may never affect the users in actual operation. If we knew with certainty that a defect would never occur in life-time use, then of course we could ignore it, but that is not the case in real situations. In fact, rarely occurring conditions can result in more serious failures. However, it is important that testing is directed towards ensuring that the quality of the system is investigated where it is the most critical and most important for users, rather than the developer's ideas of what is important for users. Random testing, or user profile testing, is a way of directing testing effort to meet this objective. An article by Hamlet (1990) seemed to indicate that random testing is as effective as partition methods.

A user profile of typical operational use is drawn up, and test inputs are generated randomly (actually pseudorandomly) from the user profile. This type of test is used for system level testing, but one of its major drawbacks is the effort in determining whether the actual results from each randomly generated input was correct or not (the Oracle problem). See also RANDOM TESTING.

Syntax Testing. Also called grammar-based testing, this is a data-driven test technique, where the input data is validated by well-defined syntax rules.

An example would be an input of the form XXyyZ, where XX could be one or two alphabetic characters from A to G, yy could be a numeric value from 1 to 99, and Z could be a punctuation character such as a comma, colon, or semicolon. The syntax can be expressed in Backus Naur Form (BNF) which defines the rules for validity. Our example would be defined as:

```
INPUT        :=XXyyZ
XX           :=LETTERS(1,2)
LETTERS      :=A/B/C/D/E/F/G
yy           :=1/2/3/4/5/6/7/8/9/10/11 .. 99
Z            :=,/:/;
```

The valid test cases would include values such as "A1," and "CD56;". Invalid cases can be constructed by negating any of the valid aspects at each level of definition. For example, no letters or three letters would negate the correct number of letters for the "XX" component. A case with letters after "G" would negate the valid letter range. For the number component, a value of 0, a negative number, or a three-digit number would negate the "yy" definition. A punctuation symbol of "?" would negate the punctuation component.

Note that since discrete symbols are defined for "Z", all the valid cases should be tested individually. The values which occur in ranges, such as letters and numbers can be tested on their boundaries.

Notice also that lower-case letters would be considered invalid according to the above definition; this may or may not be what was actually required. If this is discovered in designing the tests, this is an example of how the investigation or construction of test cases can show deficiencies or errors in a specification.

Ad Hoc Testing. Testing should be thorough, rigorous and systematic. But any testing strategy which is only systematic is incomplete. Errors are not (all) made in a systematic way, so using only a systematic approach may fail to find an important error. There is a valid role in testing for a more creative and imaginative approach to supplement (not replace) the systematic approaches. Ad Hoc testing and Error Guessing fall into this category.

One type of testing which is often erroneously called random testing is where a few values are tried just to make sure that the program is actually there and does not fall down the first time it is executed. This is called "Ad Hoc" or "trial and error" testing, but should really be called Test Readiness Testing. All test execution starts here, but should not end here.

Part of any good test plan is testing by real users. Users seem to have the uncanny knack of being able to crash a system the first time they try it; this ability can be used to good effect by involving users in early testing. Although there may be practical difficulties in involving users in module testing, it pays off by finding errors early so they can be fixed while they are still relatively inexpensive to put right. Users should be involved in designing acceptance tests at an early stage, as well as participating in the running of acceptance tests. There are benefits in involving users in other testing and verification and validation activities as well, such as reviews; the growth of psychological "ownership" of the system is an important by-product of this type of test involvement by users.

Acceptance testing (at least) should include some time for unscripted testing where users try to use the system to perform a realistic task. This type of testing checks that the system is really ready for operational use, and may find errors which are not found by the scripted and rehearsed formal acceptance tests, although this should not generally be the case if development testing was adequately carried out (including early user involvement and error guessing).

Error Guessing. A good tester often has a feel for where the tricky errors might be lurking, and can guess at the best input cases to find those errors. This intuition is based on previous experience or on common assumptions made by developers. Examples of good test cases are: division by zero, an empty file, record, or field, negative numbers, alphabetic character for numeric field, decimal point, embedded comma, minimum and maximum sizes. The test suite should contain any such test cases which are suggested; if test cases are considered unnecessary because they would "never happen", that is likely to be a good test case.

White Box: Structural Test Case Selection Techniques

Structural techniques are based on the internal structure of the software. Although the function of the software is used to determine what the predicted outcome is for a given input, the choice of test cases is driven by looking inside the "box", and choosing test items to exercise the required parts of the structure.

Structural testing is most effectively used as a way to evaluate the effectiveness of functional testing, by analyzing the structural coverage achieved by a functional test set. Once structural coverage gaps have been identified, then structural techniques are used to derive test cases to exercise the parts of the structure which have not yet been exercised.

This section looks at test case design from a structural point of view, and the following section looks at coverage measurement. In fact the two uses of structural techniques are very much inter-twined in practice, as well as being closely linked with functional techniques. They are separated here to assist the explanation of the differences.

Complete Path Testing. In any program with a loop with a variable number of iterations, there is a potentially infinite number of different paths through the program, so complete path coverage is generally impractical if not theoretically impossible. However, a number of less "strong" structural techniques give reasonable test thoroughness.

Branch or Decision Testing. Any software program can be expressed as a control flow diagram (which is like a flowchart but without the words written in the boxes). Whenever there is a condition, such as an "IF" statement, or a loop, then there will be more than one way for control to proceed, i.e. either down the "true" outcome or down the "false" outcome. The point at which the condition is evaluated is called a decision point. The number of unique ways of going from the start to the end of the program is equal to one more than the number of decision points in the program. This number (decision points plus one) is also called the Cyclomatic Complexity for the program. (McCabe, 1983)

Using the control flow graph as the diagram of the structure of the program, the first test case is derived by following one path from the beginning to the end of the graph. The next test case to be chosen should follow at least one segment of the control flow graph which has not been followed before. A method devised by McCabe, called the "Basis Test Set" is a way of devising tests where the number of test cases should in theory be equal to the cyclomatic complexity. The theory does not work out in practice, however, and is now discredited by academics.

Determining what data needs to be input in order for the program to follow a given path is called "sensitizing" the path. This can be a fairly complicated exercise in its own right.

Another way to ensure coverage of all decisions is to keep a matrix of decisions versus test cases, with a tick in each box to ensure that each decision in the code has at least one test case to exercise its possible outcomes. The statements should have one test case for True and one for

False. CASE statements should exercise each option plus the default option. Loops should be executed no times (i.e. not entered), executed once, and executed more than once, the maximum number of times if there is an upper limit. (The latter is strictly speaking more than is required for coverage, but is good practice, since errors can occur when a loop is repeated.)

Condition Testing. Condition testing is more detailed than branch testing. In branch testing, it is only the outcome of a decision which is taken into account. However, many decisions are made on the basis of compound conditions rather than simple conditions (also called predicates).

For example, the statement

```
IF A<10 AND B>250 THEN..."
```

has a True Outcome if both of the individual conditions are True (for both A and B), but has a False outcome if one of them is False. To achieve branch coverage, therefore, two tests are sufficient. For example:

```
A=1 (A<10 true), B=500 (B>250 true),
                        outcome=TRUE
A=11 (A<10 false), B=500 (B>250 true),
                        outcome=FALSE
```

To achieve condition coverage, both True and False outcomes for each of the simple conditions making up a compound condition should also be tested. Two different tests are needed to achieve condition coverage, for example:

```
A=9 (A<10 true), B=250 (B>250 false),
                        outcome=FALSE
A=10 (A<10 false), B=251 (B>250 true),
                        outcome=FALSE
```

In this case we achieved condition coverage but not branch coverage or condition combination coverage (all combinations of conditions, TT, TF, FT and FF). We would need a total of four test cases to achieve condition combination coverage. (Note that some boundary conditions were also taken into account in these example cases.)

Data Flow Testing. Data flow testing is concerned with what happens to data elements in a program (Rapps and Weyuker, 1985). A variable is "defined" when a value is stored into it, such as in an assignment or a read or input operation. (Note that "defined" is not the same as "declared" when the variable name, without a value, is made known to the compiler, although some declarations are also definitions.) A value is "used" when that value determines some processing, such as in a condition of an IF statement, or when it is printed as output. The tests are derived so that adequate definition-use associations are exercised by test cases, or existing test cases are evaluated to determine the coverage achieved in terms of data flow elements. See DATA FLOW TESTING and also Beizer (1990).

Coverage Measurement: Structural-Assessment Techniques

Coverage measurement is a way to assess to some extent the quality of functional testing. Most coverage measures are structural in nature, although functional coverage can also be done (See Functional Domain Coverage below). Structural coverage measurement is best used with a functional approach to the selection of test cases.

After a set of test cases has been derived from a specification, using one or more of the functional test techniques, then that test set is run and the structural elements used by the test set are counted.

Coverage measurement can be applied to code modules, and can also be applied at system or subsystem level. At the higher levels, the number of modules exercised by a test set may be counted, or the number of menu options exercised. At the code module or unit level, there are several different structural measures which can be used.

Note that coverage analysis leads to the use of structural test design techniques to increase coverage.

Coverage analysis is a way of extending the "width" of the test cases; functional test case design gives the "depth" to the quality of the test cases. Exercising each structured element at least once does not guarantee that the tests are good, although it is not good testing to leave some parts untested. If a structural element can be reached in numerous ways, reaching it in only one way is not good testing either. The best testing comes from a combination of functional test case design with structural test coverage assessment (and subsequent structural test case design).

Software tools to assess coverage are available commercially, and are described later. Coverage measurement is an example of a test metric. See METRICS for detailed information on other metrics.

Code Statement Coverage. The first level of code module coverage is that of program statements. Statement coverage is the number of statements exercised by the test set divided by the total number of statements in the module being measured. In a program of 100 (executable) statements, a test set which actually used 75 of those statements would achieve 75% statement coverage. Statement coverage is also referred to as a "Test Effectiveness Ratio" it level 1 (TER 1) (Woodward and co-workers, 1980) or C0 (Beizer, 1990 and others)

It is generally agreed that a thorough test of a module should exercise every statement at least once, so 100% statement coverage should be achieved at some point in the testing for every module, unless there are good reasons not to. It would certainly be strange to consider a test "thorough" if there was some code which had never been tested at all.

However, simply achieving 100% statement coverage does not give a good test set. Statement coverage only tells you that you have exercised each statement at least once, but says nothing about the quality of the test cases which have exercised each statement. You can achieve statement coverage by choosing one value in an equivalence partition without approaching any boundaries, and you may be able to omit some partitions altogether, so even with 100% statement coverage, there will still be many untested areas in the software.

It is surprising to find that what is originally considered to be a good set of functional tests often achieves only 60%–80% statement coverage (Open University, 1984). Examining the results of the statement coverage analysis, therefore, shows where additional test cases are needed in order to achieve increased statement coverage to 100%.

Branch or Decision Coverage Branch or decision coverage is similar to statement coverage, but instead of the number of statements being counted, the number of equivalent branches or decisions are counted. An IF statement has two branches, the True branch and the False branch. Case statements and loops are equivalent to branches, since they can be expressed as IF statements. If a program contains 20 branches, and a test set exercises 10 of them, then 50% branch coverage has been achieved. Branch or decision coverage is also referred to as Test Effectiveness Ratio 2 (TER2) or C1.

Typical "good" functional testing achieves 40% to 60% branch coverage (Open University, 1984). 100% statement coverage can be achieved by only exercising the "true" branches of every IF statement, so statement coverage does not imply branch coverage. However, 100% branch coverage does guarantee 100% statement coverage (at least in most modern languages).

LCSAJ Coverage. Another level of coverage (TER3), used in some tools, is the number of LCSAJ's exercised by a test set, divided by the total number of LCSAJ's. LCSAJ stands for "Linear Code Sequence And Jump" (Hennel and coworkers, 1984), and program code is composed of a number of such sequences. The number of LCSAJ's is greater than the number of branches or decisions, so this is a "stronger" measure than branch (and statement) coverage. A program which contains 40 LCSAJ's and exercises 10 of them with a test set would achieve 25% LCSAJ coverage.

The additional test cases which give LCSAJ coverage include the exercising of a loop zero, one and more than one time, some combinations of branches, and others. Typical LCSAJ coverage for "good" functional testing is 30–50%. 100% LCSAJ coverage often cannot be achieved due to impossible combinations of conditions; in that case, those which can be achieved should be, and those which cannot be achieved should be explained. LCSAJ coverage can extend the test cases derived by functional test techniques to exercise situations is not explicitly covered by branch coverage. Both branch and LCSAJ coverage can be measured using a software tool. 100% LCSAJ coverage guarantees 100% branch and statement coverage (in most modern languages). However, LCSAJ's are directly related to the layout of the code; if any changes are made to the code (even without changing its function), a different set of LCSAJ's would be generated.

Decision-Condition Coverage. Decision-condition coverage is achieved by exercising both the true and false outcomes of each condition within a decision. (Quentin, 1992) A compound decision with three comparisons would achieve decision or branch coverage by exercising only the True and False outcomes of the decision, so needing only two test cases. To achieve decision-condition coverage, each of the three components used to determine the decision also need a true and false case; this can be done in two test cases (e.g., all true, all false). Decision-condition coverage can be achieved without achieving decision coverage (as in the example above).

Decision Condition Combination Coverage. Not only is each condition evaluated to true or false, but all possible combinations of conditions are evaluated to achieve condition combination coverage. For example if there are three conditions in a decision, eight test cases would be needed for the combinations of the three conditions. If there were eight conditions, then 256 test cases would be needed. 100% condition combination coverage guarantees 100% branch and statement coverage (for modern structured languages).

Functional Domain Coverage. Sampling coverage of the functional domain is achieved by having at least one sample value from each functional equivalence partition. Boundary coverage of the functional domain is achieved by having one test case on and on each side of all equivalence partition boundaries. Functional domain coverage is more difficult to measure, since it depends on having an accurate count of equivalence partitions, which is not as easily automated as a count of structural elements. This can be automated if a specification is rigorous enough and computer-readable, or it can be done manually. It is common to have some informal check of "coverage" of system level functions, by use of a matrix of functions versus test cases.

System Level Coverage. The basic idea of coverage is to achieve an independent view of the effectiveness of the testing (the "width"), by observing how much of a given item is exercised.

The coverage idea can be extended to apply at any level of a system. For example, the percentage of sub-module calls exercised in a call tree is a coverage measure at system or subsystem level. (Commercial tools can provide this.) Design level coverage can also be defined in terms of decision coverage. The number of menu options exercised gives a screen-based coverage view. The number of business functions exercised can give a business-oriented view of testing quality.

Coverage can be defined in terms of whatever technical environment is being used. For example, the percentage of objects or inheritances tested for object-oriented systems, or the percentage of triggers or events in a fourth-generation system would provide useful information about test coverage in these development environments (Herzlich, 1992).

TESTING IN MAINTENANCE

Differences between Development and Maintenance Testing

Testing in maintenance is different from development testing both in sequence and the nature of test data.

Development tests are generally run from the lowest level first (unit, module, or component test) to the highest level (the whole system) last, a bottom-up approach to test running. Testing in development should be planned as part of the development and assembly process, so that "thorough" testing (however that is defined) is achieved before the system as a whole is released for operational use.

In maintenance, testing is performed for two reasons: planned changes and emergency fixes, and on two areas of the system: where changes are expected and where changes are unexpected (see below). Tests for planned changes or enhancements are designed when the change or enhancement is designed, with detailed testing of changes to development-style standards. Maintenance testing also includes systemwide testing of parts of the system which should not have been affected, looking for unexpected changes; this is known as Regression Testing (see REGRESSION TESTING for a more detailed discussion of this topic, and information about recent research in maintenance testing).

Tests run for emergency fixes are normally performed under severe time constraints, so that "thorough" testing in the development sense is not achievable in practice, although the ideal would be the same as for planned changes. Maintenance testing must therefore be more concerned with directing the testing effort to the most cost-effective and time-efficient areas to be tested.

Test data for development testing (and to some extent for expected changes) is generally artificially constructed, often using testing techniques (described above).

Test data for maintenance testing can be derived from real-life data, possibly with modifications or selection criteria for special cases. The advantage is that this enables testing to follow a true user profile rather than be directed by projected or imagined user profile testing. The disadvantage is that data must be selected from a very large quantity of possible test data sources, and that important tests for boundary value analysis and equivalence partitioning may therefore be missed.

The objectives of testing in maintenance are to:

- Establish confidence that the system as a whole is working correctly
- Investigate more thoroughly the areas of the system which have the highest impact if they go wrong and those most likely to go wrong, i.e., those with a history of problems or most recently changed
- Order the tests for the most cost-effective use of testing resources, using tool support where possible

Types Of Maintenance Testing

There are three types of testing which can be performed in maintenance:

- Breadth testing
- Depth testing
- Regression testing.

Breadth testing establishes a basic level of confidence in the working of the overall system but not at a detailed level. The main aim is to demonstrate that the system is working from a general overview perspective.

Depth testing investigates and probes the weak areas of the system in detail but only for selected parts of the system. This can also be called destructive testing or investigative testing. The main aim is to find errors.

When existing (tested) software is changed, additional testing is required in two areas: testing for expected chances and testing for unexpected changes. The altered or additional software should be tested for expected changes, to check that the new expected results are correct; this is depth testing. Software which has not been changed should be tested for unexpected chances or side-effects; this testing is called regression testing (Myers, 1979), because it is concerned with ensuring that the software has not regressed (gone backwards) to an erroneous state (linguistically it should be called "anti-regression" testing, but it is known as regression testing.) Regression testing can include both breadth and depth testing.

The operational use of the system is the best guide to general overall confidence levels, but testing should not simply repeat or duplicate operational use, but should also cover the "dark corners".

Documentation in Maintenance Testing

System Documentation. When changes are made to a system, and tests carried out to confirm those changes, a number of system documents are used, and the maintainer builds up a knowledge not only of the software but also of the documentation associated with the changed area. It is important to capture that new knowledge so that future changes can build on it and not have to repeat the learning process.

There are two characteristics of system documentation: accuracy and trustworthiness or reliability. If documentation is 99% accurate, but you do not know which 1% is wrong, then the documentation is untrustworthy (Reid, 1990). It is more useful to have known inaccurate but trustworthy documentation than untrustworthy documentation.

The existing state of system documentation may be good, or it may be poor. If it is good, i.e., can be relied on to give an accurate picture of what really exists, then it is important that this reliability or trustworthiness is preserved over software and documentation changes. If the existing state of the system documentation is poor, i.e. it is not trustworthy or reliable, then its reliability should be increased with every change, by annotating the fact that this part of the documentation has been checked, with the date, so that at least this part can now be relied on.

Documenting Tests. Test documentation should correspond to the known state of the software and other documentation. For example if six inputs are described on a module's specification but the test script gives only five, then one of them is incorrect. Cross-references between test documentation and requirements, designs, user manuals, etc. should be accurate and consistent. If a test is changed, the associated documentation should also be changed. It is helpful to record test running instructions and keep them with the test documentation, to ease the running of that test next time. It is more likely that a part of the system which has just been changed will be changed again than that a previously unchanged part of the system will be changed. As for development tests, the expected output should be predicted in advance of running a test.

TOOLS

General Benefits of Computer-Aided Software Testing

Computer-Aided Software Testing (CAST) is a major way to reduce the cost of manual testing. Example documented benefits include the achievement of 80% reduction in testing costs, and four-fold improvement in software release schedules (Fewster, 1991).

Computer-aided software testing can improve not only the testing process itself, but also the productivity and quality of software development as a whole. Such tools can free skilled testers to concentrate on better quality testing.

The benefits of CAST include the following:

- A large volume of tests can be run unattended, for example, overnight.
- Automating menial and boring tasks gives greater accuracy as well as improved staff morale and more productive allocation of skilled resources.
- Tests can be re-run automatically whenever the software is changed, so the regression tests can check to ensure that the software elsewhere has not been affected in undesirable ways (regression testing).
- Test data can be made consistent from one test to the next, giving confidence that the same data is being input every time.
- Tools can find errors which are difficult to find manually. Of the types of error which can be found automatically, i.e., "trivial" errors, a tool can find all of the errors it is capable of looking for.
- The tedious task of entering test data can be automated or at least need be done only once and not repeatedly.
- The quality of the testing can be addressed through assessment of the thoroughness of the test input (coverage measurement).

In summary, more thorough testing can be achieved in less time, giving increases in both quality and productivity over manual testing methods.

Applicable Areas for Tool Support

Tool support for testing is mainly in running tests rather than in designing and planning them. Tools apply mainly to the second half of the life cycle (the test running phases), although there are exceptions. The very things which are the most boring to do are the things which are most suitable for automation.

Dangers Of Testing Tools

There are two major pitfalls to be wary of in moving into the automation of software testing: the technical practices which are being automated, and the implementation of tools within the organization.

The quality of the testing being automated is critical to success: all the major success stories have in common the existence or establishment of good testing practice as well as test automation. Just as CASE tools cannot succeed if they automate poor design practice, CAST cannot succeed if it automates poor testing practice. Automated chaos is just faster chaos.

The implementation of tools within an organization is a significant exercise which needs careful planning, realistic expectations, and reasonable levels of funding and resourcing. If this aspect is neglected, tools end up as "shelf-ware" —expensive investments which provide no benefits because they simply are not used (Bouldin, 1989). The use of tools will also affect working practices.

Types of Test and Debug Tools

Market surveys give current information about commercially available tools. (Graham, 1991; Durant, 1988; Norman, 1992) The following list gives the facilities offered by software test and debug tools of different types, adapted from The CAST Report (Graham, 1991).

Capture Playback and Test Harness Tools. Capture and playback tools provide the capability to record and replay a test input script. They do not save any time the first time test data is input to the software under test, but they do have three advantages.

First, they enable the test script recorded by the tool to be replayed exactly. This enables the correction of faults to be demonstrated with confidence that the input was exactly the same.

Secondly, the tests can be replayed without supervision, so a great deal of testers' time can be saved on subsequent testing, i.e. during regression testing.

A third advantage is that most capture playback tools also allow the recorded test scripts to be edited; this enables the test script to be changed as needed for error corrections and changes to the software, for example for a new field added to a screen. A typical extension to the editing facility is the provision of a "test language", which enables the test scripts to be typed in rather than recording an actual input.

A capture playback system can be either intrusive or nonintrusive. An intrusive system resides on the same machine as the software under test; a nonintrusive system resides on a separate machine. The nonintrusive system should not affect the timing of the software being tested, but it does require the purchase of special test hardware (which may be a PC).

One of the uses of a capture playback system is for capturing those elusive errors which users seem to be so good at making, and which developers just cannot seem to reproduce. People are not very good at remembering with total exactness precisely what keystrokes they performed, in what order, and at what time intervals. Attaching a capture playback tool to a remote terminal can enable the data recorded when the strange error does occur to be observed and reproduced.

Capture/Playback tools which capture and replay a series of tests are sometimes referred to as test harnesses (or test drivers). A comparator can be part of the test harness, so that the eventual output of the set of tests is a set of discrepancy reports.

Test harness tools may also perform configuration management tasks for the test documentation, keeping track of when tests were run, with what version of the software and test input, who initiated the test, where the output results are stored, etc.

The use of a test harness tool enables large quantities of tests to be run unattended, for example overnight or at weekends. Combined with a comparator tool, it can provide the facility for regression testing of software changes to be done "properly", by actually re-running all previous tests each time a change is made.

Note that changes to the software can often have significant effects on the test scripts. The maintenance of automated tests may be a significant cost.

Comparators. A file comparator is a general tool, not necessarily restricted to software testing, but is a very useful tool in testing. One of the most important tasks in the testing process is to compare the outcome of the software under test with the expected outcome for that module; in fact the execution cannot be considered to be a real test unless that is done every time. However, the comparison of long lists of numbers or symbols is the sort of task which is difficult for people to do accurately but which is ideal for computers to do.

A test comparator tool allows two test outcomes to be compared with one another, with only the differences between the two being output from the comparator. If two files are exactly the same, the tool will find no differences, or discrepancies, so the discrepancy report may say "no differences found" for example.

The comparator can also be used to compare the outcome this time with the outcome last time, i.e., for regression testing. If the expected outcome has been written down on paper rather than recorded electronically, then the first outcome of a test could be checked against the expected outcome manually. When the test is run for a second time, then the comparison tool can check to find only the differences in the outcome between the first and second runs. This enables the boring task (checking that things are exactly the same) to be automated, while the non-routine tasks (analyzing the differences, which is not easily automated) is done manually, thus getting the most effective mix of human and automated analysis.

There are two problems with the design of a comparison tool. First, there will be some output data which is different for every test run but which does not matter, for example the time and/or date of the test. A comparator tool should allow "masking" or these "don't matter" fields, so that they are not compared.

A second problem is of the two files being compared getting out of step. If a new input item has been added to the software, it requires both a new test input and a new output. A straight comparison of the new output file with the old will produce agreement until the new output item, but everything after that will disagree, although it will be obvious by looking at it that each item is off by one. A comparator tool should therefore be able to get itself back in step, either automatically, or with specific instructions from the tester when the comparator is run.

Comparator tools are often combined with capture playback tools. In fact, a capture playback tool enables so much more output to be generated by replaying tests, that a comparator is probably an essential adjunct to successful use of a capture playback tool.

Comparator tools enable the comparison of screen output as well as printed or stored output. Used in conjunction with capture playback tools, screens can be saved at intervals (snapshots) to be compared with the same screen in a subsequent test run. Screen areas can be selectively masked for "don't matter" items of data.

The comparison of graphical information is considerably more complex than the comparison of character-based data. The more sophisticated graphical comparators work at an object level rather than only a bit-map level.

A comparator is probably the easiest software testing tool to produce in-house, although the commercial tools may well turn out to be cheaper in the long run.

Input Generators. The selection of the input cases for testing is generally done manually, following some of the test techniques described above. However, test input cases can be generated automatically for some types of tests. (See also the separate entry for Random Testing.)

For large volumes of test data to test performance under heavy load, or to stress a system beyond its design limits, it is the quantity of test data which is needed rather the quality of the individual test inputs. (One assumes that this type of testing comes after the thorough individual testing.) Tools can be useful in generating a large volume of test inputs.

A single test script can be replayed over and over, possibly at a higher speed than it was originally recorded. Test input can be generated or modified by using a pseudorandom number generator to give some variety to the input data items. The modification of data items can also be done for data files.

One other type of input generation tool can be used when the requirements for the module being tested are recorded in a formal way. For example, if the description of the module consists of various states which it can be in, and exactly what input will change the software from one state to another, what inputs are valid in which states, etc., then test cases can be generated automatically from that specification.

Static Analysis Tools. Many of the errors which are made in software development are "trivial", i.e., they are very easy for people to make. For example, spelling a variable name slightly differently in two places, omitting a punctuation mark, forgetting to read in the 14th variable, etc. However, such errors which are trivial to make often have severe and non-trivial effects on the software. A misspelled word in a printed output is a mere annoyance, but using the wrong variable name to compute how much oxygen to give a chemical reaction can have an explosive effect (literally).

One software tool which filters out many of these types of error is a compiler. If variables are pre-declared, for example, misspellings are found. However, there are a number of other things which a compiler may not detect: for example, whether you have forgotten to assign a value to a variable before using it, or if a declared procedure is actually never called.

Static analysis tools have developed out of common research, and can find a number of errors in software without dynamically executing that software. They can find all occurrences of some types of error, so they are 100% accurate for some things. They are not a substitute for testing, however, as there are other errors which are not found by static analysis (the software might perfectly perform the wrong function).

Static analysis tools perform several types of analysis, as detailed below. Not all tools perform all of the functions listed; a selection of types of facilities is given.

Complexity analysis computes the cyclomatic complexity, the measurement of the number of decisions in the module, and may also compute other complexity measures. Static analysis tools can also give a measure of the "structured-ness" of the code; if the code contains transfers of control (jumps) which cross other transfers, this indicates poor program structure (usually due to improper use of "go to"'s).

Data flow analysis detects errors and anomalies of variable usage. For example, if a variable is used in an expression before a value has been assigned to it, or if it is assigned a value which is then never used. (See DATA FLOW ANALYSIS.)

Control flow analysis detects logic errors, such as program code which is never executed, or loops which cannot be exited (infinite loops).

Information flow analysis examines the relationship of input to output variables, and can tell which input values affect a given output value, or which output values are affected by a given input value. This can be used to verify (manually) that the correct dependencies between input and output values have been achieved. A partial program can be extracted, listing only the statements which use or are affected by given variables.

Static analysis tools may also provide other functions to support formal verification techniques such as correctness proving.

Simulator. Simulator or emulator tools are used to imitate (simulate) some aspect of the real world in order to test software which cannot be tested directly in its final environment. Simulators are used when it is too dangerous, too expensive, or inappropriate to test directly, for example, aircraft guidance software, nuclear power station control, chemical process control, or financial institutions, e.g., a bank.

The simulator tool feeds input to the software under test as though that input was coming from its intended environment, and also receives the program output in a similar way to the software's environment, e.g., by intercepting control signals which are intended for special hardware devices.

Simulators are often specific to a particular environment and so are usually bespoke developments in their own right. Before a simulator can be relied upon for testing, it is important that the simulator software itself be tested rigorously.

No matter how good the simulation is, the real world will always be different, so simulation testing is not a substitute for real-world testing, but can be a useful predecessor.

Coverage Analysis. Coverage analysis tools provide a measure of how much of the structure of a module or system has been exercised by a given set of tests. System level coverage measures how many of the component parts of the system have been called by a test set. Code coverage measures the percentage of statements, branches, or LCSAJ's exercised by a test set (see Coverage Measurement above).

There are two types of coverage measurement tools, non-intrusive, which are hardware-based, and intrusive, which are software-based. With an intrusive (software) tool, the code must first be instrumented, i.e., code must be inserted to count the number of times at structure is used. This is done automatically by the tool, but it does require in additional compilation-type step, and the resulting instrumented code will be of increased size and decreased performance compared to the original code. Instrumentation is therefore normally removed before performance testing, which may result in increased time for the testing. An example of a nonintrusive tool is an in-circuit emulator.

Once the code is instrumented, the test sets (probably derived by functional techniques) are run through the code. The results are the percentage measurements achieved in whatever structure is being measured. This information can then be used by the testers to devise new test input cases which will exercise those parts of the software which have not yet been reached. When those test cases have been run through the code, a cumulative total of structures exercised is given by the tool. Some debugging tools can measure statement coverage.

Performance analysis tools can also be used for coverage analysis. If the coverage of real data is analysed, the tool gives the number of times each statement is used; those which are used the most times are the performance "hot spots". If performance needs to he improved, the greatest gains can be made by optimizing the "hot spots", since the improvements will be multiplied by the great number of times that code is normally used. Statistical profiler tools can also be used as testing tools. Since the number of times a statement (for example) is exercised can be detected, the input need not be a realistic sample of real data, but could be the test case script, to give coverage information.

Database. A test database is used when the software being tested either uses or affects data which is stored, where the output from the software does not give all of the information about what the software did (i.e., the outcome is more than the output). The test database is a sample of the database which the software manipulates. Ideally it should contain at least one example of every type of record, field and index.

A comparator tool can be used to examine the effect of the software under test on the database, by comparing the "before" and "after" states of the database. A useful database tool is one which restores a database to a specified known starting point for a series of tests, called a "sunrise" database.

A test database is often special-purpose, as it may need to be tailored to the particular application.

Debug. Debug tools enable software errors to be identified and isolated so that they can be corrected. They also allow software fixes to be tried out to some extent, to verify that the fault has been correctly identified. Debug tools generally work on only one program or module, and allow observation and manipulation of program data and logic control flow, by setting up interruptions to the normal program execution.

The debug tool is like a harness for the program under test; the program is run under the control of the debug tool.

Debug tools can operate at different levels. Machine level tools allow access only by hardware or assembler level addresses. Mnemonic level tools allow names to be used for variables and procedures, although breakpoints still need to be set with reference to assembly level. Source level tools allow all interaction with the tool to take place with reference to the source code (3GL). Screen-based tools allow "animation" of control flow, i.e. highlighting the statements in the order of execution, and data items can be monitored so that changes can be seen on the screen as they occur. Debug tools can also be integrated with editors and compilers, or with configuration management tools.

Some debug tools can perform coverage analysis for statement coverage; some can also record and playback input scripts.

Debug tools are usually specific to a particular hardware and software environment.

FUTURE TRENDS IN SOFTWARE TESTING

Software Testing Practice

The momentum which has already built up towards certification in quality standards will continue, and this will continue to increase awareness of the importance of software testing. It will become the accepted norm that software developers, to be considered worth buying from, will need to conform to standards such as ISO 9001, because all of their competitors will.

Testing will become a recognized specialization within software engineering, distinct from but closely associated with quality-related specializations.

Training in testing techniques will be provided on academic courses for software engineers, and industrial courses in testing will be widely available. Managers will be given training in the effective test management. Senior executives will be aware of the need for testing and how to assess and achieve quality through testing.

In short, the methods and techniques which are known today but not generally practised, will be put in place in industry.

The problems of testing event-driven systems and graphical user interface systems are not dissimilar to the problems of testing real-time systems which are interrupt-driven at a low level (machine) rather than a high level (user).

New software development techniques will provide new challenges for testers. Two areas which may provide particularly interesting testing problems are the testing of multimedia systems, and the testing of visualization systems.

Academic research continues to concentrate on structural and statistical approaches, but maintenance testing is also a significant area of research.

Software Testing Tools

The development of tool support for software testing will continue, with support being provided in new development environments, such as object-oriented systems, 4th generation languages and form-based design techniques, and for testing graphical user interfaces. New testing techniques will be developed in parallel with new development techniques, embodying error detection and coverage measurement.

Test case generation from specifications (requirement or design) will be done automatically as CASE tools tie up with CAST tools to form tools which really do cover all of the life cycle. However, these machine-generated test cases will need to be supplemented with test cases derived using the increased skills of trained testers.

The use of testing tools will become wide-spread, particularly in maintenance for regression testing. Automated impact analysis will enable regression tests to be linked to the changes which are being tested.

Testing tools will find ways to make life easier for testers; scripting languages now allow much more automated control of test execution, but can be prohibitively complex, requiring programming skills to write the test scripts. The equivalent in test scripting to recent developments in programming will give object-oriented testing with menu-driven user-friendly interfaces.

Tools for helping to build tests early, through a prototyping, data dictionary or visual approach may make test execution tools easier to use. Tools to make the maintenance of test data "invisible" when changes are made to software will enable regression packs to be easily maintained.

Testability Analysis and Specification

The essence of software testing is to take an independent view to that taken by those constructing the software, in order to assess the quality of that construction. Future testers will be involved in testability analysis throughout the software development process, to enable physical tests to be created easily and automatically from the tester's logical test designs. The higher the testability, the easier this will be; the tester's will act as internal consultants to developers and maintainers to specify how higher testability can be achieved.

Process Testing

Future software test engineers will be involved in testing the software development or maintenance process, not just testing the products produced by that process. This may involve monitoring test metrics in a way similar to statistical process control techniques. Information learned from "the field" will be routinely used to drive the fine-tuning of the testing process.

Human Involvement

There will always be a need for human involvement in testing, since it is human ingenuity which can most successfully find the most important aspects to test, and thereby to be most effective at ensuring software quality. As testing becomes more efficient through tool support, it will become even more challenging, creative, and enjoyable.

RECOMMENDED READING LIST

Books

The following books have a full listing in the References section following.

Myers (1979): The testing "classic" and still probably the best single book on testing philosophy. Contains the "contrary" but effective definitions of testing as looking for errors, not proving correctness. Also contains many valuable checklists. Starts with a self-assessment test which can be alarmingly revealing. The technical information is now somewhat dated, but the rest is well worth having.

Hetzel (1984 and 1988): This is the best book for managers. Its emphasis is on risk assessment, and testing throughout the software development life cycle. Contains a sample testing policy statement and a quality measurement diagnostic checklist as appendices. Check that an index is present; some copies of the book do not have one.

Beizer (1983 and 1990): The most thorough book on detailed test techniques, especially structural techniques. Contains a good taxonomy (classification) of bugs and a lot of real examples and statistics. Parts of the book are very entertaining, but other parts are rather mathematical and fairly heavy going. The section on domain testing (functional testing) is not as easy to understand as Myers, and the whole book feels fairly "academic" with its emphasis on graph theory and structural elements. This book is the "Bible" of testing techniques. The wealth of information makes this book essential for anyone who is serious about testing. This book has been updated for a 1993 edition.

Ould (1986): An excellent short summary of testing as seen from different points of view: management, users, designers and programmers. The different tasks in testing for the different people involved are outlined. Very readable and full of good information.

Kaner (1988): A very practical and down-to-earth book, written for people who test in a dynamic environment, generally under-staffed, under-funded, and held to impossible deadlines. The author is a human factors analyst, so the "people" problems which often seem to interfere with the technical work are examined and helpful suggestions are given. There is a wonderful set of appendices (over 100 pages) describing twelve different types of errors to check for—a superb resource for checklists. There were rather a lot of minor errors in my copy of the book. This book has been updated for a 1993 edition.

Journals

The Journal of Software Testing, Verification and Reliability, first published by Sigma Press 1991, taken over by Wiley (UK) in 1992: John Wiley & Sons Ltd., Baffins Lane, Chichester, West Sussex P019 IUD. The only journal specifically to address software testing.

Software Engineering Notes, An Informal Newsletter of the Special Interest Group on Software Engineering, ACM (Association for Computing Machinery), ACM Press, 11 West 24nd Street, New York, N.Y. 10036 USA. The best part of this journal is the first section of every issue, "Risks to the Public in Computers and Related Systems". This contains stories reported from the press anywhere in the world concerning adverse things which have happened where computers were involved, and covers everything from loss of life, space shuttles, air traffic control, banks, telephone systems, elections, security, military, insurance, and others. The best source for the most horrifying and most amusing stories and anecdotes.

ACM Transactions on Software Engineering and Methodology, ACM (Association for Computing Machinery), ACM Press, 11 West 24nd Street, New York, NY 10036 USA.

IEEE Transactions on Software Engineering, IEEE Computer Society, 1730 Massachusetts Ave NW., Washington DC 20036-1903 USA, European office: 13, Avenue de l'Aquilon, B. 1200 Brussels, Belgium.

Software Engineering Journal, IEEE & BCS, The Institution of Electrical Engineers, Savoy Place, London WC2R 0BL.

Information and Software Technology, Butterworth-Heinemann Ltd., PO Box 63, Westbury House, Bury Street, Guildford, Surrey GU2 5BH.

Journal of Software Maintenance, John Wiley & Sons Ltd., Baffins Lane, Chichester, West Sussex P019 1UD.

Software: Practice and Experience, John Wiley & Sons Ltd., Baffins Lane, Chichester, West Sussex P019 1UD.

Software Quality Journal, Chapman & Hall, UK Office: 2-6 Boundary Row, London SE1 8HN. First issue March 1992.

The Software Practitioner, Computing Trends, P.O. Box 213, State College, PA 16804 USA.

Software Maintenance News, now renamed *Software Management News,* 141 Saint Marks Place, Suite 5F, Staten Island, NY 10301 USA.

Standards

IEEE Standards. The following Standards are from the IEEE, The Institute of Electrical and Electronics Engineers, Inc, 345 East 47th Street, New York, NY 10017 USA. or from the European office: 13, Avenue de l'Aquilon,

B-1200 Brussels, Belgium, Tel. 32-2-770-2198, Fax 32-2-770-8505.

- ANSI/IEEE Std 729-1983, Glossary of Software Engineering Terminology.
- ANSI/IEEE Std 829-1983, Software Test Documentation
- ANSI/IEEE Std 1008-1987, Software Unit Testing
- ANSI/IEEE Std 1012-1986, Software Verification and Validation Plans

BSI Standards. The following Standards are from the British Standards Institute, BSI, Linford Wood, Milton Keynes MK 14 6LE, Tel. 0909 220022, Fax 0908 320856.

- BS5887-1980, Testing of computer-based systems
- BS5750-1990, Quality Systems (same Standard as EN29001 and ISO 9001)

The TickIT Guide, the application of BS5750 to software systems, published by the Department of Trade and Industry. Available from the TickIT Project Office, 68 Newman Street, London W1A 4SE, Tel 072 383 4501, Fax 071 383 4771.

Events

There are a number of annual conferences which specifically address software testing. Since the contact details may vary from year to year, the best way to find details of such events is to look in the journals, many of which list calendar events. *Software Engineering Notes,* described above, has a comprehensive listing which usually includes all the relevant events.

BIBLIOGRAPHY

B. Beizer, *Software Testing Techniques,* Van Nostrand Reinhold, New York, 1983.

B. Beizer, *Software Testing Techniques,* 2nd ed., Van Nostrand Reinhold, New York, 1990.

R. Bender, "Tutorial on Introduction to Requirements-Based Testing," *1st International Conference on Software Testing, Analysis and Review (STAR'92),* Las Vegas, Nev., proceedings published by SQE, Jacksonville, Fla., 1992.

B. W. Boehm, *Software Engineering Economics,* Prentice-Hall, Englewood Cliffs, N.J., 1981.

B. M. Bouldin, *Agents of Change: Managing the Introduction of Automated Tools,* Yourdon Press, Prentice-Hall, Englewood Cliffs, N.J., 1989.

J. Buckle, *Software Inspection Handbook,* Institution of Electrical Engineers, London, 1990.

T. DeMarco, *Controlling Software Projects,* Yourdon Press, Prentice-Hall, Englewood Cliffs, N.J., 1982.

J. Durant, *The Testing Tools Reference Guide,* Software Quality Engineering, Jacksonville, Fla., from 1988 twice yearly.

M. E. Fagan, "Design and Code Inspections to Reduce Errors in Program Development," *IBM Systems Journal,* **15**(3), 1976, 182–211 (1976).

M. E. Fagan, "Advances in Software Inspections," *IEEE Transactions Software Engineering,* **SE-12**(7), 744–75 (July 1986).

R. Fairley, *Software Engineering Concepts,* McGraw-Hill, Singapore, 1985.

M. Fewster, "The Manager Wants 100% Automated Testing: a Case History," *Journal of Software Testing, Verification and Reliability,* **1**(2), pp 43–45 (July–Sept. 1991).

T. Gilb, *Principles of Software Engineering Management,* Addison-Wesley, 1988, pp. 205–226, pp. 403–422.

T. Gilb and D. R. Graham, *Software Inspection,* Addison-Wesley, 1993.

J. B. Goodenough, in P. Wegner, ed., "A Survey of Program Testing Issues," *Research Directions in Software Technology,* The MIT Press, Cambridge, Mass., 1980, pp. 316– 340.

J. B. Goodenough and S. L. Gerhart, "Toward a Theory of Test Data Selection," *IEEE Transactions on Software Engineering,* **SE-1**(2), (June 1975).

D. R. Graham, *The CAST Report: Computer-Aided Software Testing,* Unicom Seminars, Uxbridge, London, U.K., 1991.

D. R. Graham, "Test is a Four-Letter Word: the Psychology of Defects and Detection," *Proceedings of the Software Testing, Analysis and Review Conference (STAR'92),* Las Vegas, Nev., proceedings published by SQE, Jacksonville, Fla., May 1992.

R. N. Hall, "Independence in Verification and Validation," in B. A. Kitchenham, ed., *Software Engineering for Large Software Systems,* Elsevier, Barking, U.K., 1990.

R. G. Hamlet and R. Taylor, "Partition Testing Does not Inspire Confidence," *IEEE Transactions in Software Engineering,* **SE-16,** 1402–1411 (Dec. 1990).

L. Hatton, "Automated Static Analysis—Wheel Tapping for Software Engineers," *2nd International Software Testing Analysis and Review Conference (STAR'93),* Monterey, Calif., proceedings published by SQE, Jacksonville, Fla., May, 1993.

M. A. Hennel, D. Hedley, and I. J. Riddell, "Assessing a Class of Software Tools," *Seventh International Conference on Software Engineering,* Orlando, Fla., March 26–29, 1984.

P. Herzlich, "New Development Technologies: Bane or Boon in Testing," presented at the British Computer Society Specialist Interest Group in Software Testing, London, U.K., Nov. 16, 1992.

B. Hetzel, ed., *Program Test Methods,* Prentice-Hall, Englewood Cliffs, N.J., 1973.

B. Hetzel, *The Complete Guide to Software Testing,* QED Information Sciences, Wellesley, Mass., 1983 and 1988.

B. Hetzel, "Software Testing: Some Troubling Issues and Opportunities," presented to the British Computer Society Specialist Interest Group in Software Testing, Dec. 6, 1991.

IEEE, *Software Test Documentation,* ANSI/IEEE Standard 829-1983, Institution of Electrical and Electronic Engineers, New York, N.Y., 1983.

C. Kaner, *Testing Computer Software,* Tab Books, Blue Ridge Summit, Pa., 1988.

C. Kaner, J. Falk, and H. Q. Nguyen, *Testing Computer Software,* 2nd ed., Van Nostrand Reinhold, New York, 1993.

B. Littlewood, "Forecasting Software Reliability," *Software Reliability Modelling and Identification,* Springer-Verlag, Heidelberg, 1988.

T. J. McCabe, *Structured Testing,* IEEE Computer Society Press, Silver Spring, Md., 1983.

G. J. Myers, *The Art of Software Testing,* John Wiley & Sons, New York, 1979.

S. Norman, *Dynamic Testing Tools: a Detailed Product Evaluation,* Ovum Reports, London, U.K., 1992.

The Open University, "Testing," Unit 7, *Software Engineering* PMT600, Open University Press, Milton Keynes, U.K., 1984.

M. A. Ould and C. Unwin, *Testing in Software Development,* British Computer Society Monographs in Informatics, Cambridge University Press, Cambridge, U.K., 1986.

S. Price, personal communication, 1991.

G. Quentin, *The Tester's Handbook,* QCC, Shoeburyness, U.K., 1992.

S. Rapps and E. J. Weyuker, "Selecting Software Test Data using Data Flow Information," *IEEE Transactions on Software Engineering,* **SE-14**(4), 367–375 (April 1985).

I. Reid, *An Enquiry into Software Engineering,* Carden Publications Ltd, Chichester, W. Sussex, U.K., 1990.

Survey of Software Testing Practices in the UK. by Software, Management Magazine and Performance Software Ltd, 1991.

E. J. Weyuker, "On Testing Nontestable Programs," *The Computer Journal,* **25**(4), 465–470 (1982).

M. R. Woodward, D. Hedley and M. A. Hennel, "Experience with Path Analysis and Testing of Programs," *IEEE Transactions on Software Engineering,* **23-6**(3), 278–286 (May 1980).

DOROTHY R. GRAHAM
Grove Consultants

TESTING TOOLS

INTRODUCTION

Throughout software development, ultimate product quality directly relates to the engineering process. In recent years, corporations have begun to pay more attention to the benefits of implementing a software development process.

A software development process is the formal process by which program objectives are transformed into program requirements, then into design specifications, implemented into code, tested, and finally placed and maintained in operational status (Boehm and co-workers, 1978). As a result of this increased interest in process, there has been an increase in the application of software test and quality assurance methodologies.

Most methodologies cannot by themselves be applied without some kind of mechanical assistance. In the past, application and operating environments were relatively simple. *Ad-hoc* testing, or manual testing, was usually sufficient to exercise the product fully. Today's applications, however, are much more complex, as are the environments in which they run.

The life span of software products realistically involves multiple versions of the software. Over a single production cycle, a product may have to be tested several times or more. Additionally, as the product undergoes several releases over the course of its lifetime, the total number of times that the software must be tested may be dozens of times. Performing *ad-hoc* testing with today's complex code, results in software that is released without undergoing a well-defined and objective testing procedure.

With code complexity continuing to increase and the need to get new releases out quickly, there is a drive to adopt tools that are practical and efficient. There is no single type of tool available to solve all of an organization's quality assurance needs. The tools you invest in should cover these areas:

Software Measurement. Provides a quantitative number for benchmark comparisons to help predict schedules and quality, and to help allocate resources to areas of code most likely to be error-prone.

Coverage Analysis. Ensures sets of tests are as diverse as possible and that a program is fully tested, measured against a range of high-quality test metrics.

Regression Testing. Automates the running of tests, and verifies the results; is used for initial testing and re-testing during program modifications to verify that modifications have not caused unintended impact.

Test Planning. Assists at the start of software development to make sure that every specified feature is fully tested. Typical features assist test planning by deriving tests from organic diagrams or, if necessary, from live code, i.e., the source text of the programs being tested.

While this order may seem reversed from what makes sense theoretically, it tracks the way most organizations actually introduce automation. This ordering is most often due to a lack of a development process and to a technical or cultural inhibition to use mechanized automation—engineers have to see the benefits with their own eyes before advancing to the next stage.

SOFTWARE MEASUREMENT

In the real world, testing is usually the last thing to do before the software is shipped. Even under the best circumstances, testing is often rushed with little time to be absolutely sure that the testing is complete. The next best thing is to focus testing efforts on the parts of the code that have the greatest potential for defects.

The field of software metrics grew out of the need by programmers and managers to be able to express the characteristics of a piece of software in quantitative terms. For instance, one metric **complexity** is a measure of how difficult or how complex a program may be. Usually the complex parts of a program are the likely places where the defects can be found. Project managers can use complexity metrics to gauge resource allocation based on procedures that are likely to be error-prone.

Metric tools try to measure software complexity not by measuring complexity itself but rather by measuring the degree to which those characteristics thought to lead to complexity exist within a program. For example, a classical measure of software complexity is the number of decision statements in the code.

There are three important stages to determine when considering software measurement:

1. Agreement on the types of metrics to be used
2. Adoption of an economical and accurate tool for measuring software properties
3. Determination of the acceptable ranges of each metric.

Types of Metrics

Because of the interest in measurement, the number of measures have mushroomed to more than one hundred metrics. While opinions on which metrics to use will always differ, some categories of metrics have emerged and remain stable today.

- **Size metrics** establish the size of the source code file. A program's size can be measured by the lines of code, statement count, or function point count. Using size metrics provides a *subjective* idea as to the number of tests needed for a program. These metrics can be very subjective. A count of the number of lines of code, for instance, would not be able to distinguish between simple or complex commands. The count also depends on the printing format. Size metrics can be used for determining effort levels, maintainability and code quality.
- **Software Science metrics** determine how difficult a program might be to work with. These metrics are based on Halstead's theory that all programs are made up of 4 parameters (Halstead, 1977):

n_1=The number of unique operators in a program (e.g., keywords).
n_2=The number of unique operands in a program (e.g., data objects).
N_1=The total number of operators.
N_2=The total number of operands.

Halstead had been able to derive a large number of interesting relationships from these four basic parameters. (See HALSTEAD'S SOFTWARE SCIENCE)

- **Code Complexity Metrics** determine the control-flow or data-flow complexity of a program. These metrics are based primarily on McCabe's cyclomatic complexity metric (McCabe, 1976). (See COMPLEXITY METRICS/ANALYSIS)

Types of Tools Available

Most metric tools work by comparing a source code file to some predefined metric standards, and then generating results. With all of them, time must be allowed to determine software's standard thresholds. Once these are setup, the metric analyzer will point to the code and program functionality that is most likely to have defects.

The following are some of today's metric analyzers: *Hindsight*™, Advanced Software Automation, Inc., Santa Clara, Calif.; *Panorama*™, International Software Automation, Inc., Fremont, Calif.; and *STW/Advisor*™, Software Research, Inc., San Francisco, Calif.

COVERAGE ANALYSIS

Coverage analysis can act as the vehicle to show where testing is incomplete. While there is no way to determine if a test suite can reveal every defect in a program, it is possible to judge test quality by measuring how tests exercise the code. A set of tests is only effective if it achieves some measurable complete criteria. Left to intuition, most testers will under-test software products by 50–75% (Goodenough and McGowan, 1979).

Coverage analyzers attack this problem by giving a numerical value to the completeness of a set of tests. Their purpose is to show what parts of the application have been tested so that test cases can be created that will exercise the parts that were not previously tested.

Types of Coverage Measures

When choosing a coverage analyzer tool it is important to determine what type of coverage information is required for your application's effectiveness. Runtime coverage information can be obtained for many different levels, but the four most common are

Statement (or line): Shows which statements in the program have been exercised. The goal is to execute all statements in the program at least once. This is the easiest coverage strategy to achieve.

Branch: Measures the number of times branches have been exercised both True and False. This analyzer tool is used most often for detailed unit testing of systems of up to several hundred functions/modules.

Call-Pair: Measures the number of times call-pairs have been exercised. It is for system interface coverage checking to make sure every interface is fully exercised. This is a procedure-to-procedure coverage metric.

Path: Measures the number of times each path or path class in a module was exercised. A path is a set of branches in which the program logic follows.

The four coverage techniques work because they disambiguate an activity that for too long has relied on programmer and/or tester intuition. The process focuses attention on untested parts of programs, and this is where the latent defects lie. Depending on the application, a tool should be selected that provides coverage at least at the branch and path levels.

Statement coverage is accepted as the minimum testing requirement and is best used at the unit level for applications with less than 5,000 lines of code. For testing to be effective, 100% coverage is preferable. Done at the unit level, it forces one to decide what code should be left untested.

Roughly speaking, statement coverage is only about 50% as effective as branch coverage. The reason: statement coverage does not account for structural statements among the statements. Eighty percent statement coverage does not mean that 80% of the statements in each path were executed (how were the remaining 20% avoided); therefore, the number of paths that were executed is indeterminate.

Since paths, not statements *per se*, transform input into output, statement coverage is not a strong coverage measure.

Branch coverage is most effective for control-flow testing at the unit level. Increased branch coverage tends to find single-segment faults, and the detection method is straightforward: simple wrong output most of the time. It is desirable to obtain at least 85% branch coverage.

Call-pair coverage is best used for system testing. Call-pair coverage tends to identify interface errors—which are almost always self-evident when the caller-callee relationship is actually exercised. Experience suggests that call-pair coverage reduces interface defects by a factor of three-to-five. Other things being equal, call-pair coverage is around a fifth as difficult to obtain per KLOC as branch coverage. Call-pair coverage, attained at a 90% or better level, will add approximately 25% more defect detections to branch coverage testing.

For critical modules—usually a selected percent of the total volume of an application—path coverage can be used to extend coverage close to the practical limit. This can be a very tricky process, so it is often limited to a few functions or applications with life-criticality, such as medical products and real-time controllers.

Completing a set of path tests can take 8 to 10 times as much work as it takes to get branch coverage for the same volume of code, but the result is more effective. Defect detection efficiencies at 90% or better have been observed, even with path coverage limited to ~75%. It should be noted that a 100% complete path-coverage test set constitutes a set of tests that match one-for-one.

The advantage of coverage analysis, however, is not without cost. Typically, one has to figure on adding 10% to 20% to the software development process cost. This cost may sound high, but the payoff in earlier defect discoveries is very often worth 10 times the cost in savings because defects do not have to be found in a later life-cycle stage (Miller, 1993).

Effectiveness of Coverage Analysis

The effect on tester productivity is impressive. By showing the instantaneous coverage in real-time, 2 kinds of effect can be observed:

- The tester can concentrate quickly on the less well-tested parts of the program. This effect increases test efficiency.
- The tester can identify which program parts relate to what is going on dynamically inside the application— an entirely new capability that tends to minimize test redundancy.

Closing the feedback loop—making it as easy as possible for programmers and/or testers to complete the test process will improve productivity. Many coverage analyzers have provided good results in early applications of dynamic test visualization, in which flow charts and call trees are animated with coverage data that is generated in real-time. This kind of animation shows very quickly what is and what is not being exercised in a set of tests. In addition, the dynamic displays make the testing process more interesting.

Coverage Analyzer Tools

In selecting a coverage analyzer tool, bear in mind that the purpose of coverage analysis is to identify where test cases did not exercise code. A coverage analysis tool should be used with proper test case selection techniques. In other words, do not use the unexercised code to come up with test cases that will force higher coverage values. Instead, look for those that will execute the unexercised code.

Test coverage tools gather usage statistics on programs as they are being exercised. This analysis is usually accomplished by instrumenting the code while it is being compiled. This means that the compiler will add code that will, when executed, record those parts of the source code that were traversed. What is recorded differs from tool to tool. Most tools record the number of times each line, branch, call-pair or path is exercised. These tools often produce an annotated listing of the source code, clearly showing what was covered by the tests.

Some of the current state-of-the-art coverage analyzers available are *Logiscope*™, Verilog, Inc., USA Headquarters, Dallas, Tex.; Worldwide Headquarters Verilog S.A., Toulouse, France; *STW/Coverage*™, Software Research, Inc.; San Francisco, Calif.; *The McCabe Tools*™, McCabe and Associates, Columbia, Md.; and *ViSTA*™, VERITAS Software, Santa Clara, Calif.

REGRESSION TESTING

Once the metric and coverage analyzer tools have been used correctly, regression test tools can be used to automate the re-running of tests. For regression testing to be most effective, a strong set of tests (e.g., one that is known to attain a high set of coverage values) should be available to be run with a single command whenever even a very small change to the product has been made (see also REGRESSION TESTING).

Most of the time, the regression tests turn up no new defects, but this is good news—and an effective confidence builder on the part of developers, testers, and product managers. When regression tests do find new defects, the investment costs in constructing the tests is more than justified by the ease (and low cost) with which the defect has been found.

Regression testing involves three main activities:

1. Capturing a test for replay.
2. Comparing new outputs (responses) with old outputs (baselines) to make sure that there are no unwanted changes.
3. Running collections of 1 and 2 sequences automatically, in the background, at a low priority. In many instances, for the true value of regression testing to be realized, some fairly sophisticated programming of the test suite must be done.

Capture and playback tools are intended to simulate a user's keystrokes or mouse movements. The tester records a session, and during the recording decides on some data to save by capturing one or more screen or screen fragments. All activities are saved to an editable script. When played back, scripts wait for expected responses, such as the appearance of menus, before proceeding. Ideally, capture/playback tools should have multiple synchronization methods for playback, not simply replicate the timing of the original input. Synchronization is necessary, as response times may vary as the system load changes or the hard disk becomes fragmented.

Comparison tools monitor the screen to compare expected results with actual results. Baseline and response files generated by tests are rarely identical, but it is rare that their differences are significant. A test case passes when actual and expected outputs are the same; a test case fails when outputs are different. Some capture/playback tools provide a comparison capability to compare during the execution of the test.

Problems arise when the user wants tests with unwanted differences to pass through, and to keep tests that should fail from succeeding incorrectly. The answer lies in programmable differencing engines, where the exceptions to be ignored are programmed in by a user-supplied control script. Differences can be masked by byte, word, line, window and pattern specifications. The ability to mask out details in saved windows by specifying a special mask file is important.

The most effective way to organize a set of atomic tests, i.e., test scripts that yield a pass or fail result, is to control them under an execution controller that provides the appropriate kind of logging and other supporting recordkeeping. Regression test suites tend to be large, and as a result it is important to have a tree structure and conditional evaluation capability built into the regression test processor. Once a test suite is organized, it can be re-used across multiple software releases and can be ported, along with the software, to multiple platforms.

In addition to capture/playback, comparison and test suite management, regression tools should provide a programming language to allow for logical evaluation, such as IF, ELSE, and WHILE conditions.

Effectiveness

The measure of effectiveness of regression testing is twofold:

1. How hard it is to construct and maintain the suite?
2. How reliably does the system run, check, and correctly identify actual errors? This is sometimes very difficult to handle because it can be tedious to program the test oracle differencing system to get the right effect.

Two factors make it possible to obtain good results from this kind of testing:

1. The ability to adapt the processing of each atomic test to changing conditions, through programmability of the test suite process itself.
2. The willingness to invest minimum amounts so that the initial test suite can assist in stabilizing the software development. This small investment is good when a product is not quite stable enough to justify the use of regression tools. One should use other means to determine that a product's behavior is fairly predictable before using regression test tools.

There are numerous cases where test suites with tests numbering in the thousands are run for days or weeks at a time, effectively trading inexpensive machine time for expensive tester salary and producing defect detections at very low per-defect cost.

Regression Test Tools

Some of today's automated regression test tools are *AutoTester*™, Software Recording Corporation, Dallas, Tex.; *Ferret*™, Tiburon Systems, Inc., San Jose, Calif.; *QA Partner*™, Segue Software, Inc., Newton Center, Mass.; *SQA:Robot*™, Software Quality Automation, Inc., Lawrence, Mass.; *STW/Regression*™, Software Research, Inc., San Francisco, Calif.; *XRunner*™, Mercury Interactive Corporation, Santa Clara, Calif.

TEST PLANNING

Test support systems that address the test planning function have to somehow automate manual functions so "intuitively satisfying" interaction ensues. One hundred percent mechanical generation of test plans and data—even if it were possible—tends to produce either unbelievable or ineffectively complex structures. In fact, sorting through the sometimes enormous complexity of a system's structure is the main challenge.

In all types of software life cycles, the organic information that exists in the early stages of product development should serve as the base for developing test plans which demonstrate that the system works properly. This strategy appears to be the best route for augmenting the test planning activity with quality automated support.

Functionality

Test planning systems should consist of the following features:

- The ability to construct a test tree that can be used directly by program testers to produce a set of tests that are reasonably small and cover all of the requirements. Starting with the requirements document (or even a manual page), individual passages are highlighted and linked to the test plan, which itself grows as the process continues. At the end, one has a tree-structured test plan and a set of relations in the database that connect every phase and group of phases to one or more tests.
- The ability to create random selections of cases and the ability to generate all possible combinations of data, if that is necessary.

Types of Tools

Test planning automation remains rich for application development. Success is relatively easy, but metrics of success are more difficult. A great deal appears to depend on the level of commitment of the user; even the most-skilled user can have a bad day and leave out a major section of the test plan. Automated test planning attempts to overcome this human limitation in a variety of ways. The idea is that by systematizing and automating the test planning process the result is more complete and more effective.

Automation support for software test planning in contemporary software support products can take many forms, depending on:

1. The nature of the information on which the test plan itself is going to be based.
2. The type of test plan format or structure that is to be produced.

It is important to point out that, when it is done correctly, the test plan will feed directly into the regression test system. This closes the loop of the test life-cycle in a very efficient way.

Test Plan Template

The most common types of test planning systems employ a **test plan template** that the user fills out in a kind of interview process with a software specification or requirements expert. This may be the software tester himself.

Using the template assures that the result (i.e., the test plan) is in the right format and, given reasonable care, good test plans with few gaps can be produced.

Semi-Formal Language Description

Another kind of product operates without requiring specific mechanical contact with a design expression, but creates the test plan through use of a mini-language. The user must understand the requirements on the system and express the impact these requirements have on a test suite in a semi-formal language (i.e., like a programming language). After the description is complete (something that through automated processing can be analyzed and reported to the test developer), the test plan is in strong enough form that actual test cases (test instances) can be generated automatically. Generated this way, assuming good attention to detail in understanding the actual specifications when the high-level descriptions are written, an experienced test planner can generate a fairly effective test plan. However, combinatoric growth in the number of test states is a possible limiting factor.

Cause-Effect Graphing

A different approach is to base tests on a logical description of the system being tested through use of a **cause-effect graph,** or **CEG.** Briefly, a CEG is a set of logical implications whose input states are named after the input states of the software product being tested, and whose output states are names describing its expected outputs. (Expected outputs can be error states as well as normal output values.)

The CEG description uses regular logical operations, such as and, or, exclusive-or, not, etc. In addition, the user can make use of collective logic operators, such as zero-or-one-of, or at-least-two-of, or one-and-only-one-of to complete the test-plan description. In some cases it is helpful to draw a picture or even to edit a picture that shows how the causes logically imply the effects.

This description is analyzed automatically and all of the logically feasible and meaningful combinations can be listed. This list forms the test plan because each input/output combination represents one of the required behaviors of the product being tested.

Programmable Solution

A final type of system that is finding effective use involves applying **programming techniques,** typically, using a language patterned after BASIC or C. The user describes the inputs to the program being tested and specifies how to decide if the output actually generated is acceptable. To employ this technique requires, of course, fairly detailed knowledge of what the product is supposed to do. The result is a group of test scripts that drive the product, evaluate the result, and report on test effectiveness.

Test Planning Tools

Some of today's automated test planning tools include: *DEC Test Manager*™, Digital Equipment Corporation, Maynard, Mass.; *SofFeSt*™, Bender and Associates, Larkspur, Calif.; *StateMate*™, I-Logix, Burlington, Mass.; *STW/Advisor & STW/Regression* Software Research, Inc., San Francisco, Calif.; *T*™, Interactive Development Environments, San Francisco, Calif.; and *Test*™, MicroSoft, Inc., Redmond, Wash.

OTHER TESTING TOOLS

The tools mentioned in this article are the most commonly used testing tools today. There are other tools that are part of the testing area which are either niche-oriented or are just starting to become popular. Examples of these types of tools include:

Test Harness Tools: These tools automatically create a test harness to execute a piece of code which is not complete, or for testing a single function of an existing program.

Error Tracking Tools: Many companies have built their own error tracking systems. Over the past two years a number of companies have released commercially available error tracking systems that interface with test systems, so that when errors are discovered they can be reported and tracked.

Test Case Generators: These tools automatically generate the data and in some cases the actual tests based on requirements specifications or design information.

Over time, more and more of the testing process will be automated with tools. As companies gain experience in a formal QA process their needs will be better defined and appropriate tools will be developed in house or by third parties if they have more generic applicability.

TRADEMARKS

AutoTester is a trademark of Software Recording Corporation. DEC Test Manager is a trademark of Digital Equipment Corporation. Ferret is a trademark of Tiburon Systems, Inc. Hindsight is a trademark of Advanced Software Automation. Logiscope is a trademark of Verilog, Inc. Panorama is a trademark of International Software Automation, Inc. QA Partner is a trademark of Seque Software, Inc. SofTest is a trademark of Bender and Associates. SQA:Robot is a trademark of Software Quality Automation, Inc. StateMate is a trademark of I-Logix. STW, STW/Advisor, STW/Coverage and STW/Regression are trademarks of Software Research, Inc. T is a trademark of Interactive Development Environments. Test is a trademark of MicroSoft, Inc. The McCabe Tools are trademarks of McCabe and Associates. ViSTA is a trademark of VERITAS Software Corporation. XRunner is a trademark of Mercury Interactive Corporation.

BIBLIOGRAPHY

B. Beizer, *Software Testing Techniques,* Van Nostrand Reinhold Co., Inc., New York, 1990.

B. W. Boehm, J. R. Brown, H. Kasper, M. Lipow, G. J. Macleod, and M. J. Merrit, *Characteristics of Software Quality,* North-Holland Publishing Company, Amsterdam-New York-Oxford, 1978.

R. H. Dunn, *Software Defect Removal,* McGraw-Hill, Inc., New York, 1984.

J. B. Goodenough and C. L. McGowan, "A Survey of Program Testing Issues," *Research Directions in Software Technology,* MIT Press, Cambridge, Mass., 1979.

W. Harrison, K. Magel, R. Kluczny, and A. DeKock, A., "Applying Software Complexity Metrics to Program Maintenance," *IEEE Computer,* 65–79 (1982).

M. Halstead, *Elements of Software Science,* Elsevier North Holland, New York 1977.

T. J. McCabe, "A Complexity Measure," *IEEE Transactions on Software Engineering,* 308–320 (1976).

T. J. McCabe, "Structured Testing," U.S. Government Printing Office, Washington, D.C., 1982.

E. F. Miller, "Automated Testing: Experience From the Field," *The Sixth International Software Quality Week Conference Proceedings,* San Francisco, Calif., May 25–28, 1993, Paper 4-A-3.

K. H. Moller and D. J. Paulish, *Software Metrics,* Chapman & Hall Computing, London, 1993.

J. B. Goodenough and C. L. McGowan, "A Survey of Program Testing Issues," *Research Directions in Software Technology,* MIT Press, Cambridge, Mass., 1979.

B. Sundermeier, "A Practical Software Testing Tool Adoption Strategy," *CASE Trends,* (June 1993).

Edward F. Miller
Deborah A. Steiner
George J. Symons
Software Research, Inc.

THAYER, RICHARD E.

Richard H. Thayer, Ph.D., is a Professor of Computer Science at California State University, Sacramento, California, where he develops and teaches a software engineering curriculum. Dr. Thayer travels widely where he consults and lectures on software project management, software requirements engineering, software engineering, and software engineering standards.

Prior to this, he served over 20 years in the U.S. Air Force as a senior officer in a variety of software positions associated with engineering, programming, research, teaching, and management. He has spent his entire professional career in computer science and data processing.

Dr. Thayer is a Senior Member of the IEEE Computer Society and the IEEE Software Engineering Standards Subcommittee. He was chair of the working group that wrote the ANSI/IEEE *Standard for Software Project Management Plans* and is chair on the working group to develop an *IEEE Standards for a Concept of Operations* document. He is an Associate Fellow of the American Institute of Aeronautics and Astronautics (AIAA) where he served on the AIAA Technical Committee on Computer Systems, and he is a member of the Association for Computing Machinery (ACM). He is also a registered professional engineer.

He has a BSEE and an MS degree from the University of Illinois at Urbana (1962) and a Ph.D. from the University of California at Santa Barbara (1979) all in electrical engineering.

He is the author of over 40 technical papers and reports on software project management, software engineering and software engineering standards and an invited speaker at many national and international software engineering conferences and workshops.

BIBLIOGRAPHY

—R. H. Thayer and A. D. McGettrick (eds.), *Software Engineering—An European Perspective,* IEEE Computer Society Press, Los Alamitos, Calif., 1993.

—with M. Dorfman, eds., *System and Software Requirements Engineering,* IEEE Computer Society Press, Los Alamitos, Calif., 1990.

—with W. W. Royce, "Software System Engineering," in R. H. Thayer and M. Dorfman, eds., *System and Software Requirements Engineering,* IEEE Computer Society Press, Los Alamitos, Calif., 1990.

—ed., *Tutorial: Software Engineering Project Management,* IEEE Computer Society Press, Washington, D.C., 1988.

—"Software Engineering Project Management: A Top-Down View," in R. H. Thayer, ed., *Software Engineering Project Man-*

agement, IEEE Computer Society Press, Washington, D.C., 1988.

—with A. B. Pyster, "Guest Editorial: Software Engineering Project Management," *IEEE Transactions on Software Engineering,* **SE-10,** (1), 2–3 (Jan. 1984).

—with A. Pyster and R. C. Wood, "Validating Solutions to Major Problems in Software Engineering Project Management," *Computer,* (Aug 1982).

—with A. B. Pyster and R. C. Wood, "Major Issues in Software Engineering Project Management," *IEEE Transactions on Software Engineering,* **SE-7**(4), 333–342 (July 1981).

—with A. Pyster, and R. C. Wood, "The Challenge in Software Engineering Project Management," *Computer,* (Aug. 1980).

THIRD GENERATION LANGUAGE

See HIGHER ORDER LANGUAGES; PROGRAMMING LANGUAGES.

TOP-DOWN DESIGN

See DESIGN.

TOP-DOWN INTEGRATION

See INTEGRATION TESTING.

TORII, KOJI (1938–)

Koji Torii was born in Osaka, Japan. He received the B.E. and M.E. degrees in communication engineering in 1962 and 1964 respectively, and the Ph.D. degree in electronics engineering in 1967 from Osaka University, Osaka, Japan. In 1967 he joined Electrotechnical Laboratory. Since 1991 he has been a Professor of a newly built national graduate university, "Advanced Institute of Science and Technology, Nara", while also being a Professor of Department of Information and Computer Sciences, Faculty of Engineering Science, Osaka University since 1984.

He has been a member of Editorial Board of *Transactions on Software Engineering,* IEEE and of Software, Computer Languages and the *International Journal of Software Engineering and Knowledge Engineering.* He served on many international conferences/workshops as a program committee member. He was a program co-chair of the 13th International Conference on Software Engineering (ICSE). He has been a member of the ICSE Steering Committee. He received the Inada Award in 1940, the Annual Best paper Awards in 1976 and 1993, respectively from the Institute of Electronics, Information and Communication Engineers (IEICE).

His research interests are software metrics, measurement-centered software development process and environments, software education and GO-game computer program. He is a member of the IEEE, ACM, IEICE, Information Processing Society of Japan (IPSJ), Japan Society for Software Science and Technology (JSSST) and Japanese Society for Artificial Intelligence (JSAI).

TOTAL QUALITY MANAGEMENT

Technical capability is no longer the principal competitive determinant in the computer and software industry. Technical capability is necessary but not sufficient for success. What differentiates the successful from the unsuccessful organization, today, is superior "world-class" systems of work processes that men and women throughout the organization understand, believe in and are a part of. These systems of clear work processes reduce bureaucracy and cycle times, increase responsiveness and innovation, and lower costs thereby assuring product, market and organizational success. This is Total Quality Management:

1. *Quality is an organization-wide process.* Quality is not a specialist function, a department, nor an awareness or testing program alone. It is a disciplined system of customer-connected work processes implemented throughout the organization and integrated with suppliers. High quality products are the result of high quality work processes. After all, if you do not improve the process, you cannot expect substantial improvement in results.
2. *Quality is what the customer says it is.* It is not what a developer, manager or marketeer says it is. If you want to find out about your quality, ask your customer. No one can compress in a market research statistic or defect rate the extent of buyer frustration or buyer delight.
3. *Quality and cost are a sum, not a difference.* They are partners, not adversaries. The quality costs of fixing failures are high compared to quality costs required to properly prevent and assure no such defects. True quality leaders are cost leaders, with 10–20% competitive cost advantages common.
4. *Quality requires both individual and teamwork zealotry.* Quality is everybody's job, but it will become nobody's job without a clear infrastructure that supports both the quality work of individuals and the teamwork among individuals and departments. Too often quality improvement activities become islands without bridges. All the left hands must work effectively with all the right hands.
5. *Quality is a way of managing.* Good management today means empowering the quality knowledge, skills and attitudes of everyone in the organization to recognize that making quality right makes everything else in the organization right. The belief that quality travels under some exclusive national passport, or has some unique geographical or cultural identity, is a myth.
6. *Quality and innovation are mutually dependent.* Quality requires product and process innovation,

and the key to successful new products is to make quality the partner of development from the beginning—not a sweep-up-after mechanism for problems. It is essential to fully include the customer in all phases of development. Paper studies cannot do the job.

7. *Quality is an ethic.* The pursuit of excellence, deep recognition that what you are doing is right, is the strongest human emotional motivator in any organization and is the basic driver in true quality leadership. Quality programs relying solely on cold metrics are never enough.
8. *Quality requires continuous improvement.* Quality is a constantly upward moving target and continuous improvement is an in-line, integral component of everyone's job responsibilities—not a separate activity. This requires more than just "better-than-last-year" internal incremental improvement. The marketplace determines what is world-class performance.
9. *Quality is the most cost-effective, least capital-intensive route to productivity.* Some of the world's strongest organizations have blindsided their competition by concentrating on eliminating their hidden plant or organization; the part that exists to find and fix mistakes and the associated waste. They have done it by changing their productivity concept from the four-letter word, M-O-R-E, by adding the quality leadership four-letter word, G-O-O-D, to create the "more good quality productivity" concept.
10. *Quality is implemented with a total system connected with customers and suppliers.* This is what makes quality leadership real in an organization—the relentless application of the systematic method that makes it possible for an organization to manage its quality and associated costs.

These ten basic benchmarks underpinning the technology of Total Quality Management make quality a way of totally focusing the organization on the competitive discipline of serving the customer—whether it be the end user or the man and woman at the next desk or workstation. They make quality the organization's way of simultaneously achieving market success, employee satisfaction and cost leadership. Perhaps most importantly, they provide the basis for managing the inevitable growth that will result from this strategy in a consistently high quality manner, replicating success after success.

Dr. Feigenbaum is the originator of Total Quality Control (TQC), the management approach that has profoundly influenced the competition for domestic and international markets in the United States, Japan and throughout the industrialized world (see *Total Quality Control*, 40th Anniversary Edition, McGraw-Hill, 1991). He introduced the concept of "Total Quality Management" in the 1983 McGraw-Hill edition of that book. He was also the first to define "Total Quality Costs" in a 1956 Harvard Business Review article entitled, *Total Quality Control*.

Dr. Feigenbaum is President and CEO of General Systems Company, Inc., a Pittsfield, Massachusetts, based international engineering firm which custom designs and implements total quality management systems in major firms throughout the world. Prior to co-founding General Systems with Donald S. Fiegenbaum in 1968, he was worldwide director of manufacturing operations and quality at General Electric. A more complete biography may be found in *Who's Who in America* and *Who's Who in the World*.

ARMAND V. FEIGENBAUM
General Systems Company
Pittsfield, MA

TOTAL QUALITY MANAGEMENT: A DOD PERSPECTIVE

Total Quality Management (TQM) has been popularized by the U.S. Department of Defense (DOD) initiative for continuously improving its performance at every level in every area. It has since become the generic term (and acronym) for a wide variety of improvement initiatives, regardless of their resemblance to the systematic approaches initiated by DOD or those further developed by Deming (1986) and Juran (1986). Improvement is directed at finding both incrementally and innovatively better solutions to such pervasive problems as cost, quality, and schedule. TQM combines fundamental management techniques, existing improvement efforts, and specialized technical skills under a rigorous, disciplined structure focused on continuously improving all organizational processes. It demands commitment and discipline while relying on people and involving everyone.

Figure 1 shows how DOD represents TQM as an integral organizational process. In this process vision is articulated in principles (organizational value structure), reflected by

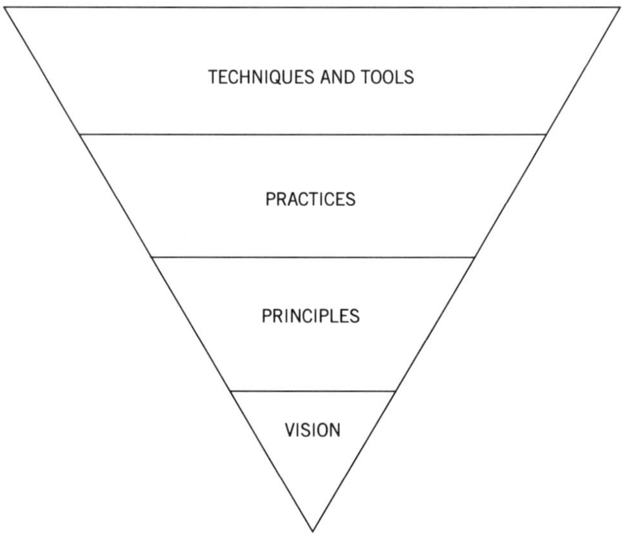

Figure 1. DOD representation of TQM as an integral organizational process.

and achieved in practices by using specific, focused techniques and tools.

VISION

The vision of a quality organization includes the business objective or "rock the organization stands on," and adds to it customer satisfaction, employee empowerment to deliver that satisfaction, supplier inclusion, and measurement to ensure facts are the basis of decisions.

PRINCIPLES

The basic TQM principles include constancy of purpose, customer focus, continuous process improvement, teamwork, and personal improvement.

Constancy of Purpose

Top leadership ensures a strong, pervasive commitment to continuous improvement. A quality culture's leadership produces, communicates, and maintains a common purpose with all personnel. Consistent goals and objectives provide focus and are realized through practicing continuous improvement and recognizing and rewarding behavior aimed at achieving the business objectives of the organization. Cost reduction, schedule compliance, customer satisfaction, and pride in workmanship all flow from an overt dedication to continuous improvement. Commitment to improvement is demonstrated by providing infrastructure and resources, and acting on recommendations to make positive changes. Top leadership must first implement the TQM concepts, practices, techniques and tools, and then let these methods filter down through the organization. Cascading deployment ensures that leaders understand, demonstrate and can coach TQM principles and practices before expecting them from their subordinates.

Customer Focus

Customer response is the absolute test of effectiveness. Although the organization's external customers are the ultimate users of products, many processes also have intermediate customers within the organization. A thorough understanding of the needs of all customers, intermediate or ultimate, not only provides the means of assessing performance, but also helps to focus the organization's future direction and establish its future goals.

Continuous Process Improvement

The primary TQM objective is unending improvement of every aspect of work. That objective is implemented through a systematic, disciplined approach that improves all processes. Emphasis is placed on preventing defects through process improvement rather than discovering them through product inspection. Process knowledge is essential for improvement. Improvement ideas are generated by those who work within a process, since only they thoroughly understand the process. Improvements can be incremental (*kaizen*) or revolutionary (innovation), depending on the process, people, technology, and environment.

Teamwork

Teamwork is essential for continuous improvement by aligning individuals' and groups' goals, objectives, and activities. Team activities build communication and cooperation, stimulate creative thought, and provide an infrastructure supporting TQM practices.

Personal Improvement

Because all products and services are produced through processes, process improvement applies to every individual in the organization. Most organizations' largest and most valuable investment is in its people. They provide the knowledge and experience on which the organization relies. They are the most essential component in continuous process improvement. Training, team-building, personal educational initiative, and empowerment are important elements in creating an environment in which people can grow, gain experience and capability, and contribute to the organization on an ever-increasing scale.

PRACTICES

TQM practices are fundamental management skills applied in a systematic framework. TQM practices can be grouped into planning, process improvement, communications, information and skills building, and supplier involvement.

Planning

Planning practices define the organization's overall direction and align its internal operations with that direction. They include evaluating the needs and desires of external customers who are the ultimate users of the organization's products, and the internal users of intermediate products and services. Deployment of planning ensures constancy of purpose throughout the organization.

Process Improvement

Continuous process improvement is essential for continuing effectiveness. Practices that encourage risk-taking, identify opportunities for improvement, and stimulate innovative ideas are crucial. The key elements in improving a process are its initial definition, documentation, and measurement. Next come incremental process improvements, and the adoption of those improvements that are found to be effective. Innovation through technology or process re-engineering provides breakaway improvements.

Communication

Effective and unfettered vertical and horizontal communication is essential to continuous improvement efforts. TQM practices remove communication roadblocks, facilitating bi-directional communication between leaders and subordinates and among peer groups, and ensuring that goals and objectives are clearly delineated and disseminated throughout the organization and its suppliers. Inconsistent signals can sabotage improvement efforts whether those signals come from leadership, customers, or suppliers. TQM practices reinforce consistent signals; leading by example, assessing performance in the context of mission, vision, plans and improvement; and rewarding appropriate behavior, usually on a team basis, from measured, significant improvement.

Information and Skill Building

Practices are taught and institutionalized in management and workers. Practices include initiating Quality Improvement or Problem Solving Process teams with proven TQM methods and concepts, such as the supplier-customer chain and process thinking.

Supplier Involvement

TQM relies on continuous improvement in acquired products and services as well as in internal processes. TQM practices address the improvement of supplier capabilities through education and technical assistance, and develop more innovative approaches to contracting and acquisition that rely increasingly on supplier continuous improvement, performance and capability.

TECHNIQUES AND TOOLS

TQM techniques and tools comprise a family of process-oriented management technologies. Their purpose is to identify issues and problems, structure and analyze data, address areas of specific concern, focus problem-solving efforts, and amplify understanding of organizational processes. They are the hands-on means for implementing TQM. Techniques and tools may be grouped under the TQM practices they support.

Planning

Planning techniques and tools include surveys, the customer value determination cycle designed to determine real customer value delivered, and plan templates. The customer value determination cycle asks you to project customer values, challenge that projected value, discover the real value, and onfirm the customer value delivered. The templates analyze user needs, expectations, and feedback and deploy them in plans. Levels of plans are documented and deployed using Hoshin planning techniques throughout the organization, its suppliers and customers, so that all employees can participate in achieving the organization's mission and vision in teams and as individuals.

Process Improvement

Process improvement relies on techniques and tools such as the Shewhart improvement cycle and streamlining. Before processes can be standardized, they must be defined and documented. Process analysis techniques provide a means for examining defects, delays and excessive variation. Techniques include the six basic tools (brainstorming, multivoting, Pareto charts, check sheets, flow charts, and force field analysis).

Communications

Tools and techniques include Interactive Skills, Meeting Management, and Expectation Setting ("Catchball" from Hoshin Planning). Recognition and team celebrations help improve the "signals" flowing in the management system. Feedback techniques that assess signals promote understanding of the environment and help to establish a sense of consistency throughout the organization. Positive signals are reinforced through recognition and reward of TQM behaviors.

Information and Skill Building

Specific TQM abilities are improved through various methods. Training exists for communications and problem-solving skills, and TQM supports a process repository (easy access to team improvement results and other activity status), management tools and measurement definitions aimed at more specific capabilities. Benchmarking, Quality Function Deployment (QFD) and other advanced techniques are added as the organization is capable of using them.

Supplier Involvement

Providing TQM information and skill building in relevant TQM tools and techniques is important to ensure supplier dedication to continuous improvement. An organization demonstrates the seriousness of its intent through its collaboration to ensure end customer quality is achieved. Techniques include quality audits and certification programs usually highly dependent on documented processes and control charting by the supplier.

SUMMARY

TQM employs top-down and bottom-up, systematic methodology to achieve the goal of continuous improvement. Measuring progress is the basis for evaluating the success of TQM efforts. TQM goals will always reflect measurable improvement in business mission achievement, rather than "hygiene factors." A process improvement cycle provides the means for translating needs into practice. After the processes by which work is accomplished are identified and defined, relevant measurement points are specified, and opportunities for improvement documented and prioritized. The most promising solutions are implemented, and their effectiveness is monitored.

If they are found to be ineffective, new solutions are tried. The process improvement cycle continues identifying opportunities for improvement, implementing solutions and monitoring their effectiveness. Shewhart's Plan-Do-Check-Act cycle shown in Figure 2 is the prototype.

Some have said TQM means empowering employees and doing away with quality assurance (QA). Ishikawa (1985) says we have to be skeptical of any claims, numbers, or other reported measurements, internal or external. This

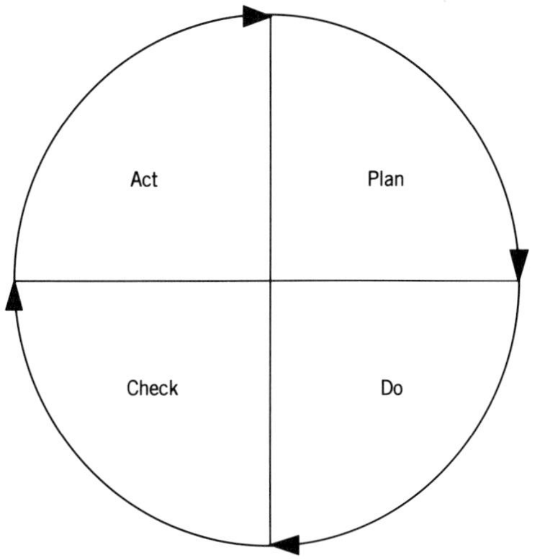

Figure 2. Shewhart's Improvement Cycle

means QA will exist under TQM although what it finds will be measurably fewer defects, delays, and aberrations from process standards.

The Software Engineering Institute (SEI) Example

The SEI is a Federally Funded Research and Development Center located at Carnegie Mellon University (CMU). It was established to (1) bring expertise and effective technology to bear on the rapid improvement of the quality of operational software in systems that depend on software, (2) accelerate the transition of state of art to state of practice in software engineering techniques and tools, (3) promulgate the use of techniques and tools throughout the United States software community, and (4) establish standards of excellence for software engineering practice. In 1992, CMU was adopted by Xerox as part of the University Challenge by Malcolm Baldrige National Quality Award winners to assist in its evolution to a quality culture. The SEI had been involved in developing TQM techniques and tools for the software community for almost five years, and had been pursuing a Juran Institute approach to its internal quality improvement initiative, but transitioned to adopt the Xerox methods within a few months.

The Xerox experience began with training in interactive skills and meeting management (IAS/MM) in April 1992. This was applied to executive meetings immediately with measurable reductions in their duration and increases in participants' satisfaction. A trip with CMU top administrators to a June week's awareness and preliminary training in concepts led to adoption of the Learn-Understand-Train-Improve (LUTI) approach for training all SEI employees in IAS/MM which took place between June and September, 1992. In addition, a pilot process team was begun using Xerox's Quality Improvement and Problem Solving Process methods (QIP/PSP) to address problems with travel reimbursement. This joint University/SEI team developed practices that reduced the average waiting time for reimbursement from 22 to 4 days.

Parallel to the five months' team effort, an assessment of the SEI culture was performed using traditional organizational dynamics instruments (surveys) employed by SEI during software improvement programs to ensure the organizational climate is appropriate for change to occur. The results in November were that the SEI mission, vision, and values (principles) were not widely known nor used in decision making, and communications were ineffective top-down and bottom-up. To ensure executives understood and signaled their determination to apply TQM principles, practices, and techniques, the five directors, their 13 direct reports, and five process team facilitator trainees were trained by Xerox in QIP/PSP practice and techniques in November and as part of the training, a prototype action plan was developed to implement TQM at SEI. The formal plan provided 2.6% of the 1993 budget for quality culture change activities and was released in December, 1992. The methods employed to plan also led to a realization that for improvements to "stick" at SEI, substantial infrastructure needed to be put in place. The plan called for establishing a Management Steering Committee for Process Improvement (MSCPI) to charter and guide process teams that were organization-wide in scope, to hire a full time "mechanic" to ensure that techniques and tools were properly implemented and to engage the directors and whole SEI in TQM practices (Deming's (1986) chapt. 16). The MSCPI was established in February, 1993 with cross-divisional and top to bottom (director to techies and support staff) representation. The TQM mechanic was hired in March 1993. In addition, a strategic planning session using elected (10% of the SEI) delegates and the directors was called for September, 1993 to redefine the mission, vision, and values of the SEI in line with TQM vision and principles.

The directors started three SEI-wide process teams (Dec. 1992, March 1993, and May 1993) while waiting for the MSCPI to organize, define its processes, request suggestions from the organization at large for process teams, and charter an initial three. The directors' teams included support staff issues on physical space; improved communications, utilization, and development; identifying the value of the SEI to the software community. The MSCPI's teams include performance evaluation (July 1993), project management (Aug. 1993), and product development life cycle planning (Sept. 1993). In the meantime, the value of the SEI process team had completed so the directors planned and initiated an executive team to work on the output and efficiency of the SEI (July 1993).

The TQM mechanic supported most of the above activities as logistics and coordination agent, but also spent time with customers and directors working on measurement issues. The quarterly reviews of programs now include program (a set of projects which develop multiple, related products) measures of success including: how does the program support achieving the SEI mission, how much does the program contribute to achieving the SEI mission, current status and trends in product technology transition (where on the technology adoption curve is each programs' product offerings), and what is the leverage achieved by the products and activities (e.g., consulting is 1:1, one SEI employee and one improved customer; training and mentoring methods is 1:10; technical reports, conference papers, and tutorials are 1:100; and televised or videotaped distribution channel courses are 1:1000).

Current efforts include improving communications via consistent use of electronic mail, electronic bulletin boards, and identifying employees' preferred mechanisms for discovering current and future events; and using the University of Tennessee's net customer value determination approach to estimate project impacts and select future products from those identified out of customer needs studies. Planned late 1993 internal efforts include transitioning to empowerment via peer reviews/inspections instead of relying on iterative quality reviews before product release; Xerox's Management By Fact (Hoshin Planning) method; communications improvements from Chris Argyris's techniques; and other University-wide improvement team and technique application efforts.

Infrastructure continues to be built by offering IAS/MM (97% of employees trained by July, 1993 despite a 10% intentional annual turnover rate), a seven basic and seven advanced tools and techniques brown bag seminar also available as a one day course, monthly QIP/PSP training, and advanced training in benchmarking, Hoshin planning, customer satisfaction identification, and empowerment techniques from Xerox, plus QFD internal training by employees. The directors also provide first item status for quality issues on their weekly meeting and periodic staff meeting agendas, and take a leading role in visibly promoting and rewarding TQM activity by employees. The Worklife Council (strategic planning and follow-on organizational capability improvements) has already had impact opening the organization to changed modes of operation.

The SEI transformation has begun with strong top leadership constancy of purpose; slow, but steady infrastructure growth; directed CPI through process teams; focused training; a good supplier partnership with Xerox; and a culture that already works to instill change in our customers. The test of time for any initiative is long term results which usually take years. If initial measured improvement is any indicator, then the SEI will be well on its way to world class in as few as three to five years.

Article was adapted from DOD5000.51G, *Total Quality Management Implementation Guide.*

BIBLIOGRAPHY

AT&T, *Quality Manager's Handbook,* AT&T Customer Information Center, Indianapolis, Ind., 1990, code 500-442.

AT&T, *Process Quality Management and Improvement Guidelines,* vol. 1, AT&T Customer Information Center, Indianapolis, Ind., 1987, code 500-049.

M. Brassard, *Memory Jogger Plus+*, GOAL/QPC, Methuen, Mass., 1989.

P. B. Crosby, *Quality is Free,* New American Library, Bergenfield, N.J., 1979.

W. E. Deming, *Out of Crisis,* MIT Press, Cambridge, Mass., 1986.

DOD 5000.51-G, Total Quality Management Guide, U.S. Dept. of Defense, Washington, D.C., 1989, vol. 1, available from National Technical Information Service, Springfield, Va. as part of TQM "Care Package".

K. Ishikawa, *What is Total Quality Control? The Japanese Way,* Prentice-Hall, Englewood Cliffs, N.J., 1985.

J. Juran, *Juran on Leadership for Quality,* McGraw-Hill Co., Inc., New York, 1986.

P. Scholtes, *The Team Handbook,* Joiner Associates, Madison, Wisc., 1988.

M. Stahl and G. Bounds, *Competing Globally Through Customer Value,* Greenwood Press, West Haven, Conn., 1991.

PETER MALPASS
ANNE WULFFRAAT
Software Engineering Institute

TOTAL QUALITY MANAGEMENT IN SOFTWARE DEVELOPMENT

INTRODUCTION

This article describes the application of Total Quality Management (TQM) methods and principles to the software development environment. Its purpose is

- to provide an introduction to TQM for software development staff
- to describe the processes needed to achieve TQM
- to illustrate the practical application of the processes through a case study

The use of TQM to gain a competitive advantage is fast becoming an acceptable practice and has been well-proven in many countries throughout the world. Probably, more has been written on the subject of quality than on any other topic in recent years. The focus of TQM is on the management of an organization and covers a wide spectrum of topics from human psychology through to business management. It is not the intention of this article to cover such a broad spectrum; there are many books and articles already available, some of which are referenced in the bibliography section. Rather, this article is an attempt to provide an overview in a language to which software developers can relate to and to put the processes of TQM into the context of their development activities.

The application of TQM to software development is very much in its infancy, (Bryan and Siegel, 1988). In the main, only the largest and most successful Information Technology companies have achieved success in translating the TQM methods and practices to the software industry.

This article aims to stimulate increased interest and provide some guidelines for the further establishment of TQM in the software development environment.

THE NEED FOR IMPROVEMENT

Competitive Pressures

The business world is an extremely competitive place. Further, the breaking down of trade barriers, the improvements in world-wide communications and the development of large international companies has produced even fiercer competition. *Only the strong survive* has never been a truer statement than at present in the industrial world.

Throughout the 1970s and 1980s, the Japanese have developed a reputation of providing high quality goods at competitive prices (Garvin, 1988) and, as a result, they have captured a significant percentage of world trade. Consequently, companies must make and sustain improvements in costs and the quality of goods and services in order to remain competitive.

Customer Satisfaction

The real motivation behind the need for improved quality of products and services comes from the customer base that is far more demanding than in the past. No longer do people accept shoddy goods that require a high level of repair and maintenance. Caring for customers gives an organization a distinct advantage over its competitors. Acquiring a new customer is more costly than retaining an existing one and so caring for current customers is paramount. Conversely, customer dissatisfaction can be very damaging. Few dissatisfied customers complain; the vast majority of them simply take their business elsewhere. *"No news is good news,"* is a dangerous attitude to adopt. The competitive advantage gained by companies offering customer satisfaction is highlighted by many contemporary writers on business management. Deming supports the argument that a satisfied customer will recommend other business (Deming, 1986); Peters and Waterman quote a number of case studies of successful companies that have achieved success through a focus on customer satisfaction (Peters and Waterman, 1982).

The Management of Change

Significant improvements only come about by fundamental changes in the way organizations are managed and by modifying the attitudes of the work-force. Recognition of the need for change is the first step in making it happen. Strong, credible threats are an effective way to promote change in attitudes. For instance, an ultimatum from a valued customer to improve product quality or lose the business is a strong motivation to change. The customer is an attractive and credible communication source and is likely to be perceived as an opinion leader. In addition, vision from the chief executive is also a powerful initiator of change.

Notwithstanding the need for improved customer satisfaction, modern technology, particularly that made available through Information Technology, creates an environment of continuous change, both in terms of customer demands and in the tools and methods used to produce goods. This scenario is especially true in the software industry where new tools and methods appear to arrive at a faster rate than it takes to train staff in their use! The exploitation of Information Technology has increased demands for more and more software solutions; but the software industry has been unable to keep pace with these demands. As a consequence, the need to manage change within the software development environment in a controlled manner is critical to the success of an organization.

WHY QUALITY?

Before commencing a discussion on *why quality?*, a definition is required. In a subjective sense, quality is described in various ways: *goodness, expense, excellence, luxury, value for money, attractiveness, prestige, comfort, satisfaction,* and so on. All of these terms lack sufficient clarity to allow the effective management of quality improvement.

The ISO definition of quality is

> *The totality of features and characteristics of a product or service that bears on its ability to satisfy stated or implied needs (ISO8402, 1986)*

This definition provides the degree of objectivity that is essential for TQM to work and recognizes the problem that requirements are not always well articulated by including the reference to implied needs; there is an expectation that products and services will satisfy industrial and social norms. A product or service is defined as being *quality* if it fully satisfies the needs. This abstraction is often stated as **conformance to requirements** (Crosby, 1979).

The concepts of TQM originated in the western world, predominantly in the U.S. through the pioneering work of the quality "gurus" such as Juran, Deming, and Feigenbaum (Bendell, 1991). Japanese industry was the first to realize the benefits of TQM and to adopt the ideas; however, throughout the 1980s, many companies in the U.S. and Europe had started to apply TQM principles in order to compete world-wide in business. The motivation for change has been helped considerably by quantifying the benefits into the language of money (Crosby, 1979). This measurement is known as the *cost of quality* and there are a number of ways in which it can be used:

- To quantify the costs of chronic waste: Software that fails to be delivered falls into this category. Fifteen per cent of software that is written is never used (DeMarco, 1982).
- To quantify the benefits of using preventive techniques to avoid problems rather than using appraisal methods and to remove defects before customer delivery. Studies have shown that the cost of prevention is less than the cost of appraisal. Appraisal methods are typically "review and test" to check for the existence of defects, followed by corrective action.

The cost of quality is one area where the experts differ in their views on a definition and on the value of such a measurement. Some relate the costs as a percentage of sales (Crosby, 1979), while others as a percentage of operating costs (Smith, 1987). Typically, cost of quality figures ignore the intangible but very real loss of goodwill from a customer. Deming is not an advocate of quality costing (Deming, 1986). However, there is irrefutable evidence that a quality-led approach to continuous improvement has positive benefits to a company.

By implementing a TQM system, a company will be able to:

Table 1. Analysis of the Composition of Software Development Organizations

Organization	Company A[a]	Company B[b]	Company C[c]
General managers (including CEO)	12	5	1
Personnel, finance and administration	21	26	5
Support services	21	5	1
Software engineers	207	88	17
Total	261	124	24
Software engineers as a percentage of total work force	79	71	71

[a]Software development group within a large computer manufacturing organization.
[b]Medium-sized software house.
[c]Small software house.

- prevent problems occurring
- reduce costs
- pro-actively manage change
- meet customer requirements
- increase customer satisfaction
- remain competitive

As illustrated by Table 1, within a typical software development organization, about 25% of the staff employed by the organization are not involved in the production of the software; for example, the chief executive, secretaries, accountants, personnel officers, computer services administration, etc. Thus, an organization may employ 75% of its staff as software engineers, assuming of course that the organization is a development laboratory without sales and marketing staff. (The term "Software Engineer" is used within this article to identify any individual who is trained and qualified in one or all of the development disciplines for the production and maintenance of software systems.) Maintenance typically accounts for 40% of the development costs (Boehm, 1981), and so only 45% of the available resource is actively working on development. Further studies show that these staff are spending 50% or less of their time actually working on design, coding and debugging, the remainder being spent on a miscellany of tasks (Brooks, 1975). Thus, an organization only spends 22% of its effort directly on software development. Although admirable, the efforts of the software engineering activities will not improve the productivity nor the quality of the remaining 78% of the organization's effort.

A BRIEF HISTORY OF QUALITY MANAGEMENT IN SOFTWARE DEVELOPMENT

One main difference between the software industry and other general industries is that the software industry is relatively very young. It is attempting to reach in 30 years a stage of maturity that has taken some industries over 200 years to achieve. Table 2 illustrates the ages of quality and provides a comparison between software and general industry. Of course, the stage any particular company has reached will vary a great deal.

Quality methods have existed since the days of the master craftsman and of the cottage industries prior to the industrial revolution. The ages indicate when a major shift was made in the general approach to achieving a level of quality in the products and services being supplied. Prior to the industrial revolution, the consumer society was very much restricted to the wealthy few who were prepared to pay premium prices for master craftsmen to make bespoke products. Quality control was achieved by the judgement of the craftsman and by individual customer acceptance (sounds a lot like software development now!).

The industrial revolution introduced mass-production that created a much larger consumer market and it also introduced the need to change the method of the control of quality. Inspection was introduced whereby all products were checked by a supervisor for conformance to a standard, before being shipped. The check may have involved precise measurement with the use of calibration equipment or it may have been judgmental (for example, a supervisor in a clothes' mill would apply a subjective standard to the stitching in a garment). (Likewise, software inspections have been predominantly subjective peer reviews as well). The increase in production rates meant that the inspection of every item being produced was no longer viable. This situation was resolved by the development of statistical sampling techniques (Grant, 1946), a procedure that reduced costs. Software quality metrics is a subject that has created a great deal of interest within the industry but their practical use in the control of product output has been very limited. The Process Maturity framework developed at the Software Engineering Institute (Humphrey, 1988) defines 5 process levels from "Initial" (level 1) up to "Optimizing" (level 5). Levels 4 and 5 are defined as using "process measurement" and "process control" respectively but no software organization has yet been recognized as reaching these levels across all its operations. As a way of reducing inspection costs further, the establishment of Quality Control Systems has ensured that production methods have been consistent. Hopefully, a consistent quality of product has been achieved as well. Standards have been introduced by organizations such as the British Ministry of Defence (DEF STAN 05-21/1) and NATO (AQAP-1), based on the best practices of the successful industrial companies. Specific standards were produced for the software industry (AQAP-13). The ISO standard for quality systems (ISO 9001) and its software derivative (ISO 9000-3) have been an evolution of these earlier standards.

In the last ten years, there has been a rapid acceleration in defining different approaches to the production of quality products that can all be categorized loosely as *Total*

Table 2. The Ages of Quality

Stage	Description	Software industry	General industry
Craftsmanship	Relies on creativity and good workmanship	1960s	pre-1800
Inspection	Supervisor checks quality prior to output	1970s	1800s
Statistical process control	Quantification of product quality; sampling techniques	Little evidence of use	1930s
Quality assurance	Use of quality system standards for processes	1980s	1950s
Conformance quality	Use of TQM to eliminate waste and save costs	1990s	1980s
Customer driven quality	Use of TQM to focus on customer care and service	Little evidence of use	1990s
Market driven quality	Focus on potential as well as existing customers	Little evidence of use	Some evidence of use

Quality Management. "Conformance quality" concentrates on meeting requirements and reducing waste within an organization. "Customer driven quality" pays attention to improving customer satisfaction, and "Market driven quality" focuses on beating the competition. Each age supplements the methods from the earlier ages that continue to be practised where appropriate.

WHAT IS TOTAL QUALITY MANAGEMENT?

Definition

The term *Total Quality Management* (TQM) is reputed to have been first adopted by the US Naval Air Systems Command as recently as 1985, to describe the Japanese-style management approach to continuous improvement. Prior to this, the term Total Quality Control had been attributed to Feigenbaum and was used as the title for his book (Feigenbaum, 1983). TQM is now widely used and is beginning to appear in many publications (Oakland, 1989). There is no universally agreed definition of TQM. Consider the following:

Total In the context of TQM, total is interpreted as meaning the involvement of everything and everyone in continuous improvement. The benefits of the improvement initiatives will be maximized if they impact all work processes; all staff operating these processes and the processes themselves, are regularly reviewed against the changing environment.

Management In the industrial world, there is a tendency to put people into compartments. Traditional conventions determine that *managers* organize, plan and regulate; *staff* (workers) cope, obey, etc. The modern approach is for managers to provide *leadership* and *support;* staff to be given *responsibility* and *trust* to carry out their tasks and duties in a professional manner. *Supervision* should be considered as a training aid and not a control process. *Management* in the quality sense is that which allows everyone to succeed in their aims. It is about the actions that are needed to plan, organize and regulate tasks. The term *manager* will continue to be used in this article to distinguish the supervisors from the *software engineers.*

Consider any organization. Its assets can be classified into three categories:

- PROCESS (the way things are done; this category includes the methods used to sustain continuous improvement)
- PRODUCT (all outputs from processes; this includes internal products and services such as memoranda, advice, improved skills, and so on in addition to the more obvious design documents produced throughout the software development life cycle and the portfolio of marketable products and services),
- PEOPLE (the individuals who operate the *processes* to produce the *products*) Within TQM, every PROCESS produces a PRODUCT.

The definition of Total Quality Management used by this article is

> *The infrastructure, tools, methods and rules which result in increased business success and customer satisfaction by enabling continuous improvements to people, processes and products.*

The key to achieving permanent improvements is to change the way things are done by removing the causes of mistakes. TQM is about having a system that supports the improvements to all items within these categories in a consistent and complementary fashion. A weak link may be the introduction of new development tools (that is, PRODUCT improvement) without the necessary PEOPLE improvement (say, through training in the use of the tools).

The Elements of a TQM System

A prerequisite to the implementation of TQM is the establishment of sound project management based on the good business practice of effective **planning, measurement, and control.** The operation of a TQM system gives added value by providing a framework for the implementation of improvements. Although the experts differ in their views on how best to implement TQM, there are a number of essential common elements as delineated by Table 3.

These elements are described below.

Continuous Improvement. Recognizing the need for change is the first step to being successful; of course, change need not only come about through the need to recover from poor quality. The entrepreneur with vision will have a head start on the competition. Once having recog-

Table 3. Common Elements of a TQM System

Continuous improvement
Definition of quality
Prevention
Commitment
Team-work
Training and education

nized the need for managing change as a core value to an organization, the next step is to establish a process of continuous improvement. The successful company is the one that intercepts change in a planned manner that prevents problems arising (being pro-active) rather than the less successful company which manages change by reacting to the problems that it causes (being reactive).

Continuous improvement is viewed as a repeatable process rather than a project that implies a defined start and end life (Crosby, 1979). Projects may be created within this process to address specific improvement initiatives (Juran, 1988).

Many attempts have been made in the past to introduce ways of improving quality; some successful and others less so. One major cause of failure has been the fact that the effects of change, once introduced, decay with time or fail to keep up with the competition or changes in requirements. Only deep-rooted cultural changes have brought about permanent and continuous improvements. The time it takes to fully implement TQM must not be underestimated; it typically takes 4 to 5 years (Crosby, 1979). "Throwing money" at a quality problem without a clear plan for where to invest it or without a clear strategy on how to implement change, will inevitably result in failure. However, there have been many successes (Crosby, 1984). For instance, one company's investment in the first year of its TQM implementation to improve the quality of its mainframe operating system, had been fully recovered three years later by reduced maintenance costs which then became a permanent annual saving. A case study on how this savings was achieved has been provided at the end of this article.

Definition of Quality. The need for an objective definition is fundamental in turning the need for improvement into a tangible and meaningful implementation. The definition of quality has been discussed earlier in this article. However, caution needs to be exercised when referring to quality as *conformance to requirements:* This definition can be misinterpreted as the need for a clear and unambiguous written statement of what is required by the customer prior to starting a development. If only life were that simple! Many customers do not know what they want and, even if they think they do, they often change their minds. The use of the phrase *stated or implied* in the ISO definition helps to focus on this issue. An implied requirement on software design could be: to *meet the current and future needs of the user, whether known or not.* The software engineer who is able to preempt changes in requirements in the design of software has a distinct advantage over contemporaries. There are other definitions; for example, Juran uses the term *fitness for purpose* to avoid the misinterpretation of *requirements,* but the intent is the same.

Prevention. *Prevention* is defined as **stopping defects being introduced** as opposed to *appraisal* which is defined as **finding and removing defects.** All tasks are a sequence of actions that can be classified as *prevention* or *appraisal.* Consider the following example. A subset of the actions to produce a module of software is:

- write the code
- static test (for example, clean compile)
- unit test

Any errors found in the unit test activity are the result of the failure to detect them in the static test activity. Consequently, static testing is viewed as prevention and unit test as appraisal. However, any errors found in the static test activity are the result of making mistakes when writing the code. In this case, static testing is appraisal and writing code is prevention. This example illustrates the fact that prevention and appraisal are not absolute but are determined by the scope of a process. In reality, both prevention and appraisal actions are carried out in most processes. The input to the process is appraised for error and actions are taken to prevent errors in the output from the process. Many studies have demonstrated that finding errors early in the development life cycle is more cost-effective than finding them later. Consequently, a preventive approach is appropriate for all activities performed by an organization, whether it be in creative design, planning, review meetings, and so on.

Commitment. For continuous improvement to be successful, not only must every individual play his or her part but top management must support and participate in the process to ensure success. Indeed, it is from the chief executive downwards that the core values should be set because individuals will behave in a way that they perceive as acceptable to their bosses. If quality is unimportant to the chief executive, it is clearly unimportant to the staff. But commitment should not be just a requirement for managers.

The people best positioned to understand processes, the causes of failure and the opportunities for improvements, are the operators (programmers). In a traditional manufacturing environment, the operators are encouraged to provide feedback to the process designers on problems and suggested improvements. In the software development environment, software engineers are in a more influential position to effect direct process change. For example, they are in a position to introduce the use of a software tool that will reduce the opportunity for error.

Team-Work. The previous section has established the principle of individual commitment from the chief executive downwards to all members of an organization. However, very few people work as individuals. Team working is essential for the successful operation of any organization. A team may consist of staff operating the same processes where they can share experiences or it may consist of staff operating a linked chain of activities. In this latter case, it is vital that the output from one process is consistent with the requirements of the input to the next process in the chain. This symmetry is best achieved by co-operation between the two operators.

Training and Education. The importance of training and education cannot be over stressed. A company's biggest asset is its work force. This status is particularly true in the software industry. Conversely, an untrained work force is its biggest liability! Once quality improvement has been established as a core value, training and education in the system to support its implementation is paramount. The ideal environment is where everyone knows what they have to do: they understand how to do it, and the minimum of bureaucracy required to maintain control. Such an environment is only realized by continual investment in training and education.

IMPLEMENTING TQM

Planning Improvements

The first step to planning improvements is for the chief executive to confirm the core values of the organization by the establishment of one or more policy statements. Policy statements are displayed to:

- confirm the company's commitment to quality
- remind all staff of the company's core values

The next step is to establish improvement goals that are achieved in one of two ways. First, initiatives may be generated by any individual or team within an organization (known as a "bottom-up" approach). This approach is based on the principle that many, small improvements will add up to significant reductions in waste and will reduce the failures to meet requirements (Imai, 1986). Further, this approach encourages all staff to get involved in making improvements; the changes are more easily identified; and the management of the changes is less complex. The choice of initiatives can be influenced by setting common goals. Second, the alternative approach is to establish improvements "top-down". Project plans are formulated to implement the changes that are needed to achieve improvement targets (Juran, 1988). This approach is likely to provide a better focus on tackling the more important issues but it has the disadvantage that it does not necessarily involve all staff and may be more difficult to manage. In practice, a combination of the two approaches should be adopted. The inclusion of improvement goals in personal objectives also provides a powerful way of gaining commitment (Humble, 1979). Some companies even go as far as to give bonuses to their managers on the achievement of the improvement goals.

The third step to planning is to establish resources for the implementation of improvements. If a bottom-up approach is used, an allowance is made in individuals' time in the same way that an allowance is made for holidays and training. The amount of time to invest depends upon the size of the company's quality problems. A minimum of about five per cent is recommended. This time equates to little more than one hour per person per week. Top-down plans require sizing and resource allocation as is the case for any project plan.

Infrastructure

The quality infrastructure is the set of fixed items within an organization that supports continuous improvement. This infrastructure may manifest itself in a number of ways:

- the appointment of dedicated staff to manage the process; for example, a quality manager
- the establishment of dedicated processes to be operated by the work force in addition to their other tasks; for example, specific improvement task groups and review meetings
- the integration of the improvement activities into the normal business processes; for example, putting quality improvement onto the agenda of existing review meetings

In practice, the infrastructure is a combination of these approaches.

Teams. Team-work is a key principle of TQM. Table 4 illustrates some of the management teams that could be put in place within the infrastructure to implement continuous improvement.
Some of these teams may be "formal" in the sense that:

- They have written terms of reference
- They have an agreed charter
- They publish minutes from meetings

Alternatively, the purposes of the teams may be addressed within the company's existing structures. In the case of bottom up initiatives, the teams may be totally informal and management will rely on trust that the members contribute positively to the continuous improvement process.

TQM Processes. There are a number of specific activities that are integrated into the infrastructure to support continuous improvement. Elements of these activities probably exist within normal business processes operated by an organization. Within a TQM system, the establishment of discrete activities ensures that actions to support continuous improvement receive sufficient focus and priority.

There are a number of risks associated with relying on normal business to address continuous improvement. These are

- The likelihood of a diversity of ways to execute the process: a common process is more likely to give a consistent result at a lesser cost.
- The trade out of activities if there is pressure to meet deadlines or reduce costs: a discrete process makes such trades more visible to senior management. Addi-

Table 4. Improvement Management Teams

Team	Purpose	Typical Membership
Steering group	To establish policies To set objectives To state direction	CEO and direct reports
Specialist steering teams	To establish strategies and plans for improvements in specific areas	Led by CEO direct reports; plus line unit representatives
Management teams	To establish and review improvement plans	Line management
Implementation teams	To implement improvement plans	Project teams; either existing ones or specific ones set up to address a particular plan
Quality circles	As "implementation teams" but initiatives defined by the circles rather than driven from the management teams	Any volunteers
Quality council	To advise improvement teams	Quality experts

tionally, it has the advantage of presenting a clearer understanding of the investment needed in the first place that helps reduce the need to trade.

These risks decrease as the TQM system matures within an organization. The activities that benefit from discrete processes are listed in Table 5. Note that these activities are concentrated on supporting continuous improvement (Collard, 1989). Elements of these activities that already exist in normal business, should be maintained.

THE APPLICATION OF TQM TO SOFTWARE DEVELOPMENT

TQM has been applied successfully to the manufacturing environment where the majority of activities are concerned with the operation of fixed procedures to achieve production quotas within budget. However, the advocates of TQM systems claim that the improvement processes apply to any business. In principle, there are no major differences between the way a software development organization is run when compared with any other manufacturing company (Cho, 1980): the same principles of management control apply. The Japanese have gone as far as applying the Factory Model to software development (Cusumano, 1991).

Mature production processes in a manufacturing organization tend to show little variation in their costs of operation between different operators and different products within a product range. However, the software production costs, as measured by lines of code per month, can vary considerably between different software engineers and between different programs. Consequently, the ability to size projects accurately is greatly impaired. The software process maturity model (Humphrey, 1988) recognizes the need

Table 5. Key TQM Activities

Activity	Description	Benefits
Control	Set improvement objectives Plan their achievement Measure and review progress Take action if necessary to remain on target	Resources made available Show commitment Demonstrate importance
Corrective action	Identify problems (opportunities for improvement) Establish implementation teams Monitor progress Evaluate effectiveness	Permanent change Management support
Recognition	Informal "thank you" Reward role models Reward achievement	Positive reinforcement Encourage others Motivate individuals
Education	Specific TQM training Market awareness Customer awareness	Improve understanding Develop skills Get requirements right
Awareness	Display measurements Communication events Publicize achievements	Keep staff informed Encourage others Maintain commitment

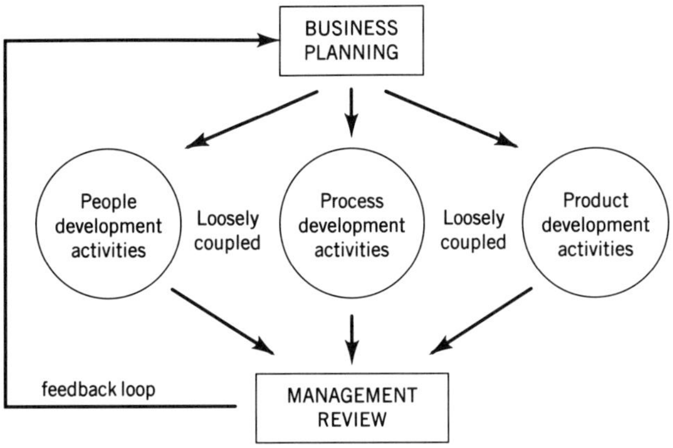

Figure 1. Balance among people, processes, and products necessary for a successful organization.

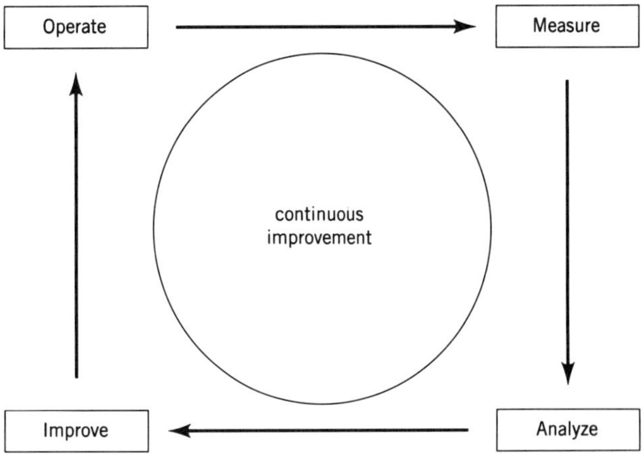

Figure 2. The process of continuous improvement.

to have greatly improved predictability for software development projects.

Also, a successful organization needs to have a balance among people, processes, and products. Each of the developments in these areas is intricately related to the other two but, in practice, the operation of them proceeds in parallel with only a loose coupling between them (Fig. 1). For example, a program to develop the skills of software engineers, filters through to product and process development activities and improves the way these activities are carried out. However, only in rare circumstances will product development be so dependent on people and process developments that it cannot proceed.

The co-ordination of activities within the three categories is achieved through traditional management practices. Typically, these are

- business planning to determine strategies, resources, and priorities
- reviews to monitor progress and assess the effectiveness of all activities

The TQM system provides the means by which improvements can be made to the processes which support all the activities of an organization.

Figure 2 illustrates a process for achieving such improvements. When *operating* a process, *measurements* are taken which are *analyzed.* This analysis identifies opportunities for *improvement* that are implemented and put into operation whereby the process is repeated. The analysis may be applied to any of the elements of a quality system (*people, process or product*).

A number of tools and methods facilitate this process and are described in the subsequent sections.

Tools and Methods for Continuous Improvement

Life Cycle Models. Life cycle models improve the understanding of how tasks operate. They identify the sequence of events and the data flow between them. Each event in a life cycle model is called a phase. The software life cycle is well established within software engineering and it will not be discussed further in this article. It addresses the *Product* development elements of the three Ps of TQM. Similar life cycle models apply to *People* and *Process* development.

People development: A typical life cycle for people development is *requirements* phase, and *operation* phase. The operation phase includes *planning* and *review.* Requirements are established through business and individual needs. The requirements may be the need to train staff in particular product knowledge, to develop personal skills, or to improve poor performers. Appraisals are an ideal way to identify the needs (Humble, 1979). The requirements are satisfied by developing a plan of action that may include training courses, coaching, and increased responsibilities. The establishment of new techniques to assist people development are covered by the process development activities.

Process development: The process development life cycle is more similar to the software life cycle. A typical life cycle includes a *requirements* phase, *design* phase, *implementation* phase, *test* phase, *installation* and check-out phase, and *operation* and maintenance phase. Requirements come from the improvement planning and corrective action activities discussed earlier. New processes or enhancements to existing ones are designed, implemented, and tested to demonstrate that the requirements have been satisfied. An introduction plan ensures the successful installation and operation of the changes. The Process Maturity Model (qv) (Humphrey, 1988) is an example of a mechanism to manage process development.

Process Models. Process modeling is a tool that provides a structure to the way that activities are described. The structure aids the understanding of the requirements of a task, the way in which it operates, and the performance standards that need to be satisfied.

A number of process models exist which allow activities to be described and managed (Crosby, 1985; Radice and co-workers, 1985).

So, what makes a good model? Each activity has a number of perspectives:

- **Operator perspective:** how the operations are carried out to produce the output
- **Designer perspective:** how requirements on an activity are agreed and how its scope and the dependen-

Table 6. The Principles of Process Modeling

Role	Plan	Task	Verify
Designer	Agree process requirements	Select language; define static test tools	Inspect design against requirements
Author	Agree process design	Document code standards	Inspect against design
Operator (programmer)	Agree product design; ensure availability of tools	Write code	Clean compile; run static tests; inspect against design
Manager (team leader)	Agree review process	Provide coaching; place actions	Check actions are progressed

cies on its operation are defined; for example, equipment and operator skills need to be articulated.

- **Author perspective:** how the design is implemented. Normally, the output from the implementation is a documented description of how the process operates, written procedures, and work instructions for inclusion into the quality system documentation.
- **Manager perspective:** how the operations are measured, controlled and reviewed.

Each activity has three basic assignments:

- **Plan:** the preparation needed to execute a task.
- **Task:** the steps needed to perform the activity.
- **Verify:** the checks carried out to ensure that the requirements of the task have been satisfied.

A good model will allow each of these assignments to be described for each of the perspectives.

Table 6 illustrates the principles of process modeling by using a simplified example of the activity writing code. In this example, the activities of the *designer* and *author* are related to developing the system for code production, whereas the activities of the *operator* (*programmer*) and *manager* (*team leader*) are related to a specific product development. Progress in the effectiveness of the code production system is reviewed by other management review processes. For example, cost reviews may identify weaknesses in the writing code activity, that need to be addressed.

Needs Analysis. A number of tools and techniques exist within the field of software engineering that analyze requirements and translate them into product specifications and design (Thayer and Dorfman, 1990). Needs analysis is equally applicable to process and people developments and existing tools and techniques are easily adapted.

Problem identification. Product faults are typically detected by testing or through operational usage. In the latter case, most organizations will have a formal process for recording and resolving faults.

Within TQM, process and people problems also need to be identified and acted upon. There are a number of ways to identify problems:

- By explicit review; for example, personal appraisals, quality system audits, project post-mortems
- By defect analysis of product faults; such analyses identify the process and people problems which caused the errors to be introduced
- By checking as part of product verification activities; for example, include process errors in software inspection reports (Fagan, 1986)

A common mistake with problem identification is to attempt to define the solution before analyzing the causes. Try the following test:

"Customer xxx is dissatisfied with his system. Last week, it failed because of a software bug." Ask the question: "What is the problem?"

Typical responses may be:

- There was a hardware incident that caused the software error
- The software failed because it had not executed that particular path before
- The software had not been installed correctly

But none of these responses are correct. The correct response is *"customer is dissatisfied with his system. Last week it failed because of a software bug."* Only with this problem definition clearly in mind will the real root cause be identified and eliminated. Fixing the specific bug may satisfy the customer ...but only until he hits the next one!

Problem Solving. A number of tools and techniques exist for analyzing the causes of problems: Pareto analysis, cause and effect diagrams, brain storming, and so on (Hutchins, 1985, Ishikawa, 1986). These tools and techniques are well documented in many of the publications on quality management and are easily introduced into the software development environment.

Design Methods. The design of processes uses the same basic skills that are needed for other design activities. However, one technique that is of particular benefit to the design of processes is "best practice benchmarking" (Gordon, 1989).

When designing a process, consider the following:

- Which company or individual performs the task best? Apply lateral thought to the answer. For example, if the plan is to improve the software distribution pro-

cess, consider companies that specialize in distribution rather than companies that specialize in software.
- Find out how the company or individual does it. There are many case studies written about successful companies. Alternatively, visit and talk to them.
- Learn and adapt the ideas to your design. Looking at bad examples also helps the learning process.

Measurement. Measurement is key to the control of software projects (DeMarco, 1982). It is also key to successful quality improvements.

Within a TQM system, measurement has a number of purposes:

- To confirm the effectiveness of the TQM system: such measurements are normally taken by independent bodies and would include such things as business performance, company ranking, and customer satisfaction surveys. Warning signals from these measurements indicate areas for improvement.
- To control projects and processes: typically, these measurements would be of costs and failure rates. Any deviations from norms would trigger the need for management attention to bring the projects or processes back under control.
- To enable corrective action: control metrics are of little value unless there are underlying data that can be analysed to determine the causes of the deviations.
- To identify opportunities for improvement (Juran, 1988): the measurement of the costs of chronic waste allows improvement targets to be set and progress to be monitored. The definition of what constitutes chronic waste is determined by industry norms where they exist, or by the specific objectives of a company. For software development, all post delivery bug fixing is waste.

Typically, control measurements are taken by the project. However, a central data collection group gives additional benefits:

- It facilitates the collection of the data for the project. For example, by developing suitable tools
- It provides trend analyses to help identify opportunities for improvements

A typical example of how measurements are taken and used is illustrated by software inspections. The data are collected by the inspection teams and used to decide whether to proceed to the next stage of development or to call for re-work and a possible re-inspection. The data are also entered into a central system that provides trend analyses. Such analyses may trigger improvements to the development processes to reduce common types of errors.

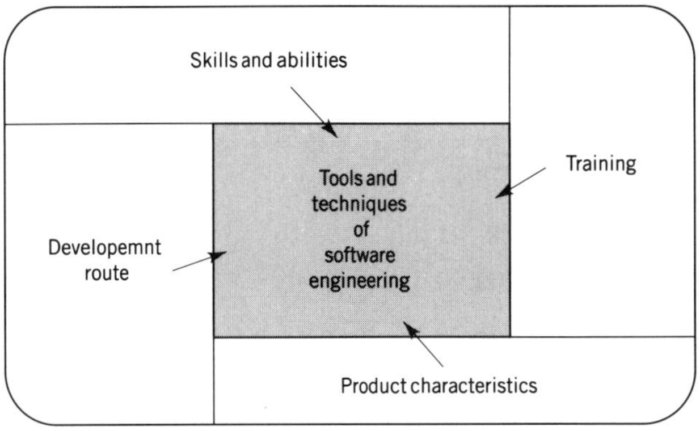

Figure 3. Effective implementation of software engineering tools and techniques.

THE ROLE OF SOFTWARE ENGINEERING IN TQM

Software Engineering is defined as **the systematic approach to the development, operation, maintenance, and retirement of software** (ANSI/IEEE Std 610.12, 1990). It manifests itself as a set of standards for tools, methods and rules to be applied throughout the software development life cycle. The effectiveness of the standards is dependent upon the skills training in their use, the environment into which the standards are to be adopted, the products to which they are to be applied and the inherent skills, abilities and attitudes of the software engineer (Fig. 3).

Assuming such a balance has been attained, software engineering is of major importance to TQM. One of the key principles of TQM is *prevention.* Software Engineering has been developed primarily to improve the productivity of the software engineer and the quality of the delivered products. This is achieved, in the main, by establishing methods and tools that automate tasks and so *prevent* software engineers from making mistakes. Clearly Software Engineering has a major impact on the ability of an organization to satisfy its customers. However, as discussed earlier in this article, software development consumes only 22% of an organization's resources so the need to establish productivity and quality improvement in other activities is as great. Within the definition of TQM (the three Ps), software engineering is primarily about tools and methods for improving PRODUCT quality.

QUALITY SYSTEM STANDARDS

Quality system standards are an accepted means of assuring the quality of delivered goods. The purpose of a quality system standard is to provide a framework that includes the selection and deployment of tools, methods and rules that, together with the engineering capability of a company, will give assurance that products will be produced in a consistent manner using acceptable industry practices. A standard does not in itself provide a guarantee of product quality. Quality system standards provide a way of addressing PROCESS issues and so form a fundamental part of any TQM system.

In the UK, a report by the Department of Trade and Industry concluded that ISO 9001 was the best existing generic standard for software development (Logica, 1988). This standard is being adopted world-wide in industry in general and a software derivative has been developed (ISO 9000-3, 1991).

A CASE STUDY

The following case study is based on ICL's development of its mainframe operating system during the 1980s. It illustrates how TQM has been applied to a large software system development project over a period of five years and the benefits that have been gained.

Consider the following scenario:

The software system has been in existence for ten years and it needs to be re-engineered to run on the latest state-of-the-art hardware platforms. However, the market requirements for the system are rapidly changing. Customers are demanding:

- increased reliability as businesses become more and more dependent upon information technology
- faster resolution of problems to eliminate or minimize the impact of defects on their business
- enhancements to use the new capabilities made possible by improving technology

The challenges facing the software engineers are to modify the system to run on the new platforms without the need for the customers to change their operational processes and to incorporate improvements that will meet the more stringent requirements being demanded.

The software engineering tool kit alone no longer was capable of meeting the new demands. A new look at the management and control processes was required.

Initial Approach

Having identified the changes in requirements, the approach was

- To size the problem
- To identify the process changes needed to secure the improvements
- To establish measures to monitor progress
- To increase staff training
- To incorporate the improvements into permanent changes to working practices.

The Plan

- An action plan was formulated to introduce both tactical and strategic changes to the development processes and people behavior. Increased emphasis was placed on total staff involvement and quality-led management control.
- Investment in quality improvement was endorsed by senior management to ensure resources were in place to implement the action plan. Four key improvements were tackled first: *document existing tasks within the software development life cycle; accelerate the rate at which the design change proposals were implemented: introduce a formal process of defect analysis; improve reliability of products currently in use.*
- A complementary program of quality education and awareness was established and delivered to all staff.
- Continuous improvement was monitored by a set of effectiveness measures, on the basis of customer performance priorities that were to eliminate system failures and to respond more rapidly to problems. Eight key metrics were defined covering software system break rates, responsiveness of support queries, development bug rates, and productivity. These metrics were put on public display, targets were established, and, progress was monitored at least monthly and often weekly.
- Management review processes were improved to give focus to the quality initiatives. Quality was put first on the agenda. Quality targets were established for all phases of the software development life cycle and progress carefully monitored.

Maintaining Momentum

- The initial successes were encouraging. Good progress had been made in reducing system failure rates and the demand for customer support had not increased in spite of a significant growth in the number of users of the system.
- Sustained performance improvement was achieved by setting more stringent targets against the eight key metrics and further process improvements were put into place.
- Further education and awareness events were developed, concentrating on the tools and methods for achieving continuous improvement.

Integration

The initial plan was managed as a focused quality improvement program but further improvements have become fully integrated into a TQM process. Note that the initiatives came first. The benefits of TQM needed to be demonstrated to the software engineers before they were persuaded to follow the process but the benefits from the cultural changes became long-lasting and deep-rooted, far outweighing the need to see a quick return. Having established this fundamental change in culture, continuous improvement was guaranteed and accelerated.

The results of implementing TQM have shown sustained and significant improvements across the eight key metrics: in three years, the software system break rate reduced by a factor of forty; response times to support queries improved by a factor of four; and development bug rates reduced by a factor of four. The improvements to the support and maintenance processes have improved productivity by 100% (per customer query) within 2 years. Software engineers now believe that the goal of error-free software that fully conforms to customer requirements, is achievable.

CONCLUSIONS

Within a TQM framework, the management of software development takes on a different emphasis with increased support for the PEOPLE and PROCESS development activities. The scope of software engineering tools and techniques is extended to provide:

- Increased awareness and understanding through measurement and process modeling
- Phase automation for all processes within the PEOPLE, PROCESS and PRODUCT development life cycles.
- Process integration using process modeling to guarantee the integrity of the development life cycles and to control its maintenance, evolution and improvement

Comparisons with best practices in other manufacturing disciplines help to reduce process variability, the key to improving software productivity and quality.

TQM is basically common sense but any company from the CEO down to its humblest employee must be passionate about wanting to change to take full advantage of what it offers. The most significant contributor to its success in software development is to exploit the talents of the software engineers; to empower them to continually seek and implement improvements to the way in which they produce software.

BIBLIOGRAPHY

ANSI/IEEE Std 610.12-1990, *IEEE Standard Glossary of Software Engineering Terminology,* IEEE, 1990.

A. Bendell, *The Quality Gurus,* DTI Booklet, 1991.

B. Boehm, *Software Engineering Economics,* Prentice-Hall, Inc., Englewood Cliffs, N.J., 1981.

F. P. Brooks Jr., *The Mythical Man Month: Essays on Software Engineering,* Addison-Wesley Publishing Co., Inc., Reading, Mass., 1975.

W. L. Bryan, S. G. Siegel, *Software Product Assurance (Techniques for Reducing Software Risk),* Elsevier Applied Science Publishers, Ltd., Barking, UK, 1988.

C.-K. Cho, *An Introduction to Software Quality Control,* John Wiley & Sons, Inc., New York, 1980.

R. Collard, *Total Quality: Success Through People,* Institute of Personnel Management, 1989.

P. B. Crosby, *Quality is Free: The Art of Making Quality Certain,* McGraw-Hill Book Co., Inc., New York, 1979.

P. B. Crosby, *Quality Without Tears: The Art of Hassle-Free Management,* McGraw-Hill Book Co., Inc., New York, 1984.

P. B. Crosby, *Quality Improvement Through Defect Prevention: The Individual's Role,* Philip Crosby Associates, Inc., Winter Park, Fla., 1985.

M. A. Cusumano, *Japan's Software Factories: A Challenge to U.S. Management,* USA: OUP, New York, 1991.

T. DeMarco, *Controlling Software Projects,* Prentice-Hall Inc., Englewood Cliffs, N.J., 1982.

W. E. Deming, *Out of the Crisis,* Massachusetts Institute of Technology, Boston, Mass., 1986.

M. E. Fagan, *Advances in Software Inspections,* IEEE Transactions on Software Engineering, July, 1986.

A. V. Feigenbaum, *Total Quality Control, 3rd ed.,* McGraw-Hill Book Co., Inc., New York, 1983.

D. A. Garvin, *Managing Quality: The Strategic and Competitive Edge,* Free Press, New York, 1988.

I. Gordon, *Beat The Competition! How To Use Competitive Intelligence To Develop Winning Business Strategies,* Blackwell, Oxford, UK, 1989.

E. L. Grant, *Statistical Quality Control,* Industrial Organisation & Management Series, 1946.

J. W. Humble, *Management by Objectives in Action,* Gower, Farnborough, 1979.

W. S. Humphrey, *Characterizing the Software Process: A Maturity Framework,* IEEE Software Management, March, 1988.

D. Hutchins, *Quality Circles Handbook,* Pitman, London, 1985.

M. Imai, *Kaizen: The Key to Japan's Competitive Success,* McGraw-Hill Book Co., Inc., New York, 1986.

K. Ishikawa, *What is Total Quality Control? The Japanese Way,* Prentice-Hall, Inc., Englewood Hills, N.J., 1985.

K. Ishikawa, *Guide to Quality Control (second edition),* Asian Productivity Organisation, 1986.

ISO 8402 - 1986, *Quality - Vocabulary,* ISO, 1986.

ISO9000-3: 1991 (E), *Quality Management and Quality Assurance Standards - Paer 3: Guidelines for the Application of ISO 9001, to the Development, Supply and Maintenance of Software,* ISO, 1991.

ISO 9001 - 1987, *Quality systems - Model for quality assurance in design / development, production, installation and servicing,* ISO, 1987.

J. M. Juran, *Juran on Planning for Quality,* Free Press, New York, 1988.

J. M. Juran, "Strategies for World-Class Quality," *Quality Progress* (Mar. 1991).

A. Kanno, "Quality Control Activities on Software Production," *JUSE Societas Qualitatis,* (Sept/Oct. 1988).

Logica, *Quality Management Standards for Software,* DTI Report, 1988.

James Martin Associates, *Improving Software Quality: Certification of Product and Process,* DTI Report, Nov., 1986.

MOD (UK) DEF STAN 05-21/1, Quality Control System Requirements for Industry, MOD, 1976.

NATO AQAP-1: *NATO Requirements for an Industrial Quality control System,* NATO, 1984.

NATO AQAP-13: *NATO Software quality control system Requirements,* NATO, 1985.

J. S. Oakland, *Total Quality Management,* Heinemann Professional Publishing, Oxford, UK, 1989.

T. J. Peters and R. H. Waterman Jr., *In Search of Excellence,* Collins, London, 1982.

T. J. Peters and N. Austin, *A Passion for Excellence - the Leadership Difference,* Collins, London, 1985.

T. J. Peters, *Thriving on Chaos,* McMillan, London, 1988.

Price Waterhouse, eds., *Software Quality Standards: The Costs and Benefits,* DTI Report, Apr., 1988.

R. A. Radice and co-workers, "A Programming Process Model," *IBM Systems Journal,* **24**(2), (1985).

M. Robson, *The Journey to Excellence,* John Wiley & Sons, Inc., New York, 1986.

S. Smith, *How to Quantify Quality, Management Today,* (Oct. 1987).

R. H. Thayer and M. Dorfman eds., *System and Software Requirements Engineering,* IEEE Computer Society Press, Los Alamitos, Calif., 1990, Chapt. 5.

P. L. Townsend and J. E. Gebhardt, *Commit to Quality,* John Wiley & Sons, Inc., New York, 1990.

R. K. Zentmyer and J. A. Zimble, "The Journey from Bureaucracy to TQM," *Quality Progress,* (Sept. 1991).

BRIAN CHATTERS
ICL

TQM

See TOTAL QUALITY MANAGEMENT.

TRANSACTION ANALYSIS

A software development technique in which the structure of a system is derived from analyzing the transactions that the system is required to process (IEEE).

TRANSFORM ANALYSIS

A software development technique in which the structure of a system is derived from analyzing the flow of data through a system and the transformations that must be performed on the data (IEEE).

TREE-STRUCTURED CHARTS

OVERVIEW

Tree-structured charts are high-level visual programming languages based on tree-structured control formalism (Aoyama, 1989). They combine visual formalism with a high-level textual description language so that designers can specify program structure more precisely and comprehensively while keeping the specifications compact. Representative tree-structured charts include GREENPRINT developed by IBM (Belady, 1980), the HCP (Hierarchical and ComPact description) chart by Nippon Telegraph and Telephone (Hanata, 1981), PAD (Problem Analysis Diagram) by Hitachi (Futamura, 1981), SPD (Structured Programming Diagram) by NEC (Azuma, 1985), YAC (Yet Another Control) II chart by Fujitsu (Aoyama, 1989) and Action Diagram by James Martin (Martin, 1989). These were introduced around 1980 and have been widely applied in Japan, while data-flow diagrams have been popular in the U. S.

BACKGROUND AND HISTORY

Influenced by structured-programming concepts, many so-called structured flow-charts were proposed in the 1970s. Tree-structured charts descended from structured flow-charts by introducing specific graphical symbols for basic control structures such as sequence, selection, and iteration. However, they incorporate other software engineering concepts such as top-down step-wide refinement and visual programming techniques. A survey reported some 20 charts proposed in this category (Tripp, 1988; Glinert, 1990). Although similar in terminology, the tree-structured chart is different from the structure charts used in structured design techniques.

CHARACTERISTICS

Tree-structured charts share the following common characteristics.

1. *Graphical control structure:* Tree-structured charts represent control structure with graphical elements. Figure 1 illustrates some basic control constructs available in YAC II. Other tree-structured charts provide the same constructs with slightly different notations. In each control structure, the control scope is explicitly defined by the symbols and lines. Since the graphical control structure is integrated with textual process descriptions, the representation is simple and compact.
2. *Hierarchical function structure:* Tree-structured charts can represent a system's hierarchical function at different abstraction levels. For example, take PAD. A module structure diagram represents the system's overall structure and the relationship among modules. Interface data definition defines the structure of the module's input and output data. Internal data definition defines the structure of data used inside the module. Finally, process description defines the detail-design algorithm. In the process description, a vertical course represents the basic process sequence, and a horizontal course represents the function hierarchy. Hence, a tree grows from top to bottom and from left to right.
3. *Pseudo-code and language independence:* Both English and Japanese pseudo-code can be used to describe each process. While some basic keywords are predefined in a dictionary, it is possible to add domain-specific pseudo-codes and terms to the dictionary. Thus the tree-structured chart is independent of programming languages.
4. *Abstraction for reuse:* Because the tree-structured chart is independent of specific programming languages, it promotes reuse at the design-specification level. The chart facilitates the binding mechanism of software components. Either part or all of a module

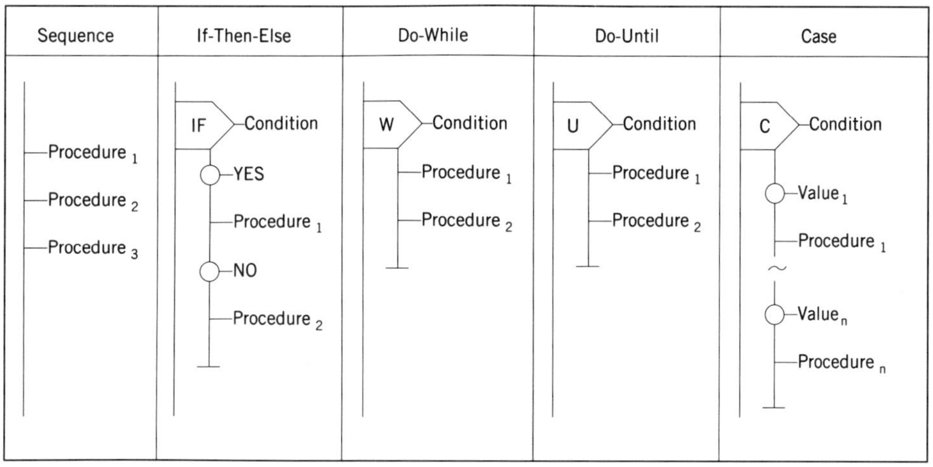

Figure 1. Basic control constructs of YAC II chart.

can be registered as a component and can be reused by referring to its-name in pseudo-code.

5. *Specification and implementation description:* Some charts support the description of both program function, i.e., the "what," in the specification part; and implementation detail, i.e., the "how," in the body part.
6. *Data-flow description:* Some charts support the description of data-flow in combining with process specification.

DEVELOPMENT SUPPORT ENVIRONMENTS

To support software development with tree-structured charts, various CASE (Computer-Aided Software Engineering) environments have been developed and used. Running on mainframe computers, UNIX workstations, and MS-DOS personal computers, the environments provide the following capabilities:

1. *Structured graphic editor:* In a syntax-directed graphic editor, the graphical elements are predefined and the cursor movement is context-sensitive. It is possible to copy, move, and delete all or part of the tree-structured chart graphically while preserving its structural consistency. Together with the editor, change management of the tree-structured chart is also supported.
2. *Source-code generator:* The environment generates source codes automatically from the tree-structured chart. The generated source codes can be in one of several languages, including Ada, C, Cobol, Fortran, and PL/I.
3. *Reverse engineering capability:* Tree-structured charts are automatically generated from source codes. This capability can help program maintenance and application of tree-structured charts in maintenance phase.
4. *Executor and debugger:* Because the tree-structured chart is executable, the environment can interactively execute the program at the chart level and graphically display the execution behavior. The environments provide test-coverage evaluator and visual debugger.

APPLICATIONS

In application development, the tree-structured charts share the mission with fourth-generation languages in the sense that they both provide high-level program representations. However, these methods differ in their use. Fourth-generation languages are used primarily for end-user programming in application domains such as business and office data processing, which do not require high performance. Tree-structured charts are used primarily by hardware and software vendors for development on a wide range of application domains, including business applications, real-time systems, telecommunication systems, and embedded computing systems. The tree-structured charts have been widely accepted in Japan for more than decade. Hundreds of projects have adopted tree-structured charts as their design specification languages; this has resulted in significant improvement of productivity and quality.

BIBLIOGRAPHY

M. Aoyama and co-workers, "Design Specification in Japan: Tree-Structured Charts," *IEEE Software* **6**(2), 31–37 (Mar. 1989).

M. Azuma and co-workers, "SPD: A Humanized Documentation Technology," *IEEE Transactions on Software Engineering* **11**(9), 945–953 (Sept. 1985).

L. A. Belady and co-workers, "GREENPRINT: A Graphic Representation of Structured Programs," *IBM Systems Journal* **19**(4), 542–553 (1980).

Y. Futamura and co-workers, "Development of Computer Programs by Problem Analysis (PAD)," *Proceedings of the 5th International Conference on Software Engineering,* Mar. 1981, pp. 325–332.

P. Glinert, ed., *Visual Programming Environments,* IEEE Computer Society Press, Los Alamitos, Calif., 1990.

S. Hanata and co-workers, "Documentation Technology for Packing Hierarchical Function, Data, and Control Structures," *Proceedings of the IEEE Compcon Fall,* Sept. 1981, pp. 284–290.

J. Martin, *Information Engineering*, Prentice-Hall, Englewood Cliffs, N.J., 1989.

L. L. Tripp, "A Survey of Graphical Notations for Program Design: A Update," *ACM SIGSOFT Software Engineering Notes* **13**(4), 39–44 (Oct. 1988).

MIKIO AOYAMA
Fujitsu Ltd.

TROUBLE REPORTS

This term is sometimes used in place of the more formal term, Problem Reports, or Software Trouble Reports. It refers to a problem assocaited with a product of development such as a document such as a document, design, code, or user feature.

See CORRECTIVE ACTION SYSTEM.

TRUSTED SYSTEMS

See SECURITY, COMPUTER.

TURSKI, WLADYSLAW M. (1938–)

Educated as an astronomer (M.Sc. in Celestial Mechanics, Lomonosov University, Moscow, 1960) Turski gained computing experience first as a "human computer" (his M.Sc. thesis on smooth Lunar landing and first publications on planetoid orbits were hand-computed). As a Leverhulme Research Fellow in 1960–1961 he visited the Jodrell Bank Radio observatory, where his research into metor stream formation led him to a massive use of electronic computing for simulation of physical processes. For this work (carried out with Prof. J. G. Davis) Turski eventually obtained a Ph.D.).

His formal computing science education was completed in two night-classes at the Electrical Engineering Department of the Manchester University, in which he learned to program the Mercury computer ("When love prevails logic fails, so the computer was made neuter" was a note pasted to its console.) On return to his native Poland, Turski joined the staff of the just created Computing Centre of the Polish Academy of Sciences, where his interests gradually shifted from astronomical and space computations to compiler building and operating system design.

In 1962 he read a paper on the KLIPA compiler for the URAL-2 computer (designed with M. Greniewski) at the ACM Conference in Syracuse, N.Y. According to the press, he was the first ever computer scientist from "behind the iron-curtain" to present a paper in the United States.

Turski's work on Algol compilers resulted in his appointment to the IFIP Working Group 2.1. on Algol in 1965. He was its Secretary to 1968, when the group split over Algol 68. Turski was in the dissenting minority which in 1969 formed Working Group 2.3. on Programming Methodology.

In 1972 Turski left the Academy of Sciences for a job in computer industry, where for 5 years he was the Director for Software and Research in the MERA (Polish Computer Manufacturers Union) Research Institute. In this capacity he supervised a number of major software projects, including the implementation of OS/360 on a Polish-made copy of the IBM360. (At the IFIP Congress in Dublin, 1986, as the responder to Fred Brooks' invited lecture, Turski started his presentation by saying "Professor Brooks is a hard act to follow, I know, I copied OS/360").

From 1977 to present, Turski is a Professor of Informatics at Warsaw University. In 1982–1987 he was also a Visiting Professor at the Department of Computing in Imperial College, London, where his collaboration with M. M. Lehman and V. Stenning resulted in the development of the LST paradigm of software life cycle. Turski's research interests are software methodology, formal foundations of program specification, and education of useful computer scientists.

He is a Distinguished Fellow of the British Computer society, Foreign Member of the Royal Academy of Engineering, a founder and the first President of the Polish Information Processing Society (two terms), and member of the Polish Mathematical Society and Polish Astronomical Society. He is a holder of the IFIP Silver Core Award (1974), and numerous other medals and diplomas.

Turski served as a consultant to UNDP and UNIDO on developing indigenous software industries in countries of the Middle East, and to several banks and insurance companies on introducing contemporary information processing services. He has had the honor to be an invited speaker at events (conferences, seminars etc.) in almost all European countries, Argentina, Brazil, Australia, United States, Canada, Egypt, Israel, and Russia.

Turski wrote over 200 papers on astronomy, mathematics, programming, software, and education. Of his several books, five are available in Western languages: *Programming Teaching Techniques* (ed.), North-Holland, 1973; *Daten-Strukturen,* Akademie-Verlag, Berlin, 1975; *Computer Programming Methodology,* Heyden, London, 1978; *Informatics, a Propaedeutic View,* North-Holland, 1985; and *The Specification of Computer Programs* (with T. S. E. Maibaum) Addison-Wesley, 1987.

U

UIMS

See User interface management systems.

ULTRARELIABILITY

Ultrareliability concerns functions for which failure entails exceptionally heavy costs, frequently including loss of life, resulting in a requirement for very low frequency of such failures. There is no clear dividing line between high reliability and ultrareliability, but the term ultrareliability generally is used to refer to failure intensities of less than 10^{-6} failures/hr (one failure per million hours). In order to give a physical feel to failure intensities, some common failure intensities and risks are noted in Table 1. Note that a failure intensity of 10^{-9} failures/hr (one failure per billion hours), which has been specified for catastrophic failures of critical functions in some applications such as aircraft control and air traffic control, implies a failure about every 114,000 years.

Note that the need for ultrareliability really does refer to *functions* rather than systems. For example, the function that shuts down a nuclear power plant in an emergency must be ultrareliable. This does not imply that the entire system must be ultrareliable; there are many routine operating and data logging functions that do not require it. In many cases it is much easier to separate software by function than hardware and focus reliability-enhancing efforts just on the critical functions.

There is an important distinction to be made in regard to reliability of hardware and software components. Reliability of hardware components is affected by factors such as aging and wear. Consequently, reliability is related to calendar time or perhaps operating time. In contrast, software reliability is affected only by the execution time of the program. The execution time of a software function is often only a small fraction of the calendar time taken by the entire system for its operation.

Table 1. Failure Intensities or Risks (per 10^6 Hours)

Space shuttle catastrophic failures during launch (*New York Times,* 1989a)	38,000
Potentially significant safety incidents, U.S. nuclear power plants, 1984-1987 (per plant operating hour) (NRC)	3,400
One failure per month	1,370
Electric light bulbs	1,000
Automatic safety shutdowns of U.S. nuclear power plants (per plant operating hour) (NRC)	500
New York City subway car (all failures) (*New York Times,* 1989c)	478
One failure per year	114
Fire in specified household (U.S. average) (*New York Times,* 1989b)	4.11
One failure per century	1.14
Death (person of age 35)	1.02

For example, planetary probes commonly involve flights of several years. Although the hardware must be ultrareliable for this time period, the critical software functions may not have the same requirements. Critical navigation and maneuver software, for example, may execute only about 10 times in a 5 year flight, with each execution lasting 3 to 5 seconds. Thus such software requires reliability over a total execution time of about 0.01 hour, a duration that is shorter than the flight by a factor of about 4×10^6.

The expense, development time, and difficulties involved in building ultrareliable functions are such that we need to take a very realistic attitude in setting failure intensity objectives. Some designers have argued that relating failure intensities to the existing "average" death rate of about 10^{-6}/hr is reasonable, on the basis that we generally "accept" that rate. The argument assumes that death is the most catastrophic event possible to a person. Thus, the acceptable intensities for other failures of lesser impact can scale up from there. Failures that would entail effects on many people would result in scaling down the failure intensity objective by the number of people involved.

It is also important that we separate functions by criticality and apply ultrahigh reliability objectives only to those functions that require them. This implies that the software architecture must be modular by function and that special care be taken to prevent interactions between modules.

The duration for which the software must function should be carefully established. The failure intensity acceptable for the software is the system failure intensity divided by the *duty cycle,* or proportion of time that the software is executing. Thus to obtain a system failure intensity of, say, 10^{-9} failures/hr for a planetary probe, where the duty cycle of the navigation and maneuver module might be 0.25×10^{-6}, we would need a module failure intensity of 4×10^{-3} failures/CPU hr.

Testing of ultrareliable functions requires a test duration that is several times the reciprocal of the failure intensity (Miller, 1989). The multiplier increases with the level of confidence required. Many have concluded that we therefore cannot certify ultrareliable software through testing. This is overly pessimistic. It is based entirely on statistical reasoning, not taking into account a number of software engineering considerations that ease the problem. In the planetary probe case we have taken as an example, a full system test necessary to demonstrate a level of 10^{-9} failures/hour would require some multiple of 10^9 hours (about 114,000 years). However, the test of the navigation and maneuver module requires only a multiple of 250 hours, which is readily achievable.

There are at least two other factors that can mitigate the testing problem. Many ultrareliable applications are implemented on relatively inexpensive embedded computers. It is feasible to test software on N machines, reducing the time duration by a factor of N. It is also possible to test software on a set of faster machines, as long as the instruction set is a superset of that of the target machine for the application. It is quite conceivable to obtain an overall speedup by a factor of 10000 (perhaps 1000 machines running 10 times as fast) by these methods.

Alternatives to the application of software reliability measurement appear worse. They all involve relying on trying to make the *process* of software engineering sufficiently rigorous that the products can be counted on to be reliable. But there is no standard software development process in place at present and there is no evidence to indicate that there ever will be. In fact, the new discipline of software process engineering virtually guarantees that there will not be. Any process is replete with opportunities for human error and hence failure. But as noted, there is nothing stable to subject to the intensive scrutiny required to insure an ultrareliable process. Even if there were, process attributes are less concrete, visible, and measurable and hence much harder to check than the product attributes software reliability measurement uses.

BIBLIOGRAPHY

D. R. Miller, "The Role of Statistical Modeling and Inference in Software Quality," B. deNeuman, ed., *Software Certification,* Elsevier Applied Science, London, 1989, pp. 135–152.

New York Times, April 9, 1989a, p. 1.

New York Times, Oct. 13, 1989b, p. B1.

New York Times, Nov. 10, 1989c, p. D24.

Nuclear Regulatory Commission Report, *USA Today,* March 21, 1989, p. 5A.

JOHN D. MUSA
AT&T Bell Laboratories

UNIT DEVELOPMENT FOLDER

See SOFTWARE DEVELOPMENT FOLDER.

UNIT TESTING

WHAT IS UNIT TESTING?

A *software unit* is a low-level component of a software system with its own specification. A unit may be as small as a commented block of code or as large as a set of coupled routines. Testing directed to a single unit is called *unit testing;* it comprises the activities of test planning, test data development, unit monitoring and execution, and evaluation of the results.

Test planning involves specifying the adequacy criterion by which to judge the test, assessing the project constraints and resources available, selecting the testing techniques that will achieve the adequacy criteria within the given constraints, and scheduling the testing process. Developing test data includes specifying test data characteristics as well as selecting test data with those characteristics. To execute the unit with the selected test data requires a *driver* for supplying the test data, monitoring the execution, and capturing the results. *Stubs* are sometimes needed to simulate the behavior of unimplemented routines that are called within the unit. The unit may need to be *instrumented* with additional code to display internal behavior. Evaluating the results determines the success of the executions as well as the degree to which the adequacy criterion was satisfied.

After finishing the test of a given unit, a decision must be made as to whether or not the unit has sufficient quality to be included in the system. The goal of unit testing is therefore to enable a more informed decision. Relevant information includes both the results of the test execution and the test *coverage.* Coverage may be specified in terms of the specification, the implementation, or a set of potential errors. Adequacy criteria are typically specified in terms of one or more of these three coverages. Each coverage gives rise to a class of testing techniques. Different testing techniques catch different types of faults; a comprehensive testing program will incorporate techniques from each of the classes as mentioned below.

SPECIFICATION-BASED TESTING

In specification-based testing, the specification is analyzed to identify required features. Tests are then constructed to demonstrate the presence of these features. Specification-based techniques include testing based on the interface of the unit, testing based on the function to be computed, and testing based on the style of the specification. Specifications implicitly partition inputs in to a set of *input domains* and the outputs into a set of *output domains.* Test data is selected from these domain descriptions. Given an input domain, extremes and midpoints are tested along with any special values associated with the function computed in the domain. Furthermore, test data is selected to produce members of each output domain, including error messages. In particular, the robustness of the unit to handle erroneous inputs is checked. Different specification techniques have engendered different testing techniques, especially for abstract data types specified by algebraic methods.

IMPLEMENTATION-BASED TESTING

In implementation-based testing one selects test data to exercise various aspects of the code. Implementation-based testing is necessitated by the fact that some of the decisions of the programmer are reflected only in the code; insufficient code coverage reduces the likelihood of discovering errors in the programmer's logic.

Implementation-based testing techniques may be classified according to the degree to which they seek to ensure that faults will produce failures. For a fault to produce a failure on a given execution, three conditions are necessary (Morell, 1990; Voas, Morell, and Miller, 1991):

1. The fault location must be *executed*; this requires reaching various parts of the structure of the program.
2. The execution must cause an *infection* (some value in the data space of the program must be corrupted).
3. The infection must *propagate* through the remaining computation to a failure.

Structural testing seeks to ensure execution of various aspects of the code's structure. For example, statement testing requires execution of each statement, branch testing requires execution of each logical sequence of statement pairs, and data coverage testing requires every data object in the program to be accessed.

Infection-oriented testing techniques seek to establish the conditions necessary for infections to occur. These techniques include requiring each clause in every condition to assume each possible value in combination (condition testing), and requiring every expression to assume several values to distinguish each expression from simpler expressions (expression testing). Other examples include domain testing, which selects test data at domain boundaries (as imposed by the program), pertubation testing, which models potential faults with vector spaces and identifies conditions which makes potential faults impossible to detect, and weak mutation testing which specifies conditions under which an infection will occur (for a given class of faults) and seeks test data that satisfies those conditions.

Propagation-oriented testing seeks to ensure potential infections propagate to failures. In path testing test data are selected to cover the execution paths of the program. Since even a small program can have a large number of paths (due to the presence of loops and/or branching), guidelines have been developed for which paths to test. Boundary and interior testing requires every loop to be executed the maximum and minimum number of times (boundary) and some number of times in between (interior) (Howden, 1975). Linear sequence code and jump criteria require successively longer logical sequences of code to be executed (Woodward, Hedley, and Hennell, 1980). Data flow testing requires covering pairs of program statements (connected along some path) in which the first statement defines a variable used by the second (Rapps and Weyuker, 1985; Laski and Korel, 1983; Ntafos, 1988). In this way, infections at the first location are given opportunity to propagate, though full propagation is not assured. Full propagation is analyzed in mutation testing, which seeks test data that distinguishes the unit being tested from slight modifications called mutants (DeMillo, Lipton, and Sayward, 1978). It is assumed that test data that catches these mutants will catch complex, inherent faults.

ERROR-BASED TESTING

In error-based testing, one selects test data based on an analysis of the potential errors that may occur in the programming process (Weyuker and Ostrand, 1980). The goal is to show that none of these potential errors were committed. Error-based testing consists of the following stages: identifying potential errors, determining their impact, selecting test data to catch the errors, executing the test data, and judging the results. If the output is correct, the errors were not committed (or the execution masked the error). Error-based testing is advantageous in that it uses all information sources to derive test data and it aims directly at the goal of testing, which is providing greater assurance that the code is fit for use.

Errors in the programming process are ultimately realized as faults, giving rise to a variant of error-based testing called fault-based testing. In this form, test data is constructed to demonstrate that prespecified potential faults are absent from the unit. Mutation testing may be viewed as a fault-based technique that considers finite faults classes. Infinite fault classes are modeled in symbolic fault-based testing (Morell, 1990) by introducing symbols (called symbolic faults) into the program to represent arbitrary faults. Execution of a symbolic fault introduces a symbolic value into the computation, which may in turn produce symbolic output that encodes the impact of any fault from the fault class. Analysis of the output determines which faults are absent from the program.

BIBLIOGRAPHY

R. A. DeMillo, R. J. Lipton, and F. G. Sayward, "Hints on Test Data Selection," *Computer* **11**(4), 34–41 (Apr. 1978).

W. E. Howden, "Methodology for the Generation of Program Test Data," *IEEE Transactions on Computers* **C-24,** 554–560 (May 1975).

W. Laski and B. Korel, "A Data Flow Oriented Program Testing Strategy," *IEEE Transactions on Software Engineering* **SE-9**(3), 347–354 (May 1983).

L. J. Morell, "A Theory of Fault-Based Testing," *IEEE Transactions on Software Engineering,* 844–857 (Aug. 1990).

S. C. Ntafos, "A Comparison of Some Structural Testing Strategies," *IEEE Transactions on Software Engineering* **SE-14,** 868–874 (June 1988).

S. Rapps and E. J. Weyuker, "Selecting Software Test Data Using Data Flow Information," *IEEE Transactions on Software Engineering* **SE-11**(4), 367–375 (Apr. 1985).

J. Voas, L. Morell, and K. Miller, "Predicting Where Faults can Hide from Testing," *IEEE Transaction on Software Engineering* **8**(2), 41–48 (Mar. 1991).

E. J. Weyuker and T. J. Ostrand, "Theories of Program Testing and the Application of Revealing Subdomains," *IEEE Transactions on Software Engineering* **SE-6**(3), 236–246 (May 1980).

M. R. Woodward, D. Hedley, and M. A. Hennell, "Experience With Path Analysis and Testing of Programs," *IEEE TSE* **SE-6**(3), 278–286 (May 1980).

LARRY MORELL
Hampton University

UNIX

The UNIX system is a computer operating system and a collection of software tools created at AT&T Bell Laboratories in the early 1970s. UNIX is a registered trademark

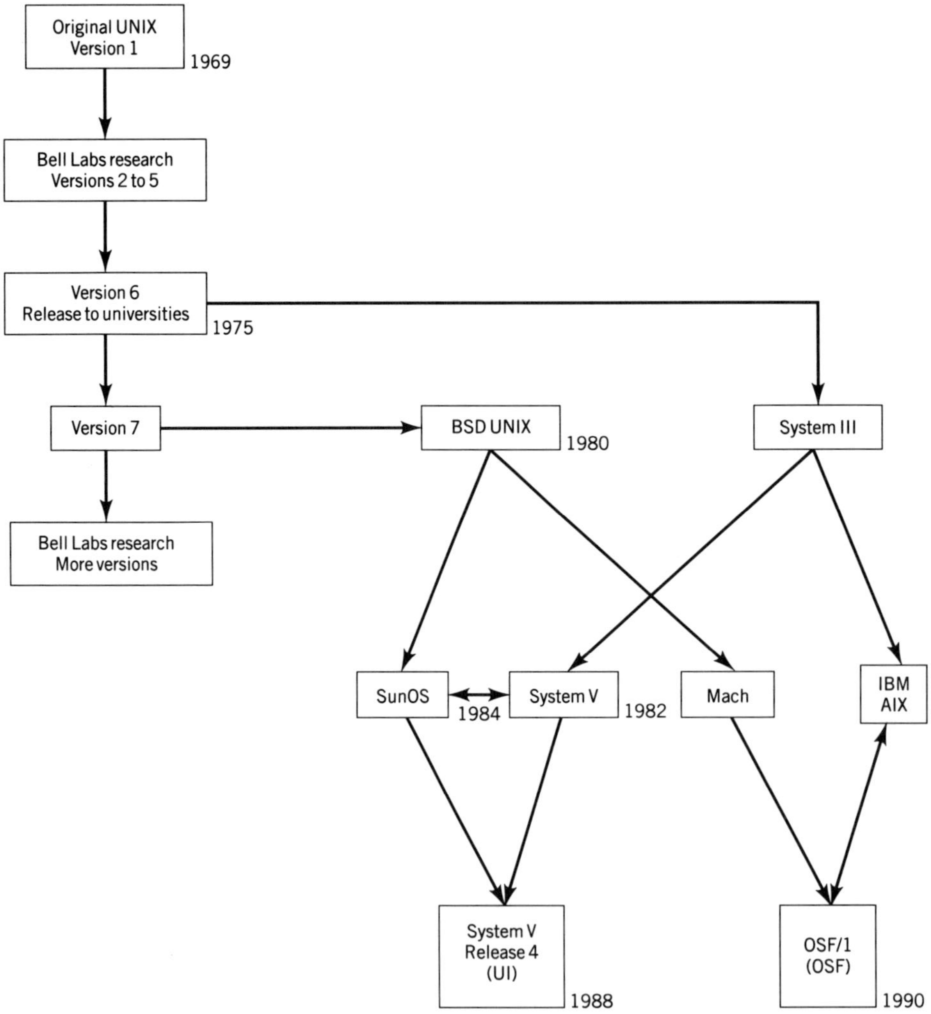

Figure 1. Milestones in UNIX system evolution.

of UNIX System Laboratories, Inc. Today the UNIX system is among the most popular and widely used computing environments, and is found on computers ranging from laptops through supercomputers. This article discusses the history and development of the UNIX system, its structure, its influence, its strengths and weaknesses as a software engineering environment, and its future.

HISTORY AND DEVELOPMENT

UNIX names a family of systems evolved by several organizations over more than twenty years. The details of this evolution are too complex to present here—this overview surveys the most important individuals and events in the development of the UNIX system. Figure 1 depicts milestones in the evolution of the UNIX system. See Computer Technology Research Corporation (1990) or Dunphy (1991) for detailed discussion of the history and development of the UNIX system.

The first version of the UNIX operating system was written by Ken Thompson of AT&T Bell Laboratories in 1969 for a DEC PDP-7 minicomputer. Thompson's goals were to provide a congenial environment for his own and his colleagues' computing research, and to create a substitute for the Multics time-sharing environment (Organick, 1972) that was lost when Bell Laboratories withdrew from the Multics project (Ritchie, 1984). Though innovative, early versions of the UNIX system were primitive by today's standards. Thompson and his colleagues used and improved the system over several years, adding features and utilities, improving the user interface, and rewriting the system in the C programming language (Ritchie and Thompson, 1978). The UNIX system has been used extensively in Bell Laboratories from its inception. The Sixth Edition UNIX System, or Version 6, was licensed outside AT&T in 1975. The UNIX system quickly gained favor in the academic community because it was innovative, powerful, free, ran on a popular platform (the DEC PDP-11), and came with complete source code.

In 1979 Thompson was on sabbatical at the University of California at Berkeley, where he worked with Bill Joy and Ozalp Babaoglu to add paging and other enhancements to the UNIX system. This work led to a new version of the UNIX system for DEC VAX computers (UCB, 1980). This version of the UNIX system, known as Berkeley Software Distribution (BSD) UNIX, hosted the TCP/IP networking software used in the ARPANET (Comer, 1988), had many useful new features (e.g., job control), and interesting new utilities (e.g., the vi screen editor). It was free, ran on a popular machine, and was released with complete source code. Like its predecessor from AT&T, this version of the UNIX system was widely adopted in the academic community. It was also the basis for many vendors' commercial versions of the UNIX system, notably Sun Microsystems' SunOS™ (Sun Microsystems, 1990). SunOS is a registered trademark of Sun Microsystems, Inc.

In the early 1980s, AT&T consolidated several internal research and development versions of the UNIX system to form its own commercial release, first as UNIX System III, then as UNIX System V (AT&T, 1992, Rosen and coworkers, 1990). Meanwhile, Thompson and other originators of the UNIX system continued their work, producing Research Versions of the UNIX system used in Bell Laboratories. Other vendors produced their own versions. By 1984 there were many UNIX system versions, all sharing ancestry in Version 6 from 1975, but largely incompatible, and a battle had begun over who would control the UNIX system, and what would become the standard version.

In 1987, agreement was reached between AT&T, Sun Microsystems, and several other vendors, to converge their versions of the UNIX system to a common standard. This agreement raised fears in the computer industry that AT&T and Sun would gain commercial advantage through control of UNIX system standards. In reaction, an alternative UNIX standardization organization, called the Open Software Foundation (OSF), was formed in 1988. OSF is an international consortium of over 100 companies including IBM, DEC, Hewlett-Packard, Groupe Bull, and Siemens AG. AT&T and Sun responded immediately by forming UNIX International (UI), a consortium of over 100 companies including AT&T, Sun Microsystems, NCR, NEC, and Unisys. OSF sponsors OSF/1, based on IBM's version of the UNIX system, AIX, and a research version of the UNIX system from Carnegie Mellon University, called Mach. UI sponsors System V Release 4 (SVR4), mainly a combination of AT&T versions of the UNIX system and Sun's SunOS. Today these two versions of the UNIX system dominate the marketplace, but most installed systems are SVR4 (often with proprietary extensions).

Despite agreement on many standards (discussed below), SVR4 and OSF/1 are very different. Because it unifies many versions of the UNIX system, SVR4 is rich and complex. SVR4 will become more complex as UI carries out its plans to enhance it with DoD level B2 security, multiprocessing, distributed processing, better system administration support, real-time features, and online transaction processing support (UNIX International, 1990). OSF/1 is simpler, and though coming later to market, offers features not yet available in SVR4. OSF/1 is based on the Mach microkernel (Black, 1990). designed for multiprocessing and distributed computing, and offers the Distributed Computing Environment (DCE) for controlling distributed computing resources. OSF/1 has powerful memory management features. OSF plans to enhance its offering to DOD security level B3, and will support AFS, a sophisticated distributed file system.

The competition between UI and OSF is complex: Though sharing a standards base, each organization offers distinct products and features. The marketplace prefers some features from one organization, and some features from the other. Competition between UI and OSF will likely continue, but areas of standardization, compatibility, and interoperability will grow.

UNIX System Standards

Despite the continuing battle over control of UNIX system standards, the UNIX community has agreed on several of them (see Cameron, 1991, for a complete survey). The most important is POSIX (qv), the IEEE Portable Operating System Interface for Computing Environments (IEEE, 1990, Lewine, 1991). POSIX specifies an Applications Programming Interface (API) stating how programs can interface with an operating system. Though based on UNIX System V and the BSD UNIX system, the POSIX API standard can be and is met by several non-UNIX systems, as well as most UNIX systems. Future POSIX agreements will specify standards for shells, tools, system administration, and so on. Both UNIX consortia endorse the Common Applications Environment (CAE) specifications from X/Open Company Limited, another international consortium of computer system vendors. X/Open published the *X/Open Portability Guide, Issue 3,* or XPG3 (X/Open Company Limited, 1988) specifying *de facto* standards for operating system interfaces, the C programming language, data management, X windows (qv), and networking. XPG4 will specify further standards for database query languages, networking, and graphical user interfaces. There is also agreement on the X windowing system (Scheifler and co-workers, 1988) as the basis for Graphical User Interfaces (GUIs), and TCP/IP (Comer, 1988) as the basis for electronic mail and news systems, networks, and client-server systems. The Network File System (NFS) is a *de facto* UNIX system standard for distributed file systems, though it is likely to be replaced or enhanced in the future. OSF has proposed an important standard for a UNIX system binary interface called the Architecture Neutral Distribution Format (ANDF) (Hurwitz, 1991).

UI and OSF continue to battle over some standards. The most heated exchanges have been over a GUI standard for the "look and feel" of windowed user interfaces. OSF sponsors Motif (Open Software Foundation, 1990), a GUI similar to Microsoft's Windows program. UI promotes OPEN LOOK (AT&T, 1989), developed by AT&T and Sun. Although Motif has the popular edge, it appears that both GUIs will persist.

The UNIX System and the C Programming Language

The UNIX system and the C programming language (Kernighan and Ritchie, 1978; Harbison and Steele, 1987) are closely related both historically and technically. The C programming language was designed by Dennis Ritchie in 1972 expressly for UNIX system programming. Over 90% of the UNIX system kernel, and virtually all its utilities, are written in C. Many UNIX software tools, like lex (Lesk, 1975) and yacc (Johnson, 1975), are built to work with C source code files. Many others, such as the text processing language awk (Aho and co-workers, 1988), share a family resemblance with C. C is specified as the standard UNIX system programming language in several standards documents, including POSIX and XPG3. C itself has been standardized by the American National Standards Institute (ANSI) and the International Standards Organization (ISO) (Plauger, 1992).

The UNIX System's Historical Strengths

The UNIX system was developed as a programming environment for a small group of computer science researchers. It was used almost from the first for electronic mail and news systems. It has been used in Bell Laboratories to support text processing applications since 1970. Thus historically the UNIX system provides strong tool support for program development, electronic communication, and document preparation, and for small groups sharing computing resources in a research environment.

UNIX SYSTEM STRUCTURE

The UNIX system consists of a kernel, a file system, a shell, and a collection of data and program files. The *kernel* is the program that handles core operating system functions, traditionally including process control and scheduling, interrupt handling, interprocess communication, main memory management, and peripheral device management (Bach, 1986; Leffler and co-workers, 1989). The kernel manages the sharing of system resources among users, ensuring that they do not interfere with each other, and that each has access to the resources they need.

The UNIX *file system* is a hierarchical arrangement of files in a directory tree with a unique root. File subsystems are mountable and dismountable, and may reside on a variety of devices. Files have only a few types, the main type being a sequence of bytes, making file processing simple and uniform. Files have owners who control read, write, and execution privileges, providing data security.

A UNIX *shell* is an operating system command interpreter. Unlike previous systems, a shell command interpreter is not a special part of the operating system, but runs like any other user program. This makes the shell flexible and modifiable, and lets users choose from several alternative shells. Shells can interpret program files, so they provide a powerful and convenient operating system programming environment. Some of the most famous and powerful features of the UNIX system are provided by shells, including input and output redirection, program pipelines, interactive job control, and command history and editing mechanisms (Rosen and co-workers, 1990). Today the most important shells are the Bourne shell (Bourne, 1978), the Berkeley C shell (Anderson and Anderson, 1986), and the Korn shell (Bolsky and Korn, 1989).

The UNIX system includes system data files for many purposes, such as user information, terminal driver data, network configuration information, and so on. These files serve as easily changed system parameters, increasing system portability and versatility. The UNIX system includes may programs called *software tools* or *utilities.* Tools range from simple but essential programs for manipulating files and controlling peripherals, to sophisticated systems for editing, checking, and formatting documents (Macdonald and co-workers, 1982), building software (Feldman, 1979), constructing lexical analyzers (Lesk, 1975) and parsers (Johnson, 1975), and managing source code (Rochkind, 1975). Since these tools are usually written in C, are not tied to the system, and interact with each other in simple ways, they are easy to change or replace.

INFLUENCE OF THE UNIX SYSTEM

Several factors combine to make the UNIX system influential. First, the UNIX system is widely distributed. As noted, it was provided by AT&T and Berkeley virtually for free, with source code. Second, because it is written in C, and makes few architectural assumptions, the UNIX system is portable: it runs on more types of computers than any other operating system. Third, its use in universities made it familiar to students who successfully encouraged its adoption when they graduated to industrial positions. Fourth, the UNIX system's simple design, flexibility, and powerful programming tools make it an ideal environment for software research and development. As a result of these factors, the UNIX system is used throughout industry and academia, runs on most machines larger than small personal computers, and is a standard environment for computer science research and development.

The nature of the influence of the UNIX system is harder to assess. One aspect of its influence is the programming philosophy it embodies. The UNIX system was the first and is still among the best examples of a *toolkit* programming environment (Dart and co-workers, 1987). In a toolkit environment, a rich collection of software tools is used to automate the software life cycle. The UNIX toolkit philosophy holds that individual software tools should be functionally simple, reusable parts combinable using the facilities of the environment (Pike and Kernighan, 1984). The software tools in the UNIX system are the reusable parts, and the shell facilities of input and output redirection, pipes, and user programmability are the means of combination. For example, suppose one wants to print a list of processes connected to a terminal in reverse order of process duration. There is no standard UNIX program to produce this listing. However, the tool ps lists the status of processes, the tool grep can filter out processes not attached to a terminal, the tool sort can order the listing by reverse process duration, and the tool lp can print the list. The following command line produces the listing:

```
ps -a | grep tty | sort -r +2 | lp
```

The success of the UNIX system popularized the toolkit philosophy, and influenced other toolkits (see ADA). Particularly important are the "small is beautiful" approach to software tools, the notion of a software filter (a tool that does a simple transformation of its input to produce its output), and the idea that simple but flexible program combination mechanisms are as important as the programs themselves.

Another aspect of the influence of the UNIX system is its ubiquity as a platform for research and development. For example, UNIX systems were the birthplace of networking software such as uucp (Nowitz and Lesk, 1980), and NFS. The client-server model of computing was pioneered and popularized on a UNIX system. The X window system (Scheifler and co-workers, 1988) was developed for the UNIX system. Many Computer Aided Software Engineering (see CASE) tools were developed first for UNIX system platforms (Cureton, 1988). Some of the best document preparation systems (Gehani, 1987; Frame Technology, 1989; Interleaf, 1989) were developed on UNIX system platforms. The features, interaction styles, computational models, and so forth, of these programs must have been greatly influenced by the UNIX system.

A final aspect of the influence of the UNIX system is its central role in the rise and popularization of electronic mail, electronic news, and the Internet. As noted, uucp and electronic mail and news were developed for the UNIX system early on. TCP/IP was mated with the UNIX system when it was implemented on BSD in 1980 and then distributed to universities that used it to link with the ARPANET. The ARPANET eventually grew into the Internet, a global network of more than 180,000 nodes (Comer, 1988). Using the Internet and the communication tools and facilities of the UNIX system, it is now possible to send electronic mail and data economically and quickly between virtually any computers in the world.

THE UNIX SYSTEM AS A SOFTWARE ENGINEERING ENVIRONMENT

A software engineering environment is an automated system supporting software development and maintenance. The UNIX system is an operating system and a collection of software tools that can be used as a software engineering environment. In surveying and evaluating UNIX system support for software engineering, the first question to settle is: What should be counted as part of the UNIX software engineering environment? As discussed above, there are competing versions of the UNIX system. Furthermore, many important commercial software engineering support tools were developed for the UNIX system, but are not properly part of it.

For this discussion, the basic UNIX software engineering environment is defined as SVR4, the most popular and complete version of the UNIX system. An enhanced UNIX software engineering environment is a version of the UNIX system enhanced with commercial software engineering support tools. The next section surveys and evaluates the basic UNIX software engineering environment. The following section suggests how to augment the UNIX system to form an enhanced UNIX software engineering environment. See Frakes and co-workers (1991) for a broader discussion of UNIX software engineering environments. See Penedo and Riddle (1988) and Dart and co-workers (1987) for other evaluations of the UNIX system as a software engineering environment. (See also SOFTWARE ENGINEERING ENVIRONMENTS).

Documentation Support	Design Support	Programming Support	Project Management Support
vi, spell, wwb, tbl, eqn, pic, grap, nroff, troff, SCCS	awk, shell programs	vi, cscope, lint, lex, yacc, make, cc, as, dis, ar, SCCS, cb, cflow, cxref, ctrace, sdb, prof, lprof	shell programs

Fundamental Services
networked file system, process control, pipes, signals, peripheral control, TCP/IP, shells, X window system, OPEN LOOK

Figure 2. Basic UNIX software engineering environment.

The Basic UNIX Software Engineering Environment

Since this is but a survey, only the most important basic UNIX software engineering environment tools are discussed, and those only briefly. See SVR4 documentation for a complete description of SVR4 software engineering support tools (AT&T, 1992).

For purposes of exposition, we consider a software engineering environment to have four components built on a base of fundamental services. The *fundamental services* foundation provides facilities for data and file management, user interface management, process control, transaction management, and so forth. The *document support* component automates the creation, evaluation, correction, and change of textual and graphical work products. The *design support* component automates creation, evaluation, correction, and change of software and system designs. The *programming support* component automates software coding and testing activities. The *project management support* component automates work estimation, scheduling, and tracking tasks. Figure 2 illustrates this breakdown for the basic UNIX software engineering environment.

The UNIX system provides a solid foundation of fundamental services, with excellent facilities for process control, file management, tool interaction, electronic communication, and graphical user interfaces. The UNIX system has been criticized for inadequate data and transaction management facilities, however. The document support component of the basic UNIX software engineering environment is strong. Generic support for writing documents is provided by the vi editor (Bolsky, 1984; Lamb, 1990), the spelling checker spell, and a collection of tools called the "Writer's Workbench" (Macdonald and co-workers, 1982) that check spelling, punctuation, grammar, and style. UNIX document generation tools, including the table formatter tbl, the equation formatter eqn, the figure generators pic and grap, and the text formatting tools nroff and troff (Gehani, 1987; Gehani and Lally, 1988) make it possible to produce high quality typeset documents. Generic support for text file version control is provided by the Source Code Control System (SCCS) (Rochkind, 1975). This collection of tools automates text file version tracking and version retrieval, and imposes a locking mechanism prohibiting simultaneous version revision (see CONFIGURATION MAN-

AGEMENT). There is weak support for editing and manipulating graphics, and it is inconvenient to incorporate graphics in text documents. There are no WYSIWYG editing or formatting tools in the basic UNIX software engineering environment.

The design support component of the UNIX software engineering environment is weak. There are no tools supporting software design methodologies. UNIX shells, especially the Korn shell (Bolsky and Korn, 1989), are powerful high level programming languages well suited to certain text processing prototypes. The awk programming language (Aho and co-workers, 1988) is also a good prototyping tool.

The programming support component is by far the strongest aspect of the basic UNIX software engineering environment. Among the many good tools supporting coding and testing are the following:

- *Program editing:* vi (Bolsky, 1984; Lamb, 1990) is a full-screen editor with special features for accelerating source code input and change. cscope supports editing of several C, lex, or yacc files at once based on cross-reference information
- *Program checking:* lint (Johnson, 1978; Darwin, 1988) is a C source code checker that finds problems ranging from genuine errors through bad coding practices.
- *Program generation:* lex (Lesk, 1975; Mason and Brown, 1990) takes a token description file as input and generates a C program implementing a finite state machine recognizer. Similarly, yacc (Johnson, 1975; Mason and Brown, 1990) takes a context free grammar and generates a C program implementing an LR(1) parser.
- *Program building*: make (Feldman, 1979; Talbot, 1990) takes a file describing program compilation dependencies and checks the modification times of program source and object files. Using this information, it recompiles just those modules affected by source code changes, and relinks just those programs whose component object files have been changed. The cc program is the C compiler; ar creates and maintains object code libraries; as is an assembler and dis a disassembler.
- *Source code change control*: the SCCS suite of programs (Rochkind, 1975) is specially designed for this task, and has special features to work with make in building programs from the most recent versions of source code.
- *Program reading*: cb reformats poorly formatted code to help program readers. cflow produces listings of C program function hierarchies. cxref produces a cross-reference for a C program. cscope provides a powerful program browsing facility based on cross-reference information.
- *Program tracing*: ctrace transforms a C program so that it prints each line as it executes, and every accessed variable, to trace the program.
- *Program debugging*: sdb is a symbolic debugger supporting controlled program execution and examination of the runtime environment.
- *Performance monitoring*: prof is an execution profiling tool that tracks how much time is spent executing each function in a C program. lprof records how often each line in a C program is executed. time reports the time consumed by application and system code, and the elapsed time for program execution.

These tools are geared to C programming, but many are generic enough to support programming in other languages as well. The UNIX shell is useful for automating many aspects of coding and testing, such as regression testing, for example.

The weakest part of the basic UNIX software engineering environment is project management support. There are no project management support tools, but some tracking and scheduling tasks can be automated with shell programs.

In summary, the UNIX operating system provides a strong foundation of fundamental services for a software engineering environment. The basic UNIX software engineering environment has a strong documentation support component, and a strong programming support component, but weak design and project management support components. Although it provides excellent support for parts of the software engineering process, the basic UNIX software engineering environment has several major weaknesses.

Enhancing the UNIX Software Engineering Environment

One great advantage of a toolkit environment is that it can be enhanced by adding or improving its tools. The UNIX system can be made into a superior software engineering environment by replacing less sophisticated tools and adding tools to fill gaps.

An enhanced UNIX software engineering environment might first improve its project management component by adding one or more project planning and tracking tools. These tools provide graphical interfaces for creating Pert and Gantt charts, finding critical paths, analyzing work loads, and so on. Next, one might obtain a CASE tool to strengthen the design support component (see CASE). CASE tools provide graphical interfaces for creating and changing data flow diagrams, structure and hierarchy charts, and state transition diagrams. They maintain data dictionaries and process descriptions, and are able to check designs for consistency and completeness.

Although these changes remedy the major weaknesses of the basic UNIX software engineering environment, other additions can strengthen it further. Various advanced programming support tools can be added as needed; examples are a C or C++language interpreter, program metrics and analysis tools, program generation tools, and software reuse and program library management tools (see REUSE). Better testing tools could be added, including tools for test coverage analysis, regression test automation, and test case tracking (see TESTING). Finally, a WYSIWYG desktop publishing system could replace or supplement the standard UNIX document generation tools.

The basic UNIX software engineering environment provides good support for the software development process.

Added software tools can enhance it into a state-of-the-art environment. Consequently the UNIX system is the preferred platform for assembling the best available software engineering environment.

FUTURE PROSPECTS

Operating System Evolution

Although the UNIX operating system was originally written for stand-alone computers, it has evolved into a network operating system that runs on different computers but allows transparent file access across a local area network, and log-in privileges from other machines on the network. As networked and distributed computing becomes more pervasive, there will be greater demand for distributed operating systems that run across an entire network and provide transparent access to all resources on a network. The UNIX system will continue to evolve in this direction, as is clear from the UI *System V Roadmap* (UNIX International, 1990), and OSF's published plans (Dwyer and Richman, 1992).

The UNIX system is evolving to meet the needs of business and government users. Because of its roots as a research and development tool, the UNIX system has lacked strength in areas important to businesses and government, particularly security, online transaction processing, and real-time processing. Both OSF and UI plan to enhance UNIX system security to the level required by U.S. intelligence agencies. UI plans to enhance SVR4 online transaction processing and real-time capabilities (UNIX International, 1990). There are already several implementations of the UNIX system providing a variety of real-time capabilities (Furht and co-workers, 1991).

Environment Evolution

The UNIX system provides good fundamental services to tool writers and program developers, but needs in this area continue to grow. Of particular concern are data repository services to support more sophisticated, especially object oriented, data stores. These services will probably be provided by adding support packages to the UNIX development environment, much as the X window system has been added to provide GUI support. A leading contender for a data repository services standard is the Object Management portion of the Portable Common Tools Environment (see PCTE) (Boudier and co-workers, 1988), a European fundamental services standard that includes specifications for an operating system and user interface API, process control and communication mechanisms, networked resource management, and data management.

Greater understanding of the software development process (Humphrey, 1989), and experience with automating it has already led to a wealth of software development tools (Kintala, 1988; Belanger and Wish, 1990). UNIX system tool evolution can be expected to continue, with emphasis on greater tool integration and interoperability, promoted by the spread of development support systems and the standardization of human and program data interfaces. The UNIX software engineering environment of the future is likely to consist of the UNIX system as the base operating system, development support systems providing a layer enhancing fundamental services, and a collection of advanced and highly integrated software tools filling out the components of the software engineering environment.

BIBLIOGRAPHY

G. Anderson and P. Anderson, *The UNIX C Shell Field Guide,* Prentice-Hall, Englewood Cliffs, N.J., 1986.

AT&T, *OPEN LOOK Graphical User Interface Style Guide,* AT&T, New York, 1989.

AT&T, *UNIX System V, Release 4 Documentation Set,* Prentice-Hall, Englewood Cliffs, N.J., 1992.

A. Aho, B. W. Kernighan, and P. J. Weinberger, *The AWK Programming Language,* Addison-Wesley, New York, 1988.

M. J. Bach, *The Design of the UNIX Operating System,* Prentice-Hall, Englewood Cliffs, N.J., 1986.

D. G. Belanger and M. Wish, eds., *AT&T Technical Journal—Issue on Software Productivity* **69**(2), (March/April, 1990).

D. L. Black, "Scheduling Support for Concurrency and Parallelism in the Mach Operating System," *Computer* **23**(5), 35–43 (May, 1990).

M. I. Bolsky, *VI User's Handbook,* AT&T Bell Laboratories, Piscataway, N.J., 1984.

M. I. Bolsky and D. G. Korn, *The Korn Shell,* Prentice-Hall, Englewood Cliffs, N.J., 1989.

G. Boudier, F. Gallo, R. Minot, and M. I. Thomas, "An Overview of PCTE and PCTE+," *Proceedings of the Third ACM Symposium on Software Environments,* Nov., 1988.

S. R. Bourne, "The UNIX Shell," *The Bell System Technical Journal* **57**(6), 1971–1990 (July–Aug., 1978).

D. Cameron, *UNIX Standards,* Computer Technology Research Corporation, Charleston, S.C., 1991.

D. Comer, *Internetworking with TCP/IP,* Prentice-Hall, Englewood Cliffs, N.J., 1988.

Computer Technology Research Corporation, *UNIX in the 1990's,* Charleston, S.C., 1990.

B. Cureton, "The Future of UNIX in the CASE Renaissance," *Software* 18–22 (March, 1988).

S. A. Dart, R. J. Ellison, P. H. Feiler, and N. Haberman, "Software Development Environments," *Computer* **20**(11), 18–14 28 (Nov., 1987).

I. Darwin, *Checking C Programs with Lint,* O'Reilly & Associates Inc., Sebastopol, Calif., 1988.

E. Dunphy, *The UNIX Industry,* QED Information Sciences, Inc., Wellesly, Mass., 1991.

J. Dwyer and J. Richman, "OSF/1," *UNIX Review* **10**(4), 43–46 (April, 1992).

S. I. Feldman "Make A Program for Maintaining Computer Programs," *Software Practice and Experience* **9**(4), 255–265 (April 1979).

W. B. Frakes, C. Fox, and B. Nejmeh, *Software Engineering in the UNIX/C Environment,* Prentice-Hall, Englewood Cliffs, N.J., 1991.

Frame Technology, *FrameMaker Reference Manual,* Frame Technology Incorporated, San Jose, Calif., 1989.

B. Furht, D. Grostick, D. Glutch, G. Rabbat, J. Parker, and M. McRoberts, *Real-Time UNIX Systems,* Kluwer Academic Publishers, Boston, Mass., 1991.

N. Gehani, *Document Formatting and Typesetting on the UNIX System,* Silicon Press, Summit, N.J., 1987.

N. Gehani and S. Lally, *Document Formatting and Typesetting on the UNIX System,* Volume II, Silicon Press, Summit, N.J., 1988.

S. Harbison and G. Steele Jr., *C: A Reference Manual,* 2nd ed., Prentice-Hall, Englewood Cliffs, N.J., 1987.

W. Humphrey, *Managing the Software Process,* Addison-Wesley, Reading, Mass., 1989.

J. Hurwitz, "OSF's ANDF," *Patricia Seybold's Unix in the Office* **6**(10), 3–14 (Oct., 1991).

IEEE, *Information Technology—Portable Operating System Interface (POSIX)—Part 1: System Application Program Interface (API) [C Language]* IEEE Std 1003.1-1900, Institute of Electrical and Electronics Engineers, Los Angeles, Calif., 1990.

Interleaf, *Interleaf Sun Reference Manual, TPS 4.0,* Interleaf Incorporated, Cambridge, Mass., 1989.

S. C. Johnson, "Lint, a C Program Checker," *Computing Science Technical Report 65,* AT&T Bell Laboratories, Murray Hill, N.J., 1978.

S. C. Johnson, "Yacc, Yet Another Compiler Compiler," *Computing Science Technical Report 32,* AT&T Bell Laboratories, Murray Hill, N.J., 1975.

B. Kernighan and R. Pike, *The UNIX Programming Environment,* Prentice-Hall, Englewood Cliffs, N.J., 1984.

B. Kernighan and D. M. Ritchie, *The C Programming Language,* Prentice-Hall, Englewood Cliffs, N.J., 1978.

C. M. R. Kintala, ed., *AT&T Technical Journal—Issue on Software Productivity* **67**(4), (July/Aug. 1988).

L. Lamb, *Learning the vi Editor,* 5th ed., O'Reilly & Associates Inc., Sebastopol, Calif., 1990.

S. J. Leffler and co-workers, *The Design and Implementation of the 4.3BSD UNIX Operating System,* Addison-Wesley, Reading, Mass. 1989.

M. E. Lesk, "Lex—A Lexical Analyzer Generator," *Computing Science Technical Report 39,* AT&T Bell Laboratories, Murray Hill, N.J., 1975.

D. A. Lewine, *POSIX Programmer's Guide,* O'Reilly & Associates, Inc., Sebastopol, Calif. 1991.

N. H. Macdonald, L. T. Frase, P. S. Gingrich, and S. A. Keenan, "The WRITER'S WORKBENCH, Computer Aid for Text Analysis," *IEEE Transactions on Communications* **30**(1), 105–110 (Jan. 1982).

T. Mason and D. Brown, *Lex & yacc,* O'Reilly & Associates Inc., Sebastopol, Calif., 1990.

D. A. Nowitz and M. E. Lesk, "Implementation of a Dial-Up Network of UNIX Systems," *Fall 1980 COMPCON,* Washington, D.C., 483–486, 1980.

Open Software Foundation, *OSF/Motif Style Guide,* Prentice-Hall, Englewood Cliffs, N.J., 1990.

E. J. Organick, *The Multics System: An Examination of its Structure,* MIT Press, Cambridge, Mass, 1972.

M. Penedo and B. Riddle, "Guest Editors' Introduction—Software, Engineering Environment Architectures," *IEEE Transactions on Software Engineering* **SE-14**(6), 689–696 (June 1988).

R. Pike and B. Kernighan, "Program Design in the UNIX System Environment," *AT&T Bell Laboratories Technical Journal* **83**(8–2), 1595–1606 (Oct. 1984).

P. J. Plauger, *ANSI and ISO Standard C: Programmer's Reference,* Microsoft Press, Redmond, Wash., 1992.

D. M. Ritchie, "The Evolution of the UNIX Time-Sharing System," *AT&T Bell Laboratories Technical Journal* **83** (8–2), 1577–1594 (Oct. 1984).

D. M. Ritchie and K. Thompson, "The UNIX Time-Sharing System," *The Bell System Technical Journal* **57** (6), 1905–1930 (July–Aug. 1978).

M. J. Rochkind, "The Source Code Control System," *IEEE Transactions on Software Engineering* **SE-1**, (4), 255–265 (April 1975).

K. H. Rosen, R. R. Rosinski, and J. M. Farber, *UNIX System V Release 4: An Introduction for New and Experienced Users,* McGraw-Hill, New York, 1990.

R. W. Scheifler, J. Gettys, and R. Newman, *The X Window System C Library and Protocol Reference,* Digital Press, Bedford, Mass., 1988.

Sun Microsystems, *SunOS Reference Manual,* Volumes I-III, Sun Microsystems, Mountain View, Calif., 1990.

S. Talbot, *Managing Projects With Make,* 2nd ed., O'Reilly & Associates Inc., Sebastopol, Calif., 1990.

UCB, *UNIX Programmer's Manual, 4.1 Berkeley Software Distribution,* Computer Science Division, Department of Electrical Engineering and Computer Science, University of California, Berkeley, Calif., 1980.

UNIX International, *UNIX System V Roadmap,* UNIX International, Parsippany, N.J., Jan., 1990.

X/Open Company Limited, *X/Open Portability Guide,* Issue 3, Prentice-Hall, Englewood Cliffs, N.J., 1988.

CHRISTOPHER FOX
AT&T Bell Laboratories

USABILITY

The ease with which a user can learn to operate, prepare inputs for, and interpret outputs of a system or component (IEEE).

USER INTERFACE

See USER INTERFACE MANAGEMENT SYSTEMS; INTERACTIVE GRAPHICS.

UNPRECEDENTED SYSTEMS

INTRODUCTION

This article addresses unprecedented systems, provides insight into the risks of such systems, and discusses how those risks might be addressed through various acquisition–development processes. The main philosophy behind risk reduction is to make unprecedented systems as precedented as practical.

Precedented systems are those for which (*1*) the requirements are consistent and well understood, (*2*) the system architecture (both hardware and software) is known to be adequate for the requirements, and (*3*) the acquisition and development teams have worked together to develop a similar previous system. Violation of one or more of these elements of definition causes the system to be unprecedented. Consequently, certain risks arise that require an acquisition–development strategy for their mitigation.

A primary assertion of this article is that precedence is one of the most important elements in the timely development of quality software. In many cases, it is more dominant than many of the more narrowly focused issues that receive more attention, such as language, tools, hardware instruction set architecture, etc. Simply stated, the concept of precedented systems means that the learning curve applies to software development, as it does in all other areas of human endeavor.

The concept of unprecedented systems came from a 1988 Air Force Studies Board Summer Study chaired by Walter Beam (1989). During that study, a number of software development successes and failures for mission-critical computer systems were briefed to the study team. The team members asked themselves what it was about the successes that made them successes and what was it about the failures that made them failures. In answering that question, the team developed the concepts of precedented and unprecedented systems. Those systems that were successfully developed were done by a team who had previously completed a similar system. When the team had no previous experience with a similar system, cost, schedule, and performance suffered substantially.

Several studies have highlighted the importance of the requirements process as well as the clarification and stability of the requirements. The relationship of the requirements to a digital system architecture and the robustness of that architecture to future change are also critical issues. The development team's experience with similar requirements and their implementing architecture are clearly critical factors associated with program success.

This article defines different types of unprecedented systems and explores in a simple way the primary risks of requirements, architecture, and team experience. The article then explores a variety of top-level acquisition processes and how they may reduce or amplify the risks.

PRECEDENTED SYSTEMS: AN IDEALISTIC CONCEPT

Three fundamental factors (a requirements factor, an architecture factor, and a team factor) determine whether a system development is precedented. For precedented systems, the system and software requirements are well defined and understood by both the government acquisition team and the industry team responsible for implementing them.

Precedented systems also have proven digital hardware and software architectures. Hardware architecture relates to the arrangement of processors, memories, input–output devices, and data buses to communicate digital information. Software architecture means the layout of functions or processes across the hardware architecture; the layering of these functions, interfaces, and protocols; the layout of major databases; and the software mechanisms that integrate the hardware architecture, including operating systems, executives, and execution concepts. A proven hardware–software architecture is one that has already been implemented for similar requirements and is known to have the capacity, throughput, and band width to meet them.

The system acquisition and development teams (including management) are clearly the crux of the system effort and key to the success of the project. A precedented system has experienced acquisition and development teams consisting of system engineers, hardware and software designers, and developers who have worked together before on a similar project, so that their processes (both formal and informal) of working together are well established. Their prior experience gives them a sufficiently clear idea of the product they are building (as well as the requirements and the environment in which it must work) to be able to communicate together clearly and easily. The development team members (both from industry and government) are usually interdisciplinary; because they have worked together before, the barriers associated with team building, interdisciplinary communications, and approaches to the development process have been lowered substantially.

Now that the key elements of known requirements, known hardware and software architectures, and an experienced team whose members understand the application and have worked together before have been defined, some examples of precedented systems will be given. Ultimately, a precedented system does not really exist. No one ever rebuilds a previous system identically. However, there are system developments that are nearly precedented, and three such examples will be discussed.

The first example is a major air defense system. This system was the third air defense system built by the contractor team. The requirements associated with the system were similar to the requirements the team had encountered on two previous developments. The extent of the requirements beyond their experience was challenging but not overwhelming. The bulk of the team had worked together before, and it was able to perform closely within cost and schedule, and to hit the ground running, so relatively little time was lost as a result of learning curve effects.

The second example is a phased-array radar warning system. Two companies worked together on this system. The prime contractor was responsible for the radar and the real-time phased-array radar control software. A subcontractor was responsible for the bulk of the remaining software, including the radar tracker, communications, and user interface software. The subcontractor's software team had just completed work on an earlier project, another phased-array radar system with characteristics similar to this new project. The prime and subcontractor had entered into a teaming relationship for the duration of the proposal effort, which lasted about 1 yr. During this time, the subcontractor provided support to the prime contractor's development of a preliminary software requirement specification that was submitted with the proposal. After contract award, the subcontractor moved its staff to colocate at the prime contractor's site. The staff was able to hit the ground running because they knew from past experience specifically what trade-offs were needed and what key issues had to be addressed. They understood the requirements well enough to point out the areas of ambiguity, deficiencies, and software cost drivers. The subcontractor was respected as a team member that facilitated the communications with the prime contractor to resolve requirements issues effectively and in a timely manner.

The third example of precedented system development resides in what are commonly called the software factories of Japan. When large Japanese companies consider entering an area of software application, such as digital controls for nuclear power plants, they attempt several initial developments of these applications through one of their subsidiaries. When they decide that they can be successful and want to compete commercially in nuclear power plant controls in a broader market, the Japanese set up a software factory. Workers in this factory are motivated to spend their careers building software for the particular application. The workers are given incentives to use as much design and code from their previous installations as makes sense. Consequently, after several control systems have been completed, the team becomes increasingly proficient in the hardware, software, and physics associated with the application. It becomes better able to predict how long it will take to develop the next system, provided it is not far removed from what it has already done. Through favorable pricing policies, customers are encouraged to keep their requirements similar to those of previous systems. The factories can reuse existing software, making it more and more mature, so that it has fewer and fewer errors. The subsequent applications are based on well-known formulations of hardware and software architectures, previous design, and shared understanding. The development process becomes repeatable and predictable, and it can be measured and fine-tuned to improve productivity and the product.

UNPRECEDENTED SYSTEMS

As discussed, a precedented system development deals with requirements and an architectural structure that are well understood, and a team that has been there before. An unprecedented system is one in which not all these elements are available to the development. It may be unprecedented because the team selected has no experience in working together or has no experience with the particular application (even if the requirements and the architecture are similar to those of jobs already performed by other teams). In this case, the system unprecedented in terms of the staffing or team. Bill Curtis (1988) explains that when a new team is put together, the members must not only understand the application but also develop the informal team respect, culture, and lines of communication. In particular, the lines of communication among system, software, and hardware engineering team members must be emphasized. Because the team has not performed a previous similar effort, members will argue about requirements interpretations and architectural designs; some will be unjustifiably overconfident of their approaches. Hence, it is important that new team members communicate extensively with one another concerning their varied disciplines and how they believe the system should be developed. In those cases in which subsystems already exist or the requirements and the architecture are clear from previous systems, the team must do its best to understand the requirements and architecture and not to deviate arbitrarily from an architecture that is known to satisfy the requirements. However, the team's interpretation of the requirements is likely to be different from the interpretation of the team that built the previous system, although that system still serves as a guide to the novice team.

An example of a system unprecedented in terms of staffing was the flight control system of a recent large aircraft. Several years into the program, it was decided that the flight control design, originally based on manual hydraulic controls with autopilot assist, had to be changed to a full-authority digital flight control system. Although the technology was available in the industry, neither the air frame contractor nor the flight control subcontractor had any experience with a full-authority system. They spent several years unsuccessfully trying to define and price the requirements. The system was then completed expeditiously by a different subcontractor that possessed the needed experience.

A second way in which a system may be unprecedented is in terms of architecture. The team may be highly experienced in the application area and understand the requirements well, but the customer or the technology may impose a new kind of hardware and software architecture on the development. An example of this might be the first use of the Ada language with the features of tasking, generics, and a new Ada run-time system. An uncertainty in execution performance is often a real risk in first-time Ada implementations.

An example of the second case of unprecedentedness (new architecture) is the revision of a large command and control system. In this program, the team understood command and control systems well; however, it had to develop a new hardware and software architecture, realizable within the constructs of a new programming language (Ada), which added risk to the development. Fortunately, the team recognized this risk. It proceeded to add resources to the project, above and beyond the government-sponsored resources, to prove early the architectural concepts on which the design was to be based. Hence, the key for controlling the software development risk caused by the unprecedented architecture was to implement and demonstrate the architecture before any other system aspect was addressed in detail. Each of these factors of unprecedentedness may be present and in varying degrees. For example, a system development may have requirements that are well understood by the government team but the development uses a new architectural concept for those requirements and a new contractor team. In this situation, considerable time is needed to arrive at a mutual understanding of the requirements. Furthermore, the architecture and the system performance remain a risk to the program until the architecture can be demonstrated.

The last case is that of highly unprecedented systems. Such systems are brand new, with no previous systems to reference to ensure that the requirements are consistent, understood, and implementable. The architecture is most likely at risk, the team must learn the application domain and its environment as part of the development, and team building must be accomplished. These difficult developments require an acquisition process and development process that mitigate all three categories of risk.

An example of a highly unprecedented system development is the Space Defense System. Only in the area of reentry has there been any precedented experience (through the Safeguard, Site Defense, and Patriot programs). The part of the Strategic Defense Initiative (SDI) that deals with early launch interception is completely unprecedented. The system itself, the architecture, the computer digital hardware, its connectivity, and the overlay of the software functions on this hardware architecture for such a system must evolve in a way that will reduce the risk of the system implementation. A team must groom its understanding through study and prototyping, build communications, and validate its process for development. In other words, it is imperative to consider the learning curve effects for highly unprecedented system developments.

Another example is a radar system based on new physical concepts to provide early warning. Although a demonstration system had been built and operated previous to the operational system, the contractual requirements for the operational system extended well beyond the demonstration system. Also, the contractor had severe communication difficulties among the system and software engineering staffs and subcontractors. In addition, the team did not have experience with the hardware–software architecture selected for this type of application. Until late in the program, the development lacked the disciplined process and the system understanding to provide adequate progress.

A last example deals with a relatively recent aircraft defensive system. The digital architecture was defined against a mild threat during the program's early days. Later, the threat was expanded to include more modern elements for which the architecture was not known to be effective. The result was that for the requirements and the environment associated with them, there was no digital system architecture known to satisfy those requirements, nor was the software team experienced in satisfying these requirements in a realistic environment. As a consequence, the defensive system was unable to satisfy the requirements placed on it.

REQUIREMENTS RISKS

For unprecedented systems, the risks associated with requirements stem from a variety of sources: poor common understanding of the requirements, incompleteness in the requirements or contradictory requirements, lack of understanding of cost impacts of specific requirements, and requirements change. The Air Force Systems Command (AFSC) Software Process Action Team (1992) addressed the requirements problems, their root causes, and potential solutions in considerable detail. Without a good understanding of requirements and the cost impacts of specific requirements and without some restraint on requirements changes, the cost and schedule baselines cannot be stabilized. Thus, when the requirements risks are perceived to be substantial, the acquisition–development process must be tailored to mitigate these risks and rebalance the cost, schedule, and performance baselines as better information becomes available during the actual development process itself.

Generally, the parties that must have a clear, common understanding of the requirements for the system (and often the requirements for the software) are the system users, their representatives, the acquisition organization, the prime contractor(s), and subcontractors developing software. In many cases, there are many people who must have a common and detailed understanding of the requirements. The AFSC Software Process Action Team recommends a specific communication structure to reduce misunderstanding of user needs. An additional approach to arrive at a more common understanding of requirements is a series of demonstrations of some of the requirements, which makes them more specific and less philosophical or general. This approach was adopted during an U.S. Air Force program to update a command center and is particularly useful for demonstrating a variety of human–machine interface requirements, as well as other system–software requirements.

A second risk deals with the incompleteness or consistency of the requirements. The process of requirements derivation really represents alternating steps of requirements and design. For example, high level system requirements are allocated to a system architecture (the definition of the architecture being a design activity). More detailed requirements are partitioned in a way to correlate with the architecture. As there are often hundreds and sometimes thousands of requirements, there is a real challenge to the participants to generate requirements that are complete and consistent. A frequent occurrence is the presentation of design information in a requirements document. When the requirements document is baselined, then the design elements become part of the requirements baseline, later inhibiting necessary design change. Prototyping and demonstration are techniques not only for communicating the requirements for a common understanding, but also a technique to improve the consistency and completeness of requirements documentation.

The *Viking* program (the NASA mission to Mars in the early 1970s) dealt with the third risk, the lack of understanding of cost impacts of specific requirements. The *Viking* system required the ground station to simultaneously process real-time data streams from two satellites orbiting Mars. When it came to implementing this requirement with NASA's available data-processing equipment, it became clear that the software was going to be complex for interleaving the data streams and ensuring that each data stream was processed separately. The solution was to have each satellite alternatively record during one revolution of the planet Mars and transmit during the next revolution, thus capturing all the data. The data streams would not have to be processed simultaneously. This simplification saved an estimated 30% of the software costs for the ground processing software, making possible the completion of the software in time to support the *Viking* program. In many cases, an understanding of the cost impacts of specific requirements would result in acceptable alternative statements of those requirements that could be satisfied at considerably less cost. Only as one acquires more details about the requirements or the design do the "cost drivers" for specific requirements become apparent.

Requirements changes in some situations are unavoidable. Clearly, if the threat has changed in such a way as to make the system obsolete, one must respond to those threat changes or cancel the system. On the other hand, some requirements change because of unforeseen assumptions or disclosures resulting from engineering study. For example, on an aircraft program, it was determined relatively late in the program that a full authority digital flight control system was necessary for the aircraft's flight safety. The enhanced mechanical system initially planned was not satisfactory and had to be replaced. This discovery prompted radical changes to the software requirements for the flight control system. So radical were these changes that they converted the flight control element of the system from something precedented, which the contractor–subcontractor knew how to do and had done before with an off-the-shelf approach, into something that the contractor–subcontractor knew almost nothing about, forcing the contractor to struggle to learn the parameters of the discipline.

It is concluded that for a highly unprecedented system, there are a variety of requirements risks that need to be curbed, and these risks are most adequately curbed by investment in prototype demonstrations and interchanges with users on those requirements before a considerable investment in the full-scale development of the system takes place. Requirements risks for highly unprecedented systems, unless properly reduced by the appropriate acquisition–development process, will translate into substantial cost, schedule, performance, or supportability risks and, in the extreme, program failure. This element of risk and its relation to the acquisition process must be addressed on a case-by-case basis so that the acquisition strategy properly mitigates the risk. One must recognize that when the requirements are unprecedented, then risks in the system architecture and team experience must also be addressed because these risks are automatically present.

ARCHITECTURE RISKS

There is a huge leap from an abstract statement of specific requirements to the layout of hardware and software architectures that can implement those requirements. By hardware architecture, it is meant primarily the organization and connectivity of digital hardware elements, such as Processors, memories, communication buses, and input–output devices. The processors may have both direct and indirect access to various memories, and may have various connectivity with each other. The processors and the input–output devices may be of the same or different types.

The software architecture is, in a sense, constrained by the hardware architecture. By the software architecture, it is meant the specific functions and the organization and structure of the collection of algorithms, data sets, and logic structures that are used. The software integrates the system, ie, it controls the communication of each element of the digital hardware to other elements of hardware and provides the software-to-software interfaces. The software architecture and the hardware architecture together comprise a static digital system architecture that must be capable of satisfying the system's functional requirements.

In addition to static architecture is the dynamic concept of execution. This dynamic architecture may be cyclic in design, with all tasks prescheduled (as is often the case for control systems); it may be demand-driven with real-time scheduling of tasks; or it may involve elements of both. Execution includes modes for startup, fault recovery, degraded performance, and shutdown. It is within this dynamic execution concept that timing, sizing, and band width in software across a distributed architecture are extremely hard to visualize. Only through analysis and measured test, through models and their verification, can the execution of the architecture be visualized, more clearly understood, and brought in line with the real-world performance requirements for the system.

When the architecture is unprecedented in relation to the system, there is a substantive risk that the architecture will break, i.e., that the architecture will be seriously inadequate to satisfy the performance requirements. When this break happens, there are few pleasant alternatives. One must either seek substantial relief from requirements, redo the hardware and software architectures, tune the software significantly, or arrive at some combination of these relief actions. All these alternatives take time and money, and substantially impact the schedule.

On many programs, there is an implicit awareness that the software involves risk, and risk reduction is performed during early phases. Such programs often implement an algorithm or one element of the system, perhaps a radar, that is presumed to be a high risk because it presses the limits of technology. But what is usually not recognized is that for unprecedented systems, the architecture itself, against the full set of requirements, is often a high risk. So it is important to address these architectural issues early, before the implementers begin on the bulk of the detailed implementation.

A clear understanding of these unprecedented architectural issues must rest on implementation in some fashion. Early on, this is done by modeling the system, including its hardware and software architecture, to discover weaknesses and bottlenecks inherent in the system architecture. Modeling is often complemented with simulation, timing and sizing studies, and analyses. However, there is the risk that the underlying assumptions and limited fidelity of modeling and analysis can yield results that miss the mark by a substantial amount. Ultimately, only through implementation with the appropriate operating system, on hardware with the appropriate characteristics, can one's intuition and analysis of the system be verified. To reduce architectural risks, developing a prototype of the hardware and the software architecture in an earlier phase of the development must be considered.

In designing the architecture, it is essential to consider not only the nominal mission but also all aspects of off-nominal system behavior. Many systems perform well against the nominal mission because it receives a considerable amount of design attention. However, when the system must recover from a hardware fault or failure, the architecture may need revision because off-nominal failure activities are usually addressed last and not considered strongly during fundamental design. Recovery from failure is an important hardware and software architectural issue that needs to be addressed early.

A sound, extendable architecture is key to system supportability after its deployment. As many of our systems must last for many decades, it may be that good architecture (i.e., flexible, extendable, portable across new technologies) will prove to be more important during acquisition than the particular functionality implied by today's requirements. The architecture is the key to cost-effective system upgrades to satisfy new requirements and accommodate new technology.

Architecture risks, therefore, have profound implications on the system. During system development, an architecture must be defined within the constraints of current hardware and software technology to meet all of the currently known requirements. In addition, the architecture should be capable of meeting future requirements for additional capability, improved performance, and as-yet unforeseen system behavior. It is little wonder that managing architecture risks are crucial to developing a long-lived system with the "right" capabilities, on time and within budget.

DEVELOPMENT TEAM RISKS

There is a substantive difference between experience and skill in relation to software teams. An experienced person will know what does and does not work in his or her area of experience. A skilled person may be bright and able to suggest new ideas, but may or may not know what does or does not work in a particular instance. On the other hand, many years of experience in one area of development may be of little use in an unprecedented development. Curtis (1987) implies that for new systems, a breadth of experience on many types of systems is more valuable than many years of experience confined to a single system. Skill and experience are important in reducing the development team risks.

Clear communication is also a key to the success of tasks like system engineering, which is multidisciplinary by definition. System engineering partitions the system, defines the executional concepts, and allocates requirements to various elements of the system, causing those requirements to flow down to hardware and software requirements. The system engineering activity that lays out the hardware architecture must be strongly correlated with its counterpart in software engineering. If the systems engineers, digital hardware engineers, and software engineers are unable to communicate clearly or do not work well together, important elements of functionality and the ability to integrate the system will be built on a weak foundation. It is particularly important in an unprecedented system for the software, hardware, and systems people to talk about risks early and continually during the program and make design decisions that will mitigate those risks. This is not unlike the more general concurrent engineering concept.

Reducing development team risks requires constant attention to interdisciplinary communications. Some individual (the conceptualizer) or group needs to be the communicator of the fundamental architectural concepts, describe what is changing in these concepts and what the latest difficulties are, explain these to the project members, and explore the potential impact on their parts of the process. These communicators often must do this orally as well as through written communication, because interpretation is so important. The acquisition–development process, particularly for unprecedented systems, must foster this intense communication and teaming process so that the staff's concepts about the system are sufficiently compatible to avoid major disconnects in the design and implementation.

Team experience is such an important factor that with the right team, the development may be precedented, whereas with the wrong team, the system becomes unprecedented. Little is done in the source selection process (particularly for less-than-major systems) to assure the government that various competitors can assemble a team that has worked together before on a similar program. The focus is usually on the companies' experience in general, rather than on the specific team's experience in the application domain of the current acquisition. It would be appropriate to consider the specific team's experience in the evaluation factors for contract awards.

A key development team risk is personnel turnover, resulting in the loss of knowledge and experience. It is extremely important that the team morale and the anticipation of success remain high, so that the people will stay with the project. One might claim that it is possible simply to document what the people do and, when personnel leave, to have the new people read that documentation, but this is not practical. Even if the project is carefully documented, it is most likely that the new person will not read the document with the understanding the author hoped for. Interpersonal communication has an important role in shaping people's understanding of what the system is, not just what is documented on paper.

The conjecture that real understanding of the system is in the people and can never be fully and adequately reflected in documentation explains the long time and expense it takes to turn over the maintenance of software to a new team. The more complex and interactive the software is, the harder the transfer is.

For a highly unprecedented system, the development team needs time to build experience and common understanding of the system and verify that experience through an iterative development process. This underscores the importance of keeping such developments funded so that there are no gaps during which key people cannot be retained on the project. Any major gaps in funding will result in a new development team having to learn these things from scratch. In other words, the concept of learning curve exists in software just as it exists in other fields of endeavor.

The development team must have experience that is consistent with the needs of the job, a high skill level consistent with the uncertainties of the job, and constant communication, high morale, and stable funding to reduce development team risks. The more experience the team has in the specific application area and with some previous implementation of a system in that area, the more precedented the system and the lower the risk.

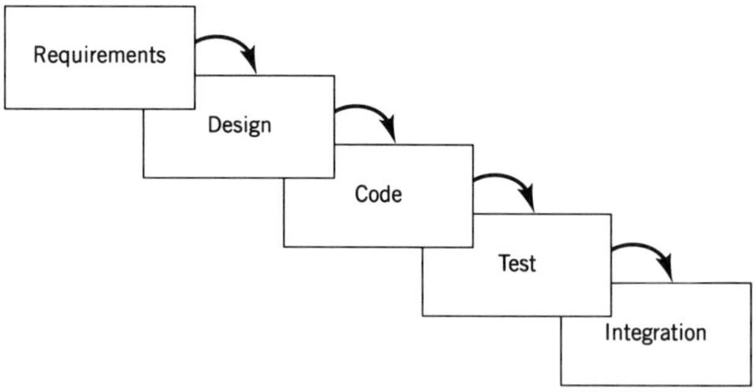

Figure 1. The waterfall model.

ACQUISITION–DEVELOPMENT APPROACHES TO MITIGATE RISK

The previous sections of this article defined risks associated with system developments with varying degrees of precedence. This section discusses the use of alternative acquisition–development approaches to mitigate the risks from these different types of unprecedentedness. Generally speaking, the traditional waterfall model is appropriate to development of nearly precedented systems; more innovative development models are better suited to highly unprecedented systems. Furthermore, rebaselining the program (reestablishing the cost, schedule, performance, and supportability objectives) is recommended from time to time as risk issues become better understood.

First, classical sequential models, which can consist of a waterfall-like model or a series of block upgrades are discussed. Second, a discussion of iterative methods, such as the spiral model and the evolutionary model are presented. Third, a risk-driven model based on early demonstrations of higher risk software is discussed. Finally, rebaselining activities during acquisition–development as the risks become resolved are discussed. These models are general. True acquisition management still lies in the selecting and tailoring the appropriate process, with the proper insertion of rebaselining activities, to match the risks inherent in each acquisition–development.

Sequential Models

Software has most commonly been developed using a sequential model in which system development proceeds by completing a given sequence of activities, in a prescribed order. Each activity entails defined outputs to document its results and its completion is a prerequisite of the proceeding activity.

The Waterfall Model. The best known sequential model is the waterfall model, for which a simple representation is shown in Figure 1. A more robust and fully defined sequential model can be found in DOD-STD-2167A (1988). Although this standard indicates that other models are permitted, little guidance is given as to what these models might be and when to use them. As can be deduced from the figure, the early portion of the model is represented primarily as a paper exercise. Software functional, performance, and derived requirements are usually developed from higher level requirements through system engineering analysis and simulation. Software and hardware architectures are defined to implement the requirements. The requirements and architecture are evaluated against higher level requirements through review of the specifications and formal design reviews. However, the most compelling evidence of this satisfaction of requirements does not occur until integration and test.

For a nearly precedented system, the team's common experience with a previous development provides the strong element of reality on which the paper exercise is based. The many hard-to-determine and hard-to-visualize elements of appropriate hardware and software architectures, such as performance issues, failure management, off-nominal modes, and test and verification processes, are already understood by the team. The team can focus on the extensions in requirements associated with the current job. Provided these extensions are limited, analysis and prototype development within the context of the sequential process can accommodate their risks. The derivation and interpretation of the supporting requirements is more precise among all team members, and their interpersonal communication is substantially better than that of a new team. Baselines that are established have a far greater basis in reality than hypothetical estimates based on less-related developments.

The waterfall model is widely understood, accepted, and used. In part, this may result from the fact that it is the easiest model to understand and that it matches the system acquisition process. Within this model, it is relatively easy to measure progress and it is probably a minimum schedule approach for developing a precedented or nearly precedented system.

The Block Upgrade Model. Under the block upgrade model, system developers recognize that the development is too ambitious or too complex at the project's outset to develop the ultimate system in a single pass through a sequential process. An attempt to develop and integrate all of the software in one pass would require a larger team, complicating the team's communication problems. It would also complicate the integration and testing activity over that of a more incremental development process.

The block upgrade model, illustrated in Figure 2, applies a sequential process to digital system development. System requirements are defined at the outset of system development, then the system development is broken up into a series of blocks, each of which represents a fieldable,

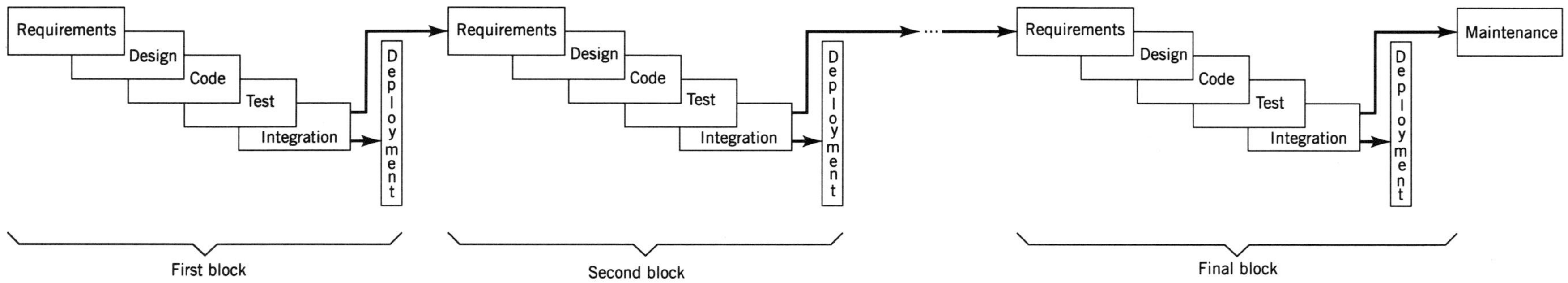

Figure 2. The block upgrade model.

operationally capable system. Each block upgrade is a substantial development project in itself, to add major new capabilities within the system requirements. In some cases the blocks are released to an extended test activity (such a flight test for an aircraft). Only after a number of blocks have been tested will the system be deployed.

Each block upgrade is developed following a waterfall-like process. System requirements are rebaselined before beginning each block, software design is extended to add the new functionality, followed by the implementation of the block's new and revised software. During early blocks, the development team builds an understanding of the system's capabilities and limitations and learns to work together. Furthermore, it learns how to overcome earlier limitations, how to design needed additional functionality, and how to improve performance. Although these discoveries cannot be incorporated into the initial block, they fill in critical information needed successfully to build the ultimate system. Also, the blocks released earlier provide a more solid foundation into which the new blocks may be integrated, thus reducing the amount of new code that must be corrected over the alternative "big bang" approach, in which everything is done at once. Furthermore, each block offers the acquisition and development teams the opportunity to revise the baselined system requirements to incorporate the needed enhancements (and potentially delete unneeded capabilities or relax over stringent requirements).

This process can be applied to develop entire systems, including the software, digital system, and other nondigital system components. It evolved informally and gradually, beginning as early as the 1960s in some cases, with the development of an initial version of the system, followed promptly by a revision to correct or add certain aspects of system functionality. More recently, this approach of preplanned extension and revision has been recognized as a software development process (Boehm, 1989). When extended across an entire system, it is referred to as preplanned product improvement.

An interesting observation is that during the early portion of the block upgrade process, team unprecedentedness is reduced. During the first block(s), the requirements become better defined and understood. However, the system architecture must be robust enough to evolve to support all of the blocks to be delivered.

Iterative Models

Iterative approaches to software acquisition have been developed to cope with the inability to specify requirements with the degree of completeness and accuracy needed to apply a sequential development process. The premise of iterative processes is that if requirements cannot be well specified before beginning the development, it will be difficult (if not impossible) to build the ultimate system functionality on the first try. Further development iterations will be needed either to add system capabilities or, in a more sophisticated iterative process, to resolve unknowns before proceeding.

For all iterative models, designing the right architecture is key. It is hoped that the architecture is well established within the early iterations. This architecture must be robust and extendable enough to accommodate the system's growth, through subsequent iterations, to the ultimate system. This can provide a real challenge to the designers of a system that is unprecedented in terms of its requirements and architecture.

The Evolutionary Acquisition Model. Evolutionary acquisition addresses the problem of the inability to define requirements fully before developing the system. The typical example of a system for which evolutionary acquisition is intended is a command center. In this example, before development begins, the users may legitimately be unable to completely define system functionality, especially the part related to external design (ie, how information should be presented). However, the users can define a set of "core" requirements and will recognize effective external design when they see it.

With evolutionary acquisition, the system acquisition team determines that the requirements for the full system are not completely known, but defines the requirements for the core system. As shown in Figure 3, the core system is developed first; successive increments add capabilities to the core system based on user feedback. The core system is actually installed in its operational environment: users try the system, use it to perform their jobs, and identify refinements and enhancements for the next development. As the developers iteratively define requirements for and implement these increments, the rest of the system is completed, one segment at a time. Each increment consists of an iterative application of the sequential process to a defined and manageable subset of the full system (National Security Industrial Association, 1987). The primary difference between the evolutionary acquisition model and the block upgrade model is that for the former, a fielding of the system is needed to further define the requirements, whereas for the latter, the requirements are known but are too big to address all at once.

Evolutionary acquisition also works to diminish unprecedentedness, but in a different way than other iterative processes. Each iteration consists of a segment for which requirements can be fully defined in advance. If some of those requirements (when implemented) do not actually meet the user's needs, there is the opportunity to revise the requirements on the next iteration. For each iteration after the first, the team is experienced at working together in the application area.

The Spiral Model. The most sophisticated of the iterative processes is the spiral model, first introduced by Boehm (1988). There has been some inconsistency among the various articles describing the spiral model which, more than anything, may simply indicate the refinement of the model as it has matured conceptually and through use. At its most basic, the spiral model consists of up-front risk reduction activities performed before beginning system development, followed by requirements definition, design, coding, and testing activities. None of these activities, however, is a

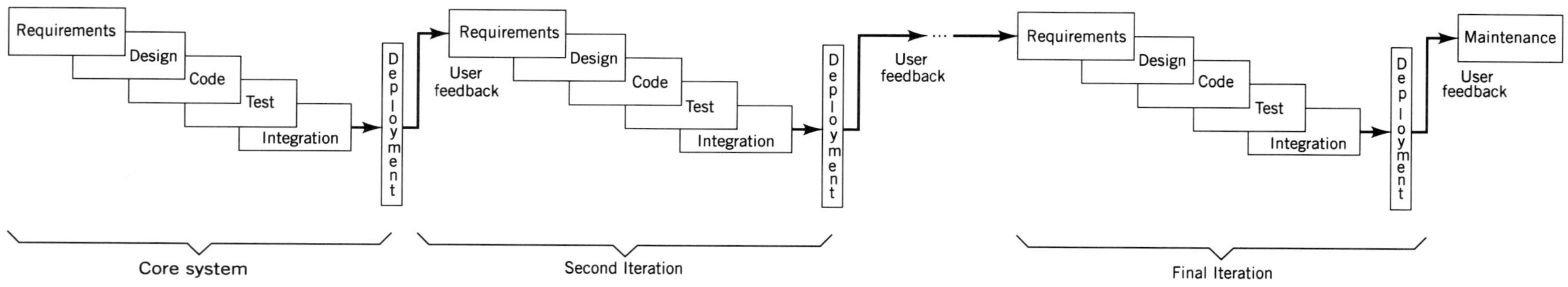

Figure 3. The evolutionary acquisition model.

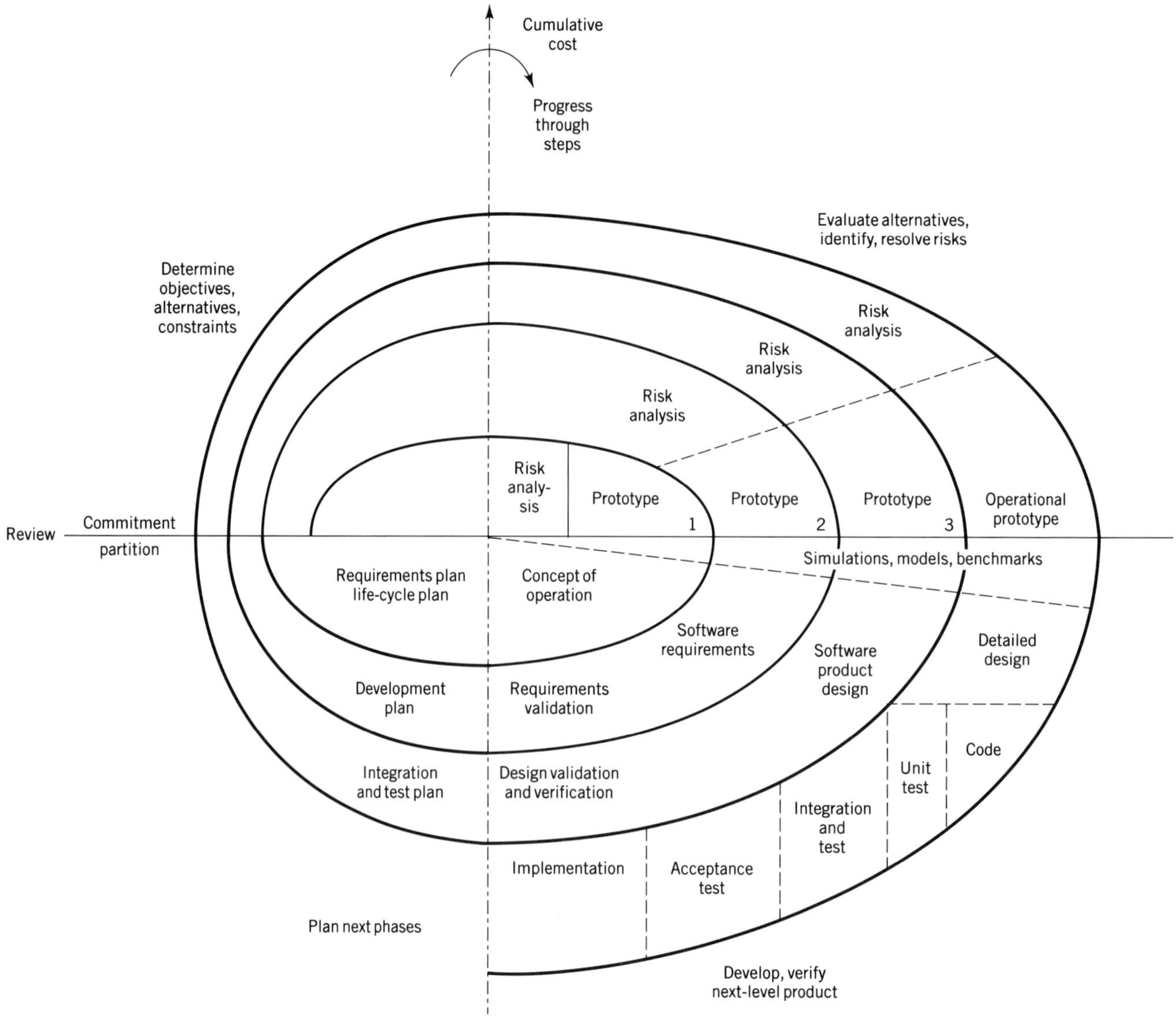

Figure 4. The spiral model.

discrete, waterfall-style step. Each activity allows iteration to previous activities and allows the development team to learn information that is vital to the successful completion of subsequent activities.

The spiral model is illustrated in Figure 4. Early applications of the spiral model used the first few iterations around the spiral to perform risk reduction activities. Then software development is started with an iteration focused on software requirements, but allowed enough design, coding, and testing to confirm the adequacy of the software requirements. The next iteration is focused on design, with enough testing to confirm the coding and refine requirements and design where necessary. The final iteration is focused on testing, and refinement of any products on previous iterations where necessary. Although this description is grossly oversimplified, it is possible to see the spiral model's two most important elements: up-front risk reduction activities and the flexibility to refine requirements and design in subsequent iterations.

More recent applications of the spiral model have increasingly integrated software risk management into the software development process. There is more emphasis on the risk reduction activities performed before beginning development, and more emphasis on structuring the software development activities themselves in accordance with a risk reduction plan. This integration of software risk management into a flexible iterative software development paradigm is the essence of the current spiral model.

The spiral model reduces unprecedentedness by focusing on risk reduction activities during early iterations and by structuring the software development activities actually to achieve reduced risks. Because unprecedentedness of requirements and architecture correlate to identifiable risks, the spiral model's incremental approach should reduce these two aspects of unprecedentedness by focusing heavily on them during the earliest iterations. The spiral model typically builds staff gradually, adding specialists at each iteration and thereby reducing the team's unprecedentedness.

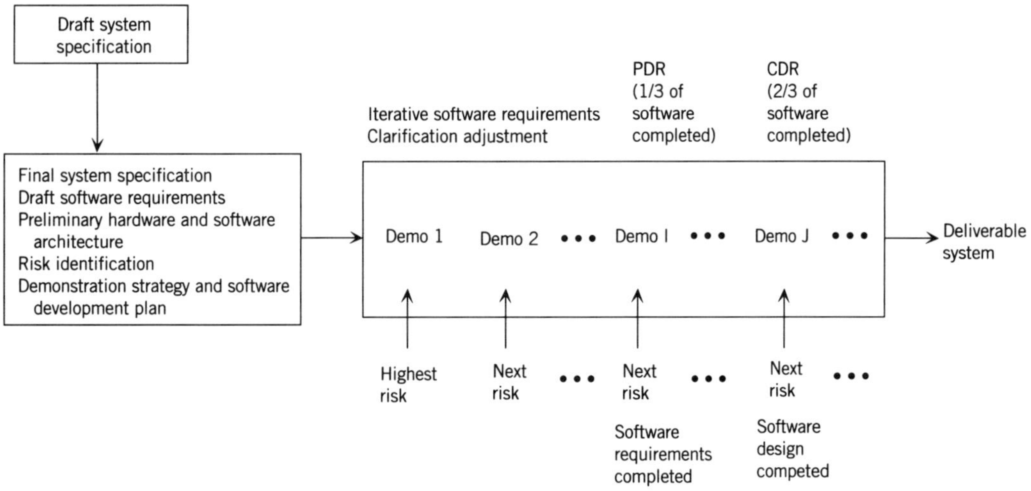

Figure 5. The risk-driven demonstration model.

The Risk-Driven Demonstration Model

A risk-driven, demonstration-oriented process is now defined in which risk analysis derives a sequence of software development increments. The increments are implemented in risk order, highest risk first, and each increment culminates in a demonstration that confirms risk containment for that increment. Depending on the risk, the demonstrations may consist of a prototype, a benchmark, a partial implementation of the system, or other tangible execution-oriented evidence of meeting system requirements.

Perhaps this risk-driven demonstration process is most easily defined by means of an example of its use. For a particular military command control system, the development was, in essence, one for which the requirements and team were precedented, but the architecture was highly unprecedented. The requirements were reasonably well understood and the team, which was very experienced, had worked together on similar command and control systems. The high risk elements were the software architecture and Ada, as this was the team's first use of Ada on a full-scale command and control application.

In addition to taking several positive steps to mitigate these risks, the development team adopted a risk-driven demonstration approach. The acquisition–development approach is shown in the schematic in Figure 5. The software requirements were drafted based on the system requirements, an architecture for hardware and software was defined, and a risk analysis was performed both identifying and prioritizing the risk. A software development plan prioritized specific implementation according to risk, with the highest risk first, and with an executing demonstration of the software at each implementation. This process brought better understanding of the detailed requirements by all participants and allowed decisions about these requirements to be based on harder evidence. The lower level requirements were adjusted when necessary.

The highest risk was the software architecture that provided the interprocessor communication skeleton. Its early implementation provided a realistic foundation for establishing system response times, while supporting revision and optimization during the course of the program. It also verified the extendability of the system architecture, including its digital hardware. The process had the advantage of substantially reducing the risk of discovering late in the development that the integrated system needed major revision. Furthermore, detailed requirements were not baselined until their feasibility and leverage were demonstrated and understood by all parties.

The risks resulting from the unprecedented architecture were reduced by the architectural team's experience. An earlier unsuccessful project and an IR&D project, which found solutions in the Ada environment, provided the Teaming experience needed successfully to implement the intercommunication structure in Ada. The team also mitigated the impact of the shortage of Ada expertise by developing tools that permitted software engineers with applications expertise to write Fortran-like Ada into which tools automatically inserted more sophisticated Ada features. Here then is an example of a process that is neither classically sequential nor iterative to handle a particular case of unprecedentedness, namely, a new system and software architecture.

Rebaselining

As a development proceeds (particularly for unprecedented systems) the relationships among cost, schedule, performance, and supportability (hardware and software) become better understood. It would be fortuitous if these four elements were to remain in balance; instead, one should plan to reestablish these baselines at key points in the program during the digital system development process. For major systems, each milestone provides an opportunity to rebaseline; however, the digital system architectural risks are seldom clearly articulated before the full-scale engineering development phase. It is essential in developing an acquisition strategy for unprecedented systems to plan for rebaselining when the appropriate risks of the system are reduced.

Rebaselining should become an accepted, integral part of the system development process. Depending on the acquisition model being used, different events might trigger rebaselining. Rebaselining could occur between each cycle

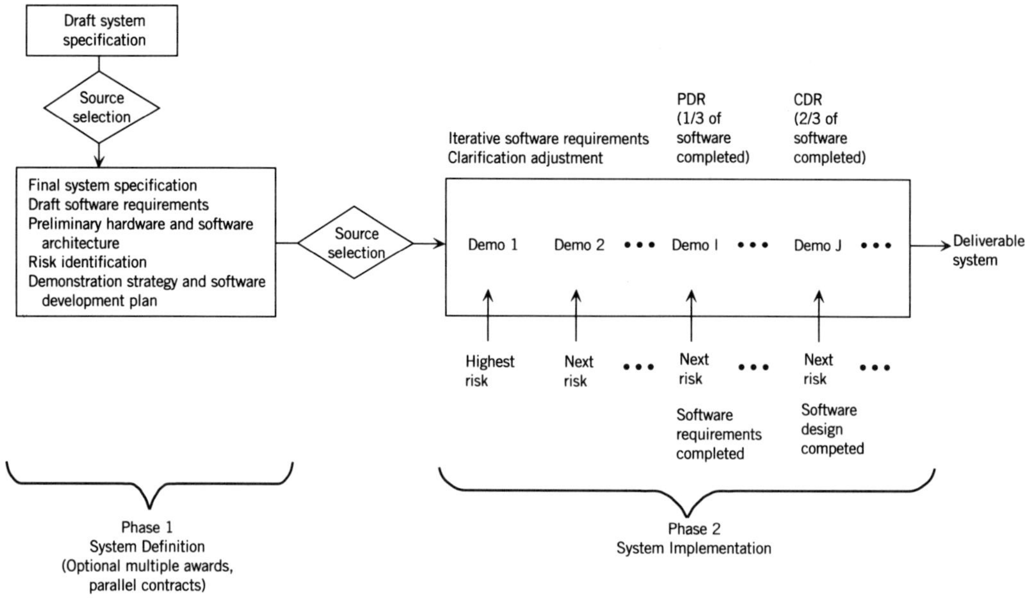

Figure 6. Using source selection to support rebaselining.

through an iterative development process or at the completion of each demonstration in a risk-driven process.

An example rebaselining approach is illustrated in Figure 6, which shows the risk-driven model with two source selections. This phased-acquisition approach gives the government and contractor the opportunity to rebaseline the major program elements after deriving the detailed software and hardware requirements, laying out the hardware and software architecture, and performing the risk analysis based on more than intuition. It is particularly important to consider rebaselining as the contractor develops a solid basis for projecting system costs. Without a clear understanding of software requirements and a reasonable understanding of the digital architecture and its risks, any cost and schedule baselines are unfounded.

Additional source selections are expensive in dollars and schedule for both the government and contractors, particularly for less-than-major programs. There may be other less expensive means to encourage good performance by contractors. Perhaps several similar programs (for the same sponsor under the same program director) could be grouped in a single line item, assessed annually, and rebaselined within the group. Using risk assessment, contractor performance, and schedule versus need date, the funding could be redistributed annually within the group of programs, along with adjustments in baselines. Some limited transfers of funds are presently permitted, but control within these larger line items, with risk reduction and improving consistency of baselines as the primary objectives, would lead to a more efficient use of resources.

Under certain circumstances, rebaselining could be incorporated into an acquisition approach employing a design-to-cost strategy. The initial phase would be to gain insight into risks for an unprecedented system development. It could consist of requirements definition, and perhaps some high level design and prototyping to define the system. Such an effort would typically be performed on a cost-type contract. Then, if there is enough funding to accomplish all essential requirements, the system development could be completed using a design-to-cost approach. The additional system insight gained during the first phase provides realistic criteria under which rebaselining is fostered. The rebaselining concept provides much-needed flexibility to address the risks associated with unprecedented systems.

In the recent past, there have been many attempts to procure unprecedented systems on a fixed-price basis before all of the risks could be properly assessed. This puts the government at odds with the contractor when the baselines are not balanced. The government stresses schedule and performance, whereas the contractor's focus is on avoiding cost overruns. The more recent trend to cost-type contracts and the recommendations for appropriate rebaselining for unprecedented systems should help ease the problems of the past.

CONCLUSIONS

In analyzing the effect of unprecedentedness on system developments, the problem of developing software on time and within cost estimates owes a large part of its existence to the failure to recognize the role of unprecedentedness and to apply processes that reduce the risks associated with the unprecedentedness of the system under development. Stated more directly, developers have too often blindly applied the sequential model to highly unprecedented system developments and missed, often repeatedly and dramatically, meeting the system's baselines. The processes discussed in the previous section of this article have the potential to improve the effectiveness of digital system acquisition and development. This final section deals with characteristics of each acquisition–development model that would reduce the risks associated with developing unprecedented systems.

The waterfall model is best-suited for precedented or nearly precedented systems. The waterfall model is based on the assumption that system requirements can be accurately baselined before development begins. Learning time needed to develop a common understanding of the system and the development process is not provided under this sequential model without jeopardizing the system's baselines. If the requirements are unprecedented, there can be no historic basis for estimating the cost of the system. There is little insight as to whether the requirements are consistent, and particularly, there is no common understanding of the requirements. Also, the cost effectiveness of specific requirements is uncertain. If the cost impact were known at requirements time, an alternate statement of requirements might be more cost effective. If the architecture is unprecedented, the total digital architecture is at risk because it may not be robust enough to satisfy all the requirements. Most devastating is the possibility that a fundamental inadequacy of the architecture will not be discovered until late in the development Consequently, major schedule and cost impacts, unplanned reduction in requirements, substantial breakage of developed software, compromised software supportability, and reduced or no system growth potential (all unpleasant and embarrassing outcomes) may result. If there is unprecedentedness in terms of the development team, the team lacks common application experience and probably has not worked together at all. Time is needed to learn the details of a common development process, establish the formal and informal lines of communication, and develop a common, consistent view of the system. There is no provision for this in the waterfall model.

The block upgrade model can reduce the effects of unprecedentedness by limiting the initial block to something known to be achievable within the baselines and by yielding subsequent block upgrades that are, by definition, more nearly precedented. If a large development can be decomposed into incrementally developed blocks, each block may be achievable at lower risk than there would be for developing the entire system at once. If the first block designs a system architecture robust and expandable enough to accommodate the full system's requirements, then architectural unprecedentedness decreases dramatically after the first block and continues to decrease with each block that is developed. Unfortunately, the architecture may remain at risk if its expandability cannot be proven in the first block. In too many cases, there is a negative proof of the architecture when a later block pressures the architecture beyond its limits. There is always the devastating possibility that a fundamental architectural inadequacy may not be discovered until it is very costly to overcome. The block upgrade model can be very effective at reducing the team's unprecedentedness if the same team can be kept together through several blocks. As in any incremental process, the development must be time-phased to avoid lags between increments, which typically increase personnel turnover and reassessment. Excessive turnover adds unprecedentedness to the development team, and even a short gap can cause a major exodus of development staff. When the next phase begins, a team with new members must redevelop its communication, knowledge of the application, and understanding of their common process.

Evolutionary acquisition offers promise for developing systems where unprecedentedness and user uncertainty lie primarily in requirements. To use an evolutionary acquisition approach, there must be a core system for which the requirements are definable and which provides a fieldable, useful capability to the system's end users. If this precondition can be satisfied, it eliminates requirements unprecedentedness from the core system. During the development of the core system, the team becomes experienced at working together, thereby eliminating team unprecedentedness from the later development iterations. As with the block upgrade model, iterations must be time-phased to avoid gaps that result in turnover. In evolutionary acquisition, the team may have to begin developing the next iteration before user feedback is received on the one just completed. Unfortunately, evolutionary acquisition cannot reduce unprecedentedness in the area of establishing an architecture known to be capable of satisfying the system requirements. Boehm and others have pinpointed the primary risk of evolutionary acquisition: that the architecture established in the core system may not accommodate the ultimate system requirements. The more unknown the requirements for the full system are, the more significant this risk is.

The spiral model was developed to reduce risks inherent in developing unprecedented systems, but there is little experience and knowledge in applying the spiral model. The spiral model has received much attention in the current literature. As a result, there is widespread discussion but limited use across industry. The spiral model has evolved into an iterative process for which the earliest iterations are focused on risk reduction. This is a strength when unprecedented requirements and architecture pose major risks and are addressed as part of the up-front risk reduction activities. There is some risk that the early iterations may not define an architecture that will accommodate the full system. The spiral model reduces team unprecedentedness after the initial project start up because it allows staff to be added gradually at each iteration, which allows the team to build up its communication and joint understanding. The spiral model's newness, however, can also add to team unprecedentedness during the early iterations. The use of a new development process, if not well understood, adds learning time and a degree of risk to the system acquisition. The spiral model's major strength, its flexibility, also makes it difficult to understand. It requires greater judgment to apply a process that is not amenable to definition via a precise and fixed sequence of activities.

The risk-driven demonstration model is specifically directed toward mitigating the risk of unprecedented architecture but also offers some of the benefits of iterative models. The risk-driven demonstration model implements the system increments in risk order, with execution-oriented demonstrations to culminate each increment. This model reduces requirements unprecedentedness by breaking the system development into pieces, each having a manageable set of unknowns in its requirements. As with the iterative models, the development becomes precedented in terms of the development team after the initial increment, provided that the increments are time-phased to avoid destabilizing time lags between increments. A primary difference in the risk-driven demonstration model accrues from implementing the system in risk order. If the architecture is unprecedented, it will most certainly be one of the highest risks in the system development, and the earliest iterations will be specifically directed toward demonstrating that the architecture is robust enough to satisfy the requirements for the ultimate system. Also, the demonstration will be execution-oriented rather than analytically based, providing more tangible evidence that the architecture will satisfy system requirements. This model offers similar advantages to the iterative models, as well as being directed toward reducing risks associated with architectural unprecedentedness. The risk-driven demonstration model is less well-known than the spiral model, meaning that there is a very limited body of knowledge about it and even less experience using it. It seems to offer promise, but its newness will increase the team's unprecedentedness due to the use of a development process that will require learning time.

Rebaselining should become an accepted part of the development process for unprecedented systems. It is appropriate whenever the requirements for the system get out of balance with the performance, schedule, resource, and supportability baselines established for the system. Whatever acquisition–development process is employed, the process itself cannot overcome unrealistic baselines. For unprecedented systems, it is highly unlikely that the baselines established when the system is merely a concept win match reality when the system begins engineering development. The more unprecedented the system is, the more likely that system development will require thoughtful and complex tradeoffs among the baseline parameters as development progresses. Acquistion-development processes must be expanded to support rebaselining by providing for periodic reevaluation and trade-offs. To make rebaselining possible, it is necessary also to change the infrastructure to institutionalize rebaselining and reward the program manager who plans realistically.

Unprecedentedness, a key indicator of risk, should be a primary factor in selecting the appropriate acquisition—development model for the system development. Current policy and compliance documents need to be expanded to embrace and facilitate more readily the application of alternative acquisition–development models. It is not enough that such documents do not prevent tailoring to match an alternative model and encourage their use in appropriate circumstances. It would also be invaluable to program offices to have a methodology that could be used to identify unprecedented aspects of and estimate the degree of unprecedentedness on their programs. Finally, acquisition personnel need guidance and training in how to apply the different acquisition–development models to reduce the risks associated with the degree and nature of unprecedentedness in the system being developed.

BIBLIOGRAPHY

Air Force Systems Command Software Process Action Team, R. Sylvestor, Chairman, Final Report, June 1992.

W. Beam, Chairman, Air Force Studies Board, Adapting Software Development Policies to Modern Technology, National Academy Press, Washington, D.C., 1989

B. W. Boehm, "A Spiral Model of Software Development and Enhancement," *Computer* (May 1988).

B. W. Boehm, *Software Risk Management*, IEEE Computer Society Press, 1989.

B. Curtis, H. Krasner, V. Shen, and N. Iscoe, "On Building Software Process Models under the Lampost," *ACM* (1987).

B. Curtis, H. Krasner, and N. Iscoe, "A Field Study of the Software Design Process for Large Systems," *Communications of the ACM* **13**(11) (Nov. 1988).

DOD Std. 2167A, Military Standard Defense System Software Development, Feb. 29, 1988.

RICHARD J. SYLVESTER
The MITRE Corporation
MARILYN J. STEWART
Logicon, Inc.

USER INTERFACE MANAGEMENT SYSTEMS

INTRODUCTION

In the early 1980s, the ready availability of computer graphics workstations, coupled with great improvements in physical interaction devices, generated the desire for more interesting and complex user interfaces than those that had been developed up to that time. Today, code to implement user interfaces make up a large percentage of the software for most computer applications. Current estimates range from 40 to 90% of the code, depending upon the type of application (Bobrow, Mittal, and Stefik, 1986; Lee, 1990; Young, 1990).

An *interactive application* is a software system that communicates with a human user. The *user interface* is the point of contact between the application and the end user. The user interface encompasses both the hardware and software that enable the user to tell the system what to do and to inform the user what the system has done (Szekely, 1988).

A *user interface management system* (UIMS) is one of several types of user interface development tools (UIDTs). Some researchers use the term UIMS as a catchall to refer to any interactive system used to create and manage user interfaces. Hix states that UIMSs "help specify, design, prototype, implement, execute, evaluate, modify, and maintain such interfaces. UIMSs are to interface development what CASE tools are to development of other system components" (1990). Other researchers use the term to refer exclusively to the runtime management capabilities of the interactive software (Myers, 1989).

The development of interactive software is sometimes more time-consuming than the development of other parts of an application. One reason is that the software underlying the display and manipulation of onscreen objects is tedious to use and difficult to learn. UIMSs and other user interface development tools were developed to speed development and to insulate the application developer from the difficulties associated with the direct use of the underlying graphics software.

There are a number of types of tools used to develop user interfaces. Before making the distinctions between

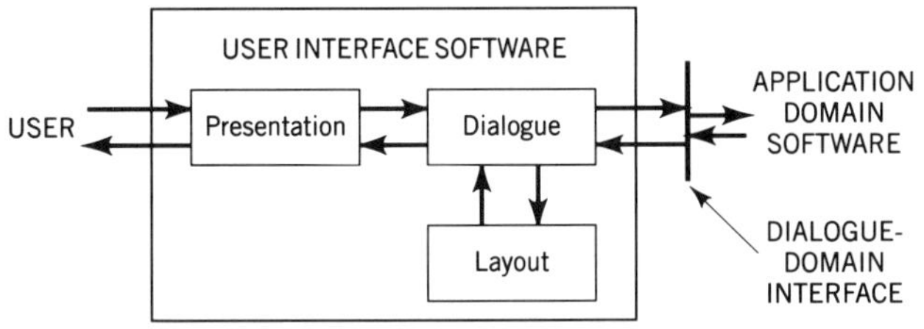

Figure 1. Components of an interactive application.

the tools, it is helpful to discuss the software components that make up a user interface and present a model to explain how these components interact.

COMPONENTS OF AN INTERACTIVE APPLICATION

An interactive application can be partitioned into three parts: application domain software, user interface software, and a dialogue-domain interface that allows communication between the two types of software (Fig. 1). Although all interactive applications contain these three parts, the degree to which they are distinct is dependent on the tool being used and the rigor of the software development process.

Application Domain Software

The *application domain software* implements the underlying functionality and purpose of the application (e.g., calculating orbit and attitude coordinates for a satellite or responding to queries about information in a data base). When separation is maintained between the user interface and application domain software, the application domain software does not specify how the results of its calculations are displayed. This function is performed in the user interface software. For example, in a flight simulator, the application domain software performs the simulation calculations and produces the raw data. The application domain developer is not concerned with how that data is displayed. It is the user interface software developer who implements a rotating dial to display simulated airspeed.

User Interface Software

The user interface software receives inputs from, and displays information to, the end user of the application. User interface software has three parts: presentation, layout, and dialogue.

The *presentation* software interacts directly with the application's end user. It collects input from, and presents output to the user. The presentation software contains the drivers that manage input devices such as the keyboard, mouse, trackball, touchscreen, or pen and stylus. The presentation software also manages the interface objects displayed on a monitor or other kinds of output (e.g., through speech synthesis).

Presentation software usually includes a windowing system, such as the X Window System™ (Scheifler and Gettys, 1986), MicroSoft Windows™ (Petzold, 1990) or Presentation Manager™ (Petzold, 1989). A windowing system provides window manipulation capabilities (e.g., moving and sizing windows) and a toolkit for use by the user interface developer. Toolkits contain common user interface objects such as radio buttons, check boxes, and label fields and the software required to manipulate them. (A radio button is an interaction object constructed from two concentric circles. A set of radio buttons provides an end user with mutually exclusive choices that can be selected with a mouse or other interaction technique.)

Toolkits can be reused for any number of user interfaces. The objects in a given toolkit help to define a common look and feel for interfaces developed using them, and the software makes programming the interface easier. Examples of toolkits are the X Toolkit (McCormack and Asente, 1988) and Next Step (NeXT, Inc., 1989).

The *layout* software defines the objects that are to be used in a particular user interface. Although the presentation component contains the entire set of available interaction objects, the layout component defines which objects have been selected for use and how they are grouped (e.g., a set of nine radio buttons arranged in three rows of three). The layout specifies the values of the attributes of each object. *Attributes* include definitions of such things as the colors, fonts, sizes, and positions of the objects displayed.

The layout also defines the hierarchy of objects that make up the interface. Lower-level objects may be contained in higher-level objects, and lower-level objects may inherit the characteristics of their higher-level objects. Inheritance of characteristics is useful because it allows reuse of software definitions, thus reducing coding effort and helping to implement a consistent look and feel across the various displays of an application or across a set of applications.

All user interface development tools address the layout of the interface. However, methods of implementing the layout differ. Some tools provide a direct manipulation editor for interactively placing objects on the screen and for defining the object hierarchy and attributes. Other tools provide a text-based language for performing these functions. A discussion of the distinctions among the types of tools is presented in the section entitled "Types of User Interface Development Tools".

The *dialogue* software represents the dynamic behavior of a user interface. The dialogue describes the application's response to a user input, specifies when to display data from the application domain software, and sequences the display of messages to prompt a user for input. For example, if a user selects a radio button with a mouse, the dialogue may respond by having the radio button change color, by having the button disappear, or by requesting and displaying data from the application domain. In summary, the dialogue includes all actions that modify the appearance of the interface or its state, transfer control to the application domain or receive control from the application domain.

Dialogue-Domain Interface

The *dialogue-domain interface* describes and controls the data exchanged between the application domain and user interface software. This is the only place that the application domain has access to data from the user interface. Additionally, the dialogue-domain interface is the only place the user interface has access to the data generated by the domain. This separation, and consequent independence, of domain and user interface software permits modification of software on either side of the dialogue-domain interface without the worry that software on the other side will be modified unintentionally. For example, properties of interface objects can be modified without any effect on the application domain code, and changes to an application algorithm can be made without affecting the user interface.

Interactive applications do not always have a dialogue-domain interface component. In fact, there is no standard definition for the dialogue-domain interface component, and applications that contain this component have implemented it in various ways. However, the basic concept is a shared data area where the dialogue and the domain each store data for access by the other. There is usually an agent that manages this data (much like a database management system) to ensure that the components storing the data will not corrupt it and will, in turn, receive correct data. User interface development tools sometimes provide the dialogue-domain interface so that the developer does not have to code it for each application.

TYPES OF USER INTERFACE DEVELOPMENT TOOLS (UIDTs)

There are several types of tools for developing user interface software. These include Toolkits, Virtual Toolkits, Layout Languages, Specialized Programming Languages, Interactive Design Tools (IDTs), and User Interface Management Systems (UIMSs). Many user interface development environments consist of integrated sets of these tools.

Toolkits

Toolkits are included in the presentation component of user interface software. Toolkits are the most basic of the UIDTs, because they deal with the graphics manipulations provided by the host windowing systems. Each toolkit has three parts: a set of interface objects that are displayed on the screen, routines to communicate with the interface objects, and a main loop (Fig. 2). Interface objects are called *widgets* by X Window System developers (McCormack and

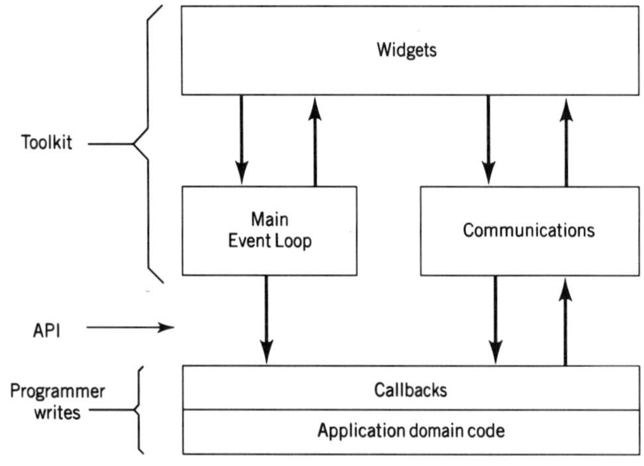

Figure 2. Using a toolkit.

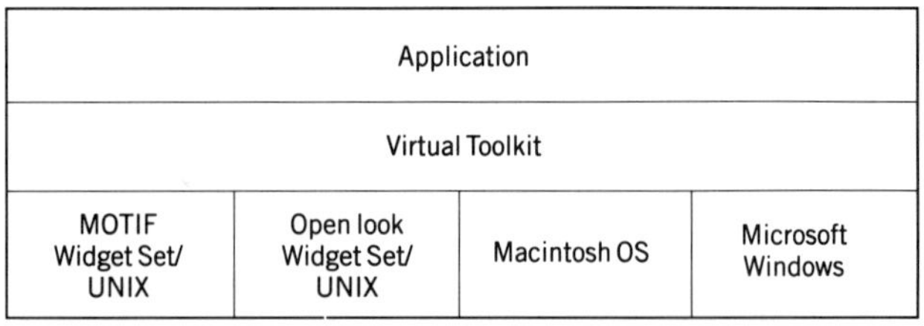

Figure 3. Using a virtual toolkit.

Asente, 1988) or alternatively, *interaction objects* (Rouff, 1991). Each widget contains functions for displaying an interface object and a set of predefined methods that define how the user interacts with it. A widget may also contain attributes or public data that allow a programmer to configure the object to look or behave in a particular way.

The communication routines provide functions for the programmer to set the public data and to call public functions in the widgets. These routines insulate the widgets' data from accidental corruption and provide an intervening layer of software so that widgets can be reimplemented without affecting the application domain code (Fig. 2).

The main loop provides an event-driven mechanism that monitors events as they occur and calls the appropriate application domain functions, which are referred to as callbacks. The *callbacks* manipulate the user interface through the communication routines and call the required functions of the application domain. The Application Programming Interface (API) defines the system programming interfaces for the application software developer.

Virtual Toolkits

Virtual toolkits are APIs that allow a programmer to move an application from one widget set to another or from one operating system to another (Fig. 3). For example, an X Window System application developed using a virtual toolkit and the Motif widget set might be ported to the Open Look widget set (Sun Microsystems, 1989) or moved to the Macintosh OS or to MicroSoft Windows. When an application is moved to a new windowing system it is recompiled with the virtual toolkit for the new system.

Virtual toolkits help to solve the problems caused by the current lack of industry standardization of platforms and toolkits. When a virtual toolkit is employed, interfaces ported from one system to another have the look and feel of the new system, even though they were developed elsewhere.

Layout Languages

Layout languages are used to describe the static look of an interface in a text-based form. The text is then compiled by a layout compiler much the same way as application domain code is compiled by a programming language compiler (Fig. 4). The compiled form of the layout, called the *resource file,* contains combinations of widget attributes and attribute values, as well as other information such as programmer-defined values. Two well-known layout languages are the User Interface Language (UIL) from OSF/

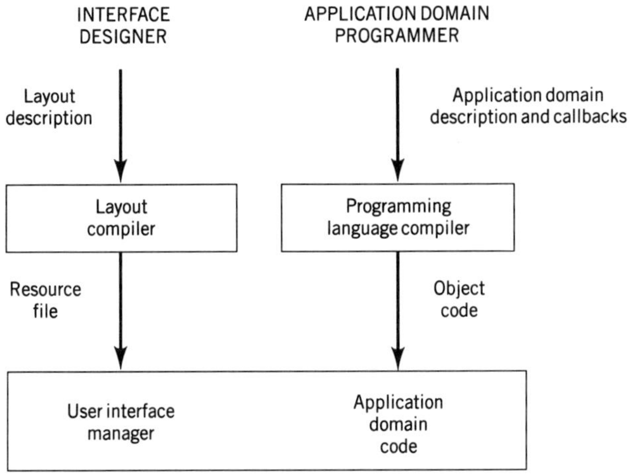

Figure 4. Using a layout language.

MOTIF (Open Software Foundation Inc., 1989) and Wcl (Smyth, 1990).

Layout languages are designed to focus on layout, and they handle dialogue in a restricted manner, if at all. Examples of the very limited types of dialogue available in some layout languages are: calling an application domain function when an event occurs in a widget or displaying another widget (e.g., a window) when an event occurs. All other dialogue, including handling of other user inputs, must be coded in the application domain component.

Specialized Programming Languages

Specialized programming languages, such as Smalltalk (Goldberg and Robson, 1989) and Winterp (Mayer and coworkers, 1990), are designed to reduce the complexity of programming directly with the underlying windowing system. These languages provide constructs that are abstractions of low-level details of the windowing system. Because of the high-level nature of these languages they are often used for rapid prototyping. However, specialized languages may restrict developers from implementing specific features of their designs because the high-level abstractions they contain deny access to lower-level attributes and functionality.

Interactive Design Tools

Although layout languages and specialized programming languages are text-based, an Interactive Design Tool (IDT) allows a designer to define the layout of a user interface interactively. Some IDTs provide a direct manipulation editor, similar to a graphics editor (e.g., MacDraw), where the widgets can be placed and sized with a mouse. IDTs generally provide forms that the user interface designer can fill in to specify attribute values and the names of callback functions.

As shown in Figure 5, a user interface designer uses an IDT to produce definitions of the layout and skeleton code for associated functions. The skeleton code is in the format of a programming language (e.g., C or Ada), a resource file, or, in Motif-based applications, User Interface Language (UIL). The application domain programmer then

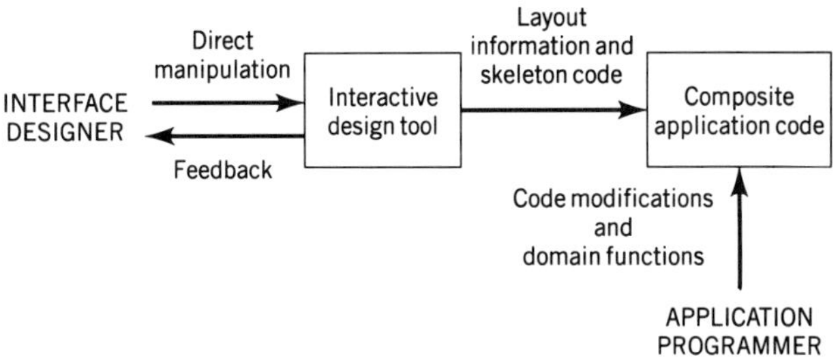

Figure 5. Using an IDT.

adds the domain functionality to the skeleton code. Builder Xcessory™ by ICS (Integrated Computer Solutions, 1990) and UIM/X™ (Visual Edge Software, 1990) are examples of IDTs.

User Interface Management Systems and Associated Models

The term "user interface management system" came into general use following the Seeheim Workshop on User Interface Management Systems (Pfaff and ten Hagan, 1985). The term has several meanings in current usage. Some researchers use it as a general catchall, referring to any integrated set of capabilities for defining and managing a user interface. Other researchers use the term UIMS to refer exclusively to the runtime management capabilities of an interactive system (Myers, 1989). A third group of developers uses the term UIMS to refer only to systems that enforce the separation of the user interface code from the application domain code according to the particular architecture known as the Seeheim model (Fig. 6).

The Seeheim model of user interface management systems was defined at the 1983 workshop in Seeheim, Germany (Pfaff and ten Hagan, 1985). Green presented a comprehensive description of the work done at the workshop and of his use of the model to develop the University of Alberta UIMS (1985).

The Seeheim model divides the user interface into three parts: presentation component, dialogue control component and the application interface model. "The presentation component is responsible for the physical appearance of the user interface including all the device interactions." (Green, 1985). In other words, it's the lexical component and is "responsible for screen management, information display, input devices, interaction techniques and lexical feedback. The dialogue control component manages the dialogue between the user and the application. This component converts the stream of input tokens originating in the presentation component into a structure representing

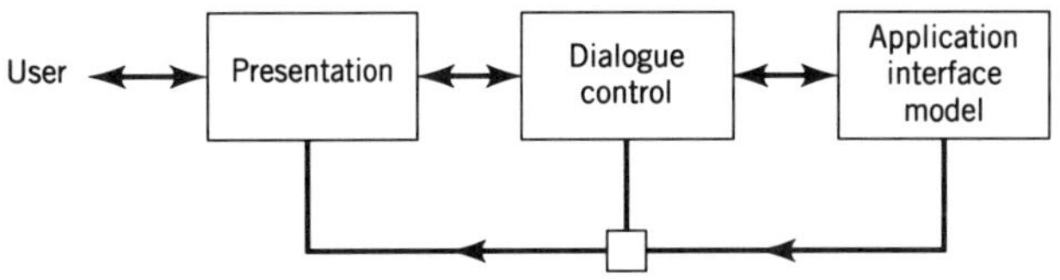

Figure 6. Seeheim model of a user interface management system (Green, 1985).

the commands and operands intended by the user. The application interface model forms the interface between the user interface and the rest of the program. It is the user interface's view of the application." (Green, 1985). The application interface model contains descriptions of the application's data structures and any routines that are accessible to the user interface.

The Seeheim model helps to focus attention on the importance of separating user interface code from domain-specific code. This separation prevents changes that occur in either the user interface domain or the application domain from impacting changes in the other domain. Additionally, the separation may encourage reuse of the application domain code with updated or different user interfaces (Gould and co-workers, 1991).

Many of the user interface management systems developed thus far have followed the Seeheim model, for example, Serpent (Bass and co-workers, 1988) and TeleUse™ (TeleSoft Corporation, 1989). However, a number of other architectural models have been proposed. Some of the more familiar ones are the Seattle model (Lantz, 1987), the Lisbon model (Duce and co-workers, eds., 1991), Olsen's model (Olsen, 1992), Model View Controller (Krasner and Pope, 1988) and PAC (Coutaz, 1987), a more modern version of the MVC concept.

A recently developed model, the Slinky Metamodel (UIMS Tool Developers Workshop, 1992), was cited by Edmonds as a creative updating of the original Seeheim concept (1992). This work is the product of a set of workshops of user interface tool developers who found available models for the runtime architecture of an interactive system inadequate for their purposes. The Slinky work argues that no single architecture will satisfy all the goals of various developers and all the requirements of various systems. For example, designing software components that are modular and reusable may be of paramount concern for one application, while optimizing the performance of the runtime system may outweigh all other considerations for a second application. These goals conflict and may require systems with different architectures.

COMMERCIAL AND RESEARCH SYSTEMS

The area of user interface design environments is an active one. In the early 1980s, the ready availability of sophisticated computer graphics workstations generated the need for fast, easy-to-use methods for creating, managing and modifying user interfaces. This section describes only a few of the commercial and research systems that have had a pronounced effect on progress in this field.

Three early systems were: The George Washington User Interface Management System (GWUIMS), Menulay, and the Functional Language Articulated Interactive Resource (FLAIR). GWUIMS (Sibert and co-workers, 1985) was an early prototyping tool that was based on an object-oriented paradigm. It was designed as a testbed for comparing user interface models. Menulay (Buxton and co-workers, 1983) incorporated the concepts of point-and-click input, differing services for novice and expert designers, and the automatic generation of the user interface code. Although Menulay had a somewhat rigid, table-driven structure that limited interactions between the semantic level and the interface, the developers pioneered significant concepts at a very early stage of the development of user interface management systems. FLAIR (Wong and Reid, 1982) had a menu-driven dialog design language and accepted input from a variety of sources, e.g., voice, tablet, light pen, and track ball. Its development is note-worthy because of the early use of a variety of interaction devices and because it was developed in private industry at a time when most research was carried out in universities.

With the development and mass production of low cost Macintosh computer systems, direct manipulation interfaces became commonplace, What You See is What You Get (WYSIWYG) became a new term in "computerese", and software developers became aware that they needed tools to help simplify the complex tasks required to develop the graphical interactions that end users had come to expect. Prototyper (Smethers Barnes, 1987) allows interface designers to rapidly place, move, and size interaction objects on the screen. Prototyper also allows limited dialogue to be defined. The designer can attach actions that display or erase windows or dialog boxes and that enable or disable menu items. Prototyper also has a test mode where the designer can pull down menu items, test the operation of interaction objects, and test causal links between objects. There is, however, no way to test the interface in conjunction with the application domain code.

HyperCard (Goodman, 1987) and SuperCard (Michael, 1989) are popular tools for prototyping interfaces in the Macintosh environment. The interface is developed as a series of cards containing icons and other interaction objects. The cards can be linked to provide transitions from one card to another. The associated development languages, Hypertalk and Supertalk, are easy-to-learn. The languages allow more sophisticated definition than the Hypercard and SuperCard editors. Limitations of these tools are that they restrict the user interface designer to the card paradigm, and they do not support multideveloper environments.

The NeXT™ Interface Builder (NeXT™, Inc., 1989) is based on Objective C (Cox, 1987), an object-oriented language. Interface Builder has the advantage of being integrated within the object-oriented NEXT environment. However, the disadvantages for some types of users are that Interface Builder requires programming expertise and also that applications are not readily transportable to other platforms.

TAE Plus™, (Szczur and Sheppard, 1993) is a NASA-developed tool that is based on the X Window System and Motif™. The TAE Plus Work-Bench is used for creating and sequencing displays. The interaction objects include real-time, data-driven display objects. TAE Plus generates C, C++ and Ada code automatically and provides application services for the runtime manipulation and management of the user interface.

Serpent (Bass and co-workers, 1988), developed at the Software Engineering Institute in Pittsburgh, is an object-oriented system that receives input from multiple types of input devices. Shared data provides the interface between Serpent and the application domain code. In this model, an object is both a presentation mechanism and an interaction mechanism. Serpent has two languages, Slang for specifying dialogue and Saddle, a database schema-like language to define the shared data.

There are several systems that allow interactive definition of the user interface dialogue in addition to the layout. One such system, Druid (Singh and Ngan, 1990), is based on a demonstration technique that allows the designer to specify what sequences of dialogue boxes and windows will appear and what application functions will be called when an event occurs. Another such system is OSU (Lewis and co-workers, 1989). OSU allows the user to interactively link buttons of one dialogue box to another dialogue box so that when a button in the first dialogue box is pressed, the second dialogue box appears. OSU linking is based on a transition diagram model where an event signals the appearance of another object and a change of state. This method allows easy linking of events to the display of objects.

Another approach to interactive definition of dialogue has been through specifications. UIDTs allow interface designers to interactively define a state machine that describes the dialogue. Two early systems were developed by Wasserman (Wasserman, 1985) and Jacob (Jacob, 1985). In these systems the user draws a state transition diagram, using nodes to represent screens and states of the interface, and arcs to indicate the next state after a particular user input. The screens themselves are defined using a layout language, and the application interface semantics are defined in a similar fashion. In Statemaster (Wellner, 1989) the user draws hierarchical state machines called statecharts (Harel, 1988). The statecharts differ from transition diagrams in that they allow grouping of states with common events and a notation to indicate concurrency. RPP is based on an executable specification called Interface Representation Graphs (IRGs) that represents layout, constraints, dialogue and the dialogue-domain interface (Rouff, 1991). In RPP, an IRG is automatically produced from an IDT augmented to define the dynamics.

Recent developments in user interface management tools have included work done with the Garnet system (Myers and co-workers, 1989) and the User Interface Design Environment (UIDE) (Foley, 1989; Gieskens and Foley, 1992). Garnet is a set of tools for creating and directly manipulating graphic objects and for handling the run-time behavior of the objects. Garnet allows development of objects with powerful constraints. For example, if two boxes are constructed with a connecting line at their midpoints and one box is moved within the display, the connecting line will appear, correctly positioned, at the new location. Additionally, Garnet allows the user interface designer to specify the operation of interaction objects by giving the system an example of the interface in action (Myers, 1988). The system infers operations from a user's manipulation of a mouse. Garnet is based on the X Window System and Motif™ but is not tied to any particular widget set. It runs on various machines and operating systems.

UIDE is a descendent of the GWUIMS. UIDE associates pre- and post-conditions with interaction objects. Preconditions indicate the state that needs to be present before an object can be used. Postconditions change the state of the user interface to reflect the action that just occurred. For example, a precondition to a *Help* button would assure that the button is disabled if the *Help* window is open. A post-condition for the *Help* button would set the help button to *disabled.* Pre- and post-conditions can also be used to generate help messages so a user can determine what a command will do, the sequence of actions that need to be done to enable a command, and for checking the completeness and consistency of the interface dialogue.

BIBLIOGRAPHY

L. Bass, E. J. Hardy, K. Hoyt, R. Little, and R. C. Seacord, *Introduction to the Serpent User Interface Management System,* Technical Report CMU/SEI-88-TR-5, ADA200085, Carnegie Mellon University, Software Engineering Institute, March, 1988.

D. G. Bobrow, S. Mittal, and M. J. Stefik, "Expert Systems: Perils and Promise," *Communications of the ACM,* 880–894 (Sept. 1986).

W. A. Buxton and co-workers, " Toward A Comprehensive User Interface Management System," *Computer Graphics,* 1–16, (March 1983).

J. Coutaz, "PAC, An Implementation Model for Dialog Design," *Proceedings of HCI Interact '87,* North-Holland, Amsterdam, 1987, pp. 431–436.

B. J. Cox, *Object-Oriented Programming: An Evolutionary Approach,* Addison-Wesley, Reading, Mass., 1987.

E. Edmonds, *The Separable User Interface,* Academic Press, San Diego, Calif., 1992.

J. Foley, W. C. Kim, S. Kovacevic, and K. Murray, "Defining Interfaces at a High Level of Abstraction," *IEEE Software* (Jan. 1989).

D. F. Gieskens and J. D. Foley, "Controlling User Interface Objects Through Pre- and Postconditions," *CHI '92 Conference Proceedings,* May 1992.

A. Goldberg and D. Robson, *Smalltalk-80: The Language,* Addison-Wesley, 1989.

D. Goodman, *The Complete HyperCard Handbook,* Bantam Books, New York, 1987.

J. D. Gould, S. J. Boies, and C. Lewis. "Making Usable, Useful, Productivity-Enhancing Computer Applications," *Communications of the ACM* **34**(1), 74–85 (1991).

M. Green, "The University of Alberta User Interface Management System," *Computer Graphics* **19**(3), 205–213 (1985).

D. Harel, "On Visual Formalisms," *Communications of the ACM* **31**(5), (May 1988).

D. Hix, "Generations of User-Interface Management Systems," *IEEE Software* (Sept. 1990).

Integrated Computer Solutions, *The Builder Xcessory User's Guide,* Integrated Computer Solutions, Inc., Cambridge, Mass., 1990.

R. J. K. Jacob, "A State Transition Diagram Language for Visual Programming," *IEEE Computer,* 51–59 (Aug. 1985).

G. E. Krasner and S. T. Pope, "A Cookbook for Using Model-view-controller User Interface Paradigm in Smalltalk-80," *Journal of Object Oriented Programming,* **1**(3), 26–49 (1988).

K. A. Lantz, P. P. Tanner, C. Binding, K. T. Huang, and A. Dwelly, "Reference Models, Window Systems and Concurrency," *Computer Graphics* **21**(2), 87–97 (1987).

E. Lee, "User-Interface Development Tools," *IEEE Software,* 31–36 (May 1990).

T. Lewis, F. Handloser III, S. Bose, and S. Yang, "Prototypes from Standard User Interface Management Systems," *IEEE Computer* **22**(5), 51–60 (1989).

N. Mayer, A. Shepherd, and A. Kuchinsky, "Winterp: An Object-oriented, Rapid Prototyping, Development Environment for Building Extensible Applications with the OSF/Motif UI Toolkit," *Xhibition '90 Conference Proceedings,* San Jose, May 1990, pp. 49–64.

J. McCormack and P. Asente. "An Overview of the X Toolkit," in *Proceedings of the ACM SIGGRAPH Symposium on User Interface Software,* Banff, Alberta, Canada, Oct. 17–19, 1988.

S. Michael, *Steve Michel's SuperCard Handbook,* Osborne McGraw-Hill, Berkeley, Calif., 1989.

B. A. Myers, *Creating User Interfaces by Demonstration,* Academic Press, Boston, Mass., 1988.

B. A. Myers, "User-Interface Tools: Introduction and Survey," *IEEE Software,* 15–23, (Jan. 1989).

B. Myers, D. Giuse, R. Dannenberg, B. Vander Zanden, D. Kosbiew, P. Marchal, E. Pervin, and J. Kolojejchick, *The Garnet Toolkit Reference Manuals: Support for Highly Interactive, Graphical User Interfaces in Lisp,* Technical Report CMU-CS-89-196, Carnegie Mellon University, Computer Science Department, Pittsburgh, Nov. 1989.

NeXT, Inc., Interface Builder, *NeXT Systems Reference Manual,* 1989.

D. Olsen, Jr., *User Interface Management Systems: Models and Algorithm,* Morgan Kaufmann Publishers, San Mateo, Calif., 1992.

Open Software Foundation, Inc., *OSF/Motif™ Programmer's Reference Manual,* Revision 1.0, 1989.

C. Petzold, *Programming the OS/2 Presentation Manager: the Microsoft Guide to Writing Applications for OS/2 Graphical Windowing Environment,* Microsoft Press, Redmond, Wash., 1989.

C. Petzold, *Programming Windows,* Microsoft Press, Redmond, Wash. 1990.

G. Pfaff and P. J. W. ten Hagan, *Seeheim Workshop on User Interface Management Systems,* Springer-Verlag, Berlin, 1985.

C. Rouff, *Specification and Rapid Prototyping of User Interfaces,* Ph.D. Thesis, Computer Science Department, University of Southern California, 1991.

R. W. Scheifler and J. Gettys, *The X Window System,* MIT Laboratory for Computer Science, Cambridge, Mass., Oct. 1986.

J. L. Sibert, W. D Hurley and T. W. Bleser, "An Object-Oriented User Interface Management System," *Computer Graphics* **20**(4), 259–268 (1985).

G. C. H. Singh and T. Y. Ngan, "Druid: A System of Demonstrational Rapid User Interface Development," *Proceedings of the 3rd Annual ACM SIGGRAPH Symposium on User Interface Software and Technology,* 1990, pp. 167–177.

SmethersBarnes, *Prototyper Reference Manual,* 1987.

D. E. Smyth, *Wcl-Widget Creation Library: A Thin Veneer Over Xrm,* Jet Propulsion Labs, Pasadena, Calif., 1990.

Sun Microsystems, Inc, *OPEN LOOK Graphical User Interface Functional Specification,* Addison–Wesley Publishing Company, Inc., 1989.

M. R. Szczur and S. B. Sheppard, "TAE Plus: Transportable Applications Environment Plus: A User Interface Development Environment," *ACM Transactions on Information Systems,* **11**(1) (Jan. 1993).

P. Szekely, *Separating the user interface from the functionality of application programs,* Ph.D, Thesis CMU–CS–88–101, Carnegie-Mellon University, Pittsburgh, Penn., 1988.

TeleSoft Corporation, *TeleUse User Interface Management System* Product Information, San Diego, Calif., May 1989.

The UIMS Tool Developers Workshop, "A Metamodel for the Runtime Architecture of an Interactive System," in *SIGCHI Bulletin,* **24**(1), 32–37 (Jan. 1992).

"User Interface Management and Design," in D. A. Duce, M. R. Gomes, F. R. A. Hopgood, and J. R. Lee, eds., *Eurographic Seminars,* Springer-Verlag, Berlin, 1991, pp. 36–49.

Visual Edge Software, *Getting Started with UIM/X,* Saint Laurent, Quebec, Canada, 1990.

A. I. Wasserman, "Extending State Transition Diagrams for the Specification of Human-Computer Interaction," *IEEE Transactions of Software Engineering* **SE-11**(8), 699–713 (Aug. 1985).

P. Wellner, "Statemaster: A UIMS Based on Statecharts for Prototyping and Target Implementation Notation for Specification," *Proceedings of ACM CHI'89 Conference on Human Factors in Computing Systems,* 1989, pp. 177–182.

P. C. S. Wong and E. R. Reid, "FLAIR: User Interface Dialog Design Tool," *Computer Graphics,* 120–125 (July 1982).

D. Young, *The X Window System: Programming and Applications with Xt,* OSF/Motif Edition, Prentice Hall, 1990.

S. Sheppard
C. Rouff
NASA Goddard Space Flight Center

V

VALIDATION

The process of evaluating a system or component during or at the end of the development process to determine whether it satisfies specified requirements (IEEE). See also VALIDATION AND VERIFICATION.

VIENNA DEVELOPMENT METHOD

INTRODUCTION

VDM (Vienna Development Method) is a Formal Method (see FORMAL METHODS) that can be used for both the specification and development of software. It is *model based,* i.e. system behavior is defined by the construction of a mathematical model with an underlying state (data) and a collection of operations on that state. It is based on discrete mathematics, i.e. set theory and logic.

The original VDM Specification Language (VDM-SL) grew out of an attempt to define formal denotational semantics for the programming PL/1 at the IBM Laboratory in Vienna. The language and method have developed much since then through both academic research and industrial application.

OVERVIEW

This section gives a technical overview via an example. The example is a trivial one and does not cover all the features of VDM but serves to give a flavor. It is written using the latest BSI-VDM-SL Standard (see Dawes, 1991).

Specification

```
types
    Person is not yet defined
state Personnel of
    MEN: Person-set
    WOMEN: Person-set
inv mk-Personnel(m,w) Δ m ∩ w =∅
init mk-Personnel(m,w) Δ m =∅∧ w=∅
end
operations
    REGISTER_MALE (man : Person)→()
    ext wr MEN : Person-set
        rd WOMEN : Person-set
    pre man ∉ MEN ∧ man ∉ WOMEN
    post MEN=↼MEN ∪ {man}
```

This specifies a personnel database which merely records who are known to the database. This information is held in the state variables *MEN* and *WOMEN* of type *Person-set* (the power set type of the *Person* type). *inv* specifies an invariant (i.e. property) on the state and *init* specifies its initial value. *mk-Personnel* is used to create a variable of the composite type personnel.

Only one operation is specified. It takes one input parameter *man* and has read/write access to MEN, but only read access to *WOMEN.* It has no output. *pre* specifies a pre-condition on the state and input parameter, and, if this is satisfied when the operation is invoked, *post* (the post-condition) specifies the final state after invocation (it would also specify the output parameter were there one). If *pre* is not satisfied upon invocation then the after state is undefined. The pre-condition uses $\overleftarrow{MEN}$ to represent the set of males in the database before invocation where as *post* uses *MEN* for this and *MEN* to represent its value after invocation. If correctly invoked, *REGISTER_MALE* adds a new *man* to the database. Other operations would also be specified. Note that the specification says what data is held and *what* the operation does, not *how*.

We are now in a position to prove theorems about the consistency of our specification. Some useful theorems are

Invariant preservation	The initial state satisfies the invariant and all operations preserve it.
Reachability	All possible states are reachable from the initial state via the operations.
Implementability	For each operation prove that a result state and output parameter exists for each input state and parameter satisfying the pre-condition (note in the example above there would be a need to define more operations in order to prove reachability, e.g., REGISTER_FEMALE).

The above *proof obligations* can be phrased mathematically and then discharged formally within a suitable proof theory or by rigorous argument. It may also be fruitful to investigate determinism, that is how many possible result states and outputs satisfy the operation for a given input (note that more than one is allowable).

Design

```
state Personnel1 of
    MEN1: Person*
    WOMEN1: Person*
inv mk-Personnel1 (m,w) Δ elems m ∩ elems w =∅
init mk-Personnel1 (m,w) Δ m =[] ∧ w =[]
end
operations      REGISTER_MALE1 (man : Person)→()
    ext wr MEN1 : Person*
        rd WOMEN1 : Person*
    pre man ∉ elems MEN1 ∧ man ∉ elems WOMEN1
    post MEN1 = ↼MEN1 [man]
```

This design begins to say more about the how of implementation than the what of specification. It uses sequences (*)

rather than sets (*elems* takes a sequence and produces the set of elements in the sequence and $\frown$ concatenates two lists). The data in the design is said to be a *refinement* or *reification* of the data in the specification. It is desirable to be able to show that this design is a *correct* implementation of the specification. In order to do this we first define the connection between the abstract specification data and reified concrete data via a *retrieve* function:

retr-MEN1 : Person* →Person-**set**
retr-MEN1 (man) $\underline{\Delta}$ **elems** (man)

Similarly for WOMEN1.

If we let *retr* represent a function from the concrete state σ1 to the abstract state σ, then to show our design is correct with respect to the specification we must consider both the data and the operation modeling. For the data we have two proof obligations:

Invariant preservation	$\text{inv1}(\sigma 1) \Rightarrow (\sigma 1 \in \text{dom } retr \wedge \text{inv}(retr(\sigma 1)))$
Adequacy	$\text{inv}(\sigma) \Rightarrow \exists\ \sigma 1 \bullet \text{inv1}(\sigma 1) \wedge \sigma = retr\sigma 1(\sigma 1)$

We also have two proof obligations per operation:

Precondition rule	$\text{inv1}(\sigma 1) \wedge \text{pre-OP}(retr(\sigma 1)) \Rightarrow \text{pre-OP1}(\sigma 1)$
Postcondition rule	$\text{inv1}(\overleftarrow{\sigma 1}) \wedge \text{pre-OP}(retr(\overleftarrow{\sigma 1})) \wedge \text{post-OP1}(\overleftarrow{\sigma 1}, \sigma 1) \Rightarrow \text{post-OP}(retr\sigma 1(\overleftarrow{\sigma 1}), retr(\sigma 1))$

This design and proof process can continue until code is produced. The code can also be proved correct with respect to the lowest level of design. The main text on VDM (Jones, 1990) gives many examples of specifications, designs, code and proofs and also covers the case where we have a retrieve relation rather than a function. It also provides a suitable proof theory. Jones and Shaw (1990) provides a number of Case Studies.

CURRENT STATUS

VDM is now taught, researched and used in many institutions and industries world-wide. There is a British Standards Institute group (BSI IST/5/50) preparing a VDM standard (see Dawes, 1991). It is one of the two most widely used Formal Methods. Z is the other, see Hayes (1992) for a comparison of the two. VDM has been used on a number of major projects in industry including:

- Looking at VDM for use in Safety Critical Software development (Hill and co-workers, 1990).
- Use of VVSL (see below) for the specification of an interface between software engineering tools (Esprit, 1988a).

VDM is also supported by a number of tools (see below).

FUTURE TRENDS

Current research directions are mainly in the development of tools to support VDM and of VDM mutants to plug perceived gaps in the expressive power of VDM.

VDM cannot express concurrent behavior explicitly and originally lacked structuring facilities and syntactic sugar for error handling (although the BSI are proposing remedies for the latter two, see Dawes, 1991). VVSL (VIP VDM Specification Language, see Middleburg, 1993) rectified all three of these. RAISE (Rigorous Approach to Industrial Software Engineering, see Raise, 1992)) extends VDM with facilities for property-oriented specification, structuring and concurrency. There are a number of ther mutants.

Tools for VDM fall into two camps: those which support just the writing of syntactically correct VDM and those which also support proofs. A number of tools are described in Prehn and Toetenel.

BIBLIOGRAPHY

J. Dawes, *The VDM-SL Reference Guide,* Pitman Publishing, 1991.

I. Hayes, "VDM and Z: A Comparative Case Study," *Formal Aspects of Computing* **4**(1) (1992).

J. V. Hill, P. Robinson, and P. A. Stokes, *Safety Critical Software in Control Systems, Computers and Safety,* IEE, 1990, pp. 92–96.

C. B. Jones, *Systematic Software Development Using VDM,* Prentice Hall International, 1990.

C. B. Jones and R. C. F. Shaw, eds. *Case Studies in Systematic Software Development,* Prentice Hall International, 1990.

C. A. Middleburg, "Logic and Specification, extending VDM-SL for Advanced Formal Specification," *Computer Science:Research and Practise*, Vol. 1, Chapman and Hall, 1993.

S. Prehn and W. J. Toetenel, eds., VDM '91, *Formal Software Development Methods,* Springer Verlag.

The RAISE Specification Language, BCS Practitioner Series, Prentice Hall International, 1992.

MICHAEL BARTLEY
Praxis

VERIFICATION

(1) The process of evaluating a system or component to determine whether the products of a given development phase satisfy the conditions imposed at the start of that phase (IEEE). See also VERFICATION AND VALIDATION.

VERIFICATION AND VALIDATION

INTRODUCTION

High integrity software is software that must be trusted to work dependably in some critical function, and whose failure to do so may have catastrophic results, such as serious injury, loss of life, or property (Wallace and co-workers, 1991). Examples include aviation, medical devices, nuclear power, weapons systems, and electronic funds transfer. Examples of catastrophes, and catastrophes waiting to happen, can be found in the annual "Risk of the Year" presentations at COMPASS (computer assurance conference for process integrity, computer security, and software safety) conferences and in major research reports (Clark and co-workers, 1991; Neuman, 1991; U.S. Congress, 1989).

In many industries, developers and customers need a standard framework of requirements that will provide reasonable assurance that the software of critical systems will be of high integrity. Software verification and validation (V & V) is one type of process contributing to this reasonable assurance. Software (V & V) (Stauffer and Fujii, 1986) is

> *"a systems engineering process employing a rigorous methodology for evaluating the correctness and quality of the software product through the software life cycle."*

Software V & V is too often ignored in today's highly competitive marketplace (Wallace and Fujii, 1989). Businesses and governments are increasingly placing their investment dollars into software systems whose successful operation is critical to their profit line and to system safety or security. The disciplines of software V & V are equally applicable for any system with software requiring quality.

Producing reliable software requires the use of both management and product standards and practices. Checking quality requires the use of each of several techniques, including review, inspection, and several types of testing. A total software quality program requires a well-planned, comprehensive application of quality engineering disciplines implemented by all participants (e.g., management, technical engineering, quality assurance team) throughout the software development and maintenance life cycle (see also MAINTENANCE; QUALITY ASSURANCE).

Traditionally, software quality assurance standards require the development process to conform to broad quality requirements involving quality procedures, major reviews, applicable standards, documentation requirements, and general software quality attributes. Most of these software quality assurance standards do not define how to evaluate software products for compliance with technical specifications for safety, security, quality enhancement, and functional and performance requirements. Software V & V fills this gap by employing activities and tasks to provide the detailed engineering assessment (including testing) for evaluating how well the software is meeting its technical specifications. Software V & V standards, when implemented in addition to other quality standards, provide a comprehensive computer assurance program for software development efforts.

To provide an understanding of software V & V and the standards which describe it, this article is divided into three sections:

1. Overview of software V & V including the software V & V techniques available in each life cycle phase to evaluate and test software.
2. Description of standards and guidelines for planning and managing software V & V.
3. Description of general project and quality assurance standards, relative to their requirements for software V & V.

The first section describes software V & V, its objectives, recommended tasks, and guidance for selecting techniques to perform the tasks. It provides historical information on software V & V; describes a minimum set of analyses and tests; and provides guidance on how and when to select specific software V & V techniques to ensure that software V & V resources can be effectively focused on the more difficult problems or areas of the software. The section analyzes two software V & V case studies to provide opinions about where software V & V was most effective.

Perspectives are provided on how software V & V practices fit into the system life cycle and on their general relationship to software life cycle processes. One issue that always arises in planning a project and its software V & V effort is project organization and the objectivity of the staff performing software, V & V tasks. Independent V & V for software (IV & V) grew out of this concern. Software IV & V may be considered to be the performance of software V & V activities by a team that is separate from the software development group. The software IV & V effort reports directly to the acquirer of the software. Members of the software IV & V team must have full access to all products of the software development effort in order to perform an independent technical evaluation of the software. Differences between software V & V and software quality assurance, and how development, software quality assurance, software V & V, and other software engineering practitioners can use software V & V techniques to produce quality software are described in INDEPENDENT VALIDATION AND VERIFICATION.

One indicator that the use of software V & V has become widespread is the fact that over time, more and more software engineering standards are requiring the use of software V & V (Wallace and co-workers; 1992a; 1992b). Standards for software V & V began to evolve in the late 1970s and early 1980s. These standards are representative of the current direction of Federal agencies and industries, businesses, and academia involved in consensus standards. Other countries and international standards organizations (e.g., British Standards Institute, Canadian Standards Organization, International Standards Organization) have recently developed, are developing, or are considering adopting software V & V standards or quality standards referencing software V & V. Bibliographies of software engineering standards may be found in Nash and Redwine (1985); CAN (1988); and Dorling (1988).

A comparison and contrast of several software V & V standards shows how each differs in requiring software V & V activities. The list of key software V & V activities identified in these standards forms a basic approach for systematically evaluating any software in determining how well the software is satisfying its performance and safety/security requirements.

General project management and software quality standards require a software V & V effort or include software V & V activities as part of their domain; some do both.

These generic project level standards reference software V & V to different levels of detail because each is focused on other project management or generic quality issues. However, each generic project level standard has recognized the value of software V & V as a means of evaluating software's compliance with its requirements (e.g., functionality, performance, safety, security, quality, external interfaces). All of the standards establish guidelines for technical review of both the interim and final products of software development and recognize that these evaluations and tests must occur at all phases of the software development life cycle. Key definitions of these standards and guidelines are highlighted to provide insight on how to use the standard relative to software V & V.

Quality software is becoming increasingly more difficult to achieve because of the larger complexities of the problem being solved and the larger scale of development efforts. The need for quality software is further stressed by the increasing use of software in critical applications not only in the obvious weapons systems but now in the control of critical day-to-day life sustaining functions. Software V & V is an effective methodology for controlling software developments and helping to build quality into the software before its release for use.

OVERVIEW OF SOFTWARE VERIFICATION AND VALIDATION

In 1961 a software error caused the destruction of a Mariner payload on board a radio-controlled Atlas booster. The Atlas guidance software had used incorrect radar data to compute navigation and steering commands. The cause was a simple programming error of misusing a hyphen on previous data rather than on the corrected, extrapolated data. This simple but expensive error led the Air Force to require independent review of the guidance equations and software implementation of all future mission-critical space launches. This need to ensure software quality and performance gave birth to the methodology of software V & V.

As the benefits of software V & V became apparent in improved software quality, including safety and security, more systems began using it. The methodology has proliferated throughout the Department of Defense (DOD) services, the Federal Aviation Administration, and the National Aeronautics and Space Administration, as well as medical and nuclear power industries. Some U.S. Government agencies, like the Department of Health and Human Services, have recently entered software V & V requirements into their policies and procedures regarding review of medical devices for approval by the Food and Drug Administration (HHS).

In many cases, software V & V is governed by standards establishing software development, project management, and software quality assurance requirements. Government and industry began to develop software V & V standards (Table 1) because managers needed a specification of this methodology for contract procurement and for monitoring the technical performance of V & V efforts.

Objectives of Software V & V

Software V & V comprehensively analyzes and tests software during all stages of its development and maintenance to:

- Determine that it performs its intended functions correctly.
- Ensure that it performs no unintended functions.
- Measure its quality and reliability.

Software V & V is a systems engineering discipline which evaluates the software in a systems context relative to all system elements of hardware, users, and other software. Like systems engineering, it uses a structured approach to analyze and test the software against all system functions and all hardware, user, and other software interfaces. It measures software against its requirements for performance, quality attributes, safety, and computer security. Each organization involved in the software development process contributes to the quality of the software.

Software quality depends on many attributes, (e.g., correctness, completeness, accuracy, consistency, testability, safety, maintainability, security, and reusability) (see also SAFETY; REUSE). In a document advising Federal agencies on software acceptance, two quality attributes, safety and computer security, are considered so important that they should be especially defined in the software requirements specification and receive special attention throughout the software life cycle (Wallace and Cherniavsky, 1990). Many systems may fail to operate safely if the software fails or if functions for software have not been defined in response to potential system hazards, either to prevent system failure or to mitigate consequences of failures due to conditions external to the software. The Computer Security Act of 1987 makes it mandatory that Federal agencies consider computer security needs in software procurements (U.S. Congress, 1988).

When performed in parallel with software development, software V & V yields several benefits:

- It uncovers high risk errors early, giving the design team time to evolve a comprehensive solution rather than forcing them into a makeshift fix to accommodate software deadlines.
- It evaluates the products against system requirements.
- It provides management with visibility into the quality and progress of the development effort that is continuous and comprehensive, not just at major review milestones (which may occur infrequently).
- It gives the user an incremental preview of system performance, with the chance to make early adjustments.
- It provides decision criteria for whether or not to proceed to the next development phase.

Software V & V is also used, because of its analytic approach, as a vehicle for locating high risk areas of the software system and for analyzing critical features (e.g.,

Table 1. History of Software V&V Standards within the United States

AFR 122-9/-10 1970	"Design Certification Program for Nuclear Weapon System and Firmware" for Air Force nuclear weapon system software (mandatory)
AFR 800-14 1975	"Acquisition Management: Acquisition and Support Procedures for Computer Resources in Systems" for acquisition of major Air Force embedded computer systems
MIL-STD-1679 1978	"Software Development" for Navy systems
JCMPO INST 8020.1 1981	" Safety Studies, Reviews and Evaluation Involving Nuclear Weapon Systems," for Navy nuclear cruise missile weapon systems software (mandatory)
ANS/IEEE - ANS-7.4.3.2 1982	" Application Criteria for Programmable Digital Computer Systems in Safety Systems of Nuclear Power Generating Stations" for nuclear power generation embedded software
FIPSPUB101 1983	" Guideline for Lifecycle Validation, Verification and Testing of Computer Software" for general guidance to computer software industry
DOD-STD-2167A and 2168 1985-1988	"Defense System Software Development: Quality Progrsm" for development of DoD mission critical computer system software
ANSI/IEEE-STD 1012 1986	" Standard for Software Verification and Validation Plans" for any software development
NASA SMAP GUIDEBOOKS 1986	" Software Verification and Validation for Project Managers" for software intensive systems
ARMY REG 50-4 1986	" Software Studies and Reviews of Nuclear Weapon Systems" for Army nuclear weapon system software
FIPSPUB132 1987	" Guideline for Software Verification and Validation Plans" for uniform and minimum requirements of V&V; adopts ANSI/IEEE 1012
ANSI/ANS 10.4 1987	" Guideline for V&V of Scientific and Engineering Computer Programs for the Nuclear Industry" for scientific and engineering programs (R&D) for the nuclear power industry
AFSCP 800-5 1988*	" Software Independent Verification and Validation" for Air Force systems with potential to cause death, system loss, more than $550K damage to equipment, or severe illness/injury
FAA STD 0-26 1989	" National Aerospace System Software Development" for National airspace system-advanced automation system
DEPARTMENT OF HEALTH and HUMAN SERVICES 1991	" Reviewer Guidance for Contolled Medical Devices" for computer controlled medical devices undergoing premarket notification [510(k)] submissions.
AF PAMPHLET 800-45* 1991	Software Verification and Validation (V&V) for Air Force (AFSCP 800-5 adopted as Air Force pamphlet)

safety and security requirements) and the relationship of those features to the entire system. Software V & V is a technical discipline using a systems engineering methodology for analyzing the entire software system and for driving better performance features into and software errors out of high risk, critical areas of the software.

An equally important concept of software V & V is to define who performs the software V & V. There are various organizational arrangements for performing software V & V; each has a specific type of contribution for the quality of the software system. A recent IEEE standard, "Standard for Software Lifecycle Processes," lays out the activities that are essential to developing software (IEEE, 1990). Software V & V is considered an integral process, that is, a process which is continuously executed concurrently with software development activities. The standard does not state who does any of the activities of software V & V; rather it states that more than one instantiation of a specific software V & V activity may occur. No one owns software V & V; it is an integral part of the software life cycle processes and activities may be performed by different organizations on the same project. There are instances when independence of the performers of the softwareV & V activities from those developing the software is important. A recent study of standards addressing assurance activities for high integrity software explains that, while several standards require or recommend IV & V, the specific requirements vary broadly. They range from an independent group executing the developer's test cases to a full analysis of all life cycle products when they are developed (Wallace and co-workers, 1992).

Applying V & V to a Software Life Cycle

In many industries (e.g., nuclear power industry) software is only one component of an individual company's business. At the top management level, the view is of the whole, not a part. Therefore, system configuration management and system validation are the engineering concepts that make sense to executives of companies within these industries. For software companies, executives think in terms of *software* configuration management (SCM) and *software* validation. The difference is nontrivial and has caused much misunderstanding in the development of standards. In many industries, software is deeply embedded in systems in which software cannot fully stand alone. In these systems, nonsoftware components often are not only plug-in but are built to precise, accredited standards. Verification of such components may consist of checking that the component has been built according to its standard; configuration management is not an issue at that level. Validation of the component occurs when the total system is validated upon completion. For software, continuous verification activities and validation of parts back to the software and system requirements occur during software development. SCM during software development provides the assurance that delivered software documentation is the software that has been verified and validated. Full functionality of software in embedded systems can only be simulated. Although it cannot be tested in real time during software development, its final validation is part of the system validation. The methodology of software V & V does not separate verification from validation.

The difference between system and software viewpoints stands out in several documents. For example, ANSI/IEEE (1982) is concerned with computer system validation and not particularly concerned with software issues. In this document, software verification means software testing; other types of software verification activities (e.g., inspection, analysis) are ignored (see INSPECTIONS). Part of the rationale for not treating verification and validation as separate functions in IEEE (1986) is to ensure that the software is examined carefully by many techniques before software testing begins. The final step of software V & V is the system validation, as in system standards. Software V & V consists of these activities applied as the software evolves to assure the internal properties of the software and the external relationships to the system.

The minimum recommended software V & V tasks which are required by the ANSI/IEEE Standard for Software Verification and Validation Plans (SVVPS) (ANSI, 1986) for the development phases are shown in Table 2. They are considered effective and applicable to all types of software applications. Tailoring software V & V for a specific project is accomplished by adding tasks to the minimum set or, when appropriate, deleting software V & V tasks. Table 3 lists some optional software V & V tasks in the life cycle phase where they most likely can be applied, and considerations that one might use to assign the tasks to software V & V. The SVVP standard requires software V & V management tasks spanning the entire software life cycle and software V & V tasks for operations and maintenance.

These software V & V tasks can be applied to different life cycle models simply by mapping traditional phases to the new model. Examples include variations of the traditional waterfall, Boehm's (1988) spiral development, rapid prototyping, or evolutionary development models (Davis and co-workers, 1988). The software V & V tasks are fully consistent with the IEEE standard for software life cycle processes (ANSI, 1990). The SVVP standard specifies minimum input and output requirements for each software V & V task; a software V & V task may not begin without specific inputs, and is not completed until specific outputs are completed. The inputs may sometimes be partial products; for example, the requirements or design of the total subsystem may be especially dependent on the requirements or design of a subsystem. When this is the case, selected software V & V tasks from Table 3 (e.g., control flow analysis) should be conducted on the subsystem before other design elements are completed. Several tasks in Table 3 are appropriate throughout the life cycle.

Management of Software V & V. Management tasks for software V & V span the entire life cycle. These tasks are to plan the software V & V process; coordinate and interpret performance and quality of the software V & V effort; report discrepancies promptly to the user or development group; identify early problem trends and focus software V & V activities on them; provide a technical evaluation of the software performance and quality at each major software program review (so a determination can be made of whether the software product has satisfied its requirements well enough to proceed to the next phase); and assess the full impact of proposed software changes. The output of the software V & V activities consists of the SVVP, task reports, phase summary reports, final report and discrepancy report.

Major steps in developing the SVVP are to:

- Define the quality and performance objectives (e.g., verify conformance to specifications, verify compliance with safety and security objectives, assess efficiency and quality of software, and assess performance across the full operating environment).
- Characterize the types of problems anticipated in the system and define how they would show up in the software.
- Select the software V & V analysis and testing techniques to detect the system and software problems effectively.

The plan may include a tool acquisition and development plan and a personnel training plan. The SVVP is a living document, constantly being revised as knowledge accumulates about the characteristics of the system, the software, and the problem areas in the software.

An important software V & V management activity is to monitor the software V & V technical progress and quality of results. At each software V & V phase, planned software V & V activities are reviewed and new tasks are added to focus on the critical performance/quality functions of the software and its system. The monitoring activity conducts formal reviews of software V & V discrepancy reports and technical evaluation results to provide a check of their correctness and accuracy. It is critical that tight internal monitoring of the quality and accuracy of software V & V results be performed, because the development group must make the necessary software changes as indicated by the software V & V results. If the V & V results are erroneous or of poor quality, the development group wastes its time and resources in review and more importantly, loses confidence in the effectiveness and helpfulness of the software V & V results. Software V & V studies (Radatz, 1981) have shown that responding to discrepancy reports and software V & V evaluation reports consumes the largest portion of a development group's interface time with the software V & V group.

Boehm and Papaccio (1988) report that the Pareto effect, that is, 20% of the problems cause 80% of the rework costs, applies to software; they recommend that software V & V "focus on identifying and eliminating the specific high risk problems to be encountered by a software project." This does not mean that software V & V should examine only 20% of the software. Rather, software V & V needs to examine the entire software, prioritize the software functions by criticality, and allocate software V & V analysis resources to those areas of the software which contain critical functions and high-risk problems (i.e., more error-

Table 2. Minimum Set of Recommended Software V&V Tasks (IEEE1012)

Phase	Tasks	Key Issues
Concept	Concept-documentation evaluation	Satisfy user needs; constraints of interacting systems
Requirements definition	Traceability analysis	Trace of requirements to concept
	Requirements validation	Correctness, consistency, completeness, accuracy, readability, and testability; satisfaction of system requirements
	Interface analysis	Hardware software, and operator interfaces
	Begin planning for V&V system testing	Compliance with functional requirements; performance at interfaces; adequacy of user documentation; performance at boundaries
	Begin planning for V&V acceptance testing	Compliance with acceptance requirements
Design	Traceability analysis	Trace of design to requirements
	Design evaluation	Correctness; design quality
	Interface analysis	Correctness; data items across interface
	Begin planning for V&V component testing	Compliance to design; timing and accuracy; performance at boundaries
	Begin planning for V&V integration testing	Compliance with functional requirements; timing and accuracy; performance at stress limits
Implementation	Traceability analysis	Trace of source code to design
	Code evaluation	Correctness; code quality
	Interface analysis	Correctness; data/control access across interfaces
	Component test execution	Component integrity
Test	V&V integration-test execution	Correctness of subsystem elements; subsystem interface requirements
	V&V system-test execution	Entire system at limits and user stress conditions
	V&V acceptance-test execution	Performance with operational scenarios
Installation and checkout	Installation-configuration audit	Operations with site dependencies; adequacy of installation procedure
	V&V final report generation	Disposition of all errors; summary of V&V results

prone). Identifying and focusing on critical and high risk areas of the software can be addressed by two software V & V methods:

- Receipt of early program deliveries for early identification of possible high risk areas of software.
- Conduct of a "criticality analysis" to identify the most critical functions of the software.

When these methods are used together, software V & V can dynamically adjust software V & V analysis to focus on the most critical areas of early program deliveries. The software V & V results can provide early feedback on the quality of early program deliveries as well as determine how well the early program deliveries perform their critical functions.

Providing early program deliveries to software V & V can be accomplished by several methods: Releasing early program prototypes; using an incremental software build approach; or handing over each module or subfunction following development unit testing. Incremental software builds are one of the most effective methods of providing early program deliveries to software V & V. These early deliveries reinforce the systematic analysis and test approach used by software V & V to examine the software in smaller pieces while progressively evaluating larger software pieces as each new piece is integrated. High risk software areas are easier to identify by using the incremental build approach because the software V & V can:

- Provide an early lead time to evaluate each engineering solution and allow time to suggest alternative solutions which can be incorporated in subsequent incremental deliveries without adversely impacting the schedule.
- Isolate each new set of requirements and evaluate their impact on the system performance.
- Provide early indications of system performance so that adjustments can be made to refine the desired performance.

Table 3. Optional Software V & V Tasks and Suggested Applications (IEEE1012)

Optional V & V Tasks	Management	Concept	Requirements	Design	Implementation	Test	Installation and Checkout	Operations and Maintenance	Considerations for Selecting Optional V & V Tasks
	Life Cycle Phases								
Algorithm analysis			•	•	•	•		•	Numerical and scientific software using critical equations or models
Audit performance									
Configuration control					•	•	•	•	When V&V is part of QA or user organizations; for large software developments to help QA or user staff audits
Functional					•	•	•	•	
In-process			•	•	•	•	•	•	
Physical						•	•	•	
Audit support									
Configuration control					•	•	•	•	When V&V is part of systems engineering or independent; for large software development
Functional					•	•	•	•	
In-process			•	•	•	•	•	•	
Physical						•	•	•	
Configuration Management	•	•	•	•	•	•	•	•	When V&V is part of user
Control flow analysis			•	•	•			•	Complex, real-time software
Database analysis			•	•	•	•		•	Large database applications; if logic stored as parameters
Data flow analysis			•	•	•			•	Data driven, real-time systems
Feasibility study evaluation		•						•	High risk software using new technology or concept
Installation and checkout testing[a]			•	•	•	•	•	•	When part of user, QA, or systems engineering
Performance monitoring								•	Software with changeable interfaces (man-machine)
Qualification testing[a]			•	•	•	•	•	•	When V&V is part of systems engineering or user
Regression analysis and testing			•	•	•	•	•	•	Large, complex systems
Reviews support									
Operational readiness							•	•	When V&V is part of systems engineering or user
Test readiness					•	•	•	•	When V&V is part of system engineering or user
Simulation analysis			•	•	•	•	•	•	Unavailable system test capability or need to preview concept for feasability or requirements for accuracy
Sizing and timing analysis				•	•	•		•	Software constrained by memory or response time
Test certification						•	•	•	For critical software
Test evaluation			•	•	•	•	•	•	When V&V is part of QA or user
Test witnessing						•	•	•	When V&V is part of QA, user, or systems engineering
User documentation evaluation		•	•	•	•	•	•	•	Interactive software requiring user inputs
V&V tool plan generation	•							•	When acquiring or building V&V analysis/test tools
Walkthroughs									
Design				•				•	
Requirements			•					•	When V&V is part of QA or systems engineering; for large software developments to staff walkthroughs
Source code					•			•	
Test					•	•	•	•	

[a]Test plan, test design, test cases, test procedures, and test execution

- Develop trend information about software anomalies and risk issues to allow time to adjust the development and software V & V resources and planning to accommodate evolving software risk issues.

A software build represents a basic program skeleton including draft documentation containing portions of the full software capabilities. Each successive build integrates additional functions into the skeleton, permitting early software deliveries to software V & V in an orderly development process. Based on discrepancy or progress reports, software program management can make the technical and management decisions to refocus the software V & V and development team onto the program's specific problem areas of the software.

Criticality analysis, a method to locate and reduce high risk problems, is performed at the beginning of a project. It identifies the functions and modules which are required to implement critical program functions or quality requirements (e.g., safety, security). The steps of the analysis are

- Develop a block diagram or control-flow diagram of the system and its software. Each block or control-flow box represents a system or software function (module).
- Trace each critical function or quality requirement through the block or control flow diagram.
- Classify all traced software functions (modules) as critical to either the proper execution of critical software functions or the quality requirements.
- Focus additional analysis on these traced software functions (modules).
- Repeat criticality analysis for each life cycle phase to observe whether the implementation details shift the emphasis of the criticality.

The criticality analysis may be used along with the cross-reference matrix of Table 4 to identify software V & V techniques to address high-risk concerns. The selection of V & V techniques to use on each critical area of the program is a method of tailoring the intensity of the software V & V against the type of risk present in each area of the software. For example, V & V would apply algorithm analysis to critical numerical software functions, and techniques such as timing analysis, data and control flow analysis, and interface analysis to real-time executive functions.

Most of the techniques in the cross-reference matrix of Table 4 are described in a publication from the National Institute of Standards and Technology (formerly the National Bureau of Standards) (Powell, 1982). In Table 4, the techniques are mapped against specific software V & V issues (Adrion and co-workers, 1982) which they address.

In general the techniques fall into the categories of static analysis, dynamic analysis, and formal analysis. Static analysis techniques are those which are the direct analysis of the form and structure of a product without executing the product (NBS, 1983). Reviews, inspections, audits and data flow analysis are examples of static analysis techniques. Methods for reviews and inspections are described in QUALITY ASSURANCE. The inspection technique, originally described in Fagan (1976), is an example of a software V & V technique that may be applied by various organizations. An analysis of the types of defects found in inspections is presented in Kelly and co-workers (1992). The static analysis techniques are traditionally applied to software requirements, design and source code. They may also be applied to test documentation, especially test cases, to verify their traceability to the requirements, their adequacy to fulfill test requirements, and their own accuracy.

Dynamic analysis techniques involve execution or simulation of a development product to detect errors by analyzing the response of a product to sets of input data (NBS, 1983). For these techniques, the output values, or ranges of values, must be known. Testing is the most frequent dynamic analysis technique. Prototyping, especially during the requirements phase, can be considered a dynamic analysis technique; in this case perhaps the exact output is not always known but enough knowledge exists to determine if the system response to the input stimuli meets system requirements.

Formal analysis is the use of rigorous mathematical techniques to analyze the algorithms of a solution (NBS, 1983). Sometimes the software requirements may be written in a formal specification language (e.g., VDM, Z) (see VDM, Z); these requirements will be verified using a formal analysis technique like proof of correctness. Such techniques are fully described in special issues of two professional publications of September 1990 (1990a, 1990b) and a companion article in another (Wing, 1990).

The cross-reference matrix for selecting software V & V techniques and tools is applicable to all phases of the software life cycle. For example, under the "feasibility" issue, Table 4 shows several techniques and tools, of which the five most commonly used are analytic modeling, criticality analysis, requirements parsing, simulations, and test data generation. Of these techniques and tools, requirements parsing, analytic modeling, and simulations give the software V & V analyst a way to parse the requirement to determine its completeness, accuracy, and correctness; to model and evaluate the desired performance analytically; and to execute test data in a simulated operating environment to determine whether the resulting performance matches the desired performance. Criticality analysis identifies the critical functions and their distribution within the system architecture. The software V & V analysts evaluate the criticality analysis results to determine whether all critical functions are properly addressed and determines how well critical functions (e.g., security, safety) are partitioned within the system to minimize interfering "cross-talk" with noncritical functions.

Concept Definition Evaluation. In this phase, the principal software V & V task is to evaluate the concept documentation to determine whether the defined concept satisfies user needs and project objectives (e.g., statement of need, project initiation memo) in terms of system performance requirements, feasibility (e.g., compatibility of hardware capabilities), completeness, and accuracy. The evaluation also identifies major constraints of interfacing systems and constraints/limitations of the proposed approach and as-

Table 4. Cross-Reference of Software V&V Issues to Software V&V Techniques/Tools

V&V Issues	Algorithm Analysis	Analytic Modeling	Assertion Generation	Assertion Processing	Cause Effect Graphing	Code Auditor	Comparater	Control Flow Analyzer	Criticality Analysis	Cross Reference Generator	Data Base Analyzer	Data Flow Analyzer	Design Compliance Analyzer	Execution Time Estimator	Formal Review	Formal Verification	Functional Testing	Inspections	Interactive Test Aids	Interface Checker	Metrics	Mutation Analysis	PDL Procesor	Peer Review	Physial Units Testing	Regression Testing	Requirements Parsing	Roundoff Analysis	Simulations	Sizing	Software Monitors	Specification Base	Structural Testing	Symbolic Execution	Test Coverage Analyzer	Test Data Generator	Test Drivers	Test Support Facilities	Timing	Tracing	Walkthroughs
Acceptance tests									■																	■	■					■				■		■		■	
Accuracy	■	■																■			■							■													
Algorithm efficiency	■	■																			■									■									■		
Assertion Violations			■	■				■				■				■				■														■							
Bottlenecks		■			■			■				■		■																	■	■	■						■		
Boundary test cases					■			■				■					■		■			■							■	■	■	■			■	■	■	■	■		
Branch and path identification					■			■				■					■		■			■							■	■	■	■			■	■	■	■	■	■	
Branch testing					■			■				■					■		■			■							■	■	■	■			■	■	■	■	■	■	
Cell structure of modules					■			■		■		■								■	■		■				■														
Checklist, (requirements, design, code)						■	■						■					■									■														■
Code reading						■	■								■			■						■																	
Component tests					■			■		■	■						■		■	■					■	■	■		■		■	■			■	■	■	■	■	■	
Consistency in computation	■												■							■					■		■	■													
Data characteristics			■							■	■	■													■																
Design evaluation					■			■	■			■	■										■														■				
Design to code correlation							■		■				■																												
Dynamic testing of assertions			■	■	■			■				■							■								■		■		■	■			■	■	■	■			
Error propagation	■	■	■	■	■			■	■			■	■		■					■													■			■					■
Environment interaction									■			■							■	■							■		■		■	■				■	■	■			
Evaluation of program paths					■				■			■				■			■														■	■		■					
Execution monitoring																			■										■		■							■			
Execution sampling														■															■		■							■			
Execution support													■						■										■		■					■		■			
Expected vs actual results					■		■	■				■				■																									
Feasibility		■							■																		■		■							■					
File sequence error								■			■	■					■												■		■	■				■		■			
Formal specification evolution				■	■			■			■				■	■		■			■			■			■														■
Global information flow					■			■			■	■								■																					
Go-No-Go decisions									■						■			■						■																	■
Hierarchial interrelationship of modules					■			■	■	■		■								■	■		■				■														
Information flow consistency						■		■	■	■		■	■					■									■														
Inspections													■					■																							■
Integration tests								■	■	■		■	■						■	■						■	■		■		■	■	■		■	■	■	■		■	

Table 4. *(Continued).*

Inter-module structure					■			■	■	■		■	■														■		■				■		■	■	■				
Loop invariants			■		■	■		■		■		■	■					■					■																		
Manual simulation																		■						■																	■
Module invocation					■	■		■		■		■	■					■		■			■		■		■														
Numerical roundoff	■	■																										■													
Numerical stability	■	■																										■													
Parameter checking						■				■										■					■								■								■
Path testing					■	■		■	■	■		■					■		■		■						■		■		■	■			■	■	■	■		■	
Physical units			■							■										■																				
Portability						■			■																															
Processing efficiency		■	■					■			■	■		■					■		■										■										
Program execution characteristics														■			■		■		■								■		■	■	■	■	■		■	■	■		
Proof of correctness						■							■			■											■							■						■	
Requirements evaluation									■											■	■						■														
Requirements indexing									■												■						■													■	
Requirements to design correlation									■																		■													■	
Retest reevaluation after change					■	■	■	■	■	■		■	■				■	■		■		■	■	■		■	■		■	■	■	■		■	■	■		■	■	■	■
Space utilization evaluation	■										■			■				■	■											■	■										
Standards check						■	■						■								■		■				■														
Statement coverage testing																	■		■		■						■		■		■	■				■	■		■		■	
Status reviews															■			■						■																	■
System performance prediction	■	■				■		■				■		■			■												■		■	■				■		■			
System tests					■	■	■						■	■			■									■	■		■		■	■				■	■	■			■
Technical reviews																■		■						■																	■
Test case preparation								■	■			■					■			■		■										■				■				■	
Test thoroughness									■								■							■								■			■	■		■		■	
Type checking						■				■										■					■															
Uninitialized variables						■				■	■	■	■				■		■				■						■		■				■	■		■		■	
Unused variables						■				■		■	■				■		■										■		■				■	■		■		■	
Variable references						■				■		■	■				■		■										■		■				■			■		■	
Variable snapshots/tracing																	■		■										■		■				■			■			
Walkthroughs																								■																	■

sesses the allocation of system functions to hardware and software, where appropriate. The evaluation assesses the criticality of each software item defined in the concept.

Requirements Analysis. Poorly specified software requirements (e.g., incorrect, incomplete, ambiguous, or not testable) contribute to software cost overruns and problems with reliability due to incorrect or misinterpreted requirements or functional specifications. Software that fully meets its requirements upon delivery often encounters problems in the maintenance phase because general requirements (e.g., maintainability, quality, and reusability) were not accounted for during the original development. The problem of outdated requirements is intensified by the very complexity of the problems being solved (which causes uncertainty in the intended system performance requirements) and by continual changes in requirements (e.g., to incorporate new technologies, new missions, changes in interfacing systems, and new people coming on the scene). The minimum software V & V tasks of traceability, requirements validation and interface analysis shown in Table 2 verify the completeness of all the requirements.

The most commonly used optional software V & V tasks listed in Table 3 for requirements analysis are control flow analysis, data flow analysis, algorithm analysis, and simulation. Control and data flow analysis are most applicable for real time and data driven systems. These flow analyses transform logic and data requirements text into graphic flows which are easier to analyze than the text. PERT, state transition, and transaction diagrams are examples of control flow diagrams. Algorithm analysis involves rederivation of equations or evaluation of the suitability of specific numerical techniques. Simulation is used to evaluate the interactions of large, complex systems with many hardware, user, and other interfacing software components.

Another activity in which software V & V plays an important role is test management. V & V looks at all testing for the software system and ensures that comprehensive testing is planned. Software V & V test planning begins in the requirements phase and spans almost the full range of life cycle phases. Test planning activities encompass four separate types of testing: component, integration, system, and acceptance testing. The planning activities result in documentation for each test type consisting of a test plan, test design, test case, and test procedure documents. When software V & V is performed by an independent organization, V & V performs all four types of testing. When software V & V tasks are embedded as part of other organizations, V & V may not perform all the testing but may review the test plans and test results produced by the development group.

Design Evaluation. The minimum set of design phase software V & V tasks involving traceability, interface analysis, and design evaluation provides assurance that requirements are not misrepresented or incompletely implemented, unwanted requirements are not designed into the solution by oversight, and requirements are not left out of the design. Design errors can be introduced by implementation constraints relating to timing, data structures, memory space, and accuracy, even though the basic design satisfies the functional requirements.

The most commonly used software V & V tasks from the optional V & V tasks listed in Table 3 are algorithm analysis, database analysis, timing/sizing analysis, and simulation. In this phase, algorithm analysis examines the correctness of the equations or numerical techniques as in the requirements analysis phase, but also examines truncation and round-off effects, numerical precision of word storage and variables (e.g., single- vs. extended-precision arithmetic), and data typing influences. Database analysis is particularly useful for programs that store program logic in data parameters. A logic analysis of these data values is required to determine the effect these parameters have on program control. Timing/sizing analysis is useful for real-time programs having response time requirements and constrained memory execution space requirements.

Implementation (Code) Evaluation. Clerical and syntactical errors have been greatly reduced through use of structured programming and reuse of code, adoption of programming standards and style guides, availability of more capable computer languages, better compiler diagnostics and automated support, and, finally, more knowledgeable programmers. Nevertheless, problems still occur in translating design into code and can be detected with some software V & V analyses.

Commonly used software V & V tasks from the optional tasks listed in Table 3 are control flow analysis, database analysis, regression analysis, and sizing/timing analysis. For large code developments, control flow diagrams showing the hierarchy of main routines and their subfunctions are useful in understanding the flow of program control. Database analysis is performed on programs with significant data storage to ensure common data and variable regions are used consistently between all call routines; data integrity is enforced and no data or variable can be accidentally overwritten by overflowing data tables; and data typing and use are consistent throughout all program elements. Regression analysis is used to reevaluate requirements and design issues whenever any significant code change is made. This technique ensures project awareness of the original system requirements. Sizing/timing analysis is done during incremental code development and compared against predicted values. Significant deviations between actual and predicted values is a possible indication of problems or the need for additional examination.

Another area of concern to software V & V is the ability of compilers to generate object code that is functionally equivalent to the source code, that is, reliance on the correctness of the language compiler to make data dependent decisions about abstract programmer coded information. For critical applications, this problem is solved by validating the compiler or by validating that the object code produced by the compiler is functionally equivalent to the source (see also COMPILER VALIDATION).

Code reading is another technique that may be used for source code verification. An expert reads through another programmer's code to detect errors. In an experiment conducted at the National Aeronautics and Space Administration Goddard Space Flight Center, code reading was found to be more effective than either functional testing or structural testing (Basili and Selby, 1987). The reason was attributed to the expertise of the readers who, as they read the code, were simulating its execution and were able to detect many kinds of errors.

Other tasks indicated in Table 4 for code evaluation are walkthroughs, code inspections and audits. These tasks occur in interactive meetings attended by a team which usually includes at least one member from the development group. Other members may belong to the development group or to other groups involved in software development. The duration of these meetings is usually no more than a few hours in which code is examined on a line-by-line basis. In these dynamic sessions, it may be difficult to examine the code thoroughly for control logic, data flow, database errors, sizing, timing and other features which may require considerable manual or automated effort. Advance preparation for these activities may be necessary and includes optional software V & V tasks of Table 3 and others shown in Table 4. The results of these tasks provide appropriate engineering information for discussion at meetings where code is evaluated. Regardless of who conducts or participates in walkthroughs and inspections, software V & V analyses may be used to support these meetings.

An entirely different approach to software code verification is Cleanroom Engineering, a method developed by Harlan Mills (Mills and co-workers, 1987). This approach refuses permission to programmers to compile their code. Rather, by designing with a box structure and using static analysis techniques, programmers thoroughly analyze their code, which is then turned over to another team to compile and test. The testing strategy is based on statistical quality control principles. Experiments with this approach indicate that this approach can be used effectively to prevent errors from entering the software (Selby and co-workers, 1987; Trammell and co-workers, 1992).

Testing. Software V & V test planning is a major portion of software V & V test activities and spans several phases. A comprehensive test management approach to testing recognizes the differences in objectives for component, integration, system and acceptance test and differences in strategies. Software V & V component testing verifies the design and implementation of software units, modules, or sub-elements. Typically, software V & V component testing is performed on only the critical components. V & V integration testing verifies functional requirements as the software components are integrated together. Special attention is focused on software, hardware, and operator interfaces. Software V & V system testing validates the entire software program against system requirements and software performance objectives. These software V & V system tests validate that the software executes correctly within its stated operating environment. The software's ability to deal properly with anomalies and stress conditions is emphasized. These tests are not intended to duplicate or replace the user and development group's test responsibilities, but instead supplement the development testing to test behavior not normally tested by the user or development group.

Acceptance testing validates the software against software V & V acceptance criteria, defining how the software should perform with other completed software and hardware. The main distinction between software V & V system and acceptance testing is that the former uses a laboratory environment in which some system features are simulated or performed by non-operational hardware or software, and the latter uses an operational environment with final configurations of other system hardware and software. Software V & V acceptance testing usually consists of a limited number of tests to demonstrate the software will execute as predicted by software V & V system testing in the operational environment. Full acceptance testing is the responsibility of the user and the development systems engineering group.

Effective testing requires a comprehensive understanding of the system. Such understanding develops from systematically analyzing the software's concept, requirements, design, and code. By knowing internal software details, software V & V testing is effective at probing for errors and weaknesses that reveal hidden faults. This is considered structural, or white-box, testing. It often finds errors for which some functional, or black-box, test cases can produce the correct output despite internal errors.

Functional test cases execute part or all of the system to validate that the user requirement is satisfied; these test cases cannot always detect internal errors that will occur under special circumstances. Another software V & V test technique is to develop test cases that violate software requirements. This approach is effective at uncovering basic design assumption errors and unusual operational use errors. The process of planning functional test cases requires a thorough examination of the functional requirements. An analyst who carefully develops those test cases is likely to detect errors and omissions in the requirements. In this sense test planning can be effective in detecting errors and contributes to the prevention of waiting until test execution to uncover some errors.

The planning process for testing must take into account the specific objectives of the software V & V for the software and the impact of different test strategies in satisfying these objectives. Frequently, the most effective strategy may be to combine two or more strategies. As an example, one project's objective may be to verify that the system will run perfectly for the 95% of the functions most likely to be used by 95% of the customers; failure may cause customer dissatisfaction but not loss of life. In another example, an unusual circumstance may cause system failure resulting in catastrophic social loss. In the first case, the use of operational profile testing supported by the Cleanroom Engineering approach may be appropriate while in the second, stress testing is essential (Mills and co-workers, 1987). When Cleanroom Engineering is used, the test plan will provide for staffing and resources by an organization different from the design and code team. The plan will also specify the test strategy, which for Cleanroom Engineering means statistical testing based on usage profiles of the system (see also CLEANROOM TESTING). That is, most of the test cases will be written to test the functions used most frequently during operation of the system. This is quite the opposite philosophy from stress testing. In stress testing, the objective is to test the response of the system to extreme conditions or to identify vulnerable points within the software; problems like these are not likely to be discovered during usage profile testing.

Other examples of test strategies include input-space, output-space, program paths, state transitions, reliability, exhaustive, and heuristic modeling. Input-space testing is based on the input data with points chosen far enough apart (e.g., limits, different characteristics) to give adequate test coverage. The assumption is that there is a sphere around each test point that will execute a latent problem. In output space, the opposite approach is based on output results, with the assumption that the transformation of output to input is known. One problem with this strategy is that the mapping from output space to input space may not be unique.

Program path testing is based in program topology and is centered on how the transfer of control is related to input and calculated variables. This strategy is similar to coverage analysis, in which the objective is to ensure that each logic path has been executed. In state transition, the strategy is to model detailed logic and focus on conditions and inputs which cause change. Reliability modeling is based on probabilities of uncovering, or not uncovering, errors. Exhaustive testing, almost never an economic or practical approach, is based on all combinations of input and output mappings. An heuristic approach is based on engineering judgment and practical experience. It requires a detailed knowledge of the software requirements, design, and code and can be used to influence how other test strategies are applied.

The most commonly used optional tasks are regression analysis and test, simulation, and user document evaluation. User document evaluation is performed for systems having an important operator interface. For these systems, software V & V reviews the user documentation to verify that the operating instructions are consistent with the operating characteristics of the software. The system diagnostic messages and operator recovery procedures are examined to ensure their accuracy and correctness with the software operations. More information and references on software testing may be found in TESTING.

Installation and Checkout Activities. During installation and checkout, software V & V validates that the software operates correctly with the operational hardware system and with other software, as specified in the interface specifications. Software V & V may verify the correctness and adequacy of the installation procedures and certify that the verified and validated software is the same as the executable code delivered for installation. There may be several installation sites with site-dependent parameters. Software V & V verifies that the program has been accurately tailored for these parameters and that the configuration of the delivered product is the correct one for each installation.

Optional software V & V tasks most commonly used in this phase are regression analysis and test, simulation, and test certification. Any changes occurring from installation and test are reviewed using regression analysis and test to verify that our basic requirement and design assumptions affecting other areas of the program have not been violated. Simulation is used to test operator procedures and to help isolate any installation problems. Test certification, especially in critical software systems, is used to demonstrate that the delivered software product is identical to the software product subjected to software V & V.

Operations and Maintenance Evaluation and Test. For each software change made in the operations and maintenance phase, all life cycle phase software V & V activities of Table 2 are considered and possibly repeated to ensure that nothing is overlooked. Software V & V activities are added or deleted to address the type of software change made. In many cases, an examination of the proposed software change shows that software V & V needs to repeat its activities on only a small portion of the software. Also, some software V & V activities such as concept documentation evaluation require little or no effort to verify a small change. Small changes can have subtle but significant side-effects in a software program.

If software V & V is not done in the normal software development phase, then the V & V in the maintenance phase must consider performing a selected set of software V & V activities for earlier life cycle phases. Some of the activities may include generating requirements or design information from source code, a process known as reverse engineering. While costly and time consuming, it is necessary when the need exists for a rigorous software V & V effort.

Effectiveness of Software V & V

Two studies to evaluate the effectiveness of software V & V as an independent organization used different data and reported on different factors. While no direct comparison of results is possible, insights on software V & V effectiveness may be gained from understanding the results of each study.

In 1982, McGarry and Page reported that software V & V was not an effective approach on these small projects at the Software Engineering Laboratory (SEL) at NASA Goddard Space Flight Center. Three flight dynamics projects ranging in size from 10K to 50K lines of code were selected. Software V & V was involved in requirements and design verification, separate system testing, and validation of consistency from start to finish. The software V & V effort lasted 18 months and used an average of 1.1 staff persons, peaking at 3 staff persons. Some results were as follows:

- Productivity of the development teams was the lowest of any previously monitored SEL project (due to the software V & V interface).
- Rates of uncovering errors early in the development cycle were better.
- Software V & V found 2.3 errors per thousand lines of code.
- Cost rate to fix all discovered errors was no less than in any other SEL project.

- Reliability of the software (error rate during acceptance and maintenance and operations) was no different from other SEL projects.

Radatz's study (1981) for Rome Air Development Center reported software V & V effectiveness results for four large IV & V projects ranging from 90K to 176K lines of code. The projects were real-time command and control, missile tracking, avionics programs, and a time-critical batch trajectory computation program. The projects varied from 2.5 to 4 years to develop. Two projects started software V & V at the requirements phase, one at the code phase and one at testing. The software V & V organization used 5 to 12 staff persons per project. Some results were:

- Errors were detected early in the development: 50% to 89% detected before development testing began.
- Large number of discrepancies were reported (total 1259) on average of over 300 per program.
- Software V & V found an average 5.5 errors per thousand lines of code.
- Over 85% of the errors affected reliability and maintainability.
- Effect on programmer productivity was positive, that is, hours of programmer time saved by the programmer's not having to find the error, minus the time required to evaluate the software V & V error report: total savings per error was 1.3 to 6.1 hours of programmer time and over 7 minutes of computer time.
- For the two projects beginning at the code phase, early error detection savings amounted to 20–28% of software V & V costs; for the two projects beginning at the requirements phase, early error detection savings amounted to 92–180% of software V & V costs.

There are several differences between the two studies. The most obvious difference is the largest project in the McGarry study was just over half the size of the smallest project in the Radatz study. Another is that software V & V found almost twice the number of errors per thousand lines of code in the Radatz study than in the McGarry study. Both studies involved projects of considerable difficulty regardless of size. Why is the discovered error rate so different between the studies? Is it reasonable to compare error rates of small projects against error rates of large projects? Was either the development group or the software V & V group more experienced in either experiment? These questions are difficult to answer but one tentative conclusion is that project parameters will affect the benefits of software V & V.

Based on the two studies, some positive effects of software V & V on a software project include:

- Better quality (e.g., complete, consistent, readable, and testable).
- More stable requirements.
- More rigorous development planning, at least to interface with the software V & V organization.
- Better adherence by the development organization to programming language and development standards and configuration management practices.
- Early error detection and reduced false starts.
- Better schedule compliance and progress monitoring.
- Greater project management visibility into interim technical quality and progress.
- Better criteria and results for decision-making at formal reviews and audits.

Some negative effects of software V & V on a software development project include:

- Additional project cost of software V & V (10–30% extra).
- Additional interface involving the development team, user, and software V & V organization (e.g., attendance at software V & V status meetings, anomaly resolution meetings).
- Additional documentation requirements, beyond the deliverable products, if software V & V is receiving incremental program and documentation releases.
- Need to share computing facilities with, and to provide access to, classified data for the software V & V organization.
- Lower development staff productivity if programmers and engineers spend time explaining the system to software V & V analysts, especially if explanations are not documented.
- Increased paperwork to provide written responses to software V & V error reports and other V & V data requirements (e.g., notices of formal review and audit meetings, updates to software release schedule, response to anomaly reports). Productivity of development staff affected adversely in resolving invalid anomaly reports.

Some steps can be taken to minimize the negative effects and to maximize the positive effects of software V & V. To recover much of the software V & V costs, software V & V is started early in the software requirements phase. The interface activities for documentation, data, and software deliveries between developer and software V & V groups should be considered as an inherently necessary step required to evaluate intermediate development products. This is a necessary by-product of doing what is right in the beginning.

To offset unnecessary costs, software V & V must organize its activities to focus on critical areas of the software so that it uncovers critical errors for the development group and thereby results in significant cost savings to the development process. To do this, software V & V must use its criticality analysis to identify critical areas and it must scrutinize each discrepancy before release to ensure that no false or inaccurate information is released to prevent the development group from wasting time on inaccurate or trivial reports.

To eliminate the need to have development personnel train the software V & V staff, it is imperative that software

V & V select personnel who are experienced and knowledgeable about the software and its engineering application. When software V & V engineers and computer scientists reconstruct the specific details and idiosyncrasies of the software as a method of reconfirming the correctness of engineering and programming assumptions, they often find subtle errors. They gain detailed insight into the development process and an ability to spot critical errors early. The cost of the development interface is minimal, and at times non-existent, when the software V & V assessment is independent.

Finally, the number of discrepancies detected in software and the improvement in documentation quality resulting from error correction suggests that software V & V costs are offset by having more reliable and maintainable software. Many companies rely on their software systems for their daily operations. Failure of the system, loss of data, release of or tampering with sensitive information may cause serious work disruptions and serious financial impact. The costs of software V & V are offset in many application areas by increased reliability during operation and reduced costs of maintenance.

GUIDELINES FOR PLANNING AND MANAGING SOFTWARE V & V

The documents in Table 5 establish guidelines for planning and managing a software V & V effort. Their activities produce information that satisfies the life cycle requirements of standards governing projects. They have the following features:

- Require software V & V to determine how well evolving and final software products comply with their requirements.
- Permit users to select specific techniques to satisfy their application needs.
- Cover a broad spectrum of software V & V activities.

NIST issued the Federal Information Processing Standards Publication "Guideline for Lifecycle Validation, Verification and Testing" in 1983 (NBS, 1983). This document was followed in 1987 with the "Guideline for Software Verification and Validation Plans" (NBS, 1987) which adopted the ANSI/IEEE standard for software V & V planning. Reference to the guideline, (NBS, 1987), includes reference to the ANSI/IEEE specifications.

Table 5. Selected Guidance for Planning Software V&V

FIPSPUB101	Guidance for Lifecycle Validation, Verification, and Testing of Computer Software
FIPSPUB132	Guideline for Software Verification and Validation Plans
ANSI/IEEE STD 1012	Standard for Software Verification and Validation Plans
AFSC/AFLCP 800-5	Software Independent Verification and Validation
ANS 10.4	Guidelines for the Verification and Validation of Scientific and Engineering Computer Programs for Nuclear Industry
JPL D 576	Independent Verification and Validaton of Computer Software: Methodology

According to Branstad and Powell (1984), standards for use by large heterogeneous communities should provide direction for specific project implementations, with information on software V & V planning, review points, verification techniques, test, and reporting. The features in the documents listed in Table 5 include organization guidelines, planning and management direction, life cycle concerns, software V & V phase requirements, and software test management. A comparison and contrast of these features leads to an approach for developing a software V & V effort based on the strengths of the guidance in the documents.

Organization

Software V & V activities may be performed by anyone responsible for assuring the quality of software. Developers perform some software V & V activities in the normal course of developing their product. Complementary, supplementary, or duplicate software V & V activities may be assigned to a software quality assurance group within the developer's company or an outside organization, usually referred to as IV & V. In the most formal arrangement, an organization independent of both the developer and the customer of the software system is contracted to perform the software V & V activities.

A master SVVP allocates the major tasks of all parties responsible for software V & V activities for assuring the quality of the software. The example of software V & V planning in Figure 1 contains several SVVPs and focuses on the distribution of test responsibilities; each SVVP contains descriptions of other software V & V tasks. In contrast, in a small project with a developer performing all the software V & V activities, the developer's SVVP may be the only SVVP and may even be included in the project plan.

The example in Figure 1 represents a more complex project. The developer is responsible for component and integration test, with integration test documentation examined by an IV & V organization. The IV & V organization is responsible for system test and for assistance to the customer for acceptance test. The customer plans for acceptance test. Developers and sub-developers may be part of the development organization who will also use the software or they may be under contract to a customer; they may be responsible for component test of their components. The master SVVP will allocate these responsibilities; the developer's SVVP will elaborate on unit test and integration test; the IV & V's SVVP will clarify its role in integration test and acceptance test and will contain complete planning for system test. This example is provided to demonstrate that a complete system approach which integrates the responsibilities of all project groups is essential to meeting life cycle requirements for the assurance of software quality.

FIPSPUB101 (NBS, 1983) permits performance of software V & V activities by developer, the same organization, or some independent group. *FIPSPUB132 / IEEE1012* does not require independence; it does require the SVVP to

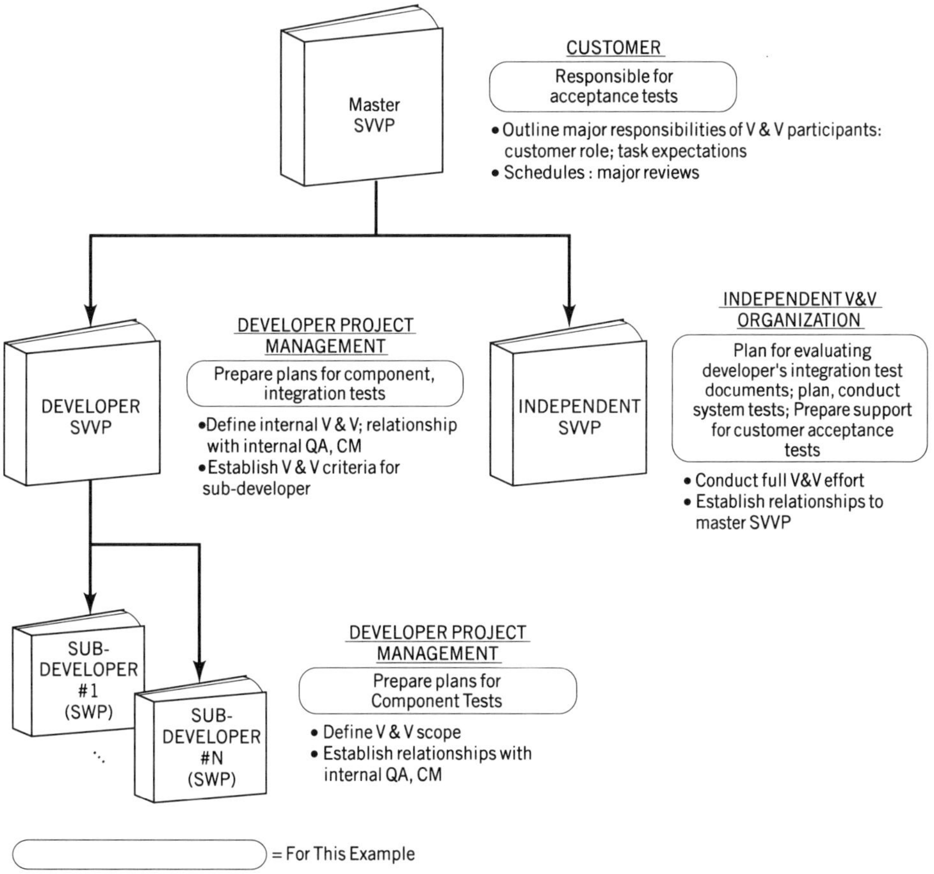

Figure 1. Example: Organizing Software V & V with Several Software V & V Plans.

"define the relationship of software V & V to other efforts such as development, quality assurance, configuration or data management, or end user." Internal and external lines of communication to software V & V must be defined; software V & V could occur independently or within one of the other efforts.

The Air Force (AF) pamphlet, "*AFSC/AFLCP 800-5* Software Independent Verification and Validation," (AF, 1988) is concerned only with software IV & V. It describes software V & V activities typically performed by an IV & V group separate from the developer's quality assurance group required by *DOD-STD-2167A* Standard, "Defense System Software Development" (DOD, 1988). The AF pamphlet provides the criteria for selecting an independent V & V group.

The software V & V activities of "Guidelines for the Verification and Validation of Scientific and Engineering Computer Programs for the Nuclear Industry," *ANS 10.4* (ANSI, 1987) may be performed by the program developer, as a task separate from development, or by an IV & V agent. The guideline contains an example of a division of software V & V responsibilities.

The "Independent Verification and Validation of Computer Software: Methodology" from the Jet Propulsion Laboratory (JPL) (Blosiu, 1983) states that software V & V activities should be performed independently of the development organization to ensure effectiveness and integrity of the software V & V effort. The document provides guidance and is flexible regarding the extent of a detailed software V & V effort.

Planning and Management

Steps for planning an effective software V & V effort include the following:

- Determining software V & V objectives and project needs by performing a criticality analysis.
- Planning and organizing the full spectrum of software V & V activities over the project.
- Managing the effort.
- Reporting on the effort.

Criticality Analysis. The requirements of the software V & V documents are based on the criticality of the software. *FIPSPUB101* recommends specific software V & V activities for three levels of software, from a small, simple project to a large, complex project. The basic set includes tasks like preparation of the software V & V plan, review and analysis of software products, and test; the final set includes correctness proofs and techniques using sophisticated automation. Each successively more detailed and comprehensive level includes activities of the level(s) beneath it.

FIPSPUB132/IEEE1012 requires an assessment of criticality of each software item. For critical software, it requires tasks of traceability, evaluation, interface analysis, test, management and reporting for each phase. It recommends the same task selection for noncritical software and provides an optional task list for all software. The planner is required to consider all tasks and to justify omission of any required task.

The AF pamphlet provides detailed instructions for conducting a criticality assessment with four levels ranging from catastrophic to negligible. The AF pamphlet defines a complete method for determining the criticality level of each software requirement and for computing the overall criticality level of the system. Software V & V tasks are selected based upon the computed criticality levels, where the scope and complexity of the V & V activities increase as the criticality increases.

The AF pamphlet defines a complete method for determining the criticality of each software requirement and for computing the system's overall criticality level. Software V & V tasks are selected by where the criticality fits into one of three tables, where scope and complexity increase as the criticality increases.

Plan Preparation. *FIPSPUB101, FIPSPUB132/IEEE 1012* and *ANS 10.4* define the minimum content information for a software V & V plan. *FIPSPUB101* provides an example plan in an appendix, and *FIPSPUB132/IEEE1012* provides a uniform format for presenting the information. Only the AF pamphlet provides guidance on estimating the costs but its scope does not include plan definition, format or content.

Management. *FIPSPUB101, FIPSBPUB132/IEEE 1012,* and *ANS 10.4* discuss the initial SVVP and updates to it. *FIPSPUB132/IEEE1012* is the only document that requires ongoing software V & V management tasks spanning the entire project life cycle. These include SVVP generation and updates, baseline change assessment for V & V activities, management reviews, review support, and reporting. The SVVP is updated because of project changes and changes indicated by findings of V & V tasks. The AF pamphlet provides strong direction in establishing initial software V & V requirements.

Reporting. *FEPSPUB101* recommends test reports, test evaluation reports, and problem reports. *FIPSPUB132/IEEE1012* requires planning for software V & V reporting and specifies content for interim and final task reports, phase summary reports, anomaly reports, and a software V & V final report after installation. The AF pamphlet makes no recommendations on reporting of software V & V activities. *ANS 10.4* specifies content requirements for a test report, for a final software V & V report after installation, and for a software V & V review report during operations and maintenance. The JPL document suggests assessment reports after each software V & V activity.

Life Cycle, Iteration, and Maintenance

FIPSPUB101, FIPSPUB132/IEEE1012, ANS 10.4, and the JPL document use reference life cycles, similar to the waterfall model, as context for presenting software V & V requirements. *FIPSPUB132/IEEE1012* identifies products for evaluation and inputs for supporting each software V & V phase task but permits other life cycles. The AF pamphlet is directly tied to the life cycle requirements and evaluation criteria of *DOD-STD-2167A* (DOD, 1988).

Iteration. Only *FIPSPUB132/IEEE1012* makes a direct statement about iteration; the issue is that changes will be made to almost every software system, if not during development, then during maintenance. *FIPSPUB132/IEEE1012* requires a SVVP to establish a "task iteration policy" and to provide for assessment of proposed software changes for their effect on software V & V tasks and the SVVP. *FIPSPUB132/IEEE1012* requires the master schedule to recognize software V & V activities are iterative.

Maintenance. *FIPSPUB101* defines software V & V activities for the operations and maintenance phase and recommends the repetition of software V & V activities of affected development phases. *FIPSPUB132/IEEE1012* requires the initial SVVP to include an estimate of anticipated software V & V activities during operation and maintenance; this estimate is updated prior to operation and maintenance. The required management task of baseline change assessments provides continuing direction for reperforming previous or initiating new software V & V tasks. *ANS 10.4* provides guidance in determining which software V & V activities are applicable during maintenance; it also provides criteria for determining how to perform software V & V on completed software that has not undergone a software V & V effort.

Software V & V Phase Requirements

Guidance documents address consistency, evaluation, and review for each phase of the life cycle.

Consistency Between Phases. *FIPSPUB101, FIPS PUB 132/IEEE1012, ANS 10.4* and the JPL document address internal consistency of software products as one objective of general evaluation activities and require traceability analysis from the system/software requirements through successive documentation. *FIPSPUB132/IEEE 1012* requires planning for traceability of all test documentation to the system requirements. The AF pamphlet addresses consistency through requirements of *DOD-STD-2167A* (DOD, 1988).

Interface Analysis. This is required at least indirectly by all the documents. *FIPSPUB132/IEEE1012* requires an analysis of the software's relationship to the total system through interface analysis of requirements documentation, design documentation, interface documentation, and the source code. *FIPSPUB132/IEEE1012* specifies that the software documentation is evaluated with hardware, software, user, and operator interface requirements, including test of the performance at these interfaces. The AF pamphlet mentions checking the consistency of external and internal interface requirements for the software requirements, the design, and the code. The JPL document provides a checklist of interface analysis questions.

Software V & V Evaluation Activities. Software V & V activities selected for any effort are based upon the characteristics of the application or system software under evaluation. The activities selected are also governed by the scope of software V & V as defined by its organizational responsibilities. None of the standards specify the set of software V & V activities or techniques to use for all applications. Most, like *FIPSPUB132,* define a recommended set of software V & V activities based on traceability, interface, and phase-by-phase activities (Table 2) which may be tailored to each user's needs by adding software V & V techniques similar to those indicated in Tables 3 and 4.

Review. All the software V & V documents address reviews of outputs of life cycle phases (e.g., concept documentation, system requirements, software management plans, user documentation). *FIPSPUB132/IEEE1012* considers conduct of formal reviews as an optional task for software V & V, but the V & V effort provides information for formal reviews as a required management task. The JPL document requires IV & V attendance at formal review meetings.

Software Test Management

All software V & V standards and guidelines include directives for general software test but *FIPSPUB101, FIPS PUB132/IEEE1012,* and the JPL document define four types of test: unit or component test, integration or subsystem test, system test, and acceptance test. *FIPS PUB132/IEEE1012* provides criteria for system test planning to determine if the software satisfies system objectives.

FIPSPUB132/IEEE1012 addresses test management by identifying objectives and a timely sequence of test planning documentation and execution for each test type. For each test type, test documentation includes plans describing the approach, tool and training needs, objectives, schedules, designs of the test structure and code, cases containing the actual test data for each test, and procedures with complete details for executing each test. With completed test documentation, testers should have resources available for executing and analyzing the tests. For small projects, separate documents may not be necessary, but the total spectrum of information is. *FIPSPUB132/IEEE1012* requires planning for tracing of all test documentation to requirements. Requirements for the SVVP overview section include identifying any special tool needs for software V & V activities, including test.

FIPSPUB101 and *ANS 10.4* contain outlines of a generic test plan. Both *ANS 10.4* and the JPL document have detailed checklists for verifying the adequacy of a test plan. *ANS 10.4* contains a checklist for verification of test results.

The AF pamphlet allocates test activities between developers and IV & V according to the level of criticality; the activities range from evaluating developers' critical test results to conducting special tests in critical areas. *ANS 10.4* defines four levels of test activities, ranging from test only by the software developer with no separate software V & V effort; to variations of test by developer and independent team as well as evaluation by independent team; and finally, complete test performed separately by the developer and by an independent team.

FIPSPUB101 recommends levels of test coverage by statement, module, and logical path coverage. *FIPS PUB132/IEEE1012* addresses functional test coverage and coverage of performance, reliability and maintainability, and user documentation. *ANS 10.4* establishes coverage requirements based on software requirements.

Summary of Software V & V Standards

As indicated by these guidance documents, a software V & V effort consists of tasks from a broad spectrum of analysis and test techniques to tailor each software V & V effort to project needs, where the basic tasks are the following:

- Traceability of software requirements through all documentation.
- Evaluation or review of interim and final software products, including user documentation.
- Interface analysis.
- Software test.

The software V & V guidance documents complement and supplement one another so that together they provide valuable direction for anyone responsible for the quality of software. The AF pamphlet addresses the major activities for determining the organization and scope of software V & V for a project. A technique which is not specifically required, but should be understood to be part of the V & V process is error analysis. Error analysis should be a requirement in all software V & V standards or sections of standards addressing V & V. Error analysis is important for uncovering a type of error (e.g., misunderstanding of trigonometry) that could appear elsewhere in the system. When the type of error is made because of a misunderstanding or a wrong specification, it is important to check other places in the program that are based on the same assumptions, especially if the same person is responsible. Otherwise, a potentially critical error could slip through. Finally, the results of error analysis could be given to those responsible for improving software processes.

Only *FIPSPUB132/IEEE1012* addresses software V & V management throughout the life cycle. Most guidance documents address planning and reporting for software V & V. The study to compare and contrast the document content of software V & V standards and guidelines led to the conclusion that the documents contribute to a systematic approach for the planning and management of a software V & V effort. In Table 6 each step of this systematic approach is mapped to those documents providing strong guidance for that step. For any project, it is important to recognize the need to tailor the requirements of these documents to different life cycles and project requirements.

Table 6. Planning Software V&V with Guidance from Software V&V Documents

	Guidance					
Procedure	AFSC 800-5	ANS 10.4	FIPSPUB 132	FIPSPUB 101	ANSI/IEEE STD 1012	JPL
Scope the V&V Effort						
Criticality assessment	■					
Organization	■	■				
Costing	■					
Plan the V&V Effort						
Planning preparation		■	■	■	■	
Objectives		■	■	■	■	■
General task selection	■	■	■	■	■	■
Minimum, required			■		■	
Optional			■		■	
Recommendations for criticality levels	■			■		
Test Management			■		■	
Test types			■	■	■	■
Objectives			■		■	
Documentation			■		■	
Coverage		■	■	■	■	■
Planning	■	■	■	■	■	■
Planning V&V for maintenance		■	■	■	■	
Manage the V&V Effort						
V&V management tasks			■		■	
Reporting		■	■		■	

GENERAL PROJECT AND QUALITY ASSURANCE STANDARDS

Many software engineering standards address primary requirements for project management and documentation requirements over variations of a similar life cycle (Fig. 2). A life cycle provides a framework of steps, usually called phases, to enable the coordination and control of development and the operation and maintenance of a software system. Software development, at a minimum, includes written requirements describing what the system must do, an overview design describing how the system will be built, a more detailed design description from which the programmers write the code, the code itself, and user documentation. The standards and guidelines described in this chapter require review of this documentation. Several also address the need for and require review of documentation for software product assurance activities: software quality assurance (SQA), software V & V including test, and software configuration management (SCM). Most also call for audits during the life cycle. The purpose of the reviews and audits is to ensure that the goals of each phase's activities have been met sufficiently to proceed to the activities of the next phase. See also CONFIGURATION MANAGEMENT; QUALITY ASSURANCE; REVIEWS AND AUDITS.

The project level standards (Tables 7, 8) are striving toward recognition that each participating group has an important role in building, reviewing, and assuring the quality of the software. The major variances among the standards and guidelines occur in the refinement of the life cycle phases, the relationship of software phases to system phases, and specific names for the phases and the products produced in the phases. Differences in specific phase and product names do not change the need for activities to provide the engineering information concerning how well the evolving software system will satisfy its requirements.

Project standards view software V & V either as a separate activity performed by different groups or as an intrinsic activity performed by the developer. In the first case, the standards require software V & V, usually with separate project documentation or with a specific section of the software management plan devoted to software V & V. A criticality assessment is a common mechanism to determine the amount of and allocation of software V & V activities among different organizations. In the second case, the standards and guidelines address software V & V as a part of project activities. Project management and documentation do not single out activities which are inherently software V & V activities but rather include software V & V

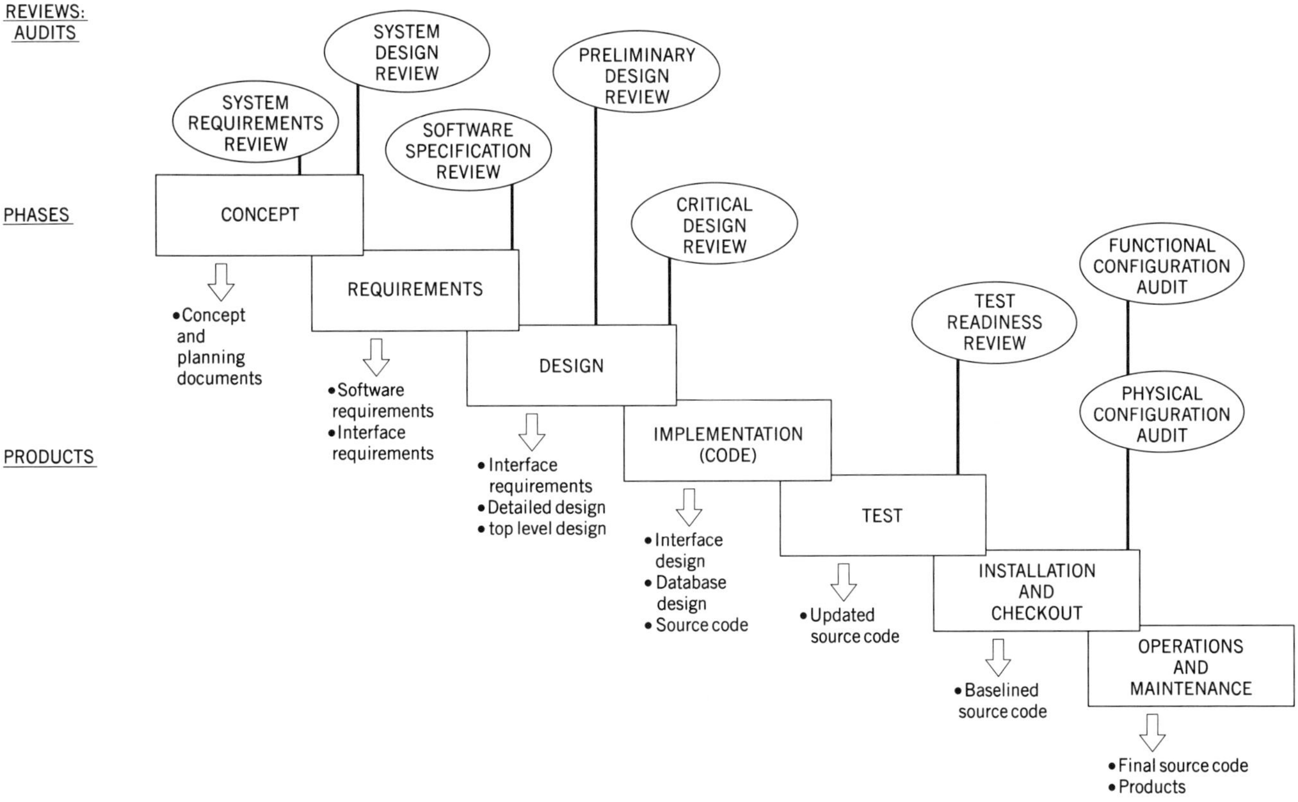

Figure 2. Example of Life Cycle Products and Review Requirements.

objectives as part of the development task (e.g., ensure that design specifications are consistent with software requirements specifications).

This article provides a brief overview of how each group of standards relates to software V & V activities. Some of the documents fit into both categories because they are used by both the buyer agency for total project management and by the developer for incorporating software V & V directly into the project.

Guidance Requiring Software V & V

The documents listed in Table 7 provide guidance to determine when and how much software V & V should be performed. In the ANSI/IEEE Standard for Software Project Management Plans (SPMP) (IEEE, 1987), project support functions such as SQA, SCM, and software V & V may be specified in a project management plan. The ANSI/IEEE Standard for Software Quality Assurance Plans (SQAP) (IEEE, 1984) specifies the minimum documentation requirements, major reviews and audits. The SVVP is one of the minimum documentation requirements to ensure that the implementation of the software satisfies system requirements. Others include the software requirements specification, software design description, the software V & V report, user documentation, and SCM plan. Reviews and audits include software requirements review, preliminary and critical software design reviews, software

Table 7. Selected Guidance for Projects Requiring Software V&V

ANSI/IEEE 1058	Standard for Software Project Management Plans (SPMP)
ANSI/IEEE 730	Standard for Software Quality Assurance Plans (SQAP)
NASA SMAP 4.3	Nasa Management Plan Documentation and Data Item Descriptions (DID) Information System and Documentation Standards
SSPO 30000	Space Station Program Definitions and Requirements (SSP)
DOD-STD-2167A	Military Standard Defense System Software Development
DOD-STD-2168	Military Standard Defense System Software Quality Program

Table 8. Selected Guidance for Projects Incorporating Software V&V

DOI	A Project Manager's Guide to Application System Life Cycle Management
DOA	A Project Manager's Guide to Systems Life Cycle Management
CAN	Software Quality Assurance Program
NUREG	Handbook of Software Quality Assurance Techniques Applicable to the Nuclear Industry
DoD-STD-2167A	Military Standard Defense System Software Development
DoD-STD-2168	Military Standard Defense System Software Quality Program

V & V reviews, functional audits, physical audits, in-process audits, and managerial review.

Drafts of NASA documentation standards for information systems (NASA, 1991) have defined basic documentation requirements for management planning, product specifications, assurance specifications, and management control and status reports. The life cycle documentation standards are intended to serve as a model for organizing and executing the management, engineering, and assurance activities of software development and sustaining engineering (maintenance). The draft version, 4.2C of August 1988 (NASA, 1988), provides documentation requirements for all software V & V implementations, whether performed by developer or an independent organization. The general project plan must address how software quality will be assured, and must address software V & V for every life cycle phase. A criticality assessment of the project characteristics determines how software V & V will be implemented for the NASA projects. When IV & V is used, it must be defined in the appropriate subsection of the product assurance plan. The published Version 4.3 of the NASA documentation standards was released in February 1989 (NASA, 1989) and contains a format for a SVVP which may be used for internal or independent software V & V. The final published version of the NASA documentation standards addresses software V & V similarly (NASA, 1991).

The Space Station Program (SSP) Definition and Requirements Document, June 1988 draft (NASA, 1988), describes Software Product Assurance (SPA) as a technical discipline responsible for requirements, criteria, and the performance of activities to oversee the software safety, reliability, maintainability, and quality assurance. Interaction with an IV & V effort is determined and monitored by the appropriate level of software management and development plans. There must be a process to assure that the software life cycle produces reliable and maintainable software. Reliability and maintainability assurance includes software V & V tasks (e.g., requirements analysis and requirements traceability analysis, design analysis, fault tolerance analysis, code evaluation, and test plan evaluation). The SPA directs that software V & V be performed as directed by a SSP Master Verification Process Requirements document for each SSP element. A Level II IV & V plan (a document type specific to the SSP) establishes basic IV & V requirements for the SSP.

In *DOD-STD-2167A* (DOD, 1988) the contractor interfaces with the IV & V agent(s) as specified in the contract. Contractors are required to perform evaluations of life cycle phase outputs. Some evaluation criteria which are applicable are internal consistency, understandability, traceability, consistency with various documents, test coverage of requirements, timing and sizing allocations, and coding techniques. While a software V & V effort is not required, the evaluation criteria are related to objectives of software V & V activities. Review of software requirements follows system requirements and system design review; software preliminary design and critical design reviews precede system design and critical design reviews. The software V & V analyses in the software documentation can provide engineering information to system level reviews on how well the software will meet system requirements.

The "Military Standard Defense System Software Quality Program" *DOD-STD-2168,* (DOD, 1988), establishes requirements for a software quality program. Contractors determine whether an item or activity meets specified criteria and maintain reports on these findings. Government agencies may serve the role of contractors in performing the software quality program. Many of the evaluation requirements (e.g., product evaluations, certification) can be fulfilled by the activities of software V & V.

Each of these documents requires evaluation of the software products for each life cycle phase, either by the developer or by some other group. The major software V & V requirements of these documents are summarized in the following:

SPMP	Software V & V addressed in project management plan.
SQAP	SVVP required.
NASA and SSP	Software V & V must be addressed and is governed by each project's characteristics.
DOD-STD-2167A	Contractor interfaces with IV & V agent whose role is determined by AF pamphlet; evaluation criteria must be satisfied by contractor and IV & V.
DOD-STD-2168	Software quality program and use of software V & V determined by contractor.

Guidance Addressing Software V & V as Part of Project Development

The standards and guidelines listed in Table 8 require software V & V activities as an inherent part of a project's life cycle activities. These activities are not necessarily named as software V & V activities but often are named at the specific task level or even are implied because the evaluation objectives are those that are found in the definition of specific software V & V tasks.

The Department of Interior developed a set of documents to manage their system life cycle (DOI, 1985). These consist of a regulatory statement, a handbook, and a detailed guide for project managers. The handbook defines the system life cycle and the major responsibilities and management decision points within that life cycle. Some required activities are those required in the software V & V standards and guidelines (e.g., unit test, system test, database validation, test procedures, user acceptance plan and validation procedures). The handbook states criteria for identifying major acquisitions for applicability. The same criteria could be applied to determine when a software V & V effort is applicable. The life cycle requirements complement those of *FIPSPUB132/IEEE1012* and can be used together. The Department of Agriculture has adapted the Interior's guidelines for use by their agencies.

The draft Canadian standard (CSA, 1988) for software quality assurance uses a significantly different approach by addressing a different level of criticality and type of software in four separate documents. Predeveloped software refers to software prior to issuance of a contract or purchase order. The documentation identifies the following requirements for each type of software:

- Critical developed software: requirements and design reviews; test plan, including acceptance test; verification plan, including identification of verification of sub-contracted components and subcontractor software quality assurance program; validation requirements to demonstrate compliance with acceptance criteria.
- Critical predeveloped software: same as for critical developed software except requirements review is not required.
- Noncritical developed software: required verification plan with verification and test activities.
- Noncritical pre-developed software: no test plan, verification plan or validation requirements.

The Handbook on Software Quality Assurance for the Nuclear Industry (USNRC, 1987) has one chapter on verification and test. Software V & V is under the responsibility of software quality assurance, although the verification tasks should be performed independent of development. The handbook describes the concepts of verification, general test and acceptance testing and suggests verification for each life cycle phase and provides checklists for each phase.

NASA, SSP, *DOD-STD-2167A* and *DOD-STD-2168* establish requirements for software evaluation that may be satisfied by an IV & V effort but they also place software quality requirements on the contractors themselves. While the intent of the Air Force pamphlet is to determine when independent software V & V is necessary, the contractors can use the AF pamphlet to determine their software V & V requirements. *FIPSPUB132/IEEE1012* fits nicely into the next step of planning and implementing a software V & V program within the contractor environment, with additional guidance coming from *ANS* and *JPL*.

The key features of guidance documents including software V & V as part of the project are the following:

DOI, DOA	Life cycle management; internal activities of unit test, system test, test procedures, database validation, user acceptance plan, and validation procedures.
CAN	Verification and test activities and performing agent determined by criticality level; separate standards.
NUREG1	Independence recommended; descriptions of software V & V techniques, test, and checklists for each life cycle phase.
NASA, SSP, DOD-STD-2167A, 2168	Contractors have responsibility for internal software quality activities; software requirements specified for each life cycle phase.

CONCLUSIONS

Software engineering technology has matured sufficiently to be addressed in approved and draft software engineering standards and guidelines. Many of these documents address project level requirements for reviews to ensure satisfactory progress at interim steps along the life cycle. Standards for software V & V require activities which produce the information that management needs to decide whether or not to allow the project to progress to the next development step and at completion whether or not to accept the product. Software V & V coexists with other quality engineering disciplines and complements many of the software engineering disciplines. A major difference between software V & V and other software quality engineering functions is that, like the developer's activities, software V & V activities examine the software in detail from a systems viewpoint. Results from software V & V analyses and tests can supply systems engineering data for every review and audit required by general project standards.

From this study of standards and guidelines it can be seen that the software V & V guidance documents can be used to complement the requirements of the project level documents.

United States businesses and industries, along with Federal agencies, spend billions annually on computer software in many of their functions:

- To manufacture their products.
- To provide their services.
- To administer their daily activities.
- To perform their short and long term management functions.

As with other products, industries and businesses are discovering that their increasing dependence on computer technology to perform these functions emphasizes the need for safe, secure, reliable computer systems. They are recognizing that software quality and reliability are vital to the U.S.'s ability to maintain its competitiveness and high technology posture in the marketplace. Software V & V is one of several methodologies that can be used for building vital quality software.

The overview of software verification and validation in this article is largely extracted from the National Institute of Standards and Technology Special Publication 500-165, *Software Verification and Validation: Its Role in Computer Assurance and Its Relationship with Software Project Management Standards* by Dolores R. Wallace and Roger U. Fujii.

BIBLIOGRAPHY

W. R. Adrion, M. A. Branstad, and J. C. Cherniavsky, "Validation, Verification, and Testing of Computer Software," *ACM Computing Surveys* **14**(2), (June 1982).

AFSC/AFLCP 800-5, Air Force Systems Command and Air Force Logistics Command Software Independent Verification and Validation Washington, D.C., May 22, 1988.

ANSI/IEEE-ANS-7-4.3.2-1982, Application Criteria for Programmable Digital Computer Systems in Safety Systems of Nuclear Power Generating Stations, American Nuclear Society, 1982.

ANSI/IEEE Std. 730-1984, Standard for Software Quality Assurance Plans, The Institute for Electrical and Electronics Engineers, Inc., New York, 1984.

ANSI/IEEE Std. 1012-1986, Standard for Software Verification and Validation Plans, The Institute for Electrical and Electronics Engineers, Inc., New York, Nov. 1986.

ANSI/IEEE Std. 1058-1987, Standard for Software Project Management, The Institute for Electrical and Electronics Engineers, Inc., New York, 1987.

ANSI/IEEE Std. 1074-1990, Standard for Software Life Cycle Processes, The Institute for Electrical and Electronics Engineers, Inc., New York, 1990c.

ANSI/IEEE Transactions on Software Engineering, Sept., 1990a.

ANSI/IEEE Software, IEEE Computer Society, Los Alamitos, Calif., Sept., 1991.

ANS/ANS-10.4-1987 Guidelines for the Verification and Validation of Scientific and Engineering Computer Programs for the Nuclear Industry, American Nuclear Society, La Grange Park, Ill., 1987.

V. R. Basili and R. W. Selby, "Comparing the Effectiveness of Software Testing Strategies," *IEEE Transactions on Software Engineering,* **13**(12), 1278–1296 (Dec. 1987).

J. O. Blosiu, *Independent Verification and Validation of Computer Software: Methodology,* National Aeronautics and Space Administration, Jet Propulsion Laboratory, Pasadena, Calif., JPL D-576, Feb. 9, 1983.

B. W. Boehm, "A Spiral Model of Software Development and Enhancement, *COMPUTER* (May 1988).

B. W. Boehm and P. N. Papaccio, "Understanding and Controlling Software Costs," *IEEE Transactions on Software Engineering* (Oct. 1988).

M. Branstad and P. B. Powell, "Software Engineering Project Standards," *IEEE Transactions on Software Engineering* **SE-10**(1), 73–78 (Jan. 1984).

CAN-CSA-Q396. 1, Software Quality Assurance Program, Canadian Standards Organization, Toronto, Ontario, Canada.

Canadian Standards Association, *A General Guide on Procurement Quality Assurance Standards and Organizations, CAN/CSA Q396* series, Draft, 178 Rexdale, Toronto, Ontario, Canada, 1988b.

D. D. Clark and co-workers, *Computers At Risk,* National Research Council, National Academy Press, 1991.

A. M. Davis, E. H. Bersoff, and E. R. Comer, "A Strategy for Comparing Alternative Software Development Life Cycle Models," *IEEE Transactions on Software Engineering,* **14**(10), 1453–1461 (Oct. 1988).

Department of Agriculture, *A Project Manager's Guide to Application Systems Life Cycle Management,* DM 3200-2; *Application Systems Life Cycle Management Manual,* DM3200-1 and *Software Management,* DM 3220-3, Washington, D.C., March 1988.

DOD-STD-2167A, Military Standard Defense System Software Development, AMSC No. 4327, Department of Defense, Washington, D.C., Feb. 29, 1988.

DOD-STD-2168, Military Standard Defense System Software Quality Program, AMSC No. A4389, Department of Defense, Washington, D.C., April 1988.

Department of the Interior, "A Project Manager's Guide to Application Systems Life Cycle Management"; *Departmental Manual Part 376 DM 10* and *Application System Life Cycle Management Handbook,* Washington, D.C., Aug. 1985.

A. Dorling, *Activities Relating to the Development of Standards Relevant to Software Quality,* ISO/IEC/JTC1/SC7 #575, ISO/IEC/JTC1/SC7 Plenary, The Hague, June 13–17, 1988.

M. E. Fagan, "Design and Code Inspections to Reduce Errors in Program Development," *IBM Systems Journal* (3), 219–248 (1976). (reprinted in *Software Quality Assurance: A Practical Approach,* IEEE Computer Society Press, 1985.)

J. C. Kelly, J. Sherif, and J. Hops, "An Analysis of Defect Densities Found During Software Inspections," *Journal of Systems and Software* (Feb. 1992).

F. McGarry and G. Page, *Performance Evaluation of an Independent Software Verification and Integration Process, SEL 81-110,* NASA Goddard, Greenbelt, Md., Sept. 1982.

H. D. Mills, R. C. Linger, and A. R. Hevner, *Principles of Information Systems Analysis and Design,* Academic Press, New York, 1986.

H. D. Mills, M. Dyer, and R. C. Linger, "Cleanroom Software Engineering," *IEEE Software,* 19–25 (Sept. 1987).

S. H. Nash and S. T. Redwine, Jr., *Information Interface Related Standards, Guidelines, and Recommended Practices, IDA PAPER P-1842,* Institute for Defense Analyses, Alexandria, Va., 1985.

Information System Life-Cycle and Documentation Standards and Management Plan Documentation and Data Item Descriptions (DID); Releases 4.2a,b,c (Draft, 1988), Release 4.3 (Feb. 1989), NASA Headquarters, Washington, D.C.

NASA Software Documentation Standard Software Engineering Program, NASA-STD-2100-1991, NASA Headquarters, Washington, D.C.

NBS, *Guideline for Lifecycle Validation, Verification and Testing of Computer Software, FIPSPUB101,* National Bureau of Standards (US), Gaithersburg, Md., 1983.

NBS, *Guideline for Software Verification and Validation Plans, FIPSPUB132,* National Bureau of Standards (US), Gaithersburg, Md., 1987.

P. R. Neumann, "The Computer-Related Risk of the Year," *COMPASS '91, Proceedings of the Sixth Annual Conference on Computer Assurance,* The Institute of Electrical and Electronics Engineers, Inc., June, 1991.

P. B. Powell, *Software Validation, Verification and Testing Technique and Tool Reference Guide, National Bureau of Standards Special Publication 500-93,* National Institute of Standards and Technology, Gaithersburg, Md., 1982.

J. W. Radatz, *Analysis of IV & V Data, RADC-TR-81-145,* Logicon, Inc., Rome Air Development Center, Griffiss AFB, N.Y., June 1981.

R. W. Selby, V. R. Basili, and F. T. Baker, "Cleanroom Software Development: An Empirical Evaluation," *IEEE Transactions on Software Engineering,* **13**(9), 1027–1037 (Sept. 1987).

Space Station Support, Space Station Program Definition and Requirements Document, *Section 9.5, SSPO 30000,* NASA Headquarters, Washington, D.C. (Draft, June 1988).

B. C. Stauffer and R. U. Fujii, "Security Evaluation of Missions Critical Computer Systems," *COMPASS '86,* (July, 1986).

C. J. Trammell, L. H. Binder, and C. E. Snyder, "ACM Transactions on Software Engineering and Methodology," **1**(1), 81–94 (Jan. 1992).

Computer Security Act of 1987, Public Law 100-235, 100th United States Congress, Washington, D.C., Jan. 8, 1988.

U.S. Congress, House Committee on Science, Space, and Technology, *Bugs in the Program,* U.S. Government Printing Office, Sept. 1989.

USNRC, *NUREG/CR-4640,* prepared by J. L. Bryant and N. P. Wilburn, *Handbook of Software Quality Assurance Techniques Applicable to the Nuclear Industry,* Pacific Northwest Laboratory, PNL-5784 for U. S. Nuclear Regulatory Commission, Washington, D.C., Aug. 1987.

USNRC, NUREG/CR-5930, *High Integrity Software Standards and Guidelines,* D. R. Wallace, L. M. Ippolito, and D. R. Kuhn, National Institute of Standards and Technology, for U.S. Nuclear Regulatory Commission, Washington, D.C., Sept. 1992.

D. R. Wallace and J. C. Cherniavsky, *Guide to Software Acceptance NIST SP 500-180,* U.S. Department of Commerce/National Institute of Standards and Technology, Gaithersburg, Md., 1990.

D. R. Wallace and R. U. Fujii, *Software Verification and Validation: Its Role in Computer Assurance and Its Relationship with Software Project Management Standards, NIST SP 500-165,* U.S. Department of Commerce/National Institute of Standards and Technology, Gaithersburg, Md. 1989.

D. R. Wallace, D. R. Kuhn and John C. Cherniavsky, *Proceedings of the Workshop on High Integrity Software,* Gaithersburg, Md., Jan. 22–23, 1991, U.S. Department of Commerce/National Institute of Standards and Technology, *NIST SP 500-190,* Aug. 1991.

D. R. Wallace, L. M. Ippolito, D. R. Kuhn, *High Integrity Software Standards and Guidelines, NIST SP 500-204,* U.S. Department of Commerce/National Institute of Standards and Technology, Gaithersburg, Md., 1992.

J. M. Wing, "A Specifier's Introduction to Formal Methods," *COMPUTER,* 8–24 (Sept. 1990).

DOLORES R. WALLACE
National Institute of Standards and Technology

VERSION

(1) An initial release or re-release of a computer software configuration item associated with a complete compilation or recompilation of the computer software configuration item. (2) An initial release or complete re-release of a document, as opposed to a revision resulting from issuing change pages to a previous release (IEEE).

VICK, CHARLES R. (1934–)

Charles R. Vick was the Director of the Ballistic Missile Defense Advanced Technology Center's Data Processing Directorate in Huntsville, Alabama from 1969 through 1981. There he initiated one of the most aggressive and visionary research and development programs of the time in life-cycle Software Engineering. He gained international recognition during the early 1970's for his work in Software Requirements Engineering Methodology and an associated Requirements Statement Language. He advanced the theory that software requirements could be stated in a machine processable context free language which provided a basis for formalized testing. In 1981 he was elected to the grade of Fellow of the IEEE for *"contributions to software engineering theory and practices."* During the 1970s he was also known for pioneering work in Distributed Computing Systems. Vick joined the faculty of Auburn University in Auburn, Alabama in 1981 where he organized and became the first Department Head of the Computer Science and Engineering Department. He left the University in 1987 to become the President and CEO of Optimization Technology, Inc., a company specializing in Software Engineering research and applications.

Some of Vick's technical publications in Software Engineering and Distributed Computing are included in the following bibliography.

BIBLIOGRAPHY

C. R. Vick, *Dynamic Resource Allocation in Distributed Computing Systems,* UMI Research Press, 1980.

—with C. V. Ramamoorthy, *Handbook of Software Engineering,* Van Nostrand Reinhold, 1984.

—The Software Development System (coauthor), *IEEE Transactions on Software Engineering* **SE-3** (Jan. 1977).

—"A First Generation Software Engineering System," *Proceedings of ACM National Conference, 1977.*

—"Requirements: Software Engineerings' Big Hurdle," (coauthor), *Proceedings of COMPSAC,* 1977

—"The Software Development System: Status and Evolution," (coauthor), *Proceedings of COMPSAC,* 1977.

VIRUSES

DEFINITIONS AND HISTORY

Computers are designed to execute instructions one after another. Those instructions usually do something useful—calculate values, maintain databases, and communicate with users and with other systems. Sometimes, however, the instructions executed can be damaging and malicious in nature. When that happens by accident, we call the code involved a software *bug*—perhaps the most common cause of unexpected program behavior. If the source of the instructions was an individual who intended that the abnormal behavior occur, then we consider this malicious coding; authorities have sometimes referred to this code as *malware* and *vandalware.* These names relate to the usual effect of such software.

There are many distinct programmed threats that are characterized by the way they behave, how they are triggered, and how they spread. In recent years, occurrences of malware have been described almost uniformly by the media as *computer viruses.* In some environments, people have been quick to report almost every problem as the result of a virus. This is unfortunate, as most problems are from other causes (including, most often, operator error). Viruses are widespread, but they are not responsible for many of the problems attributed to them.

The term *computer virus* is derived from and is analogous to a biological virus. The word *virus* itself is Latin for *poison.* Viral infections are spread by the virus (a small shell containing genetic material) injecting its contents into a far larger body cell. The cell then is infected and converted into a biological factory producing replicants of the virus.

Similarly, a computer virus is a segment of machine code (typically 200–4000 bytes) that will copy itself (or a modified version of itself) into one or more larger "host" programs when it is activated. When these infected programs are run, the viral code is executed and the virus spreads further. Sometimes, what constitutes "programs" is more than simply applications: boot code, device drivers, and command interpreters also can be infected.

Viruses cannot spread by infecting pure data; pure data files are not executed. However, some data, such as files with spreadsheet input or text files for editing, may be interpreted by application programs. For instance, text files may contain special sequences of characters that are executed as editor commands when the file is first read into the editor. Under these circumstances, the data files are "executed" and may spread a virus. Data files may also contain "hidden" code that is executed when the file is used by an application, and this too may be infected. Technically speaking, however, pure data itself cannot be infected.

The first use of the term virus to refer to unwanted computer code was by the science fiction author David Gerrold. He wrote a series of short stories about the G.O.D. machine in the early 1970s that were later merged into a novel in 1972, *When Harlie Was One* (Gerrold, 1972). The description of *virus* in that book does not fit the currently accepted, popular definition of computer virus—a program that alters other programs to include a copy of itself.

Fred Cohen formally defined the term *computer virus* in 1983 (Cohen, 1985). At that time, Cohen was a graduate student at the University of Southern California attending a security seminar. Something discussed in class inspired him to think about self-reproducing code. He put together a simple example that he demonstrated to the class. His advisor, Professor Len Adleman, suggested that he call his creation a computer virus. Dr. Cohen's dissertation and later research were devoted to computer viruses.

Actual computer viruses were being written by individuals before Cohen, although not named such, as early as 1980 on Apple II computers (Ferbrache, 1992). The first few viruses were not circulated outside of a small population, with the notable exception of the "Elk Cloner" virus released in 1981.

Although Cohen (and others, including Len Adleman, 1990) have attempted formal definitions of *computer virus,* none have gained widespread acceptance or use. This is a result of the difficulty in defining precisely the characteristics of what a virus is and is not. Cohen's formal definition includes any programs capable of self-reproduction. Thus, by his definition, programs such as compilers and editors would be classed as "viruses." This also has led to confusion when Cohen (and others) have referred to "good viruses"—something that most others involved in the field believe to be an oxymoron (Cohen, 1991; Spafford, 1992).

Stubbs and Hoffman (1990) refer to a definition by John Inglis that captures the generally accepted view of computer viruses:

1. At least a partially automated capability to reproduce.
2. A method of transfer which is dependent on its ability to attach itself to other computer entities (programs, disk sectors, data files, etc.) that move between these systems.

Several other interesting definitions are discussed by Highland (1990) in Chapter 1.

Other forms of self-reproducing or malicious software have also been written. Although no formal definitions have been accepted by the entire community to describe this software, there are some informal definitions that seem to be commonly accepted (Russell and Gangemi, 1991):

Back Doors, Trapdoors. Back doors, often called trapdoors, consist of code written into applications to grant special access without the normal methods of access authentication. They have been used for many years, and are generally written by application programmers who are seeking a method of debugging or monitoring code that they are developing. This usually occurs when a programmer is developing an application that has an authentication procedure, or a long setup, requiring a user to enter many different values to run the application. To debug the program, the developer may wish to gain special privileges, or to avoid all the necessary set-up and authentication. The programmer also may want to ensure that there is a method of activating the program should something be wrong with the authentication procedure that is being built into the application. The back door is code that either recognizes some special sequence of input, or is triggered by being run from a certain user ID. It then grants special access.

Back doors become threats when they are used by unscrupulous programmers to gain unauthorized access, or when the initial application developer forgets to remove the back door after the system has been debugged, and some other individual discovers its existence.

Logic Bombs. Logic bombs are a form of software that has been known for many years. They usually are embedded in programs by software developers who have legitimate access to the system. A logic bomb is code that checks for a certain set of conditions to be present on the system. If those conditions are met, it executes some special function that is not an intended function of the code in which the logic bomb is embedded.

Conditions that might trigger a logic bomb include the presence or absence of certain files, a particular day of the week, or a particular user running the application. It might examine to see which users are logged in, or which programs are currently in use on the system. Once triggered, a logic bomb may destroy or alter data, cause machine halts, or otherwise damage the system. In one classic example, a logic bomb checked for a certain employee ID number and then triggered if the ID failed to appear in two consecutive payroll calculations.

Worms. Worms are another form of software that is often referred to by the term virus, especially by the uninformed. Recent "cyberpunk" novels such as *Neuromancer* by William Gibson (Gibson, 1984) refer to worms by the term "virus." The media has also often referred incorrectly to worms as viruses.

Unlike viruses, worms are programs that can run independently and travel from machine to machine across network connections; worms may have portions of themselves running on many different machines. Worms do not change other programs, although they may carry other code that does, such as a true virus. It is this replication behavior that leads some people to believe that worms are a form of virus, especially those people using Cohen's formal definition of virus (which also would classify network file transfer programs as viruses). The fact that worms do not modify existing programs is a clear distinction between viruses and worms, however.

In 1982, John Shoch and Jon Hupp of Xerox PARC (Palo Alto Research Center) described the first computer worms (Shoch and Hupp, 1982). They were working with an experimental, networked environment using one of the first local area networks. While searching for something that would use their networked environment, one of them remembered reading *The Shockwave Rider* by John Brunner, written in 1975. This science fiction novel described programs that traversed networks, carrying information with them. Those programs were called *tapeworms* in the novel. Shoch and Hupp named their own programs *worms,* because they saw a parallel to Brunner's tapeworms. The Xerox worms were actually useful—they would travel from workstation to workstation, reclaiming file space, shutting off idle workstations, delivering mail, and doing other useful tasks.

The Internet Worm of November 1988 is often cited as the canonical example of a damaging worm program (Seeley, 1990; Spafford, 1989a; b). The Worm clogged machines and networks as it spread out of control, replicating on thousands of machines around the Internet. Some authors (e.g., (Eichin and Rochlis, 1989) labeled the Internet Worm as a virus, but those arguments are not convincing (cf. the discussion in (Spafford, 1989). Most people working with self-replicating code now accept the Worm as a form of malware distinct from computer viruses.

Few computer worms have been written in the time since then, especially worms that have caused damage, because they are not easy to write. Worms require a network environment and an author who is familiar not only with the network services and facilities, but also with the operating facilities required to support them once they have reached the machine.

Trojan Horses. Trojan horses are named after the Trojan horse of myth and legend. Analogous to their namesake, they resemble a program that the user wishes to run—a game, a spreadsheet, or an editor. While the program appears to be doing what the user wants, it actually is doing something else entirely. For instance, the user may think that the program is a game. While it is printing messages about initializing databases and asking questions about "What do you want to name your player?" and "What level of difficulty do you want to play?" the program can actually be deleting files, reformatting a disk, or otherwise altering information. All the user sees, until it is too late, is the interface of a program that the user thinks he/she wants to run.

Trojan horses are, unfortunately, common as jokes within some programming environments. They are often planted as cruel tricks on bulletin board systems and circulated among individuals as shared software. Note that the activity of a trojan is not necessarily damaging, but usually is unwanted.

Bacteria, Rabbits. Bacteria, also known as rabbits, are programs that do not explicitly damage any files. Their sole purpose is to replicate themselves. A typical bacteria or rabbit program may do nothing more than execute two copies of itself simultaneously on multiprogramming systems, or perhaps create two new files, each of which is a copy of the original source file of the bacteria program. Both of those programs then may copy themselves twice, and so on. Bacteria reproduce exponentially, eventually taking up all the processor capacity, memory, or disk space, denying the user access to those resources.

This kind of attack is one of the oldest forms of programmed threats. Users of some of the earliest multiprocessing machines ran these programs either to take down the machine or simply to see what would happen. Machines without quotas and resource usage limits are especially susceptible to this form of attack.

Liveware. Harold Thimbleby coined the term *liveware* to describe self-propagating software that carried information or program updates (Witten and co-workers, 1990). Liveware shares many of the characteristics of both viruses and worms, but has the additional distinction of announcing its presence and requesting permission from the user to execute its intended functions. There have been no reports of liveware being discovered or developed other than by Thimbleby and his colleagues.

Where viruses, in particular, have flourished is in the weaker security environment of the personal computer. Personal computers were originally designed for a single dedicated user—little, if any, thought was given to the difficulties that might arise should others have even indirect access to the machine. The systems contained no security facilities beyond an optional key switch, and there was a minimal amount of security-related software available to safeguard data. Today, however, personal computers are being used for tasks far different from those originally envisioned, including managing company databases and participating in networks of computer systems. Unfortunately, their hardware and operating systems are still based on the assumption of single trusted user access, and this allows computer viruses to spread and flourish on those machines. The population of users of PCs further adds to the problem, as many are unsophisticated and unaware of the potential problems involved with lax security and uncontrolled sharing of media.

Over time, the problem of viruses has grown to significant proportions. In the seven years after the first infection by the *Brain* virus in January 1986, the number of known viruses has grown to several thousand different MS-DOS viruses. The problem has not been restricted to the IBM PC, and now affects all popular personal computers. Mainframe viruses may be written for any operating system that supports sharing of data and executable software, but all reported to date have been experimental in nature, written by serious academic researchers in controlled environments (e.g., Duff, 1989). This is probably a result, in part, of the greater restrictions built into the software and hardware of those machines, and of the way they are usually used. It may also be a reflection on the more technical nature of the user population of these machines.

VIRUS STRUCTURE AND OPERATION

True viruses have two major components: one that handles the spread of the virus, and a "payload" or "manipulation" task. The payload task may not be present (has null effect), or it may act like a logic bomb, awaiting a set of predetermined circumstances before triggering.

For a computer virus to work, it somehow must add itself to other executable code. The viral code is usually executed before the code of its infected host (if the host code is ever executed again). One form of classification of computer viruses is based on the three ways a virus may add itself to host code: as a shell, as an add-on, and as intrusive code. A fourth form, the so-called *companion virus,* is not really a virus at all, but a form of trojan horse that uses the execution path mechanism to execute in place of a normal program. Unlike all other viral forms, it does not alter any existing code in any fashion: companion viruses create new executable files with a name similar to an existing program, and chosen so that they are normally executed prior to the "real" program. Because companion viruses are not real viruses unless one uses a more encompassing definition of virus, they will not be described further here.

Shell Viruses. A shell virus is one that forms a "shell" (as in "eggshell" rather than "Unix shell") around the original code. In effect, the virus becomes the program, and the original host program becomes an internal subroutine of the viral code. An extreme example of this would be a case where the virus moves the original code to a new location and takes on its identity. When the virus is finished executing, it retrieves the host program code and begins its execution.

Almost all boot program viruses (described below) are shell viruses.

Add-On Viruses. Most viruses are add-on viruses. They function by appending their code to the host code, and/or by relocating the host code and inserting their own code to the beginning. The add-on virus then alters the startup information of the program, executing the viral code before the code for the main program. The host code is left almost completely untouched; the only visible indication that a virus is present is that the file grows larger, if that can indeed be noticed.

Intrusive Viruses. Intrusive viruses operate by overwriting some or all of the original host code with viral code. The replacement might be selective, as in replacing a subroutine with the virus, or inserting a new interrupt vector and routine. The replacement may also be extensive, as when large portions of the host program are completely replaced by the viral code. In the latter case, the original program can no longer function properly. Few viruses are intrusive viruses.

A second form of classification used by some authors (Solomon, 1991) is to divide viruses into file infectors and boot program infectors. This is not particularly clear, however, as there are viruses that spread by altering system-related code, such as file system directories, and other viruses that infect both application files *and* boot sectors. It is also a classification that is highly specific to machines that have infectable boot code.

Yet a third form of classification is related to how viruses are activated and select new targets for alteration. The simplest viruses are those that run when their "host" program is run, select a target program to modify, and then transfer control to the host. These viruses are *transient* or *direct* viruses, known as such because they operate only for a short time, and they go directly to disk to seek out programs to infect.

The most "successful" viruses to date exploit a variety of techniques to remain resident in memory once their code has been executed and their host program has terminated. This implies that, once a single infected program has been run, the virus potentially can spread to any or all programs in the system. This spreading occurs during the entire work session (until the system is rebooted to clear the virus from memory), rather than during a small period of time when the infected program is executing viral code. These viruses are *resident* or *indirect* viruses, known as such because they stay resident in memory and indirectly find files to infect as they are referenced by the user. These viruses are also known as TSR (Terminate and Stay Resident) viruses.

If a virus is present in memory after an application exits, how does it remain active? That is, how does the virus continue to infect other programs? The answer for personal computers running software such as MS-DOS is that the virus alters the standard interrupts used by DOS and the BIOS (Basic Input/Output System). The change is such that the virus code is invoked by other applications when they make service requests.

The PC uses many interrupts (both hardware and software) to deal with asynchronous events and to invoke system functions. All services provided by the BIOS and DOS are invoked by the user storing parameters in machine registers, then causing a software interrupt.

When an interrupt is raised, the operating system calls the routine whose address it finds in a special table known as the *vector* or *interrupt* table. Normally, this table contains pointers to handler routines in the ROM or in memory-resident portions of the DOS. A virus can modify this table so that the interrupt causes viral code (resident in memory) to be executed.

By trapping the keyboard interrupt, a virus can arrange to intercept the CTRL-ALT-DEL soft reboot command, modify user keystrokes, or be invoked on each keystroke. By trapping the BIOS disk interrupt, a virus can intercept all BIOS disk activity, including reads of boot sectors, or disguise disk accesses to infect as part of a user's disk request. By trapping the DOS service interrupt, a virus can intercept all DOS service requests including program execution, DOS disk access, and memory allocation requests.

A typical virus might trap the DOS service interrupt, causing its code to be executed before calling the real DOS handler to process the request.

Once a virus has infected a program or boot record, it seeks to spread itself to other programs, and eventually to other systems. Simple viruses do no more than this, but most viruses are not simple viruses. Common viruses wait for a specific triggering condition, and then perform some activity. The activity can be as simple as printing a message to the user, or as complex as seeking particular data items in a specific file and changing their values. Often, viruses are destructive, removing files or reformatting entire disks.

The conditions that trigger viruses can be arbitrarily complex. If it is possible to write a program to determine a set of conditions, then those same conditions can be used to trigger a virus. This includes waiting for a specific date or time, determining the presence or absence of a specific set of files (or their contents), examining user keystrokes for a sequence of input, examining display memory for a specific pattern, or checking file attributes for modification and permission information. Viruses also may be triggered based on some random event. One common trigger component is a counter used to determine how many additional programs the virus has succeeded in infecting—the virus does not trigger until it has propagated itself a certain minimum number of times. Of course, the trigger can be any combination of these conditions, too.

Computer viruses can infect any form of writable storage, including hard disk, floppy disk, tape, optical media, or memory. Infections can spread when a computer is booted from an infected disk, or when an infected program is run. This can occur either as the direct result of a user invoking an infected program, or indirectly through the system executing the code as part of the system boot sequence or a background administration task. It is important to realize that often the chain of infection can be complex and convoluted. With the presence of networks, viruses can also spread from machine to machine as executable code containing viruses is shared between machines.

Once activated, a virus may replicate into only one program at a time, it may infect some randomly-chosen set of programs, or it may infect every program on the system. Sometimes a virus will replicate based on some random event or on the current value of the clock. The different methods will not be presented in detail because the result is the same: there are additional copies of the virus on the system.

VIRUSES UNDER MS-DOS

The IBM PC can be used as an example to illustrate how a virus is activated. Viruses in other types of computer systems behave in similar manners. MS-DOS is of particular interest, however, as the vast majority of computer viruses written to date have been for Intel-based personal computers running that operating system.

We will start by listing the various steps in the MS-DOS boot sequence that can be infected by a virus. We will not go into extensive detail about the operations at each of these stages; the interested reader may consult the operations manuals of these systems, or any of the many "how-to" books available.

The MS-DOS boot sequence has seven components:

- ROM BIOS routines
- Master boot record (MBR) code execution
- Boot sector code execution
- IO.SYS and MSDOS.SYS code execution
- CONFIG.SYS execution
- COMMAND.COM command shell execution
- AUTOEXEC.BAT batch file execution

ROM BIOS. When an IBM PC, or compatible PC, is booted, the machine executes a set of routines in ROM (read-only memory). These routines initialize the hardware and provide a basic set of input/output routines that can be used to access the disks, screen, and keyboard of the system. These routines constitute the BIOS.

ROM routines cannot be infected by viral code (except at the manufacturing stage), as they are present in read-only memory that cannot be modified by software. Some manufacturers now provide extended ROMs containing further components of the boot sequence (e.g., the MBR and boot sector code). This trend reduces the opportunities for viral infection, but also may reduce the flexibility and configurability of the final system.

Master Boot Record (MBR). The ROM code executes a block of code stored at a well-known location on the hard disk (e.g., head 0, track 0, sector 1). The MS-DOS operating system allows a hard disk unit to be divided into up to four logical partitions. Thus, a 100Mb hard disk could be divided into one 60Mb and two 20Mb partitions. These partitions are seen by DOS as separate drives: "C," "D," and so on. The size of each partition is stored in the MBR (also known as the partition record), as is a block of code responsible for locating a boot block on one of the logical partitions.

The MBR code can be infected by a virus, but the code block is only 446 bytes in length. Thus, a common approach is to hide the original MBR at a known location on the disk, and then to chain to this sector from the viral code in the MBR (i.e., a shell virus). This is the technique used by the Stoned or New Zealand virus, discovered in 1988, and still one of the most wide-spread MS-DOS viruses.

Boot Sectors. The MBR code locates the first sector on the logical partition, known as the boot sector. (If a floppy disk is inserted, the ROM will execute the code in its boot sector, head 0, track 0, sector 1.) The boot sector contains the BIOS parameter block (BPB). The BPB contains detailed information on the layout of the filing system on disk, as well as code to locate the file IO.SYS. That file contains the next stage in the boot sequence. Note that on some systems, such as PC-DOS systems, IO.SYS may be named something else.

A common use of the boot sector is to execute an application program, such as a game, automatically; unfortunately, this can include automatic initiation of a virus. Thus, the boot sector is a common target for infection. Many of the most widespread viruses are boot sector viruses.

Available space in the boot sector is limited, too (a little over 460 bytes is available). Hence, the shell virus technique of relocating the original boot sector while filling the first sector with viral code is also used here. Boot sector viruses are particularly dangerous because they capture control of the computer system early in the boot sequence, before any anti-viral utility becomes active.

MSDOS.SYS, IO.SYS. The boot sector next loads the IO. SYS file, which carries out further system initialization, then loads the DOS system contained in the MSDOS. SYS file. Both these files can be subject to viral infection. (Note that the names of these files may be different in different versions of DOS.)

CONFIG.SYS. This file is run to initialize certain machine-specific items and adjust system parameters, such as those associated with specific device drivers. This file is also subject to modification by a virus. As part of its execution, it specifies a command interpreter to be run next, usually COMMAND. COM.

Command Shell. The code next executes the command shell program (COMMAND. COM). This program provides the interface with the user, allowing execution of commands from the keyboard. The COMMAND. COM program can be infected, as can any other .COM or .EXE executable binary file.

The COMMAND.COM file is the specific target of one of the first PC viruses to appear: the *Lehigh* virus that struck Lehigh University in November 1987 (van Wyck, 1990). This virus caused corruption of hard disks after it had spread to four additional COMMAND.COM files.

AUTOEXEC Batch Files. The COMMAND.COM program executes a list of commands stored in the AUTOEXEC.BAT file. This is simply a text file full of commands to be executed by the command interpreter. A virus could modify this file to include execution of itself. Although a curiosity, such a virus would be slow to replicate and easy to spot.

Application Files. Once the system is booted and operational, viruses present in application files may be activated. This occurs when an executable file containing a virus is run. A common approach used for .COM files is to infect the programs by storing the first few instructions in the file, and then replacing them with a jump to its own code. When the infected program is run, the virus code is executed. When the virus finishes, it executes a copy of the instructions that were at the start of the program's original code, then jumps to the beginning of the unaltered program code.

GENERATIONS OF VIRUSES

Since the first viruses were written, we have seen what may be classified as five "generations" of viruses. Each new class of viruses has incorporated new features that make the viruses more difficult to detect and remove. Here, as with other classification and naming issues related to viruses, different researchers use different terms and definitions (Ferbrache, 1992, Appendix 10). The following list presents one classification derived from a number of sources. Note that these "generations" do not necessarily imply chronology. For instance, several early viruses (e.g., the "Brain" and "Pentagon" viruses) had stealth and armored characteristics. Rather, this list describes increasing levels of sophistication and complexity represented by computer viruses in the MS-DOS environment.

First Generation: Simple

The first generation of viruses were the simple viruses. These viruses did nothing very significant other than replicate. Many new viruses being discovered today still fall into this category. Damage from these simple viruses is usually caused by bugs or incompatabilities in software that were not anticipated by the virus author.

First generation viruses do nothing to hide their presence on a system, so they can usually be found by means as simple as noting an increase in size of files or the presence of a distinctive pattern in an infected file.

Second Generation: Self-Recognition

One problem encountered by viruses is that of repeated infection of the host, leading to depleted memory and early detection. In the case of boot sector viruses, this could (depending on strategy) cause a long chain of linked sectors. In the case of a program-infecting virus, repeated infection may result in continual extension of the host program each time it is reinfected. There are indeed some older viruses that exhibit this behavior.

To prevent this unnecessary growth of infected files, second-generation viruses usually implant a unique *signature* that signals that the file or system is infected. The virus will check for this signature before attempting infection, and will place it when infection has taken place; if the signature is present, the virus will not reinfect the host.

A virus signature can be a characteristic sequence of bytes at a known offset on disk or in memory, a specific feature of the directory entry (e.g., alteration time or file length), or a special system call available only when the virus is active in memory.

The signature presents a mixed blessing for the virus. The virus no longer performs redundant infections that might present a clue to its presence, but the signature does provide a method of detection. Virus sweep programs can scan files on disk for the signatures of known viruses, or even "inoculate" the system by providing the viral signature in clean systems to prevent the virus from attempting infection.

Third Generation: Stealth

Most viruses may be identified on a contaminated system by means of scanning the secondary storage and searching for a pattern of data unique to each virus. To counteract such scans, some resident viruses employ stealth techniques. These viruses subvert selected system service call interrupts when they are active. Requests to perform these operations are intercepted by the virus code. If the operation would expose the presence of the virus, the operation is redirected to return false information.

For example, a common virus technique is to intercept I/O requests that would read sectors from disk. The virus code monitors these requests. If a read operation is detected that would return a block containing a copy of the virus, the active code returns instead a copy of the data that would be present in an uninfected system. In this way, virus scanners are unable to locate the virus on disk when the virus is active in memory. Similar techniques may be employed to avoid detection by other operations.

Fourth Generation: Armored

As anti-virus researchers have developed tools to analyze new viruses and craft defenses, virus authors have turned to methods to obfuscate the code of their viruses. This "armoring" includes adding confusing and unnecessary code to make it more difficult to analyze the virus code. The defenses may also take the form of directed attacks against anti-virus software, if present on the affected system. These viruses appeared starting in 1990.

Viruses with these forms of defenses tend to be quite large and thus more easily noticed. Furthermore, the complexity required to significantly delay the efforts of trained anti-virus experts appears to be far beyond anything that has yet appeared.

Fifth Generation: Polymorphic

The most recent class of viruses to appear on the scene are the polymorphic or self-mutating viruses. These are viruses that infect their targets with a modified or encrypted version of themselves. By varying the code sequences written to the file (but still functionally equivalent to the original), or by generating a different, random encryption key, the virus in the altered file will not be identifiable through the use of simple byte matching. To detect the presence of these viruses requires that a more complex algorithm be employed that, in effect, reverses the masking to determine if the virus is present.

Several of these viruses have become quite successful. Several virus authors have released virus "toolkits" that can be incorporated into a complete virus to give it polymorphic capabilities. These toolkits have been circulated on various bulletin boards around the world, and incorporated in several viruses.

DEFENSES AND OUTLOOK

There are several methods of defense against viruses. Unfortunately, no defense is perfect. It has been shown that any sharing of writable memory or communications with any other entity introduces the possibility of virus transmission. Furthermore, Cohen, Adleman, and others have shown proofs that the problem of writing a program to exactly detect all viruses is formally undecidable: it is not possible to write a program that will detect every virus without any error.

Of some help is the observation that it is trivial to write a program that identifies all infected programs with 100% accuracy. Unfortunately, this program must identify every (or nearly so) program as infected, whether it is or not. This is not particularly helpful to the user, and the challenge is to write a detection mechanism that finds most viruses without generating an excessive number of false positive reports.

Defense against viruses generally takes one of three forms:

Activity Monitors. Activity monitors are usually programs that are resident on the system. They monitor activity, and either raise a warning or take special action in the event of suspicious activity. Thus, attempts to alter the interrupt tables in memory, or to rewrite the boot sector would be intercepted by such monitors. This form of defense can be circumvented by viruses if it is implemented in software and the viruses activate earlier in the boot sequence than the monitor code. It is further vulnerable to virus alteration if used on machines without hardware memory protection—as is the case with all common personal computers.

Another form of monitor is one that emulates or otherwise traces execution of a suspect application. The monitor evaluates the actions taken by the code, and determines if any of the activity is similar to what a virus would undertake. Appropriate warnings are issued if suspicious activity is identified.

Scanners. Scanners have been the most popular and widespread form of virus defense. A scanner operates by reading data from disk and applying pattern matching operations against a list of known virus patterns. If a match is found for a pattern, a virus instance is announced.

Scanners are fast and easy to use, but they suffer from many disadvantages. Foremost among the disadvantages is that the list of patterns must be kept up-to-date. In the

MS-DOS world, new viruses are appearing by as many as several dozen each week. Keeping a pattern file up-to-date in this rapidly changing environment is difficult.

A second disadvantage to scanners is one of false positive reports. As more patterns are added to the list, it becomes more likely that one of them will match some otherwise legitimate code. A further disadvantage is that polymorphic viruses cannot be detected with scanners.

To the advantage of scanners, however, is their speed. Scanning can be made to work quite quickly. Scanning can also be done portably and across platforms (Kumar and Spafford, 1992), and pattern files are easy to distribute and update. Furthermore, of the new viruses discovered each week, few will ever become widespread. Thus, somewhat out-of-date pattern files are still adequate for most environments. Scanners equipped with algorithmic or heuristic checking may also find most polymorphic viruses. It is for these reasons that scanners are the most widely used form of anti-virus software.

Integrity Checkers/Monitors. Integrity checkers are programs that generate checkcodes (e.g., checksums, cyclic redundancy bodes (CRCs), secure hashes, message digests, or cryptographic checksums) for monitored files (Radai, 1991). Periodically, these checkcodes are recomputed and compared against the saved versions. If the comparison fails, a change is known to have occurred to the file, and it is flagged for further investigation. Integrity monitors run continuously and check the integrity of files on a regular basis. Integrity shells recheck the checkcode prior to every execution (Cohen, 1990).

Integrity checking is an almost certain way to discover alterations to files, including data files. As viruses must alter files to implant themselves, integrity checking will find those changes. Furthermore, it does not matter if the virus is known or not—the integrity check will discover the change no matter what causes it. Integrity checking also may find other changes caused by buggy software, problems in hardware, and operator error.

Integrity checking also has drawbacks. On some systems, executable files change whenever the user runs the file, or when a new set of preferences is recorded. Repeated false positive reports may lead the user to ignore future reports, or disable the utility. It is also the case that a change may not be noticed until after an altered file has been run and a virus spread. More importantly, the initial calculation of the checkcode must be performed on a known-unaltered version of each file. Otherwise, the monitor will never report the presence of a virus, probably leading the user to believe the system is uninfected.

Several vendors have begun to build self-checking into their products. This is a form of integrity check that is performed by the program at various times as it runs. If the self-check reveals some unexpected change in memory or on disk, the program will terminate or warn the user. This helps to signal the presence of a new virus quickly so that further action may be taken.

Variations on these methods and approaches to virus removal are described more fully in the references.

If no more computer viruses were written from now on, there would still be a computer virus problem for many years to come. Of the thousands of reported computer viruses, several hundred are well-established on various types of computers around the world. The population of machines and archived media is such that these viruses would continue to propagate from a rather large population of contaminated machines.

Unfortunately, there appears to be no lessening of computer virus activity, at least within the MS-DOS community. Several new viruses are appearing every day. Some of these are undoubtedly being written out of curiosity and without thought for the potential damage. Others are being written with great purpose, and with particular goals in mind—both political and criminal. Although it would seem of little interest to add to the swelling number of viruses in existence, many individuals seem to be doing exactly that.

The writing of computer viruses is not a crime in most places. It is arguable about whether writing a virus should be a crime, just as constructing a bow and arrow is not innately a crime in most jurisdictions. It is the use of the item, and the state of mind of the user that determine the criminality. As such, it is probably the case that the deliberate release of a computer virus should be considered criminal and not simply the writing of a virus. Laws should reflect that difference. However, lawmakers will discover the same difficulty in clearly defining a virus that researchers have encountered. An overbroad definition such as Cohen's would make the authoring and release of almost any software illegal; the presence of bad laws may hurt the situation more than help it.

It is very difficult to track computer viruses once they have established themselves. Some luck may be had with tracking a computer virus to its authors if it is found very early after its release. This is currently an area of some study (Spafford and Weeber, 1992).

The best hope for the future appears to be the emergence of newer computer systems with enhanced security mechanisms. As these systems become more widespread, older viruses will be rendered harmless for lack of appropriate hosts. If appropriate measures are present in these newer systems, including hardware memory protection and integrity features, then successful new viruses may be much more difficult to write and propagate. That, coupled with the new awareness of professionals in the field may be sufficient to change the situation from that of major threat to minor nuisance.

BIBLIOGRAPHY

L. Adleman, "An Abstract Theory of Computer Viruses," In *Lecture Notes in Computer Science,* **403,** Springer-Verlag, New York, 1990.

M. Bishop, "An Overview of Computer Viruses in a Research Environment," In *Proceedings: Fourth Annual Computer Virus & Security Conference,* ACM-SIGSAC and IEEE-CS, New York, March 1991, pp. 111–137.

F. Cohen, *Computer Viruses,* PhD dissertation, University of Southern California, 1985.

F. B. Cohen, *A Short Course on Computer Viruses,* ASP Press, Pittsburgh, Pa., 1990.

F. B. Cohen, "Friendly Contagion: Harnessing the Subtle Power of Computer Viruses," *The Sciences,* 22–28, (Sept./Oct. 1991).

P. J. Denning, ed., *Computers Under Attack: Intruders, Worms and Viruses,* ACM Press, Addison-Wesley, 1990.

T. Duff, "Experiences with Viruses on Unix Systems," *Computing Systems* **2**(2), (Spring 1989).

M. W. Eichin and J. A. Rochlis, "With Microscope and Tweezers: An Analysis of the Internet Virus of November 1988, In *Proceedings of the Symposium on Research in Security and Privacy,* IEEE-CS, Oakland, Calif., May 1989.

D. Ferbrache, *A Pathology of Computer Viruses,* Springer-Verlag, New York, 1992.

C. V. Feudo, *The Computer Virus Desk Reference,* Business One Irwin, Homewood, Ill., 1992.

P. Fites, P. Johnson, and M. Kratz, *The Computer Virus Crisis,* Van Nostrand Reinhold 2 ed., 1992.

D. Gerrold, *When Harlie Was One,* Doubleday, Garden City, N.Y., 1972.

W. Gibson, *Neuromancer,* Ace/The Berkeley Publishing Group, 1984.

H. J. Highland, editor, *Computer Virus Handbook,* Elsevier Advanced Technology, 1990.

L. J. Hoffman, ed., *Rogue Programs: Viruses, Worms, and Trojan Horses,* Van Nostrand Reinhold, New York, 1990.

J. Hruska, *Computer Viruses and Anti-Virus Warfare,* Ellis Horwood, Chichester, UK, 1990.

S. Kumar and E. H. Spafford, "A Generic Virus Scanner in C++," In *Proceedings of the 8th Computer Security Applications Conference,* p. 210–219, ACM and IEEE, IEEE Press, Los Alamitos Calif., Dec. 1992.

Y. Radai, "Checksumming Techniques for Anti-Viral Purposes," *1st Virus Bulletin Conference,* pp. 39–68, Sept. 1991.

D. Russell and Sr. G. T. Gangemi, *Computer Security Basics,* O'Reilly & Associates, Cambridge, Mass., 1991.

D. Seeley, "Password Cracking: A Game of Wits," *Communications of the ACM,* **32**(6), 700–703, (June 1990).

J. F. Shoch and J. A. Hupp, "The 'Worm' Programs—Early Experiments with a Distributed Computation," *Communications of the ACM,* **25**(3), 172–180 (March 1982).

A. Solomon, *PC VIRUSES Detection, Analysis and Cure,* Springer-Verlag, London, UK, 1991.

E. H. Spafford, "An Analysis of the Internet Worm," in C. Ghezzi and J. A. McDermid, eds., *Proceedings of the 2nd European Software Engineering Conference,* pp. 446–468, Springer-Verlag, Sept. 1989.

E. H. Spafford, "The Internet Worm: Crisis and Aftermath," *Communications of the ACM,* **32**(6) 678–687, (June 1989a).

E. H. Spafford, "The Internet Worm Program: An Analysis," *Computer Communication Review,* **19**(1), 17–57, (Jan. 1989b). Also issued as Purdue CS technical report TR-CSD-823.

E. H. Spafford, "Response to Fred Cohen's 'Contest'," *The Sciences,* p. 4, (Jan./Feb. 1992).

E. H. Spafford, K. A. Heaphy, and D. J. Ferbrache, *Computer Viruses: Dealing with Electronic Vandalism and Programmed Threats,* ADAPSO, Arlington, Va., 1989.

E. H. Spafford and S. A. Weeber, "Software Forensics: Can We Track Code to its Authors?, *Computer & Security,* **12**(6), (1993).

B. Stubbs and L. J. Hoffman, "Mapping the Virus Battlefield," in Hoffman, 1990, Chapter 12, pp. 143–157.

K. R. van Wyk, "The Lehigh Virus," in Highland 1990, pp. 103–196.

I. H. Witten, H. W. Thimbleby, G. F. Coulouris, and S. Greenberg, "Liveware: A New Approach to Sharing Data in Social Networks," *International Journal of Man-Machine Studies,* 1990.

General References

Several of the items the references can be consulted for more detail. Of particular value are Cohen, 1990; Denning, 1990; Ferbache, 1992; and Hoffman, 1990. Also of use are Feudo, 1992; Highland, 1990; Fites and co-workers, 1992; Hruska, 1990, and Solomon 1991 (although the latter is already out-of-date.

EUGENE H. SPAFFORD
Purdue University

VISUAL PROGRAMMING

See PROGRAM VISUALIZATION.

VOGES, UDO (1946–)

Udo Voges joined the research staff of the Nuclear Research Center at Karlsruhe as a mathematician in 1971. Within its Institute for Industrial Data Processing and its Institute for Applied Informatics, he has worked in different areas of software engineering over the years. He received his PhD in computer science from the University of Karlsruhe.

He became well known, especially in Germany, for his work in software testing, and the development and the application of software testing tools.

The application of software in safety related environments such as nuclear reactors requires fault tolerance. Here, Voges has done some important work in software diversity and is one of the leading figures in this area. He participated in national and international projects on this topic. From 1984 to 1985 he was a Visiting Research Scientist at the University of California Los Angeles, USA, Dependable Computing and Fault Tolerant Systems Laboratory, Computer Science Department.

Voges has promoted the standardization efforts in software engineering and dependability on a national and international level.

He is actively engaged in national and international professional societies such as GI, ITG, ACM, IEEE, EFIP, and EWICS.

BIBLIOGRAPHY

U. Voges, "Zuverlässigkeit—Grundkonzepte und Terminologic," in J.-C. Laprie, *Dependability: Basic Concepts and Terminology,* Springer-Verlag Wien, 1992.

—*Software-Diversität und ihre Modellierung—Software-Fehlertoleranz und ihre Bewertung durch Fehler- und Kostenmodelle,* Springer-Verlag Berlin, Informatik-Fachberichte 224, 1989.

—, ed., *Software Diversity in Computerized Control Systems,* Springer-Verlag Wien, 1988.

—with L. Gmeiner and A. von Mayrhauser, "SADAT—An Automated Testing Tool," *IEEE Trans. Software Engineering* **SE-6(3)**, 286–290 (1980).

—with W. Geiger, L. Gmeiner, and H. Trauboth, "Program Testing Techniques for Nuclear Reactor Protection Systems," *IEEE Computer* **12**(8), 10–18 (Aug. 1979).

—"Aspects of Design, Test and Validation of the Software for a Computerized Reactor Protection System," *Proc. 2nd Intern. Conf. on Software Engineering,* San Francisco, Calif., Oct. 13–15, 1976, pp. 606–610.

VON MAYRHAUSER, ANNELIESE KATHARINA AMSCHLER (1952–)

Anneliese von Mayrhauser has made contributions in a wide range of topics in software and systems engineering including software development and maintenance tools and environments, program verification, software process definition and assessment, software reliability, performance analysis and modeling, technology and productivity assessment, project management, testing and maintenance, program understanding, and people needs throughout the software life cycle.

She has developed curricula from high school through PhD level in software engineering and contributed to a variety of industrial training courses for companies such as Motorola and AT&T Bell Laboratories.

Her research motivation is to find viable practical solutions to real problems. Not surprisingly, this has often meant "tough" theoretical problems, as actual needs and constraints do not always translate into easily tractable assumptions. She also works with the premise that people needs must drive process, technique, and tool development, not the other way around. This has distinguished her approach to a flexible process, building and maintaining software project groups, and tools built according to programmers cognition needs.

Dr. von Mayrhauser was a member of the faculty at Illinois Institute of Technology from 1980 to 1991 as Assistant and Associate Professor and Associate Chair of the Computer Science Department of its West Suburban Dan and Ada Rice Campus. She also served as Faculty Council member and on the Strategic Planning committee. Since 1991, she has been at Colorado State University as a faculty member in the Computer Science Department.

Dr. von Mayrhauser has been an active volunteer leader in the IEEE Computer Society. She has served as General Chair and Program Chair for various conferences and symposia, as member of editorial boards, as Chair for the Technical Committee on Software Engineering, as a member of the Board of Governors, and as Vice President for Conferences and Tutorials. She received several awards for her contributions.

Dr. von Mayrhauser received her Dipl. Inf. degree from University-of Karlsruhe in 1976, her MA (1978) and PhD (1979) from Duke University.

BIBLIOGRAPHY

A. von Mayrhauser, *Software Engineering: Methods and Management,* Academic Press Boston, Mass., 1990.

—"AMT—The Ada Maintenance Tool Chest," *Proc. TriAda 91,* San Jose, Oct. 1991, pp. 294–299.

—with J. Keables, *A Simulation Environment for Early Life Cycle Software Reliability Research and Prediction,* International Test Conference '92, Baltimore, Md.

—with A. Roesseler, "A Production-Based Approach to Performance Evaluation of Computing Technology," *Journal of Software and Systems* (1993).

—with A. Roeseler, "Software Process Assessment and Improvement using Production Models," *COMPSAC 93,* Nov. 5–7, 1993, Phoenix, Ariz.

—"Should CASE Care about Software Maintenance or Why We Need Code Processing," *Proc. CASE 90,* Dec. 1990, Irvine, Calif., p. 20–22.

—with E. Choi, "Assessment of Support for Program Understanding," *Proc. Symposium on Assessment of Quality Software Development Tools,* May 27–29, 1992, New Orleans, La.

—with U. Voges and L. Gmeiner, "Sadat—An Automated Testing Tool," *IEEE Transactions on Software Engineering,* May 1980, 286–290 (May 1980).

—"Simple and Fast Throughput Approximations for Generalized Stochastic Petri Nets," *Journal of Systems and Software* (1993).

W

WALK-THROUGH

See Reviews and audits.

WALLACE, DOLORES R.

Dolores Wallace leads the "Assurance of High Integrity Software" project at the Computer Systems Laboratory of the National Institute of Standards and Technology. She is responsible for research, the development of standards and guidelines, and technology transfer for Federal agencies and industry in the areas of software quality, including software management, software engineering practices, software verification and validation, software quality assurance. She has served as project leader in assisting many Federal agencies, including the Nuclear Regulatory Commission, the National Aeronautics and Space Administration and the Environmental Protection Agency, and the Department of Defense.

Ms. Wallace currently serves as the Chair of the COMPASS Board of Directors. The COMPASS organization provides an annual forum for the discussion of issues and transfer of technology related to computer assurance (e.g., software safety, process integrity). She also serves on the advisory board of the Quality Assurance Institute.

Ms. Wallace has been active within the IEEE Computer Society, having been an IEEE lecturer and officer for working groups on software engineering standards. She also served as guest editor of a special issue of *IEEE Software* on software verification and validation.

She previously worked on computer applications for the U.S. Navy Department. She has a MS degree in mathematics from Case Western University in Cleveland, Ohio.

WARE, WILLIS H. (1920–)

Willis H. Ware is a member of the Corporate Research Staff at the RAND Corporation. He joined RAND in 1952 and and has held several staff and management postions, including head of the Computer Science Department and deputy vice-president responsible for interdisciplinary research for the U.S. Air Force. He has devoted his career to all aspects of computer science-hardware, software, architecture, software development, federal agency and military applications, management of computer-intensive projects, public policy, and legislation. He has served on advisory groups to many government agencies and on taskforces or committees for the National Research Council. He currently chairs the National Computer System Security and Privacy Advisory Board, created by the Computer Security Act of 1987.

Since the mid-1960s, Dr Ware has concurrently worked in various aspects of computer security and personal privacy, particularly in regard to federal policy and national posture. In the early 1970s, he chaired a Department of Defense committee that wrote the first definitive treatment of computer security, as both a technical issue and a policy concern.

In 1972, Dr. Ware chaired (then) DHEW Secretary Elliot Richardson's Advisory Committee on Automated Personal Data Systems that examined privacy issues in the context of government use of data about people. His committee wrote the report which became the intellectual foundation for the Federal Privacy Act of 1974.

In 1975 President Ford appointed Dr. Ware to the Privacy Protection Study Commission, created by the Privacy Act, and he served as a commissioner and its vice chairman. The commission made a study of data banks in the private sector, automated data processing programs,and information systems of governmental, regional, and private organizations and reported its findings and recommendations to President Carter and the Congress on June 12, 1977. This report remains the most extensive examination of private sector record-keeping practices.

Dr. Ware is a member of the National Academy of Engineering, Fellow of the Institute of Electronics Engineers, and Fellow of the American Association for the Advancement of Science. He was the first president of the American Federation Processing Societies.

Dr. Ware received the U.S. Air Force Exceptional Civilan Service Medal (1979), the Data Processing Managment Association Computer Sciences Man-of-the-Year Award (1975), and the IEEE Centennial Medal (1984). In 1989 he received the National Computer System Security Award presented jointly by the National Systems Laboratory of the National Institute of Standards and Technology and the National Computer Security Center of the National Security Agency.

Dr. Ware's academic degrees are Ph.D. (Princeton, 1951), S.M. (MIT, 1942), and B.S. (University of Pennsylvania, 1941). All of his degrees are in electrical engineering.

WARNIER

See Design.

WATERFALL MODEL

A model of the software development process in which the constituent activities, typically a concept phase, requirements phase, design phase, implementation phase, test phase, and installation and checkout phase, are performed in that order, possibly with overlap but with little or no iteration (IEEE). See also Process models in software engineering.

WBS

See WORK BREAKDOWN STRUCTURE.

WEINBERG, GERALD M. (1933–)

For more than 35 years, Jerry Weinberg has worked on transforming software organizations, particularly emphasizing the interaction of technical and human issues. After spending between 1956 and 1969 as software developer, researcher, teacher, and designer of software curricula at IBM, he and his anthropologist wife, Daniela Weinberg, formed a consulting firm to help software engineering organizations manage the change process in a more fully human way.

He is author or coauthor of several hundred articles and more than 30 books. His earliest published work was on operating systems and programming languages, but the 1971 publication of *The Psychology of Computer Programming* is considered by many the beginning of the study of software engineering as human behavior. His subsequent works have been an elaboration of many of the software engineering topics raised in that book, through all phases of the software life cycle.

On defining problems and requirements, there are *Exploring Requirements* and *Are Your Lights On?* both with D. C. Gause. On analysis and design, there are *Rethinking Systems Analysis and Design, An Introduction to General Systems Thinking,* and *General Principles of System Design* (with D. Weinberg). On testing and measurement there are *The Handbook of Walkthroughs, Inspections, and Technical Reviews* (with D. Freedman) and *Quality Software Management,* Volume II , *First-Order Measurement.*

He has written on the role of consultants in *The Secrets of Consulting,* on programmers in *Understanding the Professional Programmer* and on management in *Becoming a Technical Leader* and the multivolume *Quality Software Management.* To many, he is best known for his workshops for software leaders, such as "Software Quality Management," "Problem Solving Leadership," and the "Organizational Change-Shop".

BIBLIOGRAPHY

G. M. Weinberg, *The Psychology of Computer Programming,* Van Nostrand-Reinhold, New York, 1971.

—*An Introduction to General Systems Thinking,* Wiley-Interscience, New York, 1975.

—*Becoming a Technical Leader,* Dorset House, New York, 1986.

—*The Secrets of Consulting,* Dorset House Publishing, New York, 1986.

—with D. Weinberg, *General Principles of System Design,* Dorset House, New York, 1988.

—*Rethinking Systems Analysis and Design,* Dorset House Publishers, New York, 1988.

—*Understanding the Professional Programmer,* Dorset House, New York, 1988.

—with D. C. Gause, *Exploring Requirements: Quality Before Design,* Dorset House, New York, 1989.

—with D. C. Gause, *Are Your Lights On?: How To Know What the Problem Really Is,* Dorset House Publishers, New York, 1989.

—with D. P. Freedman, *Handbook of Walkthroughs, Inspections, and Technical Reviews,* Dorset House, New York, 1990.

—*Quality Software Management: Systems Thinking,* Dorset House, New York, 1991, vol. 1.

—*Quality Software Management: First-Order Observation,* Dorset House, New York, 1992, vol. 2.

WHITE BOX TESTING

Testing that takes into account the internal mechanism of a system or component. Types include branch testing, path testing, statement testing (IEEE).

WILEDEN, JACK C. (1950–)

Jack C. Wileden received the A.B. degree in mathematics and the M.S. and Ph.D. degrees in computer and communications sciences from the University of Michigan, Ann Arbor in 1972, 1973, and 1978, respectively. He has been on the faculty of the University of Massachusetts at Amherst since 1978, and is currently a Professor in the Department of Computer Science there.

Prof. Wileden's research interests center on advanced software technology, particularly software system infrastructure and software development and analysis tools. In the infrastructure area, his work has focused on object management topics, including persistent object systems and name management, and on interoperability support for multilingual programming. In the tools area, he has worked on tools for describing and analyzing the module structure of software systems, and on a variety of development tools and techniques applicable to concurrent software systems. His research has been supported by ARPA, NSF and ONR and he is the author of more than forty papers in journals and refereed conferences.

Prof. Wileden is a member of the Association for Computing Machinery and a senior member of IEEE. He is currently an associate editor of the IEEE Transactions on Parallel and Distributed Systems and has previously served as an ACM National Lecturer and an IEEE Distinguished Visitor. He has presented full-day tutorials on object management and on tools for developers of distributed software systems in the U.S., South America, Europe, Australia, and Japan.

BIBLIOGRAPHY

J. C. Wileden, G. S. Avrunin, U. A. Buy, J. C. Corbett, and L. K. Dillon, "Automated Analysis of Concurrent Systems with the Constrained Expression Toolset," *IEEE Transactions on Software Engineering* **17**(11), 1204–1222 (Nov. 1991).

—with G. S. Avrunin, "Automated Analysis of Concurrent and Real-time-Software," in A. M. van Tilborg and G. M. Koob, eds., *Foundations of Real-Time Computing: Formal Specifica-*

tions and Methods, Kluwer Academic Publishers, 1991, pp. 195–215.

—with P. C. Bates, "High-Level Debugging of Distributed Systems: The Behavioral Abstraction Approach," Approach, *Journal of Systems and Software* **3,** 255–264 (1983) (reprinted in S. M. Shatz and J. P. Wang, eds., *Tutorial: Distributed Software Engineering,* Computer Society Press, Washington, D.C., 1989, pp. 205–214.)

—with A. L. Wolf, W. R. Rosenblatt, and P. L. Tarr, "Specification Level Interoperability," *Communications of the ACM* **34**(5), 72–87 (May 1991).

—with L. A. Clarke and A. L. Wolf, "A Comparative Evaluation of Object Definition Techniques for Large Prototype Systems," *ACM Transactions on Programming Languages and Systems* **12**(4), 670–699 (Oct. 1990).

—with A. L. Wolf, C. D. Fisher, and P. L. Tarr, "PGRAPHITE: An Experiment in Persistent Typed Object Management," *Proceedings SIGSOFT '88: Third Symposium on Software Development Environments,* Dec. 1988, pp. 130–142. (Received Best Paper Award)

—with A. L. Wolf and L. A. Clarke, "The AdaPIC Toolset: Supporting Interface Control and Analysis Throughout the Software Development Process," *IEEE Transactions on Software Engineering* **SE-15**(3), 250–263 (March 1989).

WIRTH, NIKLAUS

Professor N. Wirth received the degree of Electronics Engineer from the Swiss Federal Institute of Technology (ETH) in Zurich in 1958. Thereafter he studied at Laval University in Quebec, Canada, and received the M.Sc. degree in 1960. At the University of California at Berkeley he pursued his studies, leading to the Ph.D. degree in 1963. Until 1967 he was Assistant Professor at the newly created Computer Science Department at Stanford University, where he designed the programming languages PL360 and, in conjunction with the IFIP Working Group 2.1, Algol W. In 1967 he became Assistant Professor at the University of Zurich, and in 1968 he joined ETH Zürich, where he developed the languages Pascal between 1968 and 1970 and Modula-2 between 1979 and 1981.

Further projects include the design and development of the Personal Computer Lilith, a high-performance workstation, in conjunction with the programming language Modula-2 (1978–1982), and the 32-bit workstation computer Ceres (1984–1986). His most recent works produced the language Oberon, a descendant of Modula-2, which served to design the operating system with the same name (1986–1989). He was Chairman of the Division of Computer Science (Informatik) of ETH from 1982 until 1984, and again from 1988 until 1990. Since 1990 he is head of the Institute of Computer Systems of ETH.

In 1978 Professor Wirth received Honorary Doctorates from York University, England, and the Federal Institute of Technology at Lausanne, Switzerland, in recognition of his work in the fields of programming languages and methodology. In 1983 he was awarded the Emanuel Priore prize by the IEEE, in 1984 the A. M. Turing prize by the ACM, and in 1987 the award for Outstanding Contributions to Computer Science Education by ACM. In 1987, he was awarded an Honorary Doctorate by the Universite Laval, Canada, and in 1988 he was named a Computer Pioneer by the IEEE Computer Society.

In 1989, Professor Wirth was awarded the Max Petitpierre Prize for outstanding contributions made by Swiss noted abroad, and he received the Science and Technology Prize by IBM Europe. He was awarded the Marcel Benoist Prize in 1990. In 1992 he was nominated Distinguished Alumnus of the University of California at Berkeley. He is a member of the Swiss Academy of Technical Sciences and a Foreign Associate of the U.S. Academy of Engineering.

WORD

(1) A sequence of bits or characters that is stored, addressed, transmitted, and operated on as a unit within a given computer. (2) An element of computer storage that can hold a sequence of bits or characters as in (1). (3) A sequence of bits or characters that has meaning and is considered an entity in some language; for example, a reserved word in a computer language (IEEE).

WORK BREAKDOWN STRUCTURE

INTRODUCTION

Software engineering success is determined by many factors; understanding of the customer and user environment and expectations, effective application and coordination of critical resources, the accomplishment of all essential tasks required to complete and support an acceptable product successfully and the effective management and oversight of the diverse disciples required to develop, demonstrate, deliver, and release the software successfully. The success of a software project is determined as much by the effectiveness of the project management and coordination activities as it is by the technologies applied, the automated facilities used and the talent and experience of the staff involved in the project. The best software engineers cannot be successful if essential work that they rely on has not been accomplished, if resources they count on are not available or the complete set of activities that they must accomplish has not been defined, assigned, or scheduled.

The following discussion provides a brief overview of how a software project may define, allocate, and monitor work. As discussed below the work planning and management techniques described below do not apply to all projects, however they are essential components of projects which have certain complexity or organizational characteristics. The disciplines that are components of the work planning and monitoring process are

Table 1. WBS Levels

WBS Hierarchy	WBS Product or Process
Level 1	Primary product delivery requirement
Level 2	Product components, training, support . . .
Level 3	Software components, hardware components, user and product documentation components . . .
Level 4	Subsystem 1, Subsystem N, . . . software branch . . .
Level 5	Software requirements, software design, software implementation, software test and integration, software internal and maintenance documentation. . .
Level 6	Software preliminary design, software design review, subsystem detailed design, software detailed design review . . .

- Work breakdown structure (WBS)
- Work planning
- Work allocation

These disciplines are discussed below.

WORK BREAKDOWN STRUCTURE

The problem facing a software project throughout the development period is identifying exactly what tasks must be accomplished, by whom, when, and what resources are required to complete them successfully. In many cases software engineering is the most demanding example of "Just In Time" production since the ideal project will have all activities start according to a predefined schedule and when these begin all constraining activities and products, analyses, and resources must be available, correct and in the correct form for immediate application. When dealing with software project requirements even a slight delay in availability of a key piece of information which delays start of a management, technical, assurance or reporting activity can have a significant cascading effect on the project schedule.

In order to achieve this tight coordination between project activities a disciplined and effective work allocation procedure is an effective tool. The cornerstone of the procedure is the Work Breakdown Structure (WBS). The work breakdown structure serves as the basis for program scheduling and fiscal planning and provides the means to coordinate and control the diverse activities of a program toward a focused goal.

The WBS is a top-down division of hardware and software products to be produced, services and support tasks that must be accomplished if the project is to be successful, and tasks that plan, organize, manage, monitor, and control the project environment.

The WBS subdivides all required work into manageable units through the definition of various levels of hierarchy described and illustrated in Table 1. At the top level is an identification of the product to be delivered. Treeing down from the product level are the end items, which are major segments of the product or system to be developed. These then tree down into all required components of the product the specific work package instructions, and, finally, all revisions to work packages and functional planning. Use of the WBS by a program manager forces the proper allocation of work through the project from the top down.

There are typically three different forms of the WBS that can be applied to define and allocate work in a software project: the End-Item or Product division; the Functional division; and the Organizational division. An End-Item or Product WBS structure defines and allocates work based on the products to be developed. Each element represented by the WBS represents a discrete management, technical, assurance document or code product or a report which is produced to document an event.

A functionally structured WBS defines and allocates work by function rather than product. This form or organization systematically decomposes the functions to be performed into smaller discrete elements which are to executed to support development, documentation, delivery, or support of the software products to be delivered.

An organizational WBS structure decomposes the work according to the organization who will perform it. Although not normally used for software projects, this WBS form may prove useful in certain software maintenance or support activities.

Typically software projects that use the WBS employ a hybrid product and functional WBS structure to allocate work throughout the organizational structure.

The WBS is the basis for planning and defining a structure for the software project, allocating work, and tasking individual organizational elements in a coordinated and focused manner.

WBS PLANNING

The WBS is developed by analyzing the agreements that have been made by the software project, the software management, technical, assurance and reporting requirements, the project development environment, and defining the end items, project development, and support requirements of the program. These are then translated into a specific task hierarchy, which, when implemented in the program, guide the development of the system.

The WBS decomposes work throughout the project into successively lower levels and portrays this decomposition process through a hierarchical diagram. This diagram integrates the definition, assignment, and monitoring of program work by:

1. Integrating the master project schedule and subordinate schedules.
2. Assigning individual responsibilities to organizational components.
3. Accumulating costs and measuring performance.
4. Integrating technical performance planning and reporting.
5. Authorizing work.
6. Analyzing performance.

The WBS is developed by starting at the top level, which represents the products to be delivered or the functions required to interface to the customer, user or organization receiving the software. Through use of an iterative procedure, the work is decomposed downward until all the products or activities to be completed WBS have been satisfied. Although every software project, no matter how small, has to project and monitor the work to be accomplished the formality of the process and the number of WBS levels required is a function of:

- Number of discrete organizations involved.
- Cost account and work package dollar size.
- Geographical project distribution for individual task areas.
- Task duration and schedule.
- Number of milestones in each task.
- Implementation schedule and cost risk.

From the WBS a WBS dictionary may be developed which identifies, in outline form, the WBS elements and who they are assigned to. The task statements included as part of the dictionary are developed by the manager responsible for each program development area based on data describing program commitments, constraints, and planning parameters. The dictionary is used with the WBS to amplify the program developmental and organizational requirements indicated on the WBS and provide an effective method for identifying which organization is responsible for implementation of which tasks.

Task descriptions are developed concurrently with the WBS structure and the WBS dictionary. The task descriptions are related to the WBS element numbers and are based on the definition of the element used in the WBS dictionary and the work specifications submitted by the functional organization. Task descriptions are modified to conform to the contract as negotiated. Task descriptions are specific, directed toward specific organizations, may be quoted or referenced in work authorization documents, and are grouped by performing organization under applicable WBS element codes. The summary paragraph for each WBS element is prepared by program management based on the WBS dictionary.

Cost accounts represent the effort to be performed by a major organization in support of a single WBS element. They are used to accumulate summary data established by the contractor and represent the lowest level in the work breakdown structure at which actual cost are required to be recorded. The planned value of work performed is summarized in these accounts for comparison with actual costs directly into the work breakdown structure without requiring splitting costs between two WBS elements.

For large projects, work authorization to various functions such as engineering, manufacturing, or purchasing may be at a higher level than the cost account. These may be issued for periods of up to 12 months. They may consist of both authorized cost accounts and planning packages.

From the cost accounts, the next logical subdivision for planning and control is a breakdown of each end item subdivision into specific work packages. As the Table 2 illustrates, the work package describes the specific requirements, by each task, to be used in controlling development. Work packages are detailed descriptions of work to be accomplished, material items to be purchased, and subcontractor work to be accomplished to complete the contract. A work package:

Table 2. Work Packages

Key Elements	Description		
Responsible department			
Department manager			
Description of work to be performed			
Resources required			
Direct charges			
Labor category	Hours	$/Hour	Total
Management			
Technical			
Assurance			
Reporting			
Totals			
Materials (dollars)			
Travel (dollars)			
Overhead (dollars)			
Overhead added by accounting			
...			

1. Describes manageable units of work.
2. Is unique and clearly distinguished from all other work packages.
3. Is scheduled with a start and completion date, has defined, documented scope, and is controlled by budgets (expressed in labor hours, dollars, or other measurable units).
4. Work assignable to a single organizational element with any suballocation of work to be done by the assigned organization.
5. Is integrated with detailed engineering, manufacturing, and the schedules as applicable.

A work package is job specific and results in a specific set of products or services such as a report, a piece of hardware, or a service, which is in the responsibility of one operating unit with an organization. Work packages plan what must be accomplished, by whom, and under whose responsibility and estimate the resources required.

MICHAEL W. EVANS

WULF, WILLIAM A. (1939–)

William A. Wulf is currently Professor of Computer Science at the University of Virginia. He was Assistant Director of the National Science Foundation (NSF) where he headed the Directorate for Computer and Information Science and Engineering. Previously, Dr. Wulf founded Tartan Laboratories, a software company. The technical basis for Tartan was research by Dr. Wulf while he a Professor at Carnegie Mellon University.

Dr. Wulf is a Fellow of the AAAS and IEEE, and currently chairs the Computer Science and Telecommunications Board of the National Research Council. He has been on the Editorial Board of a number of publications, including the IEEE Transactions on Software Engineering.

Professor Wulf's research interests span programming systems and computer architecture. Specific research activities have included: the design and implementation of Bliss, a systems-implementation language; implementation of an early and effective optimizing compiler for Bliss, the design and construction of a 16 processor multiprocessor and its operating system, and development of a technology for the automation of the construction of high quality optimizing compilers. Dr. Wulf is the author of over 70 papers and technical reports, has written three books, and holds one U.S. Patent.

BIBLIOGRAPHY

W. A. Wulf, R. Levin, and S. P. Harbison, *Hydra/C.mmp: An Experimental Computer System,* McGraw-Hill Publishing Co., 1980.

—with M. Shaw, P. M. Hilfinger, P. M., and L. Flon, *Fundamental Structures of Computer Science,* Addison-Wesley, 1980.

—with R. Johnson, C. Weinstock, S. Hobbs, and C. Geschke, *The Design of an Optimizing Compiler,* American Elsevier Publishing Company, Inc., New York, 1975.

—with G. C. Bell, R. Cady, H. McFarland, B. Delagi, J. O'Laughlin, and R. Noonan, *A New Architecture for Mini-Computers—The DEC PDP-11,* AFIPS Conference Proceedings, 1970.

—with A. N. Habermann and D. Russell, *Bliss: A Language for Systems Programming,* Communications of the Association of Computing Machinery, Dec. 1972.

—with R. London and M. Shaw, "Abstraction and Verification in Alphaed: Introduction to Language and Methodology," *IEEE Transactions on Software Engineering,* Dec. 1976.

—"Evaluation of the WM Architecture," *Proceedings of the Fifth International Symposium on Computer Architecture,* May 1992.

X

X WINDOW SYSTEM

ARCHITECTURE

The X Window System, which originated at MIT, is a client/server window system for workstations and PCs with bit-mapped screens. The "server" is the software controlling the display, i.e., creating and managing windows, drawing text and graphics, handling mouse and keyboard input, etc. The "client" is the application program. Several clients can connect to one server simultaneously. Clients and server can run on the same computer, communicating via some means of inter-process communication, or they can run on separate computers linked by a local-area or wide-area network. Either way, the interface seen by the user (sitting at the server's display) is the same: X is said to be "network transparent" (Fig. 1). In this respect it resembles Sun Microsystems' now almost defunct Network extensible Window System (NeWS). X is also network independent: client and server may communicate via any reliable network system such as TCP/IP or DECnet, over Ethernet, token ring, X.25, ISDN, etc. The specification of what is exchanged between client and server is the X Protocol, which is a network protocol.

X clients must handle many functions that in other window systems are handled by the base window system. Clients must themselves redraw the freshly exposed portions of windows which were previously obscured. All the user interface of an application (interface components such as scrollbars, pushbuttons, menus, etc). and the logic controlling them are entirely within the client. Because of this, X can support many different user interface "look and feels," by incorporating different user interface code in different applications (Fig. 2); this is usually done by means of toolkits. Toolkits are libraries of functions for creating and managing standard user interface components. Currently the two most prevalent graphical user interface (GUI) styles are Motif, which resembles Presentation Manager and Microsoft Windows, and OPENLOOK although OPENLOOK is rapidly dereasing in importance. Much work is currently being done, on improving toolkits, for example to use C++, on providing user interface management systems (UIMSs) to allow interfaces to be built graphically and interactively, and on interpreted languages for rapid development of GUI-based programs.

Another function not handled by the server is window management, i.e., how the user controls the size and layout of the windows on the screen, how they are moved, changed into icons, etc. This function is provided by a separate client program called the "window manager." Like other clients, the window manager can run on a different computer to the server (Fig. 1). Many different window managers are available, providing a variety of user interface or management styles. The user interface of the window manager is completely unrelated to the interface(s) within the programs it manages, e.g., a Motif window manager can handle a mixture of Motif, OPENLOOK, and other applications.

Purpose-built X terminals are available. They consist of a packaged X server, CPU, graphics hardware and screen, network interface hardware and software, and mouse and keyboard. As with other terminals, the only software running in the terminal is that controlling the display (the X server, or the terminal's firmware), and all applications are run remotely on other computers. Thinking of the X server as a terminal emphasizes the client/server nature of X, and is a good way to understand the system.

BENEFITS OF X

X's architecture has many advantages. Because client and server are separate, and because X is network transparent,

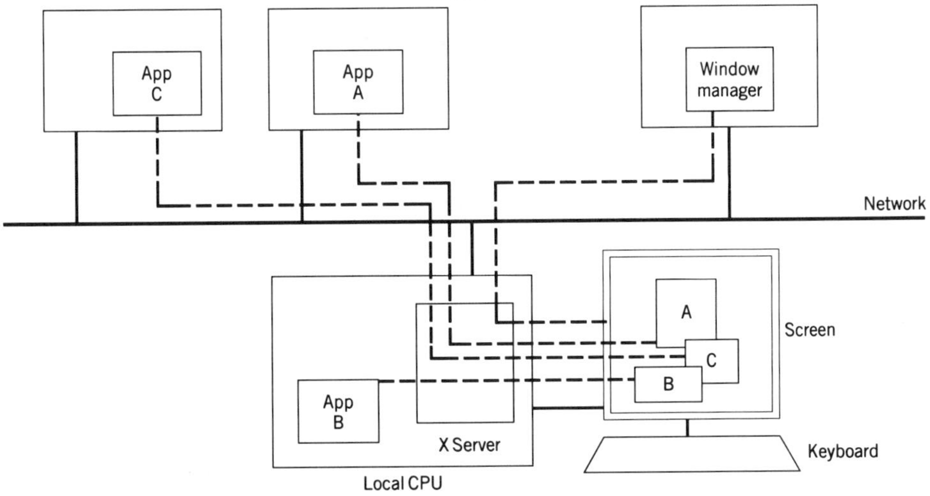

Figure 1. Client applications can run on the same computer as the X server, or remotely on other computrs, or both. The window manager can also run remotely.

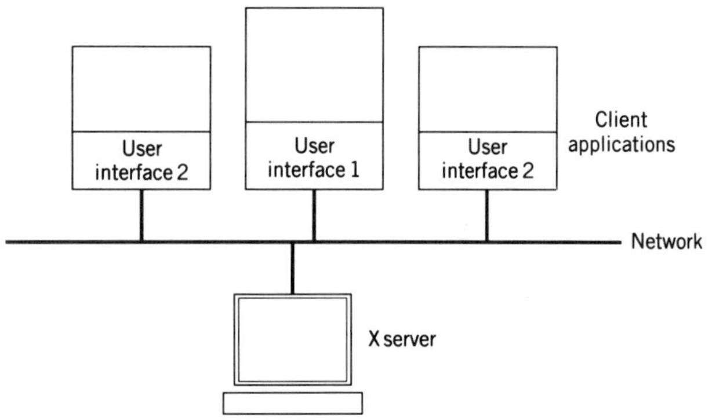

Figure 2. Applications built with different toolkits can have different user interface styles.

applications running on many different hardware platforms and operating systems can operate with one X server, on the same LAN, or over a WAN. X is available for almost every type of system, including VMS VAXes, DOS and other PCs, IBM and other mainframes, and a wide range of UNIX-based systems. X-based applications are becoming widely available also. You can easily add a new X server to your network: as soon as you plug it in, it can make use of all the existing X applications on other machines on the network. Similarly, if you provide a new X application on some host, all X servers on the network can immediately use it. X allows all the users on your network to share expensive resources (such as supercomputers, database engines, or other special-purpose machines). Special X servers can also run "on top of" other window systems, such as Microsoft Windows, Presentation Manager, or Macintosh. Since the user interface is not fixed by X but is programmable within the client, X applications can be made to resemble the others, so they integrate well on a single screen.

BIBLIOGRAPHY

General References

P. J. Asente and R. R. Swick, *X Window System Toolkit,* Digital Press, Bedford, Mass., 1990.

N. M. Mansfield, *The Joy of X: An Overview of the X Window System,* Addison-Wesley, Reading, Mass., 1993.

R. W. Scheifler and J. Gettys, *X Window System,* Digital Press, Bedford, Mass., 1990.

D. A. Young, *The X Window System: Programming and Applications with Xt, OSF/Motif Edition,* Prentice Hall, Englewood Cliffs, N.J., 1990.

Niall Mansfield
User Interface Technologies Ltd.

Y

YACC

A UNIX operating system program for generating C language Parsers from LR(1) grammars (T. Mason and D. Brown, *Lex & yacc,* O'Reilly & Associates Inc., Sebastopol, Calif., 1990).

Z

Z

Z is a formal notation with a sound mathematical basis used for the development of computer systems. It stemmed initially from the work of J-R Abrial. Z was originally developed at the Programming Research Group at the Oxford University Computing Laboratory, supported by IBM United Kingdom Laboratories Ltd., in the early to mid-1980s. Z is now used internationally in both academia and industry.

Z OVERVIEW

The fundamental mathematical basis for Z is elementary set theory (Spivey, 1988). Like several formal methods (e.g., VDM, the B Method, the Refinement Calculus) the Z notation uses typed first order predicate calculus. The Z type system is decidable.

Within industry, Z is generally used in the formal specification and design of computer software. It is a model-oriented method (see FORMAL METHODS) for abstractly describing the behavior (i.e., functionality) of sequential programs. In general, other aspects of a system such as timing or concurrency cannot be described in Z. Z consists of a core language plus powerful extension mechanisms. An extensive mathematical toolkit including relations, functions, and sequences, is built using these extension mechanisms. This toolkit is used to model the pieces of information contained in a system and the ways in which the pieces can be transformed.

Z STRUCTURING

What distinguishes Z most strongly from similar model-oriented methods (e.g., VDM) are the additional structuring mechanisms Z provides for combining parts of a model together. The key unit of structure is the Z **schema** which is a simple visual construct drawn as a stylized box. A schema is just a named piece of mathematical text consisting of a declaration part and an optional predicate part. The declaration part introduces a collection of individually named and typed schema components, whose values may be constrained and related in the predicate part.

One of the powerful Z structuring mechanisms is the **schema calculus** which allows the meaning of various schemas (represented by their names) to be combined logically to form new schemas. The contents of these new schemas can be (mechanically) produced from the definition of the schema calculus. Typically separate schemas are used to describe parts of a system's information or parts of operations on the information, and then combined using the schema calculus to describe the entire system.

Schemas can also be used as types a little like records or structures in a programming language. Using these mechanisms large systems (e.g., containing tens of thousands of lines of code) can realistically be specified.

INDUSTRIAL EXPERIENCE

Z is successfully being used in the specification and/or design of a growing number of commercial computer systems. INMOS used Z to specify the international floating point arithmetic standard (IEEE-754). This was one aspect of the formal development of the floating point unit of the T800 transputer chip (Shepherd, 1989). The largest single use of Z is probably within the IBM CICS development team (Houston and King, 1991). These and other experiences consistently show substantial reductions in bugs found in Z specified systems, from that achieved with non-formally specified systems. Furthermore improvements in product quality usually incur no extra (or even lower) cost and development timescales.

CURRENT RESEARCH

There is a very active Z research community. Several groups are developing ways of using or extending Z for object-oriented techniques (Stepney, Barden, and Cooper, 1992). Formal logics exist for reasoning about Z specifications, including some soundness proofs. There is also a trend towards combining Z with other formal methods, e.g., CSP or temporal logic (see FORMAL METHODS), to handle issues such as concurrency and timing. An emerging aspect of this final trend is the idea of using Z for specification and high level design before converting to another formal method for formal refinement to code. In addition Z is being used with various structured methods, e.g., Yourdon, SSADM, both to add precision to the structured methods and to increase the usability of Z for people inexperienced in formal methods.

TOOL SUPPORT

Although initially limited, the tool support for Z has been increasing for several years and continues to do so. Various tools exist that provide editing facilities for creating Z documents. Facilities provided include formatting and cross referencing of mathematical text, full type checking, and schema expansion (i.e., mechanical production of the contents of schemas defined using the schema calculus). Currently animators, proof checkers, and proof assistants are being developed for verifying and formally proving the correctness of Z specifications and designs. This is likely to continue with tools to support formal refinement a possibility in the next few years.

STANDARDIZATION

In the absence of an agreed Z standard, (Spivey, 1989, 1992) is widely used as a *de facto* Z standard. However, the collaborative ZIP project within the UK (supported by the UK Department of Trade and Industry) has, *inter alia,* produced a standard for both a syntax and semantics of Z

(Brien and Nicholls, 1992). It is hoped that this will form the basis for a subsequent ISO standard.

BIBLIOGRAPHY

J. Bowen, "Select Z Bibliography," in J. E. Nicholls, ed., *Proceedings of the Seventh Annual Z User Meeting,* Workshops in Computing, Springer-Verlag, London, 1993. An updated version of the bibliography is maintained on-line, send an email message containing the command "help" to archive-server@-comlab.ox.ac.uk.

S. M. Brien and J. E. Nicholls, eds., *Z Base Standard (Version 1.0),* Oxford University Programming Research Group, 1992.

I. J. Hayes, ed., *Specification Case Studies,* Prentice-Hall International, London, 1987 (2nd ed., 1993).

I. Houston and S. King, "CICS Project Report: Experiences and Results from the Use of Z in IBM" in S. Prehn and W. J. Toetenel, eds., *Proceedings of VDM 91,* Lecture Notes in Computer Science No. 551, Springer-Verlag, 1991, pp. 588–596.

D. Shepherd and G. Wilson, "Making Chips That Work," *New Scientist* **1664,** 61–64 (May 13, 1989).

J. M. Spivey, *Understanding Z: A Specification Language and its Formal Semantics,* Cambridge University Press, 1988.

J. M. Spivey, *The Z Notation: A Reference Manual,* Prentice-Hall International, London, 1989 (2nd ed., 1992).

S. Stepney, R. Barden, and D. Cooper, *Object Orientation In Z,* Workshops in Computing, Springer-Verlag, London, 1992.

JONATHAN HAMMOND
Praxis Systems plc

MARVIN V. ZELKOWITZ (1945–)

Marvin V. Zelkowitz has been a professor of Computer Science at the University of Maryland since joining the faculty as an assistant professor in 1971. He has held a joint appointment with the University's Institute for Advanced Computer Studies since 1988 and has a faculty appointment with the Computer Systems Laboratory of the National Institute of Standards and Technology of Gaithersburg, Maryland since 1976.

For over 20 years Zelkowitz has been investigating the use of software tools within software engineering environments. He developed the load and go PLUM PL/I compiler for the Univac 1100-series computer, which today would be called an integrated software engineering environment (1971–1981), he developed a syntax-editing environment for Pascal, named SUPPORT, for the IBM Personal Computer (1982–1988), and more recently he has been investigating the relationship among software engineering environments, environment frameworks and tools that execute on those environments. He most recently was editor of the NIST/ECMA report for defining frameworks for software engineering environments (1991–1993). He has an interest in software measurement and complexity theory and along with Victor Basili of the University and Frank McGarry of NASA Goddard Space Flight Center started the Software Engineering Laboratory (SEL) for the measurement, study, and evaluation of software in an industrial setting (1976).

Zelkowitz was a previous chairman of the IEEE Computer Society Washington Chapter (1978–1979), ACM SIGSOFT (1979–1981), and the Computer Society's Technical Committee on Software Engineering (1984–1986). He is a member of both the IEEE Computer Society and ACM, including SIGSOFT and SIGPLAN. He graduated from Rensselaer Polytechnic Institute with a BS in Mathematics (1967) and from Cornell University with both an MS (1969) and a PhD (1971) in Computer Science.

BIBLIOGRAPHY

M. V. Zelkowitz, with A. C. Shaw and J. D. Gannon, *Principles of Software Engineering and Design,* Prentice Hall Inc., Englewood Cliffs, New Jersey, 1979.

—with S. Cirdenas-Garcia, "A Management Tool for Evaluation of Software Designs," *IEEE Trans. on Software Engineering* **17**(9), 961–971 (1991).

—with J. Tian, "A Formal Model of Program Complexity and its Application," *J. of Systems and Software* **17**(3), 253–266 (1992).

—"The Role of Verification in the Software Specification Process," *Advances in Computers 36,* Academic Press, Boston, 1993, pp. 43–109.

INDEX

D

E

F

N

Q

R

U

V

W

X

Y

Z